A
COMPANION
TO
MELVILLE STUDIES

Portrait of Herman Melville by Joseph Oriel Eaton. Reproduced by permission of the Houghton Library, Harvard University.

A COMPANION TO MELVILLE STUDIES

Edited by
John Bryant

Greenwood Press
New York • Westport, Connecticut • London

Library of Congress Cataloging-in-Publication Data

A Companion to Melville Studies.

Bibliography: p.
Includes index.
1. Melville, Herman, 1819–1891—Addresses, essays,
lectures.   2. Melville, Herman, 1819–1891—Criticism and
interpretation—History—Addresses, essays, lectures.
3. Melville, Herman, 1819–1891—Bibliography.
4. Novelists, American—19th century—Biography—
Addresses, essays, lectures.   I. Bryant, John.
PS2386.C66   1986   813'.3   86–361
ISBN 0–313–23874–X (lib. bdg. : alk. paper)

Library of Congress Catalog Card Number: 86–361
ISBN: 0–313–23874–X

First published in 1986

Greenwood Press, Inc.
88 Post Road West, Westport, Connecticut 06881

Printed in the United States of America

The paper used in this book complies with the
Permanent Paper Standard issued by the National
Information Standards Organization (Z39.48–1984).

10 9 8 7 6 5 4 3 2 1

Copyright Acknowledgments

Innocence and Infamy: *Billy Budd, Sailor*, by Merton M. Sealts, Jr. is published here with
permission of the Wisconsin Humanities Committee. This chapter draws on a lecture given
by Merton Sealts in a seminar for lawyers presented by the Committee in 1983, funded
in part by the National Endowment for the Humanities. Along with other materials that
he prepared for the seminar, it was published by the Committee in Innocence and Infamy:
Resources for Discussing Herman Melville's *Billy Budd, Sailor* (1983).

Lyrics from *The Sea Beast*, released in 1925 by Warner Brothers, appear in "Melville in
Popular Culture" by M. Thomas Inge. Used with permission from MGM/UA.

CONTENTS

PREFACE

In 1938 Herman Melville had been dead forty-seven years. He had died in obscurity, and for three decades until the publication of Raymond Weaver's biography in 1921 he was known only to a small but growing group of academics and bibliophiles. Although public awareness of the author increased throughout the Melville Revival, his reputation did not skyrocket; editions of his works were still relatively hard to come by. Reading Melville was not so much a problem as finding him. But 1938 saw a great reduction in this (still living) problem of accessibility with the American Book Company's publication of *Herman Melville: Representative Selections*. The editor was Willard Thorp. His volume provided excerpts from all of Melville's books up through *Moby-Dick* (except *Redburn*), and samplings of Melville's poems, reviews, and letters. A lengthy introduction and thorough bibliography preceded the texts. For those graduates studying under Stanley T. Williams at Yale in the 1940s and for countless other students (undergraduate and graduate alike) reading Melville well into the 1950s, Thorp's compact anthology, quite literally a Melvillean's "bible," was a primary resource that also extended the Melville Revival throughout the land.

In organizing *A Companion to Melville Studies*, I asked Willard Thorp if he would be willing to contribute a chapter. At eighty-four, he graciously declined, but not without writing a few words that provide a clear context for this volume as a whole. I quote with Professor Thorp's permission: "I am sure the *Companion* is one book on Melville that *is* needed. We know enough now so that the contributors to the book can indeed make it a work that will endure. How different it was fifty years ago when I turned to Melville! Much of the little that we knew about the man and his works was wrong." While more insight than error has in fact come down to us from Thorp's generation of scholars, his observation that we know more now than before is an unassailable fact. That we know "enough now" to make a critical venture such as this plausible is equally true. It is not our intention, however, to create a "bible" for Melville scholars. The relative availability of reliable texts makes such a creation unnecessary. Rather we take this book to be what its title implies, A Companion. Like any companion it should provide support, direction, and enjoyment. If it endures, it shall do so, as did Professor Thorp's because it inspired another generation to surpass it.

A Companion to Melville Studies is a unique production not simply because it comprises the learning of so many noted and varied scholars but because it attempts to combine criticism and bibliography. Readers should realize from the outset that the Companion is not merely a survey of countless secondary sources, or a set of "service" pieces useful only as a display of facts. To be sure, each contributor has covered the known facts; many have added new information. But by far the more valuable aspect of each chapter is the contributor's insights into the specialized critical debates that have emerged over the years, the weaknesses and strengths of various approaches, and the suggestions for further study. We find here, then, a balance of fact and argument, and as an editor who has conversed extensively with each contributor, I can attest that each has struggled mightily to find the precise balance suited to his or her subject matter and personal approach.

The Companion, then, is not merely a fact book; it is an intellectual guide. But we would not be true to the spirit of Melville's mind, if we were to embrace a "guide book" without reservation. In Redburn, Melville's hero relies on his father's guide to the city of Liverpool and gets lost; it is outdated. In The Confidence-Man, Melville, still leery of guide books, observes that the best "maps" reveal the "feature," not the "expression" of a town, the general and lasting nature of a place, not its mutable outcroppings. Taking these cues from Melville, then, I have shaped this Companion to address both the expression and feature of Melville's life, art, and influence. That is, each chapter attempts to touch on the facts that will vary and grow as well as the natural patterns of research and inquiry that are ageless.

The reader will find two kinds of chapters here: textual (which focus on particular Melville works) and topical (which relate the Melville canon to a particular sphere of inquiry). The textual chapters are arranged chronologically in Part Two, and each touches on the problems of genesis, reception, and criticism related to the work at hand. Each provides a brief plot summary and where appropriate a discussion of the value of particular approaches, the nature of certain critical debates, and the opportunities for future study. The topical chapters are not as uniformly organized for obvious reasons, but they have been gathered in logical clusters. Part One treats aspects of Melville's life; his travels, New York associates, and the ways we have chosen over the years to view Melville biography. Part Three, following the core of textual chapters, examines the varieties of Melville's thought. Ideas loom large in Melville's work; it is curious that he did not write more essays or treatises. But fortunately he did not, for surely one of his greatest accomplishments was to render the idea or the feeling of an idea into palpable imaginative forms. Here, then, we find discussions of Melville's relation to society and language, to religion, to the mind, and to cognition. Having argued for Melville's unique combining of thought and art, it seems odd that in Part Four we separate art from thought, but the focus here is more on Melville's theories of art, as best we can determine them: his "philosophical art," his aesthetics, and his blending of comedy and tragedy. Finally, Part Five examines Melville's mark on modern culture, both "elite" and "popular," and his pervasive presence in foreign cultures and the world of books.

As editor, I did not attempt to force contributors to adopt a particular format that did not appeal to their scholarly needs or to the unique requirements of their subject matters. Thus, readers expecting a rigid uniformity of structure from one chapter to the next may be annoyed. And, although I have in overseeing the entire project, eliminated needless redundancies as they cropped up throughout the chapters, I have also allowed, indeed insisted, that different contributors reflect on the same materials so that readers can get an idea of how a single Melville fact or text can be treated by various and divergent minds. To touch only one instance, Bette Weidman's discussion of T. Walter Herbert's *Marquesan Encounters* in her chapter on *Typee* differs from Rowland Sherrill's examination of the same book from his theological angle. In short, each chapter is an invitation to a different point of view.

Each chapter concludes with its own list of works. Here may be found all works cited in the text and important additional items. These lists are not comprehensive; however, they include all major books, articles, and primary sources relevant to the particular chapter and a significant sample of minor publications. Two bibliographies go beyond this format. M. Thomas Inge's list (ch. 23) provides primary bibliography on Melville materials found in film, comics, radio, television, recordings, and popular fiction. Concluding the *Companion* is G. Thomas Tanselle's extensive list (ch. 25) of the major editions and printings of Melville's works as well as the principal research tools of Melville scholarship.

In documenting, we have used a modified version of the new Modern Language Association (MLA) reference style in which author, short title, and page number may be cited parenthetically at appropriate points in the text. Although under this system the reader is obliged to find full citations in the chapter's bibliography, this small discomfort enables us to eliminate cumbersome and costly documentation footnotes. Discursive endnotes have been kept to a minimum as well and appear if at all before each bibliography. We vary in style from the MLA convention in citing full names of authors and in preserving abbreviations for page, chapter, and item number references ("p.," "ch.," "#," etc.). Each chapter's bibliography is arranged alphabetically by author (books are mixed in with articles). Some entries, of course, will reappear in other chapters. In the *Companion*, I have used the Melville material found in the standard editions of his texts. Major reference tools such as the *The Melville Log* or the letters and all standard texts have been cited only once, at the beginning of the *Companion* in the list of abbreviations. References to these sources in the individual chapters use the specified abbreviations.

Organizing and editing a *Companion*, I have learned, is like making a rocking chair; you should never attempt it without having made one before. Not having done this type of thing before, I have had to depend a great deal on the kindness of many strangers and some friends. Happily, the strangers have become friends, and the friends are still speaking to me. Mostly. I am deeply grateful to the *Companion*'s twenty-five scholars. Each has been an active correspondent providing suggestions and encouragement. They have been patient with my editing and understanding about deadlines. They have not griped about their virtually non-existent pay. Mostly. Donald Yannella has been particularly helpful as a sounding board for ideas. Several others have provided support, encouragement, and advice throughout this project; they include Harrison Hayford, Thomas Heffernan, Robert Milder, Sanford Marovitz, Joel Myerson, Merton Sealts, Thomas Tanselle, and the late Wilson Heflin. Also aiding and abetting in this endeavor are Marilyn Brownstein and Cynthia Harris of Greenwood Press; Laura DeBonis, my typist; and Barbara Pittman, my bibliographical assistant.

I want to thank, too, the various administrators at the Pennsylvania State University, on my campus, in my department, and in the College of Liberal Arts, who encouraged me in this project and who provided for or argued in favor of my receiving released time. They are Eric Birdsall, Carol Cartwright, Michael Chaplin, Jack Crane, Vincent DeSanctis, Wendell Harris, Robert Hume, Theodore Kiffer, Thomas Knight, Joseph Michels, and Stanley Weintraub. Grants from Penn State's Faculty Scholarship Support Fund and Institute for Arts and Humanistic Studies as well as from the National Endowment for the Humanities were also indispensable.

Finally, I must thank my true Companion, Virginia Blanford.

LIST OF ABBREVIATIONS

ALS	Robbins, J. Albert, and James Woodress, eds., *American Literary Scholarship: An Annual.* Durham, N.C.: Duke University Press, 1965– . [Editorship alternates between Robbins and Woodress up to 1984. Warren French is general editor for the volume published in 1985.]
BBS	*Billy Budd, Sailor.* Ed. Harrison Hayford and Merton M. Sealts, Jr. Chicago: University of Chicago Press, 1962.
CM	*The Confidence-Man: His Masquerade.* NN Edition, Volume 10, 1984. Historical Note by Watson Branch, Hershel Parker, and Harrison Hayford, with Alma A. MacDougall.
Clarel	*Clarel: A Poem and Pilgrimage in the Holy Land.* Ed. Walter E. Bezanson. New York: Hendricks House, 1960. Rpt. 1973.
Crit. Her.	Branch, Watson G., ed. *Melville: The Critical Heritage.* Boston and London: Routledge & Kegan Paul, 1974.
Doubloon	Parker, Hershel, and Harrison Hayford, eds. *Moby-Dick As Doubloon.* New York: W. W. Norton, 1970.
ESQ	*ESQ: A Journal of the American Renaissance* (1969–). Formerly *Emerson Society Quarterly* (1955–1968). Up to 1969, issues are numbered individually. After that date volume numbers are provided.

Howard
: Howard, Leon. *Herman Melville: A Biography*. Berkeley: University of California Press, 1951.

IP
: *Israel Potter: His Fifty Years of Exile*. NN Edition, Volume 8; 1982. Historical Note by Walter E. Bezanson.

1849 *Journal*
: *Journal of a Visit to London and the Continent by Herman Melville, 1849–1850*. Ed. Eleanor M. Metcalf. Cambridge, Mass.: Harvard University Press, 1948.

1856 *Journal*
: *Journal of a Visit to Europe and the Levant, October 11, 1856–May 6, 1857 by Herman Melville*. Ed. Howard C. Horsford. Princeton, N.J.: Princeton University Press, 1955.

Lectures
: Merton M. Sealts, Jr., *Melville as Lecturer*. Cambridge, Mass.: Harvard University Press, 1957.

Letters
: Davis, Merrell R., and William H. Gilman, eds. *The Letters of Herman Melville*. New Haven, Conn.: Yale University Press, 1960.

MD
: *Moby-Dick*. Ed. Harrison Hayford and Hershel Parker. Boston: W. W. Norton, 1967.

Mardi
: *Mardi, and A Voyage Thither* (1849). NN Edition, Volume 3, 1970. Historical Note by Elizabeth S. Foster.

Mel. Diss.
: Bryant, John. *Melville Dissertations, 1924–1980: An Annotated Bibliography and Subject Index*. Westport, Conn.: Greenwood Press, 1983.

Mel. Log
: Leyda, Jay, ed. *The Melville Log*: *A Documentary Life of Herman Melville, 1819–1891*. New York: Harcourt, Brace, 1951; rpt. (with Supplement). New York: Gordian Press, 1969.

"*Mosses*"
: "Hawthorne and His *Mosses*." In *Moby-Dick*. Ed. Harrison Hayford and Hershel Parker. Boston: W. W. Norton, 1967, pp. 535–50.

NN
: Hayford, Harrison, Hershel Parker, and G. Thomas Tanselle, eds. *The Writings of Herman Melville*. Evanston and Chicago: Northwestern University Press and the Newberry Library, 1967– . [Awaiting publication are *The Piazza Tales and Other Prose Pieces, 1837–1860* (Historical Note by Merton M. Sealts, Jr.), *Moby-Dick* (Hayford, Parker, Tanselle), *Clarel* (Parker and Brian Higgins), *Poems* (Robert C. Ryan), *Journals* (Howard C. Horsford), *Billy Budd and Other Late Manuscripts* (Hayford and Ryan), and *Letters* (Lynn Horth).]

Omoo
: *Omoo: A Narrative of Adventures in the South Seas*. NN Edition, Volume 2, 1968. Historical Note by Gordon Roper.

Pierre
: *Pierre; or, the Ambiguities*. NN Edition, Volume 7, 1971. Historical Note by Leon Howard and Hershel Parker.

Poems

Collected Poems of Herman Melville. Ed. Howard P. Vincent. Chicago: Hendricks House, 1946.

Reading

Sealts, Merton M., Jr. *Melville's Reading: A Check-List of Books Owned and Borrowed.* Madison: University of Wisconsin Press, 1966.

Recognition

Parker, Hershel, ed. *The Recognition of Herman Melville: Selected Criticism Since 1846.* Ann Arbor: University of Michigan Press, 1967.

Redburn

Redburn: His First Voyage. NN Edition, Volume 4, 1969. Historical Note by Hershel Parker.

Tales

Great Short Works of Herman Melville. Introduction by Warner Berthoff. New York: Harper & Row, 1969.

Typee

Typee; or a Peep at Polynesian Life. NN Edition, Volume 1, 1967. Historical Note by Leon Howard.

WJ

White-Jacket; or, The World in a Man-of-War. NN Edition, Volume 5, 1970. Historical Note by Willard Thorp.

INTRODUCTION:
A MELVILLE RENAISSANCE

John Bryant

There are many Melvilles, each weighty and elusive, like a whale. There are the historical Melvilles—the young Ishmael cruising deep seas and the stern Abraham casting out sons; the farmer and the customs inspector; the intellectual, romancer, and poet. And there are the "phenomenal" Melvilles—those individual, invariably self-contradictory Melvilles that are the projections of our modern mind—the amiable yet Byronic Melville; the optimist and pessimist; the Christian nihilist; the democratic writer betrayed by democracy; the artist betrayed by art. A scholar might devote a life of study and come to know only a few of these Melvilles, only a fraction of the total man. Time and the very limits of our critical perspectives subvert our desire to illumine and encompass that conglomerate of Unknowns, Herman Melville.

A Companion to Melville Studies might attempt to assemble all of the available facts about Melville in hopes of pinning down as many Melvilles as possible. As "noble" a service as this may be, such an encyclopedia would become instantly dated, for new historical evidence and new approaches to Melville are emerging yearly. New Melvilles have yet to be discovered. Indeed, this growing multiplicity is at the heart of Melville's present-day appeal and continued popularity. The function of this *Companion*, then, is to assist readers in their own discovery. To be sure, "facts" abound in this volume. But the chief goal is to direct the reader of Melville toward several important, ultimately personal questions: Which Melvilles *can* be studied fruitfully; which (for the individual reader) *should* be studied, and why, and how? There is a volume to be written on each question, and, therefore, it is with a sense of humility that we offer this plump but necessarily limited companion to the community of thoughtful readers. In this introduction, I would like to share some further observations on Melville's appeal, our approach to his work, and the prospects for a renaissance or resurgence of Melville studies.

WHY MELVILLE?

Herman Melville is such a monumental presence in the canon of American literature that it seems hardly necessary to ask why we study him. He is his own reason for being. And yet anyone familiar with Melville's life knows that his career as a writer suffered a downward slope almost from the beginning, that his last thirty years were spent in obscurity, and that his modern popularity stems almost entirely from the "Melville Revival" of the 1920s and 1930s when he was rediscovered and lionized by book lovers and academics in search of something called American literature. We tend to think of Melville as a man of the 1840s and 1850s, but his works had more impact on readers beginning in the 1940s. His appeal is largely a modern phenomenon, and his popularity is far less institutionalized than one might suspect. If his posthumous career began with a Revival, it may slump into another Dark Age. It is a bit presumptuous, then, to speak of Melville's "enduring popularity," although, fortunately, the prognosis for continued study of the man and his work is strong.

One reason for Melville's appeal is evident in the very diversity of the twenty-five chapters in this volume. Something of a cosmopolitan (to borrow his expression) in thought and character, he created works that could fascinate students of divergent disciplines: anthropology, linguistics, natural science, political science, myth, philosophy, psychology and psychiatry, popular culture, even literary criticism. But it may well be that the unique facts of Melville's life hold the deeper spell over us. He is the boy who lost his father, wrote of castaways, and as a father himself lost his boys. He was an artful commoner—the perfect example of how a democracy can produce an aristocratic mind. He is also the perfect example of what a democratic marketplace can do to the creative spirit. Melville wrote furiously, ebulliently, almost ceaselessly for ten years, from 1845 to 1855 composing nine books and at least sixteen tales. Such productivity in one decade suggests the manic career of Van Gogh, another diver and enthusiast who suffered the neglect of his public. Melville though was not a suicide. Amidst exhaustion and discouragement, he quit the profession and lapsed into obscurity. Melville's "quiet" decades were a productive period giving us three volumes of poetry and such masterworks as *Clarel* and *Billy Budd*. America's neglect of Melville has become legendary, and Melville the Ignored Artist is the dominant, romantic image of the man that has most captivated American scholars.

But, of course, Melville's ultimate appeal lies in his art: his mighty lines, his concrete and surprising images, his palpable ideas, his penetration into mind and being, his exposure of that human longing for the eternal, and his evisceration of American myth. There is, too, his rich resonant voice, genial yet nervous, full of doubt and IF, but always reaching for repose. And then there is the Whale, a ludicrous image really—large, formless, ungainly. Yet Melville fashioned this "natural resource" into a massive Unknown, not unlike himself, so evocative that, after first blush, it grabs us as it does Ahab's men. The Whale or at least vague shadows of that image have penetrated the nation's popular consciousness where deep and threatening thoughts are so handily sugar-coated for public consumption. When, if that moment should ever come, *Moby-Dick* is no longer in print, there will no doubt be a restaurant of that name serving fish sticks with plastic forks. Stubb would not mind; nor Ishmael. Let us have our Whale and eat him, too.

In one form or another, whether as a man of his age, writer, or legend, Melville will persist.

APPROACHING MELVILLE

It may well be that God had a shelter for literary critics in mind when he instructed the Tower of Babel to be built. Indeed, as R. S. Crane notes, different critical approaches are like different languages, each with its own vocabulary, assumptions, choice of evidence, and methodology. On figuring the permutations that arise when we combine the many languages of criticism with the many Melvilles already alluded to, we can only marvel at the resultant babble. Making sense of it all is hard work, but it begins, I feel, with the pluralist's attempt to recognize the strengths and weaknesses of any given approach. The biographical critic, whether focusing on aesthetic or psychic growth, explores the imagination and creative process, but generally (and especially given the paucity of evidence in Melville's life) on highly speculative ground. The historicist taps into the class or cultural consciousness embodied in a work as much to criticize our own America as to unearth Melville's. The "New" Critic, perhaps the closest of readers, finds coherent wholes in a text, whether or not they exist. The poststructuralist shows how a text creates a consciousness or state of being in readers, even to the point of insisting on the failure of word and mind to interpenetrate. In all cases and from each angle, the humanities are served. Each critical language promotes a form of knowledge about ourselves: how we create, how we react to society, how art coheres, how it fails, how we read. But each approach is constrained by necessary limits. Each selects one kind of knowledge it will explore and shuts out or even denies the relevance of other kinds. As Robert Milder in another context has argued, "knowing

Melville" is a complicated affair, full of what Melville would call "man traps."

Perhaps in some future millennium, a critical apocalypse will join these and other divergent approaches into one comprehensive "language" in which the strengths of each perspective are compounded and the weaknesses, like goats, sent south. But until that time we might do well simply to acknowledge the limitations of our approach as honestly and as vigorously as we uproot the "faults" of other camps. This is not a plea for gentility or charity; it is a plea for rational discourse, or at any rate a certain self-consciousness about what our own form of rationality can and cannot do.

So often, the particular Melville we hope to know better is predetermined by the way we decide how one knows a particular phenomenon or person. Some submit that we can only know the interaction of Melville's text and the reader, that intentions and their fulfillment or failure are irrelevant in the face of the more readily accessible, measurable, and "knowable" states of being imposed on us by the written word. If it can be said that Melville exists at all, it is only like the Deist's God, who, having set so many little worlds of fiction before us, retreats into the infinite obscure. Other, more speculative thinkers are interested in Big Bangs, the electric moment of creation when Melville—the man—sat down to write. Which Melville is most worth knowing? "Melville" the creator, or "Melville" a collection of texts whose being is a reader response? There seems little hope of a rapprochement between these camps. The biographical critic is dismayed at the apparent sterility of the deconstructor whose monographs are philosophical tracts revealing more about the philosophy of language than the work criticized. The poststructuralist denies, in turn, any possibility of penetrating the intentions, much less the mind, of a man now almost one hundred years dead. One hopes to know the historical Melville; the other, Melville's text. One, the process of creation; the other, the process of reading. Which is better?

Neither and both. The two are a single process, but to develop an approach that would combine both forces seems as unlikely as finding a Unified Field Theory. But if one must choose between two equally relevant forms of knowledge, how does one select one Melville over another? Is it by whim or personal inclination? Do we as individual readers wear one Melville better than the other, like a coat? This is likely but not entirely satisfactory. We turn, then, to certain generally accepted criteria. Perhaps one approach is more *objective* than the other. But objectivity is like mead, sweet to some, poison to others. Which is more objective—the historical fact transmitted through sources of varying reliability or the textual fact, the written word, subject to varying connotations and interpretations? Both kinds of fact have separate and defensible claims to objectivity. Perhaps, then, one approach is more *useful* than the other. But this begs the question of how we define utility. Knowing Melville the creator may help us better understand the ways in which various internal and external vectors impinge on the act of creation. On the other hand, knowing how we read Melville illuminates the equally creative process of reading. Each is equally useful because each attempts to uncover states of being possible in all readers. So we come again to the rather unpromising proposition of determining which half of Solomon's baby we want, which activity is more useful to study: writing or reading.

It is possible, although not as yet visible on any critical horizon, that a coalescence of these two approaches might emerge, one that would unite biography and rhetoric, intentionality and reader response. Certainly, what Hershel Parker calls for in his notion of "New Scholarship" comes close. But there is no promise that such an apocalypse, unified field, or other fanciful, half-facetious concept would reduce critical "babble." Indeed, it would probably add only another dialect. For now, it seems best to affirm that whatever the approach, critics must not fail to ponder the rationale behind their personal pursuit of one Melville over another. We must continually inspect the criteria we adopt or inherit in judging the ultimate worth of our critical endeavors. Finally, a critic's work is only as good as his or her evidence, argument, and even (we might add) style. Only by inspecting the context of our values can we begin with integrity to present convincingly one Melville as more relevant than another.

"SOME LEGENDS IN MELVILLE SCHOLARSHIP"

Certainly, a price must be paid when an author or work achieves the legendary or "classic" status Melville now enjoys. Harold Ross's (we hope) facetious query, "Is Moby Dick the man or the whale?" (Thurber, p.77), suggests a fairly benign misapprehension compared to the more dangerous miscalculations, misreadings, and legends perpetuated among scholars. Good lies die hard. Many, despite biographical evidence, still consider Poe to have been an alcoholic or opium-chewing necrophiliac. And despite Leon Howard's low-key denials in his biography, many think of Melville as a manic depressive homosexual abusing wife and family while pining for blue-eyed Nathaniel Hawthorne. The "legends in Melville scholarship" that Sidney P. Moss complained of in his 1968 article were not so lurid. In particular, he was upset by the general view that Melville rejected Transcendentalism. As it turns out, what Moss feared to be a misleading "legend" was not so widely held, but his warning against legend-building in literary criticism is a forever timely admonition.

A case in point is that from Melville's earliest biographers onward, critics have naturally gravitated toward *Moby-Dick*. But as a consequence, we have been disposed to view Melville's earlier and later works merely as preparations for and deteriorations from that single master-work. That Melville "peaked" with his whale is a "legend" that still persists. Like any legend, it is not entirely false. But the legend of *Moby-Dick*'s absolute centrality in Melville's career has promoted a frame of mind that has allowed for the neglect of many of the later works. True, *The Confidence-Man* and *Clarel* are no longer considered "abortions" or "unreadable." But their acceptance into the Melville canon took decades, and other aspects of Melville's later years have not fared even as well. The intriguing problem of why Melville switched from fiction almost exclusively to poetry has been largely ignored, and the bulk of Melville's extant manuscripts from this later period, which contain countless insights into Melville's habits of writing, remain largely unexamined. The poems, some tales, *Israel Potter*, and late manuscript leaves have yet to be fully scrutinized. Mesmerized by *Moby-Dick*, scholars continue to find in the later works evidence of failure, retreat, and exhaustion when, in fact, the diversity and experimentation after *Moby-Dick* reveal an active, still searching, highly inventive artist, who, to borrow from Stanton Garner, "awaits discovery."

A legend in scholarship is an interpretation or hypothesis that, for some, has acquired the exalted status and immunity from attack of a fact. The notion of Melville having written "two *Moby-Dick*s" first proposed by George Stewart is one such "legend." Most evidence concerning the composition of *Moby-Dick* suggests that Melville's encounter with Hawthorne while he was completing his whaling adventure inspired him to rethink the book, to engage in what Leon Howard calls a "second growth." No matter how compelling the evidence, we must recognize that this theory is only a theory—that it is an inference derived from a combination of textual and biographical facts to account for structural peculiarities in the work. Howard's view has been useful as *one* explanation of Melville's development as a writer. But it is important to note that no conclusive external evidence has yet emerged to prove the "two *Moby-Dick*s" theory. Nevertheless, many assume it to be a fact upon which to base their reading, teaching, or interpretation. Hence, hypothesis is taken for truth, and a legend in scholarship is born. The danger in all of this is that we lose sight of how a critical hypothesis is derived. We lose sight of the complex thinking, assumptions, and logic that give the hypothesis strength. The peril of any legend in scholarship is that it allows us to ignore derivations and rationale. And there are other hypotheses which continually threaten to become legends: that after having read reviews of *Moby-Dick* Melville "wrecked" *Pierre* by changing the novel's course to include an attack on his critics, that *The Confidence-Man* was to have a sequel, that Melville drove his son Malcolm to suicide and that in later years was something of a monster in the family, that the short poem "Monody" is about Hawthorne, and so on.

Any *Companion to Melville Studies* serves us well if it can help the reader discern fact from legend. At the same time, readers must recognize that the contributors to this volume have been free to hypothesize, to wonder out loud, and to suggest fruitful areas for further discourse. Therefore, let the reader beware that the interpretations found in this volume are hypotheses designed to stimulate thought not put an end to it.

A MELVILLE RENAISSANCE

Over the past three decades, Melville studies have grown at a remarkable rate, and all signs indicate continued growth for the next decade. Moreover, in recent years a number of discoveries and publications have converged to make Melville and his work even more alluring and more accessible than in the past. It is hoped that as we approach the centenary of Melville's death, these and perhaps more findings will lead to a new surge, something of a renaissance in Melville scholarship.

Perhaps the most momentous development is the Northwestern-Newberry project which after years of bibliographical and textual analysis nears completion with the publication of one volume after another of Melville's writings. Edited by Harrison Hayford, Hershel Parker, and G. Thomas Tanselle, these volumes are invaluable not only for their textual accuracy but also for their objective historical notes (contributed by the editors and additional scholars) and their discussions of sources and (where any exist) manuscripts. Eight of the fifteen projected volumes have now been published, and each serves as the standard text for the *Companion* and for any scholar proposing serious study of or publication on Melville.

Also in recent years we have seen the unearthing of new material which may alter our views of Melville or lead to other, more valuable finds. In 1975 Reverend Walter D. Kring (of the Unitarian Church of All Souls, New York City) and Jonathan S. Carey stumbled upon evidence of Melville's Unitarian affiliation and, more significantly perhaps, of severe domestic problems between Herman and his wife Elizabeth in the very year that their son Malcolm, under cloudy circumstances, shot himself. In 1978 Amy Puett Emmers published a letter by Melville's uncle Thomas Melvill, Jr., to the author's future father-in-law Judge Lemuel Shaw, which she interpreted to mean that Herman's father Allan Melvill in his youth fathered an illegitimate daughter. The implication, of course, is that Melville incorporated this family matter into *Pierre*. An essay by Henry A. Murray, Harvey Myerson, and Eugene Taylor (1985) presents strong evidence identifying both child and mother.

On top of these, the biggest find has been the discovery of a large part of an early draft of *Typee* and a cache of letters primarily by family members, including one by a cocky Herman crowing over the birth of Malcolm. Now located in the Gansevoort-Lansing Collection in the New York Public Library (which, along with the Melville collections at The Newberry Library, Harvard, and the Berkshire Athenaeum, contains a fund of primary sources), the manuscript fragment and letter should provide us with more of an understanding of how Melville wrote. (For a discussion of the find, see Susan Davis.) Significant information about Melville can also be found in the family letters, if patient scholars are willing to examine those letters and rub them up against the facts already known about the author. Perhaps more "fragments" and "tangents" of Melville's being will emerge in the years to come as scholars, alert to what is and is not known about Melville, stumble on important, although not direct, evidence located in unlikely places: regional newspapers and journals, family records, papers, and annals.

Finally, the flotsam and jetsam of Melville's library sold after his death periodically surface in book sales or emerge from private collections. In the past two years Melville's copies of Milton, Dante, and Hazlitt have done so. His annotations in these volumes increase our understanding of his thought and reading habits.

Another impetus to a Melville renaissance is the anticipated updated edition of Jay Leyda's *The Melville Log*. The original two volume work is a chronological assemblage of available facts and documentary excerpts concerning Herman Melville. It is a unique research tool giving scholars easy access to much of the data for Melville biography. It matches up Melville's experiences and reports on or about him with relevant excerpts from the letters and works. A set of thumbnail sketches of Melville's family, friends, and associates precedes the *The Melville Log*; a listing of locations for source materials follows. An afterword, entitled "The Endless Study,"enumerates many of the biographical lacunae, each of which would occupy a scholar for some time. Nevertheless, in the thirty years since Leyda wrote, many mysteries remain unresolved simply because they have not been pursued. (See also Leyda's "Herman Melville, 1972.")

The Melville Log's first edition (1951) was the basis for Leon Howard's biography. A second printing of the *Log* (1968) includes a supplement at the end of volume 2 which corrects errors and adds many new entries. The supplement has its own index. The projected revised edition will add still more newly discovered material including much from the most recent finds, and will place each item in its proper chronology and provide a single index. Will this new edition be the harbinger of a new biography? Hershel Parker is already at work on one. Others are bound to come.

The problem with *The Melville Log* is that it is so good, so meticulous, so thorough, so reliable that a scholar might become too dependent on it, or assume that little remains to be done, or that if any area remains uninvestigated, Professor Leyda will cover it. But Leyda would be the first to insist that the *Log* is, properly speaking, not an end but a means to further study, a point of departure for future explorations that can best be accomplished by men and women of varying points of view and historical insight.

Readers who desire quarterly updates on developments in Melville studies should turn to the Melville Society's publication, formerly the *Melville Society Newsletter*, now *Melville Society Extracts*. Scrupulously edited by Donald Yannella of Glassboro (New Jersey) State College, the journal prints notes, short essays, and announcements pertaining to Melville biography, family history, and sources, and on the author's influence on the culture. Numbers 25 to 48 (1976–81) have been indexed by Sally Hoople.

If *The Melville Log* were not enough to satisfy the needs of any Melville enthusiast, various scholars have in recent years put together other reference works that together enhance our ability to gain reliable information about Melville quickly and efficiently. Brian Higgins' projected three-volume *Herman Melville: An Annotated Bibliography* provides a yearly record and brief abstracts of reviews, notices, articles, and books that mention Melville from 1846 to the present. So far only volume 1 ending in 1930 has been published (1979). Leland Phelps' recent *Herman Melville's Foreign Reputation* (1983) assembles all foreign language editions of Melville writings and, like Higgins's work, can be used to ascertain the growth of Melville's popularity. Jeanetta Boswell's *Herman Melville and the Critics* (1981), a checklist of twentieth-century criticism up to 1978, is a handy but error-ridden resource that will, along with the yearly bibliographical essays on Melville in *American Literary Scholarship*, tide scholars over until Higgins's volumes 2 and 3 are published. John Bryant's *Melville Dissertations* (1983) annotates all dissertations relating to Melville up to 1980. It supersedes similar compilations by Tyrus Hillway, Joel Myerson, Hershel Parker, and Arthur Miller, and can help graduate students and dissertation directors avoid the all-too-familiar thesis topic or find a new one.

The past decade has brought other, more specialized reference tools that display the minutiae of Melville's life and work. Gail Coffler, for instance, has assembled Melville's classical allusions. Jill Gidmark has compiled an interesting "dictionary" of Melville's sea terminology. Larger and more thorough concordances of Melville's writings are coming slowly into print. There are two *Moby-Dick* concordances. Separate concordances for *Clarel* and *Billy Budd* have appeared as dissertations, and, most recently, Larry Wegener has published a concordance of

Pierre. Only the Wegener volume, however, has drawn on a definitive Northwestern-Newberry text. Much, then, remains to be done in deriving a complete and reliable concordance of all of Melville's writings.

Each of these newer works complements several older reference tools which remain indispensable resources for the Melville scholar. As already noted, Howard's 1951 biography is still standard. Merton M. Sealts's *The Early Lives of Melville*(1974) reprints all known biographical essays and notices published during the author's life. Merrell R. Davis and William H. Gilman's edition of the letters (1960) will be revised and updated (with over thirty new letters) in a forthcoming volume of the NN edition.

Melville's Reading (1966) compiled by Sealts lists all books that Melville is known to have owned and borrowed. The product of decades of research and updating, the volume is both alluring and frustrating. It is on the one hand a record of one part of Melville's inte"..ctual activity and yet is only a fraction of what we surmise was a much larger library. The story of the dispersal of Melville's books is related in Sealts's introduction; the story of Sealts's tracking down various volumes and his correspondence with poet and Melvillean Charles Olson on book matters appears in *Pursuing Melville* (1982). This collection of Sealts's writing also provides updates on all discoveries since 1966. Mary K. Madison's 1984 Northwestern dissertation, *Mellville's Sources*, complements Sealts's *Reading* by listing all suggested or proven sources. Finally, an indispensable resource is Walker Cowen's 1965 Harvard dissertation on Melville's marginalia. Over five thousand pages long, this compilation does not appear in most libraries, and the cost of reproducing it on eight reels of microfilm is prohibitive for most individuals. However, much gold remains to be extracted from the marginalia, of which only a fraction has been reprinted in *The Melville Log.*

Reviews of Melville's work are an invaluable resource not simply for gauging the author's reputation but for discerning the audiences he had to contend with and in some sense educate to his way of writing. Few scholars, however, have studied the reviews for all of their implications. Nina Baym's *Novels, Readers, and Reviewers*(1984) does not focus on Melville or any one author, but it does provide the most comprehensive discussion to date of the critical vocabulary (a loose affair) and expectations of antebellum reviewers. Higgins's bibliography is the best listing of Melville reviews; however, Steve Mailloux and Hershel Parker's pamphlet *Checklist of Melville Reviews* (1975) is a handier compilation. Both resources are updated in the pages of *Melville Society Extracts*. Hugh Hetherington's *Melville's Reviewers* (1961) was the first to reprint a selection of reviews, but this has been superseded by Watson Branch's selection, *Melville: The Critical Heritage* (1971). Fuller collections of reviews of individual works, however, can be found as in Milton R. Stern's *Critical Essays on Herman Melville's Typee* (1982), M. Thomas Inge's *Bartleby*

The Inscrutable (1979) and Higgins and Parker's *Critical Essays on Herman Melville's Pierre* (1983). A more detailed discussion of these and other Melville reference books can be found in G. Thomas Tanselle's chapter at the end of this volume.

Now, more so than twenty years ago, scholars have at hand reliable texts and a wealth of readily accessible information about Herman Melville. And, contrary to the weary assumption that there is nothing new under the sun, the prospect for more discovery and fresh insight into Melville's art seems excellent. Our hope here is that this *Companion to Melville Studies* will guide and stimulate scholars as they embark upon their own phase of "the endless study" of Herman Melville.

WORKS CITED

Baym, Nina. *Novels, Readers, and Reviewers: Responses to Fiction in Antebellum America*. Ithaca, N. Y.: Cornell University Press, 1984.

Boswell, Jeanetta. *Herman Melville and the Critics: A Checklist of Criticism*. Metuchen, N. J.: Scarecrow Press, 1981.

Coffler, Gail H. *Mellville's Classical Allusions: A Comprehensive Index and Glossary*. Westport, Conn.: Greenwood Press, 1985.

Cohen, Hennig, and James Cahalan. *A Concordance to Melville's Moby-Dick*. 3 vols. N. p.: Melville Society, 1978.

Cowen, Wilson Walker. "Melville's Marginalia." Ph.D. Diss., Harvard University, 1965. [*Mel. Diss.*, #134.]

Crane, R. S. *The Languages of Criticism and the Structure of Poetry*. Toronto: University of Toronto Press, 1953.

Davis, Susan. "More for the NYPL's Long Vaticans." *Melville Society Extracts* No. 57 (February 1984): 5–7.

Emmers, Amy Puett. "Melville's Closet Skeleton: A New Letter about the Illegitimacy Incident in *Pierre*." In *Studies in the American Renaissance 1977*. Ed. Joel Myerson. Boston: Twayne, 1978, pp. 339–42.

Garner, Stanton. "The Melville Who Awaits Discovery." *Melville Society Extracts* No. 53 (February 1983): 2.

Gidmark, Jill B. *Melville's Sea Dictionary: A Glossed Concordance and Analysis of the Sea Language in Melville's Nautical Novels*. Westport, Conn.: Greenwood Press, 1982.

Hetherington, Hugh W. *Melville's Reviewers: British and American, 1845–1891*. Chapel Hill, N. C.: University of North Carolina Press, 1961.

Higgins, Brian. *Herman Melville: An Annotated Bibliography, 1846–1930*. Vol. 1. Boston: G. K. Hall, 1979.

———, and Hershel Parker, eds. *Critical Essays on Herman Melville's Pierre; or, The Ambiguities*. Boston, Mass.: G. K. Hall, 1983.

Inge, M. Thomas, ed. *Bartleby the Inscrutable: A Collection of Commentary on Herman Melville's Tale "Bartleby the Scrivener"*. Hamden, Conn.: Archon Press, 1979.

Irey, Eugene F. *A Concordance to Herman Melville's Moby-Dick*. 2 vols. New York: Garland Press, 1982.

Leyda, Jay. "Herman Melville, 1972." In *The Chief Glory of Every People: Essays on Classic American Writers*. Ed. Matthew J. Bruccoli. Carbondale: Southern Illinois University Press, 1972, pp. 163–71.

Madison, Mary K. "Melville's Sources: A Checklist." Ph.D. Diss., Northwestern University, 1984.

Mailloux, Steve, and Hershel Parker. *Checklist of Melville Reviews*. N. p.: Melville Society, 1975.

Milder, Robert. "Knowing Melville." *ESQ* 24 (Second Quarter 1978): 96–117.

Moss, Sidney P. " 'Cock-a-Doodle-Doo!' and Some Legends in Melville Scholarship." *American Literature* 40 (May 1968): 192–210.

Murray, Charles Joseph. *A Concordance to Melville's Billy Budd*. Ph.D. Diss., Miami University, 1979. [*Mel. Diss.*, #505.]

Murray, Henry A., Harvey Myerson, and Eugene Taylor. "Allan Melvill's By-Blow." *Melville Society Extracts* No. 61 (February 1985): 1– 6.

Parker, Hershel. "The 'New Scholarship': Textual Evidence and Its Implications for Criticism, Literary Theory, and Aesthetics." *Studies in American Fiction* 9 (Autumn 1981): 181–97.

Phelps, Leland. *Herman Melville's Foreign Reputation: A Research Guide*. Boston: G. K. Hall, 1983.

Sealts, Merton M., Jr. *Pursuing Melville, 1940–1980: Chapters and Essays*. Madison: University of Wisconsin Press, 1982.

———. *The Early Lives of Melville: Nineteenth-century Biographical Sketches and Their Authors*. Madison: University of Wisconsin Press, 1974.

Stern, Milton R. *Critical Essays on Herman Melville's Typee*. Boston, Mass.: G. K. Hall, 1982.

Thorp, Willard. *Herman Melville: Representative Selections*. New York: American Book Co., 1938.

Thurber, James. *The Years with Ross*. Boston: Little, Brown and Co., 1957.

Wegener, Larry Edward. *A Concordance to Melville's Pierre; or, the Ambiguities*. 2 vols. New York: Garland 1985.

———. "A Concordance to Herman Melville's *Clarel: A Poem and Pilgrimage to the Holy Land*." Ph.D. Diss., University of Nebraska, 1978. [*Mel. Diss.*, #487.]

Yannella, Donald, and Hershel Parker, eds. *The Endless, Winding Way in Melville: New Charts by Kring and Carey*. Glassboro, N. J.: Melville Society, 1981.

PART ONE

MELVILLE'S WORLD

MELVILLE BIOGRAPHY: A LIFE AND THE LIVES

James Barbour

As *Moby-Dick* was "in his flurry," Melville wrote a long confessional letter to his Berkshire neighbor Nathaniel Hawthorne in which he openly discussed his hopes and fears as a writer and then apologetically observed, "—I talk all about myself, and this is selfishness and egotism. Granted. But how help it? I am writing to you; I know little about you, but something about myself. So I write about myself " (*Letters*, p. 129). Melville's first biographers believed that Melville had always written about himself, particularly in his early novels, a belief that Melville planted by claiming in *Typee* to have reported incidents "just as they occurred" (p. xiv) and asserting that *White-Jacket* and *Moby-Dick* were based on his experiences in a man-of-war and "two years & more, as a harpooneer" (*Letters*, p. 109). Recent scholarship has been able to separate much of the fact from the fiction and has discovered that Melville's "unvarnished truth" was frequently lifted from literary sources or was simply a product of his imagination. This chapter on Melville biographies, then, will begin with an overview of Melville's life to establish the important people, events, and dates in his history, and the rise and collapse of his literary career—points of reference for his biographers as they trace Melville's inexorable journey from early success into isolation and silence.[1]

A LIFE

Melville was born on 1 August 1819 in New York City, the third child of Allan Melvill, an importer of French goods, and Maria Gansevoort

Melville (there were eight children eventually; Herman was the second of four boys). Father and mother came from distinguished American families of historical importance: Major Thomas Melvill had been a "Mohawk" at the Boston Tea Party and was appointed Collector of the Port of Boston by President Washington in 1789; the Gansevoorts were a successful Albany family also active in the Revolutionary War, and General Peter Gansevoort, the hero of Fort Stanwix, had prevented the British from reinforcing General Burgoyne before the Battle of Saratoga.

Allan Melvill was a well-to-do businessman and a world traveler who moved the family into increasingly larger and more comfortable homes in New York. But his business was shaky, for he had borrowed extensively from his father and the Gansevoorts; when America experienced its first postwar depression in 1830, he was forced to move the family to Albany, the first in a series of economic reversals for the family. Allan then set himself up in the fur business on money borrowed from his brother-in-law Peter Gansevoort. In the dead of winter he traveled to New York on business; on his return he crossed the Hudson River on foot in below-zero temperatures. Tired, suffering from his recent exposure, and harassed with financial concerns, he continued working. His health worsened. He soon lapsed into a state of excited delirium and died early in 1832. Herman was an impressionable twelve years of age, the age at which many of his fictional heroes are orphaned.

The father's death threw the family into genteel but grinding poverty. The mother was forced to beg from her brothers while the children were taken out of school and put to work. Herman was placed as a bank clerk, and his elder brother Gansevoort was entrusted with the family fur business. The Panic of 1837 squeezed Gansevoort out of business. Herman attempted to help the family by teaching in various district schools and by looking for employment as a surveyor on the Erie Canal. In 1839, frustrated with his inability to contribute, he made his first voyage, signing on as a crew member on the *St. Lawrence* bound for Liverpool. One of Melville's young characters in similar straits was later to observe, "Talk not of the bitterness of middle-age and after-life; a boy can feel all that, and much more, when upon his young soul the mildew has fallen; and the fruit, which with others is only blasted after ripeness, with him is nipped in the first blossom and bud. And never again can such blights be made good; they strike in too deep"(*Redburn*, p. 11).

He returned to try his luck in the West, traveling to Galena, Illinois, to visit his uncle Thomas Melvill, who after repeated failures himself had left the family farm in Pittsfield, Massachusetts. Herman saw the muddy waters of the Mississippi which he was later to use as the setting for *The Confidence-Man*; otherwise the trip was a failure, and he was back in New York by the fall of 1840. (See Tanselle, "Melville's Visit.") Without future prospects, he signed on to serve as an ordinary seaman on the whaler *Acushnet*, committing himself to a voyage of three years or more. On 3 January 1841, he sailed from New Bedford and away from the seemingly irreversible economic woes of the family. Unwittingly, he was to embark on a fortuitous series of adventures that would form the matrix of his early fiction.

By late June 1842 Melville and a friend Toby Greene, tired of the tyrannical cruelty on the *Acushnet*, jumped ship in Anna Maria Bay, Nuku Hiva, in the Marquesas. By miscalculation they made their way to a valley inhabited by the Typees, a tribe reputed to be cannibals. Melville, who suffered from "a mysterious infection of the leg" (Howard, p. 51), stayed four weeks. He lived happily among the Typees, free from the getting and spending of Western civilization that had impoverished his family, but the mindlessness of primitive paradise began to pall at about the time he was rescued by the *Lucy Ann*, an Australian whaler seeking additional crew.

The conditions here were perhaps worse than on the *Acushnet*: the captain was sick, the first mate a drunk, living conditions bad, and the ship unlucky, for it sighted no whales. When they reached Papeete, seeking aid for the captain, Melville and others refused duty and were taken to the calaboose. Released after the ship sailed, Melville and the steward John B. Troy became "omoos" (rovers or beachcombers) and went to the neighboring island of Eimeo where they worked on a potato farm until early November when Melville signed on the *Charles and Henry* as a harpooner for a run to the next port. He was discharged at Lahina on the Hawaiian Island of Maui and made the short voyage to Honolulu where he signed a contract to be a clerk and bookkeeper for a year in a merchandise store. His plans were interrupted when the *Acushnet* pulled into port. (Melville had been posted as a deserter by the captain in Lahina.) This probably prompted his decision to leave Honolulu prematurely by enlisting in the U.S. Navy for a homeward-bound cruise on the frigate *United States*. In Callao, Peru, Melville heard with interest the story of the mutiny on board the U.S.S. *Somers*: two sailors and a midshipman had been hanged for mutiny, among them the son of the Secretary of War and the seaman Elisha Small, who was run up the yardarm after exclaiming, "God bless the flag." More personally distressing news was that Melville's cousin Guert Gansevoort had been in charge of the council of officers and, at the insistence of the captain, had pressed for a guilty charge. Guert later said his decision was "*approved* of God" (*Mel. Log*, p. 161), but that did not seem to relieve his depression.

Melville's reaction to the primitive cultures in the Pacific had been positive. He found, however, that Paradise had been profoundly changed by Western culture and its emissaries. The missionaries had attempted to govern the behavior of the natives and had introduced laws without a corresponding grace. The resulting hypocrisy of the natives completed the physical devastation begun by the sailors who had introduced diseases to which the islanders had no immunity. Melville's reaction to the missions in the South Seas was compounded by his experience with authority in the navy: the officers were indifferent to the plight of "the people" and often guilty of the same offenses for which common seamen were flogged.

On 3 October 1844, the *United States* anchored in Boston harbor, and Melville was soon thereafter discharged. He returned to his family whom he entertained with stories of his adventures which they encouraged him to write down. Thus began the "unfolding" of which Melville would relate to Hawthorne in 1851: "From my twenty-fifth year I date my life. Three weeks have scarcely passed, at any time between then and now, that I have not unfolded within myself" (*Letters*, p. 130).

The first story was *Typee*, the account of Melville's month in Typee Valley, stretched to four months in the novel. His brother Gansevoort, recently appointed secretary to the American legation in England, submitted the manuscript to John Murray in London, who accepted it for his Home and Colonial Library.[2] But Murray had doubts about its authenticity, so Melville revised the manuscript and added new chapters (see *Typee*, p. 279). Clearly he supplemented his own limited knowledge of the Typees—he did not speak their language and was puzzled by a number of their practices—by interpolating authoritative material of previous Marquesan visitors into his narrative. Thus began Melville's compositional habit of borrowing from factual sources to add ballast to his narrative. But *Typee* was a popular success because he avoided the dull and sententious tradition in British travel literature; instead he told a lively romantic tale of suspense that hangs on the question of whether the Typees are cannibals, and then the discovery of the truth and a bloody escape.

The firm of Wiley and Putnam published *Typee* in America. The reviewers, although favorable, rightly questioned whether he was not a romancer rather than a historian; the religious press, predictably, objected to his treatment of the missionaries. Unexpectedly, Toby Greene surfaced in Buffalo and wrote a letter testifying to the "entire accuracy of the work" (*Mel. Log*, p. 220). Melville "expurgated" the book for a second edition along the lines suggested by his American publishers and included "The Story of Toby" as a sequel. When *Typee* was followed in 1847 by *Omoo*, an account of his wanderings in Tahiti, Melville was, in the words of James Russell Lowell, one of the "best launched" young authors of his time (Howard, p. 98).

In 1847 Melville also married Elizabeth Shaw, daughter of Lemuel Shaw, Chief Justice of Massachusetts, a friend of Melville's father, and a benefactor to the family. The couple moved to New York where they set up housekeeping with Melville's younger brother and his bride—a move that brought Melville into the circle of Evert Duyckinck, editor for Wiley and Putnam, who was about to edit his own journal, the *Literary World*. More important for Melville's own growth, Duyckinck had an extensive library from which Melville began to borrow books; he also began to purchase books against his account at the Harpers (publishers of *Omoo*). Melville was gaining an education: he avidly read Shakespeare as well as Dante, Montaigne, Coleridge, Browne, and Rabelais. Melville, who had entered "the world of the mind" (Howard, ch. 6), began a third book, an account of his Pacific travels, but he unfolded once more and changed the story to an island-hopping allegory through the world of the imagination in which his hero is engaged in a quest for happiness (a fair maiden) while he is pursued by guilt (a dark temptress). The trip is enlivened by conversations about religion, philosophy, and the ideal state. The book was completed on the eve of the French Revolution of 1848. When the news reached New York, Melville's imagination was stirred by the possibilities for social change, so he added twenty-three chapters of political allegory. *Mardi* is, as its subtitle suggests, "A Chartless Voyage," but more significantly it was Melville's response to the world of ideas and his turning away from the popular travel romances that his audience had come to expect. *Mardi* failed to sell, a lesson that was not lost on Melville. Hereafter he would make a distinction between what he was forced to write and what he wanted to write. Artistic and financial demands were wholly separate, and he could not resolve them as he admitted to Hawthorne in the midst of writing *Moby-Dick*: "What I feel most moved to write, that is banned,—it will not pay. Yet, altogether, write the *other* way I cannot" (*Letters*, p. 128).

Melville immediately returned to writing "the other way," turning out *Redburn* and *White-Jacket* in the summer of 1849. *Redburn* is a fictional reworking of Melville's summer voyage of 1839 to Liverpool. His young hero, the self-pitying Wellingborough Redburn, burdened with such a distinguished name in a democratic setting, has fallen from high estate and is introduced to a world of indifference and evil, first in the person of Jackson, a dying misanthropic sailor who jeers at all religious beliefs, and later in the slums of Liverpool where Redburn tries in vain to elicit help for a starving mother and her children. While laboring over the proofs of *Redburn*, Melville wrote *White-Jacket*, a re-creation of his experience on the *United States* with many fictional additions. The book is a detailed examination of life on a man-of-war (a floating Gomorrah) and specifically a denunciation of the flawed instruments of command and a propaganda statement about the abuses of flogging (163 floggings were recorded while Melville was on board). When the summer was over, Melville wrote to his father-in-law Lemuel Shaw that "no reputation that is gratifying to me, can possibly be achieved by either of these books. They are two *jobs*, which I have done for money—being forced to it, as other men are to sawing wood. . . . So far as I am individually concerned, & independent of my pocket, it is my earnest desire to write those sort of books which are said to 'fail.' "Melville would soon have the satisfaction of writing books that failed, but in the summer of 1849 he had written better than he knew. His "little nursery tale," the "beggarly" *Redburn* would in time become a minor classic (*Letters*, pp. 91–92, 93, 95).

Exhausted and badly in need of a vacation, Melville decided to travel to England to negotiate a better contract for *White-Jacket* and perhaps to gather background material for a projected book based on the life of Israel R. Potter, an American revolutionary who was marooned in London for forty years before returning home. Once abroad Melville missed his young family (Malcolm was born in 1849, the first of four children). By February 1850 he was back in New York, working on a whaling novel, presumably another autobiographical romance that began with his experience on the *Acushnet*. Melville described the book to his English publisher as a "romance of adventure" based on legends of the Sperm Whale Fisheries and supported by personal experience (*Letters*, p. 109). In August he reported to Evert Duyckinck that the book was "mostly done" (*Mel. Log*, p. 385); it was not published, however, until October 1851—and by then the pedestrian whaling story had been transformed into *Moby-Dick*, the greatest of American novels.

The transformation of *Moby-Dick* was perhaps the result of a meeting between Melville and Nathaniel Hawthorne. During a July 1850 visit to his Berkshire relatives, Melville invited his New York friends to meet the local literary figures, one of whom was Hawthorne, living nearby in Lenox. Melville had probably not read much Hawthorne before the meeting, but he quickly read *Mosses from an Old Manse* with great interest and was profoundly moved; the result was "Hawthorne and His *Mosses*," a review essay written for Duyckinck's *Literary World*. The meeting was, to borrow Melville's words, "a shock of recognition," for he saw in Hawthorne a writer in whom, like his beloved Shakespeare, there lurked "a great power of blackness." Both writers probed at the axis of reality and spoke "the sane madness of vital truth" ("*Mosses*," pp. 540–42). Sometime in the next few months or early in 1851, Melville made the decision that great writers must make: he decided to trust his own genius and revised his whaling novel.

The significance of Hawthorne during this period cannot be overemphasized. Melville's previous novels reflect a need for male companionship, and in the older Hawthorne he found a kindred spirit, one with whom he could share ideas—and on occasion cigars and champagne—and engage in long intellectual conversations. Melville broke through Hawthorne's famous reserve. And in the spring and summer of 1851, as Melville was revising his novel and seeing it through its final stages, he wrote a remarkably insightful series of letters to Hawthorne. He clearly recognized that he could not write to suit himself and survive as a novelist: "Dollars damn me," he wrote, "and the malicious Devil is forever grinning in upon me.... My dear Sir, a presentiment is on me,— I shall at last be worn out and perish, like an old nutmeg-grater, grated to pieces by the constant attrition of the wood" (*Letters*, p. 128). *Moby-Dick* was dedicated to Hawthorne, "In admiration for his genius." But Hawthorne left the Berkshires in November: something had come between the two men. They were to allude to each other in their fiction, Hawthorne in *The Blithedale Romance*, Melville in *Pierre* and later in "Monody" and *Clarel*, but the mutual influence of their friendship and the mystery of their estrangement remains.

Depleted by his extended struggle with the whale, Melville, perhaps anticipating the commercial rejection of *Moby-Dick*, immediately began *Pierre*, a story that he described early on as a "rural bowl of milk" (*Letters*, p. 146). *Pierre* was designed for a common reader as it combined the properties of popular potboilers: a seemingly innocent setting masking hypocrisy and arrogance, courtly love that concealed sexual attraction, seduction, disinheritance, devotion to a rejected heroine, murder, and a nightmarish conclusion. But as the story moves from its bucolic setting to a Dantesque New York, it plunges into autobiographical complexity. Pierre is a popular poet of light verse (just as Melville is a writer of South Sea romances), who is slaving feverishly to capture the everlasting elusiveness of Truth in the novel he is writing (the same effort Melville put into *Moby-Dick*). Melville was writing, in the words of Henry A. Murray, the "biography of his self-image" (p. xx). The book turns upon itself and ends in rage with murder and suicide—but its anger is also directed toward Pierre, the silly scribbler of verse who will preach Truth to a dense and indifferent world. The second half of the book reflects Melville's disappointment with the negative reviews of *Moby-Dick*.[3] William Charvat argues that *Pierre* may be taken as Melville's statement of his own loss of faith in fiction, and Pierre's suicide may be symbolic of Melville's professional self-destruction (*Authorship in America*, p. 255).

The disappointing reception of *Pierre* dimmed Melville's hopes of supporting himself as a professional writer. *Typee* and *Omoo* had been popular successes, but he could no longer write that way. And the last two novels had made great demands on him and his family: Elizabeth in a later memoir remarked that when writing *Moby-Dick* her husband "would sit at his desk all day not eating anything till four or five o'clock" (Sealts, *Early Lives*, p. 169). Melville's family worried about his health. His mother observed that he was overworking his mind and his imagination—and there were rumors of insanity. The family attempted in vain to get him a consulship.[4]

Instead Melville began a career as a magazine writer. He was invited by *Putnam's Monthly Magazine* to contribute stories at a rate of five dollars a page. His first story, "Bartleby, the Scrivener," appeared in the November and December 1853 issues. The story can be read as Melville's statement about the demise of his career as a novelist and his refusal to write the type of fiction his audience demanded. Over the next four years *Putnam's Monthly Magazine* and *Harper's Monthly Magazine* printed more than a dozen of his stories.[5]

In 1853 the Harpers gave Melville an advance for a book on "Tortoises or Tortoise-Hunting," but when their publishing house burned down, he apparently turned the material into a series of sketches which he sold to *Putnam's* as "The Encantadas." *Israel Potter: His Fifty Years of Exile*, the book he had planned as early as 1849, was published serially in *Putnam's* in 1854–55 and in book form in 1855. Melville then turned to an account he had found in the eighteenth chapter of Captain Amasa Delano's *Narrative of Voyages and Travels*. It told of Delano's boarding and rescuing the Spanish ship *Tryal*, which had experienced a slave rebellion. Melville reworked the story as an ironic allegory of nineteenth-century optimism and sent *Putnam's* the completed portion along with legal documents pertinent to the narrative. The reader for the magazine failed to see that Melville may have intended the documents as an outline of the conclusion, and, though complaining about the lack of continuous narrative, recommended that the story "Benito Cereno," be printed (Howard, p. 221). During the winter of 1855–56, Melville wrote his most modern novel, *The Confidence-Man,* an apocalyptic view of contemporary American society. Set on the Mississippi River on April Fool's Day on the steamship *Fidèle*, the book is a fugue on the theme of confidence that explores the impossibility of absolute Christian faith in an imperfect, if not evil, world. In the end the confidence man convinces an old man that a chamber-pot is a life preserver (there is no salvation for this culture) and turns out the lights.

Melville's final stories deal with despair: failed men and the failure of communication, messages not delivered, Dead Letter Offices, rotting mail boxes, characters deserted, isolated, and violated—"the imagery of defeat and physical wreckage and spiritual ruin abounds" (Lewis, p. 37). When Melville's father-in-law, aware of his mental state, proposed a trip abroad, Melville did not hesitate. He placed the manuscript of *The Confidence-Man* with the firm of Dix and Edwards and sailed for Glasgow on 11 October 1857. It was the last fiction Melville was to publish during his lifetime. And his luck held: Dix and Edwards failed before Melville could return home.

Melville looked for his roots in Scotland and then in Liverpool visited Hawthorne, who had been appointed American consul by his college friend Franklin Pierce. In his journal Hawthorne described their walk among the sand dunes outside the city:

Melville, as he always does, began to reason of Providence and futurity, and of everything that lies beyond human kin, and informed me that he had "pretty much made up his mind to be annihilated;" but still he does not seem to rest in that anticipation; and, I think, will never rest until he gets hold of a definite belief. It is strange how he persists—and has persisted ever since I knew him, and probably long before—in wandering to and fro over these deserts."(*Mel. Log*, p. 529)

Melville traveled to Egypt and Constantinople but his depression remained, and this time he did not hurry home to his family. The pyramids reminded him of death— "It was in these pyramids that was conceived the idea of Jehovah. Terrible mixture of the cunning and awful" (1856 *Journal*, p. 118)—and he questioned whether the desolation of the Holy Land was "the result of the fatal embrace of the Deity" (p. 154). There were no answers to Melville's questions. He toured Europe, went back to England and then home.

During the years 1857 through 1860, Melville tried the lecture circuit, first with moderate success and then with none. The only topic that combined his reputation with the interest of the audience was that selected for the second season, "The South Seas." When he secured only three speaking engagements for the third season, it was clear that he must try something else, but that something would not be fiction. Melville had become reclusive, turning his back on his early novels which he referred to sarcastically as "Peedee, Hullabaloo, and Pog-Dog." In 1859 Titus Coan, one of two Williams College students who visited Melville to discuss the author's early works, reported to his mother, "he would not repeat the experiences of which I had been reading with rapture in his books. In vain I sought to hear of Typee and those Paradise islands, but he preferred to pour forth his philosophy and his theories of life. The shade of Aristotle arose like a cold mist between myself and Fayaway. ... With his liberal views he is apparently considered by the good people of Pittsfield as little better than a cannibal or a 'beach-comber' " (Metcalf, p. 173).

In 1860 Melville decided to sail again, this time around the world on a ship captained by his younger brother Tom, leaving some poetry behind for Elizabeth to publish—if she could. Neither venture was realized: Elizabeth was unsuccessful, and Melville returned home from San Francisco. The Civil War broke out soon, and he attempted to gain a naval appointment. Two years later in 1863 he moved to New York City where he would remain. With the fall of Richmond he began writing a poetic sequence *Battle-Pieces and Aspects of the War*, published by the Harpers in 1866. The volume dealt with the war chronologically, beginning with the hanging of John Brown ("The Portent") and concluding with "A Meditation," a commemoration for the slain and a hope for reconciliation. The work was poorly received, and sales were disappointing.

In 1866 Melville secured a position as Deputy Inspector in the New York Custom House. (Ironically, Hawthorne was discharged from the Custom House in Salem and gained international acclaim; Melville achieved initial popularity and retreated to his New York Custom House and obscurity.) The family hoped that a "regular job" would ease the growing tensions in the Melville home, but within a year Elizabeth's minister suggested that she leave her husband. She did not. The marital problems were perhaps dissolved in grief when Malcolm, their oldest son, evidently committed suicide. The other son Stanwix had gone to sea to begin a lifetime of wandering that eventually led him to a solitary death in San Francisco in 1886.

In recent years, much to the dismay of his wife, Melville had been writing a long philosophical poem—eventually 18,000 lines and 150 cantos—based on his trip to the Holy Land. The publication of *Clarel*, a work that Melville accurately predicted was "eminently designed for failure," was privately financed by his uncle, Peter Gansevoort. Elizabeth's remark that Melville's sisters could not visit while he was writing offers an insight into the conditions in the Melville household during this period. Elizabeth continued, "If ever this dreadful *incubus* of a *book*(I call it so because it has undermined all our happiness) gets off Herman's shoulders I do hope he may be in better mental health" (*Mel. Log*, p. 747). The poem is about a religious pilgrimage taken by Clarel and a group of companions, but it actually examines the possibilities of religious faith in a century shaken by scientific discoveries and the questions raised by German Higher Criticism. Clarel's doubts, like Melville's, were not resolved, but the poem marks a quiet acceptance of self and fate. Melville's "wandering to and fro over these deserts" had ended. *Clarel* also offers a portrait of Hawthorne in Vine, one of the pilgrims. Earlier, Melville had summarized their relationship in "Monody," a poem probably written after Hawthorne's death in 1864:

> To have known him, to have loved him
>   After loneness long;
> And then to be estranged in life,
>   And neither in the wrong;
> And now for death to set his seal
>   Ease me, a little ease, my song!
>   (Poems, p. 228)

Melville retreated to the family in his final years—long his torment, but in graying years his enjoyment. With a modest inheritance from Elizabeth's family, he retired in 1885 from the Customs House to his study and the continued but unpressured writing of poetry. *John Marr and Other Sailors* was published in 1888, *Timoleon* in 1891 (both in limited editions of twenty-five copies), and *Weeds and Wildings*, his final collection, was dedicated to Elizabeth, but he died before he could see it through publication. Melville had steadily withdrawn from the literary scene in New York, although Arthur Stedman and Titus Coan, now a physician in the city, were able to form friendships with the forgotten writer, and W. Clark Russell, English author of sea novels, corresponded with him. Otherwise he had wrapped himself in silence.

When Melville died in 1891, *Billy Budd* was in manuscript, not to be published until 1924 in the early years of the Melville Revival. The *Somers* affair had again been discussed by *American Magazine* in June 1888. Perhaps the memories of the event along with various other sources of inspiration prompted Melville to expand a poem, "Billy in the Darbies," into a complex story that explored the fate of innocence in the handsome sailor Billy Budd, the nature of evil in the malevolent master-of-arms Claggart, and finally the problems that confront authority and the impossibility of human judgments in the fatherly Captain Vere who condemns the child-like Billy to death.

Billy Budd has been read as Melville's testament of reconciliation. Billy's final words—"God bless Captain Vere"—are a benediction upon his judge. The conclusion is perhaps unwarranted, for Vere is killed on his return passage in an encounter with the French ship *Athee* (*Atheist*). The book seems to affirm the mystery of human behavior and man's enigmatic motives. Man is life's central ambiguity.

In his final months Melville had marked a passage in Schopenhauer that reflected his own thoughts about fame: "the more a man belongs to posterity, in other words, to humanity in general, the more of an alien he is to his contemporaries" (*Mel. Log*, p. 832). Melville was correct: he was a writer for the ages, not for his century. This was confirmed by Melville's obituary in the *New York Times*: "There has died and been buried in this city, during the current week, at an advanced age, a man who is so little known, even by name, to the generation now in the vigor of life that only one newspaper contained an obituary account of him, and that of only three or four lines" (Sealts, *Early Lives*, p. 120).

THE LIVES

Little attention was paid to Melville's passing. Brief notices appeared in the New York and Boston newspapers, and a serialized biographical sketch in nine installments by J.E.A. Smith, an old Berkshire acquaintance, appeared in the *Pittsfield Evening Journal* (27 October 1891–25 January 1892). Arthur Stedman and Titus Coan attempted to rekindle an interest in him, Coan with an essay in the *Literary World* of Boston (19 December 1891) and Stedman with several essays and an introduction to a new edition of *Typee* (United States Book Company, 1892). A formal biography was not proposed until ten years after his death, but Frank Jewett Mather could not get the necessary financing from the Boston publishers—a measure, certainly, of Melville's popularity.

The Melville Revival began in 1917 with Carl Van Doren's reassessment of Melville's work in the *Cambridge History of American Literature*. Later at an English Department dinner at Columbia University, Van Doren asked Raymond Weaver to contribute an essay on Melville to *The Nation* to commemorate the Melville centennial. Weaver was surprised at what he found:

> being unhampered with information, I fell in with his [Van Doren's] request. I thought: "I'll read a few South Sea travel books, examine Melville's official biographies, and turn out an adequate article." The following day I visited Columbia library, to find books and books by Melville—an indecent spawning—and no "official" biographies at all. (Quoted in *Recognition*, p. viii)

Two years later, in 1921, Weaver published the first Melville biography.

Because there have been few biographies of Melville (twelve book-length studies in more than sixty years), their progression and development are easy to trace. The early biographers of the 1920s had little material to work with. Lewis Mumford complained that there was only "This journal [the 1849 *Journal*], a later one kept during his trip to the Near East, and a small sheaf of letters" (p. 118). He and others therefore relied heavily on the novels, which they read as autobiographical statements. Author and character merged together. This autobiographical and largely mythical Melville disappeared in the biographies that were published from the late 1930s to the 1950s: these biographies traced his South Sea wanderings, identified his source material, thoroughly examined his circumstances, unearthed letters—in short, they rescued him from his own fiction, surrounded him with facts, and placed him within the intellectual climate of his times. The task of "factualizing" him, as it were, was completed with the publication of Jay Leyda's *The Melville Log* and Leon Howard's *Herman Melville* in 1951, the centennial year of *Moby-Dick*. It wasn't until 1975 that Edwin Haviland Miller's *Melville* offered a psychobiographical examination to round off the external portrait that had prevailed for twenty-five years. There have been, then, two clear stages in Melville biography: the early author-character blending, and then the severing of the Siamese ligature and the factual reconstruction of the writer. Perhaps a third stage waits to be written: one that balances the factual biography of the 1950s with the inner soundings of the man, biography that utilizes a combination of approaches in what has been termed the New Scholarship.

The Melville that emerges from Raymond Weaver's pioneering biography, *Herman Melville: Mariner and Mystic* (1921), is, in part, a self-made man, the creation of his own fiction and a melodramatic figure of the failed artist defeated by the unimaginative Philistine sanity of mid-nineteenth-century America. Weaver depicts Melville as a rebel ("Devil's Advocate" is the title of the first chapter) driven eventually to despair and silence: "His whole history is the record of an attempt to escape from an inexorable and intolerable world of reality" (p. 19). Initially he escaped by writing adventure stories and later by "wrapping himself up in a vague kind of mysticism" (p. 17).

Weaver's Melville is a twice-banished Ishmael whose disillusionment "began at home" and then was completed when he was scorned by the reading public. His early bitterness is described in *Redburn*, and his vindictive presentation of his parents appears in *Pierre*—his mother, of whom Melville reportedly said, "she hated me" (p. 62), is remembered in "oral tradition" (presumably Weaver means family and friends) as "cold," "worldly," "formal," and "haughty" (p. 60). Melville escaped to the Pacific only to return to write the truth about civilization and its institutions, a naive act that led ultimately to his being rejected by the reading public. *Pierre* is an apologia of his defeat. He dared to say that the reward for virtue and truth in this world is wailing and gnashing of teeth. And the world in turn repaid Melville for his brashness. His career thereafter is aptly summarized in Weaver's final chapter titles, "The Great Refusal" and "The Long Quietus." This, in its broad outline, is the history of Melville that was generally accepted for almost two decades.

Weaver's claim that Melville's novels are a long effort toward the creation of an original character "known in life as Herman Melville" is the result of his assumption that the early novels, with the exception of *Mardi*, are "transparent chapters" (p. 133) in autobiography. Even *Moby-Dick* is used to "block in, with a considerable degree of certainty" (p. 134), Melville's whaling experience. Thus, Weaver reads the fiction as fact (in *Redburn*, for example, only the London section is questioned).

This "elevation" of fiction into history has unfortunate consequences, not the least of which is the loss of Melville the artist. Numerous errors in dating are perpetuated (Melville is thought to have sailed to Liverpool in 1837 because he is equated with the younger Redburn), and events—like Jonah—are swallowed whole. Weaver's reading of the fiction also forces him to reevaluate the Melville canon: those books that are not usable biographically are discounted; consequently, *Mardi* receives low grades, *Israel Potter* is discussed in half a page, and *The Confidence-Man* is dismissed in a peculiar sentence that is, perhaps, the key to Weaver's methodology: "published in 1857: but it was a posthumous work" (p. 348). What Weaver means is that inasmuch as Melville creates himself as a character in his own fiction, that character dies at the end of *Pierre* when Melville turns away from autobiographical fiction. Thereafter the works are "posthumous" or not self-creating. Weaver's biography ends accordingly in the year 1852; the final forty years of Melville's life are covered in only thirty-two pages.

With biographical material in short supply, Weaver is forced to dwell on the context of Melville's early adventures: histories of whaling and South Sea exploration enlarge the early years. (The biographical equivalent of filler.) Blank years in the history inevitably appear: Melville's wandering between Tahiti and Honolulu are uncharted, and the period from 1837 through 1841 compels Weaver to confess that "What he was doing and thinking and feeling must be left almost completely to surmise" (p. 113). Extensive quoting from Melville's two journals expands a biography that is remarkable for its prolonged years of silence. It is what is not known about Melville that is intriguing.

But Weaver's biography, naive in its methodology and unbalanced in its presentation, marks a beginning. *Herman Melville: Mariner and Mystic* directed the attention of the literary world to one of its forgotten authors and to *Moby-Dick*, which Weaver acclaimed as one of the world's great books. The Melville Revival was underway, rising from the depths like leviathan itself.

Melville had long been admired in England where his reputation was greater than at home. Robert Louis Stevenson mentioned him in his correspondence; W. Clark Russell praised him; Robert Buchanan proclaimed Melville to be the greatest living American novelist (but Melville's reputation was so diminished that he could not locate him in New York City); and James Billson corresponded with Melville throughout his final years. Other enthusiasts included William Morris, Henry S. Salt, who once planned to write a biography of Melville, James Barrie, who borrowed Ahab and the whale and reduced them to Captain Hook and the alligator, and D. H. Lawrence, who included *Typee* and *Moby-Dick* in his *Studies in Classic American Literature*. This interest culminated in 1926 with the publication of *Herman Melville*, a short biography for the "English Men of Letters Series," by John Freeman, British poet and essayist.

As might be expected, the Freeman biography is, in many ways, a brief rehashing of Weaver's pioneering book. Melville's history is condensed into a discussion emphasizing his early career: there are four chapters (seventy-three pages) devoted to the biography, one-fifth of which examine the years after 1851. The remainder of the book is a critical examination of the novels and the poetry. Freeman's real contribution is the study of Melville's poetry, which Weaver had ignored.

Freeman warns that, although Melville's South Pacific novels have to be read autobiographically—"the story is to be sought almost exclusively in the books" (p. 23)—caution must be exercised, for "there are frequently difficulties when an attempt is made to distinguish what is true in memory from what is true in imagination" (p. 23). Freeman also reads *Moby-Dick* and *Pierre* with greater caution than Weaver: *Moby-Dick* offers "no foothold even for [biographical] speculation" (p. 41), and *Pierre* is discredited as a gallery of family portraits, particularly of Melville's mother. "Speculative biography," he warns, "is dangerous" (p. 4).

Freeman unfortunately fails to heed his own warning, and the fiction again collapses into autobiography with embarrassing results. Freeman, for example, reads White Jacket's narrow escape from flogging and his contemplated murder of his captain as Melville's own escape, and comments that here Melville was writing "as nowhere else, his spirit's auto-biography, as painfully, as burningly, as Saint Augustine wrote his" (p. 35). It is pretty to think so, but, as Charles R. Anderson was to point out, not true. The incident was fictional, for the Log Book of the *United States* reveals that Melville kept himself off the punishments lists throughout his cruise.

In methodology, structure, and evaluation of Melville's works, the Weaver and Freeman biographies are strikingly similar. (Freeman also dismisses *The Confidence-Man* in only a few pages.) The figure of Melville that emerges from each, however, is quite different. Weaver gives us a rebel who preaches truth to a pious and hypocritical world and is banned for his audacity. Freeman presents an author of considerable imagination who invests the world with illusions and ideals only to find that reality is different; his final years are an attempt to cope with the barrenness that remained.

The last and best of the "autobiographical biographies" is Lewis Mumford's *Herman Melville* (1929). The Mumford book redresses the unbalanced structure of its predecessors: the years after 1851, particularly the New York years, are filled in (yes, there is life after *Pierre*), and the hitherto neglected texts—*Mardi, The Confidence-Man*, and the tales—are finally recognized. Mumford's biography may best be described as three books in one: an impressionistic and somewhat Freudian study, a cultural history of Melville's times in the manner of Van Wyck Brooks, and a tracking of Melville's inner development as a writer. Mumford adds few additional facts to Melville's biography and reads the early romances as personal accounts "with only the faintest disguises" (p. 109). In general he leaves factual matters as he found them. Anderson would later observe that he had found one documented fact in 150 pages of Mumford's popular Melville biography ("Romance of Scholarship," p. 263).

Mumford, however, is not as interested in spatial and temporal biography as he is in tracing Melville's intellectual and psychological development. Melville was born into a provincial, cloistered society that "finds its sources and motives within its own region" (p. 9); it was a society in a state of transformation when the author returned from the Pacific and one that would destroy itself by the end of the Civil War, replacing the "freedom . . . and local initiative" (p. 292) of Melville's youth with a strident, national materialism. This matter-of-fact culture that embraced the surfaces of life had no tolerance for Melville's "habit of questioning" the source of their verities: he "drew back the cosy hangings of Victorian parlours, and disclosed the black night outside." As an artist Melville "grappled with certain great dilemmas in man's spiritual life, and in seeking to answer them, sounded bottom" (p. 5).

Mardi "disclosed to [Melville] the nature of his own demon—that deeper other half " of Babbalanja named Azzageddi (p. 102). Babbalanja is the solid provincial who reflects the ideas of his time; Azzageddi is free and irresponsible, recognizing no conventions. Azzageddi is the other self, the unconscious who seeks to utter the truth: "All round me, my fellow-men are new grafting their vines and dwelling in flourishing arbors; while I am forever pruning mine, till it becomes but a stump. Yet in this pruning I will persist; I will not add, I will diminish; I will trim myself down to the standard of what is unchangeably true" (p. 103). *Mardi* gave Melville the courage to be an intellectual rover.

Melville's struggle after *Mardi*, as Mumford sees it, was between the conventional, social self and the hard, defiant self that arose out of Melville's deepest convictions about life. The conventional self wrote *Redburn* and *White-Jacket*. The demon wrote *Moby-Dick* ("a wicked book," Melville wrote to Hawthorne), a parable on the mystery of good and evil and the accidental malice of the universe, and "one of the first great mythologies" of the "modern world . . . its concentration upon power and dominion over nature" (p. 193). The chapter on *Moby-Dick* is, as Stanley T. Williams observed in the *Yale Review*, "Mr. Mumford at his best . . . easily the most remarkable analysis of Melville's genius at the height of its power" (p. 193).

In *Pierre* Melville attempted to arrive at the "same sort of psychological truth that he had achieved, in metaphysics, in Moby-Dick" (Mumford, p. 211); thus, he peeled off the layers of the conscious until he reached the recesses of the unconscious personality. At that point Melville found his own artistic development blocked. The fair-haired Lucy, Pierre's rejected fiancee, and the brunette Isabel, Pierre's half-sister, are the key to Mumford's analysis:

Lucy, then, may signify the naive writings of his youth, which promised him happiness, and Isabel, the mysterious child of a foreign mother, lost in an obscure youth, may stand for that darker consciousness in himself that goads him to all his most heroic efforts, that goads him and baffles him, leaving him balked and sterile, incapable of going further in literature, and yet unable to retreat to the older and safer relations with Lucy—the Lucy of Typee and Omoo. (pp. 220–21)

Timonism enclosed in the corrosive satire of *The Confidence-Man* followed. But by 1858 Melville had regained possession of himself. The Epilogue to *Clarel* indicates that he was slowly gaining peace.

Mumford's study repeats the flaws of the first biographies, reading the novels as autobiography. But Mumford hunts other game: his search is for Melville's intellectual and artistic development, and he reads the texts primarily as a record of Melville's thought. Mumford's genius leads him and the results are often brilliant. It is a book that deserves rereading, but as criticism, not strict biography.

The publication of Charles R. Anderson's *Melville in the South Seas* (1939) forced Melville scholars to reexamine the methodology of the previous biographies, for Anderson affirmed that Melville was truly an imaginative writer, creating scenes and characters *ab nihilo* and often borrowing and embellishing from sources. Anderson tells of his scholarly pursuit of Melville in "The Romance of Scholarship: Tracking Melville in the South Seas": years of research in the Library of Congress in which he discovered journals and letters from sailors on the *United States* and Muster Rolls and the Log Book from the frigate—these together with a letter from a Harvard undergraduate identifying the source of White Jacket's fall from the yard-arm persuaded Anderson that *White-Jacket* was not "all straightforward autobiography," a conclusion reinforced when Anderson examined Melville's sources for *Typee*.[6]

Anderson's *Melville in the South Seas* is limited to the three-year period from 1841 through 1844 when Melville sailed to the Pacific and wandered from the Marquesas to Honolulu and back home, the adventure that comprises *Typee*, *Omoo*, and *White-Jacket*. In abundant detail Anderson records Melville's drifting against a background that richly describes the devastating incursions of Western civilization—disease, exported Christianity, and gross displays of political power—demonstrations that could not have been lost on the impressionable young Melville.

The real value of Anderson's scholarship, however, is that it put to bed the prevailing notion of Melville as an autobiographer and enabled scholars to examine him as an artist. The affidavit of Melville's desertion of the *Acushnet* and the muster roll for the *Lucy Ann* indicate that he stayed with the Typees four weeks (much less than the stated four months in the novel), hardly enough time for him to have acquired the knowledge of the culture and customs displayed in *Typee*. Anderson's investigations revealed that Melville borrowed extensively from books on the Marquesas, including Captain David Porter's *Journal of a Cruise Made to the Pacific Ocean* (1815), "a work," Melville claimed, "which I have never happened to meet with" (p. 118; but see also Howard's suggestion that at the time Melville wrote the truth, p. 289). Other evidence indicated that certain episodes were suspect, particularly Melville's entry and escape from the valley and the cannibal practices of the tribe.[7] Melville's "residence" in Typee Valley was extremely brief, and almost all of his recorded experiences there were lived vicariously in the travel literature which he consulted upon his return. Anderson concluded that Melville could have written *Typee* without leaving home.

In *Omoo* Melville continued to rely heavily on sources. But in *White-Jacket* he displayed his mature power as a novelist. Despite his claim that he was writing "an impartial account...inventing nothing" (p. 361), Melville altered his own experiences, dramatically heightened other events, and invented or borrowed major scenes in order to appeal to a public concerned with the resolution, then in Congress, to abolish flogging in the U.S. Navy (finally passed as a proviso to the Naval Appropriation Bill in September 1850). *White-Jacket*, then, was a book designed for "some use in the world" (p. 420). Melville could no longer be viewed as a writer "of unvarnished truth," but rather as a professional writer acquainted with popular fictional forms and knowledgeable about the marketplace, who packaged his works accordingly.

An extraordinary group of graduate students were contemporaries at Yale University in the late 1940s and completed their dissertations under Stanley T. Williams. This "class"—Harrison Hayford, Merrell R. Davis, Elizabeth Foster, Walter Bezanson, Merton M. Sealts, Jr., and William H. Gilman—contributed immensely to Melville studies over the years. No contribution was more important, however, than Gilman's *Melville's Early Life and Redburn* (1951), a biographical examination of *Redburn*, previously thought to be the most autobiographically accurate of the early novels. The first half of Gilman's study examines the history of young Melville and his family within the cycles of prosperity and adversity that encompassed his first twenty-one years (the study ends where Anderson's analysis begins). Gilman is particularly helpful in describing the circumstances in which Melville matured (the curriculum at his various schools, his mother's Calvinism which was not as severe and orthodox as assumed, the Albany milieu that combined piety and materialism, the importance of the maritime profession in the Melville and Gansevoort families, the name and true sailing date of Melville's ship, the *St. Lawrence*) and in filling out the years from 1837 to 1841, one of the blank periods in Melville's biography. Gilman's portrait of Melville's mother, derived from her correspondence, corrects the image of a cold and worldly woman; instead she was "essentially a simple, domestic, and somewhat provincial woman in whom a Dutch prudence, bluntness, and reserve were softened by strong feelings of Christian charity" (p. 18). The Appendices include Melville's juvenile writings, "The Lansingburgh Fragments" and "The Philo Logos Controversy," as well as an interesting historical survey of the criticism of *Redburn*.

Gilman's major contribution is his examination of *Redburn* as a factual record in the chapter "Art and Autobiography." Gilman concludes that Melville fashioned in his young hero a satiric, more naive, slighter and younger version of himself, and, for the most part, the events of the journey—the suicide, Jackson's death, and the whole of the voyage—were total fabrications. *Redburn* was modeled after the tradition of the greenhorn sailor. Melville may have borrowed incidents from the popular literature of the day, "pages of magazines, newspapers, and obscure books, perhaps dime novels" (p. 204). Gilman advises that *Redburn* should be read as art rather than history: "It has been fashionable for some time to consider his book [*Redburn*] autobiography with elements of romance. It is more nearly correct to call it a romance with elements of autobiography" (p. 204).

In the following year Merrell R. Davis' *Melville's Mardi: A Chartless Voyage*(1952), an extensive examination of Melville's third book, was published. The first half traces Melville's life as an author during the years 1844 through 1848, beginning with his return from the Pacific and the publication of his early novels, and concluding with an examination of his literary relationship with friends and publishers, his intellectual growth during this time, and his extensive reading—all manifest in his ever-changing *Mardi*, a book that incorporated three distinct stages of composition: "The literary voyage which Melville made in *Mardi* and which he described both in letters to his publishers and in the "Sailing On" passage of that book was a chartless voyage. It began with factual narration, proceeded after alterations and repairs through the world of poetry and romance, and finally entered the world of mind" (p. 194). *Mardi* leaves much to be desired as art, but as Davis notes, it marks "a significant growth in an author who came to acknowledge an ambition to write 'such things as the Great Publisher of Mankind ordained ages before he published "The World" ' " (p. 200). *Melville's Mardi* concludes with an analysis of the three sections of the novel ("The Narrative Beginning," "The Romantic Interlude," and "The Travelogue-Satire"), a chapter on the characters and their quest, and a final interpretative section.

The autobiographical theory had tumbled and like Humpty-Dumpty was beyond repair. But Melville's history still needed "facts," and 1951, the centennial of *Moby-Dick* and *anno mirabilis* in Melville studies, saw the publication, in addition to Gilman's biography, of Jay Leyda's *The Melville Log* in two volumes and Leon Howard's *Herman Melville: A Biography*. The two men had met at the Huntington Library in 1945 at the beginning of Leyda's search. Howard, then teaching at U.C.L.A., had encouraged and helped Leyda and in 1947 committed himself to writing a narrative biography, using the information he, Leyda, and others could glean, to be published simultaneously with *The Log*. In his "Introduction" to *The Log*, Leyda described the book as a result of a pooling of information about Melville. Leyda had offered to share information with all who would toss their bits into the pool—and toss they did: Howard, Hayford, Davis, Gilman, Bezanson, Sealts, Wilson Heflin, and others contributed so that "no one person can now claim the making of this book."[8]

The Melville Log contains over five thousand entries, eight hundred pages of quotations from letters, diaries, newspaper clippings, crew lists, business documents, Melville's juvenilia and marginalia, excerpts from his books and two journals, and reviews of his books. Were it not for the bonfires that Melville and, later on, his daughter Elizabeth made of the family letters, *The Log* would be more complete and revealing. The daughter, for example, burned a shoe box full of letters (some of them love letters) from her father to her mother and only one remains. *The Log* places the material in chronological order, juxtaposing matters of large and small importance, with no obvious or apparent exclusion, emphasis, or interpretation—a universalist's heaven of information. Leyda explains his purpose in the "Introduction":

to give each reader the opportunity to be his own biographer of Herman Melville, by providing him with the largest possible quantity of materials to build his own approach to this complex figure. The only way I knew to do this was to put together everything that could be known about this life, to bring the reader close to Melville's progress through as many of his days as could be restored, so that the reader may watch him as he works, sees, reacts, worries—to make those seventy-two years, from 1819 to 1891, and a portion of the America they were lived in, in Henry James's word, *visitable*. (p. xi)

Leyda's documentary chronology of Melville's life is not, in the strict sense, a biography, but rather a "factual reconstruction" modeled after the type "employed by Russian scholars for the study of several of their writers and composers" (p. xi), an indispensable foundation for future biographers and scholars. *The Melville Log* with its compendium of facts fills in the arid spaces in Melville's history and strikes through the myths that surrounded him. It offers for the first time a full and relatively complete record of Melville's life.

Howard's biography complements *The Log:* as Howard explains, *The Log* "provides both the source material and the documentation" (p. vii), and even where more complete evidence was used, the biography was circumstantially allusive to *The Log* so that the basic source of information could be readily located. Howard, however, was able to draw inferences and show causal relationships denied to the documentary form. With the scholarship of the burgeoning school of Melville scholars available to him, Howard was able to produce a history of Melville's life that has not been surpassed. Howard's biography offers not only a balanced account of Melville's life (half the book deals with the years after *Pierre*), but also a brilliant exposition of Melville's development as an artist and a thinker.

The sole departure from conventional biography, as Howard notes, is "in the amount of attention paid to the writing of Melville's books" and in dealing "with the observable evidence of their growth" (p. viii). Howard meticulously traces Melville's reading and his use of sources through the first two novels to *Mardi*, where Melville's interests, now more philosophical, resulted in "speculative fancies, rhetorical exercises for their own sake, and whimsical representation of conflicting points of view" (p. 117) as Melville moved abruptly from a realistic story into allegory (see also Davis, *Chartless Voyage*). The compositional history of *Mardi*, of which Richard Brodhead commented, "having begun one sort of book [Melville] is often willing to throw that over in the middle and pursue an entirely new direction" (pp. 124–25), was repeated again with *Moby-Dick*. In his famous chapter, "Second Growth," Howard traces the composition of the novel, showing how Melville extensively revised a romantic whaling voyage into a dramatic struggle in which a superior intellect [Ahab] who practices "dark and evil necromancy" attempts to divert Nature from her course and control the hearts of men. The composition is an example of the artistic struggle repeated in many of Melville's novels between a calculated plan and the separate organic growth of the story.

Howard also traces Melville's philosophic quest for certainty. *Typee* and *Omoo* were powered simply by what Duyckinck called a "sailor's grudge" (p. 101) against the missionaries and the world's pretensions. In *Mardi* Melville revealed a personal conflict: "When he indulged in abstract thought, he was capable of positive belief in an ideal ... when he looked at the everyday realities of the world, he was inclined toward criticism, skepticism, and even cynicism" (p. 126). This struggle between the will to believe and the tendency to doubt supplied the emotional tension for *Moby-Dick* and *Pierre*; in *The Confidence-Man* Melville's skepticism turned to cynicism. A resolution of sorts was reached in *Clarel*: "There was no absolute certainty anywhere for a whole man. He could only be what he was meant to be" (p. 306).

For all its virtues, and they are bountiful, the Howard biography leaves the inner Melville untouched. Melville's artistic and intellectual life—the stated focus of the biography—is ably explored. The reader is given a complete view of the historical Melville: he knows Melville's daily whereabouts, his compositional habits, his contracts with publishers, his reading, his love of good conversation, all this and much more. But the soul of the man is missing. Melville as husband and father, rumors of the family's fears of Herman's insanity in the period after 1851, other tales of irascibility, drunkenness, intellectual bullying of his wife [recently enhanced by the discovery that Elizabeth considered the possibility of separation from her husband in 1867 (Kring and Carey)], these are ignored or attributed to Elizabeth's habit of translating her frustrations into concerns about her husband's health. But as Howard later admitted, "I never had any particular 'sense' of Melville and his family relationships" (Yannella and Parker, p. 23). Howard stays with the given facts; such is the strength and the limitation of this, the best of the Melville biographies.

In reviewing *The Melville Log*, Richard Chase complained that with the accumulation of factual material Melville studies had entered a period of "Know-Nothingism." He preferred and admired Newton Arvin's biography, *Herman Melville* in the American Men of Letters Series (1950):

> Melville criticism, since Mr. Newton Arvin's admirable book of two years ago, has appeared eager to content itself with any kind of approach which does not involve judgment or ideas. And in general there has been no period in the last forty years when so many critics, some of whom used to be alert and adventurous, have succumbed to a morose and prudential anti-intellectualism and have grown resentful and suspicious of any writer who makes a judgment or is interested in ideas. (pp. 478–79)

History proved Chase wrong, for Arvin's book was replaced "almost immediately" by Howard's biography (Milder, p. 173). But Chase raises an interesting question: What kind of biographies should we have? He obviously prefers biographies of ideas and judgments, that is to say, criticism and interpretation. Arvin offers both, and at times, especially in his discussion of *Moby-Dick*, he does so brilliantly (although the reader must have a tolerance for his Freudian criticism). Arvin's evaluation of Melville's career is reminiscent of the early biographers: much of the work after *Moby-Dick* is "on a lower level . . . that is lower by several wide degrees" (p. 218). Similarly, his reading of the early novels is ambiguously autobiographical: in real life the sailor Jackson on the *St. Lawrence* did not die, "but one has no difficulty in imagining that the real Jackson was as ferocious a bully" (p. 40); the amputation scene in *White-Jacket* "never took place in the world of physical action. But this does not mean it never took place in any sense" (p. 116)—whatever that means.

Arvin's biography fails as biography because he tends to divorce the books from Melville's life and offers too few facts. He states, for example, that Melville's father died because of anxiety about his business debts, which undoubtedly was a factor, but he doesn't mention that his final illness was brought on by overexposure to cold; the reader learns that Melville's older brother then became the father's successor at the family fur store without having been told that the family owned a fur store. Later Arvin discusses the first five novels without mentioning the biography; when he covers the years between 1847 and 1850, he does so in two pages and draws no connection between the failure of *Mardi* and the pressing necessity that drove Melville to write *Redburn* and *White-*

Jacket during the same summer. And Arvin's interpretations are at times questionable: for example, Melville's alleged statement that his mother hated him is twisted to mean that "Melville, on one side of his nature, hated his mother" (p. 30).

The chapter on *Moby-Dick*, "The Whale," offers an interesting evaluation of Melville's talent ("he was hardly an 'inventive writer' at all... he should rather be described... as an essentially convertive or transmutative poet" [p. 144]) and a lengthy but outstanding analysis of the novel, touching on the sources, structure, rhythms, imagery, and language, closing with a four-fold interpretation of the book (literal, psychological, moral, and mythical). Arvin's psychological reading summarizes the significant themes that he finds in Melville's life: the lure of the South Pacific, the destructive love of the mother, and Melville's inability to enjoy a satisfactory heterosexual relationship.

In his role of archetypal parent, in fact, Moby Dick is the object of an excessive and eventually crippling love, as Maria Melville was for her son; and the consequence is the vital injury symbolized by the loss of Ahab's leg, an injury to the capacity for heterosexual love. Both Ahab and Ishmael suffer in this way, but Ahab far the more terribly of the two. Ishmael, by somehow preserving a complexity of feeling toward the White Whale, has preserved also his capacity for selfless love even though it is directed toward... a member of his own sex, Queequeg, who embodies both the grandeur and limitations of the primitive, the prerational, the instinctive. (p. 174)

The intimate view of Melville, conspicuously absent in the other biographies, is supplied by the author's oldest granddaughter Eleanor Melville Metcalf in *Herman Melville: Cycle and Epicycle* (1953). Her purpose is to evoke a sense of Melville's life within the setting of family and friends by drawing on a hoard of letters (some from Melville and others to him or that mention him), diaries, journals, and reminiscences. The documents present Melville as a scion of an old and noble American family, a secretive and protective clan, with the Gansevoorts, the Shaws, the Lansings, and the DeWolfs in the background, and depict him in his various roles as husband, father, cousin, nephew, and friend. But the charm of the book and its unique value come from the personal recollection of Mrs. Metcalf and her retelling of family stories. Distinct impressions of Melville are scattered throughout its pages: how the family suffered from Melville's "bursts of nervous anger and attacks of morose conscience" (p. 159); the children's memories of bread and tea for supper because their father had bought a book or an object of art that the family could not afford; recollections of a father who gave as birthday presents books that he wanted to read; a man who suffered from "desperate irascibility" (p. 215) and took to the solace of brandy, who roused a daughter at 2 A.M. to read proof for *Clarel*, but who was remembered by his granddaughter (a nine-year old at Melville's death) as a gracious and sensitive old man.

Metcalf's biography (in its time, the fullest reprinting of Melville's letters) was supplanted by the publication in 1960 of *The Letters of Herman Melville*, edited by Merrell R. Davis and William H. Gilman, a collection of 271 known letters. Nothing however can replace the warmth and immediacy of Mrs. Metcalf's memories, as her final recollection of her grandfather illustrates:

> To go back for a moment to that "paper-piled table" in Melville's room at Twenty-sixth Street: on it stood an inclined plane that for lack of more accurate designation one must call "desk"; for though it had a pebbled green-paper surface, it had no cavity for inkwell, no groove for pen and pencil, no drawer for papers, like the little portable desks that were cherished as heirlooms in the late nineteenth century. Rather, it was open underneath; and pasted on one side wall, well out of sight, was a printed slip of paper that read simply, "Keep true to the dreams of thy youth." If we but knew what these dreams were! (pp. 283–84)

Merton M. Sealts, Jr.'s *Melville as Lecturer* (1957) completes the factual biographies of the 1950s by filling in the period from 1857 to 1860 when Melville toured the lecture circuit. Sealts gives a general outline of the lectures, an account of Melville's problems with his voice and platform manner (his articulation was slightly indistinct, and he lacked animation), traces his reception through existing newspaper reports, the majority of which were favorable, and lists Melville's annual income (he received only $110 for three engagements in his last season). In the back of the volume Sealts reconstructs the three lectures from a collation of newspaper reports. Sealts observes that the lectures reveal a Melville who turned his back on the present and the prevalent notion of progress; the best life had to offer "appeared to be receding inevitably into the past" (p. 122). The lectures, then, presaged the older Melville, who in the years after 1860, would turn almost exclusively to the past for his subject matter.

In the mid-1970's, the next and most recent Melville biographies were published: Edwin Haviland Miller's *Herman Melville: A Biography* and Merton M. Sealts, Jr.'s *The Early Lives of Melville: Nineteenth-Century Biographical Sketches and Their Authors*. Both in their way extend the search that began with Raymond Weaver in 1923: Miller by examining the interior, and Sealts by returning to the origins.

Charles N. Watson, Jr., seemed to anticipate Miller's biography when he noted that Leon Howard had "created a Melville of largely outer, rather than inner experience": "In his reluctance to 'psychologize,' Howard made Melville seem almost too 'normal,' and as a result the more volatile and even frightening depths of his nature were not sounded. A protean writer needs a protean biographer, one who can combine sound scholarship with psychological insight" ("Melville's Fiction," p. 297).

Miller's book opens *in medias res* on 5 August 1850 when Melville met Hawthorne and began a relationship that dramatically re-created patterns already established in Melville's fiction. Miller contends that the central or core myth in Melville's work is the Biblical Ishmael story that tells of the child Ishmael sent by his father Abraham into the desert along with his mother Hagar—banished to placate the will of Sarah, the cold and tyrannical wife of Abraham, and supplanted by his half-brother and the family favorite Isaac. In Melville's self-dramatization, he plays the role of Ishmael, alone in a sharkish world. The myth originates in Melville's sense of self and family: Gansevoort, the older brother, plays the part of Isaac, the favorite son; Maria Melville is both the disapproving Sarah and Hagar, the potential comforter; and it is the father Allan Melvill whose approval he seeks. Melville's father died when he was twelve; consequently, his fiction depicts his young protagonists seeking "paternal companionship" in a male whose Apollonian beauty bears a resemblance to his father. Melville found the friend and surrogate-father in Hawthorne, and the friendship prompted the most creative period in Melville's life. Finally, Melville approached Hawthorne (in what sense remains vague), and the older writer hurriedly left the Berkshires. Thereafter the two men haunt each other's writings. Miller's is the fullest exposition of the relationship between the two men, but readers interested in the subject should also consult works by Randall Stewart, Henry A. Murray, Harrison Hayford, Sidney P. Moss, and Charles N. Watson listed in the bibliography.

Miller's central myth, so painstakingly established, is frequently left behind or irrelevant when Miller discusses the individual works. *Typee*, for example, is presented as a story of "rebirth," a young man seeking to be completely sheltered by his parents; *Omoo* is passed over; *Mardi*, despite the quest, the interminable conversations, and the symbolism, is really about the re-creation of a family; in *Redburn*, where the myth is most applicable, it is ignored; and *White-Jacket* is read as an initiation story. (All the early novels are reduced to aborted rites of passage; only in *White-Jacket* is it successful.)

On the other hand, in his exposition of *Moby-Dick*, Miller brilliantly discusses the contrasting values suggested in the voices of Ishmael and Ahab (both are Ishmaels in a crippling universe), and he plumbs the depths of despair that Melville expressed in *Pierre*, a book that is really about writing a book. Pierre's fateful decision to support Isabel, whom Miller identifies with the departed Hawthorne, and to leave Lucy and his mother offers a penetrating glimpse into Melville's family situation:

It is no wonder that the book made him "mad." Upstairs he wrote of parricide, incestuous bonds, sexual anxieties, and fear of insanity. Downstairs Maria Gansevoort Melville sat in the parlor, with his wife, the daughter of Allan Melvill's childhood friend. In his study Melville expressed his dreams of taking his revenge upon his father, killing his mother, destroying a sister-wife and his betrothed. In the parlor two "toddlers" he fathered had to refrain from noisy outbursts which would disturb him, while he vented his destructive fantasies and verbalized his death fascination. After killing off Mrs. Glendenning, Melville had to dine with Maria Gansevoort Melville. Pierre kills the Apollo figure, Glendenning Stanly, whose name resembles Stanwix Melville, the recently arrived toddler. Glendenning Stanly also recalls the rival of his youth, Gansevoort Melville. (p. 233)

Melville's family, it is speculated, worried that he was upstairs mixing fiction with family history, and that the readers might not be able to tell the difference. They may have had reason to worry, for Melville may have learned of his father's having an illegitimate daughter and had written the scandal into the plot of *Pierre* alongside the recognizable family laundry (see Emmers).

Miller's biography received harsh reviews from Melville scholars who accused him of ignoring hard facts and scholarship—especially when they didn't fit his argument—and of distorting events. Robert Milder argues in "Melville and His Biographers" that Miller resolves "manifest content into latent content, so that all cognitive meaning becomes an elaborate disguise for a work's 'real' meaning" (p. 177). Actually, Miller derives his central myth from Melville's family situation and imposes it on the novels, but the myth doesn't travel well. And in reading the books, Miller is too often engaged in Freudian symbol-hunting, leaving both the myth and the ideas that inform the works behind. All this is unfortunate, for it masks the fact that Miller's reading of "Hawthorne and His *Mosses*" and of Melville's letters to Hawthorne, his explication of *Moby-Dick, Pierre,* and *Clarel,* and his discussion of Melville and his family are sensitive and deserve our attention.

Merton M. Sealts, Jr.'s, *The Early Lives of Melville* returns to the biographical sketches of the nineteenth century. The book is divided into two parts: the first surveys the biographies from 1850 to 1890, offering brief histories of the biographers; and the second reprints the documents—four contemporary essays from literary encyclopaedias; seven retrospective essays by Arthur Stedman, Melville's literary executor, Titus Coan, and J.E.A. Smith. Three family reminiscences by his wife and two of his granddaughters conclude the book.

The encyclopaedia entries reiterate the assessment of Melville in his own lifetime, praising the South Sea adventures and dismissing his later books. The Duyckincks' *Cyclopaedia of American Literature* (1855) judges *Pierre* to be a "literary mistake" in which Melville "was off the track of his true genius" (p. 94). J.E.A. Smith's portrait of Melville as a boon companion who loved the Berkshires ("a hospitable and courteous host;

a pleasant and true friend; a gentleman of graceful and dignified manner" [p. 138]) altogether misses the dark years after the failure of *Moby-Dick*. Coan's brief sketch perpetuates the notion of the later Melville who "shut himself up as a cloistered thinker and poet" (p. 119). Stedman's selections repeat the literary judgment of his day, that Melville was an autobiographical writer who failed miserably when he attempted "creative romances" or engaged in philosophical speculation. *Typee* was his most artistic work, and with "the completion of 'Moby-Dick' in 1851 his important literary work was practically ended" (p. 110). The real contribution of *Early Lives* is to give "a cumulative portrait of Melville in his final years as a gray, stalwart figure, proud and withdrawn, prey to 'moods and occasional tempers' (as one granddaughter reminisced), and profoundly alone" (Milder, p. 171).

On 28 February 1906, Stedman wrote to H.S. Salt concerning a possible biography of Melville: "—If I meditated a life of Melville, it passed out of my mind long ago. . . . As I look back, it seems to me that there would be little to tell outside of his books. After they petered out, he made his life a merely mechanical affair, you remember, & shut himself away from all events and associations. I don't believe a life would be worthwhile" (*Early Lives*, p. 58). Critical opinion of Melville has changed profoundly since then. Biographers have thought the "fiery hunt" worthwhile. They have pursued Melville through his books, across the South Seas, through ships' logs, crew lists, letters, journals, and tracked him from archives to trunks in attics and basements. And the hunt continues.

Much still needs to be done. Jay Leyda is revising *The Melville Log* to include the discoveries of the last thirty-five years (some of which are to be found in the 1969 supplement). Mysteries surrounding Melville and his family continue to escape resolution: there are still blank periods in Melville's youth; his marital problems are fascinating, particularly in the light of family rumors; Malcolm's suicide and Stanwix's failure are unexplained and inextricably linked with their father; the family's financial status from 1850 to the mid–1860s begs for a thorough examination; the years after *Pierre* are relatively obscure, particularly the reclusive New York period and Melville's increasing isolation. To my mind, the effect of the failure of *Moby-Dick* on the remainder of Melville's writing has not been explained satisfactorily. The biography of Melville—one that examines the inner as well as the outer man, that intelligently considers the cognitive as well as the psychological content of the works, that is knowledgeable of previous scholarship but not pedantic or cautious—that biography remains to be written. A major figure needs a new biography for each new generation. Until then the Howard biography will continue to serve.

There have been reports, as each biography was published, that Melville had been sighted and cornered. But the inner man still eludes us.

We cannot say that we yet know Melville, although we know infinitely more about him than we did fifty years ago. And so the hunt continues. Future Melville scholars will implore, in the words of Samuel Rosenberg, "Come out Herman Melville, Wherever You Are" (p. 177). But will he show more of himself ?

NOTES

1. There are several excellent brief summaries of Melville's life and career. The best may be Hennig Cohen's "Melville" in *Antebellum Writers in New York and the South* (1979), and Leon Howard's 1961 pamphlet *Herman Melville*. More recent biographical sketches are John Updike's *New Yorker* essay "Melville's Withdrawal" (1982) and Hershel Parker's introduction in the *Norton Anthology of American Literature* (1979). Warner Berthoff covers Melville's career from 1846 to 1856 in the first two chapters of *The Example of Melville* (1972). The Dutch patrician background of Melville's mother's family is traced by Alice P. Kenney in *The Gansevoorts of Albany* (1969; pp. 214–28 are devoted to Melville).

2. Hershel Parker discusses Gansevoort's efforts on behalf of his brother and the relationship between the two in "Gansevoort Melville's 1846 London Journal" (1965). See also Leyda, "An Albany Journal of Gansevoort Melville" (1950) and Parker, "Gansevoort Melville's Role in the Campaign of 1844" (1965).

3. Hershel Parker in "Contract: *Pierre* by Herman Melville," *Proof* 5 (1977), 27–44, also contends that, in addition to the scathing reviews of *Moby-Dick*, Melville was also hurt by the contract negotiations with the Harpers which were settled on less than favorable terms than before. Thereafter, according to Parker, the conception of the book changed, and it was considerably enlarged.

4. This and other attempts by Melville to secure a government position are discussed by Harrison Hayford and Merrell R. Davis in "Herman Melville as Office-Seeker" (1949).

5. For a complete record of when Melville's tales were written, submitted, and published, see Sealts, "The Chronology of Melville's Short Fiction, 1853–56" (1980). A somewhat revised version appears in his Historical Note to the NN edition of *The Piazza Tales and Other Prose Pieces*.

6. Anderson also published *Journal of a Cruise to the Pacific Ocean, 1842–44, in the "Frigate United States." With Notes on Herman Melville.* Two other scholarly sleuths also tracking Melville throughout the South Pacific were Robert S. Forsythe, ("Herman Melville in the Marquesas" and "Herman Melville in Tahiti") and Clarence Gohdes, ("Gossip about Melville in the South Seas"). The history, as we currently have it, was filled in by the efforts of Leyda, Howard, Heflin, Hayford, and others.

7. William Gilman notes that when Mary L.D. Ferris submitted her article "Herman Melville" to Melville's wife for correction, "the chief correction was that 'Mrs. Melville would not have been willing to call his [Melville's] old Typee entertainers "man-devouring," as he had stated that whatever might have been his suspicions, he never had any evidence that it was the custom of the tribe' " (*Melville's Early Life and Redburn*, 1951, p. 343).

8. See Howard's account of his meeting and collaboration with Leyda in "The Case of the Left-Out Letter" in his *Mysteries and Manuscripts* (1976, pp. 17–26).

WORKS CITED

Anderson, Carl L. "The Minister's Advice to Elizabeth Melville." *Melville Society Extracts* No. 54 (May 1983): 10–12.

Anderson, Charles R., ed. *Journal of a Cruise to the Pacific Ocean, 1842–1844, in the Frigate United States; Notes on Herman Melville.* Durham, N.C.: Duke University Press, 1937.

———. *Melville in the South Seas.* New York: Columbia University Press, 1939.

———. "The Romance of Scholarship: Tracking Melville in the South Seas." *Colophon* 3 (Spring 1938): 259–79.

Arvin, Newton. *Herman Melville.* New York: William Sloan Associates, 1950.

Berthoff, Warner. *The Example of Melville.* Princeton, N.J.: Princeton University Press, 1962.

Brodhead, Richard H. *Hawthorne, Melville, and the Novel.* Chicago: University of Chicago Press, 1976.

Charvat, William. "Melville and the Common Reader." *Studies in Bibliography* 12 (1959): 41–57; rpt. *The Profession of Authorship in America, 1800–1870: The Papers of William Charvat.* Ed. Matthew Bruccoli. Columbus: Ohio State University Press, 1968, pp. 262–82.

———. "Melville's Income." *American Literature* 15 (November 1943): 251–61; rpt. *The Profession of Authorship in America, 1800–1870: The Papers of William Charvat.* Ed. Matthew Bruccoli. Columbus: Ohio State University Press, 1968, pp. 204–61.

Chase, Richard. "The Real Melville?" *Nation* (1 December 1951): 478–79.

Cohen, Hennig. "Melville." In *Antebellum Writers in New York and the South. Dictionary of Literary Biography.* Vol. 3. Ed. Joel Myerson. Detroit: Gale Research Co., 1979, pp. 221–45.

Davis, Merrell R. *Melville's Mardi: A Chartless Voyage.* New Haven, Conn.: Yale University Press, 1952.

———. "Melville's Midwestern Lecture Tour, 1859." *Philological Quarterly* 20 (January 1941): 46–57.

De Marco, John, and Carolyn De Marco. "Finding the New Melville Papers." *Melville Society Extracts* No. 56 (November 1983): 1–3.

Doenges, Richard C. "The Blizzard and Tulips of '88: Clues for Dating Melville." *Melville Society Extracts* No. 56 (November 1983): 11–12.

Emmers, Amy Puett. "Melville's Closet Skeleton: A New Letter about the Illegitimacy Incident in *Pierre.*" *Studies in the American Renaissance 1977.* Boston: Twayne, 1978, pp. 339–43.

Engel, Leonard. "Melville and the Young American Movement." *Connecticut Review* 4 (April 1971): 91–101.

Ferris, Mary L. D. "Herman Melville." *Bulletin of the Society of American Authors* 6 (Summer 1901): 289–93.

Forsythe, Robert S. "Herman Melville in the Marquesas." *Philological Quarterly* 15 (January 1936): 1–15.

―――. "Herman Melville in Tahiti." *Philological Quarterly* 16 (October 1937): 344–57.

―――. "More upon Herman Melville in Tahiti." *Philological Quarterly* 17 (January 1938): 1–17.

Freeman, John. *Herman Melville*. London and New York: Macmillan Co., 1926.

Garner, Stanton. "Melville's Scout Toward Aldie." *Melville Society Extracts* No. 51 (September 1982): 5–16; No. 52 (November 1982): 1–14.

Gilman, William H. *Melville's Early Life and Redburn*. New York: New York University Press, 1951.

―――. "Melville's Liverpool Trip." *Modern Language Notes* 60 (December 1946): 543–47.

Gohdes, Clarence. "Gossip About Melville in the South Seas." *New England Quarterly* 10 (September 1937): 529–31.

Hayford, Harrison. "Melville and Hawthorne: A Biographical and Critical Study." PhD. Diss., Yale University, 1945. [*Mel. Diss.*, #24.]

―――. and Merrell R. Davis. "Herman Melville as Office-Seeker." *Modern Language Quarterly* 10 (June and September, 1949): 168–83, 377–88.

―――. "Melville's Freudian Slip." *American Literature* 30 (1958): 366–68.

Heflin, Wilson L. "Melville's Third Whaler." *Modern Language Notes* 64 (April 1949): 241–45.

Hillway, Tyrus. *Herman Melville.* New York: Twayne, 1963.

Howard, Leon. "The Case of the Left-Out Letter." In *Mysteries and Manuscripts*. Albuquerque, N.M.: By the author, 1976.

―――. "The Case of the Missing Whaler." *Manuscripts* 12 (Fall 1960): 3–9.

―――. *Herman Melville*. University of Minnesota Pamphlets on American Authors, No. 13. Minneapolis: University of Minnesota Press, 1961; rpt. *American Writers: A Collection of Literary Biographies*. Vol. 3. Ed. Leonard Unger. New York: Scribner's, 1974, pp. 74–98.

―――. *Herman Melville: A Biography*. Berkeley: University of California Press, 1951.

―――. "Historical Note." *Typee*. Ed. Harrison Hayford, Hershel Parker, and G. Thomas Tanselle. Vol. 1. Evanston and Chicago, Ill.: Northwestern University Press and The Newberry Library, 1968.

Kennedy, Joyce Deveau, and Fredrick James Kennedy. "Elizabeth and Herman." *Melville Society Extracts* No. 33 (February 1978): 4–12; No. 34 (1978): 3–8.

Kenney, Alice P. *The Gansevoorts of Albany: Dutch Patricians in the Upper Hudson Valley*. Syracuse, N.Y.: Syracuse University Press, 1969.

Kring, Walter D., and Jonathan S. Carey. "Two Discoveries Concerning Herman Melville." *Proceedings of the Massachusetts Historical Society* 87 (1975): 137–41, rpt. in Yannella and Parker.

Lawrence, D. H. *Studies in Classic American Literature*. New York: Thomas Seltzer, Inc., 1923.

Lueders, E. G. "The Melville-Hawthorne Relationship in *Pierre* and *The Blithedale Romance*." *Western Humanities Review* 4 (Autumn 1950): 323–34.

Lewis, R.W.B. *Trials of the Word: Essays in American Literature and the Humanistic Tradition*. New Haven, Conn.: Yale University Press, 1965.

Leyda, Jay. "An Albany Journal of Gansevoort Melville." *Boston Public Library Quarterly* 2 (October 1950): 327–47.

———. "The Army of the Potomac Entertains a Poet." *Art and Action: Twice A Year* 16 (1948): 259–72.

MacDougall, Alma A. "The Chronology of *The Confidence-Man* and 'Benito Cereno': Redating Two 1855 Curtis and Melville Letters." *Melville Society Extracts* No. 53 (February 1983): 3–6.

McNeilly, Dorothy V.B.D.R. "The Melvilles and Mrs. Ferris." *Melville Society Extracts* No. 28 (November 1976): 1–9.

Mansfield, Luther S. "Glimpses of Herman Melville's Life in Pittsfield, 1850–51: Some Unpublished Letters of Evert A. Duyckinck." *American Literature* 9 (March 1937): 26–48.

Metcalf, Eleanor Melville. *Herman Melville: Cycle and Epicycle.* Cambridge, Mass.: Harvard University Press, 1953.

Milder, Robert. "Melville and His Biographers." *ESQ* 22 (Third Quarter 1976): 169–82.

Miller, Edwin Haviland. *Herman Melville: A Biography.* New York: Braziller, 1975.

Moss, Sidney P. "Hawthorne and Melville: An Inquiry into Their Art and the Mystery of Their Friendship." In *Literary Monographs.* Vol. 7. Ed. Eric Rothstein and Joseph Anthony Wittreich. Madison: University of Wisconsin Press, 1975, pp. 47–84.

Mumford, Lewis. *Herman Melville.* New York: Harcourt, Brace & Co., 1929.

Murray, Henry A., ed. *Pierre.* New York: Hendricks House, 1949, pp. xiii–ciii.

Neumeier, Charles, and Donald Yannella. "The Melvilles' House on East 26th Street." *Melville Society Extracts* No. 47 (September 1981): 6–8.

Osborne, Frances Thomas. "Herman Melville Through a Child's Eyes." *Bulletin of the New York Public Library* 69 (December 1965): 655–60.

Paltsits, Victor Hugo, ed. *Family Correspondence of Herman Melville, 1830–1904: In the Gansevoort-Lansing Collection.* New York: New York Public Library, 1929.

Parker, Hershel. "Contract: *Pierre* by Herman Melville." *Proof* 5 (1977): 27–44.

———. "Introduction to American Literature: 1820–1865" *Norton Anthology of American Literature.* Vol. 1. New York: W. W. Norton, 1979, pp. 2032–44.

———, ed. "Gansevoort Melville's 1846 London Journal." *Bulletin of the New York Public Library* 69 (December 1965): 633–54; 70 (January and February 1966): 36–49, 113–31.

———. "Gansevoort Melville's Role in the Campaign of 1844." *New York Historical Society Quarterly* 49 (April 1965): 143–73.

———. "Why *Pierre* Went Wrong." *Studies in the Novel* 8 (Spring 1976): 7–23.

Rosenberg, Samuel. "Come Out Herman Melville, Wherever You Are! (The Man Who Turned to Stone)." *The Confessions of a Trivialist.* Baltimore: Penguin Books, 1972, pp. 177–219.

Runden, John P. "Columbia Grammar School: An Overlooked Year in the Lives of Gansevoort and Herman Melville." *Melville Society Extracts* No. 46 (May 1981): 1–3.

———. "Old School Ties: Melville, the Columbia Grammar School, and the New Yorkers." *Melville Society Extracts* No. 55 (September 1983): 1–5.

Sealts, Merton M., Jr. "Additions to *Early Lives.*" *Melville Society Extracts* No. 28 (November 1976): 11–13.

———. "The Chronology of Melville's Short Fiction, 1853–56." *Harvard Library*

Bulletin 28 (October 1980): 391–403; Rpt. in *Pursuing Melville, 1940–1980.* Madison: University of Wisconsin Press, 1982, pp. 221–31.

————. *The Early Lives of Melville: Nineteenth-Century Biographical Sketches and Their Authors.* Madison: University of Wisconsin Press, 1974.

————. "Historical Note." In *The Piazza Tales and Other Prose Pieces, 1837–1860.* Ed. Harrison Hayford, Hershel Parker, and G. Thomas Tanelle. Evanston and Chicago: Northwestern University Press and The Newberry Library, 1986.

————. "Mary L. D. Ferris and the Melvilles." *Melville Society Extracts* No. 28 (November 1976): 10–11.

————. *Melville as Lecturer.* Cambridge, Mass.: Harvard University Press, 1957.

Shneidman, Edwin S. "The Deaths of Herman Melville." In *Melville and Hawthorne in the Berkshires.* Ed. Howard P. Vincent. Kent, Ohio: Kent State University Press, 1968, pp. 118–43.

Stewart, Randall. "Melville and Hawthorne." *South Atlantic Quarterly* 51 (July 1952): 436–46.

Tanselle, G. Thomas. "Herman Melville's Visit to Galena in 1840." *Journal of Illinois State Historical Society* 53 (Winter 1960): 376–88.

————. "The Sales of Melville's Books." *Harvard Library Bulletin* 18 (April 1969): 195–215.

Thorp, Willard. "Herman Melville's Silent Years." *University Review* 3 (Summer 1937): 254–62.

Titus, David K. "Herman Melville at the Albany Academy." *Melville Society Extracts* No. 42 (May 1980): 1, 4–10.

Updike, John. "Melville's Withdrawal." *New Yorker* (10 May 1982), pp. 120–47.

Watson, Charles N., Jr. "The Estrangement of Hawthorne and Melville." *New England Quarterly* 46 (September 1973): 380–402.

————. "Melville's Fiction in the Early 1970's." *ESQ* 20 (Fourth Quarter 1974): 291–97.

Weaver, Raymond M. *Herman Melville: Mariner and Mystic.* New York: George H. Doran, 1921.

Williams, Stanley T. "Victorian Americans." *Yale Review* 19 (September 1929): 191–93.

Wilson, James C. The Hawthorne-Melville Relationship: An Annotated Bibliography. Kingston, R.I.: American Transcendental Quarterly, 1982.

Yannella, Donald, and Hershel Parker, eds. *The Endless Winding Way in Melville: New Charts by Kring and Carey.* Glassboro, N.J.: Melville Society, 1981.

————, and Kathleen Malone Yannella. "Evert A. Duyckinck's 'Diary': May 29–November 8, 1847." *Studies in the American Renaissance 1978.* Boston: Twayne, 1979, pp. 207–58.

2

MELVILLE THE TRAVELER

Thomas Farel Heffernan

A writer's travels are of a piece with a writer's education or marriage or debts or society, things that were important enough for Arnold, Browning, Baudelaire, and Proust, respectively, but that counted for nothing in the lives of other writers. For Herman Melville travels *were* important and counted for much. Had he not gone halfway around the world, he might still have become a major writer, but he would not have written most of the books we know him for.

Wherever Melville went—Liverpool when he was nineteen, the Pacific when he was in his twenties, Jerusalem when he was thirty-seven—his eyes drained the scenes before them of impressions that were carried home for transformation into novels, tales, and poems. These experiences he supplemented with literary impressions, for he was a constant and curious reader about all parts of the world, a mental traveler as well as a physical one. Titles in Sealts's *Melville's Reading* (1966), include many histories, guide books, and descriptive accounts of places Melville had visited in earlier years and some books about places he would visit at a later date. At times it is difficult to tell whether Melville's evident familiarity with a place owes more to his experience or his reading. His comments on Nantucket in *Moby-Dick* (ch. 14) are apt and penetrating, but, as far as we know, Melville had never been to Nantucket when he wrote *Moby-Dick*.

Melville's ultimate goal in his scrutiny of places, whether as a visitor or as a reader, was to discover their psychological geography. He was not blind to the landmarks and amenities that the guide books emphasized, and he enjoyed the diversions that new places offered, but his preoccupation was to find in each new place another entry in the great moral guide book that he was compiling in his memory for use when needed.

In the introduction to her edition of Melville's 1849–50 journal of a trip to Europe, Melville's granddaughter, Eleanor Melville Metcalf, cites a quotation from Samuel Johnson in a book given to Melville, "The use of travelling is to regulate imagination by reality; and instead of thinking how things may be, to see them as they are," and observes that "Melville might have written, 'The use of travelling is to regulate reality by imagination; and instead of *thinking*, to *see* things as they are.' For 'to see things as they are,' finally necessitated for him their transmutation by the imagination" (p. xix).

In the survey of Melville's travels that follows, part of what is said is gratuitously biographical—one does, after all, want to know that the author really did go here or there—and part is an examination of the connections between Melville's travels and writings. Sometimes those connections are so obvious that no one could overlook them. "Is that episode really autobiographical?" the first-time reader asks. "Was Melville really there?" Usually scholarship can come up with a firm answer, but ultimately the question to ask is, what governed Melville's selection when he came to write about the worlds he had traveled to? What was his regulation of reality? Out of an infinite number of possible views of Tahiti, London, Jerusalem, and Rome, why this one? Why state it so? What was the whole soul and imagination behind this phrase? An awareness of Melville the traveler is the first step toward answering those questions.

One may add that an incidental benefit in this study of Melville's travels, especially those he documented in journals, is a sensitivity to the flickering allusions throughout his work to provocative names and geographical details. What are we to make, for instance, of the repeated references to the Syrian city of Tadmor (Palmyra) in *Pierre*? Although the accumulated scholarship of two generations has explained many such references, others are obscure and tantalizing. The reader with a heightened awareness of Melville's feeling for places is wired for little alarms that are set off by allusion after allusion in his works. The most basic sources of information about Melville's travels in general are Leyda's *Log* and Howard's *Herman Melville*. Melville's *Letters* touch on some of his travels. Sources pertinent to specific voyages or periods of travel are treated below in discussions of those voyages or periods.

HIS FIRST VOYAGE

Herman Melville began his life of travel when he was six weeks old; to get away from fever-ridden New York, his mother took him and his older brother and sister to her family's home in Albany, making the first of the family visits on the New York-Albany-Boston triangle which were to be major events of the first ten years of Herman's life. It may seem nothing but a pleasantry to mention these family trips in the same discussion as a whaling voyage, but it would probably be wrong to ignore their impact altogether. A romantic riverboat trip 160 miles inland lasting twenty hours and ending with a grandmother's embrace is not part of every child's experience. For the right child that could be all that was needed to breed a taste for ships in general.

Melville's major travels, however, began nineteen years later with a trip not up, but down, the Hudson. In his fourth novel, *Redburn: His First Voyage*, the author has left a fictionalized but still informative version of "Melville: his first voyage." The real-life green hand was fresh from being a country school teacher, engineering and surveying student, and applicant for a job on the Erie Canal; he was nineteen when he came down from Albany to New York to sign on a merchant ship for Liverpool and twenty when he returned four months later. Melville's first service at sea was, in today's terms, a summer job, but its importance for the young sailor was great.

After a hasty departure from Albany and a few days' stay in New York with a family friend, Melville sailed 5 June 1839 on the *St. Lawrence*, Captain Oliver P. Brown, for a crossing to Liverpool of twenty-seven days. For readers of *Redburn*, the *St. Lawrence* is the *Highlander*, and Captain Brown is Captain Riga. Just how much the adventures recorded in the novel had in common with Melville's real experiences is discussed in William H. Gilman's *Melville's Early Life and Redburn* (1951), Leon Howard's biography (1951), Hershel Parker's "Historical Note" for the NN edition of *Redburn*, (1969), and Chapter 6 in this volume, but it may be said in general that outside the pages of *Redburn* there is no evidence that young Melville received any harsh treatment on board ship or witnessed such dramatic scenes as the death of the morally ugly seaman Jackson. As far as can be known, the voyages out and back were routine; the hardest thing about them for the green hand may have been the chores, usually given to the newest seaman on board, of clearing up around the pigs and chickens.

The *St. Lawrence* docked in Liverpool on 2 July. For the next six weeks Melville and the other sailors were occupied with light maintenance duties on the ship and had free time to walk around the city. They spent their nights on board the ship and took their meals in a boarding house ashore.

Melville took advantage of the time ashore to see what he could of the city. Liverpool, according to travelers' reports, was not the most enchanting place to visit. A growing commercial center, it had a waterfront that reminded Americans unromantically of views of New York and Brooklyn from the East River. It had relatively few attractive features; what was most in the public eye was the poverty, beggary, disease, squalor, and vice of the city, and Melville saw evidence enough of these aspects of Liverpool life in the streets around the docks. In what is probably the most remembered scene in *Redburn*, the young sailor finds a starving mother and her children dying on the street one day and a pile of lime in their place the next day (pp. 180–84). This scene is assumed to be an invention, but it would not tax credibility.

Melville may well have stood and listened to the city's street preachers as Redburn did, but Gilman, Howard, and other biographers do not consider it likely that he had any memorable cultural experiences, say, in a fee-charging reading room or art gallery. (Nor is it realistic to think that he got away to London, as did Redburn.)

Whatever Melville may have anticipated about Liverpool from hearing his father talk of it years before or his cousin Leonard Gansevoort talk of it shortly before Melville's departure from Albany (Leonard had two years earlier made the same voyage as a seaman), the city proved to be something less than delightful, probably just tolerable. By his own report Melville became quickly homesick in Liverpool.

On 13 August the *St. Lawrence* weighed anchor; seven weeks later, it tied up in New York. Melville's initiation into the life of the sea was now completed; it may not have been as culturally rewarding as he had hoped it would be, but it did one thing for him: it taught him seamanship. Now he knew the names of gear, he knew how to work in the rigging, he was used to watches, and he was used to authority.

INLAND VOYAGE TO FAIRYLAND

Fifteen months went by before Melville again signed on a ship, but in the interim he made a trip away from the sea. In the summer of 1840, possibly in the company of his friend Eli James Murdock Fly, Melville traveled to Illinois with the formal goal of visiting his Uncle Thomas Melvill in Galena. The trip, however, was probably a leisurely bit of touring undertaken as much for its own sake as for a family visit.

In the manuscript (in the Gansevoort-Lansing collection of the New York Public Library), but not the published version, of a sketch about his Uncle Thomas prepared for J.E.A. Smith's *History of Pittsfield*, Melville wrote, "In 1841 [error for 1840] I visited my now venerable kinsman in his western home, and was anew struck by the contrast between the man and his environment." This sentence is the only solid external evidence that Melville ever made the western trip. A remark made in a letter by Melville's mother and another made in a letter by Fly around the time the trip began lend some confirmation to Melville's statement; the in-

ternal evidence of a large number of references in Melville's writing—
and these create the most interest in the western trip—gives the statement
considerable confirmation and helps reconstruct details of the trip.

The trip, which has been treated at length in articles by John
W. Nichol, G. Thomas Tanselle, and Stanton Garner, is assumed to have
started in the early summer of 1840 with Melville (and Fly?) traveling
from Albany to Buffalo, on through the St. Clair River to Lake Huron,
past Mackinaw Island into Lake Michigan, and down to Chicago, probably with a stop in Milwaukee. The final 170–mile leg of the trip from
Chicago to Galena would have been made by stagecoach.

Galena, tucked away in the northwest corner of Illinois almost directly
across the Mississippi from Dubuque, Iowa, was a rapidly growing town
that owed its prosperity to its being the lead mining capital of the United
States. Apart from an allusion to the town's lead (in a 3 March 1849
letter to Evert Duyckinck), Melville has left us no words on Galena, but
he has left a description of a Mississippi scene above the Falls of St.
Anthony about 275 miles upstream from Galena which suggests that he
had taken a riverboat excursion to the Falls. The description is in a
discarded fragment of *The Confidence-Man* and emphasizes the pristine
and unviolated character of the scene: "The furred bear on the marge
seems to eye his amphibious children. Wood & wave wed, man is remote"
(p.497). The spot, if one assumes that the area described is immediately
above the Falls, is today the heart of downtown Minneapolis, which when
Melville looked it over consisted of little more than Major Plympton's
log house on the east bank and a government grist mill downstream on
the west bank.

About the rest of Melville's activity in Galena and the length of his
stay there, we can only speculate. While his return route east is also
conjectural, there are references in his writings to suggest that the route
was down the Mississippi to Cairo, up the Ohio to Wheeling, and across
Pennsylvania by land.

When all the internal evidence about the trip is collected from Melville's works, it becomes clear that the chief literary expression of the
trip is in *The Confidence-Man*. That he (apparently) covered more than
half the length of the Mississippi in the course of his riverboat travels
and never saw the river again before making it the setting of his novel
is in itself notable. The more than fifteen-year-old memories of the
Mississippi Valley were obviously indispensable to the making of *The
Confidence-Man*.

The Midwest also appears, probably as the result of Melville's experience more than his reading, in references in *Moby-Dick, Mardi, Redburn,
Clarel*, "John Marr," and the poem "Trophies of Peace," subtitled "Illinois
in 1840." One of the most telling lines about the trip is one in "The

Piazza" which Nichol has drawn attention to: the speaker, musing over waving grain fields, refers to an "inland voyage to fairy-land. A true voyage; but, take it all in all, interesting as if invented" (*Tales*, p. 386).

Melville's return from the Midwest is thought to have been in late summer or early fall 1840. By November he appeared in New York with his friend Fly, both of them living off Herman's brother Gansevoort while they looked for "situations." By mid-December both had succeeded, Fly in finding an office job and Melville in finding a berth on a whaler.

IN THE PACIFIC

When Melville sailed from Fairhaven, the town across the Acushnet River from New Bedford, he was departing for "my Yale College and my Harvard" as Ishmael described a whaling ship in Chapter 24 of *Moby-Dick* (p. 101). On his return almost four years later he had the raw material for *Typee, Omoo, White-Jacket, Moby-Dick*, and "The Encantadas" as well as images and lore for "Benito Cereno" and *Billy Budd*. College had done wonders.

The question of the autobiographical content of the stories just named will tease the reader even more than the question of the autobiographical content of *Redburn*. Was Melville really a captive of cannibals? Was he the ringleader of crewmen refusing service on an Australian whaler? Such questions are treated in the chapters on the respective novels, but three observations pertinent to them may be made at this point.

First, the stories have been sufficiently studied by now for all to agree that they are a combination of accurate autobiography, literary borrowing, and pure invention, and most episodes in the novels can be assigned to one (or more) of these categories. Second, the two novels which have to be filtered for autobiography with most care are *Omoo* and *White-Jacket*. Third, one does not want to approach the question of Melville's presence in his fiction as such a purist that he dismisses the biographical relevance of every passage which cannot be corroborated by independent evidence. Good guesses, as long as they do not claim to be more than guesses, pay off too; the juxtaposition of historical evidence and excerpts from Melville's writing assembled by Jay Leyda in *The Melville Log* is a good model of what to do with suggestive but unverifiable narrative.

The first title to mention in relation to Melville's travels in the Pacific is Charles Roberts Anderson's *Melville in the South Seas* (1939). This fundamental study was such a scholarly adventure that the author published an article on the writing of the book: "The Romance of Scholarship: Tracking Melville in the South Seas" (1938). It is a major reference which everyone working in the area must consult, but it should be corrected and supplemented at points. It contains wrong dates for Melville's Liverpool voyage (corrected in Gilman, *Melville's Early Life*), and it does not identify the ship on which Melville sailed from Eimeo, the *Charles and Henry* (first identified in Wilson Heflin, "Melville's Third Whaler," 1949). Its dating of the *Acushnet's* arrival in the Marquesas is not precise (cf. Leyda and Howard), and it does not make reference to the "abstract log" of the *Acushnet*. Abstract logs condensed essential navigational information—dates, latitudes and longitudes, meteorological data, and other important details—from ships' logs proper. The abstract log of the *Acushnet* is one of those compiled for the U. S. Navy Hydrographic Office under the direction of Matthew Fontaine Maury for use in the preparation of oceanographic charts; 324 of the Maury abstracts are in the National Archives, Record Group 27. The *Acushnet's* abstract log was first utilized by Leyda and Heflin and supplies in its limited way information about Melville's most important cruise which scholars would prefer to be getting from the never located original log of the ship.

In spite of the need for a revised edition (the 1966 reprint was revised only in its preface), *Melville in the South Seas* is an important work. Not the least of its merits is the fullest single bibliography on Melville and the Pacific, a natural starting point for research in the area; to it one should add Wilson Heflin's 1952 dissertation [*Mel. Diss.*, #46] as well as the "Historical Notes" to the NN editions of *Typee* (by Leon Howard), *Omoo* (by Gordon Roper), and *White-Jacket* (by William Thorp). The NN edition of *Moby-Dick* is in preparation. The Hendricks House *Omoo* edited by Harrison Hayford and Walter Blair modifies Anderson a good deal, and Heflin has published fresh material on Melville at sea in "New Light on Melville's Cruise in the *Charles and Henry*" (1974).

The *Acushnet* sailed from Fairhaven on 3 January 1841 under the command of Captain Valentine Pease II and headed for Cape Horn (unlike the *Pequod* in *Moby-Dick*, whose course was for the Cape of Good Hope and, for the most part, over seas which Melville never saw). There was a stop in Rio de Janeiro in March, and a month later the *Acushnet* rounded the Cape and moved into the Pacific.

Sailing down the Chilean coast (in South America "down" the coast is northbound and "up" the coast is southbound), the *Acushnet* passed west of St. Mary's Island, which was to be the setting, when Melville wrote the story fourteen years later, of "Benito Cereno," and anchored 23 June in the harbor of Santa, Peru. "Nothing about that deadly skrimmage with the Spaniard afore the altar in Santa?—heard nothing about that, eh? Nothing about the silver calabash he spat into?" asks Elijah in *Moby-Dick*, conjuring up the picture of Ahab striding to the main altar of the cathedral of Santa while mass was being celebrated and spitting into the chalice (p. 87).

The *Acushnet* left Santa on 2 July after nine days in port and moved west for three months of work in an area whose center was roughly longitude 105° W / latitude 5° S. This was the northeastern corner of what was known to whalemen as the "Off-Shore Ground," one of the most productive whaling areas in the Pacific. At the end of October the *Acushnet* turned east to the Galapagos, sailing for about three weeks through the islands and anchoring for a week at Chatham Island.

The Galapagos have had an eerie attraction for nineteenth- and twentieth-century visitors and for readers of literature on the islands; witness the continuing popularity of accounts of the Ritter-Strauch-Baroness de Bosquet regime set up there in the late 1920s and early 1930s (Ainslie and Frances Conway, Dore Strauch, John Treherne). Those adventures are weird and melodramatic, but accounts of them are passing curiosities in comparison to the timeless, unearthly picture of the islands that Melville put together in "The Encantadas" from the glimpse that the *Acushnet*'s days there afforded him.

A week after leaving the Galapagos the *Acushnet* anchored in the port of Tumbes, Peru, its abstract log shows, and reported that it had 570 barrels of whale oil on board, a satisfactory amount for eleven months' work when added to the 150 barrels shipped home from Rio de Janeiro (Nuñez). Leaving Tumbes 15 December after two weeks in port, the *Acushnet* moved west through the Galapagos and across the top of the Off-Shore Ground for a long stretch of unrelieved whaling—over six months of it.

Then on 23 June 1842, the *Acushnet* entered Taio Hae (Anna Maria) Bay on the island of Nukahiva in the Marquesas, a fateful stop for Melville. This already wilting garden of Eden was popular with whaling captains as a victualing stop. It was even more popular with seamen as an "R & R" stop, an unauthorized one, for the desertion rate on Nukahiva, testified to by the logs of a multitude of whalers, was high enough to keep at least three local crimps—procurers of crewmen—in business.

On 9 July, after two and a half weeks of looking at the island from on board ship and two days before the *Acushnet* (in *Typee* called the *Dolly*) was to sail, Melville joined the tradition and became a deserter. Accompanied by a shipmate, Richard Tobias (Toby) Greene, he slipped away during a shore liberty and set out, if we credit the account in *Typee*, on the most perilous adventure of his life: he and Toby sought to cross a low mountain range on the east side of Taio Hae Bay to reach the land, lying between the mountain and the next indentation on the coast, Comptroller Bay, which belonged to the friendly Happar (Hapaa) tribe. Heading more to the north, however, than they had intended, they fell instead into the hands of the Typees (Taipi), a cannibal people whose ultimate culinary intentions became clear after a few weeks to the otherwise hospitably received seamen. Because of the threat of being eaten and despite the sensual and indolent delights of his days with the natives, the narrator made a movie-scenario escape—all alone, for Toby, allowed to leave earlier, had not returned.

Leaving aside at this point the mass of detail in the novel which does or does not seem autobiographical, it may be noted that the chronology of *Typee* is an invention, for Melville was in fact one month on the island, not the four months described in the novel. Whatever his adventures were during that month, they probably unfolded somewhere in the southeast corner of the island where the action of the novel is set.

The month ended with Melville's enlistment on 9 August on a Sydney whaler, the *Lucy Ann*, Captain Ventom, for a voyage that was aborted less than seven weeks later in Tahiti. This turn of events was the inevitable result of the deteriorating condition of the ship, the deteriorating health of the captain, and the deteriorating morale of the crew. In *Omoo* the *Lucy Ann* appears as the *Julia*; the novel, discussed in Chapter 4, recounts the story of the cruise, the refusal of most of the crew to serve, their fussy prosecution by the local authorities, Melville's not too onerous imprisonment, his friendship with the beachcombing Dr. Long Ghost (John Troy), and the encounters of Long Ghost and Melville with various residents of Tahiti and the neighboring island of Eimeo (today Moorea). The picture of Melville's days on the islands and the episodes in the novel involving Melville's contact with the local population have received an unusual amount of independent confirmation (in sources cited by Leyda, Howard, Anderson, Hayford and Blair, and Robert S. Forsythe), so *Omoo*, whose title is explained as the Polynesian word for rover or wanderer, is read as something closer to autobiography than any other Melville novel. It was an idyllic and mildly picaresque two-month interlude, which ended with yet more duty on a whaler.

The whaler out of Eimeo was the Nantucket ship, *Charles and Henry*, Captain John B. Coleman, which Melville signed on in November, possibly as boatsteerer or harpooner. It was a six-months' cruise which took Melville over a good deal of the Pacific—the ship was reported in January 1843 west of Valparaiso and in February near the Off-Shore Ground. On 27 April it arrived at Lahaina in the Sandwich Islands; five days later Melville was discharged by agreement. Going up to Honolulu two weeks after that, he found employment first in a bowling alley according to one report (*Mel. Log*, p. 166) and then—and probably more congenially— as a clerk in the store of one Isaac Montgomery. Since he contracted to work for Montgomery for a year (for $150 and room and board) he clearly could have stayed on, but he chose not to.

In the middle of August 1843 Melville joined the U. S. Navy, signing on the frigate *United States*, then in Honolulu, for three years or the length of the cruise—it would be the latter, fourteen months, for the *United States* had already completed most of its cruise. This voyage is variously documented; Willard Thorp's "Historical Note" in the NN edition of *White-Jacket* (1970) cites most of the sources (pp. 410–11). The ship's log for the cruise is in the National Archives in Washington. An anonymous journal of the cruise was published by Anderson (*Journal of a Cruise*, 1937). Three of the journals kept as a required exercise by midshipmen on the *United States* have survived: that of William Sharp is in the National Archives, that of Alonzo C. Jackson is in the Library of Congress, and that of William H. Willcox is in the United States Naval Academy Museum; these three rather perfunctory records do not add much to the information in the ship's log. A more revealing journal was kept from 1841 to 1844 by William H. Meyers on board the *Cyane*, which sailed with the *United States*; although not reporting on life on the *United States*, it is vivid enough to give a good picture of life on other ships in the squadron (see Anderson, *Journal of a Cruise*, p. 16). The Pacific Squadron letters from the time of the cruise are in the National Archives, and the medical and surgical journal of the *United States* is in the Princeton University Library. A copy of *White-Jacket* annotated (now privately owned) by one of Melville's shipmates, Harrison Robertson, contains references to Melville as does the published *Memoirs of a Rear-Admiral* by Samuel R. Franklin, who had been a midshipman on the cruise. The one record of the cruise, of course, which has drawn attention to all the others is Melville's fictionalized account of the voyage in *White-Jacket*, where the *United States* appears as the *Neversink*. The novel and the historical reliability of its episodes are discussed in Howard P. Vincent and in Chapter 6 in this volume.

The *United States* covered some waters familiar to Melville, taking him back to the Marquesas on 6 October and Tahiti on 12 October. The ship then sailed for South America, coming into Valparaiso 21 November for two weeks, and then sailed for Callao, Peru, the port serving Lima. As a result of the *United States*'s two lengthy visits to this port, Callao became the city that Melville spent more time in than any other foreign city he ever visited—if anchorage in the harbor can be regarded as a visit; the two days' leave on which he went to Lima on New Year's Day, 1844, allowed him to get the impressions of that white city that he presented in the much discussed "The Whiteness of the Whale" chapter of *Moby-Dick*. The *United States* was at Callao from 15 December 1843 to 24 February 1844, when it was sent on a mission to Mazatlan, Mexico. It returned to Callao on 6 June and stayed until 6 July, when it was dispatched to Rio de Janeiro. On 16 August the ship reached Rio; it was nine days in that port and then proceeded home. On 3 October the *United States* reached Boston, and on 14 October Melville was discharged from the navy. His big voyage was over, three years and ten months after he left Fairhaven; more than one-fourth of this time had been passed in port.

TRAVELS OF AN AUTHOR

Once ashore Melville became, after scarcely a breathing space, a novelist of the sea; six books in six years turned his whaling, merchant, and navy experience into literature. His working days at sea were over, but on three more occasions he would take sizable sea voyages, each time—ignoring Ishmael's advice in the matter—as a passenger (*MD*, p. 14).

The first of these occasions was in late 1849, ten years after he sailed into Liverpool on the *St. Lawrence* "—*then* a sailor, *now* H. M. author of 'Peedee' 'Hullabaloo' & 'Pog-Dog,' " as he put it in his 1849 *Journal* (p. 18).

The trip was on business, and the business—finding a British publisher for *White-Jacket*—was not a pretext, for Melville put miles of walking the streets and days of calling at offices into the task before he succeeded in arriving at a satisfactory contract. Nonetheless, most of the trip was pure vacation and, clearly, a needed one. His first five novels had been produced in five years of unrelieved writing. *Mardi* took longer than any of the others, but the last of the five, the one that he was carrying to Europe with him, had been written in about three months.

The diary that Melville kept of the trip radiates pleasure in good company, plentiful drink, and assiduous prowling through big and little city streets. The companion whom Melville enjoyed most was George Adler, a professor of German at the University of the City of New York (after 1896 known as New York University) and already, in his late twenties, one of America's leading philologists. The friendship between Melville and Adler, struck up the first day they boarded ship, led to the two of them becoming inseparable companions in London and on the continent until Melville had to leave Paris to return to England. Their talk was "of the German metaphysics, & discourses of Kant, Swedenborg" (*Mel. Log*, p. 319), and many other philosophical ideas, Melville reported. Melville and Adler were in touch again after Adler's return to the United States a year later, but by then the concern of Adler's friends was how to come to his aid in the crisis of mental illness that caused him to be confined to the Bloomingdale Asylum. A vivid and appalling picture of Adler's state on his return from Europe is presented in Adler's own *Letters of a Lunatic* (1854). Bradley's "George J. Adler, 1821–1868" and Lee's note-length "Melville and George J. Adler" contain basic information on Melville's companion. Vincent Quinn is writing a book-length biography of Adler, and Sanford E. Marovitz has a study of Adler that will appear in *Studies in the American Renaissance*.

Melville sailed from New York 11 October 1849 on the *Southampton*, Captain Robert Griswold. Melville did not take a shine to the captain at first, but soon came to respect him—"[he] understands himself," Melville wrote (*Mel. Log*, p. 324)—and spent long stretches at sea socializing with

Griswold, Adler, Dr. Franklin Taylor, and a wealthy young man named McCurdy, the last welcome enough in a group but a bore when alone. Melville noticed a woman on board reading a copy of *Omoo* and glancing up at the author from time to time as if comparing notes.

Melville frequently mounted the rigging as in his old seafaring days, and on one occasion saw for the first time in his life the corposants which he would so vividly depict in Chapter 119 of *Moby-Dick*. He also went over the side, hanging on just above the water line, in an effort to save a drowning passenger—a vain effort, for the man was out of his mind and suicidal.

When Melville, Adler, and Taylor were landed at Deal, near Dover, on 5 November, Melville suggested walking the eighteen miles to Canterbury "for an appetite to breakfast." The little party settled for Sandwich, six miles away, and then entrained for London.

For three weeks Melville enjoyed London. His negotiations about *White-Jacket* with the eight publishers he mentions in his journal were spaced out through these days and did not jeopardize his leisure. A typical day would find Melville strolling alone through the city, meeting Adler or one of his other shipboard companions for dinner, going to a theater, and stopping by a pub or two before retiring.

Alone or with Adler, Melville went to art galleries, the royal gardens at Kew, Hampton Court (where he had a glimpse of Queen Victoria and Prince Albert), Regent's Park, St. Paul's, Lincoln's Inn, and a wide range of theaters, from a Charles Mathews performance at the Royal Lyceum to the burlesque "Judge and Jury" and a rowdy "penny theater" (which frightened Adler). One morning Melville rose early to attend a celebrated hanging, paying a half crown for a vantage point from which he could witness the execution of George and Marie Manning. Dickens was also in the crowd of spectators.

Howard Horsford has observed that much of Melville's time in London was spent in the most squalid parts of the city, yet almost nothing in Melville's journal indicates that he was encountering unpleasant scenes. Horsford, who is editing the journals for the NN edition, treated Melville's experiences during this visit in "Melville in the London Literary World" (1984).

Some of what Melville saw proved useful in his writing. Attending a play in a one shilling gallery gave him material for "The Two Temples." "While on one of the Bridges, the thought struck me again that a fine thing might be written about a Blue Monday in November London"; that impression turned up in *Israel Potter*. Dining at Elm Court, the Temple, prompted Melville to describe the setting as "The Paradise of Bachelors," and a view of the pomp of the Lord Mayor's show followed the next day by a view of the city's beggars being allowed the remainders of the feast was enough to make half of "Poor Man's Pudding and Rich Man's Crumbs."

On 27 November Melville set out for the continent, taking a two-week vacation within a vacation. Adler had gone on to Paris a few days before, and Melville's first concern was to look him up. When the friends were reunited they set out on a round of dining and sightseeing in the spirit of their London touring. Melville was anxious to see the celebrated actress Rachel but twice failed because of the length of the ticket lines. "Bitterly disappointed" at that, he wrote. He did enjoy a performance at the Opera Comique, however. In good guide book fashion he took in Notre Dame, the Place de la Bastille, the Madeleine, the Hotel des Invalides, the Pantheon, the Hotel de Cluny, Versailles, and other points of interest.

On 6 December Melville sat in Adler's room writing up the Parisian entries for his journal. He bade Adler farewell and left early the next morning for Brussels, Cologne, Coblenz, and points in between. This swing over to the Rhine took five days; by the morning of 13 December Melville was back in England, having taken an overnight boat from Ostend to Dover.

The two weeks that remained to Melville's London stay were characterized by somewhat more elevated socializing than before; he met John Gibson Lockhart, John Tenniel, Alexander Kinglake, Bryan Waller Procter ("Barry Cornwall"), and other literary and public figures. He entered this society wearing a coat he had purchased on his return from the continent, abandoning at last the old green coat which had begun to gain him the unwelcome notice that the white jacket of his latest novel's central character had attracted.

The sale of *White-Jacket* to Richard Bentley on 15 December was for £200. Bentley, who had brought out *Mardi* and *Redburn* in England, was the first London publisher Melville had gone to see and the most sympathetic of all of them. Because of a recent court decision weakening copyright protection for foreign books, British publishers were reluctant to take American titles, but Bentley ignored the risk and acted liberally in his relations with Melville, strikingly so in view of the disappointing sales of *Mardi*.

When planning his voyage to England, and for a while after arriving, Melville had entertained the idea of extending his trip to include Italy and the Near East. As time went by and *White-Jacket* remained unsold, however, he despaired of meeting the costs of such a trip. With the book's last minute sale he could have afforded the planned tour, but by this time homesickness was eating at him, and he was in no mood to change plans twice. He even passed up an invitation to visit the estate of the Duke of Rutland (although "I am confident that hereafter I shall upbraid myself for neglecting such an opportunity of procuring 'material' ") rather than delay his return. Melville sailed Christmas Day, 1849 on the *Independence*, Captain A. T. Fletcher, and arrived in New York on 1 February 1850.

In the year and a half that followed Melville's return from Europe two things stand out, his meeting and quick friendship with Nathaniel Hawthorne and the writing of *Moby-Dick*. The novel was published in November 1851; eight months later Melville saw, apparently for the first time, those Nantucket scenes which he had created to usher in the action of the story.

His father-in-law, Judge Lemuel Shaw, setting out to hold court on Nantucket, invited Melville along. The two left on 6 July 1852, going to New Bedford by train, Nantucket by boat for a three-day stay, Martha's Vineyard also for three days, then the rarely visited Naushon Island, and back to Wood's Hole, Falmouth, and Boston. The jaunt took a little over a week and would not be worth noting in a survey of Melville's travels were it not for the heightened significance that Nantucket now had for him. No event in his three days on the island was probably more significant for him than his meeting with George Pollard, Jr., who had been captain of the *Essex* in 1820 when that ship was attacked and sunk by a whale; from the account of the *Essex* shipwreck written by the ship's first mate, Owen Chase, Melville drew the most dramatic events of the last days of the *Pequod* in *Moby-Dick*. More important to Melville than this historical association, however, was the impression that Pollard made on him as a person. "To the islanders he was a nobody—to me, the most impressive man, tho' wholly unassuming, even humble—that I ever encountered," Melville wrote in an annotation of his copy of Owen Chase's *Narrative of the . . . Shipwreck of the Whale-ship Essex* (Thomas Farel Heffernan, pp. 195–96). Melville was years later to turn this impression into poetry when he included a sketch of Pollard in *Clarel* (pp.119–22). The visit to Nantucket is examined in Heflin's "Melville and Nantucket" (1953).

EUROPE AGAIN, THE EAST AT LAST

Melville had finished *Pierre* a few months before he made the trip to Nantucket. His next novel, *Israel Potter*, appeared serially in 1854 and as a book in 1855. In 1856, he collected some of his stories in *Piazza Tales*, and finished his ninth novel, *The Confidence-Man*. When this novel came off the press in April 1857, its author was traveling in Italy, nearing the end of a tour that finally fulfilled the longings he had felt and talked about in 1849 to see the Mediterranean and the Near East.

The keynote of the 1849 trip had been business; the keynote of this 1856–57 trip was health. One cannot study this middle stage of Melville's life without becoming aware that there was anxiety in some quarters over Melville's mental health. A popular opinion until 1975 was that Melville's mental troubles peaked in the mid–1850s, were alleviated by his 1856–57 trip to Europe, and were finally put to rest by his regular employment at the Custom House beginning in 1866. The contents of the so-called Kring-Carey find, two letters from 1867 detailing a concern on the part of his family so serious as to prompt some members of the family to try to devise a separation between Melville and his wife, were published in 1975; they indicate that the spectre of mental illness was before the eyes of everyone in Melville's circle at a later date than hitherto thought.

An instructive discussion of Melville's mental state is to be found in the pamphlet in which the two 1867 letters were published (Yannella and Parker). The student of this issue is likely to conclude that the mounting evidence of Melville's insanity is really evidence that other people thought him insane. Dark and anxious family letters cannot be ignored; they allow the direst conclusions, but they also present a picture of overreaction to what might be diagnosed today as symptoms of exhaustion.

It is not necessary to define fully Melville's psychological state at the time of his 1856 departure for Europe; one may settle for his wife's statement, recorded in a memoir. "In Oct. 1856 his health being impaired by too close application he again sailed for London" (Sealts, *Early Lives*, p. 171). Perception of this impairment, whatever it was, was apparently the reason for Melville's father-in-law's providing him the fourteen or fifteen hundred dollars needed for the trip "as advance by way of loan or a gift according to some future arrangement" (*Mel. Log*, p. 525).

It was a long trip, seven months, and is chronicled in *Journal of a Visit to Europe and the Levant*, edited and thoroughly annotated by Howard Horsford; an earlier edition of the same journal was edited by Raymond Weaver and published as *Journal Up the Straits*. Citations below are from the Horsford edition, a revision of which will appear as a volume in the NN project.

The trip and the journal began 11 October 1856 with Melville's boarding the steamer *Glasgow* for Glasgow. Note, *steamer*—at last Melville was able to enjoy the fast (two weeks) crossing which he did not feel he could afford in 1849.

The reader of the journal who has settled back to be treated to a series of impressions like those in the 1849 *Journal* will be disappointed at first, for the account of Melville's first three weeks in Europe often amounts to just a string of phrases. Ten days during which Melville traveled by some route or other from Glasgow to Liverpool are passed over altogether except for "Arrived from York, through Lancaster, at 1 P. M., having passed through an interesting country of manufactures" (p. 61).

Horsford attributes the scanty entries in this part of the journal to the exhaustion that occasioned the trip. As Melville passed from familiar England to the unfamiliar Mediterranean, his vitality seemed to return until it reached points where, as Horsford says, "one could almost chart his blood pressure by the degree of feverish illegibility in his handwriting, by the pressure of images, words, and phrases that crowd each other off the page in the compulsion to be written" (1856 *Journal*, p. 17).

Just how intense the fatigue of the first three weeks in England must have been for Melville may be gathered from the fact that he visited Nathaniel Hawthorne, then American consul in Liverpool, and gave the several days' visit less than two hundred words' mention in his journal. What passed between the two men was—at least part of the time—as profound as their 1850 conversations, but we know this only from Hawthorne's record of Melville's visit in his *English Notebooks* (pp. 432–37).

"Tired of Liverpool," Melville sailed 18 November on the *Egyptian*, Captain Robert Taitt. On 24 November when the ship cleared Gibraltar, summery weather and good spirits prevailed. The trip, which was conceived as valetudinarian, was effectively so from this point on. "Threw open my coat.—Such weather as one might have in Paridise [*sic*]" (p. 65). On the 26th the ship passed Algiers, and on the 29th it stopped at Malta.

On 2 December Melville debarked at the island of Syra, "such an isled resort / As heartless Homer might have known" (*Poems*, p. 250). His poem titled after the island is in *Timoleon* and records some of his initial impressions of the Greek world. The port scenes, the sun, the costumes are noted, but mainly the spirit of the folk: the longshoremen were "Such chatterers all! like children gay / Who make believe to work, but play" (*Poems*, p. 251).

On 5 December a slow overnight cruise took Melville to Salonica. Olympus loomed to his west and Mount Athos to his east as the ship moved up the bay of Salonica. The captain called Melville on deck at dawn for the view. Other views were offered to him, once he was ashore, by an employee of a ships' agent's firm who gave him his initial tour of the city. Left to himself in such a place, Melville tended to let one of the guide books published by his British publisher, Murray, lay out his route for him. No matter how guided, Melville made note of the same kind of detail: types of people, their trades and costumes, curious or dramatic vignettes, architecture, the openness or congestion of places, amenity and squalor.

On 12 December Melville was in Constantinople after an unduly long three-day, fog-impeded voyage from Salonica. Constantinople, Melville found, was a city where one could not go out at night "owing to footpads & assassins" (1856 *Journal*, p. 78) and where one got lost in labyrinthine streets if he went out during the day. A guide gave him a tour, and on his first full day in the city he managed to take in St. Sophia, the Hippodrome, the Cistern of Philoxenus, a couple of mosques, and neighborhoods of several characters. The day was beautiful, the water scenes glorious, the city *fourmillante* like Baudelaire's, and the spectacle engaging, but always before him was "the horrible grimy tragic air of these streets. The rotten & wicked looking houses. So gloomy & grimy seems as if a suicide hung from every rafter within" (p. 85).

Melville missed seeing the whirling dervishes but followed an Armenian funeral and in the cemetery saw a woman mourning over a grave as if speaking down into it. "This woman & her cries haunt me horribly" (p. 89). Beautiful women, an ominous Greek following him for three hours, and more tokens of crime and beggarliness made up a day in Constantinople. On another day Melville escaped from the city for the scenic short cruise to the suburb of Buyukdereh. He visited the Seraglio, crossed the Bosporus to Scutari, commented on the city's dogs, and noted the decorum of relations between the sexes. A fine site for a capital, he concluded, but the feeling of a suffocating density of population stayed with him.

On 18 December Melville left Constantinople for Alexandria. There was a stop en route of four days at Smyrna and a second visit, also of four days, to Syra, the only one of the Greek islands that Melville had had the opportunity to explore. The others he had seen from shipboard, but he had apparently talked and read about them too. His parting verdict on them was that they "look worn, and are meagre, like life after enthusiasm is gone. The aspect of all of them is sterile & dry" (p. 111).

Arriving in Alexandria, Melville found the U.S.F. *Constellation* in port and spent some time with the ship's doctor, John Alexander Lockwood, a congenial spirit whom Melville would meet again before his visit to the Mediterranean ended. On 30 December Melville went to Cairo and the next day visited the pyramids. He was vexed that he had only one full day in Cairo because of his scheduled steamer departure, and was even more vexed when departure delays kept him in Alexandria, which he found a boring place, for two days. The days were well spent, however, for he used them to write up a long journal entry on his impressions of Cairo and the pyramids. Cairo had some of the traits of Constantinople: "Crookedness of the streets...splendor & squalor, gloom & gayety" (p. 115). It was a "dust colored city" and venerable, and he would have liked more time to take it in, but the pyramids were even more engaging than the city.

The climb up was like a mountain climb, by calculated paths and ascent from cliff to cliff. It was vertiginous, a strange experience for the ex-seaman who never lost his taste for mounting a mast, and who, as Horsford observed, took advantage of every opportunity throughout this trip to go *up*, whether in tower or elsewhere, and who in Constantinople even longed to get aloft over the mazed streets of the city (p. 21). But there was another side to the pyramids too: where the summit was dizzying, the tunneled entrances to the depths were terrifying. "It was in these pyramids that was conceived the idea of Jehovah. Terrible mixture of the cunning and awful" (p. 118).

On 4 January Melville sailed from Alexandria to Jaffa, whence on landing he set out at once for Jerusalem. The author of *Clarel*, now on the scene of the long poem he was to publish almost twenty years later, began his visit to the Holy Land with several days of sightseeing concerning which he recorded little at first. The *Clarel* material was accumulating, however—some details from stops made before reaching the Holy Land were to become part of *Clarel*—and the hotel where he stayed the first night in Jerusalem would find its place in the poem.

It was not until his Holy Land visit was over and Melville found himself waiting in Jaffa for a ship to Beirut that he recorded his impressions of Jerusalem, its environs, and an excursion to the Dead Sea. It was a bleached, stony, and rubbishy land. "The mind can not but be sadly & suggestively affected with the indifference of Nature & Man to all that makes the spot sacred to the Christian" (pp. 141–42).

The sacred shrines of Christianity were duly visited. Of all of them the Church of the Holy Sepulchre drew Melville's attention most. The marble bedizened, theatrical display of the sepulchre itself repelled him and, he felt, repelled his fellow pilgrims as well. The sacred associations of the places contrasted with their surroundings grimly at times and at times comically: "Yonder is the arch where Christ was shown to the people, & just by that open window is sold the best coffee in Jerusalem" (p. 151).

Melville recorded his impressions of several missionaries who had come out from America to improve the agricultural and spiritual condition of the land. The sketches of Mr. and Mrs. Saunders of Rhode Island, Mrs. Minor of Philadelphia, and Mr. and Mrs. Dickson of Massachusetts illustrate what to Melville was the folly, futility, and pathos of introducing rationalized enthusiasm into that agriculturally and spiritually unresponsive land. This is the note on which Melville's record of the Holy Land closes. It may have seemed to him in years ahead that the best way to do justice to the leprous landscape and singular atmosphere of Jerusalem to whose "weird impression" he had offered "myself up a passive subject, and no unwilling one" (p. 145) was to people it not merely with Dicksons, Saunderses, and himself, but with a wider range of types whom fate and impulse could draw there. The result was *Clarel*, the fullness of his 1856 *Journal*.

From Jaffa Melville went to Beirut in an Austrian steamer, staying in that city from 25 January to 1 February. "Quiet days," he called them. He jotted down no unfavorable impressions of Beirut. Another Austrian steamer, slow and foul, carried him back past Cyprus, Cos, Samos, and Patmos to Smyrna. Ashore for just a few hours there, he sailed on to Scio and Syra, making his third stop at that island, and then went on to Piraeus and Athens.

Approaching Athens by moonlight, Melville had a view of the Acropolis from the road which he later recalled in two poems, which, taken together, come to about the same length as his journal entries on Athens; the journal entries on the city are written with a curiously half-interested air. Then it was on to Sicily and Naples. In Messina Melville met his friend Dr. Lockwood again and was the guest of Lockwood and the officers of the U.S.F. *Constellation* at dinner in their ward room. In and around Naples Melville made the natural tourist stops; Pompeii and Vesuvius were first, then Posilipo, Castelmarre, Sorrento, Pozzuoli, and Baiae.

An anecdote from Melville's Naples experiences is worth quoting not merely because it captures Melville's mood (and the spirit of Naples) but because his transformation of it into verse in the opening lines of "Naples in the Time of Bomba" is a tidy and typical example of the journal's shorthand growing into a rounded literary statement. The journal entry for 21 February reads:

Tumblers in narrow street. Blocked way. Balconies with women. Cloth on ground. They gave way, after natural reluctance. Merriment. Turned round & gave the most grateful & graceful bow I could. Handkerchiefs waved from balconies, good humored cries & c—Felt prouder than an Emperor. (p. 184)

After some scene setting, the poem describing these events reads:

> We jounced along till, just ahead,
> Nor far from shrine in niche of wall
> A stoppage fell. His rug or bed
> In midmost way a tumbler spread,
> A posturing mountebank withall;
> Who, though his stage was out of doors,
> *Brought down the house* in jolly applause.
> "Signor," exclaims my charioteer,
> Turning, and reining up, the while
> Trying to touch his jaunty hat;
> But here, essaying to condense
> Such opposite movements into one
> Failing, and letting fall his whip,
> "His Excellency stops the way!"
> *His Excellency* there, meanwhile—
> Reversed in stature, legs aloft,
> And hobbling jigs on hands for heels—
> Gazed up with blood-shot brow that told

The tension of that nimble play—
Gazed up as martyred Peter might;
And, noting me in landeau-seat
(*Milor*, there he opined, no doubt)
Brisk somersetted back, and stood
Urbanely bowing, then gave place;
While, tickled at my puzzled plight,
Yet mindful that a move was due,
And knowing me a stranger there,
With one consent the people part
Yielding a passage, and with eyes
Of friendly fun,—how courteous too!
Catching an impulse from their air,
To feet I spring, my beaver doff
And broadcast wave a blithe salute.
In genial way how humorsome
What pleased responses of surprise;
From o'er the Alps, and so polite!
They clap their hands in frank acclaim
Matrons in door-ways nod and smile
From balcony roguish girls laugh out
Or kiss their fingers, rain their nosegays down.
At such a shower—laugh, clap, and flower—
My horses shy, the landeau tilts,
Distractedly the driver pulls.

     (*Poems*, pp. 339–41)

The poem goes on, expressing the speaker's delight at becoming "the popular hero," and being given a triumph worthy of an emperor.

Leaving Naples Melville went to Rome, arriving the morning of 25 February. The three and a half weeks that Melville spent in Rome made it his longest stay anywhere on this trip. His first impressions, which were disappointing, were succeeded by a packed schedule of visits to archaeological, architectural, and artistic treasures, and these quickly became engrossing. They included St. Peter's, the Coliseum, the Capitoline Museum, and Protestant cemetery where Keats and Shelley lay, the Cenci palace, the Villa Borghese, the Villa Albani, St. John Lateran, every kind of neighborhood from the Pincian to the Ghetto, and a host of other places and attractions. The climax of his sightseeing came on 2 March when he went to the Vatican Museum: "Fagged out completely, & sat long time by the obelisk, recovering from the stunning effect of a first visit to the Vatican" (p. 200).

New sights and revisited ones filled up his days until on 5 March he had to retire early because of eye trouble, a complaint that was going to recur in days to come and intensify in years ahead. An American lawyer, Peter Rousse, and Rousse's sister Anna were frequent companions of

Melville, and Melville visited the studios of the American painter William Page and the British sculptor John Gibson.

More detail about art work and more critical appraisal of it appear in the Roman entries than anywhere else in Melville's journal. The lecture on "Statues in Rome" which he would be giving within a year to American audiences was apparently beginning to take shape in his mind.

Melville combined his active touring in the city with excursions outside it to Frascati and Tivoli. On 21 March after almost a month in Rome, Melville moved on. A steamer from Civita Vecchia took him to Leghorn "Nothing special about Leghorn" (pp. 215–16)—and from there he went on to Pisa and Florence. His journal notes at this point are devoted to inventories of the museums; there was little else in Florence that caught his attention. He included a side trip to Fiesole before going through Bologna, Ferrara, and Padua to Venice, where he arrived 1 April. His few days in the city on the water were spent in the same kind of well-informed sightseeing as his days in Rome and Constantinople had been— the Rialto, St. Mark's, a glass bead factory, the Academia delle Belle Arti, the Lido. Traveling through the canals was one of the chief pleasures of Melville's visit to Venice, and the experience seems to have left him relaxed and happy.

Melville left Venice on 6 April, and from this point on all of his stops on the continent were brief, usually overnight. The itinerary now was Milan, Turin, Genoa, Lucerne, Berne, Basel, Strasbourg, Heidelberg, Frankfurt, Mainz, Cologne, Amsterdam, and Rotterdam. Where he stayed, whom he met, what he saw are noted in his journal as usual, but even after he returned to London on 26 April his observations are relatively casual and inconsequential. In Oxford on 3 May his responsiveness perked up: "It was here I first confessed with gratitude my mother land, & hailed her with pride" (p. 259).

From Oxford it was on to Stratford-upon-Avon, Warwick, Birmingham, and Liverpool. "Saw Hawthorne," Melville notes—and nothing more. Hawthorne does not record the visit at all. On 6 May Melville sailed for home on the steamer *City of Manchester*; on 19 May he was back in New York.

READY TO LECTURE

Melville's decision to go on the lecture trail a few months after his return from Europe was not unrelated to the European trip itself. The journal he kept seemed to be, in some of its entries, a conscious hoarding of material for future use—one explicitly noted possibility in the journal was the use of some of the travel material in a projected sequel to *The Confidence-Man* (pp. 31–32). The combination of reasons that led him to put the material to use in lectures rather than books or magazine articles is discussed in Sealts's *Melville as Lecturer* (1957), the all-important source on Melville's lecture tours. Sealts assembled all the known newspaper reviews of Melville's three lectures (of which no manuscripts are known to remain) and from them restored all that could be restored of the lectures; the book contains the reconstructed lectures and a history of the tours. These materials are included in the NN edition of *Piazza Tales and Other Prose Pieces*. Earlier articles on Melville as lecturer were published by Merrell R. Davis, Francis V. Lloyd, and John Howard Birss.

The tours were apparently not interesting for Melville; they were business, and he went at them assiduously: "If they will pay expences, & give a reasonable fee, I am ready to lecture in Labrador or on the Isle of Desolation off Patagonia," Melville wrote to George Duyckinck on 20 December 1858 (*Letters*, p. 193). Duyckinck had visited Melville at the end of the first season of lecturing and found him "robust and fine looking" but suffering from serious back trouble (*Mel. Log*, p. 595).

For each of his three tours Melville chose a topic that drew on his experience as a traveler. This meant abandoning one amusing topic: "Daily progress of man towards a state of intellectual and moral perfection, as evidenced in history of 5th Avenue & 5 Points" (*Lectures*, p. 7). The subject settled on for the 1857–58 tour was "Statues in Rome."

Melville delivered his first lecture on this tour on 23 November 1857 in Lawrence, Massachusetts, and his last on 23 February 1858 in New Bedford. In between he spoke in Concord, Boston, Montreal, Saratoga Springs, New Haven, Auburn (New York), Ithaca, Cleveland, Detroit, Clarksville (Tennessee), Cincinnati, Chillicothe, Charlestown (Massachusetts), and Rochester (New York) (pp. 20–56). Melville's subject may seem a bit refined for audiences in some of these places—or for what one would imagine to have been the audiences—but receptions were more favorable than not. The only consistent complaint in newspaper reviews of the lectures was about the low level of the speaker's voice which left those beyond the first few rows straining to hear.

From the reconstructions of the lectures which Sealts put together one can see why Melville's handling of the subject of Roman statuary did interest a general audience: it was more psychological than aesthetic (*Lectures*, pp. 127–54). The lecture was a long study in motivation and character, both of the figures represented in the statuary and of the culture that wanted them so represented. It was the voice of a novelist and was an articulation of the way Melville did his looking when he traveled. It was the regulation of reality popularly explained.

The second lecture tour ran from 6 December 1858 to 16 March 1859 and took Melville to Yonkers, Pittsfield, Boston, New York, Baltimore, Chicago, Milwaukee, Rockford (Illinois), Quincy (Illinois), and Lynn (Massachusetts). This time the subject was "The South Seas," probably a concession to the undeniable interest of general audiences in the subject matter of *Typee* and *Omoo*. The lecture was not, as Melville advised his audiences at the start, a rehash of impressions from the two novels; it was instead a view of the great ocean as a phenomenon, a kind of philosophy of the Pacific. It was a step beyond anything said in *Typee* and *Omoo* and showed the same receptivity to the ocean that his journal remarks and earlier lecture did to contents of the Villa Albani.

Melville's third lecture, "Traveling: Its Pleasures, Pains, and Profits," was delivered in Flushing (Long Island) on 7 November 1859, South Danvers (Massachusetts) on 14 February 1860, and Cambridgeport (Massachusetts) on 21 February 1860. With this short series Melville's platform career ended.

For our present purposes the lecture on "Traveling" is one we would like to have the full text of, but it happens to be the one we know least about, for there is no record of it except in one newspaper review (pp. 181–85). From that review one can conclude that Melville's main points were that to travel well one must be young, care-free, genial, and imaginative, else one would be bored even traveling to paradise, and that travel's benefits are loss of prejudices, rebirth of the self, and vividness of experience. In the phrasing of the brief newspaper review are suggestions that the lecture contained a profound statement of the need to get the larger view of one's situation in life and the need to bring that view back home.

CALIFORNIA: THEN A BRUSH WITH WAR

There was more traveling in store for Melville a few months after his last lecture. On 28 May 1860 he sailed from Boston for California on the *Meteor*, the captain of which was his brother Thomas. How far he had originally intended to go is unclear, but a week after he arrived in San Francisco—and in spite of the interest in hearing him lecture expressed in a local newspaper—he booked passage back home on a ship to Panama, whence he crossed the isthmus and boarded another ship for New York. Melville's days in San Francisco coincided with the operation of the Pony Express, and he was able to use that short-lived service to send word east of his early return.

One thing that is known about the *Meteor* voyage and the return from California is that Melville brought a good deal of reading with him. The *Meteor* inscription appears in several titles in Sealts's *Melville's Reading*; some annotation in these volumes, apparently made on board the ship, suggests close rather than casual reading.

The last bit of Melville travel that should be singled out as particularly significant is his 1864 trip to the Civil War front outside of Washington. Melville's trip to Washington and his excursion to visit the Union forces was made with his brother Allan apparently at the invitation of his cousin

Colonel Henry S. Gansevoort. A pass signed by the Secretary of War, Edwin Stanton, authorized Melville to visit the Army of the Potomac. Getting the pass took some string pulling and the argument that Melville, being a writer, needed the trip to gather material. Anyone who has read Melville's *Battle-Pieces, and Aspects of the War* will know that first-hand experience of every aspect of the war he wrote about was no more indispensable to Melville than it was to Stephen Crane. But there is one long poem of Melville's, "The Scout Toward Aldie," which utilizes so many details of an actual scouting party that Melville rode along on that it comes close to being history. It was a situation of real danger that the scouting party moved into, and it returned with Confederate captives. Stanton Garner observes that Melville's "participation in this scout made him the only major American writer of the nineteenth century to take part in a real sense in a combat operation, and, in his narrative poem entitled 'The Scout Toward Aldie,' the only one to write about the war from the point of view of one who had done so" (*Melville Society Extracts*, No. 51, p. 5). It probably never dawned on Melville that he had gained that distinction. Knowing what we now do about Melville's role in the scouting operation, we can read the poem with particular interest. As an experiment in turning life into verse, it is small next to *Clarel* but extensive and dramatic next to the shorter poems based on travel experience such as the Neapolitan poem quoted above. On this episode in Melville's life see Stanton Garner's "Melville's Scout Toward Aldie" (1982) and Jay Leyda's "The Army of the Potomac Entertains a Poet" (1948).

THE VIEW FROM ON HIGH

The movements of Herman Melville from place to place which in this study have been called "travel" with some special formality were selected not because of their length—although all of his long journeys have been treated here—but because of their moment. All of Melville's travels from his Liverpool voyage onward had demonstrable ties to his literary work. The specific ties of this trip to that scene in a novel are usually easy to demonstrate; so is the great overall tie of all of his travel to the formation of his imagination.

Part of that great overall tie is the fact that the whole world that he encountered was what Ishmael said a whaleship was, "my Yale College and my Harvard." And at college one does not learn just facts; one learns principles. Another part of the overall tie is that Melville's imagination was kept alive in the fashion he described in his lecture, "Traveling": by departure and return, by "view[ing] the landscape from the summit" and then coming down to the base of the hill again (*Lectures*, p. 182). The view from on high is needed—it is the truth—but one does not stay at the summit. Lucy in *Pierre*, taken to a mountaintop, became distressed precisely because she saw too far. Captain Vere had the lofty view of a migratory waterfowl, but the waterfowl did not know when it crossed a frontier; the crewmen he commanded saw everything up close and sensed all the frontiers. A large part of Melville's discipline as a writer was keeping both visions acute; his travel was part of his effort to do so.

The theme of travel and quest in Melville's work is explored in John Seelye, *Melville: The Ironic Diagram* (1970). Edwin Fussell treats Melville in the context of early western travels in *Frontier: American Literature and the American West* (1965). See also Janet Giltrow, "Speaking Out: Travel and Structure in Herman Melville's Early Narratives" (1980), and Howard C. Key, "The Influence of Travel Literature Upon Herman Melville's Fictional Technique" (*Mel. Diss.*, #55).

Melville was not a travel writer, the popular misreading of his first two novels notwithstanding. Melville's acquaintance, Bayard Taylor, was a travel writer. Hawthorne's friend, G. S. Hillard, was a travel writer. But it would have been constitutionally alien to Melville to bring to home audiences impressions of anything foreign for the sake of its foreignness. In "Statues in Rome" the interest is in statues that tell tales; it is accidental that they are in Rome. If one reads Henry James's *Portraits of Places* and compares Melville and James treating the same place—Venice, for example—one may be struck by some similarities, but in the end one comes away from James with an impression that Venice is in Italy and from Melville with an impression that Venice is in the world.

WORKS CITED

Adler, George J. *Letters of a Lunatic, or, A Brief Exposition of My University Life During the Years 1853–54.* [New York?]: By the Author, 1854.

Anderson, Charles Roberts, ed. *Journal of a Cruise to the Pacific Ocean, 1842–1844 in the Frigate United States; With Notes on Herman Melville.* Durham, N. C.: Duke University Press, 1937.

———. *Melville in the South Seas.* New York: Columbia University Press, 1939; rpt. New York: Dover, 1966.

———. "The Romance of Scholarship: Tracking Melville in the South Seas." *Colophon* 3 (Spring 1938): 259–79.

Birss, John Howard. "Herman Melville Lectures in Yonkers." *American Book Collector* 5 (February 1934): 50–52.

Bradley, Lyman R. "George J. Adler, 1821–1868." *German Quarterly* 7 (1934): 152–56.

Conway, Ainslie, and Frances Conway. *The Enchanted Isles.* New York: Putnam, 1947.

Davis, Merrell R. "Melville's Midwestern Lecture Tour, 1859." *Philological Quarterly* 20 (January 1941): 46–57.

Forsythe, Robert S. "Herman Melville in Honolulu." *New England Quarterly* 8 (March 1935): 99–105.

———. "Herman Melville in the Marquesas." *Philological Quarterly* 15 (January 1936): 1–15.

———. "Herman Melville in Tahiti." *Philological Quarterly* 16 (October 1937): 344–57.

———. "Herman Melville's Father Murphy." *Notes and Queries* 172 (10 and 17 April 1937): 254–58, 272–76.

———. "More Upon Herman Melville in Tahiti." *Philological Quarterly* 17 (January 1938): 1–17.

Franklin, Samuel R. *Memories of a Rear-Admiral.* New York and London: Harper & Brothers, 1898.

Fussell, Edwin. *Frontier: American Literature and the American West.* Princeton, N. J.: Princeton University Press, 1965.

Garner, Stanton. "Melville's Scout Toward Aldie." *Melville Society Extracts* No. 51 (September 1982): 5–16; and No. 52 (November 1982): 1–14.

———. "The Picaresque Career of Thomas Melvill, Junior." *Melville Society Extracts* No. 60 (November 1984): 1–10; and No. 62 (May 1985): 1, 4–10.

Gilman, William H. *Melville's Early Life and Redburn.* New York: New York University Press, 1951.

Giltrow, Janet. "Speaking out: Travel and Structure in Herman Melville's Early Narratives." *American Literature* 52 (1980): 18–32.

Hawthorne, Nathaniel. *English Notebooks.* Ed. Randall Stewart. New York: Modern Language Association of America, 1941; rpt. New York: Russell & Russell, 1962.

Hayford, Harrison, and Walter Blair, eds. *Omoo: A Narrative of Adventures in the South Seas.* By Herman Melville. New York: Hendricks House, 1969.

Heffernan, Thomas Farel. *Stove by a Whale: Owen Chase and the Essex.* Middletown, Conn.: Wesleyan University Press, 1981.

Heflin, Wilson. "Melville and Nantucket." In *Moby-Dick Centennial Essays.* Ed. Tyrus Hillway and Luther S. Mansfield. Dallas: Southern Methodist University Press, 1953.

———. "Melville's Third Whaler." *Modern Language Notes* 64 (1949): 241–45.

———. "New Light on Melville's Cruise in the *Charles and Henry.*" *Historic Nantucket* 22 (October 1974): 6–27.

Horsford, Howard. "Melville in the London Literary World." *Essays in Arts and Science* 13 (1984): 23–42.

James, Henry. *Portraits of Places.* New York: Lear Publishers, 1948.

Key, Howard C. "The Influence of Travel Literature Upon Herman Melville's Fictional Technique." Ph. D. Diss., Stanford University, 1953. [*Mel. Diss,* #55.]

Lee, Dwight A. "Melville and George J. Adler." *American Notes and Queries* 12 (May/June 1974): 138–41.

Leyda, Jay. "The Army of the Potomac Entertains a Poet." *Art and Action: Twice a Year* 16 (1948): 259–72.

Lloyd, Francis V., Jr. "A Further Note on Herman Melville, Lecturer." *Bulletin of the Massachusetts Historical Society* 20 (July 1964): 310–12.

————. "Melville's First Lectures." *American Literature* 13 (January 1942): 391–95.

Melville, Herman. *Journal of a Visit to Europe and The Levant, October 11, 1856—May 6, 1857*. Ed. Howard Horsford. Princeton, N. J.: Princeton University Press, 1955; rpt. Westport, Conn.: Greenwood Press, 1976. [An earlier edition was published under the title *Journal Up the Straits* (Ed. Raymond Weaver. New York: Colophon, 1935; rpt. New York: Cooper Square, 1971). Ample annotations make the Horsford edition more useful. Revised editions (by Howard Horsford) of this journal and the following two will be included in the NN *Journals* volume.]

————. *Journal of a Visit to London and the Continent 1849–50*. Ed. Eleanor Melville Metcalf. Cambridge, Mass.: Harvard University Press, 1948.

————. "Journal of Melville's Voyage in a Clipper Ship." *New England Quarterly* 2 (January 1929): 120–25.

Nichol, John W. "Melville and the Midwest." *PMLA* 66 (September 1951): 613–25.

Nuñez, Estuardo. "Herman Melville en el Peru." *Panorama* 3 (1954): 3–25.

Sealts, Merton M., Jr. *The Early Lives of Melville*. Madison: University of Wisconsin Press, 1974.

————. *Melville as Lecturer*. Cambridge, Mass.: Harvard University Press, 1957; rpt. Folcroft, Pa.: Folcroft, 1970.

Seelye, John. *Melville: The Ironic Diagram*. Evanston, Ill.: Northwestern University Press, 1970.

Strauch, Dore. *Satan Came to Eden*. New York: Harper, 1936.

Tanselle, G. Thomas. "Herman Melville's Visit to Galena in 1840." *Journal of the Illinois State Historical Society* 53 (Winter 1960): 376–88.

Treherne, John. *The Galapagos Affair*. New York: Random House, 1983.

Vincent, Howard P. *The Tailoring of Melville's White-Jacket*. Evanston, Ill.: Northwestern University Press, 1970.

Yannella, Donald, and Hershel Parker, eds. *The Endless, Winding Way in Melville: New Charts by Kring and Carey*. Glassboro, N. J.: Melville Society, 1981.

3

WRITING THE *"OTHER* WAY": MELVILLE, THE DUYCKINCK CROWD, AND LITERATURE FOR THE MASSES

Donald Yannella

Among my several purposes in this chapter is a consideration of a very trying period in Herman Melville's career during the 1850s, when he began writing for *Harper's* and *Putnam's* monthly magazines. The difficulty in understanding this phase of Melville's life is representative. We must rely heavily on sources of information other than Melville himself because he was at best a fitful and sketchy recordkeeper and a person evidently given to discarding documents that would be of aid to students of his life and work. To gain some idea of what he knew about the world of journalism, I will attempt to offer a glimpse of it that is afforded by a few of the New York literati Melville knew and worked with, the Duyckinck brothers and Cornelius Mathews. His relations with them are also of concern. My principal resource, the Duyckinck Family Papers, is a massive collection on deposit at the New York Public Library. Along our way through the tough commercial publishing world these people inhabited, we will try to piece together a reasonably substantiated landscape but also be tentative and not claim too much certitude about it. It is, after all, of our making. A similar caution is suggested in considering a possible interpretation of "The Fiddler," one of the short prose pieces Melville published in the 1850s. Finally, I hope to tempt other scholars to search in manuscript archives as well as encourage them to continue the quest for new documents in barns and attics. Such materials are, after all, the heart of biography and scholarship generally. They may seem irrelevant or tangential at first glance but may prove to be useful, even enlightening.

In his remarkable and frequently quoted letter to Hawthorne on or about 1 June 1851, Melville complained about being "so pulled hither and thither by circumstances" that "The calm, the coolness, the silent grass-growing mood in which a man *ought* always to compose" could "seldom" be his. Furthermore, he was damned by dollars, and said that what he felt "most moved to write, that is banned,—it will not pay. Yet, altogether, write the *other* way I cannot. So the product is a final hash, and all my books are botches" (*Letters*, p. 128).

Calling attention to Melville's lament about being unable to write "altogether" the "*other* way," the one that paid (and still does!), helps us focus on his grappling with the dilemma which every serious writer of the modern period has confronted. Perhaps we can sharpen our image by posing a few of the questions such authors seem compelled to ask: How far does one go in responding to the taste of the reading audience— today's mass market or consumer group—without severely or utterly compromising one's integrity and that of his or her writing? Put more forcefully, should a line even be drawn between the author's need to state what he wishes and must and the expectations, requirements, tastes, or demands of his audience, editor, publisher, or all three? Stated even more simplistically, does the author write for himself or his reader? All of us have pondered and discussed these and related aspects of authorship. They are legitimate, even crucial concerns, but it is not my purpose here to formulate yet another series of possible, worthy answers to such insoluble problems, to add my voice to the continuing dialogue.

What I am going to do is offer some information which will show that Evert A. Duyckinck's crowd—including its central figures, his brother, George, and novelist Cornelius Mathews[1]—was confronting these perennial dilemmas in the early 1850s period, a crucial half-decade in American literary history; that their resolutions were quite different from Melville's, or at least the one he leaned toward; and that the gulf that separated him from the Duyckincks and Mathews on this issue may have been a factor in the estrangement that some literary historians judge is suggested by some of the evidence that has survived, or at least been recovered—or noticed—and published to date (for example, Howard, pp. 191–92, 198–200, 236; *Pierre*, pp. 375–76, 381n.3).

In the early 1850s, probably earlier, Melville was confronting several major questions about his writing career. He was faced not only with the relative failure of his long prose works in the hard, demanding, money-making marketplace, but also with the proposition—perhaps "reality" is a better term—that were his fortunes in it to improve, he would have to alter, perhaps radically, the sort of writing he had been doing. He undoubtedly confronted what appeared to be a necessity that to enhance his popularity and, therefore, improve the sales of his writings, he might have to be more flexible and hospitable to popular and commercially successful writing than he appears to have been willing or capable of being. Contemporaries and peers, such as Mathews and the Duyckincks, on the other hand, seem to have been quite able and ready to respond to the demands of the burgeoning mass market for literature in a manner that Melville may have "preferred" not to emulate.

To clarify my suggestion, allow me to review what I consider some significant pieces of information about the literary world these people inhabited; then, with these facts as my base, indulge in a bit of interpretation or speculation about the statement Melville may have been making in one of his early magazine pieces, "The Fiddler." Finally, I will conclude with some observations about the widely supposed hiatus in the relationships between the Duyckincks, especially Evert, and Melville—evidence and inferences about which may well obfuscate whatever I might succeed in illuminating in the longer part of this chapter. To paraphrase and perhaps even warp the words of Whitman, another New Yorker of the period, one almost thoroughly ignored if not repudiated by those in the part of the scene Melville and the Duyckinck crowd moved in: Will I contradict myself? Very well then I will contradict myself. My subject is large; it contains multitudes—of gaps of information! Finally, at the risk of guaranteeing the failure of my rhetorical strategy by too severely trying your patience, I warn you that I will be presenting several seemingly unrelated or poorly cut—even perhaps irrelevant—pieces as I ask you to join me in building our puzzle, our landscape.

Let me begin by considering *Holden's Dollar Magazine.*

Early in 1851 the Duyckinck brothers had acquired this monthly journal, and Evert invited Melville to contribute and even requested a daguerreotype that might serve as a model for a cut or engraving in the magazine. (Evert understood the value of promotion in the fiercely competitive literary marketplace which he had been near or at the center of for almost a decade.) In his response of 12 February Melville claimed to have no such picture to send and—anticipating that Evert might charge him with false modesty—he wrote: "The fact is, almost everybody is having his 'mug' engraved nowadays; so that this test of distinction is getting to be reversed; and therefore, to see one's 'mug' in a magazine, is presumptive evidence that he's a nobody." Standing Evert and his request on their respective heads, as a substitute for being stood on his own in the camera, Melville "respectfully decline[d] being oblivionated by" a picture of *his* "mug" in the press. Lest his friend Evert be hurt by his refusal, he admitted his "queerness," "his own distinct peculiarity," and reminded Duyckinck that in fact "We are all queer customers, Mr Duycknck [*sic*], you, I, & every body else in the world" (*Letters*, p. 121). Castaways, Renegades, Ishmaels, Pierres—all.

The vigor of Melville's response in this letter, however, may have less to do with daguerreotypes than with the sort of journal *Holden's* in fact was. Deep in the composition of his sixth and greatest book, *Moby-Dick,* this "wild Everest of art," to borrow Henry Murray's elegantly ambiguous phrase (p. xiii), this giant who had or was "now [to] come to the inmost leaf of the bulb" (*Letters*, p. 130), as he described his development several months later in a letter to Hawthorne, was being asked to interrupt his labors on *The Whale* to write a piece for what we may justly label a "pop" magazine. "I can not write the thing you want," he told Duyckinck. "I am in the humor to lend a hand to a friend, if I can;—but I am not in the humor to write . . . for Holden's Magazine." Refusing to stipulate his reasons, he told Evert that "You must be content to believe that I *have* reasons, or else I would not refuse so small a thing" (*Letters*, p. 120). And so we are left to infer, even speculate, as Duyckinck had to, about Melville's "reasons."

My suggestion is that that *Holden's* carried the same sort of aroma, intolerable to Melville at this critical point in his intense career, exuded by *Yankee Doodle*, the short-lived satire weekly run by Mathews and supported by the Duyckincks, in the summer of 1847 when Melville had contributed his Old Zack satires and a modest number of other pieces recently attributed to him by Merton M. Sealts, Jr., in the forthcoming collection of his shorter prose (NN, vol. 9). To offer something more substantial about the nature and quality—and intended audience—of *Holden's*, let us look at George Long Duyckinck's letter to the enigmatic and brilliant Long Islander, Joann Miller.[2] George was writing on 8 February 1851, four days before Melville turned down Evert's request.

"We" have been purchasing a monthly magazine which we intend to carry on in connection with the *Literary World*[,] that is[,] they will be published from the same office though the matter and plan of each will be widely different[.]

We have long had such an overflow of excellent matter for the Literary World that we have often thought of starting a magazine. In this state of affairs Holden's Dollar Magazine was offered to us for sale on favorable terms and I agreed to take it. You may not have seen the publication. It is a monthly of 48 pp double columns, subscription $1.00 a year. You see this is on the basis of the broadest popularity and it remains to be seen whether we can succeed in catering and writing for "the million"—if we are the "elegant inutilities" you once styled [us?] we certainly cannot. The Magazine requires from 8 to 10,000 subscribers to pay, and has now about half that number so you see we have some work before us— this is of course confidential. (Box 49)

But it seems, these "elegant inutilities" were quite willing to be inelegant utilities and write "altogether" the "*other* way," as Melville phrased it. We should note that with four or five thousand subscribers, *Holden's* was at the time the Duyckincks acquired it a much better seller than the *Literary World*. To understand George's comments to Miller and some information presented below, a few words about the state of the *Literary World* are in order. We might summarize the tale by considering David Davidson's connection with the weekly. Davidson was that "good fellow"

(*Letters*, p. 95) with whom Melville had spent "two evenings" in London late in 1849; the first was "at the Mitre Tavern" in Fleet Street where they enjoyed "doing" their steaks and then went on "(by omnibus) to the 'Blue Posts' " where they "had a pint of real punch at the very table" George, William Allen Butler, and Davidson "had blue posted a dinner" a few years earlier, when the younger Duyckinck and Butler, his classmate at the University of the City of New York (now New York University), were on their grand tour. The second night Davidson and Melville returned to the Blue Posts where Melville paid the tab for a steak dinner, "ending on empty pitchers," that lasted from six until eleven-thirty. Davidson reported that "We talked of you [George], of several New Yorkers, some books, [Melville's] affairs," and his "tour."[3] And they undoubtedly discussed the *Literary World.* For somewhat more than a year earlier—in 1848, that is—Davidson had offered to serve the Duyckincks as London agent and to get advertisements for *Literary World* (Davidson, letter to George Long Duyckinck, 10[?] November 1848, Box 46), an offer they accepted. In a letter to George on 6 February 1849, he reported on what he was doing as their English Connection (Box 46). But activities in behalf of them and the journal were not to be confined to England. Davidson came to the United States sometime in 1850 and by early 1852 was handling the business affairs of the journal and promoting its circulation in this country. His efforts included canvassing and drumming trips—promotion excursions—to places such as Boston, Washington, and Buffalo. But to little avail. By the end of 1852 the circulation and finances of *Literary World* were bad enough to have George entertain the possibility of closing down the operation, even though Davidson insisted that matters would improve in 1853. They did not. By the summer of 1853, notes were being called and Robert Craighead, the Duyckincks' printer as well as Melville's, was demanding payment of outstanding bills. During 1853 Davidson himself had bought into *Literary World* sufficiently to allow George to argue that its debts were his—that is, Davidson's.[4] The haggling continued through 1854, and it would seem that George won—that is, was successful in making Davidson responsible for at least some of the debts the journal had incurred in 1853.[5] (I should add here that the two were also partners in an importing business in 1853—sculpture, painting, and so forth— which was evidently more profitable[6] than *Literary World*, whose circulation never rose above about 1,500 to 1,750,[7] a far cry from George's hopes for *Holden's* as they were expressed in his 1851 letter to Joann Miller.)

All this is by way of background. Now back to George's concluding remarks in his hopeful letter of 8 February 1851 to Miller:

My idea about the matter is that the intended agencies of the affair would help the Literary World and that it would be a good mode of testing the question whether a good popular magazine (with plenty of stories and light reading) could be made to succeed without fashion plates and Laura Matilda literature. It is the cheapest magazine in the country and we mean to and I think can make it the best. No one who wants it but can afford a dollar a year for it, and it is within the possibilities that it might attain a circulation of 50,000[.] However I am not sanguine in the matter and if I fail will have the satisfaction of failing in a good cause....

You must not understand that the Lit World will be tapped for this affair. We intend to make our first undertaking as good or better, than ever....

What do we want to attract the ladies? (Box 49)

I am sure Hawthorne's complaint about "scribbling" women writers as well as recent interpreters of them such as Ann Douglas and Nina Baym, among others, are called to mind. However, my point is that Melville knew *precisely* the sort of audience the Duyckincks were trying to reach with *Holden's*, and he wanted no part of it. Perhaps *Yankee Doodle* had been enough; more likely, by 1851 the "Everest of art" was incapable of caring about reaching a mass audience and commanding fame. Back to the June 1851 letter to Hawthorne: "All Fame is patronage. Let me be infamous; there is no patronage in *that*.... I have come to regard this matter of Fame as the most transparent of all vanities" (*Letters*, pp. 129–30). Perhaps it was impossible for him to write for "the million"—the word George used in his letter to Joann Miller and precisely the word, in its plural form (even more ambitious), Evert and Cornelius Mathews had proposed as the title of a "weekly folio newspaper of the general size, quantity of matter and of the price of the Sunday Dispatch" (Box 35); the draft of this legal document is undated (though it is probably from the 1840s), and to my knowledge the newspaper was never published. Had it been, it undoubtedly would have been nothing but another variation on the popular magazine: a "weekly of elevated tone, but agreeable and amusing," as Thomas Delf described *his* suggested "Ladies Newspaper" in a letter to Evert on [1?] December 1847, shortly after the collapse of *Yankee Doodle*: "Something that should annihilate," he went on, "the infernal host of Lady's Mags &c. I am of opinion that if entered upon with due preparation, an [*sic*] well matured plan, the proper precaution, a circulation of 10,000 could be secured. The *title* would be worth 50 pr cent"(Box 18).

These contemporaries of Melville knew what they were about and were willing to attempt reaching a large audience, aggressively and even enthusiastically, by indeed writing "altogether" the "*other* way." Yes, literature was art. But it was also business. Of course, Melville knew this, too, but was, I think, unable when the chips were down to treat the enterprise, if we might call it that, as a business to turn a profit. As Melville came down from the publication of *Moby-Dick*, and as the pain of *Pierre* suffused his spirit, Evert Duyckinck—with *Holden's* already failed and the *Literary World* slipping further into the red—diversified by signing an agreement on 21 January 1852 with Appleton's to give "editorial aid and assistance in the selection of the [popular library]," a series not unlike the Library of Choice Reading and the Library of American Books—in which *Typee* had appeared—that he had edited for Wiley and Putnam in the mid–1840s. For his services Appleton would pay Evert 2 percent of the gross sales (Box 35).

There is perhaps no better illustration of the hard business instincts and practices of the Duyckincks than the story of their acquisition of the publishing firm of Justus Redfield. To begin, recall Evert's reporting from Pittsfield—where he was visiting Melville—to his wife Margaret, on 7 August 1851, that the Harpers were "to publish Melville's whale book. I have said a great deal for Redfield but it appears to have been concluded." He instructed her to pass this information to her brother, Henry Panton (*Mel. Log*, p. 420). Fewer than two years later, on 11 April 1853, Redfield was in financial trouble, and George entered a partnership with him by putting up common stocks valued at $10,000, this for a one-third share of the business; for his two-thirds' interest Redfield contributed his presses, plates, sheets, books, copyrights, engravings, store fixtures—virtually everything. Their total appraised value was $40,000. According to a memorandum of agreement between George and Redfield (Box 53), the partnership was scheduled to terminate in five years—that is, on 10 April 1858—but by May 1855 Redfield's financial woes had worsened. George, who was publicly silent through all this, and John A. Panton (another of Evert's brothers-in-law who had been admitted to the bar in 1850) got all Redfield's rights to print, publish, and sell in May of 1855, and by November 1857, after having extended even more loans to Redfield, caused him to bankrupt by calling in the notes. Redfield's assets were $50,000, including his house in Brooklyn, worth $7,500. (To be fair, we must recall that economic distress was widespread during this Panic year of 1857, and not leap to the conclusion that Panton and George had been rather callously setting up Redfield.) Intricate lawsuits occurred when it was discovered that Redfield, after indemnifying himself to John Panton in 1857, used the same collateral to secure loans from other sources.[8] John and George won, but both died shortly after, in 1863. Evert inherited George's estate, and his wife, Margaret, got her brother John's.[9] By the end of the year, Evert, serving as executor for both estates,[10] sold the plates to the publisher Widdleton—on the installment plan;[11]—and even after the sale he turned profits from what had been Redfield's stereotype plates, for example, by selecting, at Widdleton's request, which tales of Poe were to be included in a "new"— that is reshuffled and selected—edition of the *Works*.[12]

I have not meant to cast the Duyckincks in an unfavorable light. I am not arguing that they were sharks in the literary marketplace but am only pointing out that they knew how to turn a dollar, had a business instinct and talent to make money which, if it was not rare in period America, was not shared by Melville. They were attempting to cash in, and with some success, on the emerging mass market in publishing that appeared in the two decades before the Civil War. I have a sense at the same time that Melville objected to such behavior as he observed it and as it was thrust upon him, perhaps because he himself could not succeed in the literary enterprise or "preferred not to"—consciously or unconsciously. Drained after seven books in as many years of writing, he found himself in 1853 reversing the career pattern of most fiction writers, including Hawthorne, and turning to short stories and sketches for the magazines. I suspect he resented his situation deeply. If he had been put off by Evert's request to contribute to *Holden's* two years before, what must he have felt, with *Moby-Dick* and *Pierre* behind him, as he contemplated his prospects?

Having offered more fact—perhaps too much—than speculation, let me indulge in what is perhaps more speculation than fact, though "facts" aplenty I will offer: a reading of "The Fiddler."

"The Fiddler" was published in the September 1854 issue of *Harper's*. Although it appeared well after Melville had published other short pieces, it "probably" was composed and submitted in the spring and summer of 1853 (Sealts, pp. 393, 398). In the story Melville may well have been revealing his doubts and fears about the career he was about to embark on as a writer for magazines. I suggest that in his witty portrait of Hautboy he was caricaturing Cornelius Mathews, possibly offering a parody of Evert Duyckinck in his character Standard, and expressing his own trepidation and ambivalence about the compromise necessity was forcing on him to write that "*other* way." In the story he was viewing his unfolding role as magazinist with a combination of detached resignation and distress. The manic stoicism of the narrator, Helmstone, evokes, for me, the tone of Ishmael in the initial paragraph of "The Hyena" as he "takes this whole universe for a vast practical joke, though the wit thereof he but dimly discerns, and more than suspects that the joke is at nobody's expense but his own." The spring and summer of 1853 were for Melville, indeed, a "time of extreme tribulation," a period that perhaps could best be handled with a "free and easy sort of genial, desperado philosophy" (*MD*, pp. 195–96).

"The Fiddler" may have added tension to the possibly already strained relations between Melville and the Duyckincks. In all likelihood it was an utter repudiation of Mathews's work in periodical editing and writing as well as a somewhat biting attack on Evert Duyckinck's commitment not only to Mathews but also to the popular literature the Duyckinck's whole crowd seems to have been drawn toward.

The tensions between Melville and the Duyckinck Circle's values in the early 1850s have long been familiar to literary historians. His characterization of the "Young America" group in Books XVII and XVIII of *Pierre* was one response to Duyckinck (pp. 375–76). In these passages Melville/Pierre was, among other matters, agonizing about the prospect of becoming a "poor be-inked galley-slave" forced to cater to the popular magazine's "worship [of] Mediocrity and [the] Common Place" (p. 261). In effect he was reflecting on the implications of prostituting his genius to journals that puffed trash. Pierre had come to a crossroads—one Melville probably felt he himself might soon approach—and must choose between keeping "thy body effeminate for labor, and thy soul laboriously robust; or else thy soul effeminate for labor, and thy body laboriously robust. Elect! the two will not lastingly abide in one yoke" (p. 261). Or, all your books will end as "botches."

In "The Fiddler," it appears Melville was again lashing out at the popular journals, their audiences, their taste, and their contributors—even what these were pressing on their contributors. He was taking to task those wheelers-and-dealers, apparently represented to him by the Duyckincks, and especially Mathews, for their worship of Mammon and their sacrifice of genius on those altars of mediocrity, their magazines and journals, as well as their "Libraries" of Popular Books.

Before continuing, however, we should focus on a subtle but crucial distinction. My suspicion is that the satire I am about to suggest Melville was presenting in "The Fiddler" was probably directed less at them than at the literary world, and its values, which they represented. If they inhabited that mass-marketplace—which he was struggling to survive in (without writing too much that *"other* way")—they were among those in it, or were those, he knew best. He was striking out at the type more than at the people. After all, Melville was certainly of large enough mind to distinguish between systems and circumstances, and their victims, even those, such as the attorney in "Bartleby," who in order to function were forced to play the game—the "safe" sort most people are. If he was caricaturing the Duyckinck crowd, he probably saw and attacked them more as representatives than as individuals.

The most compelling evidence to support my identification of the characters occurs near the end of the story when Hautboy (Mathews) brings Helmstone (Melville) and Standard (Duyckinck) to "the fifth story of a sort of storehouse, in a lateral street to Broadway." Here, "Pressed by Standard, Hautboy forthwith got out his dented old fiddle and, sitting down on a tall rickety stool, played away right merrily at 'Yankee Doodle' and other off-handed, dashing, and disdainfully care-free airs" (*Tales*, p. 191). I find it difficult to imagine Melville choosing that particular title, "Yankee Doodle," by chance or without recalling the magazine venture of six years before. He had known Mathews since shortly before the summer of 1847 when Mathews was editing, or fiddling with, the satirical weekly *Yankee Doodle*, the one to which Melville had contributed the comic pieces on Zachary Taylor (Mansfield) and others recently identified, as noted above (Yannella, "*Yankee Doodle*"). By 1853 he had good cause to be nervous about the pending renewal of his engagement with magazines. He had witnessed the disastrous effects of popular journalism on Mathews's career, for example. The "other off-handed, dashing, and disdainfully care-free airs" Hautboy played suggest to me Mathews's efforts in popular journalism after *Yankee Doodle* folded in October 1847. Early in 1848 he had edited *The Elephant*, another short-lived satirical weekly (Yannella, " 'Seeing the Elephant' in *Mardi*") and may have had a hand in writing a spin-off play *Seeing the Elephant* (see Mathews's letter to George Long Duyckinck, 20 March 1848, Box 11.) In 1850, he edited *The Prompter*, a theatrical weekly, which enjoyed an equally short period of survival (see Mathews's statements in George O. Seilhamer, p. 31) and during 1852, at least, when Melville was struggling with *Pierre*, Mathews held an editorial position with the New York *Reveille*, a gossipy, humorous weekly published from 1851 to 1854 (Frank Luther Mott, p. 180). In addition to these tunes, Mathews also fiddled away on numerous other journalistic pieces printed in a variety of periodicals in the late 1840s and early 1850s, including *Holden's*. (Many in *Holden's*, for instance, are identified as his by Evert's pencilled initiallings in his own bound copy of the magazine now in the New York Public Library.) Mathews was a steady contributor to a number of periodicals (Daniel A. Wells, *Literary Index*, pp. 103–104)—not all his work has been identified—and was constantly mentioned in the *Literary World* ("An Index," p. 271). There he was reported, for example, on 9 February 1850 to be editing the *Weekly Review*, "an exceedingly well-filled newspaper" (p. 134); and on 30 March 1850 it was announced that he had been named editor of two book series: "The Modern Standard Drama" and "The Minor Drama" (p. 330). All this in addition to hustling and bustling, speaking here, arranging there. And not only was he writing for the *World*, he was also helping edit it in 1853.[13] This after Mathews had begun his career as an editor by working with Evert on the widely acclaimed monthly *Arcturus* (1840–42), which even Poe, no easy critic, praised (Allen F. Stein, *Cornelius Mathews*, p. 163n.16).

As a matter of fact, if Hautboy is indeed a lightly masked Mathews, an arch-representative of the world of cheap journalism—literature for the masses—Melville was accurate in assessing the disappointing quality of his subliterary work and prescient in predicting Mathews's career. Mathews, after beginning with the high hopes, visions, and enthusiasms of youth, was to end his professional life by editing weekly newspapers. *Trow's New York Directory*, in the annual appendix devoted to New York magazines and newspapers, lists him as the publisher and editor of a weekly newspaper, *The New-Yorker*, from 1858–59 through 1875–76,[14] and another, *Comic World,* for a few years (1876–78) at the end of his career. Based on my perusal of the few issues of these which I have recovered, the most generous label I can suggest for them is "uninspired." In the 1880s, sick and old, he became an occasional contributor to the *New York Dramatic Mirror,* one of the forerunners of *Variety,* and a fabricator about his role in American literature, especially drama, a mass audience medium he had been part of for some forty years (Seilhamer, pp. 25–32).

In 1853 Melville would certainly have been anxious about the prospect of spending the rest of his career engaged in petty and futile trifles, wasting his time, energy, and effort on journalistic "fiddle-faddle"— "trifling discourse; nonsence" (John Russell Bartlett, pp. 136–37). How else could he view magazine writing after having produced seven rich books, including *Moby-Dick?*

Several physical details and the setting add support to this identification of Hautboy as Mathews. First of all, the storehouse where Helmstone and Standard hear him fiddle, Melville tells us, "was curiously furnished with all sorts of odd furniture which seemed to have been obtained, piece by piece, at auctions of old-fashioned household stuff" (p. 199). Mathews had long-standing connections with the furniture and auction business, associations Melville must have known of. From 1817 until the late 1840s, *Trow's* lists Mathews's father, Abijah, who died in 1850, as a cabinet-maker and proprietor of a furniture store in Catherine Street, near Broadway. Cornelius's brother, Daniel, joined his father in the business in the late 1820s, again according to *Trow's,* and remained with him through the early 1840s. From 1843 until sometime in 1854 Daniel was variously a merchant, book dealer, broker and commission merchant, or importer. Sometime in 1854 he became a storage man and auctioneer, a business he was to continue in through the 1880s. The Mathews brothers always had offices within a few blocks of Broadway.

Hautboy possesses several of Mathews's physical characteristics, as noted by his contemporaries. Of course, Melville was too subtle to present a perfectly accurate description of Mathews. Rather, he suggests, he offers hints that are readily picked up by the careful reader. Early in the sketch Hautboy is described as "short and full" (p. 195) and later as a "short, fat fellow" (p. 198). Mathews's small stature was noted repeatedly by his contemporaries, especially critics such as Charles F. Briggs, James Russell Lowell, and Oliver Wendell Holmes.[15] I have not discovered whether Mathews was rotund during this period.[16] But the most striking discrepancy in Melville's caricature is the absence of spectacles. According to contemporary descriptions and the two portraits that have survived (one a beautifully preserved tintype, in its original frame, now in the New York University Archives), Mathews ordinarily wore glasses. On the other hand, Hautboy appears to Helmstone to be twelve, but "his hair alone betrayed that he was not an overgrown boy. From his hair I set him down as forty or more" (p. 195). Mathews's hairline was receding in the early 1840s, and he was evidently almost bald by the mid–1850s, according to the surviving portraits. Shortly after Helmstone judges him "forty or more," he pinpoints Hautboy's age as forty. Mathews was, it appears, possibly to turn forty on 28 October 1854, a month after the publication of "The Fiddler." With only one exception I have discovered (his friend Harrison Gray Fiske's obituary in the *New York Dramatic Mirror*, 6 April 1889, p. 8), Mathews's birth year has been listed as 1817. Fiske seems, in fact, to have been correct in recording it as 1814; this is borne out by Mathews's death certificate, a copy of which I have placed in his papers in the Duyckinck Family Papers, and the record of his burial in the registry for St. Ann's Episcopal Church (Episcopal Diocese of New York, "Parish Register No. 4," Burial No. 1271; located at St. John the Divine Cathedral).

I am less sure that Standard is Evert Duyckinck. Again, though, let me emphasize my point that Melville seems to have been more concerned with exposing and satirizing types rather than smacking at friends. This is especially the case with Evert. Physical description is thin and not really compelling. But Melville's choice of the name Standard does suggest Duyckinck's taste, as demonstrated, for example, by the rigorous application of principles and assumptions—standards—to Melville's recent work as it was reviewed in the *Literary World*. (By the way, I know of no external evidence to support the virtually universal inference that the Duyckincks themselves wrote the reviews in the *Literary World* of *Moby-Dick* and *Pierre*.) That Standard introduces Helmstone to Hautboy, as Duyckinck had evidently introduced Melville to Mathews less than a decade earlier, is suggestive, as is Standard's insistence on Hautboy's genius, and his sympathy—even complacency—about the little man's failure.

The depth of Duyckinck's faith in Mathews's genius and the lengths to which he went to defend him and promote his career are familiar.[17] The hit at Standard's misplaced faith in the fiddling Hautboy, if it is a comment on Duyckinck's faith in Mathews, is subtle but strong. Melville's judgment about the ridiculousness of Duyckinck's rationalizations about Mathews is driven home by Standard's own words: Hautboy "who has a hundred times been crowned with laurels, now wears, as you see, a bunged beaver.... *With* genius and *without* fame, he is happier than a king. More a prodigy now than ever" (p. 200). The utter collapse of Mathews's reputation in the dissolving New York literary scene was paralleled by his evidently constant economic difficulties, facts of a "bunged beaver" world Melville could well appreciate in 1853. Mathews was evidently of humble background and, it appears, never became a financial success. He died intestate and was buried on 28 March 1889 in an unmarked pauper's grave, a charity case, in Brooklyn's Evergreen Cemetery (Burial Register, 1889, Entry No. 105624). I have been unable to understand this unseemly end for a man who warranted extensive obituaries in New York papers such as the *Times* and *Dramatic Mirror*; the issue is further confused by the fact that six years later, on 7 and 8 February 1895, his painting collection, mixed with that of another, unnamed collector, was auctioned by the Silo Art Galleries in New York City. According to a newspaper notice (the paper, presumably New York, remains unidentified) tipped into the catalogue at the New York Public Library, the first day of sale brought $3,380. The recipient or recipients of the proceeds remains unknown. A pauper's grave is rather remarkable for a member of a family with a vault in Trinity churchyard, at the foot of Wall Street, which they used as late as the 1920s.

Bearing in mind the facts that Helmstone is a parody, an ironic self-portrait, but that Melville, ever in control, maintains a certain distance from his first-person narrator, we can nevertheless hear in the almost manic quality of Helmstone's response to "the bow of an enchanter," Hautboy's "magical fiddle," the profundity of Melville's doubts about launching his career as a magazinist and his fear about his future. Had not Mathews's career descended from serious attempts at book-length fiction in the late 1830s and 1840s to a series of ventures in popular fiction, trendy theater, and cheap journalism?

If this interpretation is accurate, it might cast some light on one of the more interesting puzzles in Melville's relations with the New York literati. After the famous Monument Mountain picnic of 5 August 1850, Mathews apparently disappears from Melville's life. His accounts of the day in the *Literary World* (25 August 1850, p. 147; 31 August 1850, p. 166; and 7 September 1850, pp. 185–86), among the handful of credits by which his name survives, mark the apparent end of his Melville connection, at least if we are to judge by surviving—or retrieved—evidence. After late 1850 the Melville papers recovered so far are silent about him. And since the handful of Mathews's papers that have survived are principally from the late 1830s and early 1840s, there has been no explanation from the Mathews end of their drifting apart. I propose that "The Fiddler" possibly marked a serious break between Mathews and Melville.

Yet the portrait of Hautboy, while hardly flattering, is not as scathing as those of other Mathews critics. Melville's picture of the fiddler's gossipy, flitting movements and occasionally frenetic gestures and speech is much gentler than, for example, Briggs's in *The Trippings of Tom Pepper*.[18] Even Sophia Hawthorne characterized Mathews as a "very chatty gossiping body" (Eleanor Melville Metcalf, p. 86). Hautboy's eye is "cheery," his countenance expresses "good humor" (p. 195). He impresses Helmstone with his "genuine enjoyment," his "happiness" and "pleasure" at the circus (p. 196). When they go to Taylor's (a reference to the "Ole Zack" pieces in *Yankee Doodle*?), Helmstone notes that "Though greatly subdued from its former hilarity, his face still shone with gladness." The little fellow possesses "a certain serene expression of leisurely, deep good sense.... Hautboy seemed intuitively to hit the exact line between enthusiasm and apathy. It was plain that while Hautboy saw the world pretty much as it was, yet he did not theoretically espouse its bright side nor its dark side" (p. 197). If this is a sarcastic comment on Mathews's almost schizoid responses to nineteenth-century American culture—his alternate celebrations and laments about the emerging urban-industrial civilization—it is a milder rebuke than he was accustomed to receiving. Rather than offering a caricature of Mathews as a strident, abrasive, and obnoxious man, the conventional period image still ascribed to him by most literary historians, Melville serves up an admittedly absurd fellow, but one whose silliness and failure are softened by a touch of pathos and a dash of affection. But I doubt that Mathews was capable of making the distinctions I am suggesting between Melville's caricature and those of his more virulent critics. They were, in the end, all dismissing him.

At the conclusion of "The Fiddler" there is an echo of Ishmael's resolve at the end of "The Hyena." When Helmstone reports that "Next day I tore all my manuscripts, bought me a fiddle, and went to take regular lessons of Hautboy"—about how to write the "*other*" way"?—he has in effect committed himself, at least for the time, "for a cool, collected dive at death and destruction, and the devil fetch the hindmost" (*MD*, p. 197). Melville's dive into the world of journalism, however, was to be only temporary; thankfully, Mathews proved no model for him. And as best as is known no forefathers have been heard to take him to task for his magazine writing, much of which is splendid, as Hawthorne's had for his "story-books": "Why, the degenerate fellow might as well have been a fiddler" (Hawthorne, p. 12).

Now, if I may have made a case for one possible reason why Melville and the Duyckincks parted for several years in the early 1850s, let me conclude by offering some information that might raise questions about the hiatus in their relationship. Here I will to some degree contradict much of what I have proposed. There is no question but that the Melville/ Duyckinck friendship cooled after early 1852. But for how long, and precisely how low did the temperature drop? Only one letter from Melville to Evert, dated 9[?] January 1852 (*Letters*, pp. 147–48), survives, or has been retrieved,[19] and it is the last document we have before Melville appears in Evert's diary in October 1856 (*Mel. Log*, p. 523), almost five years later. We must remember, however, that we are at the mercy of those who have preceded us, especially those who somehow became custodians of what for us are—or would be—important, even crucial documents. I have no idea what happened to Evert's letters to Melville. And it might be that someone, even Evert himself, discarded some of Melville's to him. But I do know that there was a fairly constant Pittsfield/New York connection from 1851 through the early 1860s: that between Sarah Morewood and George Duyckinck. Many if not all of her letters to him are in the Duyckinck Family Papers (Boxes 46 and 47), and there is not one mention in them of a break or even a disruption between him and his brother and Melville; only one of George's to Sarah, however—an innocuous note from 1851—is among the Morewood papers at the Berkshire Athenaeum. Judging from the intimacy and occasional passion of her letters, she, or some member of the family later on, may have judged it best to relegate George's to her to the trashheap or the fire.

My point is that there are undoubtedly gaps in our information about this trying period in Melville's life. Frankly, I find it hard to comprehend there having been a thorough break between Melville and the Duyckincks, especially Evert, from early 1852 to October 1856. I do not understand why the entries in Evert's diary in October 1856 are so friendly, glowing even, rich in the warmth of continued, *not renewed*, friendship. Yet there are no manuscripts I know of about or between the two for almost five years. The silence is deafening, except for one third-person report: Richard Lathers's *Reminiscences* about evenings in Duyckinck's well-known basement during Thackeray's stay in New York from November 1855 through about January 1856. And Lathers places Melville in the company (p. 51). If we accept Lathers's report, the term of the supposed break is reduced from five to four years, or from four to three—depending on how one interprets the tone of Melville's 1852 letter to Evert. We might even further reduce the term of the hiatus if we choose to read as a compliment the *Literary World's* description on 3 December 1853 of "Bartleby" as a "Poeish tale" (p. 295). It is one of a few items the author of the notice singles out for mention, though the December *Putnam's* was rich and varied in its offerings.

So the drifting apart may, indeed, have been caused to some degree by Evert's bruised feelings as a result of the Young America portions of *Pierre* and the reading I offer of "The Fiddler." Certainly, Melville was to some degree disenchanted with him and the crowd in 1852 and 1853. But our attempt to understand should also take into account what may only have been a temporary parting of friends. While Melville was in evident distress in Pittsfield around 1852 and 1853 and pausing on the threshold of what he may have thought to be his career as a magazinist, the Duyckincks were closing down the *Literary World* operation and embarking on an intense research and writing project: the *Cyclopaedia of American Literature* (1855), which would include a rather brief assessment of Melville taken from notes supplied by Allan Melville. Their roles in the literary world reversed, caught up in their new labors, separated by distance, our subjects were off in different directions. These may be factors as worthy of consideration as the quarrels I have emphasized. Admittedly, these are speculations but they are reasonable and have a basis in fact. And let me repeat that Melville scholars should exercise caution: never leap toward perceived certitude.

After 1856, Evert and Melville continued their friendship until Duyckinck died in 1878. The last person, aside from his physician, that Evert noted as having visited him during his last illness was Herman Melville.[20]

NOTES

A version of this paper was delivered on 3 October 1981 at the University of Tennessee "Melville Seminar in Honor of Nathalia Wright."

1. For biographical/critical studies, see Donald Yannella's essays in *Dictionary of Literary Biography*, on the Duyckincks, and Stein's works on Mathews, as well as Yannella's forthcoming essay. Discussions of the volatile New York literary scene in the period are in Miller and in both of Moss's books.

2. Unless otherwise noted, the manuscript materials presented here are from the Duyckinck Family Papers, Manuscripts Division, New York Public Library. To facilitate the reader's pursuit of unpublished documents, box or volume numbers are supplied for items not already, or only partially, in print.

Many of these pieces were located in 1978–79, under a grant from the National Endowment for the Humanities.

For a biographical sketch of Joann Miller, see *Mel. Log.*

3. David Davidson, letter to George Long Duyckinck, 24 December 1849, Box 46. *Mel. Log*, p. 352, offers an abridged account of the second evening. My transcription varies slightly from Leyda's in that I read the evening as ending at 11:30 rather than 7:30.

Davidson was befriended from boyhood by Washington Irving, who helped get him a position with Wiley and Putnam in 1841, and he was working for them in London as late as 1849 (*Mel. Log*, p. 333, and *Letters*, p. 95n.6).

4. For more information about Davidson, particularly his connections with the Duyckincks and the *Literary World*, see Yannella, "*Literary World*" (1986).

5. Davidson, letters to George Long Duyckinck, 14 September 1854, 2 November 1854, and 10 January 1855, Box 46.

6. This venture is discussed in Davidson, letter to George Long Duyckinck, 10 February 1854, Box 46. One should note that the financial arrangements between the two were so intricate as to make it possible that some of Davidson's continuing indebtedness to George may have stemmed from the importing business and even, perhaps, other ventures, records of which appear not to have survived. Those that do exist are incomplete. Davidson's angry letter of 10 February 1854 is the most substantial in detailing their financial connections.

7. Evert A. Duyckinck, Journal, 1847–52, "Account Book," Vol. 37. This 481–page volume contains records of several ventures, including the *Literary World*. The indication on p. 4 is that the ordinary print run was 1,750.

For other records of the *Literary World*, including accounts with Davidson and Craighead, see George Long Duyckinck's pocket diary in Box 51; this soft-covered, darkened maroon book measuring 3 3/4″ x 5 7/8″, is so described to provide information which will enable the researcher to distinguish it from the other five volumes in the box.

For more information on this subject, see Yannella, *"Literary World,"* particularly note 12.

8. The best summary of these complex events is offered in the copy of the summons and complaint (bill of particulars), dated 13 March 1860, by John A. Panton in his suit against John F. Zebley (one of the interested parties in Redfield's demise) in New York Superior Court, Box 74. See also, for example, the several undated memoranda in George's handwriting, Box 53.

9. See the document dated 12 May 1863 making Evert the administrator of George's estate and also the inventory filed in Surrogate's Court on 2 October 1865, Box 35.

10. See the notations in "Blank Books...," the soft-covered, buff-colored account book, 6 3/4″ x 8 1/8″, Box 44.

11. W. J. Widdleton, letters to Evert A. Duyckinck, 14 December 1863, 29 December 1863, and 1 November 1864, Box 20.

12. W. J. Widdleton, letters to Evert A. Duyckinck, 10 and 14 August 1866, Box 20.

13. David Davidson, letter to George Long Duyckinck, 10 February 1854, Box 46. For further detail, see Yannella, *"Literary World."*

14. The only file of *The New-Yorker* I have been able to locate covers fourteen months, April 1858 through July 1859 (Ohio Historical Society); these issues list Mathews as editor. There is one additional issue, for 10 May 1856 (Vol. 1, no. 9), in the New York Public Library. In its eight pages *The New-Yorker* offers as standard fare three pages of serialized domestic-sentimental and gothic fiction of the usual mass-appeal quality published in story weeklies such as Robert Bonner's *New York Ledger*; a page of news and gossip—domestic and foreign; theater and amusement gossip, announcements, and advertisements; editorials on a variety of items of topical interest; and fully three columns of the sort of one-line jokes and quips that had been the style in *Yankee Doodle* and *The Elephant*.

15. Mathews is described as small in Harry Franco [Briggs], p. 70, where he is satirized in the person of Mr. Ferocious in chapters 8 and 9. Mathews is the small New York critic in *Astraea*, pp. 356–57. Lowell, pp. 124–28, describes him as a "small man in glasses."

16. None of the earlier attackers mentions his being fat. The only two likenesses I have found are those in the Mathews entry in the Duyckinck's *Cyclopaedia*, where he is thin, and Seilhamer's interview, where he is corpulent. The latter is conveniently available on the fly-leaf of Perry Miller's *The Raven and the Whale* (1956). It is not clear when Mathews settled into middle-age plumpness.

17. Among the contemporary satires on Evert's support of Mathews are Franco [Briggs], pp. 72–76, 159–72, where Tibbings (Duyckinck) plays flunky to Ferocious (Mathews), and Lowell, pp. 124–28. For modern accounts of Duyckinck's puffing of Mathews's reputation, see Miller, pp. 79–85, *passim*, and Moss, *Poe's Literary Battles*, pp. 81, 103–104.

18. Pp. 69–77, 159–72; Longfellow characterized Mathews's manner as, for example, "florid and exuberant" (*Kavanagh*, p. 113); and Lowell describes him as "dodging about" and "muttering," p. 125.

19. That is, if we exclude the business communications in which Melville cancelled his subscription to the *World*; these are dated 14 February 1852 (*Letters*, p. 149) and 16 April 1852 ("A New Melville Letter").

20. *Mel. Log*, p. 768. The entry for 4 June 1878 reads only "Mr Melville" and is one of eight (the first on 13 November 1877) recorded in a brown, paper-covered booklet, measuring 2 3/4″ x 4 5/8″ and labeled by the staff at New York Public Library: "Pocket Memo bk. 1877–78," Box 25.

WORKS CITED

Anonymous, "A New Melville Letter." *Melville Society Extracts* No. 64 (November 1985): 11.

Bartlett, John Russell. *Dictionary of Americanisms, Usually Regarded as Peculiar to the United States*. New York: Bartlett & Welford, 1848.

Baym, Nina. *Woman's Fiction: A Guide to Novels by and About Women in America, 1820–1870*. Ithaca, N.Y.: Cornell University Press, 1978.

Catalogue of Oil Paintings by Foreign and American Artists: In Part from the Estate of the Late Well-Known Author and Literateur Cornelius Mathews. New York: Silo Art Galleries, 1895.

Douglas, Ann. *The Feminization of American Culture*. New York: Alfred A. Knopf, 1977.

Duyckinck Family Papers. Manuscripts Division. New York Public Library.

Duyckinck, Evert A., and George L. Duyckinck. *Cyclopaedia of American Literature*. 2 vols. New York: Scribner, 1855.

Franco, Harry [Charles F. Briggs]. *The Trippings of Tom Pepper*. New York: Burgess, Stringer, 1847.

Hawthorne, Nathaniel. *The Scarlet Letter*. Ed. Sculley Bradley et al. 2d ed. New York: W. W. Norton, 1978.

Holmes, Oliver Wendell. *The Complete Poetical Works of Oliver Wendell Holmes*. Ed. Horace E. Scudder. Boston: Houghton Mifflin, 1908.

———. "O.W. Holmes on New York 'Pseudo-Critics' in 1850." *Bulletin of the New York Public Library* 4 (1900): 365–57.

Lathers, Richard. *Reminiscences of Richard Lathers: Sixty Years of a Busy Life in South Carolina, Massachusetts and New York*. Ed. Alvan F. Sanborn. New York: Grafton, 1907.

Longfellow, Henry Wadsworth. *Kavanagh*. Boston: Ticknor, Reed, & Fields, 1849.

Lowell, James Russell. *The Poetical Works of James Russell Lowell*. Boston: Houghton Mifflin, 1897.

Mansfield, Luther S. "Glimpses of Herman Melville's Life in Pittsfield: 1850–1851." *American Literature* 9 (March 1937): 26–48.

———. "Melville's Comic Articles on Zachary Taylor." *American Literature* 9 (January 1938): 411–18.

Metcalf, Eleanor Melville. *Herman Melville: Cycle and Epicycle*. Cambridge, Mass.: Harvard University Press, 1953.

Miller, Perry. *The Raven and the Whale: The War of Words and Wits in the Era of Poe and Melville*. New York: Harcourt, Brace, 1956.

Moss, Sidney P. *Poe's Literary Battles: The Critic In the Context of His Literary Milieu.* Durham, N.C.: Duke University Press, 1963.

———. *Poe's Major Crisis: His Libel Suit and New York's Literati.* Durham, N.C.: Duke University Press, 1970.

Mott, Frank Luther. *A History of American Magazines: 1850–1865.* Cambridge, Mass: Harvard University Press, 1938.

Murray, Henry A. Introduction. *Pierre or, the Ambiguities.* By Herman Melville. New York: Hendricks House, 1962.

Sealts, Merton M., Jr. "The Chronology of Melville's Short Fiction, 1853–1856." *Harvard Library Bulletin* 28 (1980): 391–403. [Also in "Historical Note" to NN *The Piazza Tales.*]

Seilhamer, George O. *An Interviewer's Album: Comprising a Series of Chats with Eminent Players and Playwrights.* New York: Alvin Perry, 1881.

Stein, Allen F. *Cornelius Mathews.* New York: Twayne, 1974.

———. "Cornelius Mathews." In *Antebellum Writers in New York and the South. Dictionary of Literary Biography.* Vol. 3. Ed. Joel Myerson. Detroit: Gale, 1979, pp. 211–13.

Wells, Daniel A. "An Index to American Writers and Selected British Writers in Duyckinck's *Literary World*, 1847–1853." *Studies in the American Renaissance 1978.* Ed. Joel Myerson. Boston: Twayne, 1978, pp. 259–78.

———. *The Literary Index to American Magazines: 1815–1865.* Metuchen, N.J., and London: Scarecrow, 1980.

Yannella, Donald. "Cornelius Mathews." *Dictionary of Literary Biography.* Ed. John W. Rathbun and Monica Grecu. Columbia, S.C.: Bruccoli Clark, forthcoming 1986.

———. "Evert Augustus Duyckinck." In *Antebellum Writers in New York and the South. Dictionary of Literary Biography.* Vol. 3. Ed. Joel Myerson. Detroit: Gale, 1979, pp. 101–109.

———. "George Long Duyckinck." In *Antebellum Writers in New York and the South. Dictionary of Literary Biography.* Vol. 3. Ed. Joel Myerson. Detroit: Gale, 1979, pp. 109–11.

———. "*Literary World.*" *American Literary Magazines: The Eighteenth- and Nineteenth-Centuries.* Ed. Edward E. Chielens. Westport, Conn.: Greenwood Press, 1986, pp. 224–30.

———. " 'Seeing the Elephant' in *Mardi.*" In *Artful Thunder: Versions of the Romantic Tradition in American Literature in Honor of Howard P. Vincent.* Ed. Robert J. DeMott and Sanford E. Marovitz. Kent, Ohio: Kent State University Press, 1975, pp. 105–17.

———. "*Yankee Doodle.*" *American Literary Magazines: The Eighteenth- and Nineteenth-Centuries.* Ed. Edward E. Chielens. Westport, Conn.: Greenwood Press, 1986, pp. 451–56.

PART TWO

MELVILLE'S WORK

4

TYPEE AND *OMOO*: A DIVERGING PAIR

Bette S. Weidman

In a well-known autobiographical aside, Melville has Ishmael attribute his achievement to his education: "a whaleship was my Yale College and my Harvard" (*MD*, p. 101). We remember the remark not only for its witty mockery of formal credentials but for its simple accuracy. In the years during which others were undergraduates, Melville was earning a first-hand view of the world: he did not study in the Harvard course of which Thoreau remarked: "To my astonishment I was informed on leaving college that I had studied navigation!—why if I had taken one turn down the harbor I should have known more about it"(p. 52). Instead, Melville spent almost four years on sea roads and ports of call in the Pacific. He experienced a working life in the whale fishery and the U.S. Navy and an observer's life among various groups of Polynesians in the Marquesas, Tahiti, and Hawaii.

Melville saw first and read later, and his books are the record of his integration of these two ways of knowing. They are essentially about how we know, a theme in the service of which he explored many forms of literary art, including exposition, narration, dramatization, allegory; he wrote long prose works, short stories, series of connected sketches, poetry ranging from briefest lyric to book-length epic. To the vexed question of whether his first two books, *Typee* and *Omoo,* are novels or autobiographies or varieties of travel literature, let it be said at once that Melville is best defined as a writer: one who writes in order to explore what he knows. No single convention or genre can contain such a figure, as a study of his first published books amply shows.

TYPEE

Typee (1846), written shortly after Melville's return from the Pacific, is a first-person narrative offering a recollection of life in the Marquesan Islands. The speaker addresses the reader after the completion of his visit; he interweaves later events and attitudes into a dramatic and immediate representation of his Marquesan experience. This experience is set off by a double escape: first, the narrator and his friend, Toby, leave their whaling vessel in the bay of Nukuheva in protest against miserable conditions, and second, at the end of the book, the narrator escapes from ambiguously benevolent captivity among the Typees, in whose remote valley he has spent four months. Suspended between the two escapes, the body of the book is about his immersion in a strange culture. With no developed plot, character description substitutes for character development; analysis of political and moral issues takes a place unusual in a work of fiction.

The most striking feature of *Typee* is the alternation of moods in the narrator from the emotional/intuitive to the critical/analytical. The first of these moods is associated with the dramatic material of the story, the actual period of captivity and escape from the Typee Valley. The second mood reminds us that the immediacy of the story is an occasion for the maturer reflections of a writer who has distanced the events. As we read the book, we experience this regular alternation of mood and voice, the ultimate effect of which is the reader's questioning the wholeness of the speaker's sensibility. He seems permanently divided into two: the youthful sailor who fears that he will die horribly or sink into meaningless lethargy in his cultural isolation; the skeptical commentator who, from the cool vantage of a survivor, considers the social structures and moral frameworks of American and European invaders and their Polynesian victims.

We can easily document the two voices in chapters 1–4. No sooner does the narrator achieve present-tense immediacy, invoking the quality of sea, sky, and desire as he approaches the Marquesas, than he shifts to the recollection of an incident he witnessed later—her royal Majesty, Queen of Nukuheva, baring her bottom to the American fleet. He laments the contamination of Polynesia by European civilization, taking a particularly satirical view of the French, including the story of the vanquishing of Rear-Admiral DuPetit Thouars by Mrs. Pritchard at Tahiti. The prevailing tone, in the opening of the book, is skeptical; it appears to be a leisurely tale embellished with stories out of time sequence, full of frankness and low comedy, and devoted to sharpening the contrast between Europeans and Polynesians. At the end of Chapter 4, after a return to the present-tense apprehensions of the innocent narrator, we catch a glimpse of the skeptical observer of a later period remembering his impressions of a meeting between DuPetit Thouars and the King of Tior.

The journey to the interior of Typee does not begin in earnest until Chapter 7, where the naive narrator takes over. He tells his story in a manner reminiscent of literary models, dividing Happars and Typees into good and bad "savages" much in the way Cooper classified noble Delawares and venomous Mingoes. Poe is evoked as the narrator finds himself in a bewildering landscape, on a nightmare journey up and down gorges, helplessly falling, slipping down roots shaped like "dark icicles." The injured narrator makes this nightmare descent with a physically courageous companion, whose courage alternates with his; when they reach the humans in the valley the narrator takes the lead as Toby quails. In chapters 7 to 10, opposing reactions are objectified in the two characters, as opposing kinds of savages are imagined under the names *Typee* and *Happar*.

In the course of Chapter 11, the narrator begins his careful portrait of the chief Mehevi and the family of Marheyo including the beautiful maiden, Fayaway, and her brother Kory-Kory, assigned to be the narrator's attendant. As Tommo (their name for him) becomes familiar with these people, his admiration for them and their paradise grows, yet by the end of Chapter 12, his fear at a nighttime fire-lighting surfaces despite the "excess of deferential kindness" from natives and his belief that the "horrible character imputed to these Typees appeared to me wholly undeserved" (p. 97). After a skirmish with the Happars, Toby is permitted to go to Nukuheva for medicines to treat Tommo's swollen leg, an ailment that flares up and subsides throughout the book with the increase of melancholy fear or the disappearance of cultural anxiety. With Toby gone, Melville's two voices are firmly embodied in one character. In Chapter 17, for instance, the narrator, offering a full-fledged evaluation of the Polynesians as compared to that of Europeans, begins a rhetorically effective paragraph with this sentence: "There were none of those thousand sources of irritation that the ingenuity of civilized man has created to mar his own felicity" (p. 126). By the end of Chapter 18, the idyllic pleasures of the narrator evaporate into despondency. Tommo overrules the mood by deciding to enjoy himself, and the decision permits a portrait of the Polynesian day, an account of the history and monuments of Nukuheva, and a description of the Feast of the Calabashes. Whether the information concerning the feast originated in Melville's own memory or in his sources, his narrator dramatizes the role of participant-observer anthropologist in chapters 22 through 24, renewing his suspicions of the missionaries, his objections to South Seas rovers as sources of information, and his commentary on religion in Typee.

Still in the character of objective observer, he devotes Chapter 25 to physical anthropology and Chapter 26 to an account of the corrupted government of Hawaii, allowing space for a description of sexual relations and kinship beliefs, burial customs and attitudes toward work. The attack on colonialism reaches its climax in the ironic exclamation "Heaven help the 'Isles of the Sea!' "

The Anglo-Saxon hive have extirpated Paganism from the greater part of the North American continent; but with it they have likewise extirpated the greater portion of the Red race (p. 195).

Not until I visited Honolulu was I aware of the fact that the small remnant of the natives had been civilized into draught horses, and evangelized into beasts of burden. (p. 196)

The pervasive theme of anti-colonialism is the distinction of *Typee*; one has to go back to the fifteenth-century Spaniard, Bartolome de las Casas, or forward to Helen Hunt Jackson's *A Century of Dishonor* or Mark Twain's *King Leopold's Soliloquy* for as firm an indictment of colonialist destruction. The special richness and poignance of *Typee* is in the relationship drawn between the Polynesian and Native American; it is a similarity Melville will allude to again in his portraits of the three pagan harpooneers in *Moby-Dick*. Here the narrator concludes his indictment of civilization with a description of that "paragon of humility," the overstuffed missionary's spouse pulled uphill in a go-cart by her Polynesian servants. (It is, incidentally, his fourth significant image of women in this book, with the Queen of Nukuheva, the English Mrs. Pritchard, and the glorious Fayaway.)

The indictment continues where we hear the skeptical voice deriving, from its observation of the lawless Typees, an "inherent principle of honesty and charity." Tommo's consideration of Typee views of property and real estate helps him to form "a higher estimate of human nature" than he had held before, or that he can sustain after his return to life on a man-of-war. This narrator, sounding considerably more experienced than the young man held in benevolent captivity in Typee, explodes the "good/bad savage" stereotypes, willingly confesses that he does not understand what he sees, and finds "Truth . . . to be centrally located" (pp. 201, 203, 205).

"I made a point of doing as the Typees did" (p. 209), he explains, as he takes us to a midnight fishing banquet and through a natural history of the valley. But by the end of Chapter 29, he returns to emotional depression; his fear of being disfigured by tattooing haunts him and disrupts his collecting samples of language and music. "I was almost tempted to believe that I gazed upon a set of evil beings" (p. 227), he admits even after stating his positive intellectual view of Typee. But with renewed symptoms of leg injury and heightened anxiety, the emotional/

intuitive narrator returns: "In this wretched situation, every circumstance which evinced the savage nature of the beings at whose mercy I was, augmented the fearful apprehensions that consumed me" (p. 232). This is an account of culture shock in progress; all the criticism of "civilization" is forgotten in the terror of "savagery," fear of treachery, fear of isolation from home. The same narrator who mocked the French in the passages about DuPetit Thouars now links his hopes for rescue to the French fleet.

The final two chapters, after preserving one serene image of three breadfruit trees waving gracefully before Marheyo's house, give themselves up to struggle. The narrator leaves the Typees as he came to them, during a physical contest: "It was no time for pity or compunction ... I dashed the boat-hook at him." Tommo, striking his pursuer, suffers alienation, underlying which is an unexamined recognition that he could never live in Typee permanently: "The strong excitement which had thus far kept me up, now left me, and I fell back fainting into the arms of Karakoee" (p. 252). The narrative ends in a faint; the three-paragraph epilogue relates Tommo's undermined health and the still unresolved mystery of Toby's disappearance.

This is Melville's first book—a quest culminating in defeat and survival; a complex narrator whose words reveal the experience as lived (dramatized) and considered (analyzed); a setting far removed from familiar American life; a strongly stated concern for social justice. That this generalized description could apply to his masterpiece, *Moby-Dick*, as well as to his apprentice work, *Typee*, shows the unity of Melville's work. In *Typee* Melville found a flexible first-person point of view, an accommodatingly loose plot shape, a habit of explicit and unacknowledged recourse to other writers. Here he first set down images and patterns to which he would later return: the verdant isle, the leg-crippling accident, the handsome sailor/savage, the artful postscript. In *Typee*, Melville took one giant step toward *Moby-Dick*; in *Omoo* (1847), he took another.

OMOO

In contrast to *Typee*, the most striking feature of *Omoo* is the maintenance of a steady narrative voice. Neither subject to plunging or exalted moods, nor divided into the naive adventurer and the skeptical observer, the narrator remains throughout a thoughtful, detached participant. Similarly, the relationship between the narrator and the events he is relating does not shift in time as it did in *Typee*, where the writing in some passages implies immediacy and in others, distance. In *Omoo* the narrator does not undergo radical changes within himself. He is already experienced at the start of *Omoo*: he has struck violently at his captors and freed himself, and henceforth he will be especially aware of coercion and choice in his place of residence. The narrator's repeated domestications in exotic places, none of them final, are undertaken cautiously, in the form of experiments. Wherever he is, he seems to ask: what is the nature of these people? Can I regard this place as home for the time being? That is all the time there is in *Omoo*; there are no long looks back or forward. The ultimate home or destination is infinitely postponed. The anti-missionary indictment returns in this book, not as emotional or rhetorical, but as a carefully constructed argument with sources.

The eighty-two chapters of *Omoo* compared to thirty-four in *Typee* indicate the young author's capacity for development. In *Omoo* (the Polynesian word for "rover" or "wanderer"), the development is accomplished by the narrator's movement with his companion, Dr. Long Ghost, through a succession of experiences in various communities: (1) subjugation to tyrannical and disorderly shipboard life aboard the *Julia*; (2) imprisonment in the European-influenced harbor town of Papeetee; (3) participation in the free-lance labor plantation in Martair; (4) journey to the still more remote paradisal Tamai, from which they are expelled; (5) brief idyllic stay at Loohooloo; (6) halfway house visit with Christian, Jeremiah Po-Po, at Partoowye, where they try to join the court of Queen Pomaree. These successive experiments in finding a place and a way to live culminate in the combined failure and survival that leads the narrator back to shipboard, only another temporary home for a roving soul.

Fully a quarter of *Omoo* (the first twenty-six chapters) takes place aboard the *Julia* and exposes the disorder of its shipboard community: the deluded mate, Jermin; the destructive and traitorous Bembo; the incompetent and vicious Captain Guy. There is a gallery of characters, including the omen-studying Van; pathetic Rope Yarn; drunken Chips and Bungs; witty and detached Dr. Long Ghost. From the time that the narrator (known as Paul), observes the unprepossessing *Julia* from the whaleboat in which he is escaping the Typees to the turn at Chapter 26 when Jermin brings the ship into Papeetee harbor, Melville has constructed a miniature whole.

The language and images in these chapters keep readers of Melville's better known works gasping at familiar configurations: sea creatures frolicking beside a gliding ship; the instinctive enmity of Jermin and Beauty (cf. Steelkilt and Radney in *Moby-Dick*); the comparison of rats in molasses to Clarence in a butt of Malmsey (cf. Ohio bee-hunter and Plato's honey head also in *Moby-Dick*); Bungs's imitation of Lord Nelson (a figure repeatedly invoked in Melville all the way to *Billy Budd*); the black cook's tribulations; the faulty instruments; the wild story of Bembo's climb aboard a whale; the mad dance of the mutinous sailors (cf. "Midnight-Forecastle," in *Moby-Dick*). During this section of the book, the sailors' grievances and their mutinous unwillingness to serve aboard the *Julia* are clarified. The narrator and Long Ghost play leading roles in subduing violence and giving verbal expression to resentments.

The figure of one who has lost or recreated his place is firmly established in the *Julia* chapters. Sailors find themselves in the never-never land of the unresolved; they include those who will never go home or find home, endlessly traversing the endlessly revolving globe. Two characters in this section hold the theme in firmer tension: the renegade, Lem Hardy, who in accepting the blue shark tattoo on his face has created a new identity for himself, and the playful, noncommital Dr. Long Ghost, who embodies the emotional detachment, the permanent skepticism, of the rover.

The entrance into Papeetee harbor (ch. 27) provides a transition in scene and supervision, and is followed by a caricature of a French lieutenant and criticism of life on the French frigate, *Reine Blanche*. Chapters 30–38 constitute a second subunit of the book. The crew of the *Julia*, including the narrator, is delivered into the custody of the British consul and is imprisoned in the Calabooza Beretanee (British jail), under the benevolent guard of "Capin Bob," a fatherly old native who eases their restriction. In this section we meet another range of characters—the colonial administrators, French missionaries, and Tahitian collaborators. After the *Julia* sails, Capin Bob's imprisonment becomes even looser; in chapters 39–47, the mutineers remain at the Calabooza without active supervision, more as an economic burden on their jailor than as a serious detainment. Here, the narrator describes the custom of *tayo*, Polynesian friendship, and his own friend, Kooloo; he visits the European chapel and tries to penetrate the royal island of Motoo-Otoo; he attends the native church. In searching for familiar cultural situations, he describes the acculturation of the Tahitians: their religious police, moral hypocrisy, and indolent women. This whole twenty-chapter section (27–47), devoted to the narrator's supervised introduction to Europeanized Tahiti, effects a gradual loosening of his bonds as a sailor belonging to the *Julia* and culminates in a two-chapter (48 and 49) discussion of the influences of missionaries on religion, morals, and social life in Tahiti in which Melville relies on various reference works to support his powerful indictment of the effects of the missions on the wretched Tahitians.

In chapters 50 and 51, the narrative takes another turn: Long Ghost's antics discredit the mercenary colonialist, Dr. Johnson, and, following a confrontation with the weak Consul Wilson, he and the narrator leave for Imeeo, where in chapters 52–61 they encounter yet another set of characters and possibilities, dominated by the planters, Zeke and Shorty, and Tonoi, the Polynesian who lives symbiotically with them. It is another opportunity to describe a potential way of life (that of *unofficial* white men in Polynesia), while at the same time offering landscape description and historical information. But life as a plantation laborer suits neither Dr. Long Ghost, who is averse to any kind of work, nor the narrator, who senses incipient conflict with his malingering friend. They decide to leave the plantation, where the most successful crop is a transplanted work ethic, for Tamai, a paradise of fruit and women.

Only four chapters (62–65) are devoted to this remote and beautiful place where Long Ghost and the narrator witness a native dance and dodge the importunings of an old man who wants to sell them a pair of musty trousers. Another casualty of colonialism, this "goblin" (like "Long Ghost") reminds us of the degradation caused by the weakening of culture. Just as the narrator and Long Ghost are planning to settle down in Tamai, they are forced to flee from hunters of runaway seamen. They plan a new destination, the village of Partoowye, and Queen Pomaree's court.

Dating the events of this "hegira," as he calls it, from the expulsion from Tamai, the narrator and Long Ghost journey along the beach visiting three gay girls in the hamlet of Loohooloo (prefiguring Redburn's three country beauties) and enjoying an idyllic vacation of spearfishing and swinging over land and sea in a basket suspended from a cocoa-nut tree. The idyll (chs. 67–71) ends with a stop (ch. 72) at the hut of a supposedly deaf and dumb hermit, Varvy, who manufactures a killing liquor and finds speech when the narrator objects to it. This comic figure, with the "goblin," Tonoi, and "Capin Bob," is ranged along a continuum of acculturating Polynesians who match the continuum of expatriated whites. The best of both groups awaits the narrator in Partoowye, where he and Long Ghost hope to gain preferment at court. Here he is the guest of the genuinely Christian Jeremiah Po-Po and his motherly wife, Arfretee, who have succeeded in adapting to Western religion without losing morale. Among the colonizing whites, the narrator catches a glimpse of the beautiful young Englishwoman, Mrs. Bell, and meets her husband, a handsome and successful sugar planter. In final contrast to these, stand the degraded naval officer Captain Crash and the defeated Pomaree, with her history of conjugal discord, drunkenness, and disorder.

The narrator is guided through her Tahitian court, a jumble of European and native artifacts, by an uncorrupted Marquesan, Marbonna, whose physique marks his superiority. A forerunner of Queequeg, Marbonna hopes to return someday to his native island. He delivers the narrator and Long Ghost to the guidance of a young woman who shows them the household of a European married into the royal family (who does not condescend to greet them!) and takes them to the private chamber of the Queen. Matronly, careworn Pomaree will not receive them, as they observe her, surrounded by European delicacies, eating "fish and poee out of her native calabashes, disdaining either knife or spoon" (p. 310).

For nine chapters (73–81), the narrator and Long Ghost have been guests of Jeremiah Po-Po; now, their hopes of preferment at court dashed, they need a new plan. Long Ghost elects to stay on in Tahiti, while the narrator ships aboard a Vineyard whaler whose captain knows by testing his pulse that he is American. After a tender farewell to his Tahitian family, he divides his advance of fifteen Spanish dollars with Long Ghost: "Once more the sailor's cradle rocked under me, and I found myself rolling in my gait" (p. 316).

Reviewing Melville's first two works, we find that in *Typee* the anti-colonialist argument struggles against the drama of unwilling detention and escape from cannibals; in *Omoo* the anti-colonialist argument structures the work, and the narrative embellishes and illustrates it. As a result, *Omoo* is a more unified piece of work, pointing toward *White-Jacket*, which is similarly structured by social observation and protest.

The chief difference between Melville's early work and his later fiction is this: when he started out as a writer, Melville needed two books to accomplish what he would later achieve in one. *Typee* embodies more dramatic tension in its plot and theme development, but *Omoo* includes many sketches of subordinate characters, accompanied by suspended stories that stand as foils to the actual events of the book; *Omoo* also develops the dissolving narrator, less a character than a voice. In *Typee* Melville begins his confident treatment of the real world, but he extends this in *Omoo* beyond geographical and anthropological material to matters of shipboard life, richly foreshadowing the later novels. Although critics have regarded *Typee* more highly in the past, *Omoo* reveals more of the individual genius of its young author.

THE *TYPEE* MANUSCRIPTS

The importance of *Typee* in Melville studies has been enhanced by the 1983 discovery in a barn in Gansevoort, New York, of a manuscript representing thirty pages of a first draft of the book. The manuscript, part of a collection of papers originally belonging to Melville's sister, Augusta, now belongs to the Gansevoort-Lansing Collection (Melville Family Papers) of the Manuscript Division of the New York Public Library, where it joins a single leaf from the same draft, already owned by the Library and photographed and transcribed in the NN *Typee* (pp. 363–69). This manuscript leaf corresponds to a portion of Chapter 24 (pp. 106.28–107.36 in NN). The new find includes ten gathered leaves corresponding to a portion of Chapter 12, (p. 89.12 to end) and all of Chapter 13; and five loose leaves: Chapter 14, pp. 104 to 105.23; p.

107.36–109.9; pp. 109.9–110.15; pp. 110. 15–111.16; pp. 111.16–112, the end of Chapter 14 in the NN *Typee*. For further discussion of the find and the Library's handling of it, see Susan Davis (pp. 5–7).

Because there are few extant manuscripts among Melville's prose works, the discovery of several chapters of an early draft of *Typee* offers scholars a special opportunity to observe the young author at work. Although no definitive analysis can be made until the manuscript fragment has been fully transcribed and compared with published versions, a preliminary study shows a worked-over copy, including marginal insertions and strike-overs. Comparing the passage describing Tommo's first bath among the Typee girls to the final published version in the NN *Typee* offers a good example of how the author or an editor (possibly his brother, Gansevoort, or John Murray's reader, Henry Milton, or all three) revised and pruned Melville's writing. The scene in the NN edition reads as follows:

From the verdant surfaces of the large stones that lay scattered about, the natives were now sliding off into the water, diving and ducking beneath the surface in all directions—the young girls springing buoyantly into the air, and revealing their naked forms to the waist, with their long tresses dancing about their shoulders, their eyes sparkling like drops of dew in the sun, and their gay laughter pealing forth at every frolicsome incident (p. 90).

The description of the girls is a long participial phrase adding movement, light, and sound to the main action. By contrast, leaf 3 of the manuscript devotes a full sentence to this description:

The young girls springing buoyantly into the air, & revealing their naked forms to the waist, with their long tresses dancing about their bosoms & shoulders, their eyes sparkling like drops of dew in the sun & their gay laughter pealing forth at any frolicsome incident, looked among those green mossy rocks like so many mermaids splashing in the billows that washed the sea weed covered sides of their mossy lurking places.

In this earlier version the activity of the girls is converted into a conventional simile. Whoever attached the first part of it to the preceding sentence and dropped the simile took a step toward improved writing.

A comparison of the NN edition, based on the first English edition, to the new manuscript shows an elimination of conventional allusions and a preference for direct description of scene over romantic commentary. For example, consider this later deleted sentence on leaf 7 of the manuscript: "This picturesque procession carrying along such glorious specimens of tropical vegetation moving with wild chants through the sylvan defiles of the valley might have been taken for a throng of the ancient devotees of Ceres wending their way with votive offerings towards the altars of the goddess." Perhaps Melville himself later struck such a passage as destructive of the special realism toward which he aspired.

The newly-found manuscript also reveals the young Melville's tendency to verbosity. For example, "a heavy javelin dashed past me as I fled and stuck the next moment into a tree beyond where it hung quivering with the sudden resistance it had met" (ms. leaf 10) has been shortened to "stuck quivering in a tree close to me" (p. 101.27).

Perhaps most important is Melville's awkward introduction in the manuscript of Toby's story of the Happar attack. He tries to get it right twice in leaf 10, striking out the first sentence quoted here:

As I cannot remember the words made use of by Toby on this occasion, I shall accordingly relate his adventure in my own language tho' in the same putting the words in his mouth.

Though I can not recall to mind anything like the precise phraseology employed on this occasion still for the sake of unity I shall permit my companion to rehearse his own adventure in the language that most readily occurs to me.

These sentences are entirely omitted from the published text (see p. 100), where Toby tells his story in his own words without apology or explanation. The passage enlightens us about Melville's concern for authenticity. It is also a reminder of later explanations that precede Melville's suspended stories, familiar examples of which are the Town-Ho's story in *Moby-Dick* and certain disclaimers that introduce interpolated tales in *The Confidence-Man*. As early as the "first draught" of *Typee*, Melville was wrestling with the problem of the narrator's voice. His bold resolution of it in *Typee* is a hint that he will always face such issues with an alerted consciousness, resolve them in a way to promote artistic rather than documentary effect and even play with the problem (see, especially, the two ways of telling the same story in "Benito Cereno").

Students of Melville, and particularly of *Typee*, should be alerted to the forthcoming publication of the manuscript fragment. It promises to support the work called for by Hershel Parker, who noted that no one has studied so basic a subject as "the attitudes toward literary creativity which are revealed in Melville's compositional practices" (p. 421).

PUBLICATION HISTORY, EDITIONS, AND TEACHING TEXTS

Typee presents complicated problems in the establishment of a reliable text. Entitled *Narrative of a Four Months' Residence Among the Natives of a Valley of the Marquesas; or, a Peep at Polynesian Life*, it first appeared in the "Colonial and Home Library," Volume 1 in February 1846, and Volume 2 in April 1846. The book was first set in type from a now-missing manuscript corrected by the author, his brother Gansevoort, Melville's English publisher John Murray, and Murray's reader, Henry Milton (see Mary K. Madison). On 17 March 1846 an American edition, entitled *Typee* (followed by a slightly revised subtitle), was published from the English proof-sheets, expurgated of some references to religion, sexuality, and politics, by Wiley and Putnam. These revisions were made at the request of John Wiley, who was concerned about his firm's respectability; Melville accepted the changes and, for a Revised American Edition, published on 15 July 1846, removed even more material, approximately thirty-six pages of the text and the Appendix, concerning the activities of Lord George Paulet at the Sandwich Islands. In this edition, the omitted words and passages are scattered through the book, in some places just a phrase, in others a complete episode, in still others, the whole development of an idea. The end of Chapter 1, for example, omits the final two pages of comment on the Protestant mission and the comic account of the behavior of the Queen of Nukuheva. More important, the extended bitter attack on "the white civilized man as the most ferocious animal on the face of the earth" (ch. 17) is eliminated entirely, so that the passage focuses on Typee, where "there seemed to be no cares, griefs, troubles or vexations" (Dodd, Mead, *Typee*, p. 133). Because such powerful passages concerning civilized barbarity introduce extended criticism, to which the author had given careful rhetorical shape, their elimination shifts the emphasis from pointed criticism to nostalgic panegyric. Such an expurgated edition as the above-quoted Dodd Mead converts *Typee* from an important cultural document to a story-book dream for children, appropriately illustrated by glossy colored plates that romanticize the exotic scenes while ignoring Melville's verbal equivalent of black and white political cartoons.

A second English edition was published by John Murray in September 1846; it included the unbowdlerized text and Appendix concerning Lord Paulet, as well as "The Story of Toby: A Sequel to *Typee* by the Author of that Work." This sequel was based on Richard Tobias Greene's 11 July 1846 account of his experience as Melville's companion in escape Toby, published in the *Buffalo Commercial Advertiser*. The second English edition carried the title *Typee* before its subtitles.

As the closest edition to Melville's manuscript, the first English edition is the copy-text for the NN *Typee* and the accepted text for reprinting. However, the Revised American Edition was the basis for all future editions printed in this country during Melville's lifetime. Ironically, if not surprisingly, the book was available during its author's life in the bowdlerized version in his own country and in the original version in England. Many adult Americans probably read it in the 1907 Everyman's

Library, which was based on the Revised American Edition (the 1958 Everyman printed the English text).

Many public libraries in this country bought reprinted illustrated editions, such as the 1941 Dodd, Mead with full-page color illustrations by Mead Schaeffer, based on the bowdlerized text. A useful summary of the publishing history of *Typee* can be found in Milton Stern's *Critical Essays* (pp. 17–21) and in the "Historical Note" and "Note on the Text" in the NN edition (pp. 277–315). Further information and discussion are included in G. Thomas Tanselle, "Bibliographical Problems" (1974).

Although Melville himself consented to prepare the bowdlerized edition, it should be noted that he did not send it to John Murray for reprinting. The modern reader of the Revised Edition is bound to find it flat; the complexity of texture and relief from the romantic plot, afforded by the astringent social criticism of the English edition, are missing. Simplified, *Typee* is merely an adventure story with a somewhat overdramatized conclusion. Returning to the English version, especially in the NN edition, one can hear much more clearly the skeptical and incisive voice of the Melville of the next five books. It is possible that Melville was so long in being taken seriously as a major writer because the bowdlerized *Typee* misrepresented him. This history of its publication is a bitter example of the influence of short-sighted publishing practices.

Modern readers should scrutinize their local school and public library holdings to encourage the replacement of the bowdlerized text with the NN edition. Another valuable permanent hardcover edition is the Library of America volume, which reprints the NN texts of *Typee*, *Omoo*, and *Mardi*, a treasure to Melvilleans. Beware of the Constable edition of *Typee* (1922) which uses the English text but according to the NN editors "in patches apparently used the revised American edition" (p. 314). For teaching purposes, the NN paperback is the best choice; also acceptable are the Signet Classic (1964), edited by Harrison Hayford which brackets the excisions of the Revised American Edition, and the Penguin paper edition (1972), edited by George Woodcock.

The publication of *Omoo* was a far less vexed affair. It was set in type by its American publisher, Harper & Bros., in January 1847, and John Murray reset it from the American proof-sheets on 30 March 1847. Shortly after this English publication, it was available to its American readers and deposited for copyright on 16 June 1847. Thus, as the editors of NN point out, the second published edition (American) is, oddly, the one based on the manuscript. The differences between the two editions chiefly involve typographical and spelling errors. A late English issue added a memoir of Melville, maps, and engravings, but made no changes in the text. Arthur Stedman supervised an 1892 edition published by the United States Book Company, the plates from which have been used by many subsequent publishers (Kathleen Kier). The

Everyman Library edition, in which many twentieth-century readers read *Omoo*, was published in 1908. A highly regarded French translation, *Omoo, ou le Vagabond du Pacifique*, was published in 1951 by Jacqueline Foulque, an expert in Polynesian languages.

Aside from the NN, the best permanent edition of *Omoo* for the modern reader is published by Hendricks House and edited by Harrison Hayford and Walter Blair (1969). It reproduces important documents relating to Melville's whalers and the events of his jailing on Tahiti. The Hendricks House *Omoo* offers a comprehensive discussion of Melville's informational sources and an excellent critical introduction, making it an indispensable volume for students of this neglected work. The only authoritative paperback edition is the NN. For full information concerning the publishing history of *Omoo*, see the NN "Historical Note" and "Note on the Text" (pp. 319–54)

RECEPTION OF *TYPEE* AND *OMOO*

The immediate reception of *Typee* was complicated by its publishers' concerns and the consequent representation of the book. The British John Murray, offering it in his "Colonial and Home Library," a series of travel accounts, was eager to confirm its accuracy as a documentary record. John Wiley, its American publisher, was less concerned about the truth of the narrative than he was about its potential offensiveness to a genteel or religious audience. The reception of the book in each country fell, in part, into the pattern established by the publishers: in England, some reviewers suspected Melville's veracity, whereas in America, some were critical of his tone toward missionaries and his political commentary. On the whole, however, the reception was positive. Both books were favorably reviewed, *Omoo* even more widely than *Typee*. The reviews began the tradition of considering the works together. For example, Joseph Wenke's "Annotated Bibliography of *Typee* Studies" (in Stern, *Critical Essays*, pp. 261–67) lists all the reviews of *Omoo* as well because they all invoke the comparison to *Typee* as a central matter. More than 150 reviews and extended mentions appeared by the end of 1847. Most of the reviews were favorable, including those by Margaret Fuller, Nathaniel Hawthorne, C. F. Hoffman, George Ripley, William Gilmore Simms, Walt Whitman, and N. P. Willis. The violent attack by William Oland Bourne, "Typee, the Traducer of Missions," originally published in the *Christian Parlor Magazine*, is an example of the special interest reviewing that condemned the author "for his flagrant outrages against civilization" (Stern, *Critical Essays*, pp. 38–52).

John Wiley's fear of criticism by a genteel and pro-missionary audience was more a reflection of his own taste than of reality, as the reviews expressed it, but it conditioned Melville's reputation by causing the bowdlerization of the most widely disseminated edition. Those who reviewed the Revised American Edition were not reading the true *Typee*. John Murray, on the other hand, by being concerned about Melville's veracity, promoted the addition of factual material drawn from secondary sources. Although this addition changed the manuscript (before publication) markedly, it was, in my view, a positive change. It led to the development of a more versatile narrative voice in Melville and possibly provided the suggestion for his use of expository material in later works.

Several articles and anthologies help us to follow the reception of *Typee* and *Omoo* and the development of Melville's reputation. An early and still useful article by Charles Roberts Anderson, "Contemporary American Opinions of *Typee* and *Omoo*" (1937), partially summarized in *Melville in the South Seas* (1939), corrects the then conventional picture of Melville as a neglected writer. Anderson discusses the attack on *Typee* by George Washington Peck, a proponent of missionaries, and James Russell Lowell's mockery of Peck in "A Fable for Critics." He reprints sections of appreciative reviews of *Typee* and *Omoo*, such as this one from the *Anglo-American Review*: "*Typee* was something rare; but *Omoo* is still rarer." Horace Greeley also admired *Omoo*, but distorted its meaning to support his own view that the Polynesians must change "from idleness and inefficiency to regular and well-directed industry" (Mentor Williams, p. 95).

Jay Leyda's *The Melville Log* remains an indispensable reference for information about the reception of *Typee* and *Omoo* (see especially pp. 197–217). Leyda reprints critical sections of reviews along with relevant letters, such as Evert Duyckinck's letter to Hawthorne about *Typee* and Melville's letter of 2 September 1846 to John Murray concerning revisions; he also provides documentary support for autobiographical aspects of *Typee*. Reading these documents along with the narrative account of life in the New York literary world presented by Perry Miller, in *The Raven and the Whale* (1956), gives a clear picture of the young author among his early supporters and detractors.

Hugh Hetherington discusses a broad range of British and American reviews of Melville written during his lifetime in *Melville's Reviewers 1846–1891* (1961). Prefacing his eighty pages on *Typee* and *Omoo* with a valuable essay on the timing and influence of British reviews and the composition of the New York literary world, he also discusses the international copyright law finally accepted by Congress in 1891, five months before Melville's death. Hershel Parker's *Recognition* reprints significant portions of contemporary reviews and essays as well as academic essays from 1884–1912 and from the revival of interest in Melville in the 1920s. But the fullest collection of reviews of Melville's work through 1892 appears in Watson G. Branch's *Critical Heritage*. There are sixteen British and American reviews of *Typee*, including those by Nathaniel Hawthorne, Margaret

Fuller, and John Sullivan Dwight. For *Omoo*, Branch reprints seventeen reviews, including the negative one by George Washington Peck—"*Omoo* is a book one may read once with interest and pleasure, but with a perpetual recoil" (p. 132)—and the reply to it written by Jedediah B. Auld (p. 133).

A useful supplement to this book is Nelson C. Smith's reprinting in the *Melville Society Extracts* of a newly found series of laudatory British reviews that appeared in the London *Sun* in 1846 and 1847. Additional reviews of *Typee* and *Omoo* can be found by using the bibliography prepared by Joseph Wenke for Stern's *Critical Essays* (pp. 261–68). This volume also reprints five representative reviews of *Typee* (pp. 222–52). A thorough discussion of the reception of *Omoo* is offered in the Hendricks House edition.

CRITICISM

Critical writing on *Typee* and *Omoo* may be divided into two major categories: a large group of studies of American literature or of Melville's work in which his first two books are used in an introductory way, or referred to in passing to support a thesis primarily framed in relation to other works; and a small set of closer readings that reflect specific problems in interpretation.

To organize this diverse body of criticism in a useful manner, I have subdivided it, first discussing four indispensable books and reserving for last eight articles that offer close readings of *Typee* and *Omoo*. Between these sections, I have grouped selected works by kind: general works on American literature or on Melville; biographical studies; literary source and influence studies; books and articles on special topics; discussions of form and narration in Melville. I hope, in this way, to emphasize the range of critical speculation on *Typee* and *Omoo*, rather than its limits to specific critical issues that are finally unresolvable. Critics do divide over the meaning of Tommo's swollen leg and over the ending of *Typee*, but invariably this is the least valuable aspect of their study. *Typee* is like *Billy Budd* in this respect; it has invited pro-paradise and anti-paradise readings, just as *Billy Budd* has divided critics who would praise or blame Captain Vere. Similarly, *Omoo* has been treated like *Pierre*: called a failure by most, admired by a few, and generally neglected.

But *Typee* and *Omoo* have succeeded in sustaining an increasingly interesting and sophisticated discussion since the 1920s, and it seems that we are now at the crest of a thirty-year period of work, framed by the publication of James Baird's *Ishmael* (1956), and T. Walter Herbert's *Marquesan Encounters* (1980). Assisted by Milton Stern's review in *Critical Essays* (1982) and inspired by the 1983 discovery of the manuscript fragment, students of Melville are bound to recognize the remarkable vitality of his first two books.

Major Works on *Typee* and *Omoo*

Milton Stern's *Critical Essays on Herman Melville's Typee* (1982) is an indispensable reference source. In addition to five contemporary reviews and a biographical memoir, it represents *Typee* criticism chronologically, excerpting chapters from fourteen books and including five articles, a summary of publication history, and an extensive bibliography of periodicals and books arranged by decade from 1846 to 1981.

In his introductory essay, Stern describes the contributions made by various critical methodologies, also identifying important works excluded by length from his anthology. He shows that the missionary controversy surrounding *Typee* at the time of its publication transmuted itself into the critical study of Melville's primitivism, and finds that "a recognition of richly mixed yearning for and final repudiation of the primitive energies [is] the major continuum of critical thought concerning this aspect of *Typee*" (p. 8). A second critical issue Stern identifies is the degree of factual accuracy in *Typee*, in regard to both autobiography and ethnography; he concludes that "Melville's first book is recognized as a work of considerable reality, both ethnographic and literary" (p. 10). Stern also observes that the narrative quality of *Typee* has engaged readers including Robert Louis Stevenson and Jack London. *Typee* continues to be widely read, and not just by scholars. After *Moby-Dick* and *Billy Budd*, it is the most frequently mentioned of Melville's works.

Most of the essays in the Stern anthology concern themselves with deriving the philosophical argument of *Typee*, an approach that has some rewards as well as problems. These can be illustrated by reference to John Wenke's "Melville's *Typee*: A Tale of Two Worlds," written especially for Stern's volume. Working primarily with "the rudiments of *Typee*'s plot," Wenke sees the book as "the story of man's attempt to reconcile the opposing forces of freedom and necessity" (p. 250). The distance between concrete plot and such an abstraction is too great, but Wenke's smaller generalizations are useful; for example, "Tommo is Melville's first character who encounters cultural relativism" (p. 251). Wenke notes that "cannibalism becomes the narrative's central metaphor for the primitive threat to consume Tommo's contemporary identity," a useful starting point for a look at the metaphor as Melville extends it in his other work, especially *Moby-Dick*. The effect of Wenke's method, however, is to make Tommo's flight from Typee seem a reasoned part of his "search for self-hood," rather than the spontaneous reflex of panic born of culture shock.

The problems of over-argumentation are avoided by the three major books that take *Typee* and *Omoo* as their subject. Charles Roberts Anderson's *Melville in the South Seas* (1939), James Baird's *Ishmael* (1956), and T. Walter Herbert's *Marquesan Encounters* (1980) are different from each other in method and purpose, but have in common a salutary resistance to translating Melville's work too far out of its own terms. Anderson's study is biographical and historical, chiefly concerned with sources; Baird's is a comparative study of literary images, influenced by Suzanne Langer and Carl Jung; Herbert puts *Typee* and *Omoo* in the context of two other South Seas observers, studying them at the place "where interpretive social science can be joined with literary criticism" (p. 4).

   In his edition of *Journal of a Cruise to the Pacific Ocean, 1842–1844* (1937), Anderson suggests the value of searching for new source material regarding Melville's naval record in the South Seas. His *Melville in the South Seas* reports his findings and takes up the family precedent for Melville's career in the lives of his cousins, Thomas Melville and Guert Gansevoort, and his uncle Captain John De Wolf II, before turning to written sources specifically mentioned by Melville, such as C. S. Stewart's *A Visit to the South Seas in the U.S. Ship Vincennes* (1831) and William Ellis's *Polynesian Researches* (1833). Anderson uses records of the Catholic priest M. l'Abbé Mathias Gracia and tests Melville's account of Marquesan life by comparing it to early works, like David Porter's *Journal of a Cruise in the U.S. Frigate Essex* (1815), and later studies such as the information gathered in 1921 by the Bayard Dominick Expedition. He uses side-by-side comparison of passages to estimate the importance of borrowings, concluding that *Typee* is a compilation from sources (p. 191) with an uncertain autobiographical element. *Omoo*, on the other hand, Anderson finds more strictly autobiographical. Existing French Naval records substantiate even the number of mutineers. (See Hendricks House *Omoo* for the names and more specifics.) He finds Melville's account of the degradation of the Tahitians supported by other observers and detailed corroboration of his work in the writings of two visitors to the South Seas (Lieutenant Henry Wise and Henry T. Perkins) who deliberately followed him. Anderson sees *Omoo* as "a sort of traveller's portfolio": "Rather than a novel it is a series of stereopticon scenes skillfully interlarded with a gallery of grotesque portraits, the slender line of continuity being furnished by the offhand reminiscent chat of a graceful raconteur" (p. 309). I find less offhandedness and more patterning in *Omoo* than Anderson does, particularly in the gradation of communities and people, but consider Anderson's work vital on sources for corroboration of Melville's view of the South Seas. (See also Anderson, "The Romance of Scholarship.") A corrective to Anderson's claim for autobiographical accuracy in *Omoo* is the inclusion and analysis of subsequently discovered consular records and discussion of Melville's borrowings (particularly from Ellis's *Polynesian Researches*, for the second half of *Omoo*) in Hayford and Blair's introduction and notes to the Hendricks House *Omoo*.

Baird's *Ishmael* (1956) examines the "autotypes or imagistic patterns which Melville acquired in the Pacific," finding Melville an exemplar of the artist working within the symbolic system of primitivism, "a system appearing in the art of the western world during the last century" (p. 4). Defining primitivism carefully as "the mode of feeling which exchanges for traditional Christian symbols a new symbolic idiom referring to Oriental cultures of both Oceania and Asia" (p. 6), Baird sets Melville's work against the background of what is known of these cultures (for example, he explores the Polynesian custom of *tayo*, friendship) and against the work of others, such as Mark Twain, R. L. Stevenson, Paul Gauguin, Ernest Fenellosa, Lafcadio Hearn, and Rimbaud. He follows the extension of South Seas autotypes through Melville's works, proving the centrality of this material for understanding the reverberations of elements from minor women characters to the whiteness of the whale. The book is a model of the power of the literary critic, uniting scholarship and sensibility to set its subject in a new perspective. *Typee* and *Omoo* take their rightful place as seminal works, and Melville takes *his* rightful place, not as moralist, politician, or logician, but as artist, a primary symbol-maker for our time.

Marquesan Encounters (1980) is the third and most recent of these central studies of *Typee* and *Omoo*. Herbert discusses "three episodes in which early nineteenth-century Americans confronted the inhabitants of Nukuheva" to illuminate "a debate on the meaning of civilization" (p. 4). The three Americans are Captain David Porter, military man and spokesman for the Enlightenment; the Reverend Charles Stewart, Calvinist missionary; and Herman Melville, Romantic. Each one's story is "organized by a consciousness that is itself organized by ideas of what constitutes civilized life" (p. 8). Herbert studies the language and the structure of events in the three works, indicating "perceptual blind spots." His trilogy answers the question "What is American civilization?" He concludes justly that "Of the three exemplars of American civilization at the Marquesas, [Melville] tells us least about the Marquesans themselves, but most about what it meant to Americans to encounter them" (p. 21). Charles Stewart saw Marquesans as "moral monsters"; Porter (who is amazingly like Melville's own Captain Delano, in "Benito Cereno") saw them as "promising neophytes." Only Melville is capable of dramatizing the fact that consciousness interprets experience.

Melville "lays claim to and repudiates a civilized identity," his narrative voice characterized by "subtle ambivalent balancing" (p. 156). The only perspective that is possible is that of the Romantic—"a meditative outsider who at the bottom of his heart does not know what world he belongs to" (p. 158). His anxieties become the theme as he dramatizes the "encounter, the experience of contact," rather than an objectification of the Marquesans. Herbert shows how *Typee* is the beginning of Melville's career-long attempt to tell the truth through fiction; thus his book complements Anderson's, which defined the field and sorted out the materials, and Baird's, which illuminated the symbolism upon which Melville's attempt draws. Herbert's noteworthy bibliography sends the reader to anthropological studies that have been models for the author (pp. 227–30).

Biographical Studies

Raymond Weaver (1921) considered *Typee* and *Omoo* to be "transparent chapters in autobiography" (p. 133). This view has been corrected by Anderson, but Weaver's general historical background to Melville's years as a sailor is still valuable, as is his assertion that "Melville was the first competent literary artist to write with authority about the South Seas" (p. 205). The narrative biography of Leon Howard (1951) provides several important chapters that summarize Melville's experiences in the Pacific and in writing his first two books (pp. 41–111).

The most recent biographical venture in Melville studies is Michael Paul Rogin's *Subversive Genealogy* (1983), which takes Melville's works out of literary isolation and places them against the background of a biography broadened to include family and political history. Rogin discusses Melville's indebtedness to Cooper's *The Red Rover*, especially in regard to *Omoo*; the relationship between *Typee* and the political career of Melville's brother Gansevoort and the naval career of his cousin, Guert Gansevoort; and he gives meaning to the dedication of subversive *Typee* to Lemuel Shaw, among other relevant subjects.

General Works on American Literature

D. H. Lawrence's famous chapter on *Typee* and *Omoo* in *Studies in Classic American Literature* (1923) is the starting point for many subsequent critics. Lawrence finds an unresolvable conflict in Melville between his longing for a paradisal ideal and his "American" need to struggle against the world. In *Typee* this conflict is dramatized by Tommo's recurring unhappiness. Lawrence theorizes that the moral and intellectual gulf, "a gulf in time and being," between the white man and the "savage" is the cause of the swollen leg, and that a "return" to paradise means losing our places in "the consciousness-struggle, the struggle of the soul into fullness" (p. 145). Although he disclaims ideas of race superiority, Lawrence maintains the necessity of a separation between races: "But it seems to me that in living so far, through all our bitter centuries of civilization, we have still been living onwards, forwards. God knows it looks like a *cul de sac* now. But turn to the first negro, and then listen to your own soul" (p. 145). What sort of nonsense is this? Lawrence imposes his own dread of the "renegade" on Melville, claims a clear meaning for Tommo's mysterious injury ("If you prostitute your psyche by returning to the savages, you gradually go to pieces"), and even applies a reptilian image to Fayaway, whom Melville immortalized as the straight clean spar of a sailboat. One of the critical labors ahead is to disentangle Melville and Lawrence. Melville's work consistently moves toward the translation of "savage" or "racial other" to "human being"; I take that to be the meaning of Queequeg as well as Babo. It is grossly unfair to saddle him with Lawrence's racism, a racism which had political consequences that Melville abhorred. Note, for example, Lawrence's lumping of "renegades" with those " 'reformers' and 'idealists' who glorify the savages in America" (p. 146).

Read Herbert's *Marquesan Encounters* as an antidote to Lawrence, but note that Lawrence on *Omoo* is somewhat more reliable; he is the first modern critic to recognize *Omoo* as "a fascinating book; picaresque, rascally, roving...Perhaps Melville is at his best, his happiest, in *Omoo*" (p. 148).

A. N. Kaul, in his chapter on Melville in *The American Vision* (1963), takes the theme Lawrence would have Melville reject—"the 'paradisal ideal' of love...the ideal community" (p. 218) and traces its presence throughout Melville's work. Kaul emphasizes the acculturation of races, "somehow connected in Melville's imagination with the meaning of democracy" (p. 219). He finds *Typee* an angry book that holds a society based on abundance up to nineteenth-century America; its idealization of the Happy Valley appears against the dark background of civilized society. When Tommo leaves Typee, Kaul sees it as neither a repudiation of primitive social values nor a reconciliation to civilization. Although Kaul is not so clear on what it is, he takes the reader on to the exploration of new communities in *Omoo*.

No student of Melville should miss studying F. O. Matthiessen's chapters on Melville in *American Renaissance* (1941). Although there is no extended treatment of *Typee* and *Omoo* in this book, Matthiessen provides an indispensable discussion of Melville's skepticism and his concern with human suffering. Quoting the Rabelaisian picture of the Queen of Nukuheva, Matthiessen remarks of *Typee* and *Omoo*: "The personality of the author, which radiates through both of these books, suggests in its self-possession and in its robust meeting of life, something of the 'great individual' whom Whitman's poems were to announce a decade later" (p. 378).

In *The Confidence Game in American Literature* (1975), Warwick Wadlington devotes a chapter to *Typee* and *Omoo*, with special attention to *Omoo*: "*Omoo's* rhetoric is in some ways more instructive than that of

Typee concerning his developing skill" (p. 42). Wadlington takes up Matthiessen's interest in eloquence in his discussion of the mediating narrative posture—"invitational and elusive"—in *Typee* and *Omoo* that he regards central to Melville's genius. The theme of friendship discussed by Baird is treated here as part of the hazardous human connection enacted in Melville's rhetoric. *Typee* adds a suspense plot to this rhetorical stance; Wadlington pairs it with *The Confidence-Man* in its examination of the "invisibly familiar." The first book creates a more naive narrative presence than *Omoo*, yet it resists "moral reductionism" by maintaining mystery; this purposeful irresolution links it with *Moby-Dick*. Concentrating on the narrative stance in *Typee* and *Omoo*, Wadlington supports the modern critical view that Melville's first books are significant in form and style to students of the later work. By treating Melville with Mark Twain and Nathanael West, he brings Melville into refreshingly unaccustomed company.

Typee and *Omoo* in Melville Studies

Scholars concentrating on Melville's work have long recognized that the study of *Typee* and *Omoo* takes them to the heart of central issues in Melville's work, from textual and biographical problems to matters of form and theme. Consequently, nearly every book on Melville devotes some attention to them. I will briefly mention nine works—five of the 1940s and early 1950s, and four of the 1960s and early 1970s. The earliest of these post-Matthiessen studies, William Ellery Sedgwick's *Herman Melville: The Tragedy of Mind* (1944), is still one of the most durable in its view of Melville's career as an "unfolding of inward vision, a vision not so much of life as of what it is to be alive" (p. 15). This idea helped Sedgwick to disregard the old reviewers' questions of factual or autobiographical accuracy and to recognize that Melville's books represent a fusing of experience and reading. As Baird asserted and developed twelve years later, *Typee* remained with Melville as a vital symbol throughout his life. Sedgwick is less helpful on *Omoo*, which does not suit his thesis that *Typee* is paradise and the murder of Mow-Mow a symbolic act reflecting human necessity. If Tommo's escape from Typee is allegory, *Omoo* is just stalling, a dead-end position for the critic.

Richard Chase (1949) reduces the treatment of *Omoo* even further in his psychological reading of *Typee*. He regards Melville's first book as dramatic withdrawal "into the recesses of his own infantile sexuality" (p. 12), which oddly makes the murderous leavetaking a claim to maturing sexuality. *Typee*, then, is linked to Melville's later work by its expression of castration anxiety in a typical figure, "the maimed man in the glen." This analysis emphasizes the adventure plot of *Typee* and barely mentions the social criticism; it leaves the critic helpless before *Omoo*, which Chase dismisses as "slightly oafish philosophizing" (p. 176).

By contrast, Newton Arvin (1950), in his critical biography, resists the psychologizing for firmer literary study. He identifies in *Typee* and *Omoo* the first example of Melville's interest in factual information, and he places the books beside those of contemporary explorers and travelers, especially in their painterliness. He contrasts the nightmare effects of *Typee* and the "emotionally liberating current of humorous narrative" in *Omoo*. Arvin characterizes both books as pilgrimages that led to failure, but from which Melville returned with a refreshed view of his sources in myth. Of all of these general studies, Arvin's is the least thesis-ridden and the richest in opening up connections. It remains the best starting point for a novice in Melville studies.

Another well-written general view of Melville is Ronald Mason's *The Spirit Above the Dust* (1951). Mason starts out strongly, seeing *Typee* as an initial example of Melville's central theme: "innocence at every step of its universal progress to tragedy" (p. 29). He finds himself in agreement with Lawrence that Tommo's escape from Typee is "a reaction against the inertia that goes with innocence" (Lawrence's term was "precons ciousness"), but his thesis fails him in *Omoo*, which he regards as a "pot-boiler": "imaginatively, *Omoo* is a regression, a relaxation, a record lacking the intimacy of passion" (p. 33).

In *Melville's Quarrel with God* (1952), Lawrance Thompson sees Melville's first seven books as stemming from the development of his youthful adventures. He regards the first five as apprentice work, all dealing with disillusionment derived from the jolt given to Melville's Calvinist heritage by his first-hand observation of natural man. To Chase's negative view of the Typee experience and Arvin's positive view of it, Thompson offers a third interpretation: Melville was searching for a personal religious belief in which Typee became a paradise image only after it was left behind. This reading again leads to a disregard of *Omoo*.

In 1960 Merlin Bowen in *The Long Encounter* continued to find *Omoo* superficial and to attribute a "flash of deeper insight" to *Typee* (p. 15). Neither book satisfied the critic; for a fuller treatment, we must turn to Milton Stern's *The Fine-Hammered Steel of Herman Melville* (1968), which considers *Typee* as one of four central works. Stern sees *Typee* as "an order sheet for the materials Melville is to use characteristically" (p. 25). He finds it a symbolic work in which ship and land represent opposing forces of mind and body, but because Stern undervalues the openness of Melville's exploratory forms, he, too, concludes that *Typee* is incomplete. He shapes his reading of Melville's first book (*Omoo* is not included) to mesh with his view of *Billy Budd*, even comparing Tommo's instinctive murder of Mow-Mow to Vere's considered execution of Billy Budd.

Typee's conclusion has been a problem for critics: Martin Pops in *The*

Melville Archetype (1970) finds "the final sequence of events...jumbled in a way very strange for a novelist who had such a powerful grip on facts" (p. 37). Pops goes on to find *Omoo* lacking in structure and symbolic meaning; he also finds it a poor sequel to *Typee*. He reminds us that Ishmael's image of "one insular Tahiti" derives from *Omoo* and that Bembo, the New Zealander, prefigures Ahab, but then he unaccountably lets the two works go as "pleasant books with pleasant heroes" (p. 39).

John Seelye omits extended discussion of *Omoo* in *Melville: The Ironic Diagram* (1970), comparing it only briefly to the later *Israel Potter*, but he gives full consideration to *Typee* as "an elaboration in many ways on the materials of quest and consequent disillusionment found in the early 'Fragment'" (p. 13). Finding Melville's literary sources in Cervantes and Scott, he sees Tommo's return to the sea as shaping an ironic circle like that in "The Piazza." Seelye's discussion of the inability of the narrative voice in *Typee* to handle irony finally sheds some light on the troublesome finale of the book and suggests that the answers to many critical controversies may lie in closer attention to the problems of form and narration.

Melville's Form and Narration

Both Warner Berthoff's *The Example of Melville* (1962) and Edgar A. Dryden's *Melville's Thematics of Form* (1968) devote substantial attention in passing to narrative structure in *Typee* and *Omoo*. Berthoff treats the books as they serve his discussion of the various aspects of Melville's fiction; his chapter on first-person narrators is most useful in considering Tommo's voice: Melville's narrator "takes the world as he finds it and indeed discovers his voice in describing it" (p. 124). Dryden continues this discussion, focusing on the problems of memory and detachment: "By taking the view of the detached anthropologist, the narrator is able to bridge both the smaller gap between the successive sensations of his Typee experience and the larger one between the primitive and civilized worlds" (p. 38).

William Dillingham's *An Artist in the Rigging* (1972) takes *Typee* and *Omoo* out of compositional order, treating them as two very different books. Dillingham patiently uncovers the two views of Typee created by the naive and detached narrator, a potential Ishmael and "no systematizer" (p. 30). He considers the narrator of *Omoo* a Prince Hal figure, finding his identity in his work as a sailorman.

Four recent articles usefully explore questions of form and narration. Paul Witherington's "The Art of Melville's *Typee*" (1970) takes up questions of genre, concluding that *Typee* is an experimental novel divided into six major phases. Michael Clark, in "Melville's *Typee*: Fact, Fiction and Aesthetics" (1978), sees the narrator as important for what and how he sees, invoking the aesthetic principles of centrality, development, harmony, and balance. Nina Baym, in "Melville's Quarrel with Fiction" (1979), places the blame for all this critical controversy about form squarely on the author, whose literary ambitions changed over the course of a career in which he always found "genre requirements to be an impediment to his imagination" (p. 918). She identifies in Melville a progressive loss of belief in language as well as in God. In spite of Melville's praise for Hawthorne and Shakespeare, Baym asserts that he "had no great respect for fiction" (p. 910). *Typee* and *Omoo* are mere journalism in this reading, their truth referring only to "descriptive accuracy." In contrast, a more positive view of form in the early works, Janet Giltrow's "Speaking Out: Travel and Structure in Herman Melville's Early Narratives" (1980) describes *Typee* and *Omoo* as generically misclassified. Giltrow describes the formal properties of travel writing, particularly its consequences for the narrative voice. Although she overlooks the fact that Melville's plot is not his itinerary, her analysis allows for his "digressive, discursive tendencies," his scenic exposition (a much neglected subject), and his ultimate return to his audience. This article provides critical insights even if, in view of his later works, we grant Melville more imaginative shaping power; like Herbert's *Marquesan Encounters*, it reminds us of the value of placing Melville's work against other forms of prose.

Gorman Beauchamp adds to this effort in his "Melville and the Tradition of Primitive Utopia" (1981). A valuable and original suggestion, that *Typee* draws on the genre of the captivity narrative, is made by Robert K. Martin in "Enviable Isles: Melville's South Seas"(1982). Yet another venture in the genre study of *Typee* is Robert Roripaugh's "Melville's *Typee* and the Frontier Travel Literature of the 1830's and 1840's" (1981). For confirmation of the importance of form in discussions of *Typee* and *Omoo*, see "Melville's Search for Form" by James E. Miller, Jr., reprinted in the Stern anthology (pp. 154–56).

Literary Sources and Influences

In addition to the informational sources explored by Charles R. Anderson, a variety of literary sources and influences have been discussed. Henry F. Pommer's *Milton and Melville* (1950) refers only briefly to *Typee* but includes a useful general discussion of Melville's borrowings from his reading. Robert Stanton, in *"Typee* and Milton: Paradise Well Lost" (1959), adds to Pommer's two identified Miltonic echoes several deliberate, extensive, and detailed parallels. Identifying Tommo symbolically with Satan, he supports the view of D. H. Lawrence: "Modern man and Paradise are mutually exclusive" (p. 411).

"The Mythical Quest: Literary Responses to the South Seas," by Subramani (1977), identifies Melville's effect on other South Seas writers, such as Conrad and Maugham. A further resource for Melville's sources in this field is A. Grove Day's anthology, *Melville's South Seas* (1970).

Michael Clark suggests, not very convincingly, that Philip Freneau's essay on Tomo Cheeki may be "A Source for Melville's Tommo" (1979). Both works are structured by a journey between primitive and civilized cultures. In "Thoreau and Melville's *Typee*" (1980), Robert Sattelmeyer shows how Melville influenced his Concord contemporary, who recorded notes on his reading of the revised edition in his journal notebook in the fall of 1846. *Typee* is the source for Thoreau's remarks on tattooing in his censure of fashion in "Economy." Sattelmeyer notes that the upshot of Thoreau's reading of *Typee* and his visit to Maine was the major study of primitive cultures recorded in his Indian notebooks. There is no evidence that Thoreau read *Omoo*, but he did go on to read at least one of Melville's major informational sources, Ellis's *Polynesian Researches*.

One of Melville's older literary sources is the subject of Gorman Beauchamp's "Montaigne, Melville and the Cannibals" (1981); the writer finds several parallels in language and idea, notably both writers' defense of cannibals.

Specialized Book-length Studies

A number of books written within the last thirty years on special topics in Melville studies refer at some length to *Typee* and *Omoo*. These concern central characters, the problems of race and war, and Melville's humor.

John Bernstein, in *Pacifism and Rebellion in the Writings of Herman Melville* (1964), finds some aspects of his complementary themes raised in the early books, though not yet placed in opposition. His discussion is hindered by its focus on what *Typee* and *Omoo* lack, such as "intense metaphysical probing." He finds Melville dishonest at the end of *Typee* in not explaining why Tommo leaves "paradise," but follows Lawrence to the conclusion that he leaves to fight "the forces of injustice" (p. 23). The trouble with this thesis is that the narrator does not fight injustice in *Omoo* so much as observe it. Bernstein finds *Omoo* "the most sustained piece of comic writing in the Melville canon" (p. 25), but lacking in intellectual content.

Nicholas Canaday, in *Melville and Authority* (1968), asserts that "the coercing power of legal right or an assumed moral right" (p. 1) is the central theme structuring the narrative in *Typee*. In *Omoo*, he points to anti-authoritarianism as the principal theme, illustrated in the portraits of contrasting ship captains. Canaday thinks of the rovers of *Omoo* as having escaped authority, yet he does not explore the forms of communal coercion influencing them. Some, like Lem Hardy, become authority figures themselves, within their new social group. The narrator and Long Ghost are coerced into leaving Tamai by mysterious group pressure. Instead of versions of Ahab, in *Typee* and *Omoo* we have explorations of the less personally concentrated authority of culture.

Progress into Silence: A Study of Melville's Heroes (1970), by Alan Lebowitz, groups Melville's novels into threes, dismissing *Typee* and *Omoo* as slight and *Mardi* as "impossibly tedious" (p. 24), but finding Tommo interesting as a bewildered hero, "always afraid, yet never really threatened" (p. 25). Lebowitz makes the interesting observation that, in his first two books, it has not yet occurred to Melville to separate the Promethean hero from the neophyte and narrator. Unfortunately, *Omoo* is treated here as "wayward ramblings, picaresque in character" (p. 41).

Melville's indictment of American and European imperialism in *Typee* and *Omoo* is part of his reaction to then current theories of race, according to Carolyn Karcher, in *Shadow over the Promised Land: Slavery, Race and Violence in Melville's America* (1980). Here is a study that finds *Typee* and *Omoo* revealing for what they are, rather than for what they are not. Karcher sees that Melville's experience in Polynesia gave him a vision of colonialist destruction: "Never again did he judge non-white peoples by ethnocentric standards" (p. 2). She also points out that in *Typee* and *Omoo* the narrators are ambivalent about their illegal or nonconforming status; she connects this with Melville's own willingness to withdraw anti-missionary material in the revised *Typee*, but his strengthened repetition of it in *Omoo*: "Only through his art did Melville achieve an uneasy truce between his conformist and rebellious selves" (p. 11).

This book makes an interesting companion to Joyce Sparer Adler's *War in Melville's Imagination* (1981), an important book for *Typee* and *Omoo* scholars. Adler justly observes that "*Typee* and *Omoo* present the three stages of Polynesian history as Melville interpreted them" (p. 6). Early in *Typee*, in his discussion of the French takeover in Tahiti, Melville begins to develop his view of war as the greatest of evils. *Omoo* continues to examine the effects of colonialist wars, especially the "denationalizing" attacks on culture by missionaries and police. Adler points out that in both of his first two books Melville emphasized his negative view of war and imperialism despite the potential alienation of readers and publishers.

Jane Mushabac, in *Melville's Humor* (1981), turns away from theme and toward literary forms available to Melville from the "tradition of prose humor...beginning in the Renaissance with the opening of the New World frontier" (p. 2). In *Typee*, his humor, coexisting with a sense of inevitable imprisonment, plays with the model of *Rasselas*. Eventually, however, Mushabac finds *Typee* a botch, citing the leg infection and the ending as insufficiently worked out. In her study of *Omoo*, she claims the humor turns thin because Paul is too weak a character to sustain it. In her view the book is most successful in its last thirty chapters, which celebrate "an easy love of motley" (p. 72).

Edward H. Rosenberry's *Melville and the Comic Spirit* (1955), still the central work on Melville's humor, treats *Typee* and *Omoo* as expressions of the "jocular-hedonic" phase of Melville's development. Rosenberry examines Melville's gastronomic humor, his self-ridicule, and the gallery of rogues that people *Typee* and *Omoo*, and finds Long Ghost "a full-fledged American folk-hero or comic demigod . . . one of the funniest characters in our literature" (p. 21). His book is especially valuable for its attention to the language of Melville's humor and for its thirty-year-old observation that *Omoo* is "certainly his most hilarious, possibly his most underrated book": "*Omoo* alone among his books floats raft-like above the undercurrent of outer problem and inner drama that tugs even at parts of *Typee*" (p. 46).

Articles on Special Topics

Recent articles support and extend inquiry into the questions of race and war and the nature of the narrator/protagonist. Eleanor E. Simpson, in "Melville and the Negro: From *Typee* to 'Benito Cereno' " (1969), views the dark-skinned characters in *Typee* and *Omoo* as "relatively facile conventional portrayals" (p. 38). She discusses Billy Loon and Old Baltimore, excluding mention of the Polynesians.

Simpson dives into Melville's early work to pluck out characters for a study that centers elsewhere; James L. Babin, on the other hand, enters *Typee* for a longer stay, but also brings along a good deal of baggage. In "Melville and the Deformation of Being: From *Typee* to Leviathan" (1971), he finds that Tommo moves between "poles of self-consciousness and unself-consciousness," represented by the sea and the land. Babin's psychological reading emphasizes the images of descent into the valley, the language and actions of childhood care and play when Tommo is among the Typees, the sexual implications of producing fire. (See also Gerard M. Sweeney.) Tommo's period of timeless pleasure in Typee is interrupted, in this view, by a sense of spiritual loss, and his final act of will returns him to unnatural adulthood.

In "Evolving the Inscrutable: The Grotesque in Melville's Fiction" (1978), Richard M. Cook shows how Melville's protagonist in *Typee* is forced to confront his failure to understand his position by the "arresting vision of deformity" (p. 544). Cook carries this discussion of the grotesque in Melville's work on to *Redburn*, *Moby-Dick*, *Pierre* and *The Confidence-Man*; his helpful analysis should be applied to *Omoo* as well.

The most satisfying of the essays concentrating on Melville's protagonist is Wyn Kelly's "Melville's Cain" (1983). Kelly finds a procession of

Cain figures in Melville's work, from Lem Hardy in *Omoo* to Taji in *Mardi*, Ahab and Pierre. He locates references to the Biblical story, including Cain's city, in *The Confidence-Man, Battle-Pieces* and *Billy Budd*: "As both outlaw and cosmopolitan, savage and civilized man, Cain represents for Melville the paradox of human society ... and fratricide as a fact of human history" (p. 27). The article explores contemporary treatments of Cain that Melville may have known, as well as the view of St. Augustine that fratricide emerged from "diabolical envy" (p. 31). The Romantic and the Augustinian Cain are both reflected in Melville's work, with Lem Hardy "the prototype of Melville's Romantic Cain and a perhaps surprising predecessor of Pierre" (p. 32). This analysis, resting on observation of an important figure in Melville's work, is one of the few to see *Omoo* as making a contribution, entirely of its own and apart from *Typee*, to Melville studies.

Specialized Studies Concentrating on *Typee* and *Omoo*

The following eight specialized studies have *Typee* and *Omoo* as their central subjects. They expand the critical discussion summarized above and point the way to new treatments of Melville's first books.

A thirty-year-old article, Joseph J. Firebaugh's "Humorist as Rebel: The Melville of *Typee*" (1954), is still the fullest discussion of humor in the language and episodes of *Typee*. Firebaugh's astute remark, "Confidence in Melville's profundity has kept his ingratiating humor in a sort of critical quarantine" (p. 108), has been addresssed by recent critics, but they have said little about the first two books. Firebaugh relates Melville's mock-heroic irony concerning bad food and his description of savage banquets, to his theme of the "methodical cannibalism" of one race on another: "Awareness keeps Melville, even as a young man, from being the fool at the feast" (p. 111). Firebaugh points out Melville's use of incongruity and anticlimax, his strategy of comparing and contrasting the familiar with the unfamiliar (a common method of travel books), and his paraphrase and burlesque of Bible rhetoric. These humorous devices help explore "the underlying similarity of man wherever found," the institutions of matrimony and religion, and the attitudes toward work and history in his own culture.

Winston Weathers, in "Melville and the Comedy of Communications" (1963), furthers discussion of one element of Melville's humor in *Typee*—his struggle to understand and to make himself understood. The comic element is again related to a serious theme in which Typee emerges as no paradise. Weathers finds an above–average incidence of such words as *communication, language, word,* and *name* in *Typee*; he regards the tabooed Marnoo, who saved Tommo by understanding his language, as a special "communications" figure. This subject invites further study, as interference in exchanges of meaning is a pervasive concern of Melville's work, with tragic as well as comic overtones, from *Typee* and *Omoo* to the "pyramidal silence" of the sperm whale and the stammer of Billy Budd. (For a more recent discussion of the problem of communication in *Typee*, see J. Kerry Grant.)

In "False Sympathy in Melville's *Typee*" (1982), Mitchell Breitwieser finds the gap in communications less a technical or metaphysical problem than a cultural one. His argument rests on the assumption that Melville deliberately separated Tommo's voice from his own in order to reveal Tommo's faulty self-conception. Tommo is interested in the Typees only insofar as they permit him to express hostility to his own culture; his is an "exploitative view of an alien culture in terms of its usableness" (p. 398). Although this view skews the effect of the problematical narrator of *Typee*, its analysis of colonial attitudes and its attribution to Melville of Marxist perceptions are interesting. It is a good example of an odd difficulty of critics writing on *Typee* and *Omoo*: they either minimize the books as faulty apprentice works or grant the twenty-five-year-old author extraordinary wisdom and detachment. Both views lead to distortions.

A recent British view of *Typee*, A. Robert Lee's " 'Varnishing the Facts': *Typee* and the Art of Melville's Early Fiction" (1980), takes the position that Melville is a more conscious artist in his early work than he has been considered. Showing how patterns and balancing parts work to shape *Typee*, Lee discusses the central critical matters of Tommo's leg wound, cannibalism, and tattooing, finding evidence that each is treated with "analogues and parallels" that argue "Melville's designing hand" (p. 209). The question of form—are *Typee* and *Omoo* novels?—and the question of authenticity—are the events literally true or artfully retold?—have been with us in Melville criticism since 1846.

A crucial approach to the answers is made by Robert E. Abrams in his "*Typee* and *Omoo*: Herman Melville and the Ungraspable Phantom of Identity" (1975). Finding the mature Melville an artist "unencumbered by a finite, self-compromising identity" (p. 33), Abrams discovers in the early books the author's awareness of his own development "as he poured himself into the evolving narrative 'I' of these tales" (p. 34). Discovering that his identity has been determined by his culture, he dramatizes in *Typee* the loss of self that comes from falling out of one's culture. Abrams's inquiry into the identity of the "I" is central, but it leads him into some odd speculation about the way the Typees see Tommo, a point of view for which there is little textual support. Although he seems to miss the humor in Tommo's voice, he sees clearly enough that the *Omoo* narrator is a development of Tommo: "the *Omoo* hero sheds his western clothing and identity, puts on a two-tailed turban and voluminous robe, and opens himself up to destinies and roles little dreamed of along his native Hudson" (p. 49). Coming to terms with this story-telling narrator is the single most important critical issue in *Typee* and *Omoo* studies.

Abrams's attention to the relationship between *Typee* and *Omoo* is expanded in Carl William Brucker's 1980 dissertation "The Happy Prisoner: A Study of Melville's *Typee* and *Omoo*" (*Mel. Diss.*, #518). Brucker finds the books not merely sequential but complementary opposites which present similar cycles of failure. Regarding *Typee*, the gothic melodrama, as an exercise in romance, and *Omoo*, the mock-heroic parody, as an exercise in satire, Brucker calls *Typee-Omoo* a two-part novel embodying "the growth of Melville's naive protagonist," accomplished through his defiance of limits placed on his freedom by racial and cultural heritage.

The general failure to attribute importance to *Omoo* is the starting point for Edwin M. Eigner in "The Romantic Unity of Melville's *Omoo*" (1967). Eigner notes that the wanderings of Melville's narrator in *Omoo* perform a timing function, "showing . . . the various stages of the subject's development or degeneration as if in a series of still photographs" (p. 96). He compares this technique to a Hogarth progress and recommends finding the unity of *Omoo* by relating digressions to the psychological development of the narrator. Eigner identifies Lem Hardy as an "image of alienation" and Dr. Long Ghost as another potential model for the narrator: "He is the long ghost of skepticism and despair" (p. 98). There is a full discussion of Long Ghost in this article, comparing him to Plotinus Plinlimmon; he is certainly a Melville character whose portrait requires further attention.

"*Omoo*: Germinal Melville" (1978) by Steven E. Kemper also recognizes the general neglect of *Omoo*. Kemper finds its author "artistically naive," but believes that "in *Omoo* we can glimpse the 'germs' and instincts that develop into the consciously articulated symbologies, thematic concerns and strategies of the later works" (p. 420). He finds *Omoo* germinal in theme, reading back into it the "philosophical conservatism" he attributes to Melville's later works. While this conclusion seems unwarranted, there are useful brief discussions in this article of mutiny, of the "neutral territory" between savagery and civilization, of the character of the "isolato," and of authority and charisma.

But *Omoo* is equally germinal in form and language, matters that are still largely untreated in criticism. The starting point for such a study is Hayford and Blair's Hendricks House edition, with its documentary source material and useful introductory discussion which is also important for its characterization of the narrator, a story-teller both sympathetic and aloof, set firmly in the tradition of American humor.

PROBLEMS FOR FUTURE STUDY

In an essay on "Melville Criticism in the 1970's; or Who's Afraid of Wellek and Warren" (1980), Robert Milder devotes several paragraphs to the deficits of "critical monism" in *Typee* studies. Referring to R. S.

Crane's comments on interpretation of poetry, he recommends that we "approach Melville's books inductively as works whose 'peculiar principles of structure' may have no 'usable parallels either in literary theory or in our experience of other works.' See what they are, and how they function, and for what inferable end" (p. 6). This is good advice to invoke for the study of *Typee* and *Omoo*.

The ending of *Typee* still has not been satisfactorily treated, although Wyn Kelly's essay on the Cain figure, which does not mention *Typee*, might be helpful. Pair this with Robert K. Martin's distinctions among types of male friendship in *Typee* (1982). *Omoo* is still dismissed or treated as a series of random sketches and portraits, while even my brief summary of it above shows significant patterning. The function of the narrator as story-teller/artist in both books needs more elaboration, especially in regard to Melville's later development of this figure. The undramatized social criticism in *Typee* and *Omoo*, as well as its other informational or expository content, needs to be better observed as prose; it should be considered together with all the rest of the non-fiction prose included in Melville's work and viewed against the background of our diverse heritage in this form, from Burton to Thoreau to John McPhee.

In "Trends in Melville Scholarship: Dissertations in the 1970's" (1982), John Bryant reports that *Typee* has lost ground among dissertation writers in the 1970s and that texts least likely to be discussed in extra-Melville theses are *Typee* and *Omoo*. If interest in psychological interpretation of *Typee* has waned, so much the better; perhaps we are ready to redirect our critical energies to the task of seeing the two books in the context not only of Melville's work, but in that of his fellow-writers as well.

For *Typee* and *Omoo* diverge in form and theme like Mark Twain's *Tom Sawyer* and *Huckleberry Finn*, two books that have also invited the general reader as warmly as the scholar. Reversing the critical fate of Mark Twain's work, the first of Melville's pair has always captured the larger share of commentary, drawing the second volume along in a diminished position. But Melville's Tommo is a version of Twain's romantic Tom, while the narrator of *Omoo* is an anticipatory portrait of an older Huck, composing fictional identities and repeatedly lighting out for the Territory. This observation suggests the need for a fresh view of the old pairing and a restitution of *Omoo*.

WORKS CITED

Abrams, Robert E. "*Typee* and *Omoo*: Herman Melville and the Ungraspable Phantom of Identity." *Arizona Quarterly* 31 (Spring 1975): 33–50. [Also in Stern, *Critical Essays*, pp. 201–10.]

Adkins, Nelson F. "A Note on Herman Melville's *Typee*." *New England Quarterly* 5 (April 1932): 348–51.

Adler, Joyce Sparer. *War in Melville's Imagination*. New York: Columbia University Press, 1981. [Excerpted in Stern, *Critical Essays*, pp. 244–49.]

Anderson, Charles Roberts, ed. *Journal of a Cruise to the Pacific Ocean, 1842–1844, in the Frigate United States; With Notes on Herman Melville*. Durham: Duke University Press, 1937.

———. *Melville in the South Seas*. New York: Columbia University Press, 1939; rev. New York: Dover Publications, 1966. [Citations are from the revised edition.]

———. "The Romance of Scholarship: Tracking Melville in the South Seas." *Colophon* 3 (Spring 1938): 259–79.

Arvin, Newton. *Herman Melville*. New York: William Sloane Associates, 1950. [Excerpted in Stern, *Critical Essays*, pp. 99–106.]

Babin, James L. "Melville and the Deformation of Being: From *Typee* to Leviathan." *Southern Review* NS 7 (1971): 89–114.

Baird, James. *Ishmael*. Baltimore: Johns Hopkins University Press, 1956.

Baym, Nina. "Melville's Quarrel with Fiction." *PMLA* 94 (October 1979): 909–23.

Beauchamp, Gorman. "Melville and the Tradition of Primitive Utopia." *Journal of General Education* 33 (Spring 1981): 6–14.

———. "Montaigne, Melville and the Cannibals." *Arizona Quarterly* 37 (Winter 1981): 293–309.

Bergmann, Johannes Dietrich. "The *New York Morning News* and *Typee*." *Melville Society Extracts* No. 31 (September 1977): 1–4.

Bernstein, John. *Pacifism and Rebellion in the Writings of Herman Melville*. The Hague: Mouton, 1964.

Berthoff, Warner. *The Example of Melville*. Princeton, N.J.: Princeton University Press, 1962.

Birss, John Howard. "The Story of Toby, a Sequel to *Typee*." *Harvard Library Bulletin* 1 (Winter 1947): 118–19.

Bowen, Merlin. *The Long Encounter: Self and Experience in the Writings of Herman Melville*. Chicago: University of Chicago Press, 1960.

Breitwieser, Mitchell. "False Sympathy in Melville's *Typee*." *American Quarterly* 34 (Fall 1982): 396–417.

Brucker, Carl William, Jr. "The Happy Prisoner: A Study of Melville's *Typee* and *Omoo*." Ph.D. Diss., Rutgers University, 1980. [*Mel. Diss.*, #518.]

Bryant, John. "Trends in Melville Scholarship: Dissertations in the 1970's." *Melville Society Extracts* No. 50 (May 1982): 12–14.

Canaday, Nicholas, Jr. *Melville and Authority*. Gainesville, Fla.: University of Florida Press, 1968.

Chase, Richard. *Herman Melville: A Critical Study*. New York: Macmillan Co., 1949. [Excerpted in Stern, *Critical Essays*, pp. 93–98.]

Clark, Michael. "Melville's *Typee*: Fact, Fiction and Aesthetics." *Arizona Quarterly* 34 (Winter 1978): 351–70. [Also in Stern, *Critical Essays*, pp. 211–25.]

———. "A Source for Melville's Tommo." *American Transcendental Quarterly* No. 44 (Fall 1979): 261–64.

Cook, Richard M. "Evolving the Inscrutable: The Grotesque in Melville's Fiction." *American Literature* 49 (January 1978): 544–59.

Davis, Susan. "More for the NYPL's Long Vaticans." *Melville Society Extracts* No. 57 (February 1984): 5–7.

Day, A. Grove, ed. *Melville's South Seas: An Anthology.* New York: Hawthorn Books, 1970.

Dillingham, William B. *An Artist in the Rigging: The Early Works of Herman Melville.* Athens: University of Georgia Press, 1972.

Dryden, Edgar A. *Melville's Thematics of Form: The Great Art of Telling the Truth.* Baltimore: Johns Hopkins University Press, 1968.

Eigner, Edwin M. "The Romantic Unity of Melville's *Omoo.*" *Philological Quarterly* 46 (January 1967): 95–108.

Firebaugh, Joseph J. "Humorist as Rebel: The Melville of *Typee.*" *Nineteenth-Century Fiction* 9 (September 1954): 108–20.

Fletcher, Richard M. "Melville's Use of Marquesan." *American Speech* 39 (May 1964): 135–38.

Franklin, H. Bruce. *The Wake of the Gods: Melville's Mythology.* Stanford, Calif.: Stanford University Press, 1963. [Excerpted in Stern, *Critical Essays*, pp. 166–72.]

Frederick, Joan. "Feet of Clay: Authority Figures in Melville's Early Novels." *James Madison Journal* 37 (1979): 50–58.

Giltrow, Janet. "Speaking Out: Travel and Structure in Herman Melville's Early Narratives." *American Literature* 52 (March 1980): 18–32.

Gohdes, Clarence F. "Melville's Friend 'Toby.' " *Modern Language Notes* 59 (January 1944): 52–55.

Gollin, Rita Kaplan. "The Forbidden Fruit of *Typee.*" *Modern Language Studies* 5 (Fall 1975): 31–34.

Grant, J. Kerry. "The Failure of Language in Melville's *Typee.*" *Modern Language Studies* 12 (Spring 1982): 61–68.

Hamada, Masajiro. "Two Utopian Types of American Literature: *Typee* and *The Crater.*" *Studies in English Literature* (Tokyo) 40 (March 1964): 199–214.

Haverstick, Iola S. "A Note on Poe and *Pym* in Melville's *Omoo.*" *Poe Newsletter* 2 (April 1969): 37.

Herbert, T. Walter, Jr. *Marquesan Encounters: Melville and the Meaning of Civilization.* Cambridge, Mass.: Harvard University Press, 1980.

Hetherington, Hugh W. *Melville's Reviewers: British and American, 1846–1891.* Chapel Hill: University of North Carolina Press, 1961.

Jones, Bartlett C. "American Frontier Humor in Melville's *Typee.*" *New York Folklore Quarterly* 15 (Winter 1959): 283–88.

Joswick, Thomas Philip, "*Typee*: The Quest for Origin." *Criticism* 17 (Fall 1975): 335–54.

Kaplan, Sidney. "*Omoo*: Melville's and Boucicault's." *American Notes and Queries* 10 (January 1950): 150–51.

Karcher, Carolyn L. *Shadow Over the Promised Land: Slavery, Race and Violence in Melville's America.* Baton Rouge: Louisiana State University Press, 1980.

Kaul, A. N. *The American Vision: Actual and Ideal Society in Nineteenth Century Fiction.* New Haven, Conn.: Yale University Press, 1963. [Excerpted in Stern, *Critical Essays*, pp. 157–65.]

Kelly, Wyn. "Melville's Cain." *American Literature* 55 (March 1983): 24–40.

Kemper, Steven E. "*Omoo*: Germinal Melville." *Studies in the Novel* 10 (Winter 1978): 420–31.

Ketterer, David. "Censorship and Symbolism in *Typee*." *Melville Society Extracts* No. 34 (May 1978): 8.

Kier, Kathleen. "Elizabeth Shaw Melville and the Stedmans, 1891–1894" *Melville Society Extracts* No. 45 (February 1981): 3–8.

Lawrence, D. H. *Studies in Classic American Literature*. New York: Thomas Seltzer, Inc., 1923; rpt. New York: Penguin, 1977. [Excerpted in Stern, *Critical Essays*, pp. 69–77.]

Lebowitz, Alan. *Progress into Silence: A Study of Melville's Heroes*. Bloomington: Indiana University Press, 1970.

Lee, A. Robert. " 'Varnishing the Facts'; *Typee* and the Art of Melville's Early Fiction." *Durham University Journal* (UK) 72 (1980): 203–209.

Madison, Mary K. "Fanny Trollope's Nephew Edits *Typee*." *Melville Society Extracts* No. 39 (September 1979): 15.

Martin, Robert K. "Enviable Isles: Melville's South Seas." *Modern Language Studies* 12 (Winter 1982): 68–76.

Mason, Ronald. *The Spirit Above the Dust: A Study of Herman Melville*. London: John Lehmann, 1951.

Matthiessen, F. O. *American Renaissance: Art and Expression in the Age of Emerson and Whitman*. New York: Oxford University Press, 1941.

Melville, Herman. *Omoo: A Narrative of Adventures in the South Seas*. Ed. Harrison Hayford and Walter Blair. New York: Hendricks House, 1969.

———. *Omoo, ou le Vagabond du Pacifique*. Trans. Jacqueline Foulque. Paris: Gallimard, 1951.

———. *Typee*. Illus. Mead Schaeffer. New York: Dodd, Mead and Co., 1941. [Revised American Edition.]

———. Unpublished Manuscript Fragment of *Typee*. Gansevoort-Lansing Collection, Melville Family Papers, Additions. Rare Books and Manuscripts Division, New York Public Library. [Permission to quote passages from this manuscript has been given by the Office of Special Collections, New York Public Library, Astor, Lenox and Tilden Foundations.]

Milder, Robert. "Melville Criticism in the 1970's; or Who's Afraid of Wellek and Warren." *Melville Society Extracts* No. 43 (September 1980): 4–7.

Miller, James E., Jr. *A Reader's Guide to Herman Melville*. New York: Farrar, Straus & Cudahy, 1962. [Excerpted in Stern, *Critical Essays*, pp. 154–56.]

Miller, Perry. *The Raven and the Whale: The War of Words and Wits in the Era of Poe and Melville*. New York: Harcourt, Brace & World, 1956.

Mitchell, Bruce Eardley. "Women and the Male Quester in Herman Melville's *Typee, Mardi* and *Pierre*." Ph.D. Diss., Northwestern University (Education), 1979. [*Mel. Diss.*, #503.]

Mowder, William Joseph. "Identity in the Early Novels of Herman Melville." Ph.D. Diss., Indiana University, 1979. [*Mel. Diss.*, #504.]

Mushabac, Jane. *Melville's Humor: A Critical Study*. Hamden, Conn.: Archon Books, 1981.

Parker, Hershel. "Evidence for 'Late Insertions' in Melville's Works." *Studies in the Novel* 7 (Fall 1975): 407–24.

Petrullo, Helen B. "The Neurotic Hero of *Typee*." *American Imago* 12 (Winter 1955): 317–23.

Pommer, Henry F. *Milton and Melville*. Pittsburgh, Pa.: University of Pittsburgh Press, 1950; rpt. New York: Cooper Square Publishers, 1970.

Pops, Martin Leonard. *The Melville Archetype*. Kent, Ohio: Kent State University Press, 1970.

Pullin, Faith, ed. *New Perspectives on Melville*. Kent, Ohio and Edinburgh: Kent State University Press, and Edinburgh University Press 1978.

Rogin, Michael Paul. *Subversive Genealogy: The Politics and Art of Herman Melville*. New York: Alfred A. Knopf, 1983.

Roripaugh, Robert. "Melville's *Typee* and Frontier Travel Literature of the 1830's and 1840's." *South Dakota Review* 19 (Winter 1981): 46–64.

Rosenberry, Edward H. *Melville and the Comic Spirit*. Cambridge, Mass: Harvard University Press, 1955.

———. "Queequeg's Coffin-Canoe: Made in *Typee*." *American Literature* 30 (January 1959): 529–30.

Ruland, Richard. "Melville and the Fortunate Fall: *Typee* as Eden." *Nineteenth-Century Fiction* 23 (December 1968): 312–23. [Excerpted in Stern, *Critical Essays*, pp. 183–92.]

Samson, John. "Profaning the Sacred: Melville's *Omoo* and Missionary Narratives," *American Literature* 56 (December 1984): 406–509.

Sattelmeyer, Robert. "Thoreau and Melville's *Typee*." *American Literature* 52 (November 1980): 462–74.

Scorza, Thomas J. "Tragedy in the State of Nature: Melville's *Typee*." *Interpretation: Journal of Political Philosophy* 8 (January 1979): 103–20. [Also in Stern, *Critical Essays*, pp. 226–43.]

Scudder, Harold H. "Hawthorne's Use of *Typee*." *Notes and Queries* 187 (21 October 1944): 184–86.

Sedgwick, William Ellery. *Herman Melville: The Tragedy of Mind*. Cambridge, Mass.: Harvard University Press, 1944; rpt. New York: Russell & Russell, 1962. [Excerpted in Stern, *Critical Essays*, pp. 81–92.]

Seelye, John. *Melville: The Ironic Diagram*. Evanston, Ill.: Northwestern University Press, 1970. [Excerpted in Stern, *Critical Essays*, pp. 193–200.]

Simpson, Eleanor E. "Melville and the Negro: From *Typee* to 'Benito Cereno.' " *American Literature* 41 (March 1969): 19–38.

Smith, Nelson C. "Melville Reviews in the London *Sun*." *Melville Society Extracts* No. 36 (November 1978): 8–10.

Stanton, Robert. "*Typee* and Milton: Paradise Well Lost." *Modern Language Notes* 74 (May 1959): 407–11.

Stern, Milton R. *Critical Essays on Herman Melville's Typee*. Boston: G. K. Hall & Co., 1982.

———. *The Fine-Hammered Steel of Herman Melville*. Urbana and Chicago: University of Illinois Press, 1957. [Excerpted in Stern, *Critical Essays*, pp. 117–53.]

Subramani. "The Mythical Quest: Literary Responses to the South Seas." *Literary Half-Yearly* 18 (1977): 165–86.

Sweeney, Gerard M. "Melville's Smoky Humor: Fire-lighting in *Typee*." *Arizona Quarterly* 34 (Winter 1978): 371–76.

Tanselle, G. Thomas. "Bibliographical Problems in Melville." *Studies in American Fiction* 2 (Spring 1974): 57–74.

———. "*Typee* and DeVoto: A Footnote." *Papers of the Bibliographic Society of America* 64 (Second Quarter 1970): 207–209.

———. "*Typee* and DeVoto Once More." *Papers of the Bibliographic Society of America* 62 (Fourth Quarter 1968): 601–604.

Thomas, Russell. "Yarn for Melville's *Typee*." *Philological Quarterly* 15 (January 1936): 16–29.

Thompson, Lawrance. *Melville's Quarrel with God*. Princeton, N.J.: Princeton University Press, 1952. [Excerpted in Stern, *Critical Essays*, pp. 107–16.]

Thorp, Willard. " 'Grace Greenwood' Parodies *Typee*." *American Literature* 9 (January 1938): 455–57.

Thoreau, Henry D. *Walden*. Ed. J. Lyndon Shanley. Princeton, N.J.: Princeton University Press, 1971.

Vincent, Howard P. "Herbert's *Marquesan Encounters*." *Melville Society Extracts* No. 44 (November 1980): 15.

Wadlington, Warwick. *The Confidence Game in American Literature*. Princeton, N.J.: Princeton University Press, 1975.

Weathers, Winston. "Melville and the Comedy of Communications." *Etc.: A Review of General Semantics* 20 (December 1963): 411–20.

Weaver, Raymond. *Herman Melville: Mariner and Mystic*. New York: George H. Doran, 1921. [Excerpted in Stern, *Critical Essays*, pp. 62–67.]

Williams, David Park. "Peeping Tommo: *Typee* as Satire." *Canadian Review of American Studies* 6 (Spring 1975): 36–49.

Williams, Mentor. "Horace Greeley Reviews *Omoo*." *Philological Quarterly* 27 (January 1948): 94–96.

Witherington, Paul. "The Art of Melville's *Typee*." *Arizona Quarterly* 26 (Summer 1970): 136–50.

Young, Philip. "Melville's Eden, or *Typee* Recharted." In *Three Bags Full*. New York: Harcourt Brace Jovanovich, 1973, pp. 99–112.

5

THE QUEST FOR *MARDI*

Watson Branch

Mardi was Melville's first book as a writer of fiction—or so he would have us believe. In his "Preface" he declares that, because *Typee* and *Omoo*, which he calls "narratives" of his voyages in the Pacific, were received with incredulity, he decided to write what he terms a "romance" of Polynesian adventure in order to see whether the "fiction" might not be received for a "verity," the reverse of his experience with the two earlier books. While Melville is certainly underplaying the fictional and imaginative elements in *Typee* and *Omoo*, there is no doubt that *Mardi* is a very different book from them especially because it is not based on the author's personal experiences in the South Seas.

A ROMANTIC POTPOURRI

A synopsis shows just how far Melville moved away from his own adventures as a framework for his story. *Mardi* opens with the unnamed first-person narrator, a young and rather romantic American sailor, expressing his boredom aboard the *Arcturion*, a New England whaler unsuccessfully cruising the mid-Pacific. He and his comrade Jarl, a taciturn but faithful old Scandinavian, steal a whaleboat and set out at night for the archipelagoes far to the west. The narrator describes their sensations, observations, and reflections as the whaleboat *Chamois* moves ahead amid the myriad fishes and other creatures of the sea or lies becalmed in a "gray chaos" (p. 48).

After sixteen days they meet an apparently deserted brigantine, but two Pacific islanders—the Upoluan Samoa and his termagant wife, Annatoo—are hiding on board the *Parki*, sole survivors of treacherous attacks. The narrator retells Samoa's tale of betrayal and escape and then his own adventures aboard the brigantine.

After a storm drowns Annatoo and sinks the ship, the narrator, Jarl, and Samoa make their way west in the *Chamois*. Before reaching land, they encounter a large double canoe bearing Aleema (a native priest) and his three sons on their way to sacrifice Yillah, a mysterious white maiden. Determined to save Yillah the narrator kills Aleema and flees with the maiden, who recounts her fantastic history as the four sail south hoping to escape Aleema's vengeful sons.

After five days they land in the Mardian archipelago and become guests of King Media of Odo. Now declaring himself to be the demigod Taji, the narrator and Yillah live briefly in bliss until she mysteriously disappears. Taji sets out to find her and is joined by Media and a trio of companions: the philosopher Babbalanja, the historian Mohi, and the poet Yoomy. They visit many imaginary islands, including allegorical representations of real countries. The narrator describes the poetic landscapes, whimsical characters, their customs, myths, histories and legends, and relates the colloquies of the seven travelers (soon reduced to five when Samoa and Jarl are left behind). The search for Yillah provides for social and political satire as well as philosophical reflections. The tour ends when Taji encounters the poisonous Hautia, a symbol of the seductive pleasures of the material world, on her isle of Flozella. Invoking Yillah, Taji is able to resist Hautia and sets out alone, sailing "over an endless sea," (p. 654), still pursuing his lost maiden and still pursued by the sons of the slain priest.

This "romance" is a far cry from the factual "narratives" of *Typee* and *Omoo*. Although Melville undertook his third book as a sequel to the second, it became finally a potpourri of whaling life, sea adventure, romantic quest, allegory, satire, and occasional digressions of rhapsodic reflection and philosophizing. The manner in which *Mardi* grew in its author's mind and manuscript from a continuation of *Omoo* into this tantalizing and aggravating, this fascinating and boring mixture of subjects, genres, modes, and styles reveals much about Melville's creative imagination and method of composition as he began his career as a writer of fiction.

COMPOSITION

It is difficult to determine exactly when Melville began *Mardi*. Almost immediately after sending the proof-sheets of *Omoo* off to his London publisher, John Murray, on 29 January 1847, he started looking for non-literary employment, specifically with the Treasury Department in Washington, D.C., where he made an unproductive job-hunting trip in early February. Melville was anticipating his marriage to Elizabeth Shaw of Boston on 4 August 1847 and probably trying to find employment that would support them. His personal letters and comments about authorship in *Mardi* make clear that Melville was feeling financially burdened and was moved to write and publish in order to put money in his purse. So two months after he had sent Murray the proof-sheets, Melville told his publisher, "If 'Omoo' succeeds I shall follow it up by something else, immediately" (*Letters*, p. 59). The nature of the "something else" begins to come clear in mid-June when Melville asked the London publisher Richard Bentley who had made "friendly overtures" a month earlier, what value he would put on the English copyright of "a new work of South Sea adventure, by me, occupying entirely fresh ground" (*Letters*, pp. 63–64). By the end of July, Melville's hometown newspaper, the Lansingburgh (New York) *Gazette*, announced under the heading "MORE TYPEE" that he was "preparing for the press another book of adventures in the South Seas" (*Mel. Log*, p. 253), and his friend and self-appointed mentor Evert Duyckinck wrote on 23 September that Melville's third book would "exhaust the South Sea marvels" (*Mel. Log*, p. 260).

And it was just such a book that Melville proposed to Murray on 29 October: "As you may possibly imagine, I am engaged upon another book of South Sea Adventure (continued from, tho' wholly independent of, "Omoo"—The new work will enter into scenes altogether new, & will, I think, possess more interest than the former, which treated of subjects comparatively trite." Melville was not far enough along to promise its delivery on a definite date, but, he told Murray, he would "probably" send it by late spring of 1848, though "possibly" not until autumn of that year. Still he wanted to arrange "the sale of the book *now*," and he rather presumptuously suggested to the experienced publisher how to make more money on it: "Now that it strikes me, do you not think that a third book would prove more remunerative to both publisher & author" if it were not published in Murray's "Home and Colonial Library" series, as *Typee* and *Omoo* had been, but "in a different style, so as to command, say, double the price" (*Letters*, pp. 66–67). Even at this early stage Melville was evidently thinking of his new book as a lengthy money-maker though he may have sensed, too, that the new scenes he was planning to write might wander so far from his actual, first-person experiences that the book would no longer merit inclusion in Murray's series, limited to books about real-life adventures untainted by romance.

Certain it is that before the end of 1847 Melville had grown tired of writing yet another South Seas adventure story built on the commonplace events any sailor might encounter in those regions, no matter how

strange and wonderful those events seemed to the stay-at-home landsman who would read about them. His letter to Murray, written on New
Year's Day, 1848, indicates his shifted direction:

Very naturally indeed, you may be led to imagine that after producing two books
on the South Seas, the subject must necessarily become somewhat barren of
novelty. But the plan I have pursued in the composition of the book now in
hand, clothes the whole subject in new attractions & combines in one cluster all
that is romantic, whimsical & poetic in Polynusia. It is yet a continuous narrative.
(*Letters*, p. 68)

In his next sentence Melville strikes out the phrase "& its authentic"—
probably a clue that the book had progressed far enough into its Mardian
tour to qualify no longer as a tale based on real-life experience. Perhaps,
too, he felt that the slaying of Aleema was too extraordinary to be called
"authentic," and perhaps by this time he had allowed his three sailors
to discover the imaginary archipelago where his fancy could create the
romantic, whimsical, and poetic—though not authentic—world of
"Polynusia."

The basically realistic opening chapters are disrupted when the narrator and his companions encounter Aleema and finished for good when
they discover the new world of Mardi. But even after having landed his
three sailors in Mardi and having moved them on to Odo, Melville could
still have told Murray that his narrative was "continuous": the three
continue to have adventures in the South Seas, although those imaginary
South Seas contain only imaginary islands peopled by imaginary characters. But this move from sea to land indicates a major transition in
Melville's book, and the beginning of the next stage in its composition.

Whatever straightforward, descriptive, *Omoo*-ish inception *Mardi* had
when Melville first conceived of it as a continuation of his earlier book,
the published version shows the influence of his literary associations in
New York City during 1847 and 1848, especially with Evert Duyckinck,
from whom he borrowed many of the books that contributed to his
intellectual growth. "Melville reads old Books," Duyckinck wrote to his
brother, George, on 18 March 1848 (*Mel. Log*, p. 273). And the developing breadth, if not depth, of Melville's philosophical, moral, and political ideas created problems. As Leon Howard argues, Melville felt
constrained from expressing these new ideas through the character of
his sailor hero especially because the critics might consider it a glaring
inconsistency to have the narrator be a common sailor and still display
such literary sophistication (*Blackwood's* had criticized *Omoo* for this); and
so, "in a spontaneous impulse" to enlarge the outlet of his own mind,
Melville "changed the plan of his book once more by creating four
fictitious characters who could relieve him of his artistic inhibitions"

(Howard, p. 116). Melville's impulse may not have been as spontaneous as Howard thought, but at some point during the winter of 1847–48 Melville recognized that his original plan had changed so radically that the tale could in good conscience no longer still be called "a continuous narrative." Thus, he confessed to his publisher on 25 March 1848 what he knew would appear to be a gross literary transgression:

I beleive that a letter I wrote you some time ago—I think my last but one—gave you to understand, or implied, that the work I then had in view was a bona-vide narrative of my adventures in the Pacific, continued from "Omoo"—My object in now writing you—I should have done so ere this—is to inform you of a change in my determinations. To be blunt: the work I shall next publish will in downright earnest [be] a "Romance of Polynisian Adventure"—... I have long thought that Polynisia furnished a great deal of rich poetical material that has never been employed hitherto in works of fancy; and which to bring out suitably, required only that play of freedom & invention accorded only to the Romancer & poet.—However, I thought, that I would postpone trying my hand at any thing fanciful of this sort, till some future day: tho' at times when in the mood I threw off occasional sketches applicable to such a work. —Well: proceeding in my narrative of *facts* I began to feel an incurible distaste for the same; & a longing to plume my pinions for a flight, & felt irked, cramped & fettered by plodding along with dull common places,—So suddenly standing [abandoning?] the thing alltogether, I went to work heart & soul at a romance which is now in fair progress, ... It opens like a true narrative—like Omoo for example, on ship board—& the romance & poetry of the thing thence grow continually, till it becomes a story wild enough I assure you & with a meaning too. (*Letters*, pp. 70–71)

Melville's shift in direction and intention for his book led to a development and change in his cast of characters. Having introduced Media, Babbalanja, Mohi, and Yoomy for the reasons Leon Howard stated, Melville could leave Jarl and Samoa behind at one of the islands, their usefulness as satirical characters expired once their creator had finished making fun of the Viking's ignorance of native customs familiar to his Upoluan comrade. But Jarl and Samoa are not the only characters to fade out of the action. (Yillah, the lost object of the travelers' quest, seldomly appears and in name only.) Taji becomes less conspicuous in the Mardian chapters. The central, first-person singular narrator—the "I" role of the opening chapters—fades into a passive observer who only occasionally refers to himself as "I" and who fades further from the reader's consciousness and interest as the tour continues, referring to himself almost exclusively as a part of the collective "we." Only in the closing chapters, those concerned with the narrator's encounter with Hautia and his escape to pursue Yillah over the sea forever, does Taji come to the fore once again.

It is very difficult to say what state the story was in on 5 May 1848, when Elizabeth Melville wrote to her step-mother that the "book is done now, in fact (you need not mention it) and the copy for the press is in far progress" (*Mel. Log*, p. 276). But it was *not* "done," and Melville continued to write and to add material. He certainly had time—over six months—to make extensive revisions between early May and November 15 when he signed a publication agreement with the Harpers, his American publisher. As Howard notes, "Both *Typee* and *Omoo* had bulged a bit with late additions and afterthoughts inserted into the original manuscript, and *Mardi* offered infinitely more opportunities for such insertions" (p. 122).

Merrell R. Davis has identified four specific late additions—all touching on historical events:

First, the chapter about Franko (France) and Porpheero (Europe) which describes the effects of the 1848 revolutions; second, the chapters on Dominora (England) which describe the Chartists' abortive march on Parliament in 1848; third, the chapter concerned with the reception in Vivenza (the United States) of the news of the 1848 revolutions as well as the excitement over the Free-Soil Convention at Buffalo; and fourth, the chapter describing the gold rush in California. (pp. 81–82)

When in her Historical Note to the NN *Mardi* Elizabeth Foster, following Davis asserts, "During the summer and fall of 1848 the sequence describing the voyage around the real, contemporary geographical world was written and inserted, that is to say, all or most of the twenty-five chapters from 145 through 169" (p. 662), she is probably overstating the case. The allusions in *Mardi* to events occurring during the late spring and summer of 1848—the ones accurately identified by Davis—do not necessarily indicate that each chapter in which they occur was composed *in toto* directly after each event. Furthermore, those chapters appearing *between* the chapters containing the allusions may have been written before the events to which the allusions refer, unless convincing evidence can be discovered to establish otherwise.

Besides the chapters or passages noted above, there may well have been other late insertions, some of which have been discussed by scholars interested in the growth of the manuscript. Most often noted is Chapter 180, which contains a defense of the episodic structure of Lombardo's "Koztanza." As Howard says, "the Abrazza episode near the conclusion of the book was apparently composed after the political allegory and was introduced into the book because Melville felt obliged to explain his waywardness to the public very much as he had explained it in his apologetic and protesting letter to Murray during the preceding March" (pp. 127–28).

In the end Melville's "waywardness," as I have argued elsewhere (Branch), accidentally produced in *Mardi* an abundance of textual evidence (inconsistencies, repetitions, errors, and the like) that, when combined with the extra-textual evidence (especially Melville's letters), indicates five definite "stages" in the development of the manuscript. The chronology of *Mardi*'s composition can be divided in the following manner:

Stage 1: Melville recounts the adventures of the narrator and his companion Jarl on board the *Arcturion* and the *Chamois*, their meeting with Samoa and Annatoo on board the *Parki*, the death of Annatoo and sinking of the *Parki*, their fatal confrontation with Aleema, and their escape from his vengeful sons.

Stage 2: Melville moves from sea to land and continues the adventures of the narrator (now called Taji), Jarl, and Samoa, and the newly added King Media on the successive Mardian islands of Odo, Valapee, Juam, Ohonoo, and Mondoldo.

Stage 3: Melville introduces "three acquaintances," Babbalanja, Mohi, and Yoomy, revises the chapters in Stage 2 to include the three new characters, interpolates some sailing chapters between these island visits, and continues the voyage (transformed from a romantic, whimsical, poetic tour of Polynesia into a quest for happiness symbolized by the poet Yoomy's lost maiden, Yillah) on to Maramma and a series of new islands, including allegorical representations of real geographical countries, and ending at Serenia. Melville also inserts passages of inflated and highly allusive reflective writing into the Stage 1 material.

Stage 4: Melville expands the section of Stage 3 having to do with real countries to include references to events taking place during most of 1848.

Stage 5: Melville adds the narrator's confrontation with Queen Hautia, revises in the Aleema section of Stage 1 to introduce a mysterious white maiden, adjusts the chapters that follow to transfer Yillah, who has been Yoomy's lost maiden in Stages 3 and 4, to Taji, thus creating a conventional romantic love story for his narrator, and writes and inserts a series of chapters that carry forward the combined Taji-Hautia-Yillah romance.

These five stages comprise the whole of *Mardi* except for a few discrete chapters on the act of writing itself or that contain rhapsodic reflections and philosophizing by the narrator while he tells his tale, all digressions that seem not have been written at the same time as the surrounding material.

My hypothetical stages of composition obviously do not match the chronology of the story as published, and neither do they match the theories presented in earlier studies of the book's growth by Howard and Davis and such followers as Foster, Milton R. Stern, and Nina Baym.

They identify three main stages: the realistic narrative opening (chs. 1–38), the romantic interlude with Yillah (chs. 39–64), and the travelogue-satire, containing dashes of a romantic quest for Yillah, enlarged late in the compositional process by the insertion of the political and aesthetic material (chs. 65–195). My main points of disagreement with the earlier theories center on the timing of the introduction both of Yillah and Hautia and of Taji's "three acquaintances" and on the extensiveness of the late additions of contemporary material. My theory is based mainly on an analysis of textual evidence, including the shifts in narrative point of view, the fluctuations in the dramatis personae, the pattern of cross-references, and the many inconsistencies, unnecessary duplications, repetitions, contradictions, and discontinuities in the book. Despite their differences, all the theories agree that Melville did not write the book *seriatim* but, instead, inserted material into the book he had already "completed."

Melville's wife must have foreseen that her husband was going to follow his usual practice of making last-minute additions to his supposedly finished manuscript because she wrote on June 6—a whole month after she had declared the book "done"—that, even though the copying for the press was "nearly through," he could not be trusted "to finish up the book" without her when she went off to Boston (*Mel. Log*, p. 277). Indeed, it was not until 27 January 1849 that Melville's sister Augusta could write to her in Boston: "The last proof sheets are through. 'Mardi's' a book!—'Ah my own Koztanza! child of many prayers.' Oro's blessing on thee" (*Mel. Log*, p. 287).

RECEPTION

Despite Augusta's prayers, Oro did not bless *Mardi*. When the book (set from American proofs) was published in England in mid-March, by Richard Bentley after Murray refused the "romance," and in the United States in mid-April, by the Harpers, the reviews could not have pleased Melville. Most critics on both sides of the Atlantic disapproved of his effort to write something quite different from the *Typee* and *Omoo* that they had thought so good and so promising. And indifferent or negative reviews meant, Melville knew, poor sales and little income at a time when his family responsibilities had just been increased by the birth of Malcolm on 16 February.

Several of the reviewers enjoyed the opening chapters and were disappointed that the book did not continue in that vein, feeling that Melville had "failed by leaving his sphere, which is that of graphic, poetical narration" (*Crit. Her.*, p. 162), as the New York *Tribune* phrased it. "No one paints a shark better than Mr Melville" (*Crit. Her.*, p. 143), said the London *Examiner*, and the London *Athenaeum* quoted from chapters 13 and 19 and then added, "Few who read the above will contest the power of the picture: or not long to see what vision next was revealed to the adventurers" (*Crit. Her.*, p. 140). The London *Atlas* gave extracts from the first part of *Mardi* and said, "A whole chapter, narrating the passage of the boat through the sea monsters of the Pacific, is about the cleverest and tersest description of animated nature we ever encountered" (*Crit. Her.*, p. 142). Even the Boston *Post*, which thought the book "a really poor production," found "The Voyage Thither" to the Mardian islands "interesting enough" but declared that those chapters were "almost spoiled by the everlasting assumption of the brilliant, jocose and witty in its style" (*Crit. Her.*, p. 156).

The *Post* was not alone in its criticism of Melville's style. *Blackwood's Edinburgh Magazine* was totally negative: "Why, what trash is all this!—mingled, too, with attempts at a Rabelaisian vein, and with strainings at smartness—the style of the whole being affected, pedantic, and wearisome exceedingly" (*Mel. Log*, p. 311). But *Saroni's Musical Times* thought the style was the book's "sole redeeming feature. Mr. Melville possesses many of the essentials of poetry—a store of images, a readiness at perceiving analogies and felicitous expressions" (*Crit. Her.*, p. 185). His publisher's own house organ, *Bentley's Miscellany*, criticized Melville for breaking all the rules and principles of artistic style and then forgave its newly enlisted author by adding, "the subject being given, it would not be easy to find a style better fitted for recommending it to the reader": given the strangeness of Melville's subject, the review went on, nothing was left "but to give to strange thoughts and ideas a strange utterance, and by churning up language, as the gods in the Indian fable churned the ocean, to create in the reader a sense of bewilderment and dizziness, which must put to flight all wish to revert to a simple phraseology" (*Crit. Her.*, p. 148).

Melville's main support in America came from the New York *Literary World* whose editor, Evert Duyckinck, extolled at length the virtues of a book he must have felt he had a hand in creating. Praise, too, came from the *United States Magazine and Democratic Review* where another member of the Young America group, William A. Jones, declared the new work a wonderful improvement over Melville's first two books: "These works were to *Mardi* as a seven-by-nine sketch of a sylvan lake, with a lone hunter, or a boy fishing, compared with the cartoons of Raphael" (*Crit. Her.*, p. 178).

The major problem for the critics, however, was to determine exactly how to classify Melville's new book, and when they could not find a single clear generic category in which to place it, they despaired of ever figuring out what it meant. Most saw that it was mainly an allegory and a satire, but they were confused as to its ultimate purposes by the varied subjects and targets. For the *Athenaeum*, *Mardi* was a "strange book"—if "meant as a pleasantry, the mirth has been oddly left out—if as an allegory, the key of the casket is 'buried in ocean deep'—if as a romance, it fails from tediousness—if as a prose-poem, it is chargeable with puerility" (*Crit. Her.*, p. 139), and the London *Critic* declared: "It is an extraordinary mixture of all kinds of composition, and of the strangest variety of themes. There are philosophical discourse, political disquisition, the essay, scientific and humorous, touches of poetry, and episodical adventure, with descriptions of countries and people, strung together by the slight thread of a story which is not very intelligible" (*Crit. Her.*, p. 16). Some did not object to the episodic, digressive nature of *Mardi*. In fact, the *Examiner* said that for examples of "thoughtful writing" and of "very extensive reading"—in the manner of Sir Thomas Browne with a dash of Robert Burton and Laurence Sterne thrown in—the "best chapters" were those apart from the book's "ostensible purpose," such as the "essays" on Time and Temples (ch. 75), Faith and Knowledge (ch. 97), Dreams (ch. 119), and Suppers (ch. 181) (*Crit. Her.*, p. 144–45). The reviews noted resemblances in *Mardi* to a wide range of authors, though the comparisons were not always complimentary to Melville.

One who *was* unexpectedly complimentary was the French critic, Philarete Chasles. In a very long piece in *Revue des deux mondes* (which Duyckinck's *Literary World* translated and reprinted in its continuing effort to puff Melville's book), Chasles called Melville "an American Rabelais," and went on to list the variety of genres Melville used in his book. But, finally, Chasles said, "I did not understand it after I had read it, I understood it still less after I had re-read it; a key was necessary not only for the comprehension of the facts, the proper names, and the doctrines which the author introduced, but above all to the composition of such a book, which appeared to have no reason in the world to be in the world" (*Crit. Her.*, p. 164–65). And if Melville had become well known enough to attract the attention of a French critic, he was also well known enough to merit being lampooned. The London monthly *The Man in the Moon* burlesqued Melville's style (both the prose and the poetry), the plot, the characters, the subject matter, and the themes of *Mardi*—and all in the space of "A Page by the Author of *Mardi*" (*Crit. Her.*, pp. 159–61).

Before the reviews had begun to come in, Melville had dismissed *Mardi* as a step forward that itself had to be surpassed. He wrote to Evert Duyckinck on 5 April 1849:

I am glad you like that affair of mine. But it seems so long now since I wrote it, & my mood has so changed, that I dread to look into it, & have purposely abstained from so doing since I thanked God it was off my hands.—Would that a man could do something & then say—It is finished.—not that one thing only, but all others—that he has reached his uttermost, & can never exceed it. But live & push—tho' we put one leg forward ten miles—its no reason the other must lag behind—no, *that* must again distance the other—& so we go till we get the cramp & die. (*Letters*, p. 83)

But by the end of the month Melville probably knew that *Mardi* was not going to be a critical success, although he put the best face on the situation when he wrote on 23 April to his father-in-law, Judge Lemuel Shaw:

These attacks are matters of course, and are essential to the building up of any permanent reputation—if such should ever prove to be mine.—"There's nothing in it!" cried the dunce, when he threw down the 47th problem of the 1st Book of Euclid—"There's nothing in it—"—Thus with the posed critic. But Time, which is the solver of all riddles, will solve "Mardi." (*Letters*, pp. 84–85)

In early June he tried to shift some of the blame on to his English publisher, Richard Bentley, telling him that bringing out the book in England in the ordinary novel form probably disappointed many readers, who would have been better pleased had they taken it up in the first place for what it really was. Besides, Melville continued, "the peculiar thoughts & fancies of a Yankee upon politics & other matters could hardly be presumed to delight" the English critics, "while the metaphysical ingredients (for want of a better term) of the book, must of course repel some of those who read simply for amusement." Melville went on to defend his unwillingness to write the kind of book "calculated merely to please the general reader." Some of "us scribblers," he told Bentley, "always have a certain something unmanageable in us, that bids us do this or that, and be done it must—hit or miss" (*Letters*, p. 86). Like Lombardo, who was impelled by "the necessity of bestirring himself to procure his yams" (*Mardi*, p. 592), Melville saw the need to manage the unmanageable and to turn out a book that would, as the Boston *Post* had suggested, stick to " 'fact' which is received as 'fiction,' but which puts money in his purse and wreathes laurels round his head" (*Crit. Her.*, p. 156). The result was *Redburn*, a book he would soon call "beggarly" and a "little nursery tale," one written "almost entirely for 'lucre'," one, as he had told Bentley in June, that was "a thing of a widely different cast from 'Mardi':—a plain, straightforward, amusing narrative of personal experience . . . no metaphysics, no conic-sections, nothing but cakes & ale" (*Letters*, p. 86).

Eight months later, in February 1850, having published both *Redburn* and *White-Jacket*—"two *jobs*, which I have done for money" (*Letters*, p. 91)—Melville could indulge in self-irony about *Mardi* in a letter accompanying a copy of the English edition sent to its strongest advocate:

My Dear Duyckinck—Tho' somewhat unusual for a donor, I must beg to apologize for making you the accompanying present of "Mardi." But no one who knows your library can doubt, that such a choice conservatory of exotics & other rare things in literature, after being long enjoyed by yourself, must, to a late posterity, be preserved intact by your descendants. How natural then—tho' vain—in your friend to desire a place in it for a plant, which tho' now unblown (emblematicaly, the leaves, you perceive, are uncut) may possibly—by some miracle, that is—flower like the aloe, a hundred years hence—or not flower at all, which is more likely by far, for some aloes never flower.

Again: (as the divines say) political republics should be the asylum for the persecuted of all nations; so, if Mardi be admitted to your shelves, your bibliographical Republic of Letters may find some contentment in the thought, that it has afforded refuge to a work, which almost everywhere else has been driven forth like a wild, mystic Mormon into shelterless exile. (*Letters*, pp. 101–102)

This was 1850, the year in which *Moby-Dick* would be begun, and the "something unmanageable" would rise up and bid Melville to, again like Lombardo, go "deeper and deeper into himself" until he had "created the creative" (*Mardi*, p. 595) and written a book that "hit" the mark of Truth, the mark he thought he was aiming at in *Mardi*. But, as he told Nathaniel Hawthorne in June of the next year, "Try to get a living by the Truth—and go to the Soup Societies" (*Letters*, p. 127). *Mardi* certainly did not make much money for Melville: during his lifetime he received about $240 beyond the $500 advance from the Harpers and nothing beyond the 200 guineas given him by Bentley in anticipation of his share of the profits. The "child of many prayers" (*Mardi*, p. 601) turned out to be more "beggarly" (*Letters*, p. 95) than its next younger sibling, and in its fifteenth year would be disparaged in a letter by its once proud father in a comparison with Jean Paul Richter's *The Titan*: "The worst thing I can say about it is, that it is a little better than 'Mardi' " (*Letters*, p. 225).

CRITICISM

When the critics came to consider Melville retrospectively, reviewing *Mardi* as one among several works, the judgments were no more favorable than they had been at its first appearance. Fitz-James O'Brien surveyed Melville's writing twice in *Putnam's Monthly Magazine*. In February 1853 he declared that *Mardi* "is intended to embody all the philosophy of which Mr. Melville is capable, and we have no hesitation in saying that the philosophical parts are the worst." While the philosophy is "exceedingly stale and trite," the romance otherwise is "distinguished for splendor of imagery, and richness of diction. The descriptive painting in this wild book is gorgeous and fantastic in the extreme." O'Brien had not changed his opinion by April 1857, although he warned his fellow reviewers that "dull of perception, and still more dull of instinct must the critic be who does not recognize in every page of Mr. Melville's writings, however vague, and obscure, and fantastic, the breathing spirit of a man of genius, and of a passionate and earnest man of genius" (*Crit. Her.*, pp. 326–61).

Between these two assessments, Evert and George Duyckinck published in their *Cyclopaedia of American Literature* a rather condescending critical essay on Melville. They thought *Mardi* as a whole unclear, though containing "many delicate traits and fine bursts of fancy and invention," and they praised the descriptions in the first half with its "fanciful associations" drawn from the authors Melville had borrowed from Evert's library, "upon whose pages, after his long sea fast from books and literature, the author had thrown himself with eager avidity." They are more negative about the second half, where their salutary influence as mentors of this uneducated sailor is not evident: "Embarrassed by his spiritual allegories, he wanders without chart or compass in the wildest regions of doubt and skepticism" (*Crit. Her.*, p. 346).

On the other side of the Atlantic *Mardi* fared no better with those who reviewed his career. "Sir Nathaniel," writing in London's *New Monthly Magazine* (July 1853), liked the first part of *Mardi* well enough because it resembled *Typee* and *Omoo*, the only works he really approved of; "but too soon," he wrote, "we are hurried whither we would not, and subjected to the caprices, *velut aegri somnia*, of one who, of malice aforethought, 'Delphinum silvis appingit, fluctibus aprum'—the last clause signifying that he *bores* us with his 'sea of troubles,' and provokes us to take arms against, and (if possible) by opposing, end them" (*Crit. Her.*, pp. 331–32). The reviewer in the *Dublin University Magazine* (January 1856) was also "delighted and enthralled" by the first part, but he was woefully disappointed by the rest of the book: it "would be little better than insane ravings" were it not for the hints of "biting, political satire" and the energetic "poetical" language. He regrets that "so much rare and lofty talent has been wilfully wasted on a theme which not anybody can fully understand.... It is, in our estimation, one of the saddest, most melancholy, most deplorable, and humiliating perversions of genius of a high order in the English language" (*Crit. Her.*, p. 351).

For over sixty years after this mixture of praise and condemnation, *Mardi*, along with the rest of Melville's writings, was generally ignored by the critics, and it was given short shrift by those few—like Henry S. Salt and Richard Henry Stoddard—who did write about Melville near the end of the nineteenth century. With the rekindling of interest in Melville's life and works in the 1920s, *Mardi* was once again made the focus of critical attention, but it was not until 1952 that it received a full and complete examination. That year saw the publication of Merrell R. Davis's *Melville's Mardi: A Chartless Voyage*, which, as he said in his preface, "is concerned with the literary and biographical background, the genesis, writing, and meaning" of the book; and Davis fulfilled, in the most graceful and scholarly way, the promises he made. His book superseded much of what went before; it anticipated much of what would follow. Students of Melville can do no better than to read Davis's work as their open sesame into or Ariadne's thread out of *Mardi*.

In the first of the book's three main sections, Davis outlines Melville's literary apprenticeship from 1844 through 1847—especially the composition of *Typee* and *Omoo*, the influence of Evert Duyckinck, and the writing of the comic articles on Zachary Taylor for *Yankee Doodle*—and the germane aspects of Melville's personal life during this time. In the second section he examines the writing of *Mardi*, dividing it into three periods: (1) before 1848, which includes the opening chapters on the *Arcturion*, the *Chamois*, and the *Parki* and leads up to the rescue of Yillah; (2) January-June 1848, when Melville began "experimenting with a whole range of new voices which the opening world of books helped to provide," and he developed the romance of Yillah and the "travelogue-satire" (p. 66) through the islands; and (3) after June 1848, when "almost a complete section of *Mardi*, comprising 25 chapters of satire on the geographical world, must have been inserted into a book which Elizabeth Melville had already thought complete" (p. 93).

In the third section Davis treats the sources, structure, and style of what he sees as the book's three definable parts (the "Narrative Beginning," the "Romantic Interlude," and the "Travelogue-Satire"), then analyzes the several characters, and finally presents his overall interpretation of the author's intentions, the book's meanings, and artistic quality. While *Melville's Mardi* does not deal satisfactorily with all the aesthetic problems in *Mardi* (such as the shifts in narrative point of view, the disappearance of the narrator as a central character, the attenuation of the quest for Yillah, the dismissal of Jarl and Samoa, and the many inconsistencies in the text), it does give us the best single treatment of the work.

The twentieth-century critics who preceded Davis usually treated *Mardi* as disguised autobiography, as an example of Melville's fascination with the quest for truth, or as a presentation of his views on society and culture.

Raymond Weaver set the tone for the first group in 1921 when he asserted that "the riddle of *Mardi* goes near to the heart of the riddle of Melville's life" (p. 274) and read the book as a desperate quest for the lost glamor and the joy of love Melville had felt for his mother and his bride-to-be. A somewhat brighter interpretation appeared eight years later when Lewis Mumford wrote in his biography, "If Mardi throws any light upon Melville's personal relations at all, I think one must acknowledge that the light is a happy one" (p. 59), although he did allow that the book disclosed to Melville "the nature of his own demon—that deeper other half whom Babbalanja called Azzageddi" (p. 66).

A majority of the pre-Davis critics dealt with the double thrust of the book along the lines defined in 1938 by Willard Thorp: "*Mardi* is a satirical allegory, veiling the institutions and occupations of modern life, with which is interwoven a symbolic theme of a quest, among islands which resemble the nations of the western world, for a mysterious maiden named Yillah who may symbolize 'heavenly love' or the spiritual life" (pp. 409–10). Among those who chose to accentuate the quest theme were the English critic John Freeman, who saw that "*Mardi* records an unending chase" (p. 95), William Ellery Sedgwick, whose study of Melville's "tragedy of mind" declared that out of *Mardi* "there took shape for Herman Melville that apprehension of life which was his tragic vision" (p. 53), Ronald Mason, for whom the theme was "an exhaustive search for the true philosophy" (p. 40), and Nathalia Wright (1951), who declared that, as the earliest, longest, and most undisguised account of the quest for "the 'full-developed man,' " *Mardi* was the "most important single work by Melville for the study of one of his most important themes" (p. 351)—the balance of head and heart. Richard Chase, on the other hand, emphasized the socio-political aspects of *Mardi*, and Leon Howard said that the real-world section of the book records "the maturing of penetrating intelligence and a sharply realistic mind" (Howard, p. 127).

Howard was the most perceptive among those besides Davis analyzing the composition and formal structure. Others working before 1952, including Newton Arvin and F. O. Matthiessen, also examined the book's form and style, and Matthiessen concluded that in *Mardi* Melville "had reached levels where he had no first-hand experience to support him, and he had not yet gained much notion of how to blend his abstractions into symbols by his own equivalent of the metaphysical style" (p. 387).

The years 1951–52 were a watershed for Melville criticism. So many critical biographies and general surveys of Melville's writing had been done that scholars after that time began to approach *Mardi* and the other works from more limited, specialized points of view that placed the canon within the context of some particular critical strategy. There are exceptions, of course: Milton R. Stern's long and provocative chapter on *Mardi* studies its structure, narrative voice, symbolic and allegorical elements, characterizations, and final meanings. And Edward H. Rosenberry's chapter on "Philosophical Allegory" (1979) sees *Mardi* and *The Confidence-Man* as fables "utterly independent of the 'real' world" (p. 44) and analyzes the "major skeins" (p. 48) of Mardi's structure.

Rosenberry's earlier book (1955) was one of the more specialized studies of this period; it treated *Mardi* as a major step forward in Melville's development of his comic style. Other post-Davis critics also focused on *Mardi's* position in its author's growth as a literary artist. Charles Feidelson said:

Melville's development from *Typee* to *Mardi*—from a primarily objective attitude to one that is openly symbolistic—is dramatized within *Mardi* itself . . . . Seen from a distance, the voyage takes shape as the symbol of thought. What is thought *about* is a relatively minor matter; Melville's ultimate question is *how*. In the largest view the book is a study of what it entails to regard thinking as a metaphysical journey. (pp. 166–67)

Later scholars extended this idea within the scope of their special approaches, notably, James Baird in his treatment of Melville as a maker of myths and as an important example of modern primitivism; Edgar Dryden in his study of Melville's fiction as a metaphysical response to the emptiness of life; and Richard Brodhead in his reading of *Mardi* as Melville's personal quest for his own mental world: "the value of *Mardi* for its author lies not in what it is but in what his composition of it could bring into being—his own mature creative self " (p. 41). Mildred K. Travis ("Melville's Furies") draws attention to Melville's development as an artist by focusing on the canoe encounters in *Mardi* and showing how they evolve into the so-called gams of *Moby-Dick*, and Nina Baym, putting *Mardi* in the context of Melville's growing "quarrel with fiction," asserts that during its composition Melville twice "breached the genre contract with his readers" (p. 912) as he dropped his narrative of facts for romance and then shifted to political satire and commentary in his attempt, finally, "to transcend all genres" (p. 913).

Scholars who saw Melville drawing material and inspiration from identifiable sources analyzed *Mardi* along with his other works to discover how the sources were incorporated into the book. Dorothee Metlitsky Finkelstein was interested in "the role of the *Arabian Nights* in Melville's concept of 'romance' " (p. 189) and in "the Arabian character of *Mardi*" (p. 223). H. Bruce Franklin read *Mardi* as a study of myths and myth-making, drawing "upon the mythologies of the Hindus, the Polynesians, the Incas, the Hebrews, the Greeks, the Christians, the Romans, and the Norse" (p. 17), comparing them to one another and to other myths, and dramatizing what Melville saw as "the identity of Sir William Jones's four sources of mythology" (p. 52). Each of the five questors in *Mardi*, according to Franklin, has a "peculiar mythological function," and each function "must be seen in the context of contemporaneous mythology" (p. 18). In the only book-length study of *Mardi* besides Davis's, Maxine Moore asserts a unity of design based in a continuous riddle game that grew out of Melville's interest in astronomy, nautical navigation, astrology, and game theories. Much more reasonable in conception and argument is Merton M. Sealts's study of "Melville and the Platonic Tradition," which sees the author's first-hand acquaintance with the dialogues as "a major influence" on *Mardi* (p. 278): "from Plato himself, in addition to the pattern of philosophical dialogue that informs so much of *Mardi*, Melville drew seminal themes and images that first emerged there and reappeared in key passages of his later writings" (p. 281).

Some recent critics interested in Melville's social and political attitudes examine *Mardi* as if it were a statement of his deepest beliefs on those subjects, especially in regard to his native land. For example, Carolyn L. Karcher looked at the problems of slavery, race, and violence in Melville's America, and James Duban focused on the Vivenza chapters as Melville's "satirical inquiry into American expansionism and slavery" (p. 17).

More general readings, yet ones still determined by the critics' special perspectives, continue to appear. John Seelye's controlling idea of irony in Melville's writings led him to see *Mardi*'s structure as one of expanding ironic contrasts that present many valid choices, reasonable alternatives, and balanced attitudes—reflecting "the complexity of the perceived world" (p. 39). William B. Dillingham exalts *Mardi* as the most ambitious and comprehensive of Melville's early works, the only one before *Moby-Dick* to contain all three of the "basic ideas" (p. 4) expressed in "The Lee Shore": the nature of experience, the thirst for psychological freedom, and the paradox of Promethean heroism.

So the quest for *Mardi* goes on. Foster concluded her survey in the NN edition of criticism through the 1960s by saying that "most modern critics forgive the gaucheries of *Mardi* for the sake of its riches of the spirit and of language, and it is obvious that modern critics study *Mardi* as the first bold stroke of Melville's greatest work" (p. 679). (As a guide to the criticism of *Mardi* from the year of its publication until 1971, the annotated checklist by David H. Bowman and Ruth L. Bohan serves very well, categorizing the material as contemporary British and American reviews, criticism in English appearing in books and in periodicals, and criticism in foreign languages.) What was true in 1970 is true of the criticism since that time, although none of the more recent critics has exhibited the sensitivity, reasonableness, and intuitive brilliance of a Leon Howard nor the intelligence, thoroughness, and rigorous scholarship of a Merrell R. Davis.

The areas for further study of *Mardi* as a separate work are quite limited, thanks especially to Davis. For example, a new source may supplement those mentioned above and others such as the ones noted by Charles R. Anderson, William Braswell, Richard Allan Davison, A. Grove Day, David Jaffe, James Jubak, Robert Milder, Robert A. Rees, Mildred K. Travis ("Spenserian Analogues"), Nathalia Wright (1953), and Donald J. Yannella, but it is most doubtful that it will alter or appreciably enhance our understanding. Nor, probably, will yet another article on the themes in *Mardi*, an explication of some aspect of the book's meaning, like Tyrus Hillway's early pieces on Taji's "suicide," or James E. Miller's on "unmasking" the characters and social institutions in Mardi, or Travis's comparison of the pairs of lovers ("Melville's Allegory of Love"), or Philip Graham's allegorical reading of the book as the history of humankind, or those essays, like Barbara Blansett's or Stuart Levine's or Travis's ("Melville's Furies") that see *Mardi* foreshadowing later works in particular ways. Barring the unearthing of new documents from Melville's life that might illuminate *Mardi* (they would have to be more substantial than those acquired in 1984 by the New York Public Library), the approach that seems most useful is close reading of the text to discover what the style and structure (and the "aesthetic problems" I mentioned above) can teach us about its composition and Melville's shifting intentions. Building on that, we can then refine our interpretations of *Mardi* and learn more about Melville's method of writing. Of course, *Mardi* will continue to be included in future studies of Melville's works as a whole, but even this is not very promising. It will take real ingenuity to find a new approach that would justify yet another full-length treatment.

For the most part *Mardi* will continue to be forgiven its aesthetic sins and will be assumed bodily into a literary heaven not for its own merits but for the sake of its author and his great later works. The book itself is a chaos, out of which readers can create any sort of orderly universe they want, developing their own continuities and establishing their own unities: things go together because the readers say they do. Despite its apologists' efforts to explain away its artistic failings, *Mardi* must finally stand or fall on its own, and fall it does. But such a failure does not diminish Melville, for, as he himself announced, "Failure is the true test of greatness" (*MD*, p. 545). Like Pierre, "goaded, in the hour of mental immaturity, to the attempt at a mature work" (*Pierre*, p. 338), Melville had to clear away the dull and commonplace—the "earthy rubbish"—before he could discover "the fine gold of genius" within him (p. 258). With *Mardi* behind him, Melville was able at last to penetrate to the center of his soul and there find the precious ore that he would refine and shape into *Moby-Dick*.

WORKS CITED

Anderson, Charles R. *Melville in the South Seas*. New York: Columbia University Press, 1939.
Arvin, Newton. "Melville's *Mardi*." *American Quarterly* 2 (Spring 1950): 71–81.
———. "*Mardi, Redburn, White-Jacket*." In *Melville: A Collection of Critical Essays*. Ed. Richard Chase. Englewood Cliffs, N.J.: Prentice-Hall, 1962, pp. 21–38.
Baird, James. *Ishmael: A Study of the Symbolic Mode in Primitivism*. Baltimore: Johns Hopkins University Press, 1956.
Baym, Nina. "Melville's Quarrel with Fiction." *PMLA* 94 (October 1979): 909–23.
Bernard, Kenneth. "Melville's *Mardi* and the Second Loss of Paradise." *Lock Haven Review* No. 7 (1965): 23–30.

Blansett, Barbara Ruth Nieweg. "From Dark to Dark: *Mardi*, a Foreshadowing of *Pierre*." *The Southern Quarterly* 1 (April 1963): 213–27.

Bowman, David H., and Ruth L. Bohan. "Herman Melville's *Mardi: A Voyage Thither*: An Annotated Checklist of Criticism." *Resources for American Literary Study* 3 (1973): 27–72. [Lists published criticism, 1849–1971.]

Branch, Watson. "The Etiology of Melville's *Mardi*," *Philological Quarterly* 64 (Summer 1985): 317–36.

Braswell, William. "Melville's Use of Seneca in *Mardi*." *American Literature* 12 (March 1940): 98–104.

Brodhead, Richard. "*Mardi*: Creating the Creative." In *New Perspectives on Melville*. Ed. Faith Pullin. Kent, OH and Edinburgh: Kent State University Press and Edinburgh University Press, 1978.

Chaffee, Patricia A. "Paradox in *Mardi*." *American Transcendental Quarterly* No. 29 (Winter 1976): 80–83.

Chase, Richard. *Herman Melville: A Critical Study*. New York: Macmillan Co., 1949.

Cook, Richard M. "The Grotesque and Melville's *Mardi*." *ESQ* 21 (Second Quarter 1975): 103–10.

Davis, Merrell R. "The Flower Symbolism in *Mardi*." *Modern Language Quarterly* 2 (December 1941): 625–38.

———. *Melville's Mardi: A Chartless Voyage*. New Haven, Conn.: Yale University Press, 1952.

Davison, Richard Allan. "Melville's *Mardi* and John Skelton." *Emerson Society Quarterly* No. 43 (Second Quarter 1966): 86–87.

Day, A. Grove. "Hawaiian Echoes in Melville's *Mardi*." *Modern Language Quarterly* 18 (March 1957): 3–8.

Dillingham, William B. *An Artist in the Rigging: The Early Work of Herman Melville*. Athens: University of Georgia Press, 1972.

Dryden, Edgar. *Melville's Thematics of Form*. Baltimore: Johns Hopkins University Press, 1968.

Duban, James. *Melville's Major Fiction: Politics, Theology, and Imagination*. DeKalb: Northern Illinois University Press, 1983.

Feidelson, Charles. *Symbolism and American Literature*. Chicago: University of Chicago Press, 1953.

Finkelstein, Dorothee Metlitsky. *Melville's Orienda*. New Haven and London: Yale University Press, 1961.

Franklin, H. Bruce. *In the Wake of the Gods: Melville's Mythology*. Stanford, Calif.: Stanford University Press, 1963.

Freeman, John. *Herman Melville*. London: Macmillan Co., 1926.

Graham, Philip. "The Riddle of Melville's *Mardi*: A Reinterpretation." *University of Texas Studies in English* 36 (1957): 93–99.

Guido, John F. "Melville's *Mardi*: Bentley's Blunder." *Papers of the Bibliographical Society of America* 62 (1968): 361–71.

Haberstroh, Charles, Jr. "Melville's Marriage and *Mardi*." *Studies in the Novel* 9 (Fall 1977): 247–60.

Hillway, Tyrus. "Taji's Abdication in Herman Melville's *Mardi*." *American Literature* 16 (November 1944): 204–207.

————. "Taji's Quest for Certainty." *American Literature* 18 (March 1946): 27–34.

Jaffe, David. "Some Sources of Melville's *Mardi*." *American Literature* 9 (March 1937): 56–69.

Johnson, Julie M. "Taji's Quest in Melville's *Mardi*: A Psychological Allegory in the Mythic Mode." *Colby Library Quarterly* 18 (December 1982): 220–30.

Jubak, James. "The Influence of the Travel Narrative on Melville's *Mardi*." *Genre* 9 (Summer 1976): 121–33.

Karcher, Carolyn L. *Shadow over the Promised Land: Slavery, Race, and Violence in Melville's America*. Baton Rouge: Louisiana State University Press, 1980.

Levine, Stuart. "Melville's 'Voyage Thither.' " *Midwest Quarterly* 3 (Summer 1962): 341–53.

Mason, Ronald. *The Spirit Above the Dust: A Study of Herman Melville*. London: John Lehmann, 1951.

Matthiessen, F. O. *American Renaissance: Art and Expression in the Age of Emerson and Whitman*. New York: Oxford University Press, 1941.

Metcalf, Eleanor Melville. *Herman Melville: Cycle and Epicycle*. Cambridge, Mass.: Harvard University Press, 1953.

Milder, Robert. " 'Nemo Contra Deum . . .': Melville and Goethe's 'Demonic.' " In *Ruined Eden of the Present: Hawthorne, Melville, Poe*. Ed. G. R. Thompson and Virgil L. Lokke. West Lafayette, Ind.: Purdue University Press, 1981, pp. 205–44.

Miller, James E., Jr. "The Many Masks of *Mardi*." *Journal of English and Germanic Philology* 58 (July 1959): 400–13.

Mills, Gordon H. "The Significance of 'Arcturus' in *Mardi*." *American Literature* 14 (May 1942): 158–61.

Moore, Maxine. *That Lonely Game: Melville, Mardi, and the Almanac*. Columbia: University of Missouri Press, 1975.

Mumford, Lewis. *Herman Melville*. New York: Harcourt, Brace & Co., 1929.

Packard, Hyland. "*Mardi*: The Role of Hyperbole in Melville's Search for Expression." *American Literature* 49 (May 1977): 241–53.

Rees, Robert A. "Melville's Alma and *The Book of Mormon*." *Emerson Society Quarterly* No. 43 (Second Quarter 1966): 41–46.

Rosenberry, Edward H. *Melville*. London, Henley, and Boston: Routledge & Kegan Paul, 1979.

————. *Melville and the Comic Spirit*. Cambridge, Mass.: Harvard University Press, 1955.

Sealts, Merton M. "Melville and the Platonic Tradition." In *Pursuing Melville, 1940–1980*. Madison: University of Wisconsin Press, 1982, pp. 278–336.

Sears, J. Michael. "Melville's *Mardi*: One Book or Three?" *Studies in the Novel* 10 (Winter 1978): 411–19.

Sedgwick, William Ellery. *Herman Melville: The Tragedy of Mind*. Cambridge, Mass.: Harvard University Press, 1944.

Seelye, John. *Melville: The Ironic Diagram*. Evanston: Northwestern University Press, 1970.

Stern, Milton R. *The Fine-Hammered Steel of Herman Melville*. Urbana: University of Illinois Press, 1968.

Sumner, D. Nathan. "The American West in Melville's *Mardi* and *The Confidence-Man.*" *Research Studies* 36 (1968): 37–49.

Thorp, Willard. *Herman Melville: Representative Selections.* New York: American Book Co., 1938.

Travis, Mildred K. "*Mardi*: Melville's Allegory of Love." *ESQ* No. 43 (Second Quarter 1966): 88–94.

———. "Melville's Furies: Technique in *Mardi* and *Moby-Dick.*" *ESQ* No. 47 (Second Quarter 1967): 71–73.

———. "Spenserian Analogues in *Mardi* and *The Confidence Man.*" *ESQ* No. 50 (1968 supplement): 55–58.

Weaver, Raymond. *Herman Melville: Mariner and Mystic.* New York: George H. Doran, 1921.

Wright, Nathalia. "The Head and Heart in Melville's *Mardi.*" *PMLA* 66 (June 1951): 351–62.

———. "A Note on Melville's Use of Spenser: Hautia and 'The Bower of Bliss.' " *American Literature* 24 (March 1953): 83–85.

Yannella, Donald J. " 'Seeing the Elephant' in *Mardi.*' " In *Artful Thunder: Versions of the Romantic Tradition in American Literature in Honor of Howard P. Vincent,* Ed. Benjamin DeMott and Sanford E. Marovitz. Kent, Ohio: Kent State University Press, 1975, pp. 105–17.

6

REDBURN AND *WHITE-JACKET*

Wilson Heflin

In the latter part of April or early May 1849, Herman Melville made an abrupt, perhaps reckless, about-face from the ambitious creative and philosophical course he would have preferred to follow after *Mardi* and returned to the quasi-autobiographical, semi-fictional narrative modes of *Typee* and *Omoo*. He determined to exploit in two books, first his experiences as sailor on a merchantman ten years before, and then those as an enlisted man in the U.S. Navy four and a half years in the past. Whether or not he viewed these tasks with distaste, he addressed them professionally with sustained concentration at his writing desk and greater speed in composition than ever before. He was apparently driven to these endeavors by the sting of unfavorable early reviews of *Mardi* but, more pressingly, by the necessity of supporting a growing household "with duns all round him" (*Letters*, p. 95).

In about three months he had completed the first book, *Redburn*. By early September he was reading the proofs of *Redburn* and probably composing *White-Jacket*. The second book evidently took only two months, perhaps less, to finish.

Neither book, Melville felt, would contribute to the kind of reputation he wished to gain. In a letter to his father-in-law, Judge Lemuel Shaw, he spoke of them disparagingly as "two *jobs*, which I have done for money" (*Letters*, p. 91). To Richard Henry Dana, Jr., he deprecated *Redburn* as "A little nursery tale of mine," and to Evert Duyckinck he described the book as "beggarly" (*Letters*, pp. 93, 95). Melville's stated contempt for *Redburn* and *White-Jacket*, as Edward H. Rosenberry perceptively remarks, "should tell us more of him than of the books" (p.

57). "Yet in each of them," Leon Howard observed, "Melville had written far better than he knew and far better than he could have written without the experience gained from *Mardi* and from the perceptive reading which followed" (Howard, p. 135). With these two books Melville made substantial gains as a creative artist in control of his material as well as in stylistic proficiency. After them, he could chart the course to *Moby-Dick* with greater assurance.

Early biographers of Melville—notably Raymond Weaver and Lewis Mumford—accepted without skepticism the events of each of these books as facts of Melville's nautical experiences. It was not until 1939 that Charles R. Anderson separated fact from fiction in *White-Jacket* in two chapters of *Melville in the South Seas* (pp. 361–419). Depending on the very full documentation of the voyage of the frigate *United States* (1842–44), he concluded that about half of *White-Jacket* "is a straight-forward account of daily life on board a man-of-war." The narrative portion, he felt, involved "alterations of fact . . . dramatic elaboration of actual events; and deliberate invention" (p. 361). In 1951 William H. Gilman, with great skill in detection but fewer pieces of objective evidence available for analysis, carefully sorted elements of romance and reality in *Redburn*. In *Melville's Early Life and Redburn*, he came to the carefully reasoned conclusion that "It has been fashionable for some time to consider [*Redburn*] autobiography with elements of romance. It is more nearly correct to call it romance with elements of autobiography" (p. 204). Anderson's and Gilman's studies are landmarks in Melville scholarship.

Charles Anderson was reluctant to claim as a source for *White-Jacket* any book not owned or borrowed by Melville. Later investigators, however, have been less inhibited in their attributions of printed influence. In his excellent "Historical Note" to the NN edition of *White-Jacket*, Willard Thorp listed eleven important sources for the naval book and some minor ones (pp. 417–24). These sources and others are fully explored in Howard P. Vincent's *The Tailoring of Melville's White-Jacket* (1970), an important study. *Redburn* was apparently composed without much substantive help from other books than *The Picture of Liverpool*, used extensively, and Adam Smith's *Wealth of Nations*, cited briefly. Several analogous books, chief among them Frederick Marryat's *Peter Simple* and Charles Briggs's *The Adventures of Harry Franco*, have been claimed as possible influences on "the little nursery tale."

REDBURN

On 5 June 1849 Melville wrote his prospective English publisher, Richard Bentley, the following account of a new book: "I have now in preparation a thing of a widely different cast from "Mardi":—a plain, straightforward, amusing narrative of personal experience—the son of a gentleman on his first voyage to sea as a sailor—no metaphysics, no conic-sections, nothing but cakes & ale" (*Letters*, p. 86). This statement, in some respects, is about as far from the mark as Melville's promise to Sophia Hawthorne that *Pierre* "will be a rural bowl of milk" (*Letters*, p. 146). Nineteenth-century readers may have found comical the confusion and mishaps of the greenhorn sailor, Wellingborough Redburn, during his early shipboard adventures or his so often coming a cropper when his naive, country-gentlemen pretensions and illusions are shattered. But most modern critics find in *Redburn* few "cakes & ale." With the exception of those who agree with Leslie A. Fiedler that *Redburn* is a weary tale about "a *schlemiel* with an absurd name" (p. 357), twentieth-century critics predominantly take the book seriously, seeing it as "a study in disillusion, of innocence confronted with the world, of ideals shattered by facts" (Matthiessen, p. 396), or as "the initiation of innocence into evil" (Arvin, p. 103), or as a way station in Melville's development as an artist, prelusive to later, greater books. Some critics view *Redburn* as the beginning of a narrative that concludes with *White-Jacket* and see ties between the shooting-jacket of the first book and the makeshift sea-jacket of the second. William B. Dillingham finds hunger, actual and spiritual, a pervasive theme in the book (pp. 34–41).

The narrative structure of *Redburn* is uncomplicated: three main sections—the voyage to Liverpool, the stay in England, and the return to America—and two shorter sections—the preliminaries to the voyage and the aftermath.

Wellingborough Redburn, the young narrator, about fifteen years old, leaves his home on the upper Hudson River to go to New York City and from there to sail as a foremast hand on his first sea-voyage. He is the "Son-of-a-Gentleman," who died a bankrupt and left his family in straitened circumstances. Ill provided for what lies ahead, with only a dollar in his pocket, an old shooting jacket, and a gun given him by his brother, Redburn takes the steamboat to New York, finds to his chagrin when underway that the passage fee has been raised to two dollars, and arrives at the city, hungry, penniless, and forlorn. Mr. Jones, his brother's friend, takes him in and feeds him, and the next day accompanies him to the docks, where they meet the merry Captain Riga of the trading ship *Highlander*. After Mr. Jones grossly misrepresents Redburn's financial situation and speaks lordly of his distinguished kin, Captain Riga signs the lad on for three dollars a month. Redburn is rated as "boy" (green hand or landsman).

The *Highlander* sails in early June. Soon Redburn, wretched with hunger, is ordered to perform demeaning and dangerous duties, cleaning the ship's pigpen and climbing aloft to slush down the topmast. When watches are chosen, Redburn, selected last, finds himself in the larboard (port) watch, presided over by the chief mate. When the lad becomes seasick, he accepts from a Greenlander in the crew a drink of rum, this despite his temperance pledge back home. For his shipboard ignorance, he is subject to derisive abuse from the crew, and he is assigned humiliating duties by the mate. Soon after the voyage begins, a drunken sailor rushes on deck and shrieking jumps to his death in the sea. Redburn must sleep that night in the drowned man's bunk. And Jackson, a small, sickly seaman who inexplicably tyrannizes the crew and whom Redburn later comes to believe is absolutely evil, threatens to kill the boy should he ever cross his path.

One day, when Redburn, ignorant of nautical protocol, decides to visit Captain Riga sociably in his cabin, the furious mate orders him from the quarter-deck. Shipboard nomenclature constantly confuses Redburn, but he learns his duties fast, becoming at length "as nimble as a monkey in the rigging" (p. 115), and he is commended by some of his shipmates, now no longer so hostile. Jackson, whose illness becomes progressively worse, is to Redburn "a Cain afloat; branded on his yellow brow with some inscrutable curse" (p. 104). Incidents of the eastward crossing include the ramming of another ship by the *Highlander*; the sighting of whales (a disappointment to Redburn); an encounter with a water-logged derelict with three dead bodies aboard; the discovery of a boy stowaway, who is befriended by the crew; and some merriment at the expense of a stuttering passenger. After thirty days at sea, the *Highlander* reaches Liverpool.

For more than six weeks, while the ship is moored at Prince's Dock, Redburn, living ashore at an inn, has light duties aboard the *Highlander* and ample time to explore the town and the countryside. With a prosy old guidebook, once owned by his father, he seeks places visited years before by Walter Redburn. To his disappointment he finds that Liverpool has much changed and that even Riddough's Hotel, where his father stayed, no longer exists. A "sadder and a wiser boy," he concludes that "the thing that had guided the father, could not guide the son" (p. 157). He visits the docks, the pestilent booble-alleys of the town, and foreign ships in port, and is unceremoniously thrown out of a lyceum. On a narrow street called Launcelott's-Hey, he finds a destitute woman, faint from hunger, lying in a vault below the walk, holding a baby, apparently dead, and two shrunken children. Redburn tries in vain to gain assistance for them. A few days later he finds the bodies gone, quicklime in their place. The countryside provides an exhilarating contrast to squalid and beggarly Liverpool; on a delightful Sunday ramble, he is invited in for tea and muffins by a hospitable Englishman with "three adorable charmers," his daughters (p. 209).

Shortly before sailing time, Redburn befriends Harry Bolton, a slight, girlish lad, who claims a mysterious, aristocratic background and experience as a midshipman with the East India Company. Harry wishes to join the crew of the *Highlander*. Together the two go to London for thirty-six hours. At Aladdin's Palace (apparently a luxurious gaming house) Harry presumably bets and loses most of his wealth, while Redburn awaits mystified in an anteroom. They return at once to Liverpool, having seen little of London, and Harry officially becomes Redburn's shipmate.

On the return voyage to America, the *Highlander*'s foul-smelling steerage is overcrowded with some five hundred immigrant passengers, who suffer miserably in the storms that soon appear. Redburn is terrified when a sailor, brought on board earlier by a crimp, is consumed in the forecastle by the green fires of animal combustion. Harry Bolton's claims to previous shipboard experience are soon proved false; after one frightening attempt to go aloft, he vows never again to climb the rigging. Thereafter, he is tormented by merciless shipmates. Carlo, a young Italian immigrant, plays the hand-organ so beautifully that Redburn is inspired to rhapsodize about music. When a contagious fever rages among the immigrants, thirty of them die. After the pestilence subsides and the crew cleans the steerage of nauseating defilement, the chief mate compassionately nurses those convalescing. Harry, at a loss for what to do after they reach America, is promised assistance by Redburn in getting him a position in a mercantile house.

Off Cape Cod in heavy gales, the ailing, demonic Jackson, who has refused duty for some time, suddenly emerges from the forecastle to join the men aloft reefing sails, totters up the rigging to the weather end of the main topyard, and spouting blood, falls headlong to his death in the sea. After a prolonged, stormy crossing of four months, the *Highlander* reaches New York. When Redburn and Harry go to Captain Riga for their pay, he charges Redburn for lost gear and time absent from duty, giving him nothing and Harry only a dollar. Redburn tries unavailingly through a friend to get employment for Harry, then reluctantly leaves for his home. Years later, while himself a whaleman, Redburn learns that Harry is dead, having fallen overboard from a Nantucket ship and been crushed against it by a whale moored alongside.

In *Redburn*, it is sometimes difficult to separate biographical fact from fiction. The main difference between the experiences of Herman Melville and Wellingborough Redburn is that when Melville sailed to Liverpool in the trading ship *St. Lawrence*, he was a relatively mature lad, almost twenty; the fictional Redburn is at least five years younger. There are nonetheless certain parallels between the actual voyage and the imaginary one. Both the crews of the real and the fictional ship include a Greenlander, an Irishman, a sailor named Jackson, and one called Larry. The chronology in *Redburn* of the eastward crossing to Liverpool, the stay there, and the return voyage corresponds closely to that in actuality. Captain Oliver Brown was a naturalized Swede; Captain Riga is Russian. Three sailors desert both from Melville's ship and from Redburn's.

Using the official ship's papers as checks, William H. Gilman noted invented episodes and characters in *Redburn*. The three deaths of crew members—by suicide, animal combustion, and a fall from the mast— are not substantiated by the ship's records of 1839. No Miguel Saveda joined the crew at Liverpool, and there is no precise parallel to Harry Bolton. In contrast to the five hundred or so immigrants on the return trip of the *Highlander*, the official passenger roll of the *St. Lawrence* listed thirteen men, three women, and sixteen children, all of whom survived the voyage. There was no Carlo, no sets of triplet Irish boys, and only two cabin passengers. Gilman found other, lesser, instances of departure from biographical fact.

Sources and Composition

Two sources have already been mentioned: the anonymous *Picture of Liverpool* and Adam Smith's *Wealth of Nations*. The first of these sources was discovered by Willard Thorp and studied carefully in 1938. The second is of slight importance. Thorp also discovered that Melville relied, especially in the Liverpool section, on information found in the *Penny Magazine* and the *Penny Encyclopedia* (27 volumes; 1833–34). Other possible printed influences include Washington Irving's *Sketch Book*, Richard Henry Dana's *Two Years Before the Mast* and *The Seaman's Friend*, and Nathaniel Ames's *A Mariner's Sketches*.

No manuscript of *Redburn* has been found. To avoid possible copyright infringement, Melville had *Redburn* set up in type from his manuscript by his American publisher, Harper and Brothers, but had it published earlier in England by Richard Bentley.

The NN edition of *Redburn*, relying on the earliest impression of the American edition for its copy-text, is the result of extensive collation of various editions and thorough, precise study by its editors—Harrison Hayford, Hershel Parker, and G. Thomas Tanselle—of all textual problems (see their "Editorial Appendix," pp. 353–84).

Reception

Gilman provides a brief summary of early reviews and responses to *Redburn* (pp. 274–80); longer summaries appear in Hershel Parker's excellent "Historical Note" to the NN edition (pp. 332–41) and in Hetherington (pp. 135–56). Fifteen representative contemporary reviews are reprinted by Branch (*Crit. Her.*, pp. 188–216).

For the most part, American and British reviewers were enthusiastic about *Redburn*, and its sales soon exceeded those of *Mardi*. *Redburn* was praised in the American press for its vivid reality, its careful reporting, and its affinity with the writings of Defoe and Smollett; Melville was urged to write more books in this vein.

Although British reviewers were more critical of the book, some of them printed long sections from *Redburn*. Objections raised in the English press concerned Redburn's inconsistent character (sharp ashore, a simpleton aboard ship); the pictures of Liverpool and London, and especially Melville's notions of aristocracy (which it treated derisively); and the effeminate Harry Bolton (an improbable character). Yet some British reviewers found Melville's humor engaging and agreed that *Redburn* was "as perfect a specimen of the naval yarn as we ever read" (*Literary Gazette*).

From the time of its early reception until well into the twentieth century, *Redburn* was almost a forgotten work, despite the fact that it was reprinted in 1850, 1855, and 1863. A few English readers continued to praise the book, notably W. Clark Russell, John Masefield, and H. S. Salt (Gilman, p. 282). But substantial critical attention was not again aroused until after the Melville Revival.

Editions

The NN edition of *Redburn* is the preferred text for study and teaching; it has been issued in paperback. The Penguin English Library edition, available in paperback since 1977, with a useful introduction by Harold Beaver and twenty-eight pages of annotation, profits by the textual decisions of the NN editors. An inexpensive paperback edition, with no critical paraphernalia, has been available since 1957, published by Doubleday Anchor Books. Students may also find useful Robert M. Schaible's 1971 doctoral dissertation, "An Annotated Edition of Herman Melville's *Redburn*" (*Mel. Diss.*, #258). It contains a good summary of recent criticism and sixty-one pages of annotations.

History of Criticism

In a review of the reputation of *Redburn* up to 1951, William Gilman concluded that, with few modern exceptions, early reviewers wrote literary criticism superior to that of their twentieth-century counterparts (p. 279). At least they saw the book as ficton and treated it as such. The two exceptions Gilman noted were Matthiessen and Arvin. Each of these critics charted courses that commentators were to follow for a decade or so.

Matthiessen found in *Redburn* (and *White-Jacket*) the "waking of Melville's tragic sense"; "the miseries of the world became misery for him, and would not let him rest" (p. 396). Arvin saw archetypal myth in a book the "outward subject" of which is the story of a lad's first sea-voyage, but whose "inward subject is the initiation of innocence into evil" (p. 103). A good many later critics followed Arvin's lead, especially R.W.B. Lewis, who found in *Redburn* "the Adamic coloration of experience" (p. 136). James E. Miller viewed *Redburn* and *White-Jacket* as "a single whole" in which the protagonist "ultimately and deliberately discards his mask of innocence and proclaims his common bond of guilt with all humanity" (pp. 54, 56).

For at least fifteen years the mythic interpretation prevailed; then it was challenged on three fronts—by H. Bruce Franklin (1965), James Schroeter (1967), and Terence G. Lish (1967). Franklin accepted the basic initiation theme but found that Redburn, in deserting the hapless Harry Bolton, had cruelly departed from the Adamic model (pp. 190–94). Schroeter, in "*Redburn* and the Failure of Mythic Criticism," held that archetypal interpretation fails because "it is contradicted repeatedly by some of the most important tonal and structural features of the novel" (p. 283). In place of a mythic reading, he proposed a structure of "two extreme models, both counterparts of Redburn" (p. 294)—Harry and Jackson—each representing an experience that is, in ways, both attractive and hazardous. In "Melville's *Redburn*: A Study in Dualism," Lish found a number of mythic overtones in the book but rejected the "seeker" interpretation, offering instead a structure of "interwoven qualities," the most important of which is that of Redburn and Harry. He concluded that Redburn, "in clutching his innocence to his breast and denying his obligation to his darker half, defeats his own purpose as a seeker and earns the reader's contempt" (p. 120). Despite these and other attacks, the initiation theme continues to survive, though now usually divested of archetypal trappings.

For some years after Matthiessen was troubled by Melville's failure "to keep his center of consciousness in Redburn's inexperience" (p. 397), shifting from a boyish angle of vision to that of a mature narrator, critics were concerned with point of view in the book. Gilman believed Melville's narrative practice in *Redburn* was a "ruinous defect" (p. 397). Lawrance Thompson identified three points of view, the last of which was a skeptical Melville satirizing Redburn's boyish tale, his mature editorializing later in the narrative, and the book's readers (p. 75). William B. Dillingham found four Redburns in the story: an inexperienced boy to begin with, a maturer one toward the end of the book, an older narrator, and "an older actor in the events of the story who should not be there" (pp. 33–34). Merlin Bowen, in "*Redburn* and the Angle of Vision," reviewed the issue at length, concluding that there was only one narrative voice, that of an older Redburn. Warner Berthoff's position is perhaps that generally accepted today: "the one voice is used for direct participation in events, the other for recollecting them from a distance and reflecting on their significance" (p. 32). An incisive, brief account of the debate and a suggestion for its resolution appear in Hershel Parker's "Historical Note" to the NN edition of *Redburn* (pp. 318–19).

Many critics have discussed and evaluated the symbols appearing in *Redburn*. Chief among these are the glass ship (Sale), the guide book (Thorp), and the shooting jacket (Miller). Lesser symbols are the nautical picture and the rope aboard the *Highlander* that separates wealthy passengers from indigent immigrants.

WHITE-JACKET

White-Jacket defies conventional classification as to literary genre. Technically, at least, the book belongs to a type of writing that was popular in the nineteenth century but is now virtually moribund—the seaman's man-of-war narrative. Melville's book, however, differs from works of this sort in several important respects. For many years *White-Jacket* was read as a faithful segment of autobiography, but in a literal sense it is not. For those who would consider it a novel, it must be protested that the book does not qualify as to complexity of plot or depth of characterization. Yet it contains fiction of a special kind. It is full of exposition of the interior life of a man-of-war, a kind of nineteenth-century documentary, but not altogether so. It is polemical, often angrily propagandistic, but it is much more than a tract. *White-Jacket* is thus a complex of diverse parts, yet somehow more than the sum of those parts. In its way, it is as hybrid a work of art as *Moby-Dick*.

A good many sailor-writers in Melville's time got their nautical reminiscences into print, often from the presses of little-known publishers. Their books differ from *White-Jacket* in certain key respects. For one thing, the typical seamen-authors usually remained anonymous, or employed such quaint seafaring pseudonyms as "by Hawser Martingale," or "Bill Truck," or "Tom Taffrail," or often simply "Man-of-War's Man," "A British Seaman," or "A Voice From the Forecastle." Furthermore, most of the seamen-authors protested their lack of formal education and their inexperience as writers; they nearly always disavowed any pretensions to stylistic excellence. Herman Melville, by contrast, was a recognized man of letters in 1850, when *White-Jacket* was published, with four books already in print, at home and abroad, and he appended his byline to the work without concealment.

The typical seaman-narrative of the nineteenth century usually named the ship or ships aboard which the author served and often identified the commanding officer by name and the junior officers, too, unless these men were adversely criticized or attacked—in which case they were protectively referred to as "Captain R—," "Lieutenant M—," "Sailing-Master L—." The seamen-authors told the events of the voyages in which they had participated just as they had happened and insisted that all scenes were as faithfully presented as they were capable of portraying them. Again, there are differences with *White-Jacket*. The American man-of-war in which Melville was an ordinary seaman, from 17 August 1843 to 14 October 1844, was the first-class frigate *United States*, flagship of the Pacific Squadron. In *White-Jacket*, however, the frigate becomes the *Neversink* and her officers' identities are disguised under such sobriquets as "Captain Claret," "Lieutenant Bridewell," "Surgeon Cuticle," "Mad Jack," and "Selvagee."

As to the veracity of his narrative, Melville publicly addressed quite differently his American and his British readers. From the three-sentence "Note" to the American first edition of the book (there was no Preface), readers must have expected *White-Jacket* to contain straightforward autobiography: "In the year 1843 I shipped as 'ordinary seaman' on board of a United States frigate, then lying in a harbor of the Pacific Ocean.... My man-of-war experiences and observations are incorporated in the present volume." Melville spoke quite otherwise in his "Preface" to the English first edition; he was more cautious and his claims more generalized: "As the object of this work is not to portray the particular man-of-war in which the author sailed, and its officers and crew, but, by illustrative scenes, to paint general life in the Navy, the true name of the frigate is not given. Nor is it here asserted that any of the persons introduced in the following chapters are real individuals" (p. 487). Surely a serious contemporary reader with both the American and English first editions at hand would have been perplexed, and rightly so.

What American familiar with the U.S. Navy of the 1840s could have failed to identify the Commodore of the *Neversink* as Captain Thomas ap Catesby Jones, USN, described in Chapter 6 of *White-Jacket* as "a gallant old man," who, in "gun-boat actions on the Lakes near New Orleans" during the War of 1812, had "received a musket-ball in his shoulder; which...he carries about with him to this day" (p. 21)? On the other hand, who but a personal enemy of the medically competent and administratively able Surgeon of the Fleet Thomas Johnson would have thought of equating him with the eccentric and brutally inhuman Cadwallader Cuticle of the *Neversink*? The subject of documented fact and creative fiction in *White-Jacket* is complex and will be discussed further on in more detail.

As a novel, *White-Jacket* has the thinnest of plot lines, simply recounting the cruise and adventures of a national frigate, homeward-bound. It lacks any consistent, probing exploration of the nature of a human character, unless one, knowing the life of Herman Melville, reads it as a species of spiritual autobiography. Many of the characters are sharply sketched, but sketched only, not fully developed—not even matchless Jack Chase, "our noble First Captain of the Top" (p. 31). The men who people the *Neversink* are most often like the "humours" characters of a Ben Jonson or they are etched, though more skillfully, in the eighteenth-century manner of Edward Ward's *The Wooden World Dissected in the Character of a Ship of War* (1707).

In its extensive documentary aspect and large proportion of exposition, *White-Jacket* has much in common with *Moby-Dick*. With his love of hard facts, Melville explores every nook and cranny of the interior world of a man-of-war even as he later marshalled the realities of cetology in his whaling book. "I let nothing slip, however small," he writes. Sometimes his chapters are simply descriptive or explanatory, like "Cutting In" in *Moby-Dick*; however, exposition in *White-Jacket* is often followed by angry protest, by impassioned polemics, as in the four chapters on flogging. In their little sea-books, sailor-narrators of Melville's time similarly inveighed against inhumane practices of the sea.

Whatever the components of his book—narration, exposition, argument—Melville has them under firm control, and usually in precise balance. Lest elaborate shipboard routine prove tedious to the reader, he moves on to the "story"; lest he seem to protest too much in humanitarian zeal, he returns to the facts of the gun deck. One chapter moves on quite naturally and skillfully to the next. *White-Jacket* is, in fact, as Lewis Mumford observed years ago, "the best reasoned and seasoned of all [Melville's] factual narratives" (p. 278).

The very slight plot of *White-Jacket* primarily concerns the experiences of the narrator and his jacket during the homeward voyage of the U.S. frigate *Neversink* from Callao, Peru, around Cape Horn to Rio de Janeiro, and thence to Norfolk, Virginia. Some attention is also given to doings of the narrator's companions in the maintop and his friends of the After-Guard, as well as to officers of the ship. Events of the cruise constitute a third component of the narrative.

White-Jacket, the narrator, is so-named because in preparation for a winter passage round Cape Horn, he finds no more regulation pea-jackets are available, and devises from a white duck shirt an improvised, padded substitute. His jacket distinguishes him from the five hundred other seamen of the ship, all of whom wear dark, government-issued "reefers," and, in time, it acquires certain portentous, symbolic qualities for the superstitious crew and its troubled wearer. Twice it nearly causes his death.

Besides being soggy and uncomfortable in rainy weather and inadequate protection against icy storms off the Cape, the jacket, though acceptable to men of the maintop, is a source of alienation to others. When, for example, it is White-Jacket's turn to prepare food for his mess, his "duff" (a mixture of flour, raisins, and beef fat) is so unacceptable to his surly messmates, already prejudiced against his jacket, that they urge him to eat elsewhere. White-Jacket is happy to be accepted as a member of Mess No. 1, "The Forty-two-pounder Club," a group that includes Jack Chase, his friend and mentor, the captain of the maintop.

Because of the jacket, the narrator's life is first put in hazard one evening soon after the cooper of the *Neversink* has fallen overboard and drowned. White-Jacket, reclining aloft in a meditative manner high on the main-royal-yard, is thought by superstitious seamen to be the ghost of "Bungs," and they suddenly lower the halyards, almost dropping him to the spar deck far below. Much later, when the ship is off the Capes of Virginia, White-Jacket is ordered to reeve the halyards of the main-topgallant-stun'-sail. In the course of his carrying out this hazardous duty, the ship gives a plunge, pitching him over a hundred feet into the calm sea below. His accursed jacket nearly causes his death, but he rips himself free and is soon rescued by one of the ship's cutters.

Shortly after the ship has rounded the Cape, all hands are summoned to witness punishment. White-Jacket observes the flogging of four seamen, each of whom responds differently to the lash. Then he inveighs against this undemocratic, inhuman practice. Later in the voyage White-Jacket himself is ordered to appear at Captain's-mast, where Captain Claret accuses him of being absent from his duty station during a recent tacking operation. Despite his denial of knowledge of this duty, he is about to be flogged, when Corporal Colbrook and Jack Chase bravely attest to his veracity. Captain Claret surprisingly lets White-Jacket go free. White-Jacket, in his desperation, would have rushed the captain and have carried him overboard rather than suffer the lash.

Considerable space is devoted to small incidents in the maintop, where its petty-officer captain, the literate, eloquent, and sometimes magisterial Jack Chase holds court, directing the actions of White-Jacket and shipmates stationed there, and inviting others to come aloft for visits.

White-Jacket, because of a duty assignment to Carronade No. 5 beside the quarter-deck, gets to know and befriend members of the After-Guard, chiefly the profound, reclusive Nord; Williams, a Yankee "peddler and pedagogue"; Lemsford, a poet who has much difficulty composing verse on the gun-deck of a man-of-war and concealing his manuscript; and a young seaman named Frank. When the *Neversink* is at Rio, Lemsford hides his opus, "Songs of the Sirens," in one of the ship's cannons and is dismayed when the gun is fired. Frank is particularly sensitive about his lowly enlisted status aboard the ship. When a store-ship arrives with supplies for the frigate, Frank learns that his brother is a midshipman aboard the small vessel. Ordered to help transfer supplies to his frigate, Frank manages to conceal his identity and avoid recognition by his brother—such is the gulf between officers and seamen.

The Cape Horn passage of the *Neversink*, stormy and miserably cold, is especially rough on the seamen who must work aloft. Off the pitch of the Cape the frigate is becalmed, then struck by a sudden gale and nearly lost, but Lieutenant Mad Jack (White-Jacket's favorite officer) daringly countermands Captain Claret's orders and saves the ship. Fifty men go aloft in the storm to furl the mainsail. Then it snows.

The *Neversink* finally arrives at Rio for an extended stay. The crew is granted liberty ashore, perhaps because of an eloquent request by Jack Chase, and many enlisted men and officers return to the ship intoxicated. Much liquor is smuggled aboard, and there are more floggings. One ingenious smuggler is Bland, the master-at-arms (surely a blood-brother of the Jackson of *Redburn* and the Claggart of *Billy Budd*, but considerably less demonic). An "organic and irreclaimable scoundrel" and a favorite of the Captain, he is at length apprehended, cashiered, and imprisoned. White-Jacket is surprised to find that Bland, now a seaman and a member of his mess, has become very sociable, cordial, and assured. Before long Bland is restored to his position as the ship's chief policeman.

An enlisted man of the foretop, in trying to swim from the frigate on unauthorized leave, is shot in the thigh by a sentry. His wound provides an opportunity for Cadwallader Cuticle, the surgeon of the squadron, to demonstrate his professional skills to junior naval doctors in port. After a pedantic discussion over the body of the terrified seaman, Cuticle suggests amputation. Though deferentially opposed by some of his juniors, the surgeon exerts his authority and neatly severs the thigh. The seaman dies.

When the *Neversink* finally sails, she races an English frigate and a French man-of-war. In fine warmer weather the ship moves slowly to the north. As she nears home, Captain Claret invokes a recent navy regulation that all beards must be shaved. The seamen, many of whom had cultivated "homeward-bounders," protest and nearly mutiny until dissuaded by Mad Jack's manly eloquence. All submit to shearing except defiant old Ushant, captain of the forecastle, who keeps his hoary beard despite flogging and imprisonment. The *Neversink* at length arrives at Norfolk and the ship's company, paid off, disperses, White-Jacket bidding farewell to his most cherished shipmates, especially Jack Chase, his "liege lord," his "sea-tutor and sire" (p. 396).

The extensive documentation of the 1842–44 voyage of the frigate *United States*, carefully explored by Charles R. Anderson, provides many checks on how closely Melville recorded its events in *White-Jacket*. There is an abstract of the voyage in the National Archives (edited by Professor Anderson), as well as the official logbook, Midshipman William Sharp's journal, and the ship's muster roll and payroll. Two other midshipmen journals have survived: that of Alonzo Jackson in the manuscript division of the Library of Congress and that of William H. Willcox in the Naval Academy Museum. The Medical and Surgical Journal is in the Princeton University Library.

These records show that, though Melville in *White-Jacket* used a good many facts of the historical voyage (the deaths, for example, and the race out of Rio) and followed its general outline, he often departed from actuality. The real frigate's voyage ended in Boston, not Norfolk. The extended stay of the *Neversink* at Rio is in contrast to the brief, eight-day visit of the *United States*. There was no dramatic fall from a stun'-sail into the sea, no amputation, no grog expended. Events that occurred before the homeward cruise find their way into Melville's narrative. Melville, according to a contemporary navy commander, served in the After-Guard, not the maintop. John J. "Jack" Chase's career before joining the real frigate is somewhat altered. And so on.

Expositions, Polemics, and Emblems

In many chapters of the book—some with a narrative thread, some without—Melville details, from an enlisted man's point of view, the day-to-day organization and routine aboard a nineteenth-century federal frigate: the principal divisions and principal officers, the general training, eating habits, sleeping arrangements, the watches, discipline, gunnery, medicine and surgery, religious worship, and other aspects. The documentation is almost exclusively confined to the interior life in a man-of-war. Such practice in exposition served Melville well when he later turned to the cetological chapters of *Moby-Dick*.

White-Jacket has been characterized as the best-humored of Melville's books, but certainly it is not so throughout. From the early chapters on, a polemical line begins in attacking the petty abuses and procedures that made a seaman's life so hard, moves to a climax of impassioned protest in the early chapters on flogging, and drops off again to rise in full militant protest against flogging and the "Articles of War," which Melville considered an archaic, barbarous code. Melville's specific objections to general shipboard life include such long-established practices as having three meals a day crowded into eight hours; denying the night watch access to the berth deck for daytime sleeping; long cruises with little shore liberty; putting the lives of seamen in hazard while showing off the discipline and efficiency of the ship. But against the major evils of the man-of-war world, as he saw them, Melville wrote in anger.

From "the lofty mast-head of an eternal principle" (p. 147), Melville denounced flogging as "religiously, morally, and immutably *wrong*" (p. 146). It violated the principles of our nation, the rights of man, and the innate dignity of his being. For the flogged American seaman, "our Revolution was in vain; to him our Declaration of Independence is a lie" (p. 144). "Join hands with me, then; and, in the name of that Being in whose image the flogged sailor is made, let us demand of Legislators, by what right they dare profane what God himself accounts sacred" (p. 142).

Throughout *White-Jacket* runs an abiding theme of egalitarianism, perhaps the major theme of the book. It is part of the comprehensive liberal and optimistic philosophy which Melville avowed. The surviving evils of the past, he felt, thwarted the promises of America. "The Past is, in many things, the foe of mankind; the Future is, in all things, our friend" (p. 150). The intolerable world of the man-of-war was not beyond redemption."Who knows," he asked, "that this humble narrative may not hereafter prove the history of an obsolete barbarism?" (p. 282).

In view of the haste with which Melville composed *White-Jacket*, the book is surprisingly emblematic, replete with simile and linked-analogy, and freighted with allusion and theoretic overtone. Take a major symbol of the book, the jacket. It could have been a veritable garment, although it was non-regulation clothing, and pea-jackets were in plentiful supply aboard the *United States*. (Melville later wrote Dana that he had disposed of his own jacket in the Charles River on his return from sea.) Whether reality or imaginative creation, the jacket becomes a symbol of alienation and isolation, making its wearer conspicuous among other sailors, the victim of spite, unmerited ostracism, and superstitious fear. It is a symbol of uncomfortable individuality and comprehensive discomfort. In a subjective sense, it is perhaps an objective correlative for the lonely, sensitive, and aloof spirit of the young man who shipped aboard the *United States* in August 1843.

The ship may be viewed as an even more important symbol in *White-Jacket*, one explored exhaustively in its physical structure and its connotative potential. In an early chapter of the book, Melville calls attention to the microcosmic character of the *Neversink*: "For a ship is a bit of terra firma cut off from the main; it is a state in itself; and the captain is its king" (p. 23). In Chapter 18, "A Man-of-war Full as a Nut," such equivalences are fully declared:

> In truth, a man-of-war is a city afloat.... Or, rather, a man-of-war is a lofty, walled, and garrisoned town, like Quebec, where the thoroughfares are mostly ramparts, and peaceable citizens meet armed sentries at every corner.
> Or it is like the lodging-houses in Paris, turned upside down....
> And with its long rows of port-hole casements, each revealing the muzzle of a cannon, a man-of-war resembles a three-story house in a suspicious part of the town, with a basement of indefinite depth, and ugly-looking fellows gazing out at the windows. (pp. 74–75)

By implication, a man-of-war also represents a rational universe, but one sadly lacking in humanity.

Sources and Composition

Howard Vincent, in *The Tailoring of Melville's White-Jacket* (1970), has explored in depth Melville's use of literary source material. He concentrates on a skillful and intense examination of "five little-known sea books" (p. 7), showing how Melville creatively borrowed incidents, details, and colorful language from them and often transmuted his appropriations—even as Shakespeare did the chronicles of Holinshed—into the magic of literature.

Melville's five major "prompt books," Professor Vincent shows, were William McNally's *Evils and Abuses in the Naval and Merchant Service Exposed* (1839), Samuel Leech's *Thirty Years from Home, or A Voice from the Main Deck* (1843), Nathaniel Ames's *A Mariner's Sketches* (1831), "A British Seaman's" *Life on Board a Man-of-War* (1829), and Henry James Mercier and William Gallop's *Life in a Man-of-War, or, Scenes in "Old Ironsides"* (1841).

Melville used *Scenes in "Old Ironsides"* pervasively for humorous, day-to-day man-of-war occurrences. The chapters in *White-Jacket* on the grog's depletion, on "dunderfunk" ("a sea-pie" of hard biscuit, beef fat, molasses, and water), sailor-theatricals, smuggling, and the purser's auction are especially indebted to Mercier and Gallop. From McNally, Melville got ammunition for his attacks on naval abuses; in McNally's master-at-arms Sterritt, he probably found the model for Bland in *White-Jacket*. From Leech came the account of the battle between the *United States* and the *Macedonian* in the War of 1812 which Tawney recalls for comrades who had invited him to the maintop. And Jack Chase's modest yarn of the Battle of Navarino from his viewpoint as a sailor aboard the British flagship came from the pages of *Life on Board a Man-of-War*. (In fact, the actual Chase was not an eyewitness at Navarino, as Professor Vincent shows.)

Perhaps the most creative appropriations which Melville made were those, Professor Vincent observes, which resulted in Chapter 92 in White-Jacket's fall from the weather topgallant yard-arm. Drawing on similar incidents in Ames's *A Mariner's Sketches* and "A British Seaman's" *Life on Board a Man-of-War* and on poetic imagery in Schiller's "The Diver" (in Bulwer-Lytton's translation), Melville synthesized his literary raw material and produced the most famous single section of his book.

Certainly Melville's most ingenious and resourceful use of background reading came from his study of articles in *The Penny Cyclopedia*, 27 volumes. From articles on gunshot wounds, anatomy, amputation, and the like, Melville thoroughly researched the authoritative-sounding chapters in *White-Jacket* which relate to Surgeon Cuticle's amputation of a fore-topman's leg. Willard Thorp first called attention to this source. Additional discoveries have been made by Kathleen E. Kier in her "Annotated Edition of Melville's *White-Jacket*" (*Mel. Diss.*, #523).

Other sources have been suggested by Robert F. Lucid (use of *Two Years Before the Mast*), Thomas L. Philbrick (an article on impressment and a review of Collingwood's correspondence, both in the *Edinburgh Review*, and articles on flogging in the *United States Magazine and Democratic Review*), and John D. Seelye (*The Life and Adventures of John Nicol, Mariner*). Keith Huntress first called attention to the use of *Life in a Man-of-War*. A concise summary of printed influences on *White-Jacket* appears in the "Historical Note" to the NN edition (pp. 417–24).

Of the manuscript of *White-Jacket*, only a fragment, the revised Preface, is extant. This is reproduced, with genetic transcription in the NN edition (pp. 494–97). As with *Redburn*, Melville had proof-sheets printed first by Harper. These he took to London, looking for a British publisher, and there he signed a contract with Bentley. The two-volume English edition appeared in February 1850, followed about six weeks later by the one-volume Harper printing. It is the 1850 American edition that the NN editors used (with some emendations) as their copy-text.

Reception

Most of the contemporary reviews of *White-Jacket* in the journals and newspapers appeared shortly after its English and American publication, and most reviewers enthusiastically rendered, though at greater length, judgments similar to that voiced in *Godey's Lady's Book*: "We like it much."

In England, for example, the book was praised by the *Athenaeum*'s critic for its ability to convey "the poetry of the ship." An unsigned review in *Atlas* found the narrative "marked by all the sobriety of truth" and "enlivened by the sparkling and racy style which characterizes the author in his happiest moments." *John Bull* commended Melville for having written "a first rate sea-novel." And the reviewer in *Bentley's Miscellany*, as might have been expected, was highly favorable in his remarks, claiming for *White-Jacket* the highest rank among Melville's books and finding it preferable to works by Frederick Marryat, James Fenimore Cooper, and Basil Hall. Other reviewers praised the book for its realism (London *Daily News*) and its "peculiarly happy descriptions" (London *Globe and Traveller*).

American reviewers, for the most part, expressed similar warm approval. *White-Jacket* was commended in the *Southern Literary Magazine* for its "elegant learning" and "educated taste"; in the *Home Journal* for "vividness" and "truthfulness"; in *Albion* for "fancy, freshness, and power" and its appeal to serious readers; and in the *Literary World* for its "sound humanitarian lesson" and its lack of sentimentality. The reviewer in *Saroni's Musical Times*, himself a former enlisted man, attested to its authenticity. George Ripley in the New York *Tribune* described it as a "glowing log-book of a year's cruise." Reviewers of humanitarian and democratic persuasion applauded the attacks on naval abuses and the calls for reform. Melville, a *Knickerbocker* writer declared, was "on the right ground at last."

Although the critical consensus was favorable, there were minority voices of dissent. The *Britannia* reviewer, who found the book wearisome, lectured Melville and American authors in general on their dependence on "mental vigour" and lack of "mental discipline." The New Bedford *Mercury*'s critic accused Melville of "an unaccountable penchant for fine writing" and "lavender phrases." A brief notice in the *United States Magazine and Democratic Review* was inimical throughout, chiefly because of Melville's partiality for British seamen and the Royal Navy. Almost equally hostile was the critic of the Boston *Post* who objected to Melville's "autobiographical twaddle" and questioned his competence to evaluate such subjects as the "Articles of War" and corporal punishment in the navy. A few reviewers mixed praise and adverse criticism, as did George Ripley, who found "great power and interest" in *White-Jacket* as well as "bad Carlylese."

More extended accounts of *White-Jacket*'s early reception may be found in Hetherington (pp. 157–88) and in Thorp's "Historical Note" to the NN edition (pp. 429–36). Eleven reviews are reprinted in Branch (*Crit. Her.*, pp. 217–36) and short critical excerpts appear in *The Melville Log*. Hershel Parker has reproduced the Harper and Brothers advertisement, which contains favorable quotations from six British and two American reviews (*Recognition*, p. 32).

After the initial successful sales of *White-Jacket*, the rash of early favorable notices, and a few scattered reviews in the following six years, there was a long period of decline during which the book was almost completely forgotten. Harpers, in its third printing, issued only 257 copies in 1855. After Melville's death, Arthur Stedman was reponsible for an edition, printed in 1892. Like *Redburn*, *White-Jacket* had to await the Melville Revival and its aftermath to receive the attention and analysis it deserved.

Editions

The paperback NN edition of *White-Jacket* (1970) is recommended for instruction and study because of its accurate text and readable type, its "Historical Note," and textual paraphernalia. Arthur R. Humphreys has edited and written an introduction for the only annotated volume in English, published by Oxford University Press in 1966. The notes are very helpful to landlubbers, and there is an appendix containing definitions of "Some Nautical Terms." Walter Weber's German translation (*Weissjacke*) provides thirty pages of annotation. This volume, based on the Constable and Company text and containing a useful introduction, was published in Switzerland in 1948. The most recent edition (without notes) was published in paperback in 1979 by the New American Library as a Signet Classic. Its concise, incisive introduction is by Alfred Kazin.

The paperback Rinehart Edition (1967), now out of print, has a valuable introduction by Hennig Cohen. Kathleen E. Kier's 1980 dissertation devotes a great deal of attention in her 117 pages of annotation to the "densely allusive" character of *White-Jacket*. She finds that "much of Melville's seeming erudition" was due to his plundering of the *Penny Cyclopedia*.

History of Criticism

In one of the most percipient of the analyses of *White-Jacket*, Warner Berthoff (pp. 35–38) identifies the problem faced over the years by critics of the book: "I suspect that the difficulty criticism has had with *White-Jacket* is principally one of finding a standard to judge it by. Contemporary preoccupation with the art of the novel and its special norms may be at fault in this. For *White-Jacket* is not a novel. . . . Its motives are chiefly documentary and polemical" (p. 35).

For these reasons, critics, by and large, have taken other scholarly stances. After Charles Anderson's thorough dissection of fact and fiction, and *White-Jacket* was no longer considered outright autobiography, attention was focused on the sources. New sources and analogues continue to be identified (see, for example, Duban), but that area of investigation seems near its end.

On the factual level, Livingston Hunt assessed Melville's competence as a naval historian. Harrison Hayford identified Lemsford, "The Sailor Poet of *White-Jacket*," as Ephraim Curtiss Hine. Frederick and Joyce Kennedy uncovered a cache of correspondence between two prominent naval officers, Commander Samuel F. Dupont and Lieutenant Charles Henry Davis, who were outraged at the book. Dupont urged Davis to write a strong critical article, pointing out errors in *White-Jacket*, but Davis reasoned that to do so would only attract attention to a book that soon would be forgotten. Charles Anderson printed a long, hitherto unpublished rejoinder by another naval officer, Commander Thomas O. Selfridge, Sr., who was an acquaintance of Dupont and Davis. Wilson Heflin called attention to the striking parallel between the arrival of the midshipman brother of seaman Frank in Chapter 59 and the actual arrival of Midshipman Stanwix Gansevoort, Melville's first cousin, aboard the store-ship *Erie*, which carried supplies for the frigate *United States*. Heflin suggested that Chapter 59 was "intended also to be read in a special way by a limited audience, one which would include Melville's immediate family and an alienated first cousin" (p. 57).

Howard Vincent, in a pioneer interpretation in the *New England Quarterly*, called attention to the symbolism in the book, finding the jacket "a symbol of pseudo-self-sufficiency" (p. 308). His readings there are augmented by scattered critical observations in *The Tailoring of Melville's White-Jacket*. James E. Miller felt that the initiation theme that began with *Redburn* was continued in *White-Jacket* and that the actual and symbolic baptism of the protagonist in his fall into the sea contributed to his spiritual development (pp. 72–73).

In *Melville and Authority* (1968), Nicholas Canaday, Jr., analyzed "the complex institutionalized authority of the navy" (pp. 22–36), as Melville portrays it. The usually accepted view that Melville's pervasive attitude in the book is democratic is challenged persuasively in Larry J. Reynolds's "Antidemocratic Emphasis in *White-Jacket*." Priscilla Allen Zirker examined "Evidence of the Slavery Dilemma in *White-Jacket*" (pp. 477–92) and found Melville's view ambiguous. In another article, "*White-Jacket*: Melville and the Man-of-War Microcosm," she showed how naval officers, with more freedom aboard ship and on shore, wrote travel books very different from the man-of-war narratives that concentrated on the interior life of navy ships.

Problems for Future Study

No logbook of the *St. Lawrence*'s 1839 Liverpool voyage has turned up, but it is well worth the hunting, if only to provide the checks on autobiographical aspects of *Redburn* that were unavailable to Gilman. Events of Captain Oliver Brown's earlier career as a shipmaster might be revealed in maritime records of Philadelphia, a port from which he sailed on several voyages. Was there a relationship between Joseph M. Shaw, chief mate of the *St. Lawrence*, and Melville's future father-in-law, Lemuel Shaw, and could the mate have been instrumental in Melville's shipping aboard that vessel?

Study of the maritime pages of New York newspapers of 1849 and of books about Irish immigrants might yield sources for Melville's chapters on the return voyage of the *Highlander*. Contemporary English novels, such as those by Bulwer-Lytton and Disraeli, might shed light on the London chapters of *Redburn*.

Critics might well devote additional attention to some of the characters in the book. The memorable Jackson is Melville's earliest creation of a diabolical, organically evil character. To what extent could he be based, not on unhappy memories of the thirty-one-year-old Robert Jackson of the *St. Lawrence*, but on some theory of evil that came from Melville's reading? Why did not Melville develop in more detail the character of the mate, who is cruelly impatient and demanding of young Redburn, yet very compassionate toward the sick immigrants? Finally, reasons for changes in the roles of Harry Bolton might be explored. He first appears as a very equivocal character, a kind of adolescent confidence man, then as a reckless gambler, then as a shipboard incompetent, and ultimately as a helpless foreigner in a strange land. In terms of Melville's artistic intentions, how does one account for these changes?

If the "Watch, Quarter, and Station Bill" of the frigate *United States*, 1842–44, could be found, it would settle once and for all for students of *White-Jacket* whether Melville was stationed in the After-Guard, as was claimed by Rear-Admiral Selfridge, or was in the maintop, as is usually supposed. This small manuscript book, which would show all of Melville's assignments was probably among the papers of Rear Admiral James Lardner, USN, who as a lieutenant was executive officer of the ship. He was a native of Philadelphia. The papers of Fleet Surgeon William Johnson and those of Chaplain Theodore Bartow might contain reactions to the portrayals of Cadwallader Cuticle and the transcendental sea-minister in *White-Jacket*. It would seem that all the important source-hunting has been done; yet further searching of the *Penny Magazine*, nine volumes of which (weekly issues, 1832–40) were in the seamen's library of the *United States*, and the *Penny Cyclopedia* might prove rewarding.

It is difficult to predict in what directions future criticism of *White-Jacket* may turn, but there is no reason for the foreclosure of interpretation. Some of the new critical disciplines, perhaps semiotics, may provide important insights; some may also yield obfuscation.

WORKS CITED

Anderson, Charles R. "A Reply to Herman Melville's *White-Jacket* by Rear-Admiral Thomas O. Selfridge, Sr." *American Literature* 7 (May 1935): 123–44.

———. *Journal of a Cruise to the Pacific Ocean, 1842–1844, in the Frigate United States; With Notes on Herman Melville.* Durham, N.C.: Duke University Press, 1937.

———. *Melville in the South Seas.* New York: Columbia University Press, 1939.

Arvin, Newton. *Herman Melville.* New York: William Sloane Associates, 1950.

Berthoff, Warner. *The Example of Herman Melville.* Princeton, N.J.: Princeton University Press, 1962.

Bowen, Merlin. "*Redburn* and the Angle of Vision." *Modern Philology* 52 (November 1954): 100–109.

Canaday, Nicholas, Jr. *Melville and Authority.* Gainesville: University of Florida Press, 1968.

Dillingham, William B. *An Artist in the Rigging: The Early Works of Herman Melville.* Athens: University of Georgia Press, 1972.

Duban, James. "Melville's Use of Irving's *Knickerbocker History* in *White-Jacket*." *Melville Society Extracts* No. 46 (May 1981): 1, 4–6.

Fiedler, Leslie A. *Love and Death in the American Novel.* New York: Criterion Books, 1960.

Franklin, H. Bruce. "Redburn's Wicked End." *Nineteenth-Century Fiction* 20 (1965): 190–94.

Gilman, William H. *Melville's Early Life and Redburn.* New York: New York University Press, 1951.

Hayford, Harrison. "The Sailor-Poet of *White-Jacket*." *Boston Public Library Quarterly* 3 (July 1951): 221–28.

Heflin, Wilson L. "A Man-of-War Button Divides Two Cousins." *Boston Public Library Quarterly* 3 (January 1951): 51–60.

Hetherington, Hugh W. *Melville's Reviewers, British and American: 1846–1891.* Chapel Hill, N.C.: University of North Carolina Press, 1961.

Hunt, Livingston. "Herman Melville as a Naval Historian." *Harvard Graduates' Magazine* 39 (September 1930): 22–30.

Huntress, Keith. "Melville's Use of a Source for *White-Jacket*." *American Literature* 17 (March 1945): 66–74.

Kennedy, Frederick J., and Joyce Deveau Kennedy. "Some Naval Officers React to *White-Jacket*: An Untold Story." *Melville Society Extracts* No. 41 (February 1980): 3–11.

Kier, Kathleen E. "An Annotated Edition of Melville's *White-Jacket*." Ph.D. Diss., Columbia University, 1980. [*Mel. Diss.*, #523.]

Lewis, R.W.B. *The American Adam.* Chicago: University of Chicago Press, 1955.

Lish, Terence G. "Melville's *Redburn*: A Study in Dualism." *English Language Notes* 5 (1967): 113–20.

Lucid, Robert F. "The Influence of *Two Years Before the Mast* on Herman Melville." *American Literature* 31 (November 1959): 243–56.

McCarthy, Paul. "Symbolic Elements in *White-Jacket*." *Midwest Quarterly* 7 (July 1966): 309–25.

Matthiessen, F. O. *American Renaissance: Art and Expression in the Age of Emerson and Whitman.* New York: Oxford University Press, 1941.

Melville, Herman. *Redburn: His First Voyage.* Edited, with an Introduction by Harold Beaver. Harmondsworth, England: Penguin Books Ltd., 1976.

———.*Weissjacke.* Deutsch von Walter Weber. Zurich: Conzett & Huber, 1948.

———. *White-Jacket.* Ed. Arthur Humphreys. London: Oxford University Press, 1966.

———. *White-Jacket.* Introduction by Alfred Kazin. New York: New American Library, 1979.

Miller, James E. *A Reader's Guide to Herman Melville.* New York: Farrar, Straus, and Cudahy, 1962.

Mumford, Lewis. *Herman Melville: A Study of his Life and Vision.* New York: Harcourt, Brace & Co., 1929.

Philbrick, Thomas L. "Another Source for *White-Jacket*." *American Literature* 29 (January 1958): 431–39.

———. "Melville's 'Best Authorities.' " *Nineteenth-Century Fiction* 15 (September 1960): 171–79.

Reynolds, Larry J. "Anti-Democratic Emphasis in *White-Jacket.*" *American Literature* 48 (March 1976): 13–28.

Rosenberry, Edward H. *Melville.* London, Henley, and Boston: Routledge & Kegan Paul, 1979.

Sale, Arthur. "The Glass Ship: A Recurrent Image in Melville." *Modern Language Quarterly* 11 (June 1956): 118–27.

Schaible, Robert M. "An Annotated Edition of Herman Melville's *Redburn.*" Ph.D. Diss., University of Tennessee, 1971. [*Mel. Diss.*, #258.]

Schroeter, James. "*Redburn* and the Failure of Mythic Criticism." *American Literature* 39 (November 1967): 279–97.

Seelye, John D. " 'Spontaneous Impress of Truth': Melville's Jack Chase: A Source, an Analogue, a Conjecture." *Nineteenth-Century Fiction* 20 (March 1966): 367–76.

Thompson, Lawrance. *Melville's Quarrel with God.* Princeton, N.J.: Princeton University Press, 1952.

Thorp, Willard. "Redburn's Prosy Old Guidebook." *PMLA* 53 (December 1938): 1146–56.

Vincent, Howard P. *The Tailoring of Melville's White-Jacket.* Evanston, Ill.: Northwestern University Press, 1970.

———. "*White-Jacket*: An Essay in Interpretation." *New England Quarterly* 22 (September 1949): 304–15.

Zirker, Priscilla Allen. "Evidence of the Slavery Dilemma in *White-Jacket.*" *American Quarterly* 18 (Fall 1966): 477–92.

———. "*White-Jacket*: Melville and the Man-of-War Microcosm." *American Quarterly* 25 (March 1973): 32–47.

7

MOBY-DICK:
DOCUMENT, DRAMA, DREAM

Walter E. Bezanson

Moby-Dick is an absolutely stunning book, written by a young American genius, consciously speaking out from the New World at a climactic moment in his career.

It is not necessary to share this view in order to have a good time reading *Moby-Dick*. In fact, it may well be better to approach it with a show-me skepticism, thus adopting one of Ishmael's stances even before discovering it. The book, published in England and America in 1851, though widely reviewed at the time, fell into virtual obscurity until about 1920. Since then a rising chorus of praise has lifted *Moby-Dick* to the status of an American classic, and in recent decades, one of the Great Books of the Western World. Thus, along with the *Odyssey* and *Gulliver's Travels*, say, it now risks that kiss of death which popular culture usually bestows on such literature, leaving an embalmed text to academic autopsy and nervous skimming by students. In the meantime fragments of "the story"—crazy old one-legged Ahab in worldwide pursuit of the fabulous White Whale—takes up a life of its own in jokes and cartoons, restaurant menus, motel signs, and seaside souvenirs based on *Classics Comics* or cassettes of Hollywood movies.

And no wonder. For the "plot" of *Moby-Dick* is a humdinger, old as the Biblical story of Jonah and *his* whale and as recent as Faulkner's "The Bear." Chase fables and quest tales seem archetypal, widespread through folklore, fairy tale, epic narratives. Typically a hero figure at last encounters unknown powers which prove variously indifferent, divine, or demonic, depending on the teller of the tale, and the mood of the listeners. The quester may be either crippled and ultimately killed

(Ahab), or by a miracle saved (Ishmael). A powerful theme, and from the day of publication there have been those who wished that Ishmael had told his story more simply and quit. These are the readers who, one quarter through the book and shortly after Ishmael has boarded the *Pequod*, find themselves so uncomfortably at sea as to go over the side and repair to the local diner. No illusions are necessary; *Moby-Dick* will baffle the novice, stretch the apprentice, and test the veteran. Of course there is no "right" reading of Ishmael's account, as anyone knows who has sampled the mountain of commentary it has provoked. Perry Miller used to enjoy telling his Harvard colleagues that the Melville industry had replaced whaling in the New England economy; but the trade is no longer regional, monomania having spread through India and Japan, as well as England and Europe. The scholars have no exclusive fishing rights, however, and the Common Reader, if he still exists, should take courage. This is a wonderful book, full of delights and provocations of both thought and style.

GERMINATION: "I LOVE ALL MEN WHO *DIVE*"

Selecting two adventures from his nearly four years in the Pacific (1840–44)—a month's "captivity" among a tribe of Marquesan natives, and subsequent beachcombing in Tahiti and nearby Eimeo—Melville had worked up his first two highly popular and mildly scandalous narratives: *Typee* (1846) and *Omoo* (1847). With these two books he had weathered, may even have profited from, the stir over "sea-freedom" and anti-missionary sentiments. A deeper problem, at least to his English publisher, John Murray, who included both books in "The Home and Colonial Library," a series that included sober travel accounts like Darwin's *Voyage*, was to know whether Melville was writing facts or fiction. It was a problem that ragged Melville a good bit too, and would continue to do so. For he often worked best when he occupied a space midway between fact and fiction; and this he complicated still further by borrowing other writer's adventures, modifying them to his own convenience. This problem enlarged enormously, of course, with his third book, *Mardi* (1849), in which after a hundred pages of more or less realistic marine adventures, the story took off into an extraordinary mixture of allegorical romance, contemporary social-political satire, and self-discovery. When *Mardi* was savaged by most critics, Melville made a quick comeback with *Redburn* (1849); for this "little nursery tale" as he disarmingly called it in a letter to Richard Henry Dana, Jr. (*Letters*, p. 93), he had turned back to his first sea adventure, his round trip as a green hand aboard the London packet *St. Lawrence* (1839). This he followed up immediately with *White-Jacket or The World in a Man-of-War* (1850), a sturdy Dana-like account growing out of his naval enlistment and ride home from the Pacific aboard the frigate *United States*.

By the beginning of 1850, therefore, Melville had pretty well exhausted his sea experiences with the curious exception of whaling. His eighteen months aboard the whale ship *Acushnet*, leading to his island adventures, had been followed by another six months on board the Australian whaler *Lucy Ann* and the Nantucket whaler *Charles & Henry*. Yet these experiences, the most dangerous and most spellbinding phase of his adventures, had not yet been used centrally in his writing. He had made scattered references to whaling in the first five books. Writing a review of J. Ross Browne's *Etchings of a Whaling Cruise* obviously excited him, for towards the end he suddenly opened out into three paragraphs that anticipate action scenes in *Moby-Dick*. And the first eight chapters of *Mardi*, perhaps under the stimulation of the review, took place aboard the whaler *Arcturion*. But the intellectual and rhetorical turbulences of *Mardi* took Melville elsewhere just then. From our vantage point it seems as if he consciously withheld his greatest subject, waiting for the moment of his own readiness.

Two very rich interludes in 1849 deeply affected Melville's readiness for *Moby-Dick*. First came two months in Boston—February and March. Then in October, he took off for England, to market *White-Jacket*, and to explore Europe to the extent his money held out; the trip lasted four months. In between Boston and Europe, back in New York City, he raced through the writing of *Redburn* and *White-Jacket* like a man in an enormous hurry.

The Boston interlude was spent in the heart of Brahmin culture, in the large and handsome Beacon Hill home of his wife's family, presided over by Lemuel Shaw, chief Justice of the Supreme Court of Massachusetts. The social and intellectual challenges from New England to a suddenly popular young writer from New York were immense, but Melville seems to have flourished under them. He had already been checked out by the Shaw's circle of friends before his marriage to Elizabeth in 1847, and a year later by some thirty of Boston's elite at a party given by the Shaws. Present on both occasions was Richard Henry Dana, Jr., a family friend and, as the author of *Two Years Before the Mast* (1840), quite clearly the Boston author against whom Melville was to be measured. By the second meeting Dana thought he "ought to do something" for Melville and staged a proper bachelor party for him at the Parker House, Boston's best hotel and restaurant. Dana produced a group of young literati (Whipple, Woodman, Metcalf, Spooner—all long since forgotten) and "gave them cold birds, fruit champagne & hock" (*Mel.Log*, pp. 254, 278).

Now Melville was back again, and there were two more evenings with Dana at the Parker House, once to meet another Dana, once to meet a

Cabot who had been to sea. Melville must have felt flushed with victory; Dana's letter to his brother said Melville was "incomparable in dramatic story telling" (*Mel.Log*,p. 293). Playing the role of "Typee" (as he was often denominated), he was getting the same kind of bemused admiration from the Shaw coterie that he had won from the Duyckinck circle in New York. It also helped, of course, that he and Elizabeth had " come home" for the birth of their first child, Malcolm; and Melville's high expectations for *Mardi*, coming out in April, no doubt was a covert source of exhilaration in his performances. The four quite wonderful letters that he wrote back to Evert Duyckinck (*Letters*, pp. 76–84), who no doubt passed them around, showed the immense leap of his ambitions brought on by the writing of *Mardi*. He wrote eloquently of discovering Shakespeare, as if he had never heard of him before, and of what it meant to have the leisure to give himself utterly to reading the plays. "Dolt & ass that I am I have lived more than 29 years, & until a few days ago, never made close acquaintance with the divine William." On he burbled, comparing him to the Messiah (to the consternation of the orthodox Duyckinck), and ranking him with the same triumvirate of archangels—Gabriel, Raphael, and Michael—whom he would ritually name in the Extracts section of *Moby-Dick* (p. 2). These first two letters to Duyckinck mark clearly the beginning of Melville's obsessive encounter with Shakespeare, a central figure eighteen months later in Melville's excited review, "Hawthorne and His *Mosses*," and in turn an immense, unnamed presence in *Moby-Dick*.

Emerson was the other powerful voice Melville heard while in Boston. A little further along Beacon Street at the Freeman Chapel, the Concord seer and poet was giving a course of five lectures on "Mind and Manners in the Nineteenth Century," and Melville went to hear him. "Say what they will," he wrote Duyckinck (who undoubtedly was a "they"), "he's a great man" (*Letters*, p. 77). And when Duyckinck apparently teased Melville in a return letter (lost), for having surrendered to New England's peculiar pieties, Melville replied in elaborate comic defense that "I was very agreeably disappointed in Mr. Emerson"; he is "no common humbug" but "an uncommon man," not at all lost in "transcendentalisms, myths & oracular gibberish." Surely he delighted the New York group with a quip about "this Plato who talks thro' his nose"; but then he went on to classify Emerson among "the whole corps of thought-divers, that have been diving & coming up again with bloodshot eyes since the world began." It was Emerson in fact, in this second letter, who evoked Melville's famous phrase: "I love all men who *dive*" (pp. 78–79). And as he had in the previous letter, he again mingled Shakespeare and Emerson as he wrote, two voices that at times would frame a subtextual *agon* in the pages of *Moby-Dick*.

In the final letter from Boston two other suggestive themes arise. One is a moving paragraph on a mutual friend's madness, leading Melville to say: "And he who has never felt, momentarily, what madness is has but a mouthful of brains," and so on to imagining the "sort of sensation permanent madness . . . may be" (p. 83). The other theme is that of skepticism and heresy, brought excitedly to mind by his purchase of an eighteenth-century edition of Pierre Bayle's Dictionary. Monomania and skeptical views of religion and myth were to be central in *Moby-Dick*. The Boston interval marks the reaching of Melville's mind beyond the still unwritten *Redburn* and *White-Jacket* to his sixth book.

Melville's second recess from writing began 11 October 1849 when he took off for his first serious contact with Europe. He sailed with letters and guide books from his urbane and well-traveled friends, the brothers Duyckinck. He also bore documents from the Shaw-Dana-Everett powerhouse in Boston. Edward Everett—Unitarian minister, Harvard professor, editor of the *North American Review*, governor of Massachusetts, recently minister to England, currently president of Harvard—broke his rules against writing letters of introduction because of Melville's "extraordinary merit" and the claims of Shaw's friendship. Melville's daring request to his father-in-law for letters from Emerson to Carlyle and perhaps to some others apparently didn't work (Metcalf, pp. 64–65).

Most of what we know about this crucial four-month trip, just preceding *Moby-Dick*, is contained in two small notebooks Melville kept, apparently in part to be shown to Lizzie when he got home, and well edited by his granddaughter, Eleanor Melville Metcalf. An uneven, almost random, record of events and reactions, the 1849 *Journal* probably hides as much as it tells. But the sea voyage (pp. 3–18) made him wide awake and full of memories. Although the *Southampton*, an old-fashioned square-rigged packet, was more than three times the tonnage of the *Acushnet*, Melville was excited by being under sail again after five years ashore. He walked the deck day and night, climbed to the masthead the first morning "to recall the old emotions," hung down over the ship's side within a foot of the sea in a vain effort to save a suicide, performed "occasional feats in the rigging," and seems thoroughly to have enjoyed the admiration of often seasick passengers as well as one young lady who kept looking up at him while reading *Omoo*. For the first time he saw corporsants on the yardarms.

The big event of the voyage was surely his encounter with George Adler, a young German lexicographer and friend of Duyckinck's with whom Melville at once hit it off. By the second day out Melville knew Adler was "full of the German metaphysics, & discourses of Kant, Swedenborg, &c" (p. 4). Adler's impact on Melville during the next eight weeks was powerful and timely. Before they separated in Paris they saw each other almost daily (I estimate some forty-four days of conversation, drinks, dinner, sightseeing, and the like.) On at least nine occasions,

Melville specifically refers to these meetings as involving "metaphysics," or "high German metaphysics," or even (the very thing reviewers would continue to charge him with) "riding on the German horse again" (1849 *Journal*). Melville's attitude toward Adler seems to have been, beyond any personal attraction, that of an excited undergraduate turned on by an informed and eloquent teacher, even to the point of jotting down at night specific "notes" from the day's lecture in the rigging. "Spent a good part of the day aloft with Adler, in conversation" (pp. 10–11). Off the Banks, on a rainy day, Adler and another young traveler who had been in Germany, came to Melville's cabin for whiskey and talk: "We had an extraordinary time & did not break up till after two in the morning. We talked metaphysics continually, & Hegel, Schegel [sic], Kant &c were discussed under the influence of the whiskey" (p. 12). In addition to being "an exceedingly amiable man," Adler was, as Melville said, "a fine scholar whose society is improving in a high degree" (p. 9). His *Dictionary of the German and English Languages* (1849) had just been published, and in January 1851 he was to send Melville his translation of Goethe's *Iphigenia in Tauris* (*Mel. Log*, p. 403). Nothing on the trip suggests that Melville wanted to read the Germans, or proposed to; but certain of their questions about the nature of nature, about religion, man, history, and the arts, were obviously his questions too. It was to writers, however, not philosophers, that Melville turned once the course with Adler was over.

Melville went ashore in high spirits, recalling ten years earlier when he was twenty: "*then* a sailor, *now* H. M. author of "Peedee" "Hullabaloo" & "Pog-Dog" (p. 18). He kept daily records of eating and drinking, general sightseeing, five excursions out of London, and visits to eight different publishers until finally *White-Jacket* was placed with Bentley. He wrote a comic account of a very formal dinner at John Murray's, and twice was invited by George Rogers to his famous breakfasts. At dinners or parties he met enough of the current literati (Alexander Kinglake, B. W. Procter ["Barry Cornwall"], John Gibson Lockhart, and the comic writer "Arthur Crowquill") to be persuaded that he could hold his own with the best of them, that it was okay to be an American. He seems even to have persuaded the formidable Murray that the author of *Typee* and *Omoo* was both a gentleman and a sailor, named Melville.

Three of his pursuits while abroad bear meaningfully on *Moby-Dick*: theater, church services, and book-buying. In London he went to the theater nine times in three weeks; in Paris he saw "three comical comedies," went to the Opéra Comique, and twice tried to get to see the great actress, Rachel, without success; even in Germany he saw some vaudeville. Over and beyond casual sightseeing in a score of churches and cathedrals Melville attended Sunday services on six of the seven Sundays he was abroad, going to two services on two occasions; on his final Sunday in London he did not go to church because he was breakfasting with Rogers and two other writers until early afternoon. He relished book-buying and cursed his lean purse. A "much desired" copy of Rousseau's *Confessions,* and Goethe's *Autobiography* and *Letters,* pleased him. Seventeenth-century folios of Jonson, D'Avenant, and Beaumont and Fletcher, plus a pocket Shakespeare and Marlowe's plays tell us how fixed his mind was on drama. His taste for the Gothic led him to *The Castle of Otranto* and *Frankenstein.* How ravenous a reader he was when hungry: while waiting for a clerk he "ran out, & at last got hold of 'The Opium Eater' & began it in the office. A wonderful thing, that book." The next day: "Have just this moment finished the 'Opium Eater.' A most wondrous book." And the following day: went for a walk "After finishing the marvellous book" (pp. 80–81). Edward Moxon, Lamb's friend and publisher, was charmed enough by Melville, who just happened to have boned up on Lamb in the ship's library, to send Melville a set of Elia's works.

We know little of what Melville thought or did during the long five-week voyage home aboard the packet ship *Independence.* His list of book purchases and a few reading notes end his 1849 *Journal,* which he closed out soon after sailing on 25 December (pp. 83–86). He made no comments here about his next book, nor did he discuss whaling. The only leakage in his notebooks is an amusing verbal sequence of two metaphors and a pun: "Strolled through Fleet Market—butchering under hatches—blubber rooms." That night, returning very late from a bachelor drinking party: "through Oxford Street home & turned flukes." And the next day, seeing the royal carriage at Windsor Castle, inevitably, "& long live the 'prince of whales' " (pp. 41–42). One quick scene at the Market and memory flashed. During eight of the seventeen weeks away from home he was at sea. He was in daily contact with two sociable captains, both of whom told stories. Coming home, if again he spent hours aloft, there were certainly swarming memories of the Pacific, now perhaps melting with Adler's metaphysics, with the scenes and language of theaters, with the words of many sermons and whatever reflections they had stirred in his mind, and with rhythmic lines from the trunk-full of old books in his cabin, including a folio of his favorite, Sir Thomas Browne. We do not know what plans or reveries were swirling through his mind while at sea, or when he docked, 1 February 1850 in New York Harbor. But the events we have been following suggest a period of profound germination. The cresting of purpose which had begun with *Mardi* by now was driving him relentlessly toward his next book.

Adler spent more time with Melville than anyone outside his family in the period between *Mardi* and the completion of *Moby-Dick.* He wrote Duyckinck from Paris in February, some two weeks after Melville got home. He regretted Melville's departure, "but all I could do to check and fix his restless mind for a while at least was of no avail." Melville left, he thought, from homesickness, and because "the instinctive impulse of his imagination to assimilate and perhaps to work up into some beautiful chimaeras . . . the materials he had already gathered in his travels, would not allow him to prolong his stay" (1849 *Journal*, p. 139).

COMPOSITION: "A CERTAIN SOMETHING UNMANAGEABLE IN US"

When he began to write in February of 1850 Melville did not know that it would take eighteen months to complete the manuscript of *Moby-Dick*, but he was ready for the encounter. During the process of composition he kept re-shaping and re-visioning his material, trying to meet the enormous demands he was now putting on himself. Surely too there were cycles of enthusiasm and despair and there was some misjudging, obviously, on his own part, of the cost of time. He told Dana after only three months that he was "half way" and wrote his English publisher, by the end of June, that his new work would be ready "in the latter part of the coming autumn" (*Letters*, pp. 108, 109). These discrepancies here have led scholars into an intricate controversy as to whether or not there were "two *Moby-Dicks*, " or even three. This is not the place to enter or detail that argument; those interested can sample some versions of it cited in my bibliography: in chronological order, Howard P. Vincent, pp. 22–25; Leon Howard, pp. 150–179; George Stewart; James Barbour; Robert Milder; Harrison Hayford, "Unnecessary Duplicates." But I wish, as we go along, to counter the legend, too often picked up by critics and passed on to readers: that up until August of 1850, when Melville first met Hawthorne at the famous week of partying in the Berkshires, or that up until any other event one might suggest as occurring about then, Melville had been engaged in writing a straightforward account of whaling adventures and only *then*, as it were, virtually started over or totally recast what was so far done. The implication here is that Melville was *not* ready for the kind of book *Moby-Dick* became, that he despaired of picking up where he had left off with *Mardi*, that the critics, or financial need, or self-doubt, or a combination of these for six months had him tied down. But the profile that emerges from reading the documents, beginning with the almost rudely bold letter he wrote to John Murray on 25 March 1848, a virtual declaration of literary independence, takes quite another shape.

Melville's statements written to key people should be taken seriously. He is bored with "*facts*" and "longing to plume my pinions for a flight"— this to Murray about *Mardi*, which on reading the American sheets, Murray declined to publish. To Bentley, who did publish *Mardi*, he writes, with obvious comic cynicism, that *Redburn* will have "no metaphysics, no conic-sections, nothing but cakes & ale." Then, with both

Redburn and *White-Jacket* done in a rush, he dares tell his father-in-law that "no reputation that is gratifying to me, can possibly be achieved by either of these books," since they were merely "two *jobs*, which I have done for money—being forced to it, as other men are to sawing wood." And finally, from Europe, he writes back to his friend and mentor, Duyckinck, that *Redburn* seems well received, "But I hope I shall never write such a book again,"—that is, "a beggarly 'Redburn!' " (*Letters*, pp. 70, 86, 91, 95). Melville's point of view, not feigned but quite unfair to the narrative verve of *Redburn* and *White-Jacket*, was that he had wasted his new self on these two books. In the meantime he stood by *Mardi*, stubbornly, as the kind of book that he believed in, telling his publisher that "some of us scribblers, My Dear Sir, always have a certain something unmanageable in us, that bids us do this or that, and be done it must— hit or miss" (p. 86). He tells Justice Shaw "it is my earnest desire to write those sort of books which are said to 'fail.'—Pardon this egotism" (p. 92). And from London stubbornly holding his ground he writes Duyckinck: "Had I not written & published 'Mardi', in all likelihood, I would not be as wise as I am now, or may be" (p. 96).

Melville's state of mind when he reached home is nicely revealed in the letter he penned to Duyckinck the day after docking (*Letters*, pp. 101–103). He presented Duyckinck with "a fine old spicy duodecimo" edition of Butler's *Hudibras*, and, tellingly, with a three-volume edition of *Mardi* which he had brought home from England. Duyckinck had reviewed the American edition of *Mardi* the previous April, calling it a "purely original invention" and "an extraordinary book," except when "attempting to handle the problem of the universe" (*Recognition*, pp. 9– 13). Notice that Melville, in defending *Mardi*, shows the strongly "me- taphysical" turn of his mind just at the time when he was about to start his whaling book: he conceives of *Mardi* as an aloe, "now unblown (em- blematically, the leaves, you perceive, are uncut)," which may or may not flower in another hundred years. Do not cut the leaves, but wait for the flowering; meanwhile, bind the volumes in "old parchment (from some old Arabic M.S.S. on Astrology)" and keep it "sealed" with a "Sphynx" as "device" on the binding. This is the language of a "crack'd Archangel"—Melville's phrase for Sir Thomas Browne, which so de- lighted Duyckinck (*Mel. Log*, p. 273)—suggesting how richly steeped in seventeenth century mannerisms Melville was at this time; that language will underwrite the elaborately emblematic devices which flower often in *Moby-Dick*. A second significance lies in the image Melville chose to describe the fate of *Mardi*: "almost everywhere...driven forth like a wild, mystic Mormon into shelterless exile." The exile theme here links powerfully with the Ishmael theme, central to *Moby-Dick*, which he is about to begin writing.

It may be useful to divide Melville's eighteen months' work on *Moby-*

Dick into four periods: the six months before the August house parties; the August scene in the Berkshires and the writing of "Hawthorne and His *Mosses*"; the long winter of work after Melville moved his family from New York to the Pittsfield farm he bought and named Arrowhead; and the last rush, summer of 1851, to finish his manuscript. What Melville was doing and thinking about, as revealed in his letters and the volcanic "*Mosses*" essay, tell us much about his creative ambitions. Some passages virtually serve as commentary on the text of *Moby-Dick*.

Three letters of this period comment on Melville's progress on his manuscript, unnamed in the first year. On 1 May 1850, when he had been back in New York only three months, Melville wrote at some length to Dana. He owed him some kind of report on the European trip, Dana having written a letter of introduction to Moxon, publisher of the English edition of *Two Years Before the Mast*. Also he was replying to a letter from Dana, now lost, which, it seems, strongly praised *White-Jacket*, and perhaps *Redburn*. The final paragraph of Melville's letter is his first known statement about *Moby-Dick*:

> About the "whaling voyage"—I am half way in the work, & am very glad that your suggestion so jumps with mine. It will be a strange sort of a book, tho', I fear; blubber is blubber you know; tho' you may get oil out of it, the poetry runs as hard as sap from a frozen maple tree;—& to cook the thing up, one must needs throw in a little fancy, which from the nature of the thing, must be ungainly as the gambols of the whales themselves. Yet I mean to give the truth of the thing, in spite of this (*Letters*, p. 108).

But on 27 June he was writing to his English publisher about "a new work" which would be ready by "the latter part of the coming autumn." Now he spoke of the book as

> a romance of adventure, founded upon certain wild legends in the Southern Sperm Whale Fisheries, and illustrated by the author's own personal experience, of two years & more, as a harpooner (p. 109).

Neither the completion date nor the impressive role as harpooner were accurate, of course. Then on 7 August, in the midst of the famous Berkshire house party, Evert Duyckinck wrote home that "Melville has a new book mostly done—a romantic, fanciful & literal & most enjoyable presentment of the whale fishery,—something quite new" (Metcalf, p. 84).

The Dana letter is the major source for arguing that Melville was writing one kind of book until August and then another during the next year. But there are many ambiguities here. The usual assumption is that Dana's "suggestion" would obviously be that Melville do for whaling what he had done for life on a man-of-war in *White-Jacket*, and, by implication, what Dana had done for the merchant service in *Two Years Before the*

Mast. But J. Ross Browne had already done that, said Melville in his 1847 review: "Indeed, what Mr. Dana has so admirably done in describing the vicissitudes of the merchant sailor's life, Mr. Browne has very creditably achieved with respect to that of the hardy whaleman's" (*MD*, pp. 529–530). Moreover we have already seen that what Dana had responded to in the Boston supper parties was that Melville was "incomparable in dramatic story telling." Perhaps, then, his "suggestion" was that Melville do a book that captured that gift for "dramatic story telling?" As to the long middle sentence in Melville's paragraph, it simply acknowledges that Melville is struggling once again with the old problem, not of choosing between fact and fancy but of interrelating them. In fact, the central theme of the Browne review is precisely that, treated both seriously (Byron versus Dana) and comically ("the ocean . . . as the peculiar theatre of the romantic and wonderful" versus "a valetudinarian bather at Rockaway, spluttering and choking in the surf"). The two most positive statements in the Dana letter are that "It will be a strange sort of a book," and that "I mean to give the truth of the thing," both despite the blubber versus poetry problem. But the truth of *what* "thing"—the whaling experience already treated by Browne and Henry T. Cheever in *The Whale and His Captors* (1849)? Or was the "thing" Melville's own deepest range of psychic experience? The phrase suggests uncertainty, or duplicity, or both. Melville's relation to Dana was double-edged: he admired *Two Years* but could see its limits. He liked, or at least courted, Dana enough to have called him a "sea-brother" in an earlier letter (p. 93), and in the present to suggest a "Siamese link of affectionate sympathy" between them (p. 106); yet Dana and his rather imperious father—an admired second-rate poet who thought *Mardi* "an absurd book?" (*Mel. Log*, p. 298)—represented a bulwark of Boston society and orthodox attitudes that Melville at best played games with. The Dana letter is richly ambiguous.

In writing to John Murray about *Mardi*, Melville had remarked, "It opens like a true narrative . . . & the romance & poetry of the thing thence grow continually, till it becomes a story wild enough I assure you & with a meaning too" (*Letters*, p. 71). That *Moby-Dick* was already headed in the same direction is suggested by Melville's proposal to Bentley of "a romance of adventure, founded upon certain wild legends . . . " Finally, Duyckinck, who writes as though he either actually saw some manuscript, or was given paraphrases by Melville, records that Melville for six months has been working on a book that is "romantic," "fanciful," "literal," and "most enjoyable." By the time Melville met Hawthorne he had already been wrestling "with the angel—Art" for six months (Poems, p. 231).

The best accounts of that extraordinary week of festivities in the Berkshires are in *The Melville Log* (pp. 382–395), Howard's biography (pp. 154–161), and the gathering of documents in Metcalf (Ch. 6). Each version records a wonderful holiday of bright young literati, most of them in their early thirties, except Oliver Wendell Holmes, at age 41 a Brahmin deity, poet, and dean of Harvard Medical School, and old man Hawthorne, at age 46 newly famous for *The Scarlet Letter*. Duyckinck and Cornelius Mathews, playwright and comic novelist, came up from New York; Hawthorne's publisher, James T. Fields came in from Boston with his bride; the local hosts were the Melvilles, with access to the big old family house, Broadhall, and various neighbors; Hawthorne had moved to the red house in Lenox (now near Tanglewood), and Holmes was summering near by. There was much racing about the Berkshire countryside in carriages and on horseback. Picnic lunches and baskets of champagne set the mood of an amusing *fête champêtre* complete with high and hilarious talk, costumes and masquerading, lots of teasing, joking, posturing, and poet-mongering. Highlights were the trip up Monument Mountain—Melville up to his old show-off sailor tricks, "the boldest of all, astride a projecting bowsprit of rock" according to Duyckinck (Metcalf, p. 82)— and the walk down into the Ice Glen—Hawthorne hallooing mysteriously from dark caves (*Mel. Log*, p. 384). At dinner one day Holmes became witty and pontifical about "the superiority of Englishmen"; Melville—no longer intimidated by either Boston or London— "attacked him vigorously" (Metcalf, p. 82).

Three consequential events followed from the stunning impact on Melville of meeting and rereading Hawthorne that week: Melville's virtually overnight production of the famous "Hawthorne and His *Mosses*," (the best text is in *MD*, pp. 535–551); the ten letters Melville wrote to Hawthorne, all of them effusive, profound, deeply affectionate, the sixth one an endless jubilation that Hawthorne (whose letters to Melville are lost), has read and "understood" *Moby-Dick*; and of course the dedication of that book to Hawthorne "In Token of My Admiration For His Genius." The *"Mosses"* essay is so deeply related to Melville's imaginative and intellectual world while writing *Moby-Dick* as to be everyone's prime piece of contextual reading; it could be printed almost as a preface, as relevant to *Moby-Dick* as Whitman's Preface would be to his 1855 *Leaves of Grass*. Transparently showing through Melville's inordinate praise of Hawthorne, comparing him to Shakespeare and Dante, comes the image of a new generation of American writers: "genius, all over the world, stands hand in hand, and one shock of recognition runs the whole circle round" (*"Mosses*," p. 547). It is impossible to miss Melville's self-projection in the idea of "the coming of the literary Shiloh of America," in the dozen reiterations of the word "genius," in the more than two-dozen references to Shakespeare, in the insistence that "Shakespeare's unapproachability" (p. 543) is nonsense for an American. When Melville says that the modern author's problem is "not so much paucity, as superabundance of material," and that "The trillioneth part has not yet been said" (p. 544), we know for sure that Melville has moved on from Hawthorne's tightly crafted literary microcosms to his own struggle with the multiple kinds of truth that can or cannot go into a whaling manuscript. The measure of Melville's aroused psyche as he considers the power of "American genius" coalesces in a tremendous trope: "For that explosive sort of stuff will expand though screwed up in a vice, and burst it, though it were triple steel" (p. 545). The sexual excitement in this essay, and in all the letters to Hawthorne, suggest that Melville's cresting of purpose ever since *Mardi* is moving up to a cresting of power under the magic of his new relationship.

During the winter of 1850–1851 Melville did his most intense work on *Moby-Dick.* He had left the noise and confusions of New York City and bought a farm in Pittsfield, out of hunger to find "the silent grass-growing mood in which a man *ought* always to compose" (*Letters,* p. 128), and out of need to be near Hawthorne. His fine letter to Duyckinck of 13 December tells us a great deal:

> I have a sort of sea-feeling here in the country, now that the ground is all covered with snow. I look out of my window in the morning when I rise as I would out of a port-hole of a ship in the Atlantic [as on the *Southampton;* whalers have no forecastle portholes]. My room seems a ship's cabin; & at nights when I wake up & hear the wind shrieking, I almost fancy there is too much sail on the house, & I had better go on the roof & rig in the chimney.
>
> Do you want to know how I pass my time? . . . My own breakfast over, I go to my workroom & light my fire—then spread my M.S.S. on the table—take one business squint at it, & fall to with a will. At 2 1/2 P.M. I hear a preconcerted knock at my door, which (by request) continues till I rise & go to the door, which serves to wean me effectively from my writing, however interested I may be.

Then to the village by sleigh, with family. Evenings, when the others were gathered around the big downstairs fireplace, Melville sat "in a sort of mesmeric state in my room—not being able to read—[he was having eye troubles] only now & then skimming over some large-printed book."Apparently the "mesmeric state" was when imagination ran riot, for the letter continues immediately: "Can you send me about fifty fast-writing youths, with an easy style & not averse to polishing their labors? If you can, I wish you would, because since I have been here I have planned about that number of future works & can't find enough time to think about them separately.—But I don't know but a book in a man's brain is better off than a book bound in calf—at any rate it is safer from criticism. And taking a book off the brain, is akin to the ticklish & dangerous business of taking an old painting off a panel—you have to scrape off the whole brain in order to get at it with due safety—& even then, the painting may not be worth the trouble." (*Letters,* p. 117)

In a January letter he invites Hawthorne over to share "wisdom," "story-telling," and "jokes"—three attributes of his daily writing, one might add. In an April letter, after lengthy praise of *The House of the Seven Gables*, he returns to a theme of his "*Mosses*" essay and again draws a profile of Hawthorne as an aggressive and fearless truth seeker—transparently once more a self-image. "There is the grand truth about Nathaniel Hawthorne. He says NO! in thunder; but the Devil himself cannot make him say *yes*" (p. 125). One wonders how Hawthorne reacted to this assault in Carlylese. It seems clear that Melville dared write more heretically to Hawthorne than he ever had to Duyckinck. Some of the attributes of Ahab, whose character and dramatic speeches by now must have been fully exploited in the manuscript, reverberate in phrasing that, of all things, Melville assigns to Hawthorne, as a man who "declares himself a sovereign nature (in himself) amid the powers of heaven, hell, and earth. He may perish; but so long as he exists he insists upon treating with all the Powers upon an equal basis." And so on to the problem of "my sovereignty in myself," all this reminiscent of Ahab's two most defiant and imperial scenes: "The Quarter-Deck" and "The Candles" (chs. 36 and 119). More dryly Melville remarks: "We incline to think that God cannot explain His own secrets.... (*Letters*, pp. 124–125).

By June 1851 a Melville letter to Hawthorne confesses to the psychic cost of the winter's work. "My dear Sir, a presentiment is on me,—I shall at last be worn out and perish..." In spite of a winter of hard work he returns to his earlier theme: "What I feel most moved to write, that is banned,—it will not pay. Yet, altogether, write the *other* way I cannot. So the product is a final hash, and all my books are botches." In three memorable tropes he emblematizes his career. He is "like an old nutmeg-grater, grated to pieces by the constant attrition of the wood, that is, the nutmeg"; the heavy joke at the end of course refers to the phony wooden nutmegs of Yankee peddlers. In an extraordinary confession he tells Hawthorne that he had no development until his twenty-fifth year (1844, when he returned from the Pacific). Two organic metaphors emerge: he is like a seed taken from the Egyptian Pyramids after three thousand years that "grew to greenness, and then fell to mould." Modifying his image: "Three weeks have scarcely passed, at any time between then and now, that I have not unfolded within myself. But I feel that I am now come to the inmost leaf of the bulb, and that shortly the flower must fall to the mould" (*Letters*, 128–130).

But Melville's moods are cyclical, from letter to letter (and even within one letter, as with Ishmael within one chapter of *Moby-Dick*). By the end of June he is reasserting to Hawthorne a theme of the "*Mosses*" essay, grateful that there are "men like you and me and some others, forming a chain of God's posts round the world." He wants to visit Hawthorne and over brandy "talk ontological heroics together." In a flair of braggadocio he refers to "the hell-fire in which the whole book is broiled," and then cryptically concludes with a reference to the scene in "The Forge" (ch. 113): "This is the book's motto (the secret one),—Ego non baptiso te in nomine—but make out the rest yourself" (*Letters*, pp. 132–133).

MOBY-DICK EDITIONS

The Norton Critical *Moby-Dick* (1967), edited by Harrison Hayford and Hershel Parker, is the preferred text—a highly sophisticated conflation of the American and English texts, which differ markedly. The Norton text is an almost final version of the forthcoming NN *Moby-Dick*. It has been made available to most subsequently printed editions. The Hendricks House *Moby-Dick* (1952), edited by Luther S. Mansfield and Howard P. Vincent, has whale-size Explanatory Notes, running to some 265 pages. They present citations from literary sources and whaling books, biographical miscellany, and discussions of major characters and themes. A good Index (19 pages, to Notes only) provides indispensable access to the thickets of commentary, some of which are distractingly remote. The Penguin Books *Moby-Dick* (1972), edited by Harold Beaver, has a look-alike Commentary of 278 pages, drawing heavily on Mansfield and Vincent, spiced with highly subjective additions. For practical foot-of-the-page notes to Ishmael's richly allusive text, one should return to Willard Thorp's pioneering Oxford edition (1947), or to Charles Feidelson's Bobbs-Merrill edition (1964).

Each of the above editions (except Mansfield-Vincent) is amply supplied with appendices, variously consisting of maps and charts; whale ship and whaleboat sketches designating work areas, sails, and tools of the trade; and reproductions of old prints, including some described by Ishmael. The Norton edition uniquely offers technical data on the construction of its text; a nautical glossary and pictorial essay on whaling; analogues and sources; Melville's "Hawthorne and His *Mosses*"; thirteen Melville letters; and more than a hundred pages of critical materials.

ISHMAEL: "AND HE WILL BE A WILD MAN"

At a crucial unknown point, whether before writing or in the process of composition, Melville chose the names of Ishmael, Ahab, and Moby Dick. The implications were enormous for both the themes and the form of *Moby-Dick*. A reader's sense of the role played by each of these figures will shape that reader's experience with the book.

Generally the early critics dealt first with Ahab, or with the White Whale, finding there the two centers of energy in the narrative. Howard P. Vincent warned against forgetting the narrator, quoted Emerson's statement on an individual as "an encloser," and suggested that Ishmael "enfolds the entire work." This same Ishmael he also saw as "the author's surrogate among the *Pequod* crew" (*Trying-Out*, pp. 55–56). Numerous critics since then have insisted on the primacy of Ishmael-narrator, not only over sailor-Ishmael on board the *Pequod*, but over either Ahab or the White Whale as the prime mover in the book. One critic tried to discourage commentators from saying "*Melville* says this" (or that) when citing the text, or even saying *Melville-Ishmael* (Bezanson, *MD*, pp. 655–659). In his impressive and rich phenomenological reading of *Moby-Dick*, Paul Brodtkorb makes clear in his introduction that his aim is "a descriptive analysis of the Ishmaelean consciousness," and it is therefore a presupposition of his study that "Ishmael is the vessel that contains the book," that in fact "he *is* the book" (pp. 3–4). Robert Zoellner in his full-length study of *Moby-Dick* says that traditional criticism holds that Ishmael's role as narrator breaks down when Ahab and Stubb have a conversation off by themselves (Ch. 29) or more certainly when Ishmael reports the soliloquy of Ahab sitting alone (Ch. 37). But Zoellner sees no reason why readers willing to allow Ishmael the right to speculate on Ahab's purposes (Ch. 46, "Surmises") should not be willing to let him imagine a soliloquy. He thus takes up the position from the beginning that "Ishmael is *not* Melville any more than Huckleberry Finn is Mark Twain" (p. xi).

Maximizing Ishmael as narrator offers real dividends. At first, insistence on saying Ishmael rather than Melville seems like game-playing, even double talk, for no one denies that Melville wrote *Moby-Dick* as surely as he wrote *White-Jacket*. Furthermore, as good a critic as A. Robert Lee, in his close reading of the way "the tale" and "the teller" are interwoven with one another, sees "a self-aware narrative made up of narrator, point of view, a knowing tone, and a full play of equivocation and plural meanings. As a tale, *Moby-Dick* cannot function without its teller. And that teller," Lee prefers to say, is "Melville, working only in part through his designated spokesman, Ishmael" (pp. 103–104). Such critics feel that Melville can manipulate narrator Ishmael as well as any other character. Lee's "teller," one can agree, *could* serve the equivalent function; but a nameless "teller" in careless hands (not Lee's) easily becomes "Melville." What gets lost then, I would argue, is the precise profile of the narrator, who is both more and less than Melville. The profile is more in that the writing of *Moby-Dick* is itself a series of discoveries not previously part of Melville; and it is less in that an infinite number of experiences, emotions, beliefs, and ideas, which were part of Melville in the past, or were to become part of him in the future, do not find expression here. We are not reading Melville's autobiography in *Moby-Dick*, but we are reading Ishmael's.

It is obvious, yet important, to remember that we have been talking about the narrator Ishmael, not the young sailor who some years ago went whaling. The sailor, the dominant "character" of the early chapters, recedes into the crew when the *Pequod* sails, and is only intermittently brought forward by the narrator. He is pretty much an innocent, and not even particularly interesting except as the narrator, a mature and complex sensibility, examines his inner life from a distance, just as he examines the inner life of Ahab. In the remarkable chapter 42 ("The Whiteness of the Whale"), Ishmael makes it clear that the sailor Ishmael was "at times" somehow "appalled" by the whiteness of the whale. But all that was vague, nameless, ineffable—until now. It is the narrator who settles in to probe for understanding, summoning evidences from world culture in an effort to break through into meaning. The chapter is an incantatory act of imagination by the narrator, here and now in the text.

The good reader will surely develop his own sense of what terms work best in trying to encompass *Moby-Dick*, for as Melville told himself in his early letter to Dana: "It will be a strange sort of a book, tho', I fear..." What should not get lost, whatever narrative concept one adopts, is the live, powerful, dominant presence of Ishmael which surrounds the entire book. It is frequently said that Melville did not care about point of view, and of course this is true if the term is used in the sophisticated and narrow sense developed by James and his critics. The mistake would be to think the narrator indifferent to how his tale is told, his mind being on higher (or lower) things. For Ishmael's struggle with how to tell his tale is under constant discussion, is itself one of the major themes of the book. A modern reader's fascination with *Moby-Dick* might well begin with attention to Ishmael's search for forms—a sermon, a dream, a comic set-piece, a midnight ballet, a meditation, an emblematic reading. It is as if finding a temporary form would in itself constitute one of those "meanings" which Ishmael is always so portentously in search of. Also it is as if Ishmael would stop at nothing in his efforts to entertain, to show off, to perform. Caught midway in a theme of the utmost seriousness, Ishmael may turn to comedy, even to self-parody, triumphantly producing non-meaning to the bafflement of the innocent reader.

A major pleasure of the text is for each reader to try for precise delineation of the Ishmaelean consciousness, to return to Paul Brodtkorb's phrase. This need not be a strictly phenomenological enterprise, of course, though such a paradigm, like many others that have been brought to bear on *Moby-Dick*, may be useful. Warwick Wadlington's lively chapter predicating cycles of psychic growth that Ishmael goes through (intense experience, leading to estrangement, leading to new self-awareness) is interesting; his sense of Ishmael's "gamesomeness" enlivens the reader too; and, best of all, he tries to choreograph Ishmael's voice: "By turns intimate, urgent, frank, rhapsodic, but also superior, dry, and crafty" (pp. 79, 73, 94). This last game perhaps raises the stakes higher than almost any other reader activity. At first disconcerting, Ishmael's sudden twists and turns of mood and effect can become not only a delight but when trying to read his doctrines, essential to interpretation. Because there are not always clear signs of what is intended, equally good readers may disagree on effects.

Setting up one's own series of adjectives defining some of Ishmael's characteristic tones of voice can be a central critical act. If we are to ask how we should take Father Mapple's sermon (Ch. 9), whether or not to trust Ishmael's eloquent hymn to spiritual democracy (end of Ch. 26), or what to do with Fleece's forced preachments to the sharks (Ch. 64), we need to be practised in Ishmael's range of sensibilities as a whole, as well as attentive to the passage in question. The reader interested in social judgments, moral stances, or the play of psychic forces in *Moby-Dick* may find his own paraphrase embarrassingly different from that of others. For example, a common reading of the opening paragraph of the first chapter is to read Ishmael as being seriously on the edge of suicide, suffering from deep depression, "actually a suicidal neurotic" (Zoellner, p. 120). To be sure, Ishmael will project dismay, despair, perhaps anguish during his narration; is this such a moment? Are these the megrims of a sick man—"spleen" and "hypos" and "pistol and ball" and "coffins"? Or are they the marvellous energies of a raconteur in top form, a first encounter, perhaps, with Ishmael's hyena laugh, just part of the "general joke"? As he says: "There is nothing like the perils of whaling to breed this free and easy sort of genial desperado philosophy" (*MD*, p. 195–196). But Zoellner needs the suicide reading, to develop what he sees as Ishmael's progress from sickness to, at the end, health. Here thesis ignores tone.

"Loomings" (Ch. 1) is a wonderful prologue to Ishmael's book of wonders. It sets a tone, begins to establish the reader-writer contract, samples the vocabulary to come. It hints of possible events ahead and gives intimations of the form (or forms) that will carry the tale. Here is a first feeling for the high metabolism of the narrator and inklings of what kinds of things might evoke his utmost energies. All these, and more, in "Loomings." Looking for an analogy to the chapter, one might think of a rather noisy musical overture, Beethoven-like in its attack, bursting with energy, promises, threats, commands. By and large it is so aggressively comic and unabashedly assertive as to scare the wits out of a quiet reader. Are we being offered an invitation into the house of fiction, or an eviction notice? The lead-in phrases of the paragraph are imperative or brusque: "Call me...There now...Circumambulate... But look!...Once more...But here...Now, when I say...No, when I go to sea...What of it, if...Again, I always...Finally, I always...." Who is this chap Ishmael, anyway? Who does he think he is?

Ishmael, first of all, is the archetypal pariah of Biblical tradition: "And he will be a wild man; his hand will be against every man, and every man's hand against him" (Genesis 16.12). But although he is the illegitimate son of Abraham, his name, according to nineteenth-century Biblical scholars, is translated "God hears"; when his mother Hagar thirsted in the desert "God heard the lad" and provided a well of water (Genesis 21.17–19). Furthermore, God said to Abraham: "As for Ishmael . . . Behold, I have blessed him, and will make him fruitful" (Genesis 17.20). To this figure of ancient Biblical history—as well known to his audience, however, as Washington or Benedict Arnold—he gave an American voice. Mixed in with Scriptural tones and the language and rhythms of Melville's wide readings is a wildly comic strain which is fresh and boisterously American. Like Whitman's "barbaric yawp" picked up in the city streets, or, later, Twain's tall-tale manner brought back from the mining camps, Ishmael's language includes sounds from the sea frontier.

The moment when Melville took the name of the blessed pariah, the outcast beloved of God, the moment when he first wrote the name "Ishmael" into his manuscript in place of whatever else he was calling his narrator is, in my sense of things, the moment when the book we know began to exist. Under the ambiguously sacred name of Ishmael, Melville suddenly could justify his readiness, even his passion, to write like a "wild man" to release once more that "certain something unmanageable in us" of which he had warned John Murray. The Ishmael voice, with its American accent, gave Melville precisely the vantage point he wanted from which to look out upon his watery world. It was the right medium for the half-alienated but privileged genius he had become.

Ishmael is thus the discovered persona. If his opening phrase was an echo of Poe's "Let me call myself, for the present, William Wilson,"or even of Hawthorne's line in "The Gentle Boy," "Friend . . . they call me Ilbrahim, and my home is here," it has its own abrupt rhythm and resonant connotations. Vincent (p. 58) notes that Melville had used the name Ishmael for metaphor in *Redburn*, and would use it again in *Pierre*. Such uses were single allusions; now Melville was setting an over-arching theme, a book-length statement of insurgency.

Ishmael becomes the released demon, the muse incorporated into the narrator. More subtly, he is that part of Melville which is on loan, as it were, to Ishmael for the duration of the book. If we assume that the writing self for a book begins and ends with that book, then there had been no narrator-Ishmael until now; there would be none after. But it is not possible or necessary to deny the process of germination we have seen, from *Mardi* on, and especially the extension of "Ishmael" into Melville's correspondence during the composition of *Moby-Dick*. For example, put Ishmael's "fare thee well, poor devil of a Sub-Sub" (p. 2) side by side with Melville's wonderful "if ever, my dear Hawthorne" passage in his letter of 1? June 1851 (*MD*, p. 558). Though one is a comic lament and the other an heroic love poem, both have the Ishmael rhythm, and in both find "sit . . . world . . . heavens . . . together . . . strike." At times the creature possessed the creator.

Ishmael's role is like that of the membrane in cell biology: by controlling what substances move in or out, by flexible enclosure and rejection, the membrane creates order out of disorder. And by certifying his narrator as a wild man, Melville gave himself permission as he told Hawthorne to write "a wicked book, and feel spotless as the lamb" (*Letters*, p. 142), and by crossbreeding the illegitimate son of Abraham with a ring-tail roarer from Tennessee, such as Davy Crockett, he gave the New World a new voice.

DESIGNS: "A CAREFUL DISORDERLINESS"

A browser poking about an old-books store in London might find, side by side on a single shelf, a book of dreams and a collection of sermons; next to them a travel account, a book on fishing, and an autobiography; then, a novel, and perhaps a collection of Elizabethan plays, or an epic poem, with a joke book or two tucked in here and there. Call the shelf *Moby-Dick*.

For *Moby-Dick* is an unusual kind of entertainment. It may not take long for the modern reader, familiar with Joyce and Faulkner, to adjust to the discontinuities in manner and genre. Even the classicist, it has been argued, will know precedents for the structural mix (Cambon). But imagine Melville's contemporaries, accustomed to sea tales in the manner of Cooper or Marryat, or a good documentary like *Two Years Before the Mast*, wading past a page headed ETYMOLOGY and then having to go around ten pages of EXTRACTS before finding Chapter 1. In fact the English editors, being sensible folk and knowing fictions do not have Pre-pendix, shoved both sections into the back of the third volume of *The Whale*, as the English edition was titled. They simply dropped the EPILOGUE, for not obvious reasons, and also all of the short Chapter 25, for obvious ones—Ishmael's smart-ass hilarities about whale oil and coronations. Other unauthorized changes were made in the English edition wherever someone "found Americanisms, blasphemy, obscenity" (*MD*, p. 475, and for textual problems generally, see pp. 471–98). The effort to tame Ishmael did not wait for the critics.

First-time readers of *Moby-Dick* get along smoothly, in spite of some oddities such as Father Mapple's word-for-word sermon, until the *Pequod* puts to sea. For the reader as well as the *Pequod's* crew, "Merry Christmas" (ch. 22) is about over as the pilot boat withdraws, and a damp wind sets in; "a screaming gull flew overhead," and as the *Pequod* "blindly plunged like fate into the lone Atlantic" (p. 97). The reader, who is one of the "landsmen" defined early by the narrator (p. 12), is now hostage to

Ishmael, the "whaleman," in a symbiotic relationship not guaranteed to be comfortable. As " The Advocate" (ch. 24) opens, the reader is rather belligerently stood up among "ye landsmen," while Ishmael ("us hunters of whales") proceeds to indoctrinate him, want it or not. His "butchering sort of business," he asserts, is cleaner but more perilous than bloody human war. Turning the screw, Ishmael claims that veterans of human battle "quickly recoil at the apparition of the sperm whale's vast tail," a physical if somewhat ghostly threat; to which at once he adds a theological twist: "For what are the comprehensible terrors of man compared with the interlinked terrors and wonders of God!" (pp. 98–99).

The literary confrontations also now begin as we move into ten chapters of who-is-who aboard ship (chs. 26–35). A totally unexpected game called "Cetology" tells us less about whales than about some of Ishmael's eccentricities—here the mock-pedantic, with a serious hint that if whales are books, then maybe this book is a whale, and that reading either will not be easy. Then suddenly comes the great sequence of five drama chapters beginning with the announcement of Ahab's mad quest (so it appears already to the Starbuck in us all), and ending with a wild ballet at midnight, the drunken crew at each other's throats, the reader left cowering with black Pip under the windlass as the "big white God aloft" rips at the stays and yards with white squalls (pp. 154–55). A sudden deepening of the text occurs, with "Moby-Dick" and "The Whiteness of the Whale" taking us far below the surface of the adventure we thought we signed for (chs. 41, 42). Readers, it's going to be a long voyage. At this point scanning the book's horizon, from the posting of the doubloon to the first sight of Moby Dick as the three-day chase begins, is to go from Chapter 36 to Chapter 133. Many readers hold out to about Chapter 54 ("The Town Ho's Story"), a handsomely told sea tale full of dire hints about Moby Dick—published separately in *Harper's New Monthly Magazine* a month before the American edition (*MD*, p. 477)—and then abandon ship.

Yet the whole middle section of the book, aptly named "the cetological center" by Vincent, and a major object of his attention in *The Trying-Out of Moby-Dick*, is worth the work it takes. As complex in manner and intention as Cervantes, or Robert Burton, or Sir Thomas Browne, or Goethe, or Carlyle, all of whom Melville had recently saturated himself with, the cetological chapters are a special world. Nine meetings with ships (not "gams" unless crews are exchanged; see ch. 53) bring vibrant emblems to be put up against Ahab's mad quest. Some six killings are narrated with reckless brilliance, and the body of the whales being brought back to the *Pequod* for processing, provide massive anatomies over which Ishmael broods. In each of these speculations—variously a parable, a comic exposition, a meditation, a preachment—the body of the whale or a part of him—the head especially (beginning with ch. 74, seven chapters plus ch. 85), or the tail (ch. 86), or the phallus (ch. 95)—provides Ishmael sacred and profane texts for discourse. So too with a whaling artifact or process—the line or squeezing sperm (chs. 60, 94)—the first rich in facts, psychology, metaphysics, the second socially sexual. Or at intervals comes a supernatural vision (ch. 51, "The Spirit-Spout"), a memorable scene (ch. 87, "The Grand Armada"), a heart breaking event (ch. 93, "The Castaway"), or one of the great pivotal scenes after which, like a rotating stage, nothing looks the same again (ch. 96, "The Try-Works"; ch. 99, "The Doubloon"; or ch. 119, "The Candles"). So that for those who stay the voyage, by the time of the powerful three-day chase sequence, the landsman may now be whaleman enough not only to follow the events, but to feel he, too, may have won the right to survive. In a final whirl of baroque staging, like a court masque of the seventeenth century, the *Pequod* goes down. Ishmael floats free on Quee-queg's magic coffin. The drama's done.

Since its publication, many readers have wondered at the shapeless shape of this fabulous book. The sheer copiousness, the plenitude, the proliferation of inner forms, is overwhelming at times. We are given a P. T. Barnum type broadside or playbill (ch. 1); an Isaac Watts hymn revised to include whales (ch. 9), and a pastoral stanza from Watts in ironic contrast with the icy sea on Christmas eve (ch. 22); three cenotaphs on the walls of the Whaleman's Chapel (ch. 7); and a variety of sea chanteys, sailors' talk and superstitions (censored versions, mostly). We have dream recital, a Jonah sermon and a Black sermon from old Fleece. We have dependable exposition and fragments of history no safer than Baron Munchausen or Davy Crockett. The material comes to us variously with an "I" narrator, or with Ishmael somewhere in the audience with us watching the performance of his script. At times it seems only fluid system analysis and the new fractal mathematics could define this turbulence or discover the vortices.

For those for whom genre is an essential pathway to literary experience the book poses a problem. That it is not a novel by the terms of most definitions is obvious. It is to be sure a "whaling voyage" but surely not the kind Dana expected. It bears some relation to the form of the romance, as conceived by both Hawthorne and Melville, with emphasis on the possible rather than the probable course of events. Rather than seeking a form into which it might fit, however, the more fruitful exercise is perhaps to try for analogues. Thus Charles Olson in his brilliant, jagged little book, *Call Me Ishmael*, was so stirred by the Melville-Shakespeare connection that he looked for "a rise and a fall like the movement of an Elizabethan tragedy." But starting out valiantly to set up his combinations of chorus, interlude, and acts, he rapidly loses interest and moves on (pp. 66–69).

The experiment of establishing acts is worth trying, with table of contents in hand, if only for the sake of watching the chapters resist inclusive arrangements, except for the twenty or so shore chapters that open the narrative and the three final days of almost pure action. F. O. Matthiessen, as always, is provocative in discussing the ways in which the book draws heavily from drama but acknowledges that a central section of two hundred pages "delays the forward movement of his drama" (p. 419). It does not work. What does work is to develop one's own way of bracketing chapter clusters, pairs and opposites, sequences, cross-references, and any other kind of hopscotch maneuvering that establishes links or collisions for the reader. The romance, with Gothic infusions, and especially if heightened by elements of the so-called metaphysical novel, is a model some find suggestive. But none of these three forms is receptive to the kind of comedy—especially the earthy, tall-tale mode—of which Ishmael is so fond. Readers familiar with the recent generation of Latin American novels often see connections between *Moby-Dick* and "magic realism."

Still another model, for those familiar with Northrop Frye's four forms of fiction—novel, confession, anatomy, and romance—is the anatomy, a discursive satiric form of classical origins which leans toward seeing evil and folly as "diseases of the intellect, as a kind of maddened pedantry" (p. 309). The form has been made familiar to moderns, says Frye, by Rabelais, Burton, and Sterne, plus a now forgotten oddity, Southey's *The Doctor*. Melville, it so happens, borrowed Rabelais, owned *The Anatomy of Melancholy*, and was reading *Tristram Shandy* while in London (all three in *Reading*; and *The Doctor* is given more than a dozen entries in the Mansfield-Vincent *Moby-Dick* Index to annotations). The anatomy form is suggestive, and when Frye sets up combinations, as he does, with rather cheerless literalism, he finds his best illustration of the "romance-anatomy" to be, but of course, "*Moby-Dick*, where the romantic theme of the wild hunt expands into an encyclopaedic anatomy of the whale" (pp. 312–313). Anatomy, indeed, by the ton. Though the paradigm is useful, it should not allow us to forget that Ishmael's deepest anxieties—or are they enchantments—come from the Bible and Shakespeare; nor should one forget the profound confluences, in very different ways, with Emerson (for his New World aura, his Ishmaelite sense of self and of alienation, for his willingness to "dive") and with Hawthorne (the one to whom the book is dedicated, and in some sense a virtual collaborator).

One other form that readers often reach for, thinking of *Moby-Dick*, is the heroic poem or epic. Here Newton Arvin is at home with the possible relationships, not only of the two Homeric poems but especially with *The Lusiad* of the Portuguese poet Camoens. He makes provocative comparisons, in structure, subject matter, tone, and tropes, but in the end finds that what is most characteristic of *Moby-Dick* escapes epic form.

Admirers of this book are often willing to take the position that it is one of the truly original works of literature in modern times, that it is a profoundly American book, and that it comes to us out of the nineteenth century with the same kind of native force that produced *Walden*, *Leaves of Grass*, and the more than 1,775 poems of Emily Dickinson. Something came to a head in the American imagination between the time of Emerson's *Nature* (1836) and Dickinson's extraordinary creativeness during and after the Civil War. One feels both time and space in their work: that chronologically they stand at a cultural divide between the ancient Wilderness and our own time. And that they also stood in circumference to the riches of Western civilization, able to reach out to it, to take but not be taken.

Melville remained an individual talent in dealing with the tradition. One of the prices he willingly paid for his wildness was disorder. But he was careful about it. Ishmael, finding himself by self-appointment among "demigods and heroes, prophets of all sorts," seems to think the honor flows from his method: opening his chapter on "The Honor and Glory of Whaling" (ch. 82) he writes: "There are some enterprises in which a careful disorderliness is the true method" (p. 304). The particular "disorder" Ishmael will deal with in this patchwork chapter is the integration of materials from three different sources: Sir Thomas Browne, Bayle's *An Historical and Critical Dictionary* and John Kitto's *Cyclopaedia of Biblical Literature* (*MD*, p. 304n). But Ishmael's piratical pillagings and invented insurgencies take many different forms throughout his narrative; his "disorders," however well they work, are always calculated.

The chapter called "The Crotch" (ch. 63) has as its subject the notched stick in the bow of a whaleboat on which the harpoon rests. Surprisingly, Ishmael manages not to make sexual innuendos; instead he connects crotch with trees, leading him into an opening sentence which emphasizes the naturalness, one might say, of his theory of disorderly composition. "Out of the trunk, the branches grow; out of them, the twigs. So, in productive subjects, grow the chapters" (p. 246). Coleridge said it first, Whitman exploited it, Darwin made a theory out of it. Ishmael is saying: writing is like a plant growing; if the writer is of sturdy stock, if he is writing about whales and not fleas, his chapters will simply happen. Not formal gardens, one might say, but natural gardens, the form not planned ahead but discovered as one goes along; not French but English horticulture. Or even an American wilderness, at once Eden and a desert place.

Ishmael's refusal of a sustained design, his preference for letting branches, even twigs, grow as they will, leaves him nervous about his overall effect, as it should. Worried that his book will be another of Melville's botches, he defends his disorderliness with a corollary to his organic thesis. It might be called the Unfinished Tower thesis, and it occurs climactically at the end of his bookish effort at bringing order to Cetology (ch. 32). The chapter is about establishing order in the kingdom, or chaos, of whales. "I promise nothing complete, " Ishmael argues, "because any human thing supposed to be complete, must for that very reason infallibly be faulty." What he will offer therefore is "the draught of a systemitization... " (p. 118). There is mockery here, but seriousness too. When at the climax of this long chapter he returns to the idea that "I now leave my cetological system standing thus unfinished," Ishmael recovers for a similitude a strong image from Melville's recent European trip: "the vast unfinished tower" of the famous cathedral of Cologne. The great machine still resting on the top of the tower was what so fascinated Melville, as it did others; as if some day the cathedral might be finished, "the everlasting 'crane' stands on the Tower" (1849 *Journal*, pp. 61–62). Ishmael leaves his "System standing thus unfinished, even as the great cathedral of Cologne was left, with the crane still standing upon the top of the uncompleted tower.... God keep me from ever completing anything," he cries out in coda, suddenly leaping from whales to his own manuscript: "This whole book is but a draught—nay, but the draught of a draught." And then, histrionically, "Oh, Time, Strength, Cash, and Patience!" (pp. 127–28). Process is all. Incompletion becomes an aesthetic principle, is perhaps inevitable, may itself signal the towering worth of the intention.

DOCUMENT: "I HAVE SWAM THROUGH LIBRARIES... I HAVE HAD TO DO WITH WHALES WITH THESE VISIBLE HANDS"

The reader of *Moby-Dick* is intermittently exposed to Fact, Poetry, and Truth. One power of the book—and to some, its most disconcerting feature—resides in Ishmael's movements up through this scale, or back and forth among these elements, or his simultaneous presentation of all three. Any effort to define Fact, or Poetry, or Truth as Melville may have understood them from the time of *Mardi* through the time of *Moby-Dick*, would require exceptional analytical skill plus something like the fluidity characteristic of Melville's own, almost terrifying, mind-in-motion. His comments about his "development" since his twenty-fifth birthday, his sense of rapid, timeless germination, his image of layer after layer of self-exposure (and fear of the empty center) are phenomena so complex as to defy easy inventory. Transcribed into Ishmael's narrative during the period February 1850 through the summer of 1851 they become the vital center, a vortex of power that keeps Fact, Poetry, and Truth swirling. Perhaps this accounts for the sense some readers have of being engulfed by the book, of being swept up into its process of composition.

Practical criticism, rather than trying right away to unlock the Fact-Poetry-Truth dynamic, might better begin with a sequence such as the following: *Moby-Dick* as document, drama, and dream, with a glance aside toward doctrines.

Melville's personal experiences in the Pacific constitute the obvious first level of documentary validation. He had served aboard whalers, standing masthead watches (as in ch. 35), lowering for the chase and then rowing into "the charmed, churned circle" of Leviathan's death (ch. 48), working at or watching the elaborate processes of butchering, trying out, stowing down and cleaning up (chs. 67, 96, 98). His memory was stored with awesome scenes and sensory encounters, some beautiful, some repulsive. Melville's "mesmerized" evenings during composition must have run the gamut of pleasure and terror, such as veterans of combat experience years after the event, willingly, or in nightmare.

One kind of "Truth" Melville wanted was factual accuracy. By the time Ishmael got through with it, to be sure, often enough it should be squinted at; but that Melville wanted himself to verify memories, and especially to supplement his (after all) limited knowledge, is clear from his use of whaling books during composition. The decision to make available to Ishmael precise anatomical data on sperm whales, for example, quite beyond the outer blubber and, perhaps, case and jaws, that came over a whaler's sides, accounts for Melville's persistent search for Thomas Beale's *The Natural History of the Sperm Whale*, subsequently a major source book for facts and images. He had previously reviewed Browne; he got hold of William Scoresby, Jr.'s *Northern Whale-Fishery* to learn about hunting the Right Whale and apparently consulted Frederick Debell Bennett's *Whaling Voyage*, Henry T. Cheever's *The Whale and His Captors*, and Francis Allyn Olmstead's *Whaling Voyage*. Out of these books came materials which he passed through the Ishmael membrane, where they took up their guise of fact, poetry, or truth, or even parody of any of these.

All scholars are deeply indebted to Vincent's breakthrough study of Melville's use of his whaling books as sources, *The Trying-Out of Moby-Dick* (1949); other ways of reading Ishmael's cetological materials since Vincent's study include articles by J. A. Ward and Robert M. Greenberg. Provocative early critics such as D. H. Lawrence, Lewis Mumford, F. O. Matthiessen, Charles Olson, and Henry Murray, in various imaginative ways, suggest aspects of the interrelations of the whaling chapters to the book as a whole. Mansfield and Vincent's Hendricks House edition of *Moby-Dick* incorporates much whaling lore into its massive body of Explanatory Notes. The interested reader might choose a "whaling chapter" (such as 32, 33, or 35) and work through *The Trying-Out* and the Mansfield-Vincent edition to see how the Ishmael membrane works. The Norton Critical *Moby-Dick* makes available sample source studies, and provides two additional basic documents of high interest (*MD*, pp. 571–601). One is the dramatic magazine piece of 1837 by J. N. Reynolds, *Mocha Dick: or The White Whale of the Pacific*, an account bristling with analogies to *Moby-Dick*, including obviously the title. The other is a selection from the famous Owen Chase *Narrative* of how the whaler *Essex* was rammed and sunk by a giant sperm whale in the Pacific in 1820; the book and the event fascinated Melville, as is clear from his elaborate annotations to it, and its use in a footnote in the chapter Ishmael uses to validate the coming "catastrophe" (ch. 45, "The Affidavit"). The presence in *Moby-Dick* of occasional explanatory footnotes, incidentally, emphasizes the documentary guise that Ishmael insists upon—a Nabokovian touch to this "fiction," some might feel.

The documentary aspect of *Moby-Dick*, the fact that among other things it is about real whales and the kinds of ships, boats, and equipment used a century and a half ago; that Ishmael begins his narrative in New Bedford and Nantucket and takes the *Pequod* through seas, straits, and past islands that do exist on maps and charts; and that the narrator from time to time puts his hand through the membrane, as it were, to connect with his here and now (pp. 119, 172, and especially 310); all these matters, I say (to mimic the Ishmaelian style), all these matters connect the narrative, or seem to, with actuality. Thus one can read Ishmael's three chapters (55–57) about certain pictures of whales and simultaneously, if one wishes, examine exactly those same pictures in reproduction. For many readers this confirmation of text naturally reaches out into the whole world of whales and whaling available today. To go aboard the *Charles W. Morgan* today at Mystic, Connecticut, by incredible chance, is to go aboard a virtual sister ship of Melville's *Acushnet*. To go into the amply stocked whaling museums there, or in New Bedford or Nantucket, is to define ships, boats, tools of the trade, the facts and legends of the American whaling industry at the time *Moby-Dick* was written, in ways that will profoundly affect the reader's experience from then on. An even more intense context can be the "whale-watching" cruises, a dozen or so of which operate on the Massachusetts and California coasts; to lean over the bow as the massive body of a humpback whale rises slowly from sea over Stellwagen bank (off Provincetown, Cape Cod), or with a flourish of its giant flukes rolls down, and maybe later breaches, is to bring a different reader back to Ishmael's narrative. Reading modern works in the rapidly growing field of cetology, such as *The Natural History of the Whale* (1978), by a British scientist, L. Harrison Matthews, or *The Sierra Club Handbook of Whales and Dolphins* (1983), by Stephen Leatherwood and Randall R. Reeves, who are adventurous field workers as well as scholars, sharpens one's sense of what Ishmael is and is not up to. Recordings of whale songs, examples of scrimshaw, and wild life films on whales or ecological and political documents on the Save-the-Whales movement are diversionary, but of interest. However complex the critical questions raised by these contextual enterprises, one might note that *Moby-Dick* often encourages them, and in turn they inevitably change the experience of reading the book.

Ishmael means to be authentic about whales, as well as histrionic and amusing. His narrative, however, is so very literary, so full of effects, that there is danger that the reader might miss the sense of actuality he wishes to convey. Hence his remark about Moby Dick being taken "as a monstrous fable, or still worse and more detestable, a hideous and intolerable allegory" (p. 177). At times he wants what might be called photographic realism about whales and whaling procedures, as he makes clear by his detailed critiques of whaling paintings (chs. 55, 56, 57). The irony here is that Ishmael's own presentation of Moby Dick, whether through his own fantasy on whiteness, or Ahab's monomaniac obsession as projected by Ishmael, leads us away from blubber and on into an intricate series of symbolic apprehensions including "intolerable allegory."

One of Ishmael's strongest yet contrary impulses is to raise his "realistic" narrative to the level of myth. So-called "myth criticism," a popular mode during the very period when Melville was receiving a ground swell of criticism after World War II, quite naturally was attracted to *Moby-Dick* (Olson, Richard Chase, R. W. B. Lewis, James Baird, H. Bruce Franklin). The surge of myth criticism has passed, but it is quite impossible not to notice that Classical, Biblical, and American myth figures constantly appear in Ishmael's narrative. Moreover the mythmaking process is one of Ishmael's subjects, especially in chapter 41, "Moby-Dick." The *Pequod*, by name and by description, is from first sight offered as mythic vessel as well as actual whaler (p. 67). But it is of course the White Whale, from first chapter to last, about whom mythic values constantly gather. Melville's June 1850 promise to Bentley that his "romance of adventure" would be "founded upon certain wild legends in the Southern Sperm Whale Fisheries" was amply fulfilled.

Efforts to define the "meaning" of the White Whale tempt almost all readers and critics. The mythical-allegorical-symbolic implications of Moby Dick have been drawn in all directions. The most central reading is inevitably in response to Ishmael's account of the "wild rumors" and "half-formed fetal suggestions of supernatural agencies" current throughout the fisheries (p. 156)—that Moby Dick is a divine and/or demonic force. He relays "fabulous narrations" about the Whale's "hidden ways" and "mystic modes"; when to these are added superstitions claiming the Whale is both "immortal" and "ubiquitous" (p. 158), we are clearly hearing the theological vocabulary of divine attributes. Ishmael's stunning descriptions of Moby Dick's appearances (pp. 159, 221, 447) rise to epiphanic moments. In the final catastrophe Ishmael defines the whale in Calvinist terms: "his predestinating head" and "Retribution, swift vengeance, eternal malice were in his whole aspect" (p. 468). But it is through his dramatization of Ahab that Ishmael most powerfully mythologizes Moby Dick.

DRAMA: "A MIGHTY PAGEANT CREATURE, FORMED FOR NOBLE TRAGEDIES"

The figure of Ahab, once the *Pequod* puts to sea, towers over all other "characters." He is first of all a sea captain of the nineteenth century; Melville had served under five captains, and during his 1849 trip abroad became moderately intimate with two more (a wholly new relation). So that on a first level one sees him as Nantucketer, excessive in command because of his mutilated body.

But the presentation of Ahab, from the beginning, will not allow such simplification. His Biblical name, as sailor Ishmael blurts out, is "a very vile one. When that wicked king was slain, the dogs, did they not lick his blood?" (p. 77). Peleg calls him "a grand, ungodly, god-like man," and it is this double image that narrator Ishmael proposes to the reader. Clearly to the narrator, Ahab, though manic and tyrannical, is an awesome figure, wracked by physical and psychic pain, yet fearlessly committed to revenge even after he foresees his own destruction. In his sultanism and in the intensity of his purpose, he will remind modern readers of Joseph Conrad's Kurz in *The Heart of Darkness*, of Cipolla in Thomas Mann's "Mario and the Magician,"and William Faulkner's tyrant figure, Thomas Sutpen, in *Absalom, Absalom*. His special difference might be his God defiance, over and above the hubristic presumptions that he is god-like. It is through this attribute—Ahab as heresiarch—that Ishmael, himself caught up in whirls of belief and unbelief, can project an almost Satanic figure, like Milton's rebel commander, not entirely hiding his half-secret admiration.

That Ishmael for a time makes Ahab's quest his own—"Ahab's quenchless feud seemed mine" (p. 155)—is as clear as the climactic moment when Ishmael separates himself from Ahab. This occurs, many critics think, in the powerful night scene of "The Try-Works" (ch. 96). The narrator has insistently presented Ahab as a fire figure—"a man cut away from the stake" and scarred by lightning (pp. 109–110, 416), his brain blazing with "this hell in himself " (p. 174). One mad, black night, when the flaming try-works have turned the *Pequod* into a fire-ship, young Ishmael falls asleep at the helm, awakens facing the stern, and almost capsizes the ship. Narrator Ishmael now raises this heretofore "inexplicable" event to its full analogical possibilities: "Look not too long in the face of the fire, O man!. . . believe not the artificial fire, when its redness makes all things look ghastly. . . Give not thyself up, then, to fire, lest it invert thee, deaden thee; as for the time it did me" (pp. 354–355). Without developing an elaborate redemption theory, the reader can see that the narrator reads the event as symbolizing the moment when the young sailor slips out from Ahab's hot hand.

Ishmael gives Ahab a tribal shaman's role. The two largest public scenes aboard the *Pequod*, "The Quarter-Deck" (ch. 36) and "The Candles" (ch. 119), show Ahab reaching to command the souls of his crew, as if to extend his own "contract" with Fedallah. In "The Forge" (ch. 113) Ahab uses the blood of his pagan harpooners, with whom he had allied himself in "The Quarter-Deck," to baptize his new harpoon "in nomine diaboli!" (p. 404). And when he dramatically fashions a new compass needle (ch. 124), Starbuck, already diminished by Ahab, looks away; but the crew watch in "servile wonder . . . whatever magic might follow." No longer under the fire spell Ishmael notes: "you then saw Ahab in all his fatal pride" (p. 425).

Ishmael's presentation of Ahab is both a gathering in of Melville's sea experiences and projections from his reading. Scholars have seen Ahab as evoked by Melville's intense reading of Coleridge on Shakespeare (Howard), or by the reading of Carlyle's *Sartor Resartus* (Thompson). Recent brilliant essays have suggested the influence of Goethe's theory of the daemon (Milder), and of the manic figures in some of Hawthorne's tales (Brodhead). More broadly, Ahab surely reminds readers of Milton's Satan, of the pervasiveness of Byronism in romantic literature, of the "great man" theory as variously expressed by Carlyle and Emerson, and of the Ubermensch visions of Nietzsche. And finally, alas, one thinks of what happened to Wagner's ritualistic scenes, tragically reenacted by Hitler.

The single most significant aspect of Ahab, from a narrative point of view, is the decision made at some point by Melville and carried out by Ishmael, to *dramatize* Ahab. All Melville's reading in Shakespeare and his deep absorption in both Elizabethan drama and the contemporary theater in New York and abroad, provided the forms of theater used so surprisingly at intervals in *Moby-Dick*, forms which turn the deck and space aboard the *Pequod* into stage sets, and shift the language of Ahab and some of his crew away from narrative dialogue to dramatic script. Soliloquies become an established mannerism of the text. Ahab at times speaks in virtual iambic pentameter. Matthiessen is the richest critic on these matters, but there is still room for a masterful study of Melville and Shakespeare that will further illuminate *Moby-Dick*.

The emergence of the dramatic mode aboard the *Pequod* is progressive; hints of a chivalric theme (p. 100) are soon followed by chapters in which the ship's mates and harpooners are presented in the roles of "Knights and Squires" (chs. 26, 27). Ahab appears and the first use of script technique comes with him: "Enter Ahab; To Him, Stubb" (p. 111).

Climax comes with the great sequence of chapters 36–40, variations on the possibilities of pure drama. Throughout the book, Ishmael in a sense opposes his own, open-ended narrative of running speculation, comedy, and event against the more fixed drama in which he encases Ahab, creating a subtext that might be called a structural *agon* wherein an American narrator outlasts his Elizabethan tragic hero (and Melville survives his contest with Shakespeare). Captain Lear laments and defies the cosmos and berates the gods, sustains himself with Pip as Fool, and goes down following three prophecies: not from Macbeth's witches, but from Fedallah.

For one of Melville's major decisions in shaping *Moby-Dick* was to confine the Gothic strain, represented by Fedallah and crew (whose dreamlike presence may have its origin in De Quincey's "most wondrous book") and to ennoble the filthy butchering trade of whaling by bathing it in the chivalric tradition, with Ahab as King. Only drama and melodrama, the mode of excess, can speak for Ahab. Transformed under Ishmael's hand from Nantucket Captain to wicked King and suicidal Shaman, he becomes both a purgation and an act of pure style. Ahab is that unliveable strain in Ishmael's wildness too intense to survive. When Ahab dies, Ishmael floats free. "I have written a wicked book," Melville told Hawthorne, "and feel spotless as the lamb" (*MD*, p. 566).

DREAMS: "A FINE BOOK IS A SORT OF REVERY TO US— IS IT NOT?"

We are scarcely into Ishmael's narrative when he presents us with a dream—if dream it was—remembered from his childhood (ch. 4). Waking up in the Spouter-Inn to find Queequeg's arm thrown over him, Ishmael is beset with strange sensations that somehow trigger a memory—waking as a child in darkness to find that "a supernatural hand seemed placed in mine." The child lay frozen with fear, unable to move. In the morning he remembered the event with shudders, and ever since has been unable to know what it signified, or even to tell "whether it was a reality or a dream." Ishmael is interested in the dream process itself; he clearly delineates the stages of consciousness: "a troubled nightmare of a doze...slowly waking...half steeped in dreams" until he comes to "events...in fixed reality" (pp. 32–33). That he is also interested in the way daily events affect dreams is emphasized by his detailed account of having been punished by a cruel and unrelenting stepmother on the day before the dream.

Ishmael's interest in dreams is of course the continuation of a longstanding literary tradition. But it looks as though his fascination goes beyond narrative use to analytical, almost clinical, concern. A second exploration of the dream process occurs on board the *Pequod* as soon as Ahab appears. Stubb's long dream recital ("Queen Mab," ch. 31) again emphasizes the day-night connection in the dream process. Only two chapters earlier Stubb's rash proposal to Ahab that he cease patrolling the quarterdeck over the heads of the sleeping mates brought insults and humiliation: "Down, dog, and kennel!" Stubb's angry, perplexed reaction ("Maybe he *did* kick me . . . ") leads to a decision "to stash it" and see how it "thinks over by daylight" (pp. 113–114); it is also a kind of classic invitation, either by Ishmael's or Freud's terms, for a retaliation dream, and it happens. In Stubb's dream recital, which at the end over-elaborates the dialogue, the provocative area is the symbolism. Ahab kicks Stubb with his ivory leg; when Stubb tries to kick back, Ahab turns into a pyramid! Suddenly a "badger-haired old merman, with a hump on his back" appears, argues, and then "seemed somehow . . . to swim off into the air" (pp. 115–116). This seems authentic.

Along with his own primal response to dreams Melville's dream knowledge came from the literature he loved—the Book of Daniel, medieval dream visions, Shakespeare, De Quincey. Closer to home was Poe's fascination with the hypnogogic state, and with visionary apocalypse such as the vision of whiteness that concludes "Arthur Gordon Pym"; even closer was Hawthorne's penchant for submitting his characters, when under stress, to vibrating between dream and waking, unable to delimit either one. Melville's unpredictably original and altogether disastrous chapter, "Dreams," in *Mardi* (ch. 119) and the merely amusing account of Jack Blunt and his Dream Book in *Redburn* (ch. 18), make clear Melville's maturation, his Ishmaelization, by 1850.

The dividends of dream for *Moby-Dick* were enormous. Beyond specifics such as the two dreams we have noted lie a rainbow of dream-related passages. "Loomings," the opening chapter, is strewn with phrases relating to dreams and reveries, enchantments and trances, magnetic and magical and mystical vibrations. The famous Narcissus image, presumably "the key to it all," pivots on the idea of life as "ungraspable phantom"; and the chapter climaxes with the image of "one grand hooded phantom." Ishmael at his writing desk in Pittsfield, looking north from the bedroom window, in December could see the white, rolling shape of Mt. Greylock in the distance, horizontal but humped: and so the memory of giant whales rolling in Pacific waters was transformed: "one grand hooded phantom, like a snow hill in the air" (pp. 14, 16).

Once the reader acknowledges enchantment, gives in to Ishmael's need to cast verbal spells as he goes, the narrative will be seen to move in and out of dream. Document interrupts, with its air of everyday fact and the need of whaleman Ishmael to explain objects and processes. Drama takes over, to distance and ennoble the statuesque figure of Captain Ahab. But Ishmael cannot stay long with either mode before sinking down into dream, or rising toward transcendent vision.

In chapter two, standing at the door of the Spouter-Inn, Ishmael is struck by an icy wind; it blows his mind, and for three paragraphs we stand there freezing while Ishmael takes us through Euroclydon and St. Paul's tempest, an improvisation on Death, and an extended imagining on Lazarus and Dives which is half sermon, half social protest, and half (using Davy Crockett's mathematics) dream. We turn the page, stumble into the Inn's entry, and for three paragraphs are confronted with Ishmael's high spirited efforts to *read* an oil painting, smoke blackened and so "boggy, soggy, squitchy" as to be altogether undecipherable in the half-light. But Ishmael, whose nick-name might well be Daniel, proceeds to do what he will over and again do in his book: he tries to read the unreadable. The scene is comic, hardly Balshazzar's feast (a favorite allusion of Ishmael's), but none the less not unlike a dream interpretation.

Then of course there are the great dream passages, among them Ishmael's wonderful mast-head reverie (ch. 35); the sequence of dream-like images he uses in "The Whiteness of the Whale" to upset rationality and tradition (ch. 42); the never-explained apparition on moonlit nights of the spirit-spout (ch. 51), first seen by Fedallah, partly a dream figure out of De Quincey (pp. 77–97), who with his "five dusky phantoms" emerged from nowhere at the first lowering (p. 187). Immediately after the spirit-spout, while "the silent ship, as if manned by painted sailors in wax" moves on (p. 202), the *Pequod* encounters a "spectral" vessel, named the *Goney*, which Ishmael translates for us as "The Albatross" (ch. 52), lest we miss the absorption into his tale of Coleridge's dream-poem. The spirit-spout is still entrancing the crew on moonlit nights when, one lovely blue morning they see the giant squid (ch. 59), "a strange spectre," a "phantom," and "an unearthly, formless, chance-like apparition of life" (pp. 236–237); here in broad daylight, the surfacing of the subliminal strikes fear into generally fearless Starbuck.

The power that such semi-dream scenes can have, quite beyond Gothic ambiance, is clear in the passage describing Pip's wondrous descent into "the unwarped primal world" (ch. 93). There "He saw God's foot upon the treadle of the loom, and spoke it; and therefore his shipmates called him mad" (p. 347). Pip went overboard, and Pip went out of his mind; but Ishmael, by dreaming a saint's vision, transforms the event into divine madness. The pivotal experience of Ishmael in the midnight fire scene at the helm (ch. 96) can be read against Ishmael's childhood dream (ch. 4); again the sensations are "strange"; again we are in the world of the "half conscious"; and again the dream has been "ever since inexplicable" (p. 354). And at the end, the going down of the *Pequod* is more than melodrama; the detailed exactness of its absurdity is that of a nightmare.

Given the subliminal cast of Ishmael's narrative it is not strange that a large, and sometimes amateurish, body of psychological commentary has grown up around *Moby-Dick*. Among professional psychologists who have been serious about the book Henry A. Murray is preeminent, from 1929 when he wrote about Melville daring to cast himself adrift, and open himself "to a torrential spiritual insurgency" (Parker, *Doubloon*, p. 176) on to his widely reprinted centennial essay, "In Nomine Diaboli," a vigorous, even exultant, reading by a man who has loved Melville as much as Freud. Another professional reading by a Jungian scholar, Edward F. Edinger, uses the text handsomely to illustrate Jungian insights (rather than conversely), suggesting, as do many other studies, the copious uses to which this resilient book may be put.

Whether one chooses to name the narrator Ishmael or Melville, *Moby-Dick* is about the self of that narrator, his inner quest alternating with the pursuit of the White Whale. In both pursuits, dream is a constant resource.

There is another way in which dream extends itself: merging with what may be the one great all-encompassing symbol of *Moby-Dick*—the sea. Most of the passages we have cited for their oneiric power are water passages. Ishmael tells us early that, as "every one knows, meditation and water are wedded for ever." And in the book's very first anaphora (one of Ishmael's favorite ways of piling up emotions) we have a rhetorical "Why... Why..." sequence about the eternal pull of the sea— from Tennessee poet to Persian religion to Greek mythology (pp. 13– 14). The sea is deep space and deep time; it is not by chance that three poets—Lawrence, Auden, and Olson—are among the acute responders to this attribute of *Moby-Dick*. At the mast-head Ishmael offers himself as "a dreamy meditative man," with meditation here ranging from "the problem of the universe revolving in me" (one recalls Melville and Adler on the yardarms, discussing metaphysics) on to a De Quincey-like dream of pleasure: "lulled into such an opium-like listlessness of vacant, unconscious reverie... that at last he loses his identity; takes the mystic ocean at his feet for the visible image of that deep, blue, bottomless soul, pervading mankind and nature" (pp. 136, 139, 140).

But the real sea is also here, and one false move will bring the masthead sailor out of "this sleep, this dream" and into a long plunge to his death. Here as so often, Ishmael's quick shift in mood gives a sense of double vision. One moment "the inscrutable tides of God" are rocking the sea, which is rocking the ship, which is rocking Ishmael; the next, comes the threat of instant death (p. 140).

Whether or not Melville read De Quincey's now-famous distinctions between the literature of knowledge and the literature of power he committed himself, as the Dana letter suggested, to trying to combine the two. De Quincey said it couldn't be done, that the two were essentially "repelling forces" (De Quincey, p. 334n). Knowledge, he said, keeps you always on the same plane, "whereas the very *first* step in power is a flight ..." (p. 332). Melville had already made up his own mind, writing Murray, as we have seen, of his "longing to plume my pinions for a flight" (*Letters*, p. 70). Ishmael keeps the faith, as in his famous image of the Catskill eagle "that can alike *dive* down into the blackest gorges, and *soar* out of them again" (italics mine). Even when trapped in the gorges "the mountain eagle is still higher than other birds upon the plain, even though they soar" (p. 355). Diving and soaring is a central dynamic of Ishmael's book, dipping into the subliminal, riding the thermals up from dream.

Writing Sarah Morewood, the party girl of August 1850, Melville warned her against *Moby-Dick*, soon to be published: It "is of the horrible texture of a fabric that should be woven of ships' cables & hausers. A Polar wind blows through it." But he also thanked her for sending him books; at the moment distractions kept him from "falling into the reveries of these books—for a fine book is a sort of reverie to us—is it not?" (*MD*, p. 564). For in the name of Ishmael he had just completed a dream book, ranging from revery to nightmare, of his own.

EPILOGUE: "THE UNHARMING SHARKS, THEY GLIDED BY . . . THE SAVAGE SEA-HAWKS SAILED WITH SHEATHED BEAKS."

From the beginning of our inquiry it seemed clear that Melville, becoming impatient with the success of his first two books, risked in *Mardi* more than he was ready for. *Mardi* elicited Hawthorne's astute comment: "It is so good that one scarcely pardons the writer for not having brooded long over it, so as to make it a great deal better" (*Mel. Log*, p. 391). The two writers could scarcely have been more unlike, in spite of obvious admiration on both sides. Over a twenty-five year period Hawthorne practiced a highly structured craft in his ninety some short stories and sketches; he used a lucid, clean style, eighteenth-century in spirit, for his romantic probings into the buried motivations of his often deviant characters. Then along came Melville, bursting on to the American scene with racy accounts of outlandish adventure, presumably his own, narrated in an increasingly baroque style.

Melville was word-mad by the time he got into *Mardi*, restrained himself in *Redburn* and *White-Jacket*, and then once again took off—toward *Moby-Dick*. The insurgencies of his mind and imagination are reflected in his immensely varied style, whose fundamental allegiance, when not to the contemporary or colloquial, is to the seventeenth century. Reading Shakespeare, Montaigne, Burton, Browne, Goethe, Carlyle and Emerson—all of them just before or even during the planning and writing of *Moby-Dick*—gave him models for expressing his Genius; for he no longer doubted his high commission, though he sometimes despaired. One reads Melville for the sheer excitement of style, among other things. His performance is highly self-conscious, and at its best elicits powerful emotional responses. He writes like a surfer, lingering outside the swells, waiting for the big wave to appear; and when it does, he rides its crest, runs laterally beneath its curl, comes racing up the beach singing jubilates and looking about for praise; then he goes back out, to perform again.

But in writing *Moby-Dick* Melville wanted to attempt a number of different things, some of them not easily compatible with each other. Thus his genuine perplexity in the letter to Dana, the long winter of intensive work and mesmeric evenings, the seeming exhaustion and doubts trying to make everything fit in the summer of 1851. Genre makes demands but it pays back. Mixing forms may lead to the creation of a new form, or it may lead to disaster. Probably Melville did not know what he had achieved when he finished *Moby-Dick*. Had he solved the blubber versus poetry problem, raised in his letter to Dana, so that (to quote Ishmael) "fact and fancy, half-way meeting, interpenetrate, and form one seamless whole"? (p. 406) Above all had he managed "to give the truth of the thing," as he promised himself in that same letter?

He could not have been happy with what his close friend and mentor, Evert Duyckinck, wrote in the New York *Literary World* (*MD*, pp. 613–616). Duyckinck saw *Moby-Dick* as three books: Book I is an admirable and exhaustive account of the sperm whale; Book II he calls "the romance of Captain Ahab" and other characters, about which he had divided sentiments—ennobling and very literary, but too drawn out and sometimes not in good taste; and Book III he defined as long sections of moralizing and rhapsody, with "quaint conceit and extravagant daring speculation." Duyckinck was sharp in his reading, balancing praise and blame; but essentially, a conservative churchman, he was offended: "This piratical running down of creeds and opinions, the conceited indifferentism of Emerson, or the run-a-muck style of Carlyle . . . is out of place and uncomfortable." No wonder Melville kept saying that what he most wanted to write was banned, that he would die in the gutter if he wrote the Gospels, and the like. And no wonder Hawthorne's letter, now lost but apparently of unstinting praise, evoked such a flood of ecstacy from Melville: "A sense of unspeakable security is in me this moment, on account of your having understood the book (*MD*, pp. 566–568).

WORKS CITED

Allison, June W. "The Similes in *Moby-Dick*: Melville and Homer." *Melville Society Extracts* 47 (September 1981): 12–15.

Anderson, Charles R. *Melville in the South Seas.* New York: Columbia University Press, 1939.

Arvin, Newton. *Herman Melville.* New York: Sloane Associates, 1950.

Ashley, Clifford W. *The Yankee Whaler.* Boston: Houghton Mifflin, 1926.

Auden, W. H. *The Enchafèd Flood: or The Romantic Iconography of the Sea.* New York: Random House, 1950.

Baird, James. *Ishmael: A Study of the Symbolic Mode in Primitivism.* Baltimore, Md.:Johns Hopkins University Press, 1956.

Barbour, James. "The Composition of *Moby-Dick.*" *American Literature* 47 (November 1975): 343–60.

Barbour, James and Leon Howard. "Carlyle and the Conclusion of *Moby-Dick.*" *New England Quarterly* 9 (June 1976): 214–224.

Baym, Nina. "Melville's Quarrel with Fiction." *PMLA* 94 (October 1979): 909–23.

Bell, Millicent. "Pierre Bayle and *Moby-Dick.*" *PMLA* 66 (September 1951): 626–48.

Berthoff, Warner. *The Example of Melville.* Princeton, N.J.: Princeton University Press, 1962.

Bewley, Marius. *The Eccentric Design: Form in the Classic American Novel.* New York: Columbia University Press, 1959.

Bezanson, Walter E. "Moby-Dick: Work of Art." In *Moby-Dick Centennial Essays.* Ed. Tyrus Hillway and Luther S. Mansfield. Dallas: Southern Methodist University Press, 1953, pp. 30–58. Rpt. in *MD,* pp. 651–71.

Bickman, Martin, ed. *Approaches to Teaching Melville's Moby-Dick.* New York: Modern Language Association, 1985.

Blackmur, R. P. "The Craft of Herman Melville: A Putative Statement." In *The Expense of Greatness.* New York: Arrow, 1940, pp. 139–166.

Bowen, Merlin.*The Long Encounter: Self and Experience in the Writings of Herman Melville.* Chicago: University of Chicago Press, 1960.

Braswell, William. *Melville's Religious Thought.* Durham, NC: Duke University Press, 1943

Brodhead, Richard. *Hawthorne, Melville, and the Novel.* Chicago: University of Chicago Press, 1976.

Brodhead, Richard H. "*Mardi*: Creating the Creative." In *New Perspectives on Melville.* Ed. Faith Pullin. Kent, Ohio and Edinburgh: Kent State University Press and Edinburgh University Press, 1978, pp. 29–53.

Brodhead, Richard. "Hawthorne, Melville, and the Fiction of Prophecy." In *Nathaniel Hawthorne: New Critical Essays.* Ed. A. Robert Lee. Totowa, NJ: Barnes & Noble, 1982, pp. 229–250.

Brodtkorb, Paul, Jr. *Ishmael's White World: A Phenomenological Reading of Moby-Dick.* New Haven: Yale University Press, 1965.

Brooks, Van Wyck. *The Times of Melville and Whitman.* New York: Dutton, 1947.

Buckley, Vincent. "The White Whale as Hero." *Critical Review* 9 (1966): 1–21.

Buell, Lawrence. "Literature and Scripture in New England Between the Revolution and the Civil War." *Notre Dame English Journal* 15 (1983): 1–28.

Burns, Graham. "The Unshored World of *Moby-Dick.*" *Critical Review* 13 (1970): 68–83.

Cambon, Glauco. "Ishmael and the Problem of Formal Discontinuities in *Moby-Dick.*" *Modern Language Notes* 76 (June 1961), 516–23.

Cameron, Sharon. *The Corporeal Self: Allegories of the Body in Melville and Hawthorne.* Baltimore, Md.: Johns Hopkins University Press, 1982.

Chase, Richard. *The American Novel and Its Tradition.* Garden City, NY: Doubleday, 1957.

————.*Herman Melville: A Critical Study.* New York: Macmillan, 1949.

Clark, Marden J. "Blending Cadences: Rhythm and Structure in *Moby-Dick.*" *Studies in the Novel* 8 (1976): 158–71.

Coffler, Gail H. *Melville's Classical Allusions: A Comprehensive Index and Glossary.* Westport, CT: Greenwood Press, 1985.

Cohen, Hennig, and James Cahalan, eds. *A Concordance to Melville's Moby-Dick.* 3 vols. Ann Arbor, MI: University Microfilms International, 1978.

Cowan, Bainard. *Exiled Waters: Moby-Dick and the Crisis of Allegory.* Baton Rouge, LA: Louisiana State University Press, 1982.

DeQuincey, Thomas. *Confessions of an English Opium Eater.* Ed. Aileen Ward. New York: New American Library, 1966.

Dryden, Edgar A. *Melville's Thematics of Form: The Great Art of Telling the Truth.* Baltimore, Md.: Johns Hopkins University Press, 1968.

Duban, James. *Melville's Major Fiction: Politics, Theology, and Imagination.* DeKalb, IL: Northern Illinois University Press, 1983.

Edinger, Edward F. *Melville's Moby-Dick: A Jungian Commentary.* New York: New Directions, 1978.

Feidelson, Charles. *Symbolism and American Literature.* Chicago: University of Chicago Press, 1953.

Fiedler, Leslie. *Love and Death in the American Novel.* New York: Criterion, 1960.

Finkelstein, Dorothee Metlitsky. *Melville's Orienda.* New Haven: Yale University Press, 1961.

Franklin, H. Bruce. *The Wake of the Gods: Melville's Mythology.* Stanford: Stanford University Press, 1963.

Freeman, John. *Herman Melville.* New York: Macmillan, 1926.

Friedman, Maurice. *Problematic Rebel: Melville, Dostoevsky, Kafka, Camus.* Chicago: University of Chicago Press, 1970.

Frye, Northrop. *Anatomy of Criticism: Four Essays.* Princeton, NJ: Princeton University Press, 1957.

Geist, Stanley. *Herman Melville: The Tragic Vision and the Heroic Ideal.* Cambridge, MA: Harvard University Press, 1939.

Gidmark, Jill B. *Melville Sea Dictionary.* Westport, CT: Greenwood Press, 1982.

Gleim, W. S. *The Meaning of Moby-Dick.* New York: Brick Row Bookshop, 1938.

Glenn, Barbara. "Melville and the Sublime in *Moby-Dick.*" *American Literature* 48 (May 1976): 165–82.

Greenberg, Robert M. "Cetology: Center of Multiplicity and Discord in *Moby-Dick.*" *ESQ* 27 (First Quarter 1981): 1–13.

Greenberg, Robert M. "The Three-Day Chase: Multiplicity and Coherence in *Moby-Dick.*" *ESQ* 29 (Second Quarter 1983): 91–98.

Grobman, Neil R. "The Tall Tale Telling Events in Melville's *Moby-Dick.*" *Journal of the Folklore Institute* 12 (1975): 19–27.

Guetti, James. *The Limits of Metaphor: A Study of Melville, Conrad, and Faulkner.* Ithaca: Cornell University Press, 1967.

Halverson, John. "The Shadow in *Moby-Dick.*" *American Quarterly* (Fall 1963): 436–46.

Hayford, Harrison. "Unnecessary Duplicates: A Key to the Writing of *Moby-*

Dick." In *New Perspectives on Melville.* Ed. Faith Pullin. Kent, Ohio and Edinburgh: Kent State University Press and Edinburgh University Press, 1978): 128–61.

———. " 'Loomings': Yarns and Figures in the Fabric." In *Artful Thunder: Versions of the Romantic Tradition in American Literature in Honor of Howard P. Vincent.* Ed. Robert J. De Mott and Sanford E. Marovitz. Kent, Ohio: Kent State University Press, 1975.

Heimert, Alan. "*Moby-Dick* and American Political Symbolism." *American Quarterly* 15 (Winter 1963): 495–534.

Herbert, T. Walter, Jr. *Moby-Dick and Calvinism: A World Dismantled.* New Brunswick, N.J.: Rutgers University Press, 1977.

Hirsch, David H. "The Dilemma of the Liberal Intellectual: Melville's Ishmael." *Texas Studies in Literature and Language* 5 (Summer 1963): 169–88.

Hirsch, David H. "*Hamlet, Moby-Dick,* and Passional Thinking." In *Shakespeare's Aspects of Influence.* Ed. G.B. Evans. Cambridge, MA: Harvard University Press, 1976.

Hoffman, Daniel G. *Form and Fable in American Fiction.* New York: Oxford University Press, 1961.

Hohman, Elmo Paul. *The American Whaleman: A Study of Life and Labor in The Whaling Industry.* New York: Longmans, Green, 1928.

Horsford, Howard C. "The Design of the Argument in *Moby-Dick.*" *Modern Fiction Studies* 8 (Autumn, 1962): 233–51.

Humphreys, A. R. *Herman Melville.* Edinburgh: Oliver and Boyd, 1962.

Ingalls, Jeremy. "The Epic Tradition: A Commentary." *East-West Review* 1 (Spring 1964): 42–69.

Irey, Eugene F., ed. *Moby-Dick Index Concordance.* New York: Hendricks House 1978.

Irwin, John T. *American Hieroglyphics: The Symbol of the Egyptian Hieroglyphics in the American Renaissance.* New Haven: Yale University Press, 1980.

Jeffrey, Lloyd N. "A Concordance to the Biblical Allusions in *Moby-Dick.*" *Bulletin of Bibliography* 21 (May-August 1956): 223–29.

Kruse, Joachim, ed. *Illustrationem zu Melville's Moby-Dick.* Schleswig: Schleswiger Druck-und Verlagshaus, 1976.

Lawrence, D. H. *Studies in Classic American Literature.* New York: Thomas Seltzer, 1923.

Leatherwood, Stephen and Randall R. Reeves. *The Sierra Club Handbook of Whales and Dolphins.* San Francisco: Sierra Club Books, 1983.

Lee, A. Robert. "*Moby-Dick*: The Tale and the Telling." In *New Perspectives on Melville.* Ed. Faith Pullin. Kent, Ohio and Edinburgh: Kent State University Press and Edinburgh University Press, 1978: 86–127.

Levin, Harry. *The Power of Blackness.* New York: Knopf, 1958.

Lewis, R.W.B. *The American Adam: Innocence, Tragedy, and Tradition in the Nineteenth Century.* Chicago: University of Chicago Press, 1955.

Mansfield, Luther S. and Howard P. Vincent, eds. *Moby-Dick; or, The Whale.* New York: Hendricks House, 1952.

Matthews, L. Harrison. *The Natural History of the Whale.* New York: Columbia University Press, 1978.

Matthiessen, F. O. *American Renaissance: Art and Expression in the Age of Emerson and Whitman.* New York: Oxford University Press, 1941.

McIntosh, James. "Melville's Use and Abuse of Goethe: The Weaver-Gods in *Faust* and *Moby-Dick.*" *Amerikastudien* 25 (1980): 158–73.

Metcalf, Eleanor Melville. *Herman Melville: Cycle and Epicycle.* Cambridge: Harvard University Press, 1953.

Milder, Robert. "The Composition of *Moby-Dick*: A Review and a Prospect." *ESQ* 23 (Fourth Quarter): 203–16.

Milder, Robert. " '*Nemo Contra Deum*...': Melville and Goethe's 'Demonic.' " In *Ruined Eden of the Present: Hawthorne, Melville and Poe.* Ed. G.R. Thompson and Virgil Lokke. West Lafayette, IN: Purdue University Press, 1981.

Miller, James E., Jr. "Melville's Search for Form." *Bucknell Review* 8 (December 1959): 260–76.

Moore, Richard S. *That Cunning Alphabet: Melville's Aesthetics of Nature.* Atlantic Highlands, N.J.: Humanities Press, 1982.

Mumford, Lewis. *Herman Melville.* New York: Harcourt, Brace, 1929.

Murray, Henry A. "In Nomine Diaboli." In *Moby-Dick Centennial Essays.* Ed. Tyrus Hillway and Luther S. Mansfield. Dallas: Southern Methodist University Press, 1953, pp. 3–21.

Olson, Charles. *Call Me Ishmael.* New York: Reynall & Hitchcock, 1947.

Parke, John. "Seven *Moby-Dicks.*" *New England Quarterly* 28 (September 1955): 319–38.

Parker, Hershel. "Being Professional in Working on *Moby-Dick.*" *College Literature* 2 (1975): 192–97.

Percival, M.O. *A Reading of Moby-Dick.* Chicago: University of Chicago Press, 1950.

Pommer, Henry F. *Milton and Melville.* Pittsburgh, Pa.: University of Pittsburgh Press, 1950.

Rogin, Michael Paul. *Subversive Genealogy: The Politics and Art of Herman Melville.* New York: Knopf, 1983.

Rosenberry, Edward. *Melville and the Comic Spirit.* Cambridge: Harvard University Press, 1955.

Ross, Morton L. "*Moby-Dick* as an Education." *Studies in the Novel* 6 (Spring 1974): 62–75.

Sachs, Viola. *The Game of Creation: The Primeval Unlettered Language of Moby-Dick; or, The Whale.* Paris: Editions de la Maison des Sciences de l'Homme, 1982.

Sealts, Merton M., Jr. "Melville and Emerson's Rainbow." *ESQ* 26 (Second Quarter 1980): 53–78. Slightly revised in *Pursuing Melville, 1940–1980.* Madison, WI: University of Wisconsin Press, 1982, pp. 250–277.

———."Melville and the Platonic Tradition." In *Pursuing Melville, 1940–1980.* Madison, WI: University of Wisconsin Press, 1982, pp. 278–336.

Sedgwick, William Ellery. *The Tragedy of Mind.* Cambridge, MA: Harvard University Press, 1944.

Seelye, John. *Melville: The Ironic Diagram.* Evanston, IL: Northwestern University Press, 1970.

Sewall, Richard B. "Ahab's Quenchless Feud: The Tragic Vision in Shakespeare and Melville." *Comparative Drama* 1 (Fall 1967): 207–18.

Smith, Henry Nash. "The Image of Society in *Moby-Dick.*" In *Moby-Dick Centennial*

Essays. Ed. Tyrus Hillway and Luther S. Mansfield. Dallas: Southern Methodist University Press, 1953, pp. 59–75.

Stackpole, Edouard A. *The Sea-Hunters: The New England Whaleman During Two Centuries: 1635–1835*. Philadelphia: Lippincott, 1953.

Stafford, John. "Henry Norman Hudson and the Whig Use of Shakespeare," *PMLA* 66 (September 1951): 649–61.

Stanonik, Janez. *Moby-Dick: The Myth and the Symbol, A Study In Folklore and Literature*. Ljubljana, Yugoslavia: Ljubljana University Press, 1962.

Stewart, George R. "The Two *Moby-Dicks*." *American Literature* 25 (January 1954): 417–48.

Stone, Geoffrey. *Melville*. New York: Sheed & Ward, 1949.

Sweeney, Gerard M. *Melville's Use of Classical Mythology*. Amsterdam: Rodopi, 1975.

Tanselle, G. Thomas. *A Checklist of Editions of Moby-Dick, 1851–1976*. Evanston and Chicago: Northwestern University Press and The Newberry Library, 1976.

Thompson, Lawrance. *Melville's Quarrel with God*. Princeton, N.J.: Princeton University Press, 1952.

Thorp, Willard. *Herman Melville: Representative Selections, with Introduction, Bibliography, and Notes*. New York: American Book, 1938.

Trimpi, Helen P. "Melville's Use of Demonology and Witchcraft in *Moby-Dick*." *Journal of the History of Ideas* 30 (1969): 543–62.

Ujhazy, Maria. *Herman Melville's World of Whaling*. Atlantic Highlands, N.J.: Humanities Press, 1982.

Van Cromphout, Gustaaf. "*Moby-Dick*: The Transformation of the Faustian Epoch." *American Literature* 51 (March 1979): 17–32.

Vargish, Thomas. "Gnostic *Mythos* in *Moby-Dick*." *PMLA* 81 (June 1966): 272–77.

Vincent, Howard P. "*The Trying-Out of Moby-Dick*." Boston: Houghton Mifflin, 1948.

Vincent, Howard P., ed. *Melville and Hawthorne in the Berkshires: A Symposium*. Kent, Ohio: Kent State University Press, 1968.

Wadlington, Warwick. *The Confidence Game in American Literature*. Princeton, N.J.: Princeton University Press, 1975.

Ward, J. A. "The Function of the Cetological Chapters in *Moby-Dick*." *American Literature* 28 (May 1956): 164–83.

Werge, Thomas. "*Moby-Dick* and the Calvinist Tradition." *Studies in the Novel* 1 (Winter 1969): 484–506.

Woodson, Thomas. "Ahab's Greatness: Prometheus as Narcissus." *ELH: A Journal of English Literary History* 33 (September 1966): 351–69.

Wright, Nathalia. *Melville's Use of the Bible*. Durham, N.C.: Duke University Press, 1949.

———."*Moby-Dick*: Jonah's or Job's Whale?" *American Literature* 37 (May 1965): 190–95.

Yu, Beongcheon. "Ishmael's Equal Eye: The Course of Balance in *Moby-Dick*." *ELH: A Journal of English Literary History* 32 (March 1965): 110–25.

Zoellner, Robert. *The Salt-Sea Mastodon: A Reading of Moby-Dick*. Berkeley, CA: University of California Press, 1973.

Collections of Critical Essays:

Chase, Richard, ed. *Melville: A Collection of Critical Essays.* Englewood Cliffs, N.J.: Prentice-Hall, 1962.
Gilmore, Michael T., ed. *Twentieth-Century Interpretations of Moby-Dick.* Englewood Cliffs, NJ: Prentice-Hall, 1977.
Hillway, Tyrus and Luther S. Mansfield, eds. *Moby-Dick Centennial Essays.* Dallas: Southern Methodist University Press, 1953.
Lee, A. Robert, ed. *Herman Melville: Reassessments.* Totowa, N.J.: Barnes & Noble, 1984.
Pullin, Faith, ed. *New Perspectives on Melville.* Kent, Ohio and Edinburgh: Kent State University Press and Edinburgh University Press, 1978.
Stern, Milton R., ed. *Discussions of Moby-Dick.* Boston: Heath, 1960.
Vincent, Howard P., ed. *The Merrill Studies in Moby-Dick.* Columbus, OH: Charles E. Merrill, 1969.

Melville's Whaling Sources:

[Anonymous.] "Whales." *The Penny Cyclopaedia of the Society for the Diffusion of Useful Knowledge.* London: Charles Knight, 1843. Vol. 27, pp. 271–298.
Beale, Thomas. *The Natural History of the Sperm Whale.* 2nd ed. London: Van Voorst, 1839. [*Reading, #52*].
Bennett, Frederick Debell. *Narrative of a Whaling Voyage Round the Globe.* 2 vols. London, 1840.
Browne, John Ross. *Etchings of a Whaling Cruise.* New York: Harper, 1846. [*Reading, #88*].
Cheever, Henry T. *The Whale and His Captors.* New York: Harper, 1849.
Heffernan, Thomas Farel. *Stove by a Whale: Owen Chase and the "Essex."* Middletown, CT: Wesleyan University Press, 1981.
Olmsted, Francis Allyn. *Incidents of a Whaling Voyage.* New York, 1841.
Scoresby, William. *An Account of the Arctic Regions, with a History and Description of the Northern Whale Fishery,* 2 vols. Edinburgh: Constable, 1820. [*Reading, #450*].

8

READING *PIERRE*

Brian Higgins and Hershel Parker

Seldom assigned even in graduate classrooms, still passed sometimes from hand to hand as a talisman (as *Moby-Dick* once was), *Pierre* is perhaps taken up most often by readers avid to find just what kind of book Melville could have written in the months after he finished his whaling book.[1] Probably no reader has ever been quite prepared for the multitudinous and multi-directional shocks of reading *Pierre*. Nothing should deter the young or more mature but still innocent Enthusiast to Melvillean Truth from approaching the book alone, but he should be aware that old marauding Melvilleans, survivors of those shocks, now motivated by pure peacefulness and kindly fellowship with nature, have left behind in their bibliographical Barrington Isle symmetrical lounges of stone and turf where the wayfaring reader may careen, refit, and refresh himself for *The Ambiguities*. Amid old nails, rusty hoops, rusted cutlasses and daggers, and fragments of broken jars, the reader will find compilations of documents about *Pierre*, some conscientiously researched histories of its composition and publication, and some genial overviews of scholarship and criticism. But the reader, lounging off guard in romantic seats left by the not unmitigated monsters, should beware. Young reader or older hand, don't let anyone tell you he understands this book.[2]

Writing on *Pierre* since 1963 is noted in the Melville chapter of *American Literary Scholarship*. The "Introduction" to Brian Higgins and Hershel Parker's collection, *Critical Essays on Herman Melville's "Pierre; or, The Ambiguities"* (1983), is a full and accurate account of the composition, the negotiations for publication, and the motivations for and the dating of the enlargement of the book from an estimated 360 pages to an eventual 500. It supersedes the history of the composition of *Pierre* by Leon Howard in the "Historical Note" to the 1970 NN edition (except for its still-valuable discussion of literary influences) and supersedes "Why *Pierre* Went Wrong," where Parker first printed the 21 January 1852 letter from Melville's lawyer-brother Allan, which dates the enlargement. (In the interests of the history of scholarship it needs to be said that Howard's section of the "Historical Note" largely supersedes his own discussion in his 1951 *Herman Melville: A Biography*, where he did not deal with the discrepancy between the estimated length of the book in the contract and the actual length of the book as published.) The "Introduction" does not supersede Parker's "Contract: *Pierre*" for its photographic reproductions of the contract between Melville and the Harpers (including two draft passages for the contract in the hand of Allan Melville) or for its extended analysis of the terms of the contract (most important of which was a reduction of Melville's profits from the usual 50 cents on the dollar after expenses to 20 cents on the dollar). The "Gansevoort trove" acquired by the New York Public Library in 1983 (after the Higgins-Parker "Introduction" was written) sheds additional cross-light on Melville's motivations for enlarging *Pierre*. The "Note on the Text" in the NN edition by the three editors, Harrison Hayford, Hershel Parker, and G. Thomas Tanselle, provides a brief account of the 1852 Harper edition (some sets of the Harper sheets—not many: a dozen? a hundred?—were issued in London in the same year with a Sampson Low title page) and traces the book's later publication history beginning with its first reprinting in the 1923 Constable Edition. Detailed study of the words of the text is facilitated by Larry Edward Wegener's *A Concordance to Herman Melville's "Pierre; Or, The Ambiguities."* The basic tool for study of Melville's life before and during the composition of *Pierre* is Jay Leyda's supplemented, second printing of *The Melville Log*.

The NN "Historical Note" contains Hershel Parker's extensive summary and characterization of the contemporary reception in the United States (only one review is known to have appeared in England, an indication that very few copies were distributed). Previous samples of the reviews are superseded by the Higgins-Parker collection, which includes all the known reviews in their entirety, printed in chronological order. (All our page citations for reviews of *Pierre* are to this collection, cited as *Critical Essays*.) Another section of the "Historical Note" by Parker gives a brief account of the sporadic commentary on *Pierre* between 1852 and the beginnings of the Melville Revival, during which "the general literary reputation of *Pierre* was created by critics struck by the extraordinary modernity of its psychological probings and by its anticipations of modern fictional techniques" (p. 396). A longer section by Parker surveys the development of two interpretive camps, one finding in the book momentous revelations of Melville's family history as well as profound anticipations of Freudian psychology, the other (led by Robert S. Forsythe, whose edition of *Pierre* appeared in the Americana Deserta series in 1930) seeing the book first of all in its place in literary history and, second, as a literary experiment in which Melville used family members and household paraphernalia merely for convenience. Parker traces the attempts to combine these rival approaches (in particular William S. Braswell's 1936 accounting for the style in terms of Melville's life: his career floundering, Melville "was having his last fling," expecting the book "to be his final publication" ("Satirical Temper," p. 427). Parker then turns to the course of academic criticism as it burgeoned in the 1950s, when critics were concerned mainly with "the significance of literary allusions, of mythic patterns, of imagery, and of metaphors" (*Pierre*, p. 403) but, regardless of their approaches, still frequently recurred to a few major topics: "the possible sources in British, Continental, and American literature; the relationships to themes and characters in Melville's other works; and the meanings of particular symbols or passages" (p. 404). In his final section Parker reviews the critical debate over the meaning of the pamphlet on "Chronometricals and Horologicals" attributed to the philosopher Plotinus Plinlimmon (Book 14, Chapter 3), a section which twentieth-century critics have seen as central to the meaning of the entire work, some taking Plinlimmon as a spokesman for Melville, others seeing him as a satiric butt. Parker concludes that in spite of the conflicting nature of the criticism several of the major commentators "have partially indicated a way of resolving the difficulties: by accepting that on an intellectual level Melville might often if not always agree with the ideas attributed to Plinlimmon while altogether dissociating himself from the blandly rational and self-satisfied tone in which Plinlimmon is reported to express them" (p. 406).

In addition to all the known reviews, the Higgins-Parker collection contains "virtually all of the known commentary on the book from 1853 to 1917" (including extracts from the invaluable 1892 memoir of Melville by J.E.A. Smith); "most of the known commentaries, in their entirety or in large extract, from 1919 to 1929"; and a selection of later essays and chapters which the editors believe "have enhanced understanding and appreciation of the book" (p. 27). The longest pieces in this last section are E. L. Grant Watson's "Melville's *Pierre*" (1930), a brilliant summary-commentary on the book as a powerfully prescient exploration of conscious and unconscious psychology (one of the most profound and most sympathetic responses to Melville ever recorded); a substantial part of Richard H. Brodhead's chapter on *Pierre*, "The Fate of Candor" (1976), the most conscientious of several recent attempts to see the book as a companion volume to *Moby-Dick* in themes and ambitiousness; and a somewhat revised version of the Higgins-Parker "The Flawed Grandeur of Melville's *Pierre*" (1978), the most detailed attempt to anatomize the structure of the book as Melville first wrote it and the conflicting aims of some of the late-added portions. (Their "Introduction" accounts for the flaws from a biographical point of view rather than from internal evidence.) The collection also includes a significant but short essay, "New Crosslights on the Illegitimate Daughter in *Pierre*," in which Amy Puett Emmers prints a suspiciously cryptic letter from Melville's uncle Thomas Melvill to Melville's future father-in-law Lemuel Shaw; the essay was originally published in 1977 under the somewhat misleading title of "Melville's Closet Skeleton: A New Letter about the Illegitimacy Incident in *Pierre*."

The Higgins-Parker collection must be supplemented by several studies. Harrison Hayford's "The Significance of Melville's 'Agatha' Letters" (1946), is the first and still the best analysis of, and dismissal of, the possibility that Melville's letter offering Richard Bentley *Pierre* was an attempt to "mulct" his English publisher. It is also the first enunciation of a now-common reading of *Pierre* in the light of the theory Melville promulgated in his 1850 essay on Hawthorne's *Mosses from an Old Manse*—the theory that dark books, telling profound truths, could be so contrived that the superficial skimmer of pages could read them for amusement while the eagle-eyed reader read them for grand revelations about human nature and the universe. The editors of the collection could not gain permission to excerpt Murray's extremely important Introduction to the 1949 Hendricks House edition. Murray's work on *Pierre* may have antedated that of Mumford, who acknowledged Murray's help in his 1929 preface and who in the *Saturday Review of Literature* for 29 June 1929 specifically acknowledged the biographical research Murray had brought to bear upon *Pierre*. Murray's study seems to have been published out of its proper time, the boldly Freudian 1920s, for it shares many of the faults of the 1920s, such as facile identification of the fictional with the real. Nevertheless, it remains an essential provocative and exhilarative, the record of a momentous modern engagement with a momentous book. Parker's article on the contract for *Pierre* supersedes the slightly erroneous discussion of the contract in William Charvat's *The Profession of Authorship in America, 1800–1870* (1968), but Charvat's survey of Melville's career as a professional writer is still valuable, though rarely consulted. The letter Emmers first published is reprinted by Henry A. Murray, Harvey Myerson, and Eugene Taylor in a 1985 essay, "Allan Melvill's By-Blow," a title as problematical as the original title of her own essay. (The title states as indubitable fact the possibility—or even the high probability—that Melville's father had an illegitimate daughter.)

The Higgins-Parker collection ends with the editors' brief prospectus for future scholarship and criticism on *Pierre*. Most needed, they point out, are critics who "will discard the prevailing assumptions inherited from the New Criticism, so that they will not automatically feel compelled to define Melville's 'intention' in *Pierre*, as if he had had a single intention, one 'pervading thought that impelled the book,' but rather will acknowledge and analyze his dual or multiple intentions which shifted as a result of the blows dealt him by his publisher and by the reviewers of *Moby-Dick* and as a result of other, perhaps still identifiable, forces in his life" (p. 268). In the perfervid academic atmosphere of the 1980s this call for openminded readers has proved controversial. Robert Milder warns in *American Literary Scholarship (ALS), 1983* that the reader should "beware" the G. K. Hall collection: "From its Introduction, which draws on Parker's previous work and speculates broadly about the composition of *Pierre*, to its concluding 'Prospects for Criticism on *Pierre*,' which proselytizes for the 'New Scholarship' (see *ALS 1981*, pp. 60–61), the Higgins-Parker volume is an exercise in critical canon-formation that institutionalizes the editors' preferred literary method and claims unwarranted authority for critical conclusions drawn from an arguable reading of the external evidence" (p. 70). Those are serious charges, perhaps even more so than James Duban's accusation in *Melville's Major Fiction* (1983) that Higgins and Parker are guilty of "a too-facile biographical reading" (p. 181), although no self-respecting genial old Melvillean wants to be thought to take a simplistic approach to a book subtitled *The Ambiguities*.

This chapter will not be "an exercise in critical canon-formation," but it will not be an impersonal academic exercise. If it is to be a true guide, a companion on an ambiguous and arduous yet exhilarating journey, it must deal with some of the reasons that writing on *Pierre* has been, on the whole, so inconclusive and unsatisfactory, and must point toward approaches that may yet prove astonishingly fruitful. The dreariness of most writing on *Pierre* is rarely ascribable to the incompetence of individual critics but rather to the state and status of scholarship from decade to decade and the controlling assumptions of literary criticism, from the Freudian twenties, through the New Critical fifties and sixties, right into the deconstruction and post-Freudian structuralism of the 1980s. Each period displays its own prejudices and limitations. But it is no less true that each period, except perhaps the last, has taught us much—has taught us more than we always remember, as we can show by a few illustrations.

A SAMPLER OF CRITICISM

In 1929 Lewis Mumford played fast and loose with facts (saying that Melville exclaimed in one passage of *Pierre*, " 'I write to please myself' "(p. 199) and that Melville dedicated the book "to his one solitary and steadfast companion, Mt. Monadnock" [p. 200]). Even though he despised the style of parts of *Pierre*, Mumford was sympathetically alert to the possibility that the book was a genuine, although "abortive," complement to *Moby-Dick* (p. 200). Lacking facts of the composition available to us, never having read the contract, apparently, Mumford pictured Melville as settling to work "in the spring of 1852" (another factual error) in a "mood of defeat, foreboding, defiant candour" (p. 200). We need to discard our prejudices against slapdash, hubristic Freudianism in order to see that Mumford may be partly and brilliantly right: that although Melville probably began the book around November 1851 in a mood of victory, self-assurance, and, indeed, defiant candor, he enlarged the book, beginning in January 1852, in moods that ranged from defiant, sardonic candor to suicidal despair. The danger of not appreciating Mumford becomes clear if we look at one of his best formulations:

What did Melville consciously set himself to do when he wrote Pierre? He sought, I think, to arrive at the same sort of psychological truth that he had achieved, in metaphysics, in Moby-Dick. His subject was, not the universe, but the ego; and again, not the obvious ego of the superficial novelist, but those implicated and related layers of self which reach from the outer appearances of physique and carriage down to the recesses of the unconscious personality. "The novel will find the way to our interiors, one day," he wrote in Pierre, "and will not always be a novel of costume merely." (p. 211)

Melville did not write that in *Pierre*, but we lose by our irritation if it keeps us from following the argument, for Mumford's formulation is brilliant. In the interests of accuracy, we would want to change only the first sentence: "What did Melville consciously set himself to do when he wrote *Pierre*—that is, when he wrote the short version which he carried to New York City to show the Harpers, before he wrecked it under different impulses?" ("Short" is relative: *Redburn* was 390 pages in the Harper edition, and Melville had thought of it as short, at least until he "enlarged" it [*Letters*, pp. 86, 88].) And any such attempt to put accurate words into his mouth reminds us that, unlike most academics, Mumford wrote genuine English prose (what he lost in geographical accuracy, he gained in alliteration).

Stung by the insensitivity of Mumford and others who had condemned Melville for writing pages of trash indistinguishable from the trash of *Godey's Lady's Book*, William Braswell in 1950 came to the defense in "The Early Love Scenes in Melville's *Pierre*." He convincingly argued that "certain passages which have been criticized as insipidly sentimental are rather mock-romantic," meant to be humorously satirical. Yet Braswell remained perturbed: "is it fitting that a novelist go so far in mocking a hero to whom he is obviously devoted and for whom he ultimately desires the reader's deepest sympathy?" Braswell concluded that censuring Melville for such lapses "would be very different from censuring him for not writing conventional romance in an acceptable manner. Though he might justly be condemned for a perverse use of his undeniably great power as a writer, he should not be condemned for failing to do what he had no intention of doing" (p. 289). Although he is attuned to Melville's satiric tone and alert to some of the satiric targets (such as "the optimistic Emersonian belief that good is ousting evil from the universe" [p. 289]), Braswell leaves *Pierre* reduced from the grandeur claimed for it as a whole by E. L. Grant Watson and claimed for parts of it by Mumford, Murray, and others.

First in "Melville and the Common Reader" (1958) and then in a longer, uncompleted reworking of that essay in the posthumously published *The Profession of Authorship in America, 1800–1870*, William Charvat placed *Pierre* (more fully than others had done) in the context of his professional career. He saw Melville as having engaged in a "conflict with his readers, which lasted the whole ten years of his professional writing life and ended in a defeat which even in our time has not been completely reversed" (p. 204). Analyzing Melville's prefaces for clues to his sense of what he was doing and what he wanted his readers to think he was doing, analyzing Melville's correspondence with his publishers, reading Melville's contracts, using the reviews that were available to him, Charvat told a persuasive story of Melville as a struggling, opportunistic, self-deluding, willful genius trapped by a readership that had overvalued him for his forays into journalistic semi-autobiography and that persisted in undervaluing his attempts to assert himself as heir to "the great tradition of Western art which grew out of the Renaissance" (p. 217).

Charvat is often inexact in details, as when he misreads the terms of the contract for *Pierre* and makes the Harpers' skepticism about the manuscript a response to the longer work as we know it. Like Mumford, Charvat ignores the possibility that Melville's intentions shifted during the composition of the book. (He does not explicitly comment on the discrepancy between the page estimate in the contract and the length of the published book, a problem first analyzed by Leon Howard in the NN *Pierre*.) Despite such minor lapses, Charvat should be required reading for critics, since he is more sensitive to the vicissitudes of Melville's career, his aspirations, mistakes, and achievements, than later writers who have ventured onto the same terrain, such as Ann Douglas in *The Feminization of American Culture* (1977) or Nina Baym in "Melville's Quarrel with Fiction" (1979).

Charvat was an older historicist scholar persisting in the face of the triumphant New Criticism, but most writing on *Pierre* has been in the mode of the New Criticism, whether or not the critics have known or said so. Underlying most essays on *Pierre* is the conviction that a novel is by definition a work of art, perfectly unified, ready for the critic to count its images, explicate its symbols, and demonstrate that any tensions between warring elements can in fact be triumphantly justified in the critic's essay. The title of a 1974 essay by Robert Milder, "Melville's 'Intentions' in *Pierre*," is misleading. Milder means "Intention," for he declares that "*Pierre* is an intensely deliberate book" (187); the "book Melville published, 'loathsome' as it seemed to many of its first readers, is the book he set out to write" (p. 193). This is demonstrably wrong: the book Melville set out to write, in so far as it ever had an achieved existence, was the short manuscript he carried to New York, not the book the Harpers published. What is revealing in Milder's article is just how engrained had become the New Critical assumption that by definition any literary work is written under one pervading intention. In a more relentless fashion this conviction about literature governs James Duban's 1983 discussion of *Pierre*. Duban's task is to demonstrate the unity of Pierre-as-author with the rest of the book, thereby refuting such biographicizers as Higgins and Parker. A counter-tendency in another heir of the formalist new critics is apparent in Richard Brodhead's cogent study, "The Fate of Candor"(1976). Brodhead recognizes that Melville's intentions shifted in the course of writing the book, but he makes the best of a bad situation, deciding that since it is good to have such a section as "Young America in Literature," nothing that led to its being written is to be deplored. What is lost in each of these approaches—the one that identifies aesthetic unity at all costs and the one that accepts cheerfully the fact that Melville may have had his little compositional troubles as long as those troubles led him to compose more pages, imperfect or not, for us to read—is any sense of the process of composition, the day-to-day, even hour-by-hour struggle any writer has to retain control, and any sense that losing control, however heady the recklessness may at times have felt, was in the long run destructive to Melville's sense of himself as a man and as a professional writer and to any sense of triumph he had first had in what he had written as a brilliant, short psychological novel. In studiously avoiding biographical evidence, critics may seem cold-blooded formalists, heartless rationalists, when set against earlier writers such as Lewis Mumford, E. L. Grant Watson, and William Charvat.

Most studies of the 1970s and 1980s have been less significant, dealing with less genuine formal issues than Braswell had done, less profound psychological issues than the writers of the Revival had grappled with. During the 1970s there were stirrings of interest in aspects of *Pierre* which had been ruled out of order by the fear of the genetic fallacy and the biographical fallacy proclaimed by the New Critics. Such a general article as Nina Baym's "Melville's Quarrel with Fiction" (1979) has no match in the articles published in the preceding three decades. Baym focuses on *Pierre* after a survey of Melville's earlier career and follows her discussion with a section, however truncated, on his later writing. She recognizes the importance of knowing what literary models Melville might have had for *Pierre*, and implies that she has given close readings to the reviews of the book. Baym declares that Emerson's thought, especially as embodied in the "Language" chapter of *Nature*, is "the single most significant influence on the shape of *Moby-Dick*" (p. 915) and is the source of a belief which Melville disastrously repudiated in *Pierre*: in *Moby-Dick* Melville had doubted truth, in *Pierre* he doubted language itself. According to Baym, the doubt of language arose because Melville was attempting an uncongenial genre, the *bildungsroman*: "But as might have been predicted, Melville found his commitment distasteful and irksome almost from the first sentence. And with his revulsion from genre came, now, a revulsion from language itself " (p. 918). Despising the language of *Pierre* herself, much as the early reviewers had done, she misses out on the exuberance, the intellectual exhilaration, the sheer fun, of what Melville achieved. Baym's arguments are hard to deal with because the air of scholarship is so thick, until one looks closely—at all the known reviews, for instance, or at the much larger context of Romantic views of language in which Carlyle (whom she ignores) is demonstrably important to Melville, while there is no evidence at all that by the time of *Pierre* Melville had read *Nature*, and no evidence that he ever did. Merton M. Sealts, Jr., in "Melville and Emerson's Rainbow" (1980) goes over the available evidence meticulously before concluding: "I have been unable to satisfy myself that Melville ever read *Nature*" (p. 67). Furthermore, Baym's article reveals the same sort of carelessness about details that one deplores in Mumford: She says Melville died in 1892 (really, 1891); she finds it odd that Melville did not mention "Feathertop" in his essay on Hawthorne's *Mosses from an Old Manse* (not odd— it wasn't in the work Melville was reviewing).

We are probably not alone in finding that still other recent writing on *Pierre* (much of it in the form of exercises in post-Freudian structuralism or nouveau-phenomenology cum do-it-by-the-dots deconstructionism) often seems to demonstrate the adeptness of the critic with a modish literary approach rather than anything about the book or about Melville. Post-New Critical readings by Eric Sundquist (1979), who examines the book as "the record of Melville's exhaustion and burning out on the themes of authority and genealogy" (p. 145); by Edgar A. Dryden (1979), who argues that the book is "about reading and writing, about the consumption and production of literary texts" (p. 146); and by Brook Thomas (1979), who claims that the book scrutinizes "the patriarchal structure of the family and of writing" (p. 417)—all illustrate this tendency. Such criticism typically abounds in ingenious formulations like these by Sundquist: "Not the phallus of signification, but its absence, the wholesale demolition of the *object* of reference, is *Pierre's* locus of truth"

(p. 162); "what is precisely at stake in *Pierre* is whether the sexual crisis has not dissolved belief in the *object* altogether, whether authority has not taken sanction in a labyrinth of words to be read, displacing the *object* of the Father, his Word" (p. 174). Such formulations, however "precisely" edged they are, probably leave most readers, whether sophisticated young enthusiasts to theory or simplistic old biographers and bibliographers, stranded, farther remote from *Pierre* than ever.

The authors of this chapter are now, for better or worse, part of the literary history of *Pierre*, not disinterested parties and not innocent bystanders. We can turn this potential liability into an advantage by calling attention to our assumptions as well as the assumptions of others, testing assumptions and weighing relevance and substance of evidence on the topics that have absorbed the attention of critics and scholars. We will end with a discussion of the implications which biographical evidence about the composition has for future interpretation.

AUTOBIOGRAPHICAL ELEMENTS

In Melville's lifetime almost everyone seemed to have read some of his early books as fairly reliable autobiography (*Typee* and *Omoo* in particular, but often the much more fictional *Redburn* and *White-Jacket* as well, or even *Moby-Dick*). So far as we know, no one read *Pierre* as autobiographical, except in the way the New York *Sun* casually did on 16 August 1852 in telling its readers that *Pierre* had something to do "with 'an immature attempt at a mature book,' wherein, perchance, the author has taken a look at his first beginnings" (*Critical Essays*, p. 35). Later critics have recognized in Pierre's attempt to write a mature book an account, however distanced, of Melville's own attempts to do the same thing—first in *Mardi*, then in *Moby-Dick*, then in *Pierre* itself.

When he read *Pierre* in 1852, Melville's estranged friend Evert A. Duyckinck, the editor of The *Literary World*, must have recognized himself as the original for the editor of the *Captain Kidd Monthly* in "Young America in Literature," since Melville had based a passage directly on his refusal of Duyckinck's request for Melville's Daguerreotype in February 1851 (*Letters*, pp. 119–22). Duyckinck must have recognized also that that section of the book was Melville's wry backward look at the process by which American writers like himself were hyped to the public with scant regard for the genuineness of their originality, but he had his reasons for focusing his criticism on other parts of the book. J. E. A. Smith, who called his friend Melville "almost a zealot in his love of Berkshire scenery" (Sealts, *Early Lives*, p. 198, from Smith's 1879 edition of *Taghconic*), was the first to compile a list of real terrain and real household paraphernalia which found their way into the book and the first to suggest that a character might have been based on a member of Melville's family.

Since the Melville Revival, beginning with Raymond Weaver, students of Melville's life have discovered a close correspondence between some of the paraphernalia at Saddle Meadows and real items possessed by the Melvilles and Gansevoorts—paintings, drums, banners, camp-bed, and so on. More consequential to later critics was Weaver's assumption that in his portrayal of Mary Glendinning Melville was giving the inside narrative of his own relationship with his mother, Maria Gansevoort Melville. Robert S. Forsythe best represents the skeptical attitude some scholars of the 1930s took toward the relevance of both the stage properties and the family relationships: Melville was writing fiction, not autobiography, and when he made use of a captured British banner he had seen at his Uncle Peter's or when he worked into the plot a character based on his Gansevoort grandfather, he was turning real things and people to convenient fictional purposes, without importing emotional baggage along with real objects and people. For Forsythe, autobiographical elements were "almost always mere details used in heightening character or rendering settings more vivid" (p. xxii). Taking *Pierre* as a portrait of real people, places, and objects culminates, for better or worse, in Henry A. Murray's 1949 edition. Murray concludes, with only slight qualification, that "the models of the principal characters are all (with the possible exception of Mr. Ballard [a Pittsfield minister Murray links to Falsgrave]) persons to whom Melville was affectionately attached during some period of his life; and, setting aside his brothers and sisters, no one he is known to have loved has been excluded from the cast" (p. xxii).

Such relentless searching for correspondences between real people and fictional characters has struck many recent critics as reductive, if not repugnant. Yet some of the most speculative readings of real people and places into the book have proved appealing. John Seelye's 1969 suggestion that Isabel has some connection with Hawthorne cannot be disregarded, though what Melville meant by placing the Ulver cottage in a location similar to that of the little red cottage at Tanglewood is unanswered. Ever since *Typee* (where comments on the nudity or exotic costumes of South Sea maidens were plainly designed to tease his sisters) Melville had regarded his manuscripts as places to put private messages, just as for a time he read the *Literary World* as a private letter from Evert A. Duyckinck to himself. Overwhelmed by his affinity with Hawthorne as he began the book, to the point of wanting to write only for him, on an "endless riband of foolscap" (*Letters*, p. 144) stretching from Arrowhead to the little red cottage or wherever else Hawthorne might be, Melville might well have put a private message to him or about him into *Pierre*.

Around the time he prepared his edition of *Pierre* Murray had been told, by Charles Olson, of the letter which Amy Puett Emmers rediscovered three decades later. For other Melvilleans, Emmers's publication of the letter from Thomas Melvill, Jr., to Judge Shaw stunningly complicated the question of the autobiographical nature of *Pierre* by its revelation that two women with claims on the estate of Melville's father called at the Melvill house in Boston twice, shortly after his death in January 1832 and before September 1832, when Melville's grandfather died. "Mrs. A. M. A." and "Mrs. B." saw, to the best of Thomas Melvill, Jr.'s knowledge, only his aged mother and his sister Helen, Melville's aunt. When he arrived in Boston, Thomas was told of the visits and himself went to see Mrs. A. and Mrs. B. in order to dispel "the erroneous ideas they had formed of *claims*" (*Critical Essays*, p. 237) on the old Major Melvill or on Allan's estate. Thomas gave Mrs. B. some money, but denied to Shaw that he had given Mrs. A. "*some encouragement.*" He admitted to feeling sympathy for her: "From the little I saw of her, I thought her quite an interesting young person,—that it was most unfortunate she had not been brought up different—and I most deeply regret that she too, has been called to feel the disappointments & sorrows, so generally attending our earthly sojourn" (*Critical Essays*, p. 238).

Some cautionary words are in order. A few Melvilleans (including Hayford) acknowledge that the letter looks like nothing so much as a letter about a family scandal, where the very obliquity of expression is a sign of the incriminating nature of the business, but nevertheless point out that we inevitably read the letter in the light of *Pierre*. The point is that if Melville had not written *Pierre*, we might not so readily leap to the conclusion that the letter concerns an illegitimate daughter of his father's. Furthermore, while Murray, Myerson, and Taylor are extremely plausible, if not all but entirely convincing in their 1985 identification of the two women who called at the Melvill home in Boston in 1832, there is still room for lurking skepticisms. Does the Boston Directory list other households in which women with the initials B. and A. M. A. both resided? Need the women have resided at the same address? If the newly identified Miss Bent and Miss Allen were the mysterious callers, was their mission to seek redress for paternal abandonment of Miss Allen or was it for a more mundane purpose—to collect, for instance, a bad business debt? The most obvious reading of the letter is in all likelihood the correct one, but we cannot, without more evidence, be entirely sure either that Allan Melvill had a "by-blow" or, if he did, and the child was a daughter, that she was Ann M. Allen.

Speculation concerning the possibility that Melville had and knew he had an unacknowledged half-sister is of a somewhat different order from earlier speculation about real places, objects, and people familiar to Melville and their fictional parallels. If Melville really had a half-sister the family never acknowledged, who in the family (besides his Uncle Thomas, his Aunt Helen, and—part of the family even then, in intimacy—Shaw) knew about her, and who told Herman? If Herman knew a secret which almost no one else, by 1851, knew, did he think he could base a plot on it without horrifying his mother and other close relatives? Did he *want* to horrify his mother? We simply do not know for sure. To begin with, we do not know, beyond a shadow of a doubt, that there was an unacknowledged half-sister.

In his work on a biography projected for 1991, Parker is elaborating an autobiographical approach to *Pierre* which can only be sketched here as a way of discussing the limits of responsible speculation. According to this view, *Redburn*, which Melville dismissed as trash he wrote to buy tobacco with, and which modern critics have found interesting mainly for the handling of point of view, may be important to *Pierre*—perhaps more important than the two books some writers of the 1920s and 1930s saw as forming a trilogy with it—*Mardi* and *Moby-Dick*. Parker plans to suggest that Melville began exploiting his own psychological past in *Redburn* merely as an expedient, as a fast way of getting material for a narrative of a trip to Liverpool loosely based on his own, probably without realizing how dangerous memory can be. He was to write of Pierre immaturely attempting a mature work: "Not yet had he dropped his angle into the well of his childhood to find what fish might be there; for who dreams to find fish in a well?" (*Pierre*, p. 284). In *Redburn* Melville was attempting a popular book, having just immaturely attempted a mature one, and he was cavalierly dropping his angle into the well of childhood, not prepared for what fish might bite. In this view, the innocuous *Redburn* might have laid open the floodgates to the unconscious, and months may have passed before Melville paid full attention to what was emerging from that wonder world—a grand hooded phantom, like a snow-hill in the air, we assume.

Parker plans to argue that *Redburn* started the process by which Melville would get deeper and deeper into the dangerous confrontation of his own childhood, but that what accelerated the process, what so stirred Melville in the summer of 1850, and led the next year to his relentless exploration of the unconscious in *Pierre* and to the formulation of and enunciation of general psychological laws in it, was Pittsfield itself, more than Shakespeare and Milton, more even than Hawthorne, who is so frequently cited as the sole precipitant of Melville's manic state of mind in the summer of 1850. At his late Uncle Thomas's house, where he was staying that summer, Melville had witnessed his father and the uncle he had never seen before renew an intense family relationship which antedated his own birth by four decades (*Mel. Log*, p. 48). (Redburn briefly speculates about his father's leading a life independent of him, before he was so much as thought of.) On that first visit to Pittsfield he was a secure boy, accompanied by a loving father, and thereafter he associated his uncle and father as wealthy, privileged businessmen-travelers, both fluent in French, both cosmopolitans. Melville went back again in the 1830s, after his father's death, for long periods, to stay with his uncle. At the time and later he managed to think (however unrealistically) of his uncle as a refugee from Versailles: at night when his uncle brooded before the fire, the boy thought that his mind had wandered away across the ocean to the boulevards of Paris (*Mel. Log*, pp. 63–64). In that house, Paris and Pittsfield or, in his phrase (*The History of Pittsfield*, p. 400), the Tuileries and the Taghconics, merged in Melville's imagination. (In *Pierre* he was to bring together Saddle Meadows and France in the story of Isabel.) Every time he had dinner there with his Aunt Mary and cousin Robert in the summer of 1850 or later with the Morewoods, who moved into the house in the early fall of 1850, he may have encountered his father and his uncle in memory. (This is all aside from the possibility that while living in that house, very possibly, Melville learned the family secret, if there was such a family secret, which he used for the illegitimate-daughter plot of *Pierre*. The obvious guess would be that he learned about it in Pittsfield, while he was living with or near his Uncle Thomas: did the incautious Thomas tell his son Robert, and did Robert tell his younger cousin?)

Everywhere in that region were traps for Melville's "susceptible and peradventure feeble [febrile?] temperament" (*Letters*, p. 133), reminders of how his life had changed, and changed again—through death, impoverishment, bodily changes, seasonal changes, his own travels, his literary achievements, his marriage. As a fatherless adolescent on the farm (very likely he entered puberty there), or as a teenaged school-teacher (the time his sexual urges would have been the most intense) when he boarded with rustics in the hills south of town, Melville had taken an outjutting of rock as a vantage point for brooding over the steeples of Pittsfield and the natural scenery dominated by Mount Grey-lock. He passed that outcropping whenever he took the Old Lenox Road to see Hawthorne. Making a turn on a road, just as much as glancing about a room at his uncle's old place, Melville in 1850 and 1851 collided with himself as a penniless and futureless youth, a sexually wondering and sexually excited youth, just as he had collided in 1849 with his younger self, now a famous author stepping ashore in England, in 1839 a ship's boy. Small wonder, Parker suggests, that a turbulent state began building as soon as Melville arrived at Pittsfield in July 1850 (Parker, "Melville and the Berkshires," pp. 65–69). Small wonder that months later he would dedicate *Pierre* to Mount Greylock.

Perhaps Melville could take the Old Lenox Road on a visit to Haw-thorne without looking at his old observation outpost, or could look toward it without having his past violently collide with the astonishing present. But we know that Melville habitually brooded about dates of memorable events and about the strangeness of being in a place he or someone he loved had been before; and we know that he habitually speculated about the differences between two or more times he had been in the same place. We hold that a biographer should be willing to speculate on the nature of Melville's youthful thoughts as he sat or stood or lay on that outcropping. We might be wrong to think that it is human nature to strike exalted postures in exalted places, but we know, more mundanely, that Melville himself knew a good deal about posturing from exalted topographical vantage points. What a literary youth did if he found a precipice in the decade or so after Byron's death, when Melville was much in Pittsfield, was apostrophize or soliloquize from it. The odd thing would have been if Melville had *not* struck Byronic postures there. He might also have thought long, long, thoughts there, before Longfellow put the phrase into the language. Why not go further and ask if Melville in his youth had spent some time there raging at his fate in what he later recognized as fatuous threats and bargains with the gods? If he had done so, that might account for his repeatedly characterizing Pierre by *his* posturings: maybe Melville was making easy self-satirizing literary use of a store of memories. Any pattern Melville saw in his own mental processes could be used as literary material (how else did he think to make Ishmael perceive each new situation or person as a tantalizing puzzle?), and he had become preoccupied at the unfolding of his mind, first intrigued, then awed and enthralled, by what he was drawing up from the well of childhood.

This theory about the influence of Pittsfield where past and present collided is offered here to help us understand why Melville just at this time was consumed with understanding his own psychology and human psychology in general. Such speculation, we submit, is not reductive, however inconclusive it must be. We are not going to understand *Pierre* until we understand Melville—and understanding Melville means approaching him in the spirit of Lewis Mumford, E.L. Grant Watson, and Henry A. Murray as well as the spirit of Robert S. Forsythe, Leon Howard, and William Charvat.

COMPOSITION

Because the contract for *Pierre* contains the 360–page estimate, scholars have reasonably thought that the enlargement took place after the contract was signed on 20 February 1852. That is not so. The estimate dates from the drawing up of the contract around the first of the year, and it remained unchanged because contingency clauses already covered the possibility of substantial variation from 360 pages. The Higgins-Parker "Introduction" lays out the evidence that Melville brought the short

version down to New York City from Pittsfield a week or so after Christmas 1851, and within a matter of days had agreed to accept lower royalties from the Harpers than in the past and then had become absorbed
in his enlargements. There is no doubt that both the decision to enlarge
Pierre and a great deal of actual enlarging took place in New York City
during the first two weeks or so of January 1852, before Melville went
back to Pittsfield and completed the book. (He may have expressed the
final manuscript to New York City without going there; Allan signed
the contract for him.) No one who has written on the discrepancy between estimated length and actual length (either before or after 1976,
when Parker first dated the start of the enlargement in January 1852)
has doubted that what was added consisted mainly of everything that
had to do with Pierre as an author. Indeed, it seemed obvious to the
reviewer in the *American Whig Review* that making Pierre an author was
"nothing more than an afterthought of Mr. Melville's, and not contemplated in the original plan of the book, that is, if it ever had a plan. It
is dragged in merely for the purpose of making Pierre a literary man,
when the author had just brought him to such a stage that he did not
know what else to do with him" (*Critical Essays*, p. 61). This writer was
in a fury at Melville, but he was not unreasonable. (The reviewer's assumption that the book as we have it was composed sequentially—though
a middle section was an afterthought—is not unlike the working assumption of so sophisticated a scholar as Charvat. We almost instinctively
think of books as growing from page 1 to page 496—even though we
know that Melville habitually stuck long passages down into or between
chapters composed much earlier.)

Melville's motivations for enlarging *Pierre* are less clear than the dating.
Parker's 1976 and 1977 view, clarified and elaborated with Higgins in
their 1983 Introduction, was that the negotiations with the Harpers and
the simultaneous exposure to some of the most scathing reviews of *Moby-
Dick* in the January periodicals set him off. The Higgins-Parker "Introduction" contains a little new speculation. The summer before, Duyckinck had urged Melville to let Redfield publish *Moby-Dick* rather than
the Harpers. During the negotiations over *Pierre* did Melville try the
manuscript out on Duyckinck to see if Redfield could make a good offer
for it? If so, did Duyckinck react in horror? If so, was that the immediate
cause for Melville's writing him into the manuscript as the editor of the
Captain Kidd Monthly? The "Introduction" should not be taken as toting
up all of the motives that led Melville to write an account of his own
disastrous career into the manuscript that had been completed or almost
completed in a short form—witness a letter in the Gansevoort trove that
reveals that in December, in Pittsfield, Melville was already very angry
that his neighbors were gossiping about *Moby-Dick* as "more than Blasphemous." There were conscious motives and unconscious motives, eva-

nescent motives and persistent motives—some more of which may yet be identified.

MELVILLE'S INTENTIONS IN *PIERRE*

Melville had strewn *White-Jacket* with tolerant disdain for the sentimental readers of "novels and romances" (p. 10). Yet this disdain of romances coexisted with a fascination for extravagant, mannered, romantic styles and with a desire to write an extraordinary romance. The two "Fragments from a Writing Desk" which Melville wrote at nineteen provide his earliest known example of such a style. The high spiritedness of the fragments indicates that they were easy to do because once Melville got the pitch he could go on indefinitely, fun to do because he could trick the unwary reader into taking his spoofing seriously, safe to do because when he spoofed a genre he did not risk exposing himself as genuinely attracted to it and challenged by it. After his literary career was established, he fell into a variation of the style in the Old Zack sketches (1847). His letters to his first English publisher, John Murray, in 1848 suggest that Melville had long wanted to write a romance—and in his mind had done so, in parts of *Mardi*. He had planned, he wrote, to postpone writing a romance of Polynesia, though he had "long thought" that it "furnished a great deal of rich poetical material" as yet unexploited in romances and at times "when in the mood" he had thrown off "occasional sketches applicable to such a work." While proceeding in his "narrative of *facts*," however, he had begun to feel such an incurable distaste for it that "suddenly" he gave up on it and "went to work heart & soul at a romance which is now in fair progress," since he had "worked at it under an earnest ardor" (*Letters*, p. 70). It is problematical what Melville was thinking of as romantic—only the pallid imitation of *Undine* in the Yillah story? or the ranging conversations and discursions that recall Rabelais and Burton? He adopted the go-ahead style again in an agricultural report which he wrote for his cousin Robert Melvill (1850). Examples of the style, where tongue-in-cheek maudlinity looks amazingly like earnest melodrama, occur even in *Moby-Dick* (1851), in the history of the blacksmith (ch. 112). A version of the mannered, cloying style came ready to hand when he wanted to write *Pierre* as a profound book that could be read by superficial skimmers of pages as an ordinary romance, apparently merry and pellucid when not thrillingly melodramatic.

Braswell's reading of some ludicrous-sounding passages as satiric is irresistible, and it is appealing to elaborate his argument into the notion that Melville might be aiming high as a satirist—aiming as a modern Cervantes to write a satire that would laugh popular bestsellers out of the bookstores. But Melville did not have Cervantes's aesthetic objectivity or his emotional equilibrium and, more important, probably did not have that particular laudable ambition. The satire, we believe, is secondary, not primary. As Hayford, Howard, Charvat, and others have said, Melville was out for bigger game than satire, despite an abundance of satirical passages early in the book. Melville's letter to Hawthorne on 17[?] November 1851 implies that he was then thinking of writing a book greater than *The Whale*: he had "heard of Krakens" (*Letters*, p. 143). Once he had postponed such an ambition. In 1849 the failure of *Mardi* had forced him to forsake his plans to write a still more ambitious book, whatever it might have been. Instead he wrote, in a total of four months, *Redburn* and *White-Jacket*. Nothing suggests that Melville made a similar renunciation late in 1851. Rather than another book wherein he set out to please his readers at the cost of inhibiting himself, Melville was determined to write about the ideas that most concerned him, and now apparently thought he could please readers while pleasing himself. But we must try to keep it clear what form of the work we are talking about. Charvat takes the *Pierre* that we know as the Kraken book Melville meant to write. But *Pierre* as we know it is not what Melville was writing or intending to write when he said he had heard of Kraken. The Kraken book was to have been the shorter book, and for all we know that shorter version *was* the achieved Kraken book.

The themes Melville chose to deal with in *Pierre* were dangerous. What he had in mind when he started, judging from the first half of the book, was a promulgation of what he had learned of human psychology from unfolding within himself a hundred or more times since he became a writer (*Letters*, p. 130). Through this self-observation he had learned much about how thoughts, motives, impulses, impressions glide their ways through the mind, especially great minds, and how thoughts rise out of the unconscious to invade the conscious mind. He was determined to probe the psychosexual urges that operate, even if repressed and altogether unacknowledged, in family relationships. Powerfully stirred for years by the appeal of absolute obedience to Jesus and realistically aware that nominal Christianity is un-Christlike, he now confronted the possibility that absolute Christlike behavior might be not only impracticable but might always be, in the end, destructive to the enthusiastic follower of Jesus as well as to others. Daringly, perhaps recklessly, Melville decided to deal with these themes in a plot the basis of which was fornication, illegitimacy, and incest, and the conclusion of which involved murder and suicide.

Yet the dangerous nature of the themes does not mean that Melville had deliberately set out to offend his readers. Some extremely lurid books over the previous half-century, from *The Monk* to *The Quaker City*, had sold phenomenally, and (as Charlene Avallone points out in a study now in progress) *Holden's Dollar Magazine*, edited for a time by Duyckinck, had printed stories of incestuous passion and had in all seriousness offered melodramatic rant of the sort which has struck sober readers of *Pierre*, from the reviewers to the present, as intolerable. Melville was a bad judge of what he could get away with, as even the early reviews of *Moby-Dick* showed, and must have persuaded himself that his treatment of the themes would keep the simpler readers from seeing what he was doing yet would be entertaining enough on the level of action, but he was not a suicidal fool: other people were getting away with as much. Was it a matter of who they were and what was expected of them? Was it a matter of who the publisher was and how books were distributed? Was incest less horrific than blasphemy? Much of the book *ought*, we feel, to have worked on the two levels. Yet evidence suggests it did not work: not one reviewer claimed to have read happily along until he reached a page which so outraged him that all his prior good will evaporated and rage triumphed thereafter: to all appearances, those who loathed the book loathed it from the start. We are still mystified.

Under the delusion that he was appealing simultaneously to superficial and eagle-eyed readers, we would say, Melville devised elaborate strategies for disguising his themes: an authorial rhetoric whose tone was exceedingly difficult to catch; rhapsodical dialogue between characters from almost un-Americanly high or low society; abrupt shifts in style and tone; characters who played a variety of roles with each other and sometimes seemed to step into Shakespearean roles, speaking not so much in imitation of Shakespearean rhetoric as in a set of elaborations of Shakespearean scenes—shanties, lean-tos, in Melville's architectural imagery. (Melville wasn't satirizing *Shakespeare*—but no one has yet analyzed precisely what he was doing with the echoes of Shakespeare.) In the early chapters Melville exploited the device of presenting situations so ambiguous that even the most brilliant reader might not be quite sure what was going on; then, later, he would reward that attentive reader in a new scene designed to strip away the ambiguity, clarifying the tone of the early passage and confirming or correcting the reader's edgy suspicions about the fatuously idealized romantic love between Pierre and Lucy, about the dangerously intimate and artificial love Pierre and his mother share, about the mixture of Christianity and militarism in the idealization of Grand Old Pierre, about the exaltation of Beauty. A reader like Melville's friend Dr. Augustus Kinsley Gardner, a specialist in sexuality, might promptly have suspected a sexual component in a description of a boy's aesthetic responses to reading Spenser in adolescence. (See the long section on Gardner in G. J. Barker-Benfield [1976].) Surely there is something wrong, the Christian reader would feel, at Pierre's going in prayer to God only through preliminary filial recollections of his earthly father, but that reader would not necessarily know at once that Melville himself held the same Christian values and would later reveal the dangers of Pierre's idealizing of his father. The reader who had devoted any thought to the psychology of family relationships might also have been uneasy from the start at the idealization of the artificial relationship between Pierre and his mother, but would have been hard put for a time to be sure that Melville was setting up a situation that would expose the dangers of instilling in a child a pattern of falseness in the most intimate relationships of life. This complex strategy of following baffling ambiguities with dazzling clarification is so deftly handled that a modern critic is impelled to feel that it *ought* to have worked with readers who knew Melville's most recent writings. But the reality is that Melville's enunciation of his theory that a great book could simultaneously appeal to two readerships had been published in an anonymous review that only a handful of people knew was his, and only a most limited number of people who knew that Melville was the author of the Hawthorne review had also read *Moby-Dick* before reading *Pierre*. In that group were the Duyckincks, who had been distressed at the irreverence in *Moby-Dick* and with whom Melville broke off relationships as he was finishing *Pierre*, months before they reviewed it in the *Literary World*. (Maybe the Valentine's Day cancellation of his subscription to the *Literary World* was a late notification. Maybe in his mind he broke off the relationship when he wrote "Young America in Literature.") Reading backwards, as scholars of Melville, it is easy to delude ourselves about what Melville could realistically have expected, and our confusion is compounded because no one knows at all precisely what Melville had in mind as examples of lurid, stagy writing that his American and European contemporaries were getting away with.

GENRE

We have contemporary testimony to the literary models Melville was using. Pre-publication gossip in the New York *Herald* had it that in *Pierre* Melville had localized in the Berkshires "some of the ancient and most repulsive inventions of the George Walker and Anne Radcliffe sort—desperate passion at first sight, for a young woman who turns out to be the hero's sister, &c., &c., &c." (*Critical Essays*, p. 31). The *Albion* said that Lucy Tartan did not differ much "from some scores of Lucies in your book acquaintance, if it be extensive" (p. 38), and went on to condemn the pretended marriage as written in the spirit of Eugene Sue (p. 39). The eventual full review in the *Herald* said no book had ever been "such a compendium of Carlyle's faults" as *Pierre* (p. 52) and scorned Melville for "borrowing tinsel imagery of a Lamartine" and "the obscure mysticism of a Goethe or a Kant" (p. 53). The reviewer pleaded with

Melville: "The Tireis-and-Phillis tone of conversation is long since dead and buried; trouble not its ashes." Some passages were in such bad taste as to suggest to the reviewer that Melville had been under the influence of "a man who has done no good to our literature—Martin Farquhar Tupper" (p. 53). *Graham's* thought Melville had "attempted seemingly to combine" in the book "the peculiarities of Poe and Hawthorne" (p. 55). The *American Whig Review* thought *Pierre* was "precisely what a raving lunatic who had read Jean Paul Richter *in a translation* might be supposed to spout under the influence of a particularly moon-light night" (p. 63). The *Athenaeum* said the style was like "an 'upsetting' into English of the first novel of a very whimsical and lackadaisical young student at the [U]niversity of Gottingen" (p. 68), and condemned it as "Germanism at second hand" (p. 69). The Duyckinck brothers may have been drawing on their private knowledge of Melville's theory that some powerful dark books were written for two sets of readers when they speculated in the *Literary World* about what was "possibly intended by the author" (p. 42). The comment that the book might be a "mare's nest" has been misunderstood: the Duyckincks meant that it might have been designed to create a sensation, in which the first discoverers would hail it as a great rarity, only to find that it was not a rarity of the same nature they had supposed. Melville had said to his father-in-law that Time would solve the puzzle of *Mardi*. There is no reason he might not have said something of the sort to the Duyckincks about *Mardi*, if not about *Moby-Dick* or *Pierre*.

Since the Melville Revival scholars have listed a great many literary influences. The book itself points to Dante and to *Hamlet*, and other Shakespearean plays are echoed, some quite clearly, some very subtly. In his notes Murray credits his daughter with discovering a great many parallels in novels by Scott, Disraeli, Thackeray, and others (including aplenty of "such Lucies"). Higgins's 1972 article on the Plinlimmon pamphlet (revised for *Critical Essays*) suggests that Melville was drawing on the English satirists of the Augustan period for satiric strategies. (If Melville's annotated Swift had turned up in 1983 instead of his Milton, would we see the pamphlet differently? Will new revelations attend the recovery of Melville's Dante in 1985?) So far scholars such as Murray and Howard have identified many isolated parallels with English, continental, and American literature, but have provided no analysis based on a fresh reading of even all those books we know Melville read, from Scott to De Stael to Richter. We still do not have a good sense of what novels and other literary works were in Melville's mind as he planned *Pierre*. Charlene Avallone's recent discovery of likely satiric targets in *Holden's Dollar Magazine* in fiction, autobiographical pieces, and essays clarifies the situation somewhat. Melville had at hand wretched prose and wretched attempts at philosophical profundity which could have set him off, gaily, in passages of satire which subserved, nevertheless, his primary purposes—as when he satirized the worship of nature and philosophical ameliorism.

THE QUESTION OF TRYING TO MULCT THE ENGLISH PUBLISHER

Upon publication in 1846 *Typee* aroused misplaced incredulity both in England and (less often) the United States: reviewers often doubted that so pleasingly written a book could have been produced by a sailor before the mast rather than a man of education, but they never challenged Melville on the brevity of his stay in the islands and his having late in the composition resorted to printed sources to eke out his imperfect recollections of anthropological customs of the islanders and the island's flora and fauna. This initial duplicity about the length of time he had spent with the natives put Melville in a false position, vexed and even outraged at being suspected of lying when he had told the truth but apparently ungrateful that his real deceptions had not been exposed. Melville deliberately deceived readers from *Typee* onwards by presenting other people's observations as his own (gradually refining his plunderings into private jokes at the expense of the plundered); he lied (there is no other accurate word) on 27 June 1850 to Richard Bentley, his second British publisher, by claiming to have had first-hand experience of "two years & more, as a harpooneer"; and he shamelessly claimed in his narrative voice in *Moby-Dick* that he had swum through libraries looking for whaling material when he was relying on others' compilations whenever he could, such as those in the *Penny Cyclopaedia*; and it appears that he even deceived the Hawthornes, face to face, in the fall of 1850 when he said that he wrote the essay on Hawthorne (just published in two August issues of the *Literary World*) with no thought that he would ever meet the author of *Mosses from an Old Manse*. What he offered a publisher was never quite what he labeled it, what he professed to believe about the salability and potential popularity of a book was rarely quite straightforward (and often may well have been self-deceptive), what he offered the great majority of readers was rarely quite what it appeared to be; his writing was, as far as we know, the one area of his life which he defended at such cost to simple truth.

In this context we read skeptically Melville's claim to Bentley on 16 April 1852 that the completed *Pierre* possesses "unquestionable novelty," treating "of utterly new scenes & characters;—and, as I believe, very much more calculated for popularity than anything you have yet published of mine—being a regular romance, with a mysterious plot to it,

& stirring passions at work, and withall, representing a new & elevated aspect of American life" (*Letters*, p. 150). To take a moral tone toward such wishful thinking is worse than useless. Our concern should be with understanding the complexity of Melville's compulsion to protect himself from others and from acknowledgment of what he had done. As Harrison Hayford said in 1946, Melville probably "deceived himself in thinking he had submerged the profounder elements of his book far enough below the surface to allow the ordinary reader clear sailing through the romance" (p. 307n.20). More precisely, Melville probably deceived himself in that regard as he wrote the short version of *Pierre*. The self-deception required by what he wrote in 1852 is of a different and more tortured order.

THE "TWO" PLOTS: IMPLICATIONS FOR CRITICISM

James Duban (1983) has accused Parker (1976) and Higgins-Parker (1978) of "attacking *Pierre*'s unity" in the course of "a too-facile biographical reading" of the book (p. 181). Robert Milder had prepared the philosophical way for Duban by pronouncing that "the history of revision and publication" may be important "only to critics concerned with the work as it unfolded in the author's mind," and that other critics do not need to know the genesis of a work (*ALS 1981*, p. 60). Milder and Duban are not alone in their distrust of biographical evidence. Indeed, they articulate the assumption that governs almost every post-World War II reading of *Pierre*—and of course readings of other literary works as well, for they are (explicitly, in Milder's case) relying on the principles of the New Criticism, according to which biographical information cannot legitimately be brought into literary criticism. The novel you hold in your hand, according to the New Criticism, is by definition a work of art, perfectly unified, in which all images build toward thematic significance, in which all characters interact in a complicated formal structure, in which passages of description counterpoint passages of dialogue, in which scene plays off against scene. Sometimes a novel is so well designed that it would be nearly impossible to locate flaws in it and almost churlish to dwell long on any analysis of them. But very often well-known novels that we read and write about all the time are so flawed that any formal analysis designed to demonstrate unity will be wasted effort, as will any modish deconstructive analysis which at the start assumes the unity of the artifact it will proceed cleverly to demolish. The fullest demonstration of the pervasive influence of the New Criticism in all subsequent critical schools is Parker's *Flawed Texts and Verbal Icons: Literary Authority in American Fiction* (1984), which has incidental comments on *Pierre* and which analyzes the theoretical bases of assumptions held by critics such as Milder and Duban. Here we will use these two critics to focus the implications of biographical evidence for literary criticism on *Pierre*.

As Parker argues throughout *Flawed Texts and Verbal Icons*, biographical evidence and often textual evidence (evidence from manuscripts and variant texts, not simply evidence from the words of one particular printed text) can have profound implication for literary criticism in general as well as for literary theory. (Beginning theorists are urged to consult the "Conclusion: Textual Evidence and the Current Practice of Theory.") Biographical evidence, we would say, has particularly profound implications for literary criticism on *Pierre*. Anyone counting and classifying literary allusions, mythic patterns, imagery, and metaphors would do well not to assume a controlling pattern from the first word of the book to the last. Do the mythic patterns established early in the book culminate in the myth of the Titans? Does the imagery in the Pierre-as-author sections develop from the image patterns of the opening sections? If the same image clusters and metaphors occur, is it because a pattern was established at the outset to be developed throughout, or simply because the imagery and metaphors were in Melville's mind when he finished the 360–page version in December and were still there when he proceeded to enlarge the manuscript under differing intentions in January?

We venture some challenges. No one is ever going to succeed in showing that "Love, Delight, and Alarm" (Book II) brilliantly foreshadows "Pierre, as a Juvenile Author, Reconsidered" (Book XVII). No one is likely to demonstrate that the Plinlimmon Pamphlet is "central" to an interpretation of both of the two "Books" just named. No one is likely to write a worthwhile essay that demonstrates the way the Mount of the Titans section functions as a fulfillment of themes and images first set forth in the section on the Memnon Stone. No one is likely to demonstrate that image patterns found throughout the book are coherently placed from first to last, so that an image in the middle of the book is designed to recall the previous examples and to prepare for subsequent ones. No one is ever going to demonstrate the perfect unity of *Pierre* from the opening words to the last words. And to try to demonstrate such formal unity is to engage in a formalist game that dehumanizes the author and trivializes his genuine achievements.

Instead of vaunting ourselves on having discerned the lurking intention that unifies the whole book and all its parts, we should be candidly admitting what we know and what we do not know. For starters, we do not know just what the original 360–page version of *Pierre* was like. One cannot prove that in it Pierre was never said to be a juvenile author and never portrayed as immaturely attempting a mature work. But from the reviewers onward people have been violently disconcerted on arriving at the news in Book XVII that Pierre had been a juvenile author and have frequently concluded that Melville had not planned from the start to make him one. Readers have tended to assume that the work was composed sequentially, however, in the order in which we have it. But once we determine that the book was virtually completed (in the estimated length of 360 pages) at the time the contract was agreed on, and once we know that before the end of the third week of January 1852 Melville had enlarged the book so much that his brother felt called upon to tell the Harpers about the changed length, we are compelled to abandon the idea of sequential composition. Then the plausible assumption is that what Melville was doing in January and early February 1852 was adding anything that has to do with Pierre as an author and working that element of plot into portions of the work already written. We know that as he finished a book, from *Typee* onwards, Melville had habitually inserted long passages into his manuscripts without heavily revising the passages that were severed by the insertions. Chances are high that up to "Young America in Literature" (Book XVII) we have the book about, if not exactly, as it was in the short version. Chances are high that a good many portions in the remainder of the book were written before Melville decided to make Pierre an author. If we crossed out everything having to do with Pierre as an author, we might end up with a rough approximation of what Melville showed the Harpers at the turn of the year. (It would not have contained the depiction of the wrath of Pierre's fictional publishers, Steel, Flint, and Asbestos!).

Plainly, *Pierre* as we know it is the product of two major, and conflicting, impulses. And we would be wrong to rule out the possibility that it might also be the product of other, briefer, impulses. Had Melville's anger at gossip about *Moby-Dick* caused him to lose control in parts of the shorter version? If "The Journey and the Pamphlet" (Book XIV) was in that version, as it may have been, had the control over tone slipped in the paragraphs introducing the pamphlet? Furthermore, we should remember that "Young America in Literature" and "Pierre, as a Juvenile Author, Reconsidered" are hardly in the same mood as "Pierre at His Book" (Book XXV). Melville may have started the additions almost as a lark, without foreseeing that he would be led into extensive new writing: it is possible, at least, that he wrote "Young America in Literature" (we are self-consciously making the all-too-human assumption that the first Pierre-as-author passage we encounter is the first Melville wrote) thinking he would indulge himself in a little satire on himself and the publishing establishment *without* planning to go on to depict Pierre's immature struggles to write a great book. Since there is so much we do not know, we are obligated to examine our assumptions constantly as we talk about the different parts of *Pierre*.

One issue here is what parts of the book we most value. For Leon Howard (and for many perturbed or irritated by the mannered style of the opening) the most important parts of the book dealt with Pierre's attempt to write a great book. For Higgins and Parker, the book up to "Young America in Literature" is the surviving first three-fifths of a masterpiece, and the remainder of the book is of very great but less sustained power, where remnants of the original text survive, however mangled, among late-written passages that are not integrated into their contexts. We can make the point best with Pierre's dream of Enceladus. If we were commissioned to make an anthology of *Great Passages from Melville*, we would find the Enceladus scene irresistible as a specimen of magnificent Melvillean prose. Yet as readers of *Pierre* we cannot forget our earlier encounter with the Memnon Stone, cannot dismiss our sense that in a coherent novel the Enceladus scene would complexly recall the earlier scene and derive some of its power by contrast with it. Our guess is that Melville was not even recalling the earlier scene as he wrote. The Mount of the Titans seems to us *too* magnificent for its immediate context, with the result that its great power is less than it could have held in a context fully worthy of it. Now, to discuss some disastrous consequences of Melville's enlarging the book is not to "attack" the unity of *Pierre*. One attacks the unity of something one wants to diminish. To lament that Melville desecrated his own splendid achievement is not to attack the book. In the spirit of Ishmael we would throw all our costliest robes over any ignominious blemish, but we are also impelled to try, and try again, to understand the book and the author.

NOTES

1. Some readers may find use for an overview of the post-publication, critical history of *Pierre*. Rather than devise a new one, we recycle one:

Pierre; or, The Ambiguities, Herman Melville's seventh book, was a disaster for him personally and professionally. It lost him his English publisher, and reviewers of the American edition (1852) accused the book and the author of being mad. In the remainder of the nineteenth century, *Pierre* was dismissed as Melville's "late miserable abortion" [Abel Stevens in the *National Magazine* (January 1853), reprinted in *Critical Essays*, p. 73], and characterized as repulsive, insane, and unreadable. The book fared little better after it was rediscovered in the 1920s. John Freeman, Melville's first English biographer, found in it "an enormous and perverse sadness, declining to mere madness" [p. 111], and Lewis Mumford saw it as "crude melodrama" [p. 209]. Despite his interest in the psychological dimensions of *Pierre*, Henry A. Murray, Jr., judged it "the performance of a depleted puppeteer" [p. xiv]. Less restrained, another of Melville's modern critics, Newton Arvin, dismissed *Pierre* as "four-fifths claptrap, and sickly claptrap to boot" [p. 226], while Warner Berthoff characterized it as "freakish" [p. 51], and Edwin H. Miller recently declared that "Pierre is paranoid and so is the book" [p. 231]. E. L. Grant Watson has been alone in claiming that *Pierre* is a greater work of art than *Moby-Dick*, and few other critics in the twentieth century have celebrated the book as even a moderately high achievement. Yet despite all the critical uneasiness and outright disdain, *Pierre* is now recognized as one of Melville's most important works, the book nearest to *Moby-Dick* not only in time but also in the ambitiousness of its aims and in the power of at least some passages. (From the "Introduction" by Brian Higgins and Hershel Parker in *Critical Essays* [1983], p. 1).

2. In accordance with the format of these chapters, we give a summary of the plot of *Pierre*. Readers who have not read the book should skip this footnote so as not to ruin their reading experience. Survivors of *Pierre* may benefit from a reminder that the plot so outraged and appalled the reviewers that several of them printed detailed and fairly accurate summaries designed to discourage readers from attempting the book for themselves. The first of these, in the Boston *Post*, was reprinted in Philadelphia, then a rival to New York as a literary center, and may have influenced some reviewers in New York and elsewhere:

Pierre Glendinning and his proud but loving mother are living together, surrounded by everything the world, intellect, health and affection can bestow. The son is betrothed to a beautiful girl of equal position and fortune, and everything looks brightly as a summer morning. All at once, Pierre learns that his father has left an illegitimate daughter, who is in poverty and obscurity. His conscience calls upon him to befriend and acknowledge her—although, by the way, his proof of the fact that the girl is his father's offspring is just nothing at all. On the other hand, he will not discover to the world or to his mother the error of his (supposed) sainted father, and he adopts the novel expedient of carrying off the girl, and giving out that he has married her. His mother discards him and soon dies of wounded love and pride, and his betrothed is brought to the brink of the grave. She finally recovers somewhat, and strange to say, invites herself to reside with Pierre and his sister, who, as far as the world and herself were concerned, are living as husband and wife. The relatives of Lucy, as a matter of course, try to regain her, and brand Pierre with every bad name possible. The latter finally shoots his cousin who had become the possessor of the family estate and a pretender to the hand of Lucy—is arrested and taken to prison. There he is visited by the two ladies, the sister and the betrothed. Lucy falls dead of a broken heart and Pierre and his sister take poison and also give up the ghost. This tissue of unnatural horrors is diversified a little, by the attempts of the hero to earn his living by authorship, and by the "ambiguous" love between Pierre and his natural sister. (*Critical Essays*, p. 33)

The reviewer in the *Post* followed his summary with a sentence which pretty much summed up the prevailing attitude for the next eight decades: "Comment upon the foregoing is needless."

WORKS CITED

Avallone, Charlene. (Work in progress).

Barker-Benfield, G. J. *The Horrors of the Half-Known Life: Male Attitudes Toward Women and Sexuality in Nineteenth-Century America*. New York: Harper & Row, 1976.

Baym, Nina. "Melville's Quarrel with Fiction." *PMLA* 94 (October 1979): 909–23.

Braswell, William "The Early Love Scenes in Melville's *Pierre*." *American Literature* 22 (November 1950): 283–89.

———. "Melville's Opinion of *Pierre*." *American Literature* 23 (May 1951): 246–50.

———. "The Satirical Temper of Melville's *Pierre*." *American Literature* 7 (January 1936): 424–38.

Brodhead, Richard H. *Hawthorne, Melville, and the Novel*. Chicago: University of Chicago Press, 1976.

Charvat, William. *The Profession of Authorship in America, 1800–1870*. Ed. Matthew J. Bruccoli. Columbus: Ohio State University Press, 1968.

Davis, Merrell R., and William H. Gilman, eds. *The Letters of Herman Melville*. New Haven, Conn.: Yale University Press, 1960.

Douglas, Ann. *The Feminization of American Culture*. New York: Alfred A. Knopf, 1977.

Dryden, Edgar A. "The Entangled Text: Melville's *Pierre* and the Problem of Reading." *Boundary* 2 (Spring 1979): 145–73.

Duban, James. *Melville's Major Fiction*. DeKalb: Northern Illinois University Press, 1983.

Emmers, Amy Puett."Melville's Closet Skeleton: A New Letter About the Illegitimacy Incident in *Pierre*." *Studies in the American Renaissance 1977*. Ed. Joel Myerson. Boston: Twayne, 1978, pp. 339–43. [See also *Mel. Diss.* #211.]

Forsythe, Robert S. Introduction to *Pierre*. New York: Alfred A. Knopf, 1930, pp. xix-xxxviii.

Hayford, Harrison. " 'Loomings': Yarns and Figures in the Fabric." In *Artful Thunder: Versions of the Romantic Tradition in American Literature in Honor of Howard P. Vincent*. Ed. Robert DeMott and Sanford E. Marovitz. Kent: Kent State University Press, 1975. 119–37.

Hayford, Harrison. "The Significance of Melville's 'Agatha' Letters." *ELH, A Journal of English Literary History* 13 (December 1946): 299–310.

Higgins, Brian, and Hershel Parker, eds. *Critical Essays on Herman Melville's "Pierre; or, The Ambiguities"*. Boston: G. K. Hall, 1983.

———, and Hershel Parker. "The Flawed Grandeur of Melville's *Pierre*." *New Perspectives on Melville*. Kent, Ohio and Edinburgh: Kent State University Press and Edinburgh University Press, 1978.

[Melville, Herman.] Memoir of Thomas Melvill, Jr. In J.E.A. Smith, *The History of Pittsfield, (Berkshire County,) Massachusetts, From the Year 1800 to the Year 1876*. Springfield, Mass.: C. W. Bryan & Co., 1876. 399–400.

Milder, Robert. "Melville's 'Intentions' in *Pierre*." *Studies in the Novel* 6 (Summer 1974): 186–99.

Mumford, Lewis. *Herman Melville*. New York: Harcourt, Brace, 1929.

Murray, Henry A. Introduction to *Pierre*. New York: Hendricks House, 1949, pp. xiii-ciii.

———, Harvey Myerson, and Eugene Taylor. "Allan Melvill's By-Blow." *Melville Society Extracts* No. 61 (February 1985): 1–6.

Parker, Hershel. "Contract: *Pierre*, by Herman Melville." *Proof* 5 (1977): 27–44.

———. *Flawed Texts and Verbal Icons: Literary Authority in American Fiction*. Evanston, Ill.: Northwestern University Press, 1984.

———. "Melville and the Berkshires: Emotion-Laden Terrain, 'Reckless Sky-Assaulting Mood,' and Encroaching Wordsworthianism." In *American Literature: The New England Heritage*. Ed. James Nagel and Richard Astro. New York: Garland Publishing, Inc., 1981,) pp. 65–80.

————. "Why *Pierre* Went Wrong." *Studies in the Novel* 8 (Spring 1976): 7–23.

Sealts, Merton M., Jr. *The Early Lives of Melville*. Madison: University of Wisconsin Press, 1974.

————. "Melville and Emerson's Rainbow." *ESQ* 26 (Second Quarter 1980): 53–78.Rpt. in *Pursuing Melville, 1940–1980* Madison: University of Wisconsin Press, 1982, pp. 250–277.

Seelye, John D. " 'Ungraspable Phantom': Reflections of Hawthorne in *Pierre* and *The Confidence-Man*." *Studies in the Novel* 1 (1969): 436–43.

Sundquist, Eric. *Home as Found*. Baltimore: Johns Hopkins University Press, 1979.

Thomas, Brook. "The Writer's Procreative Urge in *Pierre*: Fictional Freedom or Convoluted Incest?" *Studies in the Novel* 11 (Winter 1979): 416–30.

Watson, E. L. Grant. "Melville's *Pierre*." *New England Quarterly* 3 (April 1930): 195–234.

Weaver, Raymond. *Herman Melville: Mariner and Mystic*. New York: George H. Doran, 1921.

Wegener, Larry Edward. *A Concordance to Herman Melville's "Pierre; Or, The Ambiguities."* 2 vols. New York: Garland, 1985.

9

MELVILLE'S TALES

Johannes D. Bergmann

Between the winter of 1852–53 and early 1856 Herman Melville published fifteen separate tales and sketches in *Harper's New Monthly Magazine* and *Putnam's Monthly Magazine*.[1] One other story, "The Two Temples," was rejected by *Putnam's* in early May 1854, and apparently not published elsewhere; its text has survived along with a letter of rejection from editor Charles F. Briggs. Another piece, "The Piazza," was written as the title tale for Melville's collection, *The Piazza Tales*, published by Dix and Edwards in May 1856. Republished (with small changes) from *Putnam's* were "Bartleby," "Benito Cereno," "The Lightning-Rod Man," "The Encantadas," and "The Bell-Tower." We have some evidence, through his jottings, that Melville worked during this period on other tales that were never published (Leyda, pp. x–xiii). Other ideas could have been developed either as tales or novels. The "Agatha story," about which he wrote to Nathaniel Hawthorne in late 1852, could have become a tale, but may also have been the larger manuscript he was "prevented from printing" with *Harper's* in early 1853; and "Tortoise Hunting," a book he proposed to *Harper's*, which may or may not have been similar to "The Encantadas" (*Letters*, pp. 164–65). Common sense tells us that with a career as active as Melville's during the period, and with the relatively small amount of documentation we have, it is possible, even today, that there remain published Melville stories to be discovered.

Melville had published fiction in a magazine at least once before 1853 when *Harper's* carried "The Town-Ho's Story" (*MD*, ch. 54) in October 1851. Following the nineteenth-century custom, magazines and newspapers which reviewed Melville's romances often published extensive excerpts from his books, but "The Town-Ho's Story" has the look, in *Harper's*, of a separate publication, however connected its appearance was to the Harpers' promotion of their novel *Moby-Dick*. It reads as, and is, a complete tale. Moveover, *The Confidence-Man: His Masquerade* (1857), published after the tales, but which Melville apparently began in the summer of 1855, includes chapters that are themselves self-contained pieces. In one sense, *The Confidence-Man* is an assemblage of tales and sketches, held together in our own intuition of the titular shape-shifter.

No manuscripts of the 1853–56 tales and sketches exist other than that of "The Two Temples," now preserved in the Melville Collection of the Houghton Library of Harvard University, and a recently discovered fragment in Augusta Melville's hand of the ending of "Bartleby," now in the Gansevoort-Lansing Collection in the New York Public Library. In Melville's lifetime only three of the tales seem to have been reprinted other than in *Piazza Tales*. "Poor Man's Pudding and Rich Man's Crumbs" appeared in the *Western Literary Messenger* for August 1854; "The Lightning-Rod Man" was reprinted in William E. Burton's *The Cyclopedia of Wit and Humor* (1857); and "The Bell-Tower" appeared in two collections, Rossiter Johnson's *Little Classics: Tragedy* (1874) and E. C. Stedman and E. M. Hutchinson's *Library of American Literature* (1889).

The earliest twentieth-century republication of *The Piazza Tales* was in Constable and Company's collected edition. Also in 1922, Princeton University Press brought together previously uncollected tales in *The Apple-Tree Table and Other Sketches by Herman Melville*. In 1924 "The Two Temples" first appeared in print, in *Billy Budd and Other Prose Pieces*, a volume edited by Raymond Weaver as volume 13 of the Constable edition. Other important editions of this century are Raymond Weaver's *Shorter Novels of Herman Melville* (Liveright, 1928), Egbert S. Oliver's *Piazza Tales* (Hendricks House, 1948), and Jay Leyda's *The Complete Stories of Herman Melville* (Random House, 1949). Leyda's edition contains all the tales and sketches of the 1850s with the exception of "The 'Gees," and its "Introduction" and "Notes on Sources" represent the first important scholarship on the tales. Richard Chase edited what became a popular teaching edition, the *Selected Tales and Poems* (Rinehart, 1950); it includes nine of the tales. Probably the most useful collection is still Warner Berthoff's *Great Short Works of Herman Melville* (Harper & Row, 1966). His brief headnotes to the stories (taken from Leyda's texts) unerringly identify the kind of story one is about to read and are important addenda to Berthoff's comments on the tales in his *The Example of Melville* (1962). The Berthoff collection, used throughout this chapter, also includes "The 'Gees" and "The Town-Ho's Story" as well as prose from late in Melville's career.

The most important edition of all is still (at this writing) unpublished.

It is *The Piazza Tales and Other Prose Pieces, 1839–1860*, forthcoming as Volume 9 of the NN edition of *The Writings of Herman Melville*. An extract from its "Historical Note" by Merton M. Sealts, Jr., has already appeared as "The Chronology of Melville's Short Fiction, 1853–1856." It is a carefully reasoned and convincing account of the probable chronology of Melville's composition of the tales and sketches between 1853 and 1856.

MELVILLE IN *HARPER'S* AND *PUTNAM'S*

The critical response to Melville's novel *Pierre; or, the Ambiguities* (1852) was overwhelmingly unfavorable, and by 1853 the general remarks about the body of his work were equally severe. Melville was apparently unable to place the "Agatha story" with the Harpers in the spring of 1853. Leaving aside the question of whether these events "forced" Melville to "lower" himself and turn to magazine writing for a living or whether he turned to magazine writing because he wanted to work in that form, it should be understood that Melville began his career in the magazines with a flying start. By the end of 1853 he had published both in *Harper's* and in *Putnam's*, one the most popular magazine in the United States, the other the most prestigious. More than that, he was paid five dollars a page, the highest rate generally available. From all his 1853–56 magazine writing, however, he earned an approximate total of only $1,300 (Sealts, "Chronology" p. 399).

Harper's began publication in June 1850 with a statement of editorial policy that must have been chilling to American writers trying to establish themselves in the British-dominated literary marketplace: "The magazine will transfer to its pages as rapidly as they may be issued all the continuous tales of Dickens, Bulwer, Croly, Lever, Warren, and other distinguished contributors to British periodicals" (Frank Luther Mott, p. 384). The "transfer" (which often meant "theft" because *Harper's* did not always pay for what it took) drove out Americans seeking a livelihood from their writing. *Harper's* did as promised, publishing at first very few American writers. When Melville first started sending out tales in 1853, for example, *Harper's* was serializing Dickens's *Bleak House*, which appeared month after month from April 1852 until October 1853 (David Jaffe, p. 2). After *Bleak House* finished, Thackeray's *The Newcombes* began.

Among the Americans who managed to break into *Harper's* in its early years were, in addition to Melville, Benson J. Lossing, Jacob Abbott, Caroline Chesebrough, and Fitz-James O'Brien. The Harpers chose Lewis Gaylord Clark, longtime editor of the *Knickerbocker* and writer of its "Editor's Table," to be the first writer of the popular section "The Editor's Drawer." Later, the Reverend S. Irenaeus Prime took over that job. The writer of the best department, "Editor's Easy Chair," was usually Donald G. Mitchell, but in 1853 George William Curtis joined him, even though he was still an associate editor at *Putnam's*. To the extent that the early *Harper's* used American material, the Americans represented were familiar ones in New York journalistic and publishing circles (Mott, pp. 383–405). *Harper's* published seven tales or sketches by Melville during this period.

The appearance of "Bartleby" in the highly respected New York monthly *Putnam's* must have been encouraging to a writer who had turned to the magazines to make a living. *Putnam's* began in January 1853, with Charles F. Briggs, George W. Curtis, and Parke Godwin as editors. Briggs and Curtis had convinced the cultivated George Palmer Putnam to publish a monthly that would carry *only* American fiction and non-fiction, in explicit and self-conscious contrast to *Harper's*. *Putnam's* was, in other words, the distinguished offspring of a New York movement, centered sometimes in "Loco-foco" Democratic circles and sometimes in Whig New York *Tribune* offices, which had long argued for the encouragement of American literature by not allowing English writers to be published "free" in this country and thus driving out American professionals.

The ambition of *Putnam's* seems hard to understand, however admirable. *Putnam's* was born into an American publishing world dominated by *Harper's* and, more than that, the great British novelists. Up against them *Putnam's* brought Herman Melville, Henry David Thoreau, James Fenimore Cooper, Henry Wadsworth Longfellow, and James Russell Lowell as well as John P. Kennedy, Richard Henry Stoddard, Charles Eliot Norton, Henry James, Sr., Fitz-James O'Brien, and Henry W. Herbert ("Frank Forester"). Many of the contributors, like editor Curtis, had been associated at one time or another with the New York *Tribune*. Bayard Taylor, Clarence Cook, Charles A. Dana, and George Ripley had all written for the *Tribune* before writing for *Putnam's*, and Horace Greeley himself also contributed to *Putnam's*.

Editor Parke Godwin had close ties to Greeley because they shared a passion for Fourierism which transcended Greeley's disapproval of Godwin's early Loco-foco politics. The magazine, as might be expected from all this, was strongly supported in the columns of the *Tribune*. *Putnam's* made an effort to be a national magazine and did publish articles on Southern and Western issues, but not enough to convince anyone: the magazine was New York all over. Godwin's fierce political articles written from 1853 to the magazine's last year, 1857, were then the best known and most controversial pieces in the magazine and defined an emerging New York political attitude. "Our New President" in September 1853 attacked Pierce and became notorious, as did Godwin's later "Our American Despotism," "Kansas—It Must Be Free" and "The Two Forms of Society—Which?" The Southern *DeBow's* magazine called *Putnam's* "the leading review of the Black Republican party" and the *Southern Literary*

Messenger also attacked it. The magazine's founding editors were men who had worked for years in the New York idiom, and it is difficult to imagine them editing and writing for a magazine that would not be more New York than "American" (Mott, pp. 419–31).

The magazine was highly regarded. Thackeray, according to Samuel Ward, asserted at a London dinner table that " 'Putnam's' was much the best Mag. in the world,—and was better than *Blackwood* is or ever was!" (*Mel. Log*, p. 507). In 1898 Henry James recalled his "very young pleasure" in "the prose, as mild and easy as an Indian summer in the woods," of Melville, Curtis, and D. G. Mitchell as he read their work in "the charming *Putnam*" of "the early fifties" (George Monteiro, p. 14).

Melville did not find an automatically friendly audience among *Putnam's* writers, no matter how much a part of the New York literary scene he had once been. As part of the magazine's effort to treat American literature seriously, it had published Fitz-James O'Brien's "Our Young Authors—Melville" in its second (February 1853) number, some nine months before "Bartleby." It is a painful analysis which sees Melville's career in novel writing as descending into a sort of mad self-indulgence: "His later books are a decided falling off, and his last [*Pierre*] scarcely deserves naming.... Let him diet himself for a year or two on Addison, and avoid Sir Thomas Browne, and there is little doubt but that he will make a notch on the American pine" (*Mel. Log*, pp. 466–67). Melville did concentrate and polish his craft in 1853 and afterwards and was published in *Putnam's* eight times. In fact, his contributions came to be highly valued.

He had been asked for submissions in a general letter before the magazine began (*Mel. Log*, p. 461), and "Bartleby" was one of 980 manuscripts sent in to *Putnam's* during the first year (Sealts, "Chronology" p. 397). "Bartleby," Melville must have known, has the "New York flavor" for which *Putnam's* became famous. Most revealing of the respect in which Melville's short fiction came to be held is Charles F. Briggs's letter to him rejecting "The Two Temples." On May 12, 1854, Briggs writes he is "very loth to reject" it because it "contains some exquisitely fine description, and some pungent satire," but he is afraid that its publication would "array against us the whole power of the pulpit ... and the congregation of Grace Church." The story was all too much New York. The publisher himself, George Palmer Putnam, wrote Melville the next day and apologized, asking him to send "some more of your good things" (*Mel. Log*, pp. 487–88). The magazine went on to publish six more tales as well as *Israel Potter* in two years, in addition to the two it had already published.

When it reviewed *Piazza Tales* in its issue for 31 May 1856, the *American Publisher's Circular and Literary Gazette* praised the tales as "evincing ... the excellent characteristics of their popular author," and remarked that

Melville could be given much of the credit for *Putnam's* success: the tales "were, in no small degree, instrumental in raising that journal to its present proud position—the best of all American Monthlies" (Inge, p. 37).

HISTORY OF CRITICISM

Reviewers in newspapers and magazines commented on Melville's tales and sketches when they were first published in *Harper's* and *Putnam's* and again when some of them were reissued as *The Piazza Tales* in 1856. We also know something of what a few of Melville's contemporaries thought through their private correspondence. The number of nineteenth-century comments is, of course, small compared to the hundreds of articles and chapters in books published in the twentieth century.

Little direct evidence of the newspaper reaction to the first printings has been collected, even though newspapers regularly commented on the contents of the monthlies as they came out. We know from Jay Leyda that several newspapers and magazines identified Melville as the author of some of the anonymously published pieces. Anonymity was a convention in the magazines, and identifying the authors was the literary columnist's part in the game. The *Literary World* for 3 December 1853 identifies Melville as the author of "Bartleby" and calls it a "Poeish tale" (*Mel. Log*, p. 482); *The Evening Post* for 14 February 1854 praises Melville as the author of the forthcoming "The Encantadas," published in *Putnam's* under the parody picturesque pseudonym of "Salvator R. Tarnmoor" (*Mel. Log*, pp. 484–85); and the *Morning Courier and New York Enquirer* for 31 (?) July 1854 notes that it is "whispered" that the serialized "Israel Potter" is by Melville (*Mel. Log*, pp. 490–91).

We know that Richard Henry Dana, Sr., thought well of "Bartleby" because he wrote to Evert Duyckinck on 25 January 1854 in reaction to the *Literary World* announcement that Melville was its author: "['Bartleby'] touches the nicer strings of our complicated nature, & finely blends the pathetic & ludicrous" (Inge, p. 31). James Russell Lowell praised "The Encantadas" in a letter to Charles F. Briggs, or at least so Briggs reports in his 12 May 1854 letter to Melville rejecting "The Two Temples" (*Mel. Log*, p. 487–88).

Several of the reviews of *The Piazza Tales* comment on the first reactions to the tales. The *New York Dispatch*, for example, notes in its 8 June 1856 issue that "The Encantadas" was "considered among the most interesting papers of that popular Magazine [*Putnam's*], and each successive chapter was read with avidity by thousands" (Inge, p. 44). *The United States Magazine and Democratic Review* for September 1856 notes that "The Lightning-Rod Man" had excited "great attention when originally published" (Inge, p. 52).

Of the thirty-three reviews of *The Piazza Tales* conveniently collected in M. Thomas Inge's *Bartleby the Inscrutable*, only two seem seriously negative. The *New York Daily Times* for 27 June 1856, although it praises "The Piazza" and "The Encantadas," does not think the book will "augment [Melville's] high reputation" (Inge, p. 48), and *Godey's Lady's Book* for September 1856 thinks "his style has an affectation of quaintness, which renders it, to us, very confused and wearisome" (Inge, p. 53). Other reviews seem strongly supportive of Melville's work, full of praise particularly for "Bartleby," "Benito Cereno," and "The Encantadas." Several commenting on "Bartleby" and "The Bell-Tower" argue the similarities to Edgar Allan Poe's work. Many discuss the originality of the tales, others how they suit the contemplative mood of the upcoming summer months (*Tales* is often "recommended summer reading"), and one (the Boston *Daily Evening Traveller* for 3 June 1856) notes the resemblances to the works of Dickens. As a group, the reviews express the cultural assumptions of their time: they praise Melville for the "imagination" he demonstrates and the "imagination" he can stimulate in his readers. Melville can open for his reader a world of contemplation. For these reviewers, this did not make Melville a genius but a very good contemporary magazine writer, perhaps one of the very best writing.

A tendency in twentieth-century scholarship has been to make Melville's contemporary reputation in the 1850s lower than it was to augment our own century's discovery of his work. Not only did we discover Melville, we discovered a genius, a nearly lost great artist. Editors and readers of Melville's own time were blind to that genius; we, however, are the hero-critics who understand him. Melville writes for us.

Melville's complaint to Hawthorne that "What I feel most moved to write, that is banned, —it will not pay," and as a result "all my books are botches" (*Letters*, pp. 128–29) is often quoted in modern Melville scholarship and persuades us of the inability of the larger society to recognize genius. We believe that Melville should have been able to write what he felt most moved to; if we had been the readers, he could have. However, there is a serious complication here: Melville's books, whatever he thought of them, are not "botches" despite the fact that they were the productions of economic necessity and the cultural conditions of Melville's period. They are what they are *because* of the limitations on them: there is no "freedom" in this sense in writing, and the "Melville" we read is a product of his time and place, not a twentieth-century writer living his unhappy artistic life ninety years too soon.

The twentieth century's interest in discovering a forgotten genius does not mean that Melville's fame is unmerited, but it does have certain interpretive consequences. First, the investigations of Melville have been intensely biographical—we want to understand the life of the genius. This line of investigation has led to some marvelous scholarship, like Jay

Leyda's still astonishing *The Melville Log*, which helps us understand not only Melville, but Melville in his time as well. Second, there has been a fundamental paradox in the consideration of Melville's work: Melville is a great writer and therefore wrote great books, but he was unrecognized in his time and therefore was "forced" to write what he did not want to. The awkwardness here is that this view would seem to make the works he did not feel most moved to write somehow less, not works of genius. For a time, the most convenient way of dealing with this paradox was for scholars and critics to praise *Moby-Dick* as the miraculous masterpiece which somehow sneaked into history, and to disparage the works that came after it which were the products of necessity ("history").

Newton Arvin, for example, has considerable scorn for much of the short fiction. Writing about "Cock-A-Doodle-Doo!," "The Lightning-Rod Man," "The Fiddler," "The Bell-Tower," and "Poor Man's Pudding," he says:

it is Melville whipping himself on, without a moment's support from his deeper nature, to be a disposable and pliant writer for *Harper's* and *Putnam's*, to furnish the magazines with the literary staples they will pay for, to enroll himself in the efficient ranks of the Curtises, the Mitchells, and the Warners ... The meaning Melville wishes to communicate in these sketches is ... intensely serious and deeply personal, but the fashionable little form is hopelessly inadequate to it." (Arvin, pp. 235–36)

Arvin has kinder things to say about "Rich Man's Crumbs," "Temple First," "I and My Chimney," and "The Tartarus of Maids," but the comments still seem surprisingly antiquated to scholars who are now so convinced of the complexity and interest of the tales Arvin condemns.

Other critics find the stories to have a hidden text, Melville's explanation of life to insightful twentieth-century readers. Most of what he reveals is that he is forced by economic necessity to write what he wishes not to: "Bartleby" is the story of how Melville had to "copy" the ordinary productions of his time (see particularly Leo Marx, although there are many similar readings), "The Fiddler" shows Melville learning to play harmless tunes, "The Happy Failure" has him trying to adjust, and so on. With this view, the interpreter can see Melville in a "decline" but still active in that he writes about that decline. The paradox of this line of criticism is obvious: "Bartleby" is a magnificent piece of writing about its author who refuses to copy or finally write at all anymore because he is forced to write for the magazine that "Bartleby" is in!

The autobiographical elements are often presumed to be secret for our acute twentieth-century eyes alone. These readings also point to another important line of interpretation of the tales and sketches: that Melville was engaging in "secret" writing, that the tales and sketches have a surface which is perfectly genial and acceptable to people like Curtis, Briggs, and Mitchell but that they *also* have an underneath, a "hidden meaning" (as the puzzled freshman always says) which was only available to an "underground audience" in the 1850s and to academics today. As Hershel Parker says in his 1971 "Foreword" to *The Confidence-Man*, Melville after 1852 "mastered a sort of secret writing in which he palmed off upon his genteel publishers a series of innocuous tales which concealed highly personal allegories not meant to be understood" (p. ix). It has struck few people as strange that so many readers today should understand so easily what so large a group of readers in the mid-nineteenth-century missed altogether.

Melville, like other short story writers of the period (Poe, for example), does create narrative structures that encourage readers not to rest with their easy interpretations but rather to proceed imaginatively to understand more. He asks his readers to participate and imagine beyond the "surfaces" of "Cock-a-Doodle-Doo!" "I and My Chimney," or "The Paradise of Bachelors and the Tartarus of Maids" to their references to male and female sexual organs and functions. He dares his readers to see the anti-Christian emphasis of "Bartleby," of "The Encantadas," or (perhaps) of "Benito Cereno." It is certainly a complex art, an "art of concealment" as Leyda, Parker, Dillingham and many other critics have suggested, but we need not argue that these meanings were unavailable to Melville's audience or that Melville's writings are somehow outside his own history, however great our biographical knowledge of Melville might be.

The first book exclusively on the tales was Richard Harter Fogle's *Melville's Shorter Tales* (1960). Fogle does not think that Melville's tales are as highly crafted as the novels; he shares with Arvin the conclusion that the forms are at fault: "He is too heavy for the delicate fabric of the kind of tale he is trying to write; what he really has to say is at odds with the limits he has chosen to observe" (p. 12). Fogle's book is a landmark in the scholarship on Melville's tales precisely because it takes their craft so seriously and because it treats them as a whole. Two years after Fogle's book, Warner Berthoff, in *The Example of Melville* (1962), made a much greater claim for the art of the tales: "If by some sad chance Melville had survived to us only in the stories and sketches of this brief period, there would still have been high excitement at his recovery as a serious writer, and we would still rate him as one of the few accomplished craftsmen in our nineteenth-century prose fiction" (p. 138). This general estimate of Melville's work has hardly been seriously challenged since Berthoff wrote it, although there are some exceptions (Jane Mushabac, pp. 119–22, for example).

In the late 1970's three books exclusively on the tales and sketches were published: R. Bruce Bickley's *The Method of Melville's Short Fiction*

(1975), Marvin Fisher's *Going Under: Melville's Short Fiction and the American 1850's* (1977), and William B. Dillingham's *Melville's Short Fiction 1853–1856* (1977). Bickley's book extends Berthoff 's high estimation of the tales and is another explication of Melvillean irony and narrative form, like Paul Brodtkorb's *Ishmael's White World* (1965) and John Seelye's *Melville: The Ironic Diagram* (1970). In his penetrating review of the scholarship on the short fiction, Merton Sealts points out the principal weakness of Bickley's study: Bickley explains Melville's artistic experiments but does not keep the further engagement to show how those experiments were an increase in artistic strength ("Melville's Short Fiction," p. 48).

Marvin Fisher's *Going Under* attempts to demonstrate how the stories reflect the "moral and spiritual paralysis" in the American culture of the 1850s. Fisher seems to me always worth reading, but I do not think the nature of the "reflection" of the culture is carefully enough considered. The descriptions of the actual cultural discourses of the 1850's are done only in the broadest strokes, and we do not learn enough about the relationship between what the contemporary ideology is and how it expresses itself in formal conventions.

Dillingham's book is valuable. It is careful and detailed; it surveys the body of criticism for each of the tales and sketches; it adds new source material; and it argues (not originally by 1977) that Melville was practicing the "fine art of concealment" and that his goal was delineation of character, particularly in his narrators. His readings are not always convincing, but they are stimulating. Dillingham finds, in contrast to Fisher, that Melville's interests were not primarily in representing the historical, social, political, or economic issues of his culture, but in personality, in how characters choose to live. This is a plausible thesis, although it is important to observe that the tales' not being *about* the social or economic issues does not mean that Melville's fiction might not have been governed by the contemporary cultural discourses and their consequent forms.

Although many articles have been written on the direct and indirect sources of the tales and sketches, many of those articles operate in splendid isolation. A scholar discovers another author's novel or tale, a bit of prose in a travel book, a newspaper item, or a paragraph in Robert Burton which is reminiscent of a Melville tale and then jubilantly claims a source discovered. Even when the item can be shown to be an undeniably direct source, wiser analysis often reveals that the source and Melville are working with larger conventions in a culture. To find an 1837 item about "dead letters," for example, does not mean that Melville must have read the 1837 item before he wrote about such letters in his 1853 "Bartleby" but that one must look for evidence of metaphoric discussion of "dead letters" throughout the culture (see Parker, "Dead Letters").

The huge number of academic articles on the tales and sketches is itself a cultural phenomenon, one that opens to question the whole academic critical practice. Some of the best scholarship on the tales and sketches, like Milton R. Stern's "Towards 'Bartleby the Scrivener,' " address and question the body of criticism itself, noting its divergence and attempting to account for it. To understand, as Stern shows, that "Bartleby" has fit into Gestalt after Gestalt of very different critics is to start to understand the story itself (as well as the American academic need simply to *produce* scholarship).

WINTER 1852 THROUGH SUMMER 1853

The order of publication of Melville's 1853–56 tales and sketches is not the same as their compositional order. As noted, Merton M. Sealts's meticulous analysis of the available sources has given us a probable compositional order ("Chronology of Melville's Short Fiction"). I will discuss the tales and sketches in that order, hoping thereby to indicate how they might be grouped for interpretation. I have divided the compositional continuum into four periods.

In the winter of 1852–53, Melville probably worked on the "Agatha story," which he had written Hawthorne about the previous summer (13 August 1853, *Letters*, pp. 153–61). Sealts thinks that this apparently unpublished and unsurviving story is the manuscript Melville submitted to Harper & Brothers in the spring of 1853 but was "prevented from printing" as he says without further explanation in a letter to that firm dated 24 November 1853 (*Letters*, pp. 164–65). In the spring and summer of 1853 Melville probably composed and certainly submitted to *Harper's* "Cock-a-Doodle-Doo!," published in December 1853, "The Happy Failure," published in July 1854, and "The Fiddler," published in September 1854. He also composed and submitted to *Putnam's* "Bartleby, the Scrivener," published in November and December 1853 (Sealts, "Chronology," p. 398).

All of the stories of this group are first-person accounts of an encounter between the narrator and an extraordinary character. An apparently self-confident and engaging narrator tells of his brief involvement with a man who is totally out of the ordinary. Readers are asked to understand as they read that the encounter was not like the ordinary experience of the narrator, and that is why the narrator is telling about it. The narrator assumes the reader is of roughly like mind and will be interested in the extraordinary encounter.

In "The Happy Failure: A Story of the River Hudson," perhaps the most broadly comic of the stories, a young and level-headed narrator describes rowing up the Hudson River with his extraordinary uncle to test the invention the uncle has been working on for "ten long years of high-hearted, persevering endeavor" (p. 182). The Great Hydraulic-

Hydrostatic Apparatus is a mysterious box which our unpoetic narrator complains to his uncle looks like "nothing but a battered old dry-goods box, nailed up," but to the uncle it is a device which will give him immortal renown and glory by "draining swamps and marshes, and converting them, at the rate of one acre the hour" (p. 180). The test is a failure and the uncle despairs grandiosely, but before they have drifted down the river with the current the uncle has come out of his high passion and become a happy failure, advising his nephew "never try to invent anything but—happiness" (p. 185). The failure makes the uncle "a good old man" and the narrator "a wise young one" (p. 186).

In "The Fiddler," the young and romantically self-dramatizing Helmstone, a writer, begins his narrative in full cry against his fate—his poem has been badly reviewed. "So my poem is damned, and immortal fame is not for me!" (p. 195). He rushes into Broadway where his friend Standard meets him, quiets him with some standard remarks and introduces him to Hautboy, an extraordinary grown-up boy. Hautboy's "leisurely, deep good sense" (p. 197) seems at first to calm Helmstone, but then Helmstone turns on Hautboy, thinking him ordinary—"Nothing tempts him beyond common limit" (p. 198). Helmstone then hears Hautboy play his fiddle, and the "miraculously superior" (p. 199) playing makes him change his mind again. "My whole splenetic soul capitulated to the magical fiddle" (p. 200); Helmstone gives up all grasping for fame, tears up his manuscripts, and goes to take (fiddle?) lessons from Hautboy.

In "Cock-a-Doodle-Doo! or, the Crowing of the Noble Cock Beneventano," the narrator, in angry melancholy, cursing his fellow men, his creditors, even the landscape around him, hears a marvelous cock crowing and seeks its owner. He discovers the extraordinary poor man Merrymusk, who, though totally at the mercy of his wretched economic conditions, is happy. His family is wasting away, but Merrymusk glories in his magnificent cock: "Don't the cock *I* own glorify this otherwise inglorious, lean, lantern-jawed land? Don't *my* cock encourage *you*" (p. 94)? The family dies as the narrator watches, but they die with what Melville might call "celestial radiance" (p. 96). The narrator tells us that even though he sometimes is in the "doleful dumps" he always cheers himself by crowing, "COCK-A-DOODLE DOO! OO! OO! OO! OO!" (p. 97).

In "Bartleby, the Scrivener: A Story of Wall Street," an elderly Wall Street lawyer tells of his encounter with the extraordinary scrivener Bartleby, the "strangest I ever saw, or heard of " (p. 39). The lawyer employs Bartleby to copy law documents, but after a time, Bartleby "prefers not to" participate in the work of the office and finally does not eat or move. The lawyer tries in vain to understand Bartleby so that he may deal with him: he tries to bribe, threaten, entreat, love, and hate Bartleby, all without success. Finally, rather than evict Bartleby forcefully from his office, he moves his office. Bartleby dies in the Tombs, the New York City prison. The lawyer sighs for Bartleby and humanity.

Even the "Agatha story," if it can be imagined briefly, had the core of an encounter between the ordinary observer and the extraordinary Agatha. Melville writes Hawthorne about the narrative he has heard from a lawyer named Clifford: "The very great interest I felt in this story while narrating to me [*sic*], was heightened by the emotion of the gentleman who told it, who evinced the most unaffected sympathy in it" (*Letters*, p. 154). The lawyer's story tells of a sailor, James Robertson, who was wrecked on the coast of Pembroke, Massachusetts, where a Miss Agatha Hatch was living. Robertson "was hospitably entertained and cared for" and within a year married Agatha. After two years, Robertson left Agatha Hatch, then pregnant, to look for work. From that time until "*Seventeen* years afterwards she never heard from him in any way whatsoever, directly or indirectly, not even a word" (*Letters*, p. 159). The lawyer and Melville marvel at the extraordinary patience and endurance of Agatha.

Many readers of the tales have pointed out that these tales and certain of Melville's later short pieces seem to come in pairs. Among the tales of this period, "The Happy Failure" and "The Fiddler" seem a pair as do "Cock-A-Doodle-Doo!" and "Bartleby the Scrivener." Thinking this way certainly allows for neatly balanced interpretations, like William B. Dillingham's: "In 'The Happy Failure' Melville depicts an ass trying to be a lion; in 'The Fiddler' he shows a lion trying to be an ass" (p. 159). The reversal is, in my view, all too neat: the asses and lions in Melville are always harder to sort out. One awkwardness is that the argument for pairs is backreasoned from the later tales which Melville wrote specifically as pairs, or "diptychs" as Jay Leyda calls them (*Complete Stories*, p. xx).

These four tales are often thought of as constituting autobiographical revelation by scholars who see Melville's career as a writer of tales as a decline. Leon Howard thinks "The Happy Failure" and "The Fiddler" may "have had reference to the ease [Melville] had found in writing his unambitious magazine pieces" (pp. 215–16). Edward H. Rosenberry thinks they are "mere skits," and they ask, in Melville's name, "how to be happy though unappreciated (*Melville*, p. 116).

"Bartleby" is the most frequently discussed tale of the group, and it has been subjected to many autobiographical readings—by Raymond Weaver (pp. xi, xlii); Lewis Mumford (pp. 236–39), Richard Chase (pp. 143–49), Joel Porte (pp. 152–92), and others, although the most influential autobiographical reading is undoubtedly Leo Marx's "Melville's Parable of the Walls" (1953). The scrivener is a kind of writer, Marx maintains, a "copyist" who "obstinately refuses to go on doing the sort of writing demanded of him," and "there can be little doubt about the connection between Bartleby's dilemma and Melville's own" (p. 603). Marx assumes this autobiographical "parable" at the beginning and then reads the story (naively, I think) as demonstration. More valuable than his thesis is Marx's analysis of the metaphoric possibilities in the many *walls* described in the tale.

Some nineteenth-century reviewers and twentieth-century scholars have suggested that Melville's tales of the period are based on real personages Melville knew or knew of. The *Berkshire County Eagle* of 30 May 1856, reviewing *Piazza Tales*, says that "Bartleby" is "a portrait from life," and *The Criterion* of 31 May 1856 says that it is "based upon living characters" (Inge, pp. 36–37). George William Curtis wrote in his piece "Sea from Shore" appearing in the *Putnam's* for July 1854 about a clerk "Titbottom": "Before I knew him, I used sometimes to meet him with a man who I was afterwards told was Bartleby, the scrivener" (Barton Levi St. Armand, p. 220). I would guess that the personage was not *named* "Bartleby," that Curtis used Melville's well-known name to describe a particular person somehow similar to Bartleby or even the "source" for Bartleby. Jay Leyda has suggested that Melville's Albany friend Eli James Murdock Fly, who became a "confirmed invalid" sometimes cared for by Melville, might have been a model for Bartleby (*Complete Stories*, p. 455).

Twentieth-century scholars have claimed many discoveries of sources for the four tales of this period in the works of well-known writers Melville may have been reading. Among the suggested sources of, for example, "Cock-A-Doodle-Doo!" are William Wordsworth's poem "Resolution and Independence" (Richard Chase, p. 163, and Leavis) and several of the works of Ralph Waldo Emerson and Henry David Thoreau (Egbert S. Oliver, "Cock"; Hershel Parker, "Melville's Satire"; William Bysshe Stein, "Melville's Cock" and "Melville Roasts"; R. Bruce Bickley, pp. 62–64; and Allan Moore Emery, "The Cocks"). Most argue that Melville is satirizing those transcendental writers in his story of the magnificent rooster and the crowing narrator. For "Bartleby, the Scrivener" the list of suggested sources seems endless, including at least the works of Thomas Carlyle (Mario L. D'Avanzo), Cicero (Marvin Singleton), Isaac D'Israeli (Richard Tuerck), Jonathan Edwards and Joseph Priestley (Walton R. Patrick and Allan Moore Emery, "The Alternatives").

It seems to me that the most consequential source studies for the tales of this group are those that discuss possible sources in Robert Burton's *Anatomy of Melancholy* (Nathalia Wright), Charles Lamb's Elia essays (Joel O. Conarroe), Washington Irving's tales (Seelye, "The Contemporary 'Bartleby'"; Bickley, pp. 26–44; Mushabac, pp. 110–20), and Nathaniel Hawthorne's "Wakefield" (which Melville mentions in his "Agatha" letter) and "The Birthmark" (Leo B. Levy; Bickley, pp. 26–44; Seelye, "The Contemporary 'Bartleby'"), and the works of Charles Dickens, particularly *Bleak House* (Jaffe). Taken together, these source suggestions, while not always establishing a direct link, provide important ways to understand Melville's handling of narrative tone and character (Lamb, Irving), "humors" characters (Burton, Dickens), and extraordinary characters (Dickens, Hawthorne).

Each of the tales of this first group is quite topical, each recognizable as part of a small tradition of popular stories. "The Happy Failure" has fun with a staple of American popular culture, the mad inventor. "The Fiddler," as has been demonstrated by Leyda (*Complete Stories*, pp. 467–68) and Gilman (*Melville's Early Life*, p. 316) and, more completely, by Dillingham (p. 149n), is in the genre of the child prodigy story, popular in the period. Leyda and Gilman are convinced that the prodigy Joseph Burke (1815–1902) is the sole source for Hautboy, but Dillingham quite properly points out that there were many accounts of prodigies. As is so often the case in source studies in American literature, the initial case for a source is too narrow when the contemporary convention is explained.

"Cock-A-Doodle-Doo!" alludes to the American craze in the early 1850s for fancy chickens—the "hen fever" as it was called. Beryl Rowland in "Melville and the Cock That Crew" (1981) points this out, as does Allan Moore Emery in "The Cocks of Melville's "Cock-a-Doodle-Doo!"(1976), although Emery tries (mistakenly, in my view) to fasten the story to one particular fancy chicken source, Reverend Frederick W. Shelton's "Letters from Up the River," as a series that appeared in the *Knickerbocker Magazine*. Many fancy chicken articles appear in the period, many of them perfectly aware of the symbolic possibilities of the cock. To take one simple example, Melville's New York acquaintance Cornelius Mathews published *Chanticleer: A Thanksgiving Story of the Peabody Family* in 1850. The rooster in that sentimental novel crows the family's faith in the reunion of all its prodigals; he crows particularly magnificently at the sentimentally transcendent ending of the novel.

"Bartleby, the Scrivener" would have been recognizable in 1853 as an example of several kinds of conventional stories, all associated with the character of a mysterious stranger. As John Seelye has pointed out, Melville had ample models in Hawthorne's "Wakefield," in Poe's "The Man of the Crowd," and especially in Irving's "The Little Man in Black" ("The Contemporary 'Bartleby' " [1970]). The more popular versions of the story have the extraordinary stranger appearing and finally being recognized as, or discovered to be, the lost heir of a great fortune, or the lost Dauphin himself. *Putnam's* itself made a great hit in its second issue (February 1853) with Charles H. Hanson's article attempting to prove that the Dauphin had been reared in America by Indians and was living as a missionary by the name of Eleazar Williams. The title of the article—"Have we a Bourbon Among Us?"—passed into a current catch phrase (Mott, p. 421). I point out elsewhere that "Bartleby" is possibly related to James Maitland's novel *A Lawyer's Story; Or, The Wrongs of the Orphans* (1853), a popular novel of the dauphin style narrated by a lawyer about his strange employee (Johannes Dietrich Bergmann). This is not necessarily a direct source; there were many "lawyer's stories," sentimental books about lost people whom the lawyers helped.

All the stories of this group, excluding the "Agatha" about which we can only speculate, are humorous, a fact that has been insufficiently recognized. The events are funny enough: the practical realist is forced to row his dreamy uncle's heavy worthless box upstream for its test; the absurd poet splenetically rages, is pacified, rages, and finally is pacified again by the grown-up boy; the angry melancholic learns to see hope and transcendence in the world by crowing like a rooster; the lawyer stolidly tries everything with Bartleby, even asking the motionless and conversationless scrivener whether he would like to work "going as a companion to Europe, to entertain some young gentleman with your conversation" (p. 69). The humor rises out of the contrast of two worlds—the alien one of the extraordinary character and the initially normal one of our narrator. We recognize the narrators as akin to *humors* characters (Wright, Mushabac)—eccentrics who display excess yet are familiar—Dickensian, perhaps, but knowable.

The phlegmatic narrator of Bartleby, the splenetic narrator of "The Fiddler," and the angry melancholic of "Cock-A-Doodle-Doo!" stretch the New York narrative tradition Melville shares with Washington Irving and George William Curtis and Donald Grant Mitchell ("Ik Marvel"). Melville makes two important changes. First, he removes the controlling frame narrator—the narrator, that is, who tells us about the person telling. Second (and perhaps this is a consequence of the first), Melville has pushed the humors narrator to and over the edge of acceptable eccentricity. As we read, we begin to suspect that the narrator of "Bartleby" is not simply genially phlegmatic but imaginatively insufficient; we suspect, then see, that the narrator of "Cock-A-Doodle-Doo!" is flapping just as excessively for faith as he was for melancholy. The effect of this is to destabilize the interpretive act, forcing the reader to interpret both narrator and extraordinary character. Bartleby's "Do you not see the reason for yourself?" (p. 59) becomes an interpretive challenge.

The extraordinary character is the test of the reader's interpretation: it is he who provides the void that cries out to be filled. Following our own century's interpretive imperative, Melville critics often find the extraordinary characters representative of assorted abstractions. Bartleby, for example, is a nineteenth-century alienated worker in rebellion (Louise K. Barnett, John H. Randall); he is Christ or a Christ figure (Leon S. Roudiez; Franklin, *Wake*, pp. 126–36; John Gardner; Donald M. Fiene; Seelye, *Ironic Diagram*, pp. 96–99); he is a portrait of Thoreau (Oliver, "Second Look"), he represents schizophrenia (Philip Rahv,

Christopher Bollas, Ted Billy); he represents existential philosophy (Robert Donald Spector, Margaret Jennings), and so on. The point with all the extraordinary characters—the uncle, Hautboy, Merrymusk, and Bartleby—is that we do not know, that we must imagine because that is all we have to do, but we must understand as we do so that we are not discovering Truth. We can only hope that our fire to distill the truth will not end up with Pip's "consequence".

AUTUMN 1853 THROUGH EARLY SUMMER 1854

During the autumn of 1853 and the winter of 1853–54 Melville might have worked on the "Tortoise Book" proposed to *Harper's* on 24 November 1853, although he evidently never finished it. During the winter, he probably also wrote, for *Putnam's*, "The Encantadas,"published in March, April, and May of 1854, and "The Two Temples," rejected in Briggs's 12 May 1854 letter. During the winter he also must have written, for *Harper's*, "Poor Man's Pudding and Rich Man's Crumbs" (published in June 1854) and "The Paradise of Bachelors and the Tartarus of Maids" (published in April 1855). That busy spring, he worked on *Israel Potter*, which was serialized in *Putnam's* from July of 1854 through March of 1855, and he certainly composed and submitted to *Putnam's* "The Lightning-Rod Man," published in August 1854 (Sealts, "Chronology," pp. 398–99).

During this period Melville composed pieces that were quite different in structure from the tales of the previous compositional group. The "Tortoise Book,"although we know nothing about it except our assumption that it must have as one origin the reflections on tortoises in "The Encantadas," must have been intended to be book length, and *Israel Potter* which appeared serially in *Putnam's* was published separately as a novel. The three two-part tales, "Poor Man's Pudding and Rich Man's Crumbs," 'The Two Temples," and "The Paradise of Bachelors and the Tartarus of Maids," while not longer than "Bartleby" or "Cock-A-Doodle-Doo," seem efforts to stretch the form of the tale into something more than a single telling of a single event; the form seems designed for *contrast* and for social comparison. Only "The Lightning-Rod Man" resembles in form the four tales of the first compositional group.

"The Encantadas, or Enchanted Isles" is a series of ten sketches which have as their organizing principle the Galapagos Islands. After one sketch on "The Isles at Large," the narrator, in separate sketches, describes the tortoises of the islands; the towering Rock Rodondo; the "Pisgah View" from it; the near loss of the U.S. Frigate *Essex* on the Rock in 1813; Barrington Isle; the "resort" of Buccaneers; Charles's Isle and its "Dog-King"; Norfolk Isle and the "Chola Widow" Hunilla; Hood's

Isle and the "Hermit Oberlus", and, finally, in the tenth sketch, "Runaways, Castaways, Solitaries, Grave-Stones, Etc." The narrator is dramatized, but he is often not involved in the action he describes. The encounter with the extaordinary is here in the form of the travel narrative so popular in the books and magazines of the period.

"Poor Man's Pudding and Rich Man's Crumbs" is a diptych, the first half of which describes the narrator's visit in the country with Blandmour, the poet, who fatuously comments on the beneficence of nature's ability to take care of the poor with "Poor Man's Manure" (snow) and "Poor Man's Egg" (rain). The narrator then visits a real poor family and describes the hardness of their life. We learn what we could have known already—that Poor Man's Pudding is not as good as real pudding, that the actual as opposed to the imagined or "poetic" condition of the poor is hard. In "Rich Man's Crumbs" the same narrator describes his visit to a charity "dinner" at Guildhall in London at which a starving urban mob is allowed to "feast" off the remains of a royal banquet. The horror of the scene, and the notion that some think it "charity," stupefies the narrator and he only escapes the mob with torn clothes, looking, in fact, like one of the mob himself.

In another diptych, "The Two Temples," another dramatized narrator, this one more clearly eccentric than the first, describes, in "Temple First," being turned away from a fashionable church in New York and climbing instead into its tower and peeking down on the service from a high inward window which vents all the hot air of the church. The implications are anti-hierarchical: he can hear the minister when he reads from the Bible at the "reading-desk" which is on the same level as the congregation, but he can no longer hear him when he ascends the pulpit to preach his sermon—except for one phrase the minister keeps repeating to his wealthy congregation: "Ye are the salt of the earth" (p. 155). In "Temple Second" the narrator, telling us that he is a "young physician" (p. 158), describes being in London and out of money when a man gives him his reentry stub for a performance at a London theater. In this temple he ascends to another lofty gallery and sees Macready doing Cardinal Richelieu, but the resemblance to the New York priest is remarkable! "The same measured, courtly, noble tone. See! the same imposing attitude." But there is a difference between the two temples. At the end of the "service" in the London theater the "enraptured thousands sound their responses, deafeningly; unmistakably sincere" (p. 164).

In "The Paradise of Bachelors and the Tartarus of Maids" another dramatized narrator/observer first describes eating a magnificent dinner in England and then making a visit to a paper-making factory in New England. The boozy, convivial, hearty, smoky, and most determinedly male dinner in the Temple in London is, the narrator tells us, "The very perfection of quiet absorption of good living, good drinking, good feeling, and good talk" (p. 209). It is a male collegiate dream of conviviality—measured, scholarly, drunken, infertile. The companion piece, "The Tartarus of Maids," is complex. On one level the narrator, a "seedsman," he says, is describing a visit to a paper factory in a cold and windy notch. What he finds is women working under appalling conditions in the cold: "This is the very counterpart of the Paradise of Bachelors, but snowed upon, and frost-painted to a sepulchre" (p. 214). "At rows of blank-looking counters sat rows of blank-looking girls, with blank, white folders in their blank hands, all blankly folding blank paper" (p. 215). The narrator's observation that they are "all maids," all called "girls" despite the fact that they are women, suggests one allegorical reading of the story: the factory is the female anatomy, from notch to the nine minutes it takes to produce the paper. But what these girls make is not new life but their own deaths: "So, through consumptive pallors of this blank, raggy life, go these white girls to death" (p. 218).

"The Lightning-Rod Man" seems more akin to "Cock-A-Doodle-Doo!" than to "The Paradise of Bachelors and the Tartarus of Maids." The initially reasonable narrator tells us about his encounter with an extraordinary other, a lightning-rod salesman. The salesman arrives in the midst of a violent thunderstorm and warns the narrator of the immense dangers of the storm. As the thunder crashes and lightning flashes, the salesman urges the narrator not to stand on the hearth, near the walls, anywhere: he sells lack of faith. The narrator finally rejects him: "In thunder as in sunshine, I stand at ease in the hands of my God." "Impious wretch!" foams the salesman, and the "indigo-circles enlarged round his eyes" (p. 193). The narrator violently breaks the "false" rod but warns that the salesman is still at work in the neighborhood.

The sources for the stories of this group have been well explored. Melville's use of Charles Darwin's *The Voyage of the Beagle* for "The Encantadas" is discussed by L. D. Gottlieb, H. Bruce Franklin ("The Island Worlds"), and Benjamin Lease, and the Spenserian epigraphs that begin each sketch have been identified separately by Leon Howard ("Melville and Spenser") and Russell Thomas. Melville himself points to another source—Captain David Porter's *Journal of a Cruise Made to the Pacific Ocean* (1815). He may also have used James Colnett's *A Voyage to the South Atlantic ... (1798)*, John M. Coulter's *Adventures in the Pacific* (1845), and James Burney's *Chronological History of the Discoveries in the South Sea or Pacific Ocean* (1803–17), each discussed most fully by Russell Thomas.

Melville reveals other possible sources by dedicating "The Two Temples" to the actor Sheridan Knowles (1774–1862) whose writings are thought by Beryl Rowland ("Melville Answers the Theologians," 1974) to be a source for Melville's imagery. "Poor Man's Pudding" refers to the writings of Charles Doddridge (Dillingham, pp. 127–28), and "Rich Man's Crumbs" recalls an 18 June 1814 Guildhall banquet. Dillingham finds important models for "The Paradise of Bachelors and the Tartarus of Maids" in Boccaccio and Dante (pp. 183–207).

Topical reference is evident in these tales, particularly in "The Two Temples" which was turned down because of its all too topical attack on Grace Church. "Poor Man's Pudding and Rich Man's Crumbs" takes part in a tradition of writing about the poor in the period. The second half of "The Paradise of Bachelors and the Tartarus of Maids" would have been familiar to Melville's readers because of the extensive discussion of the New England mill girls, particularly those in Lowell, Massachusetts (Fisher, pp. 70–94; Rogin, pp. 201–208). There was, of course, interest in mills and the human effects of manufacturing generally. Dickens, for example, has a piece on "A Paper Mill" in *Household Words* for 31 August 1850 in which the paper being manufactured is turned into the "I" of the narration: the impersonalization of the process is emphasized, though not with any of Melville's intensity. In addition, specific comparisons between England and America, like those in the three diptychs, were standard and popular fare in the magazines of the period.

Jay Leyda has pointed out how Melville must have used incidents in his own life for these stories. He visited the Galapagos with the *Acushnet* in 1841–42, seeing them at their "busiest social and whaling season" when he must have heard many sailors' tales about the enchanted islands. He was there again on the *Charles and Henry* late in 1842 or early 1843 (*Complete Stories*, pp. 455–56). The specific events of Melville's London trip in 1849 which lie behind "Rich Man's Crumbs," "Temple Second," and "The Paradise of Bachelors" are also described by Leyda (pp. 462–65), and Melville family tradition has it that Melville had had an encounter with a real lightning-rod salesman at the door of his house in Pittsfield (pp. xxvi–xxvii).

Arguments about the structure of the stories of this group focus, as one might suspect, on the two halves. What does one have to do with the other, why are they together? Even for "The Encantadas" there is a version of this discussion, in the question of the unity of the sketches. At least two critics (Bickley, p. 115; Fisher, p. 35) have also pointed out that the structure of "The Encantadas" specifically foreshadows the diptych. Bickley argues that the last two sketches, "Norfolk Isle and the Chola Widow" and "Hood's Isle and the Hermit Oberlus," read together as if they were a diptych, the paired stories showing the difference in the ways one can react to unbearable events.

Clearly the diptychs are *contrasts*. They—like Catherine Maria Sedgwick's *The Poor Rich Man and The Rich Poor Man* (1837) or Douglas Jerrold's *St. Giles and St. James* (1845) or Charles Dickens's *Bleak House* (1853) or the works of George Lippard, George G. Foster, E.Z.C. Judson or many daily or monthly journalists— structure themselves on opposition, reversal, social contrast. We readers will learn, we think, the difference between rich and poor, between religion and drama, between male and female, between English bachelor of leisure and American maid of work, between viciousness and enduring goodness, between England and America. It is precisely this starkness that makes Mushabac think that two of the diptychs ("Poor Man's Pudding and Rich Man's Crumbs" and "The Two Temples") announce the opposition all too clearly, that the "choppy form . . . cuts Melville off just as he is getting into his subject" (p. 120). Mushabac shares with Newton Arvin the sense that Melville is confining himself to a standard journalistic form he cannot transcend.

Writing of "the reiterated contrast to the established world" in "The Encantadas," Warner Berthoff comes to the opposite conclusion: "the writing, with this bold and simple opposition to illustrate, is solidly yet easily informative. . . . 'The Encantadas' . . . moves to some of the finest English prose in nineteenth-century literature by being, first of all, admirably efficient journalism" (*Example*, p. 77).

For critics who see the stories of the period as explicit social criticism, the contrast structure seems perfectly appropriate: it *demonstrates* a difference in social conditions and implies a world that should be. "The Two Temples" is about false religion, failed democracy, and the lack of true charity (Ray B. Browne, pp. 200–208; Fisher 51–61). "Poor Man's Pudding and Rich Man's Crumbs" shows that the true foundation of human dignity is "subverted by the insistence of the Americans, rich and poor, on behaving as though the 'ideal of universal equality' were achieved, and of the British on behaving as though it were absurd" (Vida K. Brack and O. M. Brack, p. 71). For many critics "The Tartarus of Maids" is an explicit indictment of industrialism (for example, Fisher, pp. 70–94; Rogin, pp. 201–208), and Carolyn L. Karcher finds that several of the sketches in "The Encantadas" have specific reference to American slavery (*Shadow*, pp. 109–20).

Readers who are convinced that the tales go beyond social comment often write of the *tone* of the tales in this group, as if the intensity of the pieces enriches the simple contrast of the form. Newton Arvin, for example, notes the "startling ferocity of effect" in "Rich Man's Crumbs" that "suggests an essay of Elia suddenly turning Zolaesque before one's eyes" (p. 236). Mushabac finds the same piece memorable for its "Hogarthian barbarity" (p. 120). Such commentators generally single out "The Tartarus of Maids" as the most important tale of the group. As Mushabac puts it about that tale, "the resonances transcend the form" (p. 120).

"The Encantadas" is also often thought of as transcending its pocket encyclopedia form and creating "resonances" that haunt the reader forever, just as the tortoise of the islands haunts the narrator. What the ghost tortoise asks the narrator to remember, and what we remember, is death—"Memento * * * * * [Mori]" (p. 103). The islands become "a token of the inscrutable wholeness of nature" (Seelye, *Ironic Diagram*, p. 101) which is untranscendable, unforgettable. The sketches seem an explicit rejection of the picturesque tradition in landscape painting and literary art in which the "presence" of nature fully realized by the observer makes for transcendence, a rejection keyed by the parody pseudonym printed in *Putnam's*: "Salvator [Rosa] Tarnmoor" (Sharon Furrow; Fisher, pp. 29–30). It is a fallen world that promises no resurrection (Fogle, pp. 92–115; I. Newberry: Robert C. Albrecht; and, with less theological emphasis, Dillingham, pp. 76–78).

Many twentieth-century scholars think Melville was at pains to keep these meanings "secret" from his nineteenth-century readers. The assumption is that because his meanings are complex and subtle and violate proprieties of various kinds, he cannot have meant his audience to understand. Readers like Leyda and Rosenberry have made such arguments based on biographical insights, while more recent readers like Dillingham have connected them to careful interpretations of the narrative voice. For Dillingham, for example, the narrator of "The Lightning-Rod Man" is not the reasonable man Parker takes him to be; his imputations and treatment of the salesman are excessive and so the apparent Christianity of the ending is suspect, as is the demonism of the salesman (Dillingham, pp. 168–82; Parker, "Melville's Salesman Story"). Attention to the narrator in all the diptychs also leads Dillingham to some important remarks about how the apparent structural contrast can be seen by the acute reader as masking a fundamental identity. "Poor Man's Pudding" and "Rich Man's Crumbs" are both about the narrator's education in the *language* of misperception (pp. 119–42); the two parts of "The Two Temples" are both about the wandering narrator and his discovery of a new communion in art (pp. 104–18); and the two tales in "The Paradise of Bachelors and the Tartarus of Maids" are *both* about the narrator's nearly blinding perception of the frozen white blankness of life (pp. 183–207).

SUMMER 1854 TO SPRING 1855

During the summer of 1854, Sealts tells us, Melville probably composed and submitted to *Harper's* "Jimmy Rose," published in November 1855, and "The 'Gees," published in March 1856. In the winter of 1854–55 he composed and submitted "Benito Cereno" to *Putnam's*. It was apparently in proof before 1 April 1855, though it was not published until October, November and December of 1855. In the spring of 1855 he also composed and submitted "The Bell-Tower" to *Putnam's*, and it was published in the August issue (Sealts, "Chronology," pp. 402–403).

The tales of this grouping are narrated in different ways. Melville is clearly experimenting with several different narrative voices, two of them third person, one completely unsympathetic. "Jimmy Rose" seems similar to the earlier "The Happy Failure" and "The Fiddler," but the narrator is less dramatized and more highly characterized: the revelations he makes about himself are much more subtle and involving for the reader. "The 'Gees," according to recent commentary, is a hoax whose narrator is unreliable in that his racism does not represent the attitude of his creator. "Benito Cereno" and what some think is its compositional twin, "The Bell Tower," have undramatized third-person narrators, unlike any of the other tales. "Benito Cereno" is a complex non-dramatic third-person narration; "The Bell-Tower" is dramatic allegory of the kind written by Nathaniel Hawthorne. Both deal with enslavement, literal and figurative.

"Jimmy Rose" is a New York story in which the melancholy old narrator, William Ford, tells us the story of the New York bankrupt Jimmy Rose. Rose was once the wealthy and glittering center of the most fashionable dinners where all sought his attention and where he excelled at generosity and compliments. After he lost his fortune and sought isolation, he lived the rest of his life in New York "poor as any rat; poor in the last dregs of poverty; a pauper beyond alms-house pauperism; a promenading pauper in a thin, thread-bare, careful coat; a pauper with a wealth of polished words; a courteous, smiling, shivering gentleman" (p. 322) who kept the rose in his cheeks. The old narrator holds tight to his precious memory of Jimmy Rose.

"The 'Gees" is a sketch describing an actual race of crossbred Portuguese sailors who were familiar in the Atlantic fisheries and ports. The sailor-narrator tells the racist sailor stories of the astonishing appetite and stupidity of "the 'Gees." We can hear in the narrator a boozy cruelty and casualness: "The 'Gee has a great appetite, but little imagination; a large eyeball, but small insight. Biscuit he crunches, but sentiment he eschews" (p. 356). There is a joke about a 'Gee with elephantiasis and another about how the Quakers want to send some to Dartmouth. Even the summary indicates why one might have been tempted to leave "The 'Gees" out of a collection. The assertion in the criticism, it must be obvious, is that the story is an ironical demonstration of the absurdity of prejudice.

"Benito Cereno" is the third-person narrative description of the 1799 encounter between the captain of an American sealer and general trader, Amasa Delano, with a ship carrying slaves off the coast of Chile. The ship seems in distress, and Delano boards her to offer his assistance. He spends the day on the *San Dominick* with the Spanish captain, Benito Cereno, puzzled and disoriented by the seemingly inexplicable events he witnesses: he sees the picture but cannot find the frame. Cereno tells him that the ship has weathered a great storm, lost some of its officers, and suffered disease, hence the apparent disorder and lack of discipline among the slaves. Delano proceeds as if in a trance, sometimes accepting Cereno, sometimes distrusting him. What he does not suspect, and what is finally revealed at the end, is that there had been a violent slave revolt on board the ship, that the slaves are in control and only feigning their former enslavement. Delano had been fooled all day, although his folly was his physical salvation. A set of legal depositions follows the narrative proper.

"The Bell-Tower" is a third-person allegorical tale of the "mechanician" Bannadonna's creation of a three hundred foot high bell-tower, the "noblest" in Italy. In casting the equally magnificent bell, Bannadonna murders one of his workmen in a rage and part of the victim is cast with the bell. Bannadonna is forgiven because the murder is imputed to "sudden transports of esthetic passion" (p. 225). Bannadonna himself is killed when the silent and efficient automaton he has created to ring the hour duly smites him. The magnificent "too ponderous" bell is flawed, and when first rung, it falls under its own weight; the tower itself (with a recast bell) falls victim to an earthquake one year later. "So the blind slave obeyed its blinder lord; but, in obedience, slew him . . . And so pride went before the fall" (p. 237).

Carolyn Karcher thinks the sources of "The 'Gees" can be found in the format and style of certain racist antebellum "ethnologists" (*Shadow*, pp. 160–85). We can assume, I think, because of the highly oral quality of the prose, that it is also an imitation of the "funny"stories sailors told about the 'Gees (see Rosenberry on Walter Blair's comments on its oral qualities, *Comic Spirit*, p. 200n). Dillingham finds the major sources of "Jimmy Rose"to be Melville's attitudes toward his grandfather, Major Thomas Melvill (pp. 302–307); Leyda guesses at some similarities between the second Melville family home in New York and Ford's house (*Complete Stories*, p. 468). The source for "Benito Cereno" is, as Harold H. Scudder shows, Chapter XVII of the real Amasa Delano's *A Narrative of Voyages and Travels in the Northern and Southern Hemispheres Comprising Three Voyages Round the World* . . . (1817). The differences between Delano's account and Melville's have been argued thoroughly by several commentators (see particularly Harold H. Scudder; Feltenstein; Karcher, *Shadow*, pp. 127–43; and Ward). The "mechanician" Bannadonna of "The Bell-Tower" is thought to be based on Benvenuto Cellini (Robert E. Morsberger) or, more plausibly, on Juanelo Torriano, the mechanician of Emperor Charles V who is mentioned in *Mardi, White-Jacket*, "Benito Cereno," and "I and My Chimney" (William B. Dillingham, p. 212n). Several critics have discussed the possible Hawthorne sources for this apparently "Hawthornean" allegory (Morsberger; Gerard M. Sweeney; Irving Malin; Bickley, pp. 96–100). Another critic thinks the tale is a response to a bad article on Melville by Fitz-James O'Brien which appeared in *Putnam's* in February 1855 (Wayne R. Kine). The critical commentary on "Jimmy Rose" is not extensive. Berthoff finds it "expert in performance" but says little about it (*Example*, p. 15). Other scholars find that the story exposes the "obtuseness of a society primarily oriented toward material values" (Ralph M. Tutt, p. 30) or, more interestingly, that it is a "story about a man whose adjustment to failure was made without any essential moral growth" (James W. Gargano, p. 277). William Dillingham (pp. 296–318) and Marvin Fisher (pp. 133–45) have the most extended commentaries. Both cite Barbara Seward's book *The Symbolic Rose* (1960) as source for their analyses of the rose symbolism. Dillingham finds the story a warm spot in Melville's works: the roses in Jimmy's cheeks represent Ford's ability to "see and feel the bloom of life, to know warmth as well as chill. Melville had come to cherish that spot of color, that experience of the rose" (p. 317). The story is the other side, as it were, of the cold, white blankness of the second half of "The Paradise of Bachelors and the Tartarus of Maids."

Rosenberry's comments about "The 'Gees" are blind to the racism exposed by the piece: " 'The 'Gees' is in fact the epitome of sunny surface, indistinguishable in matter and manner from *Omoo* and with no more depth of meaning in its comedy" (*Comic Spirit*, pp. 179–80). Berthoff (Tales, p. 355) guesses that the sketch may allude to the exploitative order of modern economic life, even to slavery itself; Dillingham is sure the sketch is a hoax (pp. 358–59); and Carolyn L. Karcher thinks it a clever satire on the aforementioned ethnologists (*Shadow*, pp. 160–85).

The critical history of "Benito Cereno" is long and complex. The tale's unreliable, even deceptive, narration led some readers to think it an "artistic miscarriage," as Newton Arvin called it. For Arvin the atmosphere of the tale is built up tediously with a silly portentousness; Melville is too tired to rewrite (pp. 238–41). George William Curtis, commenting on the story for *Putnam's* in 1855, said "[Melville] does everything too hurriedly now." Curtis was particularly concerned that the "dreary documents" at the end had not been worked into the narrative proper (Leyda, *Complete Stories*, pp. 468–69).

Warner Berthoff, responding to such accusations, insists that the narrative techniques of the story be examined for what they are:

... it seems only reasonable not to write off so persistent a set of compositional practices as the product of exhaustion or fumbling, but to take them as they come, for the serious virtue that may be in them; for what they positively contribute, that is, to a body of work of which it is scarcely possible not to feel the peculiar originality and expressiveness. (*Example* p. 150)

For Berthoff, the chiaroscuro, the non-dramatic tableaux, the frag-
menting of the narrative into short paragraphs are all central to the
story's "massed effect—the sense of tension increasing and diminishing,
the irregular measuring out of time, the nervous succession of antithetical feelings and intuitions" (p. 155). It is a masterpiece of narrated—
as opposed to dramatized—fiction. A postmodern, but not better, elaboration of the tale's indeterminacies is Eric J. Sundquist's "Suspense and
Tautology in 'Benito Cereno' " (1981). Milder's commentary on the mixture of the "profound and the banal" in Sundquist seems to me apt (*ALS
1981*, pp. 71–72). Another postmodern analyis is Elizabeth Wright's
"The New Psychoanalysis and Literary Criticism" (1982) in which Lacanian thought explains that fiction attempts to recover lost wholeness
but fails, and in "Benito Cereno" the multiple meanings are the author's
failure to control the wholeness intended.

The narrative indeterminacy has led to ambiguities in which the reader
and scholar as well as Amasa Delano participate. Delano himself is almost
universally condemned for his characteristically American naivete (Barry
Phillips; Allen Guttman; W. J. Pilkington; Richard Harter Fogle, pp.
116–47), but few of those critics ask whether the first-time reader shares
that naivete (not knowng in fact what is going on) and whether the
reader's naivete is a creation of a narrator who, in places, encourages
misperception. Another question for the reader is whether or not he or
she is expected to be sympathetic to the slaves. Assertions that the story
is not "about" slavery and hence that readers need not be sympathetic
to the revolt but to an innocent Cereno overwhelmed by the evil of the
humanity (Rosalie Feltenstein; Kingsley Widmer, pp. 59–90; Robert J.
Ward) are answered by powerful reminders of the abolitionist views
Melville expressed at least in *Mardi* and arguments which try to demonstrate Melville's approval of Babo and the slaves (Bernstein; Fisher,
p. 104–17; Karcher, *Shadow*, pp. 127–43).

Many of the issues of the interpretation turn on the extent to which
we can sort out the narrative points of view and determine or infer
Melville's point of view. As Dillingham argues there are (at least) four
narrative perspectives: "reportorial, official (the deposition), authorial,
and individual (Delano)" (p. 243). Dillingham writes clearly about the
perspectives, but a successful theory of how and why they interact with
one another in the single work "Benito Cereno" would demonstrate more
convincingly than Dillingham, or Berthoff or Sundquist, how the tale is
"about" evil, or indeterminacy or American slavery and how the reader
might be empowered to understand that.

"The Bell-Tower" is not admired by Melville's most distinguished
twentieth-century critics. Arvin finds it "convictionless" (p. 235), and
Berthoff thinks it "the most inept" of all of Melville's stories (p. 223).
The London *Athenaeum* had been even less kind 100 years before: "The

author who 'flames amazement' in the eyes of his readers by putting forth such grand paragraphs as [the first] must content himself with a very young public" (Inge, p. 51). However, other nineteenth-century and some twentieth-century readers have admired the tale. H. Bruce Franklin's 1966 suggestion that "The Bell-Tower" is a science fiction tale with specific reference to the institution of American slavery (*Future Perfect*, pp. 144–50) is developed by Marvin Fisher (pp. 95–104) and Carolyn Karcher (*Shadow*, pp. 143–59). Clearly, the *Putnam's* editors of the early 1850's would have been sympathetic to such allegorical readings of "The Bell-Tower" and "Benito Cereno," since Parke Godwin and other of the "black republicans" were publishing equally virulent, though non-fictional, attacks on slavery in the magazine. Dillingham, on the other hand, thinks Bannadonna a sort of hero, a "cynic solitaire," a misperceived, obsessed artist "of profound genius who is bent upon the degradation of mankind" (p. 226).

SPRING 1855 THROUGH MARCH 1856

In the spring of 1855 Melville composed and submitted "I and My Chimney," published in *Putnam's* in March 1856. It seems probable, if not certain, that it was composed after "The Bell-Tower" of my last grouping and seems also to be the first of the last compositional group, with their "domestic" narrators. In the summer or fall of 1855 Melville composed and submitted to *Putnam's* "The Apple-Tree Table," published in May 1855. By the fall he was apparently also at work on *The Confidence-Man: His Masquerade*, a novel finished in 1856 and published in April 1857. He revised (by 19 January) the magazine pieces that were collected in *The Piazza Tales*. He also composed and submitted the tale "The Piazza" for the collection. *The Piazza Tales* was published in May of 1856 (Sealts, "Chronology," pp. 402–403).

This group contains two much admired tales, "I and My Chimney" and "The Apple-Tree Table," as well as the poetic "The Piazza." These tales are all narrated by what seems a family man, somewhat like the narrator of "Jimmy Rose," William Ford. The narrators of "I and My Chimney" and "The Apple-Tree Table" have each a wife and two daughters. In "Jimmy Rose" the narrator has just "removed from the country" to an inherited city house, and his daughters are unnamed; in "I and My Chimney" the narrator lives in the country and the daughters are named Julia and Ann; in "The Apple-Tree Table" the narrator lives in the city in a purchased house and the daughters are also Julia and Ann. In "The Piazza" the narrator says he has moved to a country house, and from its north side one can see Mount Greylock, as one could from Melville's house in Pittsfield. All three stories seem initially genial and sunny, confident and adept examples of the New York tradition of the narrated tale. They are as well the high points of that tradition, embodying for all their ease a richness of suggestion and complexity, even, paradoxically, a calm despair, which is the highest development of the tradition begun with Washington Irving.

In "I and My Chimney" the narrator describes in an extended monologue his extraordinary chimney. It is the strong centerpiece of his house, an old smoker (like himself) which rests on a secure foundation in the basement. It rises up through the house impractically, refusing to allow a convenient center hall. It is ample, broad, and traditional, but the narrator's wife wants it down. Her maxim is "Whatever is, is wrong" (p. 336), and she takes up all new causes, including center halls. She, the narrator suspects, connives with mason Hiram Scribe to get the chimney removed; they try to tempt the narrator with the "calculation" that there is a secret compartment in the chimney. The narrator resists successfully, buys off Scribe, and gets from him a certificate that he has "found no reason to believe any unsoundness..., any secret closet [is] in it" (p. 351). The narrator has only won the battle, the chimney and he are still under attack, but "I and my chimney will never surrender (p. 354).

In "The Apple-Tree Table; or, Original Spiritual Manifestations," the narrator rescues an old table and a copy of Cotton Mather's *Magnalia Christi Americana* from the haunted attic of his house, much to the displeasure of his two daughters who fear the attic. The narrator laughs at that, and at Mather, until one night he sits alone at his new apple-tree table, sipping his punch and reading *Magnalia*. Mather's tales of witchcraft no longer seem so foolish and—the narrator hears a strange ticking! His wife thinks it is the punch but the next day she too hears the ticking and takes charge, vigorously managing the search for the source of the noise. "Upon occasion my wife was mistress in her house" the narrator tells us in the understatement of the story (p. 371). The source is not found; but later the narrator sees a bug coming out of the wood of the apple-tree table. That bug is lost, the narrator is not believed, but another bug repeats the performance, and all believe in the amazing birth of the bug from its 150–year dead egg in the apple-tree table.

In "The Piazza," the tale that was written to introduce *The Piazza Tales*, the narrator describes his old-fashioned country house and its scenic surroundings, a place which "in berry time" is a "very paradise of painters" (p. 383). He dreamily invokes the old New York romantic principles established by Irving—one must have time and leisure to see meaning and beauty. The imagination is a quiet one: "beauty is like piety—you cannot run and read it; tranquillity and constancy, with, now-a-days, an easy chair, are needed... in these times of failing faith and feeble knees, we have the piazza and the pew (p. 384). He has the necessary piazza built (impractically, according to his neighbors) on the north side of his house so he can walk his "sleety deck"and see Mount Greylock. Looking out, he sees a "golden sparkle" of light, in "some sort of glen, or grotto"— some sleepy hollow—in the distant mountain side. He imagines the magic life lived there at the rainbow's end, in Titania's land, and sets out to make his "inland voyage to fairyland" (p. 386). He finds Marianna, whose life of loneliness and toil leads only to death, not to transfiguration on midsummer nights. The flies and wasps in her windows are flies and wasps, and when the sun "gilds" the house, it only sets the flies and wasps astir. Marianna dreams of the golden palace in the valley—the narrator's house. The narrator goes home and is no more bound for fairyland but continues to watch the illusion from his piazza. "But, every night, when the curtain falls, truth comes in with darkness. No light shows from the mountains. To and fro I walk the piazza deck, haunted by Marianna's face, and many as real a story" (p. 395).

Merton M. Sealts suggests in his "Herman Melville's 'I and My Chimney' "(1941) that the tale is built on the medical events in Melville's life, particularly his physical examination by Oliver Wendell Holmes in June of 1855. The Pittsfield house the Melvilles lived in, "Arrowhead" (now the headquarters of the Berkshire County Historical Society), had a large central chimney and an awkward front hall. "The Apple-Tree Table" shares with other stories and books of the period, including Henry David Thoreau's *Walden* and the *History of the County of Berkshire, Massachusetts* which Melville acquired in July 1850, the folktale of the bug in the apple-tree table (Douglas Sackman; Frank Davidson; Walter Harding, *Variorum Walden*, p. 266). The story also refers to the spiritualism of the period (Fisher, pp. 124–32; Howard Kerr). The anonymous reviewer of *The Piazza Tales* for the *New York Daily News* (26 May 1856) gives the source of "The Piazza" as Tennyson's 1830 poem "Marianna" (Inge, pp. 34–36), and that poem alludes to Shakespeare's Marianna in *Measure for Measure* (Helmbrecht Breinig; Fogle, p. 89; Bickley, pp. 124–30). The incidents in Tennyson clearly constitute a source for Melville—even a fly is in the windowpane. The epigraph to Melville's tale is from *Cymbeline* (Dillingham, pp. 335–37). Other scholars think Hawthorne is a specific source, particularly his "The Old Manse" in *Mosses from an Old Manse* (Breinig; Waggoner; Fisher, pp. 13–28; Dillingham, pp. 332–35).

The most important twentieth-century criticism of these last three tales was quick to perceive that the genial surfaces—the "easy-going, sunny quaintness,"as Sedgwick says about "I and My Chimney" (p. 193), the "good nature" so prevalent in the same tale that Fogle finds it "tiresome" (p. 78)—hide more significant meanings. The argument, in other words, is that the narrative tone is at odds with the authorial intent.

The task then, of course, is to read the authorial intent through the story and the biographical sources, to unlock the "secrets" of the story by reading the symbols—the central chimney, the resurrected bug, the trip to fairyland—as symbols of crises in Melville's own life. For Merton Sealts, the chimney is "The heart and soul" of Herman Melville, the central core he is attempting to preserve against all sorts of attacks ("Melville's 'I and My Chimney' "); for Rosenberry, "The Apple-Tree Table" is a symbolic account of Melville's career, a "broadly Twainish" burlesque treatment of his inner contest between panic and philosophy (*Comic Spirit*, p. 183); and for Dillingham "The Piazza" is a highly personal account of an emotional crisis, complete with the "shock therapy" of the narrator's visit to Marianna (pp. 319–40).

The three tales are as warming for interpretations as is the chimney for its narrator's wife's eggs. The chimney, for example, is thought to represent not just Melville's "heart and soul" but also the narrator's phallus (Bickley, p. 52), "Melville's importunate integrity" (Sedgwick, p. 195), the narrator's conservatism (Fogle, p. 73), slavery, which the narrator will not give up (William J. Sowder), "All that is best left undisturbed" (Seelye, *Ironic Diagram*, p. 92), and the British Constitution (Browne, pp. 259–71). "The Apple-Tree Table" is rife with apocalyptic imagery (Malcolm O. Magaw), an indictment of spiritualism and the belief in resurrection (Karcher, "The 'Spiritual Lesson' "), and a retort to the "Conclusion" of *Walden* (Breinig). "The Piazza" is an attack on Hawthorne's aesthetics (Breinig), inspired by Hawthorne (Waggoner; Fisher, pp. 13–28), or related to Dante (C. Sherman Avallone).

All the readings seen together seem to demonstrate the need for the kind of analysis which Milton R. Stern has applied to "Bartleby." We need to focus more clearly on what it is about the symbolic method of the stories that provokes so many apparently divergent readings; that sort of analysis, well done, would tell us a great deal about the tales as well. Most readings do share a sense of the narrator (whether representing Melville directly or not) as a person with a need to conserve, to save something of his personality from the forces attacking it. The narrator, particularly in "I and My Chimney" and "The Piazza," is an isolato trying to salvage something from the wreck of his hopes. I would argue that these meanings are not necessarily "secret," however: the narrators' efforts to salvage something from total despair seem to me a meaning enriched and contained in the "surface" of the story, inextricable from it—and probably quite available to the nineteenth-century reader.

"The Piazza" has seemed to several scholars a "literary manifesto" (Roundy), a statement of the possibilities of the creative imagination (Porte, p. 153). As such it is a confident and positive final tale for the 1853–56 period. It is surely a rejection of the romantic landscape ideology (Klaus Poenicke), but it is an affectionate rejection. The narrator continues to look at his fairyland illusion, even though he is now sure it is an illusion. He is prepared as well for the "truth [which] comes in with darkness," the "real story" like Marianna's (p. 345). His creator uses, as the reviewer for the *New York Daily News* argued in 1856 (Inge, pp. 34–36) and as Warner Berthoff noted in 1966 (Tales, p. 383), a new sort of narrative prose, a narrative poetry inspired, in part, by the two poets who told a story of Marianna before Melville did.

CONCLUSION

Melville's tales and sketches are a remarkable achievement. That Melville was able to accomplish so much in those nearly four years seems to me astonishing, particularly when it is remembered that my survey here has not included *Israel Potter*, also written during this period, or *The Confidence-Man* on which he probably worked from the summer of 1855 on. To repeat Berthoff's view, the recovery of these works would have occasioned high excitement even if they had been the only Melville works known (*Example*, p. 138). The tales and sketches are certainly not evidence of a decline in craft.

The scholarship and criticism of the tales and sketches has been extensive and, at times, distinguished. The biographical and compositional groundwork would seem to have been as well and as completely done as the evidence permits, although new biographical material will continue to be discovered. We have a large group of very good readings (and a large group of bad readings). What both the scholarship and the criticism now awaits is the authoritative Northwestern-Newberry edition of *The Piazza Tales and Other Prose Pieces 1839–1860*. That edition should stimulate another round of scholarship and criticism: it may even, we can hope, stimulate some "New Scholarship" which would combine the best of historical, biographical, textual, and bibliographical scholarship with the most insightful and methodologically adept criticism.

That "New Scholarship" is something of a trip to fairyland too, of course, but surely it is an admirable goal (Parker, "The 'New Scholarship' "). For the tales and sketches, it would be a scholarship that would interpret the tales in their compositional context. It would examine the tales alongside the novels that were written during the period, *Israel Potter* and *The Confidence-Man*, and it would locate the 1853–56 work within Melville's whole career.

New Scholarship would as well come to some greater analytic determination of what the huge body of criticism about the tales itself means about Melville's work and our own academic subculture. It might also encourage the writing of more meticulous histories of the American literature of Melville's period, scholarship that continues to be slighted in favor of concentration on the major figures like Melville. We need to read *all* of *Putnam's* and *Harper's* carefully, and we need to understand Curtis and Mitchell and Godwin and Briggs on their own terms. Most of all, we need to understand the particularities of the formal conventions of the period. Much has been done; much remains to be done.

NOTE

1. They are "Bartleby, the Scrivener: A Story of Wall Street," *Putnam's* (November, December 1853); "Cock-a-Doodle-Doo! or, the Crowing of the Noble Cock Beneventano," *Harper's* (December 1853); "The Encantadas, Or Enchanted Isles," *Putnam's* (March, April, May 1854); "Poor Man's Pudding and Rich Man's Crumbs,"*Harper's* (June 1854); "The Happy Failure: A Story of the River Hudson," *Harper's* (July 1854); "Israel Potter," *Putnam's* (July 1854, and monthly through March 1855); "The Lightning-Rod Man,"*Putnam's* (August 1854); "The Fiddler," *Harper's* (September 1854); "The Paradise of Bachelors and the Tartarus of Maids," *Harper's* (April 1855); "The Bell-Tower," *Putnam's* (August 1855); "Benito Cereno," *Putnam's* (October, November, December 1855); "Jimmy Rose," *Harper's* (November 1855); "The 'Gees," *Harper's* (March 1856); "I and My Chimney," *Putnam's* (March 1856); and "The Apple-Tree Table: or, Original Spiritual Manifestations," *Putnam's* (May 1856).

WORKS CITED

Albrecht, Robert C. "The Thematic Unity of Melville's 'The Encantadas.' " *Texas Studies in Literature and Language* 14(Fall 1972):463–77.

Arvin, Newton. *Herman Melville.* 1950; rpt. New York: Viking Press, 1957.

Avallone, C. Sherman. "Melville's 'Piazza.' " *ESQ* 22 (1976): 221–33.

Barnett, Louise K. "Bartleby as Alienated Worker." *Studies in Short Fiction* 11 (Fall 1974): 379–85.

Bergmann, Johannes Dietrich. " 'Bartleby' and *The Lawyer's Story.*" *American Literature* 47 (November 1975): 432–36.

Bernstein, John. *Pacifism and Rebellion in the Writings of Herman Melville.* The Hague: Mouton, 1964.

Berthoff, Warner. *The Example of Melville.* Princeton, N. J.: Princeton University Press, 1962.

———. [Introductions to the tales]. *Great Short Works of Herman Melville.* New York: Harper & Row, 1966.

Bickley, R. Bruce, Jr. *The Method of Melville's Short Fiction.* Durham: Duke University Press, 1975.

Billy, Ted. "Eros and Thanatos in 'Bartleby.' " *Arizona Quarterly* 31 (Spring 1975): 21–32.

Bollas, Christopher. "Melville's Lost Self: 'Bartleby.' " *American Imago* 31 (Winter 1974): 401–11.

Brack, Vida K., and O M Brack, Jr. "Weathering Cape Horn: Survivors in Melville's Minor Short Fiction." *Arizona Quarterly* 28 (1972): 61–73.

Breinig, Helmbrecht. "The Destruction of Fairyland: Melville's 'Piazza' in the Tradition of the American Imagination." *ELH: A Journal of English Literary History* 35 (June 1968): 254–83.

Brodtkorb, Paul, Jr. *Ishmael's White World: A Phenomenological Reading of Moby-Dick.* New Haven, Conn.: Yale University Press, 1965.

Browne, Ray B. *Melville's Drive to Humanism.* Lafayette, Ind.: Purdue University Studies, 1971.

Burton, William E., Ed. *The Cyclopedia of Wit and Humor.* New York: n.p., 1857.

Canaday, Nicholas, Jr. "Melville's 'The Encantadas': The Deceptive Enchantment of the Absolute." *Papers on Language and Literature* 10 (Winter 1974): 58–69.

Chase, Richard. *Herman Melville: A Critical Study.* New York: Macmillan Co., 1949.

Conarroe, Joel O. "Melville's Bartleby and Charles Lamb." *Studies in Short Fiction* 5 (Winter 1968): 113–18.

D'Avanzo, Mario L. "Melville's 'Bartleby' and Carlyle." In *Melville Annual 1965, A Symposium: "Bartleby, the Scrivener."* Ed. Howard P. Vincent. Kent, Ohio: Kent State University Press, 1966.

Davidson, Frank. "Melville, Thoreau, and 'The Apple-Tree Table.'" *American Literature* 25 (January 1954): 479–88.

Dickens, Charles, and Mark Lemon. "A Paper Mill." *Charles Dickens' Uncollected Writings from Household Words 1850–1859.* 2 vols. Ed. Henry Stone. Bloomington: Indiana University Press, 1968.

Dillingham, William B. *Melville's Short Fiction 1853–1856.* Athens: University of Georgia Press, 1977.

Dryden, Edgar A. *Melville's Thematics of Form: The Great Art of Telling the Truth.* Baltimore: Johns Hopkins University Press, 1968.

Eby, E. H. "Herman Melville's 'Tartarus of Maids.'" *Modern Language Quarterly* 1 (March 1940): 95–100.

Emery, Allan Moore. "The Alternatives of Melville's 'Bartleby.'" *Nineteenth-Century Fiction* 31 (September 1976): 170–87.

———. "The Cocks of Melville's 'Cock-a-Doodle-Doo!'" *ESQ* 28 (Second Quarter 1982): 89–111.

———. "The Political Significance of Melville's Chimney." *New England Quarterly* 55 (1982): 201–28.

Feltenstein, Rosalie. "Melville's 'Benito Cereno.'" *American Literature* 19 (November 1947): 245–55: rpt. in *Melville's "Benito Cereno": A Text for Guided Research.* Ed. John P. Runden. Lexington, Mass.: D. C. Heath, 1965.

Fiene, Donald M. "Bartleby the Christ." *American Transcendental Quarterly* No. 7 (Summer 1970): 18–23.

Fisher, Marvin. *Going Under: Melville's Short Fiction and the American 1850s.* Baton Rouge: Louisiana State University Press, 1977.

Fogle, Richard Harter. *Melville's Shorter Tales.* Norman: University of Oklahoma Press, 1960.

Franklin, H. Bruce. *Future Perfect: American Science Fiction of the Nineteenth Century.* New York: Oxford University Press, 1966.

———. "The Island Worlds of Darwin and Melville." *The Centennial Review* 11 (Summer 1967): 353–70.

———. *The Wake of the Gods: Melville's Mythology.* Stanford, Calif.: Stanford University Press, 1963.

Furrow, Sharon. "The Terrible Made Visible: Melville, Salvator Rosa, and Piranesi." *ESQ* 19 (Fourth Quarter 1973): 237–53.

Gardner, John. " 'Bartleby': Art and Social Commitment." *Philological Quarterly* 43 (January 1964): 87–98.

Gargano, James W. "Melville's 'Jimmy Rose.' " *Western Humanities Review* 16 (Summer 1962): 276–80.

Gilman, William H. *Melville's Early Life and Redburn.* New York: New York University Press, 1951.

Gottlieb, L. D. "Reflections: The Uses of Place: Darwin and Melville in the Galapagoes." *BioScience* 25 (March 1975): 172–75.

Guttman, Allen. "The Enduring Innocence of Captain Amasa Delano." *Boston University Studies in English* 5 (Spring 1961): 35–45; rpt in *Melville's "Benito Cereno": A Text for Guided Research.* Ed. John P. Runden. Lexington, Mass.: D. C. Heath, 1965.

Harding, Walter, ed. *The Variorum Walden.* By Henry David Thoreau. Boston: Twayne, 1962.

Hayford, Harrison. "The Significance of Melville's 'Agatha' Letters." *ELH: A Journal of English Literary History* 13 (December 1946): 299–310.

Howard, Leon. "Melville and Spenser—A Note on Criticism." *Modern Language Notes* 46 (May 1931): 291–92.

Inge, M. Thomas, ed. *Bartleby the Inscrutable: A Collection of Commentary on Herman Melville's Tale "Bartleby the Scrivener."* Hamden, Conn.: Archon Books, 1979.

Jaffe, David. *"Bartleby the Scrivener" and Bleak House: Melville's Debt to Dickens.* Arlington, Va.: Mardi Press, 1981.

Jennings, Margaret, C. S. J. "Bartleby the Existentialist." *Melville Society Extracts* No. 22 (May 1975): 8–10.

Johnson, Rossiter, ed. *Little Classics: Tragedy.* Boston: James R. Osgood, 1874.

Kaplan, Sidney. "Herman Melville and the American National Sin: The Meaning of 'Benito Cereno.' " *Journal of Negro History* 41 (October 1956): 311–38 and 42 (January 1957): 11–37.

Karcher, Carolyn L. "Melville's 'The 'Gees': A Forgotten Satire on Scientific Racism." *American Quarterly* 27 (October 1975): 421–42.

———. *Shadow Over the Promised Land: Slavery, Race and Violence in Melville's America.* Baton Rouge: Louisiana State University Press, 1980.

———. "The 'Spiritual Lesson' of Melville's 'The Apple-Tree Table.' " *American Quarterly* 23 (Spring 1971): 101–109.

Kerr, Howard. *Mediums, and Spirit-Rappers, and Roaring Radicals: Spiritualism in American Literature, 1850–1900.* Urbana: University of Illinois Press, 1972.

Kine, Wayne R. " 'The Bell-Tower': Melville's Reply to a Review." *ESQ* 22 (First Quarter 1976): 28–38.

Lacy, Patricia. "The Agatha Theme in Melville's Short Stories." *Texas Studies in English* 35 (1956): 96–105.

Lease, Benjamin. "Two Sides to a Tortoise: Darwin and Melville in the Pacific." *The Personalist* 49 (Fall 1968): 531–39.

Leavis, Q. D. "Melville: The 1853–6 Phase." In *New Perspectives on Melville.* Ed. Faith Pullin. Kent, Ohio and Edinburgh: Kent State University Press and Edinburgh University Press, 1978.

Levy, Leo B. "Hawthorne and the Idea of 'Bartleby.' "*ESQ* No. 47 (Second Quarter 1967): 66–68.

Leyda, Jay. "An Introduction" and "Notes on Sources, &c." In *The Complete Stories of Herman Melville*. By Herman Melville. New York: Random House, 1949.

Magaw, Malcolm O. "Apocalyptic Imagery in Melville's 'The Apple-Tree Table.' " *Midwest Quarterly* 8 (1967): 357–69.

Malin, Irving. "The Compulsive Design." In *American Dreams, American Nightmares*. Ed. David Madden. Carbondale: Southern Illinois University Press, 1970.

Marx, Leo. "Melville's Parable of the Walls." *Sewanee Review* 61 (Autumn 1953): 602–27.

Mason, Ronald. *The Spirit Above the Dust*. London: John Lehmann, 1951.

Melville, Herman. *The Apple-Tree Table and Other Sketches by Herman Melville*. Princeton, N.J.: Princeton University Press, 1922.

———. *Billy Budd and Other Prose Pieces*. Ed. Raymond Weaver. London: Constable, 1924.

———. *The Complete Stories of Herman Melville*. Ed. Jay Leyda. New York: Random House, 1949. [Texts rpt. in *Selected Writings of Herman Melville*. New York: Random House, 1952.]

———. *Great Short Works of Herman Melville*. Ed. Warner Berthoff. New York: Harper & Row, 1966.

———. *The Piazza Tales*. London: Constable, 1922.

———. *Piazza Tales*. Ed. Egbert S. Oliver. New York: Hendricks House, 1948.

———. *Selected Tales and Poems*. Ed. Richard Chase. New York: Holt, Rinehart & Winston, 1950.

———. *Shorter Novels of Herman Melville*. Ed. Raymond M. Weaver. New York: Horace Liveright, 1928.

Milder, Robert. "Knowing Melville." *ESQ* 24 (Second Quarter 1978): 96–117.

Monteiro, George. "More on Herman Melville in the 1890s." *Melville Society Extracts* No. 30 (May 1977): 14.

Morsberger, Robert E. "Melville's 'The Bell-Tower' and Benvenuto Cellini." *American Literature* 44 (November 1972): 459–62.

Moss, Sidney P. " 'Cock-a-Doodle-Doo!' and Some Legends in Melville Scholarship." *American Literature* 40 (May 1968): 192–210.

Mott, Frank Luther. *A History of American Magazines, 1850–1865*. Cambridge, Mass.: Harvard University Press, 1938.

Mumford, Lewis. *Herman Melville*. New York: Harcourt, Brace, 1929.

Mushabac, Jane. *Melville's Humor: A Critical Study*. Hamden, Conn.: Archon Books, 1981.

Newberry, I. " 'The Encantadas': Melville's *Inferno*." *American Literature* 38 (1966): 49–68.

Oliver, Egbert S. " 'Cock-a-Doodle-Doo!' and Transcendental Hocus-Pocus." *New England Quarterly* 21 (1948): 204–16.

———, ed. *Piazza Tales*. By Herman Melville. New York: Hendricks House, 1948.

———. "A Second Look at 'Bartleby.' " *College English* 6 (1945): 431–39.

Parker, Hershel. "Dead Letters and Melville's Bartleby." *Resources for American Literary Study* 4 (1974): 90–99.

————. "Melville's Salesman Story." *Studies in Short Fiction* 1 (1964): 154–58.

————. "Melville's Satire of Emerson and Thoreau: An Evaluation of the Evidence."*American Transcendental Quarterly* 7 (Summer 1970): 61–67. [See also "Corrections." *ATQ* 9 (Winter 1971): 70.]

————. "The 'New Scholarship': Textual Evidence and Its Implications for Criticism, Literary Theory, and Aesthetics." *Studies in American Fiction* 9 (Autumn 1981): 181–97.

Patrick, Walton R. "Melville's 'Bartleby' and the Doctrine of Necessity." *American Literature* 41 (March 1969): 39–54.

Phillips, Barry. " 'The Good Captain': A Reading of *Benito Cereno*." *Texas Studies in Literature and Language* 4 (Summer 1962): 188–97.

Pilkington, W. J. " 'Benito Cereno' and the American National Character." *Discourse* 8 (Winter 1965): 49–63.

Poenicke, Klaus. "A View from the Piazza: Herman Melville and the Legacy of the European Sublime." *Comparative Literature Studies* 4 (1967): 267–81.

Porte, Joel. *The Romance in America: Studies in Cooper, Poe, Hawthorne, Melville, and James.* Middletown, Conn.: Wesleyan University Press, 1969.

Rahv, Philip. "Introduction." *Eight Great American Short Novels.* Ed. Philip Rahv. New York: Berkeley, 1963.

Randall, John H. "Bartleby vs. Wall Street: New York in the 1850s." *Bulletin of the New York Public Library* 78 (Winter 1975): 138–44.

Rogin, Michael Paul. *Subversive Genealogy: The Politics and Art of Herman Melville.* New York: Alfred A. Knopf, 1983.

Rosenberry, Edward H. *Melville.* London, Henley and Boston: Routledge & Kegan Paul, 1979.

————. *Melville and the Comic Spirit.* Cambridge, Mass.: Harvard University Press, 1955.

Roudiez, Leon S. "Strangers in Melville and Camus."*French Review* 31 (January 1958): 217–26.

Roundy, Nancy. "Fancies, Reflections, and Things: The Imagination as Perception in 'The Piazza.' " *College Language Association Journal* 20 (June 1977): 539–46.

Rowe, John Carlos. *Through the Custom-House: Nineteenth-Century American Fiction and Modern Theory.* Baltimore: Johns Hopkins University Press, 1982.

Rowland, Beryl. "Melville and the Cock That Crew." *American Literature* 52 (January 1981):593–606.

————. "Melville Answers the Theologians: The Ladder of Charity in 'The Two Temples.' " *Mosaic* 7 (1974): 1–13.

————. "Melville's Bachelors and Maids: Interpretation Through Symbol and Metaphor." *American Literature* 41 (November 1969): 389–405.

————. "Melville's Waterloo in 'Rich Man's Crumbs.' " *Nineteenth-Century Fiction* 25 (September 1970): 216–21.

Runden, John P., ed. *Melville's "Benito Cereno": A Text for Guided Research.* Lexington, Mass.: D. C. Heath, 1965.

Sackman, Douglas. "The Original of Melville's Apple-Tree Table." *American Literature* 11 (January 1940): 448–51.

Schechter, Harold. "Bartleby the Chronometer." *Studies in Short Fiction* 19 (Fall 1982): 359–66.

Scudder, Harold H. "Melville's 'Benito Cereno' and Captain Delano's Voyages."*PMLA* 43 (June 1928): 502–32.

Sealts, Merton M., Jr. "The Chronology of Melville's Short Fiction, 1853–1856." *Harvard Library Bulletin* 28 (October 1980): 391–403; rpt. in *Pursuing Melville 1940–1980*. Madison: University of Wisconsin, 1982, pp. 221–31.

———. "Herman Melville's 'I and My Chimney.' " *American Literature* 13 (May 1941): 142–54; rpt. in *Pursuing Melville, 1940–1980*. Madison: University of Wisconsin, 1982, pp. 11–22.

———. "Melville's Short Fiction." *ESQ* 25 (First Quarter 1979): 43–57.

Sedgwick, William Ellery. *Herman Melville: The Tragedy of Mind*. Cambridge, Mass.: Harvard University Press, 1944.

Seelye, John. "The Contemporary 'Bartleby.' " *American Transcendental Quarterly* No. 7 (Summer 1970): 12–18.

———. *Melville: The Ironic Diagram*. Evanston, Ill.: Northwestern University Press, 1970.

Singleton, Marvin. "Melville's 'Bartleby': Over the Republic, a Ciceronian Shadow." *Canadian Review of American Studies* 6 (Fall 1975): 165–73.

Smith, Herbert F. "Melville's Master in Chancery and His Recalcitrant Clerk." *American Quarterly* 17 (Winter 1965): 734–41.

Sowder, William J. "Melville's 'I and My Chimney': A Southern Exposure." *Mississippi Quarterly* 16 (Summer 1963): 128–45.

Spector, Robert Donald. "Melville's 'Bartleby' and the Absurd." *Nineteenth-Century Fiction* 16 (September 1961): 175–77.

Springer, Norman. "Bartleby and the Terror of Limitation." *PMLA* 80 (1965): 410–18.

St. Armand, Barton Levi. "Curtis's 'Bartleby': An Unrecorded Melville Reference." *Papers of the Bibliographical Society of America* 71 (1977): 219–20.

Stedman, E. C., and E. M. Hutchinson, eds. *A Library of American Literature from the Earliest Settlement to the Present Time*. New York: Charles L. Webster, 1889.

Stein, William Bysshe. "Melville Roasts Thoreau's Cock." *Modern Language Notes* 74 (March 1959): 218–19.

———. "Melville's Cock and the Bell of St. Paul's." *ESQ* No. 27 (Second Quarter 1962): 5–10.

Stern, Milton R. "Towards 'Bartleby the Scrivener.' " In *The Stoic Strain in American Literature*. Ed. Duane J. MacMillan. Toronto: University of Toronto Press, 1979.

Sundquist, Eric J. "Suspense and Tautology in 'Benito Cereno.' " *Glyph* 8 (1981): 103–26.

Sweeney, Gerard M. *Melville's Use of Classical Mythology*. Amsterdam: Rodopi, 1975.

Thomas, Russell. "Melville's Use of Some Sources in *The Encantadas*." *American Literature* 3 (January 1932): 432–56.

Tuerck, Richard. "Melville's 'Bartleby' and Isaac D'Israeli's *Curiosities of Literature, Second Series*." *Studies in Short Fiction* 7 (Fall 1970): 647–49.

Tutt, Ralph M. " 'Jimmy Rose'—Melville's Misplaced Noble." *ESQ* No. 33 (Fourth Quarter 1963): 28—41.

Waggoner, Hyatt H. "Hawthorne and Melville Acquaint the Reader with Their Abodes." *Studies in the Novel* 2 (Winter 1970): 420–24.

Ward, Robert J. "From Source to Achievement in 'Benito Cereno.'" *Anglo-American Studies* 2 (1982): 233–40.

Watson, Charles N., Jr. "Melville's Agatha and Hunilla: A Literary Reincarnation." *English Language Notes* 6 (December 1968): 114–18.

Weaver, Raymond, ed. "Introduction." *Shorter Novels of Herman Melville.* New York: Horace Liveright, 1928.

Widmer, Kingsley. *The Ways of Nihilism: A Study of Herman Melville's Short Novels.* Los Angeles: Anderson, Ritchie & Simon (for the California State Colleges), 1970.

Wright, Elizabeth. "The New Psychoanalysis and Literary Criticism." *Poetics Today* 3 (Spring 1982): 89–105.

Wright, Nathalia. "Melville and 'Old Burton,' With 'Bartleby' as an Anatomy of Melancholy." *Tennessee Studies in Literature* 15 (1970): 1–13.

10

ISRAEL POTTER: COMMON MAN AS HERO

Hennig Cohen

For Herman Melville writing was a vocation and a profession, and the conflicting pressures of both calling and craft are present in his prose fiction. He was not simply an artist who on occasion broke the bonds of a society that declined his most meaningful work and a family that compelled him to write not what he preferred but what was acceptable. He might well complain that dollars damned him and that he wrote with duns looking over his shoulder, but in fact he defied the duns or forgot them in the creative intensity of his calling, the obvious example being *Moby-Dick* (1851), or he crafted and controlled his writing so adroitly, as in *Israel Potter: His Fifty Years of Exile* (1855), that he overcame such restraints. *Israel Potter* is an instance of calculated success through professionalism. It is the quiet success of a writer who must earn his living with his pen, has some important things to say, and has learned to say them without ruffling up the spirits of his readers. It is a serious but unpretentious book, at times funny and sad and sly. It is a narrative of the character's and the author's struggle for survival and their capacity to adapt.

The response to Melville's fiction in the literary marketplace of his day is notable for peaks of public acclaim that descend into valleys of disapproval and eventually emerge on plateaus of mild approbation. Melville was sensitive to his readers' opinions even when he did not accommodate to them. The success of *Typee* (1846) and *Omoo* (1847)

Preparation of this essay was supported by a grant from the University of Pennsylvania Research Committee.

tempted him to overreach in *Mardi* (1849), a romance best remembered for what it risked and what it promised. But he knew how to sift well-meant advice, and he could learn from experience. He modified accordingly; and in *Redburn* (1849) and *White-Jacket* (1850) he was able to reestablish his reputation. They are more modest books than *Mardi*, and in this respect they foreshadow *Israel Potter*. Like *Israel Potter* they are closer to their sources, structurally straightforward, relatively relaxed and accepting; in sum, the work of a seasoned professional. Yet this was not enough. Melville in *Moby-Dick* (1851) surged upward like a whale breaching, a mighty surge he could not sustain in *Pierre* (1852), and its dismal failure forced him once more to reappraise his literary situation.

TOWARD THE MAGAZINES AND RECOVERY

In July 1852, before the disheartening reviews of *Pierre* began to accumulate, Melville accompanied his father-in-law, Judge Lemuel Shaw, to Nantucket where Judge Shaw was to hold court. While there, as Melville shortly would write Nathaniel Hawthorne, a lawyer told him about a client, the deserted wife of a sailor, whose case demonstrated "the great patience, & endurance, & resignedness of the woman of the island "(*Letters*, p. 153). It excited Melville's "most lively interest." The theme was one that had begun to attract him, and he would use it in *Israel Potter* and elsewhere. He obtained detailed information about the case and offered it to Hawthorne who tactfully suggested that Melville himself might make something of it (*Letters*, pp. 153–63). What this episode reveals is Melville's crafty eye. Here was material that could be of future use, and here was an opportunity to confront unusual ideas and to attempt new forms. So when the failure of *Pierre* required him to look to the realities of the publishing world, he was not entirely unprepared either by inclination or for dearth of substance. Besides, he was an inveterate wanderer among the literary genres and was ready to try something else. There were, for example, the periodicals. *Harper's New Monthly Magazine*, founded in 1850, was flourishing, and Harper & Brothers had published all of his novels thus far except *Typee*, the first one. Furthermore, in October 1852 he was one of the writers invited by G. P. Putnam & Co., publishers of *Typee*, to contribute to *Putnam's Monthly Magazine of American Literature*. A formidable competitor of *Harper's Monthly*, it would begin publication in January 1853. As the title advertised, it featured American literature. For the professional man of letters, the magazine offered possibilities.

He seems first to have tried *Harper's*, submitting a story based on the Nantucket sailor's wife (he called it "the story of Agatha") in early 1853. Nothing came of this, but before the year was out *Harper's* had accepted at least four of his pieces, and he was at work on "Bartleby, the Scrivener," and "The Encantadas" which *Putnam's* would serialize. The magazines paid nicely and his press notices were good. In addition, he had a reserve of ideas and impressions, many of them gathered when he was in London in 1849–50 to arrange for the publication of *White-Jacket.*

Melville the journeyman writer had even more tangible resources at his disposal. By the early fall of 1849, before he sailed for London, he had picked up the cheaply printed chapbook, *Life and Remarkable Adventures of Israel R. Potter* (Providence, R.I.: printed by Henry Trumbull, 1824. Hereafter *Life and Adventures*; reprinted in NN edition of *Israel Potter*, pp. 286–394). He would describe this little book in the dedication of *Israel Potter* as "a tattered copy, rescued by the merest chance" (*IP*, p. vii), and hint that it was a rarity. Actually it was not, as a reviewer in the May 1855 *Putnam's* would point out to support his contention that it was "an authentic narrative" (p. 548), but Melville's words are consistent with his thematic design which emphasizes his character's obscurity. There were two other editions in 1824, both "Printed by J. Howard, for I. R. Potter." Sadly we cannot be sure which of the three editions Melville owned (*IP*, pp. 277, 282–85). Nor is it necessary to accept that Melville's copy was "tattered," for this claim, too, might be a departure from the facts for literary reasons. Whether chance or some other agency placed it in his hands is also problematic, for chance, or at least the fell clutch of circumstance, plays a vital part in the narrative of Israel Potter that Melville eventually wrote, and his choice of words in his prefatory remarks may well be designed to signal this. But of several things we can be more confident. Melville's own resilient and congenial character at the time indicates that he was somewhat detached from Potter's story, moved by it but not identifying with the Potter of the chapbook. Potter's was a story that Melville in due course would ponder and use, but he did not then see it as a parallel or revelation of himself as he might in the future. He was being businesslike, putting aside something for a rainy day, and at the same time responding to themes that stirred his literary imagination and to a subject that induced familiar reverberations. For the lengthy subtitle of the *Life and Adventures* makes the point that Israel Potter was "a soldier," not an officer "in the American Revolution," and it goes on to state that he

took a distinguished part in the Battle of Bunker Hill (in which he received three wounds,) after which he was taken Prisoner by the British, conveyed to England, where for 30 years he obtained a livelihood for himself and family, by crying "*Old Chairs to Mend*" through the Streets of London.—In May last, by the assistance of the American Consul, he succeeded (in the 79th year of his age) in obtaining a passage to his native country, after an absence of 48 years. (*IP*, p. 287)

Patience, endurance, and resignation are implied in the subtitle, and also modest station. These are qualities notable in Agatha, the deserted sailor's wife, and in Bartleby, in the Chola widow of "The Encantadas," and in a number of other long-suffering, poverty-stricken outcasts who were appearing in his magazine fiction.

But the chapbook must have interested Melville for additional, more positive reasons. Israel Potter's "Remarkable Adventures" could advance his literary recovery. Its subject, if judiciously shaped to the taste of the public and the bias of his family, might become an appealing "Cooperesque historical saga of the Revolution" (Carolyn L. Karcher, p. 93), at least on the surface. Moreover, it was purportedly the autobiography of a Revolutionary War hero, a subject of much family interest. His grandfather, Major Thomas Melvill, had taken part in the Boston Tea Party and, like Israel Potter, had fought under General Putnam at Bunker Hill. In his ripe old age he had had the satisfaction of receiving the compliments of the Marquis de Lafayette for his patriotic services. Melville's maternal grandfather, General Peter Gansevoort, was known as the "Hero of Fort Stanwix" for his bloody victory over the British and Indians. His painting in his Revolutionary War uniform by Gilbert Stuart, among other family matters, found its way in *Pierre* (II, iii), and Melville himself, like his character, young Pierre, was of "double revolutionary descent...sprung from heroes" (*Pierre*, p. 20).

But proud as he was of his exalted forebears, he had his democratic side. Melville the common sailor projected his own mixed feeling about the position of the hero in a democratic context when he has his aristocratic protagonist, Pierre, take pride in "the epaulettes of the Major-General his grandfather" but has the narrator chide this "fond and foolish" young man for thus showing himself "no sterling Democrat" (p. 13). Melville had borrowed a copy of Carlyle's *Heroes, and Hero-Worship* from Evert Duyckinck in the summer of 1850 (*Reading*, no. 122), but though attracted to certain exceptional men, like Emerson he perceived hero worship as counter to the American grain. His family legends, and Pierre's, were about patrician Revolutionary heroes, founding fathers, but Melville, while aware of the possible contradictions, was sensitive to the heroism of ordinary people. In his previous books he had favored first-person narrators who were sailors before the mast and fatherless, and in *White-Jacket* and *Moby-Dick* he had raised the issue of the heroic potential of the common man. The "little narrative...on sleazy gray paper," as he described *Israel Potter* in the dedication (p. vii), was about the adventures of a Revolutionary hero who was a common soldier and ordinary American, if indeed revolutionary hero is, for Melville, the precise term.

As busy and pleasant as his trip to London was, he remained on the lookout for literary capital, and he did not forget Israel Potter. During the week before he departed, despite the rush of social engagements, finding gifts for his family, and putting the last touches on the *White-Jacket* manuscript, he bought a London map dated 1766 "to use ... in case I serve up the Revolutionary narrative of the beggar" (1849 *Journal*, p. 75). He did not need it for more than four years, until he became a magazine contributor and was considering the advantages of serial publication. By the late fall of 1853, he queried Harper & Brothers about a "book—300 pages, say ... chiefly, of Tortoise Hunting Adventure" (*Letters*, p. 164), and in correspondence the following spring refers to it and to "another Serial" (*Letters*, p. 169). The tortoise hunting adventures, whether book or serial, never materialized, but *Putnam's* printed "The Encantadas," which seems to overlap with it to a certain extent, in three installments beginning in March 1854. Melville was paid the tidy sum of $50 for each installment. It is likely that he began his version of Israel Potter's life in this interval and had it in mind when he mentioned "another Serial" to Harper & Brothers. But at the moment the firm was not interested in another serial, perhaps because, as Melville explained, the tortoises were proving "proverbially slow" (*Letters*, p. 168), and, in addition, the business of the publishing house was disrupted by a serious fire. At this point Melville turned to *Putnam's* (Merton M. Sealts, pp. 224–27).

The record of Melville's negotiations with *Putnam's* is fragmentary. He may have sounded out the magazine in response to an ingratiating request from G. P. Putnam for "some more of your good things" (*Mel. Log*, p. 488). In any event, the first document that refers to *Israel Potter* is an incomplete copy of an urgent letter to Putnam, tentatively dated 7 June 1854. Sent "prepaid by Express, to-day," it accompanied "some sixty and odd pages of MSS ... part of a story called 'Israel Potter,'" concerning which a more particular understanding need be had" (*Letters*, p. 169). These words are followed immediately by an excision in the transcript. Melville then proposes terms of payment and copyright, informs Putnam that the "story when finished will embrace some 300 or more MS. pages," and finally, no doubt with the experience of *Pierre* in mind, provides an assurance: "There will be very little reflective writing in it; nothing weighty. It is adventure" (*Letters*, pp. 169–70). Details about the "understanding" were a likely subject of the material deleted from the transcript. They may have concerned, to forestall the editors and the critics, a need to make clear how closely Melville had followed *Life and Adventures* (*IP*, pp. 182–83). Yet reviews do not suggest that this was a problem, and it could have had a positive effect. Keeping close to the facts of an authentic narrative helped to affirm the validity of the novel. Melville originally faced this problem in *Typee*, and when he wrote "Benito Cereno," published serially in *Putnam's* in 1855, he evidently saw undisguised adherence to the facts of his source as an asset, and not simply to document. He had long since discovered the usefulness of authentic fact to embody symbolic significance.

PUBLICATION AND INITIAL RECEPTION

Whatever the preliminaries, the manuscript sample Melville sent to *Putnam's*, about 20 percent of the whole, elicited prompt, affirmative attention. *Putnam's* agreed to pay him its highest rate, $5.00 per page, and scheduled it for immediate use. The first installment of "Israel Potter; or, Fifty Years of Exile" appeared in the issue of July 1854. It carried a timely subheading: "A Fourth of July Story."

As early as 3 July, it was receiving good notices. The New York *Commercial Advertiser* called it "the greatest literary attraction" in the new issue of *Putnam's*, and though it was unsigned, according to custom, identified the author and predicted that it would "be much more popular than even his admired narratives of South Sea adventures" (Quoted in *IP*, p. 209). Other newspapers were equally favorable. On 7 July *Putnam's* sent Melville its check for $50, the first of nine monthly payments that would total $421.50 (Sealts, p. 226). He had reason to be pleased.

Both Melville and *Putnam's* moved quickly to take advantage of the appropriateness of the subject to the celebration of a great national holiday, but who was responsible for subtitling it "A Fourth of July Story" has not been ascertained. It could have been Melville himself (but for an opposite view, see Walter Bezanson's "Historical Note" to *IP*, p. 209). Although he ignored this patriotic celebration in the part of the novel he sent as a sample to *Putnam's*, he grossly exploited it when he came to write his last chapter. Still, within the family circle, prior to publication, *Israel Potter* was associated with Independence Day. Thus, Melville's sister Helen Briggs in Boston writes to his sister and copyist, Augusta Melville, in Pittsfield:

I shall be quite wild to make the acquaintance of "Israel Potter," and have the Fourth of July come. I shall have George [her husband] procure me *my* Independence—namely a new novel, & a paper of candy. I wish I could help you with your copying, dear, but I can sympathize with your state of entire employment. (Gansevoort-Lansing Collection, Additions 1.17, New York Public Library)

The letter is not dated, but obviously Helen Briggs wrote it before the first installment was published, probably in June since she mentions "summer" and "warm" weather. Obviously, too, she picks up the title designation which Augusta would have used in her secretarial assistance to her brother or perhaps she had seen proof. Even then Melville alone could have provided the full magazine title or had a hand in it.

The question is trivial, for in spite of his assurance to Putnam that

Israel Potter would contain "little reflective writing," Melville could not dismiss the larger implications of a rousing narrative of historical adventure, such as the dynamics of history and the role of great men, as well as little men, in great events. He knew that the chance topicality of a story or its title didn't matter much in the long run, though, as in the instance of *Israel Potter*, it could ease the publication process and attract readers. *Putnam's* dropped the subheading after the second installment, and the serial moved through the press in an unremarkable way. Melville supplied batches of manuscript on schedule, with little regard for the nature of the serial itself as a literary mode, while the editors made use of it more in terms of their space requirements than the natural divisions of the copy he sent, their installments varying from six and a half to thirteen and a half double-columned pages. The reviews continued to be encouraging. *Israel Potter* had become a satisfactory piece of business of a professional writer, and it was being handled accordingly. On 1 February 1855, Melville's local newspaper, *The Pittsfield Sun*, reported that G. P. Putnam & Co. would be publishing the serial in book form on 1 March, a date concurrent with the last installment in *Putnam's Magazine (Mel. Log,* p. 498). In New York on that date, Allan Melville, his lawyer brother and business adviser, wrote to Augusta: "Hermans book 'Potter' will not be out for a week yet. —I was at Putnam's yesterday to get a copy but none was ready. He has sent a dedication to Bunker Hill Monument—" (Gansevoort-Lansing Collection, Additions 1.12). Explaining that the book was expected to "have a large sale," the publishing house placed a notice to the trade in the *Commercial Advertiser* of 9 March 1855 that it had "been obliged twice to postpone the day of publication . . . to arrange for a large enough quantity" (Steve Mailloux and Hershel Parker, p. 60).

   G. P. Putnam & Co. promoted it energetically through advertising and the generous distribution of review copies. It got good reviews and by 19 March was in its third printing. Putnam reported to Melville that as of 1 July 1855 the firm had 3,700 copies in print and Melville's royalties amounted to $193.27 (*Mel. Log,* p. 509). The third printing was distributed by Putnam in England through Sampson Low, Son & Co., but George Routledge & Co. published an unauthorized paperback that surely outsold it. Professionally speaking, Melville was adequately compensated, and Putnam came out well enough, but the book did not achieve an unqualified commercial or critical success. Serial publication had taken the edge off. *Israel Potter* stabilized Melville's reputation but did not enhance it.

"CONTENTS" AS PREFIGURATION

   The book retained the chapter titles of the magazine serial which presumably the editor took from Melville's original manuscript. It is hard to imagine an editor writing chapter titles for any Melville novel because they are so intimately related to his texts. *The Confidence-Man* is a conspicuous example, and *Israel Potter* is another, though less obvious, one. If the editor supplied the titles for the chapters of the serial as it was being written, then he was remarkably prescient and, furthermore, had a capacity for an occasional Melvillean mannerism and playfulness. On the whole such attention would be a departure from the cavalier treatment Putnam gave the text. The chapter titles are important because they are also the table of contents and, through certain key words and phrases, convey clues to themes, motifs, symbols, settings, structures, genres, and tonalities of the narrative to come. The table of contents is, in effect, a synopsis and a prefiguration, a result more readily attainable because Putnam's practice (cf. *Typee*) allowed a degree of spaciousness. Three entries in the "Contents" of *Israel Potter* run to more than twenty-five words, and one requires four lines of type.

The title of the first entry, "The Birthplace of Israel," suggests that the book will be a biographical account from cradle to grave, a suggestion validated by the title of the last chapter, "Requiescat in Pace." Aside from the possible ironies that the gravestone epitaph might have acquired or the function of the imagery of stone in the book or the chain of reference to tombs and entombment, this initial and terminal linkage raises questions about the structure of the narrative: whether, for instance, the structure reflects a chronological, linear progress; or whether it consists of an array of disjointed episodes; or whether, like earlier Melville novels, it turns back on itself in an implied circle that will, in due time, be confirmed thematically. Hints accrue. The name "Israel" recurs in eleven of the twenty-seven title entries. *Israel Potter* is clearly a tale of *his* adventures. This the pronoun references verify, though with one notable exception. In titles of chapters on Israel Potter's naval service under Captain John Paul Jones, the third-person singular is displaced by the third-person plural. The "he" and "his" of Israel become the "they" of Paul Jones and Israel together. One suspects a fusion of personalities, with perhaps the subordination of Israel to Jones, or a change or loss of individuality on Israel's part. These are questions that likewise deserve attention.

Note, too, that Israel's surname does not appear in the "Contents" at all. This may have something to do with brevity, which would be odd in a table of contents in which half of the titles required, in the first edition, from two to four lines of type; or perhaps it is appropriate because early on Israel is referred to "as a boy" (p. 6) and the continued use of the term serves to belittle him, to reduce his stature in the great scheme of things. But the repeated use in the "Contents" of the first name forces attention on its Biblical reference generally, allusions that are appropriate to situations in which Israel finds himself in the chapters titled

"Israel in Egypt" or "Israel in the Lion's Den." It is also significant that the first entry in the "Contents" refers primarily to Israel's "birthplace" and not the character himself. When his name is introduced in the initial chapter of the novel, it is in a phrase, "the birthplace of the devoted patriot, Israel Potter" (p. 5), that likewise emphasizes place. The second and only other mention of his name in this chapter occurs in its brief penultimate paragraph, and it also underlines his birthplace: "Such, at this day, is the country which gave birth to our hero: prophetically styled Israel by the good Puritans, his parents, since for more than forty years, poor Potter wandered in the wild wilderness of the world's extremest hardships and ills" (p. 6). The focus on "the country which gave birth to our hero" is categorical evidence that the chapter is not biographical in any immediate sense but an essay in the genre of scenic travel and that "the country" described (it is a locality and nation) is a symbolic landscape. We will discuss the travel sketch again when we consider in general the genres that Melville puts to use, but at this point it is enough to observe its pertinence to the structure of the novel. For structurally, among other things, the book is a record of Israel Potter's travels from the place he was born and back again.

This penultimate, single-sentence paragraph is also packed with prophecies (another structural feature) and indications of their significance, and it affirms that, as in much of Melville, close readings of seemingly casual passages remain to be done. The narrative voice, for example, in a rare instance employs the shopworn storyteller's epithet, "our hero," but in what sense is "poor Potter" a "hero"? In what sense, too, beyond their adherence to Puritan naming traditions, are Israel's parents "good Puritans" or for that matter, good parents? Is there a puritan strain in *Israel Potter* that should be traced, and is there a parental strain? Is "poor Potter" so called merely to introduce the poverty motif that will become important, or does it punningly evoke sympathy for the pathos of his life (Newton Arvin, p. 233)? And ours? The Biblical allusions become all too frequent, but why is the London "wilderness" in which Israel is to wander so insistently "wild"? Is this perhaps in some way related to the American Western frontier? Perhaps Melville suspected that the westward march of civilization might transform spatial wilderness into urban wilderness. Cities of Dis? Or perhaps it refers to the aesthetic and moral category of the Romantic Sublime? And stylistically, what is the effect of the devices at work in this sentence, the heavy alliteration, for instance? The word "wander" catches the eye, or is this hindsight?

To return to the table of contents, the value of following the hints it contains is demonstrable in key words like "Adventures" in the second entry, a word repeated in various forms in four subsequent entries. It reminds us of Melville's promise to G. P. Putnam that the substance of his book would be primarily "adventure." His departures from this stated intention have been remarked, for example, regarding the metaphysical brickyard sequence (James E. Miller, pp. 149–50), but bear a closer look. The word "Travels" in the third entry indicates a discursive narrative, a matter amplified in the fourth entry by the reference to "Wanderings," which has thematic application as well. A word like "Sly" in the sixth entry will be picked up in the text where it will be made to play ambiguously on Benjamin Franklin, on the Englishmen who send Israel on his illicit errand to Franklin, and throughout on Israel himself. The nuances of the more laconic headings invite consideration. For example, "The Shuttle" is appropriate to the literal facts of this chapter, Israel's movements back and forth and up and down; but it calls to mind a persistent theme, the force of fatality, and, more directly, the interwoven lives of Israel and Paul Jones, the entangled rigging that by chance will lead to severing their connection, and the weaving of the narrative itself. (One remembers "Loomings," the suggestive heading of the chapter with which *Moby-Dick* begins.) Furthermore, the shuttle reference moves backward to Benjamin Franklin, who after he shuttles Israel back to England "proceeded to whittle away at a shuttle-cock of an original scientific construction" (*IP*, p. 65). Israel is the shuttle of Fate and of Franklin, among others. The reference to "the City of Dis" (ch. 24) likewise calls up a range of possibilities that have not yet been fully investigated. One might usefully examine the Dantean presence in *Israel Potter* especially in light of the recent recovery of the translation of *The Divine Comedy* he owned and annotated (*Reading*, #174; *Christie's Catalogue*, sales no. 6028). Israel's descent into the Underworld is not only figurative and allusive, a harried animal seeking refuge in its burrow or a Dante without a Virgil as his guide. It is also literal. He is "assigned to " a "pit" in the purgatorial setting of the brickyard (*IP*, p. 155), and he is a part of a "subterranean society" residing in the London sewers (p. 163). The Underworld demands a patience and acceptance that facilitate his ultimate reconciliation to the natural universe. Does he emerge from "Avernus," from the "depths . . . the secret clefts, gulfs, caves and dens of London " (p. 153), with a salvific vision in some way comparable to Dante's?

To conclude, when one remembers that Melville was supplying copy at intervals for a story being published serially before he had finished it and that the chapter titles would become the table of contents and epitome of the book regardless of who wrote them, the table of contents turns out to be a stunning clue to Melville's conceptualization of the work before he put it down on paper. Functioning as the "Contents," these seemingly random and diverse titles suggest that from the outset Melville had a plan, a structure, in mind. How this affects our general understanding of his compositional method remains to be seen. In the more specific case of *Israel Potter*, the "Contents" invites greater attention to the structural coherence of the narrative, especially the structural details of its working parts; its thematic integrity; and the possibility of a high degree of unity in its formal variety—what one might fairly describe as the professionalism that characterizes the magazine fiction. This is a far cry from his ambitious failures, the chartless *Mardi* and the self-indulgent *Pierre*. They are more in accord with the compositional practice of the Mardian epic poet, Lombardo: "When Lombardo set about his work, he knew not what it would become. He did not build himself in with plans; he wrote right on..." (*Mardi*, p. 595). It is not enough to say that the plan of *Israel Potter* comes mainly from its basic source.

"CONTENTS" AS SYNOPSIS

The "Contents" is the skeleton of *Israel Potter*, and with a little fleshing out, a synopsis and an outline of its settings and structure. Chapter 1, devoted almost entirely to Israel's "Birthplace" in the Berkshire Mountains, introduces an environmental and genetic background—a natural setting and a pastoral, puritanic family that will have a lasting effect on Israel. His "Youthful Adventures" begin when he quarrels with his father (ch. 2). Israel is outward bound, a venturesome runaway, ready to try his luck on land or sea in a succession of occupations. He is plowing his fields when his militia company is called out and "Goes to the Wars." He fights valiantly at Bunker Hill, is wounded, and volunteers for the naval service. Taken prisoner off Boston, he is "Forced to Extend His Travels across the Sea into the Enemy's Land" (ch. 3). At this point begins his "Further Wanderings" (chs. 3–6). He escapes, is recaptured, and escapes again, and, barely surviving, is befriended by "a Good Knight of Brentford" (ch. 4). Through this good knight he obtains work as a gardener "in the Lion's Den," George III's garden at Kew, where he has an extended conversation with the British sovereign (ch. 5). He also meets "Certain Secret Friends of America," including the English politician, Horne Tooke, who "Despatch Him on a Sly Errand" with a message for "the Renowned Sage, Dr. Franklin" in Paris (chs. 6–7).

Paris is the setting for the Franklin sequence (chs. 7–12) and is, incidentally, the approximate point at which Melville begins to deviate markedly from *Life and Adventures*. Israel comes under the close tuition of Franklin, about whom he—and Melville—are ambivalent. "Another Adventurer," Captain John Paul Jones (chs. 10–11), who will loom large in due course, also appears. Returning to England, Israel finds himself virtually entombed in a tiny cell in the manor house of a Squire John Woodcock, yet another British sympathizer with America. In fear that he has been abandoned, Israel slips out through a secret passage, discovers that the Squire has died suddenly, dons the Squire's clothes, and bluffs his way out of the house. Once more on the road, he is picked up by a press gang and put aboard a British warship bound for India (ch. 13). But his luck improves. In a chapter that is a prodigy of transition, Israel finds himself "in Three Ships, and All in One Night" (ch. 14). From the British warship he is transferred to a revenue cutter which he contrives to seize singlehandedly, and from which he is rescued by Paul Jones. What follows next is a naval sequence dominated by Paul Jones (chs. 14–19). With Israel's vital assistance, "They ... Descend on Whitehaven" and "Fight the Serapis," events that move Israel to acts of ferocious bravery (chs. 18–19). But Israel is accidentally trapped on a British privateer that momentarily brushes past Paul Jones's ship. Once aboard, he manages to find a place for himself as a member of the British crew (ch. 20). When the privateer lands at Falmouth, Israel has the opportunity to see how Ethan Allen, held prisoner there, overawes his captors, before continuing his "Flight Towards the Wilderness" of London (chs. 21–22). In what has become his usual disguise, the garb of a pauper, Israel works for a time in a brickyard, a transitional (and allegorical) pause, on the outskirts of London (ch. 23), before entering this "City of Dis" (ch. 24) where he will live in exile for "Forty-five Years" (ch. 25). He subsists on the edges of poverty and is sometimes submerged in its miseries. He marries almost accidentally, works as a mender of chairs and at odd jobs when he can find them, and outlives his family except one son. In his old age, he dreams of returning to the Berkshires, and through the kindness of the American consul, he and his son manage to do so. Israel Potter, now an octogenerian, lands at Boston, on the fiftieth anniversary of the Declaration of Independence, views the Bunker Hill battlefield and its incipient monument across the way, and seeks the family homestead in the Berkshires. Nothing remains but crumbled masonry and an "old hearthstone ... half buried" that he recognizes as his proper monument. He dies soon thereafter. The final entry in the "Contents" is the epitaphic "Requiescat in Pace" (ch. 26). Whether Melville intends it as testimony to a serene acceptance or as irony, or in some degree and from different viewpoints both, are positions worth arguing. Certainly it suggests that Melville was looking far ahead, toward *Billy Budd, Sailor*, taking a long view and by no means a simple one.

SOURCES AND THEIR TRANSFORMATION

At the end of the dedication, Melville signs himself "The Editor," thus asserting the authenticity of what will follow and evading authorial responsibility. Being Melville, he allows himself a few "exceptions," admitting to "some expansions, and additions of historic and personal details, and one or two shiftings of scene," departures from the copy of *Life and Adventures* he had "rescued ... from the rag-pickers" (*IP*, p. vii).

He admits to no other source, and *Life and Adventures* stands as primary. It is so basic that the NN edition includes a facsimile with "marginal page and line numbers to indicate corresponding passages of Melville's *Israel Potter*" (*IP*, p. 285; however, not all such passages are indicated). Melville also made important use of Robert Sands's *Life and Correspondence of John Paul Jones* (1830) and James Fenimore Cooper's *History of the Navy of the United States* (1839), probably in the edition published by G. P. Putnam & Co. in 1853 (R. D. Madison, pp. 9–10), for the naval sequence and an unknown edition of the popular autobiographical *Narrative of Colonel Ethan Allen's Captivity* (1779) for the sequence on the heroic career of Allen as a prisoner of war.

The real Israel Potter, as legal documents associated with his application for a pension attest, was an illiterate (Hennig Cohen, p. 7). Melville suggests this when he writes in his last paragraph that before Israel died, he "dictated a little book, the record of his fortunes." The writer to whom the real Potter dictated his narrative was Henry Trumbull of Providence, Rhode Island, to which Potter had wandered from Boston. Henry Trumbull was a printer, bookseller, and an author of penny thrillers and other works of doubtful repute. He was not above dealing in "obscene books and pamphlets" for the sale of which one of his apprentices was arrested in 1823 (David Chacko and Alexander Kulcsar, p. 367). In the copyright notice he claims authorship of *Life and Adventures*, which he originally published. Despite its being cast in the first person, there is no reason to doubt that Potter supplied the outline and Trumbull the embellishment. Trumbull was to print a similar work, *Life and Adventures of Colonel Daniel Boon*, the same year (*IP*, pp. 277, [398]), cribbed from John Filson's famous sketch. Many of Trumbull's imprints are among the holdings of the American Antiquarian Society. These little books belong to a popular type that included the narratives of shipwrecked sailors, Indian captives, frontiersmen, criminals, runaway slaves, eccentrics, veterans of the American Revolution and other wars, and biographies of founding fathers. They were cheaply printed and often hawked throughout the country, Parson Weems being the best known of the intinerant chapbook peddlers. Melville's eclectic taste included such narratives as the wide-ranging "Extracts" which preface *Moby-Dick*, but not just for their own sake. In *Israel Potter* he exploited their legendary dimension and their significance as indicators of the nature and directions of the culture and its heroes.

Unlike Lombardo, when Melville set about his work he had something of a plan, basically Trumbull's *Life and Adventures*, but like Lombardo he may not have known what it would become. When he wrote the dedication, contrary to the evidence of the novel that lay before him, he averred that "with a change in the grammatical person, it preserves, almost as in a reprint, Israel Potter's autobiographical story" (p. vii). Still, the first chapter is an important departure from *Life and Adventures*. Its title page states that Israel Potter was "a native of Cranston, Rhode Island." Melville, as noted, shifts his birthplace to the Berkshires and devotes most of his attention to the place itself. In the second chapter he bolsters Israel Potter's Berkshire association by enlisting him in the local regiment of minute men, and for military information borrows from *A History of . . . Berkshire . . .* (1829) edited by his friend, David Dudley Field (*Reading*, no. 216). However, his account from Israel's boyhood until the Benjamin Franklin episode is a near adaptation, though with increasing freedom, of *Life and Adventures*. Franklin incited Melville's more imaginative impulses. He sketches Franklin's character, identifies it as archetypal, and relates it to a vision of the national destiny—establishing a pattern he will follow with other heroes of the American Revolution whom Israel Potter will meet during his wanderings. He uses settings to enhance his characterization, move the story, and function emblematically. And he creates discourse between Franklin and Israel Potter, often amusing, from which Israel learns useful lessons and shows himself capable of teaching the master a thing or two.

For this section Melville draws on another source, Franklin's own writings, though in what form remains uncertain. It may well be Franklin's *Works* edited by Jared Sparks (*IP*, p. 193), for he makes use of obscure facts such as Franklin's brief residence in the Latin Quarter which he could have found "in the volumes of Sparks" mentioned in the dedication. He quotes from "The Way to Wealth" which he has Israel apply in much the same way as Redburn his prosy old guide book, and he rings changes on Franklin's proverbial wisdom, for instance, "God helps them that help themselves" (p. 54) in another demonstration of his expansive use of a source. The proverb is a rationalization of Franklin's character as a self-made man. Great men create themselves, a process that has heavenly approval, as Paul Jones is quick to agree and as Ethan Allen's behavior substantiates. And if they help themselves to some of the pleasures of life that are denied to lesser folk, as they do, or manipulate others to their advantage, it's all part of a divine scheme. Israel Potter, the little man, try though he may, cannot create himself. The playing with proverbs might well be viewed within the context of the extraordinary popularity of Martin Farquhar Tupper's *Proverbial Philosophy* (1838), pithy moralizing that was an object of humor at the time. Melville bought a copy in 1847 (*Reading*, 530).

The false boot heel, which also functions as a framing device for the Franklin sequence, typifies Melville's imaginative expansion of *Life and Adventures*. Israel Potter is given a "pair of boots, made expressly" to serve as a hiding place for documents he is to carry to Franklin (*Life and Adventures*, p. 51; *IP*, p. 337). When Melville's Potter enters into Franklin's presence, "the man of wisdom" is quick to observe how uneasily he walks on the polished surface of the floor and chides him for his vanity before he recognizes the special purpose of the high heels. Israel then tells Franklin about the bootblack whose persistent solicitations appeared to threaten their secret until Israel kicked over his blacking box and ran away. Franklin's response is "a paternal detailed lesson upon the ill-advised act he had been guilty of" and a warning, in language that associates him with Melville's next novel, *The Confidence-Man*, against the "indiscriminate distrust of human nature." Israel accepts Franklin's logic and agrees to "pay the man for the damage done to his box" (p. 41). As Israel departs from London, Franklin takes a last look at his false heel, plans an improvement in its design, and dismisses him with some advice, as usual, difficult to follow: "Mind your own box. You can't be too cautious, but don't be too suspicious" (p. 65). Israel is able to learn from his encounter with Franklin, if not from his apothegms. On the boat returning to England, as he dozes, a sly rogue attempts to steal his boots. Though he has every reason, in the event, to distrust human nature, he does not, so to speak, kick over the box. Instead, he recovers the boots by talking the rogue out of countenance (pp. 65–66). The source of this comic coda to the Franklin sequence lies in Melville's imagination.

Potter's two trips to Paris as a secret courier comprise less than three pages of *Life and Adventures* (pp. 50–52; *IP*, pp. 336–38). In Melville's novel Israel Potter visits Paris only once. Franklin's reference to a second trip allows him to tempt Israel with the pleasures of Paris he had missed and, since he will no longer be of use to Franklin, the likelihood of Franklin arranging his return to America. But these are hopes deferred. Chance in the form of renewed tension between Britain and France plays its part, but the experience tests the efficacy of Franklin's proverbial wisdom: Israel learns that he cannot rely on the help of others. In the end he will also discover that neither can he rely entirely on God's help or on himself. The elaboration and departure from his sources in the Franklin sequence show that Melville was no longer content to rewrite *Life and Adventures*.

The introduction of Paul Jones into the sequence underscores this new turn. In the fabric of Israel Potter's "blue-jean career," Melville writes, "Paul Jones flits and re-flits like a crimson thread" (p. 131). The same may be said for the fabric of the story. Jones is egregious, like "the King's yarn in a coil of navy-rope" to which Melville will allude in *Billy Budd, Sailor* (*BBS*, p. 63). He is domineering, divided within himself and from the social order, a "swarthy" man dramatically presented against a backdrop of red flame and blood. His histrionics and power over Israel Potter are likewise egregious. Simply in terms of the space he engrosses, he stands out. Introduced in an interlude (chs. 10–11) within the Franklin chapters, Jones reappears as the dominant figure in the naval sequence (chs. 14–20). In all, he preempts nine of the novel's twenty-seven chapters. His origin is a passing reference in *Life and Adventures* to "that bold adventurer capt. [sic] Paul Jones; who, for ten or eleven months kept all the western coast of the island in alarm" (*Life and Adventures*, p. 60; *IP*, p. 346). The famous fight with the *Serapis* is not mentioned in this source, nor is there any indication that Potter ever laid eyes on Paul Jones. The Jones material is Melville's fabrication.

Melville's chief sources for the naval sequence, as noted, were Sands's *Life . . . of John Paul Jones* and Cooper's *History of the Navy*. Claims have also been made for John Henry Sherburne's *Life and Character of John Paul Jones* (1825; W. Sprague Holden), Nathaniel Fanning's *Narrative of the Adventures of an American Navy Officer* (1806; Howard, p. 214), and Alexander Slidell Mackenzie's *Life of John Paul Jones* (1841; Howard, p. 214), though there is good reason to argue otherwise (*IP*, pp. 195–200). Yet for all of his use of histories, biographies, and documents, Melville's imagination controls his borrowings, and the role of Israel in the naval sequence is his creation, a situation largely true of Israel's adventures after he recrosses the channel and returns to Squire Woodcock's manor house where he is entombed (ch. 12).

According to *Life and Adventures*, when Potter returns, he is "secreted in the house of 'Squire Woodcock a few days" (p. 51). This brief, bland statement is the germ for an "incident of incarceration and escape" which "bears a close resemblance to Pym's initial adventure on the *Grampus*" in Poe's *Narrative of Arthur Gordon Pym* (1838; Charles N. Watson, "Premature Burial," p. 105). More important in Melville's imaginative transformation of his source of the incident was his knowledge of the historical sites of London he had explored indefatigably, among them the Temple Church where he would have seen the so-called penitential cell of the Knights Templars, a feature of the guide books available to him, with window slits and a winding stone staircase he incorporated into his novel (1849 *Journal*, p. 27). In the Temple Church setting he found religious references more overt than those in *Pym* and turned them into a resurrection with a parodic twist. From *Pym* he may have borrowed Israel Potter's trick of disguising himself as the dead man's ghost in order to escape from his "coffin-cell" (p. 71). The result is a macabre scene that he modulates into the comic. Once headed in a comic direction, the incident becomes a grotesque farce in which Israel transforms himself into a scarecrow (ch. 13). The comic strain here and throughout is Melville's. Then, taking a hint from *Life and Adventures*—"I thought that in the city of London I should not be so liable to be suspected" (p. 53)— he once more sets Israel on his way, but contrary to his source, has him impressed into the British Navy in order to initiate the naval sequence and Israel's association with Paul Jones. Henceforth Melville moves Israel Potter about with little regard for the adventures of his original. Having, on his own, joined Israel and Paul Jones together, he sunders them with a device of his own invention. Their separation is followed by an elaborate Yankee joke with serious implications—the outcast sailor repeatedly rebuffed when he seeks a proper berth aboard a microcosmic ship bound for an uncertain destination. Melville had rehearsed this motif in *White-Jacket* (ch. 20). One might conclude that as far as his sources were concerned, Melville began by rewriting one book, allowed his imagination free play, and ended by writing another.

The imaginative transformation of Melville's source, those known and those still to be discovered, is territory for further exploration. Potter's false heels have not previously attracted much attention, but it is evident that Melville used this detail from *Life and Adventures* for a number of reasons. Other borrowings from *Life and Adventures* are used to present significant themes. For example, Melville's persistent concern with the interplay between activity and passivity is articulated in *Israel Potter* by means of repeated references to Franklin's proverb, "God helps them that help themselves." The presence of active and passive inclinations in *Israel Potter* in relationship to their occurrence in other Melville works is in itself worth investigating, as is their presence in other characters in this novel, but particularly in Israel Potter himself. Rational, carefully considered activity may well prove effective for a wise, old statesman like Benjamin Franklin and dynamic activity may bring victory to Paul Jones, but an ordinary man like Israel Potter, even when he acts to help himself, may be hemmed in by his inferior status and the limitations of larger circumstances. The direction in which Israel Potter moves, Melville indicates, is toward resignation and passivity, and the climactic indicator of this direction is a slight change Melville makes in his source.

In *Life and Adventures* Potter states that he "was almost constantly urged by my son to apply to the American Consul for a passage" home though it "must cause our separation" (*Life and Adventures*, p. 96; *IP*, p. 382). With considerable difficulty stemming from his "weakness and debility," he makes his way to the consul to plead for assistance. It is granted, though as he had anticipated the boy is sent ahead, and he must follow some time later. In Melville's version, Israel tells his son "tales of the Fortunate Isles of the Free . . . night after night," but whenever the boy asks "would his father take him there . . . ," the father would reply, " 'Some day to come, my boy.' " The narrative continues:

In these talks Israel unconsciously sowed the seeds of his eventual return. For with added years, the boy felt added longing to escape his entailed misery, by compassing for his father and himself, a voyage to the Promised Land. By his persevering efforts he succeeded at last . . . in gaining credit in the right quarter . . . In short, charitably stretching a technical point, the American Consul finally saw father and son embarked in the Thames for Boston. (*IP*, p. 166)

The most noticeable differences are that the father and son are not separated and that they land at Boston. Less obvious is that Melville has the son rather than the father initiate the action that makes possible their return. As his wanderings draw toward an end, as he returns to the place from which he began, Melville converts Israel Potter from an active, energetic, self-reliant youth to a passive old man who instinctively allows the natural currents to sweep him along.

To summarize the present situation in regard to source studies, beyond the pioneering article on *Life and Adventures* by Roger McCutcheon in 1928 and its judicious expansion by Walter E. Bezanson in 1982 (*IP*, pp. 184–205), there is room for further work on Melville's imaginative treatment of his sources. Extensions of Melville's basic source are exemplified here by the false heel episode, his deviation from a source to convey thematic material by Israel's conversion from activity to passivity, and the possibility of new sources derived from Melville's first-hand knowledge of London by the episode of Israel's entombment and resurrection (chs. 12–13). It is in the latter category that the promise of new discoveries seems most likely. The settings that Melville knew at first hand— the Berkshires where he was living when he wrote the novel; Boston and Bunker Hill with their family associations; London, Portsmouth, and Paris which he visited before he served up the old beggar; the nautical context—all of these, though looked at, may well be looked at again, especially for the ways in which Melville employed them. Maps and guidebooks should be consulted in greater depth, as well as books not just about what Melville could not know directly (the Paul Jones and Ethan Allen material) but what he did know, such as certain London streets with their turbulence and poverty, some of which, despite a map he bought, he confuses. Did he nod or did he have his reasons? Melville met Charles Knight, "author of London Illustrated, &c., and the Publisher of the Penny Cyclopedia," and bought his London guide book, works that may contain further information about his sources (1849 *Journal*, pp. 70, 80; *Reading*, no. 312; Raymona Hull, p. 80). And what about the *Penny Cyclopaedia* itself? Melville borrowed significantly from it for *Redburn* (p. 329) and took a few details from it for his description of the British coast in *Israel Potter* (p. 197), but surely there is more.

There remain small questions that might be settled, perhaps, by a search in the London Public Records Office or other British archives. Who were Sir John Millet, Squire John Woodcock, and James Bridges of Brentford? A Charles Woodcocke, who owned property there, has been identified (*Magazine of History*, p. 651n). And who was Bridges, or rather, *which* James Bridges figures in the novel, for there are several possibilities. Millet, Woodcock, and Bridges seem to have been historic personages like their associate, John Horne Tooke. Can anything be found connecting them with the historic Israel Potter? One of the most puzzling problems has to do with the relationship between Benjamin Franklin and Israel Potter. It is verified in Franklin's correspondence by a strange letter dated 14 February 1777 (*Papers of Benjamin Franklin*, pp. 333–34). The letter introduces Potter to Franklin, requests his help in aiding him to return to America, and seeks to establish communications for the ostensible purpose of aiding the American cause. It is signed with the initials "C:W:K and J:H." Do they stand for Charles Woodcocke and John Horne, as Horne Tooke was then known? Franklin was suspicious of the letter, endorsing it: "Israel Potters, pretended letter from some Gentm. in England" (p. 334), but his account books show that he advanced funds to Potter "to help him home," checked to see whether he had, in fact, departed for America, and discovered he had not. Franklin had his doubts about the real Israel Potter (Chacko and Kulcsar, pp. 380–82). Is it conceivable that Melville, too, had his doubts? Probably not, but the novel that would follow this masquerade was about an unequivocal confidence man.

ISRAEL POTTER AS FACT AND FOLK FIGURE

The question of who, or rather what, was the historic Israel Potter, is not unrelated to what Melville made of him. The initial question (and Melville avoids it) is why he, or rather first Trumbull and then he, wrote the biography. The obvious answer in the case of Trumbull was to promote Potter's repeated attempts to obtain a pension, which it is unlikely he ever received. The ultimate outcome of his efforts is not specified in Trumbull's account, though Melville assumes his appeals were denied (pp. vii, 169). A second purpose of the chapbook was to make a little money for the old beggar and for the enterprising Trumbull. In this they seem to have met with more success than they expected, for second and third editions, at a slightly higher price and set by another printer, were called for (*IP*, pp. 283–84). But one of the factors that produced *Life and Adventures*, and that Melville surely recognized, was the historic Potter's sense of his own significance. He was notable, of course, for his remarkable adventures, but as he grew older he had become something of a London character, a part of the city's colorful low life. Potter's portrait was taken by the folklorist John Thomas Smith in 1819 to illustrate his *The Cries of London: Exhibiting ... the Itinerant Traders of Antient and Modern Times* (1839; Alma A. MacDougall, p. 4). Chair menders are a recognized category of "London Street-Folk" in Henry Mayhew's classic *London Labor and the London Poor* (1851), which is likewise generously illustrated. Smith explains that Potter, "one of the oldest menders of chairs ... sallies forth by eight o'clock in the morning, not with a view of getting chairs to mend; for, from the matted mass of dirty rushes ... it must be concluded that his cry of 'Old chairs to mend' avails him but little ... he goes his rounds and procures broken meats and subsistence thus early in the morning for his daily wants" (p. 4). Smith is probably correct, but the important fact is that he found Potter worthy of regard as a folk figure, and it is a truism that folk figures are aware of their peculiar status. Potter knew his life was remarkable, and hence his story was worth the telling, and he had confirmation from Smith that he was a personage of sorts. Melville seems to have sensed and responded to these convictions on the part of the historic Potter, in addition to the potential of his adventures as substance for a professional writer with an abiding interest in the multiform pilgrim species, man.

"CONTENTS" AS STRUCTURE

Melville's basic source, *Life and Adventures*, accounts for the origin and plan of his novel, but to determine what his plan became we should look again at the table of contents. The structure of *Israel Potter* originates in the chronological order and sequence of settings of its main source, but the "Contents" reveals a decided drift toward organic growth. This is certainly compatible with the growth of Israel himself, his efforts to adapt to the environments he finds himself in, and the figurative language associated with him. Organicism is evident in his identification with trees, for example, the "soft, prophetic sighing of the pine" (*IP*, p. 8) he hears as he sets out on his wanderings; it is also evident in his death on "the same day that the oldest oak on his native hills was blown down" (p. 169). The organicism of the structure is consistent with the resolution of the narrative, which, we will discover, is largely in terms of Israel's eventual understanding of his place within the natural processes of the universe. In *Moby-Dick*, Ishmael, voicing ideas close to Melville's own and employing organic metaphor, begins a chapter with a statement about literary method and by implication its manifest form: "Out of the trunk, the branches grow; out of them, the twigs. So, in productive subjects, grow the chapters" (*MD*, p. 246). But as he often does, Melville counters his own assertion by beginning a subsequent chapter with the observation that "There are some enterprises in which a careful disorderliness is the true method" (p. 304).

The organicism that emerges in the progress of the narrative is at odds with the linear plan that inheres in its source (cf. John Seelye, p. 112). Melville saw plans as restrictive, excessively abstract and mechanical, but he found the organic disorderly. When he generalizes that "all human affairs are subject to organic disorder" (*IP*, p. 114), he is primarily indicating the innate susceptibility of the human organism to irregularity and digression, but he is at the same time recognizing the disorder that results from humankind's organic nature. In crafting *Israel Potter* he was careful, sometimes all too obvious, in his attempts to make his way between the calculated and the inspired. But this problem is not confined to *Israel Potter* or the demands of magazine fiction, or Melville. He accepted the orderly, rational, chronological, linear plan of *Life and Adventures*, but he allowed room for his version of the story to evolve, in fact, structurally—and for that matter, thematically—to circle back to its beginning in a manner that accords with the cyclic time scheme of nature. In the end, he emphasizes Israel's return to the site of his birth and more than metaphorically to his infancy—"here I, little infant, would totter...even as now" (p. 169). This is a framing device that seems carefully calculated, yet it grows logically from the organic nature of the situation. If it is retrogression, it is also regeneration.

FROM STRUCTURE TO GENRE

The array of literary forms comprising *Israel Potter*, some of them well developed and others inchoate, suggests Melville's impatience with the limitations of literary form. More positively seen, it is another mark of Melville's evolutionary procedure. He declined to be hemmed in by plans, in this case the conventions of any single genre. Instead, he followed a disorderly course among a succession of genres, from the dedication at the beginning of the book to the epitaph at the end. The dedication was an established form he had already bent to his purposes in *Pierre*. In *Israel Potter* it evolves from the completed work, at once a retrospect and an introduction, but it is also appropriate to the role of the "devoted and obsequious...Editor" (p. viii). His facetious obsequy is designed to modify the pathos of Israel's life and to satirize pretensions and heroics. The tactic is calculated irony. "The Editor" identifies the Bunker Hill Monument as a tribute to "anonymous privates" like Israel Potter who succeeded in overthrowing a monarchy but failed to enjoy their victory (Michael T. Gilmore, p. 155), and with mock respect, he addresses the stone shaft in honorifics reserved for royalty. The Editor himself assumes a lofty detachment comparable with that he attributes to "His Highness the Monument." His purpose is to attack the sovereign indifference that it personifies, and his detachment is the more feasible because he is, after all, the Editor of the editor to whom Israel had "dictated" his "little book" (p. 269). (For another view of the Editor's detachment, see Edgar A. Dryden, pp. 144–45.) The monument is shown to be as fraudulent an inversion as the genre Melville inverts in order to satirize it. It is germane that Melville admired "the plain speaking of [Samuel] Johnson...in the Rambler" (Evert Duyckinck Diary, 21–31 January 1860, quoted in *Reading*, p. 21) who denounced "the practice of indecent and promiscuous dedication" (*Rambler*, no. 136). It is likely that he was aware of the by no means unique view of President John Quincy Adams who complained in his diary: "Democracy has no monuments.... Its very essence is iconoclastic" (p. 433).

Melville methodically draws on his last chapter for the dedication, forging links to the final paragraph of the novel through information and phraseology that they share. For instance, both refer to Israel's having dictated his narrative to an editor, mention his unsuccessful efforts to obtain a pension, and state that his little book has long since gone "out of print" (*IP*, pp. vii, 169). Both are elegiac and both feature funereal references, often playfully (e.g., "true 'Potters' Field' " on p. 168, and "dilapidated old tombstone" on p. vii), and a mutability from which not even primordial stone is exempt. The "ruinous... masonry," the "half buried hearth," and the "bemossed stone jambs" that Israel finds in the end are all that remains of his family domicile (p. 169), and they have their equivalent in the dedication where the not yet completed monument, on its twenty-ninth birthday, is said to be growing "prematurely gray." Death is the end, and even granite moulders into dust. But references to the "bemossed stone jamb" among the ruins and the "ever-new mosses" on Israel's grave bespeak the natural cycle, "the consecration of moss" (p. 159) that for the editorial voice is emblematic of regeneration. Israel's valediction, "The ends meet" (p. 169), returns us to the first sentence of the dedication in which the Editor justifies posthumous biography on the grounds that "the ended lives of the true and the brave, may be held the fairest meed of human virtue" (p. vii). The biography of a "devoted patriot" (p. 5), dead and forgotten, may be as detached from life and but remain as vital as the seasonal rounds of nature, and hence this meeting of ends and beginnings may be a reward beautiful and just, "the fairest meed," *dulce et decorum*. The end is meet. Such a view of biography "may be held," but the tone of the dedication and its insinuating language intimate present inversions, mockeries, and tragicomic torsion, and those that lie ahead. Still Melville is given to qualifying his own qualifications. Ends may well be endless. Thus in *Mardi* a bard rhapsodizes: "Fellow men! our mortal lives have an end; but... it will prove but as the beginning of another race" (p. 575); in *Moby-Dick*, the quintessential natural man, Queequeg, deathly sick, approaches with calm the immortality that Ishmael calls his "endless end" (ch. 110, "Queequeg in His Coffin"); and in his late poem of calm acceptance, "Pontoosuce," on the natural processes visible in the Berkshire landscape, the end is again a beginning:

> End, ever end, and begin again—
> End, ever end, and forever and ever begin again!
>
> (*Poems*, p. 397)

"CONTENTS" AS GENRE

Melville changes his genre almost as often as Israel changes his clothing and for much the same reason—to provide a suitable guise for the oc-

casion. The variety of literary forms in *Moby-Dick* has been remarked
often, and on a much more modest scale *Israel Potter* includes a like
variety. Their presence, purpose, and origin remain to be studied but
may be indicated briefly by once more turning to the "Contents." The
dedication suggests other genres to come, among them biography, narrative of adventure, patriotic tribute, and epitaph. Actually, we observed
that the first genre of the novel proper is the picturesque travel sketch
in the tradition of William Gilpin whose numerous works have such titles
as *Essays ... on Picturesque Travel* and *Observations ... Relative Chiefly to
Picturesque Beauty in Various Parts of Britain.* This should be no surprise.
Melville was familiar with the Gilpin aesthetic, and picturesque travel
writing remained popular in mid-nineteenth-century America. Besides,
Melville was known at the time as a traveler and travel writer, would
later lecture on his travels, and publish a group of verses he called "Fruit
of Travel Long Ago" and write a poetic discourse on the picturesque.
More to the point, Israel Potter, as we have argued, is a wanderer, a
traveler. In fact, an astute critic concludes that " 'Traveling' is at once
the rationale and the chief theme" of the entire Melville canon (Charles
Feidelson, p. 173). "The Birthplace of Israel" (ch. 1) situates Israel firmly
within the natural landscape, notes its shaping influence on him, and
suggests that as a projection of the landscape he is in some degree a
national type. He is insistently an American democrat, a facet of his
character that runs counter to his capacity to adapt. Israel is the name
of a man but also a place and a people: "And we Americans are ... the
Israel of our time" (*WJ*, p. 151).

The next genre, which the editor correctly calls "a little narrative of
... adventures" (p. vii), is a sequence of biographical chapters on "The
Youthful Adventures of Israel" that comprise his military service, his
"Travels Across the Sea," and his "Further Wanderings" (chs. 3–6), ending when he meets Franklin in Paris. This is the setting for two biographical exercises of a different kind. Israel's encounter with the
legendary sage provides the editor with an opportunity for a character
sketch, "Something to Say about Dr. Franklin" (ch. 8), and his meeting
with Paul Jones produces another, "Paul Jones in a Reverie" (ch. 11).
His later glimpse of Ethan Allen will likewise lead to "Something Further" (ch. 22). The sketches are distinct from their subjects' participation
in the action of the narrative. Their purpose is to anatomize, to identify
them as representative of the culture, and to probe their motives and
the values they, as cultural configurations, embody. Founding fathers
and revolutionary heroes were routinely depicted as a combination of
the Christian gentleman and noble Roman in both the popular biographies of Parson Weems and the tomes of Jared Sparks (John McWilliams,
pp. 257–59). Melville departs from this convention in his sketches of
Franklin, Jones, and Allen. His representative men reflect the manysid-

edness of their countrymen, and he stressed their radically conflicting components and the backwoods characteristics present even in the urbane Franklin. The sketches should be read within the context of the Revolutionary War and the demand it made for a distinctive American identity (H. Bruce Franklin, p. 211). This might well add to our understanding of the ambivalent attitude toward England that the novel expresses and remind us that *Israel Potter* is to some extent an international novel well before Henry James gave the genre its ultimate definition.

Israel's "Return to the Squire's Abode" and "His Escape" from the Templars' penitential cell (chs. 12–13) is a gothic tale that soon shifts into a seriocomic ghost story that becomes a grotesque farce (ch. 13), so we have, in effect, three genres that slip from one into another. Layered within the "little narrative" that Melville took from *Life and Adventures* are elements of the genre of historical romance (Edward H. Rosenberry, *Melville*, p. 101) which have no sanction in his basic source. The extensive naval sequence involving Paul Jones (chs. 14–20) is Melville's most notable instance of romanticized history, but mixed in with it are passages of straightforward naval history and highly theatrical set pieces. This is particularly true of the account of the fight between the *Bon Homme Richard* and the *Serapis* in which Melville sticks to the facts as he found them in Sands, Cooper, and his other historic sources while giving Israel a romantic fictional role, and presenting in a very painterly fashion his melodramatic description.

The description is a verbal equivalent to the genre of the naval battle-piece, a type of history painting popular in Europe in the eighteenth century and in America, especially after the War of 1812 (Clive Bush, pp. 148–51). The *Serapis* battle was an event of sustained interest and the subject of many paintings and prints, usually illuminated by a full moon as well as gunfire and flames. Whether in print or on canvas, the sea fight was a combination of genres, authentic history and historical romance, the naval battle-piece and the theatrical spectacle, and it was visual in the extreme. To maximize its visual qualities and their significance Melville employs three angles of vision: the viewpoint of the spectators on Flamborough Head who are effectively an audience within a theater; that of the seamen involved in the conflict and thus the actors; and that of the moon rising above the scene, remote and orderly, a "Mephistopheles prompter of the stage" (p. 123). This evocative scene has been read as evidence that Melville is within the Calvinist typological tradition (Ursula Brumm, p. 19), as reflecting the sectional strife of the time and anticipating the fratricidal conflict to come (Edwin Fussell, pp. 298–99), and as denouncing the disasters of war (Joyce Sparer Adler, p. 82). It has also been read as a game in which the skill and bravery of the players rather than chance are the important factors (Robert Zaller, p. 615). Melville's scenic description in *Israel Potter* has led perceptive critics to describe it as "a series of pictures" (Warner Berthoff, p. 69), "hardly more than a heap of sketches" (Arvin, p. 245). Significantly, his two most highly regarded word pictures have subjects that stand in extreme contrast: the enduring natural landscape of the Berkshires and the horrific mechanical slaughter of the sea battle.

"The Shuttle" (ch. 20) terminates the extended naval sequence. It is a clearly defined genre, a tall tale of a slick Yankee trying to slip out of a tight situation, and it is a shift to comic relief from bloody deeds and bluster. Israel finds himself involved in an absurd quest for a place and an identity, a parody of a quest that depends for its humor on its absurdity, though this heavier element is awash in the waters of a comic folk genre. For the next forty years or more Israel will be landlocked. On his way to the city, he finds work in a brickyard (ch. 23), an occasion for a self-contained parable. Its subject is the effect of the fire in the kiln on furnace-brick, extended by implication to humanity's proximity to the vital fires of life that may, depending on the distance, severely scorch, sustain through its warmth, or prove inadequate. The brickyard episode is Melville ringing changes on Melville (Arnold Goldman, p. 80). The "slap, slap, slap" refrain of the "half jolly" brickmakers as they stir barrels of mud (p. 155) is an inversion of the mollifying "squeeze, squeeze, squeeze" of the sailors in *Moby-Dick* at their tubs of sperm (ch. 94). The depiction of the notoriously squalid and noxious business of brick-making (cf. Dickens' *Bleak House*, ch. 56), makes the chapter a variant of the local color genre, the culture of poverty. In part, so are passages of the next chapter which describes Israel's "forty year's wanderings in the London deserts" (p. 158), and in "The City of Dis" (ch. 24) which follows. The gothic and exotic qualities of Chapter 24, however, relate it to the spate of novels of the period on the mystery of cities, from Eugene Sue's *Mysteries of Paris* (1844) to Ned Buntline's *Mysteries and Miseries of New York* (1848). The title of the last chapter, "Requiescat in Pace" (ch. 26), suggests the genre of the epitaph, as noted, but there is little beyond the title and some graveyard elegizing (and the connection with the dedication) to make this much more than a suggestion. Similarly suggestive but undeveloped is the genre of the holiday story incipient in the ironic treatment of the Fourth of July (ch. 26). Melville would do much better with another holiday, April First, in *The Confidence-Man*.

PATTERNS OF CONTRAST

The paragraph with which Melville ends his first chapter, "The Birthplace of Israel," is synoptic, and to summarize what lies ahead Melville sets up a series of contrasts. These, in turn, foreshadow important events and ideas and are integrating devices that support the circularity of his structure and theme. The tone of the paragraph, elegiac and pathetic and touched with irony, also prefigures the narrative as a whole:

> How little he thought, when, as a boy, hunting after his father's stray cattle among these New England hills, he himself like a beast should be hunted through half of Old England, ... Or, how could he ever have dreamed, when involved in the autumnal vapors of these mountains, that worse bewilderments awaited him ... across the sea, wandering forlorn in the coal-fogs of London. But so it was destined to be. This little boy of the hills, born in sight of the sparkling Housatonic, was to linger out the best part of his life as a prisoner or a pauper upon the grimy banks of the Thames. (p.6)

The little boy in New England will become the old man in Old England. The pastoral ambiance of the Housatonic will be displaced by the grimy Thames. The Berkshire mist will give way to the coal smoke of London. The hunter of stray cattle will himself be pursued like a wild beast.

The pursuit motif recurs with such regularity that its recurrence becomes a structural device even as it is developed thematically. Israel is a "wild creature of the American wilderness ... hunted ... by a red coat" (p. 23); he is "driven from hole to hole like a fox in the woods" (p. 29); he "sped toward London" [like] "the hunted fox to the wilderness" (p. 153). Israel is hunted like a deer (p. 15) and a dog (p. 92) as well, both appropriate analogies, but his comparison with the hunted fox is significant for concentrating a set of crosscurrents, contrasts within a contrast, that flow through the narrative: the American rebel pursued by the British Redcoats, the wilderness denizen under threat from civilized society, a creature little better than an animal chased for sport by a red-coated, fox-hunting gentry. The gap implied here between plebeian and patrician is important because it poses the question of whether an ordinary creature, the object of the hunt, no matter how remarkable his adventures, might in any way be considered a hero and quester.

WANDERER AS HERO

The conjunction of the Berkshire boy seeking strayed cattle and the old man in London "many years after" (p. 164) dreamily replicating his original searchings has a further thematic and structural role. It informs us that, though Israel in England is hunted like a beast, he remains a seeker. (For a differing view, see Arvin, p. 246, and Feidelson, p. 182.) *Israel Potter*, among other things, is a plebeian version of the heroic quest. Its direction is not the straightforward progress of the culture hero, a Benjamin Franklin methodically heading toward a rationally predetermined goal or a Paul Jones driven by instincts too powerful to be denied. Rather, it is the wanderings of a common man shaped by the circumstances and personalities he encounters, willing and able to learn, watching for the main chance, but seldom in control of his destiny. He wanders through the landscape, not changing it but adapting to it. This is not the stuff of heroic tragedy or historical romance. Nor is the interweaving of comedy and pathos that characterizes the editorial voice. Israel, we are told in the last sentence of the synoptic paragraph, is destined to spend "the best part of his life as a prisoner or pauper" (*IP*, p. 6). Presumably they are equivalents (and they, too, are recurrent motifs that function as plot, theme, and structure) since poverty is one of the many prisons, literal and figurative, to which Israel will be confined. But Melville is having his little joke, albeit a sad one, and he offsets the pathos when he writes that Israel "was to linger out the best part of his life" in "Babylonian London," to borrow an explicit reference to captivity and exile from a closely related magazine piece, "The Two Temples" (*Tales*, p. 159). The phrase "best part" has an edge that cuts two ways, and "linger out" is a curious choice of language with its suggestion that Israel tarried in London because he was disinclined to leave. Melville's humor is usually more lively and overt than this, but even then, given Israel's miseries and frustrations, we are apt to forget that he is a comic Yankee type (Richard Chase, pp. 177–78).

The resonance of the word "wandering" encourages comment. It does not occur in *Life and Adventures*, and the Israel Potter of Melville's source, though battered by misfortune, is a conscientious planner who has specific goals. In Melville's retelling, "wanderer" is the most frequent term that the editorial voice applies to Israel, often with Biblical reference that seems more inevitable than functional. Thus, we are told at the beginning of Melville's narrative that Israel's name is prophetic because "for more than forty years" he "wandered in the wild wilderness" (p. 6), and he is referred to as "the wanderer" until and at the very end (p. 169). One effect of this is to highlight his subordination to forces, events, and personalities greater than himself at the expense of the relatively few instances when he instigates the action. These instances, which take place mainly at the beginning of his career, include his departure from home and his "youthful adventures" (ch. 2) as a farmhand, hunter, surveyer's assistant, Indian trader, and seaman—the epitome of the enterprising young American. But there is an air of happenstance in what he does, as if he were adapting to opportunities that came his way rather than seeking them. He wanders from one thing to another, establishing a pattern of acquiescence, a willingness to put on the clothing or the personality that seems to fit the occasion. Immediate circumstance is always important. He adopts the dress of a beggar or a country squire as events demand, and he takes on some of the character of Franklin, and even more, of Paul Jones, when he finds himself a planet within their respective orbits. In the terminology of folklore he is a shapeshifter, but in the broader sense his responses are passive, the adaptations of a footloose Yankee whose original efforts to get ahead are superseded by the need to survive.

Melville elaborates Israel's good humor, his quick wits, his versatility, his patience, his endurance, his bravery, in all, the Yankee qualities that reside in the comic folk type and in his basic source. He also reduces the extensive descriptions of poverty in the source to a single chapter with a laconic title, "Forty-five Years," something of a sacrifice as Trumbull knew—and Melville in *Redburn* instances—since the annals of the poor can have a certain morbid appeal. These measures, however, do not transform Israel Potter into a questing hero. In the last analysis, he is not a figure to inspire veneration or emulation. He is a curiosity.

An early biographer of Melville called *Israel Potter* "a delightful picaresque story" (John Freeman, p. 60) in spite of its London gloom and its fatality, and Melville read *Lazarillo de Tormes*, the generic prototype, in 1850 (*Reading*, #324). The picaresque is part of the story, and the comment is justified by its roguish protagonist of low degree, its comic and satiric elements, its vividness of detail enhanced by bravura touches, its episodic nature, and its attention to movement through space and time and a social scale that embraces beggars and kings. Structure and protagonist evolve in a picaresque fashion, in a wandering narrative without a logical story line about a character whose identity is uncertain.

These factors and others cited—plebeian social status, passivity, the importance of chance, the mingling of comedy and pathos, a multiplicity of roles, and most of all his apparently aimless wandering—make it hard to see Israel as quester or hero. Paradoxically, however, his wandering makes this identification possible. A highly cultivated "man of wisdom" like Franklin can attain legendary stature by means of his sagacity, and a "barbarian" Paul Jones, a noble savage, can pursue a heroic career through the power of his primordial energies. The little man, the Israel Potter, wanders about seeking a place for himself and trying to find out who and what he is. This is the commonalty's counterpart of the heroic quest.

The seriocomic chapter, "The Shuttle," clarifies Israel's role as quester. The fortunes of war put him aboard a homeward-bound British ship where his survival depends on passing himself off as a British sailor. He seeks a station in the maintop but is rejected, a process repeated as he descends level by level. When he attempts to hide himself among "the *waisters*, the vilest caste of an armed ship's company" (*IP*, p. 135), he is forced to face the ultimate question (A. Carl Bredahl, p. 55): "Who are ye?" (p. 136), and this question is repeated and extended by the officer of the deck: "Who the deuce *are* you?...Where did you come from? What's your business? Where are you stationed? What's your name? Who are you, any way?...where are you going? (p. 137). Baldly stated for the first time, these are questions that have been implicit in Israel's wanderings and give them purpose. Cross-examined, Israel extemporizes slyly, feigns madness methodically, and is dismissed by the officer to resume his "devious wanderings" (p. 141) and shape shifting. In time his antic disposition and willingness to work at whatever task presents itself win him a place in the maintop. Near the end of the voyage, the officer sees him there and remarks, "Well . . . you seem to belong in the main-top, after all." Israel responds carefully, "I always told you so, sir, . . . though, at first, you remember, sir, you would not believe it" (p. 141). These are not categorical statements on either side.

THE ENDS MEET

Israel has moved from the maintop down into the bowels of the ship, a parallel to his descent into the obscurity of the London underworld (Seelye, p. 114), but at the end of his homeward-bound passage he is back in the maintop. His elevation, tentative and uncertain, points toward the consolation he will find at home in the Berkshire Mountains where his wandering quest will end, a consolation that comes from the subdued heroism of his acceptance of the "posthumous pension . . . annually paid him by the spring in ever-new mosses and sward" (p. vii). His descent into his mossy grave is his certain elevation, "aloft from alow" in the not entirely ironic words of "Billy in the Darbies." But he differs from Billy, the handsome sailor transformed into a demigod and memorialized in a folksong by his sacrificial death. Israel comprehends and can articulate what has happened to him. Gradually, in his wandering, he comes to understand that he is a common man who has lived an uncommon life. As he nears the site of his childhood home, he "passed into an ancient natural wood, which seemed some way familiar, and midway in it, paused to contemplate a strange, mouldy pile." It proves to be the remains of "stout hemlock" cut for fuel but left "by subsequent oversight . . . to oblivious decay" (p. 168). It typifies his life, and he now knows that it is natural that he should fade "out of memory" (p. 169), out of human history, and into the cycle of natural history.

His last words are "The ends meet. Plough away, friend" (p. 169). They are addressed to a farmer whose plowshare strikes the hearthstone of the ruins of the house in which Israel was born. The ends do meet, for Israel's pattern is circular. The constellation Bootes, the Plowman, dominates the sky above the Berkshires, we are told in the descriptive sketch of Israel's birthplace. In fancy (cf. *Moby-Dick*, ch. 57, "Of Whales . . . in Stars"), those whose "eye sweeps the broad landscape beneath," presumably including Israel who was born there, themselves "seem to be Bootes driving in heaven" (p. 4). To aspire, to plow the heavens, seemed his birthright, and faced with misfortunes in his youth "he chose rather to plough, than to be ploughed" (p. 12). But in his old age he understands and accepts that his place is not in the stars but in the abiding earth. His words to the plowman testify that the wanderings of his exile are ended, and within the circular embrace of nature he can rest in peace.

RECOGNITION OF *ISRAEL POTTER*

Melville's "little book" has not exactly "faded out of . . . . memory" (p. 169), but it is probably the least discussed of his novels even though most critics speak well of it while lamenting its discursiveness and its failure to sustain the excellence of its best parts. These are usually identified as the vernacular facets of Israel's character; the subtlety of the sketches of Franklin, Jones, and Allen and their identification as national archetypes; and the vividness of the naval battle-pieces which double as commentary on physical and moral valor. The accumulated criticism and scholarship, with the exception of the NN edition, have been slight in every sense. The best tends to subordinate *Israel Potter* to its critic's larger argument. Some of it is so trivial or mediocre that it is listed in the bibliography below merely to complete the record.

The first fruits of the Melville Revival were passing observations and source studies. Thus, Lewis Mumford (1929) saw *Israel Potter* as evidence of Melville's "restored health" and "powers of invention" (p. 240), and Roger P. McCutcheon, following the obvious clues, identified "Melville's additions . . . about two-thirds of the book" (p. 163), which, with the exception of a conclusion that "seems lame and impotent, its symbolism tawdry" (p. 174), he thought praiseworthy.

As academic recognition of Melville increased, critics turned their attention to his cultural milieu, biography, and literary craft. Chase (1949), by way of Constance Rourke, treated Israel Potter as a quasi-comic figure shaped by folklore and popular culture, a view consistent with his interest in Melville's "strong young heroes," the best "of common humanity" (pp. ix-x). Arvin (1950), in a critical biography that relates Melville's psychic state to his art, saw the novel as a pathetic "symptom of Melville's fatigue" (p. 232), the scatterings of what "might conceivably have been a superb book" that failed because it lacked "serious inner coherence" (pp. 244–45). Berthoff (1962) examined the literary qualities of Melville's art and found the Berkshire travel sketch exemplary. He avers that the picturesque scene is "both composed and interpreted, so that . . . there gradually emerges a large, whole image of an entire region"; effectively, the "ground has been prepared for a story with all the authority of myth" but such a story does not follow (pp. 74–75). Two articles of this period focus directly on the novel. Robert M. Farnsworth (1961) suggests that Israel, a lesser figure but in the footsteps of the more intense Pierre, is "under greater control" and his repeated defeats appear "ironically in the soft light of pathetic comedy" (p. 126). John T. Frederick (1962) confronts the "astonishing neglect" of *Israel Potter* and Arvin's charge of "aimlessness and disunity" (p. 246) by arguing the merits of its "strategically placed ... organic symbolism" (p. 266). Two monographs on *Israel Potter* appeared in 1969, Arnold Rampersad's *Melville's Israel Potter: A Pilgrimage and Progress* which asserts that the novel is in the tradition of the medieval allegory of the journey, and Alexander Keyssar's *Melville's Israel Potter: Reflections on the American Dream*, a dream which the common man can have little hope of realizing. Related social and political issues are explicit in the discussions of *Israel Potter* in the books by Gilmore (1977), Karcher (1980), and Adler (1981).

Translations of *Israel Potter* are sparse in comparison with Melville's other works and oddly distributed. Leland R. Phelps (1983), whose listings include all printings in whole or part and are categorized by language rather than country, has located the following: Czech, two; French, six; German, seven; and Italian, Lithuanian, Russian, Slovenian, and Spanish, one each. By comparison, he found sixty-seven Spanish translations of *Moby-Dick*, fifty-six in German, fifty-three in French, fifty-one in Italian, eight in Czech, eight in Russian, two in Slovenian, and one in Lithuanian, which, contrary to other examples, followed after, rather than preceded, *Israel Potter*. The earliest translation was into German in 1946, the next into Italian in 1948. The novel has attracted effective scholarly attention, but only recently, in Britain and in Germany. Phelps lists as an article rather than a translation Emile Montegut's "Israel Potter, Legende democratique americaine," a summary of some fifty pages introduced by six pages of comment, published in the *Revue des deux mondes* (July–September 1855). Although a political conservative, Montegut was captivated by what he saw as the capacity of so young a nation to project its democratic character in legendary terms. His article is a landmark, for almost nothing of critical value on any Melville work appeared in any foreign language until the revival of the 1920s.

The most important recognition of *Israel Potter* thus far is the publication of the NN edition in 1982. Aside from establishing the text, it has Harrison Hayford's discussion of "Melville's Basic Source," Trumbull's *Life and Adventures*, a photo-reproduction of the 1824 edition, and Bezanson's fine "Historical Note" which provides definitive information on the composition, sources, publication, popular and critical reception of the novel. Bezanson summarizes and evaluates the scholarship of his predecessors so well that further comment in the present review would be supererogatory.

WORKS CITED

Adams, John Quincy. *Memoirs Comprising Portions of His Diary.* Ed. Charles Francis Adams. Philadelphia: J. P. Lippincott and Co., 1876.

Adler, Joyce Sparer. *War in Melville's Imagination*. New York: New York University Press, 1981.

Anonymous. "Editorial Notes." *Putnam's Monthly* 5 (May 1855): 545–48.

Arvin, Newton. *Herman Melville: A Critical Biography*. New York: William Sloan, 1950.

Bach, Bert C. Melville's *Israel Potter*: A Revelation of Its Reputation and Meaning." *Cithara* 7 (November 1967): 39–50.

Berthoff, Warner. *The Example of Melville*. Princeton, N.J.: Princeton University Press, 1962.

Bredahl, A. Carl, Jr. *Melville's Angles of Vision*. Gainesville, Fla.: University of Florida Press, 1972.

Browne, Ray B. *Melville's Drive to Humanism*. Lafayette, Ind.: Purdue University Press, 1971.

Brumm, Ursula. *American Thought and Religious Typology*. New Brunswick, N.J.: Rutgers University Press, 1970.

Bryant, John. "Melville's Comic Debate: Geniality and the Aesthetics of Repose." *American Literature* 55 (May 1983): 151–70.

Bush, Clive. *The Dream of Reason: American Consciousness and Cultural Achievement from Independence to the Civil War*. London: Edward Arnold Ltd., 1977.

Cecchi, Emilio. "Two Notes on Melville." *Sewanee Review* 48 (Summer 1960): 400–406.

Chacko, David, and Alexander Kulcsar. "Israel Potter:The Genesis of a Legend." *William and Mary Quarterly* 41 (July 1984): 365–89.

Chase, Richard. *Herman Melville: A Critical Study*. New York: Macmillan Co., 1949.

Christie's: Printed Books, Manuscripts and Modern Illustrated Books in Fine Bindings; Friday, November 22, 1985. New York: Christie's, 1985.

Cohen, Hennig. "The Real Israel Potter." *Melville Society Extracts* No. 53 (February 1983): 7–11.

Dryden, Edgar A. *Melville's Thematics of Form: The Great Art of Telling the Truth*. Baltimore, Md.: Johns Hopkins University Press, 1968.

Farnsworth, Robert M. "*Israel Potter:* Pathetic Comedy."*Bulletin of the New York Public Library* 65 (February 1961); 125–32.

Feidelson, Charles, Jr. *Symbolism and American Literature*. Chicago: University of Chicago Press, 1953.

Flibbert, Joseph. *Melville and the Art of Burlesque*. Amsterdam: Rodopi, 1974.

Franklin, Benjamin. *Papers of Benjamin Franklin*. Vol. 23. Ed.William B. Willcox. New Haven, Conn: Yale University Press, 1983.

Franklin, H. Bruce. "From Empire to Empire: *Billy Budd, Sailor*." In *Herman Melville: Reassessments*. Ed. A. Robert Lee. London and Totowa, N.J.: Vision and Barnes, 1984.

Frederick, John T. "Symbol and Theme in Melville's *Israel Potter*." *Modern Fiction Studies* 8 (Autumn 1962): 265–75.

Freeman, John. *Herman Melville*. New York: Macmillan Co., 1926.

Fussell, Edwin. *Frontier: American Literature and the American West*. Princeton, N.J.: Princeton University Press, 1965.

Gansevoort-Lansing Collection, Additions. New York Public Library.

George, J. L. "*Israel Potter*: The Height of Patriotism." *American Transcendental Quarterly* 7 (Summer 1970): 53–56.

Gilmore, Michael T. *The Middle Way: Puritanism and Ideology in American Romantic Fiction*. New Brunswick, N.J.: Rutgers University Press, 1977.

Goldman, Arnold. "Melville's England." In *New Perspectives on Melville*. Ed.Faith Pullin. Edinburgh: Edinburgh University Press, 1978, pp. 68–85.

Grejda, Edward S. *The Common Continent of Men: Racial Equality in the Writings of Herman Melville*. Port Washington, N.Y.: Kennikat Press, 1974.

Henchey, Richard Francis. "Herman Melville's *Israel Potter*: A Study in Survival." Ph. D. Diss., University of Massachusetts, 1970. [*Mel. Diss.*, No. 229.]

Hillway, Tyrus. "Israel Potter—Bicentennial Hero?" *Americana-Austriaca: Beitrage zur Amerikakunde* 5 (1980): 85–90.

Holden, W. Sprague. "Some Sources for Herman Melville's *Israel Potter*." M.A. Thesis, Columbia University, 1932.

Hull, Raymona. "London and Melville's *Israel Potter*." *ESQ* No. 47 (Second Quarter 1967): 78–81.

Jackson, Kenny. "*Israel Potter*: Melville's 'Fourth of July Story.' " *College Language Association Journal* 6 (March 1963): 194–204.

Jones, Walter Dickinson. "A Critical Study of Herman Melville's *Israel Potter*." Ph. D. Diss., University of Alabama, 1962.[*Mel. Diss.*, #105.]

Karcher, Carolyn L. *Shadow over the Promised Land: Slavery, Race, and Violence in Melville's America*. Baton Rouge, La.: Louisiana University Press, 1980.

Keyssar, Alexander. *Melville's Israel Potter: Reflections on the American Dream*. Cambridge, Mass.: Harvard University Press, 1969.

Lebowitz, Alan. *Progress into Silence: A Study of Melville's Heroes*. Bloomington, Ind.: Indiana University Press, 1970.

MacDougall, Alma A. "The Phoenix Rises: Northwestern-Newberry Edition." *Melville Society Extracts* No. 49 (February, 1982): 3–4.

Madison, R. D. "Melville's Edition of Cooper's *History of the Navy*." *Melville Society Extracts* No. 47 (September 1981): 9–10.

Magazine of History, with Notes and Queries. 4, Extra No. 16 (1911). [Annotated rpt. of Henry Trumbull's *Life and Remarkable Adventures of Israel R. Potter*.]

Mailloux, Steve, and Hershel Parker. *Checklist of Melville Reviews*. Los Angeles: Melville Society, 1975.

Matthiessen, F. O. *American Renaissance: Art and Expression in the Age of Emerson and Whitman*. New York: Oxford University Press, 1941.

Mayhew, Henry. *London Labor and the London Poor*. New York: Harper and Brothers, 1851.

McCarthy, Harold T. "Israel R. Potter as a Source for *Redburn*." *ESQ* No. 59 (Spring 1970): 8–9.

McCutcheon, Roger P. "The Technique of Melville's *Israel Potter*." *South Atlantic Quarterly* 27 (April 1928): 161–74.

McWilliams, John. "The Faces of Ethan Allen, 1760–1860." *New England Quarterly* 49 (June 1976): 257–82.

Miller, James E., Jr. *A Reader's Guide to Herman Melville*. New York: Farrar, Straus and Cudahy, 1962.

Mumford, Lewis. *Herman Melville*. New York: Harcourt, Brace and Co., 1929.

Mushabac, Jane. *Melville's Humor: A Critical Study.* Hamden, Conn.: Archon Books, 1981.

Neff, Winifred. "Satirical Use of a 'Silly Reference' in *Israel Potter.*" *American Transcendental Quarterly* No. 7 (Summer 1970): 51–53.

Paluska, Duane Alan. "The Dead Letter Office: A Study of Melville's Fiction, 1852–1857, with a Checklist Related to Melville's Tales, *Israel Potter*, and *The Confidence-Man.*" Ph. D. Diss., Brandeis University, 1970. [*Mel. Diss.*, #234.]

Phelps, Leland R. *Herman Melville's Foreign Reputation: A Research Guide.* Boston: G. K. Hall, 1983.

Pops, Martin Leonard. *The Melville Archetype.* Kent, Ohio: Kent State University Press, 1970.

Putz, Manfred. "Typologie und Historischer Roman: Zum skeptischen Geschichtsbild von Melvilles *Israel Potter.*" In *Mythos und Aufklarung in der Amerikanischen Literatur (Myth and Enlightenment in American Literature).* Ed. Dieter Meindl et al. Erlangen: Universitatsbibliothek, 1985, pp. 227–50.

Rampersad, Arnold. *Melville's Israel Potter: A Pilgrimage and a Progress.* Bowling Green, Ohio: Bowling Green University Popular Press, 1969.

Rogin, Michael Paul. *Subversive Genealogy: The Politics and Art of Herman Melville.* New York: Alfred A. Knopf, 1983.

Rosenberry, Edward H. "Israel Potter, Benjamin Franklin, and the Doctrine of Self-Reliance." *ESQ* No. 28 (Third Quarter 1962): 27–29.

———. *Melville.* London: Routledge and Kegan Paul, 1979.

Russell, Jack. "*Israel Potter* and 'Song of Myself.'" *American Literature* 40 (March 1968): 72–77.

Sealts, Merton M., Jr. *Pursuing Melville, 1940–1980: Essays and Chapters.* Madison: University of Wisconsin Press, 1982.

Sedgwick, William Ellery. *Herman Melville: The Tragedy of Mind.* Cambridge, Mass.: Harvard University Press, 1944.

Seelye, John. *Melville: The Ironic Diagram.* Evanston, Ill.: Northwestern University Press, 1970.

Stone, Geoffrey. *Melville.* New York: Sheed and Ward, 1949.

Trumbull, Henry. *Life and Remarkable Adventures of Israel R. Potter.* Providence, R.I.: Henry Trumbull, 1824.

Turner, Frederick W., III. "Melville and Thomas Berger: The Novelist and Cultural Anthropologist." *Centennial Review* 13 (Winter 1969): 101–21.

Virtanen, Reino. "Emile Montegut as a Critic of American Literature." *PMLA* 63 (December 1948): 1265–75.

Watson, Charles N. "Melville's *Israel Potter:* Fathers and Sons." *Studies in the Novel* 7 (Winter 1975): 563–68.

———, Jr. "Premature Burial in *Arthur Gordon Pym* and *Israel Potter.*" *American Literature* 47 (March 1975): 105–107.

Wilmes, Douglas Robert. "The Satiric Mode in Melville's Fiction: *Pierre, Israel Potter, The Confidence-Man*, and the Short Stories." Ph. D. Diss., University of Pennsylvania, 1976. [*Mel. Diss.*, #435.]

Yates, Norris. "An Instance of Parallel Imagery in Hawthorne, Melville, and Frost." *Philological Quarterly* 36 (April 1957): 276–80.

Zaller, Robert. "Melville and the Myth of Revolution." *Studies in Romanticism* 15 (Fall 1976): 607–22.

Zverov, A. "Melville and the XX-th Century." In *Romantic Traditions of the XIX-th Century American Literature and Modernity.* Ed. Ya. Zasursky. Moscow: Nauka, 1982.

11

THE CONFIDENCE-MAN: MELVILLE'S PROBLEM NOVEL

John Bryant

April Fool's Day, 1857, is a landmark in American literary history, but no one suspected it at the time. It is the publication date for Melville's ship-of-fools book, *The Confidence-Man*. That irony, the least of many in this puzzling production, was lost on Melville's first readers. And decades later, the entire novel was lost even on such ardent Melville revivalists as Raymond Weaver, who, assuming that the author had apparently suffered brain death after *Pierre*, declared *The Confidence-Man* a "posthumous work" (p. 348). To be sure, the acute exhaustion Melville had endured during the mid–1850s may have seemed like death. He had composed one serialized novel (*Israel Potter*) and seventeen tales (that we know of) in less than three years when he embarked in 1855 upon *The Confidence-Man*. By the time he had completed the meticulous revisions of his novel about the end of faith, he was ready to quit, and for good. Ironically, or perhaps, appropriately, his next venture was to the Holy Land. In England, smoking again with Hawthorne in the lee of Liverpool's sandy dunes, his back (I like to imagine) to the sea, Melville announced he had about decided "to be annihilated" as a writer (*Mel. Log*, p. 529). Thinking back over his past ten years of feverish composition, an ignored Herman Melville must have felt that *he* was the April fool to have written so well and yet communicated to so few.

If Melville's April Fool's Day joke backfired, if it became a swan song and not the clarion of a rejuvenated career, it is equally true that the novel's recent popularity has made Melville's contemporaries the fools at last. Out of place in its own day, Melville's "entropic" novel (Lawrence Buell, p. 20) has in retrospect been better suited to our entropic world shaped by two World Wars, the apparent failure of capitalist and Communist governance, the memory of one Holocaust and the threat of another, the death of God, and loss of identity. Nevertheless, Melville's last published prose fiction (one hesitates to call it a novel for its very structure—novel, anatomy, allegory, satire, comedy—is a matter of considerable debate) remains his least accessible, even for modern readers. So strained is its humor, so generalized its allegorical and satiric sources, so distant its narrator and indefinable its characters, so convoluted its style and involuted its ironies, so elusive its normative values—indeed, so complex is this work that it is even difficult to render a reasonable plot summary without in some sense betraying one's interpretive biases. Surely, then, *The Confidence-Man* is Melville's problem novel.

STRUCTURE: "SPEEDS THE DAEDAL BOAT AS A DREAM"

Something of a closet drama, *The Confidence-Man* presents on board the aptly named steamboat *Fidèle* over twenty-five significant characters—either alleged confidence men or their victims—who enter, strut and fret generally in twos or threes, and then exit. Invariably, a knave but sometimes a dupe passes from one scene to the next providing a thread of continuity to an otherwise disjointed narrative. Not until the novel's latter half does the action focus on one character, the cosmopolitan Frank Goodman. Readers rarely fail to notice the jaunty rhythms of the first half in contrast with the slow pace of the second. In attempting to tie the two halves more tightly together, many critics prefer to read the various con men as one Protean, supernatural, even Satanic con man in disguise. But only ironic hints, not conclusive evidence, support this; and certain textual peculiarities (either errors in composition or intentional red herrings) suggest that some alleged con men (the cosmopolitan in particular) have, in fact, separate identities. Melville's narrator remains utterly detached from the action, refusing to penetrate his characters' minds. Like a dramatist, he provides stage directions but little else in the way of interpretive guidance, thus leaving his puzzled readers convinced that if any confidence man truly exists in the book it is Melville himself. From its sunrise opening to its midnight end, *The Confidence-Man* is an algebraic equation with too many variables in plot, character, and narrative voice to allow for a definitive solution.

Plot and Character: "A Pic-nic *En Costume*"

The particulars are these. At sunrise on the St. Louis docks, again on April First, a deaf mute proselytizes the varied assemblage on the need for confidence. He bears some resemblance to a gentleman described on a wanted poster, but his audience, epitomized by the ship's barber's "No Trust" sign, rebuffs him. Equally abused is Black Guinea, a "negro cripple" who begs for alms. Skeptics and believers alike (among them a Methodist, the merchant Roberts, and the cynic Canada Thistle) require character references, and Black Guinea supplies a list of eight "ge'mmen" which prefigures some of the confidence men to come (p. 13). The novel proper begins when John Ringman, dressed in mourning (weeds), confronts Roberts as though he were an old friend and in a classic scam asks for a loan. Full of sorrow, Ringman succeeds with the good merchant, gives him a worthless stock tip on the Black Rapids Coal Company, and then accosts a collegian. Inveighing against Tacitus, Ringman fails to gain the young man's confidence and wanders away.

"You—Pish!" are the scornful words of a well-to-do gentleman addressing a man in gray, our next con man and enthusiastic seeker of charitable donations to the Seminole Widow and Orphans Asylum. Meeting with the scorn of Canada Thistle (again) and the reluctance of a man with gold sleeve-buttons (who in the "Wall Street spirit" contends that charity trickles down), the enthusiast finally dupes a plump lady, and the narrative moves on to the next, more sophisticated diddler.

The genial Mr. Truman, carrying a ledger book for the aforementioned Black Rapids Coal Company, signs up souls who wish to invest. The collegian, no longer shy, insists on being duped. He is. Later, Truman finds Roberts who also buys stock, and the two discuss the problem of misery. Truman denies its existence despite Roberts's examples of a miser sighted below decks, the crippled Black Guinea, and Ringman's story of woe. The latter serves as the interpolated tale of Goneril, Ringman's deranged wife. But Truman insists Ringman's story is one-sided. Somewhat persuaded, Roberts sips champagne, but, perceiving dark truths beneath the con man's geniality, he suddenly departs. Chapter 14, the first of three digressions on the nature of fiction, defends this sudden inconsistency of character. In the next chapter, Truman descends into the hold, diddles the aforementioned miser, and exits.

An herb doctor, perhaps the most broadly comic of Melville's con men, takes his place on deck and convinces a dubious invalid to eschew scientific remedies for nature's anodynes. Slowly, the self-defeatist takes heart and purchases six vials of Omni-Balsamic Reinvigorator. But when a titanic backwoodsman subsequently strikes the herb doctor to the deck, three observers argue whether the con man is a simpleton, knave, or original genius (ch. 18). The doctor's next mark is a "soldier of fortune." Truly lame but not a veteran of any war, the "soldier" seeks charity through false appeals to patriotism. His tale of neglect and deception constitutes a second interpolated tale. The old miser, vainly seeking

Truman, runs into the herb doctor and buys his worthless elixirs while the doctor tries to diddle Pitch, a Missouri backwoods skeptic. Unsuccessful, the doctor takes his leave.

Pitch remains and is accosted by the Philosophical Intelligence Officer—an employment agent who hopes to convince the Missourian to hire a young laborer. Burned too often by lazy runaways, Pitch resists the con man's punning analogies, but as the *Fidele* passes a point known as Devil's Joke, he relents. Somewhere within, Pitch's "too artless and companionable nature betrayed him" (p. 130). Chapter 24 introduces Frank Goodman and begins the novel's second half which focuses exclusively on this cosmopolitan's unsuccessful attempts to convince Pitch and five others of the need for confidence and good-natured fellowship.

Observing Goodman's failure with Pitch, Charlie Noble, an apparent Mississippi Operator, tells Goodman that Pitch is an unregenerate frontier misanthrope not unlike Colonel John Moredock, the notorious Indian-hater and subject of the novel's third interpolated tale (chs. 26–27). Goodman objects to the uncharitable comparison, and the two sit down to a bottle of port and a lengthy dialogue on friends, the press, wine, good humor and bad puns, Shakespeare (Autolycus, Polonius, Lear), surly philanthropists (Pitch), and "a new kind of monster," the genial misanthrope (p. 176). The scene climaxes when Goodman turns table on Noble and asks him for the loan that Noble was no doubt hoping to secure from Goodman. Five short chapters (31–35) mimic the rapid overturning of character and emotions caused by Goodman's "necromantic" change. Among these are Chapter 33 (another digression on inconsistent characterization, Harlequin, and fiction) and Chapter 34, Goodman's interpolated tale of Charlemont, a Hawthornesque "gentleman-madman" who returns to geniality after years of inexplicable isolation.

Upon Noble's exit, the mystic Mark Winsome warns Goodman of such operators. But as with Pitch, the cosmopolitan defends Noble as well as a passing, madman-poet who peddles a transcendental tract. Goodman is surprised by Winsome's steely disregard for "fellow-feeling" and even more distraught by the identical arguments of Egbert, Winsome's pragmatic disciple. In a remarkable scene (ch. 39), the two reenact Goodman's encounter with Noble, with Goodman playing himself and Egbert, Noble. Egbert/Noble refuses to give Goodman/Goodman a loan, citing the story of China Aster's fateful decision to accept a "friendly" loan, which serves as the novel's fifth and last interpolated tale (ch. 40). Goodman increases the intensity of his appeal, but again is refused, whereupon he storms off enraged at the heartlessness about him.

The novel concludes with four swiftly paced chapters (42–45). Goodman diddles the ship's barber into removing his "No Trust" sign and giving him a shave. He then races below decks to check a Bible reference alluded to by the barber. The penultimate Chapter 44 provides a final digression on the possibility of creating an "original" character like Hamlet, Don Quixote, or Milton's Satan. In the concluding chapter, Goodman finds the ship's Bible and an old man who professes faith in humanity but wears a money belt, purchases a counterfeit detector from a sloe-eyed boy-diddler, clings to a chamber-pot life preserver, and fears the dark. Goodman, satisfied that the Bible quotation is to be found in the Apocrypha, not the true book, extinguishes the smoky cabin light and offers to show the old man to his cabin. The novel's final words amidst the midnight gloom are "Something further may follow of this Masquerade."

Play and Replay: The Mimetic and Didactic Modes

The largest structural problem associated with *The Confidence-Man* is whether it may be classified as didactic or mimetic, whether it is a comic allegory (satire) or representation of human folly. On the surface, there seems to be little room for debate. The novel's highly emblematic characters and seemingly aimless plot preclude any serious consideration of Melville's desire to put forth flesh and blood creations. And yet, there are moments in the novel when characters such as Roberts, Pitch, and Goodman grow beyond allegory and spring to life. These are not emblems but people. Clearly, the novel is somehow a blend of didactic and mimetic forms.

The issue might best be illustrated in terms of the ways idea and action interact in both modes. In didacticism, argument dictates action; that is, the plot moves as the author's principal idea develops. In mimesis, ideas emerge along with our evolving sympathies for characters and the necessary complications of their lives. In Melville's novel the principal event or action is the confidence game, or more precisely, the continual replay of that game which induces in readers a vaguely modern sense of *deja vu*. On the simplest level, each new character conveys the same old story of knave duping fool. But Melville articulates this pattern of replay with subtle effect and in ways that can be seen to serve both didactic and mimetic ends.

Each of the major victims (Roberts, the collegian, the miser, and Pitch) is "hit" by two confidence men, or, if you assume there is only one confidence man, they are "hit" twice by the same con man dressed in two disguises. Interestingly enough, Goodman, whom we take to be a con man (perhaps *the* con man), seems in fact to be the "mark" or intended victim of Noble and perhaps even the Winsome-Egbert duo. He is as much a victim as a knave; thus, in the second half of the novel, the replays vary radically and complicate our understanding of Goodman's identity. Is he a knave, fool, or original genius? Other replays provide a deeper texture to Melville's tapestry. Goodman, for instance, strongly resembles the genial businessman Truman. The Truman-Roberts encounter with its drinking, wine imagery, and climactic character reversal parallels the Goodman-Noble chapters even down to Goodman's sudden change in character, the placement of interpolated tales (Roberts's Goneril, Noble's Moredock), and the digressions on fiction (chs. 14 and 33). The novel's most dramatic replay, however, occurs in the second half, with Goodman and Egbert's literal replaying of Goodman's encounter with Noble. (This, too, contains an interpolated tale, that of China Aster.)

Viewed didactically, these replays (typical of many allegories) might be interpreted as repeated opportunities for Melville to ring changes on Christian hypocrisy, the failure of confidence, or the lack of American moral vision. We move from one replay to the next because Melville wishes to explore a new facet of the same argument, not because a particular character's moral dilemma demands a probable and necessary development in the story. On the other hand, from a mimetic approach, the replay of events intensifies the recurrent and inevitable folly of human belief and interaction. Each replay with its intriguing variations and unexpected inversions increases our involvement in the victim or apparent victim (Roberts, Pitch, Noble, and Goodman) so that their problems of recognizing selfhood become, out of the very force of the repetition, our own. We are left in Chapter 39 with Goodman vainly playing his greatest role, himself, and yet achieving nothing but anger and frustration. It is a role with which we cannot fail to identify.

My point, here, is not to argue for one approach over the other but to suggest that Melville's novel is problematic precisely because it blends allegory and comedy, the didactic and mimetic, so seamlessly. The challenge to critics, it seems to me, is to unite both structural perspectives.

GENESIS: "THE SUN COMES OUT, A GOLDEN HUZZAR" AND "ALL THINGS ... LEAP."

Where Melville got the idea for *The Confidence-Man* and when he began to write are matters of speculation. Watson G. Branch dates the inspiration of the novel as early as May 1855 when Melville is likely to have read a newspaper report of Samuel Willis, a noted con man ("Genesis," p. 427). The evidence of an undated letter from George William Curtis to Edward Dix, now proven to be written on 29 June 1855 (Alma A. MacDougall), reveals that Melville may have proposed his book and written part of it by the early summer of 1855. Other evidence indicates that he was decidedly underway by that fall (Howard, p. 226, and Elizabeth S. Foster, p. 315). Although most agree that Melville probably planned his work to be serialized, this is only a conjecture based on the internal evidence of the novel's episodic structure and interpolated tales. The novel's last line coupled with evidence from the 1856 *Journal* suggests that Melville may have planned a sequel to *The Confidence-Man* (Howard C. Horsford).

Composition

Melville's compositional process is not known. Only one of his surviving letters alludes to the work; no journal records his progress. The twenty-six leaves of working manuscript from the novel provide local insights into the author's creativity and no real evidence of an overall procedure. Several scholars have guessed at the initial inspiration for the novel. Leon Howard believed that Melville may have found the essential "conceit" for *The Confidence-Man* at an outdoor costume party or "pic-nic *en costume*," as Frank Goodman puts it (p. 226). Foster contended that Melville's original intention was to satirize Emersonian Transcendentalism (p. lxxx), but her evidence rested on manuscript leaves that the NN editors now believe were written much later in the compositional process than Foster had surmised (*CM*, p. 294).

Given the paucity of external evidence, scholars have been reticent to propose elaborate compositional theories. Watson Branch and Tom Quirk, however, have gone to the text itself to support their fascinating ideas. Both demonstrate some impressive educated guessing, but their theories are only as strong as their divergent assumptions about the novel's structure and Melville's creative process. Branch scrutinizes the novel for inconsistencies, anticlimaxes, unfulfilled expectations, unaccountable repetitions, and visible seams in order to present Melville's somewhat adventitious method of writing. Quirk is a bit more ambitious; he examines sources and character development in hopes of understanding how Melville pulled "significance" out of raw material. In a sense, the one shows Melville's falterings, and the other his recombinations.

Branch assumes that *The Confidence-Man* is an allegory based on the disguises of one confidence man and that the allegory breaks down midway with the nonfulfillment of Black Guinea's list. He posits four structural parts to the novel: the encounters of six con men, Goodman's colloquies, the opening and closing chapters that constitute a frame for the novel, and various interpolated materials. These structural parts also constitute compositional phases. Hence, Branch argues that Melville abandoned Black Guinea's list with the introduction of Goodman, and that in completing the allegory, the author added a frame to give his novel coherence and inserted tales and digressions to expand its length. Obviously, Branch's structural assumptions affect his theory. He believes that the failure of two of Black Guinea's projected con men to show up is a compositional error that reveals a shift in Melville's original intention. But we might as easily assume that Melville intended the list to break down, thus requiring a different compositional theory altogether. Without external evidence to show that Melville made a mistake or planned the "error," the questions of original intent and compositional process remain moot. As Hershel Parker puts it, it is "far simpler to assume a basically straightforward composition" ("The Uses of Evidence," p. 124).

Quirk's theory of composition in *Knave to Knight* (1982) is equally problematic. Less interested than Branch in the novel's allegorical underpinnings (p. 60), Quirk does accept Branch's notion of a midway change in intention and of late insertions. His prime focus, however, is on the growth of Melville's "creative imagination" (p. 3). According to Quirk, Melville first perceived a satiric potential in the William Thompson criminal type and then developed that potential more broadly along cultural, philosophical, and literary lines—as he wrote. Quirk's book would make a fine critical interpretation, but his insistence on the last three words of the preceding sentence weakens his work as compositional theory. Quirk assumes, I think falsely, that the development of Melville's main character corresponds to the artist's own intellectual development, again, while he was writing. He seems to ignore the possibility that from the very beginning Melville may have conceived of his character developing as it does.

In the final analysis, the NN editors are justified in stating that both Branch's and Quirk's theories are "fruitfully suggestive" but finally "unverifiable" (p. 300). Nevertheless, they conclude that "Melville, as with most of his books, did not plan *The Confidence-Man* from the beginning in its final form but developed it in various unforeseen and not altogether seamless ways" (p. 300). Indeed, one easily gets the impression from reading Melville's longer works that they are not "well wrought urns," and it is only logical to assume that Melville played out his fictions as he went along. But even this rather cautious conclusion requires scrutiny. It is important to note that we have no definitive external evidence (such as letters, journals, or personal interviews) that reveals Melville's customary habits of inspiration and production. It may be safe to say that his works developed in "unforeseen" ways, but it is less safe, it seems to me, to suggest that Melville did not have at the beginning some sense of his book's final effect. A disjointed narrative does not necessarily mean errors, oversights, or flaws in the creative process. It is altogether possible that Melville set out to write a disjointed work even though he did not foresee exactly how the disjunctures would be created—whether by interpolations, digressions, or Black Guinea's broken down *dramatis personae*.

Unfortunately, compositional theories can only scratch the surface of the creative process. We must admire the endeavor to know Melville's imagination, but statements about Melville's composition, at this point, are necessarily speculative and should not be taken as a solid pad of fact from which to launch larger critical arguments. Like delicate crystals, such theories necessarily distort our view of Melville's creative mind even as they magnify and illuminate it.

Manuscripts

Even without its alluring critical complexities, *The Confidence-Man* would remain a focal point for modern scholars because it is one of the few prose texts in the Melville canon for which manuscripts exist. The twenty-six sheets, consisting of several early versions of Chapter 14, two lists of chapter titles, some scattered fragments, and the rejected passage known as "The River," are not as extensive as the *Billy Budd* and poetry manuscripts or the recently discovered *Typee* fragment, but they constitute a rare, albeit arrow-slit, view into Melville's creative process at a crucial moment in the artist's career. Elizabeth Foster was the first to transcribe and discuss most of these fragments. (Before her, Jay Leyda reproduced part of "The River" in *The Melville Log*.) In an appendix to her Hendricks House edition, she analyzes Melville's meticulous changes, noting the author's tendency to write expansively and then contract, to begin with a "loose structure" that yields to more tightly pruned sentences, to convert from "statement to understatement," and, more specifically, to tone down irreligious phraseology (pp. 275–76). Ultimately, Foster's focus is on style, not expurgation, and the "infinite pains" Melville endured in "achieving in his sentences that fine ironic contrast and tension between mild-mannered, leisurely surface and stern dialectic beneath." Such "tension," she concludes, "is the mode of his novel" (p. 377).

The digressive Chapter 14 is a key document in the study of Melville's theory of fiction, and the manuscript of this document affords the unique view of an artist shaping a fiction on the shaping of fiction. Presumably, critics would be attracted to these leaves, but that has not been the case. In fact, "The River" fragment including several still-undeciphered words, has drawn more attention. Edwin Fussell and John Seelye (in his 1968 edition) have provided separate transcriptions and interpretations of this intriguing, eventually rejected description of the Mississippi, and Robert Allen's transcription appears in the Norton edition (1971). But the Chapter 14 material has remained virtually untouched since

Foster. And yet a feast of new interpretations awaits those who might turn to it.

A case in point occurs toward the end of the chapter when Melville observes that the "great masters" of the psychological novel gain their appeal in part by giving their heroes apparent inconsistencies which in the end are resolved through simple shifts in point of view or contrived revelations. But such facile unravellings of the mystery of human character, Melville sarcastically notes, are comprehensible "to the understanding even of school misses" (p. 70). A look at the manuscripts, however, reveals that up until this final, published version, the phrase "school misses" had been "school boys" (p. 456). The last minute change from "boys" to "girls" may indicate a recognition on Melville's part of who the readers of fiction really were, "mere" ladies. Perhaps, however, in striking "boys" he had hoped to reduce confusion between this mindless reader of fiction and a later allusion to a "studious youth" (also characterized in earlier drafts as "sequestered," "cloistered," and "secluded"). The shift in gender, then, allows us to distinguish two kinds of naive readers: "school misses" who are easily duped by contrived fictions, and "studious youths" whose attachment to fiction is deeper but still illusory and perhaps even dangerous.

More attention to Melville's evolving text is bound to emerge with the recent publication of the NN edition of *The Confidence-Man* (1984). This excellent volume devotes about one hundred pages (five times the space given by Foster) to manuscripts. It provides photographs, genetic transcriptions, and "final versions" of each fragment sheet as well as a table listing variations between the published and final manuscript text. The editors argue conclusively that Melville's process of revision follows five phases (similar to Foster's theory) and that Chapter 14 was indeed a late insertion during the novel's composition. They differ with Foster on the usefulness of the two chapter lists in determining Melville's thematic intentions, and they provide to date the most precise transcription of "The River" with only eleven "questionable" decipherings.

EDITIONS: "WHAT IS THAT LARGE BOOK YOU HAVE"

On the surface, *The Confidence-Man* poses few problems for the textual scholar. Only two editions appeared in Melville's lifetime—one American (Dix, Edwards and Co.), the other British (Longman, Brown)—and copytext is easily assigned to the American. Melville's handwriting is notoriously bad, and since he did not supervise any phase of publication, more than the usual number of errors created by Melville's copyist (his sister Augusta) or the typesetter are bound to have crept into the text. The first American edition, although the best available, is therefore not necessarily an ideal representation of Melville's intention (if such a thing could possibly exist). That a confusing passage may be a corruption of the author's original only compounds the reader's difficulty in fully comprehending this recondite novel. The textual scholar, of course, is tempted to alter the more obvious errors, but Melville's style is so complex and original that problematic expressions might have been intended. Fortunately, the editors treated below have been scrupulous in their emendations.

Foster's 1954 Hendricks House edition is the first to be derived through rigorous textual methods. (The 1923 Constable edition is an anglicized version of Dix & Edwards.) Foster collated the two first editions of 1857, noted variants, and made thirty-five emendations of the American copy-text. The volume also contains her transcription of some of the manuscript fragments, a comprehensive introduction, and an invaluable set of explanatory notes. H. Bruce Franklin's useful introduction to the 1967 Bobbs-Merrill edition stresses the violence of Melville's America, the ambiguities of Black Guinea's list, and Melville's use of Hindu mythology. Franklin incorporates some of Foster's notes into his own extensive and equally valuable annotations which stress mythology, popular culture, and Melville's punning. He also includes his own transcription of "The River." John Seelye's introduction to the 1968 Chandler facsimile reprinting discusses the book's relation to popular culture and such figures as P. T. Barnum, Timothy Flint, and George W. Curtis. A rogue's gallery of con men from comic illustrations of the day supplements the text.

The Norton Critical Edition edited by Hershel Parker has been valuable to teachers and scholars since 1971. Parker provides three times the variants that Foster records but only minimal annotations. Extensive back matter includes a transcription of "The River," several source materials, eleven reviews, and a selected annotated bibliography of secondary criticism. Readers may not cotton to all annotations; in addition, the last item, a pamphlet published in "Comanche, Okla." does not exist. (It should be recalled that Professor Parker who hails from Oklahoma claims Indian ancestery.) Reprinted in their entirety, or virtually so, are essays by John W. Shroeder, Hershel Parker ("Metaphysics"), Harrison Hayford ("Poe"), and Howard C. Horsford. Also included are various critical excerpts and short musings prepared for the edition by Brian Higgins, Parker, Branch, and one "Samuel Willis," once a practicing con man (see *CM*, p. 283) who now, apparently, aspires to the less honorable calling of literary critic.

Volume 10 of the NN edition provides the most accurate text of *The Confidence-Man* to date and is the preferred text for teachers and scholars. Its Historical Note reviews Melville's career, the novel's composition and reception, and much of twentieth-century criticism. The Textual Record lists a dozen emendations more than the Norton, and a section of Related

Documents reproduces the manuscript fragments, relevant sections of James Hall's *Sketches* (1835), and passages from Timothy Flint's *The Mississippi Valley* (1828).

Almost without exception the editors' emendations are judicious and useful, but a particularly testy reader might take issue with their decision to drop two little commas from copy-text. In the American edition, Truman addresses the miser, thusly: "I wish, my friend, the herb doctor was here now." The NN edition drops both commas (p. 74) so that the herb doctor, not the miser, becomes Truman's "friend." The justification is twofold: Truman has previously used the formal (not friendly) term "sir" to address the miser, so that labeling the miser "my friend" would be inconsistent. And making the herb doctor Truman's friend restores the "important undercover irony" (p. 380) that Truman, who will eventually don the herb doctor mask, is essentially referring to himself as "my friend." But this emendation (or its alternate "I wish my friend, the herb doctor," adopted in the Norton edition) is debatable. For one thing, Truman calls the miser "my poor, poor sir" (p. 73) and "My dear, *dear* sir" (p. 75, Melville's emphasis), and these are not so formal or unfriendly. Second, irony already exists in the "original" text when Truman merely mentions the herb doctor by name. To call him "my friend" only intensifies an irony that is already there; thus, this particular emendation seems unwarranted. But to dwell on this matter only detracts from an otherwise thoroughly justifiable set of emendations. For instance, the editors have turned a "bold" man "bald" with good reason and changed an Indian blanket formerly "fringed with *lead* tassel-work" to the more logical (and less weighty) "*bead* tassel-work."

SOURCES: "THE BROOK SHOWS THE STAIN OF THE BANK IT PASSES THRU"

Like any writer Melville drew on his readings, personal experiences, and cultural milieu for literary material. Although he borrowed directly from certain sources, we would be hard pressed to accuse him of plagiarism. He was trapped between the Romantic bugbear of originality and the critical injunction against excess. His discussion of "original genius" in Chapter 44 hints at the constraints on his imagination in producing a new Quixote or Hamlet. One must have "much luck" (*CM*, p. 239) to stumble on something thoroughly new and to make it sell. The epigraph for this section is a marginal note in Melville's copy of Emerson's *Essays* pointing out a hint of Calvinism in the Transcendentalist's prose, but it is also an apt metaphor for the interpenetration of artist and milieu. The fluidity of Melville's mind is not only constrained but also "stained" by the banks of history and culture. The artist is in effect tainted by the necessary borrowings from his surroundings; and his literary creation can only be "akin" to genesis (p. 239), never a pure genesis in itself. Melville probably felt no Puritan guilt over any "stains" on his imagination. He wrote and borrowed to the end. Those borrowings, then, offer readers an *entrée* into Melville's creative process and the relationship with his audience. They can be grouped as classical allusions and models; cultural themes, types, and models; and contemporary allusions.

Classical Allusions and Models

According to Nathalia Wright, *The Confidence-Man* is exceeded in Biblical allusions only by *Clarel, Moby-Dick,* and *Billy Budd.* The opening references to St. Paul set the theme of charity and are met at the end with "antiphonal" allusions to the Apocrypha. Throughout, we hear Melville's favorites, the Solomonic and disillusioned "wisdom writers" (*Bible,* pp. 9, 101). Some idea of the full texture of Biblical allusion can be found in the notes to Foster's and Franklin's editions. In addition, Quirk argues that the con man's disguises mock St. Paul's "types of the faithful" as revealed in I Corinthians. The likelihood of this is strengthened by Quirk's observation that the relevant Pauline scriptures were part of the Episcopalian order of service that Melville would have read while enmeshed in his novel (*Knave to Knight,* p. 67). Margaret Bruner also provides a Biblical commentary on the man with gold sleeve-buttons.

Melville had used the ship-microcosm image in earlier works, but the ship of fools concept may derive from Sebastian Brant's *Das Narrenschiff* which, according to Edward H. Rosenberry, Melville may have read in translation or heard of through Burton's *Anatomy of Melancholy.* Rosenberry also argues in "Melville's Ship of Fools" that *Cock Lorrel's Boat* is a more likely source. Ben Jonson was another Renaissance favorite, and acting on hints from William Ellery Sedgwick and Rosenberry, Jay H. Hartman has investigated sources in *Volpone* (see also Jane Mushabac, p. 139). Quirk fruitfully examines the important Cervantes connection (*Knave to Knight,* pp. 89–101), and Mildred K. Travis and Carole Moses find hints and echoes of Spenser in their separate studies. Shakespeare is an important but rarely discussed source: Larzer Ziff briefly observes that Melville denies his Shakespearean references their "expressibility" (p. 66); Quirk argues unconvincingly that Melville patterned his five interpolations on answers to five questions posed in Hamlet's soliloquy (p. 122); and Vincent F. Petronella links the final scene (again, unconvincingly) to bits of *Macbeth.*

Supplementing Henry F. Pommer's identification of expropriations from *Paradise Lost* is Thomas L. McHaney's view that Melville modeled the con man's disguises on Satan's. Satan first appears as a golden-haired cherub, and this is good evidence that the fleecy mute can be included as one of the con men, but most of Satan's other guises (except the snake) do not fit. From a philosophical rather than purely literary angle, Fred E. Brouwer argues that Melville's con men are modeled on a logical progression of various philosophers including Shaftesbury, Berkeley, Bishop Butler, and William Paley. But the most exhaustive research into a model for Melville's novel is Helen P. Trimpi's study of Commedia Dell'Arte, the Italian tradition of Harlequin and other clowns which came to America via French and British versions and offered Melville a panoply of pantomimic characters to draw on. Melville was probably not as relentless in his borrowings as Trimpi is in her research, but it is undeniable that the novel's theatricality stems from aspects of Harlequinade, and future studies of Melville's exposure to low comedy performances on Broadway in the late 1840s would be welcome.

Cultural Themes, Types, and Models

In some form or another—either as trickster, picaro, peddler, or knave—the con man has appeared throughout the literature and lore of all cultures, primitive and modern, East and West. But the actual locution "confidence man" did not come into being until 1849 when diddler William Thompson was apprehended in New York. Thompson's epithet derives from his m.o. of explicitly asking for the confidence and then money of strangers. Jay Leyda passed along to Foster an 1855 newspaper reference to Thompson (a.k.a. Samuel Willis) who died soon after while residing in Sing Sing. Paul Smith later reported another find: Evert Duyckinck's reprinting of an August 1849 editorial in the *Merchant's Ledger* on the humanity of being susceptible to a con game. But it was Johannes Bergmann who found the earliest mention of "the original confidence man" in the New York *Herald*; in a fine essay he pulled together these and other references which show the topicality and cultural ambiguity of Melville's central character. A point noted by all of these scholars is the existence of John Brougham's play or interlude, "The Confidence Man," which delighted theater-goers in 1849. Thus far, the piece has not been found. Perhaps a script never existed, but scenarios printed on as-yet undiscovered playbills might give some inkling of the nature of the little comedy.

The recent popularity of *The Confidence-Man* has inspired a remarkable number of book-length treatments of the con man as both an ageless cultural figure and a modern literary device used by Melville, Twain, James, as well as major twentieth-century (American and European) prose writers. Some have focused specifically on the con man's roots in early American humor, in particular Johnson Hooper's Simon Suggs. While they do not discuss Melville, Kenneth S. Lynn, Walter Blair, and Blair and Hamlin Hill provide important background on the development of the con man within the American humor and tall tale traditions. Susan Kuhlmann explores the aesthetic and metaphysical potentials of these materials. More recently, William E. Lenz argues that we cannot fully understand the con man unless we recognize him as the product of a particular historical moment, the expansive "flush times" of the 1840s. As a comic device, the con man allowed readers to identify with and control their social anxieties. Despite his severe narrative distancing (which normally lessens the rhetorical effectiveness of the con man figure), Melville's "variation" on the convention succeeds (pp. 117–36). Karen Halttunen's study of attitudes toward urban con men as expressed in the manner books of the 1830s and 1850s is an important corrective to Lenz's rural orientation.

The frontier plays a complex role in *The Confidence-Man*. The "all-fusing spirit of the West" (*CM*, p. 9) symbolizes both optimism and ominous expansionism. Melville experienced the American frontier directly in his early trip to Galena (John W. Nichol; G. Thomas Tanselle) and indirectly in his reading. In "Wicked River," John Seelye provides strong parallels between Melville's river references (including "The River") and Timothy Flint's *Recollections of . . . the Mississippi Valley* (1826) and *History and Geography of the Mississippi Valley* (1828). Seelye argues that Melville's rejection of his colorful River fragment suggests that he did not feel the epical description was appropriate for his tight social satire and that his discussion is evidence of "Melville's increased craftsmanship and versatility" (p. 79). Harrison Hayford provides minor corrections to Seelye's on-target thesis, offering as well an anonymous pamphlet describing John Banvard's *Panorama of the Mississippi* as another source (*CM*, pp. 511–18). Edwin Fussell's important study, *Frontier* (1965), speculates a bit on Western sources but focuses mainly on Melville's deliberate exaggeration of frontier cliches found in James Hall's discussion of Indian-hating in *Sketches of History, Life and Manners in the West* (1835). Douglas Robillard offers additional Indian-hating sources.

Carolyn L. Karcher's "Spiritualism and Philanthropy in Brownson's *The Spirit Rapper* and Melville's *The Confidence-Man*" (1979) is not so much a source study linking the two designated texts as it is a fascinating examination of Melville's liberal America and the varying ways in which "occultism and radical social protest" merge (p. 35). Equally fascinating and yet rarely used is Ted N. Weissbuch's explication of counterfeit detectors which in Melville's day were used by banks to "puff" certain weak currencies and were therefore as unreliable as Frank Goodman says they are. Finally, it seems clear that the barber shop scene in which Goodman diddles William Cream is modeled on a standard joke motif of the day. See Hershel Parker (*CM*, pp. 264–66); Donald Yannella; Tom Quirk (*Knave to Knight*, pp. 163–65); and David R. Sewell ("Another Source").

Contemporary Allusions

Since many assume *The Confidence-Man* to be a satire and since satires are sharpest when, according to Edward Rosenheim, they attack "historical particulars" (real people, events, or controversies), it is only natural for scholars to correlate Melville's characters to specific individuals he might have known or known of. Hayford's essay identifying the crazy beggar in the Winsome episode as Poe is a model for all source hunters. In it, Hayford offers sound criteria for judging a possible source. The character and its original should share "conspicuous details of their physical appearance, of their previous careers, and of their known attitudes and philosophies" (p. 207). We might add that a comparison is more or less convincing depending on how Melville's presumed attack fits into his overall argument and whether Melville's readers would have recognized the portrait. *The Confidence-Man* is far from being a *Fable for Critics*; its satiric butts, if they exist at all, are deeply submerged. Melville may have inserted quiet thrusts at personal acquaintances and public figures for whatever private reasons, but it is equally true that no satiric thrust may have been intended, that, as Hayford puts it, "the actual persons brought into the fiction were used as available and appropriate embodiments of relevant ideas and attitudes, not simply as themselves" (p. 215).

No doubt, however, exists that Melville had Emerson in mind when he created Mark Winsome. But a small controversy surrounds the attribution. Egbert S. Oliver was the first to organize a case in terms of physical and philosophical resemblances. Less convincing, although understandable, is his assertion that Winsome's disciple Egbert is Thoreau. Using different and more reliable evidence, Foster agreed with Oliver about Winsome but strongly argued against his latter formulation. She sees Winsome and Egbert as two sides of Emersonianism, its moonshine metaphysics and its cold ethics (pp. lxxii–iv). Since Egbert does not resemble Thoreau physically or temperamentally, Foster's point about Thoreau, like her entire argument, is well taken. In "Some Legends in Melville Scholarship" (1968), Sidney Moss also attacks Oliver's slim evidence and assumption that Melville is an anti-Transcendentalist. In 1970 Parker evaluated the evidence concerning Emerson and Thoreau. He chided Moss for inventing legends that did not exist, reminded us of Foster's work, but acknowledged that, given new evidence unavailable to Foster or Oliver, there may, in fact, be some truth in connecting Thoreau to Egbert. Mercifully, nothing further has followed of this masquerade.

Oliver's identification of Goneril as flamboyant actress Fanny Kemble has also stirred controversy. Foster objects strenuously to the assumption that Melville would savagely attack the somewhat masculine actress when Kemble appeared to be an "impulsive, loving, generous woman" (p. 313).

Robert Sattelmeyer and James Barbour's unearthing of the children's magazine *The China Aster* as a model for the interpolated tale about the unfortunate candle maker of that name is a more convincing endeavor. None of the many homiletic tales in the magazine's nine volumes matches Melville's. But one, an inverted version about the *success* of a man who *refuses* a loan from a Mr. *Chandler*, may be slyly parodied in Melville's tale of a *chandler* who *fails* because he *accepts* a loan. In any event, Melville's secret purpose is to undercut those "pulpit philosophers who reduced complexities to platitudes" (p. 578).

The mute has inspired much speculation. Is he one of the con men or a symbol of ineffectual and recumbent Christianity? Paschal Reeves conjectures that the curious figure may be based on an as yet unidentified gentleman who in 1850 posed as a deaf and dumb "Herman Melville" in the Southern states. Jane Donahue Eberwein illuminates the association between the mute and Manco Capac by drawing attention to Joel Barlow's depiction of that Incan deity as a "pious fraud" in *The Columbiad*. Ernest Tuveson finds a similar source in the work of traveler von Tschudi (p. 250). The cosmopolitan has attracted even more attention. Wright compares him to Cooper's Steadfast Dodge in *Homeward Bound*; Hans-Joachim Lang and Benjamin Lease find a likely source for Goodman in Bayard Taylor; Seelye argues in " 'Ungraspable Phantom' " (1969) that the Goodman-Noble encounter parodies Hawthorne and Melville's failed friendship. Finally, in " 'Nowhere a Stranger,' " Bryant proposes that the cosmopolitan was as much an identifiable cultural type as the con man and that Melville's readers were culturally conditioned to be suspicious of any self-professed frontier cosmopolite. Born out of the eighteenth-century Enlightenment, on American soil the figure became associated with such protean and unprincipled operators as merchant Vincent Nolte and evangelist Lorenzo Dow.

William M. Ramsey ("Melville's and Barnum's Man with a Weed") cleverly ties the transmutation of Black Guinea into John Ringman (the man with a weed) to a Barnum hoax in which a Negro is made to turn white through a medicinal "weed." Trimpi, however, links Ringman to William Cullen Bryant. She also relates the man in gray to Theodore Parker, and the PIO man to Horace Greeley ("Three of Melville's Confidence Men"). Finally, William Norris provides some enticing parallels (but no smoking gun) between the man with gold sleeve-buttons and Abbott Lawrence, a Northern philanthropist who profited from Southern slavery.

RECEPTION AND REVIVAL: "YEA AND NAY—EACH HATH HIS SAY"

By 1855 Melville's readership had markedly dwindled, and some of his more loyal followers (acknowledging him as a "prose-poet") wished out loud that he would return to sea romancing. Speaking of *The Confidence-Man*, Fitz-James O'Brien blended wishful thinking and criticism to predict that the novel was "one of those books everyone will buy, many persons read, and very few understand" (*Crit. Her.*, p. 356). He was right on one count—few understood the book—but sadly in error on the other two, for almost no one bought it or read it. Presumably, Melville's brand of literary metaphysics was better suited for the ocean than the town, and certainly not a Mississippi steamboat.

Nevertheless, the reviews of *The Confidence-Man* registered neither total adulation nor contempt but on the whole a kind of troubled bemusement. To be sure, extreme pronouncements were made. One reviewer found the novel "graphic, fresh, and entertaining" (*Crit. Her.*, p. 372); another complained that it was a "tangled web of obscurity" (p. 375). But Ann Stephens's brief yet insightful notice typifies many of the responses. She appreciated Melville's improved "sinewy and compact" style but allowed that the book could just as easily be read backwards as forwards (p. 384). In short, Melville's first readers, like today's, did not know exactly what to make of *The Confidence-Man*, and their confusion over its form, style, and humor prefigured modern critical assessments.

To begin with, the earliest critics did not know what to call *The Confidence-Man*. It was neither novel (*Literary Gazette*) nor romance (*New York Times*). The reviewer for the *Athenaeum*, for instance, perceived a stage and elaborate scenery but could detect "no drama"; he called the book a "morality enacted by masqued players" (p. 371). The *New York Times* likened the book to "a Rabelaisian piece of patch work" (p. 378), and the *Westminster Review* identified the *Fidèle* as an "epitome" of the American world. At least two reviewers recognized *The Confidence-Man* as a satire either on America's money-making monomania (*Saturday Review*) or "the gullibility of the Great Republic" (*Westminster Review*). But this was not an age that relished satire, no matter how richly deserved, and an ill-tempered satire had no place among good-natured readers. Thus, Melville's style, humor, and excessive originality were significant topics for discussion.

Fitz-James O'Brien's sympathetic admonitions address the problems of tone and voice: Melville is "a man born to create, who resolves to anatomize; a man born to see, who insists upon speculation." He cannot balance head and heart, insight and style. He "persist[s] in distorting the images of his mind, and in deodorizing the flowers of his fancy" (pp. 364–65). Similarly, the *Literary Gazette* argued that Melville's rambling narrative was the result of "excessive originality." If the author wished to present his readers with the "*vrai*," he must "pay . . . some slight attention to the *vraisemblable*" (p. 375).

But not all critics agreed. The *New York Times* rejoiced in Melville's "rollicking inspirations" (p. 378). Several reviewers noted Melville's growing "mastery" over language (*Athenaeum*) and his effective use of "neutral tints" (*Leader*). But if O'Brien (whose own style could have used a bit of deodorizing itself) was advising Melville to achieve a style already evident in *The Confidence-Man*, his final comments concerning deficiencies in Melville's humor strike home. Whereas George W. Curtis might be faulted for a paltry imagination, Melville exhibits too much fancy and too little taste; he is too "grave in his gayeties" (p. 368). The *Westminster Review* agreed: *The Confidence-Man*'s "absence of humour" implied an "absence of kindliness"; it was a book written "too much in the spirit of Timon" (p. 385). The *Literary Gazette* suggested Melville's humor was a "hoax on the public—an emulation of Barnum." Anticipating modern readers who almost uniformly recognize the novel's narrator as something of a con man, the reviewer also conjectured that "the mild man in mourning [Ringman]...is an emblem of Mr. Melville himself imploring toleration for 353 pages of rambling" (p. 375).

Unfortunately, *The Confidence-Man* did not receive as favorable a critique as any of the first reviews until the 1930s and 1940s. During Melville's final years and on into the early 1900s when his work was slowly gaining recognition, the book was generally dismissed (when treated at all) as baffling, unreadable, and incomprehensible. Moreover, the Melville revivalists did little to resuscitate *The Confidence-Man* from critical neglect; indeed, some of their responses were downright vicious. Frank Jewett Mather called it "dreary" (*Recognition*, p. 168); John Freeman felt it was the "vainest of satires" and "a failure in intelligence" (pp. 140–41). Weaver ironically labeled it a "posthumous work," but Van Wyck Brooks capped them all, vilifying the novel as "an abortion" (p. 2). Carl Van Vechten was virtually alone in praising *The Confidence-Man* as "the great transcendental satire" starring Emerson as the confidence man (p. 19).

More level-headed judgments arrived with the works of Lewis Mumford (1929), Yvor Winters (1938), F. O. Matthiessen (1941) and William Ellery Sedgwick (1944). But none of these divergent critics gave the problematic novel much of a berth, and each assumed the work to be a failure. In his literary biography Mumford derides the dismal views of Mather, Freeman, and Weaver but does not address Van Vechten at all. Mark Winsome, for him, is not Emerson but simply "the original pragmatist" (p. 251). In all, the novel's title character "represents all the sweetness and morality of the race" that "had become for Melville the greatest of frauds" (p. 252). Mumford explicitly resists the temptation to read "indirect revelations of Melville's own life" into the tantalizing Goneril, Indian-hater, and Charlemont sections. But the biographer finally succumbs to temptation, speculating that the book "may be considered as Melville's own masquerade, his own bitter plea for support, money, confidence" (p. 254).

Winters argues that *The Confidence-Man* is the product not of mental disorder but of an intellectual impasse or "moral limbo" (p. 85), the same state of mind that also led to "obscurantism" in other American writers. Like *Pierre*, the novel's "absolute ambiguity" (p. 82) incapacitates our facility to judge and denies "the reasonable skepticism of the cautious and critical man" (p. 83). Winters's controversial thesis does well to ignore the biographical approach, but its assurance that "cautious and critical" people exist or that their skepticism can be "reasonable" is the kind of grand assumption that Melville was trying to subvert in his reader. Matthiessen spends little time on the novel except to complain that it should have been written by Twain or James. Melville's use of the *Fidèle* as a microcosm of American life aptly focuses attention on "a commercial society . . . increasingly corrupted by greed" (p. 410). But the author sends his characters off too quickly for his narrator to weave a fabric of social interaction.

Sedgwick's *Tragedy of Mind* (1944) does not dwell on *The Confidence-Man*'s novelistic shortcomings. Focusing on the "amazing ductibility" of Melville's consciousness, he isolates the author's "self possession" as the ability to balance those "profounder workings of the human mind" and one's sense of a "sovereign" self (pp. 7, 12, 17). Turning at first with faint praise to *The Confidence-Man*'s "strong, tough intellection," Sedgwick eventually registers a deeper appreciation for the book's subtle revelations of consciousness, especially with Moredock, that "diluted Indian-hater" whose very hatred reveals him to be "a true believer in his kind" (p. 192).

Richard Chase's celebratory essay on *The Confidence-Man* (1949) marked the end of years of neglect and scorn for Melville's problem novel and the beginning of a new age of rapt acceptance. No longer "an abortion," the comedy became Melville's "second best book" and the subject of over one hundred articles and monographs.

CRITICISM: "TRUTH-HUNTERS, AND STILL KEENER HUNTERS"

Critical interest in *The Confidence-Man* grew slowly following Chase's "rediscovery," then broke loose in the 1960s and 1970s with an average of about thirty articles a decade devoted solely to the work. The present decade shows no sign of abatement. Although a consensus of what the novel "means" or "does" is unlikely, we can at least articulate the novel's recurrent critical problems. What is the novel's genre? If allegory, is the confidence man Devil or God? If satire, what are the novel's political, social, or humanistic norms? If norms cannot be determined, what is the effect on the reader? Does the novel's apocalyptic vision signal an end or a new beginning for man? What is the nature of confidence and what are its ontological ramifications? Does the novel's epistemological dilemma suggest nihilism and the failure of language, form, and fiction? Or does the comedy contain, while it exposes, subversive impulses that ultimately reveal Melville's artistic control over his material? The following "sampler" cannot begin to abstract each of the many critical works devoted to *The Confidence-Man*; however, it does attempt to encompass the major critical perspectives associated with the book.

Myth and Folklore: "Shrewdness and Mythiness, Strangely Jumbled"

The Confidence-Man is an alembic of Western, Eastern, and native folk materials. For Richard Chase, the con man (a "portmanteau" figure uniting folk and classical heroes) reveals as much about America's immediate political dilemma as its past social rituals. The figure personifies America's lack of moral and social vision. A "false Prometheus," he maintains a cynical "neutrality" amidst controversy that "unmans" the spirit of reform. Chase concludes by exhorting his postwar colleagues wavering between Stalinism and reaction to rejuvenate their embattled liberalism. In *Form and Fable* (1961), Daniel Hoffman borrows some of Chase's terms, expands the con game into a "type of the Fall of Man" (p. 281), but finds fault in Melville's attempt to create "allegory without the superstructure of belief, and dialectic without the possibility of resolution." Thus, where Chase sees a timely moral imperative, the less polemical Hoffman finds an undeniable "satiric power," won, however, "at the cost of a larger failure...of form" (p. 310).

H. Bruce Franklin disagrees; for him, the novel is "Melville's most nearly perfect work" (*Wake of the Gods*, p. 153). With varying degrees of success, his study of Melville's awareness of nineteenth-century comparative mythology and use of Eastern myth links each con man to the progressive gods who appear in the Hindu masquerade or Huli (an April Fool's celebration). In brief, the con man is both creator (Vishnu) and destroyer (Siva). Melville's joke on both man and reader is that our Savior and Satan are One, a cosmic and comic union signalled in the novel's apocalyptic conclusion.

Allegory: "The Comedy of Thought"

In one sense, *The Confidence-Man* is the creation of a romancer trying to write a novel that became an allegory. Whatever its intended form, the final product is surely didactic, or at least partly so. Thus, the argument that the novel is an allegory of one sort or another has wide acceptance. John W. Shroeder's early study ("Sources and Symbols") established many of the terms that have shaped the allegorical perspective. Finding its roots in Bunyan and Hawthorne's "Celestial Railroad," he argues that the con men are multiple disguises of the Devil who lures us toward easy, superficial forms of faith. Only the Indian-hater can see through the deception and provide a "strong purge" for a "severe disease" (p. 314). Shroeder's careful discussion of demonic symbolism becomes reductive when he attempts to elevate the image pattern to a governing structure and moral vision. In rebuttal Roy Harvey Pearce examines Melville's respect for Indians and his scorn for his sources to argue that the author "has no more praise for Indian-hating than he does for confidence. Both are false, blind, unreasoning" (p. 948). Similarly, Fussell sees Indian-hater Moredock as a con man whose exploitation of land and humanity Melville reduces to absurdity. By cutting through Judge Hall's platitudes, Melville helps us sharpen our skepticism and become more like Pitch (pp. 319, 325). Joyce Sparer Adler agrees with Pearce and Fussell, claiming that to call Indian-hating positive is like misreading "A Modest Proposal" (p. 424).

Foster draws on the best of Shroeder and Pearce and adds insights of her own. She acknowledges the novel's devil imagery but agrees with Pearce in rejecting the Indian-hater as a hero. However, she modifies Pearce's dark assessment of the hopeless clash between hatred and confidence. Ultimately, we side with the victims whose goodness fails them (p. 341). Although Melville distrusts God and nature, he "stops short of Timonism" (see, however, Charles N. Watson) and clings to man with "a sort of last ditch humanism" (p. lxxxix). More than anyone before her, Foster outlined the novel's complex allegorical structure which she called "as formal as a fugue" (p. xci). In decoding this "cipher," she discerns a progression of satires following each con man and focusing on different defects in optimism (Shaftesburyean benevolence, utilitarianism, Emersonianism, faith, hope, charity). In all, the book reveals "the failure of Christians to be Christian" (p. liii). James E. Miller, Jr., goes further, saying that Melville's "universal allegory" shows Christianity to be unworkable.

Calling *The Confidence-Man* a "consistent allegory" and "grotesque" satire on Christians "giving lip service" to their religion, Hershel Parker, in "The Metaphysics of Indian-Hating" (pp. 322 and 326), supports the Indian-hater as moral norm by arguing that for the true Christian love is a hatred of evil. He cites Biblical authority for this paradox and concludes that this "darker side of Christianity" clarifies Melville's allegorical injunction for us all to be devil haters. Although Parker's thesis has enjoyed significant but not (according to Mary K. Madison) total acceptance, it, like many allegorical interpretations, does not account for the full rhetorical context of Melville's Indian-hating tale which, as William Ramsey reminds us in "Moot Points" (1980), is told by Noble to persuade Goodman about Pitch's misanthropy. Necessarily bound up in Noble's character, it is a "teasing tautology" and, therefore, incapable of revealing the novel's moral norm. Going beyond character altogether, Edward Mitchell looks to the novel's "repetitive activity," the transaction of confidence, for its normative values and concludes that anyone "who can neither solicit nor place confidence is outside the realm of humanity" (p. 33).

Melville's allegory can be ontological, aesthetic, or political as well as religious. Edwin Honig sees the con man as a Quixotic "reformer-imposter," progressing toward a deeper consciousness with every new disguise. Taking a similar approach, Stephen A. Barney has also argued that "the uneasy fit" of novel and allegory in *The Confidence-Man* "is not only Melville's manner, but his theme" (p. 144). Since Chase, many have read the novel as an allegory of the failure of America's democratic experiment. In this camp (which includes Fussell and Adler), we find Sumner's view that the West helps Melville depict a corrupt nation failing to avert impending civil war. Karcher insists that Melville's treatment of blacks reveals a similar prophecy of national crisis (see also Kaplan). Michael Paul Rogin ties the novel's attack on American commerce and authority to the dynamics of Melville's family life, in particular his father's business failure. In "Mercantile Philosophy" (1984), Sewell argues that Melville denies the synthesis of Christianity and commerce proposed by such boosters as Freeman Hunt of the *Merchant's Magazine*. Placing Melville's book in the developing tradition of American romance (see also Joel Porte), not allegory, Michael Davitt Bell contends that Melville's aggressive "verbal advance" on the reader (p. 235) undermines the steady "relation" of fiction to reality. The duplicity of his romance, then, is a metaphor of society's duplicity (p. 195); thus, "America" itself becomes a fiction.

Narrative Indirection: "Who's That Describing the Confidence-man?"

The biggest impediment to a definitive allegorical or political reading may well be the unreliability of the detached narrator. Drawing specific correlations between image and idea or even finding general normative values is at best problematic and, for many, impossible. It has, thus, become a commonplace to call Melville's narrator the novel's true confidence man and the reader his dupe. Lawrance Thompson first introduced the idea of Melville's narrative indirections by arguing that the author hides his blasphemies beneath the shallow Christian ramblings of a "stupid narrator" (p. 300) who cannot see the con man and our unjust God for what they are. John G. Cawelti isolates the structural cause of Melville's ambiguities and their final effect in the narrator's persistent "incomplete reversals" (p. 282). The cosmopolitan, for instance, appears to be admirable until he dupes the barber, but this reversal neither proves nor disproves his guilt. The reader is left hanging, and the novel ultimately proposes no moral. Merlin Bowen pinpoints other "tactics of indirection" but contends that Melville's ironies and ambiguities do, in fact, promote clear moral imperatives. Although "an amoral God" (p. 406), the con man is balanced by the existence of Moredock, the more palatable Pitch, and their refusal to be moderate. Much like Chase, Bowen ends by chastening us not to coexist with evil.

R.W.B. Lewis specifically identifies the narrator as a con man whose aim is to question our ability to know (see also John G. Blair, *The Confidence Man*). Edgar A. Dryden's influential study, *Melville's Thematics of Form* (1968), expands this epistemological perspective to encompass ontology and aesthetics. He argues that Melville's pronounced authorial intrusions reveal an abandonment of "truth seeking forms" (p. 151). Ultimately, Melville's "wordy" novel destroys itself as all "wise" fictions should (p. 124). Stephen E. Kemper shows how the narrator's feigned ignorance leads to a similar destruction of fiction. For Christopher W. Sten, the epistemological dilemma reaches a "perpetual state of crisis" involving "an endless series of anxiety-producing yet absurdly comic confrontations" (p. 181); hence, *The Confidence-Man* is a "New Novel" à la Robbe-Grillet. Finally, it might be argued that Melville's bewildering narrative indirections are not so much deliberate fictive ploys as acts of aggression symptomatic of a deeper pathology. Drawing upon Freud and Erikson, C. Barry Chabot argues that Melville's non-identification with a quester in the novel sets up mechanisms that release him from the anxiety of ambivalence but that create painful doubts in the reader. This is a slight switch on Edwin Haviland Miller's own Eriksonian view that *The Confidence-Man* is an expression of the "pain of parental rejection" (p. 280).

Warwick Wadlington's recondite but insightful rhetorical analysis of *The Confidence Game in American Literature* (1975) shows (*contra* Dryden) that Melville used the con man device to advance his ontological mission of "disturb[ing] ... readers into fresh vision" (p. 140). Rather than falling apart because of its self-conscious fictionality, *The Confidence-Man* cons us into a stronger sense of being while the con man becomes a creator, poet, indeed god. If Wadlington's rhetorical critique smacks of structuralism, Henry Sussman's post-structural analysis in the pages of *Glyph* smacks of rhetoric. Like too many deconstructionist pieces (see Thomas P. Joswick), "The Deconstructor as Politician" (1978) reads like a private letter to other deconstructionists about a party to which the rest of us were not invited. Sussman argues that *The Confidence-Man* dramatizes the self-destruction of a philosophical system through the stylized interactions between writers (con men) and readers (their victims). Witnessing not the "rise" but the "wake" of deconstructionism, Sussman ends, again like Chase, with an exhortation to his fellow deconstructors to throw down their metonyms and abandon the self-serving realms of academe for a wider "social context" or what Sussman calls "out there" and what I would call any place where they don't read *Glyph*.

Melville's use of language is a crucial aspect of his narrative strategy. Warner Berthoff considers Melville's "strange, halting, self-referential style" to be "the surest measure" of his message (*"The Confidence-Man,"* p. 127). Characterizing certain passages as "ponderous stuttering" (EXAMPLE, p. 166), he (along with Foster, Rosenberry, and Buell) also notes the grace and rhythm of some of the author's often paragraph-long periods. Lewis and many others, for instance, have remarked on the linguistic *tour de force* in Melville's "self-erasing" description of the man with gold sleeve-buttons (Lewis, p. 64), making that passage one of the most frequently cited throughout the criticism. Cecelia Tichi, however, argues that Melville presents us with a deliberately "debased" language that reflects deeper social debasements (principally Wall Street). Readers are charged to discern the shallowness of bad (i.e., punning) logic and the egocentric use of ethical terms. A number of works focus on the more positive aspects of Melville's word games. In " 'Touching' Scenes" (1979) William Ramsey provides a nice touch on the Goneril tale; John Wenke thinks "Charlemont" is an anagram for Charlie (Noble) and Timon (of Athens), except the *i*'s are plucked out; William Bysshe Stein runs on about the metaphysics of Melville's "logorrhea"; and John G. Blair argues in "Puns and Equivocations" (1974) that Melville uses the pun as "a weapon exemplifying the thematic core of the work" (p. 92). Finally, Rebecca J. Gaudino, observing in the novel what she considers to be "an abundance of writing utensils, readers, writers, and texts," tries to elevate a minor pattern into a major statement: "all mankind becomes a text" (p. 127).

Comedy or Despair: "Seeming to Dispense a Sort of Morning Through the Night"

Whether *The Confidence-Man* is a work of negation or affirmation is a richly contested matter. Early critics saw it as Melville's most nihilistic novel (Arvin, p. 251) and the product of "a miserable compulsion" (Matthiessen, p. 340). Since then, Melville's nihilism has been observed to encompass all realms: historical, theological, epistemological, ontological, aesthetic. But no matter how much America, Christianity, Knowledge, Being, and Fiction may be seen as dead-ends, the novel remains a comedy. True, what Melville called "our comedy" may have been wishful thinking (or sarcasm), for his barely submerged cynicism drains the novel of that "lightness of being" that allows comedy to soar. As Leon Howard puts it, Melville's satire runs afoul of its own barbs and never reaches the balance of Shakespeare's "higher and lighter" comedy (p. 229). Indeed, the Shandean humor in Melville's "philosophical leg-pull" (Rosenberry, *Comic Spirit*, pp. 146–48 and 142) can easily escape us. But such humor is a version of "camp," according to Paul Brodtkorb, Jr., in which "the strain, not the humor, . . . amuses" (p. 421). To make matters worse, Melville uses comedy self-consciously as a topic of debate, aligning wit, irony, satire, and misanthropy against humor, good nature, geniality, and philanthropy. But no matter how strained or self-conscious, the "deep thought of laughter" (*Mardi*, p. 613) in *The Confidence-Man* suggests an artistic and psychological control that transcends utter nihilism. What Matthiessen derides, then, as the novel's "diagrammatic abstraction," Rosenberry hails as "the totality of . . . comic detachment." While the existence of Melville's humor, then, is incontestable, its form and final effect remain open to discussion.

Lewis and Seelye place *The Confidence-Man* in the picaresque tradition, the former also identifying the cosmopolitan as Everyman (p. 70) and the latter contending that the novel shows "Christianity mak[ing] suckers of us all" (*Ironic Diagram*, p. 122). Arthur L. Madson attempts to apply Frye's definition of comedy (the hero's integration into society) by claiming that the con man "disintegrates" along with a disintegrating society (p. 75). Probably Alexander C. Kern's undeveloped suggestion that the novel is in Frye's terms a Mennippean prose satire or anatomy is more likely (see also Gerard W. Shepherd). As with allegory, the problem of finding normative values is crucial to a satiric interpretation. Thus, what Walter Dubler identifies as the satire's imperfect dialectic between faith and distrust (p. 306) presents problems for such a genre classification. If Melville offers no synthesis, he nevertheless articulates the conflict between two unsatisfactory Americas: the old, preoccupied with benevolence, and the new, "occupied with the practice of fraud" (p. 319). Philip Drew contends that Melville's deliberate ambiguities are functional. Although the narrator swings for and against confidence, we can discern "a consistent satire against the lack of confidence" (p. 437).

Arguing from a comedic and not satiric perspective, Stanley Trachtenberg claims that Melville "disguise[s] the limits imposed on [appearance and reality]" and "questions the jurisdiction of any norm" (p. 39). Free of "normative ideals," we enjoy the con man's role-playing; it insures sanity. For Lawrence Buell, the novel is "a carefully-constructed muddle" in which "delight *and* . . . meaning" grow out of our detached laughter in observing Melville's "sly balance between possibilities suggested and the secret withheld" (pp. 20 and 26). Elizabeth Keyser rises above the muddle to find a positive synthesis in the cosmopolitan, who, "radically distinct" from his predecessors, exhibits "a healthy balance between . . . meekness and . . . misanthropy" (p. 280).

Foster and others have argued that *The Confidence-Man* is essentially a satire against the "philosophy of geniality" rampant in the age (Joseph

Flibbert, p. 149). But some claim that Melville does not attack benevolence as a false or dangerous mentality. Tuveson, for instance, contends that Melville attempts to bolster, not condemn, the Rousseauistic philosophy of "Tout Est Bien" which was losing ground in antebellum America and falling prey to the kind of "false prophet" Melville depicts in Winsome. Tuveson concludes that confidence may be illusory, but it is also a psychic necessity. According to Bryant's "Comic Debate," this need is rooted in the "instinct" of geniality (see Sealts, "Melville's Geniality") that is as compelling as its opposing instinct of demonism. The conflict of these instincts appears in the growth of the con man and genialist in the magazine pieces which finally merge in the notion of the genial misanthrope found in *The Confidence-Man*.

Leon F. Seltzer's application of Camus to *The Confidence-Man*, although anachronistic, is nevertheless illuminating, especially as a means of accounting for Melville's nihilistic, yet affirmative, perspectives. For Seltzer, the con man is an absurd man who recognizes the "groundlessness" of confidence (indeed all existence) and yet explores the limits of reason (p. 15). Melville's comedy "laments" the invalidity of confidence while it examines the consequences of metaphysical and ethical nihilism. Richard Boyd Hauck's "Nine Good Jokes" (1981) expands on his reading in *Cheerful Nihilism* (1971) as it supplements Seltzer. In exploring the existential nature of confidence, he, too, notes that Melville "laments the impossibility of verifying" true charity but argues that "confidence must begin somewhere" (p. 279). Thus, we invent confidence as we would our own being. Along these same lines, Paul Brodtkorb views "the con man as hero." Devoid of sincerity or consistency, man's true being is best revealed in his "masquerading" (p. 428), an activity the cosmopolitan raises to an art (p. 432). We admire this "arch con man" because his motives are pure (he cheats for the sake of it) and his facility high. In "Melville's Masquerade" (1982) Wenke sees role-playing as a demonstration of the author's "self-possession" or assertion of will over literary material. Finally, Gary Lindberg's *The Confidence Man in American Literature* (1982) stresses the mimetic, not allegorical, nature of Melville's game-playing (p. 27). As America's "covert hero," the con man knows his masks are masks and exercises faith in the ability to connect the outward world of his social games with his inward world of being (pp. 3, 40, 45).

"SOMETHING FURTHER MAY FOLLOW OF THIS MASQUERADE"

Almost every critic of *The Confidence-Man* has yielded to the understandable temptation of cleverly working Melville's famous last line into a statement of the never-ending debate associated with the book. But that convention has become tiresome, and, accordingly, I began this project vowing not to end with this stale line. But I have failed. There, at the head of my conclusion sits the Melvillean's weary credo with all its vaguely nauseous hints of critical infinitude and meaningless word play. This, however, is only just, for something further most certainly will follow in the criticism of *The Confidence-Man*. Readers continue to be alive to the peculiar problems of this tight fiction that manages to encompass such disparate realms: America and the nature of being, advent and apocalypse, allegory and drama, laughter and despair. These cannot be exhausted in the secondary criticism. And I cannot presume to direct readers in any future paths of criticism except to suggest exploration in certain areas that strike me as valid and still fresh.

Here, then, are yet more problems: What effect might Melville's exposure in adolescence to revivalism have had on his characterization of Christians in *The Confidence-Man*? Can we find in the novel a consistent attitude toward the economic developments of the 1850s? How might the Broadway theatricals of the late 1840s have influenced Melville? Does Mikhail Bakhtin's study of Rabelais and Carnival or of the "dialogic" enhance our understanding of the novel's theatricality or narrative? Can Anne K. Mellor's impressive study of Romantic Irony or Thomas MacFarlane's on Originality and Imagination be used to resolve the novel's aesthetic problems? Finally, it seems clear that more use of the manuscripts and study of "The River" (if only as a distinct prose poem) are in order.

By virtue of its very problems, Melville's novel, like a Drummond Light, revolves and illuminates rather than obscures the deep structures of fiction and being. To grasp its full effect, we must, as readers, adopt in some sense the crafty yet ingenuous "cosmopolitan" sensibility in which it is offered. Thus, served up in whatever critical fashion—à la New, à la rhetorical, à la structural or post-structural—"that good dish," *The Confidence-Man*, will always delight. It is "a wine I never weary of comparing and sipping."

WORKS CITED

Adler, Joyce Sparer. "Melville on the White Man's War Against the American Indian." *Science and Society* 36 (Winter 1972): 417–42. Rev. in *War in Melville's Imagination*. New York: New York University Press, 1981, pp. 111–32.

Andrews, Deborah C. "Note on Melville's *Confidence Man*." *ESQ* No. 63 (Spring 1971): 27–28.

Arvin, Newton. *Herman Melville*. New York: William Sloane Associates, 1950.

Bach, Bert C. "Melville's Confidence-Man: Allegory, Satire, and the Irony of Intent." *Cithara* 8 (May 1969): 28–36.

Baim, Joseph. "The Confidence-Man as 'Trickster.'" *American Transcendental Quarterly* No. 1 (First Quarter 1969): 81–83.

Bakhtin, Mikhail. *The Dialogic Imagination, Four Essays.* Ed. Michael Holquist. Trans. Caryl Emerson and Michael Holquist. Austin: University of Texas Press, 1981.

———. *Rabelais and His World.* Trans. Helene Iswolsky. Cambridge, Mass.: MIT Press, 1981.

Barney, Stephen A. *Allegories of History, Allegories of Love.* Hamden, Conn.: Shoe String Press, 1979, pp. 144–71.

Bell, Michael Davitt. *The Development of American Romance: The Sacrifice of Relation.* Chicago: University of Chicago Press, 1980, pp. 194–246.

———. "Melville and 'Romance': Literary Nationalism and Fictional Form." *American Transcendental Quarterly* No. 24 (Fall 1974): 56–62.

Bergmann, Johannes Dietrich. "The Original Confidence Man." *American Quarterly* 21 (Fall 1969): 560–77.

Berthoff, Warner. *The Example of Melville.* Princeton, N.J.: Princeton University Press, 1962.

———. "Herman Melville: *The Confidence-Man.*" In *Landmarks of American Writing.* Ed. Hennig Cohen. New York: Basic Books, 1969, pp. 121–33.

Bewley, Marius. *The Eccentric Design: Form in the Classic American Novel.* New York: Columbia University Press, 1959.

Blair, John G. *The Confidence Man in Modern Fiction: A Rogue's Gallery with Six Portraits.* New York: Barnes & Noble, 1979, pp. 33–52.

———. "Puns and Equivocations in Melville's *The Confidence-Man.*" *American Transcendental Quarterly* No. 22 (Spring 1974): 91–95.

Blair, Walter. *Native American Humor (1800–1900).* New York: American Book Co., 1937.

———, and Hamlin Hill. *America's Humor: From Poor Richard to Doonesbury.* New York: Oxford University Press, 1978.

Bowen, Merlin. *The Long Encounter: Self and Experience in the Writings of Herman Melville.* Chicago: University of Chicago Press, 1960.

———. "Tactics of Indirection in Melville's *The Confidence-Man.*" *Studies in the Novel* 1 (Winter 1969): 401–20.

Branch, Watson G. "*The Confidence-Man: His Masquerade*: An Edition with Introduction and Notes." Ph.D. Diss., Northwestern University, 1970. [*Mel. Diss.*, #223.]

———. "The Genesis, Composition, and Structure of *The Confidence-Man.*" *Nineteenth-Century Fiction* 7 (March 1973): 424–48.

Brodtkorb, Paul, Jr. "*The Confidence-Man*: The Con-Man as Hero." *Studies in the Novel* 1 (Winter 1969): 421–35.

Brooks, Van Wyck. "Herman Melville." New York *Herald Tribune Books* (16 May 1926): 1–2.

Brouwer, Fred E. "Melville's *The Confidence-Man* as Ship of Philosophers." *Southern Humanities Review* 3 (Spring 1969): 158–65.

Bruner, Margaret. "Melville's 'Gentleman with the Gold Sleeve-Buttons.'" *Kentucky Philological Association Bulletin* (1981): 25–36.

Bryant, John. "Allegory and Breakdown in *The Confidence-Man*: Melville's Comedy of Doubt." *Philological Quarterly* 65 (Winter 1986): 113–30.

————. "Melville's Comic Debate: Geniality and the Aesthetics of Repose." *American Literature* 55 (May 1983): 151–70.

————. " 'Nowhere a Stranger': Melville and Cosmopolitanism." *Nineteenth-Century Fiction* 39 (December 1984): 275–91.

Buell, Lawrence. "The Last Word on *The Confidence-Man*?" *Illinois Quarterly* 35 (November 1972): 15–29.

Cawelti, John G. "Some Notes on the Structure of *The Confidence-Man*." *American Literature* 29 (November 1957): 278–88.

Chabot, C. Barry. "Melville's *The Confidence-Man*: A 'Poisonous' Reading." *Psychoanalytic Review* 63 (Winter 1976–77): 571–85.

Chase, Richard. "Melville's Confidence Man." *Kenyon Review* 11 (Winter 1949): 122–40.

Cohen, Hennig, ed. *The Confidence-Man: His Masquerade* by Herman Melville. New York: Holt, Rinehart & Winston, 1964.

Drew, Philip. "Appearance and Reality in Melville's *The Confidence-Man*." *ELH: A Journal of English Literary History* 31 (December 1964): 418–42.

Drinnon, Richard. *Facing West: The Metaphysics of Indian-Hating and Empire-Building*. Minneapolis: University of Minnesota Press, 1980.

Dryden, Edgar A. *Melville's Thematics of Form: The Great Art of Telling the Truth*. Baltimore: Johns Hopkins University Press, 1968, pp. 149–95.

Dubler, Walter. "Themes and Structure in Melville's *The Confidence-Man*." *American Literature* 33 (November 1961): 307–19.

Eberwein, Jane Donahue. "Joel Barlow and *The Confidence-Man*." *American Transcendental Quarterly* No. 24 (Fall 1974): 28–29.

Feidelson, Charles, Jr. *Symbolism and American Literature*. Chicago: University of Chicago Press, 1953.

Flibbert, Joseph. *Melville and the Art of Burlesque*. Amsterdam: Rodopi, 1974.

Foster, Elizabeth S., ed. *The Confidence-Man: His Masquerade* by Herman Melville. New York: Hendricks House, 1954.

Franklin, H. Bruce, ed. *The Confidence-Man: His Masquerade* by Herman Melville. New York: Bobbs-Merrill Co., 1967.

————. *The Wake of the Gods: Melville's Mythology*. Stanford, Calif.: Stanford University Press, 1963, pp. 153–87.

Freeman, John. *Herman Melville*. New York: Macmillan Co., 1926.

Fussell, Edwin. *Frontier: American Literature and the American West*. Princeton, N.J.: Princeton University Press, 1965.

Gaudino, Rebecca J. Kruger. "The Riddle of *The Confidence-Man*." *Journal of Narrative Technique* 14 (Spring, 1984): 124–41.

Gollin, Rita K. "The Intelligence Offices of Hawthorne and Melville." *American Transcendental Quarterly* No. 26 (Spring 1975): 44–47.

Graulich, Melody. "Melville's Most Fascinating Confidence Man." *American Transcendental Quarterly* No. 52 (Fall 1981): 229–36.

Grauman, Lawrence, Jr. "Suggestions on the Future of *The Confidence-Man*." *Papers on English Language and Literature* 1 (Summer 1965): 241–49.

Gross, John J. "Melville's *The Confidence-Man*: The Problem of Source and Meaning." *Neuphilologische Mitteilungen* 60 (September 1959): 299–310.

Halttunen, Karen. *Confidence Men and Painted Women: A Study of Middle-class*

Culture in America, 1830–1870. New Haven, Conn.: Yale University Press, 1982.

Hartman, Jay H. "*Volpone* as a Possible Source for Melville's *The Confidence-Man.*" *Susquehanna University Studies* 7 (1965): 247–60.

Hauck, Richard Boyd. *A Cheerful Nihilism: Confidence and "The Absurd" in American Humorous Fiction.* Bloomington: Indiana University Press, 1971, pp. 112–29.

———. "Nine Good Jokes: The Redemptive Humor of the Confidence-Man and *The Confidence-Man.*" In *Ruined Eden of the Present: Hawthorne, Melville, and Poe.* Ed. G. R. Thompson and Virgil L. Lokke. West Lafayette, Ind.: Purdue University Press, 1981, pp. 245–82.

Hayford, Harrison. "Poe in *The Confidence-Man.*" *Nineteenth-Century Fiction* 14 (December 1959): 207–18.

Hayman, Allen. "The Real and the Original: Herman Melville's Theory of Prose Fiction." *Modern Fiction Studies* 8 (August 1962): 211–32.

Hillway, Tyrus. *Herman Melville.* New York: Twayne, 1963.

Hirsch, P. L. "Melville's Ambivalence Toward the Writer's 'Wizardry': Allusions to Theurgic Magic in *The Confidence-Man.*" *ESQ* 31 (Second Quarter 1985): 100–15.

Hoch, David. "A Possible Source for Melville's *The Confidence-Man.*" *Melville Society Extracts* No. 48 (November 1981): 7–10.

Hoffman, Daniel. *Form and Fable in American Fiction.* New York: Oxford University Press, 1961.

———. "Melville's Story of 'China Aster.' " *American Literature* 22 (May 1950): 137–49.

Honig, Edwin. *Dark Conceit: The Making of Allegory.* New York: Oxford University Press, 1966.

Horsford, Howard C. "Evidence of Melville's Plans for a Sequel to *The Confidence-Man.*" *American Literature* 24 (March 1952): 85–88.

Howe, Irving. "The Confidence Man." *Tomorrow* 8 (May 1949): 55–57.

Ishag, Saada. "Herman Melville as an Existentialist: An Analysis of *Typee, Mardi,* and *The Confidence-Man.*" *Emporia State Research Studies* 14 (December 1965): 5–41.

Jaster, Frank. "Melville's Cosmopolitan: The Experience of Life in *The Confidence-Man: His Masquerade.*" *Southern Quarterly* 8 (January 1970): 201–10.

Jones, Dale. "The Grotesque in Melville's *The Confidence-Man.*" *Colby Library Quarterly* 19 (December 1983): 194–205.

Joswick, Thomas P. "Figuring the Beginning: Melville's *The Confidence-Man.*" *Genre* 11 (Fall 1978): 389–409.

Kaplan, Sidney. "Melville and the American National Sin: The Meaning of 'Benito Cereno.' " *Journal of Negro History* 41 (October 1956): 311–18 and 42 (January 1957): 11–37.

Karcher, Carolyn L. *Shadow Over the Promised Land: Slavery, Race, and Violence in Melville's America.* Baton Rouge: Louisiana State University Press, 1980.

———. "Spiritualism and Philanthropy in Brownson's *The Spirit Rapper* and Melville's *The Confidence-Man.*" *ESQ* 25 (First Quarter 1979): 26–36; rev. in *The Haunted Dusk: American Supernatural Fiction, 1870–1920.* Athens:

University of Georgia Press, 1983, pp. 67–97. [References in this chapter are to the original essay.]

———. "The Story of Charlemont: A Dramatization of Melville's Concepts of Fiction in *The Confidence-Man: His Masquerade.*" *Nineteenth-Century Fiction* 21 (June 1966): 73–84.

Kazin, Alfred. "On Melville as Scripture." *Partisan Review* 17 (January 1950): 67–75.

Kemper, Steven E. "*The Confidence-Man*: A Knavishly-Packed Deck." *Studies in American Fiction* 8 (Spring 1980): 23–35.

Kern, Alexander C. "Melville's *The Confidence-Man*: A Structure of Satire." In *American Humor*. Ed. O. M. Brack. Scottsdale, Ariz.: Arete Publications, 1977, pp. 27–41.

Keyser, Elizabeth. " 'Quite an Original': The Cosmopolitan in *The Confidence-Man.*" *Texas Studies in Literature and Language* 15 (Summer 1973): 279–300.

Korkowski, Eugene. "Melville and Des Periers: An Analogue for *The Confidence-Man.*" *American Transcendental Quarterly* No. 31 (1976): 14–19.

Kosenko, Peter. "The Secret Design of Melville's Confidence Man." *Melville Society Extracts* No. 48 (November 1981): 13–14.

Kuhlmann, Susan. *Knave, Fool, and Genius: The Confidence Man as He Appears in Nineteenth-Century American Fiction.* Chapel Hill: University of North Carolina Press, 1973.

Lang, Hans-Joachim, and Benjamin Lease. "Melville's Cosmopolitan: Bayard Taylor in *The Confidence-Man.*" *Amerikastudien* 22 (1977): 286–89.

———. "Melville and 'The Practical Disciple': George William Curtis in *The Confidence-Man.*" *Amerikastudien* 26 (1981): 181–91.

Lee, A. Robert. "Voices off, On and Without: Ventriloquy in *The Confidence-Man.*" In *Herman Melville: Reassessments.* Ed. A. Robert Lee. Totowa, N.J.: Barnes & Noble, 1984, pp. 157–75.

Lenz, William E. *Fast Talk and Flush Times: The Confidence Man as a Literary Convention.* Columbia: University of Missouri Press, 1985.

Lewis, R.W.B. "Afterword." *The Confidence-Man: His Masquerade* by Herman Melville. New York: New American Library, 1964; rpt. *Trials of the Word.* New Haven, Conn.: Yale University Press, 1965, pp. 61–76.

Lindberg, Gary. *The Confidence Man in American Literature.* New York: Oxford University Press, 1982, pp. 15–47.

Lynn, Kenneth S. *Mark Twain and Southwestern Humor.* Boston: Little, Brown & Co., 1959.

McCarthy, Paul. "Affirmative Elements in *The Confidence-Man.*" *American Transcendental Quarterly* No. 7 (Summer 1970): 56–61.

———. "The 'Soldier of Fortune' in Melville's *The Confidence-Man.*" *ESQ* No. 33 (Fourth Quarter 1963): 21–24.

MacDougall, Alma A. "The Chronology of *The Confidence-Man* and 'Benito Cereno'": Redating Two 1855 Curtis and Melville Letters." *Melville Society Extracts* No. 53 (February 1983): 3–6.

MacFarlane, Thomas. *Originality and Imagination.* Baltimore: Johns Hopkins University Press, 1985.

McHaney, Thomas L. "*The Confidence-Man* and Satan's Disguises in *Paradise Lost*." *Nineteenth-Century Fiction* 30 (September 1975): 200–206.

Madison, Mary K. "Hypothetical Friends: The Critics and *The Confidence-Man*." *Melville Society Extracts* No. 46 (May 1981): 10–14.

Madson, Arthur L. "Melville's Comic Progression." *Wisconsin Studies in Literature* 1 (1964): 69–76.

Magaw, Malcolm O. "*The Confidence-Man* and Christian Deity: Melville's Imagery of Ambiguity." *Explorations of Literature, Louisiana State University Studies* 18 (1966): 81–99.

Male, Roy R. "The Story of the Mysterious Stranger in American Fiction." *Criticism* 3 (Fall 1961): 281–94.

Mason, Ronald. *The Spirit Above the Dust*. London: Lehmann, 1951.

Mather, Frank Jewett, Jr. "Herman Melville." *New York Review* 1 (16 August 1919): 298–301.

Matthiessen, F. O. *American Renaissance: Art and Expression in the Age of Emerson and Whitman*. New York: Oxford University Press, 1941.

Mellor, Anne K. *English Romantic Irony*. Cambridge, Mass.: Harvard University Press, 1980.

Miller, Edwin Haviland. *Melville: A Biography*. New York: Braziller, 1975.

Miller, James E., Jr. "*The Confidence-Man*: His Guises." *PMLA* 74 (March 1959): 102–11; rpt. *A Reader's Guide to Herman Melville*. New York: Farrar, Straus & Cudahy, 1962, pp. 170–92.

Mitchell, Edward. "From Action to Essence: Some Notes on the Structure of Melville's *The Confidence-Man*." *American Literature* 40 (March 1968): 27–37.

Monteiro, George. "A Shrewd 'Confidence Man.' " *Melville Society Extracts* No. 56 (November 1983): 3–4.

Moses, Carole. "A Spenserian Echo in *The Confidence-Man*." *Melville Society Extracts* No. 36 (November 1978): 16.

Moss, Sidney, " 'Cock-a-Doodle-Doo!' and Some Legends in Melville Scholarship." *American Literature* 40 (May 1968): 192–210.

Mumford, Lewis. *Herman Melville*. New York: Harcourt, Brace and Co., 1929.

Mushabac, Jane. *Melville's Humor: A Critical Study*. Hamden, Conn.: Archon Books, 1981.

Nichol, John W. "Melville and the Midwest." *PMLA* 66 (September 1951): 613–25.

Norris, William. "Abbott Lawrence in *The Confidence-Man*: American Success or American Failure." *American Studies* 17 (Spring 1976): 25–38.

Oates, J. C. "Melville and the Manichean Illusion." *Texas Studies in Literature and Language* 4 (Spring 1962): 117–29.

O'Connor, William Van. "Melville on the Nature of Hope." *University of Kansas City Review* 22 (December 1955): 123–30.

Oliver, Egbert S. "Melville's Goneril and Fanny Kemble." *New England Quarterly* 18 (December 1945): 489–500.

———. "Melville's Picture of Emerson and Thoreau in *The Confidence-Man*." *College English* 8 (November 1946): 61–72.

Parker, Hershel, ed. *The Confidence-Man: His Masquerade* by Herman Melville. New York: W. W. Norton, 1971.

———. "*The Confidence-Man* and the Uses of Evidence in Compositional Studies: A Rejoinder." *Nineteenth-Century Fiction* 28 (March 1973): 119–24.

———. "Melville's Satire of Emerson and Thoreau: An Evaluation of the Evidence." *American Transcendental Quarterly* No. 7 (1970): 61–67 and 9 (1971): 70.

———. "The Metaphysics of Indian-hating." *Nineteenth-Century Fiction* 18 (September 1963): 165–73; rpt. *The Confidence-Man: His Masquerade.* Ed. Hershel Parker. New York: W. W. Norton, 1971, pp. 323–31. [References in this chapter are to the reprint.]

Pearce, Roy Harvey. "Melville's Indian-Hater: A Note on a Meaning of *The Confidence-Man.*" *PMLA* 67 (December 1952): 942–48.

Petronella, Vincent F. "Shakespeare and the Conclusion of Melville's *The Confidence-Man.*" *American Transcendental Quarterly* No. 55 (January 1985): 41–48.

Pommer, Henry F. *Milton and Melville.* Pittsburgh: University of Pittsburgh Press, 1950.

Porte, Joel. *The Romance in America: Studies in Cooper, Poe, Hawthorne, Melville, and James.* Middletown, Conn.: Wesleyan University Press, 1969.

Quirk, Tom. *Melville's Confidence Man: From Knave to Knight.* Columbia: University of Missouri Press, 1982.

———. "Saint Paul's Types of the Faithful and Melville's Confidence Man." *Nineteenth-Century Fiction* 28 (March 1974): 472–77.

———. "Two Sources in *The Confidence-Man.*" *Melville Society Extracts* No. 39 (September 1979): 12–13.

Ramsey, William M. "Melville's and Barnum's Man with a Weed." *American Literature* 51 (March 1979): 101–104.

———. "The Moot Points of Melville's Indian-Hating." *American Literature* 52 (May 1980): 224–35.

———. "'Touching' Scenes in *The Confidence-Man.*" *ESQ* 25 (First Quarter 1979): 37–62.

Reeves, Paschal. "The 'Deaf Mute' Confidence Man: Melville's Imposter in Action." *Modern Language Notes* 75 (January 1960): 18–20.

Reynolds, Michael S. "The Prototype for Melville's Confidence-Man." *PMLA* 86 (October 1971): 1009–13.

Robillard, Douglas. "The Metaphysics of Melville's Indian Hating." *Essays in Arts and Sciences* 10 (May 1981): 51–58.

Rogin, Michael Paul. *Subversive Genealogy: The Politics and Art of Herman Melville.* New York: Alfred A. Knopf, 1983.

Rosenberry, Edward H. *Melville.* London: Routledge & Kegan Paul, 1979, pp. 43–56.

———. *Melville and the Comic Spirit.* Cambridge, Mass.: Harvard University Press, 1955.

———. "Melville's Ship of Fools." *PMLA* 75 (December 1960): 604–608.

Rosenheim, Edward, Jr. *Swift and the Satirist's Art.* Chicago: University of Chicago Press, 1959.

Roundy, Nancy. "Melville's *The Confidence-Man*: Epistemology and Art." *Ball State University Forum* 21 (Spring 1979): 3–11.

Sattelmeyer, Robert, and James Barbour. "A Possible Source and Model for 'The

Story of China Aster' in Melville's *The Confidence-Man*." *American Literature* 48 (January 1977): 577–83.

Sealts, Merton M., Jr. "Melville's 'Geniality.'" In *Essays in American and English Literature Presented to Bruce Robert McElderry, Jr.* Ed. Max F. Schulz. Athens: Ohio University Press, 1967, pp. 3–26; rpt. *Pursuing Melville, 1940–1980: Chapters and Essays by Merton M. Sealts, Jr.* Madison: University of Wisconsin Press, 1982, pp. 155–70.

Sedgwick, William Ellery. *Herman Melville: The Tragedy of Mind*. Cambridge, Mass.: Harvard University Press, 1944.

Seelye, John. *Melville: The Ironic Diagram*. Evanston, Ill.: Northwestern University Press, 1970.

———. "Timothy Flint's 'Wicked River' and *The Confidence-Man*." *PMLA* 78 (March 1963): 75–79.

———. "'Ungraspable Phantom': Reflections of Hawthorne in *Pierre* and *The Confidence-Man*." *Studies in the Novel* 1 (Winter 1969): 436–43.

Seltzer, Leon F. "Camus's Absurd and the World of Melville's Confidence-Man." *PMLA* 82 (March 1967): 14–27.

Sewell, David R. "Another Source for the Barber Shop Episode in *The Confidence-Man*." *Melville Society Extracts* No. 60 (November 1984): 13–14.

———. "Mercantile Philosophy and the Dialectics of Confidence: Another Perspective on *The Confidence-Man*." *ESQ* 30 (Second Quarter 1984): 99–110.

Shepherd, Gerard W. "The Confidence Man as Drummond Light." *ESQ* 28 (Third Quarter 1982): 183–96.

Shroeder, John W. "Indian-Hating: An Ultimate Note on *The Confidence-Man*." *Books at Brown* 24 (1971): 1–5.

———. "Sources and Symbols for Melville's *The Confidence-Man*." *PMLA* 66 (June 1951): 363–80; rpt. *The Confidence-Man: His Masquerade*. Ed. Hershel Parker. New York: W. W. Norton, 1971, pp. 298–316.

Smith, Paul. "*The Confidence-Man* and the Literary World of New York." *Nineteenth-Century Fiction* 16 (March 1962): 329–37.

Stein, William Bysshe. "Melville's *The Confidence-Man*: Quicksands of the Word." *American Transcendental Quarterly* No. 24 (1974): 38–50.

Sten, Christopher W. "The Dialogue of Crisis in *The Confidence-Man*: Melville's 'New Novel.'" *Studies in the Novel* 6 (Summer 1974): 165–85.

Sumner, D. Nathan. "The American West in Melville's *Mardi* and *The Confidence-Man*." *Research Studies* 36 (March 1968): 37–49.

Sussman, Henry. "The Deconstructor as Politician: Melville's *Confidence-Man*." *Glyph* 4 (1978): 32–56.

Tanselle, G. Thomas. "Herman Melville's Visit to Galena in 1840." *Journal of the Illinois State Historical Society* 53 (Winter 1960): 376–88.

Taylor, Dennis. "The Confidence Man from *The Pardoner's Tale* to *The Fall*." *Arizona Quarterly* 31 (Spring 1975): 73–85.

Thompson, Lawrance. *Melville's Quarrel with God*. Princeton, N.J.: Princeton University Press, 1952.

Tichi, Cecelia. "Melville's Craft and Theme of Language Debased in *The Confidence-Man*." *ELH: A Journal of English Literary History* 39 (December 1972): 639–58.

Trachtenberg, Stanley. " 'A Sensible Way to Play the Fool': Melville's *The Confidence-Man*." *Georgia Review* 26 (1972): 38–52.

Travis, Mildred K. "Spenserian Analogues in *Mardi* and *The Confidence-Man*." *ESQ* No. 50 (1968 Supplement): 55–58.

Trimpi, Helen P. "Harlequin-Confidence-Man: The Satirical Tradition of Commedia Dell'Arte and Pantomime in Melville's *The Confidence-Man*." *Texas Studies in Literature and Language* 16 (Spring 1974): 147–93.

———. "Three of Melville's Confidence Men: William Cullen Bryant, Theodore Parker, and Horace Greeley." *Texas Studies in Literature and Language* 21 (Fall 1979): 368–95.

Tuveson, Ernest. "The Creed of the Confidence-Man." *ELH: A Journal of English Literary History* 33 (June 1966): 247–70.

Van Vechten, Carl. "The Later Work of Herman Melville." *Double Dealer* (New Orleans) 3 (January 1922): 9–20.

Wadlington, Warwick. *The Confidence Game in American Literature*. Princeton, N.J.: Princeton University Press, 1975.

Warner, Fred. "Rochberg's *The Confidence-Man*." *Melville Society Extracts* No. 52 (November 1982): 15.

Watson, Charles N., Jr. "Melville and the Theme of Timonism: From *Pierre* to *The Confidence-Man*." *American Literature* 44 (November 1972): 398–413.

Watters, R. E. "Melville's 'Sociality.' " *American Literature* 17 (March 1945): 33–49.

Weaver, Raymond M. *Herman Melville: Mariner and Mystic*. New York: George H. Doran Co., 1921.

Weissbuch, Ted N. "A Note on the Confidence-Man's Counterfeit Detector." *ESQ* No. 19 (Second Quarter 1960): 16–18.

Wenke, John. "Melville's Masquerade and the Aesthetics of Self-Possession." *ESQ* 28 (Fourth Quarter 1982): 233–42.

———. "No 'i' in Charlemont: A Cryptogrammic Name in *The Confidence-Man*." *Essays in Literature* (Macomb, Ill.) 9 (Fall 1982): 269–78.

Winters, Yvor. *Maule's Curse: Seven Studies in the History of Obscurantism*. Norfolk, Conn.: New Directions, 1938.

Wright, Nathalia. "The Confidence Men of Melville and Cooper: An American Indictment." *American Quarterly* 4 (Fall 1952): 266–68.

———. *Melville's Use of the Bible*. Durham, N.C.: Duke University Press, 1949.

Yannella, Donald. "Source for the Diddling of William Cream in *The Confidence-Man*?" *American Transcendental Quarterly* No. 17 (1973): 22–23.

Ziff, Larzer. "Shakespeare and Melville's America." In *New Perspectives on Melville*. Ed. Faith Pullin. Kent, Ohio and Edinburgh: Kent State University Press and Edinburgh University Press, 1978, pp. 54–67.

12

MELVILLE'S POEMS: THE LATE AGENDA

William H. Shurr

Melville's poetry remains the least studied of his works. Yet it contains energies and innovations, passages of remarkable power and insight as well as technical virtuosity and experimental daring, which by themselves might have made him one of the notable American writers. If he had written no prose at all, we would still have a poet in the American pantheon named Herman Melville. As it is, little is known of this aspect of his work, and the specialist who says he is interested in Melville's *poetry* sometimes feels like Emily Dickinson when she wrote "All men say 'What?' to me." It may be that we still need a larger theory of Melville the Writer that would account for the prose and poetry together before this part of his work can be assessed adequately. In view of this situation there can hardly be a tradition of Melville criticism in this area. Where a few scholars have taken a look at Melville's poetry, published a piece or two, and then moved on to other interests, it is difficult to speak of "trends" and impossible to speak of "schools."

BACKGROUND

Some of the earliest scholars to come to Melville's poetry seemed to feel the need to be controlled in their approval, judicious and reserved. In 1949 Newton Arvin placed Melville in a line with Emerson and Emily Dickinson—as colloquial, prosaic, anti-poetic, ironic. As such he sees Melville as a precursor of twentieth-century poets. (The other tradition, according to Arvin's impressions at the time, was symbolic, incantatory, and musical. It was practiced by Poe and Whitman and ended in Sidney

Lanier—reading history can be simultaneously instructive, puzzling, and cautionary.) While Arvin felt that most of Melville's poems are imperfect, he praised the range of subject matter and the occasional striking image. Nearly all of Arvin's statements are carefully qualified and counter-weighted. He ended by placing Melville somewhere between juvenile exuberance and total negativism.

The following year, Richard Chase continued the trend to evaluate Melville's poetry, giving the following catalogue of topics he found there: "metaphysical ideas, personal reminiscence and confession, art and aesthetics, history and the passage of time, mythical ideas of the powers of revival to be discerned in the universe" (p. xviii). Chase judged this poetry to be "seldom flawless, though it is nearly so in a few pieces like 'The Portent,' 'The Maldive Shark,' and 'Shiloh' " (p. xix). But in 1964 Hennig Cohen felt comfortable in publishing a collection of Melville's poetry with no hesitations or qualifications whatsoever. He praised the poetry for demonstrating Melville's "power of . . . imagination, the integrity of his intellect, the scope of his interests, the depth of his courage, and the breadth of his human sympathies" (p. xvi).

In attempting a new approach to Melville's poetry Laurence Barrett described a thinker who believed life to be formless and who was struggling to put those perceptions into the formal art of poetry. Some years later, in 1969, Jane Donahue put the perception into a more concrete context, seeing in Melville's interest in Greek and Roman art and architecture a romantic's admiration for some outer principle of artistic order with which to control and express his basically lawless imagination. Richard H. Fogle, commenting only on the later poetry, found Melville's humanistic concerns continuing into his old age and showed many lines of continuity between the poems and *Billy Budd*.

The surviving manuscripts of Melville's poetry are to be found at the Houghton Library of Harvard University. After the small editions which Melville published during his lifetime and Henry Chapin's selection *John Marr and Other Poems* (1922), the printed and previously unprinted poems were edited for the Constable edition of Melville's complete works (1924). Two small selections edited by William Plomer and F. O. Matthiessen appeared in 1943 and 1944, respectively. Howard P. Vincent's attempt at a more complete edition of the poems (Hendricks House) was published by Packard and Company in 1947. Readers of this edition (from which the poems in this chapter are cited) should be aware that they are constrained to use an extensive errata sheet and some fifty pages of textual notes, neither of which was included in every copy of the volume. Some years later, Norman Jarrard's 1960 dissertation (*Mel. Diss.*, #92) was a useful and well-annotated edition of all the published verse. Finally, the Northwestern-Newberry volume, edited by Robert Ryan, has been expected for some years now. It will bear the Center for

Editions of American Authors (CEAA) imprint and will be the definitive edition of the poems when it appears. Ryan's earlier Northwestern dissertation (1967) was a preparatory exercise for this work, an edition of *Weeds and Wildings Chiefly: With a Rose or Two* (*Mel. Diss.*, #167).

Three fine selections of Melville's verse have appeared, one edited by Hennig Cohen (1964) with illuminating notes, another by Robert Penn Warren in 1970, with a lengthy appreciative essay and notes, and a third by Douglas Robillard (1976) with a thoughtful introduction. Cohen has also provided the reader with a labor of love in his edition of *Battle-Pieces* (1964), well annotated and lavishly illustrated by contemporary artists' sketches which Melville would have seen in the news sources he used for the battles he was writing about.

Some interesting and helpful editorial work has been done, in addition to the works listed above. Merton M. Sealts, Jr., published his description of the *Burgundy Club* sketches, with a commentary, in 1958; and Eleanor M. Tilton dealt with what looked like another major unfinished sequence left among Melville's poetry manuscripts, in "Melville's 'Rammon': A Text and Commentary" (1959). Both appeared in the *Harvard Library Bulletin*. Tilton's text of "Rammon" is to be preferred for study over the version published in the Constable edition.

The only book-length critical studies devoted exclusively to the poetry (apart from *Clarel*) are William Bysshe Stein's *The Poetry of Melville's Later Years* (1970) and William H. Shurr's *The Mystery of Iniquity: Melville as Poet, 1857–1891* (1972). Stein's book is a Jungean study, the culmination of a long and intense interest in Jung's psychology as it applies to poetry. Stein's insightful readings clarify many puzzling lines and obscure allusions. The Jungean methodology amplifies the mythic and psychological dimensions of the poetry. Stein is particularly good at explicating large metaphors, like the rose, the Great Mother, the redeemer figure, and the sea, which metaphors he sees as unifying these late collections of poetry. The title of his book suggests some limitations to his study and to his estimate of the value of Melville's poetry as well. As a matter of fact the two earlier works of poetry, *Battle-Pieces* and *Clarel*, which Stein feels are failures, are given only the briefest attention in an introductory chapter. He concentrates rather on the late volumes where he finds "the wisdom of old age," though he still laments "clumsy, disconcerting lapses in imaginative expression, a seemingly inexplicable recourse to folksy archaism, trite figures, and gushing colloquialisms" (p. 12).

In *The Mystery of Iniquity*, I was unable to find any of these characteristics. I tried to survey and evaluate the whole corpus of Melville's poetic accomplishments, describing the unities of the larger collections and annotating and explicating the individual poems. The poems were studied not only as the magnificent works of art they are in themselves, but also in the context of Melville's biography during his later years. I also attempted to suggest Melville's running dialogue, in his poems, with some of the major intellectual figures of the period—with Karl Marx who was widely published in America, with Darwin, and with Schopenhauer whose works began to appear in English late in Melville's writing career but in whom he seems to have found a kindred spirit and confirmation for some of his own most deeply held opinions. A great deal of very interesting work remains to be done on this subject—Melville among the Intellectuals. Melville is the most intellectual and philosophical of our canonical writers, and he responds to the writings of the great thinkers not only in his fiction but also in his poetry. *The Mystery of Iniquity* concluded with some comments on Melville's theory and practice of poetry (Agnes D. Cannon also published on this subject, in 1975) and with some speculations about the effect this long career of poetry writing might have had on the composition of his last prose work, *Billy Budd.* That last story was the culmination of Melville's life-long study of "the mystery of iniquity"—a phrase from St. Paul which fascinated Melville.

A thorough listing of essays on individual collections or poems, up until 1971, can be found at the end of *The Mystery of Iniquity.* Since then Stanton Garner has published his investigations into the background of the Civil War poem, "The Scout Toward Aldie"; he has found a source for one of Melville's phrases in Ben Jonson, and Lucy Freibert has found another in Elizabeth Barrett Browning, attesting to the catholicity of Melville's reading; and Agnes D. Cannon published "Melville's Concepts of the Poet and Poetry" in 1975. In a special issue of *Essays in Arts and Sciences* (1976), Douglas Robillard edited a symposium of essays on Melville's poetry containing names new and old to the field. Bryan C. Short (1971) and Rachel W. Stewart (1976) have both written dissertations that consider the poetry globally.

The first sign that Melville thought of himself as a poet appeared in the songs that punctuate his third novel, *Mardi* (1849). Although these songs are full of a kind of bumptious energy, they may seem slight and amateurish to the learned ear—until one remembers the sea chanties and whalers' work songs with which Melville was most familiar, which ground themselves into his own bodily rhythms as he worked as a sailor during the years of early adulthood. Then these early poems begin to live a different kind of life, as their *genre* is perceived. Melville's original sea chanties are fully appropriate to the narrative and can easily stand comparison with the folk songs and work songs he was imitating. Nathalia Wright and Bryan C. Short have both written essays on these poems and how they function in *Mardi* but without comparing them to sea chanties and sailors' work songs.

When Melville the Writer heard English prose in its most highly wrought state, he seems to have heard it as poetry. The "Shakespearean" rhythms and diction of parts of *Moby-Dick* have long been noted. One might also notice that the intensely written short story, "The Paradise of Bachelors and the Tartarus of Maids," struggles mightily in its early pages to detach itself from the condition of poetry: "It lies not far / from Temple Bar. . . . take your pleasure, / sip your leisure, / in the garden waterward." In these early paragraphs dactyls tumble over anapests, assonance and consonance seem to draw the reader's attention to some highly metaphoric images: "some cool, deep glen, shady among harboring hills. . . . where the Benedick tradesmen are hurrying by. . . . dark, sedate, and solemn piles. . . . found in the stony heart of stunning London" (*Tales*, pp. 202–203).

One tends to think of Melville's poetry as the hobby of his later years, but he was a practicing and hopeful poet even as he was writing these lines. In 1860, when he was about to begin an extended cruise on the sailing ship of his brother Tom, he left behind him a volume called *Poems*, and he seems to have had every confidence that his family or his publisher would have no trouble seeing them into print.

The fact that these poems were not published at the time introduces some complications into the chronology of Melville's poetry. When he did publish his volumes of poetry, many years later, some of these 1860 poems must surely have been in those later collections. But there is no certainty about this, nor any way of telling how much revision might have taken place in the meantime. Given the wide span of years possible, dating individual poems or discernible strata within poems, using the Houghton Library manuscripts, will continue to engage the best efforts of literary detectives. I have made a few conjectures along these lines in *The Mystery of Iniquity*, for example in the case of "Pontoosuce" (pp. 227–29).

BATTLE-PIECES

Melville's first fully achieved appearance as a professional poet took place in 1866 with the publication of *Battle-Pieces and Aspects of the War*. Three years earlier the Melvilles had moved back from Pittsfield to New York City, and he was fully involved, mentally, with the crises of a city and a country at war. The poems are passionate encounters at very close quarters with the most important event in America's history. Individual poems are triumphs of meditative lyric precision, focusing on individual incidents of the war: draft riots in New York, the battle at Shiloh, the Wilderness campaigns, DuPont's sea victory waged with a classical naval textbook strategy, the plight of the maimed veteran, the menace to the Capitol Building itself from the nearby enemy.

In *The Mystery of Iniquity*, I found this collection a record of Melville's self-education on the subject of war. Melville began his meditations as a patriotic citizen fully believing in the righteousness of the Northern cause, the necessity for physical sacrifice, and the ultimate triumph and glorious vindication of Right. But there is a second, distinctly different level of thought in the book. One can see Melville, as his meditations move more carefully and deeply into the realities of war, coming to some quite different and more general conclusions. It is as if his basic pessimism once again asserts itself and comes into play in a concrete historical situation—his "Calvinistic sense of Innate Depravity and Original Sin, from whose visitations in some shape or other, no deeply thinking mind is always and wholly free," as he put it in his essay on Hawthorne ("*Mosses*," p. 540). War is seen, in this phase, as simply another breaking through of the permanent Evil that lies just beneath the surface of all human history.

Some of Melville's most telling and memorable phrases were created to clarify his pessimistic insights into history and human behavior in *Battle-Pieces*. The young enthusiasts went into war at Shiloh fully believing they knew who the enemy was, but "What like a bullet can undeceive" (*Poems*, p. 41, line 16). In "Malvern Hill," which records the horror of the Seven Days' Battle to capture Richmond in 1862, the soldiers appeal to nature to witness and celebrate the glory of their deeds; nature, however, is passive and indifferent to their barbarous heroics and will not stoop to grant significance or honor to man's violence and destructiveness: "*Wag the world how it will, / Leaves must be green in Spring*" (p. 45, ll. 34–35).

Battle-Pieces is not so much a plea for pacifism (though surely it is at least that, and it has a rightful place in American anti-war literature) as it is a philosophical meditation on human impotence in the face of the power of destructiveness and evil which at frequent intervals rises to take over the course of history and human events. What I take to be the central poem in this collection has no specific mention at all to the Civil War or to any war. It is "The Apparition," placed at a climactic point toward the end of the collection. It is a philosophical speculation, a meditation on the dynamics of history which are always and everywhere in action. In this poem a volcano suddenly appears with terrible destructiveness in the middle of a peaceful green pasture and then disappears just as unexpectedly. Melville presents the scene as an image of history itself and of the controlling power of evil that can suddenly manifest itself: "The unreserve of Ill was there" (p. 102, l. 6). The image, like the Civil War itself, becomes a parable of human existence:

> So, then, Solidity's a crust—
>   The core of fire below;
> All may go well for many a year,

But who can think without a fear
Of horrors that happen so?
            (p. 102, ll. 11–15)

These poems of the Civil War are emotionally moving and intellectually stimulating, characteristics that set the tone for Melville's subsequent career as a poet.

Not all critics have regarded *Battle-Pieces* so highly, as has already been hinted. Gene B. Montague believed that the poems display the problems of an amateur poet, that they show Melville's "juvenile" phase (the poet was forty-seven years old at the time), but that Melville visibly grew in the course of writing them. More recently, Carolyn Karcher, perhaps overly caught up in her thesis, faulted Melville for what she felt was his less than adequate personal descriptions of slaves and their individual tragedies in the war: "The crux of the weakness we sense in *Battle-Pieces* is that Melville's anguish is focused almost entirely on the fraternal bond linking the white men fighting for Right with those fighting for Wrong. The equally intense drama of the blacks whose fate the war was deciding, and who were laying down their lives for the Union cause by the thousands, no longer seems to touch Melville's imagination" (pp. 276–77).

Henry F. Pommer's work should be mentioned, in which he found that at least one of the lines running through *Battle-Pieces* and unifying it as well as tightening it is the undoubted presence of John Milton and the themes and figures from *Paradise Lost*. Undoubtedly, Melville gave America's Civil War greater stature and meaning, more clearly dramatized the forces he saw at work there, by allusions to Milton's account of the Civil War in Heaven, between the embodiments of extreme Good and Evil. And Fogle (1959) should be mentioned again for calling attention to the weighty and impressive prose "Supplement" to *Battle-Pieces*. He pointed out that it is a formal description of the Civil War in terms of an Aristotelian *tragedy* as well as an earnest plea to his fellow countrymen for humane resolution to the animosities generated by the war, for swift binding up of wounds. R.W.B. Lewis should also be praised for writing well about this collection; he described *Battle-Pieces* as "a tragic drama expanding in the direction of a tragic epic" (p. 26). Lewis saw the scale of the collection mounting to include the souls of the combatants as well as their bodies, including as well, finally, the idea of America itself. Finally, Robert Penn Warren's thought should be mentioned, that the Civil War "made" Melville a poet by giving him a worthy and appropriate subject (p. 9).

Melville's *Clarel: A Poem and Pilgrimage in the Holy Land* is treated at length in another chapter in this volume; here we might note just the fact of its existence and, briefly, its importance in the chronology of Melville's poetry. The surprise attaching to Melville's two-volume poem is that it has not elevated its author to the status of the American Vergil of the nineteenth century. The poem, which is about twice as long as any of the classical epics, is a narrative tour through much of what makes that century intellectually interesting, through much of what constitutes our own twentieth-century modernity. It is nothing less than an overwhelming triumph to those who are Melville's devotees and have a taste for philosophical narrative. It was nothing more than a slight ripple on the publishing scene in 1876, and it remains little more than a footnote even in the minds of many Americanists. Based on Melville's own tour of Europe, Egypt, and the Holy Land some two decades earlier, *Clarel* was a massive dramatization of the forces that were changing Western civilization from a sacred to a secular culture.

JOHN MARR

Twelve years were to pass between *Clarel* and Melville's next book, *John Marr and Other Sailors* (1888). The book was printed by Putnam's through a subsidy from Melville's uncle, Peter Gansevoort, in a small edition of twenty-five copies, to be used mainly as gifts for friends. The Melvilles were at last financially comfortable because of recent bequests from wealthier family members, and some money was available for this kind of publication. The sad irony must have confirmed much that Melville felt about the world—that at this late point in his life, when (as he wrote to an inquiring professor) he was sensibly beginning to feel a decline in vigor, he should finally achieve the kind of financial security that he so badly needed during the years of his greatest creativity. The nineteen years he had spent as "an outdoor Customs House Officer," (*Mel. Log.*, p. 818), from which position he retired in 1885, might much more profitably have been spent, from the point of view of literary economy, in the pursuit and development of his writing genius. Some of the themes and images that he might have developed more fully can be seen in the massive figures elaborated in this *John Marr* volume.

All of the poems of *John Marr* touch on some aspect of the sea, and this is the subject that unifies the volume. "John Marr," the first of these poems, is the story of an ex-sailor who has married and moved inland to assume the life of a farmer. He has grown old, his wife and children have died, and he finds himself completely isolated from the temperamentally different native farmers around him. John Marr lives a life of reverie, remembering the shipmates of long ago. But these shipmates are all dead; not even the "trumps" of the last judgment will bring back these figures of memory. The poem is a clearheaded study of crushing isolation, one of the major themes of Melville's later poetry. He has known lives of dash and exuberance, but they exist only in the fragile tissues of an old man's dying memory.

Three other monologue-narratives follow in this first section of *John Marr*, all of them concerned with the loss of youth and youth's companions, with death, and with isolation. There might have been a fourth at one time. *Billy Budd* was begun in the same way, as a sea lyric ("Billy in the Darbies") introduced by a sketch of the main character involved. Luckily, this little narrative took on a larger life of its own. (For a fuller discussion, see Sealts's chapter on *Billy Budd, Sailor.*)

The second section, "Sea-Pieces," contains two longer poems, both of them narratives of tragedies at sea. The second is especially interesting. Its title, "The AEolian Harp," calls attention to one of the favorite musical instruments of the Romantics, a guitar-like instrument which was placed in an open window and sounded as the wind blew across it. For the Romantics, such as Coleridge who has a poem on exactly the same topic, the harp was an instrument for putting one in touch with the benevolent Over-Soul whose creative currents swept through the universe. Melville's AEolian Harp, in accord with the author's darker views, rather shrieks with terror as it calls to Melville's mind another recollection from sailing days. The poem describes in vivid and menacing detail the phenomenon of an abandoned hulk that eternally sails the seas, dismasted and unmanned, unmarked, threatening instant destruction to any ship that crashes into it unawares, especially at night when all aboard might think they are sailing through clear seas.

For Melville, the ocean is an emblem of the universe, not benevolently managed as it is for most Romantics, but a place of traps and threats, menacing instant doom. The dismasted hulk is white, sluggish, vaguely alive with some kind of destructive intelligence, dangerous to man and his projects, a vicious and barbaric god of the sea. Many decades after *Moby-Dick*, the white whale was still a powerful symbol in Melville's mind.

Melville returns to the same symbolic materials in two other poems in this collection, "The Maldive Shark" and "The Berg." These are two of Melville's finest and most frequently reprinted poems. Both depict monstrous denizens of Ocean, ghastly and dangerous to man. The shark has a "saw-pit" of a mouth and the head of the Gorgon. He seems all the more menacing for the pretty little pilot-fish that accompany him and guide him to his prey. For all of his destructive power, this god of the ocean still is only "the dotard lethargic and dull,/ Pale ravener of horrible meat" (p. 200, ll. 15–16). The case is similar with the iceberg. It, too, is large, white, and instantly destructive to man. It, too, has the ocean for its home and mocks, in its "stolid" and insentient stupidity, the hopes and daring of the human race.

One has the distinct feeling, reading these poems which Melville published late in his life, that the figure of Moby Dick was a permanent fixture among the most meaningful and powerful symbols of his imagination. He is still, in these three poems, exploring a world ruled over by a vast, hulking, ultimately stupid and brutal power which has anything but humankind's best interests at heart, if there is any heart to the brute at all.

The following fact may be an insignificant coincidence, or it may give us some insight into the extensiveness of this white symbol. As Melville was developing the symbolic meaning of Moby Dick and elaborating its meaning in his mind, his habitual writing place was at a large table in a second floor room in his house in the Berkshires where he could look out the window directly in front of him across the pastures to the heavily eroded mountains on the horizon. With their arching curves they seem, even today, to be distinctly whale-shaped; Melville wrote mostly during the winter months, when there was less to do around the farm, and these whale shapes in the distance would be snowy white as he worked through the symbolism of Moby Dick. That figure of menacing power, then, is not limited to the watery world, but visits the dreams of the land-locked as well. The same conclusion can extend to the reincarnations of this hulking brute of a destructive god that cruises through Melville's later poetry. He is denizen of both land and sea, and one senses another of the strong continuities unifying Melville's writing.

There are some few hints of paradise in Melville's poetic world, but in *John Marr* they are limited to two small poems, and the limitations are even more stringent than that. "To Ned" summons up Tobias Greene the companion of his first book, *Typee*, and the island paradise they had found together in the Marquesas. But ironically the description of the island paradise, published in one of Melville's most popular books, called the attention of many to the beauties of the place and led the way to their exploitation by later visitors. Merely to describe an "Eden" is to close its doors to later explorers. And in "The Enviable Isles," another paradise is described, quite obviously similar to that in Tennyson's "The Lotus-Eaters"; it is extraordinarily beautiful and satisfying, but there are two drawbacks to the place: it exists only in the imagination, and the people who inhabit it are in a state of permanent slumber.

The reader finds the puzzling words "from *Rammon*" in parentheses after the title of "The Enviable Isles." At one time Melville had developed several pages of prose that would have framed this and other lyrics. The manuscript sheets remain and portray a scene quite different from Melville's usual subject matters, a debate among several learned folk who have come to the court of Solomon. Eleanor M. Tilton accurately described the subject of the unfinished *Rammon* as "the doctrine of personal immortality," and speculated that among all of the religious doctrines questioned by Melville this one disturbed him most deeply and personally (p. 50).

The remarkable *John Marr* volume closes with seven short "Pebbles," brief sea poems that round off the collection. Most characteristic are the compacted and conflicting sentiments of the following line: "Healed of my hurt, I laud the inhuman Sea" (p. 206, 1. 30). Land-locked for decades, Melville's imagination still returns to its original sources of inspiration.

TIMOLEON

The next volume of poems, *Timoleon*, was issued in 1891, the last year of Melville's life. The poems are meditations on life and historical figures, and, especially in the second part of the volume (in the section entitled "Fruit of Travel Long Ago"), on the places Melville had visited in Europe, Egypt, and the Holy Land during his trip of 1856–57. Once again, publication was a gesture of bitterness; only a few copies were printed, and of these there were still enough remaining in 1921 for one to be used as a gift. The volume was dedicated to the American painter Elihu Vedder, whose work Melville had admired for several decades. One of the poems in *Battle-Pieces*, "Formerly a Slave," is a meditation on the portrait of a slave woman, drawn by Vedder (*Mel. Log.*, p. 674). The painter acknowledged his presentation copy with cordiality, but with no sense that he had ever met its author. Once again a small window is opened into Melville's vast isolation. Darrell Abel clearly expressed the theme of *Timoleon*—of the poem as well as the whole volume—as the alienation of artists and intellectuals from their fellow men because of their innovative, non-conformist thinking. The article is an early classic among studies of Melville's poetry. The poem itself is aptly seen by Lawrance Thompson, along with "After the Pleasure Party" and "Camoens," as evidence for his persuasive theory that the abiding concern in Melville's writings, early and late, was his quarrel with and unmasking of the Christian God. Finally, Robert P. Shulman found similarities between "Timoleon" and *Billy Budd*, especially in the dramatized confrontations in the two narratives. Shulman speculated that both pieces mirror what must have been Melville's disappointment, late in his life, that his own fellow countrymen had not recognized his genius and probably never would.

The title poem of *Timoleon* is a study, based on Plutarch, of a misunderstood hero from antiquity. The case is a strange and knotty one, leading the reader to wonder what its special appeal was for Melville. Plutarch was concerned mainly with determining the causes of Timoleon's various successes as soldier and statesman, whether they resulted from merit, fortune, "natural causes," or some combination of these three. The Corinthian's main accomplishment was the liberation of Sicily, which had become a warren of loosely confederated tyrants backed by troops from Carthage. Timoleon gradually dislodged each of the tyrants and resettled the towns with Greek Sicilians. He lived the rest of his life in Sicily, refusing to return for honors in Corinth. Early in the essay, as a flashback, Plutarch tells how, twenty years prior to his appointment as general for the Sicilian campaign, Timoleon had been involved in the assassination of his older brother Timophanes, whom he had earlier rescued from certain death in battle. The brother subsequently became a military dictator whose harsh tyranny demanded radical solution. After the assassination, Timoleon was surprised to find that the Corinthians had grown cool toward him and that he was savagely denounced by his mother. As a result of this suspicion, Timoleon lived in semi-retirement for the next twenty years until fortune brought him forward again in the Sicilian crisis.

The issues which Melville chose to dramatize in this strange story are the following: the conflict of loyalties implicit in the assassination, and the psychology of the mother who favors the ruthless strength of the older brother and would live her life through his glorious rise. But most of the poem is devoted to the twenty years of semi-retirement during which Timoleon ponders the ways of Fate, which has isolated him after the moment of his most decisive and heroic action. The final section of the poem follows Plutarch in describing the recall to Corinth, to reward and glory—a denouement which Melville was probably not able to foresee for himself. This is a close and sympathetic reading of one of the most interesting and intelligent of the historians, and Melville is concerned at least partly to find analogues for his own situation in the prose of Plutarch; but he also offers his own splendid version of those writings of the nineteenth century which describe a hero who, like Napoleon, is somehow larger than life and the strictures limiting the ordinary life, or who tries, like Raskolnikov, to live a life beyond good and evil. Melville was attracted to ethical situations—Captain Vere's confrontation with Billy Budd is another one, as is the Lawyer's with Bartleby—where the lines of good and evil are not easily discerned.

The poem that follows is also surprising. "After the Pleasure-Party" is the lament of a mature unmarried woman who has just recently and frustratingly been awakened to sexual desire. There are some signs that the poem, at least in its initial conceptions, may date back as far as 1847— more than half a century before Kate Chopin took up the subject so successfully in The Awakening. Allen Stein has speculated interestingly on Hawthorne's powerfully drawn figure of Zenobia, in The Blithedale Romance, and her possible connections with Melville's Urania in this poem.

There are at least two major reasons why Melville took up the subject himself. The first is that it encompasses the myth of the androgyne, the platonic notion that true friends embody halves of the same soul, a notion that underlay much of Romantic and Victorian views of love and marriage. Melville speaks through Urania:

Why hast thou made us but in halves—
Co-relatives? This makes us slaves.
If these co-relatives never meet
Self-hood itself seems incomplete.
And such the dicing of blind fate
Few matching halves here meet and mate.
What Cosmic jest or Anarch blunder
The human integral clove asunder
And shied the fractions through life's gate?
                    (p. 219, ll. 92–100)

The second reason for Melville's interest in the subject, and a reason that requires a much later date for the composition of this part of the poem, is that it gives him an opportunity to incorporate thoughts from Schopenhauer's "Metaphysics of the Love of the Sexes" in *The World as Will and Idea*, which became available in translation only in 1888. Melville owned a copy of this volume as he was putting his collection together. For Schopenhauer as for Melville, the sexual passion is quite likely to lead to frustration and even to madness, or at least to extreme mental distress. Cupid's promise of eternal bliss veils the threat of howling discord—for both of these aging philosophers. Walter Sutton has wondrously clarified the subject of the poem by his information both on the myth of the androgyne and the traditional stories of Sappho, as they apply to the development of the poem. Sutton attempts to connect the bisexual and homosexual elements of the poem with similar elements in Melville's life and in his other works; the question of sexuality in Melville's works is still one of great interest, by no means settled thirty-five years after Sutton thus ingeniously broached it.

Some themes in the poem show Melville to be strikingly aware of the issues of the women's movements of his time. The speaker is an educated and articulate woman who lives alone and pursues a learned profession. Once awakened there is no outlet for her passion that is sanctioned by society. As she searches for role models provided by society, she finds only the nun, devoted but hidden away in her convent, and the armed and menacing statue of Athene, goddess of war and intellect. We have only recently begun to suspect and to study the sexuality of the pre-Freudian nineteenth century; Melville offers an area for that study which has barely been touched.

Timoleon is, more than any other of Melville's poetic volumes, a miscellany. It includes poems of remarkable intelligence and insight, without displaying the kind of overarching unity that characterizes his other collections. One poem, "The New Zealot to the Sun," sweeps through recorded history uncovering the bigotry and fanaticism displayed in man's religious activities—only to reveal the speaker, in the last stanza, as a scientist who is equally blind and fanatic when it comes to the extravagant claims of his own favorite methodology. "Art," an intense little work of only eleven lines, contains Melville's theory of artistic creation—that it requires the intense compounding of opposites. Cannon has written on Melville's aesthetic theories in her 1975 essay, and I have speculated on the subject in the last chapter of *The Mystery of Iniquity*. And still another interesting poem in this part of *Timoleon*, "The Enthusiast," describes a young idealist from a completely sympathetic point of view. The poem ends with the final heroism of which the individual is capable: "Though light forsake thee, never fall / From fealty to light" (p. 231, ll. 23–24). Melville's granddaughter remembered the poet's writing desk: "and pasted on one side wall, well out of sight, was a printed slip of paper that read simply, 'Keep true to the dreams of thy youth' " (Eleanor Melville Metcalf, p. 284).

A final poem to be noted in this first section of *Timoleon* is Melville's apparent lament for his lost friendship with Hawthorne. The relationship had been intense and emotionally exhilarating, for Melville at least, during the early 1850s when they lived in close proximity in the Berkshires. Hawthorne was the one who cooled down the relationship, and Melville seems never to have understood why his warmth was not matched by equal warmth from Hawthorne. Many years after the death of Hawthorne he published the memorial which begins with these lines:

> To have known him, to have loved him
> After loneness long;
> And then to be estranged in life,
> And neither in the wrong;
> And now for death to set his seal....
> (p. 228, ll. 1–5)

Edwin Haviland Miller (1975) has written movingly on the frustrations Melville may have experienced in his relationship to Hawthorne. It was a relationship, as this poem shows, which Melville could not let go.

The second part of *Timoleon*, "Fruit of Travel Long Ago," contains eighteen poems arranged in the reverse order of Melville's tour of 1856–57, a tour that furnished him with the most important pool of experiences for his later writing career. There are poems on Venice, Pisa, and the Milan cathedral, followed by half a dozen poems on Greek landscape and architecture. The section ends with three monumental meditations, set in Egypt, on the origins of the religious impulse. In "Venice," he finds that man builds in the same way that the coral anthozoa do; both are driven by "Pan's might," by the "Pantheist energy of will" (pp. 238–39, ll. 1, 11). "In a Church of Padua" records Melville's Protestant fascination with the Catholic institution of the confessional. The confessional box is one of those places in the physical world where one descends into the mystery of metaphysical evil. Melville describes it in terms of a diving bell, the enormous, clumsy, inverted bowl, under which laborers worked in conditions of great danger to scoop out the mud at the bottom of a river or harbor as a preliminary to setting the pilings for a bridge or other structure. The image seems especially apt for the dive into man's sinful nature which takes place in the confessional. And a curious poem, "Milan Cathedral," compares the famous *duomo di Milano* to an iceberg. One remembers that menacing white hulk and how it seemed to have much in common with the shark, the kraken, the derelict hull, and with Moby Dick himself. And one senses a sudden chill as he sees Melville finding the same characteristics in this much-celebrated example of Christian architecture. The same kind of white, hulking architecture appears in "Off Cape Colonna," a deadly promontory, site of many shipwrecks, its heights crowned by the ruins of a massive Greek temple. Deity is found where man is most at his peril, in Melville's universe.

The three Egyptian poems that conclude this series furnish a dramatic climax to these materials; they are meditations on the scorching landscape, the Great Pyramid, and the historical coincidence that Moses here developed his idea of the "Shekinah," the overwhelming manifestation of God's power and glory. Melville was still the potentially religious man that Hawthorne found him to be on the dunes outside of Liverpool (*Mel. Log*, p. 529); he ends his last volume of published poems still pondering the nature of the deity.

Or almost ends it. The last poem in the volume stands apart as "L'Envoi," words spoken by a returned traveler to his wife. The traveler likes to roam but he also likes, or at least he pretends so in this poem, to return to the mild domestic joys he shares with his wife. It may be that one of Melville's own major centers of rest and rejuvenation is recorded here. And, in fact, the collection of poems which Melville left unpublished at his death, *Weeds and Wildings*, was destined to be dedicated to his wife and to celebrate their domestic joys together. Such a sentimental picture, as fit conclusion to Melville's troubled life and equally troubled career, has its lure but also its dangers, for the recent findings of Walter D. Kring and Jonathan S. Carey corroborate stories that Melville may have threatened or even abused his wife especially in the late 1860s.

WEEDS AND WILDINGS

These painful facts furnish a distant background to the collection of poems which Melville had dedicated to his wife and which were left unpublished at his death. The companionable ease of husband and wife who have grown old together may not be the stuff of first-rate drama, but given the materials just mentioned it is an interesting *achievement* of the Melvilles, both husband and wife.

The order of *Weeds and Wildings* seems to have been still in flux when Melville died; four extant tables of contents indicate that he had not decided on the final order of the poems. There are, however, several groupings that are constant in all tables of contents; some generalizations can be made and some individual poems singled out for notice.

In the prose preface the author faces up to his approaching death. But rather than casting a cloud of melancholy over the collection, the thought sends his mind back to the early years of marriage, where he creates an idyll. The yard around Arrowhead, beautiful children, small animals and wild flowers, and the early honeymoon years of marriage are the subjects vigorously celebrated by the seventy-year-old poet. The book indeed seems to celebrate a profound center of inner peace which his wife came to represent for Melville. These are truly Melville's Songs of Innocence, achieved after probing the less pleasant aspects of human experience. One of the loveliest of these poems describes "The Dairyman's Child":

> Soft as the morning
>   When South winds blow,
> Sweet as peach-orchards
>   When blossoms are seen,
> Pure as a fresco
>   Of roses and snow,
> Or an opal serene.
>   (p. 266)

But the dark side of Melville's moon is also in this collection, as might be expected: the last stanza of "The Chipmunk" reveals that the poem is really about a baby who died in infancy; an early version of "The Little Good-Fellows" (about robins) alludes to a suicide sprawled on the forest floor; a poem called "The Blue-Bird" consoles the bird for the loss of his life with the suggestion that his color, at least, lives on in the June larkspur—small consolation for the bird; and "In the Pauper's Turnip Field" is a picture unrelieved in its misery, describing one who is in a condition of poverty so crushing that he is always at the edge of death. One recalls that it was during the Pittsfield years, which Melville tries to re-create here as Edenic, that he wrote the famous "dollars damn me" letter to Hawthorne (*Letters*, pp. 126–31). Melville's conscious themes seem to clash with intuitive feelings.

A curious poem, set apart in its own section, is called "Rip Van Winkle's Lilac." Warning signals light up as details of Rip's less than satisfying marital situation flash by in the reader's mind. One imagines Irving's story as an interesting vehicle by which Melville might explore some of his more personal experiences in marriage. But Melville's odd point in this odd poem is that the only real residue left over from Rip's whole career is the proliferation of shoots transplanted from the lilac he carefully tended at his front door. There is less about Rip and his relation to his wife than Irving gave us. More seems to be struggling to get out of this long narrative poem than clearly emerges.

The second major section of *Weeds and Wildings* is a collection of rose poems. Once again some distinctly unpleasant background noise begins to sound in this collection: Melville dedicated this volume to his wife, yet one of the few concrete bits of fact that we have about her during these later years is that she was frightfully allergic to roses. She had to leave town for several weeks each year to escape the effects of their pollenizing.

Still, the rose is used as a symbol for exploring a variety of topics: immortality, death, first love, physical beauty, mutability. One of Melville's most skillfully made and intensely felt poems is found here:

> Meek crossing of the bosom's lawn
> Averted revery veil-like drawn,
> Well beseem thee, nor obtrude
> The cloister of thy virginhood.
> And yet, white nun, that seemly dress
> Of purity pale passionless,
> A May-snow is; for fleeting term,
> Custodian of love's slumbering germ—
> Nay, nurtures it, till time disclose
> How frost fed Amor's burning rose.
>
> (p. 297)

For all of the clarity of expression here and the strength of feeling, the subject is an unusual one, hardly in the central tradition of lyric poetry as it has developed in English. In form the poem is a miniaturized sonnet; its perfect execution hints at the time and effort that must have gone into it. The inner life of a cloistered nun seems an odd subject for an American Protestant—though it was the stuff of best selling literature in such books as *The Awful Disclosures* of Maria Monk. The poem is a powerful expression of the dangers of repression, as if the inevitable explosion of sexual demands will be all the stronger for earlier denials. The perfection of expression piques the reader's mind here for its pre-Freudian insight into sexuality. The poem is a strange one, both for the mysteries of human experience it seems to open a brief window into, and for the questions it raises about why Melville himself would be interested in such a subject. One seems unable to discover a context sufficiently enlightening for these few poems of highly charged female sexuality that can be found among Melville's works.

The final poem in this collection, "The Rose Farmer," is a long narrative meditation, just over two hundred lines, presenting the thoughts of a recently retired man who has taken up rose farming as his final occupation. Some Middle Eastern details seem to suggest that Melville accepts Candide's advice that one must finally cultivate one's own garden. At the intellectual level the poem is a long discussion about whether the rose farmer should sell his blossoms immediately for the quick cash profit, or go through the long and tedious process of pressing each rose petal individually for the minute drop of concentrated "attar" that might be extracted—and possibly end up with a product that was so rarified and so expensive that it would find few, if any, buyers. The scenario is, of course, a transparent allegory of Melville the writer who feels that he has never had a fair hearing or the audience that his careful artistic productions deserved.

William Bysshe Stein's study of the history and the psychological meanings of the symbol of the rose has already been mentioned; Richard Bridgman has commented on the ways that this rose-symbol holds the poems of *Weeds and Wildings* together as a collection.

OTHER POEMS

Another sequence that exists among the works that Melville left unfinished and unpublished at his death is the long series of prose and verse pieces called *The Burgundy Club*. Melville seems to have been planning a fairly extensive poetic symposium on Italian cultural and historical materials, although presided over, in several different settings, by a genial fellow with a *French* name, the Marquis de Grandvin. The first of the two long poems in this collection gathers some of the very greatest painters for a discussion of what was in Melville's time one of the most significant and disputed terms in aesthetics and art criticism, "the picturesque." As the conversation proceeds, Melville skillfully uncovers what he takes to be the individual personalities of the great painters, as each explains his own sense of the meaning of the word "picturesque." Melville, of course, extrapolates from his own analysis of the work of each of the painters. It is interesting that the three painters whom Melville considers to be far superior to the rest, Poussin, Leonardo da Vinci, and Michael Angelo, remain aloof from the conversation and irritate the lesser painters by their olympian silence. The poem is entertainment at a high intellectual level, a guided tour through many of the painters and works the nineteenth century considered important.

The poem is immensely interesting and seems to uncover an entirely new area of Melville's interests, until one remembers that during the late 1850s when he tried the winter lecture circuit one of his lectures involved art appreciation. We also know that, for all of his financial limitations, Melville was a careful and well-informed collector of prints of famous works of art. Melville must continue to grow in the mind as the multifaceted genius he was. Merton M. Sealts, Jr. (1970) has gathered the materials that can be found concerning these lectures, but the larger subject of Melville's relations to the great artists and their works remains relatively untouched. (See, however, Morris Star's unpublished 1964 dissertation.)

The second of the two *Burgundy Club* sketches is called "Naples in the Time of Bomba," and it is a massive and intelligent tour through the most important events in the history of modern Italy. The wars of Italian liberation (from Austria) and unification are complicated; Melville's focus on the city of Naples and the figure of Garibaldi helps simplify matters considerably.

Garibaldi, a major hero in the popular imagination, seems to have had some special attractiveness for Melville. In one of his periods of exile, in the early 1850s, Garibaldi lived in Melville's own city, New York. Earlier he had been an enthusiastic member of Mazzini's *Giovine Italia*, a name paralleled in New York by the group calling themselves "Young America" to which Melville belonged. Melville himself had been in Naples in February of 1857 and had jotted notes in his Journal about the repressive military government in power then. The poem itself and the rest of the *Burgundy Club* sketches seem to have been begun in 1876–77, then laid aside until Melville picked them up again during his retirement years. Victor Emmanuel, who would come to rule over a unified Italy, and Camillo di Cavour, the astute architect of Italian unity, are also treated prominently in the poem. The speaker in the poem is a new figure, Major Jack Gentian, an American of unimpeachable democratic instincts, who is first drawn to admire and envy the city and its carefree and spontaneous people. But during a day of exploring the city he is witness to several incidents that hint at the extent of political terror that reigns over the city, which emanates from the citadel of the power that now controls it.

Major Jack Gentian, we find out in the course of the poem, is a member of the famous Burgundy Club—giving us a sense that Melville may have intended to characterize several of these members and let each narrate his own particular story for this collection, a technique not unlike Chaucer's in *The Canterbury Tales* or Longfellow's in *Tales of the Wayside Inn*.

The poem is lively and fascinating, and contains many good lines. Generalizing on history, as he had in his Civil War poems, Melville finds it to be "Hell's cornucopia crammed with crime" (p. 357, l. 171); imagining the funeral of the hero Garibaldi, he believes he can see invisible spirits there: "Pale glory walks by valor's bier" (p. 367, l. 60). Melville joins Longfellow and Margaret Fuller here (and Hawthorne, Poe, Shelley, and Byron as well) in his affection for Italian Culture, a subject so far untouched by scholarly inquiry.

Melville left about forty other poems in manuscript when he died. Many of them seem connected by tone and theme: they project the interior world of a writer growing old, feeling his age, wondering about the shape of his life, comparing his own with the finished and whole lives of other writers, discovering analogues for his feelings in literary authors and characters. Thus Montaigne in his retirement, two phases in the life of the Portuguese national poet Camoens, the deserted Falstaff, the aging Quixote, the enduring reality of Shakespeare—these are the figures that loom meaningfully before him.

One poignant poem from this last group is "My Jacket Old." The jacket is the garment Melville wore to protect his clothes during the years he was a customs inspector. He imagines it covered with dust from some of the exotic and Edenic places he had written about as a young and hopeful author. The ironies are pointed: places he touched as a young romantic wanderer and then as a creative artist, he is now allowed to touch only through their physical dust and while he is chained to the employ of Mammon.

Another poem, "In the Hall of Marbles," pursues a theme that had interested Melville throughout his life: contrary to those who read in the data of evolution signs of a constant rise in the level of man's civilization, Melville's reason and his instincts produced exactly the opposite conclusion. "In the Hall of Marbles" shows that the beauty of ancient Greek statuary, and the ideals there embodied, are no longer the "aims" of modern man: "Waxes the world so rich and old?/ Richer and narrower, age's way?" (p. 389, l. 5). It ends with a significant parallel:

> This plaint the sibyls unconsoled renew:
> Man fell from Eden, fall from Athens, too.
> (p. 389, ll. 9–10)

Other poems, like "The Dust-Layers" and "A Rail Road Cutting Near Alexandria in 1855," continue to substantiate this view.

The final poem to be considered among those that Melville left in manuscript at his death is the justly famous "Pontoosuce." The name is that of a lake in Pittsfield, a favorite of the Melville family. But the poem, like others in this group, is about decline and disintegration.

One can see from the shape of the poem that it has been carefully planned. Structurally, it divides into two parts at line 60. The first part has two sections, each developed in the same way: a descriptive treatment of the setting, philosophical musings, then the dramatically brief "all dies!" All this is preparation for the vision that occupies the second part of the poem. The issue is between the two contrary facts of existence: the death of all things in nature and the ongoing thrust of life. The achievement of the poem is the momentary stasis that is accomplished, in which these two contraries exist side by side, at least for the moment, and actually seem to form a compatible whole.

The catalyst for this achievement is a female spirit who visits the poet with the gift of perception. She is interesting because Melville was rarely visited by the totally feminine view of reality. She is more real than Fayaway in *Typee*, and she performs an integrating and harmonizing function that was never to be achieved by Clarel's Ruth. Perhaps she is closest to the Yillah of *Mardi*; but here the girl, though described in erotic terms, does not stimulate the same kind of passion that adds a frantic note to the pursuit of Yillah. The figure is interesting as one of the rare explorations of the feminine in the largely masculine world of Melville's writings.

In a sense this poem is Melville's "Tintern Abbey." Melville's "indistinct abodes / And faery–peopled neighborhoods" (p. 395, ll. 11–12) sound like the landscape as Wordsworth also perceived it. For Wordsworth there is a clear distinction between the vital principle that harmonizes the contrary propositions one must read from nature, and the feminine principle, in the person of his sister, for whom he must articulate the lessons he has learned. For Melville, nature and the feminine merge into one as the source and inspiration of this kind, and the reader fulfills the function of the confidante to whom this vision of reality is to be communicated. The two great writers part company on the identity of this feminine spirit who rules the natural universe. For Melville the lady is the personification of Death. One of his finest sentences communicates this: "The poet's forms of beauty pass,/ And noblest deeds they are undone" (p. 396, ll. 46–47). Thomas F. Heffernan has explored the Melville-Wordsworth connection further in his 1977 article.

It is obvious that the younger Melville's angry pessimism has mellowed, if at all, to a quiet melancholy in these later poems. Of their famous conversation on the dunes outside of Liverpool, Hawthorne thought Melville "better worth immortality than most of us" (*Mel. Log*, p. 529). Some of this life-long quest and some, at least, of the late melancholy are visible in the following prose lines from the Burgundy Club sketches: "Yea, and shall he also at last vanish, sailing into the boundless Nil, leaving no phosphorescent wake or magic moon-glades behind?" Suitable exit lines for a mariner and mystic.

WORKS CITED

Aaron, Daniel. *The Unwritten War: American Writers and the Civil War*. New York: Alfred A. Knopf, 1973.

Abel, Darrell. "I Look, You Look, He Looks: Three Critics on Melville's Poetry." *ESQ* 21 (Second Quarter 1975): 116–23.

————. " 'Laurel Twined with Thorn': The Theme of Melville's *Timoleon*." *The Personalist* 41 (July 1960): 330–40.

Adler, Joyce Sparer. *War in Melville's Imagination*. New York: New York University Press, 1981.

————. "Melville and the Civil War." *New Letters* 40 (Winter 1973): 99–117.

Arvin, Newton. "Melville's Shorter Poems." *Partisan Review* 16 (October 1949): 1034–46.

Barrett, Laurence. "The Differences in Melville's Poetry." *PMLA* 70 (September 1955): 606–23.

Bennett, Gaymon Lamont. "Melville's *Battle-Pieces* and Whitman's *Drum-Taps*: Two Northern Poets Interpret the Civil War." Ph.D. Diss., Washington State University, 1982. [*Mel. Diss.*, #69.]

Bridgman, Richard. "Melville's Roses." *Texas Studies in Literature and Language* 8 (Summer 1966): 235–44.

Cannon, Agnes D. "Melville's Concepts of the Poet and Poetry." *Arizona Quarterly* 31 (1975): 315–39.

Chapin, Henry, ed. *John Marr and Other Poems*. Princeton, N.J.: Princeton University Press, 1922.

Chase, Richard, ed. *Selected Tales and Poems by Herman Melville*. New York: Rinehart & Company, 1950.

Cohen, Hennig, ed. *The Battle-Pieces of Herman Melville*. New York: Thomas Yoseloff, 1964.

————, ed. *Selected Poems of Herman Melville*. New York: Anchor Books, 1964; Carbondale: Southern Illinois University Press, 1964.

Dillingham, William B. " 'Neither Believer nor Infidel': Themes of Melville's Poetry." *The Personalist* 46 (1965): 501–16.

Donahue, Jane. "Melville's Classicism: Law and Order in His Poetry." *Papers on Language and Literature* 5 (Winter 1969): 63–72.

Fogle, Richard H. "Melville and the Civil War." *Tulane Studies in English* 9 (1959): 61–89.

————. "Melville's Poetry." *Tulane Studies in English* 12 (1962): 81–86.

————. "The Themes of Melville's Later Poetry." *Tulane Studies in English* 11 (1961): 65–86.

Freibert, Lucy M. "The Influence of Elizabeth Barrett Browning on the Poetry of Herman Melville." *Studies in Browning and His Circle* 9 (1981): 69–78.

Garner, Stanton. "Melville's Scout Toward Aldie." *Melville Society Extracts* No. 51 (September 1982): 5–16 and No. 52 (November 1982): 1–14.

————. "Rosmarine: Melville's 'Pebbles' and Ben Jonson's *Masque of Blackness*." *Melville Society Extracts* No. 41 (February 1979): 13–14.

Heffernan, Thomas F. "Melville and Wordsworth." *American Literature* 49 (November 1977): 338–51.

Jarrard, Norman, "Poems by Herman Melville: A Critical Edition of the Published Verse." Ph.D. Diss., University of Texas, 1960. [*Mel. Diss.*, #92.]

Karcher, Carolyn L. *Shadow over the Promised Land: Slavery, Race, and Violence in Melville's America*. Baton Rouge: Louisiana State University Press, 1980.

Kring, Walter D., and Jonathan S. Carey. "Two Discoveries Concerning Herman Melville." *Proceedings of the Massachusetts Historical Society* 87 (1975): 137–

41; rpt. Donald Yannella and Hershel Parker, eds. *The Endless Winding Way: New Charts by Kring and Carey*. Glassboro, N.J.: Melville Society, 1981.

Lewis, R.W.B., ed. *Herman Melville: A Reader*. New York: Dell, 1963.

Matthiessen, F. O., ed. *Selected Poems*. By Herman Melville. Norfolk, Conn.: New Directions, 1944.

Meldrum, Barbara H. "Melville on War." *Research Studies* (State College of Washington) 37 (1969): 130–38.

Metcalf, Eleanor Melville. *Herman Melville: Cycle and Epicycle*. Cambridge, Mass.: Harvard University Press, 1953.

Miller, Edwin Haviland. *Melville: A Biography*. New York: George Braziller, 1975.

Montague, Gene B. "Melville's *Battle-Pieces*." *University of Texas Studies in English* 35 (1956): 106–15.

Monteiro, George. "Poetry and Madness: Melville's Rediscovery of Camoes in 1867." *New England Quarterly* 51 (December 1978): 561–65.

Plomer, William, ed. *Selected Poems*. By Herman Melville. London: Hogarth Press, 1943.

Pommer, Henry F. *Milton and Melville*. Pittsburgh: University of Pittsburgh Press, 1950.

Robillard, Douglas, ed. *Poems of Herman Melville*. New Haven, Conn.: College and University Press, 1976.

———. "Symposium: Melville the Poet." *Essays in Arts and Sciences* (New Haven) 5 (July 1976).

———. "Theme and Structure in Melville's *John Marr and Other Sailors*." *English Language Notes* 6 (1969): 187–92.

Ryan, Robert C. *"Weeds and Wildings Chiefly: With a Rose or Two,"* by Herman Melville; Reading Text and Genetic Text, Edited from the Manuscripts, with Introductions and Notes." Ph.D. Diss., Northwestern University, 1967. [*Mel. Diss.*, #167.]

Sealts, Merton M., Jr. *Melville as Lecturer*. Cambridge, Mass.: Harvard University Press, 1957.

———. "Melville's Burgundy Club Sketches." *Harvard Library Bulletin* 12 (Spring 1958): 253–67.

Short, Bryan Collier. *Herman Melville's Poetry: The Growth of a Post-Romantic Art*. Ph.D. Diss., Claremont Graduate School, 1971. [*Mel. Diss.*, #259.]

———. " 'The Redness of the Rose': The *Mardi* Poems and Melville's Artistic Compromise." *Essays in Arts and Sciences* 5 (July 1976): 100–12.

Shulman, Robert P. "Melville's *Timoleon*: From Plutarch to the Early Stages of *Billy-Budd*." *Comparative Literature* 19 (Fall 1967): 351–61.

Shurr, William H. *The Mystery of Iniquity: Melville as Poet, 1857–1891*. Lexington: University Press of Kentucky, 1972.

Star, Morris, "Melville's Use of the Visual Arts." Ph.D. Diss., Northwestern University, 1964. [*Mel. Diss.*, #131.]

Stein, Allen F. "Hawthorne's Zenobia and Melville's Urania." *American Transcendental Quarterly* No. 26 (1975): 11–14.

Stein, William Bysshe. *The Poetry of Melville's Later Years: Time, History, Myth, and Religion*. Albany: State University of New York Press, 1970.

Stewart, Rachel Whitesides. *The Conditional Mood of Melville's Poetry*. Ph.D. Diss. University of Colorado 1975. [*Mel. Diss.*, #404.]

Sutton, Walter. "Melville's 'Pleasure Party' and the Art of Concealment." *Philological Quarterly* 30 (July 1951): 316–27.

Thompson, Lawrance. *Melville's Quarrel with God*. Princeton, N.J.: Princeton University Press, 1952.

Tilton, Eleanor M. "Melville's 'Rammon': A Text and Commentary." *Harvard Library Bulletin* 13 (Winter 1959): 50–91.

Vincent, Howard P., ed. *Collected Poems of Herman Melville*. Chicago: Hendricks House, 1947.

Warren, Robert Penn. "Melville's Poems." *The Southern Review* 3 (Autumn 1967): 799–855; rpt. in *Selected Poems*.

———. *Selected Poems of Herman Melville*. New York: Random House, 1970.

Wilson, Edmund. *Patriotic Gore: Studies in the Literature of the American Civil War*. New York: Oxford University Press, 1966.

Wright, Nathalia. "The Poems in Melville's *Mardi*." *Essays in Arts and Sciences* 5 (July 1976): 83–99.

13

CLAREL

Vincent Kenny

BACKGROUND

Published in 1876, the long narrative poem *Clarel* can be traced back twenty years earlier to Melville's lowest period in physical health, earning power, and mental condition. The birth of his fourth child, Frances, in 1855 did not increase so much as underscore for Melville his financial problems already strained beyond ready solution. Tending Arrowhead as a farm was impossible, with recurrences of sciatica, rheumatism, and blurred vision combining to keep him housebound for long periods. Dissatisfaction with himself as an artist, manifest in the limited income from the novels and short stories and in the compromises he made in their writing, destroyed the self-confidence necessary for him to go on. Bringing *The Confidence-Man* to a stuttering conclusion in April 1857, after the same kind of struggle with *Pierre* in 1852, had to emphasize this dissatisfaction. The family's ongoing lack of trust in his abilities was expressed by his brother-in-law, Lemuel Shaw, Jr.: "I believe he is now preparing another book for the press. . . . I know nothing about it; but I have no great confidence in the success of his productions—" (*Mel. Log*, p. 517).

These and other factors produced in Melville a morbid condition of great concern to the Melville family-at-large. Elizabeth had called in their friend and neighbor, Dr. Oliver Wendell Holmes, at different times in 1855, ostensibly for her husband's severe rheumatism but perhaps for the ongoing depression. In September 1856 Melville's father-in-law, Lemuel Shaw, wrote to his son, Samuel:

I suppose you have been informed by some of the family, how very ill, Herman has been. It is manifest to me from Elizabeth's letters, that she has felt great anxiety about him. When he is deeply engaged in one of his literary works, he confines him[self] to hard study many hours in the day, with little or no exercise, & this specially in winter for a great many days together. He probably thus overworks himself & brings on severe nervous affections. He has been advised strongly to break off this labor for some time, & take a voyage or a journey, & endeavor to recruit. No definite plan is arranged, but I think it may result, in this that in the autumn he will go away for four or five months, . . . (*Mel. Log*, p. 521).

Shaw's observation of "severe nervous affections" may have been the diagnosis of Holmes, who had advised Elizabeth that her husband must leave the Pittsfield scene if he was to be rid of the depression. Elizabeth agreed with the Doctor and secured yet another loan from her father for projected expenses, which enabled Melville to leave for Europe. This therapeutic vacation opened him to a seven-month experience that was to be told in part twenty years later in *Clarel*.

Melville's fragmented state of mind just before departure can be seen in his marking of a passage in a recently purchased copy of *Don Quixote*. Next to Cervantes's line, " . . . a knight-errant without a mistress is like a tree without leaves, a building without cement, a shadow without a body that causes it," Melville wrote, "or as Confucius said 'a dog without a master,' or to drop both Cervantes & Confucius parables—a god-like mind without a God" (*Mel. Log*, p. 508).

Melville departed from New York on 11 October 1856 on the *Glasgow*, bound for Scotland. He landed in Greenoch on 25 October, traveling thereafter through Scotland and northern England, and visiting with Hawthorne in Liverpool on 9 November. For about a week they renewed a friendship that had slipped away since 1853. Hawthorne found a different Melville than the one he knew in Pittsfield: "He certainly is much overshadowed since I saw him last." His well-known assessments of Melville's impending "annihilation" confirmed Elizabeth's fears and Holmes's medical diagnosis (*English Notebooks*, pp. 422–35).

Melville left aboard the *Egyptian* on 18 November and arrived in Constantinople on 12 December, after stops at Malta, Syra, and Salonica. He traveled to Alexandria and Cairo before landing at his planned destination—Jaffa—on 6 January. He kept a detailed account of the trip, a journal of bleakness, impatience, and bursts of anger. Any anticipation of transcendent signs was dashed, no matter what sector of the Middle East he visited, particularly Judea: "No country will more quickly dissipate romantic expectations than Palestine—particularly Jerusalem. To some the disappointment is heart sickening. &tc. Is the desolation of the land the result of the fatal embrace of the Deity? Hapless are the favorites of heaven" (1856 *Journal*, p. 154). His entries suggest that a kind of spiritual contract had been violated: "how it affects one to be cheated in Jerusalem" (p. 142). The morbid condition Elizabeth feared earlier at Arrowhead had, if anything, deepened: "I am emphatically alone, & begin to feel like Jonah" (p. 129). "I have such a feeling in this lonely old Joppa, with the prospect of a prolonged detention here, owing to the surf—that it is only by stern self-control & grim defiance that I contrive to keep cool & patient" (pp. 130–31). He left Jaffa on 24 January, depressed by the stones, weeds, cow manure, flies, beggars, and lepers that constituted for him the Holy Land.

Melville became more the tourist after this disheartening experience. Before the return trip via Italy, he remained in the Middle East, stopping for a week in Beirut, and a few days in Smyrna, the isle of Syros, and Athens. He left for Messina on 13 February. The days lightened for him during the month in Italy. Another tour of England, particularly of Oxford, repaired some of the damage done in the Levant. Even so, Melville left Liverpool with a heavy heart.

His 1856 *Journal* records the hundreds of sites and observations during the long tour, but it also includes a pattern of sleepless nights, strained eyes, and short temper with Middle East behavior. More significantly, the entries indicate that the journey as a pilgrimage for a man with "a god-like mind without a God" was a waste. The spiritual rebirth he looked for, or needed, was not to be found in barren Judea, possibly not anywhere. He wrote a late entry in the 1856 *Journal*—possibly years after— one that summed up the difference between dreams and experience: "Seeing is beleiving. The pains lie among the pleasures like sand in rice, not only bad in themselves, but spoiling the good" (p. 268).

Melville's life, of course, did not end at this time, nor on this note. Certain critics cast Melville into a Long Quietus even earlier than this return in 1857—sometime after *Pierre*—as though an author not turning out a *Moby-Dick* each year was dead to literature. Melville, in fact, never gave up writing, although in a certain way he gave up authorship. He no longer wrote out of the inspiration and energy of the 1847–52 period. With certain exceptions, the work came out of deliberation, organized research, and stylistic preparation. In addition, he assumed an indifference to criticism and fame, and he came to know that family income was not ensured through writing. As a result, he went underground or deliberately disappeared from the public eye. But he continued to write a great number of poems and vignettes over this period, culminating in *Clarel* and in *Billy Budd*, which was completed only a few months before his death. Even more telling evidence of Melville's ongoing creative impulse is the twenty-year linkage between the events of the seven-month extended vacation and the poetic narrative of *Clarel*.

COMPOSITION AND SOURCES

In late August 1875 Melville received a check for $1,200 from his uncle, Peter Gansevoort. The gift enabled him to complete arrangements on 4 January of the following year with G. P. Putnam and Sons for the anonymous publication of *Clarel*. Ironically, on the same day, he received a telegram from Albany informing him of his uncle Peter's death. When the book was published on 3 June, it contained Melville's generous dedication: "By a spontaneous act, not very long ago, my kinsman, the late Peter Gansevoort, of Albany, N.Y., in a personal interview provided for the publication of this poem, known to him by report, as existing in manuscript. Justly and affectionately the printed book is inscribed with his name."

Melville had probably begun organization and tentative writing of the long poem shortly after the publication of *Battle-Pieces and Aspects of War* in 1866. The psychic toll the work exacted was expressed by Elizabeth in a frank letter to Catherine Lansing, on 2 February 1876:

The fact is, that Herman, poor fellow, is in such a frightfully nervous state, & particularly now with such an added strain on his mind, that I am actually *afraid* to have any one here for fear that he will be upset entirely, & not be able to go on with the printing. . . . If ever this dreadful *incubus* of a *book* (I call it so because it has undermined all our happiness) gets off Herman's shoulders I do hope he may be in better mental health—but at present I have reason to feel the gravest concern & anxiety about it—to put it in mild phrase." (*Mel. Log*, p. 747)

Augusta Melville's death thereafter on 4 April and the funeral trip to Albany exacerbated the anxiety for Melville as he worked on the galleys, determined to see this enormous project brought to a conclusion.

When the book was published, Melville's name did appear on the title page, his desire for anonymity given over to the wishes or demands of the publisher. The *"incubus"* image was nowhere apparent, or, at least, it was glossed over by the author in a formal Note of indifference that preceded his poem: "If during the period in which this work has remained unpublished, though not undivulged, any of its properties have by a natural process exhaled; it yet retains, I trust, enough of original life to redeem it at least from vapidity. Be that as it may, I here dismiss the book—content beforehand with whatever future awaits it." In the light of Elizabeth's fears and of her knowledge from long years of watch over his moods, the Note sounds like the boy in the graveyard whistling to keep up his courage. No other single work of the author had involved so much time and research; no other contained such unconcealed protests and confessions. He could not "dismiss the book" as much as fear the baying of the critics once again and regret the fact of another unpopular book carrying his name. More than any other work before this, *Clarel* demonstrated the truth of Melville's statement in a letter to Hawthorne, in June 1851: "What I feel most moved to write, that is banned,— it will not pay. Yet, altogether, write the *other* way I cannot. So the product is a final hash, and all my books are botches."[1]

The predictable negative reviews, which will be discussed hereafter, and the sale of only 478 copies caused Melville to call in the publication. Failure to gain public attention was not new. From *Mardi* on, his name had lost the *Typee* appeal, and he complained repeatedly of the fickleness of fame and patronage. In a letter to his English publisher, Richard Bentley, on 5 June 1849, he expressed the writer's problem:

You may think, in your own mind that a man is unwise,—indiscreet, to write a work of that kind, when he might have written one perhaps, calculated merely to please the general reader, & not provoke attack, however masqued in an affectation of indifference or contempt. But some of us scribblers, My Dear Sir, always have a certain something unmanageable in us, that bids us do this or that, and be done it must—hit or miss (*Letters*, p. 86).

The something "unmanageable" of *Clarel* with its two volumes of over eighteen thousand lines of poetry was immediately obvious to even the most casual of buyers. Years later, Melville wryly commented on the formidable appearance of the poem to an English admirer, James Billson: " 'Clarel,' . . . a metrical affair, a pilgrimage or what not, of several thousand lines, eminently adapted for unpopularity.—The notification to you here is ambidexter, as it were: it may intimidate or allure" (*Letters*, p. 275). The eight years between the publication and this letter distanced him from the emotions brought on by *Clarel*'s failure, enough that he could then laugh at the impossible challenge laid down by the poem. Even so, shortly thereafter he sent Billson a copy of the book.

Consistent with the bad fortune of the massive work, the manuscript of *Clarel* is missing. (It might well have gone in the cleaning out that Elizabeth managed after the funeral in 1891.) One item is extant: a handwritten copy of a song sung by the young Cypriote, one of the minor characters in *Clarel* (III, iv). E. C. Stedman had asked Melville for his engraved portrait and "one of your best known short poems" for his forthcoming illustrated edition of *Poets of America*. Melville complied with the song he called "Ditty of Aristippus," amused no doubt that this "best known" poem came from *Clarel*, the work Stedman himself had berated on 16 June 1876 in a New York *Daily Tribune* review. The original copy of the poem is now in the American Antiquarian Society, in Worcester, Massachusetts; the first stanza, in Melville's hand, has been reproduced in facsimile in *The Melville Log* (p. 805).

With only 478 copies sold and the remaining inventory soon unaccounted for, the Putnam edition became a rare item. In 1924 Constable & Co., London, brought out *Clarel*, as volumes XIV and XV of *The Works of Herman Melville*. This second issuance of the poem after forty-eight years was limited to 750 copies.[2] Thirty-six years later, in 1960, Hendricks House published a third edition of the poem, edited by Walter Bezanson. For the first time, the poem was fully available to a new readership, with scholarly notes on history and geography and a comprehensive introduction to the poem and its history.

The Bezanson edition underscores at least one of the reasons that readers of *Clarel* in earlier years were perplexed, impatient, angry, and altogether disapproving. Without explanatory notes, the poem could not carry Melville's vast erudition: bookishness dominates the reader lost in the geography and culture of the Middle East, the history of ancient and medieval times, the lives of the saints, and other references and allusions that reflect Melville's extensive ongoing reading and his major interests after the Civil War. *Moby-Dick* holds the same kind of problem for the reader unfamiliar with cetology and nautical lore. But the novel attempts to help the neophyte through lengthy explanations. In addition, the drama of the hunt can be followed easily without an understanding of those added dimensions. *Clarel*, too, tells a story, but the tension is minimal in comparison with the many layers of philosophical inquiry and judgment, rendered in a generally unattractive setting and supported by hundreds of scholarly references. In addition to these difficulties for the reader, the format of a long narrative poem poses problems beyond those in the prose of a novel.

The intimacy of the Middle East in the poem was developed partially from Melville's memory of his trip but much more from his careful study of the 1856 *Journal* (see Horsford's introduction, pp. 29–41). Consistent with his past practice, Melville also used the Bible for passages relevant to the issues under discussion. Here, however, the Bible became for him more than a source of quotations; it was a guide book of geography and theology. John Murray's *A Handbook for Travellers in Spain and Palestine* complemented the Bible, and he probably used it for commentary. But the source book he leaned on most and acknowledged as a kind of Baedeker was Arthur Stanley's *Sinai and Palestine in Connection with Their History* (1856). Melville borrowed from other authors and books mostly for the second volume (Nathalia Wright, "Source"; Walter E. Bezanson; and Horsford, p. 10), but these were his four major sources.

Consonant with the philosophical inquiry and marked erudition of the poem, Melville deliberately eschewed a lyric mood in his composition. *Clarel* is a seamless piece, integrating and complicating the many and varied parts as it moves inexorably to a tragic conclusion. It is virtually impossible, therefore, to know a little of the poem, that is, to come at it through truncated texts or through judiciously selected excerpts. The

Viking Portable Herman Melville presents three worthy exceptions: portions of "A Sketch" (I, xxxvii), in which one pilgrim tells of another's background; "Dirge" (IV, xxxi), an elegy written for one of the dead characters; and the "Epilogue" (IV, xxxv). Hennig Cohen faced the same limitations in his *Selected Poems of Herman Melville* (1964). He, too, included the "Epilogue," but he also presented many passages that depend for poetic effect and explication on the entire poem.[3] The sad fact here is that *Clarel* can be known only through sustained reading, a task that few persons have the time or inclination to undertake.

THE POEM·

The poem begins with an introduction to the central figure, Clarel. He is a young Protestant divinity student seeking in Palestine reconfirmation of a belief in Christ he has lost: " 'Can faith remove / Her light, because of late no plea / I've lifted to her source above?' " (I, i, ll. 118–20). His background is unknown and will remain so throughout the poem. He has been "long confined / Apart like Vesta in a grove / Collegiate (I, i, ll. 107–109), developing his intellect until he concludes there are no answers for him in "blind theology." The trip to the Holy Land appears to be one last attempt to recover what he had formerly accepted as a Christian way of life. His first day there discourages him, for the high expectation he had of the romantic Middle East amounts to "Thy blank, blank towers, Jerusalem!" (I, i, l. 61). Weeds and dust, sealed arches, and doors cemented fast underscore the strangeness he feels in a haunted city.

He roams through the town persuaded that a companion might lift his depression. He meets Nehemiah, an old eccentric, an American millennarian in Palestine, who has announced and awaits the Second Coming of Christ. Nehemiah offers little companionship and less instruction for Clarel, then or later, but the young man tolerates him as a guide. After a few days, they come upon a youthful humpback named Celio. Although the two never speak, Clarel feels a powerful influence coming from him. Like Clarel, except that he is an apostate Catholic, he has thrown over all the Christian beliefs that seemed to sustain him in his native Italy. He dies shortly afterwards, outside the city walls, calling out defiance to an image of Christ crucified who had brought false promises of redeeming the world. Clarel sees in him his own doubts and rebellion: the brief encounter carries premonitions of his own disaster.

Later, while accompanying Nehemiah as he hands out tracts to any and all, Clarel falls in love with Ruth, a beautiful young Jewess whose father Nathan, once a God-fearing Illinois farmer, had one day read Thomas Paine and immediately professed himself an atheist. Soon after, Nathan fell in love with Agar, a Jewish woman who persuaded him to her faith. He thereupon became militantly Jewish—more so than his wife—and insisted that they leave to farm in Judea. Over her protests, they moved there with the two children—Ruth being one of them—where he spent his life fighting Arabs and cultivating arid land.

Ruth responds in her love for Clarel, and the two plan marriage. The strictures of the Hebrew religion limit the time the lovers can be together in courtship, however, and Clarel is forced once again into walking tours with Nehemiah. On one of them, he meets the two most impressive people he will engage in Palestine: one, the sensitive recluse, Vine, and the other, a forceful personality, Rolfe. They invite him and Nehemiah to join them on a pilgrimage to Siddim, the Dead Sea, the ancient Copt monastery at Mar Saba, and Bethlehem: it is less a pilgrimage than a tour conducted for foreigners. Clarel demurs because of Ruth. He leaves them, but instead of receiving a joyous lover's embrace he finds her lamenting over her dead father, killed by marauding Arabs. In keeping with Hebrew custom, she cannot see Clarel until the end of the mourning period. He decides to join the others on the pilgrimage as a way to pass over the time: they leave on the following morning.

This ends the first of four parts. Part I introduces Clarel, gives him the companion he seeks, then immediately takes her away for a time, and hints through Celio's death and Jerusalem's desolation of the probable failure of his mission to the Middle East. However, it is little more than an introduction to the Wilderness that follows and a presentiment of the tragedy that will develop.

Clarel meets the other pilgrims: Djalea, the guide; Derwent, an Anglican priest; a rich banker from Thessalonica, and Glaucon, his future son-in-law; an Elder in the Scottish Presbyterian church; and a man dressed in black named Mortmain. Rolfe, Vine, and Nehemiah fill out the group, except for the guard troops led by Belex. The terrifying desert and the grim discussions of sin and death led by Mortmain discourage the banker and his son-in-law: they join a caravan going back to Jerusalem. But even before their departure, the Elder can take no more of the "lewd balladry" and lack of "moral gravity" (II, x, ll. 51-58), and he goes back alone to Jerusalem. Memories of Christ's forty days in the desert and of Moses's lamentation over Jericho incite fear in the pilgrims, except for Mortmain, who leaves for the night to be alone on the mountain over the black gorge of Achor. The others continue to the Crusader's Tower in Jericho, where they set up camp for the first night in the Wilderness.

On the second day, they meet a Syrian monk who tells them that he spent forty days and nights in these Quarantanian mountains to atone for his sins and doubts. Although he displays a certain serenity, the doubts have obviously persisted, no less but no more than his faith. His ambivalence matches Rolfe's, but it contrasts sharply with the extreme bias of Margoth, another person they meet on the second day. He is a geologist, a "Hegelized—/ Convert to science" (II, xix, ll. 55–56). He calls the Bible a tissue of lies and insists that the so-called Holy Land must be made over in the name of progress. Unlike the Syrian monk with his gentle appeal, Margoth repels everyone within sound of his loud voice.

On the third day the group arrives at the River Jordan where the peace of the ancient baptism is shattered by marauding Arabs. Djalea talks the bandits out of their ransom demands, and the pilgrims resume their earlier conversations. They are pleasantly interrupted by a Dominican monk. He and Rolfe engage in an amicable discussion over the merits of the Catholic Church, to the dismay of Derwent, who insists that "The world is now too civilized / For Rome" (II, xxvi, ll. 120–21). Clarel tires of the speculative talk and joins Vine. A sudden erotic emotion sweeps over him, stronger by far than anything he experienced with Celio, or even with Ruth. He senses in Vine the companion he has sought, a delight that is quickly crushed in Vine's spontaneous rejection of all personal involvement.

The pilgrimage arrives at the heart of darkness, on the shore of the Dead Sea. Sodom and Gommorah, the suicidal Maccabees, and Aaron's hermitage and death cell on Mt. Hor are evoked in the infernal setting. The macabre is intensified in their night encampment when Mortmain returns from his ghastly vigil on the mountain. He has none of the Syrian monk's equanimity after his descent. Instead, Mortmain rails again at the group. He sees evil everywhere, and he commands them all to repentance. During the night, Nehemiah dreams of God calling him home to the New Jerusalem. He rises in his sleep, walks into the Dead Sea, and drowns. The others bury him in the morning when an avalanche suddenly slides down the mountain, as though nature or God has taken note of the death.

Part II, set in the Wilderness, is completed on the fourth day of the journey. Just as the Jerusalem experience ended in the death of Nathan, so the Wilderness carries the same awful message to Clarel in Nehemiah's drowning. He finds it difficult by then, in the face of recurring death, to recall Ruth's features or to vis··alize a happy future.

Part III begins with the pilgrims moving out of the Siddim gorge. For three days thereafter they submerge the Dead Sea episode in the pleasant surroundings of Mar Saba. Comfortable sleeping quarters, good food and wine, pleasant or less troublesome conversation, and singing and dancing fill out their days. The good cheer is led by a newcomer, a merchant from Lesbos, an epicurean whose jolly ways immediately stimulate the easygoing Derwent. The Lesbian's Bacchic urgings are somewhat offset by Agath, a weatherbeaten sailor who is convalescing with the monks and whose narrated bleak experience tempers for a little while the riotous mood of the revelers.

At Mar Saba, the pilgrims wander throughout the different cells and levels of the ancient oasis in the desert. Clarel is less the tourist than the seeker, even in the genial setting: the celibate peace of the monks strikes him as more desirable than a married life with Ruth. He is more troubled in the new doubts raised than he was on arrival at Jaffa. His anxiety deepens on the seventh day of the pilgrimage when they are about to leave Mar Saba. Mortmain alone is unaccounted for, until Clarel finds him dead, his open eyes fixed on a palm tree, an eagle's feather on his lips. Mortmain is buried at once but outside the monastery walls: the monks refuse Christian burial to heretics.

Part III thus ends with the death of a major character. Mar Saba provides only a false resolution of Clarel's problems, exacerbated at the Dead Sea. Like all illusions, the institutional promise of ease only intensifies anxiety. Death is now the pervasive theme for Clarel, with each significant stop on his journey marked by another death.

The fourth part is set in Bethlehem, with Vine, Rolfe, and Clarel ironically playing out the roles of modern Magi. Another pilgrim, Ungar, joins them: a military officer from Southwestern United States, a bruised veteran of the Civil War, and now a soldier of fortune. On the eighth day of the pilgrimage, they travel through the sacred sites of the ancient city, all the while that Ungar, another Mortmain, condemns the modern age of materialism and disbelief. On the ninth night, Clarel rooms with a young businessman from Lyons. A hedonist, he is in Judea because he has been told the Jewish women are the most voluptuous and most available in the world. He is garrulous and shallow, but his sensuality suggests to Clarel that his own Puritan strictures preclude happiness. In the morning, however, after the Lyonese has gone, Clarel knows the easy solution of the flesh is no way for him, and he dismisses temptation.

On the tenth night, the company completes the circled tour and enters Jerusalem. They pass a cemetery on the outskirts of the city, where laborers are preparing two graves. They are for Ruth and Agar, dead from a combination of fever and grief over Nathan's death. Clarel defies Hebrew custom, kisses Ruth's face and hands, and remains while the bodies are buried.

Rolfe and Vine wait for five days and then reluctantly leave Clarel on his own. He wanders dazed throughout Jerusalem during Holy Week, attempting in vain once again to identify with the crucified and risen Christ. Weeks go by and Clarel is still overcome by doubts and sadness. He is alone, as he was on arrival in Palestine. When last seen, he has joined another group of pilgrims on the feast of Pentecost as they move along the Via Crucis.

Part IV, like the other three sections, ends with death. Clarel now knows its pervasiveness: attempts to escape it add to the pain of its final discovery.

RECEPTION AND REDISCOVERY

When *Clarel* appeared in June 1876, it was Melville's first publication since *Battle-Pieces* in 1866. Like *Israel Potter* (1855) and *The Confidence-Man* (1857), this fairly large collection of poems on the Civil War had few readers, and it failed to renew the interest of critics who had already dismissed Melville as a serious author. He was virtually unknown in 1876. This possibly accounts for the failure of two of the three most important weeklies—*Harper's Weekly* and *Nation*—even to note the poem's publication. The four prestigious monthlies also ignored the poem: *Harper's*, *Scribner's*, *Atlantic*, and *North American Review*.

The New York *Tribune* reviewed *Clarel* as hardly the work of the "narrator of marvelous stories of tropical life and adventure" (*Crit. Her.*, p. 399). The reviewer recognized that the medium called for a different reading, but, he wanted to know, could this be the same poet who wrote the thundering lines of "Sheridan's Ride" ["Sheridan at Cedar Creek"]? The hodgepodge effect belied the author's profound intention and accounted for an obvious failure: "It is, in this respect, a medley such as we have rarely perused,—a mixture of skill and awkwardness, thought and aimless fancy, plan shattered by whim and melody broken by discords" (p. 400). The short notice in the *World* rejected the poem as a series of wild ramblings into philosophic discourse and away from the only appealing element, the "bold, clear, and judicious" descriptions (p. 403). The *Independent* and the *Library Table* derided the book in language so vague as to suggest that the book was never read. The same distance from the poem marked the criticism in the *Galaxy*. The text was not examined at all; instead, the poet was dismissed as a practitioner of dullness. The reviewer in the New York *Times* probably read the poem, but he recommended that "a writer of Mr. Herman Melville's undoubted talent" should stay with prose; that his "genius is evidently not of the kind which must express itself in numbers" (p. 404).

Unqualified praise came in the London *Academy* review. The writer commended Melville's "hidden connexion between things outwardly separate" and the poetic language selected for the intended bleak effects and theme. He saw, however, no future for the poem: "We advise our readers to study this interesting poem, which deserves more attention than we fear it is likely to gain in an age which craves for smooth, short, lyric song, and is impatient for the most part of what is philosophic or didactic" (pp. 407–408).

Lippincott's Magazine was less impressed. The reviewer, obviously a

Typee fan, was delighted with the fact of a new publication. He found, instead of the past adventure tale that made the author great, a long dull poem, filled with erroneous conclusions and marked by wearisome pedestrian expression. He wondered why Melville could believe that others were either plagued by, or could find interest in, such philosophic and religious problems.

Impatience with dullness and unintelligibility summed up the caustic notice in England's *Westminster Review.* The writer paraphrased the allegory of the mountain producing the mouse, with his lead into Melville's poem a sarcastic wondering of how such an extraordinary undertaking would yield only absurdity: "Talleyrand used to say that he always found nonsense singularly refreshing. He would certainly have set a high value on *Clarel.*"

Except for the favorable comments in the *Academy*, *Clarel* was thus summarily dismissed in 1876. Descriptions of the terrain and feel for the Middle East culture were singled out by individual critics as worthy but were seen only as fillers for a poet who concerned himself almost exclusively with troubled matters of the soul. In an age of poetry dominated by Longfellow and Lowell, *Clarel* of necessity fell on deaf ears.

These few notices ended contemporary recognition of Melville's poem. It was not until almost a half-century later that Frank Mather rediscovered *Clarel* and judged it the work of genius: the most incisive statement of the nineteenth century's social, religious, and political issues. Two years later, Raymond Weaver modestly continued this revival of interest and emphasized the autobiographical richness of *Clarel*: "[It] is by all odds the most important record we have of what was the temper of Melville's deeper thoughts during his long metaphysical period" (p. 361). Even so, he saw problems inherent in the length and style that would prevent it from ever being popular. John Middleton Murry reviewed this rediscovered work and, like Mather and Weaver, regretted the clumsy structure and gauche expressions, but he praised the author's superior perception of the spiritual problems in the modern world.

John Freeman dissented from this new appreciation: he saw in the long, "boring" poem virtually nothing of value. He traced the fault to the author's self-imposed constraints and his failure to understand the nature of poetry: "He never learned, neither in verse, nor in prose, that his philosophy and religion, his transcendentalism and piety, are of little *essential* value in poetry, and indeed of none if by their presence they exclude imagination" (p. 169). Lewis Mumford also regretted Melville's choice to give up the prose which had enabled him to be poetic: "He was a true poet; but formal verse was not his medium; and the relentless probity of his mind, the keen reaching into the heart of the dilemma, lacked in these lengthy verses an appropriate vehicle" (p. 322). Nevertheless, Mumford praised the author's social skepticism and stoic affirmation of man in a beleaguered society, qualities that were out of step in the nineteenth century but were well understood in the twentieth. Despite his demurral on aesthetic grounds, Mumford insisted that "the precious shards" must be examined. Willard Thorp (1938) also qualified his acceptance of the poem, but he was impressed by the "Epilogue" as a forthright note of Christian hope. He saw in it Melville's self-resolve and a resolution of most of the anger and doubts that pervaded the earlier works (p. xcv).

John Freeman aside, almost all modern critics have taken the positive lead from Mather and Weaver. Disagreements continued but mostly over particular elements of the poem and not over whether or not the work had value. Most critics qualified their judgments on the basis that the poem does call for a limited audience. One who had virtually no reservation was Jean Simon. He praised the artistic fusion of nineteenth-century background—accurately depicted—and the painful soul-searching that enabled the author to deal with his own deepest problems at the same time that he shrewdly assessed the shortcomings of modern man (pp. 467–90). Henry W. Wells echoed this enthusiasm in his insistence that the "toughly imaginative" language, kept in the restraining measures carefully chosen, burned steadily with energy: "In *Clarel* style is outwardly less glowing while actually a greater fire burns within. Economy and intellectual clarity replace lavishness and mental fog" (p. 480). However, like other enthusiasts of the poem, he predicted that *Clarel* for obvious reasons would never become popular. Robert Penn Warren read *Clarel* in the same way, as a twentieth-century poem in its use of bare language and in its avoidance of sentiment. In "Melville the Poet," he judged the poem a continuance of the earlier works, with Rolfe and the Druze carrying on Melville's admiration for the enduring self-isolatoes. Later, in "Melville's Poems" (1967), he wrote that the poet worked on a personal commitment to the "truth of an idea"; he had less interest in solving profound problems than knowing if Clarel could go on with his problems unsolved.

The first full study of *Clarel* in itself and not as part of the Melville canon was Walter E. Bezanson's 1943 dissertation (*Mel. Diss.*, #19). Just as Weaver first set the course for appreciation of *Clarel*, so Bezanson led all readers into a new and fuller understanding of the poem. Here, as in "Complex Passion" (1954) and in his 1960 Hendricks House edition of *Clarel*, he relates the poem to the history and geography of the Middle East, Melville's trip in 1856–57 and pertinent entries in the 1856 *Journal*, and the author's prolific reading.

William Plomer brought out in England, also in 1943, a limited selection of Melville's poetry, which included excerpts from *Clarel*. He voiced the same complaints of form aired since 1876, but he thought the poem well worth the effort required in the reading: " . . . the reader is left with an extraordinary expression of a man of the 19th century trying to free himself from the incubus of conscience, the weight of tradition and the lumber of a whole civilization, and to look backwards or forwards, inwards or outwards, for living realities" (p. 8). In the following year, F. O. Matthiessen published his brief selection of Melville's poetry but was less enthusiastic than Plomer. He read the tragic ending and the "Epilogue" as paradoxical statements of hope; paradoxical because the harsh poetic effects rendered those statements meaningless.[4]

William Ellery Sedgwick coupled *Clarel* and *Billy Budd* as final testament pieces in his study of Melville's inner life. He saw calm acceptance in Clarel's tragedy, reflective of Melville's move from "radical Protestantism" to a spiritual but uncommitted relationship with the Catholic Church. In this, he argued, Melville was only continuing his life-long concern over the dichotomy of head and heart (pp. 216–17). Rudolph von Abele believed that reconciliation did occur, in a dominance of heart over head, but he saw no cause of it in Melville's Catholic tendencies (pp. 592–98).

Van Wyck Brooks complained of Melville's sophomoric grasp of philosophic problems, a weakness that the author had successfully concealed earlier in soaring prose. Brooks dismissed the long poem, "with its jogtrot metre and its characters vaguely drifting in and out" (p. 249). He argued that if Melville had not written *Moby-Dick*, all the other pieces, including *Clarel*, would be only literary effects and not worthy of notice (p. 172). Nathalia Wright was less concerned with the form as she was impressed by how effectively *Clarel* derived from Scripture. She also saw the poem as a culmination of Melville's life-long preoccupation with Ishmael: all of the major characters are orphaned wanderers, afflicted in loneliness (p. 57).

Wright's study of Melville's Biblical allusions appeared in the same year as Geoffrey Stone's biography (1949). Stone, arguing from a Roman Catholic viewpoint, wondered over Melville's deep concern for the Church. He saw it as little more than emotional reaction, for nowhere, including the "Epilogue," is there adherence to doctrinal matters, nor is there a belief in transcendence. Like Mumford, Stone read the poem as a long statement of life "found on the subrational level . . . mere animal persistence" (p. 296).

THIRTY YEARS OF CRITICISM

Howard Horsford's edition of the 1856 *Journal* in 1955 demonstrated how dependent Melville was on the *Journal* throughout the writing of *Clarel*. Other critics before this had noted the relationship of the two but only in passing. Horsford believes that "*Clarel*, so far as narrative goes, is virtually an elaborated recapitulation of the Palestinian section of the journal" (p. 40). He reads Parts 1 and 2 as a statement of Melville's highly personal feelings, written shortly after the journey in 1857, and Parts 3 and 4 as distanced writing, a product of the poet's scholarship, composed sometime after the conclusion of the Civil War.

In 1974 Franklin Walker published his essays on three irreverent pilgrims to the Holy Land—Melville, J. Ross Browne, and Mark Twain. Melville the pilgrim is examined through *Clarel* (pp. 133–61), although the poem is viewed only as it corresponds to entries in the *Journal*. Walker has little interest in the aesthetic merits of *Clarel*, and he explores beliefs only as they touch on the thesis of American irreverence in the Holy Land.

In his Hendricks House edition of *Clarel*, Bezanson ranges beyond scholarship to study the poem *qua* poetry. He reads the form of *Clarel* as aesthetically correct: the circular movement of the pilgrims circumscribes nineteenth-century endeavors, and the cramped lines and jogtrot meter properly depict the constricted condition of modern man. The poem supports Hawthorne's acute observation of Melville's dilemma: "He can neither believe, nor be comfortable in his unbelief; and he is too honest and courageous not to try to do one or the other" (*Mel. Log*, p. 529). Bezanson cites the ending of *Clarel* and the "Epilogue" as a continuation of the poet's concern over a loss of faith and the need to find some substitute for endurance (p. cix).

Clarel has not evoked different "schools" of readers: virtually all modern critics raise this issue of faith-despair and of *Clarel* as a key to understanding Melville's final theological and philosophical beliefs. Some of them read the poem as a kind of positive resolution: all the sound and fury of life do not "signify nothing" as much as attest to human integrity. Others understand *Clarel* as a continuation of Melville's cynicism, struck with force first in *Pierre* and *The Confidence-Man* and carried on thereafter through *Billy Budd, Sailor*. The lines drawn between these two general views are not always sharp, an effect consistent with Melville's belief that life itself ends in ambiguity.

Like other critics before and after, Richard Chase recognizes the poem's weaknesses, particularly the extraordinary length, but he is impressed by the clarity of Melville's final acceptance of "a point of view" in an age the poet judged sterile, when "life has withdrawn its richness and its ecstasy and is no longer tragic but simply progressive" (p. 256). In *Herman Melville*, Newton Arvin concurs with this reading: Melville expressed in *Clarel* a final acceptance of the inscrutability of God in the relentless dialectic of good and evil (pp. 286–87). In his biography, Leon Howard does not see the poem resolving the dilemma for Melville, who had posed the polarities always in theological terms. Instead, the older poet moved away from theology and philosophy to psychology and was thereby able to give up anger over human folly for compassionate understanding of human weakness (pp. 309–10).

As noted earlier, John Freeman had little to praise in *Clarel*. But a second English critic, Ronald Mason, considers the poem a highlight in the author's career. He shares the acceptance-reading of Chase, Arvin, and Howard but rejects the pessimism implied in their judgments: "*Clarel* is nothing less than the most substantial and significant attempt that Melville's considerable intellect was ever to make to rationalise and resolve the paradoxes which his intuition had bred in his imagination" (pp. 242–44). The title of the book, *The Spirit Above the Dust*, expresses his interpretation of the "Epilogue" as an affirmative statement and evidence that Melville in this poem, as in life, came to peace with himself, society, and God.

Dorothee Finkelstein is more reserved in her praise of the poem and less convinced of a positive meaning. She points to Melville's entry in the 1856 *Journal* that he was "utterly used up" as a clue to why the Middle East failed to stir his imagination when he came to write *Clarel*. Nevertheless, she sees in the poem an expression of Melville's abiding humanism, particularly in Part III. There, Mar Saba is described in stark contrast with the Church of the Holy Sepulchre in Part I, "which is degradation of the holiest place in Christendom...[and which] proclaims the absolute sterility and failure of religious faith...[but Mar Saba] is humanized in scenes of revelry and boon companionship, and lastly, even transcendence in the vision of the Palm" (p. 243).

In my book on the poem, I call *Clarel* an autobiography of Melville's spiritual life and show the poem's direct and indirect connections with all his other work. Like other critics, I consider the "powerfully prosaic poetry" artistically correct for the theme and judge the poem, despite the missing Elizabethan language and the ellipses of understatement, the best long poem written in the United States (pp. 96–97). Unlike Mason, I cannot find Melville's resolution of life-long problems, and I am convinced that Melville believed they could not be solved. But, like Finkelstein, I am warmed by Melville's renewed faith in humanity as he "continued this Grecian demand for nobility in the face of catastrophe" (p. 215).

Father Joseph G. Knapp has virtually unqualified praise of *Clarel*. He considers the overall tone heroic, with a clear enunciation of America at a dead-end of religious belief, but with an equally strong insistence that man cannot live in unbelief. In this, he echoes Hawthorne's words on Melville's difficulty. Accordingly, Father Knapp argues, the "Epilogue" is no mere appendage: it is the logical conclusion of the major theme— "[The] deepest wisdom is the meaning of the mystery of endurance" (p. 113). In "An Existential Gospel," Stanley Brodwin also interprets the poem as modern man's search for authenticity, a theme explored no differently by Kierkegaard and Heidegger: the "inner man" succeeds when he recognizes his own nature and moves on to the "frontiers of eternity" (pp. 375–87). A third spokesman for this existential understanding of pain as prologue to wisdom, Ray B. Browne is struck by the poet's twentieth-century emphasis on man's lonely condition and, paradoxically, on the fact of human dignity in the face of such isolation (p. 278).

William Braswell's study of Melville's religious thought begins with the author's early sturdy faith imparted by his family: belief in life after death, God's providence, order in the universe, and man alone as responsible for wreckage in the universe. Braswell traces Melville through the disenchanting years of *Mardi*, the cynical period of *Pierre* and *The Confidence-Man*, and the loss of that early faith. He is surprised, therefore, to find in *Clarel* a rehearsal of the same bleak testimony of history and experience, but one that leads ironically to a somewhat benign view of the world. He does not find an explanation in Melville's favorable comments on Catholicism and suggests that these came as an indirect result of the Oxford Movement's influence. But he reads the ending as Melville's deep conviction that there has to be a meaning for man, if not in this world, then in the next: "Christ's doctrine of love and his promise of immortality were among the lasting influences in Melville's life" (p. 122). Braswell argues from this to the logical necessity of the "Epilogue," which sums up Melville's major theme:

> Then keep thy heart, though yet but ill-resigned—
> Clarel, thy heart, the issues there but mind
> (IV, xxxv, ll. 27–28)

Although these critics vary in definitions of Melville's resolution of the faith-despair conflict, they agree in their assessment of Melville's spiritual and psychological position by the time he finished the poem for publication: human existence cannot be explained, but prevailing in the face of such ignorance is reason enough to continue. Melville's posture in the poem may preclude happiness, but it insists on dignified action at every stage of existence.

Many readers come away from *Clarel* with different reactions from the ones just now cited. Lawrance Thompson hardly notes the poem in his book on Melville, and he dismisses its poetic value. He does see it, however, as another example of Melville's abiding hatred of God. He finds the "hate-shod" Pierre and "fire-worshipping" Ahab repeated in the poem; implacable and offended characters—including Christ—in a universe betrayed by God (p. 337).

William Shurr notes this same antagonism in *Clarel*, but he traces it to Melville's contempt for man rather than God. The misanthropic expression is central to Melville's aesthetic: a view of the nature of evil in the heart of man in a corrupted universe. This was Melville's essential Calvinism stirred by a poet's imagination. Accordingly, the Dead Sea in the poem is the Bad Sea, "the magnetic center toward which the pilgrims are drawn" (p. 72). All the other elements of the "highly emblematic landscape" symbolize abandoned human beings who struggle for relief.

Merlin Bowen studies the poem in depth and agrees with Thompson that it continues alienated man's "long encounter" with God. *Clarel* is no different than the earlier expressions except that it underscores the rebellion in ways the younger Melville would not have tolerated: "...if it is Melville's last fully considered judgment that we want, we must turn to *Clarel*. And quiet though it is, that answer, in its emphasis upon endurance and affirmation, is closer to defiance than surrender" (p. 282).

This defiance effects no change, John Bernstein insists, but it is a position that Melville could not give up; hence, we identify with the three revolutionaries—Celio, Mortmain, and Ungar—who reject the possibility of a benevolent God and man's innate goodness. Each attempts to fix his life in a positive set of values but discovers very early that God and man are incompatible. Bernstein considers this the major theme of *Clarel*: man endures even in the discovery of a reality which cancels out faith and hope (pp. 188–201). John Seelye also emphasizes this existential reading: modern man achieves heroism of a kind but only when he faces up to the contingencies of life and the limited possibilities for order and peace (pp. 136–45). Bernstein and Seelye read *Clarel* as twentieth-century concern over the human predicament—man's fate—but only as it echoes a life-long expression of the author.

James Baird's study of primitivism and artists includes a brief essay on *Clarel*. Baird believes that the poem contains some "of the worst aberrations of versification in the English language," but that the "total range of poetic sensitivity triumphs over these faults" (p. 75). He considers Melville's numerous allusions to the Cross and other Christian symbols actually the use of pre-Christian material to document a stoical, Protestant acceptance of a mysterious world. Nowhere in the poem are there statements or implications of faith or hope.

Milton R. Stern also judges *Clarel* as additional evidence of Melville's naturalism, one supported by rationalism, empiricism, objectivity, and relativism. For him, the poem picks up from *The Confidence-Man* in that all the questions end in silence. It is one of the "tragedies" from which community wisdom never develops; in fact, the hero's "recognition" is the uselessness of the pilgrimage. Stern reads *Clarel* and most of Melville's work as testimony to the disappearance of idealism in the Western world (p. 272).

Patricia Chaffee points to a particular motif in *Clarel* that defines the fruitless pilgrimage through tortured imagery. This is the Kedron River, a pervasive and unifying symbol and theme, according to Chaffee. It is ominous in the beginning as it relates to the geographical labyrinth of Jerusalem and the spiritual suffering of Gethsemane. Even though hardly mentioned later on, the Kedron is always implied as a threat through its counterpart, the Jordan River and its mouth, the Dead Sea. Chaffee sees the river winding through the Wilderness and into the Dead Sea as analogous to the pilgrims' spiritual wandering to a dead-end, ironically expressed in Nehemiah's death (pp. 374–82). In part or whole, all movement in *Clarel* leads to death.

Shirley Dettlaff reads *Clarel* in the same way; that is, Melville's struggle for form was therapeutic and artistic. Like Bezanson, she notes the poet's distinction between Hellenic form and Hebraic feeling as a conscious borrowing from Matthew Arnold: Hellenic emphasis on the senses and reason producing optimism; Hebraic stress on the heart and imagination resulting in a powerful emotion of sadness. Dettlaff concludes that Melville kept a tight balance of the two throughout the poem, even though the overall effect recommends the exact opposite of Arnold's prescription (pp. 212–28).

As new readers come to *Clarel*, new insights into its multi-layered meanings and general worth, and into Melville's state of mind on the completion of the poem arise. For example, Nina Baym believes the poem discloses the author's final views on sex and in this is a rarity among Melville's works. *Clarel* begins with an erotic theme that is then carried to a final resolution. But instead of sexual culmination, the theme is a retreat from sex itself and not specifically from women or homosexuality. Baym interprets "The Recoil" (III, xxxi) to mean that Clarel does not share Mortmain's revulsion for female flesh; instead, he deliberately chooses celibacy as a positive step (pp. 315–28). Another specific reading is that of John Frederick, who recommends that the poem be read, as Newton Arvin suggests, as "a novel in verse," with unified chapters, settings, and theme. Such a reading corrects the assumed ambiguities and false readings, particularly those that identify Vine with Hawthorne and Clarel with the author (pp. 151–57).

Like most contemporary critics, Richard H. Fogle insists that a complete understanding of Melville demands a close reading of the long poem (pp. 101–16). He agrees with Weaver, who first observed that *Clarel* would not have many readers at any time. Even most enthusiastic readers, like Jean Simon and Ronald Mason, do not see a later generation of Melville votaries placing the poem next to *Moby-Dick* and "Benito Cereno." But the poem by now, more than a century after publication, is well known and admired in many quarters. That knowledge and admiration have resulted from the contributions made by the critics noted in these pages.

ANALYSIS

Warner Berthoff suggests that when Melville's confidence was gone and his doubts ran high, the earlier buoyant prose disappeared and his writing became constrained and strict (p. 50). *Clarel* particularly fits this judgment in terms of form. The inspired, self-conscious author who impelled, intruded, and commented on the action in the earlier works, for example, becomes in the poem an unobtrusive narrator, rarely more informed than the characters he observes, and almost never emotionally stirred by the unfolding events. The narrator, at first glance, appears to hold a dominant position, for the *Canterbury Tales* format promises a lively exchange of personalities. But just as there are very few tales told, so, too, the altercations and humorous byplay are among the pilgrims themselves only. In fact, when the narrator-author appends an Epilogue as consolation for the distraught Clarel, the voice and posture are unrecognizable. This accounts in part for the varied critical interpretations of these final lines, as numerous and radically different as those of *Billy Budd, Sailor.*

This submergence of ego, however, was less a loss of creative impulse than a deliberate choice of form. The prophetic element no longer served Melville. Whether this reflected an unhealthy condition in his household and his life, as the work of Kring and Carey might suggest (Yannella and Parker), or a refusal to allow his muse to take him into the dangerous channels of thought explored by Ahab and the other rebels, Melville, sometime after his return from the Middle East, chose form over inspiration:

> Not magnitude, not lavishness,
> But Form—the Site;
> Not innovating wilfulness,
> But reverence for the Archetype
> (Poems, p. 248)

Reverence and dedication are demanded of the readers as well, for the poem's eighteen thousand lines of generally linked, irregularly rhymed, tetrameters are only occasionally relieved by a change of beat or by a frolicsome song. Usually, emotions are checked with such lines, just as the imagination is too often controlled or constricted by the unrelenting expression. The fluid movement is occasionally halted by stop-and-go lines that are correct in syllables but wrong in emphasis of sound:

> Some one had done a friendly thing:
> Who? Small was Clarel's wondering.
> (I, xxxviii, ll. 49–50)

Despite these self-imposed restrictions of prosody, Melville sketched tender poignant scenes and gave his characters affective lines. For example, during the night-time Masque at Mar Saba, a muffled figure cries out in lamentation over his cutoff condition, exiled from Jerusalem and separated from "man's embrace." He is the Wandering Jew, the Ancient Mariner, Absalom, and all such lost persons. The whole canto (III, xix) intensifies the poem's theme by linking the meaning of the Masque to the frustrated pilgrims, but it also tugs at the heart like a one-act drama. The earlier Obsequies (II, xxxix) for Nehemiah, after he has drowned, range beyond the simple effects of the Masque, as they sustain in hushed tone the fear, mystery, and sadness of the bewildered onlookers. Melville similarly conveys in the governing form of the poem a felt compassion for Celio's loss of the Past and of Perfection; Mortmain's suicidal demands for societal change; Agar's unfortunate marriage; Agath and Ungar and all those who are scarred through "the mystery of iniquity." Magnitude and lavishness are not to be found in *Clarel*, and the expected artistic blemishes of a long poem are readily detected. However, the sustained image of a wasteland environment suited to the spiritual lives of the nineteenth century dominates in *Clarel*, a brilliant effect achieved not in spite of, but because of, the "constrained and strict" form.

The soaring cadences and Elizabethan imagery of the earlier novels— Melville's instinctive mode of expression—were replaced in the poem by a vocabulary of archaisms and prosaic modern idiom. Men are "carles" and "wights." Other words from the imagined past are invoked: "weened," "gyve," "keepeth," "taketh," "gryde," "amort." They are mixed freely with modern diction: "hee-haw," "cigar," "luggage," "messmate." This flat language rarely conveys meaning beyond the prosaic, that is, it rarely holds subtleties hidden in the simple expression. The nouns are especially plain: "petition," "gravitation," "conjecture," "worldings." Adjectives too often are coined merely by the addition of suffixes to nouns: "glenned," "flinty," "touchy." Verbs are used more to keep the narrative moving than to be explosive in themselves. In the interlocking pattern, one verb might do for many lines, causing ellipses and occasional obscurity. Relative pronouns and conjunctions appear only infrequently, and then only when necessary as logical indicators. Wegener's 1979 *Concordance* to *Clarel* elaborates on the text for a better understanding of Melville's usage of language in the poem.

This anti-poetic language, couched in lines not intended for euphony, would seem to account for the overwhelming negative reaction of the reading public when the poem appeared. The twentieth-century reader is more at home with this kind of poetry and praises or condemns it for other reasons. But the poem has great appeal for other qualities as well. One of them is the effective use of cluster images to advance and complement the themes. One of the major images is dust.

Clarel appears at the outset covered with dust. He finds an inscription in the lining of his trunk, emphasizing the dust and ashes of a pilgrimage. Dust covers the Tomb of the Holy Sepulchre. It layers the garbage at the Wailing Wall and creeps into the cracks of houses and pores of men. Dust manifests scorched nature at the Rim of Achor. Everywhere, dust concretizes the admonition concerning death: "By the sweat of your face shall you get bread to eat, until you return to the ground from which you were taken; for you are dirt, and to dirt you shall return" (Genesis, 3:19).

The aridity of dust is compounded by the sterility of stones, another controlling image. Clarel's first impression of Jerusalem is of blank towers, sealed windows, and blind arches: they become for him a nightmare of stones. Nehemiah's foolishness in doing God's work is seen as the old man attempts to remove the millions of stones from Jerusalem's roads. Vine pelts his own shadow with stones and builds a cairn as a "monument to barrenness" (III, vii, l. 88). Jerusalem is a "Stony metropolis of stones" (IV, II, l. 12). Stones carry the weight of death for Clarel at the burial of Ruth and Agar, when their graves are filled with gravel. Significantly, both are buried at the Gate of St. Stephen, the martyr who was stoned to death.

Sea imagery fills out the cluster of Wilderness images of dust and stone. The sea is a constant referent: "Sands immense / Impart the oceanic sense: / The flying grit like scud is made: / Pillars of sand which whirl about / Or arc along in colonnade, / True kin be to water spout" (II, xii, ll. 38–43). There is no escape on the sea for those who fear the land. It is a wasteland of water, filled with wrecks, waiting rocks, icebergs, and sharks. Like the Wilderness, it is nature without pity.

These three controlling images of the sterility of nature are added to by a fourth one of the Cross. It appears overtly and subliminally; it is revered or it is mocked, but it is never forgotten. It sums up the pain and suffering of existence. Celio literally dies before a Cross as he insists it has no redemptive function. Mortmain writes an inscription in chalk beneath the semblance of the Southern Cross: it tells sadly how the Cross of Christ Redeemed has lost all significance. The faint implication of faith is scratched out immediately thereafter by Margoth in a boast that Science has properly replaced the Cross. Vine hints at the Cross as he weaves a crown of thorns. Brother Salvaterra points out to Ungar that his sword as a Cross is a statement of devotion. Larger than all the other individual images is the liturgical pattern of Clarel's actions that connect him with the Cross: Ruth's death and his grief occur during Passion Week, with the analogy to Good Friday clearly made by the poet.

These four pervasive images control the mood and theme of the poem. There are numerous others functioning as echoes. Death, for example, overrides the whole narrative as an awful fact and as a constant metaphor. All of the deaths that occur are sad in themselves and are grim lessons to Clarel, but they serve more as dramatic preparation for the culminating death of Ruth. The entire movement of the poem is toward this experiential knowledge for Clarel. It accounts for one of Melville's rare interventions, in this case, "Dirge" (IV, xxxi), one of the most moving pieces in the poem.

Birds as images add to the tragic theme, as auguries and as diabolical symbols of nature. The use of light or its absence as sign of spiritual illumination appears throughout the poem. Colors reflect the characters' attitudes toward life, although the pinks, blues, and greens, for the most part, pale to nothing in the pilgrims' colorless world of gray and black. Towers for climbing out of drab reality, and an ancient palm tree at Mar Saba hold meaning beyond their appearance for the wanderers. The tree is like Ahab's doubloon: it has substantial value, but its larger function lies in evoking personal responses from rapt viewers.

Dust, stones, the sea, the Cross, death, birds, light and its absence, colors, trees, and towers are all poetically rich and incrementally effective: collectively, they sum up the fractured image of Jerusalem. Its reality is not Isaiah's city of light and rising glory. It is a "Ruined City," one impossible to believe was ever inhabited by God. Before he arrived, Jerusalem held for Clarel the vision of David's Holy City and the promise of living evidence of Christianity's linkage with the eternal world. He finds, instead, lepers' huts in place of "Zion's old magnificence," and desert and drought holes in the Rose of Sharon land. Jerusalem becomes for him at once the image of his own lost condition, the symbol of modern sterility, and the wreckage of history. This is expressed by Agath, when the pilgrims are on the way to Bethlehem and the sharp-eyed timoneer spies Jerusalem in the distance:

> "See ye, see?
> 'Way over where the gray hills be;
> Yonder—no, there—that upland dim:
> Wreck, ho! the wreck—Jerusalem!"
> (IV, i, ll. 188–91)

Appropriately, the choral voice of the Druze confirms the sighting and, in understatement, admires the truthful words: "Keen-sighted art thou! ...ay, it is there."

Jerusalem as a symbol of Clarel's dashed hopes and of humanity's barrenness emphasizes one of the best aspects of the poem, in the way the one and the many are fused. Melville raises political, religious, economic, psychological, and numerous other problems until the poem seems to be a symposium of ideas written by a fervid polemist. Individuals await their turns to speak, like updated students of Socrates, and their statements are cogent, deeply felt, and persuasive.

As important as these ideas are, however, they are subsidiary to the personal struggle of the main character. Rolfe, Vine, Mortmain, and the rest intensify the drama of the pilgrimage as they bring their tortured pasts and vague futures through the Wilderness, but as persons they are more functional than dramatic: their anxieties only mirror those of Clarel; their unanswered questions are the same ones that Clarel is left with at the end of the pilgrimage. The poem is arranged, accordingly, so that everyone and everything revolve around him. Melville personalized this in different ways, but the most obvious expression is in the possibilities of love as a solution for Clarel.

At the outset, Clarel deplores his unbelief and directionless actions. His room, like his soul, is a "tomb-like chamber," and his movement is "...through brakes, lone brakes, I wind:/As I advance they close behind—" (I, ii, ll. 128–29). The nightmare condition deepens in the fact of "Thy blank, blank towers, Jerusalem!" (I, i, l. 61). Like any young person afflicted by loneliness, he wishes for a friend to help him through the period of time: "Longing for solacement of mate" (I, ii, l. 12). He is thus, like anyone, susceptible to the first person who offers a gesture of affection, or to the one he believes in empathy with him. This is Celio, whose spiritual state is identical to Clarel's and whose bitter view of life is manifest in a crippled body. No words are exchanged between them; nor is there evidence that Celio shares these feelings. It is, however, academic: shortly after the episode Celio dies. Despite the thrill experienced by Clarel, nothing happens; nor could anything ever develop between them. To believe that love of two men could be felt and shared is as foolish as to think that sympathy can relieve another person's pain. The narrator comments sadly on the impossibility, calling on the sea as metaphor of his experience.

> Blue-lights sent up by ship forlorn
> Are answered oft but by the glare
> Of rockets from another, torn
> In the same gale's inclusive snare.
>   (I, xiii, ll. 1–4)

Later in the poem, when the pilgrims are in the Wilderness, a stronger impulse to love overcomes Clarel. He finds Vine behind "a leafy screen," lying on the ground and moralizing on the passing of all things. "Clarel's thrill/Of personal longing" at the sight of Vine is erotic beyond his knowing.

> How pleasant in another
> Such sallies, or in thee, if said
> After confidings that should wed
> Our souls in one:—Ah, call me *brother*!—

So feminine his passionate mood
Which, long a hungering unfed,
All else rejected or withstood.
                    (II, xxvii, ll. 106–12)

Once again, no language of love is exchanged, but Vine, quickly intuiting
the situation, turns away. In Clarel's mind, Vine rebukes him simply
with body language which says,

Lives none can help ye; that believe.
Art thou the first soul tried by doubt?
Shalt prove the last? Go, live it out.
But for thy fonder dream of love
In man toward man—the soul's caress—
The negatives of flesh should prove
Analogies of non-cordialness
In spirit.
                    (II, xxvii, ll. 123–30)

This passionate impulse and immediate rejection are ironically cast,
for Clarel has already declared his love for Ruth. His cavalier decision
to join the pilgrimage is consistent with this emotional overture to Vine.
He knows there is something wrong with his behavior: "How findest
place within thy heart /For such solicitudes apart /From Ruth?" (II, xxvii,
ll. 142–44). The question has no value at this time, however, for he has
no understanding of his heart. His response to Ruth is no different than
the one to Celio, and yet he commits the rest of his life to her out of a
need for companionship. This decision quickly slips away as he moves
into the Wilderness where he experiences the awful reality of the Dead
Sea. At Mar Saba he ruminates over this relationship with Ruth, realizes
with horror the loss of purity in their impending sexual union, and
unconsciously links her with the death that is all around him. Thus, at
Mar Saba, when the mad monk, Cyril, asks for the countersign, he
interrupts himself to tell Clarel it is "death," because he sees it in the
young man's face. As any lover would, Clarel calls out to Ruth to "abash
these mortalities," but all that he can conjure up is an image of her, like
Beatrice, chastising his mortality. Later, in Bethlehem, when Derwent
calls out the name of Ruth—he means Naomi's daughter—Clarel can
recall only the funeral of a young Armenian virgin. Ruth as a carnal
fact of sexuality is death for him, that is, the death of his ideal conception
of love. Her actual death is not an anticlimax as much as a fulfillment
of his deepest wishes and fears. This is driven home at the end of the
poem. After Rolfe, Vine, and Derwent leave Clarel in shocked mourning
over Ruth's death, the young man experiences "Illusion of grief's wake-
ful doom: / The dead walked" (IV, xxxii, ll. 86–87). He sees clearly

Nehemiah, Celio, Mortmain, Nathan, and Agar, but he has no memory of his beloved's semblance: "But Ruth—ah, how estranged in face! / He knew her by no earthly grace" (IV, xxxii, ll. 99–100). Ruth for Clarel, like love, is an ideal conception in life and death. She is final evidence of nature's awful principle: solitude is man's natural state.

In these engagements with Celio, Vine, and Ruth, Clarel activates whatever interchange does take place. With the first two, love or companionship possibilities are projections out of loneliness and are recognized by the narrator as taboo in society. They are really only monologues, too explosive to be verbalized. With Ruth, however, Clarel expresses the time-honored words of love and marriage and moves easily into the traditional solution of romance. The formula collapses on him, ironically, when he reverses the situation and judges a carnal relationship offensive, that is, personally repugnant to him. Whichever way he goes, he learns that love will answer none of his problems, nor will it relieve his pain.

Clarel feels the power of other persons on the journey, but he distances himself from them even though he is "Wishful from everyone to learn" (II, v, l. 10). One of them is Mortmain, a Swedish revolutionary and reformer who believes, paradoxically, that life holds no happiness for man. The black skull cap he wears symbolizes the hell he sees everywhere. He calls out *"Dies irae, dies illa"* (III, xix, l. 174) at the end of the Masque in chorus approval of the theme. His knowledge is like Bartleby's—painful beyond the telling. His death is like Bartleby's—a wish-fulfillment and renunciation of the human race. Despite these jeremiads, Clarel and Melville empathize over Mortmain's suffering. Clarel sees in the dead man's fixed stare "A quietude beyond mere calm" (III, xxxii, l. 21) and on his lips a mystical heroic symbol of an eagle's feather that drifted from the sky. Revolutionaries are destined for failure, but they are fundamentally good. Such failure identifies for Clarel man's tragic condition and leaves him

> feeling pain
> That such a heart could beat, and will—
> Aspire, yearn, suffer, baffled still,
> And end.
> (III, xxxii, ll. 45–48)

Ungar carries virtually the same message. His lost ideals account for his opening remarks to the other pilgrims: " 'A gun:/A gun's man's voice—sincerest one' " (IV, ii, ll. 163–64). Everywhere he sees "ever-upbubbling wickedness" (IV, xxii, l. 18) in nineteenth-century democracy's bland substitutes for the Sermon on the Mount. Democracy un-Christianized contradicts utopian theory and language, for God's absence obviates any possibility of order and peace for man. Like Ahab, he hates the single dimension of his life that forces him to these conclusions, but he has no power to change. The death of God is evident everywhere in progress, science, and irreligion, but still he cannot believe it possible.

> Transcended rebel angels! Woe
> To us; without a God, 'tis woe!
> (IV, xx, ll. 135–36)

The Melville who created White-Jacket, Redburn, Ahab, Pierre, and the other compassionate rebels changed with the decades' experience. The deeply felt Protestant belief that informed the mystical democracy of *Moby-Dick*'s "Knights and Squires" was overtaken by a social skepticism that limited for him the range of human capacity for good. Like Plinlimmon's distinction, his heart remained with the ideal of progress and equity in society, but his intellect judged it impossible in this fallen world. Mortmain and Ungar, for all of their lamentations, were in fact foolish to him for they never really gave up their ideals to deal honestly with the world as it is.

Rolfe is another charismatic influence on Clarel, different altogether from the monomaniacal Mortmain and Ungar. He appears heroic to Clarel, the perfect blend of "A genial heart, a brain austere" (I, xxxi, l. 14). He suggests what Adam must have looked like. He is a traveler, a historian; he can discuss science and religion on profound levels. He tolerates all nations and points of view. When the universally hated Margoth leaves the group, Rolfe murmurs a prayer that he will reach his destination. Altogether, this "manysidedness" appeals to Clarel as the cultivated eclecticism he might imitate himself. It is, however, too glib. Rolfe seems to encompass all things in himself—Polynesia and Medieval Europe, the Muslims and Catholics, belief in God and skepticism—until there is no final definition of him free from all the contributing elements. Clarel needs stronger convictions than this if life is to have value. Thus, he responds wistfully when Rolfe asks him what he thinks of Ungar; Clarel mistakes the question and thinks he's referring to an Arab Catholic:

> "I would
> I were his mate," in earned mood
> Clarel rejoined; "such faith to have,
> I'd take the rest, even Crib and Cave."
> (IV, xvii, ll. 44–47)

All of *Clarel* comes down to this dilemma: a wish to believe and an inability to find the way. Clarel cannot be that Arab, but he will not end his search on such a note.

> "Spurn—I'll endure; all spirit's fled
> When one fears nothing.—Bear with me,
> Yet bear!—Conviction is not gone
> Though faith's gone: that which shall not be
> It *ought* to be!"
>
> (IV, xxx, ll. 124–28)

After the failure of the Easter rite to resurrect Christ or Ruth, Clarel starts out once again on the Via Crucis, ironically on the feast of Pentecost. He had sought formulas from others on the first pilgrimage, but he knows now that they do not exist. Through the sad young seeker, Melville observes that the universe is not subject to human influence and that it has no discernible moral pattern. Each person is shaped mysteriously by forces outside his choosing. Billy Budd is taken against his will from the *Rights of Man* to the *Bellipotent* and thereby hangs his life. There is no choice in life between Bartleby's rejection and Billy's acceptance except the recognition that one goes on:

> But though the freshet quite be gone—
> Sluggish, life's wonted stream flows on.
> (IV, xxxiii, ll. 75–76)

Heroism is not denied because of this blankness: it is found precisely when one acts conscious of the possibility of relief of suffering but without the possibility of change. Like Hunilla in "The Encantadas" and Marianna in "The Piazza," Clarel goes on, no different from when he landed at Jaffa, except that he's been to the Dead Sea.

Melville, like Clarel, could not be the Arab because of the Wilderness experience, which is life itself. All evidence forces him to conclude that endurance only is the measure of a man's life. And yet, who knows, Melville asks in the Epilogue: "The spirit above the dust" may transcend the inscription on the broken shards. Life may have purpose beyond the constant rounds of the Via Crucis. Melville, accordingly, has the final word in *Clarel*, even at the risk of breaking apart the carefully observed form:

> Then keep thy heart, though yet but ill-resigned—
> Clarel, thy heart, the issues there but mind;
> That like the crocus budding through the snow—
> That like a swimmer rising from the deep—
> That like a burning secret which doth go

Even from the bosom that would hoard and keep;
Emerge thou mayst from the last whelming sea,
And prove that death but routs life into victory.

(IV, xxxv, ll. 27–34)

NOTES

1. *Letters*, p. 128. In a long letter to Evert Duyckinck, 13 December 1850, he had expressed the same concern:

But I don't know but a book in a man's brain is better off than a book bound in calf—at any rate it is safer from criticism. And taking a book off the brain, is akin to the ticklish & dangerous business of taking an old painting off a panel— you have to scrape off the whole brain in order to get at it with due safety— & even then, the painting may not be worth the trouble. (p. 117)

2. Russell and Russell reprinted the Constable edition in 1963.

3. Howard Vincent judged that some of the lyrics scattered throughout *Clarel* were written as early as 1859. Early or late, he did not include any in his edition of the *Collected Poems* (p. viii).

4. Matthiessen was even more negative a few years later. He called the poem "practically unreadable because of Melville's inexplicable choice of rhymed te-trameter as the medium for philosophic meditation.... [it] might have been formed into a whole, but again he let himself be swamped by too many indistinct characters; and their discussions of religion become as tediously abstract as the details in *White-Jacket* had been heavily concrete" (*Selected Poems*, pp. 401–12).

WORKS CITED

Arvin, Newton. *Herman Melville*. New York: William Sloan Associates, 1950.
———. "Melville's *Clarel*." *Hudson Review* 14 (Summer 1961): 298–300.
Ault, Nelson A. "The Sea Imagery in Herman Melville's *Clarel*." *Research Studies* (State College of Washington) 27 (June 1959): 72–84.
Baird, James. *Ishmael: A Study of the Symbolic Mode in Primitivism*. Baltimore: Johns Hopkins University Press, 1956.
Baker, S. C. "Two Notes on Browning Echoes in *Clarel*." *Melville Society Extracts* No. 44 (November 1980): 14–15.
Baym, Nina. "The Erotic Motif in Melville's *Clarel*." *Texas Studies in Literature and Language* 16 (Summer 1974): 315–28.
Bernstein, John. *Pacifism and Rebellion in the Writings of Herman Melville*. The Hague: Mouton, 1964.
Berthoff, Warner. *The Example of Melville*. Princeton, N.J.: Princeton University Press, 1962.
Bezanson, Walter E. "Melville's *Clarel*: The Complex Passion." *ELH: A Journal of English Literary History* 21 (1954): 146–59.

————. "Herman Melville's *Clarel*." Ph.D. Diss., Yale University, 1943. [*Mel. Diss.*, #19.]

————, ed. *Clarel: A Poem and a Pilgrimage in the Holy Land*. By Herman Melville. New York: Hendricks House, 1960.

Bowen, Merlin. *The Long Encounter: Self and Experience in the Writings of Herman Melville*. Chicago: University of Chicago Press, 1960.

Braswell, William. *Melville's Religious Thought: An Essay in Interpretation*. Durham, N.C.: Duke University Press, 1943.

Brodwin, Stanley. "Herman Melville's *Clarel*: An Existentialist Gospel." *PMLA* 86 (May 1971): 375–87.

————. "Melville's *Clarel*, continued." *PMLA* 87 (March 1972): 310–12. [Reply to Chamberlain.]

Brooks, Van Wyck. *The Times of Melville and Whitman*. New York: Dutton, 1947.

Browne, Ray B. *Melville's Drive to Humanism*. West Lafayette, Ind.: Purdue University Press, 1971.

Cannon, Agnes. "On Translating *Clarel*." *Essays in Arts and Sciences* 5 (July 1976): 160–80.

Chaffee, Patricia. "The Kedron in Melville's *Clarel*." *College Language Association Journal* 18 (March 1975): 374–82.

Chamberlain, Safford C. "Melville's *Clarel*." *PMLA* 87 (January 1972): 103–104. [Response to Brodwin, 1971.]

Chase, Richard. *Herman Melville: A Critical Study*. New York: Macmillan, 1949.

Dea, Eugene M. "Evolution and Atheism in *Clarel*." *Melville Society Extracts* No. 26 (June 1976): 3–4.

Dettlaff, Shirley. "Ionian Form and Esau's Waste: Melville's View of Art in *Clarel*." *American Literature* 54 (May 1982): 212–28.

Finkelstein, Dorothee. *Melville's Orienda*. New Haven, Conn.: Yale University Press, 1961.

Flibbert, Joseph. "The Dream and Religious Faith in Herman Melville's *Clarel*." *American Transcendental Quarterly* No. 50 (1981): 129–37.

Fogle, Richard H. "Melville's *Clarel*: Doubt and Belief." *Tulane Studies in English* 10 (1960): 101–16.

Frederick, John T. "Melville's Last Long Novel: *Clarel*." *Arizona Quarterly* 26 (Summer 1970): 151–57.

Freeman, John. *Herman Melville*. London and New York: Macmillan Co., 1926.

Gretchko, John M. J. "Herman Melville's Closet Astronomy Source." *Stonehenge Viewpoint* 52 (1983): 20.

Hawthorne, Nathaniel. *The English Notebooks*. Ed. Randall Stewart. New York: Oxford University Press, 1941.

Howard, Leon. "Clarel's Pilgrimage and the Calendar." *Melville Society Extracts* No. 16 (1973): 2–3.

Jennings, Margaret, C.S.J. "The Isolatoes in Melville's *Clarel*." *American Notes and Queries* 18 (November 1979): 53–56.

Kenny, Vincent. "Clarel's Rejection of the Titans." *American Transcendental Quarterly* No. 7 (Summer 1970): 76–81.

————. *Herman Melville's Clarel: A Spiritual Autobiography*. Hamden, Conn.: Shoe String Press, 1973.

Knapp, Joseph G. "Melville's *Clarel*: Dynamic Synthesis." *American Transcendental Quarterly* No. 7 (Summer 1970), 67–76.

———. *Tortured Synthesis: The Meaning of Melville's Clarel.* New York: Philosophical Library, 1971.

Kring, Walter D., and Jonathan S. Carey. "Two Discoveries Concerning Herman Melville." *Proceedings of the Massachusetts Historical Society* 87 (1975): 137–41; rpt. in Yannella and Parker.

Mason, Ronald. *The Spirit Above the Dust.* London: John Lehmann, 1951.

Mather, Frank Jewett, Jr. "Herman Melville." *New York Review* 1 (16 August 1919): 298–301.

Matthiessen, F. O. *American Renaissance: Art and Expression in the Age of Emerson and Whitman.* New York: Oxford University Press, 1941.

Melville, Herman, *The Portable Melville.* Ed. Jay Leyda. New York: Viking Press, 1952.

———. *Herman Melville: Representative Selections.* Ed. Willard Thorp. New York: American Book Co., 1938.

———. *Selected Poems.* Ed. William Plomer. London: Hogarth, 1943.

———. *Selected Poems of Herman Melville.* Ed. F. O. Matthiessen. Norfolk, Conn.: New Directions, 1944.

———. *Selected Poems of Herman Melville.* Ed. Hennig Cohen. New York: Doubleday, 1964.

Monteiro, George. "*Clarel* in the *Catholic World.*" *Melville Society Extracts* No. 30 (1977): 11.

Mumford, Lewis. *Herman Melville: A Study of His Life and Vision.* New York: Harcourt, Brace, & World, 1929.

Murry, John Middleton. "Herman Melville, Who Could Not Surpass Himself." *New York Times Book Review* (10 August 1924): 7.

Parker, Hershel. "The Ambiguous Portrait of Vine in Melville's *Clarel.*" *Melville Society Extracts* No. 26 (1976): 4–5.

Ra'ad, Basem L. "The Death in Melville *Clarel.*" *ESQ* 27 (First Quarter 1981): 14–27.

Requa, Kenneth. "The Pilgrim's Problems: Melville's *Clarel.*" *Ball State University Forum* 16 (Spring 1975): 16–20.

Rev. of *Clarel. Lippincott's Magazine* 18 (September 1876): 391–392.

———. *Westminster Review* 105 (October 1876): 577–78.

———. New York *Library Table* (1 August 1876): 108.

———. New York *Independent* (6 July 1876): 9.

Reynolds, Larry John. "Vine and Clarel." *Melville Society Extracts* No. 23 (September 1975): 11.

Rosenberg-Sacks, Hélène. "Allegory and Nominal Identity in Melville's Poem *Clarel.*" *Literary Onomastics Studies* 1 (1974): 40–46.

Sedgwick, William Ellery. *Herman Melville: The Tragedy of Mind.* Cambridge, Mass.: Harvard University Press, 1944.

Seelye, John. *Melville: The Ironic Diagram.* Evanston, Ill.: Northwestern University Press, 1970.

Short, Bryan C. " 'Betwixt the Chimes and Knell': Versification as Symbol in *Clarel.*" *Melville Society Extracts* No. 26 (June 1976): 4.

————. "Form as Vision in Herman Melville's *Clarel.*" *American Literature* 50 (January 1979): 553–69.

Shurr, William. *The Mystery of Iniquity: Melville as Poet, 1857–1891.* Lexington: University of Kentucky Press, 1972.

Simon, Jean. *Herman Melville: Marin, Métaphysicien, et Poète.* Paris: Boivin et Cie, 1939.

Stein, William Bysshe. *The Poetry of Melville's Late Years: Time, History, Myth, and Religion.* Albany, N.Y.: State University of New York Press, 1970.

Stern, Milton R. *The Fine-Hammered Steel of Herman Melville.* Urbana: University of Illinois Press, 1957.

Stone, Geoffrey. *Melville.* New York: Sheed & Ward, 1949.

Thompson, Lawrance. *Melville's Quarrel With God.* Princeton, N.J.: Princeton University Press, 1952.

von Abele, Rudolph. "Melville and the Problem of Evil." *American Mercury* 65 (November 1947): 592–93.

Walker, Franklin. *Irreverent Pilgrims: Melville, Browne, and Mark Twain in the Holy Land.* Seattle: University of Washington Press, 1974.

Warren, Robert Penn. "Melville's Poems." *Southern Review* n.s. 3 (Autumn 1967): 799–831.

————. "Melville the Poet." *Kenyon Review* 8 (Spring 1946): 208–23.

Wasilewski, William. "Melville's Poetic Strategy in *Clarel*: The Satellite Poems." *Essays in Arts and Sciences* 5 (July 1976): 149–59.

Weaver, Raymond M. *Herman Melville: Mariner and Mystic.* New York: George H. Doran, 1921.

Wegener, Larry. *A Concordance to Herman Melville's Clarel.* 2 vols. Glassboro, N.J.: Melville Society, 1979.

Wells, Henry W. "Herman Melville's *Clarel.*" *College English* 4 (May 1943): 478–83.

Wright, Nathalia. *Melville's Use of the Bible.* Durham, N.C.: Duke University Press, 1949.

————. "A Source for Melville's *Clarel*: Dean Stanley's *Sinai and Palestine.*" *Modern Language Notes* 62 (February 1947): 110–16.

Yannella, Donald, and Hershel Parker, eds. *The Endless, Winding Way in Melville: New Charts by Kring and Carey.* Glassboro, N.J.: Melville Society, 1981.

14

INNOCENCE AND INFAMY: *BILLY BUDD, SAILOR*

Merton M. Sealts, Jr.

As Melville's *Moby-Dick, The Confidence-Man*, and *Clarel* recapitulate in large measure the writings that immediately preceded them, so *Billy Budd, Sailor*, not only sums up the thought and art of Melville's last years but also looks back in setting, characterization, and theme over his writing as a whole.[1] Left in manuscript at his death in 1891 and unpublished until 1924, *Billy Budd* has since appeared in many editions and printings, including over a score of translations. It has generated an extensive body of strikingly divergent commentary whose opposite poles are readings in terms of either personal tragedy or ironic social commentary.

The manuscript of *Billy Budd*, which Melville's widow described as "unfinished" (*Reading*, p. 95: #. 481), comprises 351 leaves in her husband's crabbed hand, written partly in ink and partly in pencil, with some passages heavily revised; no printer could have worked directly from such disordered copy. The "Genetic Text" published by the University of Chicago Press in 1962 is now considered the standard transcription; other versions, especially those published in earlier years, differ significantly in their readings. Analysis of the manuscript has disclosed that Melville's story evolved in three major phases of composition, together with other less clearly defined stages and sub-stages. In general terms, the first phase involved concentration on Billy himself as protagonist, the second phase either introduced John Claggart or at least brought him to the fore as Billy's antagonist, and the third phase de-

Innocence and Infamy: *Billy Budd, Sailor*, by Merton M. Sealts, Jr. is published here with permission of the Wisconsin Humanities Committee. This chapter draws on a lecture given by Merton Sealts in a seminar for lawyers presented by the Committee in 1983, funded in part by the National Endowment for the Humanities.

veloped Edward Fairfax Vere as the sea commander under whom Billy is tried, convicted, and executed. This order of development, it might be noted, anticipates that of later critical discussion of the story, which also concentrated first on Billy, then on Claggart, and ultimately on Captain Vere.

SYNOPSIS

Melville's title character is a handsome sailor "aged twenty-one, a fore-topman of the British fleet toward the close of the last decade of the eighteenth century" (*BBS*, p. 44), when Great Britain was at war with post-revolutionary France. We see him first aboard a homeward-bound English merchant ship, the *Rights-of-Man*, which is stopped by a British naval vessel seeking additional crewmen through forcible impressment. The warship bears another allegorical name: H.M.S. *Bellipotent*, or "war-power." The boarding officer selects Billy Budd, who is immediately transferred from the *Rights-of-Man* to the *Bellipotent* and inducted into the King's service. Already an accomplished seaman, Billy attracts favorable notice from both officers and sailors, with a single exception: John Claggart, master-at-arms, who serves aboard the ship as a nautical chief of police. Claggart's inherently evil nature is both drawn to and repelled by Billy's "good looks, cheery health, and frank enjoyment of young life" (p. 78). The two men stand in sharp contrast as types of innocence and worldly experience. Unlike Claggart, Billy in the "simplicity" of his youthful goodness has never willed malice nor been inflamed by the jealousy that possesses the master-at-arms as he looks enviously upon the Handsome Sailor.

After failing in an attempt to entrap Billy through an intermediary, who is sent to offer Billy money if he will turn mutineer, Claggart goes to the *Bellipotent*'s captain, falsely charges Billy with fomenting mutiny, and repeats the accusation to Billy himself during a confrontation in Captain Vere's cabin. Amazed and horrified by the groundless charge, Billy is unable to speak and defend himself as the captain urges him to do; a vocal impediment that afflicts him in time of stress produces only "a convulsed tongue-tie" (p. 98), and he lashes out with his fist, striking his accuser dead with a blow to Claggart's forehead. Vere, disbelieving Claggart's charge against Billy, is nevertheless aware that the young sailor, while innocent of mutiny, has in fact struck and killed a superior officer. In the captain's own words, Billy's deed is "the divine judgment on Ananias" delivered by "an angel of God"—yet that angel "must hang" (pp. 100–101). Death by hanging is the sentence subsequently imposed upon Billy by the drumhead court that Vere quickly convenes, and the Handsome Sailor is hanged at dawn from a yard-arm of the mainmast before the entire ship's company. "At the penultimate moment, his words, his only ones, words wholly unobstructed in the utterance, were these: 'God bless Captain Vere!' " (p. 123).

Although the *Bellipotent*'s crew involuntarily echo Billy's blessing, their first response soon gives way to a threatening murmur that is promptly quelled by a strategic command from the quarter-deck. A similar murmur that arises following Billy's burial is also quieted by a drum-roll to quarters, "and toned by music and religious rites subserving the discipline and purposes of war, the men in their wonted orderly manner dispersed to the places allotted them when not at the guns." "With mankind," Vere would say, "forms, measured forms, are everything" (p. 128). Both Billy and Claggart are dead, and Vere's death is soon to follow. In an encounter between the *Bellipotent* and a French warship, the *Athée* (or *Atheist*—a third allegorical name), the captain receives a fatal wound and dies ashore at Gibraltar, "cut off too early" for a part in Horatio Nelson's memorable victories over the French at the Nile and Trafalgar. Not long before his death he is heard to murmur "words inexplicable to his attendant: 'Billy Budd, Billy Budd' " (p. 129).

Among contrasting references to Billy and his fate that conclude the story, one, a journalistic account purportedly appearing in "a naval chronicle of the time" (p. 130), exactly reverses the truth, calling Billy the ringleader of a mutiny who, when arraigned before his captain by the master-at-arms, stabs his accuser to the heart and subsequently pays the penalty of death for his crimes. The other, a sailor's ballad entitled "Billy in the Darbies," expresses in rough but eloquent verse "the general estimate" among Billy's own shipmates of "his nature and its unconscious simplicity" (p. 131). These contradictory verdicts on the Handsome Sailor are summed up in a brief comment that Melville himself wrote in and then deleted from his manuscript. Such a story, he observed, is "not unwarranted by what sometimes happens" in the actual world—a world which, like the writer in the "naval chronicle," cannot distinguish between "Innocence and infamy, spiritual depravity and fair repute" (p. 422: Leaf 344).

Even in that world where literary critics live and move and have their being, there have also been and continue to be fundamental differences of opinion about the characters and characterizations of the two antagonists and also of Captain Vere, whose problematic role in the story has come to be the primary focus of much recent criticism. Each of the three figures has been singled out as a hero by at least one commentator— Vern Wagner, for example, finds even Claggart "spiritually heroic" (p. 174)—and as a villain by others. Where did Billy and Claggart err in their appraisals of one another? Was there in fact some supporting evidence or testimony unfavorable to Billy that Claggart could have cited when he accused him of fomenting mutiny? Was Billy in *any* sense justified when he replied to Claggart's accusation with a blow, whatever his actual intention? Given the situation in the British fleet at the time of the Great Mutiny of 1797, with an engagement with the French always imminent, did Vere act responsibly or precipitously in immediately trying Billy aboard the *Bellipotent*? Was the trial conducted fairly, and were the verdict and the sentence properly arrived at—in terms not only of military necessity but also of law, of justice, and of morality? And where does Melville himself stand with respect to these questions and to their larger ethical and philosophical implications?

Since Melville's twentieth-century critics differ so strongly over such issues, one may ask further about the basis for their disagreements. Are the characters and events of the story ambiguous in themselves? Is Melville's narrative willfully equivocal? Are modern readers perhaps over-subtle, projecting their own contrasting values onto a relatively straightforward nineteenth-century fiction? Or do *all* of these elements contribute in some degree to the difficulty? These are among the problems one faces in studying Melville's *Billy Budd, Sailor*, and surveying the extensive body of criticism that has grown up about it. In addressing these issues one needs first of all to understand when and how Melville came to write the story and what subsequent scholarly analysis of the manuscript has revealed about its growth and development.

GENESIS AND GROWTH

"Billy in the Darbies" and *Billy Budd, Sailor*

The retrospective and even elegiac tone that marks Melville's last prose narrative also characterizes his third published volume of poetry, *John Marr and Other Sailors*, completed after his retirement from the customs service at the end of 1885 and privately printed in 1888. As we now know, Melville began *Billy Budd, Sailor*, in the course of his work on the *John Marr* volume, for which the ballad entitled "Billy in the Darbies" that now concludes the story was originally intended, and indeed the entire story has much in common with the sailor verse.

In describing the speaker of "John Marr," the title poem in that volume, Melville wrote an introductory prose sketch, similar to those he had composed in the 1870s and after for his "Burgundy Club" poems, "At the Hostelry" and "Naples in the Time of Bomba." Like Melville himself, John Marr is a former sailor; like Jack Gentian, Dean of the Burgundy Club, he also bears some resemblance to Thomas Melvill, Jr., Melville's paternal uncle: both spend their last years on a remote frontier prairie, lacking that "common inheritance" that would serve as a basis for mutual communication with their neighbors.[2] "Whether as to persons or events, one cannot always be talking about the present, much less speculating about the future," Melville's headnote observes; "one must needs recur to the past, which . . . supplies to most practical natures the basis of sympathetic communion." But "the past of John Marr was not the past of these pioneers," and when he "naturally" speaks to them of "some marine story or picture" he finds "no encouragement to proceed." As one of them finally tells him, "Friend, we know nothing of that here" (*Poems*, pp. 160–61).

So Marr, like Herman Melville himself in his so-called silent years, breaks off his attempts to communicate with his contemporaries and turns instead to his own private memories, recalling his shipmates of former days as though they were "phantoms of the dead":

As the growing sense of his environment threw him more and more upon retrospective musings, these phantoms...became spiritual companions, losing something of their first indistinctness and putting on at last a dim semblance of mute life; and they were lit by that aureola circling over any object of the affections in the past for reunion with which an imaginative heart passionately yearns. (p. 164)

The shipmates John Marr remembers in the verse which follows— first "merchant-sailors," then "huntsman-whalers," and finally "man-of-war's men"—appear in the chronological order of Melville's own experiences at sea: first aboard a Liverpool packet in 1839, then during his whaling years that began in 1841, and finally on the American warship that brought him home from the Pacific in 1844. Other poems in the volume make more explicit references to associates of Melville's own past. Two of them go back to the long-remembered visit of 1842 by Melville and Toby Greene (here called "the Typee-truants") to the Marquesas Islands, seen now in retrospect as "Authentic Edens in a Pagan sea" (Poems, p. 201). "To the Master of the 'Meteor' " honors Melville's sea-going brother Thomas, who had died in 1884. Another, "Jack Roy," is clearly a tribute to the admired Jack Chase, "that great heart" to whom *Billy Budd, Sailor*, is dedicated. The speaker in the dramatic monologue "Bridegroom Dick" recalls still other seamen Melville himself had known, including his cousin Guert Gansevoort, a naval officer who appears in the poem both as a hero of the Mexican War and as a key figure who keeps his own counsel concerning the *Somers* mutiny affair of 1842, a controversial event which is also "cited," though "without comment," in *Billy Budd* (p. 114).

Bridegroom Dick goes out of his way to voice the same dislike of ironclad warships expressed earlier in Melville's poetry of the Civil War, notably "A Utilitarian View of the Monitor's Fight," and again in the fourth chapter of *Billy Budd*, which deals with the "change in sea warfare" brought about by such "inventions of our time" (p. 56). As steam power took over from the sailing ships Melville had known and loved in his youth, and as ironclads like the *Monitor* and *Merrimac* rendered the old oaken warships both vulnerable and obsolete, he came to think of vessels out of the past, such as Nelson's *Victory* and the ships depicted by the artists Turner and Haden, as symbolizing cherished qualities and values that to the modern world seemed superannuated—like a once well-known author fallen out of communication with his contemporaries. As Edward Stessel has aptly said, "the wooden ships" in Melville's writing "were of his time of promise and their obsolescence was his own" (p. 75).

Another poem of the *John Marr* volume, the short sea-ballad "Tom Deadlight," is set aboard one of these old ships: a British man-of-war "homeward-bound from the Mediterranean" in the year 1810 (Poems, p. 182). As with "John Marr" and those still earlier poems Melville had attributed to the Marquis de Grandvin and Jack Gentian in his Burgundy Club manuscripts, a prose headnote introduces the speaker: in this instance a seaman facing death who is saying farewell to his messmates, like the speaker of "Billy in the Darbies." That ballad in its original form was a companion-piece to "Tom Deadlight." Its setting too was aboard a British warship "in the time before steamships" (*BBS*, p. 43)—presumably in 1797, the year of the "Great Mutiny" referred to in *Billy Budd*; Melville, as we now know, first thought of his speaker in the ballad not as young Billy but as an older man apparently guilty of fomenting mutiny, the crime for which he has been condemned to hang.

As with both "John Marr" and "Tom Deadlight," Melville drafted a prose headnote to the ballad—and as with the earlier Burgundy Club pieces, the headnote grew in length until it far overshadowed the short verse it was intended to introduce. Removing the ballad from his projected volume, Melville then developed the burgeoning headnote into what became *Billy Budd, Sailor*, his final venture in prose fiction, with the ballad headed "Billy in the Darbies" standing as its conclusion. The narrator of *Billy Budd*, it may be observed, sounds very much like the authors of these several earlier headnotes—which is to say, like Melville himself. Twice he recalls specific incidents of Melville's own visits to England: at Liverpool in 1839 (p. 43: "now more than half a century ago") and at Greenwich in 1849 (p. 66: "now more than forty years ago"); he also alludes habitually to figures of history and literature that had long engaged Melville as well. But his guarded allusion to the *Somers* mutiny of 1842, like his reference in the *John Marr* volume, contrasts strikingly with the impassioned discussion of the case in Melville's earlier *White-Jacket* (1850). Although Charles Anderson, Newton Arvin, and various later critics have taken *Billy Budd* as his further comment on the *Somers* affair, it is clear from what is now known about the genesis and growth of the story that Melville did not begin writing it with the *Somers* case specifically in mind, though in the last phase of its composition that case "was certainly a cogent analogue" (Hayford and Sealts, p. 30).

Billy and Claggart

As Melville's narrative of the condemned sailor developed apart from the *John Marr* volume, he altered his original conception of his title character as an older man, laying particular stress on a younger Billy's lack of worldly experience and delineating his appearance and character accordingly. In the story he is presented as "much of a child-man" (p. 86); the old Dansker's nickname for his young friend is "Baby" (p. 70). To the reader who knows Melville's earlier works he recalls unsophisticated youths such as Redburn and Pierre, or the young soldiers of *Battle-Pieces* (1866) whom Melville had seen as fated for tragic enlightenment. "All wars are boyish, and are fought by boys," Melville wrote in "The March into Virginia," and many youthful warriors, beginning as "Moloch's uninitiate," must ultimately "die, experienced" and "perish, enlightened" (Poems, pp. 10–11). Here Captain Vere himself terms Billy a "fated boy" (*BBS*, p. 99); in another of the war poems, "On the Slain Collegians," Melville had written of "striplings" and their "fated parts," and—in lines that seem to anticipate the very name of Billy *Budd*—compared them with

> plants that flower ere comes the leaf—
> Which storms lay low in kindly doom,
> And kill them in their flush of bloom.
> (Poems, p. 105)

In the expanded story young Billy appears as a fine physical specimen—a "Handsome Sailor"—but an inexperienced moral innocent, one who on either count might well have "posed for a statue of young Adam before the Fall" (*BBS*, p. 94). He is repeatedly likened both to other "young" figures of antiquity—Alexander, Achilles, David, Joseph, and Isaac—and to the sailor companions of Melville's own youth. The reminiscing John Marr regards all sailors as "Barbarians of man's simpler nature" (Poems, p. 166); Billy too has a "simple nature" (*BBS*, p. 52), and the narrator twice calls him a "barbarian" (pp. 52, 120), implicitly associating him not only with sailors but also with those uncivilized and un-Christianized Polynesians described in *Typee* and *Omoo*, victims of what passes for Christian civilization. Melville, it has been aptly said, "had thought of unspoiled barbarians at every stage of his writing since *Typee*" (Matthiessen, p. 501), and in *Billy Budd* he specifically compares Billy's attitude toward the Chaplain's religion to that of a "superior *savage*, so called—a Tahitian, say, of Captain Cook's time or shortly after that time" (*BBS*, p. 121). In both his appearance and his character Billy with his "simple nature" is thus reminiscent of all youthful, unenlightened, and even "savage" characters in Melville's writings from *Typee* onward.

When Melville turned from Billy to Claggart, the second of his major characters to emerge as the story developed, he in a sense moved from the world of *Typee* and *Omoo* to that of *Redburn* and *White-Jacket*, for Claggart is a further development of such figures in the latter books as Jackson and Bland. Thematically, he is the antithesis of Billy, for he is a man "dominated by intellectuality" who finds civilization "auspicious" (p. 75); the two of them are paired as Jackson is paired with young Redburn, or Radney in *Moby-Dick* with Steelkilt, and to think of the one figure apparently led Melville to conceive of its opposite as well.

Claggart and his "mystery of iniquity" (p. 108) presented more difficulty in characterization than did the simpler Billy. "His portrait I essay," the narrator remarks of Claggart, "but shall never hit it" (p. 64), and as the manuscript reveals, Melville was still in the process of retouching that portrait when he put work aside during his last illness. In seeking to get at Claggart's hidden nature he made explicit reference to both the Bible and Plato, and in writing of the man's mixture of envy and antipathy with respect to Billy he drew as well on such literary analogues as Shakespeare's Iago and Milton's Satan. Within the compass of Melville's own works, Claggart climaxes that long line of monomaniacs—men obsessed with one passionately held idea—that runs from Ahab in *Moby-Dick* through the subordinate characters in *Clarel*, to all of whom Melville had extended his sympathetic understanding, if not his approval.

Captain Vere

As in *Moby-Dick* he had ascribed "high qualities" and "tragic graces" to "meanest mariners, and renegades and castaways" (*MD*, p. 104), so in *Billy Budd*, with Billy and Claggart, Melville initially created a drama played "down among the groundlings," its stage "a scrubbed gun deck" (*BBS*, pp. 78–79). Insofar as *Billy Budd* is the story of these two antagonists, it has the democratic implications of Melville's earliest books, but with the emergence of Captain the Honorable Edward Fairfax Vere, the third and latest to develop of the story's three principal characters, the dramatic focus of its central chapters shifts from the gun-deck to the captain's cabin.

Unlike Billy and Claggart, deriving as they do from antecedents in Melville's early books, Vere is the creation of an older writer—and a more conservative thinker, in the view of critics such as Milton R. Stern, Thomas J. Scorza, and Michael Paul Rogin; his affiliations are chiefly with the work of Melville's later years. The sea-captains of the earlier fiction, Ahab included, are typically autocrats; the occasional exceptions, like Amasa Delano and Benito Cereno, are special cases. During the Civil War, when Melville visited the battle-front and came to know senior military men, he seems to have formed a higher opinion of the officer class; his sketches of the 1870s concerning Major Jack Gentian and his depiction of Captain Turret in "Bridegroom Dick"—much less the martinet than Vere—are indications that he had indeed done so. But Captain Vere, it must be remembered, was created to fulfill the demands of Melville's plot, which required a senior officer to preside over young Billy's condemnation and carry out the sentence that he suffer death by hanging; Melville must therefore have asked himself the obvious question: What kind of man *could* and *would* do what Vere *must* do?

In his efforts to answer this question Melville was led into even more troublesome psychological probing than his analysis of Claggart entailed. Late revisions in those manuscript passages that deal with Vere's state of mind at the time of Billy's fatal blow testify that he was still retouching Vere's portrait as well as Claggart's when his last illness prevented further work on the story. As the manuscript stands, Vere appears, for good or for ill, as a supremely dedicated servant of King and country, first and foremost an officer enrolled in "the host of the God of War—Mars" (p. 122). Along with Melville's Jack Gentian, another patrician figure with a background of military service, Vere too might well be called "an old-fashioned Roman" (Tales, p. 406), not only in his patriotism and devotion to duty but also in his regard for established principles and values that have come down to him from the past.

As Vere is "allied to the higher nobility," so Melville, like Ishmael, is descended from "an old established family in the land" (*MD*, p. 14); Michael Rogin's *Subversive Genealogy* interprets Vere's role as a reaffirmation of Melville's own familial values (pp. 288–316). Emphasis on the contrast between Vere's private feelings for Billy and the rigorous demands of his profession has reminded other critics—notably Brook Thomas ("Legal Fictions")—of the situation repeatedly faced by Melville's father-in-law, the eminent Massachusetts jurist Lemuel Shaw, who in more than one critical case ruled contrary to his own sympathies in order to uphold the letter of the law as he understood it.

As a defender of the old order against modern innovation, Vere again has much in common with Melville himself as seen in the writings of his later years: a man disenchanted with the prevailing faith in humanity's so-called progress—"Adam's alleged advance," as he had called it in the *Burgundy Club* sketches (Tales, p. 406)—who believed instead that human nature is essentially the same from age to age, regardless of superficial changes such as modern inventions and other supposed improvements. Both Vere and the reclusive Melville of the last decades of his life take more satisfaction in reading than in "social converse"; Vere loves "history, biography, and unconventional writers like Montaigne" (*BBS*, p.

62) as did Melville himself, and he too is "as apt to cite some historic character or incident of antiquity" (originally "cite some allusion to Plutarch, say, or Livy") "as he would be to cite from the moderns" (pp. 63, 315: Leaf 87).

Another possible analogy between Vere and Melville turns on the captain's relation to Billy Budd. Given his favorable impression of the young sailor, he clearly disbelieves Claggart's charge that Billy has been fomenting mutiny, but he nevertheless arranges a confrontation between them. In a "fatherly" tone he encourages the vocally hesitant Billy to reply to Claggart (p. 99), thus helping to precipitate the fatal blow by which Billy strikes Claggart dead. From then on, however, "the father" in Vere is "replaced by the military disciplinarian" (p. 100), but after the trial it is Vere himself, "old enough to have been Billy's father" (p. 115), who tells the young sailor of the verdict.

The narrator's repeated references to Vere as a kind of "father" to Billy, figurative or otherwise, have prompted biographically oriented critics such as Robert Penn Warren and Edwin Haviland Miller to recall that in February of 1886, when Melville was presumably at work on the poem and headnote that evolved into *Billy Budd*, his son Stanwix died in San Francisco at the age of thirty-five. Stanwix Melville, we would say today, had never found himself, and his death may also have brought to mind the earlier loss of Melville's first child, who in 1867 had ended his life at eighteen with a fatal pistol shot. Accidental or otherwise—the circumstances are cloudy—the death of Malcolm had been traumatic for the Melvilles, who were already experiencing other domestic difficulties, and was at least partly responsible for their virtual withdrawal from New York society during the later years of their marriage.

As head of the family Herman Melville was a strict disciplinarian, given to moodiness and irascibility that some of his relatives by marriage came to interpret as outright insanity. When he began to develop the story that became *Billy Budd*, as Peter L. Hays and Richard Dilworth Rust conjecture, he identified Billy with his lost sons and the bookish, moody, and sometimes irascible Vere with their strict father. Vere's actions, it will be remembered, appear irrational to the "prudent surgeon" of the story, whose supposition that the captain may actually be "unhinged" leads the narrator to speculate on the difficulty of drawing a line between sanity and insanity (pp. 100, 102). This controversial hypothesis has fascinating implications for interpreting the characters of both Billy and Vere—specifically for evaluating both the narrator's remarks about their private farewell (which he does not render dramatically) and the tone of Billy's final words, "God bless Captain Vere!"

Although this provocative theory remains one that can neither be proven nor yet disproven, it would seem to be in consonance with the retrospective character of so much of Melville's writing, especially that of the latter half of his life. With particular reference to the *John Marr* volume and the "inside narrative" that Melville then went on to write (*BBS*, p. 41), one might add the further adjective "elegiac"; the ultimate subject of *Billy Budd*, it may well be, is death. But how to read that final story, as its narrator pointedly declares, "every one must determine for himself" (p. 102), and it is tempting to say that as many interpretations have been advanced as there have been readers and critics. In opposition to anyone expressing sympathy for Vere and his conservative values— especially if he or she sees either Vere or the narrator as a projection of the older Melville—stand those who take the book as reaffirming the iconoclastic ideas they attribute to the younger author who wrote *Typee*, *Omoo*, and *White-Jacket*.

Other Sources and Analogues

In addition to broad resemblances in setting, theme, and characterization between *Billy Budd, Sailor*, and Melville's earlier writings, specific verbal parallels suggest that he may have been re-reading his own works at the time he was composing both *John Marr* and *Billy Budd*; his *White-Jacket*, *Israel Potter*, and "Benito Cereno" come readily to mind. He may also have read, or re-read, material on the *Somers* case, which was under renewed discussion in American magazines of 1887 and 1888, but there is no evidence to establish whether or how such recent analyses may have influenced his late writings.[3] For the immediate historical background of *Billy Budd, Sailor*, he is known to have consulted at least two sources: *The Naval History of Great Britain* by the British historian William James, cited in Chapter 3, and the *Life of Nelson* by Robert Southey, which Mrs. Melville described as "kept for reference" for the story (*Reading*, p. 95, #. 481). B. R. McElderry, Jr., and Richard and Rita Gollin have noted parallels in Douglas Jerrold's *Black-Ey'd Susan* and *The Mutiny at the Nore* and Captain Marryat's *The King's Own*; John Bryant adds *Working a Passage* by Charles F. Briggs. Hayford and Sealts cite Cooper's *The Two Admirals* and *Wing-and-Wing* and point to possible "unsuspected analogues" in American naval history, Melville's own experience in the American navy, and various pieces of minor sea literature (pp. 30–33).

With regard to Vere's conduct of Billy's trial and execution, Hayford and Sealts concluded—perhaps somewhat hastily—that Melville "simply had not familiarized himself with statutes of the period concerning administration of British naval justice" (p. 176), for in terms of historical fact neither a drumhead court nor a hanging could legally have taken place aboard a British warship on detached service in 1797. No naval officer of Vere's rank and assignment was authorized to try a seaman for a capital offense. Moreover, both the size and the composition of the drumhead court that Vere appoints are contrary to statute, and the

British Mutiny Act, which the captain cites as justification for his actions, actually applied only to land forces of the period rather than to the navy. Finally, even were the court's proceedings in order, its resulting sentence of death should not have been carried out before the findings in Billy's case were submitted to higher authority for review.[4] Was Vere then deliberately violating established procedures, as anti-Vere critics have charged? Did he act rather out of sheer ignorance of the law? Or was it Melville himself who either did not know or for some reason chose to disregard what he had learned—or should have learned—from naval and legal history?

"Melville's expertise in naval law and history" must indeed be *assumed*, according to Richard H. Weisberg, a man trained both in literature and in jurisprudence, who adds that in view of "the extreme accuracy of so much of the legal detail in the story" the burden of proof must therefore be on anyone who thinks differently. In "How Judges Speak" (1982), he contends "that Captain Vere's articulation and application of the law in many respects were erroneous, and that Melville intended his reader both to realize this fact and to consider its broader implications" (p. 32n.192; pp. 32 and 5).[5] Stanton Garner, who has taught naval science as well as literature, takes this line of reasoning even further. Melville, he holds, "did not simply make some mistakes in handling the facts of history." Instead, through the mouth of a designedly unreliable narrator, "he deliberately introduced errors" in order to undercut his narrator's statements ("Fraud as Fact," p. 85).

These two commentators are positing a norm, grounded on the specifics of naval law and history, against which Melville's supposed narrative strategy as an historical novelist and also Captain Vere's actions as a naval commander can both be evaluated. But in view of the actual development of the *Billy Budd* manuscript, the informed critic must keep in mind that from its very beginnings, in the original ballad, the central figure of Melville's story was a condemned man; neither his subsequently conceived antagonist nor the captain as agent of his condemnation was initially present, and indeed Vere did not emerge as a distinct character until a relatively late phase of composition. Whatever Melville may have ultimately come to think of the *Bellipotent*'s captain, he obviously did not *begin* his narrative with the intention of either attacking or defending Vere's decisions.

Who then was responsible, Vere or Melville, for the captain's departures from legal orthodoxy? Within the narrative itself, taken altogether on its own terms, the testimony of Vere's fellow officers is especially pertinent. Although these experienced professionals voice reservations about the captain's handling of Billy's case, their comments are all based on pragmatic rather than legal considerations, as though they were wholly unaware of any provisions to the contrary in British naval law.

As their several remarks about Vere are plainly meant to suggest, they feel that he moved hastily and secretly to try Billy aboard the *Bellipotent* when he might better have referred the whole affair to the admiral, but not one of them charges him with acting illegally rather than imprudently because he assumes responsibility in so crucial a matter. By introducing their testimony, Melville is inviting his reader to examine Vere's actions in the context of the story as he himself conceived it, *not* with strict reference to naval law and history. He allows Vere himself to say that he has both the option and the obligation to act, and that his appointment of a summary court "would not be at variance with usage" (p. 104). To account to the reader for Billy's trial, conviction, and execution it was imperative for Melville to allow Vere that option but require him to choose as he did. To argue that a British captain of 1797 should have declined, on statutory grounds, to try Billy is really to say that Melville himself should have written an altogether different story. What readers and critics must deal with, therefore, is the story as he actually composed it: as fiction with an historical setting—as in the earlier *Israel Potter*, for example, another eighteenth-century narrative that takes place partly on shipboard—but not with the historian's fidelity to fact.

The internal logic of *Billy Budd, Sailor*, both as Melville first conceived its basic situation and as he later developed its action, not only turned on Billy's condemnation but also required an immediate trial for a capital offense, an unqualified verdict of guilty as charged, and a prompt carrying out of the sentence. The closest analogue yet suggested for a story with these requirements involves a visit that Melville himself had made during the Civil War to the Union front, a visit that provided the basis for one of the poems in *Battle-Pieces*. While in a Virginia camp, as Stanton Garner reports in "Melville's Scout Toward Aldie" (1982), Melville or perhaps his brother Allan, a New York lawyer, "may well have been told" of a recent incident involving a Union picket who had deserted his post, joined a Confederate battalion, and then been captured by his former comrades. His brigade commander promptly convened a drumhead court, which found the soldier guilty of desertion and sentenced him to be shot on the following day. The entire brigade was drawn up to witness his execution, which was said to have made a strong impression on the troops. "It is difficult to doubt that Herman heard this story," Garner writes, noting that "the entire drumhead court and execution sequence is too close to the action of *Billy Budd, Sailor* to ignore. If he heard it, he was profoundly affected by it" (pp. 12–13).

How *Billy Budd, Sailor*, should be read and interpreted in relation to these various analogues and possible sources in its author's own experience, his reading, and his previous writing remains an open question among present-day critics, who disagree over such fundamental questions as the tone of the story and Melville's possible intentions in composing it. Apart from the manuscript itself there is no reference to *Billy Budd* among his surviving papers or in any of the biographical sketches published after his death in 1891 by Arthur Stedman, his literary executor. When Stedman, with the encouragement and support of Melville's widow, prepared four volumes of his fiction for new editions of 1892 he did not include *Billy Budd*, though bringing out a previously unknown story might well have furthered their objective of keeping Melville's name and fame alive; the obviously unfinished state of the manuscript may have dismayed either Stedman or Mrs. Melville herself. After her death in 1906 the Melville papers passed in turn to her daughters Elizabeth and Frances and then to the eldest granddaughter, the late Eleanor Melville Metcalf. The manuscript of *Billy Budd* is now in the Melville Collection of the Houghton Library, Harvard University, as a gift from Mrs. Metcalf.

EDITIONS

The first mention of *Billy Budd* in print came in Raymond Weaver's pioneering biography of 1921, *Herman Melville: Mariner and Mystic*; the first published text of the story appeared in *Billy Budd and Other Prose Pieces* (1924), edited by Weaver as Volume 13 of the Standard Edition of Melville's *Complete Works*. Weaver's freely edited transcription was republished in 1928, with numerous modifications, in his *Shorter Novels of Herman Melville*. Neither text is free of error, and each silently introduces both grammatical and stylistic emendations. Weaver's intention as editor was to provide a text for general readers rather than for scholars; "the state of the manuscript," he declared in his Introduction of 1928, prevented his offering a version that would be "adequate to every ideal" (p. xi). F. Barron Freeman's scholarly edition of 1948, *Melville's Billy Budd*, sought to provide in a single text both a literal transcription of the manuscript (including variants) and a reading version, but his valuable contributions to an understanding of the story were offset by his inadequate analysis and transcription, resulting in a mistaken account of the manuscript's genesis and growth.[6]

The Chicago edition of 1962 is based on a new and independent transcription and analysis of the *Billy Budd* manuscript. Recognizing the impossibility of providing a single text equally suitable for scholars and general readers, its editors prepared both a Genetic Text—a literal transcription of the component manuscript leaves as Melville left them—and a Reading Text; the latter, based on the Genetic Text, embodies the *wording* of the story

that in the editors' judgment most closely approximates Melville's final intention had a new fair copy of *Billy Budd, Sailor*, been made without his engaging in further expansion or revision. His inconsistent spelling, capitalization, hyphenation, paragraphing, and punctuation...have here been standardized—within the limits imposed by his own characteristic syntax—in accordance with present-day usage. (p. 213)

The Editor's Introduction surveys the growth of the manuscript, history of the text, and perspectives for criticism. Editorial notes and commentary, a bibliography, and textual notes accompany the Reading Text; a detailed analysis of the manuscript introduces the Genetic Text. The University of Chicago Press has issued convenient paperback editions of both the Reading Text (1962) and the Genetic Text (1978), each including relevant apparatus along with the Editors' Introduction in full.

Although no scholar has challenged the accuracy of the transcription constituting the Chicago Genetic Text or taken issue with either the editors' analysis of Melville's manuscript or their account of its genesis and growth, some reviewers and commentators—notably Milton R. Stern, Stanton Garner, Thomas J. Scorza, and Brook Thomas—have disagreed with the editorial principles followed in establishing the Chicago Reading Text; in 1975 Stern published a somewhat different version based on the genetic transcription in the Chicago edition, and it is his text that Scorza and Thomas have elected to cite. The Chicago Reading Text has been widely reprinted in college anthologies, however. It is also used in the third volume of Melville's prose works issued by the Library of America (1984), where a textual note by the volume editor, Harrison Hayford, observes that the *Billy Budd* manuscript has not yet been prepared for publication by the editors of the NN Edition of Melville's writings that is currently in progress.

With respect to plans for treatment of *Billy Budd* in the NN Edition, Hayford explains that divergences between the principles followed in the Chicago Reading Text and those established in the completed volumes of the new edition are "minor as to treatment of *wording*; thus differences in the wording of the eventual Northwestern-Newberry edition are likely to result merely from normal and necessary judgmental differences in the application of principles to individual problems. There will be greater divergences in the treatment of the spelling and punctuation" (p. 1448).

RECEPTION AND INTERPRETATION

Beginning with Raymond Weaver in 1921, the first critics to deal with *Billy Budd, Sailor*, treated the story as an allegorical conflict between good and evil, resolved only in tragic terms; some writers associated Billy with Christ and Claggart with Satan. J. Middleton Murry and E. L. Grant Watson, who read the narrative as Melville's spiritual autobiography, went on to call it his "last will and spiritual testament" and, in Watson's celebrated phrase, his "testament of acceptance." With the writings of Lewis Mumford, Yvor Winters, and Charles Weir, Jr., critical attention began to shift from Billy and Claggart to Captain Vere, and by 1946 Raymond Short had identified Vere as "the true hero of the novel" (p. xxxii). Meanwhile, George Arms also raised the possibility that *Billy Budd* might be "more concerned with social repercussions" than previous discussion had implied, and other critics began exploring it as social and political commentary rather than religious allegory or spiritual autobiography; some followed the lead of Anderson and Arvin in taking the story as Melville's oblique comment on the *Somers* mutiny. During the late 1940s, moreover, Herbert Schneider, Richard Chase, and Charles Olson were challenging the older view that the story and its title character are genuinely "tragic."

Vigorous reassessment of *Billy Budd* marked the decade following publication of Freeman's edition in 1948. By 1950 Joseph Schiffman, acting on a suggestion by Gay Wilson Allen, declared that the story is neither a tragedy nor a "testament of acceptance" but "a tale of irony" (p. 128). "Ironist" readings of literary works were much in fashion during the 1950s, and to other critics of the ironist persuasion (Harry M. Campbell, Arthur Sale, Karl E. Zink, Lawrance Thompson, Vern Wagner, and their successors) young Billy is a passive victim of injustice whose final words—"God bless Captain Vere!"—must be read ironically, and Vere himself, with his devotion to "forms, measured forms," is a reactionary authoritarian, as Leonard Casper argued in "The Case Against Captain Vere." A literal reversal of values had evidently taken place in discussion of *Billy Budd*: in 1959, a quarter-century after Watson had called the story a testament of acceptance, Phil Withim rechristened it "Melville's Testament of Resistance."

In 1962, when the Chicago edition of *Billy Budd, Sailor*, appeared, its two editors expressed the hope "that a comprehensive scholarly edition of the work will narrow the ground of disagreement and widen that of understanding" (p. v). What they wrote still remains a hope unfulfilled, however, for advances in literary scholarship do not necessarily produce corresponding advances in literary criticism. The critical reassessments of the 1950s, signallized by new readings not only of Melville but of literature generally, were relatively quiet preludes to the social and political upheavals on college and university campuses during the Vietnam years. Like their anti-war students, some academic professionals displayed little interest in the findings of textual scholarship, for those were times when imaginative literature—if it was to be read at all—either had to be politically "relevant" or made to seem so.

How relevance was demonstrated in *Billy Budd* can be illustrated by two essays of 1968. For Kingsley Widmer in "The Perplexed Myths of

Melville" (1968), Vere is "the second-rate mad Captain"; Billy and Claggart are "stupid goodness versus depraved rationality, a cut-down Christ against a hopped-up Satan" (pp. 33, 28). The story itself "often shows infelicities"; its concluding ballad is "not a very good poem"; only readers "confused" by Melville's emphasis on Vere's "decent and serious qualities" and "their own acceptance of arbitrary authority" will excuse the captain's "outrageous and immoral behavior" (pp. 26, 35, 32). In Charles Mitchell's "Melville and the Spurious Truth of Legalism" (1968), Billy and Claggart appear as doubles of Vere who mirror the submerged moral conflict within him between heart and intellect. "Vere becomes a Claggart by killing Billy," Mitchell asserts, thus placing reason and the law above "the moral majesty of human feeling" and so exemplifying "the principle of evil within the organization man—lawyer, captain, chief of police" (pp. 115, 125, 126).

One response open to a troubled reader was to go on liking Melville but to reject *Billy Budd* as an aberration, just as earlier critics such as Richard Chase and Charles Olson had already done. Another was to find a more sophisticated way of interpreting the story that would dissociate Melville himself from what Widmer condemned as Vere's "outrageous and immoral behavior" and from that pervasive "principle of evil" which Mitchell saw contaminating "the Establishment." Such a way had in fact been opened a decade earlier with the emergence of ironist criticism, which in turn was an offshoot of the still earlier "New Criticism" of Richards, Eliot, and Brooks and Warren. The New Critics had taught the importance of close reading and analysis of literary texts; some of the ironists, in their zeal for just such analysis, went on to distinguish Melville's opinions not only from Vere's but from those of his narrator as well, basing their whole methodology on the premise that the "I" who is speaking in *Billy Budd* cannot be trusted.

Those who assume that Melville's narrator is either biased or even obtuse, as Thompson and other ironists would have it, agree that he must be regarded as *unreliable*. Melville, they contend, is using all the devices of the accomplished ironist to undercut the narrator's version of events in order to give us the *real* "inside narrative" promised in his subtitle. An ironist is one aware of discrepancies between appearance and reality—between outward dissembling and inward intention, for example, or between what words seem to say and what they truly mean. An ironist *writer* plays upon and uses these very discrepancies so as to reveal inner truth; an ironist *reader* is one capable of responding in kind. Melville is just such a writer, the argument runs; his earlier works attest it. *Billy Budd* must, therefore, be read ironically—if only by the few who are percipient enough to do so.

That there is irony in *Billy Budd, Sailor*, is not denied by other readers, although they see the story in different terms—*tragic* irony, for example, as Richard Harter Fogle contends. Critics such as Edward H. Rosenberry also take issue with the idea of dissociating Melville so completely from either his narrator or from Vere; the captain has attracted defenders once again in the cooled-down 1970s and 1980s. Both "straight" and "ironist" readings have continued to appear over the years, with the ironists disagreeing not only with the opposition but among themselves as well: just what *is* the "*real* 'inside narrative' "? Such disagreement may reflect an inherent instability, either in Melville's text (Paul Brodtkorb, Jr., emphasizes its unfinished state) or in the nature of the critical enterprise itself.

Attempts to account for that instability have been made by a number of analysts in recent years, some with regard to changing fashions of criticism, or of whatever deeper historical or sociological forces may underlie such changes. In the 1980s *Billy Budd, Sailor,* has attracted the special attention of critics schooled in semiotics, structuralism, and poststructuralism—or "deconstruction." Barbara Johnson, who is well versed in these matters, observes that the continued critical debate over the story simply recapitulates an opposition within *Billy Budd* "between two conceptions of language, or between two types of reading": literal-minded Billy "reads everything at face value, never questioning the meaning of appearances," while the worldly wise Claggart, himself "a personification of ambiguity and ambivalence," is "properly an ironic reader." It is "precisely this opposition between the literal reader (Billy) and the ironic reader (Claggart)," she holds, that has been reenacted in the persistent division among the critics between "the 'acceptance' school and the 'irony' school," a dichotomy "already contained within the story" (*The Critical Difference,* pp. 84–85).[7] But one may also argue, with considerable historical justification, that "the real focus" of critical disagreement "lies less within Melville's text than in some extraliterary universe of discourse, be it semantic, philosophical, or political," and conclude that the contending critics have seen in his story, given its ambiguities, very much what their own predispositions and allegiances conditioned them to see.[8] So by "selecting and combining as he pleases" (to borrow Melvillean language), each commentator tends to read "his own peculiar lesson according to his own peculiar mind and mood" (*Pierre,* p. 342).

PROBLEMS FOR FUTURE STUDY

Scholars and critics wishing to minimize the subjective element in their approach to *Billy Budd, Sailor* will need to devote more attention than their predecessors to the story as the work of an older Melville—"the Melville who awaits discovery," in Stanton Garner's phrase. As the author of *Battle-Pieces* and *Clarel,* he had already given much thought to questions that also arise in *Billy Budd*: war and peace, religion and philosophy, indeed the whole course of human history. *Billy Budd* ought not to be read as an immediate sequel to *White-Jacket*, as it has sometimes been taken—nor should Captain Vere be treated like the two-dimensional Captain Claret. Coming between them are such subtle accounts of military and naval figures as those of General Glendinning in *Pierre*, of Paul Jones and Ethan Allen in *Israel Potter*, of both Northern and Southern officers in *Battle-Pieces*, and of Major Jack Gentian in the *Burgundy Club* sketches.

Many of the books that survive from Melville's library were acquired during the last quarter-century of his life, and both his reading and his writing during these years may well have more bearing on *Billy Budd* than has yet been recognized. To be considered along with possible new sources and analogues is the relation of *Billy Budd* to other late Melville manuscripts (some of them still unpublished), especially the prose-and-verse experiments scheduled for collection in a future volume of the NN Edition. With regard to the *Billy Budd* manuscript itself, both scholars and critics have too often neglected to go behind any and all reading texts of the story; there is still a need to acknowledge and assimilate what the Chicago Genetic Text and the accompanying editorial analysis have to tell them about Melville's art and Melville's thought as his story gradually took form.

As for interpretation and criticism, with its recent concentration on Captain Vere and his actions rather than on other elements of the story, it would be well for future commentators to approach Vere less as the object of ideological attack or defense and more as a dramatic character. Once Melville himself had proceeded far enough with the story to look at his captain not merely as a functional figure one needed to turn the wheels of an already determined plot, he began to treat him as a character in his own right, one who demanded to be fleshed out and made credible as a human being. The man Melville ultimately presented to us is not necessarily the cardboard figure that opposing critics have continued to treat as either a paragon of virtue or an utter monster; he is a fallible mortal, forced to make a judgment that would give pause to a Solomon. And as Leon Howard once wrote with reference to Melville's Ahab, it may well have been "the author's emotional sympathy for a character of whom he intellectually disapproved" that gave his story "much of its ambiguity and dramatic intensity" (p. xiii).

Rather than seeking either to praise Vere or to blame him—a choice explicitly left to the reader—Melville's narrative *accounts* for what Billy's captain is and does in terms of his class and military vocation. At the same time it places Vere at the pivotal point of the dialectic that runs throughout the story, whether one looks at its characterization—Billy versus Claggart—or its themes: not only good and evil but innocence and experience, frankness and concealment, nature and society, barbarism and civilization, heart and head, love and justice, what is right and what is legal, peacemaking and warmaking, the *Rights-of-Man* and the *Bellipotent*. For Melville and his art, as he himself acknowledged, such "unlike things must meet and mate" (Poems, p. 231).

Vere, after all, is captain of the *Bellipotent*, not of the *Rights-of-Man*, with the *Atheist* waiting just over the horizon. His name, like those of the ships and of Billy Budd himself, has allegorical overtones: *vir* in Latin is *man*. The best thumbnail sketch of the captain outside Melville's own narrative describes him in the way just suggested, defending not Vere and his actions but the author's impressive work of characterization. Joyce Adler's *War in Melville's Imagination* (1981) takes Vere as

the symbolic figure—not crudely, but finely and fairly drawn—of civilized man: learned, but not sufficiently imaginative; not devoid of the ability to love, but not allowing this capacity to develop; sensitive to the difference between the good and evil signified by Billy and Claggart, but the puppet of the god he has been trained to think must rule in this world. His ultimate faith is in Force, not only against the enemy, but in dealing with his own side—utilizing impressment, flogging, and hanging—and in dealing violently with his own heart (pp. 177–78).

There is a subject for future critics. The proper study of mankind, for us in our century as for Melville in his, is still man, and we too must live in what his White-Jacket called "this man-of-war world"—the world of the *Bellipotent*, where innocence and infamy are not always discernible for what they really are. Like Vere and like Melville, we also must walk its deck.[9]

NOTES

1. With permission of the Wisconsin Humanities Committee, this chapter draws on a lecture given by Professor Sealts in a seminar for lawyers presented by the Committee in 1983, funded in part by the National Endowment for the Humanities.

2. See Sealts, "Melville's Burgundy Club Sketches" (1958), and "The Ghost of Major Melvill" (1957), both reprinted in his *Pursuing Melville*, pp. 78–90, 67–77.

3. For a collection of documentary materials about the *Somers* case, 1842–1924, see Hayford, *The Somers Mutiny Affair* (1959). Hayford and Sealts, "Editors' Introduction," *BBS*, pp. 27–30, and "Notes & Commentary," pp. 181–83, survey commentary on the relation of the case to *Billy Budd, Sailor*; Michael Rogin has recently renewed discussion of that relation.

4. See Hayford and Sealts, "Notes & Commentary," pp. 175–83: notes on "a drumhead court," "the individuals composing it," "the heaviest of penalties,"

"according to the Articles of War, a capital crime," "the Mutiny Act," and "follows without delay."

5. The version of Weisberg's essay published in his *The Failure of the Word* (1984) somewhat revises his position.

6. Corrections in Freeman's transcription made by Elizabeth Treeman were issued by Harvard University Press in a pamphlet of *Corrigenda* in 1953 and used as the basis for the text of *Billy Budd* in a college anthology published in 1956. For more detailed discussion of the Weaver and Freeman editions and of other texts deriving from them, see "History of the Text" in Hayford and Sealts, "Editors' Introduction," pp. 12–24.

7. In "*Billy Budd* and the Judgment of Silence" (1982), an avowedly Marxist essay, Brook Thomas not only takes issue with Johnson's non-judgmental reading of the story but also attacks deconstructionists generally for what he sees as their conservative ideology. Both Melville and his reader, according to Thomas, "are in the position to judge Vere's judgment according to the direction history has taken. When we do so, Vere's judgment seems clearly to support a dead order" (p. 70).

8. This observation was originally prompted by reflections on opposing conclusions reached by two critics who had dealt with essentially the same elements in the story; see Merton M. Sealts, "Melville," in *American Literary Scholarship: An Annual / 1969*, ed. J. Albert Robbins (Durham, N.C.: Duke University Press, 1971), p. 52.

9. "The reader must reject or sanctify Vere's action," writes Jon M. Kinnamon, but in doing so he "exposes his own nature—the very depth of his mind and the strength of his compassion. In pondering this problem, the reader walks the deck," since like Vere "he is above all a mortal" who is "called on to make a decision that is not within his human capacity to make" (p. 172). From this point of view, Melville's story is like Plinlimmon's pamphlet in *Pierre*, which "seems more the excellently illustrated re-statement of a problem, than the solution of the problem itself" (p. 210).

WORKS CITED

Adler, Joyce Sparer. "*Billy Budd* and Melville's Philosophy of War [and Peace]." *PMLA* 91 (March 1976): 266–78. Rpt. in *War and Melville's Imagination*. New York: New York University Press, 1981, pp. 160–85.

Anderson, Charles Roberts. "The Genesis of *Billy Budd*." *American Literature* 12 (November 1940): 329–46.

[Arms, George. ("T.T.E.")] "Melville's *Billy Budd*." *Explicator* 2 (December 1943): Query 14.

Arvin, Newton. "A Note on the Background of *Billy Budd*." *American Literature* 20 (March 1948): 51–55.

Berthoff, Warner. " 'Certain Phenomenal Men': The Example of *Billy Budd*." *ELH: A Journal of English Literary History* 27 (December 1960): 334–51. Rpt. *The Example of Melville*. Princeton, N.J.: Princeton University Press, 1962, pp. 183–203.

Brodtkorb, Paul, Jr. "The Definitive *Billy Budd*: 'But Aren't It All Sham?' " *PMLA* 82 (December 1967): 600–12.

Bryant, John. "Melville and Charles F. Briggs: *Working a Passage* to *Billy Budd*." *English Language Notes* 22 (June 1985): 48–54.

Campbell, Harry Modean. "The Hanging Scene in Melville's *Billy Budd, Foretopman*." *Modern Language Notes* 66 (June 1951): 378–81.

Casper, Leonard. "The Case Against Captain Vere." *Perspective* 5 (Summer 1952): 146–52.

Chase, Richard. "Dissent on *Billy Budd*." *Partisan Review* 15 (November 1948): 1212–18.

Fogle, Richard Harter. "*Billy Budd*—Acceptance or Irony." *Tulane Studies in English* 8 (1958): 107–13.

Garner, Stanton. "Fraud as Fact in Herman Melville's *Billy Budd*." *San Jose Studies* 4 (May 1978): 82–105.

———. "Melville's Scout Toward Aldie." *Melville Society Extracts* No. 51 (September 1982): 5–16.

———. "The Melville Who Awaits Discovery." *Melville Society Extracts* No. 53 (February 1983): 2.

Glick, Wendell. "Expediency and Absolute Morality in *Billy Budd*." *PMLA* 68 (March 1953): 103–10.

Gollin, Richard and Rita. "Justice in an Earlier Treatment of the *Billy Budd* Theme." *American Literature* 28 (January 1957): 513–15.

Hayford, Harrison, ed. "Note on the Texts," *Pierre, Israel Potter, The Piazza Tales, The Confidence-Man*, Uncollected Prose, and *Billy Budd, Sailor*. By Herman Melville. New York: Library of America, 1984, pp. 1442–49.

———, ed. *The Somers Mutiny Affair*. Englewood Cliffs, N.J.: Prentice-Hall, 1959.

———, and Merton M. Sealts, Jr. "Preface," "Editors' Introduction," and "Notes & Commentary." In *Billy Budd, Sailor*. By Herman Melville. Chicago: University of Chicago Press, 1962, pp. v–vii, 1–39, 133–202.

Hays, Peter L., and Richard Dilworth Rust. " 'Something Healing': Fathers and Sons in *Billy Budd*." *Nineteenth-Century Fiction* 34 (December 1979): 326–36.

Howard, Leon, introd. *Moby Dick or, The Whale*. By Herman Melville. New York: Modern Library, 1950, pp. v–xvi.

Johnson, Barbara. "Melville's Fist: The Execution of *Billy Budd*." *Studies in Romanticism* 18 (Winter 1979): 567–99. Rpt. *The Critical Difference: Essays in the Contemporary Rhetoric of Reading*. Baltimore: Johns Hopkins University Press, 1980, pp. 79–109, 151–52.

Kinnamon, Jon M. "*Billy Budd*: Political Philosophies in a Sea of Thought." *Arizona Quarterly* 26 (Summer 1970): 164–72.

Lawry, Robert P. "Justice in Billy Budd." *The Gamut* (Cleveland State University), 6 (Spring/Summer 1982): 76–86. Rpt. *In Brief* (Case Western Reserve University School of Law), 31 (June 1984): 13–19.

McElderry, B. R., Jr. "Three Earlier Treatments of the *Billy Budd* Theme." *American Literature* 27 (May 1955): 251–57.

Matthiessen, F. O. *American Renaissance: Art and Expression in the Age of Emerson and Whitman*. New York: Oxford University Press, 1941.

Melville, Herman. *Billy Budd and Other Prose Pieces*. Ed. Raymond Weaver. Vol. 13 (1924) of *The Works of Herman Melville*. 16 vols. London: Constable & Co., 1922–24.

———. *Billy Budd, Sailor (An Inside Narrative).* Ed. Milton R. Stern. Indianapolis: Bobbs-Merrill Co., 1975.

———. *Melville's Billy Budd.* Ed. F. Barron Freeman. Cambridge, Mass.: Harvard University Press, 1948.

———. *Shorter Novels of Herman Melville.* Introd. Raymond Weaver. New York: Horace Liveright, 1928.

Miller, Edwin Haviland. *Melville.* New York: George Braziller, 1975.

Mitchell, Charles. "Melville and the Spurious Truth of Legalism." *Centennial Review* 12 (Winter 1968): 110–26).

Mumford, Lewis. *Herman Melville.* New York: Harcourt, Brace & Co., 1929.

Murray, Charles Joseph. "A Concordance to Melville's *Billy Budd.*" Ph.D. Diss., Miami University, 1979. [*Mel. Diss.,* #505.]

Murry, J. Middleton. "Herman Melville's Silence." *Times Literary Supplement,* No. 1173 (10 July 1924), p. 433. Rpt. *John Clare and Other Studies.* London: Peter Neville, 1950, pp. 209–12.

Olson, Charles. "David Young, David Old." *Western Review* 14 (Fall 1949): 63–66.

Rathbun, John W. "*Billy Budd* and the Limits of Perception." *Nineteenth-Century Fiction* 20 (June 1965): 19–34.

Reich, Charles A. "The Tragedy of Justice in *Billy Budd.*" *Yale Review* 56 (Spring 1967): 368–89.

Reid, B. L. "Old Melville's Fable." *Massachusetts Review* 9 (Summer 1968): 529–46. Rpt. *Tragic Occasions: Essays on Several Forms.* Port Washington, N.Y.: Kennikat Press, 1971, pp. 137–62.

Rogin, Michael Paul. "The *Somers* Mutiny and *Billy Budd*: Melville in the Penal Colony." In *Criminal Justice History: An International Annual.* Vol. 1 Ed. Henry Cohen. New York: Criminal and Justice History Group, and John Jay Press, 1980, pp. 187–224. Rpt. *Subversive Genealogy: The Politics and Art of Herman Melville.* New York: Alfred A. Knopf, 1983, pp. 288–316, 342–47.

Rosenberry, Edward H. "The Problem of *Billy Budd.*" *PMLA* 80 (December 1965): 489–98.

Sale, Arthur. "Captain Vere's Reasons." *Cambridge Journal* (October 1951): 3–18.

Schiffman, Joseph. "Melville's Final Stage, Irony: A Re-examination of *Billy Budd* Criticism." *American Literature* 22 (May 1950): 128–36.

Schneider, Herbert. "At Sea." In *A History of American Philosophy.* New York: Columbia University Press, 1946, pp. 293–301.

Scorza, Thomas J. *In the Time Before Steamships: Billy Budd, the Limits of Politics, and Modernity.* DeKalb: Northern Illinois University Press, 1979.

Sealts, Merton M., Jr. *Innocence and Infamy: Resources for Discussing Herman Melville's Billy Budd, Sailor.* Madison: Wisconsin Humanities Committee, 1983.

———. *Pursuing Melville, 1940–1980: Chapters and Essays.* Madison: University of Wisconsin Press, 1982.

Short, Raymond, introd. *Four Great American Novels.* New York: Henry Holt & Co., 1946, pp. xxxi–xxxiii.

Springer, Haskell S., comp. *The Merrill Studies in Billy Budd.* Columbus, Ohio: Charles E. Merrill, 1970.

Stafford, William T., ed. *Melville's Billy Budd and the Critics*. San Francisco: Wadsworth, 1961.

Stern, Milton R., introd. *Billy Budd, Sailor (An Inside Narrative)*. By Herman Melville. Indianapolis: Bobbs-Merrill Co., 1975, pp. vii–xliv.

Stessel, Edward. "Naval Warfare and Herman Melville's War Against Failure." *Essays in Arts and Sciences* 10 (May 1981): 59–77.

Sutton, Walter. "Melville and the Great God Budd." *Prairie Schooner* 34 (Summer 1960): 128–33.

Thomas, Brook. "*Billy Budd* and the Judgment of Silence." *Bucknell Review* 27 (1982): 51–78.

———. "The Legal Fictions of Herman Melville and Lemuel Shaw." *Critical Inquiry* 11 (September 1984): 24–51.

Thompson, Lawrance. "Divine Depravity." In *Melville's Quarrel with God*. Princeton, N.J.: Princeton University Press, 1952, pp. 355–414.

Vincent, Howard P., ed. *Twentieth Century Interpretations of Billy Budd*. Englewood Cliffs, N.J.: Prentice-Hall, 1971.

Wagner, Vern. "Billy Budd as Moby Dick: An Alternate Reading." In *Studies in Honor of John Wilcox*. A. Dayle Wallace and Woodburn O. Ross, eds. Detroit: Wayne State University Press, 1958, pp. 157–74.

Warren, Robert Penn, introd. *Selected Poems of Herman Melville*. New York: Random House, 1970, pp. 55–71, 79–88.

Watson, E. L. Grant. "Melville's Testament of Acceptance." *New England Quarterly* 6 (June 1933): 319–27.

Weaver, Raymond. *Herman Melville: Mariner and Mystic*. New York: George H. Doran Co., 1921.

———, introd. *Shorter Novels of Herman Melville*. New York: Horace Liveright, 1928, pp. xlix–li.

Weir, Charles, Jr. "Malice Reconciled: A Note on Melville's *Billy Budd*." *University of Toronto Quarterly* 13 (April 1944): 276–85.

Weisberg, Richard H. "How Judges Speak: Some Lessons of Adjudication in *Billy Budd, Sailor* with an Application to Justice Rehnquist," *New York University Law Review* 57 (April 1982): 1–69. Rev. and rpt. as "The Creative Use of Statutes for Subjective Ends." In *The Failure of the Word: The Protagonist as Lawyer in Modern Fiction*. New Haven, Conn.: Yale University Press, 1984, pp. 2131–76, 206–14.

Widmer, Kingsley. "The Perplexed Myths of Melville: *Billy Budd*." *Novel* 2 (Fall 1968): 25–35.

Willett, Ralph W. "Nelson and Vere: Hero and Victim in *Billy Budd, Sailor*." *PMLA* 82 (October 1967): 370–76.

Winters, Yvor. *Maule's Curse: Seven Studies in the History of American Obscurantism*. Norfolk, Conn.: New Directions, 1938, pp. 86–87. Rpt. *In Defense of Reason*. New York: Swallow Press and William Morrow, 1947, pp. 230–31.

Withim, Phil. "*Billy Budd*: Testament of Resistance." *Modern Language Quarterly* 20 (June 1959): 115–27.

Zink, Karl E. "Herman Melville and the Forms—Irony and Social Criticism in 'Billy Budd.'" *Accent* 12 (Summer 1952): 131–39.

PART THREE

MELVILLE'S THOUGHT

15

MELVILLE, SOCIETY, AND LANGUAGE

Milton R. Stern

Almost from the beginning American writing centered on a contest between two views of America, a symbolic, idealizing, mythic view, and a reportorial, disillusioning, historical view. The idealizing image—America as the City on a Hill—emerged as a typological vision of experience yet to come. For the Puritans, America literally was to be the type of the millennium, a New World specially released from all the limitations of the past. The repudiation of all history since Adam was to be an imminent realization of all highest hopes.[1] The historical assessment, on the other hand, is a report of the America actually experienced.

In its seriously considered manifestations, the idealizing impulse did not gloss over the shortcomings of the historical actuality. Puritans like John Winthrop and Cotton Mather, as well as nineteenth-century Transcendentalists like Thoreau and even Whitman, found their American present to be a betrayal of their American future and the mythic meaning of America. But their essential emphasis was on the redemption that was nevertheless to come. On the other hand, in its popular manifestations, the idealizing impulse devolves into a coercive jingoism: the American present *is* the realization of all best hopes (versions of "We Are Number One"; "America, Love It or Leave It" in all periods of American history). As Hawthorne knew, and as Melville was to discover, the difference between the Transcendentalist's celebration of the present and the religious and patriotic respectabilities of their literary market-place was the difference between spiritual largeness and narrow smugness, between intellectual risk and social prudence. But in all manifestations, whether the Emersonian credos of man's divine identity and spiritual consciousness, or the popular shibboleths intimidatingly idealizing the actual, the mythic view of America tends to be transcendental, suprahistorical.

On the other hand, the historical, sociological view is an angry dismantling of the myth. This view reveals a mortal nation, not a state of grace characteristic of the New Jerusalem. The demythologizing revelation is that of an American society deluded into unexamined Idealist certitudes that it is immune to the nonmillennialistic limitations of all other human beings in any other society. For the Idealist—that is, for the one who believes in an informing Idea of things as a metaphysical Absolute, an ultimate Reality for which the actual is merely a momentary symbolic revelation—central and final emphasis is not on this world, for this world is not the ultimate reality. But for the anti-Idealist impulse, there is a strong energy of philosophical naturalism, a secularizing tendency in which the metaphysical, the Ideal, is itself the man-made illusion, and the actualities of this world are the reality. The American literature that emerged after the Civil War ("What like a bullet can undeceive," exclaimed Melville in his poem about the Battle of Shiloh) became more intense in its disillusion in the decade following Melville's death.[2] The major energy of serious American literature came to center on debunking mythic assumptions about American society. Serious literature became more often than not a radical attack on Idealist nationalism. Melville's place in this development can be seen early, even before the Civil War, in the Vivenza sections of *Mardi* and in Pierre's bitter education into his literary marketplace.

The Idealist sense of America has its roots deep in the European imagination that gave birth to the nation, deep in the classical and the medieval redactions of racial "memories" of the primal separation from the Creating Parent—the universal translation of traumatic expulsion from the blissful womb into a fall from a lost golden time and place. The Christian mythos of European civilization projected the lost Eden of the past into a millennial—and then eternal—replacement in the future, the millennium to come as the earthly type of the heavenly eternity that awaits. There was no pain, no sin, no death—God hadn't wound the clock—until after the fall from grace, and similarly, in the eternal Heavenly Kingdom, once more there would be no Time. In short, Christianity provided an Idealist context for sandwiching historical, or fallen, man between the timeless two states of pre- and post-historical grace. American Puritan Christianity insisted fervently on the American Plantation Religious as the providential and typological encapsulation of the race, the chosen people in the chosen land. For the seventeenth-century Calvinistic energies Melville was to inherit from his mother, the true identity of American society was not in its momentary historical present but in the metaphysical reality of the ideal type it was to represent.

The American eighteenth century continued the essential myth of a separatist but redemptive America; however, in the documents that express the sense of a Chosen Society, the differences between the seventeenth-century Mayflower Compact and the essentially eighteenth-century Monroe Doctrine indicate different loci for ideal reality. Paine, Jefferson, and Franklin all expressed homage to a Primal Parent, but no one can escape the secularizing terms in which they participate in the transformation of transcendent America from the Plantation Religious to the democratic Republic. The transformation, which Melville was to inherit from the religious liberalism of his father, was a social and political translation of the benevolently rational science derived from the fixed and perfect laws of nature and of nature's God. The good society now becomes, in effect, a fully secular type of absolute divine rationality and toleration. So merged is the Deist's anti-Puritan God with nature that Idealist metaphysics gives way to Idealist physics. For all their repudiation of what they considered the corrupt supernaturalism of the past, the American revolutionary Deists maintained a concept of an informing Ideal of deliberate, cosmic plan, which accounted for the nature of the universe and the possibilities of perfectible human life on earth. Opening the door to the Romanticism that would supplant it, eighteenth-century American primitivism, like the polar Calvinism it supplanted, was a vision of experience yet to come. In this unspoiled New World, the rational New Man would establish the redeemed and redeeming society, and once again, intervening history, sandwiched between the lost primitive Eden of the past and the socially perfected natural man to come, would find its apogee and fulfillment in America.[3]

Combining the Puritan sense of symbolism, mystery, and Divine immediacy with the Deistic sense of all-accommodating Divine benevolence and the goodness of nature, American nineteenth-century Transcendentalism discovered its mode of perception in the emphasis that the European Romantics placed on intuition. The highest function of mind was the translation inward of the apprehension that Divinity is here and now in all objects, which, by that fact, become changeful physical symbols of changeless spiritual perfection. The major literary context for Melville's coming of age was Transcendentalism: it was Melville's context for reactive response. What Melville inherited from his contemporary high literary milieu was the proposition that the human race has always been in a state of grace without knowing it, has always been divine without seeing it, and was about to be delivered from blindness. Like the Puritans and radical Deists before them, the American Transcendentalists continued the emphasis on newness and imminent futurity.

So the influential New Englanders, together with their New York convert, Whitman, with assumptions and certainties very different from those of both the Puritan and the Deist, but deriving from both, could announce like Chanticleer the dawn of a new world, but not to come. It is here. Now.[4]

Nevertheless, in making this announcement, the Transcendentalist Romantics were not describing the historical present, which for them fell short of its symbolic meaning. Emerson insisted on the need to confront experience unchaperoned, and no account of American Transcendentalism is reliable that fails to note its energetic insistence on the physical, the experiential, the quotidian, "the meal in the firkin; the milk in the pan" (Emerson, "American Scholar," p. 61)—and thus Transcendentalism's drive toward realism in literary diction. Nevertheless, the Transcendentalist context remained Idealist to the end. For all that Emerson insisted on "Experience," and wrestled with "Fate" and "Montaigne," with illusion and the "lords of life," he relocated, but did not abandon, a certitude about universal Divine purpose (Jonathan Bishop, Stephen E. Whicher). That was the ultimate reality to be sought in human affairs and human society. The paradox is that because their metaphysics located reality in Spiritual Presence, in an ultimate Reality permeating all things—which is *not* the same as locating reality in the actual of itself—because their metaphysics inhabited the universe with a directive, benevolent Spirit, they were at odds with their own drive toward realism in art. For all their profound democratizing redemption of the *actual*, and for all their consequent turn toward realism in diction and materials, the Transcendentalists' metaphysics stood between them and modern existentialist absurdism. That sense of the absurd is one of the results created by a phenomenological rather than Transcendentalist view of the primacy of mind, a metaphysics in which it becomes possible to see the actual as empty of essence. Secularizing realism and anti-Idealist symbolism lead toward that view, and it is that toward which Melville felt his way in his increasingly profound reading of the actual as a sign indeed, but a sign of the hollowness, the vacancy of the cosmos (Paul Brodtkorb, *Ishmael's White World*, 1965).

The important point to take from Melville's contemporary literary context is that his readings of experience will reveal society as less "temporary" than do those of the Transcendentalists, more filled with a dread sense of the possibility that the madness of the human scene is its own reality and a sign of the *lasting* absence of benevolent direction from the ethically empty infinite vastness out there. But if, like the literary realists for whom they opened the door, the Transcendentalists could be angry about the American actuality, their Idealism allowed them escape into optimisms that would be validated in "higher consciousness." And a non-Transcendental realistic writer like William Dean Howells, who seems to certify the mundane as a reality, manages his share of American optimism in his purification of the actual, observed by him in middle-class American society. But it is significant that Howells is divided; and precisely at that point at which the nature of the actual ceases to be exemplary of the "smiling aspects" of "poor real life," he fights a holding action against the very realism he otherwise welcomes and proclaims in his literary generosities and in his protest against political injustices and social inequities in America. For Melville, however, "realism" left him with neither the philosophical escape hatch of the Transcendentalists nor the optimistic sense of the American actuality advocated by Howells.[5]

In sum, the division between the mythic and historical views of America marks an essential perceptual difference between apprehension of the fallen world as a momentarily askew sign of a divinely ordered world-to-come on the one hand, and on the other an apprehension of the vicious society of a fallen world as itself an autonomous reality and a sign not of teleological moral pattern and divine purpose, but of the extent to which our human identity is cosmically incidental, a creation of our own imperfect natures. The question to which Melville obsessively recurs in his fictions is the possibility of existential emptiness—of no essential identity of nature or man in a universe empty of God and (therefore) brimming with a plenitude of shifting forms, or temporary identities. If the metaphysics underpinning the identification of America as the New-World Redeemer Nation are the necessary acceptabilities, then there is something darkly un-American, and anti-religious in the subversive proposition that American society is the product of bitterly limited human forces. The lack of One Meaning in all things results in endless meanings for any thing; the removal of the basis for typology does the same thing to words that it does to the idea of society. It is with the function of language and the nationalistic uses of Idealist metaphysics that we begin to enter Herman Melville's view of society. His view developed in a national culture that believed that human society is perfectible and that its perfectibility either will be or already has been realized in the society produced by the New Adams of the New World.[6]

The struggle in American fiction between the two views of America is a struggle toward social realism. But the Era of Good Feeling following the War of 1812 was an era of optimistic, nationalistic fervor. Patriotic chauvinism demanded cultural nationalism. The age of Jackson and the following expansion at Mexico's expense were political expressions of the cultural nationalism fanned by periodicals like the *North American Review*. The Young America movement was at once a literary and a political insistence on expansionism; the national culture identified criticism of American society as hostile to democracy, the Republic, and God. Even Melville's ambivalent review of Hawthorne's *Mosses*, fervent in its defense of nay-saying and yet jingoistic in its literary nationalism, is a sign of how intense and insistent the pervasive patriotism was. That Melville complied quickly and fully to Wiley's bowdlerizing of *Typee*[7] reflected the ideological ambience of his literary marketplace.[8] From the very beginning there had been a national consciousness of the American identity at stake in the critical role of American literature. The greatest early literary influence on Melville, Nathaniel Hawthorne, veiled his ideas so that he could criticize America's millennialism and still be accepted as a good American burgher. One can understand the stakes and issues in Hawthorne's prefaces when he hints at the critical tensions between the literary genres: the "sketch," which idealized American actuality, earned popularity; the "novel," which instructed, earned toleration; but the "romance" was "morbid" and was generally disapproved.[9] In retrospect, the hostile responses to *Typee* were inevitable.[10]

Led by his sense that Reality is the actual and that the actual is subject to multiple and shifting meanings, Melville had to find for his themes special modes of narrative in a marketplace that would not accommodate a literary realism unmistakably expressing socially and nationalistically unacceptable speculations about the nature of God, man, and society.[11] Melville's imagination sought veils. Endlessly fascinated by the limitless possibilities of meaning once fixed relationships between God and experiential fact are removed, Melville spent his writing life in deep play with language, which became for him the darkly exuberant manipulation of the connections between human limitation and the multiple referentiality of a reference.[12] The absence of absolutely dependable meaning becomes one with the essence of moral limitations. Those limitations become both cause and sign of the killing imperfections of society. The Ahab who forges exactly his own society—a subservient extension of his own will—does so through the language that is a sign of his own certitude of absolute meaning: his address to the corposants (ch. 119) and his whipping the crew to frenzied fealty in the hunt for the white whale (ch. 36) are opposite sides of the same coin. As "The Doubloon" (ch. 99) indicates, no true basis for Ahab's certitude exists. The disintegration of absolute meaning is also the literal disintegration of the state which allows itself to be governed by absolutes. Words, meaning, unwrite themselves throughout *Moby-Dick*, whose language becomes a cautionary tale for society: through its own rhetorical pluralism, *Moby-Dick* is, among other things, an act of art as a defense against totalitarianism. But the unwriting doesn't stop there, for *Pierre* can be seen as a disassembly of *Moby-Dick*— a satiric repudiation of the power of the word to be a defense against *anything*[13] and a satiric repudiation of the power of the cosmically democratic love that permeated Ishmael's narrative. The extent to which the later works, especially *The Confidence-Man* and *Billy Budd*, can be seen as farewells to art is the extent to which we see the relationship between Melville's sense of the absence of love in the universe and (consequently) in human society and his sense of the absence of dependable meaning in signs, linguistic or otherwise. The failure of society and the absurdity of clear meaning have the same root in Melville's ontological vision. The more his works multiply meanings in exploration of meaning, the more we can glimpse the crucial disjunction between the genius of Melville's distinctive language and the reportorial nature of the language of social realism. And the more we see Melville's ironic bitterness about the Good Society.

Although Melville's connection to literary realism is strong, his greatness does not fit any formula for style in the history of literary developments; there was a constant, rich, ironic tension between his anti-Idealist perceptions and his Romantic language, which was born of Idealist assumptions, and was oriented to grand philosophizing and metaphysical speculations about the Absolute. Conversely, Melville could not say his say about society without metaphysical exploration of the reasons for his condemnation; he could not make that exploration in writing the kind of book he would wish to without plunging into the question of meaning and, consequently, of language. If literary realism and a disillusioned report of American society fit together, the very character of Melville's imagination—philosophical, symbolic, mythic—tended toward the multi-leveled dense packing of suggestion and connotation that is associated not with the literary realism that developed during the last two decades of Melville's life, but with the Romanticism that permeated the decade before and the decade in which he began to write. In examining Melville's view of society, we observe a fictive and linguistic mode whose richness and complexity derive from a tension in which the idiom of Romanticism is used to react against Romantic Idealism—and against the popular Idealist conventions of cultural nationalism—in order to express the attitudes of both social realism and modernist absurdism.

In sum, the Romantic energies of Melville's literary age flowed toward Idealist perceptions, a divine human identity, and the creation of symbolism as the expression of Absolute meaning perceived in language and nature. Those Romantic energies also flowed toward a mythic assessment of America, toward the idea of incipient Ideal in society. Melville was swept into the Romantic language celebrating consciousness at the same time that his experience disillusioned him about the concept of the ideal society. With the Mexican War, slavery, the Civil War (Joyce Sparer Adler, James Duban, Carolyn L. Karcher), and with his disappointments over the literary marketplace, he became increasingly skeptical about the divinity of man and the progress of society. When all Idealist assumptions about the nature of God and man became doubtful for him, his sense of meaning and the uses of language turned absurdist. Melville became bitterly disillusioned, ironically, through his hopefully democratic and egalitarian anger at social abuses and injustices. He began with a sense of the possibility of great nobility in humanity and ended with a conviction that governmental authority is the necessary ordering force that will keep in check the savage rampages with which the base human animal always threatens to break out into destruction.[14] But there is more to it than that, for Melville's sense of society was a complex and integral part of his sense of art. Melville's developing sense of society became his developing skepticism about the Romantic possibilities of language.

Just as there was a richly creative interaction of energies in the tension between Romantic language and anti-Romantic perception in Melville's writings, so there were polar Idealist extremes of religion claiming validation in the psyche of the very young Herman Melville. One was the Unitarianism of his father, Allan, and the other was the Dutch Reform Calvinism of his mother, Maria Gansevoort Melville.The liberal Unitarian perspectives of the father offered a benevolent universe that derived essentially from eighteenth-century American Deism: a universally redeemable humanity; a predictable, safe, fixed Nature created for man's use and instruction; and a loving God who accommodatingly allowed humanity to educate itself into a rational understanding of rational divine principles through rational comprehension of the rational laws of Nature. This cheerful perspective would encourage Herman's older brother, Gansevoort, to adopt enthusiastically all the optimistic Loco Foco nationalism of the Young America movement. With this optimism, the way is clear for entry into the house of the Transcendentalists through the porch of symbolism. All one need do is substitute Romantic mystic intuition for pragmatic rationality in a universe constantly revealing divine generosity and benevolence. But both Alan and Gansevoort would abandon Herman in deaths that came at the least rational times, revealing neither generosity nor benevolence in the scheme of things.

Conversely, the Calvinistic perspectives of the mother offered a terrifying universe that derived essentially from seventeenth-century ultra-Protestantism: a depraved humanity, a fallen Nature constantly manifesting providential energy, a jealous and wrathful God testing for and alienated by the sight of sin. It would be entirely consonant with this perspective to assume an Idealist repudiation of actual, fallen society in the certainty of the millennial society to come through God's grace. Neither Deistic nor Calvinistic pole would have led to the anti-Idealist dread so characteristic of Melville's darkest visions. And neither of the opposites was unmixed or reliable in Melville's experience; but the Calvinistic bleak view of man was to come the closer of the two in describing the meaning of that experience.

When Melville was twelve his father died. More than Melville's other books, *Redburn* and *Pierre* reflect the relationship between his father's death and his mother's rule on the one hand, and his sense of society on the other. Other chapters in this volume discuss the problems of Melville's biography and psychology and the theme of parents in the individual books. It must suffice here merely to point out the revelatory relationship between a fatherless world and social events in Melville's mind as he creates fiction that is not autobiography (William Gilman) but that projects imagined characters and events out of his memory. What remains important is the fictive construction of the family: a father whose cheerful, safe world vanishes and whose legacy and identity remain ambiguous at best, a cheat and a lie at worst; and a mother who is vain and overbearing, and whose religion is not a dark truth but a prideful respectability. As in the case of *Redburn*, what remains appropriately revelatory here are *Pierre*'s ambiguous suggestions that all the fathers were a lie and that the mother's world and legacy are no less unreliable. The typological heritage of grace and the millennial promise of salvation did not seem to work out in the "providences" of Herman's life in his mother's religious context any more than did the benevolent predictability, rationality, and safety in his father's.

Significantly, like the expulsion into the world in *Redburn*, when Pierre is expelled from his illusions about the nature of existence, the pre-experiential world of childhood is replaced by initiation into a heartless society.[15] The process in *Redburn* and *Pierre* is the same: in both books symbols at first deceive when they signify the dependability of the worlds of the parents; they become "true" when they signify the non-existence of what those worlds were assumed to be. Assumed symbolic meaning (the "Cenci" portrait in *Pierre*, for instance) becomes multiple and ambiguous to the point of meaninglessness under the impact of experience. The symbols unwrite themselves. The facts of experience always replace the assumptions with new mere facts—which frighteningly always turn out to be real and to have unstable meanings. The metaphysical implications of human society's "inhuman" viciousness and horror give experiential fact reality that supplants and surpasses the initial significatory energy of the symbols, which is to say that both *Redburn* and *Pierre* are examples of anti-Idealist symbolism, of the fictive construct as a disintegration of the Idealist myth.

Both the optimism of Unitarian liberalism and the certainties of Calvinistic damnation and grace failed Melville. What lasted was the sense of a fallen world East of Eden, the world of actual and fallen parents, a world in which the actual suggests that there never had been an unfallen state of existence. This is to say that as his late brooding about Paine and Burke indicated (see David Ketterer, Jon M. Kinnamon, and—preeminently—Thomas J. Scorza), Melville found dependability in neither Idealist system, but left them both with more disdain for the assumptions of his father's liberal Unitarianism than for his mother's orthodox Calvinism. The idea of the Fall and original sin would remain with him as a metaphor descriptive of experiential reality, and he would grow to have contempt for rationalistic eighteenth-century optimism, which he felt was produced by mere watchmaker's brains. What remained central in the metaphor of the Fall was this: the failure of both Father and Mother—Melville's recoil from both ends of the Idealist spectrum—was intimately and intricately associated in Melville's imagination with the corrupt and heartless selfishness of human society.

Melville's view of institutionalized man as stupid, hypocritical, brutal, and—most of all—deluded, became the unrevised and unrelieved norm after *Moby-Dick*. It was a view of man, the social animal, that merged in a mutually causal relationship with Melville's view of the universe as empty of final meaning, spiritual purpose, or divine and guiding presence. His anti-Idealist insistence on the disillusioning history of human society from the earliest prehistoric beginnings and in every contemporary prospect turned him back in recoil from the American insistence on the history of the yet-to-be, which he saw as a nationalistic and metaphysical delusion—a perspective that he first expressed fully in *Mardi*. It is not that any single traumatic experience changed Melville into a misanthrope. Rather, the contrast between millennialistic American nationalism, which at first he partly shared, and spectacles such as the Mexican War and the conduct of slavery, which sickened him, created in him an enormous sense of the terrifying gulf between history and the presumed Ideal. In slavery he saw the paradigm of that gulf: "the world's fairest hope linked with man's foulest crime" (Poems, p. 3). And America was but the greatest intensification of that gulf, observed in all society throughout all human history. In sum, what Melville observed in human experience jarred him into speculation about God. Melville's consequent sense of a conscienceless universe threw him back again in recoil from God to human society—in which, except for a few innocents, good hearts, and noble heroes (all dupes or victims or lost in the past), Melville presents creatures who fall far short of Romantic and liberal religious Idealist assumptions, and who are lastingly *real* in their *actual* identity. Society became for Melville the mirror reflecting its human creators: heartless, unjust, violent, exploitative, selfish, and hypocritical.

TYPEE AND OMOO

In one of the best pieces of *Typee* criticism, John Samson convincingly details the energies that dissolve the validity of the Edenic-millennialistic expectations of Tommo (and of the reading public in 1846). This examination of Romantic-Idealist perceptions of the primitive—an examination that finds an excellent companion piece in Michael Kearns's study of Melville's anti-Idealist psychology—expresses the received general sense of the book: Tommo's fall is not an escape from the circumstances of human existence, but if anything it expresses the inescapability of history (John Wenke, "Melville's *Typee*"), the inevitability of what William Ellery Sedgwick summed up as "the tragedy of mind." The "prehistoric" Typees themselves are fallen away from a greater, earlier history. Furthermore, Tommo feels an increasing, almost hysterical need to renounce "Eden" and return "home."

At first *Typee* seems to offer a pastoral alternative to Western society. The Western society that Tommo deserts is one of technology, intrusion, and artificiality: the floating factories that are the whale-hunting ships, the French and English navies, and the "civilized" manners of the missionaries. From the very first that world is associated with the absence or total consumption of fertile nature: "Oh! for a refreshing glimpse of one blade of grass.... Is there nothing fresh around us?" (p. 3). The contemporary Western world is summed up in protocol, maritime law, military force, uniforms, rules and regulations, debased seamen, brutal crews, and cowardly and despicable authority (most manifest in those special Children of God, the missionaries). And the Typee Valley seems everything that Western society is not. It seems that Tommo and Toby exchange the *Dolly* for Typee as a renaturalizing of their lives in a serene, naked society set in green and innocent nature at the idyllic dawn of time: Eden.

But human society never existed in Eden. The stone foundations of the *pi-pis*, the mysterious hillside terraces, and the *morais* reveal that there was once a greater time than the Typees know. The stones suggest two speculations. One is that they are endlessly old, "coeval with the creation of the world" (p. 154). And although Tommo immediately dismisses the Typee myth of the stones' divine origin, which, as Tommo says, "at once convinced me that... [none of the Typees] knew anything about them" (p. 155), he too emphasizes their antiquity, concluding that the green Eden had been inhabited by humanity as long ago as the oldest human cultures anywhere. The second speculation is that the Typees are a "race ... sadly deteriorated in their knowledge of the mechanic arts" (p. 155). Tommo's dismissal of the mythic elements in the Typees' nationalistic accounts of their identity, and his sense of what it is that the Typees are fallen from, sets up the interesting speculation that from the very beginning human society was entirely of this world. Furthermore, the taboo and the tattoo indicate that even in the idyllic primitive society there are protocol, artificiality, uniforms, and conformist authority. The warfare with the Happars indicates that on a much simpler level the warriors belong to the same belligerent and fallen human race as the French, the English, the whalers, and the missionaries (Wai-chee Dimock). All of the dehumanizing aspects of society are summed up in the central mystery of the valley, cannibalism.

But there is one essential difference between Typee and contemporary society, a difference that does separate the prehistoric, or mythic, condition from contemporary actuality. That difference centers on the book's obsessive return to matters of technology, communication, and mind. Tommo's leg becomes a gauge of the anxiety attendant on complete submersion in the prehistoric: there is something about life in Eden against which Tommo rebels. Tommo's resistance to tattooing, his unwillingness to literally lose "face" for his own world, is associated with his suspicions about cannibalism—the *mindlessness* of Edenic life is entirely associated with the devouring of the human. Melville explores and renounces, through Tommo's panic, a society in which individual features are lost in the supposed bliss of pre-industrial, pastoral life. Furthermore, that life turns out in many ways to be a precursor of, not a diametrical alternative to, the repressive life of the present moment. But it is a precursor lacking the mind and language for which Tommo hungers: without complexity of mind, concept, and language, full humanity is frighteningly lost. (The chimerical nature of a state of loving tranquillity is a point to keep in mind for *Mardi*'s Serenia.) *Typee* concludes with the need to return "home," despite all the ugliness of the modern state that is the "home" from which Tommo departed for the Blessed Isles. Implicitly, the anti-mythic actualities in all societies are an anti-Idealist reading of human identity (Mitchell Breitwieser). Consciously or not, Melville already was reaching toward the relationships among his anti-Idealist perception, Romantic diction, and Romantic ideology. The Ideal, as the meaning of all existence, limits all objects to a single ontological message, all words to one-dimensional signs. At the very outset of his literary career, Melville was moving toward his struggle with the possibility that multiple signification is the product of a fallen world, that the energy of art is a product of limitation and history, not of the unlimited fixity of Paradise. Language and heartless society have an intricate symbiosis.

Melville begins his career with a joyful discovery of the possibilities of language in a book whose conclusion returns us to the actual. At first Melville delighted in his play with the missionaries, in the passages descriptive of the physical setting, in the wryly amused speculations about primitive and civilized sin. *Typee*, as travelogue, was to inform its reader; as reportorial expose, it was to reform institutional practices; as fictive examination of mythic assumptions, it was to unform the myths. For the young Melville the depraved state of society remained open to change and, therefore, to the possibility of new assumptions about it; the function of art and the nature of language are at once redemptive and revelatory of human limitation. But as Melville's sense of the possibilities of human society changes to angry hopelessness, so, too, will his vision of the function of art and language.

There is that aspect of *Typee* which must be judged as travelogue (Janet Giltrow, Robert Roripaugh),[16] and fictionalized though it is, *Omoo* tries to cling tightly to the non-fiction standard demanded by Melville's English publisher, John Murray. Consequently, it is hardly more than a gleaning of leftovers by the excited and delighted new author. Nevertheless, in a curious way even *Omoo* maintains a developing connection between Melville's view of society and his sense of language.

Melville had a great penchant for beginning sentences with introductory participial phrases, as often as not creating sentences with glaring dangling modifiers. Fairly consistently, Melville's introductory participles function as temporal transitions: "The boat having gained the open sea, the ship appeared in the distance. Here the present narrative opens," says the narrator in the third paragraph of the "Introduction" of *Omoo*. The construction is transitional, transporting the reader from one moment of time to another in a flow of continuing action: "Drawing near the shore, the grim, black spars and waspish hull of a small man-of-war craft crept into view" (p. 19); or from a cause to an effect: "Upon informing Zeke of these matters, he [Zeke] seemed highly flattered with the opinion we entertained of his reputation abroad" (pp. 249–50). Grammatically, the participial construction is a fluid thing, emphasizing the process of transition from one state to another rather than the simple fixity of a completed past action. Psychologically, it suggests a state of flow, a continuation of motion. Quantitatively, it appears to be used more frequently in *Omoo* than in any other of Melville's fictions.

There is a connection between the frequent usage of participial flux, the title of the book ("omoo" means "wanderer"), the attempt to eschew fiction, and Melville's view of society. Straining to stick to his gleanings, Melville had less of the fictive mode with which to arrange his travelogue details for the purposes of imaginative discovery and philosophical speculation. He was constrained by the "factual" wanderings of Paul, né Tommo, to a repetitious going through the wanderings: he creates a narrative procedure of "having gone here, we went there." It is the flux and continuous repetition of action of a narrative that has nowhere to alight. The only clear *thematic* resting point in *Omoo* is the narrator's travelogue as social expose, a development of the missionary materials expurgated from *Typee*. There is an intensification of effects through cumulative detail in *Omoo*, but there is no development of multiple ways of looking at the assumptions made about society. In *Omoo* the missionary effort creates an unmixed effect of debasement and corruption as a result of its unmixed totalitarian stupidity. The consequent society is ridiculous. Christian principles are reduced to absurd mores, and native morality is corrupted into surreptitious rituals. In *Typee* there was a felt distance between the civilized and primitive worlds, so that Tommo was able to use the two worlds as distinct points of departure into each other.

But *Omoo* presents Typee after the conquest. There is no distance between the primitive world and the intrusive West, nor between the perceived myth and the historical actuality. The interactions of the two worlds in *Omoo* are cause and effect of each other. One can wander through them only in repetition, finding the same total limitation of social possibility everywhere. Authority can be a good-humored joke, when applied by pleasant fellows like Captain Bob, or a bad joke when applied by nasty fellows like Mr. Wilson, the consul, but it is a joke. Its ubiquity turns people and nature into jokes, and even the opulent isles become sterilized and consumed in *Omoo*. In sum, the one consistent idea of *Omoo* is that power corrupts.

What becomes, then, the only possibility of interest, as well as a necessity of narrative technique, is not revelation, but the process of transition itself, the wandering. That process also quickly becomes tired precisely because we know that the restless motion will only take us to one more example of fallen society. The language of transition paradoxically becomes *ennui*, and the participial introductions consequently become intrusive. The book is saved, ironically, by the very quality that creates its tiresomeness: the jocular monotone keeps the reader from taking the reading matter seriously enough to make it a complete bore. The condescension implicit in a joke is the perspective allowed by a narrator who wanders unfixed in any obligation. He becomes a meandering, imperialist self, the quintessential tourist, who opportunistically uses people and places for the gratification of his desires. The essence of the tourist-narrator's relationship to the world is a process of consumption, a participial flow from one human relationship to another, as and where he finds it, and formed according to use. The narrator of *Omoo* is the most identityless of Melville's narrators. With no place in society, no name is needed: there is only the impersonal immunity and freedom that tourists feel with their non-belonging.

Omoo, then, reveals the connection between Melville's sense of language and his view of society: Melville is not productive as a condescending snob. Without the democratic anger of his social protest or his vertiginous metaphysical speculations about community and evil, his language loses energy and becomes participially repetitive. For most writers the second novel is notoriously their worst, a highly educational stumbling. *Omoo* is a lesson in Melville's need for rhetorical explorations that will locate the metaphysical center of his materials. Melville must open new horizons before he closes all down in darkness. That, of course, is exactly what the writing of *Omoo* teaches Melville, and *Omoo*'s closing transitional participle is departure not into one more island instance, but into the open seas of entirely new horizons: "Crowding all sail, we braced the yards square; and, the breeze freshening, bowled straight away from the land.... By noon, the island had gone down in the horizon; and all before us was the wide Pacific" (p. 316).

MARDI

And so, "We are off !" begins *Mardi*, the next book, its first sentence picking up the Miltonic perspectives opened at the end of *Omoo*. "But whence, and whither wend ye, mariners?" Tommo-Omoo-Nameless-Taji inquires immediately (p. 3). Into historical societies allegorically presented; into imaginary societies symbolically presented; into an epistemological quest for the absolute against which all societies are metaphysically measured; into a search for imagery and language which will reveal the conflict between the Ideal and the historical-actual.

The first third of *Mardi* replays *Typee*, with Taji and Yillah setting up housekeeping. Taji seems to assume that Eden thus recaptured can replace the actual. But as *Typee* suggested, American attitudes about millennial possibility were based on nationalistic self-delusion. In fact, in *Mardi* the unearthly beauty was segregated as myth: Yillah was reared in isolation by those mythkeepers, the priests, and was educated in religious myths in order to be the perfect sacrifice to the gods. Significantly, in that supposed mythic state, language suffers. On her sacred isle, Yillah had had only a bird with whom to talk, had known references only to mythic things. When taken by Taji into the actual world, Yillah had to be instructed in the names and meanings of things. And because Eden never was, it cannot be regained. Yillah disappears and Taji fruitlessly scours Mardi in endless search for her. The true state of bliss exists in yearning imagination, in what was lost, not in the actual: its attainment is promised only by man's limitless and ubiquitous pride (Hautia). The implicit question that rationalizes the remainder of *Mardi* is, in what society will Yillah be found?

In pursuing that question, Melville completely frees himself from the non-fiction constraints of *Omoo* to reply, "In none." Setting out with the Governor (King Media), the Historian (Mohi), the Poet (Yoomy), and the Philosopher (Babbalanja), Taji (the Idealist) sets government, history, poetry, and philosophy to the test in the quest for the Absolute. At the outset of the voyage, one of Taji's observations sets our expectations for the major point of Melville's *narrenschiff* expedition: we will witness the education that experience will inflict on the governor and the poet in their optimism, very much tempered in the perceptions of the historian and the philosopher, who long have brooded about human limitation. "But to my sorrow," Taji observes, "I marked that both Mohi and Babbalanja, especially the last, seemed not so buoyant of hope, concerning lost Yillah, as the youthful Yoomy, and his high-spirited lord, King Media" (p. 197).

The means by which the voyage instructs all but the Idealist are visits to society in its various phases. Islands such as Dominora, Franko, and Vivenza, emblematic of Great Britain, France, and the United States, seem the province of the historian. Islands such as Valapee and Juam, emblematic of ontological and epistemological limitation, seem the province of the philosopher. Melville clearly favors the leading role for the philosopher. Nevertheless, in the search for the lost bliss to be regained in the Ideal to come, both history and philosophy are equal in their validity and uselessness. All experience finally comes to the same point foreshadowed in *Typee*: the continuing meretriciousness of society and the ineluctable fallen state of man.

All Mardian societies except Serenia are cannibalistically impaired and brutalized by one aspect or another of power. Nor is there any debased behavior in any of the islands that is not a consequence of innate human limitation in seeing and knowing. Man is revealed as incapable of the absolute, and divinity is only humanity's own projection. Perhaps no island visit makes that point more clearly than the visit to the Pontiff on the Vatican isle of Hivohitee. Human institutions all turn out to be empty of the absolute condition we are supposed to believe they reflect. As the sum total of its institutions, any given human society in the Mardian archipelago is a corruption in which people, one way or another, devour each other.

The one exception, Serenia, is a pure Christian pastoral society of brotherly love and self-abnegation in which there are no drives to domination. There Babbalanja chooses to stay. However, two mighty energies in the book undo the validity and credibility of that choice. One is that Azzageddi, the philosopher's interior "poor devil," and the probable spokesman for Melville's own demonic skepticism, doubts the existence of any all-disposing Plan or Planner, any absolute Consciousness on which to base an ultimate state of goodness. Without a Heavenly City there can be no credence given to the type of that City, and Serenia becomes a *polis ex machina*. The other energy militating against our belief in Serenia is that precisely because the voyage has been a deliberate examination of the limitations of human perception, knowledge, and nature, there is no way to know how the Serenians came to be something other than human. Any consideration of the relationship between Taji's quest and the visits to the islands makes it as impossible to believe in Serenia as in the recapture of the Ideal, Yillah. But unsatisfactory though it may be, the imposition of Serenia on Mardi's reader reveals an aspect of Melville's development that marks an important difference between the extent to which the early book, *Mardi*, finds society wanting, and the extent to which the later book, *The Confidence-Man*, does. The existence of *Mardi*'s Serenia implies an auctorial willingness (a yearning, perhaps?) still to imagine the possibility of an enlarged and sunnier state of human existence.

The societal possibility is figured in King Media, who begins with arrogant assumptions about absolute authority. He is as much the Idealist on the political level as is Taji on the ontological. But Media learns that power absolutely wielded creates the very social explosions that he, as the type of the Governor, fears most. He even comes to understand that the explosions are the result of misery, suffering, and injustice. We can believe in Media's reformation as we cannot believe in Serenia. Media comes to *shed* his Idealist assumptions in increasing recognition of what is necessitated by knowledge of a fallen world. He neither renounces nor repudiates power. Rather, in a mediating, middle way, by finally seeing its abuses Media comes to recognize its necessity in the establishment of justice that otherwise would not exist. It is with the promise of justice that he departs for Odo and sails majestically into the growing unrest of his own land, proclaiming that Odo, not Serenia, will be his home. In Media there is the beginning of existentialist social ethics. In effect, incipient turmoil is the only world there really is.

Mardi, too, throws light on the intricate relationship between Melville's sense of language and Melville's view of society. When *Mardi* is centered on the Idealist's quest outside of society—the first twenty chapters of the book—there is no conversation. What little discourse there is is presented from within Taji's mind. When *Mardi* is centered on the Idealist's juncture with the Ideal (Yillah), discourse between them occurs in entirely mythic language not presented as actual conversation but as legend retold from Taji's memory. There is little dialogue and very few quotation marks before Chapter 69. And, in fact, when Taji loses Yillah and devotes his life to her recapture, all he can say of his lost absolute, in the last sentence of the last chapter in which Taji had had his Yillah (ch. 64), is "But hereafter, in words, little more of the maiden, till perchance her fate be learned" (p. 195). Direct conversation picks up in Chapter 86, after we are launched into the archipelagic societies, and thereafter remains the major tactic of narration. The structure of narrative strategies in *Mardi* indicates that as long as the source of the story is confined to the Idealist perspective, Melville runs out of narrative. He has monologue, he has travelogue, he has essay. The language of story begins to fail when all that there is is metaphysics—a problem looked at in different ways by R. P. Blackmur and R. H. Brodhead. Without conflict among people and their points of view, there is neither action nor multiplicity of meaning. The Transcendentalist Emerson, choosing solitude, chose Idea over object, thereby relegating all objects to a single ultimate meaning: Spirit. The conflicting opposite, to use Emerson's term, was merely "privative," an absence of consciousness. But society, the actuality of social presence in the world of Mardi, allows Melville the relativism of perspective that will increasingly mark his stance up through *Moby-Dick*. Melville needs either a non-Idealist narrator or the density of wide experience to allow him the language with which to complete a fiction. Although the conversation in *Mardi* is often tedious, it is a tediousness quite different from that of *Omoo*. It is an extension of *new* viewpoints, of conflicting perspectives and consequent arguments, an extension carried on too long, but an extension of material that is the stuff of fiction. If in *Mardi* Melville did not yet control the presentation of ideas and allowed his book to blur into ill-disguised essay, the book nevertheless foreshadowingly explains why Idealist Ahab did not narrate *Moby-Dick* and why Melville settled on a pluralistic and relativistic vision like Ishmael's through which to glimpse the impossible tale.

Without a social reality suggesting possibilities of change in perception and therefore in meaning, the only source of multiplicity becomes interior, relegating meaning to individual mind. Once arriving at that conclusion, Melville saw, as *Pierre* demonstrated, that for him the failure of society is a sign of the failure of meaning, for the individual mind asocially tuned to its fixed perceptions becomes insanity, the inappropriate Ahabian imposition of one perception and one perception only. When collective perception turns out to be merely cannibalistic hypocrisy, there is no dependable source of meaning. The failure of society is the failure of the nature of man, the hard evidence of the limitations of mortal perception. The ultimate failure of man is a sign of the failure of the Creator. By definition, however, God cannot fail, so the sign of failure signifies the absence of God. The non-existence of the supposed Creator signifies the absence of the Reality of Idealist absolutes—which is the sign of the absence of fixed meanings, which is a sign of signs unmaking signs, which is a sign of the infinite multiplicity of signification for any sign, which is a sign of the unmaking of all meanings in the subjectivity of perceptions. The vicious circle of *Mardi* provided Melville with his central intellectual anguish, which would be the epistemological subject of all his other fictions. *Mardi* taught Melville that he needed a view of society as a sign of possible change (new oceanic horizons, Tommo, Media) or he would be trapped with a repetitious, participial narrator (Omoo and his wanderings or Taji and his despairing yearning). He needed a narrator balanced between the essentially comic act of discovering through human foibles the hope for a better, human society, born of an elated sense of the nobility of man, and the terror that comes from a recognition of cosmic Absence, a balance that is the glory of *Moby-Dick*'s Ishmael.[17]

REDBURN AND *WHITE-JACKET*

In *Redburn*'s parallelisms, indifference and hostility to poverty are the same on a passenger boat *in* America as they are on a transatlantic passenger ship *from* America, or in the Old World cities of London and Liverpool that send ships *to* America. The transition from New World to Old discloses no change in essential condition, just as the multinational crew provides no basis for hope for a change in the potential nature of society. The crew is hardly one to inspire confidence in the shibboleths of democracy and progressivism or in the egalitarian view of the common man as the salt of the earth. As he uses parallelism, so Melville uses the internationalism of *Redburn* to make the same repudiation of American mythic self-identification that he made in the Vivenza section of *Mardi*. So too, despite the existence of "ever-noble Jack Chase, matchless and unmatchable Jack Chase" (p. 397), the heroic integrity of Ushant, and the courageous and true seamanship of Mad Jack in *White-Jacket*, neither officialdom and authority—the precincts of the ruler—nor the vast masses of the workforce to be sacrificed—the precincts of the ruled—in the world-warship offer a reason to believe in social change or in improved universal human nature.

Conversely, in its narrative voice, *White-Jacket* is a culmination of perceptions prepared in Wellingborough Redburn's growing recognition of the commonality of humanity. Everyone owns a stone in the Great Wall of China: "For the whole world is the patrimony of the whole world" (*Redburn*, p. 292). Redburn has hopes for life in his return to America— "Hurra! hurra! and ten thousand times hurra! down goes our old anchor, fathoms down into the free and independent Yankee mud, one handful of which was now worth a broad manor in England" (p. 301); and White-Jacket has prayers for a world in which human beings cease their murderous mutual cannibalism—"Oh, shipmates and world-mates, all round! we the people suffer many abuses. Our gun-deck is full of complaints. . . . whatever befall us, let us never train our murderous guns inboard" (pp. 399–400). To this extent, *Redburn* and *White-Jacket* share with Melville's first three books an imagination of something better to come. That something better is articulated as the hope that the relatively unaggressive naivete of primitive man (*Typee*), that the mass debased by the incursive imperialism of civilization (*Omoo*), that the suffering population to which an enlightened king returns (*Mardi*), that the oppressed world of the deprived laboring masses (*Redburn, White-Jacket*) will someday be given a more just society. But despite his awareness of mass unrest and class injustice, Melville essentially assumes change and enlightenment from above, not from a heroic, uprising mass, not from revolution. His hope is for a someday in the future when King Media will create a humane society, or for a Final Someday in the far future when the Ultimate Ruler will decree final justice (*White-Jacket*). For when we look closely at Melville's hope for society, it is always seen in tension with a balancing opposite: the atomizing ignorance and selfishness of the mass of men indicative of the debased nature of general humanity.[18]

In *Redburn*, the ecstatic return to America marks the end of the book's communication. Except for a brief account of Harry Bolton, the function of language, the object of the narrative, is at an end: "I pass over the reception I met with at home; how I plunged into embraces, long and loving:—I pass over this; and will conclude *my first voyage*" (p. 311). The closure forecloses the obvious question: what has changed? The world to which Redburn returns is the very world that had shown him only the heartless indifference of human society to individual isolation and suffering. So, too, Tommo had returned to the world whose harsh and brutal society he repudiated when he jumped ship. Nothing has changed except the experience of the narrator. Both Tommo and Redburn had left their worlds, one by choice, one by necessity, but both return to it as their true "home." And for both there had been a failure of language. Tommo's language failed him as society turned out to be something other than he had foreseen in his expectations of paradise; reciprocally, Typee failed to communicate the possibility of a lastingly real identity for Tommo. The language of the past failed Redburn when his father's "prosy old guide-book" (p. 151) served only for an unreal world of the pre-experiential imagination. As was the case with Mohi in *Mardi*, the language of history fails to reveal a society bespeaking a condition different in essential human nature from the one the quester had fled. What Redburn comes to learn is that the human world is the same everywhere. (Therein is the heart of the matter for Melville: what had been the reason to celebrate egalitarian fraternalism becomes the reason to despair.)

By virtue of its inescapable needs, the proletariat balances its own savagery with cooperative engagement in a world of mutual interdependence from which the "kingly commons" derives an elementary and direct ability for sympathy: the crude crewmen in *Redburn* take up a collection for the poverty-stricken steerage passengers, but the pampered first-class cabin folk are not even capable of recognizing the need for sympathy. When the human beast reveals redeeming virtues in Melville's fiction, the revelation is always made within the world of work, among the ship's "people." In *White-Jacket*, the most intensely living language in the narrative voice arises at the moments when brotherhood, oneness, cooperation, love, mutuality, and interdependence are invoked—preparations for some of Ishmael's most intense language. The merger of intense *language* and theme in *White-Jacket* is fitting for a narrator whose merger of intense *drama* and theme comes at the moment when he sheds the garment which separates him from the mass of the ship's working "people." Like the distance between the crew and the first-class cabin passengers in *Redburn*, the distance between the consciousness of the ship's "people" (Melville does not allow the implications of the term to fade for a moment) and the official dicta of the *Neversink*'s officers in *White-Jacket* reveals the failure of power. The official world is full of unrealities and blind arrogance, and, therefore, untruths. In the communication of events, the language of privilege and authority is a failure: Captain Claret's smug and totalitarian deafness to all the "people's" truths are paradigmatic for the universal man-o-war world.

But the balance between potential heroism, the actual individual nobility of men revealed in the world of work, and the universal fallen state of brutish humankind revealed at every level of society is not an even one in Melville's world. The narrative voice that becomes rhetorically intense in celebration of the hopeful in human life does not maintain that intensity in certitude of that hope *in society*. Rather, the appeal for goodness is associated with the hope that arises from conventional religious Idealist assumptions. When we examine the full valedictory at the end of *White-Jacket*, the closing rhetorical intensity raises some interesting considerations about the corresponding intensity of Melvillean belief in the social or historical enactment of goodness, cooperation, and love.

Oh, shipmates and world-mates, all round! we the people suffer many abuses. Our gun-deck is full of complaints. In vain from Lieutenants do we appeal to the Captain; in vain—while on board our world-frigate—to the indefinite Navy Commissioners, so far out of sight aloft. Yet the worst of our evils we blindly inflict upon ourselves; our officers can not remove them, even if they would. From the last ills no being can save another; therein each man must be his own saviour. For the rest, whatever befall us, let us never train our murderous guns inboard; let us not mutiny with bloody pikes in our hands. Our Lord High Admiral will yet interpose; and though long ages should elapse, and leave our wrongs unredressed, yet, shipmates and world-mates! let us never forget, that,
Whoever afflict us, whatever surround,
Life is a voyage that's homeward-bound! (pp. 399–400)

These closing words function the same way that Redburn's return home does. They are fraternal but reactionary. They foreclose social revolution and the major question raised in the book, a question about injustices—about the brutal excesses of privilege and oppression (*and possibilities for change*)—in human society. That question centers on the actual, and relegates social evil to an implicit essence in human nature, almost to individual choice: "the worst of our evils we blindly inflict upon ourselves." Within the actual, there is no Melvillean vision of social or societal salvation. Like the rare, individual displays of nobility, the answer to the question of the bestiality of human society is individual—"each man must be his own saviour." The only redress of wrongs, the only change, the only Good Life, awaits the Ideal, the final "home" of the "Lord High Admiral" in the sky. That is, the intense language is out of phase with the intense experiential immediacy of universal savagery in every level of human life—and the consequently intensely heroic exception of noble humans trapped within the actuality.[19] The substitution of Idealist vision for the prevailing experiential vision in which the intensity arose, and the consequent weakening of concept to acceptably conventional pieties once again reveals the relationship of Melville's language to the Idealist stance and to the failure of society. What true rhetorical intensity exists in the book is praise of the working commonality, of the universal oneness of the entire race. As long as that remains, although there is expectation only of "participial" repetition of the fallen human state in all meridians (it *is* "a mutual, joint-stock world, in all meridians," as Queequeg seems to say in *Moby-Dick*, p. 61), there remains the possibility of balancing tension between nobility in the world of work and the universally degraded state of society. As long as that tension remains there is the possibility for successfully intense language about the contradictory plural natures of man. But when that possibility goes, there is either mere repetition of experience or the intensity of language attendant on the disintegration of fixed signs. Both of those tensions exist side by side in *Moby-Dick* for the first and last time in Melville's writing, and it is that tension of tensions that creates the glory of *Moby-Dick*'s language.

MOBY-DICK

Moby-Dick is Melville's hymn of praise to the underprivileged masses who perform the labors on which society depends. It is futile to try to group chapters as examples of rhetorical or dramatic intensity: one ends up listing almost the entire table of contents. *Moby-Dick* sustains, despite rhetoric and drama, a balance between an admiration for the working world, which allows for discernible social meanings, and a dread-filled anti-Idealism that unmakes all meanings.[20] If the morally empty universe furnishes no value, the social world furnishes all; and not all the values are bitter. The treacherous, slavish lee shore confines the open independence of the soul, but it is also "all that's kind to our mortalities" (p. 97). Unlike the Idealist, Ahab, who repudiates the lee shore and its human needs, Bulkington, the pioneer hero who cannot stand to be on land, braves the unknown depths to provide life for the community. He is the darling of the crew. He is the ultimate hero of the world of work, ever in the vanguard of the human race.

The intense language that constitutes the famous closing paragraphs of "Knights and Squires" (ch. 26) is the rhetorical expression of the thematic implications created by Queequeg (that "soothing savage") in his redemption of the initially misanthropic Ishmael—a redemption that is a reclamation into human oneness (ch. 60, "The Line") and thereby into the widest possible sympathies (ch. 94, "A Squeeze of the Hand") discovered in the necessary interdependences (ch. 72, "The Monkey-

Rope") of the world of work (ch. 98, "Stowing Down and Clearing Up"). Ishmael makes a great point of pride in being among the ship's "people" rather than on the quarter-deck, in being forward in the new air rather than aft breathing the old. As Tommo was to Typee, so Ishmael is to Queequeg; both are educated and reenergized by the primitive force of human existence, a force that in *Moby-Dick* is associated with essential labor and egalitarianism. The ship becomes the locus in which the world of work becomes the fundament and essence of all human community. What is admirable in humans is disclosed in the chapters devoted to the hazardous hunting, killing, securing, loading, and trying out of whales, chapters in which "The Honor and Glory of Whaling" (ch. 82) become the honor and glory of communal work. In celebrating the working world, *Moby-Dick* argues for human nobility and the dream of the just, democratic, egalitarian society of brotherly love.

But as in all the books preceding *Moby-Dick*, there are indications that the masses are divided by cowardice and selfishness and that the commonality is endlessly manipulable. As Melville wrote in a famous passage in his 1 [?] June 1851 letter to Hawthorne, "It seems an inconsistency to assert unconditional democracy in all things, and yet confess a dislike to all mankind—in the mass. But not so" (*Letters*, p. 127). In this context, *Moby-Dick* is also a study of totalitarianism. "Midnight, Forecastle" (ch. 40) introduces the xenophobia, racism, chauvinism, and general savagery of humanity, just as the group of chapters from "His Mark" (ch. 18) through "The Lee Shore" (ch. 23) indicates its hypocrisy, greed, shallowness, and conformity. But most important, the noble knights and squires—as the chapters from "The Quarter-Deck" (ch. 36) through "Midnight, Forecastle" (ch. 40) and as "The Forge" (ch. 113), "The Quadrant" (ch. 118), and "The Candles" (ch. 119) show—are too easily put into jack-boots and armbands. For Melville, the other side of the coin of democracy is that individuals in the organized mass cannot resist the charismatic leader of the great crusade. With the exception of Ishmael, whose shouts of obeisance had gone up with the rest, all fall prey to authority. When that authority becomes total, coercing acquiescence in spirit and mind as well as body, the occasional uneasiness of the mass is quelled and all conform in a mission unto death. What occasional mass uneasiness there is in *Moby-Dick* is either based on mere superstition or economic concerns. And Ahab knows that as long as he can assuage concerns about "cash—aye, cash" (p. 184) he need not worry about the greater issues of ethics and legality. We are heroes; we are sheep. Ahab knows he can overawe the masses; that he has nothing to fear from the good citizen, for the good citizen (Starbuck), despite all, will obey; that he has nothing to fear from man's easygoing, good-humored comfort (Stubb); that he has nothing to fear from unimaginative mediocrity (Flask).

Most frightening in Melville's political insight is that the totalitarian leader expresses the subconscious will of the mass. The "subterranean miner," the subconscious, drags people along by their deepest fears and needs. There is no final, rational accounting for the inadequacy which makes people allow the crazy misuses of the commonwealth, for that limitation is in the very nature of things: "How it was that they so aboundingly responded to the old man's ire—by what evil magic their souls were possessed, that at times his hate seemed almost theirs... how all this came to be... to their unconscious understandings...—all this to explain, would be to dive deeper than Ishmael can go" (p. 162).[21]

Melville gives the metaphysical concerns the same unity of rhetoric, event, imagery, and theme that he provides for social concerns. It is sufficient here to note that energy-centers for metaphysical levels, such as "The Mast-Head" (ch. 35), "The Whiteness of the Whale" (ch. 42), "The Castaway" (ch. 93), "A Bower in the Arsacides" (ch. 102), "The Try-Works" (ch. 96), and "The Doubloon" (ch. 99), are all concerned with the nature and existence of the Ideal and with the related matter of the possibility of absolute meaning. The undercurrent of dread that drives the surface flow of *Moby-Dick* is generated by the constant implication that there is no First Cause that cares but also that (metaphysically as well as socially) we are what we make ourselves to be. Consequently, enormous force passes into the social implications of the book, for by our very nature, there is no likelihood that the essence of human existence will change. The Ishmael who begins the story does so as a misanthropic outcast; the Ishmael who concludes the action is a lone orphan adrift in a blank sea.

When one considers the freezing implications of the non-existence or inoperativeness of Ideal Reality in conjunction with what the book suggests about the generality of humankind, then both the social and the metaphysical levels coincide in a dark undercurrent that is stronger than the surface celebration of and admiration for the human. Yet so powerful are the rhetoric and the events in which the admirable enters our consciousness that *Moby-Dick* becomes a great climactic balance between the celebration of humankind and the repudiation of it. Tonally, the book balances exultation and despair. A book about meanings, *Moby-Dick* creates multiple possibilities of evaluation (of the whale, the doubloon, the ocean, the shore). *Moby-Dick* balances the power and the absurdity of language. *Mardi*'s Donjalolo is reintroduced in Pip of "The Doubloon," the Pip who comments on the problems of perception by conjugating the verb "to look" as each man evaluates the worldship's "golden navel," the Pip who completes his conjugations by concluding that we are all bats. In sum, *Moby-Dick*, in both humor and rage holds democratic joy and misanthropic despair in a relationship that invites dread more than hope. The equipoise of human potency and limitation teeters on the speculation that there is no absolute perception or fixed meaning possible, that " 'All is vanity.' ALL" (p. 355). The power of *Moby-Dick* is the tenuousness of these balances; thereafter the substratum rises from the depths of dread and emptiness and becomes the surface, as well, of the entire human world. After *Moby-Dick* there is only annihilation, the emptiness of all meanings. *Moby-Dick*, in its metaphysical theme, is a blacker, more terrifying book than it is usually seen to be, and it is the book that raises the consideration that when we talk about "Herman Melville" we are talking about two Melvilles. One is the man who maintains respect and love for the world of work in human society. This Melville says that we must learn to "lower or shift" our "conceit of attainable felicity" (p. 349) from absolutes to the social, the only world of available meaning. The second Melville cracks the sinews and cakes the brain; he speculates that there is no Cause, no Meaning in the infinite multiplicity of existence. The first Melville, riding on the shoulders of the second, maintains a precarious balance, the abyss of gravity pulling at him increasingly as its annihilating force makes itself fully felt in the dreadful depths of *Moby-Dick*; and after *Moby-Dick* he falls off and disappears. There is no human society good enough and strong enough to save him. The wonderfully weary, humorous, world-bullied Ishmael is heard thereafter only in disappearing echoes in a few of the tales, and what is left is the second Melville, the essential one who had been there all along, striding with increasingly mad fury into the consuming darkness of *Pierre* and *The Confidence-Man*.

PIERRE AS THE CONFIDENCE-MAN

The complexity of *Pierre* and *The Confidence-Man* is a paradox, for it results from an essentially absolutist stance: all is initially zero. The integers of affixed meaning dissolve and become a viscous and shifting mass. We are left with an absolute absence of absolutes. *Moby-Dick* begins in the unknown, the mystery of zero, and builds it into multiple and shifting and growing meanings. *Pierre* and *The Confidence-Man* begin in apparent meanings and unmake them through multiple contradictory possibilities into zero.

Pierre begins with a known world. Saddle Meadows sums up eighteenth-century agrarian promise (the legacy of the fathers) in an edenically pleasant existence. The past is known (the fathers were gentlemen and heroes), the present is known (Mrs. Glendinning dotes on her Pierre), and the future is known (Lucy Tartan will be the loving wife and beautiful hostess). Time, like the butler, Dates, exists but to serve. Sexual identities are so perfectly in place in this pastoral Good Society of ladies and gentlemen that undercurrents of anomaly make no ripples on the surface (the bride to be is submissive to the husband's mother;

Pierre is lady-in-waiting to his mother; Pierre and his mother play a game of brother and sister). Social identities are also perfectly in place, hiding the undercurrents that will change all the surfaces: the mild, blue-eyed, gentlemanly, revered Christian forebear was, exactly as *The Confidence-Man*'s courtly, blue-eyed Colonel Moredock is to be, a killer, a murderous Indian-hater.

But new experience discloses the mythic state of society in Young America to be an illusion. The fathers are sexual deceivers and thereby social disrupters. The "real" brother and sister play a heavily sexual game of husband and wife. The mother withholds her love, and Pierre is turned out of his heritage and promise in the land of subservient Dates. The most basic institutions, family and religion, turn out to be compounded of selfishness and hypocrisy. Furthermore, charity and sympathy cease to function in the world of work: Ned and Delly are disowned by the proprieties whose social language functions with the same arrogant untruth as the language of officialdom in all of Melville's fictions. The world accepts only the language of fixed, known meanings and the values of appearances. As long as the young, pre-experiential Pierre writes his pretty sonnets about "Tropical Summer," he is an accepted author; but when he tries to write the truth about society's illusions, he is shunned.

The urban world is no better than the heartlessness underlying the Typee-like idyll of Saddle Meadows' pastoral myth. Just as all aspects of the pastoral turned mean and hostile, so unexceptionally every aspect of life in the contemporary city is an introduction to stoniness, darkness, and isolation. The mob scene at the police station, the calculating rapacity of the cold-hearted, "very intelligent" landlord of the rooming house, the shuttered and barred coldness of the house Pierre expected his cousin to prepare for him all speak eloquently of the extent to which society indifferently is willing to cannibalize the dissenter. Pierre consequently dedicates himself to language, to writing which will expose the miserable truth about human life. He believes in The Truth beneath the false surfaces. He believes in the reformative power of language: through destructive expose, art will redeem and reconstruct.

However, *Pierre* has no roof, no basement floor. There is no fixed, single Truth to tell. The elusiveness of human identities indicates that the reversal of illusions is no more fixed and true than the illusions themselves had been. Pierre's own motives as "brother" to Isabel are mixed at best. The fathers, the mother, Lucy, all change; and Isabel herself is the epitome of the mystery of identity. "Heaven hath no roof," the Hollow of God's Hand is "a Hollow, truly!" and "appallingly vacant as vast is the soul of a man" (p. 285). All appearances frighteningly distort and flow and remake themselves in repeated demonstrations that existence precedes essence. Like Enceladus, Pierre has neither face nor prospect of victory and can only endlessly and vainly attempt to gain the realm of the Ideal. It is dreadful enough to say that God does not exist, but *Pierre* does not stop at that: the very articulation of the anti-Idealist position is itself the product of an unknowable identity. Plinlimmon, about whom swirl mists of unknowability, recommends Horologicals rather than Chronometricals, admitting that the absolute virtue of the moral Chronometer is superior to this fallen world's best sense of the moral time. But the only possibilities we have are the relative standards of Horologicals: the actuality of the time and place we occupy: Plinlimmon's recommendation serves only to make Dates subservient again to universal human hypocritical selfishness. Time-serving is not the same as saving the times. Pierre is tormented by the cool, sneering materialism which produces as its own rationale the very kind of philosophical speculation that Pierre pursues in order to find a truth unencumbered by the materialistic falseness of conventional absolutes and fixed identities. Unmoored from any reliable society or any reliable human goodness, Pierre is, in his own words, "neuter now."

The neutering results from the existential relationship of Absolute, society, and self. All the horological identities prove unreal to Pierre: he is not "brother" to his mother, not "husband" to his putative sister, not bridegroom to his betrothed, not son to his "father," whichever father that be, however pictured. He has only his own newly born identity-lessness with which to build a self. But the only model for a true self that he, in his bitterness, can accept, is Absolute, a chronometrical self. And society totally repudiates chronometrical identities: in Melville's fictive societies, the type of Christ is crucified as often as he reappears. Pierre's making of himself is an incestuous and hermaphroditic Idealism in which he attempts to beget himself upon himself. Not recognizing the existential irony, he attempts to beget a sky-assaulting self in retribution against a cosmos and Deity that remove all reliable meaning from life, just as his writing attempts retribution against all of society's falsehoods and hauteur, its Falsgraves and Glendinnings. In the act of writing an assault on his own former illusions, Pierre discovers that without an absolute to cite as the source of existence, he has nothing but himself, the total of his perceptions. And all his perceptions must be illusions because at every new perception there is a new counter-experience to make the new assumptions invalid. God does not give Pierre his spiritual essence, a chronometrical identity that lasts. There is no moral society to give Pierre a horological identity that is acceptable.[22] Self, like God, becomes an appallingly vacant thing. So Pierre becomes the Fool of the Absolute, to use his own terms, the zero that makes Vice and Virtue equal shadows—"a nothing" (p. 274).

The shattering of society's appearances had thrown Pierre on the Absolute in shuddering recoil from his entire human heritage. But the shattering of the possibility of certainty about the Absolute shows Pierre how necessary society is. Yet the greatest agony, which drives Pierre into a frenzy of irony and despair, is that by its very nature, society becomes the horror to be replaced. Both Absolute and society are projections of the human self, mutually sustaining in Edenic illusion, mutually annihilating in disillusion, mutually reflecting a chimerical human self suspended between the reflected illusions and disillusions that very self creates. Consequently, Pierre realizes that his writing, art itself, cannot fix The Truth. Because anything means everything, nothing means anything. Art is absurd, words are useless, and, once again, Plinlimmon's sneering, selfish, self-centered, self-concerned *silence* becomes the only operative—and totally repugnant—identity.

It is exactly the shape-shifting selfhood, in which humanity becomes its own illusion, that is the subject of *The Confidence-Man*. *Israel Potter* and the tales, which intervene between *Pierre* and *The Confidence-Man*, are studies in the loss of identity inextricably associated with the failure of society. There is no space here for an examination of these works, but a suggestion will indicate the continuity and development of relationship between Melville's sense of society and language. The dark mortality underlying both racism and loss of identity—the deceptions of history—are at the heart of "Benito Cereno," in which Babo's ultimate silence dramatizes the falseness of all assumptions about all societies. Capitalism and the Dead Letter Office but serve to suggest an underlying universal inefficacy of communication: silence is what "Bartleby the Scrivener" is about. The loss of easy assumptions and the reign of silence are one with the failure of society in "The Paradise of Bachelors and the Tartarus of Maids," and in "The Two Temples." Society and identity are inextricable from each other in "Poor Man's Pudding and Rich Man's Crumbs," and in *Israel Potter* the rapacity of Young American nationalism, fractured identity, and an ending of cold, dead, silent loss all become one. All appearances, as in "The Piazza," prove to be something other than one expected, and as "The Bell-Tower" indicates, human institutions crumble through the flaws inherent in human limitation. There can be no more certainty than the safety promised by "The Lightning-Rod Man," and this suggestion will conclude with what "The Encantadas" unremittingly insists on: as expectations of society crumble, as the self is thrown back on itself, what lasts is either a hermitic and insane separateness or an indomitable integrity of suffering, for which silence is the only voice for mortal creatures, be they widows or tortoises.[23]

In *The Confidence-Man*, organized society provides institutional perspectives (Christianity, capitalism) through which the illusion of identity is maintained (Gary Lindberg). On the *narrenschiff Fidèle*, one must have faith that there are definable identities, or everything perceptibly dissolves into illusion. But to have faith in the definable identities is to have faith in illusion. Illusion is inescapable: the terrifying irony is that we struggle, through our social perspectives, to keep ourselves from seeing that everything is illusion, for that way lies nonbeing, annihilation; yet it is only in the illusion of identity that we protect ourselves from illusion. All society becomes confidence in an illusion. Everyone is an illusion. Ironically, everyone is the confidence man. In the last novel published in his lifetime, Melville enters the realm that Twain did at the end of *The Mysterious Stranger*, a phenomenological unreality, or emptiness, that is itself the nature of reality. Thus, we begin with known identities (types of Christ, for instance, like the man in cream colors) and have confidence in the illusion that we believe in and act from Christian principle. However, in the hard savagery of our social actualities, we know that if we "really" acted according to Christian precept, we would be the victims of an illusion. We crucify Christ, which is to say that we remove the very Chronological by which we agree as a society to identify ourselves, in order to live by the horologicals which as a society we know are the "true" springs of our conduct. So we viciously dismiss the very first avatar of our illusion, the mute, a Christly, dumb creature of faith, dressed in the *almost* pure whiteness of cream colors. Every request for confidence is a request based either on the illusion of official (chronometrical) identity (love, charity, trust), or on the illusion of our actual (horological) identities (hatred, greed, mistrust, hypocrisy). The misanthropes and Indian-haters recognize the horologicals as the savage truth of identity. They have no sentimentality, no "illusions." But given the endless and protean flow of possibility of identity, they remain with a fixed illusion about "real" human identity. The grim horror of the book is that at least *that* illusion is operative in human society.

The Confidence-Man presents society as repetitiously false and vicious. Its point is to make a joke, but unlike *Omoo*, it does so in metaphysical as well as social dimensions. Do what one will, one cannot help but declare confidence, one way or another, in illusion. Because everyone is a confidence man, everyone is the confidence man's dupe, and the joke is that only the self-consciously deliberate Confidence Man knows it, and knows, therefore, that one way or another the confidence trick is bound to succeed. And even the "real" Confidence Man gives as much as he takes, turns us toward chronometricals as well as toward horologicals. Is he good? Is he evil? Is he other than us? As the book progresses there are many times when it becomes increasingly difficult to say who is the "real" Confidence Man, and that is just the point. One may say with equal truth that the "real" Confidence Man is that joker, God, or that joker, the Devil. In either case he is "really" the projection of our own deluded, illusory selves.

But if ALL is illusion, why do we remain with one illusion—depravity—

in the demonstrations of society and human nature? Logically, there is no reason why we should: philosophically, Melville's discovery of nihility can be a relief. But psychologically, it is bitter. It is an exaggeration to see, as Lawrance Thompson did, that Melville's work is a coded diatribe against a God that Melville could not forgive. Probably closer to the mark is that Melville's discovery that a human being is only a human being left him with an unforgiving sense of anger against a cosmos that neither knows nor cares about identity, nor provides it. And it left him with a joke—the bitter laughter of outrage and despair at history's ubiquitously persistent social spectacle of human stupidity and baseness. Melville's sense of self-delusion as the only reality is a sense of human diminution, of a Fall indeed, and there is a psychological rather than a philosophically logical basis for Melville's continued vision of society as vicious. The ending is a necessary foreclosure, for with all identities, all language, all meanings coming back to zero to begin endlessly again, there can only be a metaphysical repetitiousness paralleling the social-travelogue repetitiousness of the earlier books. Because *everything* "further may follow of this Masquerade" (*CM*, p. 251) all over again, nothing further may follow of this Masquerade in narrative. The limitlessness of illusion is the limitlessness of the unmaking of meanings. The limitlessness of illusion is the limitation of language (Cecelia Tichi, Henry Sussman). It is probably that discovery, dramatized in Pierre's career and wrought out to its full turn in *The Confidence-Man*, that sent Melville into the "silent years" in which he wrote no narrative fiction until *Billy Budd*.

POETRY AND *BILLY BUDD, SAILOR*

With his "ontological heroics" concluding in emptiness, Melville should have chosen annihilation, but philosophers rarely enact the conclusions they reach. Despite Hawthorne's report in 1856 that Melville had "pretty much made up his mind to be annihilated" (*Mel. Log*, p. 529), Melville turned in his poetry to something simpler than endless meaning-multiplicities of the "colorless, all-color (*MD*, p. 169). During the language-journey of his incredible prose years, Melville's social consciousness grew from brief, open attacks on oppressive sectors of society (missionaries, political and military authorities), to larger, symbolic attacks on society, democracy, totalitarianism, humankind. Melville began with the hope of reform and ended with the need for repression. His final conservatism was an expression of his conclusion, not his journey, and as such it was simpler than the marvelous turmoil of values that balanced and conflicted in his swirling prose speculations. Consequently, the language of his conservatism is simpler, lacking the wild grandeur and turbulence of his earlier work. One expects more energetic language in poetry than in prose, but as the vehicle of his conservative conclusions, Melville's poetry for the most part is in emotionally and metaphysically quieter and simpler language than his prose.

Poetry, in which Melville became increasingly absorbed after the outbreak of the Civil War, became his expression of his sense that bestial humanity required confrontation by the grim, self-sacrificial heroes who had learned the Swiftian lesson that Melville expressed in "A Reasonable Constitution":

> What though Reason forged your scheme?
> -'Twas Reason dreamed the Utopia's dream:
> -'Tis dream to think that Reason can
> Govern the reasoning creature, man.
> (*Poems*, p. 411)

Melville is not only specifically repudiating More's Utopia and Plato's Republic, but he is also identifying the *a priori* nature of the eighteenth-century rational liberalism that deserted him with the world of his fathers.

What remained for Melville was a final reality of depravity that required government. In poems like "Art," "Greek Architecture," and "Du Pont's Round Fight," art and government become alike. Both impose order on chaos, the reality of existence. "The House-Top," one of Melville's best and bitterest poems, makes a clear statement that all the democratic, egalitarian expectations for a redeemed human identity are chimerical: human beings are chaotic brutes. Only through imposed order is any kind of decency available. Law and art become one for the angry and disillusioned reasons that order and art become one.

In these terms, *Clarel* subsumes all of Melville's poetry within it. False faith, the desire for faith, bitterly honest loss of faith, unruly humanity, leprous society, the need for imposed law—all of Melville's disillusion comes together here in a poem that is a pilgrimage in search of a foundation for the good society. It is a poetic *Mardi*, unable to locate a believable Serenia. *Clarel* also recapitulates the prose fiction in another way: finally, all human beings are alone. There is no lasting friendship in Melville's world.

One of the most important thoughts to carry away from the poetry is that chronologically, ideationally, and even in composition ("Billy in the Darbies"), Melville's last work, *Billy Budd*, derives directly from the poetry, which incorporated Melville's brooding on the *Somers* affair (Jane Donahue; Milton R. Stern, "Introduction" to *Billy Budd, Sailor*).

In *Billy Budd* we begin again in known identities which are absolute and fixed in their mythic connotations—Billy is a type of Christ: he raises populations from strife to sweetness; he is a prince of peace; he is a type of prelapsarian Adam (the book's specific imagery), and he is also marred and fallen man (the stutter). Claggart is a type of Satan (the book's specific imagery). These opposing absolutes enact their enmity once again in the *narrenschiff*, this time in the indomitable, bellipotent ship of a man-of-war world. Where does Billy come from? Only "God knows, Sir" (*BBS*, p. 51). And Claggart is the "mystery of iniquity." Evil uses the language of the official world of authority—Claggart kills Billy through the Articles of War. Claggart is seen as noble victim and Billy as villain in the official published versions of the event. But redemptive identity has no socially effective language. Billy is noted for his stutter, and he kills Claggart through the Typeean spontaneity of alingual primitive forthrightness; he strains for words that will not come. There are no words that limited man can utter except to express his limited state, the discrepancy between his intentions and the social effect of his actions. "Speak, man!" begs Vere. "Speak! Defend yourself !" (*BBS*, p. 98). When asked, in effect, why the "mystery of iniquity" (p. 108) should have sought to reduce noble Billy to his identity as fallen man, Billy can only "relinquish the vain endeavor" for language and turn "an appealing glance" of "dumb expressiveness" toward Vere. Announcing the impossibility or unreliability of any answer to the question, Vere concludes the witness's role by saying, "Budd, if you have aught further to say for yourself, say it now." And there is only one answer that Budd can make: "I have said all, sir" (p. 108).

So has Melville. Claggart is associated with the city, the urbane man; Billy is associated with the natural, the precivilized man. From *Typee* through *Billy Budd*, both identities cause death (James R. Hurtgen, Jon M. Kinnamon, Lee T. Lemon, Charles A. Reich). But just as the Typee-types of Billy are not nearly as vicious as Western, civilized society, so fallen, imperfect Billy is all goodness and light compared to civilized Claggart and to the society in which Claggart represents the nature and function of law and official order. Now the general population, the ship's "people," are unreliable rather than noble. They spy on each other, they curry favor, they attempt entrapment. They are crew members who love Billy, but who cannot or will not try to save him. Even the Dansker, the man of long experience with the quality of human society, who knows what is going on, will not put himself at risk by enlightening Billy. And there are crew members who can be perverted and bought for any foul act. On the cld warship of human society, as in all of Melville's other *narrenschiffen*, we are in a totally fallen world that encompasses noble and heroic creatures, but whose overall quality is miserable debasement. A world at war becomes a fitting concluding paradigm for Melville's sense of history and society.[24] The chronometrics (Good and Evil, Billy and Claggart) result in a complication of the working of society. The Governor—the enlightened Media, Vere—is the other side of the horological coin that also bears the print of Plinlimmon. Plinlimmon chooses

horologicals as a sneering rationale for his own selfishness. Vere, however, puts *himself* at risk in choosing horologicals as the self-sacrificial
necessity of the only operative time there is. Thereby Melville returns
at the very end of his career to the problem he glancingly touched in
Typee at the very beginning: if the human reality is the actual, if all
history and all societies are a world that had never been in a state of
grace in the first place, then the contemporary world is the summation
of the only world there is. To think otherwise is the primary and ultimate
illusion.

Vere's argument to the court martial is an explanation of the necessity
of horologicals. The chronometric absolute must await the Ideal condition. Meanwhile, either we preserve the ship or get sunk. There have
been many arguments about whether Vere is a totalitarian apologist for
the repressive world of officialdom or is a self-abnegating governor who
sacrifices the absolute he yearns for in order to preserve what he is
responsible for: the well-being of the only world there is, peopled by an
unreliable mass.[25] For once let us forego this argument in order to focus
on another point. *Whatever* Vere is seen to be, both the chronometrics
and the horologicals fail in *Billy Budd*. Melville watches Vere's actions
come to nothing. And nothing is settled by the absolute identities, whose
qualities continue after their deaths in repetitious opposition: the crew
turns Billy into a deity whose voice still sounds in present tense in the
ballad with which he is revered; the savage cowardice of the mass and
the savage repressiveness of officialdom perpetuate everything Claggart
represented.

Vere's choice, like all human action, turns out to be participial, with
the world continuing exactly as before, killing Vere in the process. Vere's
attempt to use officialdom for wise governance is an illusion, for the
official version given in "News from the Mediterranean" and in the
conversation of the surgeon and the purser are what survive to misin-
form the world's people. Although the attendant and, through him, the
senior officer of marines, heard Vere's dying invocation of "Billy Budd,
Billy Budd," no one heard the meaning of Vere's unremorseful accents.
For the purposes of this survey, the bitter sum of *Billy Budd*, regardless
of whatever critical skirmishes might rage around the evaluation of Captain Vere, is that society remains unregenerate. There is no narrative
that makes any difference. *Billy Budd* is Melville's final act of unwriting,
for it is a narrative that dramatizes why it need never be written. Entirely
gone now is the possibility of change or hope. Gone is the energy of joy
and humorousness that culminated in *Moby-Dick*. Again, there is nothing
further to follow from this masquerade but its own reenactment. The
redeemed social state, the end of "the" war, become illusions. History
becomes a misinterpreted misrepresentation of the ever-shifting, participial present.

In that continuing present, whose forms and incidents change but whose essence never does, friendship and nobility fade into memory and loneliness. There is a *memory* of Jack Chase, but not his presence. Retrospectively, one sees the process in development throughout Melville's works. Tommo loses Toby; the Omoo-wanderer loses Dr. Long Ghost; Taji loses Jarl; Redburn leaves Harry Bolton (who dies as it turns out); White-Jacket begins and ends his book an isolato; Ishmael loses Queequeg; Pierre loses everybody; there is neither unequivocal friendship nor nobility in *The Confidence-Man*, and Billy Budd, the center of adoring friendships, has no friends. What friendships do exist in Melville's writings usually have a "chummying" relationship of pragmatic utility, a fellow-tourist connection as we travel aboard the world-ship. Again, the great exception is *Moby-Dick*, and even there Queequeg's death-casket serves as Ishmael's lifebuoy. It is strange, this essential friendlessness in Melville's works, and it brings us back again to speculations about the man himself. One wonders anew about Melville's emotional composition; about his relationship with Hawthorne; about his relationship with his family, in which his sons and wife, at least, were dramatically estranged at one time or another; about his relationships with his friends—*were* there any, even considering people like his brother-in-law, John Hoadley, Evert Duyckinck, and his uncle Peter Gansevoort? But speculations of this sort will remain inconclusive, for as much as we know about Melville's life and surroundings, we know too little about the man himself.[26]

Something within that enigma, Herman Melville, caused him to lose faith in human society. There is something in the intensity of his repugnance in his novels since *Moby-Dick* that seems almost pathological. Although grim darkness has long been recognized in Melville's work, a consideration of Melville and society suggests a darker Melville than is usually acknowledged. Rivalling Swift in savagery and surpassing Swift in metaphysical richness, Melville's work is the intensification of an enraged, despairing cry *de profundis*. By the time of *Pierre*, the consistent savagery of society came to bespeak for Melville the consistent savagery of the human animal. That in turn bespoke the uselessness of trying to change human perception and further hinted that savagery is the only consistent meaning in a valueless universe otherwise unfixed in any meaning. In the case of human savagery, art can be only pointless. In the case of cosmic emptiness, art can be only repetitious. In both cases it is absurd. Corrupt and cannibalistic society's disclosure of the corrupt and cannibalistic human is disclosure of an essence, a paradoxically absolute anti-Absolute. And so the anti-Idealist searchings of the fictions became the fixed, classicist conservatism of the poetry and *Billy Budd*. As the celebration of the democratic nobilities in the heroic world of work were nostalgically consigned by Melville to a time lost and gone ("O, the navies old and oaken,/ O, the Temeraire no more!"), he replaced them with loathing for an unreliable mass of creatures who are always potentially dangerous and who require tight control. Driven by the greatest imaginative genius in nineteenth-century American literature, Melville's developing farewell to art in the continuity of his prose fiction became, in his poetry, a renewed welcome to art. But that welcome, for all its high qualities, simplifies the possibilities of meaning. Melville's final certainty about the unregenerate nature of humanity, and the loss, therefore, of complexities arising from the earlier and brighter visions of the possibilities of human society, was one with his sense of absurdity. A perennial reopening of the question of Melville's Timonism, a question that probably never will be conclusively settled; the limitations of democracy and the sources of totalitarianism; the possibility of meaning and the existence of God; and, encompassingly, the problem of the absurdity at the limits of art and language—nothing less than these are at issue in an understanding of Melville's view of society.

NOTES

1. This topic provides a long bibliography in its own right. Some of the classic treatments are by Loren Baritz; R.W.B. Lewis; Leo Marx (*The Machine in the Garden*); F. O. Matthiessen; Charles Sanford; Henry Nash Smith (*Virgin Land*); and Ernest Tuveson. For a full focus of the topic on Melville, a few of many possible examples are found in the work of James Duban; Harry Slochower ("The Quest for an American Myth: *Moby-Dick*"); and Milton R. Stern ("*Moby-Dick*, Millennial Attitudes, and Politics"). The centrality and significance of the topic are suggested not only by the huge bibliography that could be assembled for it, but also by the fact that most commentary on Melville touches the subject in one way or another. An interesting perspective on the topic is by Bruce Kuklick. See also Marvin Fisher (*Going Under*) and Marius Bewley as examples of the many essays considering Melville's relationship to the mythic ideal. For a consideration of the earliest application of mythic expectations, see John Bakeless and John Bartlett Brebner. For Puritan typology, Perry Miller's *The New England Mind* remains the classic study, and Sacvan Bercovitch (*The Puritan Origins of the American Self* and *The American Jeremiad*) are extremely valuable. See also Mason Lowance, Jr., and Michael T. Gilmore.

2. A useful exploration of the subject by a Melvillean is Warner Berthoff's *The Ferment of Realism* (1965). There are many commentaries on Melville and the Civil War and Melville's view of his society at mid-century. An introductory, miniature sampling of the commentary from early to relatively recent includes Matthew Josephson, "The Transfiguration of Herman Melville" (1928); Ralph Henry Gabriel (1940); Alice L. Godard (1946); Dorothy F. Grimm (1948); Willard Thorp (1950); Alan Heimert (1963); Darrell Abel, "The American Renaissance and the Civil War" (1966); Paul Deane (1968); Frederick W. Turner (1969); Charles Nicol (1970); Kingsley Widmer, *The Ways of Nihilism* (1970); Jean Fagin Yellin (1970); Marvin Fisher, "Melville's 'Tartarus' " (1971); Louise K. Barnett (1974, 1975); Edward Stone (1975); Carolyn L. Karcher, "Melville's 'The 'Gees' "

(1975) and *Shadow Over the Promised Land* (1980); H. Bruce Franklin, "Herman Melville: Artist of the Worker's World" (1977); Joyce Adler, *War in Melville's Imagination* (1981); and James Duban (1983).

3. The eighteenth-century precursor to Romanticism is delineated by many historians, but the emphasis I borrow here is from a perspective such as that in Vernon L. Parrington's old but still stimulating study (Volume 1, book II, part 2, and book III; and Volume 2, book I, parts 1, 2, and 3). I continue to find instruction in old, classic standards by Carl L. Becker.

4. The effects of provincial New England optimism were far-reaching because they were metaphysical reflections of the nation's growing sense of Manifest Destiny. See Larzer Ziff (especially chapters 2 and 4). For the philosophical and social matrix of the contexts of optimism surrounding Melville, see Sherman Paul, *The Shores of America* (1958); Jonathan Bishop; and Van Wyck Brooks, *The Flowering of New England* (1936) and *The Times of Melville and Whitman* (1947).

5. Here again, the materials are overwhelming. Perhaps as good a brief introduction to the topic as any can be found in three old but still highly serviceable essays by Reginald E. Watters. Melville's philosophical sensibility engaged a profound awareness of what literary realism could suggest about Ideality, and what, in turn, cosmic moral emptiness could suggest about the hopelessness of society and, finally, the hopelessness of language.

6. The effects of his society on Melville are, in one way or another, a topic in almost everything ever written about Melville, especially in the biographies, in James Duban's and Michael Rogin's books, and in special-topic studies such as those by Nicholas Canaday, John Bernstein, and Perry Miller (*The Raven and the Whale*). For two focused, brief, and mutually supplementary statements, see Charles Boewe; also Van Wyck Brooks ("The Literary Life in America"), and William Charvat.

7. One would like to think that Melville succumbed to censorship against his will, and we see him wince in his private correspondence, as in a letter of 28 July 1846, to his friend, Evert Duyckinck: "The *Revised* (Expurgated?—Odious word!) Edition of Typee ought to be duly announced." But in fact Melville was even willing to *sell* the idea of "odious expurgation," as is made quite clear in a 15 July 1846 letter to his English publisher, John Murray:

This new edition will be a Revised one, and I can not but think that the measure will prove a judicious one.—The revision will only extend to the exclusion of those parts not naturally connected with the narrative, and some slight purifications of style. I am persuaded that the interest of the book almost wholly consists in the *intrinsick merit of the narrative alone*— & that other portions, however interesting they may be in themselves, only serve to impede the story. The book is certainly calculated for popular reading, or for none at all.—If the first, why then, all passages which are calculated to offend the tastes, or offer violance to the feelings of any large class of readers are certainly objectionable. (*Letters*, pp. 43, 39)

8. For the critical reception of *Typee*, see Stern, "Introduction," *Critical Essays on Typee* (1982).

9. A good overview of the topic is in J. Donald Crowley's excellent introductory essay to and selections of Hawthorne's critical reception. See also Stern, "Romantic Values and American Fiction" (1977).

10. For discussions of Melville's abandonment of conventional perceptions in

Typee, see Michael S. Kearns and especially John Samson. A recent introduction to the topic is in Nicholaus Mills, who traces a line of recoil and disillusion from Cooper to Hawthorne to Melville to Twain ("The Crowd in Classic American Fiction"). See also Nathalia Wright, Michael Millgate, and Sacvan Bercovitch's "Melville's Search for National Identity: Son and Father in *Redburn, Pierre*, and *Billy Budd* (1967). See also A. N. Kaul and see Lewis Mumford's treatment of Melville's tragic sense. For a connection between the national and the psychosocial dimensions of the search for the father, see Richard Chase.

11. Miller, *The Raven and the Whale* (1956), and Duban are again recommended for general social context. See also Theodore P. Greene for a study of the periodical marketplace. The problem of diction, realism, and Romanticism in Melville's essayistic uses of fiction are discussed by Richard H. Brodhead and Joel Porte as well as by F. O. Matthiessen in their rich studies of ideology and idiom. It is clear that by the time he had completed *White-Jacket*, Melville already had been aware of the discrepancy between what he wanted to write and what the market would bear. Nevertheless, he was also aware that the market notwithstanding, he managed to express his feelings in conventional and relatively realistic narrative styles. In his famous and oft-quoted letter to his father-in-law (October 6, 1849) about *Redburn* and *White-Jacket*, he said, "And while I have felt obliged to refrain from writing the kind of book I would wish to; yet in writing these two books, I have not repressed myself much—so far as *they* are concerned; but have spoken pretty much as I feel.... So far as I am individually concerned, & independent of my pocket, it is my earnest desire to write those sort of books which are said to 'fail' " (*Letters*, pp. 91–92). *Redburn* and *White-Jacket* did contain much plainly spoken questioning of prevailing economic, political, and military practices. But except for *Mardi*, it was not until the books following *White-Jacket* (1850) that Melville created heavily symbolic questionings of God, society, the possibility of knowledge, and the possibility of progress. An excellent study of Melville's style and language is Warner Berthoff's *The Example of Melville* (1962).

12. Indeed, an entire—and brilliant—book by Charles Feidelson has been dedicated to the proposition that it was the possibilities of symbolism rather than the possibilities of democracy that created the nexus for writers of the American nineteenth century. For a discussion of Melville's abandonment of art, see Alan Lebowitz.

13. For an intelligent discussion of this point, see Edgar Dryden and especially John Seelye.

14. This is another topic that has generated disputes among Melvilleans. See Alexander Keyssar's work for the suggestion that in Melville's writings the American myth of the common man is undercut by an American reality in which neither the lives nor the deaths of common men were either meaningful or redemptive. For a statement of *Billy Budd* as a farewell to a spiritually ordered world, see Bernard Rosenthal. See also Leo Marx, " 'Noble Shit': The Uncivil Response of American Writers to Civil Religion in America"; John V. Hagopian; and especially Jane Donahue. For the view that Melville's hopeful assessment of man did not change, see Ray B. Brown; see also Henry W. Wells. For a view of Melville's changed vision of man and authority from early books to late, see Theodore Gross; see also Norris Merchant, B.M. Wainger, and John Bernstein.

15. See not only the biographical studies by Newton Arvin, Richard Chase,

and Edwin Miller, but also Henry Bamford Parkes for a discussion of immaturity and isolation in Melville's characters. For an examination of the idea that society is evil as a corollary of expulsion into vagrancy, see V.S. Pritchett. For Dutch Reform Calvinism, see Arvin, pp. 31–35, and T. Walter Herbert, *Moby-Dick and Calvinism.*

16. Robert K. Martin links homosexuality with the "fantasy island" of travel literature. Indispensable to a study of Melville's South Seas fiction are Charles R. Anderson's *Melville in the South Seas* (1939) and Herbert's more recent *Marquesan Encounters* (1980). For a view of the early work as an adumbration of the political tone Melville was to give his travels, see Steven E. Kemper. For a cross-section of commentary on *Typee*, see Stern, *Critical Essays on Typee.*

17. There is no room to explore here the problems posed for fiction by the subject of the individual alone in the universe, a theme especially common since the nineteenth century. For statements somewhat related to the problem, see the studies by Darrell Abel (" 'Laurel Twined with Thorn' "); Merlin Bowen; and Rose Clavering. The limitations of perception and the problem of meaning have been noted in everything Melville wrote. For a few examples, see John Samson (*Typee*); Merrell Davis (*Melville's Mardi: A Chartless Voyage*); Paul Brodtkorb (both works cited); Gary Lindberg; John Wenke ("Melville's Masquerade"); John W. Rathbun (*"Billy Budd"*); John Seelye (especially on the tales); Milton Stern ("Toward 'Bartleby the Scrivener' "); and Robert Zoellner.

18. For views of Melville as a writer looking forward to the uprising of the working class, or other revolutionary overthrow of the present order, see Louise K. Barnett, "Bartleby as Alienated Worker" (1974); H. Bruce Franklin, "Herman Melville: Artist of the Worker's World" (1976); John Carlos Rowe; and Kingsley Widmer (especially), *The Ways of Nihilism* (1970). For the counterview that despite apparent egalitarianism Melville's "voice" bespeaks suppression of aggressive responses to circumstance, see Michael Davitt Bell. See also Maurice Friedman (*Problematical Rebel*); Edward Stone; Larry J. Reynolds ("Kings and Commoners").

19. For a statement of lost brotherhood in *Redburn*, see Terrence G. Lish, and for anti-democratic elements in *White-Jacket*, see Larry Reynolds, "Antidemocratic Emphasis in *White-Jacket*" (1976). Excellent background introductions to these books are by William Gilman and by Howard P. Vincent (*The Tailoring of Melville's White-Jacket*). For a statement introductory to Melville's condemnation of general human nature, see the Melville chapter in Daniel G. Hoffman (*Form and Fable in American Fiction*). Hoffman offers a companion piece in the topic of man's civilized possibilities versus his selfish immorality in "Melville's 'Story of China Aster' " (1950).

20. A brief sprinkling of useful examples for chronological consideration of the opposing weights: Sherman Paul, "Melville's 'The Town-Ho's Story' " (1949); Newton Arvin (1950); Harry Slochower, "*Moby-Dick*: The Myth of Democratic Expectancy" (1950); Henry Nash Smith, "The Image of Society in *Moby-Dick*" (1953); Norman Holmes Pearson (1962); Michael J. Hoffman (1969); Robert Zoellner (1973); Larry J. Reynolds, "Kings and Commoners in *Moby-Dick*" (1980); and Bainard Cowan (1982). See also Jonathan Arac; T. Walter Herbert, *Moby-Dick and Calvinism* (1977); and Milton Stern, "*Moby-Dick*, Millennial Attitudes,

and Politics" (1969). Two especially good overviews of *Moby-Dick* are by Walter E. Bezanson and Warwick Wadlington.

21. The political evaluation of Ishmael can take many interesting turns. See, for instance, T. N. Weissbuch and Bruce Stillians; David H. Hirsch; and Cecil M. Brown.

22. See Canaday, both works cited. A useful context is provided by David Brion Davis.

23. "Bartleby" has attracted more critical attention than any other item of Melville's work published between 1851 and 1857. There are several collections of criticism of some of the works, such as those by Howard Vincent and M. Thomas Inge on "Bartleby." Especially focused on Melville and society, the following tiny handful of works is representative of the dozens of commentaries on the tales and on *Israel Potter* (which does not receive as much attention as the tales): Bert C. Bach; Paul Deane; Marvin Fisher (" 'Bartleby,' Melville's Circumscribed Scrivener"); H. Bruce Franklin ("Herman Melville and Science Fiction"); Maurice Friedman, "Bartleby and the Modern Exile"; Kenny Jackson; Leo Marx ("Melville's Parable of the Walls"); Beryl Rowland; W. R. Thompson; Margaret M. Vandehaar; Robert J. Ward; for an oversimplifying but interesting and useful overview, see Charles N. Watson. See especially Fisher (*Going Under*); William B. Dillingham; and Alexander Keyssar.

24. For the view that Melville lost hope for a world without war, see Barbara Meldrum. Some commentators (Charles Weir) see evil and goodness reconciled. For a view of the matter similar to Wendell Glick's, see Rudolph Von Abele.

25. The evaluation of Vere is perhaps the most vexed question in all of Melville criticism. Sample views of Vere as villain can be found in Christopher Durer; Hiromi Itofuji; Charles Mitchell; Evelyn Schroth; Kingsley Widmer ("The Perplexed Myths of Melville's *Billy Budd*"); and Ralph W. Willett. Sample views of Vere as hero-victim can be found in Edward M. Cifelli; David Ketterer; Edward H. Rosenberry; and in Stern, ed., *Typee and Billy Budd* (1958). See also the conflicting views of Karl B. Zink and Wendell Glick. The fullest overview of law and justice in *Billy Budd*, derived from a historical survey of pertinent political theory, is Scorza's *In the Time Before Steamships* (1979). See also the notes in the Hayford and Sealts edition of *Billy Budd*.

26. Mysteries in point are furnished dramatically by the suicide (?) of Melville's son, Malcolm; by the estrangement (?) of his son, Stanwyx; and by the implications of the materials uncovered by Kring and Carey (Donald Yannella and Hershel Parker). We probably never will know "the truth" about Melville and the existence or extent of Timonism in his personality.

WORKS CITED

Abel, Darrell. "The American Renaissance and the Civil War: Concentric Circles." *ESQ* No. 44 (1966): 86–91.

———. " 'Laurel Twined with Thorn': The Theme of Melville's *Timoleon*." *The Personalist* 41 (July 1960): 330–40.

Adler, Joyce Sparer. *War in Melville's Imagination*. New York: New York University Press, 1981.

Anderson, Charles R. *Melville in the South Seas*. New York: Columbia University Press, 1939.

Arac, Jonathan. *Commissioned Spirits: The Shaping of Social Motion in Dickens, Carlyle, Melville, and Hawthorne*. New Brunswick, N.J.: Rutgers University Press, 1979.

Arvin, Newton. *Herman Melville*. New York: William Sloane Associates, 1950.

Bach, Bert C. "Melville's *Israel Potter*: A Revelation of Its Reputation and Meaning." *Cithara* 7 (November 1967): 39–50.

Bakeless, John. *The Eyes of Discovery: America as Seen by the First Explorers*. New York: J. B. Lippincott, 1950.

Barbour, James. "The Composition of *Moby-Dick*." *American Literature* 47 (November 1975): 343–360.

Baritz, Loren. "The Demonic Herman Melville." *City on a Hill: A History of Ideas and Myth in America*. New York: John Wiley & Sons, 1964.

Barnett, Louise K. "Bartleby as Alienated Worker." *Studies in Short Fiction* 11 (1974): 379–85.

———. *Ignoble Savage: American Literary Realism, 1790–1890*. Westport, Conn.: Greenwood Press, 1975.

Becker, Carl L. *The Declaration of Independence: A Study in the History of Political Ideas*. New York: Harcourt, Brace, 1922.

———. *The Heavenly City of the Eighteenth Century Philosophers*. New Haven, Conn.: Yale University Press, 1932.

Bell, Michael Davitt. *The Development of American Romance*. Chicago: University of Chicago Press, 1980.

Bercovitch, Sacvan. *The American Jeremiad*. Madison: University of Wisconsin Press, 1978.

———. "Melville's Search for National Identity: Son and Father in *Redburn*, *Pierre*, and *Billy Budd*." *College Language Association Journal* 10 (March 1967): 217–28.

———. *The Puritan Origins of the American Self*. New Haven, Conn.: Yale University Press, 1975.

Bernstein, John. *Pacifism and Rebellion in the Writings of Herman Melville*. The Hague: Mouton & Co., 1964.

Berthoff, Warner. *The Example of Melville*. Princeton, N.J.: Princeton University Press, 1962.

———. *The Ferment of Realism: American Literature 1884–1919*. New York: Free Press (Macmillan), 1965.

Bewley, Marius. *The Complex Fate: Hawthorne, Henry James, and Some Other American Writers*. London: Chatto and Windus, 1952.

Bezanson, Walter E. "Moby-Dick: Work of Art." In *Moby-Dick Centennial Essays*. Ed. Tyrus Hillway and Luther Mansfield. Dallas: Southern Methodist University Press, 1953.

Bishop, Jonathan. *Emerson on the Soul*. Cambridge, Mass.: Harvard University Press, 1964.

Blackmur, R. P. "The Craft of Herman Melville." *Virginia Quarterly Review* 14 (Spring 1938): 266–82.

Boewe, Charles. "Romanticism Bracketed." *ESQ* No. 35 (1964): 7–10.

Bowen, Merlin. *The Long Encounter: Self and Experience in the Writings of Herman Melville*. Chicago: University of Chicago Press, 1960.

Brebner, John Bartlet. *The Explorers of North America, 1492–1806*. New York: Doubleday & Co., 1933.

Breitwieser, Mitchell. "False Sympathy in Melville's *Typee*." *American Quarterly* 34 (Fall 1982): 396–417.

Brodhead, Richard H. *Hawthorne, Melville, and the Novel*. Chicago: University of Chicago Press, 1976.

Brodtkorb, Paul, Jr. "*The Confidence-Man*: The Con Man as Hero." *Studies in the Novel* 1 (Winter 1969): 421–35.

———. *Ishmael's White World: A Phenomenological Reading of Moby-Dick*. New Haven, Conn.: Yale University Press, 1965.

Brooks, Van Wyck. *The Flowering of New England, 1815–1865*. New York: E. P. Dutton, 1936.

———. "The Literary Life in America." In *American Literary Criticism, 1900–1950*. Ed. Charles Glicksberg. New York: Hendricks House, 1952.

———. *The Times of Melville and Whitman*. New York: E. P. Dutton, 1947.

Brown, Cecil M. "The White Whale." *Partisan Review* 36 (1969): 453–59.

Browne, Ray B. *Melville's Drive to Humanism*. Lafayette, Ind.: Purdue University Press, 1971.

Canaday, Nicholas. *Melville and Authority*. Gainesville: University of Florida Press, 1968.

Canaday, Nicholas. "Melville's *Pierre*: At War with Social Convention." *Papers on Language and Literature* 5 (Winter 1969): 51–62.

Charvat, William. "Literary Economics and Literary History." In *English Institute Essays, 1949*. Ed. Alan S. Downer. New York: Columbia University Press, 1950.

Chase, Richard. *Herman Melville: A Critical Study*. New York: Macmillan Co., 1949.

Cifelli, Edward M. "*Billy Budd*: Boggy Ground to Build On." *Studies in Short Fiction* 13 (Fall 1976): 463–69.

Clavering, Rose. "The Conflict Between the Individual and Social Forces in Herman Melville's Works: *Typee* to *Moby-Dick*." Ph.D. Diss., New York University, 1954. [*Mel. Diss.*, #60.]

Cowan, Bainard. *Exiled Waters: Moby-Dick and the Crisis of Allegory*. Baton Rouge: Louisiana State University Press, 1982.

Crowley, J. Donald. *Hawthorne: The Critical Heritage*. New York and London: Barnes & Noble, 1970.

Davis, David Brion. *Homicide in American Fiction, 1798–1860: A Study in Social Values*. Ithaca, N.Y.: Cornell University Press, 1957.

Davis, Merrell. *Melville's Mardi: A Chartless Voyage*. New Haven, Conn: Yale University Press, 1952.

Deane, Paul. "Herman Melville: Four Views of American Commercial Society." *Revue des Langues Vivantes* (September-October 1968): 504–507.

Dillingham, William B. *Melville's Short Fiction, 1853–1856*. Athens: University of Georgia Press, 1977.

Dimock, Wai-chee. "*Typee*: Melville's Critique of Community." *ESQ* 30 (First Quarter 1984): 27–39.

Donahue, Jane. "Melville's Classicism: Law and Order in His Poetry." *Papers on Language and Literature* 5 (Winter 1969): 63–72.

474   Milton R. Stern

Dryden, Edgar. *Melville's Thematics of Form: The Great Art of Telling the Truth.* Baltimore: Johns Hopkins University Press, 1968.

Duban, James. *Melville's Major Fiction: Politics, Theology, and Imagination.* De Kalb: Northern Illinois University Press, 1983.

Durer, Christopher. "Captain Vere and Upper-Class Mores in *Billy Budd.*" *Studies in Short Fiction* 19 (Winter 1982): 9–18.

Emerson, Ralph Waldo. *The Selected Writings.* Ed. Brooks Atkinson. New York: Modern Library, 1950.

Feidelson, Charles. *Symbolism and American Literature.* Chicago: University of Chicago Press, 1953.

Fisher, Marvin. " 'Bartleby,' Melville's Circumscribed Scrivener." *Southern Review* 10 (January 1974): 59–79.

———. *Going Under: Melville's Short Fiction and the American 1850s.* Baton Rouge: Louisiana State University Press, 1977.

———. "Melville's 'Tartarus': The Deflowering of New England." *American Quarterly* 23 (Spring 1971): 79–100.

Franklin, H. Bruce. "Herman Melville: Artist of the Worker's World." In *Weapons of Criticism: Marxism in America and the Literary Tradition.* Ed. Norman Rudick. Palo Alto, Calif.: Ramparts Press, 1976, pp. 287–309.

———. "Herman Melville and Science Fiction." *Future Perfect: American Science Fiction of the Nineteenth Century.* New York: Oxford University Press, 1966.

Friedman, Maurice. "Bartleby and the Modern Exile." Melville Annual, 1965, *A Symposium: "Bartleby the Scrivener."* Ed. Howard P. Vincent. Kent, Ohio: Kent State University Press, 1966, pp. 64–81.

———. *Problematical Rebel: Melville, Dostoievsky, Kafka, Camus.* Chicago: University of Chicago Press, 1970.

Gabriel, Ralph Henry. *The Course of American Democratic Thought.* New York: Ronald Press, 1940.

Gilman, William. *Melville's Early Life and Redburn.* New York: New York University Press, 1951.

Gilmore, Michael T. *The Middle Way: Puritanism and Ideology in American Romantic Fiction.* New Brunswick, N.J.: Rutgers University Press, 1977.

Giltrow, Janet. "Speaking Out: Travel and Structure in Herman Melville's Early Narratives. *American Literature* 52 (March 1980): 18–32.

Glick, Wendell. "Expediency and Absolute Morality in *Billy Budd.*" *PMLA* 68 (March 1953): 103–110.

Godard, Alice L. "A Study of Herman Melville's Social Criticism as Reflected in His Prose Writings." Ph.D. Diss., University of Illinois, 1946.

Greene, Theodore P. *America's Heroes: The Changing Models of Success in American Magazines.* New York: Oxford University Press, 1970.

Grimm, Dorothy F. "Melville as Social Critic." Ph.D. Diss., University of Pennsylvania, 1948.

Gross, Theodore. "Herman Melville: The Nature of Authority." *Colorado Quarterly* 16 (Spring 1968): 397–412.

Hagopian, John V. "Melville's L'Homme Revolté." *English Studies* 46 (October 1965): 390–402.

Heimert, Alan. "*Moby-Dick* and American Political Symbolism." *American Quarterly* 15 (Winter 1963): 498–534.

Herbert, T. Walter, Jr. *Marquesan Encounters: Melville and the Meaning of Civilization.* Cambridge, Mass.: Harvard University Press, 1980.

———. *Moby-Dick and Calvinism: A World Dismantled.* New Brunswick, N.J.: Rutgers University Press, 1977.

Hirsch, David H. "The Dilemma of the Liberal Intellectual: Melville's Ishmael." *Texas Studies in Literature and Language* 5 (Summer 1963): 169–88.

Hoffman, Daniel G. *Form and Fable in American Fiction.* New York: Oxford University Press, 1961.

———. "Melville's 'Story of China Aster.'" *American Literature* 22 (May 1950): 137–49.

Hoffman, Michael J. "The Anti-Transcendentalism of *Moby-Dick.*" *Georgia Review* 23 (Spring 1969): 3–16.

Hurtgen, James R. "*Billy Budd* and the Context of Political Rule." In *The Artist and Political Vision.* Ed. Benjamin R. Barber and M.J.G. McGrath. New Brunswick, N.J.: Transaction Books, 1982.

Inge, M. Thomas, ed. *Bartleby the Inscrutable: A Collection of Comments on "Bartleby the Scrivener."* Hamden, Conn.: Archon Books, 1979.

Itofuji, Hiromi. "Another Aspect of *Billy Budd.*" *Kyushu American Literature* 10 (1967): 29–40.

Jackson, Kenny. "Israel Potter: Melville's 'Fourth of July' Story." *College Language Association Journal* 6 (March 1963): 194–204.

Josephson, Matthew. "Libertarians and Others." *Portrait of the Artist as American.* New York: Harcourt, Brace, 1930.

———. "The Transfiguration of Herman Melville." *Outlook* 150 (19 September 1928): 809–11, 832, 836.

Karcher, Carolyn L. "Melville's 'The 'Gees': A Forgotten Satire on Scientific Racism." *American Quarterly* 27 (October 1975): 421–42.

———. *Shadow Over the Promised Land: Slavery, Race, and Violence in Melville's America.* Baton Rouge: Louisiana State University Press, 1980.

Kaul, A. N. "Herman Melville: The New-World Voyager." *The American Vision: Actual and Ideal Society in Nineteenth-Century Fiction.* New Haven, Conn.: Yale University Press, 1963.

Kearns, Michael S. "Phantoms of the Mind: Melville's Criticism of Idealistic Psychology." *ESQ* 30 (First Quarter 1984): 40–50.

Kemper, Steven E. "*Omoo*: Germinal Melville." *Studies in the Novel* 10 (Winter: 1978): 420–30.

Ketterer, David. "Some Co-ordinates in *Billy Budd.*" *Journal of American Studies* 3 (December 1969): 221–37.

Keyssar, Alexander. *Melville's "Israel Potter": Reflections on the American Dream.* Cambridge, Mass.: Harvard University Press, 1969.

Kinnamon, Jon M. "*Billy Budd*: Political Philosophies in a Sea of Thought." *Arizona Quarterly* 26 (Summer 1970): 164–72.

Kuklick, Bruce. "Myth and Symbol in American Studies." *American Quarterly* 24 (October 1972): 435–50.

Lebowitz, Alan. *Progress into Silence: A Study of Melville's Heroes.* Bloomington, Ind.: Indiana University Press, 1970.

Lemon, Lee T. "*Billy-Budd*: The Plot Against the Story." *Studies in Short Fiction* 2 (Fall 1964): 32–43.

Lewis, R.W.B. *The American Adam: Innocence, Tragedy, and Tradition in the Nineteenth Century*. Chicago: University of Chicago Press, 1955.

Lindberg, Gary. *The Confidence Man in American Literature*. New York: Oxford University Press, 1982.

Lish, Terrence G. "Melville's *Redburn*: A Study in Dualism." *English Language Notes* 5 (December 1967): 113–20.

Lowance, Mason, Jr. *The Language of Canaan: Metaphor and Symbol in New England from the Puritans to the Transcendentalists*. Cambridge, Mass.: Harvard University Press, 1980.

Martin, Robert K. " 'Enviable Isles': Melville's South Seas." *Modern Language Studies* 12 (1982): 68–76.

Marx, Leo. *The Machine in the Garden: Technology and the Pastoral Ideal in America*. New York: Oxford University Press, 1964.

———. "Melville's Parable of the Walls." *Sewanee Review* 61 (Autumn 1953): 602–27.

———. " 'Noble Shit': The Uncivil Response of American Writers to Civil Religion in America." *Massachusetts Review* 14 (1973): 709–39.

Matthiessen, Francis O. *American Renaissance: Art and Expression in the Age of Emerson and Whitman*. New York: Oxford University Press, 1941.

Meldrum, Barbara. "Melville on War." *Research Studies* (State College of Washington) 37 (June 1969): 130–38.

Merchant, Norris. "The Artist and Society in Melville." *Views* 4 (1957): 56–57.

Milder, Robert. "The Composition of *Moby-Dick*: A Review and a Prospect." *ESQ* 23 (Fourth Quarter 1977): 203–16.

Miller, Edwin Haviland. *Melville*. New York: George Braziller, 1975.

Miller, Perry. *The New England Mind: The Seventeenth Century*. Cambridge, Mass.: Harvard University Press, 1939.

———. *The New England Mind: From Colony to Province*. Cambridge, Mass.: Harvard University Press, 1953.

———. *The Raven and the Whale: The War of Words and Wits in the Era of Poe and Melville*. New York: Harcourt, Brace, 1956.

Millgate, Michael. *American Social Fiction: James to Cozzens*. New York: Barnes & Noble, 1965.

Mills, Nicolaus. "The Crowd in Classic American Fiction." *Centennial Review* 26 (Winter 1982): 61–85.

———. "Prison and Society in Nineteenth Century American Fiction." *Western Humanities Review* 24 (Autumn 1970): 325–31.

Mitchell, Charles. "Melville and the Spurious Truth of Legalism." *Centennial Review* 12 (Winter 1968): 110–26.

Mumford, Lewis. *Herman Melville*. New York: Harcourt, Brace, 1929.

Nicol, Charles. "The Iconography of Evil and Ideal in 'Benito Cereno.' " *American Transcendental Quarterly* No. 7 (Summer 1970): 25–31.

Parkes, Henry Bamford. "Poe, Hawthorne, Melville: An Essay in Sociological Criticism." *Partisan Review* 16 (February 1949): 157–65.

Parrington, Vernon L. *Main Currents in American Thought*, 3 vols. New York: Harcourt, Brace, 1927.

Paul, Sherman. "Melville's 'The Town-Ho's Story,' " *American Literature* 21 (May 1949): 212–21.

———. *The Shores of America: Thoreau's Inward Exploration.* Urbana: University of Illinois Press, 1958.

Pearson, Norman Holmes. "The American Writer and the Feeling for Community." *English Studies* 43 (October 1962): 403–12.

Porte, Joel. *The Romance in America: Studies in Cooper, Poe, Hawthorne, Melville, and James.* Middletown, Conn.: Wesleyan University Press, 1969.

Prichett, V. S. "The Beat Generation." *New Statesman: The Weekend Review* 56 (6 September 1958): 292–96.

Rathbun, John W. "*Billy Budd* and the Limits of Perception." *Nineteenth-Century Fiction* 20 (June 1965): 19–34.

Reich, Charles A. "The Tragedy of Justice in *Billy Budd.*" *Yale Review* 56 (Spring 1967): 368–89.

Reynolds, Larry J. "Antidemocratic Emphasis in *White-Jacket.*" *American Literature* 48 (March 1976): 13–28.

———. "Kings and Commoners in *Moby-Dick.*" *Studies in the Novel* 12 (1980): 101–13.

Rogin, Michael Paul. *Subversive Genealogy: The Politics and Art of Herman Melville.* New York: Alfred A. Knopf, 1983.

Roripaugh, Robert. "Melville's *Typee* and Frontier Travel Literature of the 1830s and 1840s." *South Dakota Review* (Winter 1982): 46–64.

Rosenberry, Edward H. "The Problem of *Billy Budd.*" *PMLA* 80 (December 1965): 489–98.

Rosenthal, Bernard. "Elegy for Jack Chase." *Studies in Romanticism* 10 (Spring 1971): 213–29.

Rowe, John Carlos. *Through the Custom-House: Nineteenth Century American Fiction and Modern Theory.* Baltimore: Johns Hopkins University Press, 1982.

Rowland, Beryl. "Sitting Up with a Corpse: Malthus According to Melville in 'Poor Man's Pudding and Rich Man's Crumbs.' " *Journal of American Studies* 6 (April 1972): 69–83.

Samson, John. "The Dynamics of History and Fiction in Melville's *Typee.*" *American Quarterly* 36 (Summer 1984): 276–90.

Sanford, Charles. *The Quest for Paradise: Europe and the American Moral Imagination.* Urbana: University of Illinois Press, 1961.

Schroth, Evelyn. "Melville's Judgment on Captain Vere." *Midwest Quarterly* 10 (Winter 1969): 189–200.

Scorza, Thomas J. *In the Time Before Steamships: Billy Budd, the Limits of Politics, and Modernity.* De Kalb: Northern Illinois University Press, 1979.

Sedgwick, William Ellery. *Herman Melville: The Tragedy of Mind.* Cambridge, Mass.: Harvard University Press, 1944.

Seelye, John. *Melville: The Ironic Diagram.* Evanston, Ill.: Northwestern University Press, 1970.

Slochower, Harry. "*Moby-Dick*: The Myth of Democratic Expectancy." *American Quarterly* 2 (Fall 1950): 259–69.

———. "The Quest for an American Myth: *Moby-Dick.*" *Mythopoesis: Mythic Patterns in the Literary Classics.* Detroit: Wayne State University Press, 1970.

Smith, Henry Nash. "The Image of Society in *Moby-Dick.*" In *Moby-Dick Centennial Essays.* Ed. Tyrus Hillway and Luther Mansfield. Dallas: Southern Methodist University Press, 1953.

————. *Virgin Land: The American West as Symbol and Myth*. Cambridge, Mass.: Harvard University Press, 1950.

Stern, Milton R., ed. *Billy Budd, Sailor: An Inside Narrative*. Indianapolis, Ind.: Bobbs-Merrill, 1975.

————, ed. *Critical Essays on Herman Melville's Typee*. Boston: G. K. Hall, 1982.

————. "*Moby-Dick*, Millennial Attitudes, and Politics." *Emerson Society Quarterly* 54 (First Quarter 1969): 51–60.

————. "Romantic Values and American Fiction." In *American Fiction: Historical and Critical Essays*. Ed. James Nagel. Boston: Northeastern University Press and Twayne Publishers, 1977.

————. "Toward 'Bartleby the Scrivener.'" In *The Stoic Strain in American Literature*. Ed. Duane J. Macmillan. Toronto: University of Toronto Press, 1979.

————, ed. *Typee and Billy Budd*. New York: E. P. Dutton, 1958.

Stone, Edward. "The Whiteness of the Whale." *College Language Association Journal* 18 (March 1975): 348–63.

Sussman, Henry. "The Deconstructor as Politician: Melville's *Confidence-Man*." *Glyph* 4 (1978): 32–56.

Thompson, Lawrance. *Melville's Quarrel with God*. Princeton, N.J.: Princeton University Press, 1952.

Thompson, W. R. "Melville's 'The Fiddler': A Study in Dissolution." *Texas Studies in Literature and Language* 2 (Winter 1961): 492–500.

Thorp, Willard. "American Writers as Critics of Nineteenth-Century Society." In *The American Writer and the European Tradition*. Ed. Margaret Denny and William Gilman. Minneapolis: University of Minnesota Press, 1950.

Tichi, Cecilia. "Melville's Craft and Theme of Language Debased in *The Confidence-Man*." *ELH: A Journal of English Literary History* 39 (1972): 639–58.

Turner, Frederick W., III. "Melville's Post-Meridian Fiction." *Midcontinent American Studies Journal* 10 (Fall 1969): 60–67.

Tuveson, Ernest. *Redeemer Nation: The Idea of America's Millennial Role*. Chicago: University of Chicago Press, 1968.

Vanderhaar, Margaret M. "A Re-Examination of 'Benito Cereno.'" *American Literature* 40 (May 1968): 179–91.

Vincent, Howard P., ed. *A Symposium: "Bartleby the Scrivener."* Kent, Ohio: Kent State University Press, 1966.

————. *The Tailoring of Melville's White-Jacket*. Evanston: Northwestern University Press, 1970.

Von Abele, Rudolph. "Melville and the Problem of Evil." *American Mercury* 65 (November 1947): 592–98.

Wadlington, Warwick. "Ishmael's Godly Gamesomeness: Selftaste and Rhetoric in *Moby-Dick*." *ELH: A Journal of English Literary History* 39 (June 1972): 309–31.

Wainger, B. M. "Herman Melville: A Study in Disillusion." *Union College Bulletin* 25 (January 1932): 35–62.

Ward, Robert J. "From Source to Achievement in 'Benito Cereno.'" *Anglo-American Studies* (Salamanca) 2 (1982): 233–40.

Watson, Charles N., Jr. "Melville and the Theme of Timonism: From *Pierre* to *The Confidence-Man*." *American Literature* 44 (November 1972): 398–413.

Watters, Reginald E. "Melville's 'Isolatoes.' " *PMLA* 60 (December 1945): 1138–48.

———. "Melville's Metaphysics of Evil." *University of Toronto Quarterly* 9 (January 1940): 170–82.

———. "Melville's Sociality." *American Literature* 17 (March 1945): 33–49.

Weir, Charles, Jr. "Malice Reconciled: A Note on Herman Melville's *Billy Budd*." *University of Toronto Quarterly* 13 (April 1944): 276–85.

Weissbuch, T. N., and Bruce Stillians. "Ishmael the Ironist: The Anti-Salvation Theme in *Moby-Dick*." *ESQ* No. 31 (Second Quarter 1963): 71–75.

Wells, Henry W. "An Unobtrusive Democrat, Herman Melville." *South Atlantic Quarterly* 43 (January 1944): 46–51.

Wenke, John. "Melville's Masquerade and the Aesthetics of Self-Possession." *ESQ* 23 (Fourth Quarter 1982): 233–42.

———. "Melville's *Typee*: A Tale of Two Worlds." In *Critical Essays on Herman Melville's Typee*. Ed. Milton R. Stern. Boston: G. K. Hall, 1982.

Whicher, Stephen E. *Freedom and Fate: An Inner Life of Ralph Waldo Emerson*. Philadelphia: University of Pennsylvania Press, 1953.

Widmer, Kingsley. "The Perplexed Myths of Melville's *Billy Budd*." *Novel* 2 (Fall 1968): 25–35.

———. *The Ways of Nihilism: A Study of Herman Melville's Short Novels*. Los Angeles: California State Colleges Publications, 1970.

Willett, Ralph W. "Nelson and Vere: Hero and Victim in *Billy Budd, Sailor*." *PMLA* 82 (October 1967): 370–76.

Witte, W. "The Sociological Approach to Literature." *Modern Language Review* 36 (1941): 86–94.

Wright, Nathalia. "The Confidence Man of Melville and Cooper: An American Indictment." *American Quarterly* 4 (Fall 1952): 266–68.

Yannella, Donald, and Hershel Parker, eds. *The Endless Winding Way in Melville: New Charts by Kring and Carey*. Glassboro, N.J.: Melville Society, 1981.

Yellin, Jean Fagin. "Black Masks: Melville's 'Benito Cereno.' " *American Quarterly* 22 (Fall 1970): 678–89.

Ziff, Larzer. *Literary Democracy: The Declaration of Cultural Independence in America*. New York: Viking Press, 1981.

Zimmerman, Michael. "Herman Melville in the 1920s." *Bulletin of Bibliography* 19 (September-December 1964): 117–20 and 24 (January-April 1966): 139–44.

Zink, Karl B. "Herman Melville and the Forms—Irony and Social Criticism in *Billy Budd*." *Accent* 12 (Summer 1952): 131–39.

Zoellner, Robert. *The Salt Sea Mastodon: A Reading of Moby-Dick*. Berkeley: University of California Press, 1973.

16

MELVILLE AND RELIGION

Rowland A. Sherrill

Some of the most vexing issues confronting students of Herman Melville's life and work involve the question of the place of religion in his
literary career, and, frequently, the scholarship has posed the possibility
that deciphering the character of Melville's religious vision might well
represent the best critical keys for unlocking specific works and, indeed,
the career itself. Few elements of Melville's thought and expression have
attracted so much close attention and diverse opinion. Melville has been
labeled a "mystic," a savvy kind of Calvinist, a Christian existentialist, a
"primitive pagan," a Romantic theologian, a Protestant prophet, an atheist, and a nihilist. The sheer range of interpretations, however, suggests
that, as old Horace was fond of saying, "*grammatici certant, et adhuc
sub judice lis est*" ("the critics wrangle, and the question remains unanswered").

Of course, the vagaries of Melville's life and literary expression have
themselves created the conditions for this wide diversity, and the matter
is not likely to be settled with any finality. The South Seas Melville, whose
experience with so-called primitive religious communities enabled him
to develop dramatic contrasts between tribal and civilized religious life,
cannot be exclusively identified with the narrators through whom those
contrasts reach the reader. As difficult as it is to isolate an authorial point
of view from any fiction, it is all the more difficult to draw conclusions
about which work might represent "the essential Melville" or which interpretation might best portray Melville's varied works. Furthermore, when
the issue of "religion" becomes entangled in the already complex critical

situation, those critics who are not only brave but also reflective must surely have reason to pause, at least, before they proceed.

From time to time in the corrigible tradition which criticism itself compromises and which it continues to "rewrite," some stock-taking becomes useful, and it is the purpose of the present chapter to undertake this more modest task on the matter of "Melville and Religion." By tracking down the problems that have confronted and occasionally stunted critical interpretation, by suggesting necessary discriminations in the ways religion should be discussed in general in relation to literary expression, and by marking out the religious implication in the case of Herman Melville, literary scholarship can meet religious studies to contribute to the possibility of refined critical perspectives. To point to such purposes implies that the four sections that follow will operate at a necessarily general level, but even the sweeping character of such a discussion might serve to put particular points of view into critical relief and to provoke a new sense of critical complexity.

The first section briefly reviews the attenuations that have haunted interpretive response. Three distinguishable areas of critical concern and argument emerge. Thus, the second, third, and fourth sections consider Melville in relation to the religious situation of his age, Melville's thought in relation to the religious traditions, and Melville in relation to some theoretical perspectives on religion. Such a survey of the alternative forms of inquiry can provide Melville scholars with some requisites for a more precise discourse about religion by literary critics. In the measure that it clarifies the multiform character of "religion" in its bearing on Melville, it can lead to an estimate of the interpretive territory ahead within each alternative.

MELVILLE, RELIGION, AND THE CRITICAL ISSUES

Perhaps the most frequent disequilibrium in discussing the question of Melville's religious background, thought, and expression has stemmed from the partial conceptions of religion with which criticism has at various points operated. In some cases, religion has been identified too exclusively, or narrowly, with "church" or with "doctrine" or with some historical "orthodoxy." Thus critics often seem to have convinced themselves that they are treating Melville and religion when, in fact, they have ignored a full array of phenomena that might well contradict their attenuated conceptions. In other cases, religion has been reduced from the outset to a particular style of religious outlook—theistic or mystical or evangelical—and the critics have been willing to conclude that Melville cannot therefore be approached at all in terms of religious factors in his life and work. Other stunted critical perspectives have likewise refused the full question of Melville and religion by depicting religion at large as nothing other than some species of irrationality, grim creed, or intolerance. Religion, of course, has in one way or another involved all of these things—blind and thoughtless passion, self-characterizing outlooks, and, indeed, fanaticism and prejudice—but it is not to be adequately understood solely on the basis of any one of these. The kind of critical labor that begins with attenuated ideas of religion is bound either to end with proportionately attenuated results or to blockade itself altogether from approaching the religious dimensions of Melville's life and work. It will at all events be forever poised to raise the extraneous question or prompted to jump at the premature conclusion.

But a second order of interpretive dilemma emerges—namely, the points of view that deal with religion normatively. Although such perspectives have at times been beleaguered by the kinds of partial definitions of religion remarked above, the critical modes that explicate Melville's works in this vein are distinguishable in their evaluating the works on the basis of the critics' partisanships with "right belief " and, finally, on dealing with the Melville behind the works in a more or less *ad hominem* manner. Religion is one of those subjects about which virtually no religious person is neutral, and all too often—especially among the respondents to Melville's works in his own time—the elements of religious bias have overwhelmed the interpretations. *Mardi* or *Pierre* or *Clarel*, in their abundance and ambiguity, become under such bias simply "proof-texts" for enlisting Melville on behalf of the critic's convictions or, more often, for identifying Melville as a heretic. A pattern of this kind of response might well have been set from the beginning. For many of Melville's contemporaries, no doubt convinced of the completely autobiographical character of the early fictions, the question of Melville's "belief " or "heresy" came to the fore immediately: the man who had lived with cannibals had also attacked Christian belief, a conclusion which, as is well known, created the pressures leading to an expurgated second edition of *Typee*. Such early normatively religious approaches were in some respects legitimated by the critics who "rediscovered" Melville in the 1920s and 1930s. Again, the works were understood as autobiographical expressions, and the animating critical purposes referred to Melville's life, including exactions of normative ideas of religion or normatively religious ideas on the issue of Melville's belief. Indeed, such a style has persisted, albeit in increasingly sophisticated ways.

Now, of course, this kind of critical approach is not only predictable in the case of Herman Melville, but has also in fact been useful in clarifying the relationship of Melville to whatever conception of religion or orthodoxy the critic in question is posing as normative. In the hands of Raymond Weaver or Randall Stewart, to cite rather different critics, such committed criticism manages to illumine Melville's religious life and thought—Weaver, on the basis of his presiding idea of what is authentically religious, and Stewart, on the basis of his own controlling reading of Christian doctrine. The value of such work ought not to be gainsaid. Indeed, even Melville's much less subtle early reviewers provide their own kinds of information, although their lessons have more to do with the character of the contemporary audience than with Melville himself.

It is easy enough to detect a normatively Christian moral outlook at work in the matter of literary judgment, and the critic may be granted his or her standpoint. But when biases go undeclared and when normative predispositions are in some ways hidden that partisan views result. D. H. Lawrence's estimate of Melville in *Studies in Classic American Literature* (1964) provides a case in point. Regardless of their evocative power, Lawrence's critiques of Melville are founded on normative ideas of "spirit." But, if his norms seem hidden at some moments, the impressionistic character of his writing alerts the reader by instilling a wariness that might not be duplicated as one follows the apparently "scientific" or descriptive approaches of an Edward F. Edinger, for instance, whose normative conception of religion is disguised by a Jungian lexicon. And the point again is that approaches that feign neutrality or that camouflage normative ideas cannot answer the question of "Melville and Christianity" or "Melville and Religion" except on the slant.

Another distinguishable dilemma lies in the confusion of imaginative expression with religious belief or the obliteration of required distinctions between religious ideation and literary discourse. This has resulted in the all-too-quick identifications of a focal character with Melville himself, without the necessary effort expended to discern, say, Pierre's thoughts, gestures, and assertions from Melville's own self-disclosures. With some other critical approaches, this tendency appears when the literary "ideas" are forced too rudely into the service of locating Melville's self-characterization. Ishmael's flirtation with a Transcendentalist mood in "The Mast-Head" (ch. 35) in *Moby-Dick* leads quickly to his alarm at the prospect of personal annihilation and to the retort to "Pantheists" which closes the chapter, and this miniature play might well issue up the rudiments of an "idea." But this "lofty" little drama is only one small episode in an unfolding pattern of Ishmael's experience which puts that scene in relief. And the "idea" of the faults in Transcendentalism, at last, is not at all a fully characterizing one for Ishmael, unless interpretation ignores other scenes, like those presented in "The Tail" (ch. 86) or in the narrator's musings on the spouting of the whale, in which Ishmael adopts recognizably Transcendentalist postures. If the "idea" of "The Mast-Head" is not a controlling one for Ishmael it clearly cannot be isolated to prove that Melville rejected Transcendentalism wholecloth, even if it can be used cautiously to interrogate Melville's responses to this religious alternative as a resource for his own belief.

In identifying character with author or attributing literary "idea" to authorial belief without critical tact, there is perhaps a more significant general confusion of imaginative discourse with religious discourse. However much a literary character might be thought to be the embodiment of some religious viewpoint, that character's meaning, moment, and implication must be settled in the imaginative framework of which the character is a part. And, to whatever degree a literary *idea* might be considered to contain or to draw to itself some order of religious meaning, it must first be understood as a *literary* idea, shaped by the pressures of its imaginative context, before it can be "translated" into the discrete orders and terms of religious discourse. Committed religious discourse seeks to state reality, to express the actualities of life, to explain spiritual necessity. It attempts to tell *the* truth, and, as it discloses authorial belief, it wants to claim the auditor's permanent assent to the "world" it discerns. But imaginative discourse explores possibility, organizes a hypothetical version of reality, proposes meaning according to its own inner principles of intelligibility. It attempts to tell *a kind of* truth, and, as it might reveal an author's momentary and working self-conception, it wants to elicit the temporary engagement of the auditor with the "world" it devises. In these respects at least, religion requires an understanding conditioned by faith, while literature attempts to elicit faith in the imagination. As literary expression asks for what Coleridge called "a willing suspension of disbelief," religious expression stems from belief. These discrete realms of discourse often borrow from each other in resources and techniques, and, in some cases, they might thoroughly interpenetrate one another. But with their different originating motives and affective aims, they are not finally identical even when they are most fully reciprocal or co-extensive.

The most crucial point in these preliminary distinctions between literary and religious ideation and discourse is also perhaps the most obvious one. While religious meaning can emerge from literary discourse, it appears in the context of authorial imagination. Melville himself seems to have understood this. The narrator of *The Confidence-Man* can assert that "it is with fiction as with religion: it should present another world, and yet one to which we feel the tie" (p. 183). As keen as the observation is to the similar transformative powers of religion and literature, the context of the statement nonetheless makes it clear that even the narrator does not confuse the "world" in which religion has faith with the "world" of fiction in which the reader must be "not unwilling to drop real life, and turn, for a time, to something different" (p. 182).

MELVILLE AND THE RELIGIOUS SITUATION

Throughout Herman Melville's lifetime the religious realm in America was in a continuous state of turbulence and transition. Even what has been called "mainstream Protestantism" was hardly univocal: doctrinal channels were altered, at first, by the new "national situation" and were redirected, then, by their confluence with deep cultural currents; orthodoxy quickly went through a series of bifurcations that sent religious institutions and communities washing down sectarian tributaries; popular piety burst open in revivalist waves that refused the now redirected old channels; religion itself in some respects was dammed by secularism to make a reservoir of values and sentiments with which to irrigate America's private and public life.

A less metaphorical and more precise historical depiction of Protestant thought in Melville's America is that it moved from the old Calvinist doctrine of God's "wonder-working providence," fading even at the opening of the century, through the doctrines of self- and social-perfection in mid-century, to the doctrine of progress, under the aegis of the "new theology" and the Social Gospel movement, stirring in the last two decades of the century. Joseph Haroutunian and Perry Miller (*Errand into the Wilderness*) have provided differing accounts of what they both consider "the passing of the New England theology" or the demise of the Puritan legacy: Haroutunian sees the influence of Enlightenment thought and its offspring in a new "moralistic" Christianity as they gradually displaced the strongholds of Puritan piety in America; Miller understands the erosion more in terms of an increasingly liberal tendency interior to New England theology which, willy-nilly, conceded more ground to antinomian impulses on the one side and to Arminian pressures on the other. In any event, by 1825, although the old Calvinism remained housed in Congregationalist centers and other scattered pockets of refuge, its hegemony had been demolished, and it was forced to compete not only with its own liberal progeny, Unitarianism, but, by 1840, with the energetic denominations (Presbyterian, Methodist, Baptist) covering the front, revivalism, new religious movements like Mormonism, an array of utopian visions, religio-cultural alternatives like Transcendentalism, and significant Catholic immigration. This new pluralism did not lead to a new equanimity. Within Protestantism, doctrinal debate howled, and theological controversy raged. Amidst all this Herman Melville passed through his early years.

The mid-nineteenth century saw popular Protestantism, perhaps weary of doctrinal strife, begin to reconsolidate under the pressures of the general cultural phenomena of industrialism, urbanism, and immigration, to accommodate itself to the American experience and find separate spheres for the churches and for "privatized" religion. Although liberal and conservative camps maintained themselves, personal emphases blurred the once-strident debates on doctrines—at least in popular piety—and the emergent evangelical strain, confusing civic virtues and Christian morality, centered on individual reform, salvation by good citizenship, grace detected in middle-class success. Propriety became a hallmark of moral perfection, and America itself traveled a course of divinely ordained as well as historically manifest destiny. Such popular surges made religion in America prosper at the center of the culture while refined theological reflection was pushed to the peripheries in newly formed seminaries. As religion saturated the domestic character of bourgeois America and its pulpits, sophisticated theological endeavor "professionalized." Within this domestication of Protestant energies, Melville came fully of age and lived most of his adult life.

In the final quarter of the nineteenth century, a consolidation of the evangelical realm had become more or less complete, but one large division within Protestantism remained intact. As Martin E. Marty has pointed out, "one [dominant] Protestant party had become individualistic, while the other [rarer form] was social" (p. 178). The party of "private" Protestantism emphasized personal moral life and individual salvation in another world. The efficacy of revivalism was now channeled by the aims of "saving" personal, moral life and not, as earlier, by social issues; in its practical shapes, it was a religion of decorum, nestled comfortably in hearth and home. The party of "public" Protestantism sought to apply the Christian message for reformation of the social order and to preach the "social gospel." Not content to await the millennium, nor convinced that American life was basically in good, moral shape, these social Protestants used secular theory in their diagnosis of the public problems (of industrialism, social justice, urban life, economics). This schism within American Protestantism—which cut across denominational lines—emerged fully and increased dramatically during the last two decades of Melville's life.

When one considers Melville's life and work in relation to the general religious milieu, a host of problems arise—not the least of which is the matter of determining how each specific epoch in this history might be pertinent. The problems range from the most immediate religious environment—the familial traditions in which the young Melville was reared—to his mature responses to the nineteenth century. With respect to the possible influences on him, of course, the inquiry touches the complexities of what students of religion refer to as the "social experience of religion."

At one level, this approach involves the sociology of knowledge and defines the religious construction of social reality in the corporate religious subjectivity, which had power in Melville's childhood. Stemming from family traditions, church environment, and local social values, such an "objective," socially-constructed world figured decisively in Melville's formative and later years, even as he resisted its determining influence. This *was* the "world" in its religious coloration against which he pushed and in relation to which his personal identity had to be achieved. To decipher this specific religious dimension biographical and historical research can detect the authoritative religious presence for Melville. It determines the kind of doctrinal views, theological interpretations, moral injunctions, and ritual practices, which "arrived" to him either formally, through official church life, or, informally, through social and familial emphases.

More difficult is the matter of interpreting how such circumstantial stuff might have played on Melville's psychological life. Summatively considered, this category of inquiry has to do with the historical manifestations of religious life in the nineteenth century and with the degrees to which family and society were consistent or contradictory with one another, and with the ways this "social experience" might have absorbed Melville and his literary imagination. It should be remembered, however, that what is at stake is not Melville's personal encounter with God or spirit but, rather, his experience with religion's social matrices. To whatever extent this bore on him personally, it is distinctive in kind from an encounter with a numinous reality.[1]

The Melville Log provides ample evidence that in young Herman's household the idea of "providence" figured prominently. Even if pushed through clichéd usage, however, the idea clearly was not foreign to Allan Melvill who, shortly after the birth of his son, Herman, on 1 August 1819, hoped that "we shall not be unmindful of these repeated blessings of Providence" (*Mel. Log*, p. 3). Repeated allusions to "the hand from which all favours come," to "the particular direction of Providence," to "the favor of Providence" (pp. 5, 10, 11) and so on, suggest that, however cosmopolitan Allan Melvill might have been, his habits of discourse at least were steeped in that Dutch Reformed community to which he was conjoined at least by marriage. Among other items, the idea of providence, nurtured early, clearly remained an element of his emotional and intellectual life. After a conversation with Melville in November 1856, Nathaniel Hawthorne recorded in his *English Notebooks* that Melville was forever persisting after "knowledge of Providence and futurity and all that lies beyond human ken" (*Mel. Log*, p. 529).

The social aura of religion surrounding Melville's life and career has been considered in various important critical pieces. T. Walter Herbert's *Moby-Dick and Calvinism* (1977) saturates itself in the familial religious traditions in which Melville was reared—the Dutch Reformed Church of the Gansevoort lineage and the liberal, largely Unitarian, impulses of the Melvilles. Drawing on the "sociology of knowledge," Herbert argues that Melville internalized the conflict between these religious "worlds," and, thus, the critical clash in his personal consciousness duplicated the largest public religious debate of the time between orthodox and liberal camps. Not only did he suffer privately the same kind of private tension expressed in a public form by Edward Beecher's *Conflict of the Ages* (1854), but he also tested both traditions against his own observations and experience. Plying the tools of "psychohistory," Herbert seeks to demonstrate that Melville "dismantled" both sets of familial religious views in *Moby-Dick*, unable as he was to accept the theocentric ideas foundational for each in the face of what he regarded as failures of providence in his own family history. For Herbert, then, Melville's master-work embodies the familial tension and the "personal crisis in a form that illuminates the crisis of his age, [with the literary effort] anticipating the imminent collapse of the theocentric world view" and putting him on the side of an "ancient charter of religious doubt" (pp. 18–19).

Without the recourse to biography and history Lawrance Thompson's earlier treatment similarly demonstrates Melville's so-called "quarrel with God." *Moby-Dick*, Thompson believes, was an explosion of "anti-Christian insinuations" (p. 159) elicited by the author's sense that the deity was a malevolent creator. Working through the rhetorical layering of the book, Thompson sees Ishmael's narration as "allegorical triple-talk" designed to placate Christian readers at the same time as it commends Ahab's efforts to destroy the white whale or Christian God. Identifying Ahab's satanic defiance with Melville's own sentiments, Thompson concludes that the "underlying theme in *Moby-Dick* correlates the notions that— God in his infinite malice asserts a sovereign tyranny over man and that most men are seduced into the mistaken view that this divine tyranny is benevolent and therefore acceptable" (p. 242). Since Thompson is not sufficiently patient to distinguish Christianity in general from a strident kind of Calvinism in particular, his conclusion probably outruns his analysis: he fails to see that Melville's "quarrel" was not so much with God as with a socially manifest conception of God. Nonetheless, the analysis, chastened a bit, can indicate how Melville's rhetoric of fiction in *Moby-Dick* might be thought pressed into the service of exposing a dark Calvinism residually present in Melville's time.

Other critics, also taking note of Melville's resistance to the main religious alternatives of mid-nineteenth-century America, have adopted different strategies and reached different conclusions about Melville's relation to Calvinism. William H. Shurr (*Rappaccinni's Children*) argues that the visions of writers are shaped by what they resist and that Melville, in some respects formed by the "Calvinist world," used Ahab to push the "logic" of that world past the boundaries of intelligibility. *Moby-Dick* transforms Ahab's Promethean heroism—from its humanistic to its satanic character—and exposes the madness of one not only conditioned by such a world but also embodying its dark necessities. In an earlier work (1972), Shurr discusses the poetry's continuous efforts to plunge down into "the mystery of iniquity." Major themes in this poetry are the lost Eden, the cannibalistic character of the natural order, and the "corroboration of Calvin's creed" about the innate depravity of human beings. Whether Melville's focus is narrowed to small Civil War scenes in *Battle-Pieces* or widened to the symbolic terrain of the Holy Land in *Clarel,* the degeneration of history, landscape, and riot of human action is posed (according to Shurr) against the confident post-Civil War Christianity. If a vestigial Calvinism could lead Ahab to enlist in fire-worship, its deeper fundamentals would stand by Herman Melville in later life as the surest counter to the naïve religious sentiments he saw all around him.

One such important instance of this "use" of Calvinism is close at hand. Melville was acutely conscious of the religious dimensions of American Transcendentalism which, refusing even the confines of liberal Unitarianism, emerged and flourished for a time before mid-century. A number of critics have concentrated on Melville's love-hate relationship with respect to this movement, but little doubt apparently remains about its influence on him and his work simply by virtue of the presence of Transcendentalist notions on the American scene.[2] And the upshot of this cumulative interpretive work might well be that his ambivalence respecting the movement worked in a strange reciprocity with his equally mingled attitudes toward the more "orthodox" currents of American Protestantism as he alternately used the resources of each in order to criticize and surpass the other.

Of course, Melville was touched by social religion beyond the American scene. Several critics have been interested, for instance, in the ways his South Seas experience affected or reflected his religious life and literary expression. Daniel Aaron and Charles Roberts Anderson provide the pioneering work on Melville's experience of missionary work in Oceania. Shifting attention from "Melville and the Missionaries"—a focus which in some ways yields interpretive results similar to those having to do with Melville's responses to evangelical Protestantism in the stateside social realm—T. Walter Herbert, Jr. (1980) has more recently argued that Melville's "Marquesan encounter" can be understood as a "psycho-social drama," a "text," with Melville's embodied romanticism confronted by the alien social reality of native life in terms that created psychic upheaval for him and that generated deep challenges to the idea of civilization structured into his unconscious life. The dynamics and implications of this dramatic "text" begin to come to the fore, when seen in relation to the psychic discordances revealed in two parallel "texts"—the embodied Calvinism of Charles Stewart and the Enlightenment embodiment of David Porter. The three "representative" Americans pose the three major forms of religious self-understanding in mid-nineteenth-century America, and their collisions with the sheer "otherness" of life in the Marquesas can help unmask some of the rifts in those American forms of religious subjectivity.

Several interesting facts bear on the critical issue of Melville and religion. First, a good deal more critical work with this focus has been given over to Melville's social-religious experience during the first half of his life than to those decades following *Moby-Dick*. This could be a result of a common twentieth-century idea, tutored by the psychologists, that the essential values of a personality are most deeply formed in childhood, after which they remain largely unchanged. Or it could result from a consensus of critical notions having to do with when Melville's "major phase" ended. Or it could result from an assumption that the period in American religious history following the Civil War is somehow less commanding or influential in Melville's case because it was ostensibly less turbulent. Second, it seems clear that, although a substantial body of critical inquiry has sought to decipher Melville's historical experience of religion, such scholarly work has gone almost invariably to the most predictable "places" one looks for "social religion"—to the institutions, groups, rhetorics, and practices associated with "orthodox" or mainline expressions of religious life. This has most often meant that critics have located Melville in what *seem* in retrospect to have been the most visible regnant communities. If these "facts" hold, they indicate neglected areas of potential importance in sizing up Melville's encounter with social religion and thus suggest areas for future work.

With respect to the second half of his life, the widespread convictions about Melville as a life-long learner and keen social observer ought to dictate more critical attention to religion between 1865 and 1890 and to the ways in which the dramatic alterations in American religion after mid-century had bearing on Melville's imaginative life. Perhaps, this attentiveness will come as American religion historians themselves continue to refine their own accounts of this period. What might prove especially useful is the measure Melville took of the Protestant community as it accommodated and indeed participated in the new cultural attitudes. Shaped by a special inculcation of evolutionary outlooks and other forms of "new science," Protestantism began to refashion its millennialist drives under the new rubric of "progress" as it charted a new course or at least found new channels for its dream of American religious empire. Although some critics have "worried" Melville in relation to Darwin in particular, Melville scholarship has yet to reckon fully with Melville's attitudes toward the developments T. Dwight Bozeman describes in *Protestants in an Age of Science* (1977).[3]

A second area of potentially fruitful investigation of Melville's relation to the religious history of the age is a more local one. Melville was both an inveterate New Yorker and a notorious "borrower," but little attention has been given to the question of how he might have used some of the highly publicized features of quasi-religious energy in his home area. For instance, so many fires of revival passed through the upstate area of New York in the first half of the nineteenth century that it came to be called "the burned-over district," and the *genus loci* of the place for some is in its having proved a spawning ground or an open field for new religious movements like Mormonism, for visionary utopian dreaming, and for seances and "spirit-rapping" by the Fox sisters in midcentury. Howard Kerr, in a well-documented treatment of the variety and character of the last of these, has considered Melville briefly in relation to American "spiritualist" movements of the age, and, without reference to Melville, Werner Sollors has more recently proposed how aspects of it were absorbed by the general consciousness of the culture. While there is little to indicate that Melville might have been deeply affected by these revivalist and "occult" movements, they were widely discussed and "ripe" for the picking by a man who, as Perry Miller (in *The Raven and the Whale*) has proposed, was tuned enough to the popular realms to draw in *Moby-Dick* on the raging debate about the relative virtues of New England versus Manhattan chowder. As such movements revealed aspects of the character of American religious life even in caricature, Melville might have made use of them in his wrestling with the terms of contemporary experience in *The Confidence-Man*, *Moby-Dick*, or *Pierre*.

A third area is also related to less formal, religious expression which, in this case, is closer to his own vocation. Like Hawthorne, he was acutely aware of the scores of popular novelists on the scene as they competed for an audience, but little thorough work has been done on Melville's relation to that portion of the tradition devoted to religious matters. David S. Reynolds's recent book might well inspire a remediation for it presents an extensive survey of the "pious fiction," its techniques, cultural contexts, and religious agenda during a time (1790–1850) when an increasing "faith in fiction" began to supplant America's pulpit rhetoric, doctrinal stridency, and sectarian competitions. Preferring dramatic forms of religious demonstration to precise theological reasoning, the popular American religious imagination overcame its old Puritan bias against literary presentation, and the publication of popular American religious fiction reached groundswell proportions. Although Reynolds gives Melville only scant mention, he isolates formulas and conventions which more "serious" artists might have used and transformed for their own purposes. For instance, in Reynolds's analysis of the popular characterizations of pure, young women in relation to "angel-visions" one can hear echoes of Melville's Lucy in *Pierre* and of the darker angel, Isabel, who are introduced finally to a more complex world than any of the pious fictions were able to see.

These observations about possible areas of future inquiry are not meant to suggest that no work remains to be done on mainstream religion in the period.[4] They are designed, rather, to suggest that attention to these predictable "places" of religion cannot begin to contain all that is pertinent for this dimension of the subject. In order to broach these relatively neglected areas, critics will need to extend their sense of what might constitute religiously significant evidence and to broaden their critical vision to see religious drives and outlets where they have frequently not looked.

MELVILLE AND THE RELIGIOUS TRADITION

When one moves from the immediate social religious scene to the larger religious tradition, the character of the inquiry changes as well. The problems to be solved with the immediate religious scene have mainly to do with Melville's own spiritual history and biography in terms of what he literally experienced and of how his literary expression relates to that public and social experience. The matter of Melville's relation to the religious tradition, on the other hand, pushes criticism toward intellectual history and the history of forms, toward questions of continuity and change, of intellectual influence, and of structural paradigms and parallels. Behind the social forms which bore so heavily on Melville's personal life, there stretched two full centuries of Protestant tradition in America, whose own lineage cannot be fully understood apart from the history of Christianity with its own even deeper roots in the complex entanglement of ancient Near Eastern with Western civilization. The contemporary religious communities which stood at the end of this continuum belonged to a particular part of this tradition, but there can be little doubt after surveying Melville's reactions to these communities that he frequently understood their complex legacy better than they did themselves. This inheritance reached forward in the continuity and change of controlling doctrine, the historical course of theological reflection, the persistence of certain modes of religious reflection, and the sweep of themes and metaphors of self-conception.

Some general works have characterized Protestant thought in Melville's day. Along with Martin E. Marty, Sydney E. Ahlstrom's monumental *Religious History of the American People* (1972) provides a rich panorama of religious periods, and his anthology (*Theology in America*, 1967) reflects the important course of the nation's theological intelligence. Claude Welch enables the student to see the American theological scene in relation to the wider, context of Anglo-European religious thought in the nineteenth century, and M. H. Abrams's *Natural Supernaturalism* (1971) provides an important cultural-historical account of crucial shifts and alterations in Christian thought in the period. Miller (*Errand into the Wilderness*, 1964) and Haroutunian, among others, explore in general terms the history of American Protestant thought from the Puritan settlements to the nineteenth-century formations. From another angle, Sacvan Bercovitch (*Puritan Origins*, 1975) traces continuities of Puritanism in the American character and, in a more recent essay, argues generally for what he calls "The Biblical Basis of the American Myth." Nathan O. Hatch and Mark A. Noll have collected essays that explore the formative power of the Biblical tradition in America, and Herbert N. Schneidau's *Sacred Discontent* (1976), measuring the influence of the Bible in Western civilization in a very particular way, proposes the nature and terms of the continuity of the "prophetic" impulse in the literary and cultural tradition. Each of these general works provides a special understanding of some features of the broad religious traditions pertinent in Melville's career.

Individual critics have studied Melville, of course, in terms of the more specific elements that belong to this encompassing lineage. An early work by William Braswell, which pinned its argument on an understanding of Melville's reading without benefit of Leyda and Sealts, has been largely superseded by more recent explorations but remains an interesting argument about Melville's movement toward skepticism.

Some critics have sought to demonstrate how Melville's recoil from the religious alternatives in his age was the catalyst that drove him to older elements of American Protestant self-understanding. Sacvan Bercovitch, Michael T. Gilmore, and Rowland A. Sherrill locate different forms of recourse. For Bercovitch (*American Jeremiad*, 1978), Melville's literary expression belongs to a prophetic tradition of discourse—the jeremiad—which, distancing itself from larger communal conventions of belief and behavior, can appear at any moment to criticize the community's historical failures by measuring aspects of its public life against its own essential, originating vision. Thus, Melville accedes to what Bercovitch calls "the national myth"—the deep interfusion of Protestant millennialist dreams with the American civil experience which consecrates the experience of the country. His imaginative work challenges the contemporary religious community for falling short of the ideals implicit in its own mythic self-conception.

According to Gilmore, Hawthorne and Melville used their fictions to keep alive a delicately balanced idea derived from Puritanism. Against a legacy fully embodied in and continuous from Benjamin Franklin, which "secularized" the national vision (by maintaining a Puritan conception of "prudence" while dismissing a correlative "piety"), both "undertook in their fiction to salvage the [full] metaphysical vision" (p. 35) of the Puritan fathers. As the two "appropriated Calvinism's grammar of thought" (p. 6), each in his own way was able to repossess in fiction the Puritan ideal of "the middle-way"—namely, that notion of "inner-worldly sainthood"—which they thought was repudiated by American Protestantism in their age. For Sherrill ("Flood-Gates," 1977), Melville's resistance to orthodox and liberal Protestantism, as both configured in the social realm of mid-century, occurred in terms of what he regarded as their facile epistemological assumptions and their resulting, faulty theological assertions, but this resistance only drove him to push the art of the romance and some assumptions of Romanticism to their extremities in *Moby-Dick*. In this, he sought to fashion a genre for expressing a more radical Protestant imagination of experience. In all three views, then, Melville's encounter with his religious communities sent him in search of older and deeper traditions.

A number of critics have also worked on the particular terms of continuity or structural consonance that Melville's thought shares with American Puritanism and the Reformation heritage. Working within the ambit of Perry Miller, Ursula Brumm (*American Thought*, 1970) poses the continuity as a matter of Melville's transforming the "typological" mode of interpretation for use in his own more symbolic art. In so doing, he placed himself not only in company with Biblical understanding and with medieval forms of exegesis but also with Puritan extensions of this interpretive theory: he found images, shadows, and emblems of "divine things" not only in scripture but also in nature and history. William B. Dillingham devotes a portion of his work on Melville's artistry to a consideration of the main rudiments of Calvinist thought from which Melville derived "an understanding of basic human nature and a sense of man's perilous position in life" (p. 139). In somewhat more particular terms, T. Walter Herbert, Jr. ("Calvinism," 1969) has studied Melville's "Calvinist connection" on the matter of the struggle with evil in *Moby-Dick*. Thomas Werge develops a view of Melville's master-work in the afterglow of Calvin and suggests the theological parallels of Melville and Luther on the matter of "the masks of God" ("*Moby-Dick*" and "Luther and Melville"). Along similar lines, Rowland A. Sherrill (*Prophetic Melville*, 1979) argues that Melville's emerging "idea of transcendence" in the mature works belongs in continuity with a radical tradition of Protestant reflection on the meaning and implication of "the hidden god" (pp. 85–107). A somewhat different view of Melville in the lineage of Christian thought appears in M. O. Percival's Kierkegaardian reading of *Moby-Dick*, but, as with most of the others, the Melville found there is remarkable for his depth and subtlety of theological thought.

In other efforts, critics have been more interested in the influence of the Biblical legacy. For some—like Bercovitch (*American Jeremiad*) and Sherrill (*Prophetic Melville*)—this endowment mainly supplied Melville with a general mode of prophetic self-understanding and with the forms for his own kind of jeremiad, but for others the formative power of the Hebrew Bible and the New Testament exacted more specific pressures and enabled more particular possibilities for Melville's literary work. The fullest treatment remains Nathalia Wright's *Melville's Use of the Bible* (1969) which explores the Biblical inheritance and its implication for Melville's imagery, his characters and types, his pervasive themes and controlling plots, and the drives and flights of his style. This was no merely literary-technical resource for Melville, she contends, for the influence went "beyond quotation and allusion, beyond allegory to true inspiration" as the writer not only echoed the mighty Biblical record but "recreated what he found there in terms of his own time and language" (p. 19). In a partly dissenting view, Edwin Cady more recently concludes that, however much Melville might have plundered the stock of Biblical material, his uses were largely subversive: he was, Cady contends, "a great biblical unscriptural writer" (p. 38).

The focus for some explications has pointed critical inquiry toward much more specific Biblical elements, themes, and figures in the Judaeo-Christian tradition. Ursula Brumm ("The Figure of Christ," 1957) and Vincent Freimarck, among others, have suggested how the fundamental designs of *Billy Budd* draw on the gospel-narratives of the New Testament to present Billy as a "Christ-figure" and how Melville's own self-disclosures might be revealed in the emphases and transformations he generates in this presentation. William Rosenfeld thinks a complex resurrection theme figures powerfully in the concluding passages of *Moby-Dick*, and John R. May is interested in apocalyptic motifs in *The Confidence-Man*. Other critics find Melville's recourse to the Hebrew Bible more important: Lawrance R. Thompson believes Melville's essential vision is akin to a dark reading of *Ecclesiastes* (pp. 148f); C. Hugh Holman is persuaded that the dramatic narrative of *Job* sets the situation for *Moby-Dick* in which Ishmael's "reconciliation" must be accomplished; Nathalia Wright (1965) thinks *Moby-Dick* is structured in a fundamental way around a choice between the whale in *Jonah* or the whale in *Job*; and Janis Stout explores Melville's literary responses to *Job* in more general terms.

Perhaps the most frequently discussed Biblical theme in the criticism is the narrative and various theological interpretations of the lost Eden and the Fall, a Biblical "episode" which has been thought to establish a rudiment of Melville's understanding of reality. Clearly respectful of the "touch of Puritanic gloom" and "that Calvinistic sense of Innate Depravity and Original Sin" he found in Hawthorne, Melville claimed in "Hawthorne and His *Mosses*" that these consequences of the Fall were elements from which no "deeply thinking mind" could be entirely free (*MD*, p. 540).

The exactions of the idea of the Fall on Melville's literary imagination, however, have been a matter of debate among the critics, no doubt because some of Melville's *personae* find the Fall more deeply determinative when contemplating corruptions of human nature in, say, the draft-riots of "The House-Tops" or the cannibalistic character of the world in "The Maldive Shark" than others who focus on the graceful beauty of Fayaway in *Typee* or the pristine countenance of Billy Budd.

Charles Moorman and Richard Ruland, for instance, locate what each argues is Melville's rendition of "the fortunate fall"—Moorman in *Pierre*, Ruland in *Typee*—and, thus, propose for Melville a more ameliorative version of this traditional theme than those critics who place Melville in a stricter Calvinistic lineage. For Richard Harter Fogle, Melville presented his deepest meditation on "the order of the fall" in *Billy Budd* and did so within the framework of a Romantic vision that relies on yet a different theological outlook. Many critics have noted the theme of the lost Eden, the nostalgia for paradise, or the drives of the Adamic impulse in the thought of American writers. R.W.B. Lewis (*American Adam*, 1955) has been particularly attentive to this last characteristic of the national literature and to Melville's generative contribution to its power. Kenneth Bernard has suggested how *Mardi* represents Melville's particular replication of the Fall as a contemporary account for his age. Some recent essays, collected by G. R. Thompson and V. L. Lokke, provide more refined interpretations of the powerful hold of the Eden myth on the imaginations of the so-called dark Romantics—Hawthorne, Poe, and Melville. Many of these critics also argue that the terms for human life established by the nature of the Fall, as Melville saw it, are fundamental in his assessments of life's subsequent state as the literary works test and measure various characters' efforts to seize principles of redemption in the structures of their experience.

Melville's relation to immediate and more distant moments in the Judaeo-Christian tradition also appears, for another group of interpreters, as a matter of resistance or subversion: Franklin Walker thinks Melville drew on the theme of pilgrimage in a debunking manner; Ray B. Browne finds "Melville's drive to humanism" in the effort to loose himself from the constrictions of Protestant ideas of dependent man and sovereign god. For others, Melville's relation to the tradition occurred less at the level of repudiation than as a matter of predicament or crisis: John T. Frederick, for instance, portrays a Melville who sensed himself caught in a closure on the efficacy of the tradition, or, for another kind of example, Arnold Rampersad finds a "pilgrim's progress" in *Israel Potter* which will not render the traditional redemptive denouement. Still others probe Melville's syncretic imagination at work in his borrowing or testing elements from "old heresies" and alternative religious traditions: J. C. Oates explores Melville's Manicheanism; Mukhtar Ali Isani works on Zoroastrian elements; and Helen P. Trimpi traces Melville's interests in demonology and witchcraft as they ponder the religious complexities in the structures of *Moby-Dick*. Convinced that Melville belongs not so much to a specific theological and doctrinal legacy as to a more general tradition of religious understanding and response, critics like Vincent Buckley find Melville's crucial commitments revealed in an essential sacramentalist apprehension of the world.

An even more tacit relation of Melville to the traditions of religion appears in those critical interpretations that center on the moral dimensions of his literary work. Although the critics themselves do not always inquire thoroughly into the theological foundations of the moral imagination, the interpenetrating realms of religion and morality become visible in *Billy Budd,* for instance, as Wendell Glick studies the conflict of ethical systems in the moral situation posed in the narrative, or as C. A. Reich considers Melville's ambivalence toward the meaning of "justice" in the same work, or as John D. Barbour explores how the literary form itself issues a critique of the ideas and forms of "virtue," or as Charles Mitchell plots the contradictory demands of law and morality.

Whether these critics conclude that Melville's various relationships with the religious tradition were rebellious or cordial, plain or paradoxical, clear or covert, their work cumulatively suggests Melville's deep engagement with the world of religious and theological ideas. But at least two problems in these works need to be surmounted. First, perhaps because a focus on a writer's relation to the past deals primarily in temporal terms, the criticism of Melville and the religious tradition has treated themes, as if they were created sheerly for the sake of a continuum which, though coursing through history, seems *ahistorical.* In this way a writer may be thought to "belong to the ages," but he must also seem not to belong to any particular age or to exist in it only as a disconnected intellect. The point is that Melville's absorption, uses, quarrels, and transformations of the tradition have their fullest significance only when seen as fully *historical* engagements that were worked out in a specific context of need and circumstance. Second, criticism has tended to "abstract" religious ideas, themes, images, from their literary contexts—that is, to treat the matter too exclusively in terms of intellectual history without due regard to the special pressures applied on these "ideas" by the authorial situation and the literary context. In short, it is one thing to define the "fire-worship" in *Moby-Dick* in relation to Zoroastrianism or the theme of "the hegira" in *Omoo* as circuitous evidence of Melville's awareness of Muslim thought. It is quite another thing to account for the kind and implication of such evidence within the matrices of the works or to mark out their significance in discerning Melville's relation to the traditions of religious faith and ideation.

But beyond these tendencies toward critical abstraction there are also useful areas of further investigation which can take interpretation past its fairly uniform "standard" questions respecting tradition and its scriptures, theological classics, and hegemonic themes. With scholarship in the field of religion growing more adept over recent decades in discerning camouflaged expressions of religion, at least two areas of inquiry could prove significant.

One centers on what Robert Bellah has called "Civil Religion in America" or what might be described as a national religious tradition.[5] Although a good deal of debate continues about the appropriate ways to define this phenomenon, interpreters agree that in post-revolutionary America there emerged a form of religious sensibility—drawn from older elements but figuring in the nascent republic—which cut across sectarian and doctrinal lines among religious communities, which, in a complex fusion of civil ideals and rhetoric with religious myths and meanings, invested the "idea" of America with religious meanings for a passionately faithful community. The images of "covenant" for describing the divinely elected status of American corporate life and the dreams of millennial fulfillment for projecting the spiritual destiny of the American people, the argument runs, have in many respects controlled Americans' interpretation of the national experience ever since. Although Sacvan Bercovitch has worked to elucidate the regnant *mythos* and symbols of this national religion and the ways American writers have been caught up in its "aura," and although Leo Marx has argued that the major literary figures have pitted themselves against such a "tradition," literary critics have only begun to gain entry to the nature and dynamics of American civil religion, and the scholars of religion have thus far been more concerned with pulpit and political rhetorics than with imaginative discourse. With Melville, "millennialist" passages toward the end of *Redburn*, reflections on the United States in *Mardi*, challenges to nationalism in *White-Jacket*, the "democratic prayer" and the meditations on American social existence in the "Knights and Squires" chapters of *Moby-Dick*, and the "complications" of America in *Israel Potter* (among other significant clues) suggest both Melville's ambivalence toward the "consecration" of America and the need for further inquiry into his engagement with this civil-religious tradition.

A second area of additional study focuses on the effect of secularism on religious authority. Indeed, in Melville's day this constituted a crisis of authority. Melville was, of course, keenly attuned to such collisions of "tradition" and "modernity". His demonstrable acumen with respect to this general break should make critics think that his own crucial moment in the history of religious faith deeply conditioned any recourse he might have had to earlier moments in the tradition. Melville's captivation by the theme of the Fall, his use of *Job*, and his appeal to typology are not simply evidence of the power of religious traditions, but are also signals of Melville's efforts to test these features of the tradition for what they might render or for how they might be sustained in an era which was generally bent on ignoring or repudiating them. If the contemporary renditions he created do not always clarify his personal commitments as much as critics might desire, they nonetheless testify to an historical vigilance, to a discernibly modern intensity, and to a profound, existential engagement regarding the religious crisis of his time.

Although any future study might be convincing about Melville's remarkable erudition in religious matters, they may not reveal Melville's religiousness. Significant critical work understands both the formative power of religious traditions and the fact that the questions of tradition always cross with questions of contemporary experience and self-understanding for an author; it keeps steadily in view how traditions hold the truth and propose meaning for religiously serious people and how the authority and efficacy of the tradition are always at stake for intellectually serious people. For Melville, whose seriousness on both counts seems beyond dispute, the sheer power of the tradition was not understood simply in its providing a reservoir of literary images, out of an antique time, but rather was felt in all those decisive claims with which his own "angel," his art, had to wrestle.

MELVILLE'S ART AND THEORIES OF RELIGIOUS EXPRESSION

To discuss the religious scene of Melville's age and his encounter with it in the realm of social experience is to decipher something of the author's "religious situation," and to trace out the discernible evidence of his having been influenced by the religious tradition is to piece together strands of the author's "religious consciousness" formed by primary experience and cognitive reflection. In both cases, the forms of inquiry relate to literary-historical questions, bent on detecting the conditions and resources of the literary performance at its crossroads with religious experience and religious tradition in Melville's career. Although such inquiry is crucial for understanding Melville's dealing with religion in its historical manifestations, there is another form of inquiry which is more interested in religion in "essence" and which questions how Melville's literary expression discloses his essentially religious imagination. Of course, one ought not to insist too strenuously on the distinctions between religion in its manifestations and in its essence, between its historical contents and its defining form, or between its variable appearances in practices and its abstract existence in theory, for to do so would be to "platonize" the matter utterly. The latter in each case can only be conceived on the basis of the evidence held out by the former, and the former, in each case, is chained to its historical specificity, its potentially "accidental" character, its own configurations and their necessarily narrowed range of reference.[6]

For heuristic purposes, however, the distinctions can be important because, with them, it becomes possible to consider the ways a fundamental and more general religious apprehension of reality and response to experience can be found within, behind, or beneath the historically manifest "stuff" of religion. There are a number of theories of what fundamentally constitutes religion and its characteristic modes of apprehension and response, of what figure in its centrally defining sources and features (its *sine qua non*), and of how religion can be differentiated from other modes of understanding reality. But, in general, the questions animating these theories revolve around the issues of developing models or discerning paradigms of "religion" itself which are as appropriate for and as inclusive as possible of the manifold data of religious life.

When such theories are converted to methods of approach (as with Melville), their basic questions are necessarily altered in a particular way, and they draw to themselves an additional set of complications. They grow more particular in practice because they are less concerned with clarifying the nature of religion than with the task of tracing one man's religious nature. Considering the assumptions about religion at a definitional or theoretical level, then, critical inquiry of this order calculates how Melville's imagination performs in fundamentally religious ways; in short, how his nature as a religious man is consonant with a more general model of religion. The paradigms may be proposed in terms of the unconscious patterns of behavior, traits of perception and cognition, or styles of expression, but in each case they promote a particular point of access to Melville's enlistment in the fundamentals of religious life as the theory construes them. The task grows more complex, however, because the theory at work, regardless of its originating terms and predictive approach, must also have the capacity to deal in a refined way with the special kind of evidence it faces in Melville's imaginative texts and with the knotty problem of how works of the imagination might intelligibly be thought to disclose an essentially religious, authorial nature. When St. Augustine struggles with the gnarled stuff of theodicy in the autobiographical mode of the *Confessions*, the character of the evidence and the disclosures of a primary religious sensibility are simply a good deal more overt for most theories of religion—whatever other complexities might be involved—than, say Milton's similar struggle in *Paradise Lost*. But Milton's clearly stated intention, his imaginative orientation toward mythography, and his theologically informed vision make his opus more highly expressive indeed of a paradigmatically religious nature when it is compared to Melville's *Moby-Dick* and what might be thought its peculiar theodicy. But the point, again, is that the theorist of religion who would approach Melville must be prepared, in theoretical terms, to accommodate the complications presented by imaginative expression.

Although most critics of Melville and religion would not cast the theoretical issues so directly, they are necessarily confronted with these issues in one form or another regardless of the respective theory. In dealing with such inquiry, of course, a fully elaborated inventory of definitions cannot be taken: the theories of religion which have been used are too numerous, and, in many cases, the specific theory at work has remained largely unannounced in the practical engagement with Melville. Nevertheless, broad categories appear in some characteristic theories of religion.

Some critics have used the psychological perspective on religion to gain access to Melville's works, mind, and personality. Henry A. Murray's pioneering Freudian approach reveals the frustrations of erotic life Melville suffered and released through Ahab, "the Captain of the Id," who wages battle not only against the cultural superego but also against religion and its superintending authority. According to this view, Melville, through his artistic expression, channeled that religious eroticism which his unconscious life required to deal with his aggression. In a more recent study, David Simpson also borrows from Freud, but he is more interested in the ways various psychological and anthropological theories of "fetishism" can help detect the nature of the religious energies at work in the psychic structures of imaginative expression. In *Moby-Dick*, the phallic worship, which plays a controlling part in Melville's figurative representations, reveals an "intrinsic paganism," stands at odds with the idols of contemporary civilization, and challenges important features of Romantic epistemology. Drawing on Freudian and Jungian theories, William Bysshe Stein uses psychoanalytical interpretations to illumine the poetry. The patterns of the poems stem from psychological necessities, Stein argues, as Melville's sense of the futility of existence and the delusions of historical understanding gradually yielded to the possibility of a reconciliation with life. For that, however, Melville used the poetry itself to develop his own kind of Dionysian understanding of the superiority of natural life over civilized life and of a perdurable cyclical apprehension of time over the delusions about tradition and linear history.

A similar Jungian conception that genuinely modern religious individuals always atone for their break with the failed tradition by generating new images of spiritual possibility underlies the work on Melville by Edward F. Edinger, Martin Leonard Pops, and James Baird. For Edinger, Melville made "an American Nekyia," a descent into the personal and cultural consciousness, required to plumb unspent resources. Collective life and personal life, endangered in their alienation from the archetypical "core," find the means for their own healing because of Melville's ability to dive where unnamed spiritual energies reside and to "ventilate" these psychic recesses through images in *Moby-Dick*.[7] Less devoutly Jungian in its recourse to the vocabulary of psychoanalysis, Pops's *The Melville Archetype* (1970) nevertheless follows Melville's progress as modern man "in search of a soul." The quest for the sacred, seen in these terms, involves Melville's efforts to locate that fully integrated vision of spirit in the world, a "new sacramentalism," which in turn enables his own individuation. Anticipating Pops, James Baird's work on Melville, in a more eclectic fashion, also sees Melville driven to recover a sacramentalist understanding of reality after having suffered the Protestant "cultural failure" of symbolic understanding. Melville's struggle to restore the immediacy and efficacy of the symbolic mode turned him toward what Baird calls "existential primitivism," toward traits of perception and imagination both elemental and authoritative in religious life.[8]

Others less interested in the psychological theory of religious expression have, like Baird, argued that Melville's religious nature can be detected in the ways that the structures of his literary presentations reveal fundamental structures of religious consciousness at the controlling center of his imagination. For these critics, therefore, religion is more a matter of a distinctive kind of perception and valuation of experience than of psychic sources and mechanisms. Working in the vein of literary biography, Raymond M. Weaver locates in an early study what he regards as structures of dualism in Melville's consciousness which generated a mystical craving for identity that was never completely satisfied. Ronald C. Mason, with a similar starting point, finally ascribes these forms of mind to an incipiently Christian understanding, though they were exercised more deeply in Melville than in conventional Christianity. In quite a different manner, R.W.B. Lewis (*Trials of the Word*, 1965) identifies a sense of the "authority of [the idea of] failure" as the structural crux of Melville's consciousness in the works after *Moby-Dick*: the commanding character of this perception in Melville ramifies in the deeply apocalyptic vision of human life as it edges into a darkness so total that the mind again touches on the ultimate. James E. Miller, Jr., isolates the structuring principle of "the quest" and, although asserting that Melville ought to be regarded as a psychological writer and not as a religious one, is convinced that the quest motif is expressed in essentially religious terms and answers to radically religious needs: the voyages of discovery which form the central organizing patterns of the fictions are pursuits of solidarity and love, the redemptive means that exist at a level deeper than doctrine can penetrate. For Sherrill (*Prophetic Melville*), Melville's rendering of time and his symbolic experience, as these work in vital intersections to structure the mimetic element of *Moby-Dick*, are significant indices of a consciousness committed to the reality of a numinous presence in life. In a similar vein, Vincent Buckley insists that the dramatic logic of the book pushes past anything Christian, un-Christian, or anti-Christian in its concern for a less particular metaphysics which, in turn, gives way to a reverence before the amplitude and mystery of the sheer forces of life.

Some critics have studied the evidence of Melville's language, style, and technique in ways that seek to illuminate his essentially religious character as a writer and, in this study, have used working conceptions of the unique character of religious utterance. According to R. P. Blackmur, Melville took recourse to sermonic styles in *Moby-Dick* and *Pierre*. His visionary insights could not be contained in fully dramatic modes and conventions but, rather, arrived in the strength of his "putative immensity," an aura of emotive relation and meaning created out of an intimate, weighted manipulation of works to communicate the intensities of reality past "belief" and beyond "convention." Although agreeing that the reader's sense of Melville, the man, is a result of the putative effect of the literary work, Charles Feidelson does not agree that Melville's success lay in manipulation of language to make empirically indefensible assertions about reality. For Feidelson, rather, Melville took the voyage of the "symbolistic" imagination in which the writer, like his Ishmael, accepts the provisional life created by the conviction that "some certain significance lurks in all things" (ch. 99). This acceptance demands the capacity of vision to see what inheres in reality and requires the symbolic capacity to discover and discern more than the rhetorical capacity to devise the meaning of its encounter with experience. James L. Guetti is interested in the situation of language in this encounter. Concentrating on *Moby-Dick*, he thinks that Melville's profound awareness of an ineffable spiritual truth is revealed in the perspectives on language and imagination which characterize Ishmael's responses to experience. The "special vocabularies" the narrator employs to define the whale all hit limits beyond which they cannot go, but Ishmael's "failures" finally succeed to give partial form to the ineffable as his "wild suggestings" and objective descriptions begin to merge, as his fabulous and expansive vocabulary develops in a way to impart to it a literal reality. For John Seelye, the key to Melville's vision of the mysterious flux of eternity is to be gained by studying the diagrammatic contrasts, the stylistic indirections, the syntactic qualifications, with which the author posed viewpoints: the quests of the various narrator/protagonists, understood in the context of the diagram, are heroic in romantic terms but ultimately quixotic and ironic as they suggest some *discordia concors* only to contradict it.

Still another and related form of critical inquiry concerns the cognitive dimension of religion or what might be called the operations of "metaphysics." Although critics of this stripe have necessarily attended to structures and stylistics, they have been most keenly interested in the ways Melville's works, in depicting specific elements of experience, emerge from an encompassing vision of reality. This has meant, in some interpretations, a concentration on the particular "worlds" depicted in the fictions as those worlds are predicated on a world-view or a cosmology. In other interpretations, the attention has been on the methods Melville used in his depictions as they reveal his epistemological assumptions. For A. D. Van Nostrand, a movement from the particular to the cosmological can be located in the ways that specific clusters of events in *Moby-Dick* are linked: in each, "the essence of the action is the contradicting man contradicted by an inscrutable universe" (p. 113), and, in their repetition, they magnify the conflict to propose it as a universal principle of reality. While F. O. Matthiessen's *American Rennaissance* (1941) had earlier identified a similar sense of tragic conflict at the center of Melville's vision, Matthiessen argues that Melville understood a still deeper cadence in the cosmos, an equilibrium sustained in the world which balanced the forces of tragedy. Edwin M. Eigner isolates "the metaphysical novel" as a special category of narrative in the hands of Dickens, Bulwer, Hawthorne, and Melville, and argues that it purposefully presents the realm of experience in materialistic and positivistic terms only to demolish and replace that conception of reality with the perspectives of a romantic and mystical epistemology. Also thinking that Melville began with the world of material existence, Edgar A. Dryden proposes that Melville's art of fiction was consistently undertaken in an acutely self-conscious manner: wary throughout his career of his implication in a world of lies, Melville's evasions of facts for the unifying elements of fiction emerged from and expressed a "metaphysics of emptiness," a recognition that left him, according to Dryden, convinced of the unreality of his fictions and of the inability of fiction to speak the truth.

Among the critical ways and means for thinking about Melville in terms of the theories of religion, then, the efforts have necessarily had to involve the question of how literary expression might be thought the vehicle for essentially religious drives, traits, habits, or concerns. Whatever the perspective in understanding religion—as a function of psychological life, as a category of certain kinds of consciousness and perception, as an especially charged and referential kind or usage of language, or as a cognitive effort to apprehend and express reality in essential terms—the case of Melville has proved both abundant and complex. Despite such "divisions," the most successful critical treatments have frequently combined several of the theoretical perspectives and their corollary notions of imaginative life and expression, and they have displayed the kind of sensitivity that permits Melville's unique density and complexity of expression to have an amending effect on the perspectives brought to bear.

Beyond the kinds of short-sightedness detected when a univocal perspective has been applied too slavishly to Melville's works, however, there are other problems or at least limitations. Two should be mentioned here as representative of some unnecessary abbreviated critical practices. First, especially among psychological theorists, the inclination has occasionally been to understand literature exclusively in its expressive dimension and to see all literary expression in those terms, without due regard, that is, for its formal dimensions—its properties of narration, plot, and genre. Such an approach, of course, has the virtues of its own intensity, but it delivers a Melville whose religiousness is crimped. And the point is that some additional discriminations with respect to literary forms might well yield richer insights into the psychological and metaphysical conventions. For a second, obverse instance, the theoretical perspective has in some cases been too constricted in its attention to the formal properties through which the operations of the metaphysics or the substances of consciousness appear. In this, the criticism has at different points approached the literary works in terms of their interior, unifying logic with Melville's religiousness made too much a matter of what the formal devices of the works represent in an iconic fashion. Although efforts of this critical character can frequently trick out hidden structures within the autotelic "unity" of the work, the tendency to consider the literary object as purely self-referential takes Melville's religiousness out of the world and confines it within the well-wrought text. What is missing is the situation of Melville's art in the densities of literary, religious, and cultural history—that is, in the contexts and circumstances that produce the conditions for consciousness. Surmounting these two general kinds of critical limitations—the one not sufficiently keen to the formal character of literature, the other captive to it—requires a recognition that the tasks of studying Melville in these various terms are commensurable and indeed critically reciprocal. A symposium of viewpoints which is historical and theoretical, substantial and formal, can enliven and enrich the inquiry by bringing it out of lonely standpoints.[9]

MELVILLE AND RELIGION

After an extended discussion of the varieties and complexities involved in posing the question of "Melville and Religion," one might well grow irritable for conclusive answers in some respects. But, as with the work of the narrator of *Billy Budd*, no "architectural finial" is to be found: the "ragged edges" remain, and the question deepens. The effort to place Melville in his historical religious perspective generally leaves us with the portrait of a restive man, driven by questions of ultimacy and discontented with the religious paradigms of the age. Informed about and formed by Western religious traditions, he nevertheless tested and challenged the most fundamental metaphors, myths, and meanings of Judaeo-Christian understanding on the basis of criteria forged out of the respect he possessed for his own experience and imagination. That experience and imagination took him into an encounter with old, unnamed spiritual energies and equipped him for visionary flights, created a craving for community and drove him into isolation, presented him with images of "attainable felicity," and forced him to see the human record of failure. Compelled to develop a special acumen in understanding and relating to reality which is the common trait of religious sensibility, he sought in his art to imagine that "something more" which William James designated as the object of religious desire and sought with his art the prophetic voice "to speak the truth."

The character of Melville's speaking in and to his age extends the force of his speaking beyond his age. Perhaps instinctively, he seemed aware that his voice would find its auditors: slightly more than six months before his death he scored in his copy of *The Wisdom of Life* Schopenhauer's observation that "the more a man belongs to posterity, in other words, to humanity in general, the more of an alien he is to his contemporaries; since his work is not meant for them as such, but only for them in so far as they form part of mankind at large" (*Mel. Log*, pp. 332–33). Never having lost his conviction about the "common continent of man," Melville spoke to the last out of a sense of the continuity of human conversation about the great mysteries and out of the belief that "the subtlest secrets of the sea" awaited those willing to go out far enough and in deep enough.

The fact that Melville continues to draw critics into conversation about religious ideas and meanings in part gives him classic stature in the tradition, and the conversation with the classics does not close any more than it yields conclusive answers. What it holds out, rather, and what generations of critics learn to relish is the invitation to spend time with a mind and imagination in action, in frequent ambiguity, in full engagement. If the expressions of this mind and imagination do not possess the formal and precise austerity of fully systematic thought to be captured and categorized in permanent conclusions, we should not be disappointed—unless, that is, we are convinced, along with Starry Vere, that " 'forms, measured forms are everything.' "

NOTES

1. The distinction between the personal experience of the supernatural and the social experience of religion was, of course, insisted on steadfastly by William James in his *Varieties of Religious Experience*. Although James disdained the social experience of religion as derived and "secondary," most recent students of religion respect the power and importance of that experience. In a recent study, for instance, Larry D. Shinn provides a useful introduction to the dynamics and claims of such experience. Rudolf Otto's work remains the classic treatment of the character of the personal encounter with the holy.

2. Critics who intermittently discuss Melville's "brushes" with Transcendentalism are too numerous to mention here, but students should consult Perry Miller (*Nature's Nation*, 1967) and Michael J. Hoffman for representative viewpoints. More recent work by Catherine Albanese (*Corresponding Motion*, 1977),

who discusses Transcendentalism as a *religious* movement, might provoke new inquiry in this area by students of Melville.

3. On Melville and Darwin, see H. Bruce Franklin ("Island," 1967) and Benjamin Lease for especially interesting views.

4. In placing Melville in relation to the American theological scene in the age, for instance, one might well begin by considering the work of his contemporary, Horace Bushnell, who, in less anguished ways than Melville, suffered the tensions between liberal and orthodox views, who has been discussed in terms of his "romanticism," who distrusted the Transcendentalist alternative, and whose work on religious language grappled with its symbolic character. David L. Smith offers a useful introduction to Bushnell and the secondary literature in these regards.

5. This key article appeared first in the Winter issue of *Daedalus* in 1967 and has since been widely reprinted (see Russell E. Richey and Donald G. Jones). Studies of American civil religion are scattered, but two collections of essays—one authored by Robert Bellah and Phillip E. Hammond, another edited by Richey and Jones—supply some representative ideas of and approaches to the phenomenon. John F. Wilson points out the issues and complications in the "civil religion" thesis, and Catherine Albanese (*Sons of the Fathers*, 1976) provides the most extensive study of the emergence and character of civil religion in colonial and revolutionary America. In a recent work, Charles Mabee discusses the terms in which *Moby-Dick* might be thought a biblically founded critique of this American *mythos*.

6. Students of religion are familiar with this set of issues, whose full complexity cannot be discussed at any length here. For a succinct outline of several issues that face those concerned about "theory and method" in religious studies, see Charles Elliott Vernoff, and for a more extended and subtle exploration of some of these matters, see Paul Wiebe.

7. H. Bruce Franklin (*Wake of the Gods*, 1963) and Gerard M. Sweeney also concentrate on Melville and myth, but they are less intent on his unconscious retrieval of archetypal symbols and patterns than on his intellectual and self-conscious appropriations. Viola Sachs's recent book argues that Melville was a mythographer whose "double text" in *Moby-Dick* corresponds at once to the mythic life of Christian civilization and to the primeval landscape of the aboriginal New World.

8. The theme of "primitivism" and the characterization of the primitive Melville are approached from different angles in Klaus Lanzinger and Ray B. West, Jr.

9. The call for such a recognition—to those bent on interpreting Melville's works in the light of some theoretical perspective on or assumptions about the nature of religion—suggests the need for literary criticism to extend itself more fully toward work in the field of "religion and literature," especially that work which assays the possibilities of the field at the level of theory and method. Four collections of essays represent a beginning point, for they contain some of the foundational work in the field, broad samples of the variety of ideas and approaches, and key bibliographic guides to other works. An early collection, edited by Stanley Romaine Hopper, concentrates on the literature of the modern period and presents essays under the headings of religion and the artist's situation,

religion and the artist's means, and religion and the artist's beliefs. More specifically concerned with the nature and terms of a "Christian Poetics," Nathan A. Scott, Jr., gathers essays that inquire into the relationships between religion and literature and theology and literary criticism, with emphases on aesthetics, imagination, evaluation, belief, and form. The critical anthology edited by Giles B. Gunn contains essays on the approaches to the relationship of literature and religion afforded by modern critical orientations, on the religious dimensions of literary presentation, and on the appropriation of literature by religious thought. A more recent general collection, under the editorship of Robert Detweiler, provides an entrance in its essays to key problems, movements, and emphases of the field and to some of the richest areas of current inquiry. Taken together, then, these anthologies offer sketches at least of some working models in religion and literature and of the general parameters which belong to that field. Its intellectual and methodological prospects, posed in theoretical terms, can lend the elements of an increased self-consciousness and the location of cross-disciplinary interpretive standpoints to critics who want to engage the questions of the religious character and dimensions of Melville's literary art.

WORKS CITED

Aaron, Daniel. "Melville and the Missionaries." *New England Quarterly* 8 (September 1935): 404–408.

Abrams, M. H. *Natural Supernaturalism*. New York: W. W. Norton, 1971.

Ahlstrom, Sydney E. *A Religious History of the American People*. New Haven, Conn.: Yale University Press, 1972.

———, ed. *Theology in America: The Major Protestant Voices*. Indianapolis, Ind.: Bobbs-Merrill, 1967.

Albanese, Catherine. *Corresponding Motion: Transcendental Religion and the New America*. Philadelphia: Temple University Press, 1977.

———. *Sons of the Fathers: The Civil Religion of the American Revolution*. Philadelphia: Temple University Press, 1976.

Anderson, Charles Roberts. *Melville in the South Seas*. New York: Columbia University Press, 1939.

Baird, James. *Ishmael: The Symbolic Mode in Primitivism*. Baltimore: Johns Hopkins University Press, 1956.

Barbour, John D. *Tragedy as a Critique of Virtue: The Novel and Ethical Reflection*. Chico, Calif.: Scholars Press, 1984.

Bellah, Robert, and Hammond, Phillip E. *Varieties of Civil Religion*. New York: Harper, 1980.

Bercovitch, Sacvan. *The American Jeremiad*. Madison: University of Wisconsin Press, 1978.

———. "The Biblical Basis of the American Myth." In *The Bible and American Arts and Letters*. Ed. Giles Gunn. Philadelphia: Fortress Press, 1983, pp. 221–29.

———. *The Puritan Origins of the American Self*. New Haven, Conn.: Yale University Press, 1975.

Bernard, Kenneth. "Melville's *Mardi* and the Second Loss of Paradise." *Loch Haven Review* No. 7 (1965): 23–30.

Blackmur, R. P. "The Craft of Herman Melville: A Putative Statement." In *The Lion and the Honeycomb*. New York: Harcourt, 1955, pp. 124–44.

Bozeman, T. Dwight. *Protestants in an Age of Science: The Baconian Ideal and Antebellum Religious Thought*. Chapel Hill: University of North Carolina Press, 1977.

Braswell, William. *Melville's Religious Thought*. Durham, N.C.: Duke University Press, 1943.

Browne, Ray B. *Melville's Drive to Humanism*. Lafayette, Ind.: Purdue University Press, 1971.

Brumm, Ursula. *American Thought and Religious Typology*. Trans. John Hoaglund. New Brunswick, N.J.: Rutgers University Press, 1970.

———. "The Figure of Christ in American Literature." *Partisan Review* 24 (Summer 1957): 403–12.

Buckley, Vincent. *Poetry and the Sacred*. London: Chatto & Windus, 1968.

Cady, Edwin. " 'As Through a Glass Darkly': The Bible in the Nineteenth-Century American Novel." In *The Bible and American Arts and Letters*. Ed. Giles Gunn. Philadelphia: Fortress Press, 1983, pp. 33–55.

Detweiler, Robert, ed. *Art/Literature/Religion: Life on the Borders*. Chico, Calif.: Scholars Press, 1983.

Dillingham, William B. *An Artist in the Rigging: The Early Work of Herman Melville*. Athens: University of Georgia Press, 1972.

Dryden, Edgar A. *Melville's Thematics of Form: The Great Art of Telling the Truth*. Baltimore: Johns Hopkins University Press, 1968.

Edinger, Edward F. *Melville's Moby-Dick: A Jungian Commentary*. New York: New Directions, 1978.

Eigner, Edwin M. *The Metaphysical Novel in England and America: Dickens, Bulwer, Hawthorne, Melville*. Berkeley: University of California Press, 1978.

Feidelson, Charles. *Symbolism and American Literature*. Chicago: University of Chicago Press, 1953.

Fogle, Richard Harter. "*Billy Budd*: The Order of the Fall." *Nineteenth-Century Fiction* 15 (December 1960): 189–205.

Franklin, H. Bruce. "The Island Worlds of Darwin and Melville." *Centennial Review* 11 (Summer 1967): 353–70.

———. *The Wake of the Gods: Melville's Mythology*. Stanford, Calif.: Stanford University Press, 1963.

Frederick, John T. *The Darkened Sky: Nineteenth-Century American Novelists and Religion*. Notre Dame, Ind.: University of Notre Dame Press, 1969.

Freimarck, Vincent. "Mainmast as Crucifix in *Billy Budd*." *Modern Language Notes* 72 (November 1957): 496–97.

Gilmore, Michael T. *The Middle Way: Puritanism and Ideology in American Romantic Fiction*. New Brunswick, N.J.: Rutgers University Press, 1977.

Glick, Wendell. "Expediency and Absolute Morality in 'Billy Budd.' " *PMLA* 68 (March 1953): 103–10.

Guetti, James L. *The Limits of Metaphor: A Study of Melville, Conrad, and Faulkner*. Ithaca, N.Y.: Cornell University Press, 1967.

Gunn, Giles B., ed. *Literature and Religion*. New York: Harper, 1971.

Haroutunian, Joseph. *Piety Versus Moralism: The Passing of the New England Theology*. New York: Henry Holt, 1932.

Hatch, Nathan O., and Noll, Mark A., eds. *The Bible in America*. New York: Oxford University Press, 1982.

Herbert, T. Walter, Jr. "Calvinism and Cosmic Evil in *Moby-Dick*." *PMLA* 84 (1969): 1613–19.

———. *Marquesan Encounters: Melville and the Meaning of Civilization*. Cambridge, Mass.: Harvard University Press, 1980.

———. *Moby-Dick and Calvinism: A World Dismantled*. New Brunswick, N.J.: Rutgers University Press, 1977.

Hoffman, Daniel. "Moby Dick: Jonah's Whale or Job's?" *Sewanee Review* 69 (Spring 1961): 205–24.

Hoffman, Michael J. "The Anti-Transcendentalism of *Moby-Dick*." *Georgia Review* 23 (Spring 1969): 3–16.

Holman, C. Hugh. "The Reconciliation of Ishmael: *Moby-Dick* and the Book of Job." *South Atlantic Quarterly* 57 (Autumn 1958): 477–90.

Hopper, Stanley Romaine, ed. *Spiritual Problems in Contemporary Literature*. New York: Harper, 1957.

Isani, Mukhtar Ali. "Zoroastrianism and the Fire Symbolism in *Moby-Dick*." *American Literature* 44 (1972): 385–97.

Kerr, Howard. *Mediums and Spirit-Rappers and Roaring Radicals: Spiritualism in American Literature, 1850–1900*. Urbana: University of Illinois Press, 1972.

Lanzinger, Klaus. *Primitivismus und Naturalismus im Prosaschafen Herman Melvilles*. Innsbruck: Universitätsverlag Wagner, 1959.

Lawrence, D. H. *Studies in Classic American Literature*. New York: Thomas Seltzer, 1923.

Lease, Benjamin. "Two Sides to a Tortoise: Darwin and Melville in the Pacific." *The Personalist* 49 (1968): 531–39.

Lewis, R.W.B. *The American Adam*. Chicago: University of Chicago Press, 1955.

———. *Trials of the Word: Essays in American Literature and the Humanistic Tradition*. New Haven, Conn.: Yale University Press, 1965.

Mabee, Charles. *Reimagining America: A Theological Critique of the American Mythos and Biblical Hermeneutics*. Macon, Ga.: Mercer University Press, 1985.

Marty, Martin E. *Righteous Empire: The Protestant Experience in America*. New York: Dial Press, 1970.

Marx, Leo. "The Uncivil Response of American Writers to Civil Religion in America." In *American Civil Religion*. Ed. Russell E. Richey and Donald G. Jones. New York: Harper, 1974.

Mason, Ronald C. *The Spirit above the Dust: A Study of Herman Melville*. London: Lehmann, 1951.

Matthiessen, F. O. *American Renaissance: Art and Expression in the Age of Emerson and Whitman*. New York: Oxford University Press, 1941.

May, John R. *Toward a New Earth: Apocalypse in the American Novel*. Notre Dame, Ind.: University of Notre Dame Press, 1972.

Miller, James E., Jr. *Quests Surd and Absurd: Essays in American Literature*. Chicago: University of Chicago Press, 1967.

Miller, Perry. *Errand into the Wilderness*. New York: Harper, 1964.

———. "Melville and Transcendentalism." *Virginia Quarterly Review* 29 (Autumn 1953): 556–75. Rpt. in *Nature's Nation*. Cambridge, Mass.: Belknap Press of Harvard University, 1967.

————. *The Raven and the Whale: The War of Words and Wits in the Era of Poe and Melville*. New York: Harcourt, Brace, 1956.

Mitchell, Charles. "Melville and the Spurious Truth of Legalism." *Centennial Review* 12 (March 1968): 110–26.

Moorman, Charles. "Melville's Pierre and the Fortunate Fall." *American Literature* 25 (March 1953): 13–30.

Murray, Henry A. "In Nomine Diaboli." *New England Quarterly* 24 (December 1951): 435–52.

Oates, J. C. "Melville and the Manichean Illusion." *Texas Studies in Literature and Language* 4 (Spring 1962): 117–29.

Otto, Rudolf. *The Idea of the Holy*. Trans. John W. Harvey. New York: Oxford University Press, 1958.

Percival, M. O. *A Reading of Moby-Dick*. Chicago: University of Chicago Press, 1950.

Pops, Martin Leonard. *The Melville Archetype*. Kent, Ohio: Kent State University Press, 1970.

Rampersad, Arnold. *Melville's Israel Potter: A Pilgrimage and a Progress*. Bowling Green, Ohio: Bowling Green University Popular Press, 1969.

Reich, C. A. "The Tragedy of Justice in *Billy Budd*." *Yale Review* 56 (Spring 1967): 368–89.

Reynolds, David S. *Faith in Fiction: The Emergence of Religious Literature in America*. Cambridge, Mass.: Harvard University Press, 1981.

Richey, Russell E., and Donald G. Jones, eds. *American Civil Religion*. New York: Harper, 1974.

Rosenfeld, William. "Uncertain Faith: Queequeg's Coffin and Melville's Use of the Bible." *Texas Studies in Literature and Language* 7 (Winter 1966): 317–27.

Ruland, Richard. "Melville and the Fortunate Fall: Typee as Eden." *Nineteenth-Century Fiction* 23 (December 1968): 312–23.

Sachs, Viola. *The Game of Creation: The Primeval Unlettered Language of Moby-Dick; or, the Whale*. Paris: Editions de la Maison des sciences de l'homme, 1982.

Schneidau, Herbert N. *Sacred Discontent: The Bible and Western Tradition*. Baton Rouge: Louisiana State University Press, 1976.

Scott, Nathan A., Jr., ed. *The New Orpheus: Essays Toward a Christian Poetic*. New York: Sheed & Ward, 1964.

Seelye, John. *Melville: The Ironic Diagram*. Evanston, Ill.: Northwestern University Press, 1970.

Sherrill, Rowland A. " 'Flood-Gates of the Wonder-World': Melville's Religious Drive and the Generic Question of *Moby-Dick*." *Journal of the American Academy of Religion* 45 (December Supplement 1977): 1227–62.

————. *The Prophetic Melville: Experience, Transcendence, and Tragedy*. Athens: University of Georgia Press, 1979.

Shinn, Larry D. *Two Sacred Worlds: Experience and Structure in the World's Religions*. Nashville, Tenn.: Abingdon, 1977.

Shurr, William H. *The Mystery of Iniquity: Melville as Poet, 1857–1891*. Lexington: University Press of Kentucky, 1972.

————. *Rappaccini's Children: American Writers in a Calvinist World*. Lexington: University Press of Kentucky, 1981.

Simpson, David. *Fetishism and Imagination: Dickens, Melville, Conrad.* Baltimore: Johns Hopkins University Press, 1982.

Smith, David L. *Symbolism and Growth: The Religious Thought of Horace Bushnell.* Chico, Calif.: Scholars Press, 1981.

Sollors, Werner. "Dr. Benjamin Franklin's Celestial Telegraph, or Indian Blessings to Gas-Lit American Drawing Rooms." *American Quarterly* 35 (Winter 1983): 459–80.

Stein, William Bysshe. *The Poetry of Melville's Late Years: Time, History, Myth, and Religion.* Albany: State University of New York Press, 1970.

Stewart, Randall. *American Literature and Christian Doctrine.* Baton Rouge: Louisiana State University Press, 1958.

Stout, Janis. "Melville's Use of the Book of Job." *Nineteenth-Century Fiction* 25 (June 1970): 69–83.

Sweeney, Gerard M. *Melville's Use of Classical Mythology.* Amsterdam: Rodopi, 1975.

Thompson, G. R., and V. L. Lokke. *Ruined Eden of the Present: Hawthorne, Poe, and Melville.* West Lafayette, Ind.: Purdue University Press, 1980.

Thompson, Lawrance R. *Melville's Quarrel with God.* Princeton, N.J.: Princeton University Press, 1952.

Trimpi, Helen P. "Demonology and Witchcraft in *Moby-Dick*." *Journal of the History of Ideas* 30 (October-December 1969): 543–62.

Van Nostrand, A. D. *Everyman His Own Poet.* New York: McGraw-Hill, 1968.

Vernoff, Charles Elliott. "Naming the Game: A Question of the Field." *Bulletin of the Council on the Study of Religion* 14 (1983): 109–13.

Walker, Franklin. *Irreverent Pilgrims: Melville, Browne, and Mark Twain in the Holy Land.* Seattle: University of Washington Press, 1974.

Weaver, Raymond M. *Herman Melville: Mariner and Mystic.* New York: Doran, 1921.

Welch, Claude. *Protestant Thought in the Nineteenth Century, 1799–1870.* New Haven, Conn.: Yale University Press, 1972.

Werge, Thomas. "Luther and Melville on the Masks of God." *Melville Society Extracts* No. 22 (May 1975): 6–7.

———. "*Moby-Dick* and the Calvinist Tradition." *Studies in the Novel* 1 (Winter 1969): 484–506.

West, Ray B., Jr. "Primitivism in Melville." *Prairie Schooner* 30 (Winter 1956): 369–85.

Wiebe, Paul. "An Encyclopedia of Religious Studies." *Journal of the American Academy of Religion* (1984): 343–57.

Wilson, John F. *Public Religion in American Culture.* Philadelphia: Temple University Press, 1979.

Wright, Nathalia. *Melville's Use of the Bible.* Durham, N.C.: Duke University Press, 1949.

———. "Moby Dick: Jonah's or Job's Whale?" *American Literature* 37 (May 1965): 190–95.

17

MELVILLE AND THE MIND

Martin Bickman

> Perhaps the principal creative work of the last three decades has
> been the critical rediscovery and reinterpretation of Melville's *Moby
> Dick* and its promotion, step by step, to the position of national epic.
> —Malcolm Cowley, *The Literary Situation*

Cowley's mention of both creativity and rediscovery raises, yet blurs, the
issue of whether we are constantly creating Melville in our own image
or uncovering aspects of the work and the person that become apparent
only as our own angles of vision broaden and multiply. Although we
cannot draw distinctly the line where one rainbow color ends and another
begins, we can see both processes interweavingly at work in the making
of the psychological Melville. Unless we are either complete solipsists or
complete positivists, we can see our own reflections as well as Melville's
in the large body of psychological criticism that surrounds him—larger
than that around any other American author.

This interplay between remaking and revealing, projection and discovery, is seen in what can be called the Doubloon aspect of Melville's
best work, the ambiguous, open-ended nature of its languages and structures, that encourages a number of specific interpretations and general
approaches. Although some theorists see similar qualities in all literature,

*I would like to thank my research assistant on this project, Janet Somerville, whose
own dissertation on writing and reading in *Moby-Dick* is a substantial contribution to Melville
studies. I am also grateful to Henry A. Murray for discussing informally with me several
aspects of this chapter.

even all discourse, Melville's texts in particular are like another of his most famous images—the coffin lifebuoy that embraces such opposites as life and death, inscribed with visible yet ultimately unreadable hieroglyphics. These markings copied by Queequeg from his own body suggest the ways in which we ourselves can embody wisdom but cannot articulate it fully, the ways in which we ourselves are the answer to the Sphinx's riddle but cannot speak it. The coffin lifebuoy has form, but it is also the hollowness, the undefined emptiness at its core, that lets it support life. The very awareness that there is more to our being than can be expressed in words charges those words with ambivalence, incompleteness, multiplicity, and resonance.

But we must also acknowledge a more intrinsic factor, the tantalizingly close connections between the life and the work. Although the mistakes of earlier biographers and critics in reading the novels too literally as autobiography have now been noted and largely corrected, the more subterranean symbolic connections continue to allure. Indeed, the more oblique connections are even more fascinating and generate, of course, much more speculation and interpretation. The single fact, for instance, that Melville's father may have had an illegitimate daughter engenders limitless ways to understand the impact on the son and his fictions.

Beyond direct and oblique relations with the life, however, there is a more general inherent psychological dimension in Melville's work. His thematic concerns include the complexities and self-conflicts in human motives and actions, the psychological roots of religion and metaphysics, the relation of language and narrative to consciousness. One frequently reads in the critical literature that Melville anticipates Freud and Jung, but this formulation is slightly patronizing and out of focus; it is more just and accurate to see Freud as post-Romantic or post-Melvillean, for Freud and his followers did not discover the unconscious, but systematized and consolidated much that had been already learned in the nineteenth century and before. Melville was immersed in and contributed to the currents of thought that helped produce psychoanalysis— the Enlightenment demystification of religion that merges into Blake's formulation that "all deities reside within the human breast," the post-Kantian emphasis on the shaping powers of the mind in perception, the Romantic fascination with depths and with the symbol as a way to apprehend these depths. One of the tasks of this chapter is to explore Robert Milder's hint that "Melville has more to tell us about psychology than psychology can tell us about him" ("Knowing Melville," p. 99).

This chapter begins with a brief look at Melville himself as a psychological critic and some of the early intuitions in the first decade of the Melville Revival of the psychological aspects of the fiction. The second section examines the career of Henry A. Murray, the key figure in relations between Melville and psychology. Murray is engaged in two main activities—a detailed, factual biography written from psychological perspectives and an elucidation of the works. These two activities have been continued by other hands but unfortunately often without Murray's attempt at coordination and synthesis, so sections three and four are concerned separately with psychoanalyses of the works and psychobiographies of the man. The fifth section deals with some of the more recent and promising ways psychology and literature have been combined, and gives what is necessarily but the draught of a draught as to how these leads might be pursued.

A LONG FOREGROUND

Given the psychological bent of Melville's mind, it may be most fruitful to begin examining the psychological criticism on Melville with his own criticism on Shakespeare in "Hawthorne and His *Mosses*":

But it is those deep far-away things in him; those occasional flashings-forth of the intuitive Truth in him; those short, quick probings at the very axis of reality:—these are the things that make Shakespeare, Shakespeare. Through the mouths of the dark characters of Hamlet, Timon, Lear, and Iago, he craftily says, or sometimes insinuates the things, which we feel to be so terrifically true, that it were all but madness for any good man, in his own proper character, to utter, or even hint of them. Tormented into desperation, Lear the frantic King tears off the mask, and speaks the sane madness of vital truth. ("*Mosses*," pp. 541–42)

The basic duality here involving, on one side, appearance, conventionality, sanity, and, on the other, a reality that is more authentic but also mad and maddening is bodied forth in related spatial images: near/far, surface/depth, mask/face. Implicit in the imagery is the notion that while art partakes of both aspects, it conceals while it reveals, or rather gives us a way of revealing that is more guarded and thus more effective. The artist is at once a truth-teller and a dissembler—a dissembler, in fact, in order to tell the truth. As Emily Dickinson writes: "The Truth must dazzle gradually/Or every man be blind—" (#1129, p. 507). We also see in the passage above a yoking—some would say a confusion—between psychological and metaphysical truth, between a capitalized universal Truth in the Platonic sense of a less accessible "far-away" ontological realm and a "deep" personal, subjective truth that varies to some extent from mind to mind. While this ambiguity has sometimes been confusing—to Melville and to his readers and critics—it has also been fruitful, leading to an exploration, particularly in *Moby-Dick* and after, of the psychological roots of belief, to a more holistic examination of the mind where affect and intellect, lived experience and idea, are related.

D. H. Lawrence, who at the very dawn of the Melville Revival wrote the first book on American literature with a depth and intensity equal to its subject, views Melville and his contemporaries in ways strikingly similar to the way Melville views Shakespeare and Hawthorne: "You *must* look through the surface of American art, and see the inner diabolism of the symbolic meaning. Otherwise it is all mere childishness" (*Studies*, p. 83). Beneath the appearances of crowd-pleasing geniality and smiling innocence there are disruptive, dark forces, barely discernible. In Lawrence's formulations, however, the dimension of depth is usually hidden from the authors as well, so in trusting the tale and not the teller, in seeing beyond the masks of "blue-eyed darling Nathaniel" (p. 83) and company, it is the critic who uncovers for the first time what gives the work its vitality and ultimate significance.

Lawrence devotes two of the late chapters in *Studies in Classic American Literature* (1923) to Melville's works, one on *Typee* and *Omoo*, the other on *Moby-Dick*. In the first of these chapters, Lawrence, knowingly or not, echoes the end of Chapter 50 in *Moby-Dick* in viewing the Pacific and its islands as "aeons older" than the rest of the world (p. 132), sleeping, preconscious, but also dreaming, "idylls: nightmares" (p. 133). Melville was at his best and truest when he wrote from this realm, which is linked to "a sort of dream-self, so that events which he relates as actual fact have indeed a far deeper reference to his own soul, his own inner life" (p. 134). More specifically, *Typee* recounts the struggles and paradoxes of a man trying to recoil from Western civilization, even from consciousness itself, but realizing in this very movement that it is impossible: "we cannot turn the current of our life backwards, back towards their soft warm twilight and uncreate mud" (p. 137).

As one would expect, Lawrence is impatient with Melville's conscious philosophizing in *Moby-Dick*, which he sees as that of "rather a tiresome New Englander of the ethical mystical-transcendentalist sort," and praises, in the form of many extended quotations, the writer who captures so well "the sheer naked slidings of the elements" (p. 146). Yet Lawrence detects a psychological allegory in the novel, a reading that, for whatever truth it contains, gives too Lawrentian a twist to Melville's subtle and contradictory accumulation of associations; the whale, for Lawrence, is "the last phallic being of the white man. Hunted into the death of upper consciousness and the ideal will" (p. 160). Lawrence's psychology is, of course, distinctively his own, but it can be viewed as an amalgam of inverted Freudianism (where *ego* is, there *id* shall be) and an earthy Jungianism in which a general "blood-consciousness" transcends our individual minds and selves. And yet if Lawrence's interpretation is finally oversimplifying, his essays are a labor of deep recognition and affinity to a man like himself strongly allured to the primal, the unconscious, but unwilling to abandon his penetrating intellect in its quest.

Surprisingly, Lawrence mentions Melville's most Lawrentian book *Pierre* only in passing, boiling its convolutions down to a maxim: "the more you try to be good the more you make a mess of things" (p. 142), so it remained for others to suggest what a psychological book it is. Raymond M. Weaver in the first modern biography of Melville, a book Lawrence had read, notes that "in its probings into unsuspected determinants from unconsciousness, it is prophetic of some of the most recent findings in psychology" (p. 341). Toward the end of the decade, interest in *Pierre* accelerated, partially caused by and partially reflected in reissues of the book by Dutton in 1929 and by Knopf in 1930. Although the editor of the Dutton edition, John Brooks Moore, stressed in his introduction the aspect of social criticism, it is the psychological dimension that reviewers and critics such as Carl Van Vechten and Lewis Mumford repeatedly underscored. A comment by S. Foster Damon is typical: "Melville was interested in the thing [incest] for its own puzzle; and that one shift of emphasis makes all the difference. His book is no longer drama but psychology; the gap between him and his contemporary, Hawthorne, is the gap that separates Calvin and Freud. Melville had learned that the problems of the soul are not to be analyzed horizontally in the Conscious, but vertically in the Subconscious. He had learned that dreams are worth fishing for" (p. 116).

This revisionary view culminates in E. L. Grant Watson's 1930 article on *Pierre*, an analysis that places the book at the center of Melville, not only as greater than *Moby-Dick* but even "a far better artistic whole" with a "style less flamboyant" (p. 232). Here is not the place to follow Watson's psychological allegory based on a metaphysics compounded of Neoplatonism, Gnosticism, and Jung, but it is relevant to note that he appropriates Melville's language—and with it the wavering between psychology and philosophy—from the *"Mosses"* essay:

[Melville's] greatness as a psychologist is not to be surpassed by any other writer. There are deep, far-away things in him, and his greatness is revealed not only in what he writes but in what he leaves unwritten. He suggests more than can be written; and as this world of Becoming is a symbol of God's vaster transcendental Universe of Being, so Melville's books shadow-forth and are themselves symbols of that same transcendental universe. His works indicate remote distances beyond actual expression, and of these distances we become increasingly aware as we go deeper into *Pierre*. (pp. 208–209)

Distances and depths merge and converge, but Watson's language suggests destinations as well as directions. The oxymoronic phrase "shadow-forth," of course, is not from the *"Mosses"* essay but from the devastatingly agnostic last paragraph of "The Whiteness of the Whale" (*MD*, p. 169), an irony suggesting how criticism tends to conventionalize and stabilize meanings, turning images into ontologies. It remained for Henry Murray to separate psychology from metaphysics in *Pierre* so that they could then be related more clearly and productively.

HENRY MURRAY AND THE UNWRITTEN LIFE

Henry A. Murray, M.D., Ph.D. (in biochemistry), has published only four major pieces on Melville, and those relatively late in his long career—a hundred page introduction to his edition of *Pierre* (1949); an essay on *Moby-Dick*, "In Nomine Diaboli" (1951); "Bartleby and I" (1966); and "Dead to the World: The Passions of Herman Melville" (1967). And yet without him, the three factors mentioned at the beginning of this essay—the Doubloon aspect of Melville's texts, the subterranean connections between the life and the books, and Melville's own position as a psychologist—might have remained dissolved, uncrystallized, in a boggy, soggy solution. Murray's centrality stems from his simultaneous excellence and influence in two fields, his vocation as professor of psychology and director of the Harvard Psychological Clinic and his avocation as one of the first and most avid scholars in the Melville Revival. In a review of Moore's 1929 edition of *Pierre*, Lewis Mumford refers to Murray "whose researches into the actualities of Melville's life have gone even farther than either Mr. Weaver's or my own" ("Catnip and Amaranth," p. 1141); and in the preface to his 1929 book, the first attempt at a full inner life, Mumford adds: "Mr. Weaver's generosity is equalled only by that of Dr. Henry A. Murray, Jr., who shared with me his knowledge of certain Melville letters otherwise inaccessible—an act of pure chivalry, since Dr. Murray is himself at work on a biography of Herman Melville" (p. vi). In *Call Me Ishmael* (1947), Charles Olson thanks both Raymond Weaver and Henry Murray, "the other true biographer" (p. 40), and in his poem "Letter for Melville 1951," in which virtually every other Melvillean of the time is excoriated, Olson writes of Murray,

> who loves him as a doctor knows
> a family doctor, how
> his mother stayed inside him, how
> the compact came out hate, and what
> this kept him from, despite
> how far he travelled.
> (p. 308)

Murray's biography of Melville is still being written as Murray enters his ninety-third year. Edwin Shneidman, a colleague and editor of Murray's latest collection of essays, *Endeavors in Psychology* (1981), suggests in this volume that Murray has had something of a writing block in regard to Melville rooted in an aspiration for perfection on this deeply personal topic. To this I would add that Murray's active mind has always been reluctant to fix and formulate the enigmatic volatility of Melville's, that like the sperm whale Melville's amplitude and complexity fated his to be "the unwritten life" for Murray. But in the four pieces mentioned above, Murray provides us with the draught of that life that may be just as valuable, in its provisional convergences of the life and the art and in its intense concentration of insight, as any book-length study would have been.

Howard P. Vincent deserves credit for drawing out a significant part of Murray's Melville scholarship and speculation through the bold step of inviting him to edit *Pierre* as part of the Hendricks House edition of Melville. One of Murray's first—and most controversial—points in his introduction is aimed at explicating the subtitle: "Moral conflict, if radical and stubborn, results in a division, an inflexible dualism, in all branches of feeling and thought, which so influences the sufferer's apperceptions, that every significant object becomes *ambivalent* to him" (p. 414).[1] In viewing the apparent ethical and ontological problems in the novel as masks or symptoms of its hero's psychological difficulties, Murray follows the lead of Raymond Weaver, who wrote that Melville's "deepest interest came to be in metaphysics: which is but misery dissolved in thought" (p. 16), and of Melville himself, who wrote of Pierre that he "disguised" his afflictions "under the so conveniently adjustable drapery of all-stretchable Philosophy" (*Pierre*, p. 339).

Murray's analysis suggests why *Pierre* is central to understanding Melville as a psychologist and as a subject for psychology. At the structural and thematic heart of the book is the transition between surface and depth, mask and face, sanity and madness articulated in the "*Mosses*" essay. Key to this interpretation is that it is the feminine in the figure of Isabel that affects this transition. Murray does not merely identify Isabel with Jung's notion of the anima, but demonstrates dynamically and in detail its workings: "Isabel's effect, then, has been to increase rapidly the permeability of Pierre's mind to elements which are beyond the reach of ordinary thought. This has amounted to a temporary flooding of consciousness—an extreme expansion with numerous insights and self-revelations, and a blurring marked by illusions and delusions" (p. 443).

The ambivalent effect of Isabel on Pierre is analogous to the effect on Melville of writing such a deeply probing and personal book. On the one hand, Melville reaches his insights only through his "unconditional surrender" (p. 475) to forces in his own unconscious: "Melville, opening his mind to undercurrents of feeling and imagery, discovered the Oedipus complex" (p. 431), and in a sentence that culminates the critical tradition noted in the last chapter of viewing *Pierre* as a psychological study, Melville "stands out from the bulk of his contemporaries, as a seer among children, a forerunner of Henry James, Proust, and the whole modern school of psychological novelists" (p. 474). But on the other hand, the book's intense concern with the dimension of depth creates its flaws as a novel. The characters surrounding Pierre are drawn not objectively but in terms of their psychic valence to the central figure. Furthermore, in *Pierre* "visualizations are weak, because appearances are not in focus. The author has given up his long-standing interest in 'presentational immediacy' (as Whitehead would say) in order to concentrate on the essence of things" (p. 475). Murray does not see much distance between Melville and Pierre, a particularly harsh judgment when coupled with the following view of the protagonist: "the hateful dispositions for which the hero blames and damns the once-beloved objects of his environment are precisely those which have been hitherto repressed with the most difficulty in himself. Everything he condemns in the external world is a projection of his shadow self" (p. 472). And yet Murray himself has pointed out how aware Melville was of the dynamics of what we now call projection, as the discussion of his next piece will suggest.

John Logan describes the *Pierre* introduction as "long, windy, repetitious, uneven" and "which itself reads like a nineteenth-century novel, occasionally brilliant" (p. 325). While this is too harsh a judgment, it skirts the truth that Murray comes at his subject as Ishmael the whale, from a series of different angles and contexts, and that the sum of the parts is more impressive than the whole, the sense of supple and informed performance more than any extractable insight.

A different strategy shapes Murray's most famous—perhaps most notorious—Melville piece, his article on *Moby-Dick*, "In Nomine Diaboli," reprinted at least six times in forums ranging from literary collections to psychology textbooks. Here the argument is too compressed, too stark and elliptical, so that what appears most frequently in summaries and what most readers remember is the rather stiff and forced set of equivalences at which Murray arrives: Ahab as insurgent Id battling Moby Dick as oppressive cultural Superego, with Starbuck completing the triad as rational Ego. But as in Lawrence's chapter on *Moby-Dick*, this reductive formula is balanced and enriched with an intensity of response and a vigorous, personal language. Murray begins his essay with an autobiographical account of his long fascination with the book, one that began before his formal work as a psychologist: "In the procession of my experiences *Moby-Dick* anteceded psychology; that is, I was swept by Melville's gale and shaken by his appalling sea dragon before I had acquired the all-leveling academic oil that is poured on brewed-up waters.... Lacking these defenses I was whelmed. Instead of my changing this book, this book changed me." (p. 83). The chronology here is important for what it suggests about the relations between Melville and psychology: the reading of *Moby-Dick* was itself a crucial factor that turned Murray toward the depths of the mind, toward his contact with Freud and his more personal involvement with Jung.

One passage in particular points to an aspect of Melville's priority, a hidden avenue through which Melville's insight into the mind became a practical tool of psychology:

Here, in short, was a man with the mythmaking powers of Blake, a hive of significant associations, who was capable of reuniting what science had put asunder—pure perception and relevant emotion—and doing it in an exultant way that was acceptable to skepticism. Not at first, but later, I perceived the crucial difference between Melville's dramatic animations of nature and those of primitive religion makers; both were spontaneous and uncalculated projections, but Melville's were in harmony, for the most part, with scientific knowledge, because they had been recognized as projections, checked and modified. (p. 84)

If Henry Murray's name has any associations for the non-literary lay person, it is as the developer of the Thematic Apperception Test (TAT), although this is a distinction Murray has come to dislike as much as Melville dreaded his identification as the author of *Typee* and *Omoo*. The instrument, first described in a 1935 article written with Christiana Morgan and made available as a test for the entire profession in 1943, shows the joining of scientific precision with a respect for the fantasizing powers of the mind that is central to Murray's work as a psychologist. In the TAT, the subject is shown a series of ambiguous pictures and is asked to tell stories about them; the stories are then analyzed to discover the subject's own underlying core concerns. Although Murray does not acknowledge a direct link between his immersion in Melville and this procedure, it is difficult to dismiss the words of Polonius viewing an undelineated cloud, quoted in the "Extracts" of *Moby-Dick*: "Very like a whale." Equally suggestive is Ishmael's confrontation with the ambiguous, perhaps unreadable picture in the Spouter Inn, which is "defaced" just as we are later told the whale is de-faced. And "The Doubloon" itself (ch. 99), is a striking demonstration of how individuals read their own value systems and deep obsessions into any mutely complex art work.

The story of Melville and projective testing circles back on itself in Edwin Shneidman's study "The Deaths of Herman Melville" (1968), in which Melville's books are examined and scored very much as TAT data both for frequency of references to death and the way these references cluster in five categories: death of the chief protagonist; death of other characters; death in nature; discourses on death, historic references to death; wishes, thoughts, threats of death related to characters other than the protagonist. The article is long on suggestive information, short on convincing interpretations, but the presence of the data allows readers to draw their own conclusions. *Moby-Dick* is significantly the highest in the death references, both in total number and in mentions per page. Shneidman, perhaps following Newton Arvin's lead and his own interests as a thanatologist, suggests an author obsessed with death before his time, drastically out of phase with "normal" life patterns. But as Murray himself points out, normalcy may not be the best yardstick for measuring genius, and we can draw more imaginative conclusions. Because the greatest percentage falls into the category of "discourses on death," these references may be seen more positively as an occasion—Melville's deepest book—where personal and social taboos and repressions are most relaxed, where acceptance of the human as a physical being and death as a process complementary to life are most apt to surface. In any case, Shneidman, building on Murray's technique, offers a quantitative model for the analysis of literature which might profitably be used alongside our more subjective studies.

In Murray's next Melville piece, "Bartleby and I," the story serves as Doubloon to eight characters in search of a Meaning, including two critics, the attorney, and the author himself. Although to some extent the medium is the message here and all interpretations are seen as partial but valid, biased, sometimes complementary, some of them are more illuminating than others. Interestingly, the psychologist is the least helpful, with his diagnostic categories, whereas the biographer, who suggests among other things, that Melville's marriage was his own wall, is the most informative and provocative.

The last major piece, "Dead to the World: The Passions of Herman Melville," is the most longitudinal study, an incipient psychobiography similar to the more strictly psychoanalytical ones discussed in the fourth section of this chapter. Murray, however, is more intimate with facts about the life—for example, that Herman was cutting three teeth at the age of three months—and finds it surprising and exceptional, instead of inevitable, that Melville's life corresponds so well with Freud's theories: "It happens that there is a remarkably close correspondence between psychoanalytic theories and the dynamic forms of Melville's imagination. . . . furthermore, it is apparent that in many instances Melville was conscious or half-conscious of the import, in a psychoanalytic sense, of what he was communicating" (p. 508). Indeed, a dissertation (*Mel. Diss.*, # 149) appearing three years after Murray's paper was delivered, supports this claim in detail, although somewhat mechanically and clumsily (Carol L. Bagley).

In "Dead to the World," we see Murray characteristically using various kinds of data and the insights of various branches of psychology—the systems of Freud and Jung, clinical observations, and empirical studies— in formulating and supporting his hypotheses. Although, as T. Walter

Herbert, Jr. has pointed out with some justification (pp. 13–15), this mixing of systems leads to conceptual difficulties, it generally gives Murray's work a more fluid, less procrustean vision than most other psychological analyses. Although logically Freud and Jung cannot be reconciled, each system highlights aspects of the psyche's workings; each sees, or rather blindly gropes, different parts of the same elephant and at our present state of knowledge we need both, supplemented by all the other psychological data we can get. In addition, Murray is almost constantly aware of the limitations of perspective inherent in the discipline itself; he persistently widens the sphere of inquiry by wondering, for example, whether Melville should have been subjected to psychological treatment: "If the culture—society and its churches—was actually inimical to the realization of an individual's personal life, as Melville ... believed it to be ... should a man who saw the culture as the Enemy be persuaded by the implications of a seductive professional technique to throw in his sponge and surrender to it?" (p. 501)

PSYCHOANALYSES OF INDIVIDUAL WORKS

The most prolific genre of psychological studies is the analysis of a single work conducted from within a single psychological framework. Because of this proliferation and of the close similarities in assumptions and methodologies among the studies, it will be more helpful to examine closely two representative pieces, one from a Freudian and one from a Jungian perspective, than to offer a complete but skimming survey of the work done.

As we have seen, Henry Murray achieves a certain range and flexibility by drawing on a variety of psychological systems and methods. The analyses we are now examining are often written by practicing therapists such as Edward F. Edinger or by literary critics such as Morton Kaplan with an ideological commitment to a given system; both groups, then, tend to see that system as having privileged access to truth. In one of our representative pieces, an article with the promising title "The Enigma of *Moby-Dick*" (1958), James Kirsch writes: "It is only with the help of Jung's psychology that we can understand the experience of Melville" (p. 145). If the psychological system one uses is seen as having greater ontological validity than all the other fictions we or Melville make to grasp the world, then all one need do is to translate the latter in terms of the former, and sadly it is only this transposition that too many of the items on the bibliography achieve.

In "The Psychological Depths of Melville's 'The Bell-Tower' " (1973), Jacqueline A. Costello and Robert J. Kloss soon make it clear that it is these depths and not the surface—the language and narrative structure—that form the true story. The task of the critic is to pierce through or delve below what Freud calls the manifest content, what the dream or story seems to be about, to get at the latent content, what the story is "really" about. The distance between manifest and latent content is created by censoring devices such as displacement and distortion, which the mind uses to hide from itself the disruptive, unacceptable contents it must repress to live in civilization. Specifically here, and most often in classical Freudianism, the repressed drives are Oedipal: "As the narrative develops, Bannadonna's true ambitions and his real crime become clear; he is enacting those forbidden fantasies common to all men but taboo to all societies. He seeks to supplant his father as his mother's lover and, ultimately, to subjugate and even eliminate his mother in his quest to create 'life' on his own. Retribution for this sin can only be castration; it is not merely appropriate, it is necessary" (p. 254).

Since neither Bannadonna's parents nor the act of castration appear in the story itself—indeed, since Bannadonna is in one sense a man made out of words, his parents ink and paper—the authors might seem presumptuous in thus isolating his "true" ambitions and "real" crime. In using this methodology, however, the critic is helped by those tools crucial to the creative artist—metaphor and allusion. Bannadonna's work on the phallic bell tower evinces a drive to dwarf his father's masculinity since "the tower is likened to Babel, which in the Bible represents man's futile attempt to outdo God, the Father" (p. 255). Similarly, the vector of incest is revealed by Bannadonna's refusal to accept natural limitations such as gravity (p. 256). What begin as suggestive resonances harden in the course of the analysis to rigid equivalences (tower = phallus, God's law = father, nature = mother), so at the end Bannadonna is seen as suffering a "castration-death" (p. 257), a hyphenated phenomenon that confounds the very relations between the symbolic and the literal, the manifest and latent, that such an analysis at its best should clarify.

A related methodological question is that of whose unconscious urges are being displaced and symbolized. Bannadonna himself is responsible for the shape and structure of the tower, but nature and natural law exist as elements both in the narrative and in the world in some ways unshaped by the main character. Who, for example, puts the maternal valence on them—Bannadonna, the narrator, a shared cultural symbology, the individual reader, or the critic? The lack of answers emerges in sentences like the following: "Melville continually relies upon sexual imagery because he is aware, consciously or unconsciously, of its enormous affective power" (p. 260). One asks what kind of awareness would be "unconscious" and, more importantly, why the analysis had to be made in the first place if the imagery is recognizably sexual. Like many traditional psychoanalyses, the end forgets its beginnings; once we have reached the latent meaning, the untanglings of symbolisms, the right placings of displacements, become dispensable, and the dialectic between indirection and directness, repression and revealing loses its energy in the triumph of the "answer." Even if these problems of methodology were resolved, or even made productively self-conscious, there would still remain the problem of boredom. In a generally favorable review of Frederick Crews's *The Sins of the Fathers*, Henry Murray complains that all the book's ingenuity and wealth of detail lead invariably to the same conclusion in work after work, that "nearly all of the rich symbolic stuff in Hawthorne is explainable in terms of an unresolved Oedipus complex—that genetically-given catchall to which orthodoxy relegates by fiat the whole enormous population of neurotics" (p. 312).

James Kirsch, in the article quoted above, chooses to "limit" himself to "the problem of Man's obedience to God, or rather to its psychological aspect—the relationship of the ego to the self—as it unfolds in *Moby-Dick*" (p. 132). Since this relation is as central to Jungian thought as the Oedipus complex is to Freudian thought, it deserves elaboration here. Jung sees the "ego" as merely one psychic complex but also the one we consciously identify with ourselves: our sense of being a simple, separate person. It is the task of the early part of life to form this ego and to separate it from the vast, unconscious psychic realm that constitutes the rest of the "self." Later in life, however, we must realize that the ego is only a small part of the self, and that it must get back in touch with the entire being (a process called "individuation," becoming an undivided psyche at a more conscious level) through an encounter with its other aspects such as the shadow (the repressed darker elements that are often imaged as a "double" figure the same sex as the ego), the anima or animus (the contrasexual aspects repressed or ignored as the ego builds its "identity"), and finally those archetypal symbols such as the wise old man or woman that represent the entire self.

Kirsch sees this process not only as a thematic element but also as the method of the work itself, a process of "active imagination" in which the subject "allows the images of the unconscious to come to the surface—images in which the ego participates quite consciously" (p. 132). The very act of writing, then, is an act of individuation, and the Jungian sense of a symbol as the bridge between the conscious and the unconscious is more dynamic and potentially more fruitful than the Freudian. Ideally, a Jungian critic would trace imagery and language through a work or canon to see how it becomes increasingly self-aware, how it elaborates and comments on itself (the Jungian term is "amplify"), as it clearly does within a chapter such as "The Whiteness of the Whale" (*MD*, ch. 42).

In practice, however, Kirsch's analysis, like virtually all Jungian readings, turns into an allegory as static and predictable as the Freudian work. What begins as only the psychological aspect of the problem of the individual's relationship to God turns out to be really the problem itself; the enigma of the universe becomes a clinical case study. Interpreting "The Candles" (ch. 119), Kirsch writes: "Ahab most daringly asserts the right of the ego to exist and to dispute its unconditional dependence on the unconscious. . . . Furthermore, it becomes clear that this ego, as symbolized by Ahab, is one which is largely identified with the archetype of the anima. This contamination between ego and anima, as expressed by the term 'queenly personality,' creates an inflation, perverts the ego and makes it power-mad" (p. 141). Often when a psychological critic claims "it becomes clear" it is helpful to be especially skeptical. From this evocative, almost opaque chapter—"darkness leaping out of light" (p. 417)—Kirsch extracts a clear lesson based on an analogy between conventional religion and conventional psychology: just as the individual should not defy God or try to abrogate His powers, the ego should not mistake itself for the entire psyche.

Significantly, the paragraph from which the above passage is quoted ends on an appeal to the authority of the most conventional character in the book, Starbuck: "When Starbuck reminds Ahab that God is against him and begs him to return, Ahab grabs the burning harpoon, the symbol of the ego's power now increased tenfold through the magic of fire" (p. 141). But it is this vision that Ahab, as well as Ishmael and the very structure of the book, put into question. There is nothing in the world of the novel to contradict the notion that right worship is defiance, that Ahab's metaphysics, as best we understand it, could not indeed be correct. As with Freudian maneuvers, what begin as suggestive metaphors harden into clear interpretations sounding suspiciously like conventional wisdom, itself a contradiction in terms. The very subversiveness of the Jungian and Freudian insights into the unconscious are checked in their applications; as the followers of Jacques Lacan like to put it, the discovery of the unconscious itself becomes subject to repression: "the unconscious which, according to the very definitions on which psychoanalysis is founded, is the realm of free instinctual energy and knows no stability, or containment, or closure, is immobilized and domesticated by its professional observers. This extraordinary agent of dispersal and surprise becomes an ordinary counter within an ordinary conceptual game" (Malcolm Bowie, p. 119).

Furthermore, traditional psychological criticism has not followed some of the leads cf Freud and Jung in seeing how writers and texts tend to interpret themselves. Rather than seeing the work as an arena where the conscious mind encounters, struggles with, and shapes unconscious factors initially alien to it, many psychological critics view it simply as Edward Edinger does, "as though it were a dream which needs interpretation and elaboration of its images for their meaning to emerge fully" (p. 1). In treating *Moby-Dick* in this way, Edinger triangulates a given image or allusion with a similar myth outside the text or with analogous dreams from patients. While there are some bright sparks struck off in this abrasion, what is lost is a sense of the ways in which the book interprets and amplifies itself with its own analogies ("The Town-Ho's Story"), dreams ("Queen Mab"), visions (Ishmael's phantom hand), and parallel myths already embedded in the text (Job, Jonah, Prometheus, Christ, Satan, St. George).

On the positive side, however, the best of these psychological analyses can give us fresh ways to reorganize our sense of a text and to treat what the older New Critics saw as "ambiguities" arising from vague ontological or aesthetic demands as ambivalences rooted in basic tensions in the human psyche. The analyses of *Moby-Dick* by David Leverenz (both his long essay on the book and his later questioning of his questionings in "Where Children Strove" and "Class Conflicts") and by Sharon Cameron have the salutary effect of grounding the novel's situation in the physicality of its narrator and setting, and of suggesting that Ishmael's—and other critics'—flights into philosophizing should be examined not only for what they say but also for how they function as evasions and defenses. The best psychological criticism, in other words, teaches us to be alertly suspicious instead of giving us a new set of certainties.

PSYCHOBIOGRAPHIES: HARMS AND THE MAN

If psychology is to merit the attention of Melville scholars, it must meet the challenge of providing a coherent, inclusive narrative of Melville's life that establishes causal connections through time and lateral relations with the writings. Although no one can claim complete success here, the body of psychobiographical writings holds up better and has more to offer the general scholar than the analyses of individual texts discussed in the previous section. The book-length studies of Edwin Haviland Miller (1975) and Michael Paul Rogin (1983) are the most widely known, but a cluster of articles that precede them deserve note.

Significantly, the earliest of these, Frederick Rosenheim's "Flight from Home," appeared in 1940 in the first volume of *American Imago*, a journal that has gone on to publish five more articles involving Melville and psychology, reflecting perhaps the predelictions of its longtime editor, Harry Slochower. Rosenheim isolates related factors, both of which he sees as Oedipal and both of which are to become *leitmotifs* in future psychobiographies: the supposition that because of his many younger siblings young Herman was thrust away from the maternal breast early and had to endure repeatedly the role of the onlooker as his mother's milk and love were deflected to others; and the death of the father when Herman was at the crucial Oedipal age of twelve, a consummation in some sense devoutly to be wished and therefore a powerful source of guilt when it became a reality. The flight from home, then, makes sense in these terms: "A strong trend in Melville was to give up his fight for mother, to atone for the 'murder' of his father, to bring him back to life and to be loved by him" (p. 26). Rosenheim gives no citations for his bibliographical sources, but it is apparent he did not engage in the kind of original scholarship that delights Henry Murray. Unfortunately, the reliance on secondary sources, even after the scholarly information in them has been superseded, is a trademark of most psychobiographical work on Melville. Yet Rosenheim's formulations themselves—given the state of psychoanalytic theory in 1940, before psychological symbiosis and separation from the mother in infancy had been more clearly delineated from later Oedipal patterns—were plausible and suggestive.

Although Rosenheim is not cited in Charles Kligerman's "The Psychology of Herman Melville" (1953), the article follows a similar format in beginning with a brief "factual" biography—based here largely on Mumford—followed by a psychoanalytic reorganizing of material from the life and the works. What is significant in terms of the history of Melville scholarship is that Kligerman anticipates virtually every insight in Miller's psychobiography. Kligerman notes that the Ishmael-Hagar story is not only a frequent allusion but also a mythic motif that underlies Melville's inner experience of his life. He points out that the frustration in early feeding may account for the profusive oral imagery in the writing, a point suggested earlier by Murray but also extended later by Miller. And Kligerman sees the "passionate vehemence" (p. 133) with which Melville turned to Hawthorne as compounded of the urge to rediscover the father and to play the role of passive female in a homoerotic relationship.

Miller's *Melville*, then, might not have been as surprising to the psychological community as it seems to have been in the world of Melville scholarship. Since the book's shortcomings have been pointed out frequently and at length—the factual errors, the thinness of original scholarship, the failure to integrate its biographical theories with its readings of the texts—I will observe here only a few of its generally overlooked strengths. It does flesh out in rich and plausible detail—the fashionable term now is "thick description"—psychoanalytic insights that in their original presentations seemed more reductive. In addition, Miller's depiction of Melville's failure in human relations is unflinching without being shrilly debunking or overly harsh. Particularly moving is Miller's chapter on Malcolm's suicide and Herman's responsibility in the matter, a story corroborated and documented more clinically by Shneidman's article published a year later, "Some Psychological Reflections on the Death of Malcolm Melville."

Whatever its shortcomings in execution, one has to admire the ambitious integrative project of Rogin's *Subversive Genealogy* (1983) to relate the fortunes, vocations, and politics of the Gansevoort-Melville families to the ideological and psychological tensions in Melville's fiction. As a political scientist, Rogin is more adept and convincing in drawing connections between family and national history and individual psychology than in relating both to the fiction itself; his readings usually feel like a series of stitched footnotes, veering away from the texture of the text.

What is needed is not a new psychobiography of Melville but a study that neither deliberately excludes psychological insights as does Leon Howard's nor relies as exclusively on them as does Miller's. As suggested above, such a study would have to take account of recent work done by Margaret Mahler and others on the psychological birth of the infant, its separation from symbiosis with the mother, a process distinct from and more crucial than later Oedipal conflicts. (Fortunately, a readable introduction to both the theory and the empirical work based on it has been written by Louise J. Kaplan.) The only piece on Melville that uses this work is a suggestive but skimpy essay by a psychiatrist, William H. Sack, which moves too quickly from childhood conflicts between autonomy and merger to "The Mast-Head" in *Moby-Dick* (ch. 35). Even more important, our ideal study would not only apply psychological theories to Melville but would also use the ineluctable specifics of the life and works to test, evaluate, and critique the theories themselves. As Wallace Stevens says, "The squirming facts exceed the squamous mind" (p. 167), and we need a biography and criticism willing to enter into a dialectic between the two.

TEXTUAL POLITICS AND OTHER NEW DIRECTIONS

In reviewing the history of Melville and psychology, one is struck by a sense of promises unperformed, potentials unrealized, opportunities missed. Many of the auspicious leads of Lawrence and Murray have not been followed up, nor have later critics built fruitfully on each other's insights as much as each setting up his or her own shop. Yet the climate now is extremely encouraging. There is more interest in interdisciplinary work and methodological self-consciousness. Freud's own texts are read and analyzed in literature classes, Jung's work is taken seriously—too seriously by some—important new theoretical work, such as that by Shoshana Felman and Meredith Anne Skura, has shown that in joining literature and psychology literature need not be the junior partner, that psychology itself can be the object of rhetorical and mythic analyses.

This concluding section focuses on three of the most promising areas in which literature and psychology can illuminate each other: reader-response criticism, the relations between literature and psychology in the history of thought, and postmodern readings of Freud and Jung. The first category is the smallest in terms of work already done with Melville, only a brief but powerful article by Stephen A. Black. As in some other important recent work, Black combines a practical interest in pedagogy with critical theory, especially as he argues that an examination of a reader's psychological interactions with the text is a way of getting beyond the limitations of both subjectivist and objectivist paradigms. As an example, he gives his own reactions and associations to "The Try-Works" chapter of *Moby-Dick* to observe: "As I think back upon the chapter I am struck, as always, by the sequence of narrative modes— from flat exposition, to sensuous imagery, to regression, and finally to self-examination—and think that Melville must relax his grasp on reality in order to obtain pleasure from the act of writing; I also think that obtaining pleasure seems to produce mixed feelings of guilt and exaltation in Melville" (p. 273).

Black would agree that his own article is meant to be only illustrative and that we need a more extensive investigation of the psychology of Melville's reader, on the scale of but not duplicating the methodologies of the work on Milton done by Stanley Fish and Robert Crosman. Such a study might take as its starting point the ideas of David Walker in *The Transparent Lyric* (1984). Walker wants to refocus attention from the sensibility of a posited speaker to the mental actions performed by the reader working directly on the material. His definition of the transparent lyric—as "a poem whose rhetoric establishes its own incompleteness; it is presented not as completed discourse but as a structure that invites the reader to project himself or herself into its world, and thus to verify it as contiguous with reality" (p. 18)—has a special relevance to a book in which the subject of the opening sentence, "Call me Ishmael," is "you" and where a self-awareness of our attempts to construct this Ishmael and his world may be more instructive than assuming a character already there to psychoanalyze.

A second fruitful direction is to probe Melville's own positions on psychological issues, especially in the context of the psychologies of his time. Historical studies, especially those by L.L. Whyte, Henri F. Ellenberger, and Walter Kaufmann, show us the variety and surprising sophistication of eighteenth- and nineteenth-century theories of psychology; and pieces by Henry Nash Smith, Paul McCarthy, Michael Shannon Kearns, Gerard W. Shepherd, and Joan Magretta are particularly helpful in delineating Melville's stances toward these theories. There is an interesting convergence in the last two articles, where both critics argue that Melville's growing awareness as a psychologist accounts for the artistic failures of *Pierre*. Magretta says that "Melville never resolved the problem of how to reconcile the irrational roots of human nature with the rationale of narrative structure" (p. 239), and Shepherd discusses "the narrator's very ponderings of Pierre's early transitions which render even tentative authority impossible, because the truth-teller realizes his own psyche is as conditioned and self-deceptive as Pierre's"

(p. 86). One of the implications of this work is that Melville's knowledge of the mind came from two main sources, models and theories already available and his own discoveries made in the process of his writings, and that when the two conflicted—as they often did—Melville opted for the latter, but not without leaving traces of both in the works. It would be useful to place Melville as a psychologist more directly and generally in the history of ideas; my own formulations in *The Unsounded Centre* (1980) that the American Romantics were on the cutting edge of psychological discovery, where metaphysical terms and ideas begin to turn into a phenomenology of consciousness, need refining and extending.

The most controversial and least understood of recent strategies in reading Melville is the application of post-structuralist theories, most importantly for our purposes Jacques Lacan's reformulation of Freud. Although a range of writers such as Sharon Cameron, John Irwin, Eric Sundquist, John Carlos Rowe, and David Simpson have been influenced by Lacan, Nancy Blake, Régis Durand, Brook Thomas, and Elizabeth Wright have given us the most directly and purely Lacanian readings. It will be most instructive to follow Wright's article, which is deliberately constructed as an exposition of theory coupled with two practical examples.

Wright begins by pointing out that, whereas the older psychoanalytic critics sought unity in "an omniscient authorial *un*conscious" (p. 89) just as the old New Critics saw the work itself as unified, holding in tension all ambiguities, post-structuralists see literature as reflecting the divisions in the self:

Fiction is what the subject, whether reader or writer, flies to in an attempt to reconstitute his lost wholeness, only to discover that language is the very thing which betrays him, since it is what he acquired to symbolize his lack. Hence his desire to make the word fit the world will be constantly undercut. What the critic can search for is the breakdown of this wholeness, as it reveals itself in a structural intentionality which does not reside in a latent or manifest content, but cuts across the two (p. 90).

One would expect, then, Wright's analysis of "Young Goodman Brown" and "Benito Cereno" to show us these dynamics operating in the text; instead—and this is endemic to the genre of post-structuralist readings— Hawthorne and Melville are shown to be knowing and saying the same things Lacan knows: "For Young Goodman Brown sin is *merely* what the father names, because there has been no proper identification with a father" (p. 95).

Post-structuralist writers are very aware of gaps and fissures, between sign and referent, language and meaning, but one of the largest unseen gaps in their own enterprise is that between the radically liberating possibilities offered by their theories and their own rather predictable, often jargon-ridden explications which tend to just thematize these ideas in the work being analyzed. To be fair, the project of these writers is not to give us better tools for the analysis of specific works but, as Wright points out, to understand in more general terms the workings of language and its relation to psychic development. Still, we should expect from the new theories more specific ways of reading texts that show us language not merely as reflecting psychic processes but as creating them, as the central factor in structuring the mind.

Less well known but equal in its potential for literary criticism is the re-visioning of Jung's thought by James Hillman in a series of books, the most relevant of which for Melville studies are *The Dream and the Underworld* (1979) and *Healing Fiction* (1983). As in Lacan's theories, the self is decentered and multiple, viewed from the perspective of what Hillman calls a "new polytheism." Furthermore, the self tries to heal its rifts through the making of narratives, myths about itself, which can harden into neuroses if they are taken literally rather than metaphorically. The only direct application, Ralph Maud's article "Archetypal Depth Criticism and Melville" (1983), is disappointing partly because he follows too literally what he takes to be Hillman's injunction against close reading. One hopes that Hillman himself, who began his career as a novelist and Joyce scholar, may someday take up the challenge of Melville.

What these new approaches share is a sense of language, imagery, and narrative not as transparencies to be read through to some deeper meaning but as themselves central loci, nodes of psychological organization. Only when we have assimilated the insight that the main psychological event in Melville's life was writing itself will we be able to move the relation of Melville and psychology into a new dimension.

NOTE

1. All references to the four major Melville articles by Murray are for convenience made to the collection *Endeavors in Psychology* instead of to the original places of publication.

WORKS CITED

Abrams, Robert E. " 'Bartleby' and the Fragile Pageantry of the Ego." *ELH: A Journal of English Literary History* 45 (Fall 1978): 488–500.

Adams, Michael Vannoy. "Ahab's Jonah-and-the-Whale Complex: The Fish Archetype in *Moby-Dick*." *ESQ* 28 (Third Quarter 1982): 167–82.

Arvin, Newton. *Herman Melville*. New York, Sloane Associates 1950.

Atlas, Marilyn Judith. "A Psychobiographical Approach to *Moby-Dick*." Ph.D. Diss., Michigan State University, 1979. [*Mel. Diss.*, #490.]

Bagley, Carol L. "Melville's Trilogy: Symbolic Precursor of Freudian Personality Structure in the History of Ideas." Ph.D. Diss., Washington State University, 1966. [*Mel. Diss.*, #149.]

Baird, James. *Ishmael*. Baltimore: Johns Hopkins University Press, 1956.

Barber, Patricia. "Melville's Self-Image as a Writer and the Image of the Writer in *Pierre*." *Massachusetts Studies in English* 3 (Spring 1972): 65–71.

Beja, Morris. "Bartleby and Schizophrenia." *The Massachusetts Review* 19 (1978): 555–68.

Bergler, Edmund. "A Note on Herman Melville." *American Imago* 11 (Winter 1954): 385–97.

Bickman, Martin. *The Unsounded Centre: Jungian Studies in American Romanticism.* Chapel Hill: University of North Carolina Press, 1980.

Black, Stephen A. "On Reading Psychoanalytically." *College English* 39 (November 1977): 267–74.

Blake, Nancy. "Mourning and Melancholia in 'Bartleby.'" *Delta* (Montpelier, France) 7 (1978): 155–68.

Bollas, Christopher. "Melville's Lost Self: *Bartleby*." In *The Practice of Psychoanalytic Criticism*. Ed. Leonard Tennenhouse. Detroit: Wayne State University Press, 1976, pp. 226–36.

———. "Melville's Man: The Character of Breakdown." Ph.D. Diss., SUNY-Buffalo, 1977. [*Mel. Diss.*, #439.]

Boudreau, Gordon V. "Of Pale Ushers and Gothic Piles: Melville's Architectural Symbology." *ESQ* 18 (Second Quarter 1972): 67–82.

Bowie, Malcolm. "Jacques Lacan." In *Structuralism and Since: From Levi-Strauss to Derrida*. Ed. John Sturrock. Oxford: Oxford University Press, 1979, pp. 116–53.

Cameron, Sharon. *The Corporeal Self: Allegories of the Body in Hawthorne and Melville*. Baltimore: Johns Hopkins University Press, 1981.

Carothers, Robert L. "Herman Melville and the Search for the Father: An Interpretation of the Novels." Ph.D. Diss., Kent State University, 1969. [*Mel. Diss.*, #194.]

Chabot, C. Barry. "Melville's *The Confidence-Man*: A 'Poisonous' Reading." *Psychological Review* 63 (Winter 1976–77): 571–85.

Chase, Richard. "An Approach to Melville." *Partisan Review* 14 (May 1947): 285–94.

———. *Herman Melville: A Critical Study*. New York: Macmillan Co., 1949.

Christy, Wallace McVay. "Journey to the Center: The Archetypal Nature of Melville's 'Piazza.'" *Higginson Journal* 20 (1978): 21–28.

———. "The Shock of Recognition: A Psycho-Literary Study of Hawthorne's Influence on Melville's Short Fiction." Ph.D. Diss., Brown University, 1970. [*Mel. Diss.*, #225.]

Costello, Jacqueline A., and Robert J. Kloss. "The Psychological Depths of Melville's 'The Bell-Tower.'" *ESQ* 19 (Fourth Quarter 1973): 254–61.

Cowley, Malcolm. *The Literary Situation*. New York: Viking Press, 1954.

Crosman, Robert. *Reading Paradise Lost*. Bloomington: Indiana University Press, 1980.

Damon, S. Foster. "Pierre the Ambiguous." *Hound and Horn* 2 (January-March 1929): 107–18.

Dickinson, Emily. *The Complete Poems of Emily Dickinson.* Ed. Thomas H. Johnson. Boston: Little, Brown, 1960.

Durand, Régis. " 'The Captive King': The Absent Father in Melville's Text." In *The Fictional Father: Lacanian Readings of the Text.* Ed. Robert Con Davis. Amherst: University of Massachusetts Press, 1981, pp. 48–72.

Eby, E. H. "Herman Melville's 'Tartarus of Maids.' " *Modern Language Quarterly* 1 (March 1940): 95–100.

Edinger, Edward F. *Melville's Moby-Dick: A Jungian Commentary.* New York: New Directions, 1978.

Ellenberger, Henri F. *The Discovery of the Unconscious: The History and Evolution of Dynamic Psychiatry.* New York: Basic Books, 1970.

Ellison, Jerome. "How to Catch a Whale: Evil, Melville, and the Evolution of Consciousness." *Michigan Quarterly Review* 3 (1954): 85–89.

Emery, Allan Moore. "The Alternatives of Melville's 'Bartleby.' " *Nineteenth-Century Fiction* 31 (September 1976): 170–87.

Faber, M. D. "The Painted Breast: A Psychological Study of Melville's *Pierre.*" *Psychoanalytic Review* 66 (1979–80): 519–51.

Fagin, N.B. "Herman Melville and the Interior Monologue." *American Literature* 6 (January 1935): 433–34.

Felman, Shoshana. *Writing and Madness: (Literature/Philosophy/Psychoanalysis).* Trans. Martha Noel Evans and the author. Ithaca, N.Y.: Cornell University Press, 1985.

Fiedler, Leslie A. *Love and Death in the American Novel.* New York: Criterion Books, 1960.

Fine, Ronald Edward. "Melville and the Rhetoric of Psychological Fiction." Ph.D. Diss., University of Rochester, 1966. [*Mel. Diss.*, #152.]

Fish, Stanley. *Surprised by Sin: The Reader in Paradise Lost.* New York: St. Martin's Press, 1967.

Fisher, Marvin. " 'Bartleby,' Melville's Circumscribed Scrivener." *Southern Review* 10 (January 1974): 59–79.

Floyd, Nathaniel L. "*Billy Budd*: A Psychological Autopsy." *American Imago* 34 (Spring 1977): 28–49.

Franzosa, John. "Darwin and Melville: Why a Tortoise?" *American Imago* 33 (Winter 1976): 361–79.

Gibbs, Charles Kenneth. "Myth and Creativity in *Moby-Dick.*" Ph.D. Diss., University of Massachusetts, 1973. [*Mel. Diss.*, #311.]

Gordon, David J. "The Quest for Guiltlessness: Melville's *Billy Budd.*" *Literary Art and the Unconscious.* Baton Rouge: Louisiana State University Press, 1976, pp. 123–52.

Grenander, M. E. "*Benito Cereno* and Legal Oppression: A Szaszian Interpretation." *Journal of Libertarian Studies* 2 (1978): 337–42.

Haberstroh, Charles J., Jr. *Melville and Male Identity.* Cranberry, N.J.: Associated University Presses, 1980.

———. "Melville, Marriage and *Mardi.*" *Studies in the Novel* 9 (1977): 247–60.

———. "*Redburn*: The Psychological Pattern." *Studies in American Fiction* 2 (Autumn 1974): 133–44.

Halverson, John. "The Shadow in *Moby-Dick.*" *American Quarterly* 15 (Fall 1963): 436–46.

Hayford, Harrison. "Melville's Freudian Slip." *American Literature* 30 (November 1958): 366–68.

Hennelly, Mark. "Ishmael's Nightmare and the American Eve." *American Imago* 30 (Fall 1974): 274–93.

Herbert, T. Walter, Jr. *Moby-Dick and Calvinism: A World Dismantled*. New Brunswick, N.J.: Rutgers University Press, 1977.

Hillman, James. *The Dream and the Underwold*. New York: Harper & Row, 1979.

———. *Healing Fiction*. Barrytown, N.Y.: Station Hill, 1983.

———. *Re-Visioning Psychology*. New York: Harper & Row, 1975.

Hyman, Stanley Edgar. "Melville the Scrivener." *New Mexico Quarterly* 23 (Winter 1953): 381–415.

Irwin, John. *American Hieroglyphics: The Symbol of the Egyptian Hieroglyphics in the American Renaissance*. New Haven, Conn.: Yale University Press, 1980.

Jeske, Jeffrey, M. "Antony as a Source for Pierre: The Saga of the Male Psyche." *American Transcendental Quarterly* No. 50 (Spring 1981): 117–28.

———. "Macbeth, Ahab, and the Unconscious." *American Transcendental Quarterly* 31 (1976): 8–12.

Justman, Stewart. "Repression and the Self in 'Benito Cereno'." *Studies in Short Fiction* 15 (Summer 1978): 301–16.

Justus, James H. "*Redburn* and *White-Jacket*: Society and Sexuality in the Narrators of 1849." In *Herman Melville: Reassessments*. Ed. A. Robert Lee. New York and London: Barnes and Noble, and Vision, 1984, pp. 41–67.

Kaplan, Louise J. *Oneness and Separateness: From Infant to Individual*. New York: Simon & Schuster, 1978.

Kaplan, Morton, and Robert Kloss. "Fantasy of Passivity: Melville's *Bartleby the Scrivener*." *The Unspoken Motive: A Guide to Psychoanalytic Criticism*. New York: Free Press, 1973, pp. 63–79.

Kaufmann, Walter. *Discovering the Mind: Goethe, Kant, and Hegel*. New York: McGraw-Hill, 1980.

Kearns, Michael Shannon. "Anatomy of the Mind: Mid Nineteenth Century Psychology and the Works of Nathaniel Hawthorne, Charlotte Bronte, Charles Dickens, and Herman Melville." Ph.D. Diss., University of California, Davis, 1980. [*Mel. Diss.*, #522.]

———. "Phantoms of the Mind: Melville's Criticism of Idealistic Psychology." *ESQ* 30 (First Quarter 1984): 40–50.

Kellner, R. Scott. "Sex, Toads, and Scorpions: A Study of the Psychological Themes in Melville's *Pierre*." *Arizona Quarterly* 31 (1975): 5–20.

Kirsch, James. "The Enigma of *Moby-Dick*." *Journal of Analytical Psychology* 3 (1958): 131–48.

———. "The Problem of Dictatorship as Represented in *Moby-Dick*." In *Current Trends in Analytical Psychology: Proceedings of the First International Congress for Analytical Psychology*. Ed. Gerhard Adler. London: Tavistock, 1961, pp. 261–74.

Kligerman, Charles. "The Psychology of Herman Melville." *Psychoanalytic Review* 40 (1953): 125–43.

Lawrence, D. H. *Studies in Classic American Literature*. New York: Thomas Seltzer, 1923.

———. *The Symbolic Meaning: The Uncollected Versions of Studies in Classic American Literature*. Ed. Armin Arnold. Fontwell, Arundel, England: Centaur, 1962.

Lesser, Simon O. *Fiction and the Unconscious*. Boston: Beacon Press, 1957.

Leverenz, David. "Anger and Individualism." *Psychoanalytic Review* 62 (1975): 407–28.

———. "Class Conflicts in Teaching *Moby-Dick*." In *Approaches to Teaching Melville's "Moby-Dick."* Ed. Martin Bickman. New York: Modern Language Association, 1985, 85–95.

———. "*Moby-Dick*." In *Psychoanalysis and Literary Process*. Ed. Frederick Crews. Cambridge, Mass.: Winthrop, 1970, pp. 66–117.

———. " 'Where Children Strove at Recess': English Professors and Psychoanalytic Criticism." *College English* 44 (1982): 451–58.

Logan, John. "Psychological Motifs in Melville's *Pierre*." *Minnesota Review* 7 (1967): 325–30.

McCarthy, Paul. "Facts, Opinions, and Possibilities: Melville's Treatment of Insanity Through *White-Jacket*." *Studies in the Novel* 16 (Summer 1984): 167–81.

McSweeney, Kerry. "Melville, Dickinson, Whitman and Psychoanalytic Criticism." *Critical Quarterly* 19 (Spring 1977): 71–82.

Magretta, Joan Barbara Gorin. "The Iconography of Madness: A Study in Melville and Dostoevsky." Ph.D. Diss., University of Michigan, 1976. [*Mel. Diss.*, #425.]

———. "Radical Disunities: Models of Mind and Madness in *Pierre* and *The Idiot*." *Studies in the Novel* 10 (Summer 1978): 234–50.

Marcus, Mordecai. "Melville's Bartleby as a Psychological Double." *College English* 23 (February 1962): 365–68.

Maud, Ralph. "Archetypal Depth Criticism and Melville." *College English* 45 (November 1983): 695–704.

Milder, Robert. " 'Knowing' Melville." *ESQ* 24 (Second Quarter 1978): 96–117.

———. "Melville and his Biographers." *ESQ* 22 (Third Quarter 1976): 169–82.

Miller, Edwin Haviland. *Melville*. New York: George Braziller, 1975.

Miner-Quinn, Paula Lois. "Pierre's Sexuality: A Psychoanalytic Interpretation of Herman Melville's *Pierre, or, the Ambiguities*." *University of Hartford Studies in Literature* 13 (1981): 111–21.

Monteiro, George. "Poetry and Madness: Melville's Rediscovery of Camoës in 1867." *New England Quarterly* 51 (1978): 561–65.

Moore, John Brooks, ed. *Pierre*. New York: E.P. Dutton, 1929.

Mumford, Lewis. "Catnip and Amaranth." *Saturday Review of Literature* 5 (1929): 1141.

———. *Herman Melville*. New York: Harcourt, Brace, 1929.

Murray, Henry A. "Bartleby and I." In *Bartleby the Scrivener*. Ed. Howard P. Vincent. Kent, Ohio: Kent State University Press, 1966, pp. 3–24. Rpt. in *Endeavors in Psychology*, pp. 482–97.

———. "Dead to the World: The Passions of Herman Melville." In *Essays in Self-Destruction*. Ed. E.S. Shneidman. New York: Science House, 1967, pp. 7–29. Rpt. in *Endeavors in Psychology*, pp. 498–517.

———. *Endeavors in Psychology*. New York: Harper & Row, 1981.

———. "The Freudian Hawthorne." Review of *The Sins of the Fathers* by Frederick Crews. *American Scholar* 36 (1967): 308–12.

———. "In Nomine Diaboli." *New England Quarterly* 24 (1951): 435–52. Rpt. in *Endeavors in Psychology*, pp. 82–94.

———. Introduction. *Pierre, or the Ambiguities*. New York: Hendricks House, 1949, pp. xiii-ciii. Rpt. in *Endeavors in Psychology*, pp. 413–81.

———. "Prelude." *Melville and Hawthorne in the Berkshires: A Symposium, Melville Annual, 1966*. Ed. Howard P. Vincent. Kent, Ohio: Kent State University Press, 1968.

———. Review of *Herman Melville* by Lewis Mumford. *New England Quarterly* 2 (1929): 523–26.

———. Review of *Pierre; or, The Ambiguities*. Ed. Robert S. Forsythe. *New England Quarterly* 4 (1931): 333–37.

———. Review of *The Trying-Out of Moby Dick* by Howard P. Vincent. *New England Quarterly* 23 (1950): 527–30.

———. "Timon of America." Review of *Herman Melville* by Lewis Mumford. *Hound and Horn* 2 (1929): 430–32.

———, with Christiana D. Morgan. "A Method for Investigating Fantasies: The Thematic Apperception Test." *Archives of Neurology and Psychiatry* 34 (1935): 289–306.

Olson, Charles. *Call Me Ishmael*. New York: Reynall & Hitchcock, 1947.

———. "Letter for Melville 1951." In *A Controversy of Poets*. Ed. Paris Leary and Robert Kelly. Garden City, N.Y.: Doubleday, 1965, 304–11.

Pedrini, Lura N., and Duilio T. Pedrini. "Melville's Attitudes Toward Women as Reflected in His Novels." *Psychiatric Quarterly Supplement* 39 (1965): 231–40.

Petrullo, Helen B. "The Neurotic Hero of *Typee*." *American Imago* 12 (Winter 1955): 317–23.

Pops, Martin L. *The Melville Archetype*. Kent, Ohio: Kent State University Press, 1970.

Rogers, Robert. "The 'Ineludible Gripe' of Billy Budd." *Literature and Psychology* 14 (Winter 1964): 9–22.

Rogin, Michael Paul. *Subversive Genealogy: The Politics and Art of Herman Melville*. Berkeley: University of California Press, 1983.

Rose, Edward J. " 'The Queenly Personality': Walpole, Melville, and Mother." *Literature and Psychology* 15 (Fall 1965): 216–29.

Rosenheim, Frederick. "Flight from Home: Some Episodes in the Life of Herman Melville." *American Imago* 1 (1940): 1–30.

Rowe, John Carlos. *Through the Custom-House: Nineteenth-Century American Fiction and Modern Theory*. Baltimore: Johns Hopkins University Press, 1982.

Rubin, Larry. "*Billy Budd*: What Goes on Behind Closed Doors." *American Imago* 37 (1980): 65–67.

Sack, William H. "Melville and the Theme of Individuation in *Moby-Dick*." *Melville Society Extracts* No. 55 (September 1983): 7–9.

Sandberg, Alvin. "Erotic Patterns in 'The Paradise of Bachelors and the Tartarus of Maids.' " *Literature and Psychology* 18, 1 (1968): 2–8.

———. "The Quest for Love and the Quest for Revenge in Herman Melville." Ph.D. Diss., New York University, 1970. [*Mel. Diss.*, # 235.]

Schneck, Jerome M. "Hypnagogic Hallucinations: Herman Melville's *Moby-Dick*." *New York State Journal of Medicine* 77 (1967): 2145–47.

———. "Karl Kahlbaum's *Catatonia* and Herman Melville's *Bartleby the Scrivener*." *Archives of General Psychiatry* 27 (1972): 48–51.

Shepherd, Gerard W. "Pierre's Psyche and Melville's Art." *ESQ* 30 (Second Quarter 1984): 83–98.

Shneidman, Edwin S. "The Deaths of Herman Melville." In *Melville and Hawthorne in the Berkshires*. Ed. Howard P. Vincent. Kent, Ohio: Kent State University Press, 1968, pp. 118–43.

———. "Orientations Toward Death: A Vital Aspect of the Study of Lives." In *The Study of Lives: Essays on Personality in Honor of Henry A. Murray*. Ed. Robert W. White. New York: Prentice-Hall, 1963, pp. 200–27.

———. "Some Psychological Reflections on the Death of Malcolm Melville." *Suicide and Life Threatening Behavior* 6 (1976): 231–42.

Shulman, Robert. "The Serious Functions of Melville's Phallic Jokes." *American Literature* 33 (May 1961): 179–94.

Simpson, David. *Fetishism and Imagination: Dickens, Melville, Conrad*. Baltimore: Johns Hopkins University Press, 1982.

Skura, Meredith Anne. *The Literary Use of the Psychoanalytic Process*. New Haven, Conn.: Yale University Press, 1981.

Slochower, Harry. "Freudian Motifs in *Moby-Dick*." *Complex* 3 (1950): 16–25.

———. "The Quest for an American Myth: *Moby-Dick*." In *Mythopoesis*. Detroit: Wayne State University Press, 1970, pp. 223–45.

Smith, Henry Nash. "The Madness of Ahab." In *Democracy and the Novel: Popular Resistance to Classic American Writers*. New York: Oxford University Press, 1978, pp. 35–55.

Steele, Jeffrey. "Emerson, Hawthorne, Melville, and the Unconscious." *Melville Society Extracts* No. 51 (September 1982): 3–4.

Stein, William Bysshe. "Melville's Eros." *Texas Studies in Literature and Language* 3 (Autumn 1961): 297–308.

———. "Melville's Poetry: Its Symbols of Individuation." *Literature and Psychology* 7 (May 1957): 21–26.

———. *The Poetry of Melville's Late Years: Time, History, Myth and Religion*. Albany: State University of New York Press, 1970.

Stevens, Wallace. *The Palm at the End of the Mind*. Ed. Holly Stevens. New York: Alfred A. Knopf, 1971.

Strauch, Carl F. "Ishmael: Time and Personality in *Moby-Dick*." *Studies in the Novel* 1 (Winter 1969): 468–83.

Sundquist, Eric. *Home as Found: Authority and Genealogy in Nineteenth-Century American Literature*. Baltimore: Johns Hopkins University Press, 1979.

Sutton, Walter. "Melville's 'Pleasure Party': The Art of Concealment." *Philological Quarterly* 30 (July 1951): 316–27.

Thomas, Brook. "The Writer's Procreative Urge in *Pierre*: Fictional Freedom or Convoluted Incest?" *Studies in the Novel* 11 (Winter 1979): 416–30.

Van Vechten, Carl. "The Later Work of Herman Melville." *Double Dealer* (New Orleans) 3 (January 1922): 9–20.

Vernon, John. "Melville's 'The Bell-Tower'." *Studies in Short Fiction* 7 (Spring 1970): 264–76.

Walker, David. *The Transparent Lyric: Reading and Meaning in the Poetry of Stevens and Williams*. Princeton, N.J.: Princeton University Press, 1984.

Watson, E. L. Grant. "Melville's *Pierre*." *New England Quarterly* 3 (April 1930): 195–234.

Weaver, Raymond M. *Herman Melville: Mariner and Mystic*. New York: Doran, 1921.

Whyte, L. L. *The Unconscious Before Freud*. New York: Basic Books, 1960.

Wright, Elizabeth. "The New Psychoanalysis and Literary Criticism: A Reading of Hawthorne and Melville." *Poetics Today* 3 (Spring 1982): 89–105.

18

MELVILLE'S COGNITIVE STYLE: THE LOGIC OF *MOBY-DICK*

Edwin S. Shneidman

From the first exciting moment that one looks at *Moby-Dick* from a logician's point of view, it is startlingly clear that the book (as a living entity) and Melville-Ishmael (as driving intellects) have rich and textured *ways* of *thinking* that are consistent with and advance the main psychological thrust and message of the book. After dramatically telling us who his logician is ("Call me Ishmael"), Melville begins the journey with an extended syllogism, or sorites.[1] First he summarizes the argument in a rather straightforward and beguiling fashion:

Some years ago—never mind how long precisely—having little or no money in my purse, and nothing particular to interest me on shore, I thought I would sail about a little and see the watery part of the world. It is a way I have of driving off the spleen, and regulating the circulation.

But then, Melville-Ishmael becomes explicit and reveals the bitter underlying meaning of this sorites:

Whenever I find myself growing grim about the mouth; whenever it is a damp, drizzly November in my soul; whenever I find myself involuntarily pausing before coffin warehouses, and bringing up the rear of every funeral I meet; and especially, whenever my hypos get such an upper hand of me, that it requires a strong moral principle to prevent me from deliberately stepping into the street, and methodically knocking people's hats off—then, I account it high time to get to sea as soon as I can.

In case any reader has lost sight of the argument (that getting away, egresssing, is Ishmael's substitute for knocking people's heads in, for committing mayhem or *murder*), Melville-Ishmael tells us straightforwardly: "This is my substitute for pistol and ball. With a philosophical flourish Cato throws himself upon his sword: I quietly take to the ship" (*MD*, p. 12).

The argument can be restated this way: When my bodily humors (hypos) are such that they make me feel like committing murder, I (Melville-Ishmael), instead, commit a partial or symbolic suicide by burying myself for an extended time in a ship at sea. Furthermore, by a subtle process that intermixes fate (or chance) and my conscious (and unconscious) selections, I make this egression on a ship that is ruled by a crazy captain-monarch whose madness takes the form of a monomaniacal murderously revengeful impulse that is coupled with a self-destructive capacity to destroy not only himself but all his crew around him, myself included.

No one now can miss the point: *Moby-Dick* is about *suicide*, specifically suicide *as an alternative to murder*. The first chapter is about it; the last chapter is about it. Self-destruction is the psychological topic that frames the entire work. All of the glorious text in between is interstitial to the "book ends" of self-sought death.

And still further *Moby-Dick* is about the covert, subintentioned, beneath-the-surface ways ("...as if the infatuated man sought to run more than half way to meet his doom..." (*MD*, p. 220)], in which a person can demean, truncate, limit, narrow or diminish himself. It is about the moieties of life, "living on with half a heart and half a lung" (*MD*, p. 160), short of death itself. It is about the unconscious elements, "the gliding great demon of the seas of life" (*MD*, p. 162), in self-induced destruction. The exploration of this world of the sub-surface stream of the mind makes this book an endlessly unfathomable excitement.

A HISTORY OF LOGIC

The history of logic is a long and interesting one.[2] Here, in an admittedly oversimplified view of Western logic, I have identified five major names or sets of names.

Aristotle dominates logic as Mt. Everest might dominate the plains of Kansas. He is the source of the concept of the syllogism. Refinements and improvement of his system have constituted most of the art and science of logic in the Western world for the past 2,500 years. Other than prayer, the principal occupation of the monasteries of the Middle Ages seems to have been a cerebral beadcounting of the Aristolelian syllogistic forms. What is considered to be correct, reasonable, sensible, or logical today is usually defined in terms of the traditional Aristotelian rules for reasoning. The bulk of Artistotle's logic is *deductive* consisting of identifying all the statements (as either true or false) that are implied or imbedded in premises or syllogisms.

Inductive logic, however, is another rather different kind of reasoning. It flows from any number of actually observed facts to one empirical generalization or conclusion. Two giants are identified with this approach. *Francis Bacon*, who spoke of the kinds of rational lapses people are liable to make when they attempt these inductions, linked such errors to false Gods and called them Idols—Idols of the Cave, of the Tribe, of the Marketplace, and of the Theater. Second, *John Stuart Mill*, in *The System of Logic* (1843), propounded a set of basic rules (or Canons) for establishing causality inductively. These are the Methods of Difference, of Agreement, of Agreement and Difference, of Residues, and of Concomitant Variation.

Since the nineteenth century there has been a major refurbishing of Aristotelian logic, sparked in large part by the insight that mathematics is itself a form of logic. Associated with this development are Frege, Boole, De Morgan, Peirce, Peano, Russell, and Whitehead, and the "Vienna Circle" (Carnap, Wittgenstein, Reichenbach)—all of whom believed that the single proper function of philosophy was to clarify language. Their doctrine of Logical Positivism, which totally eschews the traditional topics of philosophy (such as cosmology, epistemology, ethics, aesthetics), has had an enormous impact on Western thought, perhaps, in part, because of the sanctified position in which we moderns hold mathematics and precision.

Not many people think of *Freud* as a giant among logicians. Some, myself included, believe that one of Freud's major contributions is to the world of thought and logic. His emphasis on unconscious processes and on the concept of ambivalence showed us that the dichotomy deemed to be absolutely basic to Aristotelian thinking (*A vs.* non-*A*) was not necessarily psychologically sound. One could both love and hate at the same time; a person could simultaneously wish to die and entertain fantasies of rescue and intervention. Freud changed Aristotle's monologic to a more psychologically sophisticated dualogic. For our purposes what is especially interesting is that Melville anticipated Freud in this important respect.

Most of us take it for granted that Greek-European-American logic is the only logic of the world. Of course, this is not so. There are ancient Eastern logics that are predicated on styles of thinking that are fundamentally different from Western ways of reasoning. Hajime Nakamura's monumental book, *The Ways of Thinking of Eastern Peoples*, for instance, explicates the dimensions of Japanese, Chinese, and Indian logics. Indeed, the Whorf-Sapir hypothesis (that our thinking is inescapably filtered through our language) should alert us that there are at least as many basic logics as there are language types, so we might expect a

Standard Average European logic, an Arabic logic, a Chinese logic, a Hopi logic, an Eskimo logic, and so on.

There is much more then to deductive logic than classical Aristotelian syllogistic reasoning. Human beings employ many ways of coming to conclusions that are simply not accounted for in traditional logic. Furthermore, many gambits of reasoning that receive poor marks in the Aristotelian system are better understood not as "errors" but as "idiosyncrasies of reasoning," that is, as part of cognitive style in which these idiosyncrasies seem to work quite well and to "make sense" to the person who employs them. In this chapter I will distinguish at least four kinds of deductive logic. I call these (1) Denotative Deductive Logic, (2) Connotative or Conditional Deductive Logic, (3) Non-summative Deductive Logic, and (4) Paralogic.

DENOTATIVE DEDUCTION

Denotative Deductive Logic is the traditional Aristotelian logic. It depends solely on its formal structure. In this system, language sentences are represented by their denoted place, for example, Subject (S) or Predicate (P), etc. All Ss are equal; all Ps are equal. Any P is equal to any other P. There is no flexibility about it. The well-known syllogism about Socrates's mortality is equally and inflexibly true of Plato, Descartes, Smith, Jones, or anybody. It simply asserts that when all S is P (all men are mortal) then every S is P (any man is mortal).

Using Subjects and Predicates, we may generate four kinds of propositions: Universal affirmative (all S is P), universal negative (no S is P), particular affirmative (some S is P), and particular negative (some S is not P). Traditionally, these are labeled A, E, I, and O propositions, respectively.

A syllogism consists of two propositions and a conclusion, each one of them being an A, E, I, or O statement. There are then sixty-four possible combinations (called *moods* of the syllogism)—AAA, AAE, AAI, and so on—of which only sixteen are logically valid. (Sound reasoning is supposed to be confined to these sixteen moods of the syllogism.) The other combinations contain logical errors and are considered invalid.

Not unexpectedly, *Moby-Dick* has some interesting examples of straightforward valid Aristotelian syllogisms. They occur throughout the work. When, for instance in Chapter 17, Ishmael wishes to enter his room at the inn, he discovers Queequeg performing Ramadan. Here is a paraphrase of his AAA syllogism:

1. The room was locked even though sufficient time has elapsed for Queequeg to have completed his ritual. ("Towards evening, when I felt assured that all his performances and rituals must be over, I went up to his room and knocked

at the door; but no answer. I tried to open it, but it was fastened inside. 'Queequeg,' said I softly through the key-hole: —all silent. 'I say, Queequeg! why don't you speak? It's I—Ishmael.' But all remained still as before. I began to grow alarmed. I had allowed him such abundant time; I thought he might have had an apoplectic fit.")

2. Through the key-hole, Ishmael espies the shaft of Queequeg's harpoon. ("I looked through the key-hole; ... I was surprised to behold resting against the wall the wooden shaft of Queequeg's harpoon. . . .")

3. Ishmael knows that Queequeg never leaves his room without his harpoon. ("That's strange, thought I; but at any rate, since the harpoon stands yonder, and he seldom or never goes abroad without it.")

The syllogistic conclusion: "therefore he must be inside here, and no possible mistake" (*MD*, p. 78).

But this straightforward syllogism is not totally straightforward. Curiously, it has a conditional quality about it. Queequeg "seldom or never goes abroad without it" (*MD*, p. 78). The word "seldom" introduces a continuum in the "always-never" dichotomy, but Melville treats the situation as though it were a dichotomy when he adds: ". . . and no possible mistake" (*MD*, p. 78). Figure 1 shows a schematization of the syllogism, employing the traditional Venn circles.

Another, much more dramatic example is from Chapter 44, "The Chart."

Often, when forced from his hammock by exhausting and intolerably vivid dreams of the night, which, resuming his own intense thoughts through the day, carried them on amid a clashing of phrensies, and whirled them round and round in his blazing brain, till the very throbbing of his life-spot became insufferable anguish; and when, as was sometimes the case, these spiritual throes in him heaved his being up from its base, and a chasm seemed opening in him, from which forked flames and lightnings shot up, and accursed fiends beckoned him to leap down among them; when this hell in himself yawned beneath him, a wild cry would be heard through the ship; and with glaring eyes Ahab would burst from his state room, as though escaping from a bed that was on fire. Yet these, perhaps, instead of being the unsuppressable symptoms of some latent weakness, or fright at his own resolve, were but the plainest tokens of its intensity. For, at such times, crazy Ahab, the scheming, unappeasedly steadfast hunter of the white whale; this Ahab that had gone to his hammock, was not the agent that so caused him to burst from it in horror again. The latter was the eternal, living principle or soul in him; and in sleep, being for the time dissociated from the characterizing mind, which at other times employed it for its outer vehicle or agent, it spontaneously sought escape from the scorching contiguity of the frantic thing, of which, for the time, it was no longer an integral. But as the mind does not exist unless leagued with the soul, therefore it must have been that, in Ahab's case, yielding up all his thoughts and fancies to his one supreme purpose; that purpose, by its own sheer inveteracy of will, forced itself against

Figure 1
Examples of Aristotelian Syllogistic Reasoning

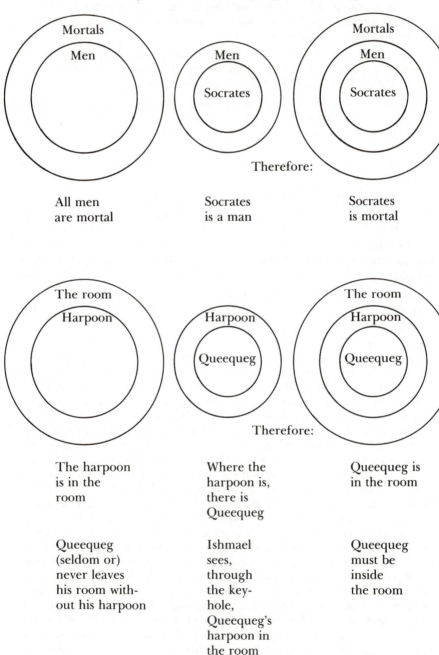

gods and devils into a kind of self-assumed, independent being of its own. Nay, could grimly live and burn, while the common vitality to which it was conjoined, fled horror-stricken from the unbidden and unfathered birth. Therefore, the tormented spirit that glared out of bodily eyes, when what seemed Ahab rushed from his room, was for the time but a vacated thing, a formless somnambulistic being, a ray of living light, to be sure, but without an object to color, and therefore a blankness in itself. God help thee, old man, thy thoughts have created a creature in thee; and he whose intense thinking thus makes him a Prometheus; a vulture feeds upon that heart for ever; that vulture the very creature he creates (*MD*, pp. 174–75).

The syllogism in this chilling paragraph may be paraphased as follows:

1. In each human being, there are two aspects of the self: "The characterizing mind" and "the eternal living principle or soul."

2. In times of great emotional intensity, these two (which should, in their normal functioning, be united) can become separated by a psychological chasm and thus become dissociated from each other.

3. In extreme cases of such dissociation (such as Captain Ahab's), by sheer power of will, one of the two elements, specifically the unsouled mind, can assume a grim (but empty) existence of its own.

4. *Therefore*, the manifestations of the tormented spirit that others see is but a hollow vessel; a man without a soul; an empty being. Such a man is a blankness, a nullity doomed by his self-created, self-destroying psychological vulture.

Melville's extraordinary passage is filled with prefigurings. In one paragraph, Melville anticipates Eugen Bleuler (1857–1939), who coined the term "schizophrenia," implying a schism between thought and feeling, a cleavage or fissure between the basic mental functions of intellect and emotion. Furthermore, it presages Jung's (1875–1961) notions of the persona, the shadow as well as existential ideas of the hollow man, the empty person, the meaningless life, the estranged individual, the affectless human ("All visible objects, man, are but as pasteboard masks. But in each event—in the living act, the undoubted deed—there, some unknown but still reasoning thing puts forth the mouldings of its features from behind the unreasoning mask" [*MD*, p. 144].) It also anticipates the basic psychoanalytic concept of the Unconscious proposed by Freud (1856–1939) and, then necessarily, of various layers of personality functioning ("Hark ye yet again—the little lower layer" [*MD*, p. 144] and "how all this came to be ... how to their unconscious understandings ... all this to explain, would be to dive deeper than Ishmael can go" [*MD*, p. 162].) In all, this passage, like a frigate filled with a thousand ideas, is indeed a fully packed syllogism.

Even these few syllogisms give us some idea of Melville's deductive logical style. *Moby-Dick* is filled with logical arguments. The book itself can be seen as one immense sorites.

The major premise of *Moby-Dick* might go something like this: There is a natural order in the universe, an order between one individual and another and between the individual and nature. (By implication, there are strict limitations to any individual's autonomy and power.) The first minor premise would be: To depart from or to challenge this natural order always results in some corrective redress or balance by nature, usually felt as retaliative punishment by the offending individual. The second minor premise: Ahab's monomaniacal, revengeful drive could have remained his own crazy business, but his overwhelming hubris openly taunted the Fates and thus became a matter between him and the natural order. Conclusion: Ahab had to be punished; he had to be destroyed, even if it meant the death of almost everyone around him. The admonition "Look not too long in the face of the fire, O man!" (*MD*, p. 354) can also be read as "Beware! Do not over-tempt the Fates. You may go only so far, even (or especially) in your megalomania."

But there are other *kinds* of logic in *Moby-Dick*. Let us try to harpoon two or three of them.

CONDITIONAL DEDUCTION

There is, of course, more to deductive logic than the classical textbooks say. There is a kind of logic, conditional logic, that purists would never admit. Connotative or *Conditional Deductive Logic* is reasoning which embodies the notion that the correctness of reasoning may depend on the time or place or circumstance. These "circumstances" may even include the emotional, psychological, or ethical state-of-mind of the logician. In other words, the logic depends, in part, on the connotative overtones of the words. Symbols alone will not do—not all Ss or Ps are alike.[3]

Logic itself is contextual or conditional. This idea is as unacceptable to Aristotelian logic as the idea that the sum of a group of numbers depends on anything other than invariable addition. But thinking (reasoning, coming to conclusions) is more complicated than mathematics precisely because it is touched by psychological and other contextual factors. All these notions lead us to a second, closer look at the seemingly least important word in the syllogism, the bridge-word "therefore."

First, however, a brief but necessary aside. Among the 216,014 words in *Moby-Dick* there are 17,560 different word forms. From among these, I have selected a set of twenty-five "logical words" including key conjunctions or conjunctive adverbs ("therefore" and "hence") and such words as "both" and "half" that reflect Melville's concern with simultaneous opposites, oxymorons, moieties, and ambivalences. The twelve "logical words" used most frequently are then (629 times), half (137), both (124), because (92), therefore (67), since (65), hence (32), thinking (28), concluded (19), thereby (28), whereas (18), and whenever (15).[4]

At first, the most innocuous word in the syllogism seems to be a simple conjunction. When someone says "therefore," we assume that that person has come to some sort of decision or resolution. "Therefore" implies that the speaker has not only been thinking but, more than that, coming to conclusions. It is the pivot-word in the syllogism.

It is generally believed that not much need be said about "therefore." There is relatively little discussion of it in Western logic. It is simply that automatic process—the colorless conjunction—between the premises and the conclusion. It is viewed as a sort of clearing of the throat after the "whereas," the signal before one gives the punch line (the conclusion) of the cognitive resolution. It turns out that "therefore" does not always indicate a totally simple or automatic or innocuous operation.

By examining Melville's use of "therefore" and "hence" we can better understand his style of thinking—the ways in which he is traditionally Aristotelian and the ways in which he is idiosyncratically, uniquely Melvillean in his thinking. Not unexpectedly, most of Melville's usage of "therefore" is straightforwardly syllogistic, as in the following example:

Now, the Pequod had sailed from Nantucket at the very beginning of the Season-on-the-Line. No possible endeavor then could enable her commander to make the great passage southwards, double Cape Horn, and then running down sixty degrees of latitude arrive in the equatorial Pacific in time to cruise there. Therefore, he must wait for the next ensuing season. (*MD*, p. 173)

There are many instances in *Moby-Dick* of this kind of not-very-exciting syllogism and sorites, all of them grist for any schoolman's mill.

But Melville was capable of a much more subtle kind of "thereforing." And it is in these non-Aristotelian variations of syllogistic reasoning, specifically in his conditional, almost Persian ways of thinking that Melville creates a new language and a new logic and adds to the tone of *Moby-Dick* that sense of special inevitability and doom.

Melville's strength as a subtle logician does not lie in his traditional syllogisms. It begins to show itself in the nuances he gives to the reasoning process, his conditional uses of "therefore" (and "hence"). In the following example, Queequeg's illiteracy, an idiosyncratic circumstance in the world rather than a universal logical rule, shapes the logical structure.

Shaking off the sleet from my ice-glazed hat and jacket, I seated myself near the door, and turning sideways was surprised to see Queequeg near me. Affected by the solemnity of the scene, there was a wondering gaze of incredulous curiosity in his countenance. This savage was the only person present who seemed to notice my entrance; because he was the only one who could not read, and, therefore, was not reading those frigid inscriptions on the wall. (*MD*, p. 40)

Father Mapple provides another telling example of conditional thinking:

"Shipmates, God has laid but one hand upon you; both his hands press upon me. I have read ye by what murky light may be mine the lesson that Jonah teaches to all sinners; and therefore to ye, and still more to me, for I am a greater sinner than ye". (*MD*, p. 50)

In this case, the "therefore" has more intensity (as if one had turned up the volume on a rheostat) for Father Mapple than it does for others— "still more to me" (*MD*, p. 50). All men are sinners, but some men are greater sinners than others. And what Jonah teaches to all sinners, he teaches much more to those who are greatest sinners: "God had laid but one hand upon you; both his hands press upon me" (*MD*, p. 50).

And reasoning can even depend on even more subjective states. Indeed, the very logic by which Ahab is able to track and find the object of his hate contains a way of reasoning that is interfused with personal, experiential, intuitive, conditional elements.

In addition, philosophical elements condition the logical flow. In Chapter 72, "The Monkey-Rope," the narrator muses as follows:

So strongly and metaphysically did I conceive of my situation then, that while earnestly watching his motions, I seemed distinctly to perceive that my own individuality was now merged in a joint stock company of two: that my free will had received a mortal wound; and that another's mistake or misfortune might plunge innocent me into unmerited disaster and death. Therefore, I saw that here was a sort of interregnum in Providence; for its even-handed equity never could have sanctioned so gross an injustice. And yet still further pondering— while I jerked him now and then from between the whale and the ship, which would threaten to jam him—still further pondering, I say, I saw that this situation of mine was the precise situation of every mortal that breathes; only, in most cases, he, one way or other, has this Siamese connexion with a plurality of other mortals. If your banker breaks, you snap; if your apothecary by mistake sends you poison in your pills, you die. (*MD*, p. 271)

All this is prologue to the main act. The psychological nuances in Melville's paragraphs on death and suicide and Melville's daring notion of partial suicide (like burying oneself in a whaling ship at sea) are a kind of subintentioned or unconscious way of cutting oneself off from life, short of overt death. Consider:

Death seems the only desirable sequel for a career like this; but Death is only a launching into the region of the strange Untried; it is but the first salutation to the possibilities of the immense Remote, the Wild, the Watery, the Unshored; therefore, to the death-longing eyes of such men, who still have left in them some interior compunctions against suicide, does the all-contributed and all-receptive ocean alluringly spread forth his whole plain of unimaginable, taking terrors, and wonderful, new-life adventures; and from the hearts of infinite Pacifics, the thousand mermaids sing to them—"Come hither, broken-hearted; here is another life without the guilt of intermediate death; here are wonders supernatural, without dying for them. Come hither! bury thyself in a life which, to your now equally abhorred and abhorring, landed world, is more oblivious than death. Come hither! put up *thy* gravestone, too, within the churchyard, and come hither, till we marry thee!"

Hearkening to these voices, East and West, by early sun-rise, and by fall of eve, the blacksmith's soul responded, Aye, I come! And so Perth went a-whaling. (*MD*, p. 402)

Continuing to focus on this issue of subintentioned death wherein the individual plays a latent or covert role in hastening his own demise, let us examine the final chapters of *Moby-Dick*, especially as they touch on Ahab's death.

There is a certain persuasive logic to the manner of Ahab's death, which might be called a victim-precipitated homicide; he dared, and made, the murderous death-white whale kill him. He could not rest until he was so taken. He invited death by the risks that he ran. He permitted suicide. To what empty purpose would any further voyages have been, if he *had* killed the symbol of his search, the object of his hate? His death on that voyage by Moby Dick came at the right time, for in his unconscious wish it was perfect, the only, the "appropriate" death.

After forty solitary years at sea, Ahab had little in the way of self-possessions or personal belongings. His wife, he said, was already a widow; his interest in the possible profits from the voyage was nil; his withdrawal from meaningful material possessions (and his loss of joy with them) is perhaps best indicated by his flinging his "still lighted pipe into the sea" (ch. 30) and dashing his quadrant to the deck (ch. 118), both rash acts for a captain.

In Ahab's conscious mind, he wanted to kill, but we know that self-destruction can be "murder in the 180th degree." Figuratively speaking, the barb of his harpoon was pointed toward him; his brain thought a thrust, but his arm executed a retroflex. Was his death an "accident?" If he had survived his psychodynamically freighted voyage and had returned unharmed to Nantucket's pier, that would have been a true accident. Men can die for nothing—most men do—but a few big-jointed men can give their lives for an internalized something. Ahab would not have missed this opportunity for the world.

What further evidence can be cited bearing on the issue of subintentioned cessation? With his three harpooneers before him, with their harpoons turned up like goblets, Ahab commands, in this maritime immolation scene: "Drink, ye harpooneers! drink and swear, ye men that man the deathful whaleboat's bow—Death to Moby Dick! God hunt us all, if we do not hunt Moby Dick to his death!" (*MD*, p. 146) Kill or be killed; punish or be punished; murder or suicide. The two are intertwined in one inexorable logic.

NON-SUMMATIVE DEDUCTION

There is more; the little lower layers. Let us go down to a deeper tier, to a more submerged stratum, to a sub-sub-sub-basement, where psychologists (not librarians) dwell. In this spirit, I propose that there is still a third kind of deductive logic, one that is an integral piece of the inner logical life of Melville-Ishmael. What I call *Non-summative Deductive Logic* asserts that one thought can actually be a half, or two, and that the two can even be contradictory while embraced in the same thought. In other words, moieties, ambivalences, and oxymorons can all be integral parts of the flow of thought.

One of two key words can signal a major shift in emphasis. Words like "both" and "half" tell us that we are dealing with modes of logic that are clearly outside the ordinary Aristotelian mold. At the Try Pots Inn, when Ishmael answers Mrs. Hussey's query, "Clam or Cod?" with " 'Both,' says I; and let's have a couple of smoked herring by way of variety" (*MD*, pp. 64, 66), he is asserting the possibility of the simultaneous presence of *A* and non-*A*, and something even more thrown in for variety. It is decidedly non-Aristotelian. On a much more profound level, the line "On life and death this old man walked" (*MD*, p. 200) clearly asserts the possibility of psychological simultaneity of logical opposites.

The use of "both" is critical in Melville's expanded logical style and his understanding of ambivalence.

Melville knows that it is humanly possible, even if it is logically strained, that "even Christians could be both miserable and wicked"; that one can "boldly dip into the Potluck of both worlds" (*MD*, p. 57); and that there is no rule of nature that one has to choose, as a rule of life, between clam or cod. " 'Both,' says I." This seemingly innocuous statement reflects more than gustatory greediness. It is a paradigm of life itself. In a single act, we can do something that has two different uses. Queequeg's tomahawk pipe can both brain his foes and soothe his soul (*MD*, p. 93); the whaleboat hull is "both balanced and directed" by one central keel (*MD*, p. 455); and Ahab plunges his harpoon into Moby Dick with both steel and curse (*MD*, p. 468). The point is that Ahab and every one of us have within us different warring forces: good and evil, light and dark, land and sea, order and disorder, love and hate, flesh and ivory limbs. Without these contradictory psychological richnesses, we would be as two-dimensional as "pasteboard masks."

In a sense, the converse of simultaneity-of-opposite ("both") is a moiety ("half"). "Half" suggests fractions, partials, moieties. It implies ambivalences, ambiguities, dualities, and, by extension, duplicities. (This expanded logic shows the way of *Moby-Dick* and of works beyond *Moby-Dick*; *Pierre*, "Bartleby," "Benito Cereno," *The Confidence-Man*, and *Billy Budd* would have no life without it.)

Melville's writings have their fair share of moieties, partials and parts, especially in relation to death, specifically partial death.

... some deep men ... are left living on with half a heart and half a lung.... (*MD*, p. 160)

His voice was like that of one with lungs half gone—hoarsely suppressed, a husky whisper. No wonder that, as in this state he tottered about, his private servant apprehensively followed him. (*Tales*, "Benito Cereno," p. 245)

Now, which was Samoa? The dead arm swinging high as Haman? Or the living trunk below? ... For myself, I ever regarded Samoa as but a large fragment of a man, not a man complete.... And the action at Teneriffe over, a great Nelson himself—physiologically speaking—was but three-quarters of a man. (*Mardi*, p.78)

Melville understood the importance of the non-Aristotelian coexistence of *A* and non-*A*. Was Socrates mortal or immortal? In a sense (by virtue, in part, of this very question): both. Was Ahab's goal survival or self-destruction? "On life and death this old man walked" (*MD*, p. 200). Even these few illustrations illuminate the close relationship between the style of logic and the basic theme in *Moby-Dick*. A suicidal person such as Ahab is basically ambivalent, thinking with simultaneity-of-opposites. He wants to flee unbearable circumstances, and, at the same time, he has active fantasies of magical intervention to be like a Catskill eagle:

And there is a Catskill eagle in some souls that can alike dive down into the blackest gorges, and soar out of them again and become invisible in the sunny spaces. And even if he for ever flies within the gorge, that gorge is in the mountains; so that even in his lowest swoop the mountain eagle is still higher than other birds upon the plain, even though they soar. (*MD*, p. 355)

In the Aristotelian sense, *Moby-Dick* is not a logical book and Ahab is not a logical character. We can reasonably conclude that Melville was not, himself, a logical person when he wrote it—for which we can be eternally grateful.

Part of Melville's marvelous illogicality stems from the fact that he was a self-taught depth psychologist. It may be as accurate to say that Melville was a pre-Freudian as it is to state that Freud was a post-Melvillean. Melville wrote about the unconscious in 1851, five years before Freud was born. When in *Moby-Dick* the author-narrator says, "what the White Whale was to them or ... to their unconscious understandings ... " (*MD*,

p. 162) or "through infancy's unconscious spell..." (*MD*, p. 406) or the phrase "the little lower layer..." (*MD*, p. 144) he is telling us that he understands the dualities, the admixtures, the contradictions, the ambivalences, the ambiguities, and the layers of the human mind.

Ambivalence is the non-Aristotelian idea that contradictories can coexist psychologically, like the simultaneous feelings of love and hate toward the same person. (Nowadays, ambivalence is considered to be an essential psychoanalytic idea.) The first-cousin of ambivalence is the oxymoron. It involves a union of opposites for epigrammatic effect. Among the best known examples in English are from *Romeo and Juliet*: "Feather of lead, bright smoke, cold fire, sick health" and, of course, "parting is such sweet sorrow." Melville's oxymoronic gem is his short poem "Art" wherein

> unlike things must meet and mate...
> And fuse with Jacob's mystic heart,
> To wrestle with the angel—Art.
> (*Poems*, p. 231)

There are two points about the logic in this poem. The first is that the juxtaposition of opposites—after conflict, sacrifice, and struggle—creates something tangible and worthwhile, Art. The second point reinforces the first. Jacob's wrestling with the angel (*Genesis* XXXII:25–33) results in both a blessing (his new name, Yisrael) as well as an injury (in "the hollow of his thigh"). Reflecting on the latter, we think of symbolic castration. So again, castrative injury, sacrifice, sweat, blood, tears, effort, pain, loss are all part of the price of their opposites: victory, creativity, and almost everything in life that has value—Art and Love. These values not only have their opposites, but, as part of a larger opposite, have their "price." Ahab, for instance, certainly wounded, perhaps, even killed the object of his hate, but at a price that a more rational man—one who is not crazy, not wildly vindictive, not obsessively hateful, not rigidly monomaniacal—would have prudently long before decided not to pay.

To exist with the knowledge of ambivalences, dualities, and oxymorons is a more complicated challenge than to live in the more simple world of the sixteen valid moods of the Aristotelian syllogism. And even more frightening, for unlike the ordered Aristotelian world, there are no magic talismanic formulas to guide us. Melville tells us as much in his profound summation in Chapter 114 of the human course of life itself, that there is no single set of fixed stages of life—totally at odds with what Shakespeare and countless others (Erik Erikson, in our time) would have us believe.

...the mingled, mingling threads of life are woven by warp and woof; calms crossed by storms, a storm for every calm. There is no steady unretracing progress in this life; we do not advance through fixed gradations, and at the last one pause: —through infancy's unconscious spell, boyhood's thoughtless faith, adolescence' doubt (the common doom), then scepticism, then disbelief, resting at last in manhood's pondering repose of If. But once gone through, we trace the round again; and are infants, boys, and men, and Ifs eternally. (*MD*, p. 406)

I believe that the greatest oxymoronic passage in *Moby-Dick* is the stunning opening paragraph of "The Funeral":

'Haul in the chains! Let the carcase go astern!'
The vast tackles have now done their duty. The peeled white body of the beheaded whale flashes like a marble sepulchre; though changed in hue, it has not perceptibly lost anything in bulk. It is still colossal. Slowly it floats more and more away, the water round it torn and splashed by the insatiate sharks, and the air above vexed with rapacious flights of screaming fowls, whose beaks are like so many insulting poniards in the whale. The vast white headless phantom floats further and further from the ship, and every rod that it so floats, what seem square roods of shark and cubic roods of fowls, augment the murderous din. For hours and hours from the almost stationary ship that hideous sight is seen. Beneath the unclouded and mild azure sky, upon the fair face of the pleasant sea, wafted by the joyous breezes, that great mass of death floats on and on, till lost in infinite perspectives. (*MD*, p. 261–62)

What is to be noted especially in this superlative passage is the breathtaking shift in mood between the first eight lugubrious sentences and the last lilting sentence—from horror and rapaciousness to the most pacific calm. Indeed, the last sentence itself contains this same dramatic contrast in the shift in tone between the first three phrases and the last two. It is the connotative tension in this passage that rivets and chills us. This description is a paradigm, if not of the actualities, then of the omnipresent tensions (whatever their character) in our own lives. In *Moby-Dick* it is the logic of tension and the aberrant ways in which these tensions are reduced that, together, provide the central implicit drama beneath the surface of the written text.

PARALOGIC

As though all this were not enough, there is still one more kind of logic we must consider. It is an openly flawed way of reasoning, a cryptologic, an illogic, a crazy logic, a *paralogic*. The topic of paralogical thinking in *Moby-Dick* has to be of some special interest to us, even though it may be somewhat painful to look too closely at it. Let us look briefly but openmindedly at the issue.

"N.B.," wrote Melville in March of 1877 at the bottom of a letter to his brother-in-law John C. Hoadley, "*I ain't crazy*" (*Letters*, p. 260). He underlined the words for emphasis. But his disclaimer has not prevented a swirl of controversy about his mental health. Independent of this, the family tried to get him to see an alienist, the esteemed Dr. Oliver Wendell Holmes. Recently, some newly found correspondence from Elizabeth Melville and Melville's brother-in-law, Samuel Shaw has revealed rather explicitly that in 1868 Melville was viewed as having more than ordinary perturbation (Walter D. Kring and Jonathan S. Carey, Donald Yannella and Hershel Parker). While there is no evidence, in my opinion, that Melville suffered from what we today would call schizophrenia, it none-theless provides an intellectually engaging exercise to turn to the topic of "language and thought in schizophrenia." In doing this I am not for a moment attempting to imply the oversimplistic notion that insanity and genius are identical, or that they are similar or just a hair's breadth apart. It is more sensible to say that there are "differences." Both the insane person and the genius are, almost by definition, "different" from the sane and the ordinary; but they are different in radically diverse ways. Principally, the genius is effective and makes sense, whereas the insane person is not and does not.

In "The Specific Laws of Logic in Schizophrenia" (1964), Elhard von Domarus puts forth the view that schizophrenic thinking involves er-roneous reasoning in terms of attributes of the Predicate (instead of thinking, as most of us do, in terms of attributes of the Subject) and it commits the error of the "undistributed middle term."

A few examples should clarify the principle. A female patient claims that she is the Virgin Mary. Elucidation of her thinking reveals that her basic syllogism is the following: The Virgin Mary was a virgin; I am a virgin; therefore I am the Virgin Mary. Another example: A patient on a closed ward continually shouted that he was Switzerland. Various per-sonnel asked him if he had Swiss ancestry, if he had been to Switzerland or if he wished to visit there—all of which served only to irritate him and disturb him further. "You don't understand," was his agitated reply. Then one day, in response to his shouted assertion, "I am Switzerland!" a new doctor on the ward told him that he would do everything he could to get him out of the locked ward. The patient's demeanor changed immediately and dramatically. "At last," he said, "someone understands me." The syllogistic reasoning, in terms of attributes of the predicate was this: Switzerland loves freedom; I love freedom (I want to get off this locked ward); therefore, I am Switzerland (see Figure 2).

Not all examples of reasoning in terms of the attributes of the Predicate have such fervent content. In Chapter 82, "The Honor and Glory of Whaling," Melville provides a rather benign and innocuous example, in which the latent syllogism can be schematized as follows:

A most noble episode in English history is that St. George was in actuality battling against a great whale.

Figure 2
Examples of Reasoning in Terms of Attributes of the Predicate; or, Fallacies of the Inadequately Distributed Middle Terms

I. It is as though the person thought this way:

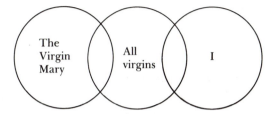

II. What the person actually does is this:

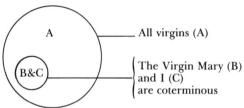

A	B	C	Therefore:
Those who are virgins	The Virgin Mary	I am a Virgin	I am The Virgin Mary
Those who are swift	Some Indians are swift	Some stags are swift	Some Indians are stags
Those who love freedom	Switzerland loves freedom	I love freedom	I am Switzerland
Those who have grand designs & immutable needs	The Fates have grand designs & immutable needs	I have grand designs & immutable needs	I am of the Fates– the Fates' Lieutenant

III. What the person should logically do is this:

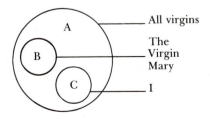

St. George's whale might have crawled up out of the sea on the beach; and considering that the animal ridden by St. George might have been only a large seal, or a sea-horse; bearing all this in mind, it will not appear altogether incompatible with the sacred legend and the ancientest draughts of the scene, to hold this so-called dragon no other than the great Leviathan himself. (*MD*, p. 305)

Therefore (reasoning in terms of attributes of the Predicate), all Nantucket whalemen are comparable to St. George and by good rights ought to be considered to be knights of the most noble order of St. George and should not be looked down on by anyone.

Thus, then, one of our own noble stamp, even a whaleman, is the tutelary guardian of England; and by good rights, we harpooneers of Nantucket should be enrolled in the most noble order of St. George. And therefore, let not the knights of that honorable company...[ever] eye a Nantucketer with disdain, since even in our woollen frocks and tarred trowsers we are much better entitled to St. George's decoration than they. (*MD*, p. 305)

Melville is clearly spoofing. He knows that the syllogism "St. George killed a whale; Nantucket whalers kill whales; therefore Nantucket whalers are equal with St. George" doesn't quite "hold water." But other times, Melville-Ahab uses an identical flawed logic in a totally serious way, filled with urgency and passion. What are we to make of the logic of this tirade by Ahab: "Swerve me? The path to my fixed purpose is laid with iron rails, whereon my soul is grooved to run" (*MD*, p. 147). A locomotive runs on rails; my soul runs on rails; therefore—it has a wild Whitmanian ring—I am a locomotive.

And, again, in a great credo passage from "The Chase—Second Day":

Starbuck, of late I've felt strangely moved to thee; ever since that hour we both saw—thou know'st what, in one another's eyes. But in this matter of the whale, be the front of thy face to me as the palm of this hand—a lipless, unfeatured blank. Ahab is for ever Ahab, man. This whole act's immutably decreed. 'Twas rehearsed by thee and me a billion years before this ocean rolled. Fool! I am the Fates' lieutenant; I act under orders. Look thou, underling! that thou obeyest mine. (*MD*, p. 459)

The underlying syllogism of this passage takes its very strength from the attributes of the Predicate: The Fates have grand designs and immutable needs; I have grand designs and immutable needs; therefore, I am part of the Fates, "the Fates' lieutenant."

All this, and several syllogisms cited above, are diagrammatically represented in Figure 2. The diagram makes it evident that while some of *A* is *B*, and some of *C* is *B*, *A* is not *C*. Paralogical thinking makes the mistake of believing that because *A* and *C* can be mentioned in the same breath (in relation to *B*) they are co-equal. It is the *wish* to do so even in the absence of the necessary logical supports that creates this fantasized bridge. It is the logic of yearning and of passion, not the logic of common sense.

Again, in "The Chase—First Day," just prior to the one that contains the passage about the Fates' lieutenant, Ahab, in response to a statement by Starbuck about an omen, declaims:

Omen? omen?—the dictionary! If the gods think to speak outright to man, they will honorably speak outright; not shake their heads, and give an old wives' darkling hint.—Begone! Ye two are the opposite poles of one thing; Starbuck is Stubb reversed, and Stubb is Starbuck; and ye two are all mankind; and Ahab stands alone among the millions of the peopled earth, nor gods nor men his neighbors! (*MD*, p. 452)

Confused in his logic, Ahab desires to be straightforward in his speech in order to communicate his deeper emotional needs. He does not seem to care that what he says contains a truly megalomaniacal bit of tortured reasoning. Here is what he implies: The extended universe—*all* that one can imagine—is made up of two and only two units: (a) *All* humankind (represented by their monotonous duplicated opposites, Starbuck and Stubb), and (b) one Ahab—"nor gods nor men his neighbors!" (*MD*, p. 452) Does Ahab really mean that he is somehow outside humankind?— "that man makes one in a whole nation's census—a mighty pageant creature formed for noble tragedies" (*MD*, p. 71).

Ahab is so wrought up that he does not care how far he goes; he seems to have the need to show just how desperately he feels by making overextended assertions to the world: "Talk not to me of blasphemy, man; I'd strike the sun if it insulted me.... Who's over me? Truth hath no confines" (*MD*, p. 144). And it does not matter if such a man has some defects:

Nor will it at all detract from him, dramatically regarded, if either by birth or other circumstances he have what seems a half wilful over-ruling morbidness at the bottom of his nature. For all men tragically great are made so through a certain morbidness. Be sure of this, O young ambition, all mortal greatness is but disease. (*MD*, p. 71)

But what kind of morbidness or disease or madness did Ahab have? In the Preface to *Language and Thought in Schizophrenia*, the noted American psychiatrist Nolan D. C. Lewis, speaking of schizophrenia, says that:

Among those presenting features repeatedly emphasized in this connection are (1) fundamental or fancy-born inconsistencies more or less foreign to normal or average life; (2) shut-in tendencies, with a sense of something wrong or unusual going on in the environment; (3) indulgence in vague artistic fantasies, with daydreaming and partial withdrawal from reality...; (4) automatic and dissociated thought processes, often with projection...; (5) odd mental influences, with transformation experiences; (6) grotesque incongruities of judgment, with accounts of fantastic episodes; (7) scatterings of thought and speech... combined with oddities of statement and fantastic action; (8) impulsive episodes and vagueness, with shifts of emotional reactions...or with other evidence of marked disorganization in language such as neologisms...(pp. viii-ix)

With a few slight shifts of emphasis, this explication of schizophrenic language and thought sounds like a harsh description of the goings-on in *Moby-Dick*. Some examples of all eight of the symptoms are present. On these grounds, a schizophrenic "syndrome" might be said to be present in *Moby-Dick*. But we would be illogical to say so.

The language and thought in *Moby-Dick* are not schizophrenic. There are a thousand differences, but the vital difference is that what Melville says, albeit in his idiosyncratically bold and lofty way, *makes sense*. From a strictly traditional point of view, the text of *Moby-Dick* is filled with logical mistakes, but it does not make *aesthetic* or *psychological* errors; rather it uses all these devices to heighten tension, to create grand efforts, and to *further communication*. It is the opposite of schizophrenic gibberish; it is Art which, by taking risks and stretching the "limits of governable imagination," communicates projectively with each active mind that confronts it.

Melville tells us that Ahab is special; Melville knew that *he* was special. A special person creates a special "bold and nervous lofty language" (*MD*, p. 71), a language that obviously is different from everyday talk and yet enables him to communicate while retaining some important measures of independence to speak-and-think his own way. It is a language-and-logic which is effective precisely because of the special modes of thought and persuasive logic that it so cunningly employs.

That is what a great writer is: a person who creates a new language, a fresh way of thinking and talking, a different style of language and thought; one who possesses an idiosyncratic way of seeing the world and reports his vision in a unique way. Possessing more than a fresh-sounding cadence or an individualized different accent or dialect, a great writer needs the unhesitating talent to be an Aristotle and forge a style of *logic* copyrighted in a private patent office of which he or she is the sole proprietor and the most enthusiastic defender. Every great author is his or her own logician, eligible to be included in the select company of Aristotle, Avicenna, Bacon, Mill, and Whitehead. There are *many* styles of logic in the world, most of them yet to be formulated. Any standard textbook of logic would, if it were read, cripple the mind of a potential Proust or Joyce. Melville knew that standard philosophy and logic have to be diluted to meet *individual* tastes: "Adler & Taylor came into my room.... We talked metaphysics continually... under the influence of the whiskey" (1849 *Journal*, p. 12). More importantly, Melville also knew the larger corollary truth: "There are some enterprises in which a careful disorderliness is the true method" (*MD*, p. 304). A great writer must think his or her own logic, forge a new genre; be a true "original." The names are few. In nineteenth-century America we have Whitman, Poe, Clemens, Dickinson, and, rising above all, "like a snow hill in the air," Herman Melville.

NOTES

1. The typical form of the syllogism consists of three statements (each with a subject and predicate); the first two are premises, and the third, which follows logically from them, is the conclusion. A commonly quoted syllogism is: All men are mortal; Socrates is a man; therefore Socrates is mortal. An extended syllogism with three or more premises (the number is almost unlimited) is called a sorites.

2. See Alonzo Church's excellent discussion of the history of logic in the *Encyclopedia Britannica* (1973).

3. Quoting from "The Sun Epistle" by the thirteenth-century Persian logician al-Qazwini-al-Katibi and from the tenth-century Persian philosopher Avicenna, Nicholas Rescher points out that the Persians introduced temporal and quantitative qualifiers of the basic Aristotelian absolute categories of "all" and "none," such as "necessarily," "perpetually," "non-necessarily," or "non-perpetually." In the Persian logic of centuries ago there were four basic modal relationships:

A. A chronically constant necessary correlation (i.e., *A* is necessarily true when *B* is true).

B. A chronologically constant correlation (i.e., *A* is true whenever *B* is true).

C. A chronologically occasional correlation (i.e., *A* is true at some time when *B* is true).

D. A chronologically occasional possibility correlation (*A* is possibly true at some time when *B* is true).

Thus, it can be seen that there are two dimensions in Arabic logic that are not at all prominent in Western (Aristotelian) logic: (1) a temporal dimension of ubiquity and occasion; and (2) a possible dimension of necessity (certainty) and probability.

4. Other "logical words" used with less frequency are argument, conclude, concluding, conclusion, deduction, denote, denoted, denotes, follows, inasmuch, premised, and whereupon. See *A Concordance to Melville's Moby-Dick*, ed. Hennig Cohen and James Cahalan, Ann Arbor, Mich.: University Microfilms, 1978. A more recent concordance is by Eugene F. Irey, New York: Garland, 1982. There

are also, in dissertation form, concordances for *Clarel* (Larry Wegener; *Mel. Diss.*, #487) and *Billy Budd* (Charles Murray; *Mel. Diss.*, #505).

WORKS CITED

Church, Alonzo. "Logic, History of: Modern Logic." *Encyclopedia Britannica*. 1973 ed.

Cohen, Hennig, and James Cahalan, eds. *A Concordance to Melville's Moby-Dick*. 2 vols. Ann Arbor, Mich.: University Microfilms International, 1978.

Kring, Walter D., and Jonathan S. Carey. "Two Discoveries Concerning Herman Melville." *Proceedings of the Massachusetts Historical Society* 87 (1975): 137–41.

Lawrence, T. E. *Seven Pillars of Wisdom*. New York: Garden City Publishing Co., 1935.

Lewis, Nolan D. C. Preface. In *Language and Thought in Schizophrenia*. Ed. J. S. Kasanin. New York: W. W. Norton, 1964.

Murray, Charles Joseph. "A Concordance to Melville's *Billy Budd*." Ph.D. Dissertation, Miami (Ohio) University, 1979. [*Mel. Diss.*, #505]

Nakamura, Hajime. *The Ways of Thinking of Eastern Peoples*. New York: UNESCO, 1967.

Rescher, Nicholas. *Temporal Modalities in Arabic Logic*. New York: Humanities Press, 1967.

von Domarus, Elhard. "The Specific Laws of Logic in Schizophrenia." In *Language and Thought in Schizophrenia*. Ed. J. S. Kasanin. New York: W. W. Norton, 1964, pp. 104–14.

Wegener, Larry Edward. "A Concordance to Herman Melville's *Clarel*: A Poem and Pilgrimage to the Holy Land." Ph.D. Dissertation, University of Nebraska, 1978. [*Mel. Diss.*, #487]

Yannella, Donald, and Hershel Parker. *The Endless, Winding Way in Melville: New Charts by Kring and Carey*. Glassboro, N.J.: Melville Society, 1981.

PART FOUR

MELVILLE'S ART

19

"ONTOLOGICAL HEROICS": MELVILLE'S PHILOSOPHICAL ART

John Wenke

> You can conclude nothing absolute from the human form, barber.
>
> (*CM*, p. 226)

SOUNDINGS

However much *Typee* bears the unmistakable mark of its maker, especially as it takes the protagonist into an alien but alluring geographical and psychological wilderness, Herman Melville nevertheless found himself in subsequent flight from what he took to be the shallow escapism of mere travel narrative. The idea of being a "man who lived among the cannibals" repelled him (*Letters*, p. 130), as did the notion that he would prostitute his talent for dollars. In a letter to his father-in-law, Judge Lemuel Shaw, Melville registered distaste for *Redburn* and *White-Jacket*—"two *jobs*, which I have done for money—being forced to it"; he then stated his desire "to write those sort of books which are said to 'fail' " (pp. 91–92). Put another way, Melville felt drawn to a commercially disastrous literary hybrid that provided a forum for his expansive intellectual inquiries. For Melville, then, these putatively failed books were predominantly concerned with "philosophy," a term that has broad, shifting connotations in his critical lexicon.

Philosophy encompasses the "best wisdom that has ever in any way been revealed to our man-of-war world" (*WJ*, p. 186), especially as it emerges in various strains of idealism. Philosophy reflects the activities of such minds that wrestle with the "Problem of the Universe" (*Letters*, p. 125; also pp. 121, 124, 256). These thought-divers explore a sea of consciousness, a world of "flux and reflux" (*Mardi*, p. 512).[1] In their undespairing skepticism they achieve the "pondering repose of If... and Ifs eternally" (*MD*, p. 406). Philosophy also refers to one's dogged yet genial capacity to endure with a sense of practical resolution: "to grin and bear it" (*MD*, p. 15). On occasion philosophy could become a term of derision—a sign of self-righteous hypocrisy or mental constipation. The chaplain of the *Neversink* propounds abstruse philosophical conundrums without ever addressing the ironic disparity between the Sermon on the Mount and the Articles of War. Ishmael celebrates Queequeg for his "calm self-collectedness" and "Socratic wisdom," but goes on to mock self-styled metaphysicians: "So soon as I hear that such or such a man gives himself out for a philosopher, I conclude that... he must have 'broken his digester' " (*MD*, pp. 52–53).

If for Melville the very notion of philosophy has various significations, it was probably because his reading was so eclectic. With no set curriculum he was drawn to a number of schools. Like Pierre, who becomes a fledgling philosophical novelist, Melville enjoyed a "varied scope of reading, little suspected by his friends, and randomly acquired by a random but lynx-eyed mind, in the course of the multifarious, incidental, bibliographic encounterings.... this poured one considerable contributary stream into that bottomless spring of original thought" (*Pierre*, XXI, i, p. 283). Melville's "contributary stream" definitely included Plato (Merton M. Sealts, Jr., "Platonic Tradition"), Seneca, Plutarch (Sealts, "Ancient Philosophy," pp. 136–38), Montaigne (Aretta J. Stevens), Robert Burton, Thomas Browne, Goethe, Coleridge, Emerson, and Carlyle. He had a glancing acquaintance with Proclus (Sealts, " 'Neoplatonical Originals' ") and David Hartley. He was possibly conversant with Epictetus and Marcus Aurelius (Sealts, "Ancient Philosophy," pp. 159–60). From Pierre Bayle's *An Historical and Critical Dictionary* (James Duban), Melville gleaned much of his knowledge of Pyrrho, Zoroastrianism, Gnosticism, Manichaeism, and Spinoza. Later in life Melville was carefully reading Aristotle, Arnold, and Schopenhauer.[2]

Philosophical influences cannot be limited to documented sources in books owned or borrowed. Any reader of Melville will encounter an extensive and precise range of allusion to such figures as Pythagoras, Heraclitus, Democritus, Zeno of Citium, Diogenes, Cato, and Tacitus among the ancients, and Descartes, Hobbes, Locke, Pascal, Rousseau, and Kant among the moderns. On the basis of available evidence, it is impossible to determine where or how Melville became conversant with the "Vatican" of names or how much knowledge he had of a particular philosophy or movement at any particular time. No record exists, for example, of Melville having read Kant. But he did assimilate a sound knowledge of the German idealist, probably from secondary sources. Coleridge's *Biographia Literaria*, which Melville purchased on 8 February 1848, devotes part of Chapter IX to Kantian philosophy. On his 1849 voyage to England Melville had ample opportunity to pick the brains of George J. Adler, a specialist in German Idealism. In his journal Melville writes, "He is author of a formidable lexicon, (German & English); in compiling which he almost ruined his health. He was almost crazy, he tells me, for a time. He is full of the German metaphysics, and discourses of Kant, Swedenborg &c. He has been my principal companion thus far" (*Mel. Log*, p. 319). Whether acquired through primary or secondary sources, Melville's knowledge of Kant provides focus for satire in *Pierre* (see pp. 267, 293, 300) and material for analogy in *Moby-Dick*. For Ishmael the strained "counterpoise" of the sperm whale's head and the right whale's head reflects the potentially overwhelming difficulties of intellectually attempting to balance Locke and Kant (p. 277). In regarding this moment critics tend to speculate on the allusion's relationship to various philosophical contexts. Michael E. Levin suggests that "Only a man at home with his metaphysics could so deftly balance an empiricist against a rationalist" (p. 64). Sealts finds the allusion more revelatory of the contemporary conflict between "adherents of John Locke's empirical philosophy . . . and the so-called Transcendentalists of New England" ("Platonic Tradition," p. 318). Paul Brodtkorb expansively considers the relationship between "Kantian epistemology" and the phenomenological implications of Ishmael's narrative voice—his experiences reconstituted "in the form of language" (pp. 11–18). The complexity and tenuousness of tracking Melville's adaptations of Kantian thought should at least give pause to critics confronting Melville's "multifarious, incidental, bibliographic encounterings." Seemingly blessed with an amazing memory, Melville could have developed a working knowledge of various schools from fragments picked up here and there. In fact, two of Melville's major influences constitute in themselves eclectic philosophical histories. Plato's dialogues, for example, routinely provide discussions of alternative positions: Socrates and his companions consider the doctrines of Anaxagoras, Cadmus, Heraclitus, Parmenides, Pythagoras, and the Sophists. Thomas Browne's dazzling, allusive technique transforms every page of *Religio Medici* into a debate among competing positions. Browne makes graceful reference to Plato, Aristotle, Pythagoras, Solomon, Epicurus, the Stoics, Seneca, Zoroaster, Moses, Cicero, and Plutarch, among many others.

Given Melville's direct and indirect familiarity with many thinkers and schools, his frequent cataloguing of names, and the unknowable relationship between influence and the creative process itself, one must be content, at present, to consider the effects of this process of assimilation rather than to search expectantly for a set of skeleton keys. In his fiction and poetry, names often function as synoptic metaphors, which resonate with associational possibilities. At the outset of *Moby-Dick*, for example, Ishmael remarks, "With a philosophical flourish Cato throws himself upon his sword; I quietly take to the ship" (p. 12). Melville knew that Cato, on the night before his suicide, had read the *Phaedo*, Plato's great meditation on death and immortality. Rather than escaping, Socrates drinks the hemlock; rather than enduring defeat, Cato falls on his sword. A reader of both the *Phaedo* and "Seneca and the Stoics" (*MD*, p. 15), Ishmael abjures Cato's solution and seeks psychological therapy in that mystic coalescence of "meditation and water" (p. 13). His accommodating sensibility allows him to choose a subjugated life and jocosely ask, "Who aint a slave?" (p. 15). Melville's references to philosophers have more restrictive associations as well. At times he evokes a popularized reduction. For example, Heraclitus and Democritus stand for the "weeping philosopher" and the "laughing philosopher," respectively. He seemed to have known more about each thinker, but in his work their names usually provide handy tags, which encapsulate a particular emotional response to experience. Diogenes suggests man-hooting waggery, while Timon represents bitter misanthropy. Seneca evokes stoical endurance and practical resolution. Solomon is the man of sorrows whose wisdom is woe. Melville associates Pythagoras with metempsychosis and Goethe with pantheism.

Characteristic of Melville's eclectic philosophical absorption is his refusal to declare allegiance to any school. Mark Winsome may have had his Egbert, but Melville was no transcendental disciple. Consequently, no single paradigm will do justice to the variations, the nuances, the contradictions of Melville's thought. Melville knew the beauties of "the *all* feeling" (*Letters*, p. 131; Melville's italics) and the dangers of hovering over "Descartian vortices" (*MD*, p. 140). He could—and did—excoriate Plato and all Philosophers (*Pierre*, XIV, ii, p. 208); he could—and did— celebrate "Plato's aristocratic tone" (*Clarel*, IV, xx, l. 102; p. 478). In the absence of ideological fixity, the nature of Melville's philosophical sensibility becomes most intelligible when examined in relation to his shifting response to idealism. While the post-Platonic schools of Pyrrho (skepticism) and Zeno of Citium (stoicism) revised Platonic formalism in order to meet practical exigencies of the here-and-now, they never became fully dissociated from the Academy; similarly, Melville's own complex of metaphysical speculations has an animating center in idealism, which in turn stirs the counteracting claims of skepticism, stoicism, cynicism, materialism, and Manichaeism. In *Mardi*, *Moby-Dick*, *The Confidence-Man*, and *Clarel*, Melville generates an intense interplay of competing philosophical voices.

At bottom, though, Melville was an artist, not a metaphysician. Consequently, this chapter focuses on Melville's self-education as it issues in the fruits of his aesthetic labors. The making of *Mardi* looms as the preeminent event in Melville's creative life. For the first time he was trying to assimilate philosophical materials into an experimental piece of fiction. For Melville, the aesthetic process brought about a fusion of disparate entities. In *Mardi*, however, fiction and philosophy meet, but they do not quite mate. Like the fictional Lombardo's epic *Koztanza*, *Mardi* "lacks cohesion; it is wild, unconnected, all episode" (p. 597). Despite (or because of) its flaws *Mardi* will provide our central text. Here the record of influence is most clear because it is least assimilated. It is precisely this quality of unrefined vent which so usefully allows one, first, to examine the explosive emergence of Melville's philosophical sensibility; and, second, to indicate ways in which elements of character, theme, and technique become reformed in subsequent works. In *Mardi* Melville mines the raw materials of his greatest fiction: Taji represents an early version of Ahab and Pierre; Babbalanja prefigures the speculative Ishmael; Yillah anticipates the symbolic qualities of the white whale and Isabel. Indeed, Melville's art achieves its greatest resonance when "philosophy" becomes inseparable from a character's identity, world-view, and action. How, for example, does the idealistic quest exhaust Taji in mind and body? How do Ishmael and Ahab appropriate Platonic thought? To what extent does Charlie Millthorpe's good-hearted but shallow transcendental optimism highlight the murderousness of Pierre's deranged absolutism? Do Joseph Priestley on necessity or Jonathan Edwards on the will provide *any* clue toward explaining Bartleby's enigmatic preferences? Why is Ungar drawn to Hobbes? What does it mean to Billy Budd's fate that Captain Vere reads and admires the matter-of-fact philosophy of Montaigne? Philosophical concepts in *Mardi* hang loosely and draw attention to themselves, often awkwardly. After *Mardi* Melville's materials become fused into the "completed fabric" (*MD*, p. 185) of philosophical art.[3]

Melville never resolved "the Problem of the Universe." There was no Serenia; safe havens and insular Tahiti's were forever astern. Lacking neat systems or an easy faith, Melville's work offers a complex record of his repeated immersions into the depths of his creative consciousness. In writing to Evert A. Duyckinck, Melville noted, "I love all men who *dive*" (*Letters*, p. 79; Melville's italics), and to this extent, surely, he loved himself. Like Lombardo, Melville "wrote right on; and so doing, got deeper and deeper into himself" (*Mardi*, p. 595). Melville's imagination drove him to find forms capable of expressing his thoughts. His major books, therefore, tend to be expansive. It seemed to be his view that, in writing, one threw "oneself helplessly open" (*Pierre*, XVIII, i, p. 259). Herman Melville courted this helplessness; it did not take him long to realize that lingering in Typee meant literary and intellectual stagnation. The "world of mind" lay open (*Mardi*, p. 557).

MELVILLE AND HIS LEARNING

The Albany Academy exposed young Melville to a strongly classical curriculum (David K. Titus). As Sealts suggests, he "possibly learned something of the old philosophers in 1830–1831 while enrolled in the Fourth Department... where the standard preparatory course included 'Universal, Grecian, Roman and English history' " ("Platonic Tradition," p. 280).[4] Sealts's "The Records of Melville's Reading" supplements the biographical, critical, and genetic studies of Leon Howard, William Gilman and Merrell R. Davis. Nevertheless, still fertile areas remain for evaluative reconstruction. For example, the extent of Melville's knowledge and application of Plutarch's *Lives,* which he mentions in *Redburn* (p. 67), awaits full consideration. Like Redburn, Melville probably examined "our old family Plutarch" in his father's well-stocked library. Here the young boy developed some familiarity with Shakespeare, Milton, and Coleridge, among others. Throughout his irregular schooling the Bible was a primary text—a resource for language, theme, image, and character (Nathalia Wright, *Melville's Use of the Bible*). As Thomas A.Werge and T.Walter Herbert have argued, the theology of the Dutch Reformed Church, especially such Calvinistic doctrines as total depravity and predestination, shaped the development of the boy and stimulated the thought of the man, especially in *Moby-Dick.*

In Melville's view, however, he did not begin to grow intellectually until after he returned from his life at sea. In a letter to Hawthorne he writes, "My development has been all within a few years past.... Until I was twenty-five, I had no development at all. From my twenty-fifth year I date my life. Three weeks have scarcely passed, at any time between then and now, that I have not unfolded within myself" (*Letters,* p. 130). After moving to New York City in 1847, Melville gained access to extensive collections in Evert Duyckinck's library and the New York Society Library, of which he became a member on 17 January 1848. He also purchased many books from Gowan's Book Store and his publishers (Sealts, "Ancient Philosophy," pp. 4–5, 16–19). During this period Melville deepened the creative dependence on source material, which had begun with *Typee* and which would continue throughout his career.

Especially in the months following January 1848 Melville's critical "digester" was working overtime. He was forging, in effect, a coalescence between the diverse claims of travel narrative and philosophical speculation. Melville's reading during this period betrays a divided affinity: Bougainville, Barnard's *Voyages,* Rabelais, and Tegner's translations of *Frithiof's Saga* merged in Melville's mind with Plato, Proclus, Ossian (Davis, p. 66), Seneca, Montaigne, Shakespeare, Burton, Browne, Hartley, and Coleridge.[5] At the time Melville was probably becoming familiar with a history or manual of philosophy and perhaps even perusing Evert Duyckinck's college philosophy notebooks (Sealts, "Ancient Philosophy," pp. 30–32).

FORGING PHILOSOPHICAL ART: TRAVELOGUE BECOMES DIALOGUE

Melville's eclectic reading impelled him, it seems, to alter his plans to write another travel book. On 25 March 1848 Melville informed his publisher, John Murray, that his work-in-progress "opens like a true narrative" but "the romance & poetry of the thing thence grow continually, till it becomes a story wild enough I assure you & with a meaning too." Murray had a well-known distaste for fiction of any kind, and he must have decided quickly that *Mardi* had no place on his list. The romance certainly does not open like a "true narrative"; rather, from the earliest chapters, Melville's "play of freedom & invention" issues in the narrator's wild, rhapsodic speculations. Melville indeed leaves behind "dull common places" and seems to project his own impatience with everyday expectations into the narrator (*Letters*, pp. 70–71). It is not often noted that the overreaching philosophical self appears almost full-blown in the early pages of *Mardi*. The narrator defines his aspirations distinctly in terms of intellectual fulfillment. If Tommo deserts the *Dolly* because his belly is not adequately satisfied, then the narrator of *Mardi* resolves to desert the *Arcturion* because his mind is malnourished. A fine man in all nautical respects, the captain cannot "talk sentiment or philosophy." Nor can his shipmates "page me a quotation from Burton on Blue Devils" (*Mardi*, p. 5). In desiring a world of extreme erudition and expansive consciousness, the narrator longs for a "dream-land" (p. 7) to the west—a geographical space exotic enough to satisfy his voracious, frenzied appetite for the unknown.

The chapter, "A Calm," in this respect, succinctly demonstrates the fusion of the narrator's intellectual aspiration and the author's aesthetic experimentation. The dullness of workaday sea-life (and for Melville the banality of travel narrative) stand in direct conflict with the wild possibilities for pursuing speculative vistas (and for Melville the profundity of writing *truth*). The calm at sea stirs a flurry of thought: it "unsettles his mind; tempts him to recant his belief in the eternal fitness of things; in short, almost makes an infidel of him" (p. 9). A calm induces skepticism, which in this meditation gives way to a need, rejected by the narrator, to adopt a pose of stoical endurance. This scene provides the first self-conscious expression in Melville's work of the tangled relationship between skepticism and stoicism, on the one hand, and the opposing psychological imperative to pursue a condition of absolute felicity, on the other. Even this early, the narrator has "eternity . . . in his eye" (p. 654). In a fascinating passage, which echoes elements of style and theme in Browne's *Religio Medici* (pp. 15–16, 24), the narrator articulates his preoccupation with merging the immediate time-bound world of sense experience with the exotic, eternal world of enraptured thought. The narrator's meditation on Jarl's ancestry and the interrelationship among mortals culminates in his densely allusive vision of a federated and congenial afterlife, replete with cameo appearances by many of the great dead:

> All of us have monarchs and sages for kinsmen; nay, angels and archangels for cousins.... Thus all generations are blended: and heaven and earth of one kin .... All things form but one whole; the universe a Judea, and God Jehovah its head. Then no more let us start with affright. In a theocracy, what is to fear? ...No custom is strange; no creed is absurd; no foe, but who will in the end prove a friend. In heaven, at last, our good, old, white-haired father Adam will greet all alike, and sociality forever prevail. Christian shall join hands between Gentile and Jew; grim Dante forget his Infernos, and shake sides with fat Rabelais; and monk Luther, over a flagon of old nectar, talk over old times with Pope Leo.... Then shall the Stagirite and Kant be forgotten, and another folio than theirs be turned over for wisdom; even the folio now spread with horoscopes as yet undeciphered, the heaven of heavens on high. (pp. 12–13)

In offering a jocular but learned display, the narrator, soon to proclaim himself the demigod Taji, seeks to absorb and contain disparate philosophies of experience. In *Mardi*'s early chapters Melville lays the groundwork for his subsequent practice of revealing a character's emerging sensibility through the adumbration of conflicting philosophical complexes. Uncharacteristically, the narrator here reveals qualities not only of the egomaniacal absolutist but also of the flexible genialist. At this point he desires the ultimate but still feels federated with other men.

Mardi very quickly becomes a "freewheeling island-hopping symposium" (Richard H. Brodhead, p. 36; also see John Wenke, "Isles of Man"), a rambling, discursive, unintegrated series of ideological externalizations. In order to express his expansive learning, Melville appropriates the technique of the philosophical dialogue, which is congenial to *Mardi*'s loose, episodic structure. The questers consider such issues as art, inspiration, Oro (God), right reason, preexistence, freedom, necessity, fate, and practical ethics. Each man propounds his particular angle of vision. When they tire of a subject they push on to the next island and the next discussion. Among the five questers ostensibly seeking Yillah, an ethereally beautiful maiden and symbol of the absolute, the philosophizing babbling-angel, Babbalanja, is most protean, most energetic, in exploring the "mystery of mysteries" (*Mardi*, p. 389).[6] Associated with ancient and obsolete authors, especially the sage Bardianna, Babbalanja is "intent upon the essence of things; the mystery that lieth beyond...that which is beneath the seeming.... I probe the circle's center; I seek to evolve the inscrutable" (p. 352). Along with his demon-self, Azzageddi, Babbalanja might well be seen as a frantic, comic reincarnation of Socrates. Sealts most fully explores this parallel as well as the more extended presence of the socratic in Melville's work ("Ancient Philosophy," pp. 39–47 and "Platonic Tradition," pp. 283–94, 330–35). Focusing on *Moby-Dick* Levin compellingly argues that Ahab becomes an inverted Socrates. Except for Thomas J. Scorza, who links Claggart and Socrates and (wrongheadedly) identifies Melville as an "enemy of Socrates and Socratism" (p. 177), critics tend to agree.that Socrates represents for Melville a figure of heroic self-possession and profound wisdom. Even when most vehemently opposed to the Platonic idealism that Socrates espouses, Melville has nothing but praise for Socrates the man. Melville's sympathy for Babbalanja is similarly divided. However unsystematic his views, Babbalanja is most socratic in his love of truth. But his incessant questioning is both comically self-deflating and neurotically self-lacerating. To his sorrow Babbalanja lacks the firm faith that characterizes Plato's mentor. In his shifting ruminations Babbalanja reflects an early formulation of the endlessly searching relativistic philosopher, whose descendants include Ishmael, Clarel, and Rolfe. On the contrary, the absolutistic strain generates from Taji through Ahab, Pierre, Mortmain, and Ungar.

Consciously or unconsciously, Melville persistently associated travel and talk. Thus, his most singlemindedly philosophical works—*The Confidence-Man* and *Clarel*—employ the travelogue as a primary means for staging elaborate philosophical exchanges. As in *Mardi*, the literal journeys in *The Confidence-Man* and *Clarel* provide the excuse for metaphysical wrangling, shifting settings, diverse interlocutors. In *The Confidence-Man* the journey down the Mississippi River is mere plot device; the essential focus of the novel is ideas. Here the master manipulator himself determines topics for discussion. In *Clarel* philosophical dialogues generate from complexes within characters, from the desolate present-day settings, and from various Biblical associations.

For Melville the philosophical dialogue often demonstrates the indeterminacy of the quest for *Truth*. In *Mardi*, for example, Media petulantly chides Babbalanja, "And to what end your eternal inquisitions? You have nothing to substitute. You say all is a lie; then out with the truth" (p. 428). *The Confidence-Man* insistently explores (and distorts) the relationship between language and reality, words and things. Retentive, detached, mystifying, the narrator indulges in cunning equivocation and knavish word play. He provides partial descriptions of surfaces and avoids entering the minds of his actors. The confidence-man himself undermines the self-knowledge, reason, and will of his victims. Here the dialogue sophistically enmeshes shallow believers in a "web of tautologies" (William M. Ramsey, p. 228), rather than leading them on a search for truth. In an excellent article Cecelia Tichi considers Melville's strategy of obfuscation: "Thematically...the repeated verbal cony-catching damns the crass American Wall Street spirit and its debased cultural ramifications. But such structural and thematic explications cannot account for Melville's obsessive insistence that his reader tends closely not to dynamic action, but to equivocating and obfuscating narrative, and to quasisocratic dialogues rife with jingoism, choplogic, false analogy, and words that change meanings as easily as the confidence man slips into new disguises" (p. 640). This book of talk, Melville's last piece of fiction to be published in his lifetime, reveals at the very least the failure of moral categories to explain the meaning of surfaces. In fact, as Franklin points out, Pitch's "discussion about innate knowledge and innate virtue with the man from the 'Philosophical Intelligence Office'... is a carefully constructed parody of Plato's *Meno*" (p. 216). What becomes most sophistical in the narrative is the perversion of analogy. Indeed, Plato's world-view hinges on the notion that the material, timebound world is an imperfect copy of the immaterial, external realm. The Sophists, however, held that all words and ideas were relative, that man (not God) was the measure of all things, that correspondence between word and thing was arbitrary. In *Phaedrus*, which Melville knew well, Socrates's discussion of deception could have warned the dupes on the *Fidele* against having an injudicious confidence in mere likenesses:

He, then, who would deceive others, and not be deceived, must exactly know the real likenesses and differences of things.... And if he is ignorant of the true nature of any subject, how can he detect the greater or less degree of likeness in other things to that of which by the hypothesis he is ignorant?... And when men are deceived and their notions are at variance with realities, it is clear that the error slips in through resemblances.... Then he who would be a master of the art must understand the real nature of everything; or he will never know either how to make the gradual departure from truth into the opposite of truth which is effected by the help of resemblances, or how to avoid it. (pp. 265–66; B. Jowett)

True to form, the man from the Philosophical Intelligence Office cites false analogy after false analogy in order to prove that bad boys, like bitter wine aging naturally into fine wine, will inevitably (naturally) become good men. After admitting that the arguments are "a kind of reasonable" (*CM*, p. 127), the unusually self-possessed Pitch passes from having conditional confidence to offering "perfect and unquestioning confidence" (p. 128). In his successive dialogues the confidence-man manipulates the meaning of words, preying on what Pitch correctly identifies as the "mystery of human subjectivity" (p. 129). Daniel G. Hoffman briefly examines the relationship between *The Confidence-Man* and the Platonic dialogue, focusing on the way in which interpolated stories, like Platonic myths, "dramatize depths of experience" beyond the limits of rational discourse. Clearly, then, the relationship between language and truth constitutes the central philosophical problem in *The Confidence-Man*. In the last fifteen years it has received increasing attention, as evidenced in the work of Edgar A. Dryden (pp. 149–95), Christopher W. Sten, Steven E. Kemper, William Ramsey, John Wenke ("Melville's Masquerade"), and Gary Lindberg (pp. 15–47). Sten considers the "dialogue of crisis" not in its sophistical origins but as a reflection of Melville's proto-existentialism. What still needs fuller consideration is the way in which the nexus between philosophy and language relates both to the preceding fiction, especially *Moby-Dick* and *Pierre*, and Melville's poetics, especially in *Clarel*.

While the philosophical dialogue has its most significant manifestation within the travelogue, it also has more incidental uses: the dialogue allows Melville to heighten dramatic intensity, usually by interpolating theatrical techniques. To take the most important example, "The Quarter-Deck" chapter of *Moby-Dick* is introduced with stage directions. Ahab does indeed enter: he assembles the crew and poses leading questions. As an "inverted Socrates" (Levin), Ahab uses his rhetorical skill to mold the crew to his will. Except for Starbuck. Ahab must take their particular dialogue out of the public arena of emotional acclamation and consider "a little lower layer." In responding to Starbuck's charge of blasphemy, Ahab identifies his metaphysical justification for wresting the voyage from its marketplace imperative: a malicious agency animates the "pasteboard" mask of material forms. If man would challenge this demonic force, he must strike "through the mask" (*MD*, pp. 143, 144).

Melville frequently uses the philosophical dialogue to combine jest and earnest. To Babbalanja's surprise, for example, the sage Doxodox turns out to be an incomprehensible recluse given entirely to philosophical obscurantism, some materials of which Melville gleaned from Proclus (Sealts, " 'Neoplatonical Originals'," pp. 80–86). After quizzing the imposter, Babbalanja makes fun of his gibberish. In perverting the philosopher's office, Doxodox becomes far more than simply Babbalanja's satiric butt: he directly prefigures the cold-hearted Mark Winsome, who is likewise fond of "using some unknown word" (*CM*, p. 193). In this novel Frank Goodman is probably Melville's most eloquent and gifted rhetorician. As Socrates often does, Frank Goodman employs the philosophical dialogue to unmask his interlocutors. For example, Frank Goodman exposes the shallow hypocrisy of Charlie Noble (pp. 139–88), and then he reveals the smug misanthropy of Mark Winsome and Egbert (pp. 189–224). Much later in his career Melville combines whimsicality and earnestness when pursuing the metaphysical enigma of Claggart's "depravity according to nature" (*BBS*, p. 75). The narrator interpolates a dialogue he claims to have had many years before. He was a young man, and his interlocutor was an old socratic scholar. The wise old man instructs the naive young man in the deceptiveness of appearance: one needs more than mere "knowledge of the world" to comprehend the psychological involutions of "certain phenomenal men." One must develop "finer spiritual insight" by examining such authorities as the Hebrew prophets and Plato.[7] Thus, Plato's definition of "Natural Depravity: a depravity according to nature"—illuminates Claggart's selectively applied but essential evil. Here the dialogue allows Melville to highlight philosophical terms that illuminate the "point of the present story" (p. 76). In "Poor Man's Pudding and Rich Man's Crumbs" and "The Lightning-Rod Man," the dialogue format also combines humorous, polemical, and metaphysical purposes.

Melville scholarship awaits a full-scale treatment of his recurrent adaptation of the philosophical dialogue: How and when does it serve or fail to serve Melville's fusion of philosophical and aesthetic materials? Could Melville's polemical concerns in *White-Jacket*, for example, be seen as a dialogue with an implied reader? Why does the technique of argumentation become more prevalent—as in *The Confidence-Man* and *Clarel*—as Melville's work becomes less accessible to the popular tastes of his literary marketplace? Can these dialogues, then, reflect projected conversations that the author might be having with himself? The problematic issue of narrative voice, especially in *Moby-Dick*, may in fact have its roots (if not its resolution) in Melville's insistence on making a single narrator the mouthpiece for divergent, often contradictory, standpoints. In pursuing such matters, it may be daunting to recognize the nagging centrality of Bardianna's assertion, the "question is more final than any answer" (*Mardi*, p. 284).

PLATONIC ADAPTATIONS: MATTER AND SPIRIT

If Melville's multiple applications of the philosophical dialogue constitute his primary technique for fusing philosophical speculation and art, then Platonic thought itself offers him a compendium of ideas and images to absorb, evoke, and re-form. Without question, Plato is the preeminent influence on the philosophical themes of *Mardi* in particular and Melville's career in general. Critical commentary, for once, is disproportionate not in quality but in quantity. As Sealts argues, "Although Melville's allusions to Plato, Plato's Socrates, and various Platonic dialogues far outnumber his references to other philosophers, published scholarship has taken relatively little notice of his significant debt to Plato since K. H. Sundermann in 1937 pointed out a number of passages in *Mardi* and its successors that unmistakably reflect Platonic thought" ("Platonic Tradition," p. 279). Sealts's monumental "Melville and the Platonic Tradition" offers a compelling and sensitive study of source, influence, and interpretation. In juxtaposing Melville, Plato, Browne, and others,

Sealts demonstrates the range and complexity of Melville's lifelong debt to Platonic thought. Sealts assiduously establishes a record of fact and provides a model of informed speculation. According to Sealts the more "transcendental" passages in *Mardi* did not generate from Melville's reading of Emerson, which he did not seriously begin until sometime between February 1849 and August 1850 (see Sealts "Emerson's Rainbow" pp. 255–63). But Melville *was* reading a number of Platonic dialogues, certainly *Phaedrus, Phaedo, Timaeus,* and the *Republic,* and perhaps *Crito,* the *Apology, Meno,* and *Cratylus.* During the composition of *Mardi,* Melville apparently was reading Plato in the Taylor-Sydenham translation. In 1850 Melville acquired the Gowan edition of the *Phaedon.* About this time he also began purchasing the Bohn edition of *The Works of Plato* (1848–54) which he apparently retained throughout his life. None of Melville's personal copies of Plato has yet been found.

Sealts locates four major Platonic concerns in *Mardi* which recur in later works. Using *Phaedo* and *Republic,* Melville applies the Platonic concept of knowledge as recollection in order to consider the relationship between a writer and the writer's cultural heritage. Sealts also examines *Phaedrus* as source for Melville's musings on poetic inspiration and divine frenzy. The "hierarchical character of Platonic thought," as found in the *Republic,* becomes reflected in King Media and points ahead to the deepening of Melville's political conservatism. Melville's familiarity with Platonic myths and Neoplatonic thought is embodied in the questers' considerations of the tripartite soul, daemonic tutelage, the afterlife, and the creation of the world. Of special note in Sealts's treatment of Platonic sources is his examination of bird imagery as it both figures the soul's flight from the material world and symbolizes the poet's office as inspired seer and sayer ("Platonic Tradition," pp. 281–97).

Throughout his career Melville was fascinated by Plato's attempt to explain the totality of existence, especially insofar as the philosopher sought to reconcile the apparent conflict between matter and spirit, phenomena and soul. This philosophical complex pervades Melville's art. For example, Babbalanja frequently meditates on the mysterious conjunction of body and soul: "Oh, Man, Man, Man! thou art harder to solve, than the Integral Calculus—yet plain as a primer; harder to find than the philosopher's-stone—yet ever at hand; a more cunning compound, than an alchemist's—yet a hundred weight of flesh, to a penny weight of spirit; soul and body glued together, firm as atom to atom, seamless as the vestment without joint, warp or woof—yet divided as by a river, spirit from flesh.... I give thee up, oh Man! thou art twain—yet indivisible; all things—yet a poor unit at best" (*Mardi,* p. 433). Plato's metaphysical dualism posits a fundamental split between the phenomenal world, which consists of matter and is restricted by limits of space and time, and the ontologically Real, which constitutes spirit, the *Ontos,* the final Truth, the Forms. The record of one's senses indicates that the physical world constantly changes; Plato's ontologically Real world transcends space and time permutations. While the phenomenal world is tangible and perceptible through the senses, the ideal world is intangible and can only be conceived of in the mind. Two orders of being—phenomenal and noumenal—correspond to two forms of knowing—sensory and philosophical. The sensual man attaches himself to the phenomenal world and believes that this relative world of appearances reveals things as they are. The philosophical man, however, weans himself from the impingements of the physical world and seeks to purify his soul in pursuit of the True and the Good.

Melville seldom merely applies a Platonic image or complex. In forming character, developing ideas, or structuring symbols, Melville usually tailors Platonic elements to fit his specific needs. In *Mardi* Melville adapts the concept of transmigration to the demands of his political satire in the "Vivenza" episode. "The Voice from the Gods" links transmigration of the soul to the evolutionary displacement of monarchy by republic and republic by tyranny: "In nations, sovereign-kings! there is a transmigration of souls.... And though crimson republics may rise in constellations, like fiery Aldebarans, speeding to their culminations; yet, down must they sink at last, and leave the old sultan-sun in the sky; in time, again to be deposed" (p. 527). With Ahab, Plato's body/soul dichotomy helps to explain the germination of his monomania. If Ahab's spirit is "god-like," then his body is "ungodly" (*MD*, p. 76). He violently rebels against crippling mortal impediments. His soul is "shut up in the caved trunk of his body" (p. 134). His physical maladies incite spiritual exasperations: "... his torn body and gashed soul bled into one another; and so interfusing, made him mad" (p. 160). It is the "infixed, unrelenting fangs of some incurable idea" (p. 162) that lead him to repudiate the limited, contextual social felicities of brotherhood as well as the utilitarian, mechanistic economic imperatives of the Nantucket marketplace. Indeed, Ahab's "proper and inaccessible being" is "strained, half-stranded" by the physical restrictions of "such a craven mate.... My body" (pp. 458–59).

While the critical debate over the nature of Melville's idealism is too extensive to be considered here in detail, one can find representative points of view in the studies of F.O. Matthiessen, Howard Vincent (pp. 154–58), S. A. Cowan, Sheldon W. Liebman, A. N. Kaul, Carl F. Strauch, and Rowland A. Sherrill. At the heart of Melville's sense of the Platonic (and Christian) dualism between matter and spirit resides the nature of being. In a superb essay Sanford E. Marovitz explores Melville's conflicting "ideas on the nature of *Being*" as they reflect his "ambivalence over the foundation of religious and philosophical Truth" (p. 11). Beginning with Melville's mystifying assertion to Hawthorne—"But it is this

Being of the matter; there lies the knot with which we choke ourselves" (*Letters*, p. 125, Melville's italics)—Marovitz discusses the idea of "Being" in a multiplicity of possible connotations. He discusses, in effect, the broad range of Melville's philosophical influences, focusing most carefully on Plato, Plotinus, the Great Chain, Coleridge, Carlyle, and Emerson.

PLATONIC RESONATIONS: ETHICS AND SYMBOLISM

The dichotomy between the phenomenal and the noumenal, and its concomitant formulations in the conflicts between the many and the one, becoming and being, constitutes the central philosophical complex in the works of Herman Melville. The Platonic dualism has its vexing ethical counterpart in the separation of earthly law and divine law—a problem that surfaces in *Mardi, White-Jacket, Moby-Dick, Pierre, The Confidence-Man*, and *Billy Budd*. In *Pierre*, Plinlimmon's pamphlet succinctly, if problematically, examines the dissociation between "chronometricals" or "Heavenly Truth" (XIV, iii, p. 211) and "horologicals" or common sense practicality. Plinlimmon asserts that man must never try to "regulate his earthly conduct by that . . . heavenly soul." To do so would be to commit "a sort of suicide as to the practical things of this world" (p. 213). The Sermon on the Mount, then, has nothing to do with *realpolitik*. Ethical standards are relative to the practical exigencies of the moment. Plinlimmon advocates a "virtuous expediency" (p. 214), a position that justifies smug self-righteousness. As Leon Howard and Hershel Parker made clear, "Critics are still confused . . . by the meaning of the setpiece which constitutes the philosophical crux of the novel" (*Pierre*, pp. 406–407). Milton Stern (*The Fine-Hammered Steel*, pp.189–95) and Brian Higgins offer the most probing examinations of this enigmatic philosophical crux. What does seem clear is that Melville assertively tries to avoid identification with Plinlimmon's view. Melville's narrator points out that the pamphlet is "a very sleazy one as to paper." It is also "metaphysically and insufferably entitled" (*Pierre*, XIV, i, p. 207). In distancing himself from its doctrine, Melville waggishly undercuts his own disclaimer and whimsically directs the reader to take the pamphlet as he pleases:

. . . [It] seems to me a very fanciful and mystical, rather than philosophical Lecture, from which, I confess, that I myself can derive no conclusion which permanently satisfies those peculiar motions in my soul. . . . For to me it seems more the excellently illustrated restatement of a problem, than the solution of the problem itself. But as such mere illustrations are almost always universally taken for solutions (and perhaps they are the only possible human solutions), therefore it may help to the temporary quiet of some inquiring mind. . . . At the worst, each person can now skip, or read and rail for himself. (XIV, ii, p. 210)

Melville's most prevalent Platonic adaptation runs counter to the static dichotomizing of "Chronometricals & Horologicals." What seems most to fascinate Melville is not the dissociation of visible and invisible spheres, but their mysterious, suggestive interplay. The Platonic notion that reality is "mind-like" (Levin, p. 62) finds issue in Melville's penchant for analogy and symbolism.[8] Ahab succinctly propounds the haunting mystery of a world in which subjective and objective realms interpenetrate: "O Nature, and O soul of man! how far beyond all utterance are your linked analogies! not the smallest atom stirs or lives in matter, but has its cunning duplicate in mind" (*MD*, p. 264). Objects and actions in the whaling world—the whale line, the doubloon, the weaving of the sword mat, the monkey rope—stand for such complexes of thought as the imminence of death, the relativity of perception, the interweaving of freedom, fate and chance, the interdependence of mortals. Objects reflect spiritual entities. As Ishmael observes, "And some certain significance lurks in all things, else all things are little worth, and the round world itself but an empty cipher" (p. 358). In an even more Platonic strain Ahab exclaims, "Oh! how immaterial are all materials! What things real are there, but imponderable thoughts?" (pp. 432–33). The doctrine of correspondence or "linked analogies" often serves Melville's characters as they try to make sense of an inscrutable world. Nature, however, does not provide the Melvillean seeker with easy answers to difficult questions. Instead, the analogical method reiterates the puzzle of human existence. For example, when Babbalanja argues that the butterfly provides an inadequate illustration of the soul's survival after bodily death, he points out the dangers inherent in man's search for "positive warranty": "... the analogy [man's soul and the butterfly] has an unsatisfactory end. From its chrysalis state, the silkworm but becomes a moth, that very quickly expires. Its longest existence is as a worm. All vanity, vanity, Yoomy, to seek in nature for positive warranty to these aspirations of ours. Through all her provinces, nature seems to promise immortality to life, but destruction to beings. Or, as old Bardianna has it, if not against us, nature is not for us" (*Mardi*, p. 210).[9]

Later, in "The Chapel" (*MD*, ch. 7), Ishmael considers the issue of immortality, but he appropriates a more applicable image directly from Plato. H. N. Couch points out that Ishmael's celebration of man's "shadow" as his "true substance"—"Methinks that in looking at things spiritual, we are too much like oysters observing the sun through the water" (*MD*, p. 41)—parallels a passage in *Phaedo*. Sealts builds on Couch's discovery and demonstrates conclusively that "Melville's memory had ranged elsewhere in the *Phaedo* and *Phaedrus*" ("Platonic Tradition," pp. 302–303). Significantly, Ishmael forges his analogy from the Platonic dialogues most concerned with death and the soul's survival. While Ishmael's affirmation here is unmistakably Platonic, it does not betray an unwavering commitment to Platonic resolutions. Rather, Ishmael reveals the drive of his imagination to establish an appropriate response to the present mood and matter. In this instance he is seeking relief from the ominous oppression—the doom and gloom—evoked by the mourners in the chapel and the marble tablets on the wall. Ishmael's culminating expression—"And therefore three cheers for Nantucket; and come a stove boat and a stove body when they will, for stave my soul, Jove himself cannot" (*MD*, p. 41)—must first be understood within its immediate narrative context. Ishmael's knowledge of Plato supplies him with images through which he fashions a therapeutic response to the "unceasing grief" reflected around him. Ishmael's imaginative process displaces the static self-laceration of the mourners. Certainly, his speculations about the spiritual world are not always so effusive and optimistic. When exploring the mystery of whiteness, for example, Ishmael is frightened by the very thought of "invisible spheres." Indeed, Ishmael suspects that universal vacuity lurks behind the material forms of this world (p. 169). Ahab's fusion of Platonism and the analogical method leads him both to eclipse the Platonic faith in absolute beneficence and to engage in cosmic defiance. His belief that "all visible objects . . . are but as pasteboard masks" impels him to strike through the visible forms in order to assault the "unknown but still reasoning thing" that maliciously operates "from behind the unreasoning mask" (p. 144).

Very frequently indeed, Melville evokes Platonic images for the purposes of drawing distinctly anti-Platonic inferences. In fact, Melville's preoccupation with the power of malicious agencies owes a great debt to his readings in Pierre Bayle's *Dictionary*. In a letter to Evert Duyckinck, Melville revealed the drive of his imagination to fuse such disparate resources as Plato and Browne, on the one hand, and Bayle, on the other: "I bought a set of Bayle's Dictionary the other day, & on my return to New York intend to lay the great old folios side by side & go to sleep on them thro' the summer, with the Phaedon in one hand and Tom Brown in the other" (*Letters*, pp. 83–84). In his essays on Zoroastrianism, Gnosticism, and Manichaeism, Bayle explored evil as an active principle in the universe. Bayle thus appealed to Melville's skepticism and iconoclasm. According to Millicent Bell, Bayle was a "master of doubt," who attacked the "ancient and modern Platonists." Bayle supplied Melville "with an arsenal of destructive logic against the Goethe . . . or the Emerson" (p. 628), who seemed to Melville benignly unresponsive to manifestations of evil. Bell's essay is the most successful treatment of Bayle's influence on Melville. While Bayle's *Dictionary* was the most important secondary source for Melville's philosophical thought, its relationship to the evolution of Melville's art awaits comprehensive consideration. In pursuing the matter, however, scholars will inevitably be left to informed speculation—careful guesstimates of Melvillean adaptation. As Sealts argues, "Melville's borrowing from Bayle ... can be illustrated only by broad comparisons; the technique of citing parallel passages is entirely inapplicable" ("Ancient Philosophy," p. 196). As excellent discussions by Dorothee Finkelstein, J. C. Oates, Thomas Vargish, H. Bruce Franklin (pp. 17–98), and John T. Irwin (pp. 285–349) indicate, this problem of fixing the scope of influence also complicates the consideration of Melville's debt to the more exotic philosophies and mythologies of the Near and Far East.

RELATIVISM AND ABSOLUTISM

The analogical and symbolic methods, which are generated from (but not restricted to) Plato, come to inform Melville's exploration of human psychology. By repudiating the transcendental insistence on the absolute existence of the Good, Melville establishes the epistemological context of shifting meanings and relativistic values. Thus, the "story of Narcissus" (*MD*, p. 14) and "The Doubloon" in *Moby-Dick* (ch. 94) together constitute an epistemological crux. The image Narcissus sees in the fountain is no more (and no less) than a self-reflection. To believe that this self-image yields universal signification is to risk the fate of Narcissus: it is to fall in love with self and then to drown—to lose oneself in the tormenting, mild, self-reflecting pool of a watery vortex. As "The Doubloon" reveals, the world of material actuality offers one text but many readers. Melville's use of correspondence presents not a fixed equation of material fact and spiritual truth; rather, it offers a way of reading reality symbolically, which becomes manifest through multiform psychological projection. We know ourselves *through* the meanings *we* ascribe to the dumb blankness of experience. Ishmael knows that what he reads is a self-projection, but Ahab and Pierre do not. Under the Memnon Stone Pierre dares the "Mute Massiveness" (VII, v, p. 134) to fall on him. When it does not, he mistakenly assumes that his psychological intimations and self-generated preconditions somehow correlate with divinely ordained mandates. Pierre sees as he does, Melville suggests, because he has an unconscious but overpowering predilection to view things that way. In *Pierre* Melville conflates the self-destruction imaged in "story of Narcissus" and the perceptual relativism of "The Doubloon" chapter. The narrator considers Pierre's early fascination with the face of Isabel:

... his profound curiosity and interest in the matter—strange as it may seem—did not so much appear to be embodied in the mournful person of the olive girl, as by some radiations from her, embodied in the vague conceits which agitated his soul. *There*, lurked the subtler secret: *that*, Pierre had striven to tear away. From without, no wonderful effect is wrought within ourselves, unless some interior, responding wonder meets it. That the starry vault shall surcharge the heart with all rapturous marvelings, is only because we ourselves are greater miracles, and superber trophies than all the stars in universal space. Wonder interlocks with wonder; and then the confounding feeling comes. (III, ii, p. 51; Melville's italics)

Thus, psychological causality is as unfixable as the readings anyone might project. Again, Melville's conflation of philosophical and psychological complexes highlights the mysteries and ambiguities of life. For Melville the greatest mysteries are within man: "Say what some poets will, Nature is not so much her own ever-sweet interpreter, as the mere supplier of that cunning alphabet, whereby selecting and combining as he pleases, each man reads his own peculiar lesson according to his own peculiar mind and mood" (XXV, iv, p. 342). Like Taji and Ahab, Pierre proceeds from poorly informed categorical fixities and then creates the iron inflexibility of purpose which he identifies as fate. By mistaking self-deluded will for fate, the absolutists drive themselves to murderous self-defeat. The failure of idealism to sustain Pierre links the novel's philosophical underpinnings and psychological explorations. As the narrator notes, "and then the confounding feeling comes" (p. 51). For Melville, the philosophical idealism provides a generative force behind his symbolic method and his psychological examinations, especially insofar as epistemology informs ontology, and ontology precedes and then justifies self-deluding action.

Philosophical complex and fictional counterpart fuse climactically as Melville's absolutistic questers pursue the idealistic lure. As Stern argues, "Melville takes as a central character the individual who makes a philosophical voyage, which is symbolized by a physical journey.... Characteristically it is a search for ultimate truth and being, a final triumph for man's cosmic status" (*The Fine-Hammered Steel*, pp. 10–11). Wright argues that Melville's plots enact "the quest for the absolute amidst its relative manifestations... all his themes represent the delicate and shifting relationship between its truth and its illusions" (*Melville's Use of the Bible*, p. 77). Taji, Ahab, and Pierre all crave the Absolute as represented by Yillah, Moby-Dick, and Isabel, respectively. Yillah, for example, comes from a "shadowy isle," which reflects the Platonic realm of the soul's preexistence. To Taji, Yillah represents "the substance of this spiritual image.... the earthly semblance of that sweet vision, that haunted my earliest thoughts" (*Mardi*, p. 158). Like Ahab's whale shoved near, Yillah and Isabel are associated with infinite and indecipherable significations. Like Moby-Dick's hieroglyphic marble-whiteness, Isabel's being reflects "one infinite, dumb, beseeching countenance of mystery" (*Pierre*, III, ii, p. 52). In responding to the absolutistic lure, the questers link metaphysical speculation and dramatic action and consequently enact Melville's version of the Prometheus myth (See Richard Chase, pp. 45–48;

Gerard M. Sweeney, pp. 35–70). The quester's hallmark is defiance strengthened by egomania. Ahab declares, "I'd strike the sun if it insulted me" (*MD*, p. 144). Heaven-assaulting questers like Ahab foolishly believe that, by lashing out at a material object, a mortal can do damage to the immaterial Form it represents. Driven by love and hate, they confuse the terms of Plato's dualism, mistaking the Ideal for an entity that can somehow be reached in the world of history, society, and limit. As Stern argues, the quester compulsively brings about his own ironic self-defeat: The "idealistic vision results in personal vision; personal vision results in separation of self and community; separation results in monomania; monomania results in a sterilizing and frantic quest for the attainment of vision according to the dictates of self" (*The Fine-Hammered Steel*, p. 12).

From the Promethean perspective it may be "better to sink in boundless deeps, than float on vulgar shoals" (*Mardi*, p. 557). But the questers do sink, and their search for the absolute always leads to disaster. Melville's idealistic lure invariably hides some form of death: "The whirlpool ... prefigured [Yillah's] fate" (*Mardi*, p. 159); Moby Dick is a death-dealing monster; Isabel longs for the extinction of individual consciousness. "I hope one day to feel myself drank up into the pervading spirit animating all things. I feel I am an exile here" (*Pierre*, VI, iv, p. 119). If the lure is related to death, then the questers usually become murderers. A notable exception is Nathan in *Clarel*, and he is murdered. Indeed, Melville's most consistent attitude toward the all-alluring idealistic quest is that it can be self-exhausting, if not self-annihilating. "The Mast-Head" in *Moby-Dick* (ch. 35) offers the least problematic instance of the incompatibility between philosophical idealism and workaday actuality. With "Descartian vortices" swirling below and "unconscious reverie" revolving within, a "sunken-eyed young Platonist" on the mast-head needs literally to watch his step. "At last," Ishmael ponders, "he loses his identity; takes the mystic ocean at his feet for the visible image of that deep, blue, bottomless soul, pervading mankind and nature; and every strange, half-seen, gliding, beautiful thing that eludes him; every dimly-discovered, uprising fin of some undiscernible form, seems to him the embodiment of those elusive thoughts that only people the soul by continually flitting through it." In this meditation Platonism merges with the pantheistic "All" feeling usually associated with the Neoplatonic tradition and appropriated by Romantics like Goethe. The key for Melville is that "elusive thoughts" dissolve as the "identity comes back in horror" (*MD*, pp. 139–40). The sailor awakens in the fall from the mast-head to confront his death by drowning.[10] To gaze excessively into the tormenting ocean of ideality or to look "too long in the face of the fire" is to risk the "fatal contingency" (*MD*, p. 354.) So it goes for Taji, Ahab, Pierre, Celio, and Mortmain.

This conjunction of philosophical quest and self-exhaustion appears as early as *Mardi*. A beautifully written enigma, "Dreams" (ch. 119) presents a self-portrait of Taji *after* the story has left him chasing Yillah into eternity. Taji suffers the physical and psychological self-immurement that comes from having his mind swamped with knowledge. Written in the present tense, divorced from even an ostensible relationship to narrative events preceding and succeeding it, "Dreams" presents Melville's judgment on Taji's unrestricted search for truth. It reveals Taji to be a victim of his expansive learning, a prey to the competing claims of contentious, unintegrated voices. His journey into the world of mind gives him access to many nations, times, places, authors. Consequently, Taji identifies with all knowledge. He becomes, as it were, lost in an intellectual vortex. His learning is too much for him to bear: " . . . my soul sinks down to the depths, and soars to the skies; and comet-like reels on through such boundless expanses, that methinks all the worlds are my kin, and I invoke them to stay in their course. Yet, like a mighty three-decker, towing argosies by scores, I tremble, gasp, and strain in my flight, and fain would cast off the cables that hamper" (*Mardi*, p. 367). Full "with a thousand souls" he struggles with a library of voices. The theater of the mind depicts an endlessly self-defeating drama of dialectic. He consorts with Homer, Anacreon, Hafiz, Shakespeare, Ossian, Milton, Petrarch. In his mind "St. Paul . . . argues the doubts of Montaigne; Julian the Apostate cross-questions Augustine; and Thomas-a-Kempis unrolls his old black letters for all to decipher." His play of mind includes such figures as Zeno, Democritus, Pyrrho, Plato, Proclus, Verulam, Zoroaster, Virgil, and Sidney. Taji's "memory is a life beyond birth; my memory, my library of the Vatican, its alcoves all endless perspectives" (*Mardi*, pp. 367–68). In this remarkable chapter Taji's boundless thought has become self-restricting, his intellectual absolutism self-exhausting. The mental growth of this "universal absorber," while perhaps stunning in its allusive reach, nevertheless reveals a basic incompatibility between the common sense world affirmed at times by Bardianna and Ishmael and the alluring infinite symbolized by that "uprising fin of some undiscernible form" (*MD*, p. 140).

PHILOSOPHICAL COUNTERFORCES: STOICISM AND SKEPTICISM

Melville does not, then, affirm either the categorical assertions of the philosophical idealist or the categorical displacement of the ideal as described by Plinlimmon's pamphlet. Rather, he tends to celebrate the human need to forge a balance between experiential and intellectual extremes, to accommodate disparate possibilities for selfhood, to maintain flexibility and freedom within limits prescribed by natural existence.

Ishmael, for example, is at home among strange beings and strange creeds. His accommodating sensibility could not have been formed simply by remaining in Manhattan. Rather, he pursues the "ungraspable phantom of life" (*MD*, p. 14), and by so doing he learns that "in all cases man must eventually lower, or at least shift, his conceit of attainable felicity" (p. 349). In Melville's work stoicism and skepticism offer such lowered conceits and thereby constitute major philosophical counterforces to idealism; consequently, they usually provide behavioral paradigms which lead one to balance, for example, the extreme poles of idealism and nihilism. The stoic remains uncompromised; he maintains dignity in the face of outrageous exasperations. In "Cock-A-Doodle-Doo!" the figure of Merrymusk sawing wood in a snowstorm reflects his dogged endurance. The skeptic remains uncommitted and, like Ishmael, on occasion tends to suspend judgment: "Doubts of all things earthly, and intuitions of some things heavenly; this combination makes neither believer nor infidel, but makes a man who regards them both with equal eye" (*MD*, p. 314).

Stoicism as a philosophy primarily concerns itself with practical affairs; it provides an attractive alternative to the absolute quest. Indeed, Babbalanja, who tends to drive himself crazy with incessant speculation, discovers "A Happy Life" while rooting through Oh-Oh's pile of antiquarian tracts and rhapsodizes over the down-to-earth pagan wisdom (*Mardi*, p. 338). As William Braswell indicates in "Melville's Use of Seneca" (1940), Melville took this material directly from Seneca's *Morals by Way of Abstract*. The Senecan abstract offers an encapsulated version of stoical philosophy, emphasizing its common sense fairness—its geniality, steadiness, and sobriety. In combining good-natured acceptance with dogged resolution, stoicism offers a practical response to the vicissitudes of life. In Melville's view the stoical hero not only endures adversity but also controls passion and achieves self-mastery. While in *Mardi* Melville extracted Seneca in whole chunks, perhaps indicating that stoicism had not yet become absorbed into his creative consciousness, he later projects various attributes of stoicism into characters as diverse as Ushant, Ishmael, Queequeg, Pierre, Bartleby, and the lawyer, Merrymusk, the narrator of "I and my Chimney," and Marianna in "The Piazza."[11]

For the skeptic the locus of reference is not so much the need to steady the self as the need to remain open to multiple ways of perceiving the "flux and reflux" of experience (*Mardi*, p. 512). To the skeptic the world is in a state of constant change and human subjects must wrestle with their continuing incapacity to rest with a fixed sense of truth. Ishmael broods over the "pondering repose of If . . . . and Ifs eternally" (*MD*, p. 406). While Melville's recurring insistence on the primacy of the subjective amid a world of shifting phenomena reflects romantic and proto-existential qualities, it must also be viewed in light of his probable knowledge of the pre-socratic conflicts between the Eleatics and Heracliteans. The Eleatics, followers of Parmenides (c. 540–470 B.C.), held that the ultimate substance—Being—was unchanging. On the contrary, Heraclitus (c. 544–484 B.C.) posited that the world was in a state of continual flux. Melville could have been familiar with this conflict. In *Cratylus* and *Theaetetus* Plato considers the Heraclitean doctrines. Throughout ancient philosophy the notion that change is the only constant usually appears in the phrase, "All things flow" (See Robert S. Brumbaugh, pp. 43–49). In one of his fragments Heraclitus writes, "You cannot step twice into the same river; for fresh waters are ever flowing in upon you" (John Burnet, p. 136). In a striking passage in *Mardi* Babbalanja echoes the essence of Heraclitean thought and may even be paraphrasing some version of Heraclitus's words: "But the balsam-dropping palms, whose boles run milk, whose plumes wave boastful in the air, they perish in their prime, and bow their blasted trunks. Nothing abideth; the river of yesterday floweth not to-day; the sun's rising is a setting; living is dying; the very mountains melt and all revolve:—systems and asteroids.... Ah gods! in all this universal stir, am *I* to prove one stable thing" (pp. 237–38; Melville's italics). How Melville evolved his philosophy of "flux and reflux" remains a matter of speculation, especially insofar as the Heraclitean/Pyrrhonic strain resonates in *Ecclesiastes*, Seneca, Montaigne, and Browne.[12] What *is* crucial in *Mardi* and subsequent works is the way in which Melville's skepticism generates an ongoing—and incessantly unresolved—search for an informing standard. It might be said that irresolvable questions provide interpretive cruxes in *Mardi, Moby-Dick, Pierre*, "Bartleby," "Benito Cereno," *The Confidence-Man, Clarel*, and *Billy Budd*.

The skeptical sense also leads Melville to repudiate philosophers in particular and in general. In *Pierre* the narrator sneeringly decries those thinkers, who claim to have found the "Talismanic Secret": "Certain philosophers have time and again pretended to have found it.... their vain philosophy [is] let glide away into practical oblivion. Plato, and Spinoza, and Goethe, and many more belong to this guild of self-impostors, with a preposterous rabble of Muggletonian Scots and Yankees, whose vile brogue still the more bestreaks the stripedness of their Greek or German Neoplatonical originals" (XIV, ii, p. 208). Clearly, such repudiations of "philosophy" should not be taken to reflect Melville's final judgment. In 1852 Melville's outrage may have been conditioned by his own exhaustion, similar to Pierre's as he attempted to "deliver what he thought to be new, or at least miserably neglected Truth to the world" (XXI, i, p. 283). Melville apparently composed *Pierre* in about four months. In relation to the narrative itself, Melville does not seem to be repudiating philosophy *per se* as the tendency of mind that grossly perverts idealistic thought into monomania. Certainly, Plato never intended his doctrine of Ideas to serve as a utilitarian remedy for abuses in the here-and-now. Rather, it provided a system of ideas and images, which helped man to explain his mediate position in the soul's quest for wisdom. The utopic *Republic*, in fact, turns on one very problematic conditional clause: *when* philosophers become kings.

"ONTOLOGICAL HEROICS"

Regardless of Melville's occasional disgust with the guild of philosophers, he nevertheless continued his vigorous exploration of the world of mind and the problematics of being. But as Sealts aptly notes, "the course of his love never did run smooth" ("Platonic Tradition," p. 336). If Hawthorne frequently lamented the anti-art bias in a literary marketplace that expected the customary, then Melville had even greater cause to bewail the anti-philosophy bias among reviewers, readers, family, and friends. In writing to Hawthorne, Melville discussed the dissociation between "Truth" and what would pay: "But Truth is the silliest thing under the sun. Try to get a living by the Truth—and go to the Soup Societies.... Dollars damn me.... What I feel most moved to write, that is banned,—it will not pay. Yet, altogether, write the *other* way I cannot. So the product is a final hash, and all my books are botches" (*Letters*, pp. 127–28; Melville's italics). Melville here was echoing his critics; they disliked even his self-professed dilution of metaphysical fiction. Even one of Melville's more sensitive and appreciative commentators became fed up with what he took to be Melville's aberrant speculations. In a review-essay of February 1853, Fitz-James O'Brien dismissed the "wild, inflated, repulsive" *Pierre* to praise *Mardi* with backhanded compliments: "*Mardi*, we believe, is intended to embody all the philosophy of which Mr. Melville is capable, and we have no hesitation in saying that the philosophical parts are the worst." The consensus came to be that Melville "totter[ed] on the edge of a precipice" (*Mel. Log*, pp. 466–67), that he had perverted his healthful talent to make *Typee*s, that he did so by indulging what O'Brien later called "metaphysical and morbid meditations" (p. 565).

Despite such charges, Melville did not capitulate to public tastes. In more playful moods he could whimsically project his own sense of exclusion (and self-acceptance) into his characters. In "I and My Chimney" the narrator would rather stand stoically with the ancients than fall to the frivolity of the moderns. The narrator identifies with all things old (*Tales*, p. 337). Consequently, he engages in an ongoing conflict with his modernizing wife, who "like all the rest of the world, cares not a fig for my philosopher jabber. In dearth of other philosophical companionship, I and my chimney have to smoke and philosophize together" (p. 353).

In a still humorous but more biting manner, the agent for the Black Rapids Coal Company ironically adopts the voice of self-deluding optimism, which so easily dismisses the darker view of life. Melville encapsulates the complacent yea-saying perspective, which found his art so viscerally disturbing. Here the confidence man feigns disgust. He vents his spleen against the depressive philosophical "bears," those destroyers of confidence, who are associated with Timon, Diogenes, Seneca, Tacitus, and Heraclitus:

And do you know whence this sort of fellow gets his sulk? not from life; for he's often too much of a recluse, or else too young to have seen anything of it. No, he gets it from some of those old plays he sees on the stage, or some of those old books he finds up in garrets. Ten to one, he has lugged home from auction a musty old Seneca, and sets about stuffing himself with that stale old hay; and, thereupon, thinks it looks wise and antique to be a croaker, thinks it's taking a stand 'way above his kind. (*CM*, p. 49)

Melville's satires of shallow optimism and its humorous, if troubled, self-awareness indicate that, by 1857, he had no audience able or willing to understand and appreciate him. Of all his works of fiction *The Confidence-Man* seems to be the kind of book Melville may have felt "most moved to write" (*Letters*, p. 128), one written mostly to himself.

After publishing *The Confidence-Man*, Melville bade farewell to his career as a public fiction-writer. He was, however, by no means silent. He continued to engage in "ontological heroics" (*Letters*, p. 133) in conversation, in the margins of books, in correspondence, and most significantly in *Clarel* and *Billy Budd*. A few brief examples reveal Melville's ongoing passion for metaphysics. On 1 October 1856, before embarking for England and the Holy Land, Melville spent an evening with Evert Duyckinck. This night of "sailor metaphysics," according to Duyckinck, led to "a good stirring evening" (*Mel. Log*, p. 523). In 1859 two collegians, on a literary pilgrimage to Pittsfield, found Melville in an expansive mood. To their chagrin John Thomas Gulick and Titus Munson Coan were not treated to sunny tales of Fayaway and Polynesia but to the "shade of Aristotle" (p. 605). On that day Melville expounded upon the decadence of modernity and the splendors of antiquity. In his journal Gulick perceptively writes,

Though it was apparent that he possessed a mind of aspiring, ambitious order, full of elastic energy and illuminated with the rich colors of a poetic fancy, he was evidently a disappointed man, soured by criticism and disgusted with the civilized world and with our Christendom in general and in particular. The ancient dignity of Homeric times afforded the only state of humanity, individual or social, to which he could turn with any complacency. What little there was of meaning in the religions of the present day had come down from Plato. All our philosophy and all our art and poetry was either derived or imitated from the ancient Greeks.

Coan notes, "... he was in full tide of discourse on all things sacred and profane" (*Mel. Log*, p. 605). The portrait that emerges here is not that of a silent, brooding recluse but an animated man who has counted his losses. While certainly not content, Melville knew where he stood and was committed to following the bent of his mind.

Although the relationship between Melville's learning and the art of his last three decades defies encapsulation, a few observations are nevertheless in order. Throughout these years of reading and re-reading, he came back to Emerson with great interest. On 22 March 1862 Melville purchased Emerson's *Essays: First Series* and *Essays: Second Series*. As Melville's marginalia indicate, Emerson raised his ire. He especially seemed to enjoy disputing Emerson's more fatuous remarks (*Mel. Log*, p. 648–49). While annoyed by Emerson's apparent dismissal of evil, Melville had great respect for his nobility of intellect. Plato was also on Melville's mind. A poem perhaps intended for a projected volume of poems that was not published (ca. 1860) leads, for example, to direct commentary on Plato's *Republic*. "A Reasonable Constitution" emphasizes the somber, classicist views of human nature that pervade his poetry, especially "The House-top," and find explicit issue in Ungar's diatribes in *Clarel* (see Jane Donahue):

> What though Reason forged your scheme?
> 'Twas Reason dreamed the Utopia's dream:
> 'Tis dream to think that Reason can
> Govern the reasoning creature, man.
> (*Mel. Log*, p. 617)

Melville goes on to remark: "Observable in Sir Thomas More's 'Utopia' are First its almost entire reasonableness. Second its almost entire impracticability. The remark applies more or less to the Utopia's prototype 'Plato's Republic' " (p. 617). Plato appears a number of times in *Clarel*, usually by way of Rolfe's speculations. As Sealts points out, Rolfe is a "partial self-portrait of Melville" ("Platonic Tradition," p. 330). Reflecting Melville's own view of himself as philosopher-sailor-rover, Rolfe "supplemented Plato's theme/ With daedal life in boats and tents, / A messmate of the elements" (*Clarel*, I, xxxi, ll. 19–21; p. 99). Of special note in Melville's later years is his attraction to Matthew Arnold (see Bezanson). After 10 July 1869 he read and commented on Arnold's essays on Spinoza and Marcus Aurelius (*Mel. Log*, p. 704). Melville's debt to Aristotle and Schopenhauer, both of whom he was reading while composing *Billy Budd*, still needs to be fully assessed.

These sporadic remarks, in their unavoidable brevity, hopefully suggest the need for a full intellectual biography of Melville. Along with areas of special critical concern noted above, one could fruitfully examine Melville's relationship to the methods and themes of Montaigne, Hobbes, Coleridge, and Carlyle. Students of Melville would greatly profit from a translation and reissue of K. H. Sundermann's groundbreaking study of Melville and Plato. What is especially vexing—and well beyond the scope of the present study—is the relationship, perhaps a divided allegiance, between the philosophical tradition represented by the Platonists and the Judaeo-Christian tradition represented by the Bible. But the problem I find most engaging—and which focuses my ongoing research on this subject—is the very fusion of philosophy and art, the making of Melville's philosophical art. How do his metaphysical preoccupations help shape his developing aesthetic and how do his works of art, in turn, re-form the philosophical materials which they contain? Such a concern directs one's gaze to Melville's practice of bringing together (at different times) disparate genetic entities—travel narrative, romance, satire, polemic, autobiography, biography, novel, poem—in the cause of expressing his metaphysical preoccupations. Thankfully, the way for our continuing pursuits has been brilliantly cleared by Sealts, Braswell, Leyda, Davis, and Howard.

In trying to tell the finally untellable story of Melville's philosophical art, this chapter began by considering Melville's flight from Typee Valley adventure in the "world of mind" (*Mardi*, p. 557). In many ways Melville's movement away from the lush verdure of Typee and the demands of adventure narrative had its most complex culmination in the desert Holy Land pilgrimage depicted in *Clarel*. Approximately ten years in the making, *Clarel* offers a compendium of Melville's life-long religious and philosophical preoccupations. Clarel, Rolfe, and their numerous companions exhaustively wrangle over such topics as God, man, science, faith, good, evil, idealism, skepticism, pantheism, metempsychosis. In the course of these dialogues Melville makes learned reference again and again to such figures as Plato, Zeno, Cicero, and Pyrrho, among the ancients, and Bacon, Spinoza, Hobbes, and Kant, among the moderns. Interestingly, this engagement with pressing questions of life and mind achieves no resolution. It seems as though *Clarel* amounts to a long elaboration of Media's remarks to Babbalanja: " . . . final, last thoughts you mortals have none; nor can have; and at bottom, your own fleeting fancies are too often secrets to yourselves. . . . Thus with the wisest of you all; you are ever unfixed" (*Mardi*, p. 370). One of the "wisest," Rolfe reflects the unsettled fate of thinking man; multiple perspectives converge in a "fold of doubt":

> Is this the man
> Whom Jordan heard in part espouse

> The appeal of that Dominican
> And Rome? and here, all sects, behold,
> All creeds involving in one fold
> Of doubt? Better a partisan!
> Earnest he seems: can union be
> 'Twixt earnestness and levity?
> Or need at last in Rolfe confess
> Thy hollow, Manysidedness!
> (*Clarel*, III, xvi, ll. 257–66;
> pp. 344–45)

Like Rolfe, Melville had the self-stimulating curse of "Manysidedness." As Hawthorne brilliantly noted, his friend "can neither believe, nor be comfortable in his unbelief; and he is too honest and courageous not to try to do one or the other" (*Mel. Log*, p. 529). Throughout his life and work Melville persisted in asking ultimate questions of a God whose voice was silence and whose dumb ambassador was recurrently figured in the Sphinx. Ahab's sphinx is a severed whale's head, whose eyes have seen but whose mouth cannot speak (*MD*, p. 264). In the "Epilogue" of *Clarel*, "The ancient Sphinx still keeps the porch of shade" while man continues the "strife and old debate":

> The running battle of the star and clod
> Shall run forever—if there be no God.
> (IV, xxxv, ll. 4, 12, 16–17, pp. 522–23)

The Sphinx is silent, as all sphinxes are and must remain. Nevertheless, Melville kept pursuing the strange, frightening, and exasperating mysteries of being. He found that man was suspended somewhere between his shifting experience of the phenomenal world and those teasing intimations from the invisible spheres. Although the phantom of life was certainly ungraspable, it could not be let alone. As Ahab tells Captain Boomer, "What is best let alone, that accursed thing is not always what least allures" (*MD*, p. 368). As Melville saw it, thinking man was relentlessly driven to engage in "reason's endless battle." Melville's philosophical art celebrates his own self-ennobling exploration of man's chronic but futile quest to solve the puzzle of existence:

> What may man know?
> (Here pondered Clarel) let him rule—
> Pull down, build up, creed, system, school,
> And reason's endless battle wage,
> Make and remake his verbiage—
> But solve the world! Scarce that he'll do:
> Too wild it is, too wonderful.
> (IV, iii, ll. 109–15; p. 418)

NOTES

1. Many of Babbalanja's meditations echo passages from Sir Thomas Browne. When discussing the wonders of nature, Browne in *Religio Medici* employs the phrase "flux and reflux" (Part I, section 15, p. 24). For extensive discussions of Browne's influence on Melville, see Matthiessen, pp. 100–30; Sealts, "The Platonic Tradition," pp. 282–99; Ruth M. Vande Kieft; and Sanford E. Marovitz, pp. 12–13. In *Mardi* the poet Vavona appears to be an alias for Browne. Interestingly, in a letter to his brother George, Evert Duyckinck relates that Melville "has borrowed Sir Thomas Browne of me and says finely of the speculations of the *Religio Medici* that Browne is a kind of 'crack'd Archangel' " (*Mel. Log*, p. 273). In *Mardi* Babbalanja refers to Vavona as "archangel" twice and as "crack-pated god" (p. 394).

2. Except when noted parenthetically, the full citations for primary sources are numbered and listed alphabetically in Sealt's *Reading*. Space prohibits discussion of Melville's relationship to all the figures mentioned above. For discussions of Montaigne, see William Ellery Sedgwick, p. 235; W. G. Kilbourne; Thomas J. Scorza, p. 179; Gorman Beauchamp; for Burton, see Nathalia Wright, "Old Burton"; for Carlyle, see Mario L. D'Avanzo and James Barbour; for Arnold, see Walter E. Bezanson; for Schopenhauer, see William Braswell, *Melville's Religious Thought*, pp. 14–15, 117–18; Walter Sutton, Kenneth Ledbetter; Olive L. Fite.

3. My notion of "philosophical art" no doubt deserves a chapter-long explanation. In taking the broadest view, one could argue that just about any work of art is "philosophical" insofar as it has ideas and reflects some kind of worldview. In this chapter, however, philosophical art reflects a synthesis of creative process and metaphysical traditions; the artist appropriates ideas, arguments, images, and thinkers from recognizable schools. While Melville responds most fully to the tradition of philosophical idealism, he nevertheless subordinates his philosophical materials and impulses to the aesthetic process. A novelist, Michael E. Levin argues, concerns himself with trying to show what "it is like to experience the world as the [philosophical] system represents it" (p. 61). Sealts argues that Melville "developed from an author who entertained philosophical ideas into a full-fledged philosophical novelist" ("Platonic Tradition," p. 316). Both Edgar A. Dryden, pp. 3–29, and Edwin M. Eigner, pp. 1–12, consider the issue of metaphysical fiction.

4. In *Melville's Religious Thought* Braswell writes:

The problem of chronology is also baffling. To take one example: The New York Public Library recently acquired ... an old school book entitled *The English Reader* in which "H. Melvill" is written in several places.... There are no dates in the book, but one assumes that Melville studied it when he was a boy.... Among the dialogues are Lord Lyttleton's "Locke and Bayle" ("Christianity defended against the cavils of skepticism") and Fenelon's "Democritus and Heraclitus." There is a piece of Addison on the immortality of the soul, and there are selections from Milton and Cowper. Did the readings in this volume make lasting impressions on the youthful Melville? Did he later read a great deal more by the authors represented here? If so, when? (pp. 9–10)

5. Except when noted parenthetically, the full citations for primary sources are numbered and listed alphabetically in Sealt's *Reading*.

6. Howard writes, "As a romantic heroine and the object of an adventurous quest, Yillah resembles the heroines of Keats' *Endymion*, Shelley's *Alastor*, and Byron's *The Island*; but the details of her watery background, her rescue from a heartless old man, and her mysterious disappearance make her more akin to the sentimental German's [La Motte-Fouque's] water sprite than to the fair maidens of the English poets" (pp. 113–14).

7. Wright makes an important distinction:

Now in his belief in the existence of this world beyond the world of sense Melville has often been called, and even called himself, Platonic. Like the Platonists, he did believe truth resided in the unseen world of ideas and conceptions rather than in the world of material manifestations. But in his essentially romantic conception of this invisible sphere he was closer to the Hebrews than to the Greeks. Order, rhetoric, and logic did not represent the primal truth to him as did elemental and undisciplined energy . . . . to the Hebrews this world was vague. (*Melville's Use of the Bible*, p. 184)

8. Melville was alert to a range of influence that extended from Plato and his successors to the contemporary German, English, and American idealists. As Sealts notes, "Certain aspects of Ahab's idealism . . . seem less like that of the Platonic dialogues than what Melville himself had encountered in the thought of his nineteenth-century contemporaries . . . . this is essentially the conception of symbolic correspondence between matter and spirit to be found in Carlyle and Emerson" ("Platonic Tradition," p. 310). Matthiessen argues, "The tendency of American idealism to see a spiritual significance in every natural fact was far more broadly diffused than transcendentalism. Loosely Platonic, it came specifically from the common background that lay behind Emerson and Hawthorne, from the Christian habit of mind that saw the hand of God in all manifestations of life" (p. 243). Matthiessen later suggests that, with the Transcendentalists, Melville "agreed that spirit is substance, but when he contemplated the mystery of the unseen, he began to diverge from the transcendental conclusion that its effect on man was necessarily beneficient" (p. 405). For related discussions, see Newton Arvin, p. 166; Charles Feidelson; Perry Miller; Howard P. Vincent, pp. 151–63; Milton Stern, *The Fine-Hammered Steel*, pp. 1–29; A. D. Van Nostrand, pp. 113–40; Sheldon W. Liebman; Hershel Parker; Luther S. Mansfield; Michael J. Colacurcio; Edward J. Rose; Martha Banta; and Philip D. Beidler.

9. Professor Albert J. Rivero has pointed out to me that Melville may possibly be punning on "psyche"—the Greek word for both soul and butterfly.

10. For important discussions of the Melville seeker becoming lost in the infinite, see Matthiessen, p. 406; Vincent, pp. 157–58; Stern, *The Fine-Hammered Steel*; Sealts, "Platonic Tradition," p. 286; Strauch, pp. 468–70; Seelye.

11. In the margin of his copy of Seneca's *Epistle XII* Melville remarks,

Surely, if these things were recorded in Holy Writ, what force they would carry. It is indeed undeniable, that in Seneca & other of the old philosophers, we meet with maxims of actual life, & lessons of practical wisdom which not only equal but exceed any thing in the Scriptures.—But behold the force of example, & its omnipotence over mere precepts however lofty. Seneca's life belied his philosophy; But that of Christ went beyond his own teachings. (*Mel. Log*, p. 285)

It should also be noted that Melville did not see stoicism as a somber or penitential philosophy of life. Rather, the stoic knew how to laugh. As Babbalanja says, "All sages have laughed,—let us; Bardianna laughed,—let us"; Demorkriti laughed,—let us . . . Rabeelee roared,—let us" (*Mardi*, p. 613). Part of Ishmael's stoical sense becomes expressed in his ability to "grin and bear it" (*MD*, p. 15). See also "The Hyena" in *Moby-Dick* (ch. 49).

　　12.　For Melville and Pyrrho, see Braswell, *Melville's Religious Thought*, pp. 51–52; Bell notes, "The association between the science of vision and religious disbelief lay before [Melville] in Bayle's article on Pyrrho. Now skepticism in Bayle's day was commonly known as Pyrrhonism, after the Greek philosopher who taught 'the art of disputing everything' " (p. 647).

WORKS CITED

Anderson, Charles Roberts. *Melville in the South Seas*. New York: Columbia University Press, 1939.

Arvin, Newton. *Herman Melville*. New York: William Sloane Associates, 1950.

Banta, Martha. "The Man of History and the Mythy Man in Melville." *American Transcendental Quarterly* No. 10 (1971): 3–11.

Barbour, James and Leon Howard. "Carlyle and the Conclusion of *Moby-Dick*." *New England Quarterly* 49 (1976): 214–24.

Beauchamp, Gorman. "Montaigne, Melville and the Cannibals." *Arizona Quarterly* 37 (Winter 1981): 293–309.

Beidler, Philip D. "*Billy Budd*: Melville's Valedictory to Emerson." *ESQ* 24 (1978): 215–28.

Bell, Millicent. "Pierre Bayle and *Moby-Dick*." *PMLA* 66 (September 1951) 626–48.

Bezanson, Walter E. "Melville's Reading of Arnold's Poetry." *PMLA* 69 (June 1954): 365–91.

Branch, Watson G. "The Genesis, Composition, and Structure of *The Confidence-Man*." *Nineteenth-Century Fiction* 7 (March 1973): 424–48.

Braswell, William. *Melville's Religious Thought: An Essay in Interpretation*. Durham, N.C.: Duke University Press, 1943.

———. "Melville's Use of Seneca in *Mardi*." *American Literature* 12 (March 1940): 98–104.

Brodhead, Richard H. "*Mardi*: Creating the Creative." In *New Perspectives on Melville*. Ed. Faith Pullin. Kent: Kent State University Press, 1978, pp. 29–53.

Brodtkorb, Paul, Jr. *Ishmael's White World: A Phenomenological Reading of Moby-Dick*. New Haven, Conn.: Yale University Press, 1965.

Browne, Thomas. *The Works of Sir Thomas Browne.* Vol. I: *Religio Medici.* Ed. Geoffrey Keynes. Chicago: University of Chicago Press, 1964.

Brumbaugh, Robert S. *The Philosophers of Greece.* New York: Crowell, 1964.

Burnet, John. *Early Greek Philosophy.* 1st ed., 1892; London: A. & C. Black, 1930.

Chase, Richard. *Herman Melville: A Critical Study.* New York: Macmillan, Co., 1949.

Colacurcio, Michael J. "A Better Mode of Evidence—The Transcendental Problem of Faith and Spirit." *ESQ* No. 54 (First Quarter 1969): 12–22.

Couch, H. N. "Melville's *Moby-Dick* and the *Phaedo.*" *Classical Journal* 28 (1933): 367–68.

Cowan, S. A. "In Praise of Self-Reliance: The Role of Bulkington in *Moby-Dick.*" *American Literature* 38 (January 1967): 547–56.

D'Avanzo, Mario L. "Melville's 'Bartleby' and Carlyle." *Melville Annual* No. 1 (1965): 113–39.

Davis, Merrell R. *Melville's Mardi: A Chartless Voyage.* New Haven, Conn.: Yale University Press, 1952.

Donahue, Jane. "Melville's Classicism: Law and Order in His Poetry." *Papers on Language and Literature* 5 (Winter 1969): 63–72.

Dryden, Edgar A. *Melville's Thematics of Form: The Great Art of Telling the Truth.* Baltimore: Johns Hopkins University Press, 1968.

Duban, James. "The Translation of Pierre Bayle's *An Historical and Critical Dictionary* Owned by Melville." *Papers of the Bibliographical Society of America* 71 (1977): 347–51.

Eigner, Edwin M. *The Metaphysical Novel in England and America: Dickens, Bulwer-Lytton, Melville, and Hawthorne.* Berkeley: University of California Press, 1978.

Feidelson, Charles, Jr. *Symbolism and American Literature.* Chicago: University of Chicago Press, 1953.

Finkelstein, Dorothee Metlitsky. *Melville's Orienda.* New Haven, Conn.: Yale University Press, 1961.

Fite, Olive L. "Billy Budd, Claggart and Schopenhauer." *Nineteenth-Century Fiction* 23 (December 1968): 336–43.

Franklin, H. Bruce. *The Wake of the Gods: Melville's Mythology.* Stanford, Calif.: Stanford University Press, 1963.

Guttman, Allen. "From *Typee* to *Moby-Dick*: Melville's Allusive Art." *Modern Language Quarterly* 24 (September 1963): 237–44.

Hauser, Helen A. "Spinozan Philosophy in *Pierre.*" *American Literature* 49 (March 1977): 49–56.

Herbert, T. Walter, Jr. *Moby-Dick and Calvinism: A World Dismantled.* New Brunswick, N.J.: Rutgers University Press, 1977.

Higgins, Brian. "Plinlimmon and the Pamphlet Again." *Studies in the Novel* 4 (Spring 1972): 27–38.

Hoffman, Daniel. "*The Confidence-Man*: His Masquerade." *Form and Fable in American Fiction.* New York: Oxford University Press, 1961. Rpt. in *Melville: A Collection of Critical Essays.* Ed. Richard Chase. Englewood Cliffs, N.J.: Prentice-Hall, 1962, pp. 125–43.

Irwin, John T. *American Hieroglyphics: The Symbol of the Egyptian Hieroglyphics in the American Renaissance.* New Haven, Conn.: Yale University Press, 1980.

Kaul, A. N. *The American Vision: Actual and Ideal Society in Nineteenth-Century Fiction.* New Haven, Conn.: Yale University Press. 1963.

Kemper, Steven E. "*The Confidence-Man*: A Knavishly-Packed Deck." *Studies in American Fiction* 8 (Spring 1980): 23–35.

Kilbourne, W. G., Jr. "Montaigne and Captain Vere." *American Literature* 33 (January 1962): 514–17.

Ledbetter, Kenneth. "The Ambiguity of *Billy Budd*." *Texas Studies in Literature and Language* 4 (Spring 1962): 130–34.

Lee, Dwight A. "Melville and George J. Adler." *American Notes and Queries* 12 (1974): 138–41.

Levin, Michael E. "Ahab as Socratic Philosopher: The Myth of the Cave Inverted." *American Transcendental Quarterly* No. 41 (1979): 61–73.

Liebman, Sheldon W. "The 'Body and Soul' Metaphor in *Moby-Dick*." *ESQ*, 50 supplement (1968): 29–34.

Lindberg, Gary. *The Confidence-Man in American Literature.* New York: Oxford University Press, 1982.

Mansfield, Luther S. "The Emersonian Idiom and the Romantic Period in American Literature." *ESQ* No. 34 (First Quarter 1964): 23–28.

Marovitz, Sanford E. "Melville's Problematic '*Being*.'" *ESQ* 28 (First Quarter 1982): 11–23.

Matthiessen, F. O. *American Renaissance: Art and Expression in the Age of Emerson and Whitman.* New York: Oxford University Press, 1941.

Miller, Perry. "Melville and Transcendentalism." *Virginia Quarterly Review* 29 (Autumn 1953): 556–75; rpt. in *Nature's Nation.* Cambridge, Mass.: Harvard University Press, 1967, pp. 184–96.

Oates, J. C. "Melville and the Manichean Illusion." *Texas Studies in Literature and Language* 4 (1962): 117–29.

Parker, Hershel. "Melville's Satire of Emerson and Thoreau: An Evaluation of the Evidence." *American Transcendental Quarterly* No. 7 (1970): 61–67. [See also "Corrections." *ATQ* No. 9 (1971): 70.

Patrick, Walton R. "Melville's 'Bartleby' and the Doctrine of Necessity." *American Literature* 41 (March 1969): 39–54.

Plato. *The Dialogues of Plato.* 2 vols. Trans. B. Jowett. Intro. Raphael Demos. New York: Random House, 1937.

———. *Phaedon: or, a Dialogue on the Immortality of the Soul.* Trans. Madam Dacier. New York: William Gowans, 1849.

———. *The Works of Plato.* 6 vols. Trans. Henry Cary, Henry Davis, and George Burges. London: Henry G. Bohn, 1848–54.

———. *The Works of Plato.* 5 vols. Trans. Floyer Sydenham and Thomas Taylor. London: T. Taylor, 1804.

Pochmann, Henry A. *German Culture in America: Philosophical and Literary Influences, 1600–1900.* Madison: University of Wisconsin Press, 1950.

Ramsey, William M. "The Moot Points of Melville's Indian-Hating." *American Literature* 52 (May 1980): 224–35.

Rose, Edward J. "Melville, Emerson, and the Sphinx." *New England Quarterly* 36 (June 1963): 249–58.

Rosenberry, Edward H. "Israel Potter, Benjamin Franklin, and the Doctrine of Self-Reliance." *ESQ* No. 28 (Third Quarter 1962): 27–29.

Roundy, Nancy. "Melville's *The Confidence-Man*: Epistemology and Art." *Ball State University Forum* 21 (Spring 1979): 3–11.

Scorza, Thomas J. *In the Time Before Steamships: Billy Budd, The Limits of Politics, and Modernity*. DeKalb: Northern Illinois University Press, 1979.

Sealts, Merton M., Jr. "Herman Melville's Reading in Ancient Philosophy." Ph.D. Diss., Yale University, 1942. [*Mel. Diss.*, #18.]

———. "Melville and Emerson's Rainbow." *ESQ* 26 (Second Quarter 1980): 53–78 Rpt. in *Pursuing Melville, 1940–1980*. Madison: University of Wisconsin Press, 1982, pp. 250–77.

———. "Melville and the Platonic Tradition." In *Pursuing Melville, 1940–1980*. Madison: University of Wisconsin Press, 1982, pp. 278–336.

———. "Melville's 'Neoplatonic Originals.' " *Modern Language Notes* 67 (February 1952): 80–86.

———. "The Records of Melville's Reading." In *Pursuing Melville, 1940–1980*. Madison: University of Wisconsin Press, 1982, pp. 31–57.

Sedgwick, William Ellery. *Herman Melville: The Tragedy of Mind*. Cambridge, Mass.: Harvard University Press, 1944.

Sherrill, Rowland A. *The Prophetic Melville: Experience, Transcendence, and Tragedy*. Athens: University of Georgia Press, 1979.

Shulman, Robert P. "Montaigne and the Techniques and Tragedy of Melville's *Billy Budd*." *Comparative Literature* 16 (Fall 1964): 322–30.

Stein, William B. "Melville's *The Confidence-Man*: Quicksands of the Word." *American Transcendental Quarterly* No. 24 (Fall 1974): 38–50.

Sten, Christopher W. "The Dialogue of Crisis in *The Confidence-Man*: Melville's 'New Novel.' " *Studies in the Novel* 6 (Summer 1974): 165–85.

Stern, Milton R. *The Fine-Hammered Steel of Herman Melville*. Urbana: University of Illinois Press, 1957.

———. "Towards 'Bartleby and Scrivener.' " In *The Stoic Strain in American Literature: Essays in Honour of Marston LaFrance*. Ed. Duane J. Macmillan. Toronto: University of Toronto Press, 1979, pp. 19–41.

Stevens, Aretta J. "The Edition of Montaigne Read by Melville." *Papers of the Bibliographic Society of America* 62 (First Quarter 1968): 130–34.

Strauch, Carl F. "Ishmael: Time and Personality in *Moby-Dick*." *Studies in the Novel* 1 (Winter 1969): 468–83.

Sundermann, K. H. *Herman Melville's Gedankengut: Eine kritische Untersuchung seiner weltanschaulichen Grundideen*. [*The Scope of Melville's Thought*.] Berlin: Arthur Collignon, 1937.

Sutton, Walter. "Melville and the Great God Budd." *Prairie Schooner* 34 (Summer 1960): 128–33.

Sweeney, Gerard M. *Melville's Use of Classical Mythology*. Amsterdam: Rodopi, 1975.

Tichi, Cecelia. "Melville's Craft and the Theme of Language Debased in *The Confidence-Man*." *ELHL: A Journal of English Literary History* 39 (December 1972): 639–58.

Titus, David K. "Herman Melville at the Albany Academy." *Melville Society Extracts* No. 42 (May 1980): 1, 4–10.

Travis, Mildred K. "Echoes of Emerson in Plinlimmon." *American Transcendental Quarterly* No. 14 (Spring 1972): 47–48.

Vande Kieft, Ruth M. " 'When Big Hearts Strike Together' ": The Concussion of Melville and Sir Thomas Browne." *Papers on Language and Literature* 5 (Winter 1969): 39–50.

Van Nostrand, A. D. "The Linked Analogies of *Moby-Dick*." In *Everyman His Own Poet: Romantic Gospels in American Literature*. New York: McGraw-Hill, 1968, pp. 113–40.

Vargish, Thomas. "Gnostick Mythos in *Moby-Dick*." *PMLA* 81 (June 1966): 272–77.

Vincent, Howard P. *The Trying-Out of Moby-Dick*. Boston, Mass.: Houghton Mifflin, 1949.

Wadlington, Warwick P. *The Confidence Game in American Literature*. Princeton, N.J.: Princeton University Press, 1975

Watson, Charles N., Jr. "Melville and the Theme of Timonism: From *Pierre* to *The Confidence-Man*." *American Literature* 44 (November 1972): 398–413.

Wenke, John. "Melville's *Mardi* and the Isles of Man." *American Transcendental Quarterly* No. 53 (Winter 1982): 25–41.

———. "Melville's Masquerade and the Aesthetics of Self-Possession." *ESQ* 28 (Fourth Quarter 1982): 233–42.

Werge, Thomas A. "*Moby-Dick* and the Calvinist Tradition." *Studies in the Novel* 1 (Winter 1969): 484–506.

Widmer, Kingsley. *The Ways of Nihilism: Herman Melville's Short Novels*. Los Angeles: California State University Press, 1970.

Wright, Nathalia. "Melville and 'Old Burton' with 'Bartleby' as *An Anatomy of Melancholy*." *Tennessee Studies in Literature* 15 (1970): 1–13.

———. *Melville's Use of the Bible*. Durham, N. C.: Duke University Press, 1949.

20

MELVILLE'S COMEDY AND TRAGEDY

Edward H. Rosenberry

> Man is the only animal that laughs and weeps;
> for he is the only animal that is struck with
> the difference between what things are, and
> what they ought to be.

If the discussion of Melville's comedy and tragedy had to be confined to one sentence, my choice would light on that familiar opening statement from William Hazlitt's 1819 essay, "On Wit and Humour." It assumes the humanistic view, which must be the ground for any searching consideration of Melville's work; it points to a common source of the two impulses, and a source likely to be found at the core of Melville's meanings; and it formulates a dichotomy, one of the most characteristic and revelatory movements of Melville's mind. What Hazlitt adds in the next paragraph may serve as justification for a certain enlargement of the topic: "To explain the nature of laughter and tears is to account for the condition of human life; for it is in a manner compounded of these two! It is a tragedy or a comedy—sad or merry, as it happens."

That tragedy and comedy constitute an either/or relationship is open to questions that will need to be addressed as we proceed, but the inclusive scope of the two is a logical proposition of radical simplicity and importance. We confront it emblematically every time we enter a theater presided over by the immemorial masks of joy and sorrow; but, in fact, it is axiomatic of our response to any aesthetic experience. Tragedy and comedy are two modes of thought, and the only ones available to us as we make or perceive images of the life we live and assign emotional values to them (L. J. Potts, p. 10). Such a sweeping perspective of the subject invites attention to many areas of study addressed by other writers in this volume, as well as to the extensive literature of research and criticism that has preceded it. Only a small fraction of the confined remarks to follow can be adequately attributed to specific sources, so broadly indebted are they to accumulated writings that tend to lose their identity as they grow in the mind.

The first obligation of this essay, to define comedy and tragedy in some critically useful fashion, may be its most difficult one, and the more difficult as the comic and tragic impulses approach each other on the continuum of their common axis. It has often been remarked that any fool can tell night from day, but the person has not been found who can tell when one becomes the other. The dilemma, in one sense a very pragmatic one, was faced with disarming candor by a former Justice of the Supreme Court in the case of pornography: "I can't tell what it is, but I know it when I see it." Melville dealt with the question as an artist should: he adopted patterns of imagery, most familiarly but not exclusively "bright" and "dark," to create the desired emotional directives. It will be part of the task in hand to relate these patterns to the ideas and values they express, and part of its method to draw evidence as largely as possible from Melville's writings, including letters and his all-important essay on Hawthorne. At the same time it should be recognized that such an effort must focus on principles and examples, necessarily passing over a multitude of cases and alternative assessments on which the greater literature of the subject enlarges.

Pending these explorations, we may attempt an oblique definition—perhaps the only kind possible—of the comic and tragic visions by taking a fresh look at some familiar lines of Sir Walter Ralegh:

> What is our life? A play of passion,
> Our mirth the music of division.
> Our mothers' wombs the tiring-houses be,
> Where we are dressed for this short comedy.
> Heaven the judicious sharp spectator is,
> That sits and marks still who doth act amiss.
> Our graves that hide us from the searching sun
> Are like drawn curtains when the play is done.
> Thus march we, playing, to our latest rest,
> Only we die in earnest, that's no jest.
> (p. 51)

It is possible to conclude that Ralegh is equating comedy with life and tragedy with death, an equation common enough in our newspapers and conversations; but his metaphor makes the point, rather, that comedy is what we dress up for and play at, and that the drama of life reveals its other face when the masquerade is done and we are face to face with ultimate reality. In the same way, we incline to see those smiling and weeping masks that symbolize theater as standing for its complementary genres, an equation that teaches us that what makes us smile is comedy and what makes us weep is tragedy. We overlook the point that laughter and tears are common effects of comedy and tragedy rather than their essences. It is the springs of those responses that Ralegh's poem hints at and that readers of Melville find so compelling in his writings: what we call comedy is our role-playing or game-playing—played according to our own rules, which may account for the smiles that normally accompany it; what we call tragedy is the end of the show, the clearing of the boards, the abrogation of our theatrical code, the striking of a music not of our making.

Indeed, there is something fundamentally misleading about regarding tragedy as a literary genre at all since genre itself is a game created entirely by man-made rules. When Melville lamented the impossibility of "be[ing] at all frank with his readers" (*Letters*, p. 96), he was in fact chafing against the self-imposed limitation of the arts which bound him to the same old game. Comedy and tragedy for Melville were not forms but ideas, metaphysical categories, or (given his expressed penchant for "heart" over "head") simply feelings. It may help to recall Stephen Dedalus's famous definition of tragedy in *A Portrait of the Artist as a Young Man*: "the feeling which arrests the mind in the presence of whatever is grave and constant in human sufferings."

The image of the "arrested" mind, the mind in constant motion, implies the continuum that unites tragedy with its opposite, that signals the beginning of tragedy where game-playing stops. When the drunken masquerader Fortunato in Poe's "The Cask of Amontillado" is struck by the seriousness of his host's intention in walling him up, his casual adventure crosses the line—always a point of no return—that divides comedy and tragedy. Of course, the reader who is aware of the uninterrupted game-playing of *his* host, the author, will not share the dire perception of the victim, and the story will remain for him what Melville called *The Confidence-Man*, a "comedy of thought." So long as one feels oneself in the presence of a masquerade the curtain has not quite rung down on comedy. Lear's fool keeps on his cap and bells and sustains his bitter banter, but the old man, his regal game-playing over, sheds even his clothes to reduce himself to what his tragic perception sees as "unaccommodated man...a poor, bare, forked animal" (III, iv, l. 101). His very madness signals his release from the inhibiting illusions of sanity, a release of thematic significance in many of Melville's writings. Like Lear, Melville's ideal tragic hero "tears off the mask, and speaks the sane madness of vital truth" ("*Mosses*," p. 542).

More than madness, it is the nakedness of Lear and of his revelatory view of man that points to the essence of tragedy as Melville understood and practiced it. There is no artifice left to it, no "accommodation," but only a confrontation with the self from which there is no turning aside. When this state of affairs is reached in the career of an imaginary character, and when—a vital proviso—that extremity is communicated in its unalloyed totality to the sensibility of the reader, then the aesthetic experience of tragedy occurs.

At the beginning of a penetrating essay on "Tragedy, Comedy, and the Esthetic Experience," Simon O. Lesser quotes the following relevant passage from I. A. Richards's *Principles of Literary Criticism*:

It is essential to recognize that in the full tragic experience there is no suppression. The mind does not shy away from anything, it does not protect itself with any illusion, it stands uncomforted, unintimidated, alone and self-reliant. The test of its success is whether it can face what it is before it . . . without any of the innumerable subterfuges by which it ordinarily dodges the full development of experience . . . . The essence of Tragedy is that it forces us to live for a moment without them. (p. 246)

No one acquainted with Melville's letters to Hawthorne can fail to hear in these sentences an echo of Melville's most definitive, though still imprecise, statement on tragedy:

There is a certain tragic phase of humanity which, in our opinion, was never more powerfully embodied than by Hawthorne. We mean the tragicalness of human thought in its own unbiased, native, and profounder workings. We think that into no recorded mind has the intense feeling of the visible truth ever entered more deeply than into this man's. By visible truth, we mean the apprehension of the absolute condition of present things as they strike the eye of the man who fears them not, though they do their worst to him,—the man who . . . declares himself a sovereign nature (in himself) amid the powers of heaven, hell, and earth. (*Letters*, p. 124).

By no means all that Melville meant by "tragedy" is expressed or implied in these casual remarks; but several characteristic ideas are plain, and the plainest of these are the identification of tragedy with truth and the recognition that truth, faced without reservation or self-deception, is painful. Chapter 27 of *Typee* recorded an early and starkly simple instance of the loss of innocence that truth entails:

I will frankly declare, that after passing a few weeks in this valley of the Marquesas, I formed a higher estimate of human nature than I had ever before entertained. But alas! since then I have been one of the crew of a man-of-war, and the pent-up wickedness of five hundred men has nearly overturned all my previous theories. (p. 203)

Tragedy thus becomes the inevitably dominant milieu for the writer who saw his profession as "the great Art of Telling the Truth." In applying that definition to the two writers he most admired, Hawthorne and Shakespeare, he described their special genius, in his now famous phrase, as a "great power of blackness": a "Calvinistic sense of Innate Depravity and Original Sin, from whose visitations, in some shape or other, no deeply thinking mind is always and wholly free" ("*Mosses,*" pp. 542, 540). In the identical vein, one thinks of the reflection of Ishmael on his harrowing intuitions at the midnight try-works: "The truest of all men was the Man of Sorrows, and the truest of all books is Solomon's, and Ecclesiastes is the fine hammered steel of woe." Indeed, in the broadest frame of reference, "that mortal man who hath more of joy than sorrow in him, that mortal man cannot be true—not true, or undeveloped" (*MD*, p. 355). The afterthought in Melville's sentence is significant. The constitutionally "jolly" mind, like Stubb's, is not so much false or hypocritical as simply a stunted product (in I. A. Richards's phrase) "of the innumerable subterfuges by which it ordinarily dodges the full development of experience."

No theme in Melville's writings is more insistent than that of tragic truth, but it is embodied more typically in images than in statements. The idea of "blackness" as the master force of literature exemplifies the image he most frequently used: darkness as opposed to light. The try-works chapter is largely elaborated in these terms. The "blackness of darkness" forms the setting for a terrifying experience in the false light of fire, and truth returns with the sun, "the only true lamp—all others but liars!"

Nevertheless [Ishmael importantly adds] the sun hides not . . . all the millions of miles of deserts and of griefs beneath the moon. The sun hides not the ocean, which is the dark side of this earth, and which is two-thirds of this earth. (*MD*, pp. 354–55)

The image of contrasted brightness and darkness, repeated with habitual frequency in Melville's writings, is here combined with another image, which has above all others the effect of *leitmotif*: the metaphoric juxtaposition of land and sea. Volumes have been and will yet be written on this most characteristic Melvillean trope; suffice it here to call attention to its special significance to his comic and tragic visions. The *locus classicus* of that relationship, as every reader of *Moby-Dick* knows, is the famous "six-inch chapter" (23, "The Lee Shore") in which Ishmael is made to moralize on the compulsive voyaging of the shadowy Bulkington. Citing the navigational principle of seeking deep water in a storm, Melville points to a "mortally intolerable truth":

that all deep, earnest thinking is but the intrepid effort of the soul to keep the open independence of her sea; while the wildest winds of heaven and earth conspire to cast her on the treacherous, slavish shore.... In landlessness alone [he adds] resides the highest truth, shoreless, indefinite as God—so, better is it to perish in that howling infinite, than be ingloriously dashed upon the lee, even if that were safety! (*MD*, p. 97)

The flight of Ishmael from his land-locked depression to the suicidal risks of the whaling voyage reflects precisely this cast of mind. So, in general, do the thematic movements of all the maritime adventurers portrayed in Melville's novels and poems, from the youthful narrator of *Typee* who turns his back on a paradise of indolence to his elder counterpart recalling in verse those "Enviable Isles" peopled by "unconscious slumberers mere" (*Poems*, p. 203). *Mardi*'s Taji may be taken as a psychological archetype, starting his fictional career in a rowboat in mid-ocean and ending it in a canoe headed for deep water.

Other images of lesser prominence but great cumulative force illuminate the tragic-comic dichotomy. Everywhere in Melville the drunken man is a self-evading figure of comedy, the sober man open to the insights of tragic truth; and while Melville loved a sociable drink and often waxed satirical over self-conscious asceticism, still, on balance, he felt that "the too-sober view is . . . nearer true than the too-drunken" (*CM*, p. 117). Fire imagery, especially in *Moby-Dick*, is strongly symbolic of tragic vision; on the other hand, in "I and My Chimney" and elsewhere fire is related to the domestic hearth and broadly comic values. Mask imagery, already alluded to, also looks both ways. Most memorable is Ahab's use of the figure to characterize "all visible objects . . . as pasteboard masks," and therefore to see it as the task of the truth-seeker to "strike through the mask" (*MD*, p. 144). But just as familiar is the titular "masquerade" of *The Confidence-Man*, in which the metaphor of disguise is a prevailingly comic device, though admittedly with tragic overtones. "We laugh, when children," Hazlitt has written, "at the sudden removing of a pasteboard mask; we laugh, when grown up, more gravely at the tearing off the mask of deceit." Ultimately, he adds, the response is a recoil of terror when something hostile or malignant is revealed behind the mask. The unveiling of Aranda's skeleton hanging from the figurehead of Benito Cereno's ship is a case in point.

Even more eloquent than the mask is what Ahab refers to as "the dead, blind wall [that] butts all inquiring heads at last" (*MD*, p. 427). It is an image that figures prominently in the description of the whale himself ("The Battering Ram") and in the somber fates of Bartleby and Pierre. One comic version of it does occur in the second sketch of "The Encantadas," where the Galapagos tortoise indulges in a "strange infatuation" of butting "like a battering-ram against the immovable foot of the foremast" (*Tales*, p. 105); but the dominant form of the image is the one found in "The Berg" in which ships are wrecked against a "dead indifference of walls" (*Poems*, p. 204), or in *Clarel*, where the young student enters the tragic world of the poem by seeing before him,

> Like the ice-bastions round the Pole,
> Thy blank, blank towers, Jerusalem.
> (I, i, l. 60, p. 4)

Clarel, of course, is a tissue of tragic images, many of them Biblical, and, consequently, many of them atmospherically associated with the waste land, where "Sands immense/ Impart the oceanic sense" (II, xi, l. 38, p. 178). Similarly, the volcanic wastes of the Galapagos Islands in "The Encantadas" serve the metaphoric purpose: "In no world but a fallen one could such lands exist" (*Tales*, p. 100). And nowhere in Melville's work does the atmospheric imagery of the tragic vision function more tellingly than in "Benito Cereno," from the symphony in gray with which it opens to the intuition of blackness ("The negro") with which its drama of despair effectively closes.

Implied in many of these images—darkness, masks, the sea—is one master metaphor that unites them all in the controlling gesture of Melville's tragic impulse: the act of penetrating surfaces by stripping away, by digging, by diving. Truth, for Melville, was a tantalizing *raison d'etre*, always hidden and beckoning behind some enigmatic veil, lost to sight in the "blackness of darkness," or buried at incalculable depths of ocean, earth, or self. Like Ahab, Pierre senses that the truth his nature demands is a monstrous presence "with visor down," challenging him to "strike through . . . and see thy face, be it Gorgon!" (*Pierre*, III, vi, p. 65–66) The tragic course of his life is set by the resolution taken at that moment: "From all idols, I tear all veils; henceforth I will see the hidden things; and live right out in my hidden life." Elsewhere Pierre's compulsive searchings take the form of exploring caves or catacombs or pyramids or endless shafts in the earth or underground rivers, and ultimately, of course, the frustrating depths of his own mind: "and the deeper and the deeper that he dived, Pierre saw the everlasting elusiveness of Truth" (XXV, iii, p. 339). As early as *Mardi*, Melville had adopted that image for the writer ("he wrote right on; and so doing, got deeper and deeper into himself "), the only difference being that the more youthful model "at last was rewarded for his toils" (*Mardi*, p. 595). The full tragic potential of the metaphor is best sensed in the version he applied to himself in describing to Hawthorne his inner development to the point of completing *Moby-Dick*: he was like a bulb, he wrote, that had been unfolding since the start of his writing career but had now reached "the inmost leaf " and "shortly . . . must fall to the mould" (*Letters*, p. 130).

Because Melville's unique milieu was the sea, it is ocean depths that his imagination most characteristically plumbed in pursuit of ultimate reality. The whale itself, of course, came to hand as the natural vehicle for the diving metaphor. "Of all divers, thou hast dived the deepest," Ahab ponders; and he adjures the "mighty head ... which ... has moved amid this world's foundations" to "speak ... and tell us the secret thing that is in thee" (*MD*, p. 264). That the secret is incommunicable is owing less to the nature of the whale than to the nature of the secret. When little Pip was "carried down alive to wondrous depths ... and the miser-merman, Wisdom, revealed his hoarded heaps," Pip "saw God's foot upon the treadle of the loom, and spoke it; and therefore his shipmates called him mad. So man's insanity is heaven's sense" (*MD*, p. 347). White-Jacket, too, in his fall from the yard-arm (*WJ*, pp. 391–94), had his most profound "life-and-death" experience at the bottom of his frightful plunge, and achieved a symbolic resurrection by cutting away his jacket as Ishmael was to do by clinging to the coffin of Queequeg. Melville's own "ponderous task" in *Moby-Dick* was seen in terms of this controlling image: "to grope down into the bottom of the sea ... ; to have one's hands among the unspeakable foundations, ribs, and very pelvis of the world; this is a fearful thing" (*MD*, p. 118). It was an aspiration closely mirrored in his contemporaneous praise of Hawthorne's "great, deep intellect, which drops down into the universe like a plummet" ("Mosses,"p. 539).

Arthur Koestler relates this metaphysical diving to the myth of the "night journey," of which the legend of Jonah (so prominent a feature of Melville's imaginative world) is an ancient exemplar. "The journey," Koestler writes, "always represents a plunge downward and backward to the origins and tragic foundations of existence, into the fluid magma, of which the trivial plane of everyday life is merely the thin crust" (p. 372). Once, late in his own tormented life, Melville (in "The Apparition") employed volcano imagery similar to Koestler's—"Solidity's a crust—/ The core of fire below" (*Poems*, p. 102)—and the connotations are sugges-tive of the dark mystery at the heart of his tragic vision. The poem implies the loss, waste, and suffering connected with personal catastro-phe, once again an emotional ground on which tragedy and truth are united. "He knows himself, and all that's in him, who knows adversity," Melville wrote in *Mardi* (p. 594); and in *Pierre*, "not to know Gloom and Grief is not to know aught that an heroic man should learn" (IX, iii, p. 169).

In a larger frame of reference, the fire imagery in the volcano recalls, as the sea cannot, the Biblical "mystery of iniquity" that so fascinated Melville and fueled his "sense of Innate Depravity and Original Sin" (*MD*, p. 540). In at least four novels: *Redburn, White-Jacket, The Confidence-Man,* and *Billy Budd*—five, if we count "Benito Cereno"—he created

overtly satanic characters which represented to his allegorizing imagination a "depravity according to nature" (*Tales*, p. 457; *WJ*, ch. 44). And
in *Mardi*, though he did not personify it there, he wrote that "evil is the
chronic malady of the universe; and checked in one place, breaks forth
in another" (p. 529). Most direct is his picturing of the man-of-war in
White-Jacket as "this old-fashioned world of ours afloat, ... charged to the
combings of her hatchways with the spirit of Belial and all unrighteous-
ness" (p. 390).

One further aspect of Melville's tragic vision needs to be understood:
this Pauline "mystery of iniquity," which he cited in *Clarel* (II, xxxv, l.
24, p. 261) and again in *Billy Budd*, is only seen "in freaks of intimation,"
in sudden insights and fleeting moments of truth. This artistic and psychological fact is no doubt implied in the diving metaphor, but a perfect
gloss is provided by the analysis in the *"Mosses"* essay of the means by
which Shakespeare's tragic genius manifests itself: "It is those deep far-
away things in him; those occasional flashings-forth of the intuitive Truth
in him; those short, quick probings at the very axis of reality." And the
reason for this almost subliminal expression, he continues, is that "in
this world of lies, Truth is forced to fly like a scared white doe in the
woodlands; and only by cunning glimpses will she reveal herself"
(*"Mosses"*, pp. 541–42). "Glimpses," indeed, are all Bulkington is expected
to catch of Ishmael's "mortally intolerable truth" (*MD*, p. 97). Ishmael
himself finds whatever truths come his way by "flashings-forth"—at the
mast-head, at the end of a monkey-rope, and most notably at the helm
the night the try-works inverted his body and opened his mind for a
moment of tragic understanding. Pierre, doomed to an unremitting
succession of spiritual crises, has tragic insights enough to enlighten a
regiment of self-lacerating protagonists. Redburn, a more promising
youth, marks his progress to maturity by such revelations as the bitter
dignity of his own social isolation, the displacement of hatred by pity for
the diabolic Jackson, and the shattering spectacle of privation and death
in a Liverpool slum. In "Benito Cereno" ("The negro") and "Bartleby"
("I know where I am") occur moments of tragic illumination (*Tales*, pp.
314, 371) reminiscent of Kurtz's "The horror!" in *Heart of Darkness*.

Not surprisingly, the tragic vision, being essentially poetic in character,
appears in purest form in Melville's poetry. *Clarel*, let it be said at once,
is an extended exploration of the tragic spirit, richly deserving study on
its own terms; but it lacks the lyric concentration to make Melville's
darkness visible. At least two poems in *Battle-Pieces*, a collection unified
by a deeply felt theme of national tragedy, show flashes of the sort of
epiphany that is matched in the more familiar prose perhaps only by
"Benito Cereno." In "Commemorative of a Naval Victory" Melville insists
on the darkness at the heart of triumph and seals his tragic perception
with a metaphysical image of great force:

> There's a light and a shadow on every man
>   Who at last attains his lifted mark—
>   Nursing through night the ethereal spark.
> *   *   *
>   —The shark
> Glides white through the phosphorous sea.
> (*Poems*, p. 115)

"The College Colonel," which should be re-read in its entirety in this connection, is arguably the finest (if not most typical) portrait of the tragic hero in the works of Melville. Although he notably lacks the pyro-technical theatricalism of more famous nay-sayers, he too is an "isolato":

> An Indian aloofness lones his brow;
> He has lived a thousand years...
> (*Poems*, p. 79)

Returning wounded from battle, he passes uncheered through cheering throngs, conscious only of the devastating experiences that have brought home "Ah heaven!—what *truth* to him" (p. 82).

With extraordinary delicacy Melville demonstrates in this poem that the tragic vision finally cannot be expressed. Most delicately of all, Melville embodied this subtle sense of tragedy in the wordless eloquence of the wind-harp. He described his own character as poet in terms of that instrument in the preface to *Battle-Pieces*; and in *John Marr and Other Sailors* it is the eerie wail of the "aeolian harp" that serves him, in the poem of that name, as an objective correlative for the tragic truth sym-bolized by the deadly drifting of a hulk at sea.

> Well the harp of Ariel wails
> Thoughts that tongue can tell no word of!

The "plaintive" sound seemed in the poet's inner ear

> ...less a strain ideal
> Than Ariel's rendering of the Real.
> (*Poems*, p. 196, 194)

Perhaps that melancholy music is as near as imagination can hope to carry us to the heart of Melville's tragic truth. For a Keats it would have sufficed. But Melville was not a Keats. Had he possessed more of Keats's *"Negative Capability"*—the capacity of "being in uncertainties, mysteries, doubts, without any irritable reaching after fact and reason" (Keats, 22 December 1817, III, p. 9), he might have had a tragic sense as man-ageable as Hawthorne's. Instead, as we know from Hawthorne's oft-quoted remarks on their Liverpool meeting in 1856, he was a hopeless captive of a compulsive need to have answers to "everything that lies beyond human ken," and could "never rest" in either belief or unbelief. Whatever he may have meant by telling Hawthorne that he had "pretty much made up his mind to be annihilated" (*Mel. Log*, p. 529), it was something very different from the sort of aesthetic distancing that Keats had in mind in seeking to be "an[ni]hilated" (Keats, 27 October 1818, III, p. 234). In that fact we have the root and spring of Melville's personal tragedy and the tragic response to life that he fathered on his imaginary progeny. Like a victim of some dreadful immune deficiency, Melville had no defenses against failure, which above all other phenomena of human life is dramatized in his writings. "The myths of failure touch us with the tragedy of life," Joseph Campbell has written (p. 206), and it is that class of myth that Melville lived out and wrote out in comic as well as tragic versions.

As an author Melville both courted failure and scorned success. Turning his back on " 'Peedee' 'Hullabaloo' & 'Pog-Dog' " (*Mel. Log*, p. 325), he expressed an "earnest desire to write those sort of books which are said to 'fail' " (*Letters*, p. 92). Indeed, in the *"Mosses"* essay he raised to a principle the notion that "failure is the true test of greatness" (*MD*, p. 545). Yet the bitterness of *Pierre* attests to the pain and despair he felt when he responded to his "devouring profundities" and was then predictably condemned for refusing to be "entertainingly and profitably shallow in some pellucid and merry romance" (XXII, iv, p. 305). Caught between the two, as between Free Will and Necessity, he complained to Hawthorne that "the product is a final hash, and all my books are botches." He wanted fame but couldn't tolerate patronage, so he perversely wished to be "infamous: there is no patronage in *that*" (*Letters*, pp. 128–29). He valued the "insular Tahiti" (*MD*, p. 236) of the soul at peace, and portrayed it movingly in the imagery of the "Grand Armada" (*MD*, ch. 87); but his major protagonists all rejected spiritual stability in favor of *sturm und drang* and the philosophical program of "The Lee Shore" (*MD*, ch. 23). The rhetoric of self-destructive bravado common to all three of these characters breathes the very essence of Romantic tragedy: Taji preferred to "sink in boundless deeps, than float on vulgar shoals" (*Mardi*, p. 557); Ahab threatened to "strike the sun if it insulted [him]" (*MD*, p. 144); Pierre swore with a "breath of flame [to] breathe back [his] defiance" (XXVI, vi, p. 360).

It is, of course, the familiar posture of Melville's acknowledged prototypes, Prometheus and Milton's Satan. Familiar, but extraordinarily difficult to emulate successfully. Melville took enormous risks to endow the "meanest mariners" with "tragic graces" (*MD*, p. 104), and, while it is universally conceded that he won the gamble in *Moby-Dick*, there can be few readers in these days who will find their disbelief suspended in the presence of Taji or Pierre. Melville learned valuable lessons from Hawthorne, but he did not—could not—learn the cool principle of self-appraisal that caused Hawthorne to label some of his own best writing "absurdities": namely, that "in writing a romance, a man is always ... careering on the utmost verge of a precipitous absurdity, and the skill lies in coming as close as possible, without actually tumbling over" (James T. Fields, pp. 89, 56). If Melville's plunge into tragedy sometimes fell over the precipice, it was a fault entirely in keeping with his virtues. "I love all men who *dive*," he said, thinking of Emerson, who, while hardly a tragic writer, seemed to him of all his contemporaries most liable to absurdity (*Letters*, p. 79). Unhappily for the Romantic writer, the absurdity that results from failed tragedy is not, by way of compensation, a creditable form of comedy. Indeed, comedy is as severely damaged by absurdity (in Hawthorne's sense) as tragedy. The issue, involving not only *Mardi* and *Pierre* but also *The Confidence-Man* and a number of shorter works, invites critical questions that are perhaps too rarely raised. It may be too late to ask whether Bartleby, a patently "absurd" character, has gained a certain factitious sanction from a dimension of that term unknown in the 1850s. Some responsible attention has already been directed to the question of latent "absurdism" in Melville (e.g., Elaine Barry, Richard Boyd Hauck), but it is the sort of problem that tends to be a candle to avant-garde moths.

Bartleby, to judge by the mass and confusion of commentary on him, has been as great an embarrassment to the critic as to the elderly lawyer who didn't know what to do with him. That he has the air of a tragic figure no one disputes. At any rate, his story perfectly illustrates Pierre's formula for life: "A play, which begin how it may, in farce or comedy, ever hath its tragic end; the curtain inevitably falls upon a corpse" (*Pierre*, XII, iii, p. 197). Yet Bartleby stands a pole apart from Melville's "man of greatly superior natural force," that "mighty pageant creature, formed for noble tragedies" (*MD*, p. 71). Did the "tragic dramatist" in Melville mean to "depict mortal indomitableness" (*MD*, pp. 129–30) as much in the whispered refusals of a mousy clerk as in the thunderous No! of a Yankee captain? Surely each in his own way answers to Father Mapple's prescription and "stands forth his own inexorable self ... against the proud gods and commodores of this earth" (*MD*, p. 51). If they share as well that "certain morbidness" (*MD*, p. 71) Melville saw in the tragic character, it is simply a different kind of pathological excess. What seems to be lacking in Bartleby is a *cause* of suitable magnitude; yet his justification is at bottom perhaps no more solipsistic than Taji's, Ahab's, or Pierre's. What strikes us about this featureless rebel against the system is his sudden flowering in the narrator's final words into a figure of universal isolation and defeat. The "humanity" he is invoked to represent is nominally the same as that represented by another silenced victim of an overriding destiny—Hunilla, the Chola widow of "The Encantadas": "Humanity, thou strong thing, I worship thee, not in the laureled victor, but in this vanquished one" (*Tales*, p. 132).

On this other more shadowy path of tragedy passes a parade of downcast figures, each with his own peculiar "crucifixion in his face" (*MD*, p. 111). To name only the first to come to mind: Israel Potter, Benito Cereno, Harry Bolton in *Redburn*, the old man who closes the last episode of *The Confidence-Man*, Mortmain and Ungar of *Clarel*, and even—though the suggestion is calculated to stir volleys of protest—even Captain Vere. Unless he is, as many have seen him, the villain of the piece, Vere can only be the tragic hero of *Billy Budd*. With the possible exception of Hunilla, who had only to endure, Vere is the only member of this loosely denominated group who can properly be called heroic. But I have argued the case for Vere elsewhere ("The Problem of *Billy Budd*") and cannot pause to take it up here.

The controversy that continues to surround such characters as Vere and Bartleby is as good testimony as we may need to the ambiguities that characterize Melville's writings and plague the interpretation of much of his work. Of all these ambiguities the one that has proved most troublesome is the confusion of those putative opposites, comedy and tragedy. Although no critic has yet claimed to discover a significant amount of humor in *Billy Budd*, and one (Jane Mushabac) has even demoted it for that lack, many have insisted on a controlling presence there of humor's cousin-german, irony. Did Melville really intend the death of Innocence to have tragic sanction? Or was he insinuating a sardonic critique of the sort of world in which such a conclusion could be drawn? Irony, like the confidence man's "Protean easy-chair," can be adapted to support nearly any posture the critic chooses to assume. It is the form of comedy closest to tragedy and, therefore, of enormous importance to the interpretation of literature. It is also the form of comedy most resistant to objective assessment and for that reason has figured in the largest claims and smallest proofs in the annals of Melville criticism. Something further will follow of this matter.

Irony apart, comedy is still more difficult to define than tragedy. Being of the essence of play, it tends not to stand still for such solemn operations as definition and classification. Still, there has been no shortage of efforts to identify the comic spirit and its voices in Melville: three books have appeared to date (Edward H. Rosenberry, 1955; Joseph Flibbert; Mushabac) and a score of articles, not to speak of a growing body of commentary in general studies of American humor. The literature on Melville's tragic art, by contrast, appears both earlier and slighter: a scattering of essays, such as those by George C. Homans and Robert E. Spiller, and two books—Stanley Geist's, excellent but only essay-length and limited to *Moby-Dick* and *Pierre*, and William Ellery Sedgwick's, still the standard work on the subject. The appearance is deceptive, of course, but the reasons for it are instructive. First is the fact that the tragic mode is clear and dominant—once one reads past the comic flash of *Typee* and *Omoo*—and therefore discussion of it is spread over the entire critical and biographical literature. Second, a once-assumed absence or scarcity of humor in Melville's books (Clifton Fadiman) placed that aspect in a defensive posture challenging to succeeding generations of scholars and critics. Finally, the inherent game-playing quality of comedy has posed another and sometimes counterproductive challenge to close-reading critics who have labored to wring from the texts some astounding extensions of meaning (e.g., Robert Shulman, Gerard M. Sweeney).

Half a century of study of the Melvillean genius has at least established that it is neither comic nor tragic but a unique blend marked by a point of view and rhetorical style that owe their character to the presence and interaction of both. Despite Melville's impassioned identification of truth with the tragic vision, he was not unaware that the "wisdom that is woe" may easily become the "woe that is madness" (*MD*, p. 355). Tragedy may be the profoundest truth, but it cannot be the whole truth, as Aldous Huxley has persuasively argued in our own time. There are two important reasons for this. The more objective of these, and the one Huxley stresses, is that tragedy can never be more than a fractional description of total reality, the more circumscribed and distorting as it focuses on individual catastrophe. Looking at Brueghel's painting of "The Fall of Icarus," W. H. Auden perceived "how everything turns away/ Quite leisurely from the disaster . . . how it takes place/ While someone else is eating or opening a window or just walking dully along. . . . " ("Musee des Beaux Arts"). Koestler makes the same point in writing of "the Tragic and the Trivial" (pp. 377–80).

This reason, a matter of perspective, is the one Ahab is made to acknowledge in Chapter 46 ("Surmises") when he orders the pursuit of ordinary whales during the search for his particular nemesis in order to provide his crew "food for their more common, daily appetites" (p. 184). It is also Melville's own artistic plan in *Moby-Dick*, which indulges in many chapters of cetological and metaphysical play en route to its cataclysmic finale. In the light of this principle, it may be argued that the real tragedy of Taji and Pierre and Bartleby is their very insistence on the totality of tragedy in human life. It is a concentration that dehumanizes them. Bartleby's wall speaks no more of the constriction of his world than of the rigidity of his response to it. It is no accident that the end of all three of the characters I have mentioned, and perhaps of Ahab as well, is suicide. The nature of their failure is precisely their inability to see "two sides to a tortoise" (*Tales*, p. 103), as Melville put it in "The Encantadas." Given the fact that the Galapagos tortoise does not in fact have a bright side (I have inspected them "with these visible hands"), it must have seemed important to Melville to invent one to illustrate his point. "What plays the mischief with the truth," he reasoned, "is that men will insist upon the universal application of a temporary feeling or opinion" (*Letters*, p. 131).

What such an observation brings us to is a second, though closely related, reason that tragedy is not—and Melville knew it could not be—the whole truth. This is the troublesome subjectivity of the tragic vision and, by necessity, of the comic vision as well. No artist could have known better than Melville that all facts are "doubloons," subject to the vagaries of the beholder and their own intrinsic ambiguities. Even something as concrete as the whale's peaking of flukes seemed to him dependent on "what mood you are in" for the associations it calls to mind—"devils" or "archangels" (*MD*, p. 317). Concerning something as constitutionally emotional as tragedy and comedy, he denied neither his "Blue Devils" on the one hand nor his "infirmity of jocularity" (*Letters*, pp. 135, 193) on the other; the first thing to go, when one gives rein to these imps of the perverse in one's nature, is any show of philosophical consistency. It will not do to forget that the Ishmael who scorns Rabelais in favor of Solomon at one point (*MD*, p. 355) is the same Ishmael who at another time praises a good joke and a good joker as "rather too scarce a good thing" (*MD*, p. 35); or that his creator, having echoed that admiration of *Ecclesiastes* in writing to Hawthorne, could at another time and in another mood play the fool with his own most earnest opinion:

> A Spirit appeared to me, and said
> "Where now would you choose to dwell?
> In the Paradise of the Fool,
> Or in wise Solomon's hell?"
>
> Never he asked me twice:
> "Give me the fool's Paradise."
> (*Poems*, p. 390)

To identify Melville with one mood to the exclusion of the other would be to reduce the admirer of Hawthorne and Shakespeare to an admirer of their "power of blackness" alone. In fact, the first thing he found to praise in Hawthorne's *Mosses* was "a wild moonlight of contemplative humor . . . so spiritually gentle, so high, so deep . . . the very religion of mirth." Yet even on that ground we cannot look for definitive consistency. The author who is credited here for displaying "no rollicking rudeness, no gross fun fed on fat dinners, and bred in the lees of wine" ("*Mosses*", pp. 540, 538), is elsewhere seen to be "lacking . . . plump sphericity" and needing "roast-beef, done rare" (*Letters*, p. 121).

Perhaps in a loose way the range of Melville's own comic voice is marked out in these contrasting views of Hawthorne's. While no critic has thought to praise Melville's humor for its spirituality, many have remarked its pervasive metaphysical character, full of puns, allusions, and sly analogies, often spun out in sheer exuberance to paragraph and even chapter length. Literary exercises of this kind, especially in *Mardi* and *The Confidence-Man*, often owe heavy stylistic debts to Rabelais and the English humorists, which have been studied and reported (Rosenberry, Mushabac). At the other extreme, he was equally at home with the "uncivilized laughter" of his shipmates over "their unholy adventures, their tales of terror told in words of mirth" (*MD*, p. 353). This native, more unstudied dimension of Melville's humor, its folklore aspect, has also come under scholarly scrutiny (Constance Rourke, Richard Chase, Rosenberry). Despite the disposition of enthusiastic investigators to locate the "key" to Melville's art in this or that special quality, neither of these models is more characteristic of Melville than the other, nor indeed any identifiable species of comedy than any equally identifiable manifestation of tragedy. Melville's was a complex personality expressing itself in a complex art; he could not be content, like Jane Austen, to "let other pens dwell on guilt and misery" (*Mansfield Park*, ch. 48). In Melville's chiaroscuro world,

> . . . if all's not bright,
> Allow, the shadow's chased by light,
> Though rest for neither yet may be.
> (*Poems*, p. 313)

This is the Melville that Hawthorne knew, who "will never rest . . . and has persisted ever since I knew him . . . in wandering to and fro" (*Mel. Log*, 529). What has only begun to be understood in Melville is this restlessness of mood, the movement and interplay of the light and shadow on his pages.

Some relevant facts, however partial, we have. We know, first, that Melville was both a social man and an "isolato." Both aspects of his character are by now thoroughly documented by his biographers, though not all have been able to make the two halves cohere in a credible whole. Reginald E. Watters in a pair of landmark articles many years ago commenced the exploration of these opposing traits in the writings, and in the intervening years at least three major studies (Merton M. Sealts, Marjorie Dew, John Bryant) have elaborated on the implications of the "geniality" about which Melville had so much to say. The traits themselves are normally and no doubt correctly aligned so as to relate solitude to the tragic vision and sociality to the comic; there is generally less success in engrafting them on particular characters, who like their creator are unlikely to represent them in a pure form. Even Ahab "has his humanities," though he lacks "the low enjoying power" (*MD*, p. 147); and Bartleby, while pathologically unsocial, is in some ways comical for that very reason.

In trying to sort out the social man and the isolato we ought to exercise special caution in coupling sociability and its opposite with another favorite Melvillean dichotomy, head and heart. Watters tried the reverse of Walpole's familiar dictum that life is a comedy to one who thinks and a tragedy to one who feels; but fallacy and inconsistency beset both paths of reasoning. The issue becomes purposely confused in the concepts of the "surly philanthropist" and the "genial misanthrope" in *The Confidence-Man* (p. 154), and in "I and My Chimney" Melville has left us a confoundingly convincing comic portrait of the genial misanthrope. If we add to these cases the figures of Redburn and White-Jacket, comically isolated in their outlandish attire, we are forced to modify easy generalizations about the tragic isolato. Even he can have a sense of humor.

Ishmael, named to enforce his identification as an isolato, is such a one. His credentials as a genial man are established in the Spouter Inn, both in and out of bed. Whatever solitude may oppress him at the masthead or the try-works, he finds compensatory solace at the monkey-rope and the sword-mat, and is able to joke about them all. Most tellingly, he is able to joke about the imminence of his own death by means of a special kind of comic sense which has a unique affinity to tragedy itself. This "queer" humor, the God-mocking and self-mocking laughter of "The Hyena" (*MD*, ch. 49), is a second important fact at hand to help in understanding the interaction of the bright and dark in Melville. It is only fair to add, however, that it is capable of wildly disparate developments: the sanative balance of Ishmael's "Catskill eagle" (*MD*, p. 355) on the one hand, the hysteria of Pierre and the madness of Babbalanja's private demon, Azzageddi (*Mardi*, chs. 155, 183), on the other.

A third kind of knowledge available to a study of Melville's peculiar amalgam of modes is that he used various techniques of satire and burlesque to comment on matters of serious and often tragic import. Up to a point—the point to which they have been studied and constitute a body of knowledge—these are standard literary devices in which Melville was fairly skilled (he was neither Swift nor Twain) and of which his total output can show, at best, originality and control, as in *The Confidence-Man*, and, at worst, an abject absence of both, as in the early political sketches of "Old Zack" which he did for *Yankee Doodle* in 1847. Typically, Melville's frequent excursions into satire and burlesque lack the continuity of topic and tone to form a general character in any book except *The Confidence-Man*. On the other hand, in nearly every book except *Billy Budd* there are lively and sometimes brilliant set-pieces, such as those on missionaries in *Typee*, politics and social customs in *Mardi*, the "man-of-war world" in *White-Jacket*, the literary life in *Pierre*, even Benjamin

Franklin in *Israel Potter*. Where the topic is sustained, as in the case of "confidence," the tone is sustained as well, but the structure remains episodic and the artistic effect is that of a theme and variations rather than of the "symphony" he achieved in *Moby-Dick*.

What is not well enough understood is the way Melville's comic and tragic visions work together to produce the unique literary voice that is his. He had a happy stroke of success in describing that collaboration in Hawthorne, but no one has done as well for him. Like Hawthorne, who in *The House of the Seven Gables* perceived a paradoxical strength in the "tragic power of laughter" (ch. 11, p. 198), Melville was captivated by the ironic and ambiguous "elements of the tear which much laughter provoketh" (*Mardi*, p. 352). Both writers recognized that, in the words of Baudelaire, "Laughter and tears are both equally the children of woe" (W. K. Wimsatt, p. 287).

We keep coming back to the doubloon, which is not seeing "two sides to a tortoise," but seeing the same side two ways, like the equivocal drawings of M. C. Escher, or the famous rabbit/duck figure invoked to telling effect by Paul Brodtkorb (p. 163). Arthur Koestler, discussing this unsettling convertibility in *Insight and Outlook* (1949), points out that even Oedipus Rex "can be made to appear as a prize fool who kills his father and marries his mother, all by mistake; the tragedy is turned into a French farce without altering its cognitive layout" (p. 241). In the same way, with far less cognitive alteration, Bartleby may be at once a sacrificial lamb (or at least goat) and a vaudeville comic with a dead-pan "tar-baby" routine (Robert E. Abrams). Surgeon Cuticle (*WJ*, chs. 61–63) and other characters I think of as Children of Oberlus ("Encantadas," Sketch Ninth) are at the same time clowns and avatars of the devil. The legendary Indian-hater is only the most provocative of an entire cast of ambiguities peopling *The Confidence-Man* and driving critics to extremities of frustration (John G. Blair, William M. Ramsey). It is a perplexity Melville himself may have anticipated with relish when he made two slippery characters in that slippery book conclude a conversation about a brutal practical joker with this exchange:

> "Funny Phalaris!"
> "Cruel Phalaris!"
> (p. 142)

It is easy—too easy—simply to sense irony in all this equivocation. Melville criticism has supported a battalion of ironists, many on quite false scents, since the days of Lawrance Thompson and Joseph Schiffman. What we need now may be, not less attention to irony, but more attention to its rhetorical and contextual means, its tone of voice, its affective characteristics, as opposed to logical constructs erected on putative biographical or thematic continuities and assumptions of the very inversion of intent that is to be proven. The critic who is prepared to look at Melville's comic and tragic modes as directives to the readers with whom he longed to establish a "frank" relationship could do worse than to reexamine some of the problematic novels and tales as the sort of texts that Stanley Fish termed "self-consuming artifacts": the kind of work that builds on dialectal counter-currents and in and through its resulting complexity "invites us," in Fish's tidy formulation, "[not] to carry the truth away, but to be carried away by the truth" (p. 75).

Every writer on comedy and tragedy recalls the challenge of that puzzling dialogue at the end of Plato's *Symposium* in which Socrates, having reduced Aristophanes and Agathon to a late postbanquet stupor, wins their "drowsy assent" to the heterodox proposition that "the genius of comedy was the same with that of tragedy" (W. K. Wimsatt, p. 6; Henry Alonzo Myers, p. 110). Perhaps the point is simply, as Wimsatt argues, that "we ought to recognize a closer union than we do between the comic and the tragic" (p. 290). Surely we should do so in the case of an author who believed that "mirth and sorrow are kin; are published by identical nerves" (*Mardi*, p. 613), and who understood

> What unlike things must meet and mate:
>   *   *   *
> And fuse with Jacob's mystic heart,
> To wrestle with the angel—Art.
> (*Poems*, p. 231)

What we may overlook is that art is a reciprocal process, that Melville's familiar poem implicitly describes not only what the writer must do to produce his book, but also what the reader must do to reap the full experience of it. In no respect is this strenuous task more urgent than in responding to the affective forces of comedy and tragedy, which together control the cognitive and emotional arsenal of the artist.

WORKS CITED

Abrams, Robert E. " 'Bartleby' and the Fragile Pageantry of the Ego." *ELH: A Journal of English Literary History* 45 (1978): 488–500.

Arvin, Newton. *Herman Melville*. New York: William Sloane Associates, 1950.

Austen, Jane. *Mansfield Park*. Boston, Mass.: Houghton Mifflin, 1965.

Barry, Elaine. "Herman Melville: The Changing Face of Comedy." *American Studies International* 16 (Summer 1978): 19–33.

Bezanson, Walter. "*Moby-Dick*: Work of Art." In *Moby-Dick Centennial Essays*. Ed. Tyrus Hillway and Luther S. Mansfield. Dallas: Southern Methodist University Press, 1953.

Blair, John G. "Puns and Equivocation in Melville's *The Confidence-Man.*" *American Transcendental Quarterly* No. 22 (Spring 1974): 91–95.

Bowen, Merlin. *The Long Encounter: Self and Experience in the Writings of Herman Melville.* Chicago: University of Chicago Press, 1960.

Braswell, William. "Melville's *Billy Budd* as an 'Inside Narrative.' " *American Literature* 29 (May 1957): 133–46.

Brodtkorb, Paul, Jr. *Ishmael's White World: A Phenomenological Reading of Moby-Dick.* New Haven, Conn.: Yale University Press, 1965.

Bryant, John. "Melville's Comic Debate: Geniality and the Aesthetics of Repose." *American Literature* 55 (May 1983): 151–70.

Campbell, Joseph. *The Hero with a Thousand Faces.* New York: Pantheon, 1949.

Chase, Richard. *Herman Melville: A Critical Study.* New York: Macmillan Co., 1949.

Cook, Richard M. "Evolving the Inscrutable: the Grotesque in Melville's Fiction." *American Literature* 49 (January 1978): 544–59.

Dew, Marjorie. "Black-hearted Melville: 'Geniality' Reconsidered." In *Artful Thunder.* Ed. Robert J. DeMott and Sanford E. Marovitz. Kent, Ohio: Kent State University Press, 1975, pp. 177–94.

Fadiman, Clifton. "Herman Melville." *Atlantic Monthly* 172 (October 1943): 88–91.

Feibleman, James. *In Praise of Comedy: A Study in Its Theory and Practice.* New York: Russell & Russell, 1962.

Fields, James T. *Yesterdays with Authors.* Boston: Houghton Mifflin, 1886.

Firebaugh, Joseph. "Humorist as Rebel: The Melville of *Typee.*" *Nineteenth-Century Fiction* 9 (September 1954): 108–20.

Fish, Stanley E. *Self-Consuming Artifacts: The Experience of Seventeenth Century Literature.* Berkeley: University of California Press, 1972. [Appendix: "Literature in the Reader: Affective Stylistics," pp. 383–427. Rpt. from *New Literary History* 2 (1970): 123–62.]

Flibbert, Joseph. *Melville and the Art of Burlesque.* Amsterdam: Rodopi, 1974.

Geist, Stanley. *Herman Melville: The Tragic Vision and the Heroic Ideal.* Cambridge, Mass.: Harvard University Press, 1939.

Hauck, Richard Boyd. *A Cheerful Nihilism: Confidence and "the Absurd" in American Humorous Fiction.* Bloomington, Ind.: Indiana University Press, 1971.

————. "Nine Good Jokes: The Redemptive Humor of the Confidence-Man and *The Confidence-Man.*" In *The Ruined Eden of the Present: Hawthorne, Melville and Poe.* Ed. G. R. Thompson and Virgil Lokke. West Lafayette, Ind.: Purdue University Press, 1981, pp. 245–82.

Hawthorne, Nathaniel. *The House of the Seven Gables.* Ed. Fredson Bowers. Columbus, Ohio: Ohio State University, 1965.

Hazlitt, William. "On Wit and Humor." In *Lectures on the English Comic Writers.* London: J. M. Dent & Sons, 1910.

Homans, George C. "The Dark Angel: The Tragedy of Herman Melville." *New England Quarterly* 5 (October 1932): 699–730.

Huxley, Aldous. "Tragedy and the Whole Truth." In *Music at Night and Other Essays* (1931). London: Chatto & Windus, 1949.

Jones, Joseph. "Humor in *Moby-Dick.*" *University of Texas Studies in English* (March 1946): 51–71.

Kaufman, R. J. "Tragedy and Its Validating Conditions." *Comparative Drama* 1 (1967): 3–18.

Keats, John. *Poetical Works and Other Writings.* Ed. H. B. Forman. London, 1883.

Koestler, Arthur. *Insight and Outlook.* New York: Macmillan Co., 1949.

Krieger, Murray. *The Tragic Vision: Variations on a Theme in Literary Criticism.* Chicago: University of Chicago Press, 1960.

Lesser, Simon O. "Tragedy, Comedy, and the Esthetic Experience." *Literature and Psychology* 6 (November 1956): 131–39.

Levin, Harry. *The Power of Blackness.* New York: Alfred A. Knopf, 1958.

Mason, Ronald. *The Spirit Above the Dust: A Study of Herman Melville.* London: John Lehmann, 1951.

Matthiessen, F. O. *American Renaissance: Art and Expression in the Age of Emerson and Whitman.* New York: Oxford University Press, 1941.

Milder, Robert. " '*Nemo Contra Deum . . .*': Melville and Goethe's 'Demonic.' " In *Ruined Eden of the Present: Hawthorne, Melville and Poe.* Ed. G. R. Thompson and Virgil Lokke. West Lafayette, Ind.: Purdue University Press, 1981, pp. 205–44.

Mushabac, Jane. *Melville's Humor, a Critical Study.* Hamden, Conn.: Archon Books, 1981.

Myers, Henry Alonzo. *Tragedy: A View of Life.* Ithaca, N.Y.: Cornell University Press, 1965.

Potts, L. J. *Comedy.* London: Hutchinson's Universal Library, 1948.

Ralegh, Sir Walter. *The Poems of Sir Walter Ralegh.* Ed. Agnes Latham. Cambridge, Mass: Harvard University Press, 1951.

Ramsey, William M. "The Moot Points of Melville's Indian-Hating." *American Literature* 52 (May 1980): 224–35.

Rosenberry, Edward H. *Melville.* London: Routledge & Kegan Paul, 1979.

———. *Melville and the Comic Spirit.* Cambridge, Mass.: Harvard University Press, 1955.

———. "The Problem of *Billy Budd.*" *PMLA* 80 (December 1965): 489–98.

Rourke, Constance. *American Humor.* New York: Harcourt, Brace & Co., 1931.

Schiffman, Joseph. "Melville's Final Stage, Irony: A Re-examination of *Billy Budd* Criticism." *American Literature* 22 (1950): 128–36.

Sealts, Merton M., Jr. "Melville's 'Geniality.' " In *Essays in American and English Literature Presented to Bruce R. McElderry.* Ed. Max F. Shulz. Athens, Ga.: University of Georgia Press, 1967, pp. 3–26. Rpt. in *Pursuing Melville.* Madison: University of Wisconsin Press, 1982, pp. 155–70.

Sedgwick, William Ellery. *Herman Melville, the Tragedy of Mind.* Cambridge, Mass.: Harvard University Press, 1944.

Sewall, Richard B. *The Vision of Tragedy.* New Haven, Conn.: Yale University Press, 1980.

Shulman, Robert. "The Serious Function of Melville's Phallic Jokes." *American Literature* 33 (May 1961): 179–94.

Shurr, William H. *Rappaccini's Children: American Writers in a Calvinist World.* Lexington, Ky.: University Press of Kentucky, 1981.

Spiller, Robert E. "Melville, Our First Tragic Poet." *Saturday Review* 33 (25 November 1950): 24–25.

Spivack, Charlotte K. "Tragedy and Comedy: A Metaphysical Wedding." *Bucknell Review* 9 (1960): 212–23.

Stern, Milton R. "Melville's Tragic Imagination: The Hero Without a Home." In *Patterns of Commitment in American Literature*. Ed. Marston LaFrance. Toronto: University of Toronto Press, 1967, pp. 39–52.

Stewart, Randall. "The Vision of Evil in Hawthorne and Melville." In *The Tragic Vision and the Christian Faith*. Ed. Nathan Scott. New York: Association Press, 1957, pp. 238–63.

Sweeney, Gerard M. "Melville's Smoky Humor: Fire-Lighting in *Typee*." *Arizona Quarterly* 34 (1978): 371–76.

Thompson, Lawrance. *Melville's Quarrel with God*. Princeton, N.J.: Princeton University Press, 1952.

Watters, Reginald E. "Melville's 'Isolatoes.' " *PMLA* 60 (December 1945): 1138–48.

———. "Melville's 'Sociality.' " *American Literature* 17 (1945): 33–49.

Weathers, Winston. "Melville and the Comedy of Communications." *Etc: Review of General Semantics* 20 (December 1963): 411–20.

Wimsatt, W. K., ed. *The Idea of Comedy*. Englewood Cliffs, N.J.: Prentice-Hall, 1969.

21

MELVILLE'S AESTHETICS

Shirley M. Dettlaff

If, after perusing the *Companion*, the student of Melville feels over-whelmed by the sheer volume of Melville criticism and fears that nothing new, unless it is totally perverse, can be said about Melville, he can approach this chapter with some hope. For work needs to be done in the area of Melville's ideas about art—the notions that Melville explicitly stated or fairly obviously implied, those ideas about the nature and func-tions of art that constitute an aesthetic. Even in the areas that have attracted most comment—Melville's beliefs about symbolism and his the-ory of fiction—there is still no definitive study. There is no one com-prehensive study covering the full range of the ideas that Melville expressed in his fiction and poetry, nor is there a developmental one analyzing the changes in his theories during his lengthy career.

Major reasons for this lack of thorough inquiry are that Melville's pronouncements about art are often scattered, sketchy, and enigmatic. Although he certainly pondered some of the great issues of aesthetics and held definite beliefs, there is no evidence that he systematically or fully articulated them. Melville did not write lengthy prefaces or literary manifestos. Instead, he dispersed public statements throughout his fic-tion, poetry, a few critical reviews, and a lecture; he also made private comments in letters, two journals, and marginalia. This wide dispersal has precluded easy access to all of Melville's statements about art. More-over, the offhand quality of many of these remarks has fostered a doubt,

*I would like to thank Hershel Parker and Brian Higgins for their helpful comments on this chapter.

reinforced by Melville's distrust of elaborate intellectual constructs, that he consciously subscribed to any coherent set of related aesthetic concepts. And the fact that these remarks are sometimes cryptic or figurative has occasionally made it difficult to determine the exact nature of Melville's ideas. Modern critical attempts to clarify or supplement these statements by inferring Melville's theories from his practice solely on the basis of textual evidence use a method fraught with risk. Such problems in accessibility and methodology have, up to now, apparently hindered critical consensus and definitive studies of Melville's aesthetics.

There are, in fact, many studies, but few are full-scale or well-known analyses. With some notable exceptions, the most influential Melville critics or scholars have not concentrated on Melville's ideas about art, although they may bring up the topic while discussing a related one. Therefore, much criticism is rather sketchy and lies hidden in studies dealing with other aspects of Melville's thought or practice. A large amount of less important criticism languishes in the half-life of obscure journals or unpublished dissertations. Partially because of their inaccessibility, new studies may repeat what they have said or be unaware of their position in a developing line of inquiry. Another problem has been that Melville's theories of art have not usually been studied by those who are specialists in both literary criticism and in Melville. Experts in literary theory may not know Melville's work, his life and times, and the body of criticism about him well enough to discuss his theories with some degree of confidence. On the other hand, the Melvillean, assuming that he knows the entire canon, including *Clarel*, may not have sufficient knowledge of aesthetics in general and of nineteenth-century aesthetics in particular to reconstruct the theoretical background needed to interpret correctly Melville's often sketchy remarks.

Major sources of Melville's explicitly stated aesthetic theories are "Hawthorne and His *Mosses*" (1850), a two-part essay published in the *Literary World*; the "Agatha" letters to Hawthorne in 1852; and chapters 14, 33, and 44 of *The Confidence-Man* (1857). In addition, there are important statements in *Mardi* (1849), *Pierre* (1852), "The Piazza" (1856), *Clarel* (1876), and *Billy Budd, Sailor* (1888–91). Individual lyric poems also comment on art, especially those published in *Timoleon* (1891), like the often quoted "Art" and "In a Garrett." Less formal observations appear in other letters, in the journals that Melville kept during his journeys to Europe in 1849–50 and to the Levant in 1856–57, and in his marginalia, which have been compiled by Wilson Walker Cowen in his eleven-volume dissertation, "Melville's Marginalia" (*Mel. Diss.*, #134). Jay Leyda's *Melville Log* is a readily available source for many of the above. Melville's lecture "Statues in Rome" (1857) has been reconstructed by Merton M. Sealts, Jr., in *Melville as Lecturer* (1957) and will reappear in the NN edition of *The Piazza Tales*.

Because criticism about Melville's aesthetics is often inaccessible, I do not claim to be exhaustive in reviewing here everything that has ever been written about Melville's ideas about art; however, I have tried to present the major critical comments about the most important issues as well as many of the less well known. Since I take up only works dealing with Melville's aesthetic ideas rather than his practice, I have excluded such outstanding studies as Warner Berthoff's *The Example of Melville* (1962) and Walter E. Bezanson's Introduction to the Hendricks House edition of *Clarel* (1960). Melville's ideas about tragedy and comedy are discussed in chapter 20. Important areas of Melville's aesthetics that critics have addressed and that I have reviewed include organic form, symbolism and allegory, myth, the sublime and the beautiful, the imagination, fiction, poetry, and the fine arts. A few studies also deal with specific influences on Melville's ideas about art. First, I have cited works that can introduce the student of Melville to some of the major nineteenth-century issues in aesthetics and literary criticism that form the context of Melville's thinking about art.

NINETEENTH-CENTURY CRITICAL BACKGROUND

There are too many important background studies of European and English Romantic aesthetics to list here, except for a few extremely influential works that can provide a point of departure for further research. In volumes 1 and 2 of *A History of Modern Criticism, 1750–1950* (1955), Rene Wellek surveys the German theorists who influenced the English and American Romanticists as well as such English writers as Coleridge. M. H. Abrams, in *The Mirror and the Lamp* (1953), discusses theories of poetry that are central to Romantic aesthetics. Important articles dealing with the problem of defining Romanticism include Arthur O. Lovejoy's "On the Discrimination of Romanticisms" (1924), Rene Wellek's "The Concept of Romanticism in Literary History" (1949), and Morse Peckham's "Toward a Theory of Romanticism" (1951). These studies have been reprinted in *Romanticism: Points of View* (1970) edited by Robert F. Gleckner and Gerald E. Enscoe. The aesthetics section in Chapter 1 of *The English Romantic Poets: A Review of Research and Criticism* (1972), edited by Frank Jordan, Jr., is also a good place to begin research.

But anyone looking for a thorough general study of American Romantic literary criticism is out of luck. The situation has improved since Norman Foerster observed in his 1928 Preface to *American Criticism* that no definitive survey of American criticism could be written until special periods and problems were more thoroughly investigated. Since then some clear light has been shed on philosophical, aesthetic, and cultural sources of American critical theory; on major periodicals and their policies; on influential critics as well as important authors; and on the waxing and waning of specific critical theories. However, no one volume thoroughly analyzes the aesthetics or literary theories in America that Melville was exposed to during the period of his greatest intellectual growth from 1845 to 1860.

Because the few early twentieth-century studies of American criticism stress the major writers such as Emerson, Poe, and Whitman who, unlike Melville, wrote sustained explanations of their literary theory, works like Norman Foerster's *American Criticism* and George E. DeMille's *Literary Criticism in America* (1931) are not especially helpful to the Melville student. One early study that is still valuable, indeed, a model, is William Charvat's *The Origins of American Critical Thought, 1810–1835* (1936), which clearly identifies the sources, periodicals, critics, and specific critical tenets of American criticism during the first few decades of the century. Although its scope does not include the actual flowering of Romanticism, Charvat's study gives a good sense of the major philosophical and aesthetic influences on American critics during the beginning of this period. Charvat not only traces some ways in which Romantic criticism evolved from the Scottish Common Sense School; he also discusses the influences of Wordsworth, Coleridge, Hazlitt, and both Friedrich and A. W. Schlegel. Charvat's tracing of the critical reactions to major English Romantics such as Byron, Shelley, Keats, and Coleridge is suggestive for the student of Melville. Helpful, too, in conveying a sense of the general background are Charvat's brief sketches of important centers of critical activity, major periodicals, and influential critics.

F. O. Matthiessen's *American Renaissance* (1941) is the best of the subsequent general surveys. In his judicious accounts of Emerson, Thoreau, Hawthorne, Melville, and Whitman, Matthiessen intersperses among discussions of their works well-informed analyses of their aesthetic theories, dealing with such Romantic concerns as the organic principle, the distinction between allegory and symbolism, the definition of romance, and the creation of myth. Two essays in *The Development of American Literary Criticism* (1964), edited by Floyd Stovall, are relevant. Harry Hayden Clark's "Changing Attitudes in Early American Literary Criticism: 1800–1840" (1964) is good at identifying some of the major concerns of Romanticism: individualism and subjectivity, intuition and imagination, beauty, sympathetic and historical criticism, and organicism; but it is rather general and meant to be supplemented by G. Harrison Orians's "The Rise of Romanticism, 1805–1855" in *Transitions in American Literary History* (1954), edited by Clark. Also in Stovall, Richard Harter Fogle's "Organic Form in American Criticism: 1840–1870" focuses on the ways in which the major Romantics differ in their attempts to achieve that reconciliation of opposites which is an essential characteristic of organicism. R. P. Adams's "Romanticism and the American Renaissance" (1952) applies Morse Peckham's definition of Romanticism to the Americans, categorizing Melville's *Moby-Dick* as an example of "positive" Romanticism. Clarence Arthur Brown's anthology, *The Achievement of American Criticism* (1954), offers thumbnail sketches of the critical theories of such major Romantics as Emerson and Melville and such minor ones as Whittier and Longfellow. Henry Pochmann's *German Culture in America* (1957) summarizes the major German critical theories that were popular in America during the Romantic period and identifies the critics that were using and disseminating them.

Other volume-length surveys are not very helpful. In *Forces in American Criticism* (1939) Bernard Smith focuses on sociological factors influencing criticism rather than aesthetic ones. John Paul Pritchard's *Criticism in America* (1956) lacks a strong theoretical framework. John W. Rathbun's more recent *American Literary Criticism, 1800–1860* (1979), the first volume in a series, concentrates on the practice of American critics during this period and mentions briefly the underlying major theories as well as the influence of Coleridge and Carlyle. Max I. Baym's ambitiously titled *History of Literary Aesthetics in America* (1973) seems superficial and unsystematic in its treatment of Melville's period.

Literary nationalism is one of the specific aspects of literary criticism during Melville's most active years that has attracted scholarly research. Still the best for an understanding of the criticism in the New York area of the period, John Stafford's *The Literary Criticism of "Young America"* (1952) outlines the major theories of criticism and literature of that political-literary movement with which Melville was closely associated during the late 1840s. Perry Miller's thoroughly engrossing study in *The Raven and the Whale* (1956) of the literary wars that Young America fought focuses almost entirely on the personalities and politics that contributed to New York's literary preeminence in the 1840s; although it recounts the campaign for literary nationalism, it sheds little light on purely aesthetic issues or, for that matter, the aesthetic roots of the movement. Chapter 3 in Benjamin Spencer's *The Quest for Nationality* (1957) is helpful on this point, mentioning briefly the critical theories and influences supporting the evolution of this important movement. John Paul Pritchard's *Literary Wise Men of Gotham* (1963), which concentrates on critical activity in New York during this period, has not been as influential.

Pioneering background studies by modern scholars on the evolution of theories concerning the sublime in England include Samuel H. Monk's *The Sublime* (1935) as well as Marjorie Hope Nicholson's *Newton Demands the Muse* (1946), which traces the effects of Newton's *Opticks* on English aestheticians, and her *Mountain Gloom and Mountain Glory* (1959), which follows the development of the "aesthetics of the infinite" as it shifts emphasis from a Supreme Deity to mountains and oceans. Also helpful are Ernest Tuveson's "Space, Deity, and the 'Natural Sublime' " (1951), his *The Imagination as a Means of Grace* (1960), and W. J. Hipple's *The Beautiful, the Sublime, and the Picturesque in Eighteenth-Century British Aesthetic Theory* (1957). In his Introduction to *The Romantic Novel in England* (1972) Robert Kiely discusses Burke and Kant as sources for the aesthetic theories underlying the Gothic novel. In *The Romantic Sublime* (1976) Thomas Weiskel gives a valuable and provocative interpretation of Burke and Kant, extending their discussions by using modern semiotic and psychoanalytic models. Studies of American theories about the sublime include William Charvat's *Origins* as well as Perry Miller's "The Romantic Dilemma in American Nationalism and the Concept of Nature" (1956) and Charles L. Sanford's "National Self-Consciousness and the Concept of the Sublime" (1961), both of which discuss the nineteenth-century effort to unite the sublime and the beautiful. In Chapter 3 of *Nature and Culture* (1980) Barbara Novak discusses changing concepts of the sublime as they relate to American landscape painting between 1825 and 1875. Blake Nevius's *Cooper's Landscapes* (1976), Dennis Berthold's "C. B. Brown, *Edgar Huntley*, and the Origins of the American Picturesque" (1984), and Richard S. Moore's *That Cunning Alphabet* (1982) are some of the recent studies suggesting how widely known and influential such concepts as the sublime and the picturesque were during the nineteenth century.

Melville's ideas about fiction involve the history and definition of the romance. Studies that trace the history of the romance from its development in England through its popularity in nineteenth-century America include G. Harrison Orians's "The Romance Ferment After *Waverley*" (1932); Charvat's *Origins* (1936); Perry Miller's "The Romance and the Novel" (1967); John Caldwell Stubbs's *The Pursuit of Form* (1970); Michael Davitt Bell's *The Development of American Romance* (1980); and Sergio Perosa's *American Theories of the Novel: 1793–1903* (1983). In *The Instructed Vision* (1969) Terence Martin briefly discusses the romance within the context of the Scottish Common Sense philosophy and its influence on the creative imagination.

In the 1950s critics subtilized the traditional definition of romance and distinguished between the romance as an American genre and the novel as an English one. Lionel Trilling originally sketched out this distinction in two essays printed in *The Liberal Imagination* (1950), "Manners, Morals, and the Novel" and "Art and Fortune." He claimed that American fiction writers did not favor the novel, which unlike the romance, stresses "reality" and social texture. Both Marius Bewley in *The Eccentric Design* (1959) and Richard Chase in *The American Novel and Its Tradition* (1957) developed Trilling's thesis, but Chase's elaboration has been more influential. Chase notes that many American novels are "romances" or "novel-romances" since, unlike the novel, they "veer toward mythic, allegorical, and symbolistic forms" (p. 13), stressing improbable, highly colored, often symbolic action and two-dimensional characters who are often abstract and ideal. Joel Porte's *The Romance in America* (1969) assumes this definition.

The 1970s saw critical reactions, with David H. Hirsch's *Reality and Idea in the Early American Novel* and Nicolaus Mills's *American and English Fiction in the Nineteenth Century* (1973) questioning these familiar distinctions between the American romance and English novel. In "Another Look at the American Romance" (1981), Robert Merrill argues that Chase's definition of the romance is valid but not his claim that the romance constitutes the major American fictional tradition. In "A Theory of Genre: Romance, Realism, and Moral Reality" (1981), Robert C. Post redefines the novel and the romance. Nina Baym's "Concepts of the Romance in Hawthorne's America" (1984) asserts that even during Hawthorne's day there was no generally accepted definition of the term "romance" nor a consensus that Hawthorne's longer fictions were romances rather than novels.

EARLY GENERAL STUDIES OF MELVILLE'S IDEAS ABOUT ART

In the late 1930s and early 1940s appeared the first sustained studies of Melville's theories of art. The most influential of these is F. O. Matthiessen's landmark study, *American Renaissance*, which focuses on the highlights of Melville's ideas as they relate to the major aesthetic concerns of the period. Pointing out that Melville had "none of Poe's equipment as a theorist" (p. 387), Matthiessen tends to treat Melville's ideas as derivative and not fully deliberate, but he does credit Melville with being an innovator in his practice of art, if not in his theory. He dismisses Melville's early Romantic theories about inspiration, the dependence of form on content, and the equivalence of the poet and philosopher, which are expressed in *Mardi*, as notions that were merely absorbed from Emerson or Carlyle, among others. Matthiessen stresses the relationship of Melville's more mature ideas to those of Hawthorne, seeing both authors as prone to allegory and symbolism because of the spiritualizing tendencies of the Puritan mind as well as their Christian literary heritage. But while pointing out this similarity and Melville's debt to the older writer, Matthiessen acknowledges the differences between the two friends. In his full discussion of the question of allegory and symbolism in Chapter 7 (see below), he categorizes Hawthorne as the allegorist and Melville as the symbolist. And although he considers Melville's objections to surface verisimilitude in *The Confidence-Man* as partly influenced by Hawthorne's ideas about romance, he points out that Melville there "formulated more exactly the kind of heightened reality they both wanted in their fiction" (p. 269). Matthiessen indicates, in Chapter 14, that Melville also surpassed Hawthorne in the use of myth, even though Melville's was only "an instinctive awareness" that myth provided a vehicle for exploring "the pastness of the present, of its illimitable shadowy extensions backward to the roots of history, to the preconscious and the unknown" (p. 654). Although Matthiessen's account of Melville's aesthetics is sketchy, his erudition and sound judgment have made this work an early influential guide.

K. H. Sundermann's "Kunstlerisches und Kunsttheoretisches" in *Herman Melvilles Gedankengut* (1937) is another early general study, but unlike Matthiessen's work, its influence has been negligible. It is unusual in bringing up early and in one place many of Melville's aesthetic concerns, such as the relationships among the poet, historian, and philosopher; the creative process, originality; realism; the picturesque and the beautiful; criticism and fame. However, its treatment of these subjects is not always incisive or thorough. At best, Sundermann tends to summarize rather than to analyze, as when he dwells on Melville's ideas about the creative process, quoting many of Melville's statements about the mysterious power of inspiration and the need for experience to fertilize it; at worst, he does not get to the heart of the matter, as when he deals with the imagination but ignores many of Melville's references to this faculty and fails to mention Coleridge's obvious influence.

ORGANIC FORM

The first specific lines of inquiry into Melville's aesthetics developed in response to allegations that critics had made about Melville's vagaries of form and to his use of symbolism. Despite their admiration for Melville's many virtues, even some of his earliest advocates during the Melville Revival in the early part of this century felt it necessary to acknowledge or defend the "irregularities" in his writing (Carl Van Doren, p. 323; Lincoln Colcord, p. 562; Lewis Mumford, pp. 176–81). The supposed aesthetic problems in Melville's work just mentioned by these early critics were fully and systematically presented by Leon Howard in "Melville's Struggle with the Angel" (1940) and R. P. Blackmur in "The Craft of Herman Melville" (1938), with Howard citing examples of Melville's technical limitations and Blackmur accusing Melville of "malpractice" in such conventions of dramatic form as plot, characterization, and dialogue.

Some notable defenses of Melville's art in the 1950s proposed the Romantic doctrine of organic form as the theoretical underpinning for his unconventional practices. In "Form as Function in Melville" (1952), exploring an area that Matthiessen did not develop, Nathalia Wright defended Melville's form as the result of his having discovered, like Emerson, Thoreau, and Whitman, the principle of organic form as a structural theory. She adduced evidence from Melville's fiction to prove his belief that, while creating, the author participates in the living process of nature and thus must reject superimposed order and the formal unities. Since life, which is inextricably complex, is the content that determines the form, the work of art should not be simply or neatly organized into a complete whole. Wright also asserted that in his poetry Melville enunciated "a theory of functional style" (p. 334), according to which a plain style should accompany realistic subject matter. Although in his excellent "*Moby-Dick*: Work of Art" (1953), originally read as a paper at a *Moby-Dick* centennial celebration in 1951, Walter E. Bezanson focused on Melville's practice of art, he concluded by citing the principle of organic form as Melville's rationale for his narrative method, as did Wright, asserting that an examination of *Moby-Dick*'s structure reveals it to be "unceasingly genetic, conveying the effect of a restless series of morphic-amorphic movements" (p. 57). Richard H. Fogle's section on Melville in "Organic Form in American Criticism: 1840–1870" (1964) is neither a systematic analysis of Melville's organicism, like Wright's article, nor a specific application of the theory to a particular work, like Bezanson's; instead, it is a judgment of Melville's organicism in relation to that of other Romantics. Defining organic form "as a comprehensive reconciler of opposites" (p. 84), Fogle compared the early Melville with Whitman, especially, because he emphasizes life and affirmation, but noted that in *Pierre* Melville began to stress the opposites of darkness and negation, without ever, Fogle tentatively concluded, resolving the "conflict between his concept of form and his concept of organic expansivism" (p. 105). A really thorough analysis and history of Melville's ideas about Romantic organicism remains to be written.

After the middle 1950s the grounds for defending Melville's practice shifted from the doctrine of Romantic organicism to a modernist interpretation of Melville's symbolic method, one that developed out of an increasing interest in Melville's symbolism.

SYMBOLISM OR ALLEGORY?

One issue that Matthiessen raised in 1941 and probably thought he had laid to rest involved the distinction between allegory and symbolism as it applied to Melville. After giving a brief history of the terms and stressing that both arise from the same concern for the spiritual significance of the physical fact, Matthiessen observed that, although neither Hawthorne nor Melville consciously subscribed to Coleridge's distinction between symbolism and allegory, or between the imagination and fancy, their typical practice reveals a similar differentiation. Matthiessen concluded: "Symbolism is esemplastic, since it shapes new wholes; whereas allegory deals with fixities and definites that it does not basically modify.

As a result *Moby-Dick* is, in its main sweep, an example of the reconcile-
ment of the general with the concrete, of the fusion of idea and image;
whereas, even in *The Scarlet Letter*, the abstract, the idea, is often of
greater interest than its concrete expression" (p. 250). Pointing out the
modern preference for the symbol, Matthiessen declared that, despite
Melville's comment about "hideous and intolerable allegory" in *Moby-
Dick*, Melville did not share this modern bias and in fact practiced allegory, although often passing beyond it to what moderns distinguish as
symbolism.

However, the 1940s saw a growing emphasis on Melville as consciously
symbolic. In his "Symbolism and Allegory in Melville" (1944), Ronald
Mason elaborated on Melville's symbolism, judging *Moby-Dick* to be Melville's "half-unconscious apotheosis of symbolic method" (p. 145), one
which led him to those practices in *Pierre* and *The Confidence-Man* that
have puzzled critics but have made him a precursor of such moderns as
Kafka. Mason incorporated this view of Melville's symbolism in his well-
received *Spirit Above the Dust* (1951). Raymond W. Short's "Melville as
Symbolist" (1949) suggested that Melville quite consciously distinguished
between allegory and symbolism, providing Ishmael's reaction to the
Spouter Inn painting as a model of the correct way to react to a work
of art like *Moby-Dick*. Short pointed out that Ishmael's initial allegorical
interpretations, with definite, single meanings, do not lead him to the
core of the picture: "The gigantic fish which in its own meaning comprises the host of particular fancies" (p. 103). Probing further into what
he inferred as Melville's theory of the symbol, Short also used Melville's
statement about the truly "original character" in *The Confidence-Man* as
evidence that Melville was trying to create, through the accumulation of
meanings in what is a mythic story, an "ur-symbol," which, like Adam,
Eve, and Satan in *Genesis*, is ambiguous, containing "all possibilities"
(p. 112).

Charles Feidelson's enormously influential landmark in Melville criticism, *Symbolism and American Literature* (1953), extended and deepened
the discussion of Melville's symbolism. Feidelson's first accomplishment
was to place Melville within the nineteenth-century American epistemological revolution led by Emerson and other American Transcendentalists against Puritan and Lockean rationalism. Feidelson argued
that Emerson went beyond German Transcendentalism to cope with the
peculiarly modern philosophical problem of knowledge, concentrating
on "the Kantian emphasis of form and method" (p. 114) and thereby
attempting to work out a method of knowing that would transcend and
reconcile both empirical and idealist categories of thinking. This method
of "organic apprehension," which is richer than and precedes rational,
ordered modes of thought, is a poetic, symbolic one in which the mind
and nature function in the act of knowing to progress organically from

the facts of nature to their significance. Melville's use of the voyage as a "metaphysical journey," a symbol for this process of thinking in the poetic, organic mode, reveals his kinship with American Transcendentalists. However, Feidelson pointed out, Melville was unlike Emerson in never forgetting that the attempt to understand the *Ding an sich* is ultimately futile.

Extending his discussion of Melville's epistemological doubt to its effect on his aesthetic theory, Feidelson argued that Melville, believing reality to be unknowable, made the symbolic process itself his theme. Ishmael's obsessive attempts to enter into the symbolic process and understand the significance of experience represent the attempt that Melville himself made in writing *Moby-Dick* to interpret reality as "instinct with significance" (to use Melville's own phrase in his first "Agatha" letter to Hawthorne), a task that he could not completely accomplish and thus passed on to the reader. All that the artist can do is record the process of creation in which, for the moment, the conflict between "subjective intention" and "objective fact" is resolved by a "mediating fiction," a resolution that is really illusory. Therefore, Feidelson concluded, Melville denounced the well-made novel in *Pierre*, just as Andre Gide did many years later. Feidelson's imputation of the French symbolic method to Melville caused him to stress the purely linguistic and arbitrary existence of the work of art and to substitute for the doctrine of Romantic organicism another way of justifying Melville's vagaries of form, an existential rationale for the anti-novel that subsequent critics like Paul Brodtkorb, Jr., and Edgar A. Dryden developed in the 1960s in their discussions of Melville's theory of fiction.

Feidelson's study gave such prominence to Melville's symbolism that studies of the allegory/symbolism issue in the 1950s and 1960s almost routinely dismissed allegory and praised Melville's conscious practice of symbolism. In his "Ahab's 'Intolerable Allegory' " (1955–56) Charles H. Cook's major point—that Ahab is condemned because he insists on turning the whale's ambiguity into a single meaning—proposed that Melville not only realized the distinction between symbolism and allegory but deliberately condemned allegorizers for oversimplifying reality. William York Tindall, in *The Literary Symbol* (1960), asserted that the true symbol does not even have multiple, individual, clear—even if contradictory—meanings; instead, it has no definite meaning at all, and therefore the inscrutable painting at the Spouter Inn is a better model for interpreting the whale than the doubloon episode. William K. Wimsatt and Cleanth Brooks relied on Feidelson's interpretation in their brief discussion of Melville as symbolist in *Literary Criticism* (1957, pp. 587–88). Book-length studies on other or related aspects of Melville published during the late 1950s repeated the basic distinction between allegory and symbolism, as did Milton Stern's *The Fine-Hammered Steel of Herman Melville* (1957) and

Richard Chase's *The American Novel and Its Tradition* (1957), whose essay "The A vs. the Whale" summarized the prevailing view but prudently warned overeager symbolists that pure allegory is rare and the truly poetic symbol an anomaly in a novel.

The end of the 1950s saw attempts to tip the balance a little more toward allegory while still acknowledging the primacy of Melville's symbolism. Actually, already in 1951 in his sketchy "The Allegorical Principle," Edward Bloom used Melville's own comments about allegory to place him in the allegorical tradition without commenting about the allegory/symbol distinction. But in the article "In Defense of Allegory" (1958), Edwin Honig launched the general attack on proponents of the Coleridgean symbol which he continued in *Dark Conceit* (1959), proposing that, although Melville belittled allegory in *Moby-Dick*, his letter to Sophia and his comments in *Pierre* suggest that Hawthorne's influence made Melville look more favorably on this literary mode. Albert S. Cook, in "Romance as Allegory: Melville and Kafka" (1960), argued that, although the whale is symbolic, it invites allegorizing because so many other elements in *Moby-Dick* are allegorical. And Paul Brodtkorb, Jr., in Chapter 7 of *Ishmael's White World* (1965), extended slightly the discussion of both Melville's allegory and his symbolism. Distinguishing between two types of allegory—explicit (e.g., "The Monkey-Rope") and implicit (the *Pequod* as microcosm)—Brodtkorb claimed that in *Moby-Dick* both are "discontinuous," not "an unbroken sequence of systematic meaning throughout the book" (p. 140), since that would violate "Ishmael's sense of processional meaning" (p. 143). The truer method, however, the literary method of temporal as opposed to doctrinal truth, is symbolism. Brodtkorb suggested that Melville's symbol is like T. S. Eliot's objective correlative in providing a focus for emotional response. In keeping with his "metaphysical view of the nature of being" (p. 143), Melville presents the whale in such a way as to state nothing definite intellectually but to arouse feelings of awe and dread in the novel's characters and in its readers that made them attach corresponding intellectual tags such as Evil or God to the whale.

Making a distinction between the simile and "the metaphorical or symbolic" (p. 37) like the one many other critics make between symbol and allegory, James Guetti's "The Languages of *Moby-Dick*" in *The Limits of Metaphor* (1967) also stressed Melville's belief that attempts to express reality by all the resources of language are inconclusive, revealing the artificiality and circularity of language while paradoxically implying, in a negative way, that an ineffable reality does in fact exist. Guetti suggested that for Melville the ultimate truth is that "reality can only be expressed suggestively and negatively as the incommunicable" (p. 41), and therefore the simile, rather than the metaphor or symbol, best represents the relationship between language and reality. Although Gordon

E. Bigelow's "The Problem of Symbolist Form in Melville's 'Bartleby the Scrivener' " (1970) does not deal with Melville's expressed statements about symbolism, the six characteristics Bigelow ascribed to the symbols in the story—"symbolic pregnance," "meaning as process or flow," "metamorphosis," "perspectivism," "presence and coalescence," and " 'field' or tensive context"—based as they often are on the theory and practice of other Romantic writers, suggest further lines of inquiry into Melville's practice in other works and to some possible theoretical grounding for the practice.

Not until the 1970s did critics attempt to ground speculation about Melville's theories more fully in the nineteenth-century milieu and its traditions. Duncan S. Harris's dissertation, "Melville and the Allegorical Tradition" (*Mel. Diss.*, #313), signalled a turn toward historicism, a reaction against what Harris considered the narrow, solipsistic formalism that Feidelson's definition of Melville's symbolic method engendered in critical studies of the 1960s, a critical approach which Perry Miller's 1953 review of Feidelson, "The Doctrine of the Symbol" (1953), warned against. Arguing that Feidelson's preoccupation with Melville's works as autonomous linguistic structures ignored the strong element of didacticism present there also, Harris asserted that in *Mardi* Melville followed such authors as Browne, Burton, and Rabelais in using the allegorical form of the romance-anatomy (as defined by Northrop Frye) and soon after developed fictional techniques that enabled him to undercut straightforward allegory. Hawthorne's influence also enabled Melville to use the form for a double purpose—to present a literal, enjoyable fiction and to express a dark, troubling truth.

Continuing the movement toward historicism, critics in the early 1980s related Melville's philosophy more closely to his aesthetics, pointing out that, although Melville was supposed to have put into practice the theory of the Coleridgean symbol, he certainly did not accept the metaphysics underlying the aesthetic doctrine. Aware of recent attempts to clarify our understanding of nineteenth-century ideas about symbol and allegory (especially those by Angus Fletcher and Edwin Honig), Michael Davitt Bell, in *The Development of American Romance* (1980), offered no new definition of symbolism and allegory in his account of their relationship to romance, but argued in Chapter 6, somewhat sketchily, that the romance, as a deviant, revolutionary attitude toward life as well as a form of art, is not basically compatible with the philosophical assumptions underlying either traditional allegory or Romantic symbolism. He asserted that while Melville originally may have believed in the possibility of Romantic symbolism, he gradually realized the implications of the fundamental "disrelation" of romance and used it instead of symbolism to explore current cultural problems as well as basic metaphysical ones.

In *Exiled Waters* (1982) Bainard Cowan explored more thoroughly the differences between the Romantic theory of the symbol and Melville's use of tropes. Influenced by Walter Benjamin, Cowan redefined allegory as "a cultural activity that arises at moments of crisis in the history of a literate people, when a text central to the people's identity can neither command belief any longer nor be entirely abandoned" (p. 7). Cowan pointed out that the Romantic era was just such a period and that Melville was keenly aware of the disjunction between Biblical text and contemporary attitudes, but that Melville also differed from the Romantic symbolists, who could experience a "moment of unification" (p. 52) with nature. Instead, as a Romantic allegorist he found nature ultimately inaccessible and saw only "writing on the body of nature" (p. 52), hieroglyphs which he assumed were meant to be decoded but which he found impossible to understand.

All of this interest in Melville's ideas about symbolism has illuminated the salient points of the topic, but an area that still needs work includes the eighteenth- and nineteenth-century theories of the symbol and allegory that Melville may have known. Surely we have not yet discovered everything possible about Melville's understanding of, for example, Coleridge's, Goethe's, and Carlyle's theories of symbolism.

MYTH

Long before Raymond Short's assertion in 1948 that Melville had created in *Moby-Dick* an "ur-symbol," critics had noted Melville's mythic tendencies: Lewis Mumford, for example, in *Herman Melville* (1929) described *Moby-Dick* as "one of the first great mythologies to be created in the modern world" (p. 193), and F. O. Matthiessen praised his ability to use myth. But most studies of Melville's use of folklore, legends, and myth during the 1950s and 1960s, when myth criticism in general flourished, focused on the meaning of Melville's myths rather than on his theories. Since Melville made very few explicit statements on the subject, critics have had to infer from his practice what his purpose or theory might be. Studies of American folklore in Melville usually reveal that Melville used folk elements to reflect his culture in both its regional forms and its national attitudes. Following Constance Rourke's *American Humor* (1931), Richard Chase in *Herman Melville* (1949) further examined Melville's use of popular folktales and stereotypes to show how closely related he was to contemporary society despite his criticism of it. R.W.B. Lewis's *The American Adam* (1955) claimed that the basic structure of Melville's works—the journey of an innocent youth into an evil world—reflects Melville's awareness of the Adamic myth which underlay the cultural dialogues of his day and his ability to infuse a mythic dimension into contemporary experience. And Daniel Hoffman's *Form and Fable in American Fiction* (1961) discussed in greater detail the specific myths and rituals that Melville used in *Moby-Dick* in order to represent his culture. Excellent as these studies are in the areas they examine, they do not explore how much Melville knew about nineteenth-century theories of myth.

Nor do the studies of Melville's mythology that have focused on his use of myths from around the world discuss Melville's theories beyond a rather general level. James R. Baird's *Ishmael* (1956) and Martin Leonard Pops's *The Melville Archetype* (1970) reveal more about twentieth-century psychological theory or myth criticism than they do about Melville's theories. However, one can, without getting caught up in Jungian mysticism, agree with Baird's point that Melville, like many other Romantics, reverted to more primitive archetypes and "autotypes" because of the failing authority of traditional Christian symbols and his own need to express himself symbolically. James E. Miller, Jr., in *A Reader's Guide to Herman Melville* (1962) arrives at a similar conclusion but from a different route. See Miller's "Melville's Search for Form" (1959) for a fuller, earlier discussion. H. Bruce Franklin in *The Wake of the Gods* (1963) also deals with Melville's use of world mythology, focusing on the ways in which Melville "discusses, compares, evaluates, and parodies particular myths of the world and dramatizes the mythmaking process" (p. 204), but he points out that since, from his readings in Pierre Bayle and Thomas Maurice, Melville knew both the Christian and skeptical theories of myth, it would be an interesting topic for another study to explore more fully and precisely Melville's knowledge of mythological theory.

Robert D. Richardson's chapter on Melville in *Myth and Literature in the American Renaissance* (1978) is just such a study, although a brief, rather general one that deals mainly with *Mardi* and *Moby-Dick*. Richardson argues that Melville knew about sixteen different theories of myth and that he oscillated between the two prevailing attitudes toward myth: rationalist skepticism, which he may have picked up from Bayle among others; and romantic acceptance, which he may have seen in George Grote's *History of Greece*. Richardson also suggests but does not demonstrate that, from his reading of Goethe, Hoffman, Ossian, Richter, Carlyle, and others, Melville surely knew of Romantic efforts to turn myth into literature. Richardson interprets *Moby-Dick* as an example of Melville's ambivalence toward myth, which caused him, on the one hand, to illustrate its deceptive qualities but, on the other, to apply a mythic dimension to a modern story or character in order to create a powerful imaginative appeal. Richardson suggests that it is by this "mythic investiture" that Melville may have been trying to "imbue the visible with the invisible" (p. 212) to achieve that "same sort of meeting ground between the actual and the imaginary that Hawthorne talked about" (p. 213) in explaining his concept of romance. Although Richardson's reading of *Mardi* and *Moby-Dick* are not entirely new, his suggestions that Melville knew of and was reacting to contemporary theories of myth offer possibilities for further research into an area that clearly fascinated Melville.

Other questions that come to mind are the following: to what extent did Melville, as an associate of the Young America crowd, know directly or indirectly contemporary German ideas about nationalistic myth in literature? Can we demonstrate that he knew some of Goethe's and the Schlegels' theories in this area? Did he see a relationship between the mythic and the sublime? Did his response to Higher Criticism affect his literary use of myth in *Clarel* and in his other poems?

THE SUBLIME AND THE BEAUTIFUL

In the late 1960s critics began exploring the relationship of eighteenth- and nineteenth-century conventions of the sublime and the beautiful to Melville's aesthetics. The earliest of two important short studies of this topic, Klaus Poenicke's "A View from the Piazza" (1967) is a rich, well-informed article that briefly surveys the development of the concepts of the beautiful and the sublime in the seventeenth and eighteenth centuries, and traces back to Edmund Burke's *A Philosophical Enquiry into the Origin of our Ideas of the Sublime and the Beautiful* Melville's fundamental dichotomy in "The Piazza," especially his opposition between the color and light/dark imagery. Poenicke argues that Melville depicts Marianna as a victim of her "sublime" environment in order to stress the eighteenth-century distinction between the sublime and the beautiful and thus criticize nineteenth-century American efforts to obscure it. In "Melville and the Sublime in *Moby-Dick*" (1976), Barbara Glenn also asserts that Melville's use of Burke's distinction reveals his rejection of contemporary thought, specifically in *Moby-Dick*, a Romantic theodicy. Glenn points out many parallels between Melville and Burke—especially the use of the ocean, the leviathan, darkness, and obscurity to evoke terror—that suggest how thoroughly and profoundly Melville may have been directly affected by Burke's study. However, Melville's use of the sublime can also be traced to indirect influences such as the gothic romance and the tradition of the sublime in painting. Sharon Furrow's "The Terrible Made Visible" (1973) explores the influence on Melville of two artists associated with the sublime—Salvator Rosa and Piranesi (see below).

Beauty, which in eighteenth- and nineteenth-century aesthetics is often related to the sublime, has not been carefully examined in those articles that mention Melville's ideas about this concept. Although both Poenicke and Glenn indicate that Melville was Burkean in subordinating the beautiful to the sublime, Max I. Baym's "Herman Melville" unaccountably asserts that Melville's was basically a quest for beauty. Without defining this term, or relating it to the sublime, Baym concludes that Melville used the power of the imagination to combine hatred and cruelty to create a kind of beauty. Richard Kuhns in "The Beautiful and the Sublime" (1981) asserts that Kant's definitions of these terms influenced nineteenth-century writers to undertake the familiar quest in search of beauty, meaning, or "at-homeness." In the section on *The Confidence-Man*, Kuhns reaches the familiar conclusion that, according to Melville, "the making of books...never achieves the redeeming beauty of art, since art itself is falsehood" (p. 302). Apparently unaware of any of the preceding studies of the beautiful and the sublime, Frank G. Novak, Jr., in " 'Warmest Climes But Nurse the Cruelest Fangs' " (1983), lists categories and instances of the "binary opposition between beauty and terror" (p. 332) in *Moby-Dick* and, searching for a frame of reference to give these facts significance, concludes that they reveal twentieth-century beliefs about the way the human mind operates.

The most thorough and comprehensive study of both the sublime and the beautiful in Melville is Richard S. Moore's recent volume *That Cunning Alphabet* (1982). It is based on a dissertation from which were excerpted two earlier notes, "Burke, Melville and the 'Power of Blackness' " and "Piranesi, 'The Blanket,' and the 'Mathematical Sublime' in *Moby-Dick*." In the book Moore creates a broad frame of reference for the sublime, the beautiful, and the picturesque, discussing not only the philosophical and psychological theories behind these aesthetic concepts but also their manifestation in nineteenth-century landscape and seascape painting and literary genres such as the sketch, the tale, and the romance. Building on Poenicke's and Helmbrecht Breinig's (see below) interpretations of "The Piazza," Moore discusses the sketch as a paradigm of Melville's aesthetics, which were opposed to official American attempts to mitigate the significance of the Burkean or horrific sublime by fusing it with the beautiful in the picturesque or by turning it into the moral sublime. In the sketch, Moore argues, Melville reveals his skepticism about art, sensational experience, aesthetic conventions, and a beneficent God immanent in nature.

Moore points out that the aesthetics of nature presented in "The Piazza" were foreshadowed in Melville's earlier works and rather fully presented in *Moby-Dick*, to which Moore devotes a lengthy section of his study. Moore's reconstruction of some of the aesthetic background that Melville knew and reacted to while writing the novel is informative. Pulling together the findings of other scholars, Moore relates literary nationalism to the moral sublime and its literary counterpart, the romance. He tracks down the artistic and literary antecedents of Melville's Spouter Inn painting and suggests that the painting was possibly influenced by J.M.W. Turner and his champion, John Ruskin. Also groundbreaking is Moore's discussion of Moby-Dick as the Kantian sublime, "an ageless, formless, dimensionless cipher of Kant's 'rude nature' involving unimaginable 'magnitude' " (p. 141). Moore stresses Melville's belief that the sublime and the beautiful cannot be reconciled, that beauty is always qualified by terror and is thus ambiguous. He concludes that, even though Melville's ethics are not transcendental, his aesthetics are. Ishmael insists that the whale and its whiteness have significance, but since Melville is unsure of what that significance is, he continually counterbalances the horrific and moral sublime to suggest that "the noumenal Absolute is ultimately beyond any moral apprehension whatsoever" (p. 170). After *Moby-Dick*, Moore notes, Melville gradually turned inward, away from an aesthetics of nature.

Moore's book is a significant contribution to our understanding of Melville's aesthetics, stressing as it does the importance of the sublime in his early works and its relationship to other aesthetic concepts in his theories. It also suggests how fruitful a study of the contexts can be in deepening our understanding of a text and guiding our interpretation of it. A similar study needs to be done for Melville's later works, tracing his ideas about the sublime in the poetry and noting especially how they relate to the controversial issue of his attitudes toward form and beauty. Subsequent studies of Melville's symbolism, myth, and imagination also need to take into consideration what was clearly a central aesthetic issue for him—the nature of the sublime and its relationship to the beautiful.

THE IMAGINATION

No study even approaches a definitive examination of Melville's ideas about the nature and function of the imagination. His beliefs are often mentioned or implied in discussions of larger issues, such as his symbolism, his use of the sublime, and his theories of fiction and poetry. Several articles do concentrate on the relationship of the imagination to reality. Helmbrecht Breinig's "The Destruction of Faeryland" (1968) is a very well-informed contextual study identifying Melville's "The Piazza" as his mature comment on American romantic uses of an imaginative "faeryland" to gain a perspective on real life, namely, those of Irving, Thoreau, and Hawthorne. Breinig argues that in this "narrative sketch" Melville especially criticizes Hawthorne's belief in a "neutral territory" between the ideal and real worlds, and suggests that while some illusion is required in order to live, one's dreams, like Marianna's, most "grow out of the actuality of her existence" (pp. 280–81). Breinig concludes that Melville is one of the first moderns because he makes "the destruction of fairyland . . . a basis for the development of art" (p. 283). A less complex piece that also sees Melville as stressing reality is Nancy Roundy's "Fancies, Reflections and Things" (1977). Like Breinig, Roundy considers "The Piazza" a "literary manifesto, exploring both epistemology and art" (p. 540). Using M. H. Abrams's classic distinction between two types of imagination, Roundy asserts that Melville's story criticizes the narrator's transcendental imagination as lamp and advocates instead Marianna's imagination as perception or mirror. Joyce S. Adler's "The Imagination and Melville's Endless Probe for Relation" (1973) establishes no aesthetic framework for her assertion that Melville's "Romantic Imagination" does not reject his "contemporary world" but instead seeks "*relation*: between concrete and abstract, particular and general, changing and continuing, finite and infinite, causes and effects, reality and sham" (p. 38).

The best discussions of Melville's ideas about the creative process are sections in larger studies by Ferdinand Schunck and Merton M. Sealts, Jr. In a portion of a chapter on Melville's theory of poetry in *Das lyrische Werk Herman Melvilles* (1976), Schunck competently sketches out the development of Melville's ideas on this subject. He sees the poem "Art" as crucial in revealing Melville's mature belief that the true creative process is a dialectical one which fuses opposites. He contrasts Melville's early Romantic stress on the subjective quality of poetic inspiration and an extreme organicism with a later attempt to achieve balance by acknowledging the complementary need for classical principles of order, proportion, and symmetry in the work of art itself. Sealts (see below) delves more deeply into Melville's early reliance on Plato's ideas about poetic inspiration in *Mardi*.

The topic is also brought up in a few studies that examine Melville's portrait of the artist in *Mardi*. Richard H. Brodhead focuses briefly but insightfully on Melville's ideas about the creative process near the end of his essay "*Mardi*" (pp. 49–52), where he points out the maturing of Melville's ideas on this subject between *Mardi* and *Pierre*. In the later work, according to Brodhead, Melville becomes more skeptical about totally spontaneous creativity and acknowledges the need for formal training; he learns also that the artist's writing to discover himself leads not to "a paradise of creative fullness but the nightmare of a central emptiness" (p. 51). Brodhead's brief treatment draws attention to the need for a study of the changes in Melville's ideas about the creative process during this crucial period of his career. John Paul Montgomery's 1972 dissertation, "The Creative Process and the Image of the Artist in Melville's *Mardi*" (*Mel. Diss.*, #288), applies to Melville's third novel the modern theory of "process literature" (p. 76), a notion prefigured by the Romantics and popularized by Charles Feidelson in the twentieth century. Montgomery traces in it Melville's awareness of polar opposites and his attempts to synthesize them in an open-ended form. Montgomery recognized in a footnote that a study of Coleridge's influence on Melville's ideas should be undertaken, despite the complexity of the task. Only peripherally concerned with aesthetic theory, Barbara Meldrum's

"The Artist in Melville's *Mardi*" (1969) emphasizes the destructive effect to his entire being when the artist gives full rein to his creative energies and denies physical reality.

When one considers the importance of imagination in Romantic aesthetics, it is surprising that critics seem to have only scratched the surface of Melville's interest in the subject. Just what were Melville's ideas about the origins and nature of the imaginative process and how did they develop as he matured? In addition to Plato's contribution to Melville's early ideas about poetic inspiration, exactly what notions about the imagination were influenced by Coleridge? To what extent may his ideas about the imagination have been influenced by Shelley, Carlyle, Emerson, Keats, Goethe, Schiller, or Arnold? Why and to what extent did Melville become disillusioned about the Romantic or transcendental imagination? Did Melville subscribe to more than one theory of the imagination? How do his ideas about the imagination relate to his interest in the sublime?

THEORY OF FICTION

Except for Charles Feidelson's study on symbolism, Melville's theory of fiction occasioned only a few passing flurries of interest before the late 1950s. These early presentations, which center on chapters 14, 33, and 44 of *The Confidence-Man*, sketch out what is now a critical commonplace—Melville's rebellion against the popular fictional conventions of his time. In portions of his Introduction to *Herman Melville: Representative Selections* (1938), the best of these early works, Willard Thorp characterizes Melville as a conscious artist who, in daring to express the truth, "set himself deliberately against the main current of fiction-writing at the time" (p. xliv). To demonstrate Melville's rejection of realistic conventions of surface verisimilitude, Thorp briefly summarizes the above-mentioned chapters in *The Confidence-Man* dealing with consistency of character, "fidelity to real life," and originality of character. Thorp also analyzes Melville's "Agatha" letter of 13 August 1852 to Hawthorne in order to illustrate Melville's fictional method of building an imaginative superstructure upon a factually true story. Nathalia Wright's "Form as Function in Melville" interprets Melville's comments in *The Confidence-Man* chapters as evidence of his commitment to the organic principle. In his introductory remarks to the section of *The Achievement of American Criticism* that reprints the *Confidence-Man* chapters and "Hawthorne and his *Mosses*" (pp. 167–70), Clarence Brown simply highlights the ideas in these works, interpreting the review mainly as an example of Melville's perceptive judgment of Hawthorne and his own enthusiastic nationalism.

Two much more thorough studies in the late 1950s and early 1960s

can still be recommended, both of which discuss Melville's pronouncements about fiction as his attempt to reconcile his personal search for
truth and developing artistry with the expectations of the reading public.
William Charvat's groundbreaking study of Melville's quarrel with his
contemporary readers—"Melville and the Common Reader" (1958)—
has not been superseded. In it Charvat traces Melville's increasing disappointment with his readers in his early novels to his outright hostility
and intent, from *Pierre* on, to deceive them. Especially interesting is
Charvat's account of Melville's discovery of his own genius and his ways
of relating his insights to the reader. Charvat is one of the first to recognize the importance of Melville's admiration for Shakespeare's strategy
of slipping dark truths about life in among the more crowd-pleasing,
sensational elements of his dramas as a way of resolving the conflict
between the artist's vision and the public's taste. Charvat leaves open to
question the possibility that Melville did eventually achieve a "truce with
the insensitive public" (p. 281).

Allen Hayman's "The Real and the Original" (1962), which adheres
rather closely to Melville's expressed statements in "Hawthorne and His
Mosses," *The Confidence-Man*, and the "Agatha" letters, remains valuable
as a systematic, non-thesis-ridden presentation of Melville's theory of
fiction. Stressing that Melville's concern with the "great Art of Telling
the Truth," as enunciated in the review of Hawthorne, is crucial to an
understanding of Melville, Hayman gathers some illuminating examples
of Melville's use of that troublesome word "Truth" in other works and
in general allows Melville's definitions to speak for themselves. Melville's
truth, he adds, does not mean the surface authenticity of realism but
rather the "truth to the human heart" of Hawthorne's concept of romance. And Hayman discusses Melville's ideas about consistent and original characters in *The Confidence-Man*, which he supplements with
comments from Melville's other works, as also stemming from Melville's
desire to probe at "the very axis of reality." Hayman elaborates somewhat
on Thorp's explanation of Melville's account of his symbolic method in
the "Agatha" letter. For all its competence, however, Hayman's cautious
empiricism leaves the reader looking for a clearer understanding of
Melville's ideas than Melville's words themselves often give and for relationships to be drawn between Melville's critical statements and broader
aesthetic concerns.

Such theoretical probing was not missing in Charles Feidelson's earlier
Symbolism in American Literature (1953), whose modernist analysis of Melville's symbolic method greatly influenced subsequent studies of Melville's fictional theory as well. For instance, Richard Chase (1957) echoes
Feidelson when he claims that in *Moby-Dick* Melville's aesthetic sense
provided his skeptical intellect with the symbols to express the contradictory quality of life. Afterwards, he asserts, Melville lost his belief that

the intellect and imagination could produce such a synthesis. In *Ishmael's White World* (1965), Paul Brodtkorb, Jr., extends Feidelson's interpretation to Ishmael's motives for telling stories and to his use of form. Arguing that the phenomenological method is applicable to Melville because its roots lie in nineteenth-century Romanticism, Brodtkorb speculates that Ishmael's story-telling is his aesthetic response to a Kierkegaardian despair, that "Ishmael is compelled to report and create meaning in what happened to him both despite, and because of, his sense of the uncertainty of meanings available to temporal man" (p. 138). Thus, to tell the entire truth—that no meaning is certain—he must at the same time undercut the meaning of his own story with irony, hyperbole, and outright lies and, in effect, deliberately sabotage the presentation of a clearly articulated form.

Applying the Feidelson-Brodtkorb approach to "Hawthorne and His Mosses," which he takes as the key to Melville's fictional theory, Edgar A. Dryden, in the first chapter of *Melville's Thematics of Form* (1968), subjects the review to the closest reading as literary criticism thus far. Stressing that Melville's metaphysics influenced his aesthetics and that his "theory of fiction is based on a vision of life as an empty masquerade" (p. 21), Dryden asserts that according to Melville the "masters of the great Art of Telling the Truth" like Shakespeare and Hawthorne created fictional worlds in order to face and express indirectly the dark truths of reality, which if looked at directly would drive them mad. Dryden's assumptions about Melville's metaphysics also underlie his interpretation of the digressive chapters in *The Confidence-Man*. Since the 1960s most studies of these chapters treat them as another ironic part of this difficult novel rather than as literary theory (John G. Cawelti; Merlin Bowen; Bert C. Bach); however, Dryden does both. (Textual analyses of Melville's revisions of Chapter 14 warn that all of these chapters do indeed require close scrutiny. Elizabeth S. Foster first studied the revisions in the 1954 Hendricks House edition of *The Confidence-Man*. In the recent Northwestern-Newberry edition of *The Confidence-Man*, Harrison Hayford and Alma A. MacDougall present full transcriptions of the drafts and evidence of the time of their composition.) Dryden cautions that the narrator's pleas for confidence in these chapters are just another instance of the book's theme and must be judged by Melville's practice, which undercuts his expressed statements about the relation between the fictional and real worlds. Dryden concludes that Melville saw no difference between the two, both being equally illusory. Dryden's study is the most fully developed presentation of this modernist interpretation of Melville's fictional theory.

The belief that in his later fiction Melville lost faith in art predominated in studies about the relationship between fiction and reality after Dryden, although few studies made significant additions to this interpretation.

Alan Frederick Zoellner's dissertation "The Splendid Labyrinth" (*Mel. Diss.*, #467) does elaborate the argument that in *Pierre* Melville became skeptical about the transcendental theory that language can unite contraries and in *The Confidence-Man* created the title character as "a counter-image to Emerson's poet" (p. 2). But Peter A. Obuchowski's claim in "*Billy Budd* and the Failure of Art" (1978) that this last novel reveals Melville's despair about the efficacy of words and art is neither well informed nor well argued.

Richard H. Brodhead's *Hawthorne, Melville, and the Novel* (1976), which can be recommended as a lucid, comprehensive account of Melville's major ideas as put forward by the critics of the last thirty years, dwells on Melville's theory of fiction and agrees with Dryden that in *Pierre* Melville developed a metaphysical nihilism and a sense that imaginative constructs "are not excellent falsehoods but out-and-out lies" (p. 189). However, Brodhead does not extend our understanding of the modernist position concerning Melville's theory in the later novels, nor does he break any new ground in his discussion of the earlier theory. In Chapter 6 he explains fully the traditional view that, before *Pierre*, Melville's attempts to dive to the heart of reality were propelled by a powerful imagination that could not be bound by superficial conventions of form or verisimilitude and thus left forms open-ended. Brodhead's forte here is clear, thorough textual explication rather than studying contextual relationships or speculative probing into larger aesthetic concerns.

Nina Baym's "Melville's Quarrel with Fiction" (1979) is a more provocative study. Ever since Raymond M. Weaver in *Herman Melville* (1921) stigmatized the years following *Pierre* as "The Long Quietus," critics have tended to slight Melville's later productions. Matthiessen, for example, suggested that *Israel Potter* and *The Confidence-Man* reveal "signs of exhaustion in Melville's vitality" (p. 491). Feidelson and the modernist interpreters of Melville's fictional theory have deepened this prejudice by attributing his withdrawal from fiction writing to his philosophical doubts about language, apparently forgetting that the poems use language and that *Clarel* is a very lengthy narrative. Despite her disclaimer, Baym perpetuates this prejudice in the two arguments she develops to prove that Melville became disillusioned with language and literature. One argument is that for a time Melville's was an "Emerson-derived notion of language as proceeding from a divine Author or Namer" (p. 910), but when Melville lost faith in the Absolute he also lost faith in the truth of the universe and the meaning of language. Emerson's supposed influence on Melville is not well supported by evidence, however. Baym's other argument, that Melville was habitually impatient with fictional genres, including the romance, and finally abandoned them altogether in general disgust for language, is an interesting development of Blackmur's original point. But Baym surely overstates her case. Apparently unaware of Melville's interest in form during the years in which he wrote poetry, she can only characterize Melville's concern for fiction in *Billy Budd* as "most curious" and evidence of "a truce in Melville's quarrel with fiction" (p. 921).

For Michael Davitt Bell in *The Development of American Romance* (1980), the cause of the supposed exhaustion in Melville's later fiction is a specifically historical and uniquely generic one, not the more general one of language. According to Bell, it is a problem inherent in using the impulse behind the romance as well as its form. Using a psychological and sociological approach to Melville's crisis of art, Bell develops more fully in Chapter 8 an argument only adumbrated in his 1974 article "Melville and 'Romance:' Literary Nationalism and Fictional Form." Bell asserts that Melville originally used the Romantic impulse, the desire to "sacrifice the relation" between objective and subjective reality, in order to express revolutionary inner truths. However, by *Moby-Dick*, Bell adds, Melville developed doubts about revolutionary ideals and began to use the romance to explore other questions about the realities behind the appearances of nature, of the self, and of language. As long as he was able to generate and explore these oppositions, to express their tension, Melville expanded and vitalized the romance. But having "followed the imperative of subjective mimesis, the impulse of sincerity, into the imprisoning arabesque trap of language" (p. 195) in the late fiction, Melville lost that impulse and the ability to create the earlier vital oppositions.

Opposed to the somewhat doctrinaire modernist approach to the later fiction is a more traditional interpretation that Melville, unlike some twentieth-century theorists, did not totally reject the efficacy of art as a path to truth but, like some other Romantics, did question it. In Chapter 1 of *The Ironic Diagram* (1970), John Seelye argues persuasively that, because of an ironic vision in part influenced by Shakespeare, Cervantes, the Schlegels, and Coleridge, Melville "was impelled by his uncertainties to create forms which would encompass them" (p. 2). Melville's idea of form is the union of opposites in paradoxes to suggest that truth is a question rather than an answer, that the exact nature of reality is a mystery which man may be incapable of understanding but which he, as a noble fool, is compelled to pursue.

Joel Porte's *Romance in America* (1969) sees *The Confidence-Man* as "a lecture with illustrations, as it were, on the theory and practice of romance" (p. 156). Unlike Dryden, Porte considers the digressive chapters the "theoretical backbone of his seemingly formless exercise" (p. 167), in which Melville uses his own voice to persuade the reader to enter the realm of romance, to search for truth, however uncertain the path, however ambiguous and confusing the dark hints of romance as opposed to the clear faith of the Bible. Porte's claim that Melville retained his belief in art as a way of seeking or revealing truth, even if limited and unsure, is more an assertion than a thoroughly developed argument. Another work based on this same assumption, Peter Harris's dissertation "Melville: The Language of Visible Truth" (*Mel. Diss.*, #385) is too ill-focused to argue persuasively that Melville believed language, despite its shortcomings, capable of presenting the "visible truth." Joe Drake Gilliland's discussion, in his 1979 dissertation "Herman Melville's Portraits of the Artist" (*Mel. Diss.*, #494) tends to summarize prevailing views in a general way.

Two studies seem blissfully unaware of the modernist interpretation. Ignoring previous studies in this area, notably Feidelson's, Thomas Edward Lucas's "Herman Melville: The Purpose of the Novel" (1972), a revision of his earlier (1963) dissertation, asserts Melville's faith in art and focuses on his questions about the truth in an attempt to prove that "fiction, in Melville's eyes the most true of all mediums, can at best state problems whose solutions are inscrutable" (p. 660). Worse yet, Sergio Perosa's discussion of Melville in Chapter 3 of the recent (1983) *American Theories of the Novel*, a kind of throwback to the early 1960s, is unaware that Melville suffered a crisis of art much less that there is some critical disagreement about the nature of that crisis. Although Perosa competently traces some of Melville's early beliefs about fiction, the latest criticism on Melville's aesthetics that he acknowledges in his notes is Hayman's 1962 study.

Recently, more groundwork has been laid to provide an actual attack on the modernist position. In the 1977 dissertation "Dialectics of Consciousness" (*Mel. Diss.*, #462), Mark Andrew Siegel cites the marginalia on Balzac as evidence of Melville's commitment to the realist's faith that art can present an ordered world, although Siegel agrees that Melville was also attracted to the anti-realist doubt that art and language can convey truth. Siegel concludes that to the end Melville was "neither realist nor modernist, but a transitional sensibility caught between both" (p. ii). In "Melville's Comic Debate" (1983), John Bryant asserts that, far from losing faith in art in his later fiction, Melville was deliberately following an "aesthetics of repose," a belief that he implied in "Hawthorne and His *Mosses*" and stated in his lecture "Statues in Rome." Bryant argues that Melville's discussion of the "great Art of Telling the Truth" in the essay emphasizes concealing the darkness of truth just as much as it stresses its "blackness," and that, following Hawthorne's example, Melville therefore tried to fuse with his dark skepticism an impulse of geniality to create the "tense repose" (p. 155) that he later admired in the statue of Laocoon. As evidence that this was Melville's aesthetic goal, Bryant traces Melville's development of the "genial misanthrope" from his early experimentation in *Pierre* and the magazine stories to his success in *The Confidence-Man*.

However, none of these studies deals head on or exhaustively with the modernist belief that Melville totally lost faith in art during the later fiction. A formidable but interesting study which remains to be written would examine both textual and contextual evidence to try to resolve the differences between the modernist and traditional interpretations of Melville's theory in the later fiction, especially in the light of new evidence concerning the growth of the digressive chapters in the NN edition of *The Confidence-Man.* Just how thorough was Melville's skepticism about fiction or art as a path to and expression of truth during this period? Did any genre theory coincide with a personal distaste for fictional form to influence his retreat from fiction writing?

POETICS

Strictly speaking, the term "poetics" here is a misnomer since Melville wrote very little specifically about poetic theory and probably identified the poet with the artist in general. The majority of the studies reviewed here deal with Melville's theories of art or literature as they relate to or are expressed in his later poetry and sometimes in *Billy Budd*, with occasional references to the earlier portrait of Yoomy in *Mardi* or to a basic document such as "Hawthorne and His *Mosses.*"

The most well-informed, comprehensive, and judicious general study of Melville's ideas about poetry and the poet is unfortunately not in English but in the first chapter of Ferdinand Schunck's *Das lyrische Werk Herman Melvilles.* Like many other critics, Schunck considers the cornerstone of Melville's theory of art the belief, which Melville enunciated in the poem "Art," that art requires the synthesis of opposites. In *Mardi* and in "Hawthorne and His *Mosses*" Melville presented the ideal artist as one who unites the complementary principles of the heart and the head, of beauty and truth. And the ideal work of art is like the rose Babbalanja describes in *Mardi*: enclosed within its beautiful petals lies the pearl of truth. With a firm grasp on this essential idea of Melville's and repeated warnings that Melville should not be labeled either a romantic or a classicist, Schunck discusses in some detail Melville's ideas about the creative process as they developed over his long career, and his theory of the symbol. Schunck also places Melville's ideas within the context of some Renaissance theories and draws brief parallels between Melville's ideas and those of Coleridge, Emerson, Carlyle, Pater, and Arnold. Even though Schunck's study is too much a summary to break much significant new ground, it can be recommended as a good starting place—for those who read German.

The next best summary is given by William H. Shurr at the beginning of the last chapter of *The Mystery of Iniquity* (1972). In a few pages Shurr incisively highlights Melville's major ideas about art as expressed in his late poetry. Shurr briefly discusses Melville's belief that the artist expresses dark, mysterious truths in symbols and that art is a "mystic" struggle to fuse opposites, as it was for Coleridge. Because the artist's lonely pursuit of truth, his "diving" into the depths of reality, may produce "some ultimate horror" (p. 244), writing "becomes a technique of concealment as much as communication and revelation, and the work produced is a quasi-gnostic document whose meaning is revealed only to the initiated" (p. 245). Insightful as it is, Shurr's brief sketch does not present the full range of Melville's ideas on this topic.

In "Melville's Concepts of the Poet and Poetry" (1975), a distillation of four chapters of her dissertation, Agnes D. Cannon attempts the first full-scale attack on Melville's poetics, but the essence and relative importance of Melville's ideas sometimes elude her. Generalizing about Yoomy in *Mardi* and Rolfe and Vine in *Clarel*, Cannon defines Melville's poet as gentle, sensitive to beauty, ideally balanced as to heart and head, artistically honest, torn between a need for solitude and a need for companionship, and able to produce Coleridge's "willing suspension of disbelief." In addition, Cannon declares that Melville considers the poet to have six roles: entertainer, mouthpiece for humankind's emotions, interpreter of ideas, seer, potential savior of humankind, and mythmaker. Relying too uncritically on Melville's marginalia concerning the nature of poetry and ignoring some of his expressed statements in *Clarel*, Cannon comes to the odd conclusion that "Beauty, to Melville, was the supreme raison d'etre for poetry." (p. 333).

A few articles dealing with more limited areas of Melville's theory have focused on Melville's interest in form. In "The Differences in Melville's Poetry"(1955), Laurence Barrett asserts that one reason Melville's poetry strikes the reader as different is that in it Melville was trying to make the form reflect thought and mood. Melville's early scorn for form in *Mardi* gave way to appreciation as he experimented with metrical patterns, line lengths, stanzaic forms, and rhyme patterns in his later poetry. Barrett is safe when he asserts that Melville undoubtedly believed that form is ancillary to truth. But when he speculates more generally and claims that Melville discovered "that forms, measured forms, are the resolution of the dissociation of sensibility and that in them alone lies the answer to the inability to believe or to be content in unbelief" (p. 622), Barrett moves into shaky ground supported rather weakly by a few statements from *Billy Budd*. Bryan Collier Short's more recent "Form as Vision in Herman Melville's *Clarel*," (1979) builds on Barrett's belief that Melville developed a faith in art when he realized that the search for truth was futile. Short argues that even before *Clarel* Melville had substituted a "disciplined objectivity for deep diving" (p. 557) in his poetry and in his long poem used the same method. But in many of the lyrics in the narrative and in the epilogue Melville, following the principle of organic form, progressed to another state in which he distanced himself from the "stale pilgrimage" in order to present a different vision. Short's conclusion, that "The lesson of Melville's changing art in *Clarel* is that truth-seeking, whether transcendental or objective, too easily produces a truth which is useless while ignoring opportunity after opportunity for beauty and satisfaction" (p. 568), ignores the main thrust of Melville's dialectical method in *Clarel* as well as counterstatements expressed in the poem.

One reason some critics believe that Melville completely changed his attitude toward form in his poetry years is that in some of his late lyrics Melville sounds very classical. Jane Donahue's "Melville's Classicism" (1969) examines a few short poems, especially those in *Timoleon*, that reveal Melville's interest in the classical values of form, harmony, unity, order, and rules in art. But Donahue concludes that, although Melville believed in an interplay of classical and romantic elements, "he was essentially a romantic whose spirit rejected any definite limits of theme or culture" (p. 71). Shirley M. Dettlaff's more recent "Ionian Form and Esau's Waste" (1982) argues that although during the period in which Melville was writing *Clarel* he clearly developed a strong interest in form, he defined art in the poem as a synthesis of both "Nature's Terror" and "ordered form," giving form a somewhat subordinate role. Melville's reading in such modern Hellenes as Goethe, Schiller, and Arnold may have partially influenced him to value more highly than he had before a classical notion of form and beauty, yet in *Clarel* he still advocated that art reveals the characteristics of the Burkean sublime—an indeterminacy and inconclusiveness that seem incompatible with clarity and form. Nor did Melville follow the Hellenes in believing that art should elevate the reader to an ideal realm or produce joy in him.

The most pressing need is for a comprehensive study, in English, of Melville's later ideas about art as presented in his poetry, including *Clarel*. His letters, readings, and marginalia should be scrutinized in order to explore the full range of his thoughts about art while he was writing poetry. The question of just how important a role form played in his later theory requires fuller treatment. To be researched also is the possibility that a theory of poetry that he espoused influenced Melville's switch to this genre during most of his later writing.

FINE ARTS

Melville's interest in painting, sculpture, architecture, and music has long been acknowledged by biographers and critics as has been the importance of the fine arts in his works and aesthetics. A growing number of studies deal with the ways that the individual fine arts function in his works and occasionally touch on their relationship with Melville's artistic theories. One article, Robert K. Wallace's "Melville's Prints and Engravings at the Berkshire Athenaeum," a forthcoming publication that cannot be adequately reviewed here as this chapter goes to press, is very valuable for its observations about Melville's lifelong study of art, its annotated catalogue of nearly 300 unframed prints and engravings in Melville's personal art collection, and its bibliography. See also Schless (1960), Star (1972), Coffler (1980), Robillard's two 1983 articles, and Wallace (1985).

An important, even if reconstructed, document, Melville's lecture "Statues in Rome" is no longer as neglected by critics of Melville's aesthetics as it was in 1957 when Merton M. Sealts, Jr., decried that fact in the introduction to *Melville as Lecturer* (1957). Although Sealts does not rigorously analyze Melville's few comments about the art of Greece and Rome, he asserts that writing about his ideas "assisted materially in their ordering and shaping" (p. 19). Sealts claims that Melville's attitude toward ancient art reveals the same predilections seen in his earlier fiction—"a firm grounding in realism and a strong concurrent tendency to 'spiritualize' the actual world by means of symbolic representation of some ideal conception or 'fable' " (p. 16).

Morris Star's 1964 dissertation "Melville's Use of the Visual Arts" (*Mel. Diss.*, #131), the most ambitious attempt to study Melville's knowledge and use of paintings, prints, sculptures, and architecture, is good for the overview of the subject it provides. Although the chapter on Melville's aesthetics is sketchy and has been superseded, the other chapters provide valuable information about Melville's acquaintance with art throughout his career, including the books about art that he purchased, the artists that he knew, and the repositories of art that he visited in his travels. Star is the first to dwell on Melville's use of the picturesque as influenced by the painters Salvator Rosa and Claude Lorrain, and of the Gothic as influenced by the novelists Horace Walpole and Ann Radcliffe. Melville's discerning but infrequent use of studio techniques such as focal point and complementary colors is analyzed. Star's detailed discussions of the many ways in which Melville uses images drawn from art—to support theme, to concretize and contrast, to create symbols, and so forth—also provide the reader with information about the individual works of art that Melville knew well enough to include in his writing. As a brief addendum to the list of works that Melville knew, John M. J. Gretchko's note, "The Glassy-eyed Hermit" (1981), tracks down an allusion in Chapter 1 of *Moby-Dick* to one of several paintings by Hieronymous Bosch entitled *The Temptation of St. Anthony*. Howard P. Vincent's "Ishmael, Writer and Art Critic" (1969) discusses Melville's use of pictorial art, specifically the Spouter Inn painting, for literary purposes—to divert the reader, celebrate the whale, and represent the book that Ishmael has written.

Apparently unaware of Star's pioneering study of Melville and the picturesque in art, Sharon Furrow, in "The Terrible Made Visible"

(1973), delves into the subject a little more thoroughly and explores Melville's interest in the sublime as that type of the picturesque which evokes terror. She points out that Melville was influenced by Salvator Rosa's wild landscapes and Piranesi's dungeons in the images he used, especially in *Moby-Dick, Pierre*, "The Encantadas," and *Clarel*, to "represent the inner life, the soul, and the darker, primeval regions of the personality and of nature itself" (p. 237). Richard S. Moore's *That Cunning Alphabet* should be consulted as the most wide-ranging study of Melville's use of the sublime and the picturesque now available. One would think that Melville's knowledge of the picturesque in "At the Hostelry," one of the Burgundy Club sketches, would have been studied by now, but that is not the case. The only treatment is in *The Mystery of Iniquity*, where William H. Shurr gives a detailed description of the poem and some background information, including a very brief history of the term in England and in America. Shurr's purpose is not to analyze Melville's theories, but his suggestion that Richard Payne Knight's definition of the picturesque as fusion parallels Coleridge's and Melville's beliefs about art indicates just one possible area for further examination. A study of the different meanings of the picturesque that Melville knew and used during the later part of his career is needed to supplement Moore's research into Melville's earlier years.

In "The Cottage and the Temple" (1969), Vicki Halper Litman argues that Melville, like nineteenth-century architectural theorists such as Andrew Jackson Downing, interpreted buildings as reflections of their owners' characters. However, Litman points out, Melville was also critical of the convention, sometimes depicting structures ironically and clearly mocking the cult of the pleasantly picturesque. Litman proposes that the two architectural models that Melville used to represent two poles in his thought are the farmhouse, a "symbol for the non-utopian view of earthly possibilities," and the Greek temple, a "symbol of perfection in artistic creation" (p. 636). Gordon V. Boudreau's "Of Pale Ushers and Gothic Piles" (1972) studies the architectural imagery in *Moby-Dick* from a mythic-theological point of view. Boudreau argues that *Moby-Dick*, like Poe's "The Fall of the House of Usher," is a gothic romance in which a central gothic edifice suggests a view of life. But unlike Poe, who uses the rock of a gothic manor house as tomb to suggest the dead-end rationalism of the eighteenth century, Melville uses the rock of the gothic cathedral to suggest a vision of spiritual rebirth. According to Boudreau, Ishmael's use of images relating to gothic cathedrals when he describes the Whaleman's Chapel, the *Pequod*, and most important, the whale indicates that Melville has intuited the sacred meaning beneath the tradition and applied to the story of the whale "the cultural myth still energized for Melville by the figure of Christ" (p. 80).

In "Ancient Greek and Roman Pieces of Art in Herman Melville's

Iconography" (1983), Ekaterini Georgoudaki analyzes Melville's references to ancient architecture and sculpture in his short poems, going
over a little more thoroughly a subject earlier mentioned in Jane Donahue's discussion of poetics. Georgoudaki concludes that Melville considered the ancients superior to nineteenth-century men in their ability
to harmonize disparate elements in art and in nature and in some of
their pre-Christian values as well. She suggests that Melville's praise of
Greek and Roman art reveals his faith in all art. Maxine Turnage's
"Melville's Concern with the Arts in *Billy Budd*" (1972) is more an interpretation of Melville's last story than an analysis of his aesthetics. Turnage asserts that the story dramatizes Melville's regret that in the late
nineteenth century two components of art—the beautiful (Billy) and the
didactic (Claggart)—have become separated and mutually destructive,
unable to achieve the synthesis so gloriously represented in the Handsome Sailor of Liverpool and Lord Nelson.

Harry R. Stevens's "Melville's Music" (1949) does little more than list
or paraphrase instances in which Melville alludes to music or musical
instruments in his works. Occasionally, observations about Melville's purpose and techniques are made but not elaborated. Stevens points out
that Melville used music in *Pierre* to "develop the content of the subconscious memory," "probe the realities of emotion," and "communicate
to his readers . . . emotional transformations" (p. 415), but he does not
analyze the devices that Melville uses to achieve these goals. Just a few
questions that Stevens's article leaves unanswered suggest areas for future study. How much did Melville know about popular and classical
music, about different styles and types, and about musical techniques?
What were the sources of his knowledge? Exactly how and why did he
use music in his works? Was he following literary models in using music
in the ways he did? How did his use of music as well as the visual arts
fit into his aesthetics?

INFLUENCE STUDIES

None of the following are complete studies that concentrate solely on
a specific influence on Melville's aesthetics but are instead sections of
articles, books, or dissertations that bring up the subject. And only a few
try to prove direct sources for Melville's ideas. Since Melville wrote little
about artistic theories and was eclectic in his borrowing, it is difficult to
prove actual filiation; therefore, most scholars or critics are content to
establish affinities between Melville's ideas and those of the writers that
we know he read. However, patient scholars can do some detective work
and determine with greater probability and precision than we now have
the specific configurations of the influences on Melville's artistic theories.

Plato's general influence on Melville has long been acknowledged, of course, but a model of what can be done to work out the details has been provided by Merton M. Sealts, Jr., in "Melville and the Platonic Tradition" (1982). In just a small portion of the essay (pp. 284–87), Sealts explores how Plato's ideals about poetic inspiration may have affected Melville's early works. While noting Plato's indirect influence through such writers as Sir Thomas Browne, Sealts carefully establishes verbal parallels between passages on the creative process in *Mardi* and in the *Phaedrus*, which along with other works by Plato Melville may have begun reading in early 1848. Similarities include the concept of a spiritual realm of essences and preexistent souls; the poet's and philosopher's inspiration as a kind of madness, a temporary return to this world, which is induced by love and is unintelligible to ordinary mortals; and the imagery of wings and flying to symbolize this spiritual transport.

Samuel Taylor Coleridge's enormous influence on Melville's aesthetics has apparently been taken for granted as a pervasive but indistinguishable part of the general Romantic attitude. Therefore no full-scale attempt has been made to disentangle the Gordian knot of direct and indirect influence. A case in point is a 1967 dissertation on the Romantic novel, "Coleridge's Definition of the Poet and the Works of Herman Melville and William Faulkner" (*Mel. Diss.*, #159), in which Lewis Franklin Archer makes no effort to prove how much of Coleridge's theory Melville actually read, nor does he systematically adduce statements by Melville which clearly demonstrate the influence. Instead, asserting that the broad outline of Coleridge's position influenced the Romantic novel, Archer highlights Coleridge's basic doctrines about the poet and concludes that, like Coleridge, Melville had a double vision of life, seeing both good and evil, reacting with both head and heart. According to Archer, Melville also felt a need to reconcile these opposites in symbolic literature, but substituted a faith in art for Coleridge's belief in God as the ground for his reconciliation. A work that brings up just one aspect of Coleridge's influence is John Seelye's brief discussion of romantic irony in Chapter 1 of *Melville: The Ironic Diagram*. Seelye does not claim to study the sources of Melville's aesthetics but does assert that the interpretation of Shakespeare that Melville derived especially from Coleridge and the Schlegels greatly influenced his view of the artist as one who combines opposites into an inclusive whole and through stylistic indirection gives dark hints about terrifying truths. Seelye's point warrants a more complete study tracing parallels between the Schlegels, Coleridge, and Melville in order to stress, clarify, and explore these key notions in Melville's aesthetics.

Thomas Carlyle may be another important source for Melville's ideas that is difficult to measure since his influence on American Romantic criticism was widespread and may have reached Melville indirectly as well as directly. In her 1975 dissertation "Thomas Carlyle and the American Renaissance" (*Mel. Diss.*, #374), Julia Deener Brent takes up the direct relationship between Carlyle's ideas about art and Melville's in a few pages (pp. 193–200) and claims that Melville's comments and practice concerning the nature of symbolism and the role of the artist as truth-teller in *Moby-Dick* substantially agree with Carlyle's. Brent points out, however, that in *Pierre*, Melville ridicules Carlyle's belief in the man of letters as hero. Brent's brief foray into this subject suggests that further study is needed, since Melville read a great deal of Carlyle and knew his ideas well.

The influence of other English Romantics on Melville's thinking about art has been generally acknowledged but not studied in much detail. Melville's possible reaction in *Pierre* to Percy Bysshe Shelley's *In Defence of Poetry* is mentioned by Leon Chai in one section of "Melville and Shelley" (1983, pp. 38–41). Although his discussion of the similarities and differences between the two authors reveals nothing new about Melville's aesthetics, Chai does explore an early notion of Melville's which has not attracted much notice—his belief in the spiritual community of great writers. One also wonders to what extent Melville knew and reacted to William Wordsworth's critical tenets. And one wonders, too, how he reacted to the critical impressionism of Charles Lamb, William Hazlitt, and John Keats. Has the influence of Matthew Arnold's ideas on Melville been completely explored?

The German influence on Melville's aesthetics has been largely ignored, perhaps because much of it was also second-hand, reaching Melville through Coleridge and Carlyle. Yet Melville read a great deal of Goethe and Schiller, and was interested in other German writers as well. In a discussion of poetics Dettlaff has brought up briefly the influence of Johann Wolfgang von Goethe, Friedrich Schiller, and Matthew Arnold on Melville's ideas about art in *Clarel*. But more thorough studies of the German Hellenes' influence on Melville, especially during the early years, need to be done. Except for Seelye's brief discussion, there has been no attempt to trace the possible influence of August Wilhelm Schlegel or Friedrich Schlegel on Melville's thought, in spite of the fact that their influence on nineteenth-century American aesthetics was considerable and Melville claimed to have spent one night of his journey to England discussing "Hegel, Schegel [*sic*], Kant" with George Adler (*Mel. Log*, p. 322). In addition to what has already been suggested concerning Melville's knowledge of German theories concerning the imagination, symbolism, and myth, what did Melville know about German theories concerning tragedy or the novel? Is it possible that his unorthodox form in *Mardi* and *Moby-Dick* was influenced by the theories of the Schlegels? To what extent did the German romance influence Melville's ideas about this genre? Do we know all that we can about Kant's influence on Melville's aesthetics? What were Melville's reactions to Arthur Schopenhauer's aesthetics?

Very little has been done to explore the influence of American theorists on Melville's aesthetics. Nathaniel Hawthorne's influence on Melville concerning the theory and practice of the romance has been taken for granted (see Matthiessen, Brodhead, and Bell) as a general one, apparently not warranting detailed demonstration. In "Melville and Emerson's Rainbow," Sealts has recently established when and how much of Ralph Waldo Emerson Melville read and how some of Emerson's ideas may have affected him, but what do we know about Melville's reactions to the essay *The Poet* and to Emerson's poetry? In addition, what did Melville know of and how did he react to the critical theories held by the critics and reviewers of American as well as English periodicals? Can we track down any models of literary criticism that he was following in his own literary reviews?

Clearly, then, there is still room for research into the specific influences on Melville's aesthetics as well as into the individual tenets he held. Previous studies have identified most of those tenets and have concentrated on symbolism, fiction, and the sublime. But we can learn more about his ideas concerning myth, the imagination, poetics, and the fine arts. It is becoming apparent that Melville's aesthetic concerns were varied, detailed, and sophisticated. His early interest in the subject persisted throughout his entire career, as he continued to read works dealing with aesthetics and reflect on the nature and purpose of art. Since there is, of course, a relationship between his theory and his practice, discovering all that we can about Melville's aesthetics can help us understand his often enigmatic works.

WORKS CITED

Abrams, M. H. *The Mirror and the Lamp: Romantic Theory and the Critical Tradition.* New York: Oxford University Press, 1953.

Adams, R. P. "Romanticism and the American Renaissance." *American Literature* 23 (1952): 419–32.

Adler, Joyce S. "The Imagination and Melville's Endless Probe for Relation." *American Transcendental Quarterly* No. 19 (1973): 37–42.

Archer, Lewis Franklin. "Coleridge's Definition of the Poet and the Works of Herman Melville and William Faulkner." Ph.D. Diss., Drew University, 1967 [*Mel. Diss.*, #159.]

Bach, Bert C. "Melville's Confidence-Man: Allegory, Satire, and the Irony of Intent." *Cithara* 8 (May 1969): 28–36.

Baird, James R. *Ishmael: A Study of the Symbolic Mode in Primitivism.* Baltimore, Md.: Johns Hopkins University Press, 1956.

Barrett, Laurence. "The Differences in Melville's Poetry." *PMLA* 70 (September 1955): 606–23.

Baym, Max I. *A History of Literary Aesthetics in America.* New York: Frederick Ungar, 1973.

Baym, Nina. "Concepts of the Romance in Hawthorne's America." *Nineteenth-Century Fiction* 38 (March 1984): 426–43.

———. "Melville's Quarrel with Fiction." *PMLA* 94 (October 1979): 909–23.

Bell, Michael Davitt. *The Development of American Romance: The Sacrifice of Relation.* Chicago: University of Chicago Press, 1980.

———. "Melville and 'Romance': Literary Nationalism and Fictional Form." *American Transcendental Quarterly* No. 24 (Fall 1974): 56–62.

Berthoff, Warner. *The Example of Melville.* Princeton, N.J.: Princeton University Press, 1962.

Berthold, Dennis. "C. B. Brown, *Edgar Huntly,* and the Origins of the American Picturesque." *William and Mary Quarterly* 41 (January 1984): 62–84.

Bewley, Marius. *The Eccentric Design: Form in the Classic American Novel.* New York: Columbia University Press, 1959.

Bezanson, Walter E., ed. *Clarel: A Poem and Pilgrimage in the Holy Land.* By Herman Melville. New York: Hendricks House, 1960.

———. "*Moby-Dick*: Work of Art." In "*Moby-Dick*" *Centennial Essays.* Ed. Tyrus Hillway and Luther S. Mansfield. Dallas: Southern Methodist University Press, 1953, pp. 30–59.

Bigelow, Gordon E. "The Problem of Symbolist Form in Melville's 'Bartleby the Scrivener.' " *Modern Language Quarterly* 31 (1970): 345–58.

Blackmur, R. P. "The Craft of Herman Melville." *Virginia Quarterly Review* 14 (Spring 1938): 266–82.

Bloom, Edward. "The Allegorical Principle." *ELH: A Journal of English Literary History* 18 (1951): 163–90.

Boudreau, Gordon V. "Of Pale Ushers and Gothic Piles: Melville's Architectural Symbology." *ESQ* 18 (1972): 67–82.

Bowen, Merlin. "Tactics of Indirection in Melville's *Confidence-Man.*" *Studies in the Novel* 1 (Winter 1969): 401–20.

Breinig, Helmbrecht. "The Destruction of Fairyland: Melville's 'Piazza' in the Tradition of the American Imagination." *ELH: A Journal of English Literary History.* 35 (1968): 254– 83.

Brent, Julia Deener. "Thomas Carlyle and the American Renaissance: The Use of Sources and the Nature of Influence." Ph. D. Diss., George Washington University, 1975. [*Mel. Diss.,* # 374.]

Brodhead, Richard H. *Hawthorne, Melville, and the Novel.* Chicago: University of Chicago Press, 1976.

———. "*Mardi*: Creating the Creative." In *New Perspectives on Melville.* Ed. Faith Pullin. Kent, Ohio and Edinburgh: Kent State University Press and Edinburgh University Press, 1978, pp. 29–53.

Brodtkorb, Paul, Jr. *Ishmael's White World: A Phenomenological Reading of "Moby-Dick".* New Haven, Conn.: Yale University Press, 1965.

Brown, Clarence Arthur. *The Achievement of American Criticism: Representative Selections from the Three Hundred Years of American Criticism.* New York: Ronald Press Co., 1954.

Bryant, John. "Melville's Comic Debate: Geniality and the Aesthetics of Repose." *American Literature* 55 (May 1983): 151–70.

Cannon, Agnes D. "Melville's Concepts of the Poet and Poetry." *Arizona Quarterly* 31 (1975): 315–39.

Cawelti, John G. "Some Notes on the Structure of *The Confidence-Man*." *American Literature* 29 (November 1957): 278–88.

Chai, Leon. "Melville and Shelley: Speculations on Metaphysics, Morals, and Poetics in *Pierre* and 'Shelley's Vision.' " *ESQ* 29 (First Quarter 1983): 31–45.

Charvat, William, "Melville and the Common Reader." *Studies in Bibliography* 12 (1958): 41–57. Rpt. in *The Profession of Authorship in America, 1800–1870: The Papers of William Charvat*. Ed. Matthew J. Bruccoli. N. p.: Ohio State University Press, 1968, pp. 262–82. Reprinted here also is an earlier, longer version of this essay, entitled "Melville," pp. 204–61.

———. *The Origins of American Critical Thought, 1810–1835*. Philadelphia: University of Pennsylvania Press, 1936.

Chase, Richard. *The American Novel and Its Tradition*. New York: Doubleday, Anchor, 1957.

———. *Herman Melville: A Critical Study*. New York: Macmillan Co., 1949.

Clark, Harry Hayden. "Changing Attitudes in Early American Literary Criticism, 1800–1840." In *The Development of American Literary Criticism*. Ed. Floyd Stovall. Chapel Hill, N.C.: University of North Carolina Press, 1955; rpt. New Haven, Conn.: College and University Press, 1964, pp. 15–73.

Coffler, Gail. "Melville, Dana, Allston: Analogues in *Lectures on Art*." *Melville Society Extracts* 44 (November 1980): 1–6.

Colcord, Lincoln. "Notes on 'Moby Dick.' " *Freeman* 5 (23 August 1922): 559–69; (30 August 1922): 585–87.

Cook, Albert S. "Romance as Allegory: Melville and Kafka." In *The Meaning of Fiction*. Detroit: Wayne State University Press, 1960, pp. 242–59.

Cook, Charles H., Jr. "Ahab's 'Intolerable Allegory.' " *Boston University Studies in English* 1 (Spring-Summer 1955): 45–52.

Cowan, Bainard. *Exiled Waters: "Moby-Dick" and the Crisis of Allegory*. Baton Rouge: Louisiana State University Press, 1982.

Cowan, Wilson Walker. "Melville's Marginalia." Ph. D. Diss., Harvard University, 1965. [*Mel. Diss.*, #134.]

———. "Melville's Marginalia." In *Studies in the American Renaissance, 1978*. Ed. Joel Myerson. Boston: Twayne, 1978, pp. 279–302.

DeMille, George E. *Literary Criticism in America*. New York: Russell & Russell, 1931.

Dettlaff, Shirley M. "Ionian Form and Esau's Waste: Melville's View of Art in *Clarel*." *American Literature* 54 (May 1982): 212–28.

Donahue, Jane. "Melville's Classicism: Law and Order in His Poetry." *Papers on Language and Literature* 5 (Winter 1969): 63–72.

Dryden, Edgar A. *Thematics of Form: The Great Art of Telling the Truth*. Baltimore: Johns Hopkins University Press, 1968.

Engell, James. *The Creative Imagination; Enlightenment to Romanticism*. Cambridge: Harvard University Press, 1981.

Feidelson, Charles, Jr. *Symbolism and American Literature*. Chicago: University of Chicago Press, 1953.

Fletcher, Angus. *Allegory: The Theory of a Symbolic Mode*. Ithaca, N.Y.: Cornell University Press, 1964.

Foerster, Norman. *American Criticism: A Study in Literary Theory from Poe to the Present*. New York: Houghton Mifflin, 1928.

Fogle, Richard H. "Organic Form in American Criticism: 1840–1870." In *The Development of American Literary Criticism*. Ed. Floyd Stovall. Chapel Hill, N.C.: University of North Carolina Press, 1955. Rpt. New Haven, Conn.: College and University Press, 1964, pp. 75–111.

Foster, Elizabeth S. ed. *The Confidence-Man: His Masquerade*. By Herman Melville. New York: Hendricks House, 1954.

Franklin, H. Bruce. *The Wake of the Gods: Melville's Mythology*. Stanford, Calif.: Stanford University Press, 1963.

Frye, Northrop. *Anatomy of Criticism: Four Essays*. Princeton, N. J.: Princeton University Press, 1957.

Furrow, Sharon. "The Terrible Made Visible: Melville, Salvator Rosa, and Piranesi." *ESQ* 19 (Fourth Quarter 1973): 237–53.

Georgoudaki, Ekaterini. "Ancient Greek and Roman Pieces of Art in Herman Melville's Iconography." *Epistimoniki Epetirida tis Philosophikis Scholis tou Aristoteliou Panepistimiou Thessalonikis [Scholarly Journal of the School of Literature of the Aristotelian University of Thessalonika]* 21 (1983): 84–95.

Gilliland, Joe Drake. "Herman Melville's Portraits of the Artist," Ph.D. Diss, Arizona State University, 1979. [*Mel. Diss.*, #494.]

Gleckner, Robert F., and Gerald E. Enscoe, eds. *Romanticism: Points of View*. Englewood Cliffs, N.J.: Prentice-Hall, 1970.

Glenn, Barbara. "Melville and the Sublime in *Moby-Dick*." *American Literature* 48 (May 1976): 165–82.

Gretchko, John M. J. "The Glassy-eyed Hermit." *Melville Society Extracts* No. 48 (November 1981): 14–15.

Guetti, James. *The Limits of Metaphor: A Study of Melville, Conrad, and Faulkner*. Ithaca, N.Y.: Cornell University Press, 1967.

Hamalian, Leo. "Meville's Art." *Explicator* 8 (March 1950): Item 40.

Harris, Duncan S. "Melville and the Allegorical Tradition." Ph.D. Diss., Brandeis University, 1972. [*Mel. Diss.*, #313.]

Harris, Peter. "Melville: The Language of the Visible Truth." Ph.D. Diss., Indiana University, 1975. [*Mel. Diss.*, #385.]

Hayman, Allen. "The Real and the Original: Herman Melville's Theory of Prose Fiction." *Modern Fiction Studies* 8 (August 1962): 211–32.

Hipple, W. J. *The Beautiful, the Sublime, and the Picturesque in Eighteenth-Century British Aesthetic Theory*. Carbondale: Southern Illinois University Press, 1957.

Hirsch, David H. *Reality and Idea in the Early American Novel*. The Hague: Mouton, 1971.

Hoffman, Daniel. *Form and Fable in American Fiction*. New York: Oxford University Press, 1961.

Honig, Edwin. *Dark Conceit: The Making of Allegory*. Evanston, Ill.: Northwestern University Press, 1959.

————. "In Defense of Allegory." *Kenyon Review* 20 (Winter 1958): 1–19.

Howard, Leon. "Melville's Struggle with the Angel." *Modern Language Quarterly* 1 (June 1940): 195–206. In *Recognition*, pp. 223–36.

Jordan, Frank, Jr. *The English Romantic Poets: A Review of Research and Criticism.* 3d edition. New York: Modern Language Association of America, 1972.

Kiely, Robert. *The Romantic Novel in England.* Cambridge, Mass.: Harvard University Press, 1972.

Kuhns, Richard. "The Beautiful and the Sublime." *New Literary History* 13 (1981) 287–307.

Lewis, R.W.B. *The American Adam: Innocence, Tragedy, and Tradition in the Nineteenth Century.* Chicago: University of Chicago Press, 1955.

Litman, Vicki Halper, "The Cottage and the Temple: Melville's Symbolic Use of Architecture." *American Quarterly* 21 (Fall 1969): 630–38.

Lovejoy, Arthur. "On the Discrimination of Romanticisms." *PMLA* 39 (June 1924): 229–53.

Lucas, Thomas Edward. "Herman Melville: The Purpose of the Novel." *Texas Studies in Literature and Language* 13 (1972): 641–61.

Martin, Terence. *The Instructed Vision: Scottish Common Sense Philosophy and the Origins of American Fiction.* Bloomington, Ind.: Indiana University Press, 1961.

Mason, Ronald. *The Spirit Above the Dust: A Study of Herman Melville.* London: John Lehmann, 1951.

————. "Symbolism and Allegory in Melville." *Penguin New Writing* 22 (1948): 140–50.

Matthiessen, F. O. *American Renaissance: Art and Expression in the Age of Emerson and Whitman.* New York: Oxford University Press, 1941.

Meldrum, Barbara. "The Artist in Melville's *Mardi*." *Studies in the Novel* 1 (Winter 1969): 459–67.

Merrill, Robert. "Another Look at the American Romance." *American Philology* 78 (May 1981): 379–92.

Miller, James E., Jr. "Melville's Search for Form." *Bucknell Review* 8 (December 1959): 260–76.

————*A Reader's Guide to Herman Melville.* New York: Farran, Straus, and Cudahy, 1962.

Miller, Perry. "The Doctrine of the Symbol." *Virginia Quarterly Review* 29 (1953): 303–305.

————. *The Raven and the Whale: The War of Words and Wits in the Era of Poe and Melville.* New York: Harcourt, Brace, 1956.

————. "The Romance and the Novel." In *Nature's Nation.* Cambridge, Mass.: Harvard University Press, 1967.

————. "The Romantic Dilemma in American Nationalism and the Concept of Nature." In *Errand into the Wilderness.* Cambridge, Mass.: Harvard University Press, 1956.

Mills, Nicolaus. *American and English Fiction in the Nineteenth Century.* Bloomington: Indiana University Press, 1973.

Monk, Samuel H. *The Sublime: A Study of Critical Theories in XVIII- Century England.* New York: Modern Language Association of America, 1935.

Montgomery, John Paul. "The Creative Process and the Image of the Artist in Melville's *Mardi*." Ph.D. Diss., Ohio University, 1972. [*Mel. Diss.*, #288.]

Moore, Richard S. "Burke, Melville, and the 'Power of Blackness.' " *American Transcendental Quarterly* No. 29 (Winter 1976): 30–33.

———. "Piranesi, 'The Blanket,' and the 'Mathematical Sublime' in *Moby-Dick*." *Melville Society Extracts* No. 47 (September 1981): 1–3.

———. *That Cunning Alphabet: Melville's Aesthetics of Nature*. Amsterdam: Rodopi, 1982.

Mumford, Lewis. *Herman Melville*. New York: Harcourt, Brace, 1929.

Nevius, Blake. *Cooper's Landscapes: An Essay on the Picturesque Vision*. Berkeley: University of California Press, 1976.

Nicolson, Marjorie Hope. *Mountain Gloom and Mountain Glory: The Development of the Aesthetics of the Infinite*. Ithaca, N.Y.: Cornell University Press, 1959.

———. *Newton Demands the Muse: Newton's Opticks and the Eighteenth Century Poets*. Princeton, N.J.: Princeton University Press, 1946.

Novak, Barbara. *Nature and Culture: American Landscape and Painting 1825–1875*. New York: Oxford University Press, 1980.

Novak, Frank G., Jr. " 'Warmest Climes But Nurse the Cruellest Fangs': The Metaphysics of Beauty and Terror in *Moby-Dick*." *Studies in the Novel* 15 (Winter 1983): 332–43.

Obuchowski, Peter A. "*Billy Budd* and the Failure of Art." *Studies in Short Fiction* 15 (Fall 1978): 445–52.

Orians, G. Harrison. "The Rise of Romanticism, 1805–1855." In *Transitions in American Literary History*. Ed. Harry Hayden Clark. Durham, N.C.: Duke University Press, 1954, pp. 161–244.

———. "The Romance Ferment After *Waverley*." *American Literature* 3 (January 1932): 408–31.

Peckham, Morse. "Toward a Theory of Romanticism." *PMLA* 66 (March 1951): 5–23.

Perosa, Sergio. *American Theories of the Novel: 1793–1903*. New York: New York University Press, 1983.

Pochmann, Henry. *German Culture in America*. Madison: University of Wisconsin Press, 1957.

Poenicke, Klaus. "A View from the Piazza: Herman Melville and the Legacy of the European Sublime." *Comparative Literature Studies* 4 (1967): 267–81.

Pops, Martin Leonard. *The Melville Archetype*. Kent, Ohio: Kent State University Press, 1970.

Porte, Joel. *The Romance in America: Studies in Cooper, Poe, Hawthorne, Melville, and James*. Middletown, Conn.: Wesleyan University Press, 1969.

Post, Robert C. "A Theory of Genre: Romance, Realism, and Moral Reality." *American Quarterly* 33 (Fall 1981): 367–90.

Pritchard, John Paul. *Criticism in America*. Norman: University of Oklahoma Press, 1956.

———. *Literary Wise Men of Gotham*. Norman: University of Oklahoma Press, 1963.

Rathbun, John W. *American Literary Criticism, 1800–1860*. Boston: Twayne, 1979.

Richardson, Robert D. *Myth and Literature in the American Renaissance*. Bloomington: Indiana University Press, 1978.

Robillard, Douglas. "Melville's *Clarel* and the Parallel of Poetry and Painting." *North Dakota Quarterly* 51 (Spring 1983): 107– 20.

———. "The Visual Arts in Melville's *Redburn.*" *Essays in Arts and Sciences* 12 (March 1983): 43–60.

Roundy, Nancy. "Fancies, Reflections and Things: The Imagination as Perception in the 'The Piazza.' " *College Language Association Journal* 20 (1977): 539–46.

Rourke, Constance. *American Humor: A Study in National Character.* New York: Harcourt, Brace & Co., 1931.

Sanford, Charles L. "National Self-Consciousness and the Concept of the Sublime." *The Quest for Paradise: Europe and the American Moral Imagination.* Urbana: University of Illinois Press, 1961.

Schelling, Hannah-Beate. "The Role of the Brothers Schlegel in American Literary Criticism as Found in Selected Periodicals, 1812–1833." *American Literature* 43 (January 1972): 563–79.

Schless, Howard H. "Flaxman, Dante, and Melville's *Pierre.*" *Bulletin of the New York Public Library* 64 (February 1960): 65–82.

Schunk, Ferdinand. *Das lyrische Werk Herman Melvilles.* [*Herman Melville's Lyrical Work.*] Bonn: Bouvier, 1976.

Sealts, Merton M., Jr. "Melville and Emerson's Rainbow." *ESQ* 26 (Second Quarter, 1980): 53–78. Rpt. in *Pursuing Melville, 1940– 1980.* Madison: University of Wisconsin Press, 1982, pp. 250–77.

———. "Melville and the Platonic Tradition." In *Pursuing Melville, 1940–1980.* Madison: University of Wisconsin Press, 1982, pp. 278–336.

———. *Melville as Lecturer.* Cambridge, Mass.: Harvard University Press, 1957.

Seelye, John. *Melville: The Ironic Diagram.* Evanston, Ill.: Northwestern University Press, 1970.

Short, Bryan Collier. "Form as Vision in Herman Melville's *Clarel.*" *American Literature* 50 (January 1979): 553–69.

Short, Raymond W. "Melville as Symbolist." *University of Kansas City Review* 15 (August 1949): 39–49.

Shurr, William H. *The Mystery of Iniquity: Melville as Poet, 1857– 1891.* Lexington: University Press of Kentucky, 1972.

Siegel, Mark Andrew. "Dialectics of Consciousness: Melville and the Realistic Imagination." Ph.D. Diss., Rutgers University, 1977. [*Mel. Diss.,* #462.]

Smith, Bernard. *Forces in American Criticism.* New York: Harcourt, Brace & Co., 1939.

Spencer, Benjamin. *The Quest for Nationality: An American Literary Campaign.* Syracuse, N.Y.: Syracuse University Press, 1957.

Stafford, John. *The Literary Criticism of "Young America": A Study in the Relationship of Politics and Literature, 1837–1850.* Berkeley: University of California Press, 1952.

Star, Morris. "Melville's Markings in Walpole's *Anecdotes of Painting in England.*" *Papers of the Bibliographic Society of America* 66 (July-September 1972): 321–27.

———. "Melville's Use of the Visual Arts." Ph.D. Diss., Northwestern University, 1964. [*Mel. Diss.,* #131.]

Stern, Milton. *The Fine-Hammered Steel of Herman Melville.* Urbana: University of Illinois Press, 1957.

Stevens, Harry R. "Melville's Music." *Musicology* 2 (July 1949): 405–21.

Stubbs, John Caldwell. *The Pursuit of Form: A Study of Hawthorne and the Romance.* Urbana: University of Illinois Press, 1970.

Sundermann, K. H. *Herman Melville's Gedankengut: Eine kritische Untersuchung seiner weltanschaulichen Grundideen.* [*The Scope of Herman Melville's Thought.*] Berlin: Arthur Collignon, 1937.

Thorp, Willard. *Herman Melville: Representative Selections, with Introduction, Bibliography, and Notes.* New York: American Book, 1938.

Tindall, William York. *The Literary Symbol.* Bloomington: Indiana University Press, 1955.

Trilling, Lionel. *The Liberal Imagination: Essays on Literature and Society.* Garden City, N.Y.: Doubleday, 1950.

Turnage, Maxine. "Melville's Concern with the Arts in *Billy Budd.*" *Arizona Quarterly* 28 (1972): 74–82.

Tuveson, Ernest. *The Imagination as a Means of Grace: Locke and the Aesthetics of Romanticism.* Berkeley: University of California Press, 1960.

———. "Space, Deity, and the 'Natural Sublime.' "*Modern Language Quarterly* 12 (March 1951): 20–38.

Van Doren, Carl. "Contemporaries of Cooper." In *Cambridge History of American Literature,* 3 vols. Ed. William Peterfield Trent, et al. New York: G.P. Putnam's Sons, 1917, pp. 307–25.

Vincent, Howard P. "Ishmael, Writer and Art Critic." In *Themes and Directions in American Literature.* Ed. Ray B. Browne and Donald Pizer. Lafayette, Ind.: Purdue University Press, 1969, pp. 69–79.

Wallace, Robert K. "Melville's Prints and Engravings at the Berkshire Athenaeum." [forthcoming in *Essays in Arts and Sciences.*]

———. "Teaching *Moby-Dick* in the Light of Turner." In *Approaches to Teaching Moby-Dick.* Ed. Martin Bickman. New York: MLA, 1985, pp. 135–40.

Weaver, Raymond M. *Herman Melville: Mariner and Mystic.* New York: Doran, 1921.

Weiskel, Thomas. *The Romantic Sublime: Studies in the Structure and Psychology of Transcendence.* Baltimore: Johns Hopkins University Press, 1976.

Wellek, Rene. "The Concept of Romanticism in Literary History." *Comparative Literature*: 1 (Winter 1949): 1–23 and (Spring 1979): 147–72.

———. *A History of Modern Criticism, 1750–1950.* Vols. 1 and 2. New Haven, Conn.: Yale University Press, 1955.

Wimsatt, William K., and Cleanth Brooks. *Literary Criticism: A Short History.* New York: Random House, 1957.

Wright, Nathalia. "Form as Function in Melville." *PMLA* 67 (June 1952): 330–40.

Zoellner, Alan Frederick. "The Splendid Labyrinth: Language, Consciousness, and the Contraries in Melville's Later Fiction." Ph.D. Diss., Indiana University, 1977. [*Mel. Diss.,* #467.]

PART FIVE

MELVILLE: HIS MARK

22

MELVILLE AND THE MYTHS OF MODERNISM

Kingsley Widmer

In Woody Allen's movie *Zelig* (1983), the chameleon anti-hero has been traumatized into his shifting conformity, he wryly informs us, by his utter embarrassment at not having read *Moby-Dick*. The epilogue notes that, after a life of therapeutic struggle, Zelig had finally started to read Melville's book but dies without finishing it. Thus, he of perplexed identity slips around what has become a touchstone of modern American sensibility, as does writer-director-actor Allen as he burlesques the mythically central Melville. *Zelig* may be viewed as a postmodernist parable of the role of Melville which was created by literary modernism.

While the nineteenth-century author can hardly be held responsible for the modernism he predates, Melville's portentous role, so evident behind the joking play in *Zelig*, is considerably the creation of a number of modernist poet-prophets, overreaching writers who used Melville's works as part of their dialectic with twentieth-century culture. In effect, they made Melville into a protomodernist. A somewhat peculiar Melville emerges, usually the alienated artist as metaphysical adventurer and visionary. Not for most of the modernists was Melville a faltering popular fictionist, ambivalent traditionalist family man, jocular autodidact, dour customhouse clerk, and a figure considerably of his Eastern Provincial American place and ugly mid-nineteenth-century times. If a good bit of the specificity of Melville is lost—and, especially for the reader, much of Melville's humor—something larger has often replaced it. As a result of modernism, Melville became not only a visionary artist and soulful symbol of American cultural pathos but also the fulcrum of a great modern myth. Thus, he was indeed something to reckon with, or to flee from.

In contrast, recent academic studies tend to show a Melville not only imbedded in his own times but of a backward-looking sensibility. In this scholarly emphasis, Melville was much involved in his familial heritage and in moral-political arguments of an earlier history. (See such historicist studies as Michael Paul Rogin and James Duban.) Paradoxically, the efforts to place Melville in his time, and in earlier ideologies, presupposes the large importance given Melville by the modernists as a prophet of later times. But my concern here is less with the scholarly institutionalization of Melville than with its source in some of the arguments of significant artist-intellectuals identified as modernists. In most informed judgments Melville was a minor author—if taken into account at all—until the years following World War I when, for two generations, he became a pivotal figure in American consciousness.

The nineteenth-century writer not only supplied apocalyptic metaphors for modernists struggling with Western cultural traditions but also contributed to a mythic desire for American cultural grandeur. Once considered the faltering author of rather obscure works, Melville became identified as the new American Homer and Dante and Shakespeare. While the modernism which helped produce this change has receded from its highwater mark, the cultural reevaluation it engendered self-generatingly continues. It may thus not be surprising that a current Jungian interpreter of modernist British poetry portentously announces, when he turns to American literature, that Melville "is the revolutionary forbearer [sic] of twentieth-century sensibility" (Ralph Maud, p. 696.)

APOCALYPTIC MELVILLE

A crucial figure in establishing Melville-as-modernist was the renegade British author D. H. Lawrence. He fortuitously read a friend's copy of *Moby-Dick* in 1916 (*Collected Letters*, p. 424). As part of his rage against Britain and the Great War, he was reaching out for various other writings and values. His un-British stretch was conditioned by prophetic purposes, influenced by such modernist prophets as Nietzsche (Kingsley Widmer, "Dark Prophecy"). By 1918 Lawrence was publishing versions of a group of essays he had sketched out on nineteenth-century American writers, though he did not publish in a periodical the one he had apparently done on *Moby-Dick*. In 1922 he collected the rewritten essays as *Studies in Classic American Literature*. Prior to his final revisions he had evidently read Raymond M. Weaver's *Herman Melville: Mariner and Mystic* (1921), the rather unprobing study sometimes credited with the "Melville Revival," since he echoes several of its points (Armin Arnold, pp. 28–

29). Weaver, however, neither started nor much shaped Lawrence's apocalyptic Melville.

Lawrence's often sharply critical essays on American literature are not scholarly nor are they, in most conventional senses, literary criticism. Rather, they come out a curious combination of personal essay, jeering polemic, and prophetic religious rumination which became somewhat hysterically wisecracking in the critic's exacerbated revisions while living in America (compare *Studies* with the earlier versions now published as *The Symbolic Meaning*.) For Lawrence, America's nineteenth-century writers "reached the pitch of extreme consciousness" (p. 2). We may connect this with modernism, but in the repressive order of their times that consciousness necessarily took form in "subterfuge" and "double meanings" which need to be exposed. Here was a program for what was to become an interpretive industry! (Edmund Wilson may have given some impetus to it in the World War II period by including all of the *Studies* in his *Shock of Recognition*, followed several years later by the popular separate reprinting of the *Studies*.)

In a brief survey essay, "The Spirit of Place," Lawrence insists on "saving the American tale from the American artist" (p. 13) since the story can reveal the truth often obscured by the lying American writer in his national pose of innocence, optimism, and freedom. In sad fact, Americans exist in terrible isolation in their purely negative freedom from authority and community. They come out recreant Europeans lacking creative positive freedom, and thus full humanity.

This stands especially pertinent to Melville. In the first of his two chapters on Melville, primarily on *Typee* and *Omoo*, Lawrence finds the underlying Melville anti-human, expressive of the "Viking" and "Northern" anti-life values in contrast with warmer blooded Mediterranean culture. Whatever its applicability to Melville, this contrast has been emphasized as early as Lawrence's prewar Italian sketches and continued in his middle-period fictions (*The Lost Girl*, etc.). The contrast of "Northern" and "Mediterranean" sensibilities has, of course, a long European history, and holds a major place in other twentieth-century European writers, too (Forster and Ford, Giono and Camus, et al.). As Lawrence saw it, the dominating Northern European recreant Americans, who negatively fled European culture, developed an extreme Northern fear of sensuality and human responsiveness. So with Melville; "Never did a man instinctively hate human life, our human life . . . more than Melville did" (p. 145). His South Sea adventures were a desperate and faltering attempt to escape the Northern puritanism, a search for the paradisically ideal in the primitive. Here Lawrence also identifies with the desperate quest, with good reason. But: "We can't go back. And Melville couldn't" (p. 149).

Lawrence's Melville also tried in the picaresque *Omoo* to identify with the rebelliously roguish but was afraid of it. Bound to the anti-life American pursuit of the "ideal," Melville was trapped in religious moralism and restriction, including conventional marriage and a life of disillusionment, after he dallied in his early fictions with fleeing it. (Lawrence, of course, had long been fleeing his own repressive and puritanic provincial upbringing.) Citing *Pierre* (probably second-handedly), Lawrence insists that Melville shows "the old pure ideal in itself becomes an impure thing of evil" (p. 154). Even without the bad *Pierre*, Lawrence views Melville as "writhing" all his life because of his demands for the ideal in morality, marriage, friendship, and belief. Thus Melville denied rich, tangible human responsiveness— "He refused life" (p. 155).

This negative side of the modernist mythic Melville—larger, and no doubt simpler, than life—was to be restated by many later writers influenced by Lawrence. However extremely he put it, surely Lawrence perceives something importantly Melvillean. Many have noted of Melville his drastic inadequacy in presenting male-female relationships, the peculiarly twisted male relationships, and, more generally, the often guiltily punitive and anxiously forlorn emphasis. But other issues should be recognized here. Through much of his writing, artistic and prophetic, Lawrence engaged in the modern existential attack on Christianity and the essentialist idealism related to it. He viewed Western idealism as a fundamental falsity—dualistic, rationalistic, anti-sensual, unholistic. He sees Melville as caught up in the same issues. Lawrence repeatedly announces that he himself has given up idealism, but concludes that Melville has not. In his fractured and sweeping comments, then, Lawrence views Melville as a symptomatic victim of the duplicitous American form of Western diseased consciousness.

Lawrence's longer chapter on *Moby-Dick* takes a more exalted view of Melville's struggles of consciousness. He relished quoting at length some of the novel's better representative passages because it is "a great book," a "surpassingly beautiful book." But at the same time he is the hardnosed critic: "Nobody can be more clownish, more clumsy and sententiously in bad taste, than Herman Melville even in a great book like *Moby-Dick*" (p. 157). He reasonably senses that Melville is often "not sure of himself," "amateurishly" ponderous, sometimes a "solemn ass," and quite unable to deal with "human contacts" (p. 158). This is more freely responsive than the usual learned criticism.

Curiously but typically, Lawrence turns some of his negative criticism into positive. Melville's very lack of full human dimensions—*Moby-Dick*'s abstractionism—provides much of the power in profoundly recording "the extreme transitions of the isolated, far-driven soul" (p. 159). Such explorations appear to Lawrence to be the special province of classic American literature. He is also acutely aware of the strange but representative Americanness of *Moby-Dick* in its combination of the documentary and the metaphysical. He notes the exaggerated efficiency of

"American industry" (whaling) combined with an antithetical poetic overreaching—"all this practicality in the service of a mad, mad chase" (p.
162). Lawrence makes other suggestive points. He is (so far as I am
aware) the first to emphasize the "phallicism" of "The Cassock" chapter.
He also praises Melville's powerful poetry of non-human nature, so
different from Romantic subjectivism and Victorian sentimentalization
(a direction in which Lawrence's nature descriptions had been moving).
Melville, in sum, was the great poet in American prose.

The heart of the poem of *Moby-Dick*, as Lawrence sees it, shows the
destructively "extended consciousness" of "northern monomania," with
the *Pequod* as the "symbol of this civilized world of ours" (p. 172). Melville's deeper purpose is to reveal our—not just his— "fatality," the
"Doom of our white day." American culture, despite its guise of energetic
innocence, reveals this doomed civilization in its farthest reaches.

"What then is Moby Dick?—he is the deepest blood-being of the white
race." The quest of the *Pequod* is to destroy that being, guided "by the
maniacal fanaticism of our white mental consciousness" (p. 173). As
Lawrence's concluding elliptical interpretation adds, "Jesus, the Redeemer, was Cetus, Leviathan. And all the Christians his little fishes" (p.
174). Apparently, then, Melville pursuing the white whale was out God-
killing—necessarily so, since our great white father is the enemy of sensual human wholeness. Melville thus exposed, for those willing to see
through the tale's subterfuges, the necessary nihilism of humanly abstracting Western civilization.

Lawrence's interpretation is not altogether consistent—for example,
the white whale is both deepest "blood-being" and Christian God (antithetical terms in Lawrence)—but the plausible response might be that
such commentary does not aim to be systematic but suggestive and provocative. The main suggestion is that Melville, in spite of his terrible
limitations and idealistic self-defeat, struggled into a tale revealing the
nuclear conflict of white American consciousness, its abstracting doom.
And what of America since its prophet? As Lawrence mockingly noted
earlier, it is just mostly "post-mortem effects" (p. 173).

Surveying all of Lawrence's fictions, I am not aware of any significant
allusion to Melville. "Influence," then, is not the appropriate issue. Imaginative recreation seems more to the point. Lawrence's Melville, of
course, has been drastically selected to hyperbolically emphasize only a
few issues in the early books and *Moby-Dick*. But that was Lawrence's
purpose toward a larger statement about America, an apocalyptic mythology with Melville as culture hero.

NEO-ROMANTIC MELVILLE

Hart Crane, a half-generation younger, admiringly read D. H. Lawrence's *Studies in Classic American Literature*, as we see in his letters (R.W.

Butterfield, pp. 132 ff.). Following other references in his letters, we may surmise that Crane read *Moby-Dick* as early as 1920, before the academic Revival and before Lawrence's book, and may have re-read it a number of times before his early self-destruction in 1932. References in his letters and poems also indicate that he probably read *Typee*, *Omoo*, *White-Jacket*, perhaps some of the other fictions, and the poems in *Battle-Pieces*. Becharmed with Melville's ornate style and portentous symbolism, Crane saw him not only as a crucial forbear for his own visionary poetics but also as an especially American hero of consciousness, a native Rimbaud. Typically, Crane saw the white whale (after a reported third and fourth reading) as "a metaphysical image of the universe" (as quoted in John Unterecker, p. 739). There seems to be nothing more specific; Crane's images and ideas often must remain essentially obscure.

Best known of Crane's specific responses to visionary Melville is his sixteen-line lyric poem "At Melville's Tomb" (*Collected Poems*, p. 100), apparently written in 1925. One of Crane's less involuted ironies relates to the title, for while the tangible Herman Melville may be buried on land, his real entombment is in the sea—the sea not as an actual place but as the mythic eternal resting place of mariners. Dead mariners' transcendent yearnings produce cosmic "silent answers" that "crept across the stars." Though one of Crane's calmer poems, it, too, is one of his strange arguments for a visionary reach without a recognizable vision.

"At Melville's Tomb," many commentators have noted, draws on the finale of *Moby-Dick*, the "circuit calms" following the sinking of the *Pequod*. It posits that the dead mariners carry a special knowledge: they "bequeath / An embassy" and have as the "calyx of death's bounty" a "livid hieroglyph." In sum, they have a sacramental cosmic vision, however incommunicable from their watery grave. But much of the fame of this rather obscure poem has to do with Crane's attempt at its explication and justification. So with his letter to the editor of *Poetry* where the poem and related correspondence were first published (Philip Horton, pp. 329–34). In answer to a query about the line "Frosted eyes there were that lifted altars," Crane replied "that a man, not knowing perhaps a definite god yet being endowed with a reverence for deity—such a man naturally postulates a deity somehow, and the altar of that deity by the *action* of the eyes *lifted* in searching" (*Complete Poems*, p. 239). Apparently the fixed dead vision ("frosted") of mariner Melville expresses such non-explicit sacramental vision. While less transcendental readers than Crane may doubt the reverence of the Melville of *Moby-Dick*, except by way of blasphemy, Crane's compacted exaltation of his predecessor as a "fabulous shadow" with quite unknowable knowledge remains self-definingly protected by its very oblivion.

Crane elsewhere used Melville, as in two lines from *Battle-Pieces*— "O, the navies old and oaken, / O, the Temeraire no more!"—as an epigraph to the "Cutty Sark" section of *The Bridge* (*Collected Poems*, p. 27). Possibly the quote may have had some private significance to Crane, but the communicable one would seem to be simply, and vaguely, a sense of loss of the past. Yet here, and elsewhere in Crane, there may be a more general significance. Crane, though no mariner, had what can plausibly be called an obsession with sea imagery. With no American Homer, Camoens, or the like, available in the direct cultural heritage for mythic frame and allusive density, what else than Melville? A society deterministically bounded by seas may, in its poets' minds, yearn for the maritime reference points and drama. Modernism self-consciously aimed to expand the cultural heritage, and thus Melville serves as a sea-culture hero. Crane so treated him.

We need not rehearse the various other echoes and parallels of Melville in Crane's poems since the larger relationship seems evident. One well-known critic has called the Crane-Melville connection a "multiple and profoundly illuminating affinity" (R.W.B. Lewis, *Critical Essays*, 1982, p. 83; for further examples of possible Melville influence, see his *The Poetry of Hart Crane*, 1967). However, the relationship appears forced, with little literary, moral, or metaphysical affinity, except perhaps homosexuality. In the 1920s Crane stumbled on Melville as a symbol-searching forbear, and he desperately turned him into a natural but unfulfilled mystic like himself. Further encouraged by reading Lawrence, and the early studies emphasizing Melville as a portentously unusual figure, he was prepared to find an affinity that may have had little literal substance. Thus are literary heritages sometimes forced. Crane wanted a rebellious and maritime American symbolist with transcendental yearnings, and that is the one he found. Thus he contributed to the myth of an obscure Melville which frightens the Zelig-sort of reader.

Still, Crane's mystical-romantic longings were also marked by an effort at intense honesty. As he wrote in his most ambitious poetic effort, *The Bridge*, "Dream cancels dream in this new realm of fact" (*Collected Poems*, p. 32). By twisting and heightening his fragments (including the fragmented past containing Melville), Crane wanted to turn the overpowering compulsive actuality of America into affirmative myth. (See Widmer, *Literary Rebel*, 1965, pp. 111 ff.) The naturalistic reality—including the incommunicable from dead mariner Melville—remained stronger. The key to this may be less in the obscurely overreaching metaphors than in the disenchantment of Crane's last years, as with the "key" in his final volume's title poem "Key West" (*Collected Poems*, p. 113). In this bitter but controlled piece of invective, his earlier mechanical dreams of ecstasy have become "apish nightmares" that lead only to a "dead conclusion." Accepting the hard self of disillusionment ("my salient faith annealed me"), in a universe indifferent to meaning ("skies impartial"), he now has a more precise illumination ("frugal noon"). No Melvillean hieroglyphs and altars here. The compulsion and fraud of the American actuality turned dreams to nightmares, sacramental mythos to machined fake, and left only the despairing rage of the isolated wanderer. Like Melville in his conversation with Hawthorne in England, Crane has accepted "annihilation" (*Mel. Log*, p. 529). "Monody shall not wake the mariner," Crane wrote in the penultimate line of "At Melville's Tomb." Nor finally for Crane will anything else; there is no mystic transcendence. (Perhaps that is why "Key West" has not been given its due—R.W.B. Lewis doesn't even mention it in a whole book on Crane's poetry.)

CHRISTOLOGICAL MELVILLE

A sharp contrast to Crane's transcendental-yearning Melville might be the use made by a slightly younger W.H. Auden. Resident in America on the way to becoming a U.S. citizen, the British poet may also have been looking for usable American ancestors. Since Auden was also converting back to Anglo-Catholicism, much of the American literary heritage (Transcendentalism, for example) was not to his taste. Always an extremely tendentious poet and ideologist, Auden finds, or makes, a Melville who is the proponent of the traditional Christian moral order.

"Herman Melville," Auden's forty-one line elegy (*Collected Shorter Poems*," pp. 145–46), first published (and apparently written) in 1939, emphasizes the aging figure. Melville had, the poem starts, "sailed into an extraordinary mildness." This Melville had given up adventuresome edenic hopes and arrived at "the new knowledge" that "Goodness existed." Unlike the Melville of Lawrence and Crane, this is a post-Romantic figure, and one who was to become academically popular in the conservative 1950s—the reconciled old Melville and ideologist of Christian submission.

Moby-Dick comes into the third stanza of Auden's elegy with its "maniac hero" hunting "the ambiguous monster that had maimed his sex." This Freudian interpretation, carrying over part of Auden's earlier ideology, however, is subordinated to a simpler, traditional moral emphasis. For the later Melville has discovered that "Evil is unspectacular and always human" (in contrast to spectacular Ahab/Moby-Dick). "Goodness," too, is an "every day" thing. By implication (in the context of Auden's other writings), Melville, the New York Custom House clerk, has turned into Soren Kierkegaard's Christian-as-postman (a major metaphor of the "ethical stage" in *Either/Or*.) Oddly, this ordinary goodness takes symbolic form in Billy Budd destroyed by lover Claggart (and later Vere). With this old ethical sense, Melville had recovered from the nightmare vision of *Moby-Dick* and, like his Billy, knew that "Even the punishment was human and a form of love." For Auden, this Christian ethic signals Melville's return to the certainty of his childhood religion (as with Auden) on which he had always really depended. "Reborn, he cried in exultation and surrender / 'The Godhead is broken like bread. We are the pieces.' " The poem's coda to this ritualized ethic is that Melville then sat down and "wrote a story" (*Billy Budd*) around the convert's knowledge of orthodox good and evil.

A decade later, Auden more elaborately extended his mythicizing of Melville in a speculative prose work, *The Enchafèd Flood* (1950), subtitled "The Romantic Iconography of the Sea." The mode became especially fashionable toward the end of the modernist movement in America— the allegorization of literature in a quasi-theological argument. Neither quite reasoned literary criticism nor moral prophecy, it submerged both in an "anagogical method" of using literature for old didactic ends. In an arbitrary selection of romantic words about the sea (and desert parallels), Auden looked for that which "stands for"—a manner somewhat derisively known elsewhere as "symbol hunting." *Moby-Dick*, of course, seemed highly suitable material for such gaming, and Auden bluntly enlists "Melville-Ishmael" in his dogmatic pursuit by announcing that his predecessor saw the allegorical symbol as "a declaration of the power and majesty of God, which transcends any human standards" (p. 65). Certainly this stands as an extreme projection of Auden. On the basis of such ineffable understanding, Auden catalogues some of the materials of *Moby-Dick*. His moral-divine pattern appears to be considerably indebted to such Christian allegorists as Kierkegaard and Charles Williams (George W. Bahlke, pp. 69 ff.).

For his characterization of the "Romantic Hero," Auden combines Ishmael and Ahab in a disapproving typology that emphasizes melancholy, isolation, and despair. In sum, Melville shows that Romanticism defeats itself. It serves as an ethic of futility: "Nor does Ahab believe for a moment that if he succeeds in killing the White Whale, he will be any happier" (*Flood*, p. 114). So where lies human happiness? In submission. Auden's allegorical exposition makes Father Mapple's sermon "the essential clue to the meaning of the whole book" (p. 119). Melville wants us to learn, like Jonah, submission of the self to the absolute deity. Auden simply ignores any possible complexity or ambiguity in Melville's art and thought. Thus, his rather pedantic allegorization of the characters in *Moby-Dick* just carries out the given moral. Starbuck suffers from inadequate transcendence, Stubb from inadequate suffering, Flask from inadequate sensitivity—three variations on the same point of unredemption. The rest of Melville's materials can be lined up with similar neatness. In his condition of "castration," Ahab is "perhaps the greatest representation" of "defiant despair" in literature (p. 137).

Auden also repeats the view given a decade earlier in his Melville elegy, allegorizing *Billy Budd* as the proper conclusion to *Moby-Dick*. Melville showed the change in Billy "from the unconscious Adam into the conscious Christ" (p. 147). It is an astonishing reading. Again, no perplexities and contradictions are allowed in the holy canon. The transcendental crux covers all. Melville went from the nightmare of evil, the Romantic Hero, in *Moby-Dick*, to the vision of Christian redemption, the "Religious Hero," in his final fiction. Such terms, however, come out mere ideological sleight-of-hand. As Charles Olson, among others, noted, there can be no Christian tragic hero, only the saint (*Human Universe*, p. 115). In Auden, as perhaps more subtly in such sources of his as Kierkegaard, the religious hero comes forth as just a recostumed romantic hero, which undercuts the issue.

Auden's allegorization of Melville no doubt has the convenience of dogmatic neatness. Curiously, it lacks much of literary concern; though a skillful poetic craftsman, Auden says nothing of Melville's details, style, or other tangible sensibility. A crass religiosity overrides everything but the one convert paradigm. But perhaps Auden should not be credited, or blamed, for the widespread mid-century popularity of such Christian allegorization of Melville. He and others were simply twisting what had become a fashionable literary figure to their own mythic purposes. The narrow Christian neo-orthodoxy had been cultivated for a generation in the anti-romantic (Eliotic) side of Anglo-American modernism. The proponents of that religious mythology may have been led to incorporate Melville within it partly because he had been taken up in quite different ways by the apocalyptic and romantic modernists. The now mythically large Melville could be used in antithetical ways by selectively choosing his ambiguities in a kind of cultural heritage co-optation.

We can note several similarities in the re-creations of Melville by these modernists despite their drastic differences. All three poets valued Melville as a prophetic hero. All three viewed him as an extreme romantic, whether demonic (Lawrence), mystical (Crane), or finally Christian-redemptive (Auden). All treated Melville as much larger than his place, time, and mixed qualities might seem to call for, thus giving him an eternal relevance. The high place of Melville in the American literary canon by mid-twentieth century must reflect such exalted, mythical, usage. A multitude of lesser exalted usages—theatrical, cinematic, operatic, as well as the literary and subliterary—confirm the cultural apotheosis.

THREE MORALISTIC MYTHOGRAPHERS OF MELVILLE

An ex- and anti-modernist poet and moralist on Melville also reinforces some of the myth—Yvor Winters. Though now generally regarded as a minor poet-critic digging a quite narrow neoclassical vein, including often its archaic diction, forced syntax, and exclusionary perspective, Winters was an influential figure. He engendered a school of frosty poets, and his moralistic literary views had considerable reverberations. At a highpoint in the historical expansion of Melville's reputation, Winters wrote a squib: "To Herman Melville in 1951": "Saint Herman, grant me this: that I may be / Saved from the worms who have infested thee" (*Collected Poems*, p. 183). I have no way of determining if the worms included Auden, whose *Enchafèd Flood* was published the preceding year, but, given Winters's many polemics in poetry and prose, he certainly intended many of the legion of crawling academic interpreters on Melville's literary corpus.

Literary corpses were not in short supply in Winters's frequently simple dogmatism. In his early writings (in the 1920s), he had been a small modernist poet, experimenting with forms, though a traditionalist scholar (Renaissance and Romance philology), but he developed revulsion against modernism, poetically and intellectually, and became an absolutistic moral and theistic curmudgeon. His fullest discussion of Melville is included in his 1938 *Maule's Curse: Seven Studies in the History of American Obscurantism* (later incorporated into *In Defense of Reason*, pp. 151–343). An earlier critical volume attacked obscurity in modernist poetry, including that of Hart Crane (*Primitivism and Decadence*). In the later volume he broadens the definition of obscurity to make it fundamental to the history of American sensibility. Maule's curse (the metaphor taken from Hawthorne's *The House of the Seven Gables*) derives, he claims, from the moral muddles of American puritanism, though he makes it pandemic to include Calvinistic determinism, romantic reactions, and a variety of resultant despairing moral relativisms. Curiously, Melville, "the greatest man of his era and of his nation" (*Defense*, p. 173), seems the hero of Winters's discontent. For while Melville succumbed to American cursed confusion in *Mardi* and *Pierre*, he morally overcame it in such works as *Moby-Dick* and "Benito Cereno."

In "Herman Melville and the Problems of Moral Navigation," Winters seasons simple summary and lengthy quotations with flat judgments. The white whale is "the chief symbol and spirit of evil" (*Defense*, p. 201). Ahab's "sin, in the minor sense, is monomaniac vengeance; in the major, the will to destroy the spirit of evil itself, an intention blasphemous because beyond human powers and infringing upon the purposes of God" (p. 211). Calvinism should be blamed: "Ahab is the magnificent fruition of Maule's curse. Melville . . . escaped the curse by comprehending it" (p. 220). In Winters's moralistic twist, a romantic-appearing Melville thus turns out to be anti-romantic.

Winters's allegorical platter is crudely one-dimensional; for example, Starbuck is simply "the critical intellect." He also misses most of the points with the admired "Benito Cereno," which he sees as simply large human "evil in action, as shown in the negroes, and of the effect of that action, as shown in Cereno" (p. 222). That ignores dominant Delano and all subtlety and irony, including that of Melville's concern with the Yankee captain as representative, benevolently rationalizing American. *Pierre* and *The Confidence-Man* show a disgusting temporary lapse in Melville's "morality" so that "truth is absolute ambiguity" (p. 227). Much of *Mardi* is immoral romanticism. *Israel Potter* "is one of the few great novels of pure adventure in English" (p. 233). Not much justification for these valuations is even suggested. *Billy Budd* is Melville's "final masterpiece," despite the "rusty" novelist displaying "a little structural awkwardness" (p. 230). Vere's "solution" of killing Billy so as to support "public order" is good; indeed, it was "likewise the solution of Socrates" (p. 231).

The weirdly forced socratic allusion also appears in Winters's poem, "To a Portrait of Melville in My Library," probably written in the late 1930s (*Collected Poems*, p. 170). Here Melville is credited with a "dreadful heart that won Socratic peace!" How Vere's murdering Billy, or Melville's writing a tortuous story about it, makes a martyred Socrates remains unclear. The sonnet's constraints may further obscure Winters's response to Melville. Apparently, he should be seen as the "unmoved" presiding spirit of "Wisdom and wilderness," whimsically presented in the library by "Plato and Aristotle" and an "ancient powder horn." Those may be metaphors for Winters's prejudices (Davis, p. 3), but the supposed Melville-Winters affinity, based on a recognition of "malevolent and demonic evil which is associated with instinct, chaos and the unknown" (Davis, p. 182), confuses Winter's simple revulsions with Melville's ambiguous fascinations.

Winters's Melville poem concludes, "The midnight trembles when I hear thy voice, / The noon's immobile when I meet thine eyes." The adoration is as quaint as the manner. Perhaps Winters's Melville should be credited with conversion to the traditional absolute: "thou rose reborn"—or is this praise for the Melville Revival which he later condemned? Yet Winter's obscurantist exaltation of Melville may have had some historical influence.

More interesting and suggestive was another poet-scholar on Melville, Charles Olson. He came out of that strain of modernist aesthetics developed by Ezra Pound and William Carlos Williams, though neither of them showed any interest at all in Melville. Olson was a central character in the literary group often identified as "the Black Mountain poets," and something of a cult figure of literary vanguardism following World War II. He was also a Melville devotee and scholar whose influential book treated Melville as a prophet of change in American consciousness and used him for what he saw as his own prophetic vision.

After writing an M.A. thesis on Melville (Wesleyan, 1933), Olson did original research on Melville's reading and annotations, especially of Shakespeare. His early statement on Melville's reading appeared as an article, "Lear and Melville" (1938), and was centrally used by F.O. Matthiessen (one of Olson's teachers) in his later highly regarded interpretation of Melville (*American Renaissance*, 1941). But Olson's view of Melville was both more personal and more cosmic than the conventional traditions of academic criticism in his time allowed. Strongly influenced by Lawrence's *Studies* (and by some of Lawrence's poorer cranky writings), Olson wished to treat Melville as a prophet and mythic source. He reportedly wrote a long book on Melville, never published, and then, under the aegis of editor-writer Edward Dahlberg (see below), finally published a rather different book, *Call Me Ishmael* (1947), a curious little essay that elliptically combines dry influence-scholarship (Shakespeare, whaling narratives) with gnomic and ecstatic pronouncements. "I am willing to ride Melville's image of man, whale and ocean to find in him prophecies, lessons he himself would not have spelled out" (p. 13). Olson had only a small interest in the historical Melville and in the actual texts of his works, subordinating them to his own later self-described role as "mythographer." For this, he credits Melville with discovering a new, primal and distinctly American sense of "space" which he used to create a "myth, *Moby-Dick*, for a people of Ishmaels" (p. 15).

Again, we have a rebellious, obscurely overreaching Melville whose free-floating metaphors can provide takeoff platforms for hop-skip-and-jumps into a supposedly different American consciousness. Olson's inconsistent and vague key metaphor of "space" (Ann Charters, pp. 48–49) may link with his hobbyish interest in mid-nineteenth-century geometries, but, more pertinently, I suggest, comes out of the Hegelian dialectic in which "quantity" turns into "quality." Thus by loose analogy, the spatial quantity of America, such as the Great Plains, the vast Pacific reaches, and the whale, become a quality, that is, a change in consciousness unique to American culture. So Melville becomes the true poet-prophet by announcing a different awareness based on a new sense of an open universe and society.

Although the space analogy is not much explored, Olson does raise a number of other insightful points. Melville's documentary obsession—whaling as an "industry"—may be viewed as a way of projecting the America that was developing, a maniacal commercial-technological society. The *Pequod*, with its mixture of races and human types, provides an image of democracy, yet with its rigid hierarchy, tyrannical captain, and exploited labor, it also provides an image of democracy's defeat. The very conquest of the vast—the whales, the Pacific, the American space—also led to a defeat of the traditional consciousness, which was the basis of America. Melville may not have been aware of the change he recorded, but it is there for the mythically imaginative reader.

For Olson, Melville's use of Shakespeare's tragedies not only gave an Elizabethan breadth to a simple whaling tale, and expressed his "disillusion in the treacherous world" (p. 44), but also gave recognition to the American tragic impulse to try to dominate the world. As one of the more learned commentators on Olson concludes, he ignores much of *Moby-Dick* "because Melville's work is only a means to his own visionary pronouncements" (Paul Christensen, p. 40). Yet Olson also does suggest an intriguing Melville, one who "wanted a God," and so made "his whale . . . his God" (*Ishmael*, p. 82).

With brilliant gnomic utterance, Olson adds: "Melville was agonized over paternity. . . . He demanded to know the father" (p. 82). Olson's version of Melville's psychoreligious torment over fatherhood does make provocative sense of the biography. Following Lawrence, Olson sees a Melville overwhelmed by familial guilt—"the ethical and northern Melville" (p. 92)—which came to dominate his life and writings. His Holy Land trip (1856) "sealed Melville in a bitterness of disillusion from which he never recovered" (p. 99). Surrounded by conventional guilty Christianity, he "surrendered to it"; "the result was creatively a stifling of the myth power in him" (p. 102). Melville's later writings are failures that but compound his isolato silence. Olson not only notes the absence of heterosexual love in Melville, as Lawrence and others had, but also adds the lack of homosexual love in his fictions from *Pierre* to *Billy Budd* since the leading males are only pale and passive images. A despairing Melville without virility and love is but a victim of America.

Although Olson yokes the earlier Melville, of *Moby-Dick*, with Homer and Dante, just what myth he projected of the supernal consciousness of American space remains obscure. As with Hart Crane, we again have a visionary without a specific vision, though Olson may be said to have gone beyond Crane in seeing Melville as a major figure of defeat by an uncongenial society and religious culture. This is not much modified by Olson's later use of Melville including a polemical poem, "Letter to Melville 1951," which mocked academic scholars (as did Winters the same year) for their institutional exploitation, and three review-essays on Melville (reprinted in *Human Universe*, pp. 105–22). In "David Young, David Old" he mocks *Billy Budd* as a "pitiful thing" inadequately presenting the "homosexuality resident to all three" leading characters (p. 107). In "The Materials and Weights of Herman Melville" Olson again attacks most of the prevailing academic studies and exalts only Lawrence (p. 112). Returning to his earlier "space" metaphor, he propounds that Melville was the first to recognize in the modern senses "physicality" and "totality." Murkily restating the point in "Equal, That Is, to the Real Itself," he takes analogies from physics to suggest that Melville went beyond the old notions of discrete space, dualistic psychology, and rationalistic thinking to fields of force, complementarity, and some sort of cosmic organicism (perhaps from Alfred North Whitehead). Somehow,

Melville provided the first major "redefinition of the real since Homer" (p. 117), though what it is remains quite unexplained.

The allusions to Melville in Olson's multi-volume *Maximus Poems* (I have not checked them all)—a Pound-Williams style pastiche of details about Gloucester, with free associations—adds little to the sense of Melville, except to confirm Olson's obsessions. But perhaps his sensibility was essentially fractured and idiosyncratic and thus not open to more coherent statement in prose or poetry. Still, *Call Me Ishmael* affected a generation's mythic view of Melville. It was also a provocative example of personal-prophetic response as an alternative to other modes of literary study—a continuation of Lawrence's contribution.

The related efforts of Olson's editor-mentor, Edward Dahlberg, may be less persuasive. Dahlberg had been a naturalistic-autobiographical fictionist, with *Bottom Dogs* (1929) and several proletarian novels in the 1930s, who in revulsion against his earlier values and style became a would-be prophetic writer of poetic prose (Widmer, "American Poetic Naturalism"). Just as he rewrote the naturalistic *Bottom Dogs* into the ornate *Because I Was Flesh* (1963), giving himself a mythic cast, he attempted rewriting the mythos of American literature. In *Do These Bones Live* (1941), an early collection of his fractured dithyrambic ruminations on writers as prophets, Melville stands as a central figure, linked in a grossly allusive, imitation Elizabethan style with Old Testament prophets, Cervantes, Shakespeare, Dostoyevsky, and classical mythology. (I am using the revision of the 1941 version, *Can These Bones Live*.) Melville becomes part of a prophetic continuity.

Obviously influenced by Lawrence—not only *Studies* but in both broader and more personal ways—Dahlberg continues Melvillean prophecy in a rather literal sense. He views Melville-Ishmael as the prototype of the alienated American artist, such as himself (*Bones*, p. 45). Dahlberg's Melville is at war with American puritanism (in a more sensual way than Winters's was), using his white whale as a "spermal demon" (p. 122) and coming forth with "ejaculatory blasphemies" (p. 123). While Melville longed for a larger sexuality, in his early work he mostly created "arrested phantoms of sensuality" (p. 129). He ended in *Billy Budd* with a Christianized sodomistic fantasy. Melville, then, is prophetic for American culture mostly as a victim of it.

Dahlberg again recast his version of Melville more harshly in "*Moby-Dick*: An Hamitic Dream" (see *Alms for Oblivion*, 1964; reprinted in the *Dahlberg Reader*). He confesses that "I once loved this cyclops" (p. 170), Melville, but came to reject him because of his dangerous lack of manly sensuality. The theme of the meandering and ornate comments is that Melville's works are the fantasies of a repressed homosexual, including ugly "misogyny" (pp. 173, 191). Because of his repression, "Melville's separation from the human race was as deranged as Bartleby's" (p. 174). "*Moby-Dick*, a verbose and tractarian fable of whaling, is a book of monotonous and unrelenting gloom" (p. 175). Dahlberg simply ignores Melville's humor, among other things. He also decides *Moby-Dick* is a rough draft badly in need of revision (in exact reversal of Olson's view), with obvious inadequacies of character development, repetitious rhetoric, and disconnected metaphors—traits of his own writing—and is therefore "shabbily written" (p. 181). Thus the prophecy must be shabby, too.

Dahlberg, of course, here practices an art at least as old as Enlightenment Biblical criticism in his new-found iconoclasm toward a prophetic text gone sour. "I must impugn *Moby-Dick* as inhuman literature" (p. 194). The rest of the case deploys his usual mythological pedantry in which he plays on Melville as Ishmael and Ishmael as the descendant of Ham, supposedly the first sodomite. In creating the white whale, Melville was projecting a "Titanic sodomite serpent" (p. 176). After this (and early cannibalistic sexuality, incest yearning, etc.), he ended with the "perverted Christian" homosexual spiritualization of *Billy Budd* (p. 196). But Melville also hated his homoeroticism, and the "tawdry writing . . . is to some extent willful self-hatred" (p. 197). Melville, then, is doubly perverse, a "Pauline invert" who puritanically made *Moby-Dick* "the bestial Bible of modern Ham" in the "worship of the male sperm" (pp. 200–201). Thus Melville is a dangerous source of modern homosexual mythology and an incentive to the perversion undermining heterosexual manliness and fuller humanity.

We may grant to Dahlberg that Melville's sexuality should be recognized as more peculiar than often acknowledged, and that some of both popular and learned modern responses to Melville might well be seen as homoerotically cultish (especially those to Budd as the "Handsome Sailor" and to lovingly vicious Vere), but the case seems overdone and personally askew. (Dahlberg had developed an animus toward Olson to whom his view is indebted.) Still, there may be larger motives in attacking what had become a Melville mythology. With unintentional irony, the one book-length study of Dahlberg praisingly concludes that he is much like Melville in his "literary pattern" (Fred Moramarco, pp. 153–54). Dahlberg can also be seen, as can Melville, as less demythologizing than remythologizing. He does give a more specific restatement, however twisted by rancor, of Lawrence's view that Melville was full of "hate" for our human life, though Dahlberg no longer has the positive side of Lawrence's responses to the "great" author of *Moby-Dick*. It may also be salutary to recognize, though rarely done by pietists of the mythic, that mythicizing cuts both ways; that which can be mythically deified, as was Melville by a number of modernist writers, can readily be demonized by the same hyberbolic impetus. The holy texts can easily be turned to scurrillous tracts. Only a slight twist in perspective is needed for larger-than-life heroism to become a threatening anti-life evil. With such as Dahlberg, the mythicizing of Melville just comes full circle.

LATER MODERNIST POLEMICIZING OF MELVILLE

For Robert Lowell, Melville's works fuse with history to become current American reality. *Moby-Dick* provides a major line of historical reference in the early poem "The Quaker Graveyard in Nantucket" (included in *Lord Weary's Castle*, 1946; cited herein, *Selected Poems*, pp. 6–10). This is the most praised poem of Lowell's baroque Catholic-convert period, and in manner and motif the basis of his reputation as mid-century successor to the earlier Anglo-American modernists in poetry. An elegy supposedly for a cousin who died at sea in World War II, "Quaker Graveyard," like *Lycidas* (from which it partly derives), is also an exercise in condemnation. It savages the New England Quakers, with no reference to their pacifism, as sanguinary sailors (as Melville had) and as a part of America's violently exploitative culture. Stylistically, this work practices the ornately involuted, allusive, and elliptical techniques of T. S. Eliot and Allen Tate (Ian Hamilton). Theologically, it exercises an apocalyptic Catholicism, with mystical Mariolatry, which tortuously justifies the violent ways of God in a paradoxical piety which concludes "The Lord survives the rainbow of his will."

In a number of explicit allusions to *Moby-Dick*, the simplest level of association depends on the *Pequod*'s having been owned by Quakers and sailed out of Nantucket, hence the linkage with the graveyard. However, as in Hart Crane's elegy to Melville, the true maritime burial is at sea where the dead sailors find the nothingness of "Ahab's void." Even in the Quaker graveyard "the bones / Cry out in the long night for the hurt beast / Bobbing by Ahab's whaleboats in the East." The reader is to associate somewhat arbitrarily Ahab's pursuit of the white whale with the whole Quaker industry and that more generally with American idealized violence, culminating in World War II.

Lowell's interpretation of Moby Dick, as elliptical as much of the rest of the poem, suggests that the "whited monster" comes from the "fabled news of IS" (that is, pure imponderable being). Ahab, then, was out to kill an ambiguous God. Although the Quaker mariners believe, even in violent death, that God is on their side, they are "three-quarters fools" who are "packing off to hell." They failed to reckon with God's peculiar will, which includes a savage nature and the sheer waste of human life— "We are poured out like water" in Lowell's not very consolatory religion. In the disproportions of human suffering, the very graveyard "bones cry out for the blood of the white whale." But no one can find solace in the bloody order which whaling represents. Whale harpooning is a kind of crucifixion, and Lowell merges wounded Christ, resurrected Jonah

(His allegorical predecessor in the traditional forced Christian typology), and the whale: "Hide our steel, Jonah Messias, in Thy side." Such tortuous cosmic order cannot be defied, even dismembering the final "red-flag hammered in the mast head."

Lowell is quoted as saying that Milton's Lucifer and Melville's Ahab "stand behind American ambition and culture" in their combination of idealism and violence. "To Lowell modern war is as demonic as Ahab's rebellion against God" (Steven Axelrod, pp. 57–58). Lowell proposes as an answering grace a traditional Catholic pietism, but his British Our Lady of Walsingham, an uncomely and uncharming (as well as inappropriate) intercessor—"Expressionless, expresses God"—seems to be an intentionally puritanic cold succor. Lowell's pessimism, except for a harshly willful assertion of arrogant traditional faith, seems as extreme as Melville's, which may have been the source of Lowell's attraction to Melville.

The convert later deconverted from such Christian grace but retained his preoccupation with American violence and Melville. Lowell's later writing also stands considerably separate from modernist styles, including his own earlier one, as in his adaptation for the stage of "Benito Cereno." Completed in 1964, Lowell's version shifts his vehemence to political evil, particularly the American "civil rights" and foreign imperialism issues of the mid–1960s—part of his reconversion, of himself and Melville, to left-liberalism. Lowell's *Benito Cereno* serves as dramatic capstone of three plays (the others adaptations of Hawthorne stories) collectively titled, with heavy irony, *The Old Glory* (pp. 135–214). In its time, this crude play was fashionably exalted, in the sense that in combination Lowell and Melville confirmed a cultural continuity with which to evaluate America.

Melville's "Benito Cereno" subtilized the original mercenary and chauvinistic Yankee skipper Delano, on whose account of the events he heavily draws, in order to give an ironic portrayal of a well-intentioned but ultimately naive and too-optimistic representative American. In later ideological language, it has been said that Melville provided a "definitive portrait" of what has "come to be called the 'white liberal' "; Lowell politicized Melville's innocent so that the "white liberal has become a fascist" (Robert Ilson, pp. 135–42). Instead of Melville's perplexing national character, the benevolently rationalizing mixture of innocence and calculation lacking a deeper sense of moral fatality, Lowell's is a ranting, bloodthirsty, egomaniacal chauvinist.

The later version of Melville's Delano is a conservative ideologue who proposes that "we need inferiors" and Americans really "all want slaves." Lowell's slaves play the "Marseillaise" and talk in Jacobin style about revolution. Other gratuitous additions include allegorical dumbshows, such as a Spanish sailor dipping naked white dolls in tar, and a gross ending with the black's forcing of whites to kiss the dead slavemaster's skull, the black leader (Melville's Babo) putting on a crown, and Delano unnecessarily emptying his anachronistic six-shooter into the black. Melville's famed ambiguity and irony never had much acceptance in Lowell's repeated use of him.

While Lowell's crude operatic play may be of little interest in itself, its mythic role is another matter. The play's views of the American past as bloodthirstily racist and crassly chauvinistic are hardly Melville's, but he is enlisted in the overdue recognitions of the 1960s. Such ideological correction provides much of the purpose of Lowell's retelling. From the original Amasa Delano's *Narrative* through Melville's ironic character exploration into Lowell's guilty ideologizing, we have more than a century-and-a-half of the same retold tale. One recent devout commentator on Lowell has noted of this: "The Benito Cereno matter may become to American literature what the Trojan War was to Greek writers from Homer to Euripides" (Richard Fain, p. 150). Granted, Euripides might plausibly be taken as classical literature's prototype of the modernist in his formal experimentation, skeptical irrationalism, and humanistic iconoclasm, but it may be hard to see Lowell as much of a Euripides. While the Benito Cereno incident seems a bit thin to be blown into anyone's Trojan War, a good many do seem ready to cast Melville as the American Homer.

There is a curious cultural pathos in the strained efforts of critics—as well as the overweening poet-prophets from Lawrence to Lowell—using Melville as the fulcrum for balancing a large and ostensibly tragic American mythology. So uncritically enhanced was the role given to Melville's writings that not only the ambitious *Moby-Dick* in all its eccentricity, but a magazine melodrama ("Benito Cereno") and a confused rambling draft of a story (*Billy Budd*) were given the status of high tragic drama. But that is part of the mythic Melville that literary modernism, in spite of being an iconoclastic movement, helped create.

MERIDIONAL MELVILLE

These seven twentieth-century Anglo-American writers poetically exalting Melville for their own purposes do not, of course, exhaust the modernist re-creation. Let me briefly note a French tradition. Jean Giono, an exuberantly poetical Provencal novelist and affirmative prophet, not only wrote on Melville but also assisted in the first complete French translation of the *Moby-Dick* he so admired (published 1941). Jean-Paul Sartre responded with some typical, lofty reflections on Melville (*Ecrits*, pp. 634–37), and Albert Camus subsequently made *Moby-Dick* one of his favorite novels (Germaine Bree, pp. 119, 197, and 247). In his first important existential essays, *The Myth of Sisyphus*, Camus notes of *Moby-Dick* that it is a "truly absurd work" (p. 83), meaning that it modernistically confronts the essential nihilism. Camus later wrote an exalting essay on Melville (first published 1952) which insists on the American's exceptional power as a "mythic" writer. He held that *Moby-Dick* should be "seen as one of the most overwhelming myths ever invented on the subject of the struggle against evil, depicting the irresistible logic that finally leads the just man to take up arms against creation and the creator, then against his fellows and against himself" (*Essays*, p. 289). Camus's Melville is a poet who goes beyond radicalism.

This was part of Camus's ambitious formulation of the modern moral dilemma of justified rebellion becoming excessive destruction, as in *L'Homme Revolté*, though he refers there only in passing to Melville (*The Rebel*, p. 80). Camus, in sum, saw Ahab's rightful revolt turning into total nihilism in the great myth of the "Homer of the Pacific." And he wanted to see such as Melville answering the nihilism with life-affirmative "meridional" values (pp. 279 ff.; Widmer, *Literary Rebel*, pp. 167–74). Ironically, the existential moralist twists Melville to his supposedly Mediterranean values when most of the other prophetic modernists saw the American as a quintessentially "Northern," guilt-ridden idealist. In either case, Melville's myth has been turned to an ancient Western cultural warfare.

A Melvillean ambiguity seems more evident in Camus's remarks on *Billy Budd*. This he strangely sees as a "flawless story" belonging with the Greek tragedies because "Melville tells us of his acceptance for the first time of the sacrifice of beauty and innocence so that order may be maintained" (*Essays*, p. 292). But, he interestingly adds, we cannot know if Melville, that visionary adventurer, was simply exploring or if his despair finally led him to this "worst blasphemy" against the humanely human and its essential imperative to rebel.

Camus, at this time ideologically engaged against more dogmatic philosophies, wanted a life-affirmative Melville, one not committed to "sombre allegories" such as the Kafkaesque and the Sartrean. His is a Melville full of rich literary variety and "health, strength . . . and human laughter" (*Essays*, p. 293). Like Lawrence (but unlike most of the others discussed above), Camus also delights in Melville's protean and positive responses to nature. His Melville affirms immediate existing experience, though in an un-American meridional temperament. The reader of Camus may also reasonably suspect that the affirmations here turn out as thin and pyrrhic as those of Mersault in *The Stranger* or the "hero of the absurd" in *The Myth of Sisyphus*. The modern existential claims for positive values seem rather desperate, but, then, Melville's existential desperation—the absence of deity, the extremes of alienation, the ambiguous idealism, the stoic defiance—may underlie much of his modernist appeal. (Further examples, and applications, of Melville-as-existentialist—including a critique of philosopher Hannah Arendt's allegorization of Billy Budd as a Jacobin Christ in her *On Revolution*—may be found in Widmer, *Ways of Nihilism*.)

POSTMODERNIST MELVILLE

The modernists created a mythic Melville considerably for their own moral and prophetic purposes but that figure now has an existence of its own—really, several of them. A handful of contemporary postmodernist literary responses to Melville might annotate the point. (I am selecting from only the better known writers, and ones strongly indebted to modernist traditions.) For example, Philip Roth, a prolific, sophisticated joker in novelistic forms, starts out *The Great American Novel* (1973) with "Call Me Smitty," for his burlesque Ishmael. In parodying Melville's work, it also affirms its premier role. What follows is an ornate and raucously jokey sports narrative that soon includes a heavy-handed parody of Hemingway writing a parody of *Moby-Dick* as a baseball story (pp. 41–45).

Such arch bemusement with American myths is not confined to American jokers. William Golding, the British Manichaean allegorist (*Lord of the Flies*), went in for a different humor in his slight costume tale, *Rites of Passage* (1980). As he acknowledged to a learned interviewer, he had Melville's Billy Budd in mind when he made his innocent Billy on a sailing voyage a sodomized fool (James R. Baker, pp. 162–63).

Robert Stone, a younger contemporary American novelist (*A Flag at Sunrise*), half-seriously expounds in a recent essay on the "American Dream" (1984) that it consists of such mythic figures as the Wizard of Oz, Uncle Sam, God, and the White Whale. For that last, "there was raised up among us a prophet" whose whale, in spite of its whiteness, "stands for all those people whose color was Other. He stands for all that was natural, wise, unowned, unsubdued, and ultimately un-American. For many, those properties mark him as Evil. For others they mark him as Good." "*American Man*" in Melville's myth "pursued the unsubduable to their mutual undoing" (p. 51). Stone admits that much of this is a bit arbitrary, but there "are almost as many interpreters of this story as there are people who finish reading it." Woody Allen's Zelig, then, didn't understand that *Moby-Dick* is to be read, if one can finish it, for any new or old or fanciful interpretation one needs. Isn't that what myths are for?

Melville's myth, like the mythic exaltation of Melville, has reached a late-stage of usage—decadence?—when it is so widely subject to postmodernist playfulness. Nor is the freeplay with dream-mythic Americans confined to *Moby-Dick*. Novelist and essayist Elizabeth Hardwick has twisted Melville's forlorn scrivener to her parochial purposes in her entitling meditation, *Bartleby in Manhattan* (1983). With the smug provincialism that has often characterized the last two generations of established New York intellectuals, she sees the tale that Melville *metaphorically* subtitled "A Story of Wall Street" as most essentially about Manhattan. Hardwick also seems to miss most of Melville's questioning, irony, and mockery. For her, the story's lawyer "is a far better man than he knows himself to be" (p. 220). Melville, of course, elaborately mocks the narrating lawyer's better intentions turned into self-interest psychology, and the rest of his pseudo-benevolent rationalizing, in what is perhaps the most devastating portrayal of a smug liberal mentality in our literature. But to benevolently rationalizing Hardwick, Bartleby's "resistance to amelioration" and other confines seems to express "Manhattanism" and a "fraternal melancholy" appropriate to the sometime cultural capital of America.

While Hardwick's account is more obtuse than most (at least since Leo Marx's) about much of what goes on in the story, she is hardly alone in adapting what may be Melville's most enigmatic tale to special purposes. Readings range from an emphasis on madness through Marxism and Buddhism and Christology to the Kafkaesque and the merely cantankerous, among others, to make Melville's "Bartleby" an outstanding playground of forlorn modernist theories. (After three published exercises in interpretation of "Bartleby," I ended up making him a saintly existential rebel—*Ways of Nihilism*, Chapter 4; the most detailed and strongest counterstatement to my view is that of Milton Stern.) "Bartleby," too, has served as myth material to conjure with.

Finally, for a good example of the modern legacy of Melville, and a good discussion on its own merits, I suggest John Updike. Reference here is not to his passing playful use of Melville in his fictions (as with late-Melville as a model for non-writing writers in *Bech Is Back*) but to his long essay, "Melville's Withdrawal," in *Hugging the Shore* (1983). He accepts the high modernist evaluation of Melville and "the assumptions that *Moby-Dick* is a masterpiece and that Melville in his endowment of ability and ambition is second to no American writer of fiction" (p. 80).

Updike's Melville is also a protomodernist in that some of his later works, such as *Pierre* and *The Confidence-Man*, are "uncanny foreshadowings of aspects of modernism," partly because they "were written with Melville's instincts in rebellion; they are protest novels cast in a would-be popular vein, and brim with tensions the author cannot express" (p. 105). That seems a crucial insight, derived from the later conditions of modernist culture, into the dilemma of those works. Updike also aptly specifies why *Pierre* is "grindingly, ludicrously, bad" (p. 85). While he does not discuss "Bartleby," he makes the interesting observation that *Billy Budd* is a tale in which "a counterfeit Christ legend is shown in the coining, and Billy goes to death blessing his condemner as credulous men everywhere go down to their doom praising God" (p. 103). Now there is a Christian moralist who has not missed the imperative sense of irony in looking at Melville's last fiction.

The non-academic critic, not confined by methodological dogmatism, can range from style to myth to biography, as Updike does in also pointing to the autobiographical impetus behind executioner father-figure Vere in father-Melville after his two sons became early fatalities. More broadly, he rightly notes Melville's horrific and damaging early history—the failed and mad father, the domineering mother (and then wife), the genteel poverty, the probably unaccepted homosexuality—all of which contributed to Melville's central message "that God was dead and life a cruel fraud."

Given his cultural time and place, this view could not be "warmly received even if Melville had himself taken more joy in it" (p. 105). Melville did not retreat from writing primarily because of money (as Marxiological critics have claimed); in fact, Updike believes that Melville may have been "one of the best paid American authors" of his time (p. 89). Melville withdrew into "public silence and private poetry" largely because of the incompatibility of his deepest views with the dominating American ideology.

The artist in conflict with culture is, of course, one of the central and distinguishing traits of modernism (see Widmer, *Edges of Extremity*, 1980). Melville had rejected the pathological "optimism" of mainstream American culture. In briefest summary, that may be a considerable part of why the modernists, from Lawrence on, rediscovered Melville. Since that conflict still importantly exists in our culture, it may also be a major reason why Melville remains pertinent.

Updike's suggested interpretation of *Moby-Dick*, though insufficiently elaborated, also belongs in the best modernist tradition. The white whale is not mystical but represents "the awful absence of God, the Calvinist God," and thus "becomes, in a way, God. Moby Dick represents the utter blank horror of the universe if Godless, a horror so awesome as to excite worship" (pp. 97–98). That, I believe, remains the existential center of Melville, which the modernists rediscovered and made so much of, in their varying ways.

No wonder Woody Allen's frightened conformist Zelig intuitively resisted completing *Moby-Dick*. Whatever the historical Melville might have been, it was the modernist's Melville who was at issue, and often still is. And that is the mythic larger-than-life Melville, the tragic American Homer, the prophet of the doom of white consciousness, the obscurely transcendent mariner, the guilty convert from romantic evil, the homoerotic mythographer of vast spaces and sins, the visionary explorer of American darknesses and pessimisms—and the rest of the large re-creations. The lineaments of this myth, I have suggested with varying emphasis in terms of the different practitioners of it, sometimes violated the mixed realities, common coherence, and adequate humanity. But perhaps Melville did, too. And these modernists are often interesting and important in themselves even when re-creating Melville—suggestive, provocative, sometimes even profound. The Melville myth from the modernists is a significant part of our cultural legacy and one we, and Melville's writings, would be poorer without.

WORKS CITED

Arendt, Hannah. *On Revolution*. New York: Viking Press, 1963.

Arnold, Armin. *D. H. Lawrence and America*. New York: Philosophical Library, 1959.

Auden, W. H. *Collected Shorter Poems*. New York: Random House, 1964.

———. *The Enchafed Flood, or The Romantic Iconography of the Sea*. New York: Random House, 1950.

Axelrod, Steven Gould. *Robert Lowell, Life and Art*. Princeton, N.J.: Princeton University Press, 1978.

Bahlke, George W. *The Later Auden*. New Brunswick, N.J.: Rutgers University Press, 1970.

Baker, James R. "An Interview with William Golding." *Twentieth Century Literature* 28 (Summer 1982): 130–70.

Bree, Germaine. *Camus*. New Brunswick, N.J.: Rutgers University Press, 1959.

Butterfield, R. W. *The Broken Arc: A Study of Hart Crane*. Edinburgh: Olivier, 1969.

Camus, Albert. "Herman Melville." 1952. In *Lyrical and Critical Essays*. Ed. Philip Thody. New York: Alfred A. Knopf, 1969, pp. 288–94.

———. *L'Homme Revolté*. Paris: Gallimard, 1951. *The Rebel*. Rev. trans. Anthony Brower. New York: Alfred A. Knopf, 1969.

———. *The Myth of Sisyphus*. New York: Alfred A. Knopf, 1955.

Charters, Ann. *Olson/Melville, "A Study in Affinity."* Berkeley, Calif.: Oyez, 1968.

Christensen, Paul. *Charles Olson, Call Him Ishmael*. Austin: University of Texas Press, 1979.

Crane, Hart. *Collected Poems*. Ed. Waldo Frank. New York: Liveright, 1933.

———. *Complete Poems and Selected Letters and Prose*. Ed. Brom Weber. New York: Liveright, 1966.

Dahlberg, Edward. *Alms for Oblivion*. Minneapolis: University of Minnesota Press, 1964.

———. *Because I Was Flesh: The Autobiography of Edward Dahlberg*. Norfolk, Conn.: New Directions, 1963.

———. *Bottom Dogs*. London: Putnam, 1929; rpt. New York: Simon & Schuster, 1930.

———. *Can These Bones Live*. New York: New Directions, 1960. [An earlier version appears as *Do These Bones Live* (1941) which was also published under the title *Sing O Barren*.]

———. "*Moby-Dick*: An Hamitic Dream." *The Edward Dahlberg Reader*. Ed. Paul Carroll. New York: New Directions, 1967, pp. 170–201.

Davis, Dick. *Wisdom and Wilderness, The Achievement of Yvor Winters*. Athens: University of Georgia Press, 1983.

Duban, James. *Melville's Major Fiction*. DeKalb: Northern Illinois University Press, 1983.

Fain, Richard. *Robert Lowell*. 2d ed. Boston: Twayne, 1979.

Giono, Jean. *Pour Saluer Melville*. Paris: Gallimard, 1941.

Golding, William. *Rites of Passage*. London: Faber, 1980.

Hamilton, Ian. *Robert Lowell, A Biography*. New York: Random House, 1982.

Hardwick, Elizabeth. "Bartleby in Manhattan." In *Bartleby in Manhattan, and Other Essays*. New York: Random House, 1983, pp. 217–31.

Horton, Philip. *Hart Crane*. New York: Viking Press, 1937.

Ilson, Robert. "*Benito Cereno* from Melville to Lowell." In *Robert Lowell*. Ed. Thomas Parkinson. Englewood Cliffs, N.J.: Prentice-Hall, 1968, pp. 135–42.

Kierkegaard, Soren. *Either/Or*. 2 vols. Trans. D. F. and L. M. Swenson. Princeton, N.J.: Princeton University Press, 1949.

Lawrence, D. H. *Collected Letters*. 2 vols. Ed. Harry T. Moore. New York: Viking Press, 1962.

———. *The Lost Girl*. 1920. London: Heinemann, 1950.

———. *Studies in Classic American Literature*. New York: Thomas Seltzer, Inc., 1923; rpt. Garden City, NY: Doubleday, 1953.

———. *The Symbolic Meaning: The Uncollected Versions of Studies in Classic American Literature*. Ed. Armin Arnold. New York: Viking Press, 1964.

Lewis, R.W.B. "Crane's Visionary Lyric: The Way to *The Bridge*." In *Critical Essays on Hart Crane*. Ed. David C. Clark. Boston: G. K. Hall, 1982, pp. 73–92.

———. *The Poetry of Hart Crane*. Princeton, N.J.: Princeton University Press, 1967.

Lowell, Robert. *Benito Cereno*. In *The Old Glory*. Rev. ed. New York: Farrar, Straus & Giroux, 1968.

———. *Lord Weary's Castle*. New York: Harcourt, Brace, and Co., 1946; rpt. in *Selected Poems*. New York: Farrar, Straus & Giroux, 1976.

Matthiessen, F. O. *American Renaissance: Art and Expression in the Age of Emerson and Whitman*. New York: Oxford University Press, 1941.

Maud, Ralph. "Archetypal Depth Criticism and Melville." *College English* 45 (November 1983): 695–704.

Melville, Herman. *Bartleby the Scrivener: A Casebook*. Ed. Stanely Schatt. Dubuque, Ia.: Kendall/Hunt, 1972.

———. *Moby-Dick*. Trans. [into French] Jacques Lucien, Joan Smith, and Jean Giono. Paris: Gallimard, 1941.

Moramarco, Fred. *Edward Dahlberg*. New York: Twayne, 1973.

Olson, Charles. *Call Me Ishmael*. New York: Reynal & Hitchcock, 1947.

———. *Human Universe and Other Essays*. Ed. Donald Allen. New York: Grove Press, 1967.

———. "Lear and Moby-Dick." *Twice a Year* 1 (Fall-Winter 1938): 165–89.

———. *Letter for Melville 1951*. Black Mountain, N.C.: 1951.

———. *The Maximus Poems, 1–10*. Stuttgart: Jonathan Williams, 1953.

———. *The Maximus Poems, 11–22*. Stuttgart: Jonathan Williams, 1956.

————. *The Maximus Poems: Volume Three*. Ed. Charles Boer and George F. Butterick. New York: Grossman, 1975.

Rogin, Michael Paul. *Subversive Genealogy: The Politics and Art of Herman Melville*. New York: Alfred A. Knopf, 1983.

Roth, Philip. *The Great American Novel*. New York: Holt, Rinehart & Winston, 1973.

Sartre, Jean-Paul. "*Moby-Dick* d'Herman Melville." In *Ecrits de Sartre*. Ed. M. Contat and M. Rybaka. Paris: Gallimard, 1970, pp. 634–37.

Stern, Milton. "Towards 'Bartleby the Scrivener,' " *The Stoic Strain in American Literature*. Ed. Duane J. MacMillan. Toronto: University of Toronto Press, 1979, pp. 19–41.

Stone, Robert. "American Dream." *Harper's* 268 (March 1984): 49–51.

Unterecker, John. *Voyager, A Life of Hart Crane*. New York: Farrar, Straus & Giroux, 1969.

Updike, John. "Melville's Withdrawal." *Hugging the Shore*. New York: Alfred A. Knopf, 1983, pp. 80–106.

Weaver, Raymond. *Melville: Mariner and Mystic*. New York: George H. Doran, 1921.

Widmer, Kingsley. "American Poetic Naturalism: Edward Dahlberg." *Shenandoah* 16 (Autumn 1964): 69–74.

————. *The Art of Perversity: The Shorter Fictions of D. H. Lawrence*. Seattle: University of Washington Press, 1962.

————. "Dark Prophecy: The Nietzschean Matrix." In *D. H. Lawrence and Tradition*. Ed. Jeffrey Meyers. Amherst: University of Massachusetts Press, 1985.

————. "Desire and Negation: The Dialectics of Passion in Lawrence." *D. H. Lawrence, Centenary Essays*. Ed. G. Salgado. London, 1985.

————. *Edges of Extremity: Some Problems of Literary Modernism*. Tulsa, Okla.: University of Tulsa Monographs, 1980.

————. "The Learned Try-Works: A Review of Melville Scholarship." *Studies in the Novel* 5 (Spring 1973): 117–24.

————. *The Literary Rebel*. Carbondale: Southern Illinois University Press, 1965.

————. *The Ways of Nihilism: Herman Melville's Short Novels*. Los Angeles: Ward-Ritchie Press, 1970.

Wilson, Edmund. *The Shock of Recognition*. Garden City, N.Y.: Doubleday, 1943.

Winters, Yvor. *The Collected Poems*. Ed. Donald Davie. Chicago: Swallow Press, 1978.

————. *Maule's Curse, Seven Studies in the History of American Obscurantism*. In *In Defense of Reason*. Denver: Alan Swallow, 1947, pp. 151–343.

————. *Primitivism and Decadence*. In *In Defense of Reason*. Denver: Alan Swallow, 1947: 15–150.

23

MELVILLE IN POPULAR CULTURE

M. Thomas Inge

Herman Melville has twice enjoyed a position of prominence in American popular culture. The first period was during his own lifetime when, as the author of such commercially successful works as *Typee* (1846) and *Omoo* (1847), he was known as "the man who lived among the cannibals." Not until the 1920s when biographical and critical attention made him the subject matter for a new myth did Melville then become in the popular mind emblematic of the neglected genius, the creative mind too advanced for his own age and destroyed by a callous, unappreciative audience. He came to represent the danger and tragedy of being an artist in a democratic, capitalistic society, where pleasing the tastes of the mob and making money counted for more than producing a classic work of literature. That there is more exaggeration than truth in this popular view of Melville is beside the point—the American mythmaking process has a way of asserting itself by creating necessary belief systems that have little relevance to reality.

Whatever the truth may be, few American writers have a larger presence in our popular culture, the chief contenders being Edgar Allan Poe and Mark Twain (Twain is viewed less as a writer than as a public treasure or an icon representing the American character.) Millions of Americans who have never read a line by Melville know the names of Moby Dick, Captain Ahab, or Billy Budd. His works have been repeatedly adapted to film, radio, television, records, comic books, and children's literature. Themes, names, and images are drawn from his fiction in popular literature, games, toys, puzzles, shop and restaurant names, popular songs, riddles, jokes, advertisements, and a variety of commercial products. To many, *Moby-Dick* represents the great unread American novel, like *War and Peace* a challenge which many undertake but few finish, yet probably the most revered work of fiction by anyone who cares about writing and American culture. It has inspired so many other works of literature, from science fiction and pulp novels to mainstream works of fiction, poetry, and drama, that the story of Ahab's pursuit of the white whale seems permanently imbedded in the national consciousness. A writer has but to begin his narrative, "Call me Jonah" (or whatever name is appropriate; this line begins *Cat's Cradle* by Kurt Vonnegut, Jr.), and the reader is reminded of Ishmael's great adventure. Surely Harold Ross, founder of *The New Yorker*, was kidding when he asked his often quoted question, "Is Moby Dick the whale or the man?" (Thurber, p. 77). So widely known is the basic plot structure of *Moby-Dick* and so frequently has it been adapted to the media that there are people who think they have read the novel without having gone near the actual text.

Why Melville and his fiction have had such a powerful appeal for the ordinary American is not easy to answer. Perhaps it has to do with the deep strain of romanticism that persists in American thought and that tends to sympathize with the misunderstood and the alienated, both elements in the mythology about the man as artist. Perhaps the towering reputation of *Moby-Dick*, a work in the American grain which pushes humanity to the outer limits of the universe, the last frontier indeed, is what grips the imagination of a nation unused to the geographic and economic limitations of modern society. Perhaps his creation of a solitary, irredeemable egomaniac in Ahab, determined to fling a challenge in the face of God, appeals to the folk mind as have other superheroes who populate our mythology—Davy Crockett, Daniel Boone, John Henry, and, for the twentieth century, Superman. Whatever the reasons, and they must be complex, if we are to ascertain and understand them, we must turn to popular culture rather than the works themselves or biography. That is where Melville continues to have a striking vitality which has taken on a life of its own. To follow this path is clearly a step toward understanding ourselves, our dreams, and therefore the things that make Americans distinctive.[1]

FILM

If the biographies of Melville by Raymond M. Weaver and John Freeman in 1921 and 1926, respectively, brought the author's works to the attention of the literary establishment, it is John Barrymore who stimulated an awareness of *Moby-Dick* in the popular mind. Barrymore made a silent (1926) and a sound (1930) version, both of which proved to be two of his most popular films, though totally unfaithful to Melville. Barrymore began to feel he was permanently cast as Ahab: "I played many a part before I reached my dream roles in *Hamlet* and *Moby-Dick*," he once noted. "*Hamlet* I played until Ophelia went nuts. *Moby-Dick* I played until I went nuts" (James Kotsilibas-David, p. 99). Coincidentally, the five years in which both versions were made also spanned Barrymore's courtship and marriage to Dolores Costello, whom he selected as the leading lady in the silent version because he thought her to be "the most preposterously lovely creature in all the world" (p. 52). Thus one of Hollywood's most sensational romances became entwined with Melville's novel (or the title anyway) and accounts for some of Barrymore's most passionate scenes on the screen during his fabled career.

Uncertain perhaps of the box-office drawing power of the original title, the first version of *Moby-Dick* was called *The Sea Beast*. In this very indirect dramatization, the only surviving effort to bring any of Melville's works to the silent screen, Ahab Ceeley (Barrymore) and his half-brother Derek (George O'Hara) are both in love with Esther Harper (Dolores Costello), the pious daughter of the Reverend John Harper of New Bedford. Ahab has her love, however, and they pledge to wed just as he and Derek ship out on *The Three Brothers*, while she travels with her father on a missionary assignment to Port Louis in Mauritius. When in pursuit of the legendary Moby Dick, Derek, consumed with jealousy, pushes Ahab overboard to fall victim to the whale, a crude papier mache monster as best Hollywood could muster at the time. Like many sailors before him, Ahab loses his leg to Moby Dick, of whom it is said in the film, "The Great White Whale is the devil's self." Just before the encounter, the captain of *The Three Brothers* notes in his Sunday sermon, "This day, perhaps, shipmates, the Lord may send the great mad fish called Moby Dick against us. But he cannot prevail against a pure heart." This is a prediction of how the movie will end.

Ahab returns to Esther at Port Louis with great trepidation over his lost leg. Derek lies to Ahab, however, that he and Esther have actually been in love for more than a year, but both had lacked the courage to tell him. Demoralized and betrayed, Ahab returns to sea and burns the tattoo of her name off his arm with a red-hot harpoon. He becomes a legend in New Bedford as the strict and cruel captain of the *Pequod*. Dressed in a black stovepipe hat and cape, he strikes fear into the hearts of his crew, and when a seagull excretes on his hat, laughter among the crew is quelled by one penetrating glance. For three years he travels the high seas around the world in pursuit of Moby Dick and revenge. His sole companions are two devilish pagans—the Chinese Fedallah and the cannibal Queequeg.

The lovelorn Esther continues to await the return of Ahab at Port Louis unaware of Derek's lie. Her father has failed to frighten the natives into salvation with threats of hellfire, so they set sail for New Bedford with the lingering Derek trailing along. In a typhoon, Derek is lost overboard. As if psychically aware of her danger, the crazed Ahab has a vision of Esther in which her ethereal hands touch his head. The crippled, insane Pip, who had witnessed Derek pushing Ahab overboard, now reveals that it was his own brother who fed Ahab to Moby Dick. Derek is found afloat on the sea and is rescued by the crew of the *Pequod*. When Ahab confronts him, Derek pulls a knife, they struggle, and Ahab throws his brother overboard to drown. Although hardly qualified by now as one of "pure heart," Ahab prevails against Moby Dick and heroically slays him. He returns to New Bedford, discovers that Esther survived the typhoon, and they sink into each other's arms with visions of happiness together forever.

The film consists primarily of staged tableaus and dwells interminably on the lovers' glances and enraptured stares. (Barrymore had these filmed first, the more quickly to court the young Miss Costello.) There is also a bizarre business about Ahab's physical handicap. It begins with the shot of Ahab peeking out of the porthole to observe the whole, healthy legs of those on the dock, including the feet of his beloved Esther (he is trying on his wooden leg for the first time). When he finally departs the ship under cover of night, we see several dockside scenes of drinking and revelry which focus on dancing, prancing legs, while Ahab hobbles with another peg-legged companion. He seeks out Esther at the Governor's ball and is once again cruelly reminded of his disability as he watches the dancers twirl around the floor. When she views him with shock, he quickly retreats. An odd perversity works in these scenes beyond any sympathy for the handicapped.

Another grotesque touch occurs near the beginning when we are told that "Of all the wild crews, the whale ship crews were the wildest," and to prove the point, we are given by way of titles the words to a grim sea chanty:

> They call me hanging Johnny,
>   Hooray! HOO-ray!
> Because I hang so many,
>   Hooray! HOO-ray!
> I hung my dear old mother,
> And I hung my baby brother,
>   So hang, boys! Hang!
> I hung my sister Sally
> And I swung her in the galley,
>   So hang, boys! Hang!
> I hung my uncle Paddy,
> And I hung my old grandaddy,
>   So hang, boys! Hang!

The likes of such a ditty would not be seen again until the cruelty jokes and Tom Lehrer's songs of the 1950s. These are the only intriguing aspects of an otherwise aborted effort to film Melville's masterpiece. As the plot summary makes clear, there are few relationships between the novel and *The Sea Beast* outside the use of names, and having Ahab slay the whale subverts the meaning of the original.

When *The Sea Beast* opened on Broadway, it brought in $20,000 a week and ran longer at the Warner theater than any previous Warner Brothers film. At least one publisher, Grosset & Dunlap, anticipating possible sales of the novel riding on the film publicity, issued a special edition (deleting the Etymology and Extracts) of *Moby-Dick* late in 1925, according to the title page, "Illustrated with Scenes from the Photoplay a Warner Bros. Screen Classic Starring John Barrymore." The eight stills dispersed throughout the book probably did little to aid the puzzled reader who found the novel not at all the romance the movie led one to expect. Even more puzzling, however, is the presence of an introductory appreciation by someone named S. R. Buchman, who says of Melville in a grammatically peculiar sentence, "A seething brain, slightly unstable but brilliant, has, together with acute vision, a tendency to introspection, and disease of cynicism give us titanic circumstances and characters that will never be forgotten" (p. ix). Buchman, who seems to have had nothing to do with the film, makes the preposterous statement that "in the present production, renamed 'The Sea Beast,' every important element has been transcribed with absolute sincerity, and is a clear reflection of the spirit originally infused into the work by Melville" (p. xi). Torturous syntax aside, this must stand as one of the most patently false claims in the history of film criticism. Arnold Bennett, who caught the film one Sunday afternoon in March of 1926, found it a "filthy and preposterous thing and humiliating to watch" and was so annoyed that he walked out before it was over (p. 140).

Those who wanted to read a summary of the film script rather than the real article had to wait until 1934 when Whitman Publishing Company issued "Big Little Book" No. 710, *The Story of Moby Dick: The Great White Whale*, a 154–page retelling of the script for *The Sea Beast* with movie stills on every other page. Nevertheless, the title page claimed it was "Adapted from the Novel by Herman Melville."

John Barrymore made his first talking picture in 1929, and anxious to try out his dramatic voice with proven and familiar material, he returned to *Moby-Dick* in 1930. This time he used the title of the novel, but like the first version, the search for the great white whale is merely a device to separate lovers in a traditional triangle and thus functions as an appendage to the main plot.

This, too, is the story of two brothers, Derek (Lloyd Hughes) and Ahab Ceeley (Barrymore), the one a quiet, landloving clerk and the other a rowdy, tattooed, sea-going swab who performs acrobatic antics for the entertainment of his fellow seamen (a good deal like the comic strip character Popeye who had just been introduced to the funny papers in *Thimble Theater* by Elzie C. Segar the year before). They both are in love with Faith Mapple (Joan Bennett), daughter of the local minister in Providence for whom Derek works. Ahab withdraws when he thinks that Faith prefers Derek, but just as he leaves for sea again, she confesses her love and they pledge to marry on his return from the three-year whaling voyage he has signed onto. It is on this trip that Ahab encounters Moby Dick and loses his leg to another crudely constructed Hollywood whale. (A method for constructing realistic sea beasts would not be perfected until *Jaws.*)

Upon his return, Ahab mistakes Faith's shock for rejection, which is confirmed by Derek who lies about her true feelings in an effort to save her for himself. She had, in fact, specifically sent Derek to reconfirm her love for Ahab. He leaves for sea again, unaware that Faith has sworn eternal love and promised herself to await his return as long as she lives. For seven years he searches for Moby Dick, finally as the owner of his own ship *The Shanghai Lady*. Derek is shanghaied by mistake along with others to replace the continually deserting crew members, and he tries to kill Ahab to deter him from his insane search. Finally Ahab finds the whale, kills it, and returns to Providence surprised to find Faith waiting with open arms. They embrace for the fade-out.

While the film is the worst kind of romantic melodrama, it too has certain effective gothic touches—the ugly, misshapen crew (some in Lon Chaney makeup); the excruciating burning of Ahab's raw stump with a hot iron; Ahab's being splashed with blood as he plunges the harpoon into Moby Dick's back; and a very black, decorated Queequeg, constantly praying to his little heathen idol. Some of the scenes of Ahab, in his black coat and hat, would seem to have been inspired by the Rockwell Kent illustrations. Derek is cruelly punished by having Queequeg break his back, but he is totally forgotten after Ahab orders Starbuck to take him below and "Do what you can for him—he's my brother."

Film historian Arthur Knight has noted in *The Liveliest Art* (1957) that this version made particularly effective use of the new technique of opening and closing the screen frame to add dramatic momentum to large scenes of action:

In the first talking version of *Moby Dick* (1930), for example, as the long boats pulled away from the mother ship, the screen began slowly to expand, the masking moving majestically back and up to reveal an ever wider view of the limitless sea. The entire pursuit of the great white whale takes place on this enlarged screen until finally the monster turns on his pursuers. Then, just as the massive jaws are closing down on Captain Ahab, the sides of the screen contract, cutting off the possibility of escape. At such moments, with the movement of the frame intensifying both the psychological and visual impact of the story, the screen did more than passively reflect the scene; it became at last an integral part of the action. (p. 332)

Once again, the film was a smash at the box office, the most successful of five pictures made by Barrymore under a million-dollar contract with Warner Brothers, perhaps because the public wanted to hear the great profile's seductive voice. A reviewer for *Theatre Magazine* found that "Altogether *Moby Dick* is a highly creditable, moving record of Melville's stirring tale," but everything else he said demonstrated no knowledge of the novel whatsoever. It is difficult to determine at this late date what odd impressions and distortions of the novel existed in the public mind as a result of the Barrymore productions. In any case, it would be a quarter of a century before anyone else would dare to undertake to film the great novel again.

The next attempt to film a Melville work was a peculiar one indeed. Allegedly based on *Omoo*, the film *Omoo-Omoo (The Shark God)* (1949) begins with what are supposed to be the words of Melville on the screen, dated 15 January 1879 and read by a voice-over narrator who says he is about to relate the strangest of all his experiences on the high seas, something that happened in 1874. When he concludes, "This is the story of the Omoo tabu and the Shark God," we should know what we are in for: a low-budget, grade-B sea and jungle adventure that has no relationship to Melville's book. The uncertainty of the title (why the repetition of *Omoo* and why the necessity to add a subtitle in parentheses?) is but a reflection of the muddled uncertainty of the script and direction.

Despite the opening narration, Melville does not appear in the film. Instead a Doctor Humphrey Long (George Meeker), an alcoholic physician who has signed on the schooner *Julia* bound for Tahiti, continues the narrative. A captain ill from some strange malady, his attending daughter Julie, a surly crew breaking out in fights, and the discovery of a Tahitian stowaway are supposed to add mystery but only draw from the largely unknown cast an incompetent and uninspired performance. As the plot develops, we find that the Captain had stolen and hidden on an earlier trip the two large black pearls which were the eyes of the Shark God worshipped by the native Omoo people. They have since fallen on hard times because the god can no longer see the difference between good and evil. The Captain is returning to retrieve them for his fortune, not realizing that he is dying from the tabu of having stolen the pearls. He is killed by two greedy members of the crew, and the curse is passed to the daughter Julie. To make a boring story short, Julie returns the pearls, peace is restored to the Omoos, and Julie plans to marry the honest sailor who rescued her.

The film was spiced up by two totally irrelevant additions—an underwater fight between a moray eel and an octopus (one can see the sides of the glass aquarium in which it is taking place and someone stirring the octopus up with a stick) and a fight between two tigers which stalk each other and pay no attention to the crowd of people gathered to watch in the jungle. The best that *Variety* could say for the feature was "Dressing up the lobby and boxoffice with reeds and palm leaves may prove helpful in stimulating biz, but . . . this 'exploitation' entry [is] merely something to round out a double bill." Except for the names of a few characters—an ill Captain Guy, a sailor named Chips, and the physician Dr. Long (Long Ghost in the novel)—the name of the ship *Julia*, and the word "Omoo" (which in Melville is not the name of a tribe but the Marquesan word meaning rover or wanderer), the shameless scriptwriters, George D. Green and Leon Leonard, have borrowed nothing from Melville. To say this film was based on the book was an outright falsehood, but this had been known to happen before in Hollywood.

By 1951 there was an increasing fascination over having another go at *Moby-Dick*. In that year, at least seven motion picture companies expressed interest in such a project: Argosy Pictures, Bing Crosby Enterprises, Film Group, J. Arthur Rank, David O. Selznick, Edward Small, and Warner Brothers (*Melville Society Newsletter* [*MSN*] No. 7). Perhaps this general interest was what encouraged John Huston finally to move ahead in 1953 with his version which he had been planning as early as 1942, when he began writing a script with the intention of starring his father, Walter Huston, as Ahab. Then World War II intervened (Stuart Kaminsky, p. 101).

Huston had always considered *Moby-Dick* the "great American novel," except perhaps for *Adventures of Huckleberry Finn*, and he wanted a script writer equal to the task of creating a faithful adaptation. He finally settled on popular science fiction author Ray Bradbury, whose fiction Huston felt had a "poetic quality" and a "soaring spirit" which he admired (Gerald Pratley, pp. 103–105). The story goes that Bradbury asked for a day to decide because he had never read *Moby-Dick*, having tried as a boy but given up in despair (Kaminsky, p. 102). In any case, he accepted the proposition and joined Huston in Ireland where Bradbury worked to reduce Melville's 135 chapters to a script of 148 pages with 54 plot events that could be filmed. With Bradbury writing and Huston approving or discarding, it took some 1,200 pages of outlines and screenplay to reach the final script. When Huston put his name on the screen credits as co-author, Bradbury was upset and instituted an appeal with the Screen Writers' Guild to have Huston's name removed, but the appeal failed (Kaminsky, p. 103).

Huston has always praised the script Bradbury produced, and Bradbury himself has said, "I'm very proud of the screenplay," and the "film is almost magnificent." Recognizing in his own and Melville's work the influence of Shakespeare, Bradbury says that he and Huston aimed for a combination of "the Shakespeare approach which is sheer language and the cinematic approach which is pure image." His gift to the film, he felt, was "to make metaphors that are clear and that fuse many dissimilar things together" (Thomas Atkins, pp. 49–50). While critics of the film would disagree about success in his intention, many might agree that Bradbury has stripped the novel down to its pure narrative form but with respect for Melville's intentions. In fact, one academic critic, Perry Miller, who felt that Melville's novel got away from his original intention in the throes of inspiration and composition, has noted, "Curiously enough, Mr. Huston's film, in an effort to make the drama of Ahab's monomaniac hunt for the malignant whale comprehensible to modern audiences, works back from the romance as it now stands to the original conception" (Miller, p. 2).

Huston's own intention appears most succinctly in a statement he made over twenty-five years later:

One could not hope merely to transfer the novel to the screen. Melville's book has that wonderful, random, disparate quality. Authors of the last century could indulge themselves more, the way Melville did with those chapters on the flensing of whales. He allows himself to slip under the influence of Shakespeare, too, and goes into the dramatic form. So, calling the picture *Moby Dick* is, in a sense, only a means of identification. The essential, however, is Melville's philosophic argument. Ahab speaks for Melville, and through him he is raging at the deity. This point, by the way, was never commented on by any critic who saw the picture, not even those who championed it. They failed to recognize that the work was a blasphemy. The message of Moby Dick was hate. The whale is the mask of a malignant deity who torments mankind. Ahab pits himself against this evil power. Melville doesn't choose to call the power Satan, but God. I thought the picture was quite good when it was released. But it went against the critics' preconceptions. And what they wrote influenced the way the picture was received by audiences. They seemed to expect Ahab as a raging madman, the way Charles Laughton [John Barrymore] played him in an earlier version. I rejected that. Then there were those who thought of *Moby Dick* as an adventure story. No kid of ten is going to read *Moby Dick*. It takes the hard application of an adult mind to appreciate Melville. It is anything but an adventure story. (Joseph E. Persico, p. 13)

The script was the least of Huston's worries. That took one year to complete, the filming took a second year, and the editing and scoring a third year. Just a few of the many difficulties Huston encountered are related in the first two chapters of seaman Alan Villiers's *Give Me a Ship to Sail*, where he describes his efforts to keep the recreated *Pequod* afloat, a "miss-rigged and ill-balanced little brute, product of a non-maritime art department and a trawler yard at Hull" (Villiers, p. 5), during the filming in 1954. He tells of the loss of the artificial white whale, the uncooperativeness of nature, and Huston's drive for authentic action. Villiers joined Huston only because "I believed in his endeavor to make a real sea film of *Moby Dick*, such as never had been tried before" (Villiers, p. 14). After numerous difficulties, accidents, and insurmountable problems, Huston finally gave up and headed for a studio to finish the film. Villiers later served as technical adviser for the Ustinov version of *Billy Budd* in 1962.

Huston's *Moby Dick* is clearly the most devoted effort to translate into film the letter and spirit of Melville's novel, which in its stylistic and philosophic depths ultimately defies any sort of adaptation. Bradbury obviously stood in awe of the original and fashioned a script that often uses Melville's own language, or a semblance of it anyway, and remains faithful to the plot. The earlier producers of the Barrymore versions found it impossible to bring the film to its original tragic conclusion, but Huston hesitated not a moment. Given the total lack of love interest and the pessimistic mood of the film, it is a wonder it did well at the box office. Perhaps the exciting chase scenes carried the film. Certainly the unusual use of color to establish mood and the expert photography of Oswald Morris and Freddie Francis make viewing the film an engaging experience.

Huston used authentic sea chanties, work songs, and folk traditions of the mariner's world to lend credibility to his fictional world, and his re-creations of New Bedford and the Spouter Inn seem appropriate, though not historically accurate. In the beginning credits, Huston acknowledges the assistance of the Mystic Seaport Marine Historical Association, the Old Dartmouth Historical Association, and the British Museum of Oceanography. The intent of such credits may be to lend the film a pedigree of authenticity, however, rather than acknowledge actual assistance which was heeded.

Water and the sea are established as the main images at the start, as well as the overpowering presence of natural forces. These are underlined by the violent storm which drives Ishmael into the inn, the monologue on the whale by the sailor at the bar, the image of Ahab passing outside in his black clothing, the ominous entrance of Queequeg into Ishmael's bedroom with the shrunken head, Father Mapple's church with rows of memorial tablets for those destroyed by whales (including an entire whaler, the *George Herriot*), and the sermon on Jonah as remarkably rendered by Orson Welles. The prophecy delivered at dockside by the mad Elijah adds a note of the supernatural.

Gregory Peck's gentle voice, better suited to wise and rational characters or noble lawyers, seems ill-suited at first to the imposing figure he strikes, a stern authoritarian Lincoln in black. But he warms up to the role and soon matches voice with appearance. Ahab's egomania is made clear, as well as the inscrutability of the universe. A good many of the thematic threads of the film are the very philosophic dichotomies which so engaged Melville—blasphemy vs. piety, egomania vs. social responsibility, individualism vs. authority, survival vs. death, violence vs. pacifism, civilization vs. savagery, and man vs. nature.

The whale is a bit on the mechanical side, as one would expect, but much more realistic than those used in the earlier films. This one appears to have been influenced by the wonderful animated whale in Walt Disney's *Pinocchio*, particularly the scene in which its jaws open camera front to swallow up the boat containing Ahab. The viewer is reminded of a similar scene in the Disney film in which the puppet is swallowed by the whale.

Reviewers were overwhelmingly positive: "a brilliant film" (*Time*); "a mighty spectacle, whose very failings are majestic" (*Newsweek*); "one of the great motion pictures of our times" (Bosley Crowther, *New York Times*); "one of the great motion pictures of all time" (*Senior Scholastic*); "a kind of monumental work" (Hollis Alpert, *Saturday Review*); and "a hell of an exciting piece of movie-making" (John McCarten, *The New Yorker*). One reviewer found it a "good work and possibly is as much of *Moby Dick* as can be transferred to the screen" (Robert Hatch, *The Nation*), while another went so far as to say that "Ray Bradbury's screen play . . . is in some ways an improvement on the original book" (Robert Bingham, *Reporter*).

Many praised the technical craftsmanship which went into the details of whaling, as well as the innovative cinematography—both color and black and white prints were made from the original Technicolor negative and then superimposed in the printing process to create the effect of color steel engravings. Almost to a person, however, the reviewers found Gregory Peck inappropriate or inadequate for the part of Captain Ahab. The New York Film Critics Award was given *Moby Dick* for best direction, and Huston was named best director of the year by the Motion Picture National Board of Review. Indicators of its broad popular appeal were adaptations of the film into a comic book version in the Dell series, a typical *Mad* magazine satire called "Morbid Dick," and a foto-novella version in Italy (composed of stills from the movie with dialogue balloons lettered directly onto them in comic book fashion).

When academic critics began to close in on the film, however, it became a different story. George Barbarow found the film mechanical, uninspired, and completely lacking in the evocative beauty of Melville's style: this "film-drama substitute for *Moby Dick*, constructed without conscious style, and thus without distinction, evokes no wonder-world at all" (p. 273). Milton Stern, in "A New Harpoon for the Great White Whale" (1956), found the film "a very bad *Moby Dick*" (p. 565), but went on here, as in his longer essay "The Whale and the Minnow: *Moby Dick* and the Movies" (1956), to enumerate instructive ways it could be used in the classroom to teach an appreciation of the novel. Stern's essays were based on a reading of the film script, as was that of Tyrus Hillway. In fact, Hillway recounts how he was consulted and allowed to criticize the script in 1954 as the project was in progress, for the most part to little avail. Finally, he felt that the film was unfair to the public, to Melville, and perhaps to the whale: he concluded, "Having withstood several generations of nearly complete neglect before the twenties, Melville's reputation should prove tough enough to withstand this assault from Hollywood" (p. 298).

While the attitude of most Melville scholars has remained the same for the almost three decades since Huston's effort, perhaps the most fair-minded statement was made by William Murray in his review for *The Village Voice*:

The virtues of this "Moby Dick" are many ...; above all, a literate script that is faithful to Melville and makes effective use of some of the most strikingly poetic passages in the text. Whatever faults this movie may have are owing, after all, to a commercial framework within which every American director has to work. Rather than perish on his artistic principles, Huston has always chosen to make his movie, compromising but yielding as little of himself as possible. That he remains an artist is a tribute not to his talent, but to his detachment. Ignore the aesthetes and see this movie. (p. 6)

One might add that the film is to be evaluated on its own terms as a cinematic experience: to say that it is not the novel is not only to state the obvious but also is finally irrelevant. Among all the Melville adaptations to popular culture, it appears to be the most conscientious in its allegiance to the spirit of Melville's work.

Whatever its strengths or weaknesses, Huston's *Moby Dick* has retained a high reputation among the public as *the* definitive film adaptation, such that no one else has dared to take it on. There is another adaptation, however, one that is unique in conception and that was undertaken, completed, and released while Huston was in the throes of editing and scoring. This is a half-hour color film called *Herman Melville's Moby Dick*, produced and directed by Jerry Winters and released commercially on 23 May 1955, at the Paris Theatre in New York, on a double bill with *The Great Adventure*. Using a series of paintings by artist and Melville-devotee Gilbert Wilson, a script read by actor Thomas Mitchell, and original music by Richard Mohaupt, Winters produced a striking and effective tribute to the novel. Melville's words and Wilson's conceptions of the main characters keep the production close to the original and make an engaging introduction to Melville's major thematic concerns. While the film was well received, the mounting publicity over Huston's film seems to have pushed Winters's from public attention.

In the flush of excitement over the praise *Moby Dick* received just after its release, Huston announced his intention to film Melville's *Typee* (Kaminsky, p. 108) with Gregory Peck and jockey Bill Pearson in the lead roles, but this proved to be a joke on his part. Oddly enough, however, the next Melville screen adaptation was indeed *Typee*. At least one other person had the same idea, since the Melville Collection at the Newberry Library contains an undated mimeographed copy of a screenplay for *Typee* by Philip Ansel Roll which features Melville himself as one of the lead characters. As far as anyone knows, this script was never filmed.

An adaptation of *Typee* did appear in 1958 under the title *Enchanted Island*, a Technicolor romance vehicle for the popular Dana Andrews and Jane Powell. There were, again, few connections between the book and the film, except for a vaguely similar plot, the use of the name Fayaway, and the setting among the Polynesian tribes Happar and Typee. It is more a retelling of the Captain John Smith and Pocahontas legend than a version of Melville, although it reflects the traditional pattern of conflicts between civilization and primitive life and repeats all the stereotypes of noble savages and untainted primitive beauties, cultural myths which Melville helped establish in his early works but which Hollywood had carried to new levels of visual power and influence.

The setting is Nukuheva in 1842. The film opens with natives happily at play on the beach as visiting sailors take shore leave and rush to the waiting arms of local maidens and drinks from a resident Scot entrepreneur named James Dooley. Lifting two of the maidens from among Dooley's daughters and nieces, two sailors, Abner Bedford (Dana Andrews) and another named Tom (Tommo and Toby in the book), speak dialogue unfortunately characteristic of the film: Ab says, "My girl can only say yes." Tom replies, "That's a girl worth having." The grim captain, who suspects that sin is rampant on the island, commands the crew to return to the ship. Ab argues for permission to stay; the captain relents but warns them that the natives inland are cannibals and they should not be tempted to desert. At Dooley's beach bar, a fight erupts between the captain and Ab which requires that he desert. Tom, who is wounded in the fray, joins him.

The two sailors head into the jungle hoping to find the friendly Happars and avoid the deadly Typees. Back at the beach the captain makes a deal with Dooley to bring them back. Weak from his wound, Tom is helped into a cave full of human bones. In a discussion about Ab's desire for freedom and women, he says "A man is never free of women until he has one of his own." This is as philosophic as the movie becomes. Dooley discovers them and makes a counterdeal to lead them to a safe place for their wages. Fearing betrayal, they escape again and come upon an idyllic village to which they are led by a beautiful maiden, Fayaway. They discover the people to be the dreaded Typees.

The next morning Fayaway (Jane Powell) brings food, and a relationship between her and Ab obviously begins. Tom is cured by the medicine man, and when Dooley shows up to retrieve them, they refuse to leave. Ab and Fayaway witness the execution of a man who has stolen the love of another man's wife, his first initiation into their brutal system of justice. Ab and Tom become pets of the island girls, and they relax until a Happar war party arrives. Having grown tired of the pampering, they at first start to escape during the battle, but then Ab cannot allow another warrior to spear the chief Mehevi and acts to save his life. They now become friends and trusted braves. Ab courts Fayaway with Mehevi's approval (he is her grandfather, and we find that she has Anglo blood). When Ab appears inclined to stay, Tom escapes alone. Ab concludes that he finds in Fayaway the freedom he has been looking for, so they marry in a tribal ceremony.

Paradise is interrupted when parts of Tom's clothing begin to appear in the village. Mehevi reveals that Tom was killed to keep Typee safe from the outside world. Ab and Fayaway are sentenced to death when Ab breaks a tabu in discovering the fate of Tom. Ab's original ship suddenly returns, and Ab escapes taking Fayaway with him. Once Ab is on board, Fayaway turns back and is wounded by her own people. Ab retrieves her, and the captain plans to marry them properly in a Christian ceremony. Impressed by Ab's spunk and devotion, the captain forgives his desertion and concludes that married men make better sailors anyway.

Enchanted Island mercifully attracted little or no attention from the critics or the movie-going public. *Variety* noted that it "features some spectacular location scenery as background and practically nothing but confusion in the foreground," but "It isn't fair to blame the actors for the debacle."

In 1962 film production of *Billy Budd* was inspired by the successful Broadway dramatization written by poet Louis O. Coxe and his Princeton classmate Robert H. Chapman. First produced unsuccessfully in 1949 as *Uniform of Flesh*, the play was revised as *Billy Budd* and opened for a long run on 10 February 1951 at the Biltmore Theatre in New York. The play was broadcast over television in the Dupont Show of the Month series on 25 May 1959. It was primarily the play, rather than the short novel, that Peter Ustinov turned to in 1962 for his motion picture.

Of all Melville's works, it would seem that *Billy Budd* most effectively lends itself to dramatic treatment and easy adaptation to the film medium. The characterizations are explicit and clear, the conflict lends itself to argumentation and debate, and the outcome is likely to move the reader. The issues raised—freedom vs. authority, individual liberty vs. the good of the group, temporal law vs. divine justice, and human goodness vs. innate depravity—are central to the survival of society and civilization. The film script written by Ustinov, Dewitt Bodeen, and an uncredited Robert Rossen benefited by having been filtered through the structure and strictures of Coxe and Chapman's drama. Ustinov's direction and control are admirable, and the motion picture emerged as what many consider a minor masterpiece in American filmmaking.

The casting was impeccable—Ustinov's Vere is appropriately sensitive but strictly devoted to his duties as an officer in time of war; Robert Ryan is perfectly sinister as Claggart in one of the most credibly evil roles during his career as a heavy; Melvyn Douglas is well-suited by age and temperament to the Dansker's role as a prophet and seer into the darker recesses of the human soul; and Terence Stamp in his first and perhaps most accomplished role of his career is the innocent, good-natured peacemaker Billy Budd. Even the secondary and minor roles are well cast, and several worthy performances are found among the ship's crew, without even a glimpse of a female except for the wooden blind justice which serves as a figurehead for the ship.

Melville's tale, however, is more in the direction of a parable, with almost allegoric characters engaged in the Biblical drama of seduction and the fall of man in the Garden of Eden, as interpreted by John Milton, whose influence pervades the text. Ustinov, therefore, to make the characters credible for the purposes of dramatic engagement, moves in the direction of making them more human and three dimensional in their presence. Thus Billy Budd stammers, he says, "Because I sometimes can't find the words for what I feel," making the speech impediment, which is his single mark of imperfection in the novel, into a lack of facility for finding the proper words to express himself. The touch of original sin becomes a more understandable lack of skill in rhetoric and speech. Lest we consider him effeminate, his fight with Jenkins demonstrates his masculinity and physical power. He becomes less angelic and symbolic and more corporeal and fully rounded.

Ustinov is first seen with a book and his spectacles to underline the scholarly side of Captain Vere. Claggart's evil nature is demonstrated by a variety of actions, as in his mistreatment of Jenkins (forcing him to clean up the spilled soup and finally sending him sick to his watch and death) and his taunting of the crew to disobey with flogging as punishment. Claggart even bares his back to the crew and calls them pigs because they lack the courage to strike back. Each character is given full development to make him credible before the symbolic drama begins.

In many ways the film becomes a polemic for fair treatment and just dealing with impressed men during time of war. Concern over mutiny and dissent and the natural rights of man are a part of Melville's story, but the focus there becomes finally a matter of the struggle between divine good and original sin. The film must move into the arena of the natural forces that move ordinary men in the real world. In a conversation between Claggart and Billy, which has no counterpart in the novel, Claggart almost yields to Billy's natural goodness and genuine human interest; he shows a side almost ready to accept brotherly love, but moves quickly to eradicate the emotion. Melville's Claggart, however, is incapable of even the inclination toward such feeling.

Billy Budd garnered largely positive reviews, most critics finding it well acted, expertly directed, and impressively filmed. There were a few naysayers, however: Jay Jacobs in *The Reporter* preferred the play to the movie, and Stanley Kauffmann in the *New Republic* found it a failure from start to finish, with the script ill-proportioned, the editing clumsy, the directing incompetent, and Ustinov comically unbearable. In the only critical essay fully devoted to the film, "Melville's Sailor in the Sixties" (1977), Robert L. Nadeau finds a series of faults which he blames on Ustinov without recognizing their source in the Coxe and Chapman play. Nadeau also posits several interpretations of Melville's original text with which many scholars would disagree, implying that Melville's intentions in the incomplete and contradictory story have been agreed on among critics. The only redeeming virtue he can find is that the film may have struck a responsive chord in the rebellious youth of the 1960s, which does little to explain its continued popularity on the rental circuit in more conservative times.

It is strange that the most frequently filmed piece of fiction by Melville, next to *Moby-Dick*, is his short story "Bartleby the Scrivener," but two of the efforts were noncommercial educational films and therefore do not qualify for discussion here. The tale's action becomes increasingly static as the hero gradually prefers not to participate in the affairs of the world, and its conflict becomes increasingly internal as the lawyer-narrator wrestles with his own conscience and the limits of one's sense of responsibility for other human beings. There is not a lot to be staged.

In 1971 a commercial *Bartleby* was released in Britain, under the direction of Anthony Friedman, and starring two accomplished actors, Paul Scofield and John McEnery. It was released in the United States a year later (but a review print was not available for discussion in this chapter). According to reviews, Friedman updated the story by moving it to contemporary London and turning Bartleby into an audit clerk in an accounting office. He somehow extended the action to an hour and eighteen minutes by adding business like Bartleby's being taken to a hospital ward where he is diagnosed as suffering from malnutrition, anemia, and low blood pressure. By making Bartleby a point-of-view character, and allowing him an inner life beyond his few words in the story, he becomes representative of the modern alienated individual rather than the enigma of Melville's creation. Despite these alterations toward clarity, most reviewers felt that the film was too esoteric for general audiences, but nearly everyone had praise for the stunning performances of McEnery and Scofield, the first remarkable for his calculated restraint in a role that could easily become pathetic, and the second impressive for the subtle bewilderment and amiable humanity he conveyed. While she praised it as an honorable labor of love, Pauline Kael in *The New Yorker* concluded, "The film has little to recommend it but the two actors, Melville's dialogue, and the remnants of his great, spooky conception" (p. 92). No doubt other producers will yet have another go at this one.

COMICS

The American comic book, which originated in 1933, was less than a decade old but at a peak of wide popularity when the first adaptation of Melville was undertaken. This is the *Classics Comics* version of *Moby Dick*, No. 5 in the series, with illustrations by Louis Zansky. It follows the plot of the original closely, with more details included than any subsequent comic book version (faithfulness was a criterion largely followed in the *Classics Comics*, often to their detriment as comic art), but little effort was made to include any of the novel's larger ideas. There is a slight nod toward the book's cetology since technical information is included about the differences between right whales and sperm whales, as well as the diagram of the *Pequod* and maps charting the ship's progress. The art is often wooden and uninspired, but occasionally Zansky turns out a nicely designed panel (he was better with ships than human forms). A single-page biography of Melville follows the story with an illustrated version of Emerson's "Concord Hymn" on the last page. It proved to be one of the *Classics Comics* bestselling issues, going through thirteen reprintings between 1942 and 1954.

With confidence in its continued popularity, the Gilberton Company commissioned entirely new art and a painted cover (as opposed to the line-drawn cover used earlier) for a new edition in 1956, which would see another ten reprintings through 1971. With a total of twenty-four printings, *Moby Dick* was one of the three most popular of the *Classics Comics* (known as *Classics Illustrated* after 1947), with only *Ivanhoe* and *Robin Hood* surpassing it with twenty-six printings each. In addition to British and Irish editions, the *Moby Dick* issue was translated and published in numerous countries including Denmark, Germany, Greece, Holland, Iceland, Norway, and Sweden. There was at least one other effort to compete with the *Classics* adaptation at the height of its popularity; this was *Features Presentation Magazine* No. 6 (June 1950) devoted to a rendition of *Moby Dick* by talented artist Wallace Wood (a copy was not available for review here).

Another Melville title was undertaken by *Classics Illustrated* in 1947 with the publication of issue No. 36: *Typee*, illustrated by Ezra Whiteman and adapted by Harry Miller. While this adaptation is also faithful, with no concessions to simplify the vocabulary (a few footnotes are even included), the art is stiff and primitive and does not match the competence of the text. Nevertheless, it went through six printings until 1969 (it had received a new painted cover in 1960). Entirely new art was commissioned for a new edition probably around 1961 just before Gilberton ceased publishing new versions. It is a pity that the new rendition was never published as the drawing was done by the inspired comic book artist Luis Dominguez, and the text adds material from the novel (even including the endnote Melville added about Richard Tobias Greene). Although the art is closer to book illustration than the comic book, the adaptation is a faithful and effective one. The original art and printer's proofs were discovered and published by W. J. Briggs in his fan publication *The Classics Reader*, No. 11 (September 1980).

The Argentines, who have always found comic books of great interest, made at least one attempt to adapt *Moby-Dick*. This rendition by artist Carlos Roume appeared in the publication *Pimpinela: Obras Completas y Grandes Historietas* in July 1952. It is workmanlike but not particularly distinguished.

The most beautifully rendered comic book of *Moby-Dick* was issued by an educational publisher, Pendulum Press, in 1973. It is a black and white 8″ by 5 1/4″ paperback edition published as a part of the *Now Age Illustrated* series designed to improve reading skills and strengthen vocabulary for young readers. With a text by Irwin Shapiro, art by Alex Nino, and the editorial supervision of Vincent Fago, each a seasoned contributor to commercial comic books, this version achieves a mood and style appropriate to Melville, with its emphasis on grotesque caricature, careful detail, and cinematic point-of-view. This is comic book story-telling at its finest. A regular-sized comic book edition in color was issued as number 8 in the *Marvel Classics Comics* series in 1976, but the color merely serves to detract from Nino's fine penwork and the story has been abbreviated by seven pages to fit a forty-eight-page format.

A similar educational effort to improve reading skills was undertaken in 1977 by King Features syndicate's *King Classics*, with motivational posters, teacher's guides, exercises, lesson plans, and dramatizations on cassette tapes, for use in the classroom. According to promotional materials, the texts were written by Marion Kimberly, a reading specialist and professor of education. Number 3 in the series is *Moby Dick*. The artist is not identified, and the story is laid out in a cramped, stilted comic strip format, with no effort made to take advantage of the artistic potential of the full comic book page. The dialogue seems to have been modernized (vocabulary is at the fourth-fifth grade level), as when Ishmael says at first sight of Queequeg, "Oh boy! Look at my bed partner! He looks like a real character." The narrative is oddly developed and poorly explained; the text often does not fit the balloons, and the whole gives the appearance of having been poorly translated from another language (the books were copyrighted by Editorial Bruguera and printed in Barcelona, which suggests a Spanish origin). The characters appear to have been modeled after the actors in John Huston's film, especially Ahab after Gregory Peck. In fact, Ahab's death is modeled after Huston's rather than Melville's account, with the mad captain tangled in the ropes and harpoons around the whale's body. Children are not likely to be inspired to better reading by this botched adaptation, the unfortunate result of well-meaning educators who have no appreciation for the special qualities of comic book art.

A foreign and strikingly different adaptation of *Moby-Dick*, which in many ways has more integrity and style as comic art than all the others, is the one published by Ediciones Larousse in Spain in the *Maravillas de la Literature* series, with text by Carlos R. Soria and art by Chiqui de la Fuente. This is a full-color forty-four page version published in a large 8 1/2 by 11″ paperback. The distinctive feature is that the drawings are done in the style of caricature and humorous cartooning (what is sometimes called the "big foot" style) rather than realism. Although the Spanish-language text takes a few liberties with the novel, and some comic interludes have been included out of animated cartoons or slapstick comedy, this approach does not trivialize the subject. Rather, it adds an appropriate touch of the grotesque and a spirit of comic pathos to a tale about insanity and egomania, among other things. An earlier Spanish-language comic book version of *Moby-Dick* by Pedro Alferez is discussed, accompanied by reprints of three pages, in Kruse's *Illustrationen zu Melvilles "Moby Dick*," the catalog for the 1976 exhibition held in Schleswig. This catalog is also an important source of information about the entire history of illustrated editions of *Moby-Dick*.

Aside from its typical parody of the Huston film in 1956, *Mad* magazine took a crack at the real article in one of its original paperbacks of 1981, *Mad Clobbers the Classics*, written by Larry Siegel and illustrated by Angelo Torres. One of the eleven classics satirized is "*Mopey Duke* by Helmsman Marvel," and the spoof proves to be as uninspired as the title. In no way a true satire of Melville or the novel, it is an exercise in silliness and no representation of the *Mad* style of wit at its best.

In addition to the direct adaptations of *Moby-Dick* to the comic book format, any number of comic book stories over the years have used parts of the novel, its ideas, or its plot structure as a source of inspiration. The concept of a half-crazed figure of authority in pursuit of an ambiguous brute force to a disastrous conclusion holds a basic or elemental appeal for the popular imagination. Only a few examples can be discussed here.

Man Comics No. 3 (1950) includes a story about a white-bearded whaler chasing a "killer" sperm whale, but the whale is gray rather than white. The only story in which the pursued beast communicates with its pursuer is "Dreadful Discovery" in *Uncanny Tales* No. 53 (March 1957), drawn by Angelo Torres. Two scientists in search of information about the brain capacity of the white whale receive telepathic communications from one which warns them away before it threatens destruction. In an interesting atomic-age conclusion, they decide against revealing the whale's intellectual superiority for fear it will discourage man's efforts to maintain dominance through scientific inquiry. The Legion of Super-Heroes take on Leviathan in a colossal battle in outer space in the year 2965 in "The Super-Moby Dick of Space" in *Adventure Comics* No. 332 (May 1965), with story by Edmond Hamilton and art by John Forte.

In "Waters of Darkness, River of Doom," *Ka-Zar, Lord of The Hidden Jungle* No. 6 (November 1974), with art by John Buscema and story by Gerry Conway, a Tarzan-like warrior named Ka-Zar defeats a giant behemoth which earlier had maimed a barbarian and sent him on an insane search to revenge the loss of an arm and an eye. *Kamandi, The Last Boy on Earth* No. 23 (November 1974), written and drawn by Jack Kirby, is but one chapter in an epic struggle in the twenty-first century which features a character named Ahab who is destroyed by a black killer whale. A more direct use of Melville occurs in "Call Me Ahab," written by Don F. Glut and drawn by Frank Bolle, in *Grimm's Ghost Stories* No. 24 (July 1975). Ken Henrick, a contemporary adventurous boater, goes out too far, encounters Moby Dick, and is rescued by the spirits of Ahab and his crew on the *Pequod* which linger near the whale. Henrick is persuaded to complete the task of slaying Moby Dick so the spirits can rest, which he does, and when the ship fades away, he stays alive only by clinging to a wooden leg tossed him by the ghostly Ahab.

The most ambitious and original use of the plot pattern and themes of Melville's *Moby-Dick* in a comic book narrative is found in the eight-part series, "Abraxas and the Earthman," written and illustrated by Rick Veitch, and published in sequential issues of the adult comic magazine *Epic Illustrated*, beginning in issue No. 10 (February 1982) and ending in issue No. 17 (April 1983). The parallels with the novel, the circumlocutions of the plot, and the number of characters are too complex for a brief summary here. Basically, it concerns two earthmen who are shanghaied by Captain Ratwang to assist his pursuit of Abraxas, the great red whale, to which he lost a limb. Finally, however, the story concerns the mystic unity of the universe, and while Ratwang goes down to defeat, "the gap between the mortal and immortal realms of existence" is bridged. In a letter to this writer (7 June 1983), author-artist Veitch has written:

Is "Abraxas and the Earthman" an extension of "Moby Dick" either philosophically or thematically?—*Both*, of course, because I see the philosophy and theme intertwined in the archetypal conflict between Ahab and the whale. I think anyone who has taken a freshman lit course must be consciously aware that there is powerful symbolism evident here, so powerful in fact that even little children instinctively recognize there is more to "Moby Dick" than just a battle between man and beast. There is a crippled Ahab that walks the decks of all our psyches, screaming vengeance against *whatever it is* (God? creativity? our own untapped potential?) that lives hidden beneath the waves of the unconscious, and is personified in the great white whale! My story means to say that in the century since Melville constellated this archetype the relationships between the captain, the whale, and the *witness* (Ishmael in Moby Dick, Isaac in my story) have gained considerably, to the point that the whale and the witness at the end become joined in a symbiotic union. The message is that in this day and age if we can transcend our Ahab tendencies then *whatever it is* that the whale symbolizes becomes accessible to us (though dangerous in many ways).

Veitch's full-color art work is impressive, and while it draws on a wide range of sources from fantasy and comic art, he brings to the comic page a vision uniquely his own and one that is respectful of Melville's. The series constitutes a graphic novel that should be published in one volume.

A series of stories by Walt Disney Studios in *Moby Duck*, a comic book issued from October 1967 through February 1978, features a duck character by that name, captain of a small boat on which various Disney characters serve—Goofy, Gyro Gearloose, and Gladstone Gander, among them. Moby Duck has been known to chase whales, but none of the stories contain any Melville references.

A useful guide to plot patterns, settings, and subjects in six of the comic books mentioned above (including the *Classics Comics* and *Marvel Classics Comics* adaptations) is *Moby Dick Comics: A Preserved Context Index to Several Adaptations and Take-Offs on Moby Dick by Herman Melville*, a pamphlet written and privately published by Randall W. Scott, librarian in charge of the Popular Culture Collection at the Michigan State University Library.

Although an adaptation of *Moby-Dick* to the pages of the funny papers would seem like an unlikely idea, it has been tried at least a couple of times. Coulton Waugh's *Dickie Dare* (originated by Milton Caniff in 1933 before *Terry and the Pirates*) was an adventure strip about young Dickie's involvement with pirates, criminals, spies, and gun-runners on the high seas. In a sequence published 21–27 September 1954 (by then actually drawn by Waugh's wife Mabel Odin Burvik), Dickie's older soldier-of-fortune companion Dan Flynn retells in brief the story of the novel, and then in 1956 the comic strip featured a fuller version which lasted four weeks or twenty-eight episodes. *The Imaginary Adventures of Little Orvy* by Rick Yager (longtime artist and writer for the *Buck Rogers* series) was a humorous Sunday feature about a youngster who daydreams his way into various adventures. In a sequence during March and April of 1960, Little Orvy dropped in on the *Pequod* and helped Ahab chase Moby Dick.

While such adaptations are rare, references to and appearances of Moby Dick and Captain Ahab in humorous comic strips and panel cartoons are quite common. The one strip where Melville references have most frequently been found over the last thirty-five years is *Peanuts* by Charles Schulz. Often these references occur in sequences having to do with Snoopy as aspiring writer, author of *It Was a Dark and Stormy Night* and other unpublished novels. On 29 April 1975, for example, Schroeder hands back a manuscript to Snoopy and says, "Your novel starts too slowly...you need a more powerful beginning." In the final panel, Snoopy types, "Call me Ishmael." Two weeks later, on 12 May, Schroeder tells him, "You know what Herman Melville said? He said, 'To produce a mighty book you must choose a mighty theme.'" After absorbing this advice, Snoopy types the title for his new novel, "The Dog."

References to *Moby-Dick* are likely to appear in comic strips with a classroom setting. In a sequence in *Shoe* by Jeff MacNelly, 4 May 1983, the Perfesser's nephew, Skylar, is at his school desk writing: "Book Report: *Moby Dick* by Herman Melville. For one of the all-time classics of literature...this is a surprisingly good book." The next day Skylar continues: "*Moby Dick* is the story of one man's obsession with finishing off a mysterious, huge, white whale—something this reviewer can really identify with." In the 11 February 1984 sequence of *Elwood*, an entire class has their hands up. The teacher responds, "Okay, okay, okay... everybody can go see the school nurse!" Then she thinks to herself, "That's amazing! In all the years I've been teaching, that's the first time I've seen a whole class get sick at the same time." On the blackboard is the following: "English Final Exam: Conjugate all the verbs in 'Moby Dick' (you have 50 minutes)." The assignment is nonsense, of course, but presumably just the mention of *Moby-Dick* will strike fear into the hearts of students everywhere.

Other references occur in a variety of contexts. On 27 January 1984, Johnny Hart's B.C. sights a whale and shouts "Thar she blows!" The ugly broad says, "Why is it always 'Thar *she* blows' and never 'Thar *he* blows'?" B.C. responds, "'Cause I'm writing a book called 'Moby Jane'!" A gravedigger in T. K. Ryan's comic western *Tumbleweeds* on 17 November 1982 writes in his log, "2:30 p.m.—At half fathom depth—Course: due South—Weather holding—smooth shoveling—All clear fore, aft and abeam—." Claude Clay, the undertaker, thinks, "I wish I'd never loaned him 'Moby Dick.'" Tom Wilson's Ziggy visits a bookstore where the salesman holds up a book called "Moby Disk" and says, "It's the story of an epic struggle between man and computer" (18 July 1984). In Gary Larson's absurdist panel *The Far Side*, a child looks gleefully into an aquarium on 14 May 1983, where six black and one white tropical fish swim about at a pet shop. Says the doting mother, "Well, little Ahab . . . which one is it going to be?" In another *Far Side* panel of 7 February 1984, a struggling writer sits at his desk with a pile of abandoned first pages for a novel *Moby Dick* scattered around him, some of which read, "Call me Bill," "Call me Al," "Call me Larry," "Call me Roger," and "Call me Warren."

Both Melville and *Moby-Dick* have inspired thousands of gag cartoons in such magazines as *The New Yorker, Playboy, Punch*, and *Saturday Evening Post*, among the best known. There are too many to be summarized here, but usually they have to do with Melville receiving editorial advice or working on his novel, with Ahab entangled in the lines of the harpoons around Moby Dick (a la Huston's film), or with the difficulties of reading the book. In many of the men's magazines, the cartoons often take an erotic or salacious turn. An entire anthology could be compiled of depictions of Melville and his works in popular comic art, editorial cartoons, gag cartoons, and caricature. If scholars have taken Melville too seriously, then America's comic artists have compensated by finding inexhaustible uses for him in their humor and satire. It largely is a comedy of appreciation, however, rather than ridicule. The joke is often on the reader unable to come to terms with the magnitude of the writer and his ideas.

RADIO, TELEVISION, AND RECORDINGS

Radio

The radio network system was born when the National Broadcasting Company began operations on 15 November 1926. Almost from the start, drama was a natural and frequent fare for filling the airwaves, and fairly early along, adaptations of literary works seemed to be a way of adding culture and quality to the comedies, soaps, and mysteries that formed the bulk of broadcasting schedules. Because so little of the material was preserved, however, anything like a comprehensive survey of Melville adaptations for radio is not possible, but records and tapes of a few do still exist.

The earliest recorded adaptation was the two-part, sixty-minute version of *Moby-Dick* done for the notable CBS experimental theater, *The Columbia Workshop* (John Dunning, pp. 144–45), which aired 19 and 26 October 1946. (Tapes and a copy of the script are available in the archives of the Museum of Broadcasting, 1 East 53rd Street, New York 10022.) Like nearly all the radio adaptations, this version emphasizes the dramatizable events of the novel and incorporates a minimum of the philosophy, thus making the story into the tale of a demented man out to wreak revenge on a brutal beast of the sea. It was good enough stuff to fascinate the listener, however, with sound effects emulating storms at sea, the murmurings of an unsettled crew, and the sinking of a ship by a powerful whale. For technicians, it was a glorious assignment, but there is nothing particularly distinctive about the production, other than an unwillingness to tamper with or expand on Melville.

In the late 1940s all three major networks attempted radio adaptations of *Moby-Dick (MSN* No. 3). Versions of the novel were heard on *Adventure Parade* (Mutual), a daily fifteen-minute serialization with all the voices done by host-storyteller John Drake (Dunning, p. 6); *CBS School of the Air: Tales of Adventure No. 3*; and *Tell It Again* (CBS), a Sunday afternoon program for young listeners. In 1949 *The NBC University Theatre of the Air* offered *Moby-Dick* as a sixty-minute home-study course in conjunction with the University of Louisville and Washington State College. *Moby-Dick* also aired on Mutual's half-hour *Family Theatre* (Dunning, pp. 193–94; *MSN* No. 5, p. 3), CBS's *Hallmark Playhouse* (Dunning, pp. 263–64), and *NBC Star Playhouse* with Frederic March as Ahab (*MSN* Nos. 9 and 12).

The 1950s also saw three efforts to dramatize "Bartleby the Scrivener": twice on Sir Laurence Olivier's *Theatre Royal (MSN* No. 10, Spring 1954, p. 3 and *MSN* No. 13) and Ronald Colman's *Favorite Story* on ABC (Dunning, p. 199; *MSN* No. 12). A dramatization of *Billy Budd* was aired in 1963 on Helen Hayes's *General Electric Theatre* with a repertory company that included Cyril Ritchard, Peter Ustinov, Joseph Cotten, Agnes Moorehead, and Dina Merrill (Dunning, pp. 272–73).

Perhaps the most interesting broadcast of *Moby-Dick* occurred in 1971 when the entire text of the novel was read aloud over station WBAI in New York by volunteer radio listeners, beginning at 7:15P.M. Christmas Eve and ending shortly after midnight on Christmas day (*Melville Society Extracts* No. 10, p. 7). Three recent dramatizations of works by Melville have been done by WGBH Public Broadcasting in Boston: *Moby-Dick*, produced in a five-part series of one-hour programs in 1979 on the *Masterpiece Radio Theatre*, hosted by Julie Harris; a two-part version of *Billy Budd* in 1983 written by Marvin Mandell, produced and directed by Everett C. Frost, with Robert Brustein as Captain Vere for *The Spider's Web* program; and a two-part version of "Bartleby the Scrivener" for the same program, written, produced, and directed by Erik Bauersfield (Everett C. Frost).

The most poetically inspired adaptation of *Moby-Dick* for the radio has never been aired in America. This was the text written by British poet Henry Reed for the Third Programme of BBC, broadcast on 26 January 1947 and performed by a cast featuring Sir Ralph Richardson, Cyril Cusack, Bernard Miles, James McKechnie, and others. The full text was published by Reed as *Moby Dick: A Play for Radio from Herman Melville's Novel*, also in 1947. Using blank verse and dropping Ishmael as the narrator (he goes down with the ship), Reed tried, he said, "so far as possible to let Melville speak for himself, and leave the listener himself to judge of his 'meaning' " (Reed, p. 8). He also noted that "It is upon the book's symbolism and tragedy alone that an adaptor must concentrate" (Reed, p. 7). The script Reed crafted is highly literate and lyrical, imaginatively constructed, and moving in its pace and sweep of action. One reviewer found Reed's version a "most intelligent adaptation" (*TLS*). How well it played over the airwaves we can only guess, but the published script demonstrates a devotion to the integrity of Melville's novel.

Television

As with radio, information about television adaptations of Melville's works is hard to come by and very incomplete. Of the productions mentioned below, only two are known to exist on tape and are available for viewing at New York's Museum for Broadcasting. These are the 1959 *Billy Budd* and 1978 *Bartleby the Scrivener*.

When "Hallmark Hall of Fame" set out to do its version of *Moby-Dick* in 1954, it cared enough about the integrity of the script to appoint newspaperman Edwin Gilcher, a close reader of Melville, as literary adviser. The director, Albert McCleery, flew Gilcher to Hollywood for pre-production sessions to assist him in rendering a version that was faithful to the novel. Gilcher set about restoring as much of Melville's original language to the script as possible and correcting errors in the script and the casting. (This information was provided by Mr. Gilcher who owns copies of the early and the final versions of the script.) When the live production was aired on 16 May 1954, Jack Gould in the *New York Times* praised McCleery's ingenuity in overcoming the space limitations of a studio (the whale does not appear and the sea had to be suggested), but noted that the necessary pace of action and abbreviation of the development of Ahab's character prevented the viewer from becoming emotionally involved. The sum total failed to add up to the novel, but then this was an expected criticism. With Gilcher's assistance, it does seem to have been more faithful than it would have otherwise been.

Later that same year, a six-week series of half-hour dramas based on *Moby-Dick* was undertaken by CBS on its "Camera 3" program beginning 16 October (*MSN* No. 10, Autumn 1954, p. 2). On 10 March 1955, ABC broadcast a version of *Billy Budd* on the "Pond's Theater" (*MSN* No. 11).

The "Dupont Show of the Month" version of *Billy Budd* of 25 May 1959 was an adaptation of the Coxe and Chapman play. For the time, it was a compelling production, though no match for the 1962 film. Don Murray, hair dyed blonde, made a handsome enough Billy Budd, and Roddy McDowell was an effectively obsequious Squeak, but Alfred Ryder had too much of the humane and rational in his Claggart to work well in conveying the evil side of his character, and James Donald's Vere was a bit too officious and authoritarian. Given better support for Murray's sensitive performance, the whole might have been better (and given the problems of live drama, it could have been much worse). The Melville Society declared it an "outstanding performance" (*MSN* No. 15, p. 2).

Although it was entitled *Moby Dick* and broadcast in the NBC "Great American Novel" series in 1969, this television production was actually a documentary on the fishing industry with reportage by Charles Kuralt and reading from Melville's novel by actor George C. Scott. The reviewer for *Variety* found that the readings merely got in the way of what was a splendid documentary of considerable artistic merit and noted that it "captured the rhythm of the ebb and flow of a lifestyle on the frontier of nature so basic that it is part of our collective unconscious." Earlier programs in this series had revisited the modern worlds of Sinclair Lewis's *Babbitt* and John Steinbeck's *Grapes of Wrath*, an interesting concept had they gone on to examine the modern world of whaling rather than fishing for halibut.

An adaptation of "Bartleby the Scrivener" had been attempted on 22 December 1966 over WOR-TV (*MSN* No. 19), but a first-rate production in color was accomplished by the Maryland Center for Public Broadcasting, in association with the Center Stage of Baltimore, and first broadcast on 29 May 1978. Although the backgrounds were obviously Baltimore rather than Wall Street, the costumes and settings evoke Melville's nineteenth-century world. Nicholas Kepros as the lawyer plays for a slightly comic effect, as do Patrick Hines as Turkey, Robert Hitt as Nippers, and Tim Zechel as Ginger Nut. They serve, therefore, as an effective counterpoint to Joel Colodner's solemn, lethargic Bartleby. The production depends primarily on overvoice rather than dialogue, the lawyer narrating the story in retrospect, often addressing the viewer in the midst of the action. This brings the method of narration closer to Melville's. Indeed, the intention of script writer Israel Horovitz was to produce a dramatic text that Melville himself might have written. The high production values and effective use of serio-comic style make this the most attractive and engaging of all efforts to translate "Bartleby" into visual media.

Elements of the plot and characters of *Moby-Dick* frequently show up on the Saturday morning television screen in several of the animated cartoon series. A "Mr. Magoo" feature, in which Magoo plays Ahab, was done sometime in the 1960s and is often repeated. Episodes of "Rocky and His Friends" have involved a search for "Maybe Dick, the Mournful Whale." In "Archie, Jughead, and Herman" (*Melville Society Extracts* No. 25) Kenneth Roemer reports on an episode of the *Archie* animated television series based indirectly on *Moby-Dick* and finds that it "isn't bad pop Melville." References to Melville and his novel have been sighted on episodes of the "Mary Tyler Moore Show, " "Flipper," "Love Boat," and "Hill Street Blues," among others, but more specific information is not available. These references attest to the assumption that everyone knows about Melville and his fictional whale, whether or not they have read the book. He is a part of America's cultural consciousness.

Recordings

According to an examination of the Melville Collection's recordings at The Newberry Library, most albums are either dramatizations of adaptations or readings of selections by distinguished actors. Since few of them are dated, a chronology is not possible.

Around 1945, Decca issued an album of four 78 rpm records (later reissued on LP) entitled *Charles Laughton as Captain Ahab, Moby Dick*, a dramatization of a text prepared by Brainerd Duffield with music composed and directed by Victor Young. Duffield's script was published as "Moby Dick: A Modern Adaptation," with a note indicating that it had also been broadcast over CBS by Orson Welles and that an expanded version was to be staged in London and Paris in April of 1949 with a musical score by Bernard Herrman. The published script follows the same basic pattern as have all radio versions focusing on a few select moments of dramatic tension. The only innovation is a final speech by Ahab from beyond his watery grave in which he hails Moby Dick as the "baronial tyrant of the sea . . . my conquerer." Other readings from *Moby-Dick* include those by Robert H. Chapman, Louis Zorich, and a cast including Charlton Heston, Keir Dullea, and George Rose.

The narration of Thomas Mitchell for the 1953 Jerry Winters film, *Herman Melville's Moby Dick*, was released as *The Story of Moby Dick*. Also related are *Whaling and Sailing Songs From the Days of Moby Dick* sung by Paul Clayton, *The Rutgers Glee Club Presents Three Whale Songs from Moby Dick* (1983), and *James Mason Reads Herman Melville's Bartleby the Scrivener*.

CHILDREN'S AND POPULAR ADULT LITERATURE

Children's Literature

Efforts to produce children's versions of Melville's works began very early with an S. G. Goodrich's 1847 adaptation of *Typee* in *Robert Merry's Museum* (*MSN* No. 5). Most adaptations for young readers have been published in this century, however. Of the fifty-nine publications listed in the "Abridgments and Adaptations" section of G. Thomas Tanselle's *A Checklist of Editions of Moby-Dick 1851–1976* (1976), at least twenty are versions designed for classroom and instructional use and another ten are illustrated children's books for trade distribution (excluding comic book adaptations). Reducing a novel of more than 240,000 words and

135 chapters to a simplified text of less than six or eight chapters is bound to alter severely the impact of the original. One abridger, Frank L. Beals (Tanselle, #83), felt that students couldn't identify with Ishmael, so he retold the story in the third person. As a consequence, at the conclusion Ishmael goes down with the ship and no one survives. In some cases, what is of interest about the children's adaptations is the ways various illustrators have interpreted Melville's text.

The most imaginative uses of Melville material in children's literature occur in books that incorporate characters and themes from the novels. For example, in *How Old Stormalong Captured Mocha Dick* (1942), Irwin Shapiro combined the legendary stories of Alfred Bulltop Stormalong, "the greatest sailor who ever lived," with a story about his pursuit of the great white whale. Defeated by Mocha Dick on his first day out, Old Stormalong deserts the sea to become first a farmer and then a cowboy but returns when he cannot adapt. He tracks down Mocha Dick, mounts the whale like a bucking bronco, and rides until it collapses and dies of a broken heart. In Ermanno Libenzi's *Robin and the Pirates* (1975), the young hero Robin is stolen by pirates and in the course of his adventures meets many figures from world literature, including Moby Dick. To assist the friendly whale, Robin sends the pursuing mad Ahab in the wrong direction.

The most intriguing and complex use of *Moby-Dick* as an integral part of a novel for young readers is found in Scott O'Dell's *The Dark Canoe* (1968). From the epigraph which uses a quotation from Melville's novel to the conclusion which turns on the narrator's effective use of that quotation to turn aside a mad quest, the novel is richly resonant with the style and spirit of Melville and serves as a latter day tribute to an earlier masterpiece. Told through the eyes of young Nathan Clegg, the plot, involving a voyage to discover the facts about the sinking of the whaler *Amy Foster*, parallels the pursuit of the white whale when Nathan's disfigured older brother, Caleb, who knows the text of *Moby-Dick* by heart, evidently identifies in some distorted, insane way with Captain Ahab. Quotations from Melville's novel, which Nathan is in the process of reading, and the discovery of what appears to be Queequeg's floating coffin, the "dark canoe" of the title, figure prominently in the narration. Seldom does adolescent fiction reach such poetic heights.

Jean Gould's *Young Mariner Melville* (1956) is described as a biography for young readers, but actually it is a fictional re-creation of the life and adventures of Melville with narration and dialogue partly based on the author's own words from his fiction and letters. It begins with Melville at nineteen shipping out to sea, on the *St. Lawrence*, then moves back to the early years before continuing with the maritime adventures. Most of the book's 280 pages are devoted to Melville's adventures at sea, often relying heavily on the fiction and accepting too readily fiction as fact, with the final four chapters devoted to a highly telescoped overview of his literary career. Although of questionable value as an authentic biography, it can serve effectively to introduce the young reader or adolescent to Melville's early adventure novels.

Popular Adult Fiction

Another gauge of the widespread familiarity Melville enjoys in the popular mind is the number of popular novels that employ him and his work in their themes or structures. There is no catalogue of such material, so a few recent examples must suffice.

The Wind Whales of Ishmael (1971) by science fiction novelist Philip Jose Farmer begins where *Moby-Dick* ends, with Ishmael clinging to Queequeg's coffin until he is rescued by the *Rachel*. The entire ship suddenly falls through a rift in time and space, apparently because of the mystical carvings on Queequeg's coffin, and Ishmael finds himself in a strange Earth of the future, where the Pacific Ocean once rested, with dragonlike whales that soar through the skies and consume lesser creatures. A beautiful Fayaway-type Tahitian maiden, Namalee, appears out of *Typee* to accompany Ishmael, who combines in character all of Melville's fictional heroes. To rebuild Namalee's lost city, destroyed by the Purple Beast of the Stinging Death, they set out to recover its stolen gods from an enemy nation; Ishmael earns the title of Grand Admiral, the hand of princess Namalee, and the stature of a god. During the course of his adventures, Ishmael comes to two conclusions: "The essential human has not changed," in spite of the passage of thousands of years, and "What the white whale had been to Ahab, time was to Ishmael. . . . Man could only live as well as he could with the greatest beast, Time, and then go into timelessness, still wondering, still uncomprehending" (pp. 52 and 150). Neither the narrative nor the symbolism of the novel, however, adequately supports these philosophic conclusions. More concerned with describing beasts and ships that visually are unimaginable than with meaning, the novel merely uses Melville to lend weight to an otherwise thin piece of fantasy fiction.

In "Herman Melville: Space Opera Virtuoso" (1980), John Kessel provides a tongue-in-cheek biography of a science fiction writer in the 1930s named Herman Melville, author of the first real science fiction epic *Starry Deeps*, or *The Wail*. It's as if Kessel has sketched satirically what Melville's career would have been like had he been born a hundred years later. Despite the title, the intent of "Call Him Ishmael" (1984) by George Baxt is clear in the opening lines: "His name is Ishmael. Remember Ishmael? Not Melville's young whaler, but the young man who made headlines for several months three years ago? Ishmael is going to kill me. That's why I'm rushing to complete this story. Time is running out" (p. 20).

The remainder of the brief crime mystery has little to do with Melville, but without the famous first line of *Moby-Dick* to bank off of, the story would lose its cleverness and point.

Woody Allen's famous story "The Whore of Mensa," is a characteristic *tour de force* in which Melville is central. This is a burlesque detective story about the investigator who breaks up a ring of prostitutes who cater to intellectuals starved for meaningful conversation with the opposite sex. When the narrator contacts the madam (who has an M.A. in comparative literature) and asks to discuss Melville, the following conversation ensues:

> "*Moby-Dick* or the shorter novels?"
> "What's the difference?"
> "The price. That's all. Symbolism's extra."
> "What'll it run me?"
> "Fifty, maybe a hundred for *Moby-Dick*. You want a comparative discussion—Melville and Hawthorne? That could be arranged for a hundred." (p. 34)

Despite his expressed disdain for the academic establishment, Allen clearly has read his literary criticism.

GENERAL CULTURE

References to Melville and reflections of his presence in American popular culture are found in nearly every imaginable aspect of society and its leisure life. Only a few of these can be touched on here.

Moby Dick Restaurants have been seen on Madison Avenue and in West Nyack, New York; at Westport Point, Massachusetts (with Ahab's hot dog stand located at nearby Baker's Beach); and at the Hotel King Kamehameha in Kona, Hawaii. The stay-at-home diner could at one time purchase the Taste O'Sea Moby Dick TV dinner, with whale-shaped cod fillets ready to be unfrozen. Holiday Inns once ran a chain of Billy Budd Restaurants throughout the country, and a Billy Budd's Sub Shop was located at Weymouth, Massachusetts.

There is a Moby Dick Motel in Cape Cod; a Moby Dick Inn on Nantucket Island; a Moby Dick Bookshop in Redondo Beach; a Bartleby's Bookshop in Bethesda; a Moby Dip Ice Cream Store in Margate, New Jersey; a Bartleby's clothing store for women in Richmond, Virginia; and a Moby Dick night club in Chicago. Among gay bars is the Moby Dick in San Francisco, the Captain Ahab in Hong Kong, and the Moby Dick in Sydney, Australia. In Kaanapali, Maui, one can have a drink at the Pequod Bar in the Maui Surf Resort before having dinner in the Quee Queg Dining Room.

Moby Dick Marine Specialities in New Bedford is a large wholesaler of nautical and related gifts and products including wooden statues of a convivial Captain Ahab, Moby Dick carved wooden boxes, and a Moby Dick Scrimshaw Kit. Taylor Gifts of Wayne, Pennsylvania, once offered by mail a scale model whittling kit to build the *Pequod*, and Whale Gifts of the Center for Environmental Education in Washington, D.C., offers a brass Moby Dick letter opener. A few years ago Old Stone Mill Corporation of Adams, Massachusetts, retailed a Moby Dick pattern of wallpaper.

Among toys for children is a Springbok jigsaw puzzle from Hallmark Cards, "Moby Duck: The Immortal Classic by Melvin Hornbill," which forms a satiric drawing of a crew harpooning a giant yellow plastic duck of the bathtub variety. Keyway Books of New York published in 1977 an activities book for children ages five to twelve in which *Moby Dick* is retold through games, puzzles, pictures to color, and do-it-yourself drawings. *A Golden Stamp Classic: Moby Dick*, issued in 1956 by Simon and Schuster of New York, included forty-eight color picture stamps to be placed in the text, an adaptation by Emma Gelders Sterne. This item was apparently very popular. In addition to a British edition, The Newberry Library Melville Collection includes translations published in France and Mexico. Slightly different in format is *Moby Dick: Pictures to Stick*, from Young World Productions in Holland. There are eight drawings with descriptions beneath, partly to be colored but with four pages of mucilage backed sheets from which stickers are removed to be pasted on the drawings in designated areas. What exactly a child is expected to make of all these toys is unclear. They do not function as very reasonable introductions to the novel, and the bare story line would not seem to have much appeal for young readers unfamiliar with the work itself.

Such would also seem to be the case with jokes that circulate among children in the oral tradition. The most popular of these is the riddle, "What's purple and lives at the bottom of the sea?" The answer is "Moby Grape." Two adult-oriented jokes have been heard. "What periodicals does Ahab subscribe to?" The answer: "*The Whale Street Journal* and *Ports Illustrated*." And if someone says "I'm impressed," the proper response is "So was Billy Budd." Perhaps the joke category should also include the "Billy Budd Button Award" which for several years after 1971 was given by the *Library Journal*, in the spirit of the life-long illiterate character of Melville's novel, to the worst children's picture book published during the year. (The "Huckleberry Finn Pin" went to the worst book for older children.)

In addition to frequent use on menus and toys, the image and name of the great white whale will suddenly come afloat in unusual places. In 1976 Watersavers, Inc. of Cleveland marketed a device that would save water if installed in a toilet tank. With no apparent sense of ambiguity,

Figure 1
John Barrymore, "The Great Profile," as Captain Ahab, in *The Sea Beast*, a
Warner Bros. film released in 1925.

Figure 3
A scene from "Abraxas and the Earthman," story and art by Rick Veitch, published in *Epic Illustrated*, 1982–83. Reprinted with permission of Rick Veitch.

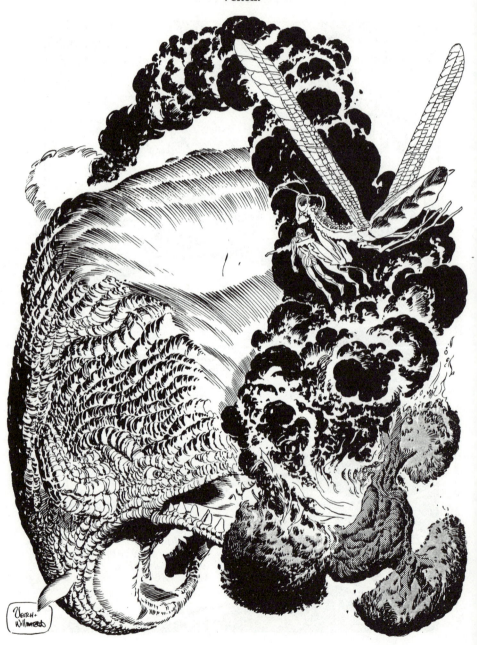

Figure 4

References to *Moby-Dick* in two contemporary comic strips: *Elwood* of February 11, 1984 and *Shoe* of May 5, 1983. Reprinted with permission of Tribune Media Services, Inc.

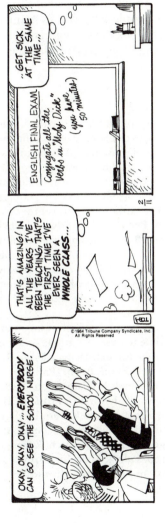

the manufacturer called the item "Moby Dike." Metro Area Transit of Omaha, Nebraska, operates a special bus service for the elderly and handicapped called "Moby" (Mobilization for Special Customers), advertised as a "whale of a service." In a more appropriate vein is the "Moby Dick Trail," a directional sign system installed by the Office of Tourism of New Bedford to lead visitors to historic sites in the city, many of which relate to the life and works of Melville. What all of this suggests is that no matter the extent to which people are actually familiar with the works of Herman Melville, his creations have long ago passed into the wider pool of popular knowledge, and Moby Dick himself has become a part of American folklore.

NOTE

1. A special word of gratitude is due Professor Harrison Hayford, who cheerfully rummaged with me through several boxes of material in his office at Northwestern University one afternoon in pursuit of loose fish. Also helpful were the staff of the Motion Picture and Television Reading Room at the Library of Congress, The Newberry Library which allowed access to the Melville Collection, and the staff at the Museum of Broadcasting in New York. A grant from the Southern Regional Education Board helped subsidize my travel for research at The Newberry Library and the Museum of Broadcasting. Edwin Gilcher kindly supplied information about his role in the 1954 television production of *Moby Dick* and loaned me copies of the working scripts. Jerry Winters loaned me a print of his excellent 1953 film *Herman Melville's Moby Dick*, and Royal Von Puckett generously provided copies of several comic books. Jens Peter Becker sent from Germany a copy of *Illustrationen zu Melvilles Moby-Dick*, and Rick Veitch kindly answered some questions about his work.

A host of other people have provided various kinds of information and help, and I am indebted to each for taking the time to assist: Charlene Avallone, John Baldwin, Ray Barfield, Judith E. Barlow, Mike Barson, Diana Bloom, Ray Bradbury, W. J. Briggs, Tom Bross, Ray B. Browne, Frank Burns, Patrice L. Buxton, Belfield Carter, Nicholas Carter, Stanley Clifford, William Cobb, Michael Finnerty, Benjamin Franklin Fisher IV, Perry Frank, Everett C. Frost, W. G. Heath, Nancy Joyner, Anthony S. Keys, Maureen Krop, Don deKoven, Linda Lapides, Virginia McLoughlin, Ivan Melada, Eti Mlinarski, William G. Scheller, Prudence C. Schofield, Randall W. Scott, Robert Page Slocum, Ray Storch, Karen Thomas, Martin Torodash, Yvonne Trinkwater, Tad Tuleja, Malcolm Usrey, Patricia L. Ward, Jeff Wanshel, Sarah Maupin Wenk, and Catherine Yronwode.

PRIMARY WORKS CITED

Film

[All American films listed here are available for review in the Motion Picture and Television Reading Room of the Library of Congress.]

The Sea Beast (1926)

Warner Brothers Pictures. 15 January 1926. Silent, black and white. 35mm. 10 reels.

Director: Millard Webb. Adapted by Bess Meredyth. Photographer: Byron Haskins. Additional photography: Frank Kesson. Assistant Director: George Webster.

Cast: John Barrymore (Ahab Ceeley), Dolores Costello (Esther Harper), George O'Hara (Derek Ceeley), Mike Donlin (Flask), Sam Baker (Queequeg), George Burrell (Perth), Sam Allen (sea captain), Frank Nelson (Stubbs), Mathilde Comont (Mula), James Barrows (Reverend Harper), Vadim Uraneff (Pip), Sojin (Fedallah), and Frank Hagney (Daggoo).

Adaptation

The Story of Moby Dick: The Great White Whale. Adapted from the novel by Herman Melville. Illustrated with Scenes from "The Sea Beast." A Warner Brothers Picture Featuring John Barrymore. Racine, Wisconsin: Whitman Publishing Company, 1934.

Moby Dick (1930)

Warner Brothers Pictures. 14 August 1930 (New York Premier). 20 September 1930 (released). Sound (Vitaphone), black and white. 35 mm. 9 reels.

Director: Lloyd Bacon. Screenplay and dialogue by J. Grubb Alexander. Photographer: Robert Kurrle. Recording Engineer: David Forrest.

Cast: John Barrymore (Ahab), Joan Bennett (Faith Mapple), Lloyd Hughes (Derek), May Boley (Whale Oil Rosie), Walter Long (Stubbs), Tom O'Brien (Starbuck), Nigel DeBrulier (Elijah), Nable Johnson (Queequeg), William Walling (blacksmith), Virginia Sale (old maid), Jack Curtis (first mate), and John Ince (Reverend Mapple).

Omoo-Omoo (The Shark God) (1949)

Esla Productions (Leonard S. Picker and George Green), released by Screen Guild. 14 June 1949. Black and white, 57 minutes.

Director: Leon Leonard. Producers: Leonard S. Picker and George D. Green. Screenplay: George D. Green and Leon Leonard. Photographer: Benjamin F. Kline. Editor: Stanley Frazen. Music: Albert Glasser. Assistant Director: Johnny Grubbs. Sound: Richard Tyler. Wardrobe: Adele Palmer and Robert H. Ramsey. Set Decorations: John McCarthy, Jr. and George Milo. Makeup: Bob Mark. Hair Stylist: Peggy Gray. Optical Effects: Consolidated Film Industries.

Cast: Ron Randell (Jeff Garland), Devera Burton (Julie), Trevor Bardette (Captain Roger Guy), Pedro de Cordoba (Tari), Richard Benedict (First Mate Richards), Michael Whalen (Chips), Rudy Robles (Tembo), George Meeker (Doctor Humphrey Long), Lisa Kinkaid (Tala), and Jack Raymond (Texas).

Herman Melville's Moby Dick (1953)

Giralda Pictures International. 23 May 1953. Eastman color. 30 minutes.
Director and Producer: Jerry Winters. Music: Richard Mohaupt. Drawings:
Gilbert Wilson. Narrator: Thomas Mitchell.

Moby Dick (1956)

Moulin and Warner Brothers Pictures. 27 June 1956 (world premier at New
Bedford, Massachusetts). Technicolor. 116 minutes.
Director and Producer: John Huston. Associate Producer: Vaughan N. Dean.
Screenplay: Ray Bradbury and John Huston. Photography: Oswald Morris. Second Unit Photography: Freddie Francis. Editor: Russell Lloyd. Art Director:
Ralph Brinton. Special Effects: Gus Lohman. Music: Philip Staunton. Sound
Recording: John Mitchell and Len Shilton. Storyboard: Stephen Grimes.
Cast: Gregory Peck (Captain Ahab), Richard Basehart (Ishmael), Leo Genn
(Starbuck), Harry Andrews (Stubb), Bernard Miles (Manxman), Melvyn Johns
(Peleg), Noel Purcell (Carpenter), Edric Connor (Daggoo), Joseph Tomelty (Peter Coffin), Philip Stainton (Bildad), Royal Dano (Elijah), Seamus Kelly (Flask),
Friedrich Ledebur (Queequeg), Tamba Alleny (Pip), Orson Welles (Father Mapple), and James Robertson Justice (Captain Boomer).

Adaptations

Moby Dick. A Movie Classic. New York: Dell Publishing Co., 1956. [Comic
book, No. 717.]
Moby Dick con Gregory Peck. I Vostri Film, Numero Speciale. Supplemento al
No. 33. 25 December 1956. [Italian fotonovela.]

Enchanted Island (1958)

A Benedict Bogeaus Production for RKO Radio, released by Warner Brothers.
1958. Technicolor. 94 minutes.
Producer: Benedict Bogeaus. Director: Allan Dwan. Screenplay: James Leicester and Harold Jacob Smith. Music: Raul LaVista. Title song: Robert Allen.
Photography: George Stahl. Art Director: Hal Wilson Cox. Editor: James Leicester. Special Effects: Lee Zavitz. Assistant Director: Nacio Real. Sound: Weldon
Coe. Special Photographic Effects: Albert M. Simpson. Wardrobe: Georgette.
Makeup: Burris Grimwood.
Cast: Dana Andrews (Abner Bedford), Jane Powell (Fayaway), Don Dubbins
(Tom), Arthur Shields (Jimmy Dooley), Ted DeCorsica (Captain Vangs), Friedrich Ledebur (Chief Mehevi), Augustine Fernandez (Kory Kory), Francisco Reignera (Medicine Man), and Les Hellman (First Mate Moore).

Billy Budd (1962)

Anglo-Allied Productions, released in the United States by Allied Artists. 1962.
Cinemascope, black and white. 123 minutes.
Executive Producer: A. Ronald Lubin. Director and Producer: Peter Ustinov.
Screenplay: Peter Ustinov, Robert Rossen, and DeWitt Bodeen. Based on the

play by Louis O. Coxe and Robert H. Chapman. Photographer: Robert Krasker. Production Designer: Don Ashton. Art Director: Peter Murton. Production Associate: Arthur S. Ferriman. Editor: Jack Harris. Music: Antony Hopkins. Production Supervisor: Albert Jaeger. Production Manager: Victor Peck. Assistant Director: Michael Birkett. Technical Adviser: Alan Villiers. Casting Director: Robert S. Leonard. Camera Operator: John S. Harris. Sound Editor: Charles Crafford. Sound Recordists: Charles Poulton and Len Shilton. Continuity: June Faithfull. Costume Designer: Anthony Mendelson. Wardrobe: Ron Beck and Laura Nightingale. Makeup: Bob Lawrence. Hairdresser: Harry Montsash.

Cast: Robert Ryan (John Claggart), Peter Ustinov (Capt. Edward Fairfax Vere), Melvyn Douglas (The Dansker), Terence Stamp (Billy Budd), Ronald Lewis (Jenkins), David McCallum (Lieut. Wyatt), John Neville (Lieut. Ratcliffe), Paul Rogers (Lieut. Seymour), Lee Montague (Squeak), Thomas Heathcote (Payne), Ray McAnally (O'Daniel), Robert Brown (Talbot), John Meillon (Kincaid), Cyril Luckham (Hallam), and Niall MacGinnis (Capt. Graveling).

Bartleby (1971)

Pantheon Film Production, released in the United States by Maron Films. 1971. Eastman Color. 78 minutes.

Producer: Rodney Carr-Smith. Director: Anthony Friedmann. Screenplay: Anthony Friedmann and Rodney Carr-Smith. Photographer: Ian Wilson. Music: Roger Webb. Editor: John S. Smith. Art Director: Simon Holland. Sound: Ron Sheffield and Barrie Copeland. Production Manager: Bryan Coates. Assistant Director: Malcolm Johnson.

Cast: Paul Scofield (The Accountant), John McEnery (Bartleby), Thorley Walters (The Colleague), Colin Jeavons (Tucker), Raymond Mason (Landlord), Charles Kinross (Tenant), Neville Barber (First Client), Robin Asquith (Office Boy), Hope Jackman (Tea lady), John Watson (Doctor), Christine Dingle (Patient), Rosalind Elliot (Secretary), and Tony Parkin (Clerk).

Comic Books

Adventure Comics No. 332 (May 1965): 17 pages. "The Super-Moby Dick of Space." Story by Edmond Hamilton, art by John Forte. New York: National Periodical Publications.

Adventures of the Big Boy No. 165 (1971). "On the Trail of Moby Dick." Garden City, N.Y.: Illustrated Features Corp.

Classic Comics (later *Classics Illustrated*) No. 5 (September 1942): 62 pages. "Moby Dick by Herman Melville." Art by Louis Zansky. New York: Gilberton Co.

Classics Illustrated No. 36 (April 1947): 40 pages. "Typee by Herman Melville." Story by Harry Miller, art by Ezra Whiteman. New York: Gilberton Co.

The Classics Reader No. 11 (September 1980): 5–49. "Typee by Herman Melville." Art by Luis Dominguez. Toronto: W. J. Briggs.

Epic Illustrated Nos. 10–17 (February 1982–April 1983): 78 pages. "Abraxas and the Earthman." Story and art by Rick Veitch. New York: Marvel Comics Group.

Feature Presentations Magazine No. 6 (July 1950). "Moby Dick." Art by Wallace Wood. New York: Fox Features Syndicate.

Grimm's Ghost Stories No. 24 (July 1975): 7 pages. "Call Me Ahab." Story by Don F. Glut, art by Frank Bolle. Poughkeepsie, N.Y.: Western Publishing Co.

Kamandi, the Last Boy on Earth No. 23 (November 1974): 20 pages. Story and art by Jack Kirby. New York: National Periodical Publications.

Ka-Zar Lord of the Hidden Jungle No. 6 (November 1974): 18 pages. "Waters of Darkness, River of Doom." Story by Gerry Conway, art by John Buscema. New York: Marvel Comics Group.

King Classics No. 3 (1977): 32 pages. "Moby Dick by Herman Melville." Story by Marion Kimberly. New York: King Features Syndicate.

Mad Clobbers the Classics. "Mopey Duke by Helmsman Marvel." Story by Larry Siegel, art by Angelo Torres. New York: Warner Books, 1981, pp. 5–33.

Man Comics No. 3 (February 1950). New York: Marvel/Atlas Comics.

Maravillas de la Literature No. 5 (1982): 46 pages. "Moby Dick de Herman Melville." Guion de Carlos R. Soria, dibujos de Chiqui de la Fuente. Madrid: Ediciones Larousse.

Marvel Classics Comics No. 8 (1976): 48 pages. "Moby Dick by Herman Melville." Story by Irwin Shapiro, art by Alex Nino. New York: Marvel Comics Group. Reprinted from *Now Age Illustrated* series.

Moby Duck Nos. 1–30 (October 1967–February 1978). Walt Disney. Poughkeepsie, N.Y.: Western Publishing Co.

Now Age Illustrated No. 64–1030 (1973): 56 pages. "Moby Dick by Herman Melville." Story by Irwin Shapiro, art by Alex Nino. West Haven, Conn.: Pendulum Press, 1973. Abridged and reprinted in *Marvel Classics Comics* series.

Pimpinela: Obras Completas y Grandes Historietas, Año 2, No. 11 (July, 1952): 33 pages. "Moby Dick de Herman Melville." Art by Carlos Roume. Buenos Aires: Editorial Codex.

Uncanny Tales No. 53 (March 1957): 4 pages. "Dreadful Discovery." Art by Angelo Torres. New York: Prime Publications.

Radio, Television, and Recordings

Radio

MOBY-DICK (1946). *The Columbia Workshop.* CBS, 19 and 26 October 1946. Director: Ernest Kinoy. Music: Norman Lockwood. Cast: Neil O'Malley (Ahab), Sidney Smith (Ishmael), Charles Irving (Starbuck).

MOBY-DICK (1946). *Adventure Parade.* Mutual, 1946. Voices: John Drake.

MOBY-DICK (1947). *Third Programme.* BBC, 26 January 1947. Producer: Stephen Potter. Director: Bee Samuel. Adapted: Henry Reed. Music: Antony Hopkins. Cast: Sir Ralph Richardson, Cyril Cusack, Bernard Miles, James McKechnie, Lawrence Honray, Valentine Dyall, and Brian Weske. [See Henry Reed, *Moby Dick: A Play for Radio from Herman Melville's Novel.* London: Jonathan Cape, 1947.]

MOBY-DICK (1947). *CBS School of the Air: Tales of Adventure No. 3.* CBS, 21

October 1947. Director: Albert Ward. Adapted: Frank Ernest Hill. [Script in Melville Collection, Newberry Library.]

MOBY-DICK (1948). *Tell It Again.* CBS, 13 June 1948. Director: Ralph Rose. Ahab: Marvin Miller. [Tape Available through AM Treasures, Box 192, Babylon, New York 11702.]

MOBY-DICK (1948?–1953?). *Hallmark Playhouse.* CBS. [Tape available through AM Treasures.]

MOBY-DICK (1949). *NBC University Theatre of the Air.* NBC, 10 April 1949. Director: Andrew C. Love. Adapted: Ernest Kinoy. Ahab: Henry Hull. [Tape available through Metacom, Box 11041, Minneapolis, Minn.]

MOBY-DICK (1949). *Family Theatre.* Mutual, 13 July 1949.

MOBY-DICK (1953). *NBC Star Playhouse.* NBC, 8 November 1953; rebroadcast 15 November 1956. Ahab: Frederic March.

BARTLEBY THE SCRIVENER (1954). *Theatre Royal.* NBC, 14 February 1954. Starring Lionel Merton.

BARTLEBY THE SCRIVENER (1956). *Favorite Story.* ABC, 25 November 1956. Directors: Jerry Lawrence and Bob Lee. Narrator: William Conrad.

BARTLEBY THE SCRIVENER (1957). *Theatre Royal.* Mutual, 6 June 1957.

BILLY BUDD (1963). *General Electric Theatre.* 1963. Cast: Cyril Ritchard, Peter Ustinov, Joseph Cotten, Agnes Moorehead, Dina Merrill.

MOBY-DICK (1979). *Masterpiece Radio Theatre.* National Public Radio, 1979. Director: Eleanor Stout.

BILLY BUDD (1983). *The Spider's Web.* National Public Radio, 1983. Producer, Director, Writer: Erik Bauersfield.

Television

MOBY DICK (1954). "Hallmark Hall of Fame." NBC, 16 May 1954. 60 minutes. Director: Albert McCleery. Adapted: Howard Rodman. Story Editor: Ethel Frank. Music Director: Jules Seidman. Costumes: Grady Hunt. Scenic Consultant: Spencer Davies. Technical Director: Silvio Caranchini. Lighting Director: Boris Isaacson. Makeup: Fred Williams. Literary Adviser: Edwin Gilcher.

Cast: Victor Jory (Captain Ahab), Hugh O'Brien (Starbuck), Lamont Johnson (Ishmael), Harvey Stephens (Stubb), Thomas B. Henry (Fedallah), Nestor Paiva (Captain Peleg), Earl Lee (Elijah), Charles Mauu (Queequeg), John Hamilton ("Jeroboam" Captain), Tim Graham (Carpenter), Howard McNeelly (Pip), Stevan Darrell (Tashtego), James Logan ("Rachel" Captain), John Larch (First Sailor), Steve Mitchell (Second Sailor).

MOBY DICK (1954). "Camera 3." CBS, 16 October to 20 November 1954. [A six-week series of half-hour sequences.]

BILLY BUDD (1955). "Pond's Theater." ABC, 10 March 1955.

BILLY BUDD (1959). "Dupont Show of the Month." CBS, 25 May 1959. 60 minutes.

Producer: David Susskind. Director: Robert Muligan. Adapted: Jacqueline Babbin and Audrey Gellen from the play by Louis O. Coxe and Robert Chapman.

Cast: James Donald (Captain Vere), Don Murray (Billy Budd), Alfred Ryder (Claggart), Roddy McDowell (Squeak).

BARTLEBY (1966). "American Story Classics." WOR-TV (New York), 21 December 1966. 30 minutes.

MOBY DICK (1969). "Great American Novel." NBC, 2 April 1969. 60 minutes.
Producer: Arthur Barron. Executive Producer: Perry Wolff. Cameraman: Jerry Sims. Film Editor: Lawrence Silk.
Narrator: George C. Scott. Reporter: Charles Kuralt.
BARTLEBY THE SCRIVENER (1978). Maryland Center for Public Broadcasting in Association with Center Stage of Baltimore. 29 May 1978. 60 minutes. Color.
Producer: Michael B. Styer. Directors: Tom Barnett and Stan Wojewodski. Teleplay: Israel Horovitz.
Cast: Nicholas Kepros (Employer), Joel Colodner (Bartleby), Patrick Hines (Turkey), Robert Hitt (Nippers), Tim Zechel (Ginger Nut), Roland Bull, Saul Caplan, Russell T. Carr, Bryan Clark, Ralph Cosham, Dan Szelag, Doug Roberts, Richard Deangelis, Richard G. Holmes, Robert Minford, Shana Sullivan.

Recordings

Charles Laughton as Captain Ahab. Moby Dick. By Herman Melville. Adapted by Brainerd Duffield. Music (Composed and Conducted): Victor Young. Story with Music and Sound Effects. Four 78 rpm records in album. Decca Records, Album No. Da–401. [1945]. Rerelease 33 1/3 rpm. Decca Records, DL9071. Text by Brainerd Duffield published as "Moby Dick: A Modern Adaptation," *Line*, 1 (April-May 1948): 32–40.
James Mason Reads Herman Melville's Bartleby the Scrivener. Lively Arts Recording Corp., 30007. Jacket Notes by Joe Goldberg. 33 1/3 rpm.
Moby Dick by Herman Melville. Read by Robert H. Chapman. Spoken Arts, 850. 33 1/3 rpm.
Moby Dick or the Whale by Herman Melville. Selections Read by Louis Zorich. With an introduction by Ann Charters. Folkways Records, FL 9775. 1965. 33 1/3 rpm.
Moby Dick by Herman Melville. Charlton Heston, Keir Dullea, and George Rose, readers. Caedmon, TC 2077. 1975. Two 33 1/3 rpm records.
The Rutgers Glee Club Presents Three Whaling Songs from Moby Dick. F. Austin Walter, Director. Rutgers Glee Club. 1983. 33 1/3 rpm.
The Story of Moby Dick. Narrated by Thomas Mitchell. Dot Records, DLP–3043. 33 1/3 rpm. Soundtrack of the Jerry Winters film of 1953.
Whaling and Sailing Songs from the Days of Moby Dick. Sung by Paul Clayton. Tradition Records, TLP 1005. 33 1/3 rpm.

Children's and Popular Adult Literature

Allen, Woody. "The Whore of Mensa." *Without Feathers*. New York: Random House, 1975.
Baxt, George. "Call Him Ishmael." *Ellery Queen's Mystery Magazine* 83 (June 1984): 20–28.
Farmer, Philip Jose. *The Wind Whales of Ishmael*. New York: Act Books, 1971.
Goodrich, S. G. "Typee." *Robert Merry's Museum* 14 (October-December 1847): 109–14, 135–39, 173–78.

Gould, Jean. *Young Mariner Melville*. Illus. Donald McKay. New York: Dodd, Mead & Co., 1956.

Kessel, John. "Herman Melville: Space Opera Virtuoso." *The Magazine of Fantasy and Science Fiction* 58 (January 1980): 47–51.

Libenzi, Ermanno. *Robin and the Pirates*. Trans. Isobel Quigley. Illustrations by Adelchi Galloni. New York: Platt & Munk, 1975.

O'Dell, Scott. *The Dark Canoe*. Illustrated by Milton Johnson. Boston: Houghton Mifflin, 1968.

Shapiro, Irwin. *How Old Stormalong Captured Mocha Dick*. Pictures by Donald McKay. New York: Julian Messner, 1942.

SECONDARY WORKS CITED

Atkins, Thomas. "An Interview with Ray Bradbury." In *The Classic American Novel and the Movies*. Ed. Gerald Peary and Roger Shatzkin. New York: Frederick Ungar, 1977, pp. 42–51.

Barbarow, George. "Making Believe It Is *Moby Dick*." *Hudson Review* 9 (Summer 1957): 270–74.

Becker, Jens Peter. "John Hustons *Moby-Dick*." In *Illustrationen zu Melvilles "Moby-Dick*." Ed. Joachim Kruse. Schleswig: Schleswig-Holsteinischen Landemuseum, 1976, pp. 113–17.

Bennett, Arnold. *The Journal of Arnold Bennett 1921–1928*. New York: Viking Press, 1933, p. 140.

Bodeen, DeWitt. "The Adapting Art." *Films in Review* 14 (June-July 1963): 349–56.

Bohn, William S. "The Vineyard Looks at 'Moby Dick.' " *The New Leader* 39 (30 July 1956): 5.

Buchman, S. R., Introd. "Moby Dick—the Book and the Sea Beast—the Picture, An Appreciation." In *Moby Dick or The White Whale* by Herman Melville. New York: Grosset & Dunlap, 1925.

Cook, Margaret Seligman. "Something Further *Did* Follow: More on Melville in the Comic Books." *Melville Society Extracts* No. 56 (November 1983): 10.

de Laurot, Edouard. "An Encounter with John Huston." *Film Culture* 2 (1956): 1–4.

Dunning, John. *Tune in Yesterday*. Englewood Cliffs, N.J.: Prentice-Hall, 1976.

Freeman, John. *Herman Melville*. London: Macmillan and Co., 1926.

French, Brandon. "Lost at Sea." In *The Classic American Novel and the Movies*. Ed. Gerald Peary and Roger Shatzkin. New York: Frederick Ungar, 1977, pp. 52–61.

Frost, Everett C. Letters to author, 12 and 27 January 1984.

Fuller, Stanley. "Melville on the Screen." *Films in Review* 19 (June-July 1968): 358–63.

Hill, Derek. "*Moby Dick* Sets New Style in Color Photography." *American Cinematographer* 37 (September 1956): 534–35, 555–56.

Hillway, Tyrus. "Hollywood Hunts the White Whale." *Colorado Review* 5 (Winter 1957): 298–305.

Inge, M. Thomas. "Melville in the Comic Books." *Melville Society Extracts* No. 50 (May 1982): 9–10.

Jameson, Richard T. "Midsection: John Huston." *Film Comment* 16 (May-June 1980): 25–56.

Kaminsky, Stuart. *John Huston: Maker of Magic.* Boston: Houghton Mifflin, 1978.

Knight, Arthur. "The Director." *Saturday Review* 39 (9 June 1956): 29–30.

———. *The Liveliest Art: A Panoramic History of the Movies.* New York: Macmillan Co., 1957.

Kotsilibas-Davis, James. *The Barrymores: The Royal Family in Hollywood.* New York: Crown Publishers, 1981.

Kruse, Joachim, ed. *Illustrationen zu Melvilles "Moby-Dick."* Schleswig: Schleswig-Holsteinischen Landemuseum, 1976.

Kunert, Arnold. "Ray Bradbury on Hitchcock, Huston and Other Magic of the Screen." *Take One* 3 (1973): 15–24.

Melville Society Newsletter No. 3 (10 November 1947): 1.

Melville Society Newsletter No. 5 (June 1949): 3.

Melville Society Newsletter No. 7 (June 1951): 3.

Melville Society Newsletter No. 9 (Winter 1953): 3.

Melville Society Newsletter No. 10 (Spring 1954): 3.

Melville Society Newsletter No. 10 (Autumn 1954): 2.

Melville Society Newsletter No. 11 (Spring 1955): 2.

Melville Society Newsletter No. 12 (Spring 1956): 3.

Melville Society Newsletter No. 13 (Summer 1957): 3.

Melville Society Newsletter No. 15 (Spring-Summer 1959): 2.

Melville Society Newsletter No. 19 (January 1967): 2.

Melville Society Extracts No. 10 (January 1972): 7.

Melville Society Extracts No. 25 (February 1976): 15–16.

Miller, Perry. " 'Moby-Dick': An Evaluation." *Berkshire Eagle* (Pittsfield, Mass.), 31 August 1956, p. 2.

Nadeau, Robert L. "Melville's Sailor in the Sixties." In *The Classic American Novel and the Movies.* Ed. Gerald Peary and Roger Shatzkin. New York: Frederick Ungar, 1977, pp. 124–31.

Persico, Joseph E. "An Interview with John Huston." *American Heritage* 33 (April/May 1982): 8–15.

Pratley, Gerald. *The Cinema of John Huston.* South Brunswick and New York: A. S. Barnes, 1977.

Rev. of *Bartleby* (film 1971). *New Yorker* 48 (4 March 1972): 91–92. [Pauline Kael.]

Rev. of *Billy Budd* (film 1962). *New Republic* 147 (10 November 1962): 25. [Stanley Kauffmann.]

———. *Reporter* 27 (6 December 1962): 42. [Jay Jacobs.]

Rev. of *Enchanted Island* (film 1958). *Variety* 212 (5 November 1958): 6.

Rev. of *Moby Dick* (television 1954). *New York Times* (19 May 1954): 54.

Rev. of *Moby Dick* (film 1956). *Nation* 183 (14 July 1956): 46. [Robert Hatch.]

———. *New York Times* (5 July 1956): 18. [Bosley Crowther.]

———. *New Yorker* 32 (14 July 1956): 83. [John McCarten.]

———. *Newsweek* 48 (2 July 1956): 72.

———. *Reporter* 15 (9 August 1956): 47–48. [Robert Bingham.]

———. *Saturday Review* 39 (9 June 1956): 28. [Hollis Alpert.]

———. *Senior Scholastic* 68 (10 May 1956): 37.

———. *Time* 68 (9 July 1956): 78.

———. *Village Voice* 1 (17 October 1956): 6. [William Murray.]

Rev. of *Moby Dick* (television 1969). *Variety* 254 (2 April 1969): 50.

Rev. of *Moby Dick: A Play for Radio from Herman Melville's Novel* by Henry Reed (radio play 1937). *Times Literary Supplement* (London) No. 2392 (6 December 1947): 632.

Rev. of *Omoo-Omoo (The Shark God)* (film 1949). *Variety* 175 (22 June 1949): 6.

Roemer, Kenneth. "Archie, Jughead, and Herman." *Melville Society Extracts* No. 25 (February 1976): 15–16.

Scott, Randall W. *Moby Dick Comics: A Preserved Context Index to Several Comic Adaptations and Take-Offs on Moby Dick by Herman Melville.* Lansing, Mich.: Randall W. Scott, 1979.

Stern, Milton. "A New Harpoon for the Great White Whale." *Clearing House* 30 (May 1956): 564–65.

———. "The Whale and the Minnow: *Moby Dick* and the Movies." *College English* 17 (May 1956): 470–73.

Stone, Edward. "Ahab Gets the Girl." *Melville Society Extracts* No. 21 (February 1975): 3–4.

———. "Ahab Gets the Girl, or Herman Melville Goes to the Movies." *Literature/Film Quarterly* 3 (Spring 1975): 172–81.

Tanselle, G. Thomas. *A Checklist of Editions of Moby-Dick, 1851–1976.* Evanston and Chicago: Northwestern University Press and Newberry Library, 1976.

Thurber, James. *The Years with Ross.* Boston: Little, Brown and Co., 1957.

Veitch, Rick. Letter to author, 7 June 1983.

Villiers, Alan. *Give Me a Ship to Sail.* New York: Charles Scribner's Sons, 1959.

Weaver, Raymond M. *Herman Melville: Mariner and Mystic.* New York: George H. Doran Co., 1921.

24

HERMAN MELVILLE: A WRITER FOR THE WORLD

Sanford E. Marovitz

> *We have the breadth of both tropics before us, to sail over twice; & shall round the world.*
>
> *(Letters,* 28 May 1860.)

Surely there is magic in the web of it, that "queer handkerchief, mockingly embellished with all the gay flags of all the known nations of the world," with which Melville's pale Usher in *Moby-Dick* dusts his old lexicons and grammars (*MD*, p. 1). If not, how else could he have prophesied the global reception that his leviathan of a novel would meet in the next century? But "mockingly" embellished? Why so? Perhaps it is but another manifestation of those little tricks the Fates hold in store for Ishmael and us all in "this strange mixed affair we call life"; possibly it is meant to serve as a small joke on the unknowing Usher or even Ishmael, but not—for this once—on the author himself. Whatever the reason, several of those nations whose flags embellish the handkerchief are presented a little farther down in "Etymology" beside the word for *whale* as written or spoken in the language of their people both ancient and modern, insular and continental. According to an approximate count of foreign publications related to Melville (see Table 1), the Usher's embellished

*I am heavily indebted for data used throughout this chapter to Leland R. Phelps and his invaluable bibliography, *Herman Melville's Foreign Reputation* (1983). For their assistance, I should also like to thank Annalucia Accardo (University of Rome), Masao Tsunematsu (Shimane University), Arimichi Makino (Meiji University), and Richard Colles Johnson (The Newberry Library).

Table 1
Distribution of Foreign Melville Publications

Language	Primary Native	Primary English	Secondary Native	Secondary English	First Translations or Foreign Editions
Hebrew	6	0	9	0	*Billy Budd* (1950)
Greek	14	1	4	4	*Billy Budd* (1952)
Italian	148	12	422	11	*Typee* (1931)
English (British Commonwealth)	—	75	—	279	*Typee* (1846)
Danish	20	0	37	1	*Typee* (1852)
Dutch	27	1	13	20	*Typee* (1847)
Swedish	35	2	93	8	*Typee* (1879)
Icelandic	2	0	1	0	*Moby-Dick* (1956)
English (non-English-speaking lands)	—	86	—	263	*Redburn* (Paris 1850)
French	122	7	253	19	*Typee* (1926)
Spanish (incl. Latin America)	109	0	73	1	*Moby-Dick* (1940)
Japanese	81	37	687	46	*Moby-Dick* (1939)
German	160	17	416	60	*Typee* (1847)
USSR (incl. various constituent langs.)	28	0	52	4	*Typee* (1929)

handkerchief may be taken to symbolize Melville's global recognition from the earliest European reviews and translations of *Typee* to editions and commentaries of the 1980s. In order that the tongues in Ishmael's table better correspond with today's nations, a few small changes have been made. The table shows, indeed, that Melville is a writer not only for America but for the world.

Melville was often reviewed abroad, occasionally at some length, and quickly translated. But his foreign reputation also declined rapidly and with so enduring an effect that, apart from a few important exceptions, the general disregard for his writings persisted even after the Melville Revival. Although Raymond M. Weaver's biography was immediately followed in London by the "Standard Edition" of the *Works* (1922–24), Melville remained a nearly forgotten author in most of Europe until World War II ended and a broad surge in his reputation became evident. But once the surge had begun, it strengthened quickly, especially among the Italians, Japanese, and Germans. Paradoxically, those very nations who had opposed the United States have added much since the war to our understanding of Melville. That his writings have become more attractive to foreign students as well as professional scholars is evident in more than forty-seven dissertations on Melville by international doctoral candidates (see *Mel. Diss.*).

> *... at 5 in the morning was wakened by the Captain in person, saying we were off Dover.*
>
> (*Journal*, 5 November 1849.)

By the time Melville left ship not at Dover but at Deal on the morning of 5 November 1849, four of his books had already been published in England, and he was carrying with him the proofs of a fifth, *White-Jacket*, which would be accepted by Richard Bentley before he returned to New York early the next year. He was excited when he first set foot on British soil. If his desire to place his new novel and to see the scenes of which he had heard and read so much was foremost in his mind during that sojourn, he was also well aware that *Typee* was first brought before the public in England, that it had been well received there (as was *Omoo*), and that *White-Jacket*, too, was likely to appear there before the American edition would be published. Indeed, it was Melville's practice, as it was with many of his contemporaries, to publish first in London rather than New York because of pirating problems generated by the lack of an international copyright law.

One of Melville's first acts in London was to inquire at a bookshop about *Redburn*, which was just off the press. On that day he also noted "something about Redburn" in *Bentley's Miscellany (1849 Journal*, p. 23) and a "long story about a short book" in *Blackwood's*; he found the favorable review "comical" because he was certain that *Redburn* was "trash." Whatever Melville felt about his fourth book, the anonymous *Blackwood's* reviewer found it far superior to *Mardi*, lacking the "obscurity and nonsense" of the earlier romance and benefiting from a "natural" style (*Redburn*, p. 334).

Mardi aside, Melville's early work through *The Whale* was widely approved by reviewers, though inevitably there were complaints. Charles Anderson pointed out long ago that in his biography of Melville, Weaver seemed purposely to have misled readers into believing that *Typee* and *Omoo* had been treated scornfully by British reviewers when he focused on "the one really hostile attack" in England on the two narratives; the abusive pieces he cited, from the *Eclectic Review* (April 1846, October 1850), disclosed outrage over Melville's overt anti-missionary stance, especially in *Omoo*. But overall, the reviewers were certainly favorable, though *Blackwood's*, the *Dublin Review*, and the *Athenaeum* looked skeptically on the two books as unlikely products of a novice writer. Nevertheless, the question of a possible hoax led to considerable praise over the quality of the first novel, and in noting that the *Athenaeum*—one of the most important literary weeklies—devoted four articles to *Typee* alone, Anderson suggests in "Melville's English Debut" that, although its reviews of his work were often unfavorable, it "probably did more to foster Melville's English reputation than any other single agency." He adds that the *Athenaeum* "followed Melville's career to the end" and gave separate reviews to each of his books (p. 32).

The British reaction to *Mardi* was mixed. In surveying the commentary, Elizabeth S. Foster has noted that in Britain, Melville's third book "was received promptly and on the whole not unfavorably," with praise drawn chiefly by the adventures in the first part and criticism by its "transcendentalism," incomprehensibility, rhapsodic language, and occasional impiety. Melville, of course, had entered the world of the romance with great enthusiasm. Sensitive to criticism, he nevertheless met the "broadside" fired at *Mardi* with stoicism, convinced that the hostility had come from reviewers seeking merely to be entertained, that his romance would "reach those for whom it is intended," and that it "has not been written in vain" (*Letters*, pp. 85–86). By the time he wrote of his attitude to Bentley, he was probably about halfway through the composition of *Redburn*, which would be published the following September, and *White-Jacket* would be completed by the end of that summer. Both of these narratives have more in common with his first two autobiographical fictions than with *Mardi*, and like those earlier works, too, both were well received in England. Hershel Parker notes that British reviewers were especially impressed over "the early comical scenes with Redburn and later dramatic scenes with Jackson" (*Redburn*, p. 339), though many found the Harry Bolton episode implausible and Bolton himself out of place. He also points out that reviewers were inclined to compare Melville with Defoe and Frederick Marryat as authors of travel-adventure fiction. *White-Jacket* drew even fewer complaints in England than *Redburn*. According to Willard Thorp, the British were especially pleased over Melville's favorable representation of the Royal Navy and the moving details of life at sea (pp. 429–30, 435).

When *The Whale* came out in England two years later, the reviews followed its publication almost immediately. Hugh W. Hetherington indicates that the British reviewers tended toward extremism in their positive and negative reactions, and the overall response was far more hostile in England than in the United States. To be sure, the earlier charges of rhapsody, confusion, and incomprehensibility that had been tendered against *Mardi* reappeared in critical responses to *The Whale*, but a number of critics acknowledged feelings of awe and astonishment together with occasional bewilderment (Hetherington, p. 223). Part of the bewilderment is understandable. Because Bentley inexplicably omitted the Epilogue in the British edition, several reviewers wondered how

Ishmael was alive to tell his story if he went down with the *Pequod* and the rest of the crew. Only the Epilogue explains it. Still, Melville was praised highly for his imagination and achievement with *The Whale* in several major London newspapers: "Melville is on the right track now," and in his novel "we see a concentration of the whole powers of *the man*" (*Morning Herald*, 20 October 1851; *Doubloon*, pp. 1–2); "three [volumes] more honourable to American literature . . . have not yet reflected credit on the country of Washington Irving, Fenimore Cooper," et al. (*Morning Advertiser*, 24 October 1851; *Doubloon*, p. 7); "Of all the extraordinary books from the pen of Herman Melville this is out and out the most extraordinary. . . . [F]ew books . . . contain as much true philosophy and as much genuine poetry" (*John Bull*, 25 October 1851; *Doubloon*, p. 9); in *The Whale* Melville casts "the spell of a magician who works wildly, recklessly, but with a skill and a potency which few . . . will be disposed either to deny or resist" (*Atlas*, 8 November 1851; *Doubloon*, p. 22); and *The Whale* "may be confidently recommended as among the freshest and most vigorous [writing] that the present publishing season has produced" (*Weekly News and Chronicle*, 29 November 1851; *Doubloon*, p. 56). These laudatory extracts better characterize the overall British responses to *The Whale* than the sarcastic and defamatory ones, and surely they belie any notion that the reviewers were generally too narrow or conventional to accept the novel's innovations.

But the same cannot be said about the British reception of his following works. Steve Mailloux and Hershel Parker list only one, sharply sarcastic, British review of *Pierre*, in the *Athenaeum*. The same weekly was among the three that assessed *Israel Potter*, again unfavorably (2 June 1855), and it may have been the only British journal to review *The Piazza Tales*. Two years later, however, in a surprising departure from its norm, it found *The Confidence-Man* "[f]ull of thought, conceit, and fancy, of affectation and originality" (11 April 1857; *Recognition*, p. 97). Similarly, the *Westminster Review* perceived that *The Confidence-Man* shows Melville "in a new character—that of a satirist, and a very keen, somewhat bitter, observer. . . . [It] is a remarkable work, and will add to his reputation" (1 July 1857; *Recognition*, pp. 98–99). On the whole, the British reviews "were much longer and more thoughtful than any of the American comments" (*Crit. Her.*, p. 318). Although Melville continued to enjoy a small following in England during the ensuing decades of the century, his work after *The Confidence-Man* attracted little public attention. In 1876, however, *Clarel* was thoughtfully, if briefly, reviewed in the London *Academy* as "a book of very great interest . . . [with] poetry of no mean order." The anonymous reviewer encouraged readers to study the work, "which deserves more attention than we fear it is likely to gain" (19 August 1876; *Recognition*, pp. 112, 114). He was right on both counts.

In all, approximately 85 percent of the British notices of Melville's work (published in the colonies as well as the homeland) appeared in relation to his first six novels, and of the remaining 15 percent, roughly two-thirds are devoted to *Israel Potter* and *The Confidence-Man*. *Battle-Pieces* and the later small volumes of poetry, privately printed, were ignored by the British press.

During the 1880s, however, Melville's subdued but persistent literary reputation among a relatively few influential devotees began to draw new attention to his work through their occasional essays and references to him in the press. Especially important in this respect was W. Clark Russell's short overview of maritime fiction. Russell, author of *The Wreck of the Grosvenor* and other notable sea fiction, praised Melville in his "Sea Stories" essay (1884) as a great but unsung writer, the chief one among the poets of the sea (*Recognition*, pp. 117–20). Melville received Russell's praise warmly and maintained a correspondence with him through most of the remainder of the decade (*Letters*, pp. 284, 378). A year later Robert Buchanan, who had unsuccessfully sought Melville while in the United States, praised him in a poem (entitled "Melville") as a "sea magician" who would remain immortal for writing *Moby-Dick* (*Recognition*, p. 121).

In 1889 H. S. Salt, the English biographer of Thoreau, published an essay on Melville praising the early travel narratives in particular. Salt found *Moby-Dick* better balanced than *Mardi*, although his observation that "the death of the white whale...rises to a sort of epic grandeur and intensity" leaves him open to questions on the care with which he read it (*Recognition*, p. 129). Later in the same year Melville received a letter of inquiry and praise regarding his work from Archibald Mac-Mechan, a young Professor of English in Halifax. He replied courteously, and although MacMechan later indicated that he intended to visit the author in New York, there is no record of his ever doing so. Nevertheless, he clearly kept Melville in mind, for ten years later he attempted to fulfill another intention he had expressed earlier—that is, to restore Melville's literary reputation by bringing the strengths of his art to public notice. In "The Best Sea-Story Ever Written," he praises *Moby-Dick* point by point for its poeticizing of the whaling industry, its effective construction, its "Americanism [in] theme and style," its consistent Melvillesque manner of speech, its "free-flowing" and at times Rabelaisian humor, and its "bringing to the landsman the very salt of the sea breeze" (1899; *Recognition*, pp. 137–45). In praising *Moby-Dick* so diversely as "the epic and the encyclopedia of whaling," MacMechan was clearly if inadvertently pointing to numerous topics that would serve as access points into the novel for many scholarly enterprises of the present.

Although it was not until more than twenty years later that Melville's reputation in England again commenced to rise among a broad reading public, for some it had never waned. In reviewing Weaver's biography for the London *Spectator* (6 May 1922), J. St. Loe Strachey alleged that the biographer did "not seem to realize how strong the feeling about Melville has always been in England," thus testifying to his enduring readership there despite the obscurity of his publications since the early 1850s. In 1922 the London firm of Constable and Co., Ltd., began publishing the "Standard Edition" of Melville's writings, still the most complete to date. Before it was finished two years later, D. H. Lawrence devoted two impressive chapters to Melville in his *Studies in Classic American Literature* (1923). In discussing *Typee* and *Omoo*, Lawrence portrays Melville as an alienated figure, "a Viking going home to the sea," and a man who could neither "accept [nor] belong to humanity." Seeking but never finding "the perfect fulfilment of love," Melville "was always in Purgatory, ... born for Purgatory," dissatisfied with the natural paradise of the South Seas and the domestic paradise of home and mother as well. In correspondence with his characteristic ideas on race and blood, Lawrence interprets the white whale as "the deepest blood-being of the white race," a representation of the "last phallic being of the white man." These, however, are among the few striking observations in a chapter overstocked with lengthy extracts from the novel.

Another significant British contribution to Melville studies appeared in 1926 when John Freeman brought out his critical biography, *Herman Melville*, for the English Men of Letters series; it was the first full-length English study devoted to Melville. Though a relatively brief volume now obviously impaired—as is Weaver's, from which he drew—by an excessive dependence on the travel narratives as autobiography, Freeman's compact and perceptive account doubtlessly helped to foster Melville's growing reputation on both sides of the Atlantic. The first half of the book is chiefly biographic, and the second half offers a critical study of the works. Freeman portrays Melville as a "myth-maker, a creator, [and] a poet" with a highly rhythmical, even musical, prose style (pp. 182–83), though only in *Moby-Dick* are all the powers effectively united. He is especially acute in recognizing at so early a date Melville's tendency toward suppression of emotions and discomfitting thoughts. That Melville believed in democracy but was naturally inclined toward aristocracy is an observation that Freeman's perspective as an Englishman under a monarch may have influenced, for it is echoed by Ronald Mason twenty-five years later in the next full-length critical work on Melville written in England; both authors overemphasize those allegedly aristocratic leanings. The critical readings of the works are now conventional ones, though Freeman rightly believes *Typee* to have been marred by Melville's willingness to comply with the demands of his American publisher to bowdlerize it after the first printing in order to avoid offending people over certain blatantly anti-missionary and sexually suggestive passages. He finds little literary worth among the writings after *Moby-Dick*, but "Benito Cereno," "The Encantadas," and *Billy Budd* are exceptions, and in his mind the last of these stands as evidence of Melville's spiritual restoration, his *Paradise Regained* in contrast to *The Whale*, his *Paradise Lost* (p. 131).

Since the 1920s Melville has continued to draw modest attention from scholars in the British Isles and perhaps a little more than that in Canada. Only two doctoral dissertations dealing with Melville's work have been written in England, and neither focuses exclusively on Melville. Doctoral candidates at Canadian universities, however, have produced eleven dissertations, the first in 1951, and only two of them treat additional authors. But in choice of topic and approach, these dissertations closely resemble those written in the United States, and it is doubtful that one could distinguish a decidedly Canadian perspective among them. Perhaps this recognition testifies further to Melville's universality as a writer of and for the world, however much his works may be saturated with his own background in the United States and aboard American vessels.

In each of the past three decades at least one useful volume has been added to the expanding library of Melville criticism published in Great Britain. Already mentioned is Ronald Mason's critical study of 1951, *The Spirit Above the Dust: A Study of Herman Melville*, written by a novelist and critic with training in the law. Mason's reading is a detailed and appreciative one in which he has specifically attempted to minimize the relation of the writings to the man. Mason takes into consideration the broad context of the author's life and thought in exploring the works, but he seriously underestimates the significance of "the actual events of Herman Melville's life, except in so far as they are directly recorded or reflected in his books" (p. 13). Consequently, reflections from the life in the work are perceived, but significant implications of biographical events and circumstances are overlooked because the associations are neither overt nor direct. In 1951, too, came the premier of Benjamin Britten's opera *Billy Budd*, with libretto by E. M. Forster; it opened late in the year at Covent Garden. Enormously successful over the past three decades, the opera quickly became a standard in the repertory not only of the Royal Opera but of New York's Metropolitan Opera as well. Eleven years later A. R. Humphreys published a concise introduction to Melville which only briefly discusses the tales and *Billy Budd* and gives no attention to the poems. It seems to have been aimed more toward undergraduates in the United Kingdom than toward readers who have already gained at least some familiarity with Melville's writing.

In contrast, a recent British volume on Melville is actually an Anglo-American partnership. Edited by Faith Pullin at Edinburgh University, *New Perspectives on Melville* (1978) collects essays by six British and six American scholars, two of whom—Brian Higgins and Hershel Parker— joined forces on a study of *Pierre*. Not all of the British essayists provide a decidedly transatlantic point of view, though several do. For example,

Arnold Goldman discusses Redburn and Israel Potter as illustrations of Americans who cannot adapt to changed circumstances; he sees them both as representing an unfulfilled quest for paternity. Q. D. Leavis scrutinizes the writings of the mid–1850s, identifying such likely British influences on Melville as Wordsworth, in "Cock-A-Doodle-Doo!," and Swift and Pope, in *The Confidence-Man*. Eric Mottram and Eric Homberger in separate chapters deal with Melville's confrontation with and response to order, form, and authority; both essays draw from numerous sources to provide informative, suggestive, and at times provocative insights into Melville's self-conflicts. The remaining three British essays, by Faith Pullin (on *Typee*), A. Robert Lee (on "the telling" of *Moby-Dick*), and C. N. Manlove (on style in *Billy Budd*), add significantly to the critical literature on the novels in question by analyzing the intricate structure of each and carefully explaining its function in developing the theme. Still more recent than Pullin's volume is *Herman Melville: Reassessments* (1984), edited by A. Robert Lee, comprised of ten new essays by British and American authors on nearly all of Melville's writing with separate chapters on the short fiction and the poetry. According to the editor's short introduction, the dual purpose of the volume is to "reaffirm" Melville's contemporary literary significance and to offer new approaches to his work (p. 10).

Although a number of critical essays have appeared separately since the 1920s, their specific topics and approaches, like the Canadian dissertations, give little indication of their authors' national backgrounds. It is impracticable to attempt dealing here with such contributions individually, of course, but if an excellent example may represent the whole, Elaine Barry's "Herman Melville: The Changing Face of Comedy" (1978) will suffice very well. A Professor of English at Monash University in Victoria, Australia, the author perceptively traces the course of Melville's humor through his canon. At first only a device to add "spice" and amusement to his adventure narratives, she says, the comic element attains psychological and philosophical values as early as *Mardi*. In *Moby-Dick* Melville explores the very "nature of humor and the [manifold] humorous perspective" thematically, and in the work that follows he reveals a world of the absurd characterized by dark ironies and artificial linguistic assumptions that become subject to his subtle mockery. One of the most thoughtful and informative articles that has yet appeared on Melville's humor, Barry's essay illuminates it not from an Australian point of view but an objective and universal one.

Other criticism may be found in the introductory matter and notes of later British editions than the Constable set of 1922–24. Among these are the Oxford edition of *White-Jacket*, edited and introduced by A. R. Humphreys in 1966, and the Penguin editions of *Redburn*, *Moby-Dick*, and *"Billy Budd, Sailor" and Other Stories*, all three of which were edited by Harold L. Beaver and published in 1972. Beaver's editions are accompanied by extensive critical and textual notes as well as an introduction and extracts from assorted relevant documents. The text of his edition of *Moby-Dick* is similar but not identical to that of Hayford and Parker in the Norton Critical Edition, 1967, and the data in his notes appear often to be derived from the Hendricks House edition, 1951, edited by Mansfield and Vincent, whose aid he acknowledges. At times helpful and at others disturbing, his interpretive notes too often show more imagination than elucidation of the text. Nevertheless, Beaver's broad familiarity with Melville's life and writing is apparent, and the proliferation of the relatively inexpensive Penguin editions has undoubtedly introduced sound, complete, and well-supported texts of selected Melville fiction to a host of new readers, especially students, throughout Europe and to some extent the Far East as well.

All told, then, since the 1920s Melville's writing has continued to attract some scholarly attention in the United Kingdom, but compared with the critical scrutiny given his work in the United States and among graduate schools in Canada, it is limited indeed. Nevertheless, the sporadic criticism and occasional new editions published in England, such as those of Oxford and Penguin, confirm a continuing interest in Melville's writing to the extent that his literary reputation in Great Britain and the English-speaking nations of the Commonwealth is probably secure.

> ...*On Tuesday—the 27th November—rose early, paid my bill—... & down to London Bridge stairs for the Boulogne boat....Passed by the Goodwin Sands, Deal, South Foreland, Dover, & then across the Channel to Boulogne.*
> (*Journal*, 27 November 1849.)

On the evening of 28 November 1849, the day he arrived in Paris from Boulogne, Melville stopped at Galignani's Reading Room on the Rue Vivienne and subscribed to the library services there. In 1850 the Galignanis would collaborate with Jules Baudry to bring out a condensed and pirated Parisian edition of *Redburn* in English, the last English edition of that novel to be issued before its author's death and the only one of Melville's works to be published in the original language in a non-English-speaking country during the nineteenth century. Apart from a few review extracts and a short passage used as an illustration in a reader and translation guide, none of Melville's works were translated into French until 1926, more than seventy-five years after the original English editions were introduced in France immediately following publication in England.

The first French translation was a much-abridged edition of *Typee* (*Un Éden cannibale: Récit des Îles Marquises*, 1926) by Théo Varlet and published by Gallimard. Three years later a new translation by Miriam Dou-

Desport came out as *Typee* (Paris: Librairie des Champs-Élysées, 1929), and five more versions appeared in the sixteen years that followed the close of the war in 1945, all but one of which were abridged; the exception was a collaboration by Varlet and François Ledoux in 1952, also published by Gallimard. Though greatly abridged, the original Varlet translation was "a milestone," according to Henry Yeager, to whose study of Melville's reception in France I am much indebted here. Varlet's was the first of the French editions, and it was favorably received by the public (p. 35). As in England, Weaver's biography had stimulated interest in Melville's works following the long period which Yeager calls "the forgotten years," 1860–1920. Nevertheless, only two other French translations were brought out during the Revival years, and both were abridgments of *Moby-Dick*. Published individually in the 1930s were *Billy Budd*, "Benito Cereno," "Hood Island and Oberlus" (*sic*, Sketch Ninth from "The Encantadas"), all translated by Pierre Leyris, and "The Lightning-Rod Man," by Henri Parisot. In 1939 came the first full-length French translation of *Moby-Dick* by Lucien Jacques, Joan Smith, and Jean Giono, illustrated by Alexandre Noll (Saint-Paul a.-M.); and Pierre Leyris's translation of *Pierre*, published by Gallimard, a new edition of which was brought out in 1967. Leyris's version is still the only one that has yet appeared in French. Only two items were added to the list of French translations during the war years, and both were revisions of earlier versions of *Moby-Dick*. Numerous publishing houses have brought out the Jacques, Smith, and Giono translation using various formats since its first appearance in 1939. From 1945 on, translations of nearly all the writings, including many of the poems and Part II of *Clarel*, have been coming out fairly rapidly.

The critical reception of Melville's work in France was similar to that in England and elsewhere in Europe. The reviewers were generally pleased with the vigor and originality of *Typee*, though parts of *Mardi* and *Moby-Dick* were not understood, and the critics began growing hostile. After the publication of *Pierre*, Melville was largely ignored in France to the extent that from the late 1850s to the mid–1920s his name rarely appeared in the French press. But his initial reception is worth dwelling on. Philarète Chasles, critic and knowledgeable reader of English literature, reviewed *Typee* in the Parisian *Journal des Débats* (22 June 1846). In praising its freshness if not its profundity, Chasles charted the course that French criticism of Melville was to take (Yeager, p. 14). Three years later an anonymous reviewer of *Typee*, *Omoo*, and *Mardi*, probably Chasles, says of *Mardi*, in particular, that "it speculates, it philosophizes, it sings the destiny of America." So long and glowing is the review that Evert Duyckinck asserted the following year that it had opened up Europe for Melville, and he accompanied this claim with a translation of the essay published in two consecutive issues of his journal, the New

York *Literary World* (*Mardi*, p. 669). Early in 1853 E. D. Forgues praised *Moby-Dick* in the *Revue des Deux Mondes* (1 February 1853), ranking it as distinctive among American romances (Yeager, p. 20), and two years later Émile Montegut translated several passages of *Israel Potter* in the same journal (July-September 1855), reviewing that novel as an account of contemporary American manners, a narrative that exposes the character of the United States as yet in a formative stage manifesting "a love of democracy and national pride" (Yeager, p. 20). It was Chasles, however, who first emphasized Melville's Americanism as well as his dual nature—the skeptical, rationalistic observer in contrast to the moody, wild, melancholic romantic. Despite these few favorable reviews after *Typee*, Melville was largely disregarded by the early French critics. Yeager attributes the neglect of his work during the "forgotten years" to the reluctance of critics to look seriously at a non-traditional manner of writing, their snobbishness, the general paucity of—as they saw it—noteworthy literature being published in America at the time, and their limited literary judgment (pp. 20–21).

The translations of the 1920s inspired reviews and occasional articles, including an essay by Régis Michaud, "Herman Melville, coureur des mers," in *Nouvelles Littéraires* (25 December 1926), in which Melville is portrayed as having "invented a new myth" (Jane V. Moriarity, p. 78). But the most important of these pieces was probably René Galland's "Herman Melville et *Moby Dick*" (1927). Much of this essay provides an interpretive reading in which the *Pequod* represents humanity, Ahab its conscience, and the white whale inscrutable malice. Yeager argues that the review was advanced for its time because it was the first in France to break away from the traditional nineteenth-century views of that novel (p. 37).

During the 1930s French critics began to look still more seriously at Melville and to associate his own mental state with his fiction (Yeager, p. 53). In the middle of that decade Jean Simon published the first of his several commentaries on Melville; three years later he completed the first French dissertation on Melville (Paris, 1938) and published it the following year under the original title, *Herman Melville, marin, métaphysicien et poète*. Comprising four main parts—an historical introduction, a biography, a critique of the work, and a long section on Melville's originality—it has been assessed by both Moriarity and Yeager as enduring in both insight and scholarship. Two years later one of the early translators of *Moby-Dick*, Jean Giono, brought out his fictionalized biography, *Pour saluer Melville* (1941), which has gone through dozens of editions and reprints since its initial publication. Its principal value has been in bringing Melville's work to the attention of a wide popular audience both in Germany, where it was translated, and in France.

Apart from Giono's popularized biography and an unsuccessful 1949 staging of *Moby-Dick* in Paris—the program for which included a brief preface by Albert Camus—the 1940s added little of consequence to the list of writings on Melville in France. After 1950, however, interest in Melville increased dramatically. Seven French dissertations have been written since 1951, and in the past thirty-five years, approximately 80 percent of the translations and over 70 percent of the critical items have appeared. Moreover, the critiques have become more specific and diverse in their approaches. In his survey, Yeager observes that a common point of view held during the early part of this period was that such nineteenth-century American writers as Melville and James had more to offer French readers than many contemporaries and that modern writers like Faulkner could not be dissociated from Hawthorne and Melville (p. 98).

Camus, for example, found much to admire in Melville. In an essay of 1952 he compares Melville as mythmaker and poet to Shakespeare and the Bible, emphasizing his balance of "spiritual experience" with "expression and invention." No less important is that in Melville he "constantly finds flesh and blood"—unlike Kafka, he says, whose symbolism is largely disengaged from the material reality of experience ("Herman Melville," pp. 292–93). Clearly, Melville's substantiality draws Camus to his myth and romance; Melville speaks to him in the mid-twentieth century.

Perhaps the best extended French study of Melville is Jean-Jacques Mayoux's well-illustrated critical biography, *Melville par lui-même* (1958). Although most of the attention is given to *Moby-Dick*, many of the insights throughout are excellent, and the book received a favorable reception among the reviewers. Like Mayoux, André Le Vot, in a superb essay of 1964, "Melville et Shakespeare," emphasizes the importance of Melville's reading to the development of his fiction, especially his poring over Shakespeare and particularly with reference to *Moby-Dick*.

Obviously, it would be unrealistic to attempt summarizing or evaluating each of the many items on Melville published over the past three decades in France, but a few words on some of the more noteworthy studies might convey a sense of the various directions followed by French scholars during this period. Two journals have published special issues devoted entirely to Melville: *L'Arc*, No. 41 (1970), comprises thirteen short and mostly impressionistic articles on a variety of Melvillean subjects. In addition, two consecutive numbers of *Delta*, Nos. 6–7 (1978), edited by Phillipe Jaworski, focus entirely on "Bartleby"; both include a few English essays among the many in French, and although useful material may be found in parts of the collection, on the whole little originality is evident. None is lacking, however, in the works of Viola Sachs, who has discovered in *Moby-Dick* what she believes to be a code, and in 1975 she explained her attempts to crack it in *La Contre-bible de Melville: Moby Dick déchiffré*. In a more recent edition, in English, *The*

Game of Creation: The Primeval Unlettered Language of Moby-Dick or, The Whale" (1981), she discloses that Melville's novel includes "a double, ciphered text," an inverted version of the Scriptures. To the uninitiated, her method of combining numerology, orthographical transpositions, and other types of wordplay is not unlike the kabbalistic system of *gematria* applied to secular literature instead of the Torah, but perhaps her approach will bring "the ungraspable phantom of [*Moby-Dick's*] life" a little closer to realization, and if at length it does, she will have many of us skeptics in her debt.

Regardless of whether American readers are inclined to accept or reject certain of the views expressed by the French critics, it is clear from the amount of attention Melville has been receiving in France that his voice, as Camus suggested more than thirty years ago, remains modern and relevant to scholars there. His star seems not likely to diminish in magnetic intensity for some years to come.

> *About 9 o'clock we arrived at Cologne, in the dark, and taking a "bus" drove to a Hotel. . . . I intended taking the boat at 10 1/4 in the morning, & so slept sweetly dreaming of the Rhine.*
>
> *(Journal,* 8 December 1849.)

By the time Melville arrived in Cologne late in 1849, *Typee* and *Omoo* had been available in German translation for two years, and a German *Redburn* would be brought out the following year. He was fortunate in his early German translators, the first of whom was Rudolph Garrigue, whose version of *Typee* was published by G. Mayer in Leipzig in 1847. Garrigue spent much of his life as a book agent and dealer in the United States. Charlotte Weiss Mangold—whose detailed account (1959) of Melville's reception in Germany has been of great help to me here—believes that Melville may have known him personally because of remarkably coincidental circumstances in their lives, but she has discovered nothing that would confirm their acquaintance. Surely the most ironic of the coincidences is that when Garrigue died during a visit to Europe in September 1891, his death notice and Melville's were listed in the same obituary column of the New York Daily *Tribune* (Mangold, pp. 3–5). In 1847 G. Mayer also brought out a German edition of *Omoo*; it was translated by Friederich Gerstäcker, a traveler and author of numerous accounts of his global wandering. In one of the two Swiss dissertations on Melville, Josef Walter traces his influence on Gerstacker's work (Fribourg, 1952). When *Redburn* was rapidly translated by Louise Marezoll and published in 1850 (Grimma: Verlags-Comptoir), it seemed to hold "a special appeal for German readers" and was consequently reprinted the following year (Mangold, p. 27). These three travel narratives were the only works by Melville to appear in German before 1927.

In that year an abridged translation of *Moby-Dick* was published with new German versions of *Typee* and *Omoo*, all three by the same house in Berlin, Th. Knaur Nachfolger, but because they were issued as items in a series of such popular American fare as the westerns of Zane Grey and Max Brand (Frederick S. Faust), they were largely ignored by critics of serious literature (Mangold, p. 49). Translations of "Benito Cereno" and *Billy Budd* first appeared in 1938, and two Swiss editions of *Moby-Dick* in German were published in 1942 and 1944. The first of these was an abridgment by Margarete Möckli von Seggern, illustrated by Otto Tschumi with a series of twenty-four plates. Unfortunately, relatively few copies of this edition were published because it was issued for a book club, but several examples of Tschumi's highly imaginative illustrations may be seen in *Illustrationen zu Melvilles Moby-Dick,* edited by Joachim Kruse in 1976. The 1944 Swiss edition of *Moby-Dick,* translated by Fritz Güttinger, was the first complete German version of that novel; published in Zurich by Manesse as part of the firm's Library of World Literature, it was quickly acclaimed a classic by German critics as the war drew to a close.

The first complete translation of *Moby-Dick* published in Germany itself was brought out in 1946, translated by Thesi Mutzenbecher and Ernst Schnabel (Hamburg: Classen & Goverts). Between that time and 1979 some eighty-four additional German versions of *Moby-Dick* were published in assorted translations, abridgments, and adaptations. In this respect, however, the publication history of *Moby-Dick* in Germany resembles that of Melville's work as a whole, for approximately 90 percent of such editions and adaptations have come out since the war's end. Moreover, the list of his writings in German translations continues to grow annually with very encouraging consistency; new editions of *Typee, White-Jacket, Moby-Dick, Israel Potter, Billy Budd,* and a few of the stories have appeared, for example, during the past decade.

Although books by American authors were generally popular in Germany during the last half of the nineteenth century, critical commentary on Melville was short and superficial after the favorable initial response to his early fiction. Furthermore, the Melville Revival in the United States, Great Britain, and France sparked by Weaver's biography, does not seem to have touched Germany; even the publication in 1927 of three of his novels in German was more the result of a search for non-German adventure fiction than the effect of new critical inspiration. When Carl Gustav Jung assessed *Moby-Dick* in 1930 as "the greatest American novel," his remark was overlooked at the time; according to Mangold, in fact, his comment was "the last critical mention to appear on this novel until 1946" in Germany (p. 63).

Other works by Melville, however, were being read in Germany and commented on there during the Nazi period. Mangold professes that foreign books were popular among Germans at this time, and as the second half of the 1930s commenced, they became more popular still. Although disturbed, Nazi officials apparently made no serious effort to prohibit importation of this non-German literature. German critics responded favorably to the new translations of "Benito Cereno" and *Billy Budd* in 1938, both of which were categorized vaguely as "conditionally acceptable" by the Nazi regime, though harsher restrictions were placed on *Typee* and *Omoo* (Mangold, pp. 68–69). "Benito Cereno" and *Billy Budd* were praised, she observes, for the quality of the translation as well as for Melville's presentation—his exploration of evil, his symbolism, and his exciting narratives. Perhaps unwilling to create unnecessary disturbances among otherwise patriotic readers over a relatively minor domestic quibble while planning to gain control over Europe and completely Aryanize their own nation, the Nazis at this time evidently did not impose their fascist literary views on the critics. Of the nine critics Mangold discusses in detail from this period, she says that "[i]n no case did political theories react upon their reviews" (p. 80).

After the war as American authors gained increasing attention throughout Europe, "a genuine renaissance of Melville interest" occurred among German readers (Mangold, p. 126). Critical attention shifted "from exposition to analysis," and the Mutzenbecher-Schnabel translation of *Moby-Dick* (1946) helped make that novel the most acclaimed of Melville's works in Germany within a short time. Mangold perceptively suggests that for German readers Melville's novel correlated with the times through which they had just passed and were still passing, that they saw Ahab's madness and defeat in direct relation to a megalomaniacal Third Reich, and that despite the destruction of ship and crew, the idea at the close of the Epilogue—that "the great shroud of the sea rolled on"—affirmed the continuity and sublimity of natural existence (p. 129). Sara Elizabeth Ballenger observes that German critics after the war began to regard *Moby-Dick* more profoundly and diversely, exploring the multitude of approaches that may be taken in interpreting that novel. The consensus among such critics, she says, indirectly concurring with Yeager's observations on the French critics of the same period, "is that Melville belongs to the twentieth century rather than to his own because of his treatment of the basic problems of modern man," who has been disillusioned from his earlier simplistic views of progress (p. 51). In contrast to Camus's allusion, however, Heinz Oliass one year earlier had compared Melville with Kafka to illustrate his modernity. Whereas Camus emphasizes Melville's imaginative vitality through empirical association, Oliass focuses on the dark irony present in both authors. Although much of the German criticism of this generation is thoughtful, it is often impressionistic and abstract to a fault, Mangold argues, and the articles in which it appears are usually short and poorly developed.

A similar complaint among American critics occurs with regard to much of the criticism published in France and other European countries. By now it should be clear, however, that American and European critics are not inevitably asking the same questions or approaching the works of their authors on the same level. Consequently, their observations necessarily differ in many profound respects, not only in the details and the angle of vision but also in the whole manner of interpretation and understanding. However vague and impressionistic were these postwar European critics, one clear benefit they provided was to stimulate a broader and more serious interest in Melville's work across the Atlantic.

A case in point here is Jean Giono's fictionalized biography of Melville (Paris, 1941). It was translated as *Melville zum Gruss* by Walter Gerull-Kardes, who also wrote an introduction for it. Soon after the translation appeared in 1946, it did much to foster, through its immense popularity, the new interest in Melville that began to surface with America's postwar occupation.

Criticism from 1950 on has followed established directions and explored new ones. On the one hand, Fritz Volquard Arnold discusses Melville in relation to Kafka, Shakespeare, and metaphysics in an essay of 1950 illustrated with lithographs by Will Sohl (see Joachim Kruse, pp. 82, 84, 223). The Calvinist element in Melville is the subject of Curt Hohoff's "Herman Melvilles weiser Wal," an article in which the Hawthorne association is emphasized. Cruising new waters, however, Harro Heinz Kuhnelt is the first among the Austrian and German critics to focus attention on the importance of humor in *Moby-Dick*, a subject that had been largely overlooked in those countries, in favor of darker and more overtly significant themes until his essay appeared in 1955.

Most of the approximately 250 items published on Melville in Austria and Germany from 1955 to the early 1980s are short introductions and afterwords to accompany new translations. Many of the rest, not surprisingly, resemble American criticism in focusing on Melvillean topics more narrow and specific than had been evident in the past. For example, most of the seventeen dissertations written in Germany and one of the two from Vienna were completed during this period, and they address the same kind of limited topic as those of American doctoral candidates—such themes as loneliness or destiny traced through selected fiction, and Melville's use of the first-person narrator. Several German Americanists have compared Melville's writing with that of his contemporaries, including Hawthorne, Cooper, and Poe. In 1959 Klaus Lanzinger brought out a monograph on primitivism and naturalism in Melville's work, and Ursula Brumm's essay on the typological orientation of his fiction is a major contribution to Melville studies; it constitutes a chapter in her book, published originally in 1963 and now, fortunately, available in translation as *American Thought and Religious Typology* (1970). Brumm sees nearly all of Melville's leading figures as types whose characters are entirely determined by fate rather than as individually developed portraits. She finds in Melville a strong legacy from the Calvinism in his background and observes that his struggle against its dogmas suffused his life and writing with Biblical reverberations. Although she does not refer to Camus in drawing her conclusions, she, too, recognizes the profundity and vitality Melville achieves through linking his art to the world of actual experience. With this in mind, she calls him "a symbolic realist, that is, a writer for whom the actual world and experience are keys for a deeper, supernatural meaning. He had an innate conviction that everything contains a transcendental meaning," she continues, no longer, however, in tandem with Camus. "Even though he quarreled with the God of the Calvinists, he never doubted that the world with all its features was a divine creation" (p. 196).

Melville and Shakespeare are again associated in a long essay of 1964 by Hans-Joachim Lang, who has written three impressive English articles on Melville's fiction as well as many in German. Max Frank's dissertation (Tubingen, 1965) was published in 1967 as *Die Farb-und Lichtsymbolik in Prosawerk Herman Melvilles [Color and Light Symbolism ...]*. A handbook to "Benito Cereno" was edited by Marianne Kesting and published in 1971; it includes several items translated from English, a text of the story, historical source material, and critical references. According to Diether Lauenstein, the secret of the white whale lies in Melville's knowledge and use of the Old Testament in *Moby-Dick*, a theory which is the subject of his book published in 1973. Three years later Ferdinand Schunk's dissertation (Bonn, 1975) on Melville's short poetry, "Das lyrische Werk ... ," was published, also in Bonn, by Bouvier, and the following year Ludwig Rothmayr's dissertation on man and fate in Melville's novels (Regensburg, 1976) was published by Peter Lang.

The publication in Germany of sound and varied writings on Melville both in English and German, including translations of his works, shows no likelihood of abating in the near future. In addition, more attention is now being given to the less familiar tales and poems, many of which have only recently been translated. And surely no less important a sign of the continuing, deepening interest in Melville among German readers is the sustained production and publication of dissertations. The record looks very promising, indeed, for Melville studies in Germany.

> *Passed within a third of a miles of Cape St: Vincent. . . . The whole Atlantic breaks here./ . . . Entered the Strait of Gibraltar at 4. P.M. . . . Spanish coast in sight.*
>
> (*Journal*, 23–25 November 1856.)

As Melville sailed past Cape St. Vincent and east through the Straits beside the Spanish coast, could he have prophesied that before the end of the next century more than 250 editions, adaptations, and commentaries related to his work would be published in the languages of Portugal and Spain? Perhaps so. No doubt the flags of those two nations were embellished among the rest on the handkerchief of his pale Usher.

But the language references alone are misleading as a guide to the sources of publication for both Portuguese and Spanish work on Melville. Of the nearly forty Portuguese translations and adaptations of his fiction, for example, only approximately 30 percent were published in Portugal (mostly Lisbon); the remaining 70 percent were brought out either in São Paulo or Rio de Janeiro, as were all but two of the secondary items, excluding introductions to accompanying texts. The percentages for the Spanish translations and commentary are different, however, and over twice as many Melville items have appeared in that language, including sixty-six different versions of and extracts from *Moby-Dick*. Of more than a hundred primary items, just over half were published in Spain (Barcelona or Madrid), including a selection of four *Obras (Typee, Moby-Dick,* "Benito Cereno," and *Billy Budd*) translated by José María Valverde (Barcelona: Planeta, 1968). The rest, including a great many illustrated and abridged juvenile editions, were brought out by Latin American publishers, mostly in Buenos Aires with a small selection from Mexico City and isolated examples from Havana, Santiago, Rio Piedras (P.R.), and others. All of the separate secondary items, however, are Latin American in origin.

With only occasional exceptions, the secondary literature published in both languages is general and introductory in nature. Apart from commentaries accompanying the translated texts, the majority of these items serve as broad introductions to Melville in literary histories and encyclopedias, though a few more specific pieces exist. For example, after completing an M.A. thesis on *Moby-Dick* in Brazil, Giovanni Bonardelli published two short English articles on that novel in a Brazilian journal, *Revista UNIMAR* (1974, 1978). Carlos Daghlian's study, "Persuasive Techniques in *Moby-Dick*" (São Paulo, 1972), which discusses Melville's "two rhetorical techniques" in that novel (one for characters addressing each other, and the second for Ishmael addressing the reader), is the only dissertation on Melville that has yet been completed in Portuguese (*Mel. Diss.*, #274). In the following year the only Spanish dissertation on Melville—a study of *Pierre* by Angeles Palacin—was accepted at the University of Madrid, and a few well-focused articles on the fiction have appeared in that language; three since 1967 were written by Cándido Pérez Gállego, including one each on *Typee*, *Moby-Dick* as political allegory, and Melville's travel theme. A worthy collection of nine essays by José de Onís, *Melville y el mundo hispanico [Melville and the Hispanic World]* was published in 1974. Enthusiastically received, the essays reveal how Melville was influenced by aspects of Hispanic culture, including *Don Quixote*, and how he in turn influenced certain Spanish-American novelists of the twentieth century.

> *Think of it! Jerusalem & the Pyramids—Constantinople, the Aegean, & old Athens!*
>
> (*Journal*, 15 October 1849.)

Melville stopped for several days in many parts of Greece—the islands, Athens and environs, Thessaloniki (then occupied by the Turks), and elsewhere—and found much there to admire and ponder. Unfortunately, few Greek scholars have reciprocated.

Of the handful of translations and adaptations published, three are in the form of *Classics Comics*, including the Greek version of *Typee*. Six different translations of *Moby-Dick* have been published, none of which is complete. The nearest to it is a serialized edition, translated by Aglaïa Mitropoulou for the literary journal *Néa Estía* and published in twenty-three issues through 1957–58. The same translation was brought out in an illustrated edition for young readers in 1959 and is still available in reprint. A second more drastically abridged translation is also being marketed for children, and an older edition, shorter still, has reduced the mighty folio whale to the merest sextodecimo quasi-cetacean bearing little resemblance to Melville's original. A *Moby-Dick Classics Comics* is the fifth adaptation. The most recent translation, by A. K. Christodolou, is also the most remarkable. It is a dual-language edition with a comprehensive but profound introduction and extensive notes all in Greek. The first volume of this ambitious work covers only the preliminary material and the opening nine chapters of *Moby-Dick*, yet it comprises four hundred pages. Begun in 1983 and published in Volos by Zodio, this leviathan of a project, when completed, will constitute a long overdue tribute to Melville in Greece and will surely gain many new readers there.

The tales and *Billy Budd* have fared better, and the available translations, particularly the three most recent ones, are noteworthy: *Billy Budd and Bartleby* (1977), by Roula Pateraki; *Bartleby the Scrivener and Three Other Stories* (1980), by Menis Koumantareas, and the more inclusive *Benito Cereno and Other Stories* (1980), by Nikos Vardikas with a short introduction and chronology. In addition to "Benito Cereno," it includes the first Greek translations of "Cock-A-Doodle Doo!," "The Bell-Tower," "John Marr," and "Daniel Orme."

In the secondary literature, there are two inconsequential introductions to the abridged translations of *Moby-Dick*, and a substantial review of the Pateraki translation of *Billy Budd and Bartleby*, written by Nora

Anagnostaki, wife of the renowned poet Manolis Anagnostakis and an important figure herself among contemporary Greek writers. Although American literature as a whole has received little scholarly attention in Greece, three recent items by Ekaterini Georgoudaki should be noted. The first is her dissertation "Melville's Artistic Use of His Journeys to Europe and the Near East" (1980), in which *Clarel* and the other poetry receive most of the attention. The second is a perceptive essay on the late poems, "Ancient Greek and Roman Pieces of Art in Herman Melville's Iconography," published in 1983 at the Aristotelian University of Thessaloniki, where she teaches. Her rewarding study of *Billy Budd*, in which she discusses Billy as a sublime mythic hero, appeared in the same journal. Perhaps her work and the recent translations of *Moby-Dick* and the short fiction will stimulate further interest in his writing among serious Greek readers of American literature. *Ei.* . . .

Despite the dearth of Melvilleana published in Greece, there are still fewer items in Turkey, and of the seven translations and adaptations that have been noted, five are different editions of *Moby-Dick*, by Sabhatin Eyuboğlu and Mina Urgan, two of which are nearly complete, though like many putatively complete foreign versions they lack the "Etymology" and "Extracts." The few other translations include an abridgment of *Typee*, two very brief adaptations of *Moby-Dick*, and a judicious selection of the tales that brings together "Cock-A-Doodle Doo!" (the title story), "Poor Man's Pudding and Rich Man's Crumbs," "The Happy Failure," "The Apple-Tree Table," and "Jimmy Rose," all translated by Tahsin Yücel and published in 1955. The only Turkish secondary literature is an introduction by Irfan Sahinbas to the first edition of the Eyuboğlu-Urgan translation of *Moby-Dick*. John Bryant, however, notes that a dissertation in English on selected fiction of Melville was completed by Esim Erdim at the University of Ankara in 1973; entitled "Appearance and Reality in Herman Melville," it portrays Melville as an artist seeking "aesthetic rather than ethical resolutions" to worldly problems (*Mel. Diss.*, #308). Evidently, however, nothing on or by Melville has been published in Turkish since 1972, though the prolific German Melville scholar Hans-Joachim Lang brought out an essay in English the following year, "Poe in Melville's *Benito Cereno*," which appeared in *English Studies Today* (Istanbul).

Work in Arabic on Melville is also decidedly limited, possibly because a large percentage of the literate population of the Arab nations can take advantage of materials published in English, French, or German. Consequently, there is little real need for translations and criticism on a foreign author in the native written language of their own countries. Complete Arabic translations of *Billy Budd*, by Mostafā Tāha Habīb (1960), and *Moby-Dick*, by Ihsān 'Abbās (1965), were published in Cairo and Beirut, respectively, but they seem to be the only versions in those languages; secondary literature in Arabic on his work is virtually non-existent, though 'Abbās discusses the "Islamic Influence on *Moby-Dick*" in English briefly in *Al-Aadaab*, a Beirut publication of 1965. Three different Persian versions of *Moby-Dick* were brought out in Tehran, including an abridgment (1956), a complete translation by Parvīz Dāriyouch (1965), and a short, illustrated children's edition (1965). It may be a while before we can reasonably expect more scholarly attention to Melville from Iran.

Among the diversified Indian population, Melville has gained only limited attention, and all of that has come in the past two decades. Secondary material on his work has appeared only in English, apart from a few introductions to particular translations. Numerous versions of *Moby-Dick* have been published in several different Indian languages, though of his other works none but *Typee* and *Billy Budd* have been translated into Gujarati (1967) and Marathi (1966); a single edition of *Moby-Dick* is also available in each of these languages, both dating back to 1962. Leland R. Phelps lists other translations of *Moby-Dick* in Bengali, Hindi, Oryia, Tamil, Telugu, and Urdu in a variety of complete and abridged texts and in many different formats. The Indian secondary material is all in English, mostly in the form of short pieces brought out during the past twenty years, though several items were written by Americans visiting the country, perhaps in the universities. Taken together the articles from India reveal no special trend or perspective. P. S. Sastri is the author of a short monograph on Melville, written as one of a series on critical approaches to American authors (1972), and R. K. Gupta published five essays on Melville between 1967 and 1974, three of which came out in the *Indian Journal of American Studies* in Hyderabad. Gupta is also the author of one of the few dissertations on Melville written by Indian doctoral candidates; his was a study of *Pierre* (*Mel. Diss.*, #124). More recently, Lakshmi Mani included Melville with Cooper and Hawthorne in her analysis of the apocalyptic content in the work of these three American romancers (*Mel. Diss.*, #286), and in the only Melville dissertation completed at an Indian university thus far, "The India of Melville and Mark Twain: A Study in Geo-Cultural Symbolism," Mohamed Elias traces patterns of imagery related to India that he discerns in Melville's fiction and *Clarel* (*Mel. Diss.*, #473).

Of all the languages into which Melville's fiction has been translated and in which it has been critically discussed, Hebrew is possibly both the oldest and the youngest. Melville's modulated enthusiasm over his visit to the Holy Land glimmers through the pages of his journal for those weeks. But at that time, of course, he did not hear Hebrew spoken. Some ninety-one years after that visit early in 1857, Hebrew became the national language of the new state of Israel, and only two years later, the first translation of Melville into Hebrew was published in Tel Aviv. It was *Billy Budd*, translated and introduced briefly by Avraham Regelson in

1950, and published by Am Oved; "Benito Cereno" and "The Encanta-das" are also included in the volume. In another two years came the first Hebrew edition of *Moby-Dick*, by Elijah Bortniker, with illustrations by Rockwell Kent; published by N. Newman in Tel Aviv. In 1981, Keter (Tel Aviv) published a full new translation in two volumes by Aharon Amir with an afterword by Zefira Porat and selected Kent illustrations. Also, two short illustrated adaptations (sixteen pages and forty-eight pages) were published by Mizrahi in the same city in 1969. Josef Rebikov's trans-lation of *Typee* had been brought out several years earlier (1961) by the same publisher.

In addition to a few introductory pieces and a brief article of 1965 by Avraham Yehoshua Bick relating Melville to Hemingway in terms of fate and will, the only secondary writing of consequence on Melville in Hebrew are the afterword to the Amir *Moby-Dick* and three other essays by Zefira Porat, two of which are chapters in her book, *Prometheus bayn ha-Kannibalim [Prometheus Among the Cannibals]* (1976). Chapter 5 investi-gates the theme of mystery in *Moby-Dick*, and Chapter 6 is a study of three character types in *Clarel*: the Promethean Rebel, the Wandering Jew, and the False Christian. Here she seems to be applying Ursula Brumm's ty-pological thesis to Melville's long narrative poem. Three years earlier, her English essay on irony, tragedy, and innocence in *Billy Budd* appeared in *Scripta Hierosolymitana* [Jerusalem] (1973). Porat's studies are possibly the best and most recent on Melville published to date in Israel.

> *Coasts of Calabria & Sicily ahead at day break....Fine sail in the straits.*
> *At 1 P.M. anchored in harbor of Messina.*
> *(Journal, 13 February 1857.)*

Melville spent two months in Italy in 1857 from mid-February to mid-April. The profound appeal that country held for him is evident in the extent and detail of his journal observations from those weeks and from his first lecture, "Statues in Rome," which he delivered several times on the lyceum circuit later that year and early the next. A glance through the list of publications in Italian by and about Melville quickly discloses that his attraction to Italy has not been a unilateral one; indeed, among the non-English speaking nations of the world only Germany and Japan have produced a longer bibliography pertaining to him. But unlike the case in England and France, his reputation in Italy is altogether a twen-tieth-century phenomenon, for whereas Melville was a noted author in those two countries when he visited them late in 1849—as a result of the editions, translations, and reviews of his work published there—the same was not true in Italy. Instead, the first translations and commen-taries date to the early 1930s. First were translations of *Typee*, by Bice Pareto Magliano (1931) and Esa Cugini (1937). A third Italian version, by Bruno Tasso, appeared in 1944, and at least eleven more translations and adaptations of that narrative have been published in Italy since then. The only other of Melville's works translated before 1940 is *Moby-Dick*, a complete version of which came out in two volumes published in 1932, translated by Cesare Pavese; by 1966 it was in the eighth edition. Beyond this, fifty or more translations, abridgments, and adaptations of this novel had been published by 1977. By the mid-1970s nearly all of Melville's work was available in Italian, including most of the poems and large segments of *Clarel* as well as selections from the letters and journals. Both "Benito Cereno" and *Billy Budd* had been translated at least a dozen times by 1978, and each had been published in some twenty different editions. One of the most telling and important Melville publications in Italy of recent years is a two-volume edition of *Selected Works (Opere scelte)*, edited by Claudio Gorlier, which incorporates in most cases translations that were brought out previously. Published in 1972 and 1975, the selection includes *Moby-Dick, Pierre, The Confidence-Man*, several tales, a large number of poems in dual-language format, some letters, and other expository pieces.

Like the Italian translators, the critics, too, were stimulated to begin looking seriously at Melville's work early in the 1930s, about a decade after the Revival had commenced in Britain and the United States. Phelps has compiled the titles of more than four hundred secondary items on Melville in Italian up to 1978, and since then, of course, additional commentaries have been published. Although the large number of such items is in itself indicative of the strong, growing interest in Melville's work among Italians, especially since the end of the war, most of the secondary entries are brief prefaces or afterwords for translations, reviews of American books and editions of the works, and general biocritical remarks about Melville from a page or two in length to a chapter in a survey or history of American literature. Nevertheless, the importance of such items in bringing Melville's work before a wider public cannot be overstated. Moreover, among the many short and often conventional statements are numerous sound critical pieces focusing on particular aspects of individual works.

Many of those smaller items were written by a select few critics, and as early as 1951 Cesare Pavese, the first Italian translator of *Moby-Dick*, consolidated several of his published prefaces and other short pieces into a section on Melville in his *La Letteratura americana e altri saggi [American Literature and Other Essays]*, published in Turin by Einaudi. Twelve years later, the noted comparatist Glauco Cambon did the same with three of his earlier essays, which he brought together in the Melville chapter of *La Lotta con Proteo [The Struggle with Proteus]*, first published in Milan by Bompiani in 1963; the essays have been translated into both English and German. Of some seventeen pieces published by Luigi Berti on Melville between 1940 ("Annotazione al *Moby-Dick*") and 1963 (a review of the Hayford-Sealts *Billy Budd*), only a few are not reviews or introductions to his translations, yet they all contributed significantly in fostering Melville's reception in Italy. Similarly, although most of Emilio Cecchi's publications on Melville are in the form of short and often reprinted pieces, it was Cecchi who introduced him to an Italian readership in 1931 with a single-page article on *Moby-Dick* in a Milan newspaper. Alfredo Rizzardi, in contrast, has published fewer articles on Melville, but three years after his first one appeared in a Bologna journal in 1950, he began to focus his critical attention on the poetry. In 1955 be brought out the first extended discussion of the poems in Italy—"La Poesia di Herman Melville"—in the opening volume of *Studi americani*, which has since become the major scholarly serial for Italian Americanists. Although earlier translations of the poems into Italian were made in 1946 and 1947 by Luigi Berti (also the translator of *Pierre* [1942]), Rizzardi's collection of 1960, preceded by his essay revised as an introduction, remains the fullest one to date. The dual-language selection in Volume 2 of *Opere scelte* is also a judicious and substantial one.

There are a good many Italian Melvilleans whose works should be mentioned here, though space limitations preclude giving their articles the attention that several of them deserve. Among Elemire Zolla's longer essays, for example, are studies of *Pierre* (1957) and *Clarel* (1964) in *Studi americani*; he has also made a partial translation of *Clarel*. In addition to a broad introduction to Melville in *Studi americani* (1957), Agostino Lombardo has published two bibliographical items on Melville criticism (1959, 1961), only the latter of which, however, deals exclusively with Melville; like Pavese and Cambon, he has gathered a number of his smaller pieces together into a Melville section in a collection of his essays on American literature, *Il Diavolo nel manoscritto* (Milan: Rizzoli, 1974). The most recent bibliographical listing, by Giuseppe Lombardo, covers the years 1972–77 and appears in *The Blue Guitar*, a Messina annual. Gabriele Baldini's *Melville o le ambiguitá* (1952) was the first critical book devoted entirely to Melville published in Italy; the next one, however, did not follow for nearly a quarter century, when Giuliana Scalera McClintock's study, *Billy Budd e la negazione dell'innocenza*, was brought out in 1976. In 1970 Marcello Pagnini's volume on critical theory included a substantial study of *Moby-Dick* in terms of theme and structure, and another extended analysis of that novel, by Mario Corona, was published in *Studi americani* seven years later. Corona's essay, "*Moby-Dick; or, The Whale*: analisis di un titolo" (1977), is said to be part of a forthcoming book on the first twenty-five chapters of the novel. His major purpose in the essay is to analyze Melville's title by studying sound values in relation to the disposition of letters and then to show that the title alone contains the structure of the book in an ambiguous but nevertheless decipherable form. There is something akin here to Viola Sachs's code-breaking in France, though the basic theories are considerably different. In 1977 Leonardo Terzo brought out an essay on "Bartleby" in which his thematic reading is a conventional one, but his analysis becomes more valuable when he points to six narrative stages according to which the scrivener's decline has been structured. The same author's penetrating monograph, *Retorica dell'avventura: Form e significato in Moby Dick*, was published the following year (1978). The first of its two sections offers a structural analysis of *Moby-Dick* in terms of comic romance (through Ishmael) and tragic romance (through Ahab) interwoven with the comprehensive description ("anatomy") of whaling which casts a shadow of uncertainty and irony over all else; the second section is a stylistic analysis of the opening six paragraphs of Chapter 1.

The most recent Italian book on Melville and surely the most theoretically oriented is a collection of ten essays (some published previously) called simply *Melvilliana* (1983). Edited and introduced by Paolo Cabibbo, who is a collaborator on one of the essays and the solo author of another, the collection focuses closely on "the strategies of Melville's narrative discourse," which changed considerably over the extent of his long career. The essayists deal with "three turning points of Melville's macrotext: *Typee* and *Redburn*, *The Piazza Tales*, [and] *Billy Budd*." In short, they provide a deconstructionist view of the fiction, which they see as open to infinite possibilities of interpretation and understanding as a consequence of the openness of language itself. Among the essayists, Donatello Izzo, for example, analyzes the multiplicity of *Typee* by identifying the three narrative perspectives—that of the participant, the narrator, and the author—to reveal its unresolvable complexity. Paolo Cabibbo and Paolo Ludovici study "Bartleby" through Melville's paradoxical use of the pervasive negation and double negation. "The Encantadas" is seen by Annalisa Goldoni as depicting islands that are simultaneously endlessly changing and yet changeless, the paradox resolvable only through the reader's imagination. Mario Materassi bases his structural interpretation of "Benito Cereno" on linguistic shifts in its opening three paragraphs; Donatello Izzo believes that because critics of *Redburn* have been reading that novel too literally, they have been missing Melville's ironic purpose of undercutting conventional narrative techniques and philosophical assumptions; and Giorgio Mariana explains in a comprehensive concluding essay how Melville's work as a whole may be better understood if read from a deconstructionist perspective. In addition to individual insights to be gained from this volume is the recognition that Melville's writing is being read in Italy from new theoretical approaches as well as from traditional ones, and the strength of his literary reputation there seems to be growing, a very encouraging observation, to be sure.

Entering Holland, began to look like a great heath . . . immense pastures, light
green. Adventure after hotel in Amsterdam, where we arrived at 3 1/2 P.M.
                                                    (Journal, [23] *April* 1857).

En route back to England from his travels through the Middle East
and Italy, Melville passed through Germany and spent a few days during
the spring of 1857 touring the Netherlands, where one of the two earliest
translations of *Typee* had been published by Erven F. Bohn in Haarlem
(1847), but he passed through the city without leaving the train. That
two-volume translation by an unknown hand was the only one of Melville's works to come out in Dutch until 1929, when the first of many
versions of *Moby-Dick*, by Johan W.F.W. Buning, was published in Amsterdam by Querido; two editions of that original one have followed it.
A Dutch translation of *Billy Budd* (1950), by John M. Palm, and three
of "Benito Cereno" have appeared, the last one with the five other *Piazza
Tales*, translated by Jean A. Schalekamp and published in 1977 by Spectrum. Only these four works of the Melville canon have been translated
into Dutch thus far. Secondary material in Holland is also sparse and
general in content; the articles and chapters characteristically are short
pieces entitled simply "Herman Melville." Approximately twice as many
English articles and other brief items have been published in Holland
as in Dutch, partly due to the presence of *English Studies* in Amsterdam
and Mouton in the Hague, which bring out the work of many non-Dutch
scholars.

In Scandinavia and Finland the response to Melville has also been
limited, with most of its diminutive strength in Sweden. In Denmark the
last translation of *Typee* came out in 1852, though modern ones exist in
Norway, Sweden, Finland. Of Melville's remaining fiction, in Iceland
Moby-Dick alone has been published (sans the "Etymology" and "Extracts"), and in the other four countries *Billy Budd* has come out as well.
Redburn has been translated only into Norse and Swedish; "Bartleby"
and a few other stories variously appear in Denmark, Sweden, and Finland, and *Mardi* has been translated only into Swedish. Although secondary items on Melville have been published with some regularity in
Sweden, they reveal more general than scholarly interest, and in the
other four nations of the region criticism is virtually non-existent.

So, hurrah for the coast of Japan! Thither the ship was bound. . . . / . . . and
all before us was the wide Pacific.
                                                    (Omoo, pp. 313, 316.)

We know that Ishmael and the *Pequod* penetrate "the heart of the
Japanese cruising ground" (*MD*, p. 405), but there is no record of Melville's ever being there before them except in his "wonder-world" of

imagination. Nevertheless, if reading and critical attention may be presented in terms of light, "that unblinkingly vivid Japanese sun," which to Ishmael "seems the blazing focus of the glassy ocean's immeasurable burning-glass" (*MD*, p. 411), surely symbolizes a degree of interest in Melville's writing second only to that in the United States. The most recent list of primary and secondary titles in Japan adds more than a hundred items to the Phelps bibliography, which includes approximately 750 entries. Compiled by Arimichi Makino for a well-illustrated volume commemorating the completion of the translated *Collected Works of Herman Melville* in thirteen volumes, "A Bibliography of Melville Studies in Japan" (in Japanese) is based on the earlier checklists by Masao Tsunematsu and Sanford E. Marovitz on the same subject. Published in English in 1978, their first list was augmented and reissued in a Japanese edition by Tsunematsu alone the following year. Because an abundance of new Japanese publications on Melville has been brought out during the last five years, however, Makino's new compilation is both welcome and needed.

Surveying Japanese Melville studies for *Extracts* in 1978, Tsunematsu and Marovitz observed that a major shortcoming in that area would probably soon be rectified, and time has proved them correct. They noted then that, although numerous translations and "retellings" of *Moby-Dick* had been published since 1941, when Tomoji Abe brought out the first one, most of Melville's longer fiction and much of the poetry had not yet been translated. A large part of that problem has been eliminated already because all of the fiction is now available in Japanese through the new eleven-volume edition of the novels, translated in its entirety by Noboru Sakashita, and the corresponding two-volume edition of the tales, translated by Ginsaku Sugiura, all thirteen volumes published between 1981 and 1983. Each volume of the longer fiction includes an introduction or afterword by a noted Japanese Melville scholar. Also published in 1983 was a reprint of the sixteen-volume Constable edition of *The Works* in bindings nearly identical to the original and an excellent new translation of *The Confidence-Man*, by Masashi Yamamoto, in a scholarly edition that includes short essays by the translator on Melville and that novel (Tokyo: Seibido). Only the poems now remain to be published in Japanese.

In addition to Makino's bibliography, the commemorative volume for the collected edition, *Whale and Text: Melville's World* (1983), includes thirteen chapters with a foreword by the editor, Kenzaburo Ohashi, a renowned Americanist in Japan, who has been publishing on Melville since at least 1960. His is also the concluding essay, on Melville's acceptance in that country. Four of the chapters are translations from American studies, and the rest vary considerably in topic and approach from the general to the specific. They include "Melville and the Modern

Spirit in the Western World," by Hidekatsu Nojima; "Melville and America," by Sho Yamamato; "Melville and Hawthorne," by Ginsaku Sugiura; "A Mosaic *Moby-Dick*," by Toshio Yagi; "Melville and the Trickster Myth," by Masao Yamaguchi; "A Reading of 'After the Pleasure Party,'" by Masao Shimura; "Inside the Author's Brain," by Nobuo Kojima; and "Ahab and *Moby-Dick*," by Meisei Goto. Kojima and Goto are well-known novelists. These titles have been itemized here to illustrate the breadth of interest in Melville among Japanese scholars today.

Although the oldest and probably best known Japanese book on Melville, *Herman Melville* (1934), was written by Tomoji Abe, a highly regarded novelist and scholar, it is exceptional in that nearly all of the important Melville scholarship from that country has come out after World War II. Nearly all of the dozen postwar books on Melville discuss his work as a whole, and most treat the fiction thematically. Among others, these include Takehito Terada's *The Silence of God: A Critical Study of Herman Melville* (1968), Tatsuo Kambara's *A Solitary Pilgrimage: A Study of Herman Melville* (1975), Taizo Tanimoto's *Herman Melville's Tragic Ambiguity and Beyond* (1977, in English), and, most recently, Ginsaku Sugiura's *Melville: Voyager to Annihilation* (1981), in which the author discusses Melville's canon from a postmodernist perspective. Also during the past several years have come three Melville dictionaries, the first by Shigeru Maeno, *A Melville Dictionary* (1976), and a more recent by Teiji Kitagawa, *A Moby-Dick Dictionary* (1981). In 1981 Maeno also brought out a helpful source list in English, *The Source of Melville's Quotations*, which includes, according to his Preface, "the sources of more than six hundred quotations, variants, and echoes . . . with the originals," except for the originals of the "Extracts" in *Moby-Dick*. Maeno's most recent book is a collaboration with Kaneaki Inazumi, *A Melville Lexicon* (1984), by far the most thorough and extensive listing to date. Melville's most industrious translator, Noboro Sakashita, has nearly completed another such resource.

The articles and chapters or sections of books that have been published on Melville in Japan during the past four decades are remarkable in their diversity as well as their number. Despite what would seem to be an almost prohibitive impediment to intensive and perceptive scholarship on Melville's fiction, the great differences in language and cultural background have deterred his devotees very little. Even more surprising where such profound differences exist, the longest and most complex of Melville's writings have generally drawn the most attention. Makino lists sixteen critical essays for *Typee* and three for *Omoo* but twenty-four for *Mardi*; he lists nine for *Redburn* and two each for *White-Jacket* and *Israel Potter* but 163 for *Moby-Dick*, fifty-nine for *Pierre*, twenty-five for *The Confidence-Man*, forty for *Billy Budd*, and dozens more for the tales, including thirty for "Bartleby" and twenty-seven for "Benito Cereno."

In addition to these items are the many introductions and afterwords for the scores of translations, adaptations, abridgments, and "retellings" in English that have been published with notes in Japanese for use in English-language classes. The abundance of secondary literature on Melville in Japan is too vast and rich for adequate summary.

Moreover, now that the fiction has been translated in its entirety and the new lexicons are available, there is every reason to expect that the scholarly interest in Melville's work as well as that of the general reader will increase even more rapidly than has been true in the past few decades. Many Americanists in Japan have published significantly on Melville over the years; in addition to those whose names have already been mentioned as authors and translators, for example, are Keichi Harada, Hisashi Hayashi, Takao Minamizuka, Kenji Noguchi, Taro Shimada, Manabu Sogabe, and Mizuo Sokuseki, each of whom has several essays on Melville to his credit. The future for Melville studies in Japan is a bright one from all indications, an "unblinkingly vivid Japanese sun," without question.

Outside of Japan, the attraction to Melville's work is extremely limited in the Far East. Only one full-length Chinese translation of *Moby-Dick* exists among several abridgments published in Singapore, Taipei, and Hong Kong. The complete text was translated by Zou Yung and published in 1957 by the New Literature Publisher in Shanghai with the Rockwell Kent illustrations. An abridgment of *Typee* was also published in Shanghai, and a translation of "Bartleby," by Yu Kuang-chang, was brought out in Hong Kong in 1972 by World Today Press. The secondary material in Chinese on Melville is negligible.

In Korea there are four versions of *Moby-Dick* in translation, though one is only an extract of a few pages and another is a simplified adaptation. The two substantial editions are by Byong-tak Yang (1960) and Ka-hyŏng Yi (1973). Nothing else by Melville has been translated into Korean. For a short time in the late 1960s Melville's writing drew some scholarly attention there, though only Byung-ok Kim wrote more than one essay: "Moral Antithesis in *Billy Budd*" and "The Magic of Ahab and Wish Fulfillment," published in *English Language and Literature* in 1969 and 1971, respectively. Apart from a short bibliographical piece, the only item about Melville published in Korea since 1971 is a discussion of "Bartleby" by Sung-kyu Cho in 1979.

Several countries of Southeast Asia have brought out abridged translations of *Moby-Dick* only, one each in Malaysia, Indonesia, Burma, and Thailand; in Vietnam three versions of *Moby-Dick* and two of *Billy Budd* have been published, all dating to the 1950s and 1960s. The Vietnamese translation of *Moby-Dick* (1968) was made by the Vietnamese Translation Center in Saigon during the height of the American presence in that country. No separate secondary material on Melville has been discovered in any of these languages of Southeast Asia.

> *But cheer up my boy! Once in the Bay of Kamschatka, and we'll be all afloat with what we want, though it be none of the best.*
>
> (*Mardi*, p. 6.)

In most of the Eastern and East-Central European nations, Melville apparently did not become known until the period of the Second World War or soon after. Translations of several of the major works have been published in Bulgaria, Czechoslovakia, Poland, Hungary, Yugoslavia, Romania, and Russia, but except for Russian criticism and an occasional monograph written by a scholar from one of the other countries named, secondary material on Melville from Eastern and East-Central Europe provides limited critical insight where it exists at all. In Bulgaria, for example, translations have been made of *Typee* (1967), *Moby-Dick* (1962), and three of the tales (1975), but there is no critical or biographical literature whatsoever. In Czechoslovakia, where secondary material is also minimal, translations of *Typee* (1941) and *Omoo* (1948) led to other versions in the 1950s, and an illustrated edition of *Moby-Dick* (1933) was followed by S. V. Klíma's translation (1947), often reissued in collaboration with Maria Konelová from 1956 on. Konelová has also made the only Czech version of *Israel Potter* (1955). Melville's one story in Czech, "Benito Cereno," was published with *Billy Budd* in 1978. Slovakian versions also exist of *Typee* (1965) and *Moby-Dick* (1958), both by Jozef Kot, and of *Billy Budd* (bound with *The Piazza Tales*) (1970), by Ján Mihál; all three Slovakian editions were published in Bratislava.

The first response to Melville in Poland occurred earlier than elsewhere in Eastern Europe apart from Russia. Polish abridgments of *Typee* and *Moby-Dick* were brought out in 1882 and 1929, respectively, and at least eight references to Melville appeared in Polish publications between the beginning of the century and 1935, seven of which are from the last few years of that period, when the Melville Revival was occurring elsewhere. But as in much of Europe, the Polish interest in Melville commenced with the end of the war, and all but two of the translations were published since then, mostly in Warsaw, including the principal one of *Moby-Dick* (1954), by Bronislaw Zieliński, who also translated a more recent edition of *Typee* (1963) and *Billy Budd* (1966). The only translation of *White-Jacket* (1974), by Marian L. Pisarek, was published in Gdansk. A radio adaptation of "Bartleby," Melville's one story in Polish (1962), was performed in 1974. In fact, "Bartleby" seems to have been a particular attraction for radio adaptations; versions of it were broadcast in several countries, including Denmark, Greece, and Norway, as well as Poland. Polish secondary material on Melville is slight.

In Hungary only two each of Melville's novels and stories have been translated, including two full-length versions of *Moby-Dick*. The first, in 1929, was done by Soma Braun, and the other, originally an abridgment of 1958, by Imre Szász, who brought out a two-volume edition five years later and the only translation of *Billy Budd* (1970). The one important example of Hungarian Melville criticism is a volume in English on *Moby-Dick*, by Maria Ujhàzy, *Herman Melville's World of Whaling* (1982); it shows extensive background reading, a good familiarity with the facts of Melville's life, and acute perception applied to his chief novel. The volume comprises three major sections: Part I provides a thoughtful and comprehensive résumé of reviews and critical responses, 1846–77; Part II offers a compact but nevertheless informative biographical sketch to early 1850, when Melville began the writing of *Moby-Dick*; and Part III includes three chapters subdivided into short sections with individual subtitles, each tracing a specific theme, motif, character, structural device, or other feature of the novel. The conclusion strongly brings out the predilections of a basically socialistic critic toward reading *Moby-Dick* as an attack on "private enterprise and ownership, self-reliance and faith in divine providence" in favor of democracy among the "kingly commons" in a sharkish, materialistic world (pp. 170–71).

The Yugoslav response to Melville resembles Hungary's in that only one major critical study of his work has been published there, though the number of his titles in translation is much larger, as is the list of secondary references. His fiction has been translated into both Serbo-Croatian and Slovenian, with *Typee* and two versions of *Moby-Dick* appearing in each. *Omoo, The Confidence-Man*, and *Billy Budd* have also been published in one or the other of the two languages as have a few of the stories. The only substantial piece of secondary literature published on Melville in Yugoslavia is a book in English by Janez Stanonik, in which the white whale is related to the legend of Mocha Dick, *Moby-Dick: The Myth and the Symbol. A Study in Folklore and Literature* (1962).

Melville's reception in Romania is somewhat easier to define than in many other areas because it is so clearly dominated by the work of two writers. Petre Solomon has translated and provided introductions to four of Melville's novels, including *Billy Budd* and a selection of tales in 1967, *Redburn* and the third Romanian version of *Moby-Dick* (with notes and glossary) in 1973, and *White-Jacket* in 1976. He also wrote the preface for Crişan Teodore's translation of *Typee* in 1960. The other dominant figure in Romanian Melville studies is Marcel Pop-Cornis, who began publishing on his author in 1969. His dissertation (Timişoara, 1979), "From Herman Melville to Thomas Wolfe: The Poetics of the Symbolic-Epopeic American Novel," is the only Romanian doctoral study thus far to deal even in part with Melville's work. Since completing it, Pop-Cornis has published several essays on Melville's fiction in relation to the contemporary American novel, most recently (1981) in terms of reader-response theory. A revision of the dissertation was published in 1982 as *The Anatomy of the White Whale* with the original subtitle (Phelp's translation). The only other Romanian critic who has written significantly on Melville is Sorin Titel, who published two articles on the fiction in 1973 before bringing out his monograph, *Herman Melville: The Fascination of the Sea*, two years later (Phelps's translation). These two books of the past decade, the translations of the 1960s and 1970s, and the existence of a recent dissertation in which Melville's writing is of great importance suggest that there may be a wider and more serious readership in Romania for his work than is evident from the relatively few noteworthy items that have been published there.

In Eastern Europe Russia was the first nation to respond in any way to Melville's writing. The Chasles article of 1846 on *Typee* was translated from the French for publication in a Moscow journal in 1849, and Phelps has discovered two anonymous items on Melville from the early 1850s. In addition, extracts from *Moby-Dick* were brought out in Russian as early as 1853. But this initial reaction lasted less than a decade. With the exception of a brief reference to Melville in a Russian history of nineteenth-century American literature, a translation of *Typee* from 1929, and two short encyclopedia items of the 1930s, Melville's literary reputation in Russia may be said to have commenced in the mid-1940s, and it was not until after the war that Russian critics began to read his fiction in a political context. In 1983 Emily Tall surveyed in "Herman Melville in the Soviet Union" the overall reception of Melville in Russia since the mid-nineteenth century, and readers interested in the prevailing attitude of the USSR toward his writing should read her valuable essay.

As in Romania, Melville studies in Russia appear to be dominated by two names, those of Anna Bernštein, a translator; and Yuri Kovalev, a critic and scholar who began publishing on Melville and American Romanticism in 1964. Although Bernštein is not the only translator of Melville into Russian, she is surely the leading one, having brought out the first complete version of *Moby-Dick* in that language in 1961 and of *Typee* in 1967. She also collaborated on the only selection of Melville's tales in Russian (1977), which includes *Billy Budd* in addition to "Bartleby," "Benito Cereno," and "The Encantadas." Russian translations of *Omoo* (1960), *Israel Potter* (1966), and *White-Jacket* (1973) have also been published, the last of which includes a long afterword by Yuri Kovalev, who sees that narrative as a nexus linking the genre of the sea novel with Melville's own development as an artist (Tall, p. 4).

Among Melvillean critics in the USSR Kovalev is preeminent not only for the number of items he has produced, Tall says, but also for his knowledge and breadth of vision (p. 4). He began publishing on Melville several years before completing his dissertation (Leningrad, 1971), "Problems of American Romanticism in the 1840s: Herman Melville and His Time," a study that led to the publication of his book *Herman Melville and American Romanticism*, the following year. Since then he has brought out two essays on *Mardi* (1973, 1975) and the afterword to *White-Jacket*, but apart from an introduction to a later edition of Bernštein's *Moby-Dick* (1981), nothing of his on Melville has appeared since 1975; after that year, Tall writes, "there has been no new scholarship on Melville [in Russia] as far as I could ascertain" (p. 2). What makes Kovalev's criticism especially valuable, she says, is that he is "relatively free of the grating self-righteousness of other [Russian] critics," who characteristically apprehend and assess literature according to a strict Marxist ideology. This is a major problem with Russian literary critics, she believes, because fiction is regarded from a limited social, economic, and historical perspective rather than a detached aesthetic one, and relativistic psychological approaches are altogether forbidden (pp. 2-3). Consequently, the Russian critics find much to praise in Melville's condemnation of exploitation and Christian missionaries in *Typee* and *Omoo*, the political satire in *Mardi*, the exposé of naval abuses in *White-Jacket*, and the mistreatment of the common man in *Israel Potter* (pp. 4-6). *Moby-Dick* is appreciated for its power and philosophical depth, which is not plumbed much below the level of allegory, however; Ahab is seen as the rebel hero struggling against the manifestation of evil in the white whale (p. 5), and Ishmael appears to be in a critical penumbra.

Although little criticism of Melville has been published in Russia in the past decade, it is not unlikely that his work is still being read seriously by students and professional scholars. Between 1968 and 1975 five dissertations were written on Melville at four Russian universities, and perhaps it is not too much to assume that interest in his writing, which at the moment seems dormant, will soon reawaken in the USSR.

> *You feel you are among the nations.*
>
> (*Journal*, 13 December 1856.)

A worldwide voyage over vast seas of print testifies that the great crew who goes a-sailing for Melville is, to be sure, an "Anacharsis Clootz deputation from all the isles of the sea, and all the ends of the earth." (*MD*, p. 108) It also suggests that if the Americans in that crew are the most numerous, they are nevertheless but contributors like the rest on a grand international voyage, a productive—indeed, an autogenous— cruise with common goals of enlightenment and pleasure gained through a better understanding of Melville's life and art. These ends are successfully attained only little by little on a winding, tacking, sometimes backtracking, largely uncharted, yet ever-progressive course. Paradoxically enough, the voyage is most productive not when the hands are all working together under the guidance of a single captain, no matter how loud his voice may be, but rather when each has his own task to follow in his own way, though not without taking occasional sideward glances at the activities of his shipmates.

Looking down on these activities as if from the masthead, one might attempt to identify certain recent trends and characteristics among select groups in the crew by distinguishing according to nationality, but except for the obvious turn toward lexicography and compilation made by the Japanese in the past ten years and the strong deconstructionist tendency among Italian Melvilleans, also during that period, international scholars even from the same countries have been widely diverse in their approaches. Nevertheless, a few generalizations may be attempted. First, it appears that on the whole, European scholars have traditionally regarded Melville more from philosophical and cultural perspectives than from those of the close textual analysis of language and imagery or the interpretation of intricate symbolic patterns which have preoccupied many American critics. In Italy, however, this would not hold true, and in France one noted critic has gone in exactly the opposite direction by attempting to expose the code that Melville allegedly employed in composing *Moby-Dick*. Second, much of the international attention given to Melville has resulted in short publications, quick biocritical overviews in textbooks and serials that do little more than introduce him to a broad reading public. This cannot be said accurately of Japan, however, where many of the publications on Melville are truly analytical and comparative essays. Third, Melville's reputation in foreign countries followed a pattern similar to that in the United States until the Melville Revival. But for the most part it was not until after World War II that readers in Europe and Asia took a sudden general interest in American literature and Melville. Soviet criticism now seems to have reached a point of stasis probably because of contemporary political hostility rather than a genuine loss of literary interest, and it remains to be seen whether it can be revitalized if relations between the United States and the Soviet Union become more cordial. Fourth, modern Melville scholarship abroad is dominated by a relative handful of countries, ironically in three cases the very countries with whom the United States was at war less than half a century ago. Although his work has been accepted with great favor in France, that nation is nevertheless fourth on the scale of Melville's appreciation overseas, behind Japan, Germany, and Italy, from all three of which abundant imaginative scholarship continues to emerge. Regarding a tangential matter, a fifth generalization that holds true for over half of the nations in which *Moby-Dick* has appeared in translation pertains to the illustrations: of those that often accompany the text, graphics by Rockwell Kent are the most popular—despite the large number of artists abroad who have created effective and occasionally brilliant plates for that novel. Phelps lists twenty-five editions in fourteen languages (1933–75) in which some or all of the Kent illustrations were used, and a few of those plates seem to have become nearly as ubiquitous as the text of the novel itself. Sixth and finally, it is safe to say that *Moby-Dick* is known in the original or in translation over most of the literate world and that much of Melville's other fiction, if less universally familiar than his greatest novel, has been widely and favorably received as well.

After all the foregoing, then, it can hardly be doubted that the queer handkerchief belonging to Melville's pale Usher, with its embellishment of gay flags from "all the known nations of the world" (*MD*, p. 1), prophesies truly, after all. Like the author himself, it "speak[s] a world's language" (*Mardi*, p. 13). Surely, there *is* magic in the web of it—and it mildly reminds us of his immortality.

WORKS CITED

Abe, Tomoji. [*Herman Melville*. British and American Men of Letters Series.] Tokyo: Kenkyusha, 1934.

Anderson, Charles. *Melville in the South Seas*. New York: Columbia University Press, 1939.

———. "Melville's English Debut." *American Literature* 11 (1939): 23–38.

Arnold, Fritz Volquard. "Das Werk Herman Melvilles." *Thema* No. 7 (Fall 1950): 24–27.

Baldini, Gabriele. *Melville o le ambiguitá*. Milan: Ricciardi, 1952.

Ballenger, Sara Elizabeth. "The Reception of the American Novel in German Periodicals (1945–1957)." Ph.D. Diss., Indiana University, 1959. [*Mel. Diss.*, #83.]

Barry, Elaine. "Herman Melville: The Changing Face of Comedy." *American Studies International* 16:4 (1978): 19–33.

Beaver, Harold, L. ed. Introd. *"Billy Budd, Sailor" and Other Stories* by Herman Melville. London: Penguin, 1972.

———, ed. Introd. *Moby-Dick* by Herman Melville. London: Penguin, 1972.

———, ed. Introd. *Redburn* by Herman Melville. London: Penguin, 1972.

Brumm, Ursula. "Herman Melville." In *American Thought and Religious Typology*. Trans. John Hoaglund. New Brunswick, N.J.: Rutgers University Press, 1970.

Buchanan, Robert. "Melville." In "Socrates in Camden, With a Look Round." London *Academy* (15 August 1885): 102–103.

Cabibbo, Paolo, ed. *Melvilliana*. Rome: Bulzoni, 1983.

Camus, Albert. "Herman Melville." Trans. Ellen Conroy Kennedy. In *Lyrical and Critical Essays*. Ed. Philip Thody. New York: Alfred A. Knopf, 1968, pp. 288–94.

———. "Melville: Un Createur de Mythes." In *Doubloon*, pp. 247–49.

Cecchi, Emilio. "Incontro con *Moby Dick*." *Corriere della sera* (27 November 1931): 3.

Chasles, Philarète. "Séjour de deux Américains chez les Taipies dan l'ile de Noukahiva." *Journal des Débats* (22 June 1846): 1–2. [Translation in *Doubloon*.]

Corona, Mario. "*Moby-Dick; or, The Whale*: analisi di un titolo." *Studi americani* 23–24 (1977): 7–61.

Erdim, Esim. "Appearance and Reality in Herman Melville." Ph.D. Diss., Ankara University, 1973. [*Mel Diss.*, #308.]

Frank, Max. *Die Farb—und Lichtsymbolik in Prosawerk Herman Melvilles. Jahrbuch für Amerikastudien*, suppl. 19. Heidelberg: Carl Winter, 1967.

Freeman, John. *Herman Melville*. New York and London: Macmillan Co., 1926.

Galland, René. "Herman Melville et *Moby Dick*." *Revue Ango-Américaine* 5 (October 1927): 1–9.

Georgoudaki, Ekaterini. "Ancient Greek and Roman Pieces of Art in Herman Melville's Iconography." *Scholarly Journal of the Faculty of Philosophy of the Aristotelian University of Thessaloniki* 11 (1983): 85–95.

———. " 'Billy Budd, Sailor': An Affirmation of the Transforming and Synthesizing Power of Man's Mytho-Poetic Imagination." *Scholarly Journal of the Faculty of Philosophy of the Aristotelian University of Thessaloniki* 12 (1984):123–41.

———. "Melville's Artistic Use of His Journeys to Europe and the Near East." Ph.D. Diss., Arizona State University, 1980. [*Mel. Diss.*, #520.]

Giono, Jean. *Melville zum Gruss*. Trans. [from French] Walter Gerull-Kardes. Hamburg: Claassen and Goverts, 1946.

———. *Pour saluer Melville*. Paris: Gallimard, 1941.

Hetherington, Hugh W. *Melville's Reviewers: British and American, 1846–1891*. Chapel Hill, N.C.: University of North Carolina Press, 1961.

Hohoff, Curt. "Herman Melvilles weiser Wal." *Hochland* 42 (February 1950): 239–50.

Humphreys, A. R. *Melville*. Edinburgh and London: Oliver and Boyd, Ltd., 1962.

Jung, C. G. "Psychology and Literature." In *The Spirit in Man, Art, and Literature*. Trans. P.F.C. Hull. *Collected Works of C. G. Jung*. Princeton, N.J.: Princeton University Press, 1966, Vol. 15, 84–105.

Kambara, Tatsuo. [*A Solitary Pilgrimage: A Study of Herman Melville*.] Tokyo: Kobian-Shobo, 1975.

Kesting, Marianne. *Melville: Benito Cereno*. Dichtung und Wirklichkeit, No. 32. Frankfurt am Main, Berlin, and Vienna: Ullstein, 1971.

Kitagawa, Teiji. *A Moby-Dick Dictionary*. Tokyo: Hokuseido, 1981.

Kovalev, Yuri. Afterword. *White-Jacket*, by Herman Melville. Trans. [into Russian] I. A. Lixačev. Leningrad: Nauka, 1973.

———. [*Herman Melville and American Romanticism*.] Leningrad: Xudozestvennaja Literatura, 1972.

Kruse, Joachim ed. *Illustrationen zu Melvilles Moby-Dick*. Schleswig: Schleswiger Druck-und Verlagshaus, 1976.

Kühnelt, Harro Heinz. "Der Humor in Melvilles *Moby-Dick*." *Wiener Beitrage zur englischen Philologie* 62 (1955): 111–21.

Lang, Hans-Joachim. "Melville und Shakespeare." In *Shakespeare: Seine Welt—Unser Welt*. Ed. Gerhard Müller-Schwefe. Tubingen: Max Niemeyer, 1964, pp. 134–81.

Lanziger, Klaus. *Primitivismus und Naturalismus im Prosaschaffen Herman Melvilles*. Innsbruck: Universitätsverlag Wagner, 1959.

Lauenstein, Diether. *Das Geheimnis das Wals: Melvilles Moby Dick und das Alte Testament*. Stuttgart: Urachhaus, 1973.

Lawrence, D. H. *Studies in Classic American Literature*. London: Thomas Seltzer, 1923.

Le Vot, André. "Melville et Shakespeare: la theme imperial dans *Moby Dick*." *Études anglaises* 17 (October-December 1964): 549–63.

Lee, A. Robert, ed. *Herman Melville: Reassessments*. London and Totowa, N. J.: Vision, and Barnes and Noble, 1984.

Lombardo, Giuseppe. "Criticism of H. Melville, 1972–77." *The Blue Guitar*. Facoltá di Magistero: Université degli Studi de Messina, 1982.

MacMechan, Archibald. "The Best Sea Story Ever Written." *Queen's Quarterly* 7 (October 1899): 120–30.

Maeno, Shigeru. *A Melville Dictionary*. Tokyo: Kaibunsha, 1976.

———. *The Sources of Melville's Quotations*. Tokyo: Kaibunsha, 1981.

———, and Kaneaki Inazumi. *A Melville Lexicon*. Tokyo: Kaibunsha, 1984.

Mailloux, Steve, and Hershel Parker. *Checklist of Melville Reviews*. N.p.: Melville Society, 1975.

Makino, Arimichi. "A Bibliography of Melville Studies in Japan." In *Whale and Text: Melville's World*. Ed. Kenzaburo Ohashi. Tokyo: Kokusho-Kankokai, 1983, pp. 9–64.

Mangold, Charlotte Weiss. "Herman Melville in German Criticism from 1900–1955." Ph.D. Diss., University of Maryland 1959. [*Mel. Diss.*, #87.]

Marovitz, Sanford E., and Masao Tsunematsu. "Melville Studies in Japan." *Melville Society Extracts* No. 36 (November 1978): 1–6.

Mason, Ronald. *The Spirit Above the Dust: A Study of Herman Melville*. London: John Lehmann, Ltd., 1951.

Mayoux, Jean-Jacques. *Melville*. Trans. John Ashbery. New York and London: Grove Press and Evergreen Press, 1960.

———. *Melville par lui-même*. Paris: Aux Editions du Seuil, 1958.

Melville, Herman. [*The Collected Works*.] Trans. [into Japanese] Noboru Sakashita and Ginsaku Sugiura. 13 vols. Tokyo: Kokusho-Kankokai, 1981–83.

———. *Opere scelte*. Trans. [into Italian] Cesare Pavese, et al. Ed. Claudio Gorlier. 2 vols. Milan: Mondadori, 1972, 1975.

———. *The Works*. 16 vols. London: Constable and Co., Ltd., 1922–24; rpt. Tokyo: Meichofukyukai, 1983.

Metcalf, Eleanor M. *Herman Melville: Cycle and Epicycle*. Cambridge, Mass.: Harvard University Press, 1953.

Moriarity, Jane V. "The American Novel in France, 1919–1939." Ph.D. Diss., University of Wisconsin, 1954. [*Mel. Diss.*, #62.]

Ohashi, Kenzaburo, ed. [*Whale and Text: Melville's World*.] Tokyo: Kokusho-Kankokai, 1983.

Oliass, Heinz G. "Herman Melville." *Welt und Wort* 6 (1951): 221–24.

Onís, José de. *Melville y el mundo hispánico (Nueve conferencias y un prólogo)*. Editorial Universitaria: Universidad de Puerto Rico, 1974.

Phelps, Leland R. *Herman Melville's Foreign Reputation: A Research Guide*. Boston: G. K. Hall, 1983.

———. "*Moby-Dick* in Deutschland." In *Illustrationen zu Melvilles Moby-Dick*. Ed. Joachim Kruse. Schleswig: Schleswiger Druck-und Verlagshaus, 1976, pp. 83–92.

Pop-Cornis, Marcel. [*The Anatomy of the White Whale: The Poetics of the Symbolic-Epopeic American Novel*.] Bucharest: Univers, 1982.

Porat, Zefira. *Prometheus bayn ha-Kannibalim* [Prometheus Among the Cannibals]. Tel Aviv: Am Oved, 1976, chs. 5–6.

Pullin, Faith, ed. *New Perspectives on Melville*. Kent, Ohio and Edinburgh: Kent State University Press and Edinburgh University Press, 1978.

Rizzardi, Alfredo. "La Poesia di Herman Melville." *Studi americani* 1 (1955): 159–203.

Russell, W. Clark. "Sea Stories." London *Contemporary Review* 46 (1884): 343–63.

Sachs, Viola. *La Contre-bible de Melville: Moby-Dick déchifré*. Paris and The Hague: Mouton, 1975.

———. *The Game of Creation: The Primeval Unlettered Language of "Moby-Dick; or, The Whale."* Paris: Editions de la Maison des Sciences de l'Homme, 1981.

Salt, H. S. "Herman Melville." *Scottish Art Review* 2 (June-December 1889): 186–90.

Simon, Jean. *Herman Melville: marin, métaphysicien et poète*. Paris: Boivin, 1939.

Smith, Nelson C. "Four New London Reviews." *Melville Society Extracts* No. 40 (November 1979): 3–6.

———. "Melville's Reputation in the Colonies." *Melville Society Extracts* No. 42 (May 1980): 13–14.

———. "Melville's Reviews in the London *Sun*." *Melville Society Extracts* No. 36 (November 1978): 8–12.

Stanonik, Janez. *Moby Dick: The Myth and the Symbol, A Study in Folklore and Literature*. Ljubljana: Ljubljana University Press, 1962.

Sugiura, Ginsaku. [*Melville: Voyager to Annihilation*.] Tokyo: Tojusha, 1981.

Tall, Emily. "Herman Melville in the Soviet Union." *Melville Society Extracts* No. 54 (May 1983): 1–8.

Tanimoto, Taizo. *Herman Melville's Tragic Ambiguity and Beyond*. Tokyo: Kobian-Shobo, 1977.

Tanselle, G. Thomas. *A Checklist of Editions of Moby-Dick, 1851–1976*. Evanston and Chicago: Northwestern University Press and the Newberry Library, 1976.

Terada, Takehito. *The Silence of God: A Critical Study of Herman Melville*. Tokyo: Chikuma-Shobo, 1968.

Terzo, Leonardo. "Lettura di 'Bartleby.' " *Studi americani* 23–24 (1977): 63–86.

———. *Retorica dell'avventura: Form e significato in Moby Dick*. Milan: Cisalpino-Goliardica, 1978.

Titel, Sorin. [*Herman Melville: The Fascination of the Sea*.] Contemporanul nostru. Bucharest: Albatros, 1975.

Tsunematsu, Masao. ["A Bibliography of Herman Melville Studies in Japan."]

Memoirs of the Faculty of Law and Literature: Literature (Shimane University) No. 2 (1979): 253–302.

———, and Sanford E. Marovitz. "A Bibliography of Herman Melville Studies in Japan." *Memoirs of the Faculty of Law and Literature: Literature (Shimane University)* No. 1 (1978): 13–68.

Ujházy, Maria. *Herman Melville's World of Whaling*. Budapest: Akadèmiai Kiadò, 1982.

Weaver, Raymond M. *Herman Melville: Mariner and Mystic*. New York: George H. Doran, 1921.

Yeager, Henry. *La Fortune littéraire d'Herman Melville en France*. Liege: Presses Universitaires de Liege, 1970.

25

MELVILLE AND THE WORLD OF BOOKS

G. Thomas Tanselle

When in 1885 the New York booksellers Leon & Brother issued what is generally regarded as the first dealer's catalogue devoted to American first editions, Melville was represented by four titles (*Typee, Omoo, Israel Potter,* and *The Piazza Tales*), each priced at $1.50, whereas the long lists for Hawthorne and Longfellow included *The Scarlet Letter* at $12.50 and *Evangeline* at $25. The situation had not altered much by 1903, when another famous dealer, Patrick K. Foley of Boston, brought out another large catalogue of first editions, in which his Melvilles ranged from $1.25 to $3, while his *Scarlet Letter*, labeled "Genuine first issue," was listed at $25. By the early 1930s, however, Goodspeed's could price *Moby-Dick* ("the finest copy that we have seen") at $900, and Dutton's could ask $1,000 for the "remarkably sound and fine copy" from Paul Hyde Bonner's library; and in 1936 Maggs offered *The Whale* (in an entry headed "One of the great masters of English prose") at £225. The trend has continued in the intervening half-century. After *Moby-Dick* brought $4,250 and *The Whale* $17,000 in the Stockhausen sale at Parke-Bernet in 1974 (where *The Scarlet Letter*, incidentally, fetched $500), one is not surprised to see Quaritch ask $11,000 for a "superb" copy of *Moby-Dick* in 1984.

The dramatic rise of interest in Melville in the twentieth century—which is the central fact about his reputation—is, of course, mirrored in the antiquarian book market, just as it is in the quantity of commentary on him and the number of editions of his works. But the sharp increase in the prices of first printings of Melville's books points to several further interrelated facts of fundamental significance. Interest creates demand, but prices go up significantly only if supply is small in relation to demand. That copies of the original editions of Melville's books are in particularly short supply is a reflection of his contemporary reputation. The point is not merely that his books generally were unpopular and did not call for large editions. A fact of equal importance is that there was no motivation, when his books were more readily available than they are now, for preserving them; he was not, in other words, a "collected" author in the nineteenth century, and copies of his books were not paid attention to as "first editions." (The Harper fire of 1853, which did destroy a small portion of the first impression of each of the books from *Mardi* through *Pierre*, along with a larger portion of the 1852 printings of *Typee* and *Omoo*, is not a principal cause of their scarcity.) An object that is expensive, or thought to be potentially valuable, has a better chance of surviving than other objects; by the late nineteenth century a tradition of collecting Longfellow and Hawthorne, for example, had developed, but Melville's books were not sought for or looked after in that way.

The upshot of this chain of events is that the availability of the central primary materials for the study of Melville—the books themselves—is reduced. Each copy of a printed edition, being a separate entity, is a separate piece of historical evidence; one cannot responsibly talk about either the physical features or the text of an edition as a whole without attempting to survey the range of evidence preserved in the surviving copies of that edition. As bibliographical and textual scholars (in the tradition of Graham Pollard, R.B. McKerrow, W.W. Greg, and Fredson Bowers) have been demonstrating for the past century or so, the textual history of a work cannot be divorced from the history of the physical means by which its text has been transmitted. A text, in the form of inked type-impressions, is one of the physical characteristics of a printed book; and even if uniform in all copies, it may have been affected by the process of production in a way that can be reconstructed through clues remaining in the finished product. Furthermore, since the copies of an impression are produced sequentially, they may differ from one another, as the result either of alterations made intentionally, or of changes that occurred inadvertently, during the course of printing; and copies of different impressions, which *a fortiori* may differ, are not always recognizable as such, for their title pages and other readily noticeable features may be identical. The proportion of surviving copies therefore has a direct bearing on the degree of confidence with which one can comment on both the publishing and the textual history of a work. Thus do present-day prices of Melville's books tell a story that is crucial not only to biographers and other historians of his reputation, but also to that larger group of scholars and readers who simply wish to read his works with as full an understanding as possible.

And thus are all aspects of the book world interrelated. It matters what editions, and what copies, of Shakespeare and Rabelais, of Thomas Beale and William Scoresby, Melville read, just as it matters what copies of what editions of his own writings were read by various commentators. The line connecting a copy of a book Melville read to the expropriation or adaptation of its text in one of his own works, and then from a copy of an edition of that work to the interpretation of its text by a critic who read that copy, is a direct one, if only it can be discerned. In the pages that follow I shall survey what has been written about these interlocking matters, ranging from Melville's own reading and book-buying to the collecting of and commentary on the books he wrote, including the efforts to establish reliable texts of his works for future readers.

MELVILLE IN THE BOOK WORLD OF HIS TIME

For a writer, the world of books is a central fact of existence, both as a source of intellectual stimulation and as the arena in which to prove oneself. Some of the books Melville owned and read can be known because copies with his signature and marginalia have been located; and library records, booksellers' statements, and Melville's letters and journals provide titles of other books that at least passed through his hands and that possibly he read. Although various stray references to such books had appeared in print before 1948, the starting point since that time for all research on Melville's reading has been the work of Merton M. Sealts, Jr. In 1948–50 he published "Melville's Reading: A Check-List of Books Owned and Borrowed" in six installments in the *Harvard Library Bulletin* (and added a supplement in 1952); the whole work, revised, was published in book form in 1966 (with two further supplements appearing in the *Harvard Library Bulletin* in 1971 and 1979); and a revision of the introductory essay and a consolidated supplement to the 1966 book were included in *Pursuing Melville 1940–1980*, Sealts's 1982 collection of essays. Sealts's list provides a meticulous record of "books" known to have been owned or borrowed by Melville—on the basis of documentary evidence external to Melville's own works, except in the case of books he reviewed—along with those known to have been owned or borrowed by members of his family while living with him. This work, for nearly four decades now, has been basic to all investigation into Melville's intellectual development. There is no end to such a listing, of course: books annotated by Melville continue to turn up, the most spectacular example being his copy of the 1836 printing of the Hilliard, Gray (Boston) edition of Milton, which was sold for $100,000 at Phillips in New York on 27 March 1984. It is to be hoped that Sealts will continue his exemplary record and provide another supplement in due course.

The "books" listed by Sealts actually consist of three kinds of items: copies (the particular copies Melville used, when they survive and have been identified), editions (when the editions he owned or borrowed can be inferred, even though the actual copies are not known to survive), and works (when the particular editions have not been identified). All efforts possible should be made to upgrade the latter two categories. Identification of a copy is obviously preferable to that of an edition, not simply because notes or markings by Melville may be present in it, but also because copies of an edition frequently vary—and thus, without knowing the copy Melville had access to, one cannot be sure of the text he read (if in fact he actually read the copy). Until his copy of a work is located, however, knowing the edition is certainly better than merely knowing the title of the work, because—generally speaking—textual differences are likely to be greater between different editions than between different impressions, or copies of an impression, of the same edition (that is, the same, or substantially the same, typesetting). Rather more opportunities exist for inferring editions than for locating copies, of course. And such work is extremely important for scholarly editors, and therefore for all serious readers, of Melville's own writings: an editor attempting to establish a text of a passage in which Melville quotes, or paraphrases, or draws on, another work needs to know precisely what text of that work Melville was using or recalling, for it may provide clues to erroneous words in the printed texts of his work (erroneous because they differ from the source at points where, one concludes, he intended no change). Access to such source texts can thus affect one's interpretation of a passage; copies and editions of books that Melville may have read are basic documents not only for elucidating his intellectual biography but also for reading his works.

If further search for these copies and editions is one way that Sealts's basic list can be supplemented, there are several others, one of which Sealts himself has dealt with admirably. He has provided, as the introductory essay to *Melville's Reading*, a narrative account of what has been learned about Melville's sources of supply for books, his habits of bookstore browsing, and the disposition of his library after his death—all of which furnishes a view of the second-hand book trade in New York in the late nineteenth century. (In 1935 Oscar Wegelin had set down his recollections of Melville's visits, in the last year of his life, to John Anderson's bookshop; and in 1977 Frederick James Kennedy published a 1900 letter of Samuel Arthur Jones that recalled Melville's appearances in Albert and Samuel Luyster's bookshop in the 1870s. Lathrop C. Harper's reminiscences of Melville's visits to his shop in the 1880s were first published by Sealts.) This excellent essay should be read in its latest revision, in *Pursuing Melville* (1982), a volume that contains additional relevant information in the exchange of letters between Sealts and Charles Olson. Another way to supplement Sealts's list is to locate and examine contemporary records of titles available at places where Melville would have had access to them: an interesting instance, reproduced by Wilson L. Heflin, is the catalogue of the library on board the *Charles and Henry*. Still another way—and a particularly important one—is to assemble a list of works that Melville was aware of (whether at first or second hand), as his writings show, but that have not been identified from external evidence as works he owned or borrowed. Such a list, complementary to Sealts's, fortunately has now been produced by Mary K. Madison (in a 1984 Northwestern dissertation, soon to be published by Northwestern University Press). The line between obvious references to sources and possible instances of allusion or influence is not distinct, and Madison's procedure is to record the works that have been cited in scholarly and critical discussions of sources—in such studies as (to name the best-known) Howard P. Vincent's books on *Moby-Dick* and *White-Jacket*. Her listing joins Sealts's as a basic book for Melville studies. (The sources of some of Melville's quotations had previously been recorded by Shigeru Maeno, in 1981.)

The scholarship treating Melville's use of and reaction to the writings of others has thus proceeded smoothly; the same cannot be said for the treatment of the contemporary reception accorded his own works. A number of the contemporary reviews had been variously reported, quoted, or analyzed (as in Mentor L. Williams's 1950 article and in Leyda's *Melville Log*) by 1961, when Hugh W. Hetherington's *Melville's Reviewers* appeared (based on a 1933 dissertation, the first one wholly devoted to Melville). The Hetherington book, however, has been shown to contain many errors of fact and many misquotations and misinterpretations of reviews (see Hershel Parker's 1970 discussion). It remains the only book-length narrative account attempting full coverage of the reviews, but it has been supplanted in various respects. Steve Mailloux and Hershel Parker took an essential step in 1975 by producing a *Checklist of Melville Reviews*, the longest list that had been published. Four years later their list was superseded by the first volume of Brian Higgins's listing of commentary on Melville, which not only adds to the total but provides a skillful abstract of each review. Higgins's book, with occasional supplements in *Melville Society Extracts*, is now the basic record of reviews. Critical surveys of reviews appear in the historical essays appended to each volume of the NN edition, and Watson G. Branch has published a comprehensive introductory essay surveying the reviews in his *Melville: The Critical Heritage* (1974). Texts of some of the significant reviews have been made available in such collections as Branch's book and Hershel Parker's *The Recognition of Herman Melville* (1967); all the then known reviews of *Moby-Dick* are printed in Hershel Parker and Harrison Hayford's *Moby-Dick as Doubloon* (1970), supplemented by Parker in *English Language Notes*; and all those of *Pierre* are included in Higgins and Parker's *Critical Essays on Herman Melville's Pierre* (1983). In reading the reviews, one should remember that some also formed part of Melville's reading and may have affected his subsequent writing; they, like the books and other newspaper and magazine pieces he read, are possible "sources" that illuminate his writings, as well as his biography. James Duban has recently pursued this point, searching through contemporary publications for passages that may have caught Melville's attention.

Melville's place in the world of books is defined not only by his reading and by the reviews his own books received, but also by his relationships with publishers and magazine editors. Those relationships are naturally taken up, in greater or lesser degree, in the biographies of Melville and in Leyda's *Melville Log*. The fullest treatment of these matters, however, occurs in the historical essays in the NN edition, which attempt to draw together all available evidence. A few separate essays, combining data from extant publishers' records, also exist: William Charvat's study of "Melville's Income" (1943) examines Melville's will, the appraisal of his estate, and his income from books, magazine pieces, and lecturing; Charvat's famous essay on "Melville and the Common Reader" (1959) draws on Charvat's wide knowledge of publication history (this essay and the earlier one are reprinted, with a much longer but still unfinished version, in the posthumous collection of his papers); and my essay "The Sales of Melville's Books" (1969) tabulates the sizes of the various printings of Melville's books published by Wiley & Putnam, the Harpers, John Murray, and Richard Bentley, as well as the numbers of copies sold and Melville's earnings, on the basis of the publishers' statements to Melville now in the Harvard collection. Several of Melville's extant letters deal with publishing arrangements, and Melville's 1849 *Journal* (published by Eleanor Melville Metcalf in 1948) furnishes some details regarding his relations with Murray and Bentley, just as Gansevoort Melville's letters of 1845 and journal of 1846 (edited by Hershel Parker in 1965–66) and John R. Brodhead's diaries of 1846–49 (discussed by David Potter in 1947) provide information about the English publication of *Typee* and *Omoo*, respectively. (Melville's brother Gansevoort and Brodhead were successively his agents for dealing with Murray.) Portions of Gansevoort's diary had earlier been published by Victor Hugo Paltsits (1943); some of Melville's letters to Brodhead and to Bentley had been included by John H. Birss in a 1948 *New Colophon* article; and further letters to Bentley, as well as letters (from Gansevoort, Allan, and Herman) to Murray, had formed the appendixes to Davis's 1952 book on *Mardi*. In 1953 Bernard R. Jerman put Bentley's side of the correspondence into print. The Harper contract for *Moby-Dick* has been reproduced and carefully analyzed by Harrison Hayford (1971); that for *Pierre* has been similarly treated by Hershel Parker (1977). A good picture of Melville's association with *Harper's* and *Putnam's* magazines emerges from Sealts's careful study (1980) of the chronology of Melville's magazine pieces (and from his earlier note on the publication of *The Piazza Tales*).

General accounts of Melville's publishers and their printers, even when Melville is not the focus, supply useful background: Francis Bond Head on William Clowes (printer of *Typee* in England), Samuel Smiles on Murray, Jacob Abbott and Eugene Exman on the Harpers, Royal A. Gettmann on Bentley, Giles Barber on Galignani (who pirated *Redburn*). The Bentley *List of the Principal Publications* provides prices and dates of publication and allows one to see the Melville titles in the context of Bentley's output as a whole. (Publishers' current catalogues—or a publication like the Longman *Notes on Books*—are, of course, also useful in this way.) Some of the surviving Harper materials have been described in print, with comment on Melville: Edwin and Virginia Price Barber survey the Harper contract books and related documents now in the Rare Book and Manuscript Library of Columbia University, abstracting the provisions of the contracts with Melville and certain other authors; Douglas C. Ewing provides a brief account of the Harper archive at The Pierpont Morgan Library, alluding to the seven Melville letters it contains (one of which—dated 24 November 1853—is reproduced, transcribed, and discussed by Herbert Cahoon in the volume displaying a sample of the Morgan's holdings of American literary autographs); and the *Secretary's News Sheet* of the Bibliographical Society of the University of Virginia notes the Harper ledger recording the melting in 1887 of the plates of *Mardi* and *Pierre*. Still broader studies of the nineteenth-century publishing situation are also important for understanding what Melville confronted—such works as Charvat's Rosenbach Lectures, J. A. Sutherland's and Guinevere L. Griest's books on the publishing and circulating of Victorian fiction, Charles E. and Edward S. Lauterbach's and Douglas C. Ewing's articles on the three-volume novel form, Simon Nowell-Smith's and James J. Barnes's books on Anglo-American copyright, and James D. Hart's and Richard D. Altick's analyses of the reading public. Further general accounts of American publishing, as well as works on the Harpers, T. B. Peterson, G. P. Putnam, and John Wiley, are listed in my *Guide to the Study of United States Imprints* (1971).

Even after all this research, there is still much that we do not know about the publishing world Melville found himself in. It may be that most of the surviving references to Melville's publishing arrangements have already been turned up in the Harper papers at Columbia and the Morgan and in the possession of the firm; in the Bentley papers at the British Library; the records still in the possession of the Murray, Routledge & Kegan Paul, and Longman firms; the copyright materials at the Library of Congress and the Public Record Office; and the Melville family papers at Harvard and the New York Public Library. But these collections, and others, need to be studied further for the details they can provide of standard publishing practice. Some of our specific questions will perhaps never be fully answered: why, for instance, Bentley lavished on *The Whale* one of the most elaborate, and presumably expensive, bindings that any three-decker was given (even though the whales on the spines were wrong), when Melville's three previous books had made no money for him. But more general questions about the way Melville was treated by his publishers in comparison to the treatment accorded others can be answered by more research in the papers relating to other writers. What is often frustrating about published accounts of publishing firms is the lack of precise details about contractual arrangements, but they can be accumulated by persistent digging. Placing the details of Melville's contracts in a larger context is essential for biographical and critical analysis, as Hershel Parker recognizes in "Why *Pierre* Went Wrong" (1976) and some of his other essays on *Pierre* (such as Brian Higgins and his introduction to their collection of essays on the book), which investigate with particular thoroughness the implications of contractual provisions for understanding the compositional history of a work. Higgins and Parker may well be right in asserting that the *Pierre* contract conveyed "a somber warning" (p. 11) to Melville, but whether that meaning was intended by the Harpers is hard to know in the absence of more detailed information about other contemporary Harper contracts. This effort to learn about the publishing context will naturally be helped by the publication, with appropriate annotation and commentary, of important primary documents: we shall know more, for example, about the New York *Literary World* circle, and be better able to assess Melville's place as reviewer in it, when Donald Yannella's edition of the Duyckinck diaries (preserved in the New York Public Library) is published. Records of allusions to Melville in contemporary periodicals contribute similarly to the picture; we now have such records for the *Literary World* (provided by Buford Jones) and *Harper's* (by Daniel A. Wells), in addition to the references that have long been available in *The Melville Log*.

A class of evidence that provides one more glimpse of Melville in the book world of his time consists of the inscriptions he placed in copies of the books that emerged from this publishing process. If many of the more substantial benefits of authorship were denied him, he allowed himself the satisfaction, as most writers do, of signing copies—a minor pleasure that is not insignificant and that may produce quite revealing results. No one would argue that Melville's presentation inscriptions are as important as his wonderful marginalia in some of the copies of books recorded by Sealts. (Those marginalia have been made available in Wilson Walker Cowen's 1965 dissertation.) But his inscriptions can be helpful in more ways than one might expect, not only for evidence of his personal relationships but—among other possibilities—for facts relevant to the compositional history of his works and other matters of dating. To cite one instance, the copy of *The Whale* that Melville inscribed in 1853 for Henry Hubbard, a shipmate on the *Acushnet*—a copy, discovered in 1976, that fetched $53,000 at auction in 1977—raises considerable doubt as to whether Hubbard had visited Melville in 1850 and therefore whether his visit played any role (as has sometimes been claimed) in reviving Melville's memories during the composition of *Moby-Dick*. I have explained this point in detail in a 1982 article on two Melville association copies, meant to illustrate how such copies can be made to yield useful information. At present there is no guide to, or edition of, Melville's presentation inscriptions—a lack I hope to remedy in due course. The interval between reading books by others and inscribing copies of one's own books encompasses the travail of composition and the frustration (as it often enough is) of dealing with publishers and their editors; the artifacts reflecting these encounters with the world of books epitomize this sequence of events and reveal their interrelationships and essential unity. Melville's case is no exception.

THE COLLECTING AND RECORDING OF MELVILLE'S BOOKS

After Melville's death a brief surge of interest in his work was stimulated, or possibly reflected, by Arthur Stedman's new editions of *Typee*, *Omoo*, *White-Jacket*, and *Moby-Dick* for the United States Book Company and Murray's new illustrated printings of *Typee* and *Omoo*. The availability of these books surely encouraged some readers to pursue Melville further and in the process to become collectors, but they formed a small band. One documented example is Samuel Arthur Jones, the homeopathic physician who collected Carlyle and Thoreau (among others) and published in 1894 the first significant bibliography of Thoreau. Jones's interest in Melville was aroused by Henry S. Salt, the English biographer of Thoreau and early devotee of Melville (Salt's 1892 essay on Melville was adapted to serve as an introduction in Murray's 1893 *Typee* and *Omoo*); and Jones bought some important copies of Melville's books (including Allan Melville's copy of *Moby-Dick* with a trial title leaf, carrying the "Whale" title and the Harper imprint, pasted in) from an 1896 catalogue of the A. S. Clark bookselling firm—that catalogue the product apparently of another devotee, for the Clark catalogues repeatedly make approving comments on the Melville books that turn up. I have discussed Jones's copies (now at the University of Illinois) and cited the sources of information about Jones in the article on association copies mentioned above. Melville's books were hardly collectors' items in the 1890s, as the Clark prices show ($2 to $4, even when the copies were thought to come "from the library of the author"), but the process of preserving significant evidence, begun by Allan, was kept alive.

Nearly a generation earlier the bookseller-bibliographer Joseph Sabin had listed five of Melville's books, with rudimentary indication of size and pagination and some mention of later printings, in the eleventh volume (1879) of *A Dictionary of Books Relating to America*—perhaps the earliest inclusion of Melville in a work of bibliographical scholarship. By the end of the century Melville's books had been listed a few more times, as a result of the growing interest in collecting American authors, the American counterpart of the attention being paid by English collectors to the writers of their own century. This movement was manifested in the 1885 Leon & Brother catalogue and, the same year, in the first separately published American author bibliography (Beverly Chew's *The Longfellow Collectors' Hand-Book*). If Melville's work was not widely collected at this time, it was nevertheless listed, for the two principal manuals for American collectors were remarkably comprehensive: one by Herbert Stuart Stone (1893), a collector and publisher, the other by Patrick K. Foley (1897), a book dealer. There was also Selden L. Whitcomb's manual for students of American literature (1894), which included a Melville checklist (omitting *John Marr* and *Timoleon*, though both Stone and Foley knew about them). The bibliographical detail in these works was minimal, scarcely more than city and year of publication (with Stone mentioning the publisher as well), but they did make lists of Melville's books readily accessible. Another list, though hardly very accessible, was printed (under the title "Herman Melville's Works") in the *New York Times* in 1901, with some comments by Melville's widow. No other significant checklist appeared for a decade and a half, until Carl Van Doren prepared one for the first volume (1917) of the *Cambridge History of American Literature*—to which he also contributed a discussion of Melville that was influential in inaugurating the "Melville Revival." Although he later (1928) called his list "the first extended bibliography" of Melville's writings, it was not much fuller than the previous listings, except that it noted some of the later printings and editions and cited a few of Melville's contributions to periodicals.

In the early 1920s the situation suddenly changed. First came Raymond M. Weaver's biography in 1921, with an appended listing that included the successive printings of the original editions of Melville's works, plus the later editions, and a record of his appearances in periodicals. The next year is a key year in Melville's bibliographical history, for it marked the appearance of Michael Sadleir on the scene, though his enthusiasm for Melville had obviously been developing over several years. His firm, Constable, began publishing under his supervision a uniform set of Melville's writings in that year, and also in 1922 Sadleir included Melville among the eight authors he covered in *Excursions in*

Victorian Bibliography (the others were Collins, Disraeli, Gaskell, Marryat, Reade, Trollope, and Whyte-Melville). The Melville section of this book (prefaced with a brief but eloquent essay on Melville as one of "the ageless, raceless family of the lonely giants") and the expanded version of it that appeared in the twelfth volume of the Constable Edition the following year are the first bibliographies of Melville that pay attention to physical details (the most that the earlier lists had done was to offer vague indications of size, such as "12mo" or "pp. 272"). In the 1922 version Sadleir transcribed title pages and gave leaf measurements, pagination, contents, and brief binding descriptions, with occasional appended notes; in the 1923 expansion he marked line endings in the transcriptions, provided signature collations (in the form "B-P in twenty-fours"), and described the bindings in more detail. Giving signature collations for modern books was uncommon at the time, but anyone who knows Sadleir's role in the history of twentieth-century bibliography will not be surprised that he recognized their importance. Sadleir was not only a publisher and a novelist but also a book collector and a student of book history. This combination of interests no doubt helped him to see the interconnections between the production history of books and the textual history of the works they contain—the connections, in other words, that the scholarly exponents of the "new bibliography" had been discovering over the previous two decades in their study of English Renaissance books. Sadleir's later bibliographical work and the many bibliographical publications that he had Constable bring out were grounded on the belief that a bibliography is a partial history of the book trade and that an understanding of "book structure" (as he called it) is fundamental to all studies of book history. His ideas were given greater currency through a circle of his friends in the English book trade—including John Carter, Percy Muir, and Graham Pollard—who brought this approach to their dealings with collectors and to their own writings. Together they showed the way for the bibliography of modern books to build on a scholarly foundation, and thus they began to close the gap that had developed in the previous half-century between the serious historical study of fifteenth-, sixteenth-, and seventeenth-century books and the superficial listing of points for the growing band of collectors of modern books.

One more important Melville bibliography appeared in the same year as Sadleir's first one, and it, too, was a responsible piece of work, written by Meade Minnigerode, an Englishman resident in the United States, and published by an American book dealer, Edmond Byrne Hackett of the Brick Row Book Shop (New York). Minnigerode's inclusion, in the same volume, of a large group of extracts from Melville letters (they occupy, in fact, the first half of the book) suggests that he placed descriptive bibliography in the context of serious biographical study—a point further borne out by his inclusion in the bibliography of a list of Melville's lecture engagements. His descriptive entries, like Sadleir's, provide title-page transcription and records of pagination and contents (for some English editions he had not seen, he simply reprints Sadleir's 1922 descriptions); but he also reports publication prices, typographical errors, some textual variants, and later printings (sometimes with the number of copies) and editions. His list of periodical appearances is longer, by five items, than Weaver's. Minnigerode's bibliography was a creditable job for its time, and it stood for the next half-century as the most substantial bibliography of Melville's work.

The boom in the collecting of "first editions" in the 1920s spawned a number of books about collecting and checklists of collected authors, and by the latter part of the decade Melville had become so well established with collectors that his name nearly always turned up in such volumes. For example, John T. Winterich's *A Primer of Book Collecting* (1926) illustrates one meaning of "association copy" by recalling Eden Phillpotts's character Albert Redmayne (in *The Red Redmaynes* of 1922), who kept his brother's "well-thumbed" copy of *Moby-Dick* "for sentiment" (pp. 44–45); and Winterich's *Collector's Choice* (1928) mentions *Moby-Dick* as the key work for "the Melville collector" (p. 65). The most influential writer on book collecting at the time, A. Edward Newton, refers to *Moby-Dick* several times in *This Book-Collecting Game* (1928), calling it "America's supreme contribution to world literature" (p. 275) and providing photographs of the binding of both *The Whale* and *Moby-Dick*. (His account and the illustrations were reprinted the same year in *The Format of the English Novel.*) In 1929 Merle Johnson's *High Spots of American Literature* included an entry for *Moby-Dick*, consisting of a title-page transcription and a few brief comments; the state of knowledge concerning the publication history of Melville's books (as well as the superficiality of the approach to collecting represented by those who dutifully searched for "firsts" of books on lists of "high spots") is illustrated by Johnson's statement, "Some claim the London edition as first issue: I cannot confirm this" (p. 57). The title page of *Moby-Dick* was reproduced in two more collectors' guides the next year: in Richard Curle's *Collecting American First Editions* (which refers to Melville several times, noting in particular the scarcity of copies of his books) and in Nolie Mumey's *A Study of Rare Books* (which asserts that the red binding of *Moby-Dick* is "much sought after by the Melville collector" [p. 374]).

Of the three checklists that appeared in these years, the first, by Meade Minnigerode, is the best known. Published originally in *Publishers' Weekly* for 18 November 1922, it was reprinted in *American First Editions* (1929), a collection of checklists of 105 authors, brought together by Merle Johnson. This volume was avowedly an extension of Foley's 1897 work and contains equally brief entries (consisting of title, city, year, and points); its compactness and comprehensiveness, despite its lack of bibliographical sophistication, made it an enormously popular book among collectors, and it has gone through a succession of revised editions (and printings of them). The next checklist, in Jacob Schwartz's *1100 Obscure Points* (1931), provided much more bibliographical detail (even if the motivation for assembling it, as suggested by the trivializing title, was perhaps less scholarly than one might wish). And the following year B. M. Fullerton included Melville in his *Selective Bibliography of American Literature, 1775–1900*, a listing that gives almost no bibliographical detail, except for some statements on the order of "yellow end papers are preferred" (said of *Mardi*). The superficial view of collecting that underlies this work is revealed in Fullerton's explanation for his word "preferred": "The bibliographical differences in Melville's works above noted are treated as matters of preference rather than as mandatory requirements for the reason that the processes of assembly for binding were easily open to variation" (p. 194). Although Fullerton apparently sees that the historical facts do not support the notion of a single binding or endpaper color with priority, he nevertheless cannot bring himself to say that various colors might have equal status and that collectors ought to concern themselves with assembling the whole range of artifacts documenting particular publishing histories.

Some view of the collectors interested in Melville—and of the copies changing hands and their prices—can be obtained by searching the successive volumes of *Book Auction Records* and *American Book Prices Current*. For example, the most substantial groups of Melville editions in pre-1910 sales turned up in the collections of Charles W. Frederickson and Charles A. Searing; a Melville letter appeared as early as 1890 in a Libbie sale catalogue, and a volume owned by Melville was so catalogued for the sale of Thomas J. McKee's library in 1900–1902. These comprehensive auction records, of course, lead one to the auction catalogues themselves, where there may be prefatory biographical accounts of collectors and almost certainly will be further details about the particular copies involved (sometimes with photographs, or quotations from inscriptions or other manuscript material). Dealers' catalogues are similarly rich repositories of bibliographical detail, but they have never been provided with thorough consolidated indexes. (Like all other material, they are to be used with caution: Samuel Loveman's Bodley Book Shop catalogues in the 1960s, for instance, list a number of Melville "association copies" that actually contain forged signatures, a fact indicative in itself of Melville's stature as a collected author.) Great collections of dealers' catalogues, like the one at the Grolier Club, preserve the raw material, but there is no efficient way to extract the relevant information. (Daniel McGrath's *Bookman's Price Index* covers only a small and idiosyncratic selection of catalogues from 1963 on.) I have myself been attempting to survey Melville entries in dealers' catalogues, with the idea of producing eventually an essay on Melville in the antiquarian book market; such an essay would certainly not substitute for an adequate index, but it would identify many significant catalogues, and it would bring together in a single picture information both from dealers' and from auction catalogues.

The view thus obtained can be augmented by dealers' and collectors' reminiscences and biographies. Edwin Wolf and John F. Fleming's biography of Rosenbach, for instance, tells of his buying from John Drinkwater a copy of *Moby-Dick* signed by Hawthorne; and David A. Randall's memoirs (Randall was in charge of Scribner's rare book department in New York in the 1930s, 1940s, and 1950s, when John Carter was his London counterpart) contain a whole chapter on Melville, in which occur the names of many prominent collectors, such as Robert Honeyman, Owen Young, Katherine deB. Parsons, Frank Hogan, C. Waller Barrett, and H. Bradley Martin. Although John Carter pays little attention to Melville in his *Taste and Technique in Book-Collecting* (1948), that book provides a brilliant account of the history of bibliophily and contributes essential background for any more restricted study. Some published catalogues of collectors also record bibliographical details about Melville's books: the two-volume catalogue (1950) of Carroll A. Wilson's collection (which Randall had helped to form) devotes twelve pages to Melville, with entries for the books (some in wrappers) and for some manuscript material (the *Omoo* round robin, a poem, a letter to Bentley) and copies of books owned by Melville; and Sadleir's great catalogue *XIX Century Fiction* (1951) describes *The Whale* (Sadleir calls it "one of the rarest of three-deckers"). About the same time as these two catalogues, several institutional collections were described, in celebration of the centennial of *Moby-Dick*: Gordon H. Mills wrote a brief account of the first printings of Melville at the University of Texas; Herbert Cahoon compiled an excellent listing of the Melville holdings (including Melville's contributions to periodicals) in the New York Public Library (later the presentation copy of *The Whale* to John C. Hoadley was singled out in John D. Gordan's 1965 Berg Collection exhibition catalogue); and Howard C. Rice, Jr., and others prepared a substantial catalogue of a Princeton exhibition devoted entirely to *Moby-Dick* (with sections on posthumous editions, abridgments and adaptations, and translations). In 1954 the American Academy of Arts and Letters published a catalogue of its exhibition on *The Greate Decade in American Writing 1850–1860*, the Melville section of which records important items drawn from the collections of Harvard, the New York Public Library (and its Berg Collection), the Rosenbach Foundation, Yale, and H. Bradley Martin. (For brief descriptions, from this period, of another notable collection, see the 1953 inventory of the Melville Room in the Berkshire Athenaeum and the 1957 account in the *Bay State Librarian*.)

Lists for "high-spot" collectors and manuals for beginning collectors were, of course, not limited to the 1920s: they have continued to appear and continued to mention Melville, two of the best known of the former being Whitman Bennett's chronology of American books (1941) and the "Grolier hundred" (1947), and of the latter the guides of Reginald Brewer (1935) and Colton Storm and Howard Peckham (1947). But serious bibliographical work took other forms, and two strands of it, ultimately intertwining, can be discerned. One is the product of the book trade, of scholarly booksellers, whose audience in the first instance is collectors. I. R. Brussel in 1936—in the second volume of *Anglo-American First Editions*, a pioneer work (part of Sadleir's justly celebrated Bibliographia series) on the transatlantic publication of books in English—set forth a table comparing the English and American publication dates of Melville's books, the former from Sadleir, the latter from the copyright records. Two years later John Carter, in *More Binding Variants* (part of another Sadleir series), discussed the first and second bindings of *The Whale*, calling the first one "the most stunning and successful piece of bravura treatment on any mid-century three-decker of my experience" (p. 24).

A more significant occurrence involving a book-trade bibliographer, as events turned out, was Jacob Blanck's publication, in 1936 and 1942, of two revised editions of Johnson's *American First Editions*. His work on this standard checklist of American authors led directly to the *Bibliography of American Literature (BAL)*, a project that he and the collector J. K. Lilly, Jr., devised in 1943. (See the account in the autobiography of David Randall, who played a central role in forming Lilly's collection.) The *BAL* began publication in 1955, and Melville fell alphabetically in the sixth volume, which appeared in 1973; but before then *Publishers' Weekly*, for which Blanck was in charge of the rare-book department, printed two significant bibliographical discussions of *Moby-Dick*, the first by Randall in 1940 (a description of the American and English first editions) and the second by Blanck himself in 1947 (on the American binding and endpaper colors). The plan of the *BAL* provided for title-page transcription, collation of signatures and pagination, specification of dimensions and bindings, and a record of relevant dates (such as those of copyright entry, advertisement, entry in *Publishers' Weekly*, and review) for first printings, along with sections on later printings and on books with contributions by the author in question. As a result it is more detailed than works of its scope generally are; but it was never meant to preclude the production of more detailed bibliographies of individual writers, at least the principal ones. Even on its own terms, the *BAL* can legitimately be criticized, especially for its deficiencies in covering major collections, its inconsistencies, its neglect of relevant published sources, and the indefensibility of its rationale governing "reprints." (My comment on this matter appeared in *Papers of the Bibliographical Society of America* (*PBSA*) in 1979.) General criticisms have been voiced by Warner Barnes and Joel Myerson, among others; for the Melville section in particular, I pointed out its failings in 1978. Nevertheless, despite its many problems, the *BAL* unquestionably offers the most sophisticated primary bibliography of Melville's books that has yet appeared.

The other strand of Melville bibliography has been the work of Melville scholars, a small group of whom (especially in earlier years) were perforce Melville collectors as well. These scholarly collectors were as interested in later printings as in firsts, understanding that copies of all printings are necessary to document the publishing history of an author. The most influential of such collectors has been Harrison Hayford, whose collection now forms the nucleus of the great Melville collection at The Newberry Library. On the basis of his own copies, those of other scholars, and the listings in Minnigerode, Sadleir, and published catalogues, Hayford produced a checklist of pre-1892 printings that he distributed in mimeographed form in the late summer of 1964 as an appeal for information "in connection with a complete new edition of the works of Herman Melville" and to "make possible a descriptive bibliography." Its appearance was a key event in the history of Melville scholarship, both because it recognized the inseparability of textual and bibliographical research and because it inaugurated what came to be known as the Northwestern-Newberry Melville Project. The determination of what exists and the systematic collation or inspection of surviving copies are basic to the production of a bibliography as well as an edition; and as work on the NN edition has proceeded over the last two decades, the material for a descriptive bibliography has been simultaneously accumulating.

Some bibliographical byproducts of this work have appeared in print from time to time—such as the notes Sidney Ives and I wrote for *PBSA* clarifying the comments Bernard De Voto had once made about certain Harvard copies of *Typee*. Of such byproducts, one of the most important is the census of pre-1892 copies published in the *Book Collector* in 1970 by Richard Colles Johnson, who is in charge of the Melville Collection at the Newberry; an expanded version of Hayford's list, it attempts to record all British, Canadian, and U.S. institutional holdings, and it remains the most convenient and reliable source of information about the successive nineteenth-century printings. (Details in it were neglected by the *BAL*, which similarly did not make use of Johnson's interesting record of pre-1892 anthologies that contain selections from Melville). Another of these byproducts is my checklist of editions of *Moby-Dick* to 1976, published on the occasion of an exhibition at The Newberry Library commemorating the 125th anniversary of the book's first publication. That the Newberry collection provided the material for this exhibition indicates that its scope encompasses posthumous editions (in fact, all printings of them) as well as all printings during Melville's lifetime: all have their uses for an editor and in any case are part of the history of the editing and publishing of Melville's work. Indeed, multiple copies of many of the printings are present on the Newberry shelves and are necessary to illustrate (and to facilitate the further discovery of) variations, both in text and in physical features, among copies of a single impression; as Johnson remarked in 1970, such variants "have been discovered in a quantity altogether sufficient to justify the acquisitiveness" (p. 334). Collections conceived with such comprehensiveness are uncommon but indisputably important; additional comment on their significance, with special reference to the Newberry Melville Collection, appears in my essay on "Non-Firsts."

The publicity given by the Melville Project to the scholarly value, and often the scarcity, of non-first printings has occasionally been reflected in the book trade—as when the Current Company, in a 1980 catalogue devoted entirely to Melville (and including many later printings and editions), offered a copy of the scarce 1871 Harper printing of *Moby-Dick* (the last printing from the original Harper plates) for $450. (The price for this printing went up to $600 two years later in a Jenkins catalogue.) A few perceptive and scholarly dealers, I should add, had long since understood the significance of non-firsts: one of the best of such dealers, John S. Van E. Kohn, issued a Melville list from the Seven Gables Bookshop in 1952 containing many of them. The importance of such printings is still by no means generally recognized; but if Melville's books can serve (because of his present status and the scarcity of his nineteenth-century printings) to call attention to the matter, the cause of the preservation of bibliographical evidence will be much advanced.

Among all these bibliographical offshoots, the central contribution of the Melville Project from a bibliographical point of view has been the editorial matter in the NN edition, particularly the "Note on the Text" in each volume, which reports many of the physical details that are the basic material for a descriptive bibliography (and which supplies many of the points reported in the *BAL* Melville section). The NN Melville Project, like the edition that is resulting from it, is a perfect demonstration of the reciprocal relationship between physical bibliography and textual study. The descriptive bibliography that I will prepare—which I envisage as a detailed history of the production and publication of the physical forms in which Melville's writings have appeared—will, I trust, further illustrate the indivisibility of these pursuits and the fundamental reliance of scholarship on collecting.

Meanwhile, the collecting continues: new material occasionally surfaces, and previously known items find new homes. The most significant recent surfacing was the discovery—in a Gansevoort, New York, barn in 1983—of a large cache of Melville family papers that included thirty pages of a draft of *Typee* and three letters from Melville and four to him (one from Hawthorne). The wide publicity given to this find reflects Melville's present standing both in literary history and in the rare-book and manuscript world. Melville manuscript material is notoriously scarce, and the bulk of what exists is in two libraries, the New York Public Library (Catherine Gansevoort-Lansing's assemblage of Gansevoort and related family papers, and the Duyckinck Collection, which includes the manuscripts of Melville's contributions to the *Literary World*) and the Houghton Library at Harvard (the papers presented by Eleanor Melville Metcalf, including the late unpublished manuscripts). The new material clearly belonged with the Gansevoort papers, and fortunately the New York Public Library was able to purchase it. The fullest account of this episode, conveying some sense of the excitement produced in the antiquarian book world by any mention of Melville manuscripts, has been written by Donald L. Anderle, the Associate Director for Special Collections at the Library; and Susan Davis, the curator of manuscripts, has published an inventory of the new papers. A recent example of the shift in location of known material is furnished by the Parkman Dexter Howe collection. Melville scholars had been acquainted with Howe's library (which focused on New England authors) because it contained the leaf (formerly in the Carroll Wilson collection) that has the *Omoo* round robin on one side and a few lines of *Mardi* on the other. In 1980 the University of Florida purchased the collection from Howe's heirs and in 1983 published the first fascicle of a handsome and thorough catalogue under the general editorship of Sidney Ives. I shall be preparing the section on the Melville holdings, which include a run of first printings, in book and periodical form, with the New York *Typee* and *Omoo* in wrappers. The Howe catalogue will occupy a place on the Melville scholar's shelf next to Sadleir and Wilson. The assiduity with which Melville materials—books as well as manuscripts—are now searched for cannot resurrect what was destroyed in the years of neglect, but it can help to prevent further loss. Some of the splendid materials that have turned up recently—such as the Hubbard *Whale*, the annotated Milton, and the Gansevoort hoard—serve to reinforce the fact, which scholars and collectors have always known, that the discovery of significant evidence from the past has no end.

THE PUBLISHING AND LISTING OF COMMENTARY ON MELVILLE

Books inevitably beget more books, and any author of the stature that Melville has attained is bound to be the subject of an enormous body of commentary. One measure, in fact, of writers' shifting reputations is the fluctuation in the number of books and articles about them. When Harrison Hayford spoke of the "dimensions" of Melville at the opening of the Newberry *Moby-Dick* exhibition in 1976, one of the dimensions he had in mind was the sheer bulk of the writing about Melville, as now brought together physically in rows of shelves and file drawers in the Newberry Melville Collection, which is the unparalleled repository of such material (in addition to the printed copies of Melville's own works). Guides to this mass of printed matter are clearly a necessity, even though the proliferation of guides adds further to the bulk. Records of "secondary" material have traditionally been constructed differently from those of the primary literature, at least as far as separate (non-periodical) publications are concerned: although they are often called "bibliographies," they do not generally involve much bibliographical research, for the entries in them are intended only as references, not as accounts of the printing and publishing of physical objects. One can see why it has seemed natural to record secondary works in checklists of simple references (annotated or not), brought together in various subject-matter or chronological groupings, and to reserve the techniques of descriptive bibliography for the primary works. But of course the practice is illogical, for the secondary works—like the primary ones—are pieces of printed matter and may—like them—contain variants and other textual problems resulting from the processes of production through which they have passed. (The same anomaly is found within most descriptive bibliographies of primary material, where full physical descriptions of books are followed by enumerative lists of contributions to periodicals.) Collectors have not generally been very concerned with secondary works, although the line between the two categories of material is not always obvious, as when a book or article quotes from unpublished letters or manuscripts and thus provides the first publication of certain passages of the author's writing. In any case, the secondary literature joins with the primary to define the total area dominated by a given writer within the universe of printed matter. There is nothing wrong with treating the two separately, for convenience, so long as we recognize their relatedness and understand that all printed texts, those of commentators as well as those of the authors commented on, must be approached with the same alertness to the possibility of variation among copies and the same awareness of how physical processes of production affect texts.

In the three decades between Melville's death and the publication of Weaver's biography, so little reference to Melville appeared in print that the question of recording it did not arise. A few noteworthy essays did appear, but Carl Van Doren was not doing an injustice to the secondary literature when he listed only seven biographical and critical pieces in the *Cambridge History* in 1917. Patient searching in later years has of course turned up many more, most of them insignificant; but, even so,

Higgins's total for the twenty-nine years from 1892 through 1920 is only 254, a number that was more than matched in the ensuing eight years. Because the beginning of the Modern Humanities Research Association (MHRA) and Modern Language Association (MLA) annual listings (1921 and 1922, respectively) coincided with the beginning of the Melville Revival, the need for a separate checklist of Melville scholarship was not particularly pressing in the 1920s, and it is not surprising that such work did not effectively begin until well into the 1930s. The earliest extensive listing of writings about Melville was the work of Willard Thorp, who prepared the list, twenty-nine pages of annotated entries, to accompany his landmark study that introduced his 1938 volume of "representative selections" from Melville for the American Writers Series. (That series, under the supervision of Harry Hayden Clark, was indispensable to the scholarly study of American literature in the 1930s and 1940s; another book produced under Clark's direction contained the longest listing before Thorp's—Walter Fuller Taylor's *A History of American Letters* of 1936, to which Harry Hartwick contributed the "bibliographies," including three solid pages, in paragraph form, of references to Melville scholarship.) Jean Simon's book on Melville, the year after Thorp's, offered a sizable listing, but Thorp's list remained the basic one for ten years, until it was joined by the *Literary History of the United States*, with Thomas H. Johnson's *Bibliography* volume and its seven-page section on Melville. The *Literary History* list, largely uncritical in its commentary, did not supplant Thorp but did extend the coverage to the late 1940s. (Its coverage has been extended twice since, in 1959 and 1972, by Richard M. Ludwig.)

Soon after the appearance of the *Literary History*, Gordon Roper supplemented its Melville coverage by circulating mimeographed sheets for 1949–50. The Melville Society (founded by John H. Birss, Tyrus Hillway and Harrison Hayford in 1945) then formally set up a Bibliographical Committee—consisting of Stuart C. Sherman (chairman), Birss, and Roper—to produce checklists of current scholarship. This group issued two mimeographed lists from the Providence Public Library, one of six leaves for 1951 and the other of twenty-eight leaves for 1952–57. Before the latter appeared in 1959, three more comprehensive but unannotated lists were made available, Lewis Leary's of seven pages (in *Articles on American Literature, 1900–1950* in 1954), Milton R. Stern's of forty pages (appended to his 1957 book *The Fine-Hammered Steel of Herman Melville*), and Norman E. Jarrard's of forty-three leaves (originally circulated in December 1958; a slightly expanded version was distributed a year later by the Melville Society as its first "Special Publication"). The Sherman-Birss-Roper lists, however, contributed to what can now be seen as the central card file, the one presently at the Newberry and thus the one underlying Brian Higgins's work. Birss's file, incorporating material from Robert S. Forsythe (with whom he had planned to produce a full bibliography), came—via M. Douglas Sackman and John Kohn—to Harrison Hayford; Roper's file then joined it, when Maurice Beebe used both to put together a long, though still selective, checklist for a special issue of *Modern Fiction Studies* (*MFS*) in 1963. (Much of Birss's other material, including many early offprints, was offered for sale in a 1973 catalogue from the dealer Kenneth Starosciak.) This combined file, placed in the Newberry collection by Hayford (and there kept up to date), has served both as a guide for developing the collection and as a record reflecting its growth.

In the sixteen years between the *MFS* list and the first volume of Higgins's work growing out of the Newberry holdings, several unrelated guides to Melville secondary material were published: Michael P. Zimmerman's list of items from the 1920s (deriving from his 1963 dissertation); J. Don Vann's list covering the decade 1958–68 (designed to supplement the Sherman-Birss-Roper and the Stern lists); Howard P. Vincent's more selective checklist (1969); two attempts in 1971, by Theodore L. Gross and by James K. Bowen and Richard VanDerBeets, to provide thoroughly annotated selective lists, the former with extensive critical comment and the latter with abstracts; and Beatrice Ricks and Joseph D. Adams's book-length listing (1973), aiming at completeness for the period 1900–72 (with "selected" earlier references) but in fact omitting many items and committing numerous other errors and inconsistencies (such as—among the hundreds that seem to exist—the failure to identify certain reprints: Patrick K. Foley and Herbert Stuart Stone, for instance, are entered as publications of 1969 and 1970, with no indication that they first appeared in 1897 and 1893, respectively). The abysmal failure of the Ricks-Adams book points to a truth not recognized in many of the "bibliographies" published by firms specializing in such works (those publishers assuming, not incorrectly, that librarians of serious reference collections will have to order the books, regardless of their quality): that responsible lists of secondary literature cannot simply be compiled but must be the product of scholars who use and understand the material. The publishers of the Ricks-Adams list, whether or not in acknowledgment of their error, have in fact redeemed themselves by publishing Brian Higgins's splendid *Herman Melville: An Annotated Bibliography*, the first volume of which (covering 1846–1930) appeared in 1979. This work, when completed in two more volumes (1931–60, 1961–), will supersede the others mentioned here: its first volume is remarkably thorough; it is arranged chronologically (in contrast to the pointless alphabetical arrangement followed unthinkingly in most of the other checklists); it contains a thoughtful and well-written summary of each entry; and it is well indexed. One could scarcely ask for anything better (except in one respect: the long index entries should have been subdivided by topic); Melville scholars are fortunate to have Higgins's 1979 volume in hand and the promise of two more on the same plan.

Another approach to the secondary literature, which has resulted in some excellent guides to Melville scholarship, is represented by the critical survey in essay form. In 1956 the American Literature Section of the Modern Language Association published a collection of eight such essays, edited by Floyd Stovall and entitled *Eight American Authors*, for which Stanley T. Williams wrote the chapter on Melville. His essay served admirably as the basic critical guide for the next fifteen years, until in 1971 a new edition (under James Woodress's editorship) was published, with a new Melville chapter prepared in exemplary fashion by Nathalia Wright. In the meantime the American Literature Section had inaugurated a series of annual volumes, called *American Literary Scholarship* (*ALS*), that provided the same kind of critical survey for the output of each year. It, too, was edited by James Woodress (later alternating with J. Albert Robbins and even later, Warren French), and its coverage began with 1963, the year in which a new printing of the original *Eight American Authors* appeared, brought up to date with supplementary checklists by J. Chesley Matthews. The caliber of the Melville chapters is shown by the roster of scholars who have produced them: Willard Thorp for the first four years, Merton M. Sealts, Jr., for the next five, Hershel Parker for the succeeding nine, Robert Milder for the next three, and Brian Higgins beginning with the 1984 volume. These essays—the Wright essay supplemented by those in *ALS*—are a perfect complement to Higgins's approach. Thus what may be the two most valuable ways of bringing the material under control—the comprehensive listing, with abstracts, and the selective survey, with critical commentary—are, in Melville's case, well provided for.

Obviously, however, guides to smaller segments of the total body of research and criticism can also have their uses. For example, there have been checklists devoted to single works of Melville, such as Joseph Wenke's list for *Typee* (with 878 entries, not annotated despite the title of the list), David H. Bowman and Ruth L. Bohan's annotated list for *Mardi*, Parker and Hayford's for *Moby-Dick*, Donald M. Fiene's and Bruce Bebb's for "Bartleby," Watson G. Branch's for *The Confidence-Man*, and William T. Stafford's for *Billy Budd* (plus the Hayford-Sealts unannotated list in their edition). James C. Wilson has provided an annotated list on "The Hawthorne-Melville Relationship" (1982). Two significant categories of material that have often not been well represented in the other treatments are dissertations and foreign-language publications. The Melville Society has taken particular responsibility for recording the dissertations (with abstracts), by sponsoring a series of publications: Tyrus Hillway's list of 1953 was revised and expanded by Hershel Parker in 1962, was further extended by Joel Myerson and Arthur H. Miller, Jr., in 1972, and in the hands of John Bryant emerged in 1983 as a full-fledged book, reporting on the astonishing total, from 1924 through 1980, of over 530 dissertations (wholly or in significant part on Melville) and containing Bryant's careful survey of the trends thus displayed. The foreign-language materials have been the special province of Leland R. Phelps, who has tirelessly searched for them (editions of Melville's works as well as commentary) for several decades. His first checklist appeared (in two parts) in 1960–61 as the second of the Melville Society "Special Publications"; his much-expanded listing of 1983 (produced with Kathleen McCullough) fills a 331–page volume and records material in forty-eight languages. (For Japanese studies, Phelp's work supersedes the substantial Tsunematsu-Marovitz list of 1979.)

It is not my task here to trace the shifts in emphasis and critical fashion that are reflected in the development over the years of this vast body of commentary. A start in that direction is made by the *ALS* essays; and the three major lists of secondary material—Higgins, Bryant, and Phelps—facilitate a historical approach by being chronologically arranged. Indeed, in the introduction to his first volume Higgins provides a marvelously concise and authoritative general account to 1930. The full story of Melville's reputation will, of course, eventually have to include various nonbook materials as well—recordings, films, videotapes, computer disks. And books and articles continue to multiply at a frightening rate: the number appearing each year now exceeds the number produced in any ten-year period during the first three decades after Melville's death. One can attempt to keep up with them by recourse to the usual current reference books; in addition, perusal of the selective annotated lists in the quarterly numbers of *American Literature* and regular reading of *Melville Society Extracts* can help to fill the gap between the end of a year and its coverage in the MLA list (or the longer gap before the appearance of *ALS* and the MHRA list). In the continual sifting of material, addenda to Higgins will inevitably turn up: Higgins himself has already published a supplement to his first volume in *Extracts*, as has Gary Scharnhorst and John M.J. Gretchko. The existence of Higgins's work has not brought—and never will bring—the process of duplicative listing to a halt: in 1981 Jeanetta Boswell published an alphabetical unannotated checklist covering 1900–78, a work that has only a short period of usefulness, for although it is preferable to the Ricks-Adams list it is doomed to be superseded by Higgins. In another post-Higgins publication, Mary K. Madison has listed all the books and pamphlets exclusively devoted to Melville or containing "substantial" discussion of him, reaching the impressive total of 243 (through 1981).

Such figures as this, or the 3,215 items in Boswell, or the 531 in Bryant, suggest the value of bringing copies of all these works together in one place. The Melville Collection at the Newberry aims for completeness, in secondary as well as primary materials, and it has both benefited from and assisted the work of Higgins and Phelps, who have been closely associated with it (an example of the kind of reciprocal development envisaged from the start). Besides the books and pamphlets, its shelves contain virtually all the dissertations devoted entirely to Melville and a comprehensive file of the periodical literature, either in offprint or photocopy form. The presence of all this material in one room is an incalculable advantage—for the effort of retrieving it from its scattered locations in the stacks of a large library (assuming a library that contained all of it) is enough in itself to inhibit scholarship. The Newberry collection establishes a model of a humane way to deal with the bulk of material now associated with major authors: every writer of the first rank ought to be provided with the equivalent of a Newberry Melville Collection. Furthermore, the Newberry collection sometimes has multiple copies of multiple printings (as well as later editions) of secondary works, with some protected from use, so that dust jackets and bindings can be kept in their original condition, or near to it. This attention does not overvalue the secondary material; it simply recognizes that books about Melville are products of the publishing process, just as those by him are. The collection is thereby a model in more respects than one, demonstrating an enlightened approach to collecting. Harrison Hayford is more responsible than anyone else for this great assemblage; and his creation, enriched over the years by the generous cooperation of The Newberry Library, the perceptiveness of its curator, Richard Colles Johnson, and the contributions of numerous Melville scholars and collectors (among them James Albert FitzSimmons, H. Howard Hughes, and Howard P. Vincent) must be regarded as the central reference tool for the study of Melville.

POSTHUMOUS EDITIONS OF MELVILLE'S WORKS

At the time of Melville's death, most of his books were out of print in the United States; only *Pierre* and *Battle-Pieces* survived in sufficient stock to be available from Harper's for a few more years. Harper's had kept Melville's six books preceding *Pierre* in print for a considerable period, however, despite slow sales. The firm's last accounting to him, on 4 March 1887, showed that the stock of *Omoo*, *White-Jacket*, and *Moby-Dick* had been exhausted during the two and a half years since the previous statement; and the copies remaining of *Typee* (16), *Mardi* (30) and *Redburn* (18) were gone by the time of Harper's 1892 catalogue. In England, Murray did keep *Typee* and *Omoo* in print until after Melville's death, but Bentley had difficulty disposing of the first printings of the next four books and certainly did not reprint them. And the later books did not have a long life in print: Putnam let *Israel Potter* go out of print after three impressions in 1855 and sold the plates to T. B. Peterson, who published one more impression in 1865; Dix & Edwards, publisher of *The Piazza Tales* and *The Confidence-Man*, was in financial trouble at the time of the appearance of the latter and, after a reorganization, failed a few months later; and Longman published a single impression of *The Confidence-Man* in England. Nor did the three publishers who brought out unauthorized editions—H. J. Gibbs (*Typee*, 1850), George Routledge (*Typee, Omoo*, 1850; *Israel Potter*, 1855), and A. & W. Galignani (*Redburn*, 1850)—keep Melville's books available for very long.

The process of bringing Melville's books back into print began just after his death, and the proliferation of new editions down to the present is a principal element in the history of his reputation. One must recognize, however, that an examination of the texts of those editions—not merely the number of editions and the size of their sales—is relevant to the study of reputation; for the particular texts of an author's work that are widely circulated inevitably affect the reactions of large numbers of readers and thus have a bearing on the author's reputation and influence. The sales of many twentieth-century editions of Melville's books have been impressive: the first two volumes of Melville in the Library of America, for example, sold just about as many copies in the two years 1982–84 as were sold of Melville's first seven books by his authorized publishers during his lifetime (that is, roughly 50,000 copies). Fortunately, the texts of the Library of America volumes are reliable; but the texts of many other editions, such as some of the classroom paperbacks read by thousands of students year after year, have not been so carefully produced, and many people's opinions of Melville have been based on the reading of defective texts.

Among those people are some who have put their views into print in critical articles and books and who have thereby enlarged the influence of the editions they had read. This fact should make obvious the central importance, for any scholarly study of an author, of knowing the history of the production of editions of that author's work. Regardless of whether one is interested in the history of the author's reputation, one must decide what editions to read and cite, and one must be concerned with what editions other critics (whose work one also reads and cites) were reacting to. Editions can vary from one another simply because of typographical errors or because of alterations introduced to correct seeming errors in previous editions; and critics have often been misled by taking such readings on faith, without checking into the authority of the texts they used. Variations between editions of certain of Melville's works arise from another source as well: seven of his books (the first six plus *The Confidence-Man*) were originally published in separate American and English editions, and most of the contents of another book, *The Piazza Tales*, had previously been published in *Putnam's Monthly Magazine*.

(The other books distributed in England, *Pierre* and *Israel Potter*, did not have separate English editions: copies of the American editions were issued with cancel title pages for Sampson Low.) The two original printed editions in each case contain numerous variations, in wording and in punctuation, and later editions naturally vary according to which of the original texts they are primarily based on. All the original English editions of Melville's books except *The Confidence-Man* were officially published a few weeks earlier than the American (because the English publishers felt that prior publication strengthened their claim to copyright); but only the first of them (*Typee*, first published as *Narrative of a Four Months' Residence Among the Natives of a Valley of the Marquesas Islands*) was set from the manuscript supplied by Melville, all the others being set from proof-sheets (or possibly, in the case of *The Confidence-Man*, final sheets) of the American editions.

Thus, the English edition of *Typee* and the American editions of the other six books are the ones closest to the final manuscripts. And when the variant readings—at points of difference between the two editions in each case—both appear to be Melville's (rather than one being a compositor's error or a change by the publisher's reader), either one could theoretically be later, depending on whether Melville made revisions on the proofs to be sent abroad that were not made on the other set, or whether he made additional revisions after sending one set abroad. Only in the instances of *White-Jacket* and *Moby-Dick*, it turns out, did Melville have much opportunity to make revisions for the transatlantic editions; and such revisions as he made are mixed with alterations initiated by the transatlantic publishers. (Bentley's office was particularly vigilant in bowdlerizing *Moby-Dick*.) The history of *Typee* is further complicated by the fact that the American publisher, Wiley & Putnam, insisted after publication that Melville revise the book to soften his criticism of missionaries and his remarks on political and sexual subjects. Indeed, the publisher had already made a few changes in this direction in the first printing. As a result, an expurgated "Revised Edition" of *Typee* circulated in the United States while the original text remained in print in England. As for *The Piazza Tales*, five of the six pieces it contains were set from the sheets of the original *Putnam's* printings (which had been set from manuscript), incorporating some revisions by Melville along with publishing house alterations. These basic facts about the textual history of Melville's books must be kept in mind by anyone wishing to evaluate particular posthumous editions; they form the essential background for tracking the story of the development of those editions.

The first new editions of any of Melville's books after his death appeared the next year, in the fall of 1892, when the United States Book Company brought *Typee*, *Omoo*, *White-Jacket*, and *Moby-Dick* back into print. The four volumes were edited by Melville's literary executor, Arthur Stedman, who had begun (in the words of Merton M. Sealts's thorough account in *The Early Lives of Melville*, 1974) "a systematic campaign to revive and enhance his dead friend's nearly forgotten literary reputation" (p. 51). Stedman's name, however, appeared only in the *Typee*, to which he contributed an introduction based on three previous biographical pieces he had published on Melville. His only comments there on his editorial method are that he had restored the passages omitted from the previously published American texts of *Typee*, "save for a few paragraphs excluded by written direction of the author," and that he had been able, with the help of Titus Munson Coan, to "harmonise the spelling of foreign words in 'Typee' and 'Omoo.' " The Stedman papers in the Columbia University Library contain an undated note, in Melville's wife's hand, headed "Memoranda for re-issue of 'Typee' (made by Mr. Melville)," which may be the "written direction of the author" referred to by Stedman. What weight should be given to these directives is not clear (see the discussion in the NN *Typee*, pp. 312–14); but in any case Stedman made many additional alterations, a few of which are clearly needed corrections, and his edition also contained a large number of new readings resulting apparently from compositorial error. If Stedman's *Typee* is for these reasons unreliable, Stedman should nevertheless be given credit for returning to the text of the English edition of *Typee* and thus making many passages readily available in the United States for the first time since 1846. His other three volumes are less praiseworthy: the *Omoo* unfortunately followed the English rather than the American edition; and although the *White-Jacket* and the *Moby-Dick* were based on the American texts, they (like the *Omoo*) contained many compositorial errors and attempted improvements (which, in the case of *White-Jacket*, eliminated three sizable passages). Stedman's editions remain of interest because of his connection with the Melville family, but there is no evidence (nor did he suggest) that he was following any instructions directly or indirectly from Melville other than the memorandum regarding *Typee*. His editorial methods seem lax and misguided by today's standards, but there is no doubt (as some of his emendations show) that he had read these four works thoughtfully and that he performed an important service to Melville's reputation in overseeing the production of these editions.

Stedman's editions have a further significance in that they have been particularly long-lived, despite the failure of the United States Book Company in early 1893: first Tait, Sons & Co. distributed the United States Book printings, and then the plates were used by a succession of publishers—the American Publishers Corporation in the 1890s, Dana Estes & Co. in the next decade, and L. C. Page & Co. from the teens through the early 1950s (with some Page printings in the 1920s bearing the St. Botolph Society imprint, and some of the St. Botolph sheets issued with D. D. Nickerson title pages). The editions also circulated in England, first in Putnam issues of United States Book (1893) and Dana Estes (1901) printings (the 1901 issue of *Moby-Dick* containing an introduction by the Australian sea novelist Louis Becke) and then in the 1920s in printings by Jonathan Cape. In the fall of 1893, a few months after the appearance of the first Putnam issues, the Murray firm brought out new printings of its original British editions of *Typee* and *Omoo*, embellished with a memoir by Henry S. Salt and with illustrations. Before the end of the decade, Scribner's published another new edition of *Moby-Dick* (1899, reprinted in 1900 by Sampson Low, Marston in London), following the American text. In 1902 D. C. Heath in Boston brought out an edition of *Typee* with an introduction by W. P. Trent, and in 1904 John Lane in London published new editions of *Typee* and *Omoo*. From then through 1920, only five further editions of Melville's books appeared, but four of them were important because they formed part of two standard series, widely distributed on both sides of the Atlantic: *Typee* and *Moby-Dick* were included in "Everyman's Library" in 1907 and *Omoo* in 1908 (the first in the revised American text, the second in the English text, and the third in the American); and *Moby-Dick* (American text, introduced by Viola Meynell) appeared in "The World's Classics" of Oxford University Press in 1920. In the thirty years preceding the explosion of interest in the 1920s, therefore, only four of Melville's books (*Typee, Omoo, White-Jacket,* and *Moby-Dick*) were accorded new editions, but three of those four (all but *White-Jacket*) appeared in multiple editions.

The most imposing monument of the Melville Revival of the 1920s is Michael Sadleir's Constable edition, presenting Melville's works in sixteen handsome volumes, in a limited edition of 750 sets, published in 1922, 1923, and 1924. Although the texts of these volumes leave much to be desired, there can be no doubt that the act of bringing the bulk of Melville's writings back into print, and so early in the decade, was a major contribution to the Revival. Sadleir's place in the history of Melville's reputation, and in the affections of Melville enthusiasts, is secure. Originally planned as twelve volumes, containing all Melville's prose published in his lifetime in book form (that is, his first ten books, with *Mardi* and *Moby-Dick* each occupying two volumes), the set was expanded in 1924 with the addition of a volume of uncollected prose pieces (edited by Raymond M. Weaver and publishing *Billy Budd* for the first time), two volumes of *Clarel*, and a volume of the shorter poems (including a number not previously published). It is therefore a virtually complete edition of Melville's writing (lacking only the letters, journals, marginalia and inscriptions, some of the unpublished verse, and some prose pieces subsequently attributed to him), and it remains the only such edition to this day. It was therefore often thought of as standard—indeed, it proclaimed itself "Standard Edition"—and was frequently so cited, at least until the appearance of the first Hendricks House volumes in the late 1940s.

Unfortunately, no textual policy was stated in the Constable edition, and investigation reveals that the texts are unreliable. There seems to be no rationale underlying its use of American or English texts as the basic ones to follow, since the English is used for *Omoo* as well as *Typee*, but the American for the other books. *Typee* is in fact a special case, further illustrating the confusion: although the Constable *Typee* generally follows the English edition, there are patches in which printer's copy for it seems to have been the American revised edition. The problems posed by the Constable texts are more considerable, however, for they frequently incorporate new punctuation and spelling (routinely substituting British forms) and contain a number of substantive variants, some of them obviously compositorial slips that were never caught. Such a slip resulted in what has become one of the most famous and widely cited examples of a critic being misled by a faulty text: F. O. Matthiessen, in *American Renaissance* (p. 392), analyzed with admiration the phrase "soiled fish" in *White-Jacket*, unaware that "soiled" was a compositorial error in the Constable text and that what Melville wrote was "coiled." (Matthiessen's error was noted in the pages of *American Literature* in 1949 by John W. Nichol.) The Constable edition, for all its historical importance, makes no contribution toward the establishment of reliable texts of Melville's works. (Some further information about this edition is provided by Philip Durham in a 1957 article on its genesis.)

During the remainder of the decade, through 1930, each of Melville's prose books except *The Confidence-Man* was accorded at least one further edition, and some of them appeared in a number of new editions—*Moby-Dick*, for instance, in eleven (plus eleven abridgments for school use), and even *Mardi* in four. There has been no other period of such intense activity in republishing so many of Melville's books. Most of the editions, however, gave no attention to textual matters and are significant only because they were widely distributed and thus helped markedly to increase the accessibility of Melville's books. Three more of his books (*Typee*, *Omoo*, and *White-Jacket*) were included in "The World's Classics" in 1924; *Moby-Dick* was added to "The Modern Library" in 1926; and Pickwick Publishers in 1928 brought out a large volume entitled *Romances of Herman Melville* (containing Melville's first six books and *Israel Potter*), which played a significant role in disseminating some of his less well-known books. The period also saw the production of one of the handsomest of all editions of Melville, the 1930 Lakeside Press *Moby-Dick* with illustrations by Rockwell Kent, now an established classic of modern bookmaking. (Of the later finely printed editions of Melville's works—undertaken by the Limited Editions Club and the Arion Press, among others—the only one with significant scholarly usefulness, though it is of no textual importance, is the Wreden edition of "The Encantadas"—printed by the Grabhorn Press in 1940—which contains the annotations of a naturalist, Victor Wolfgang van Hagen, who knew the islands.)

In the 1920s one attempt was made at an American collected set (which, unlike the Constable, was not to be a limited edition), but only four volumes appeared. Under Raymond M. Weaver's direction, Albert & Charles Boni began "The Pequod Edition of Herman Melville's Collected Works," publishing *Redburn* and *Israel Potter* in 1924 and *Mardi* and *Moby-Dick* in 1925. More significant, however, was Weaver's volume of *Shorter Novels*, published by Horace Liveright in his "Black and Gold Library" in 1928 and reprinted several times (and still in print), for it gave *Billy Budd* a wider exposure than the Constable volume could do. Weaver's 1928 text of *Billy Budd* differed in many places from his 1924 text but apparently did not result from a fresh systematic examination of the manuscript (it reproduced errors from 1924); in any case Weaver was more interested in smoothing out the roughness of an unfinished manuscript than in presenting a faithful transcription of what Melville wrote. The growing interest in the 1920s in pulling together fugitive Melville material is reflected in the two volumes that Henry Chapin edited for Princeton University Press in 1922, *The Apple-Tree Table and Other Sketches* and *John Marr and Other Poems*; preceding the Constable edition of this material by two years, the former volume collected ten periodical pieces into book form for the first time, and the latter volume provided a convenient one-volume selection of Melville's poetry (and the first edition of any of it after his death). In the same year Minnigerode published, with his bibliography, the first substantial gathering of Melville's letters (a larger group than Julian Hawthorne's and James Billson's). The most scholarly editorial effort of this period, however—indeed, the first serious work of textual scholarship devoted to Melville—is Robert S. Forsythe's edition of *Pierre* for Knopf's "Americana Deserta" series in 1930. Whether or not one concurs in his "correction" of errors and his "systematizing" of spelling and punctuation, one must recognize that he was carefully following an explicit editorial rationale and that he provided a list of the 338 emendations he made. His work was praised two years later by William S. Ament in the course of making the next substantial contribution, an attempt to analyze some differences between the American and English texts of *Moby-Dick* and to criticize some of the posthumous editions.

During the next three decades (through 1960), *Typee* and *Moby-Dick* continued to reappear in numerous new editions (nineteen of them for *Moby-Dick*, exclusive of abridgments and adaptations), but there was only a sparse scattering of new editions of Melville's other books (only one new edition of *Israel Potter*, for instance, and none of *Mardi*). It is worth observing, however, that *The Confidence-Man*—having had no edition other than the Constable since its original appearance—finally began to attract attention in this period, with the Lehmann edition in England in 1948 and the Grove Press edition in the United States the following year. Most of these editions gave no attention to textual matters, but there were a few notable exceptions, such as Willard Thorp's edition of *Moby-Dick* for Oxford University Press in 1947; although Thorp did not record his emendations, he did explain that he followed the American first edition without attempting to regularize or modernize punctuation and capitalization. (His edition was also the first unabridged one to offer scholarly annotation.)

The significant textual work of these decades largely falls into two categories, the first of which is the continuing effort to bring into print previously unpublished or uncollected material and to make the short pieces easily available. This activity is manifested by the discovery and republication of some of Melville's periodical pieces by John H. Birss ("A Thought on Book-Binding" in the *New England Quarterly* in 1932), Luther S. Mansfield ("Authentic Anecdotes of 'Old Zack' " in *American Literature* in 1938), and Willard Thorp ("Etchings of a Whaling Cruise" in *Herman Melville: Representative Selections* in 1938); by the transcription of Melville's 1849 *Journal* (edited by Eleanor Melville Metcalf in 1948), his 1856 *Journal* (edited first by Weaver in 1935 and again—much more effectively—by Howard C. Horsford in 1955), and his journal of 1860, which first appeared in the *New England Quarterly* in 1929, retranscribed by Jay Leyda for *The Portable Melville* in 1952; by the reconstruction of Melville's lectures by Merton M. Sealts, Jr., in 1957; by the publication of Melville's letters, at first singly or in small groups (as in Thorp's 1938 and Leyda's 1952 volumes) and then in a splendid collected edition by Merrell R. Davis and William H. Gilman in 1960; by F. Barron Freeman's re-editing of *Billy Budd* in 1948 (a highly flawed text, reproducing many of Weaver's errors but nevertheless achieving greater fidelity to the manuscript than Weaver did); and by the preparation of collections of Melville's poems (by Plomer in 1943 and Matthiessen in 1944), tales (by Leyda in 1949, with its Modern Library derivative in 1952), and poems and prose together (by Thorp in 1938, Chase in 1950, and Leyda in 1952). Three of these latter collections deserve special mention: both Thorp's *Herman Melville: Representative Selections* (1938) and Leyda's *The Portable Melville* (1952) served in their time as pioneering and indispensable repositories, containing thoughtfully wide-ranging and responsibly presented selections of material, some of it published for the first time; and Leyda's *The Complete Stories of Herman Melville* (1949) is an important contribution to the textual study of Melville, its texts reflecting careful collation of the extant documents and perceptive (though silent) emendations.

The other major textual activity of the time was the production, under the general editorship of Howard P. Vincent, of the first volumes of the Hendricks House Edition, projected as a fourteen-volume set to be available both with textual notes and in a "trade edition" without those notes. Three volumes appeared in quick succession in the late 1940s: *Collected Poems* (edited by Vincent, 1947), *The Piazza Tales* (Egbert S. Oliver, 1948), and *Pierre* (Henry A. Murray, 1949). And three more appeared at wider intervals in the next decade: *Moby-Dick* (Luther S. Mansfield and Vincent, 1952), *The Confidence-Man* (Elizabeth S. Foster, 1954), and *Clarel* (Walter E. Bezanson, 1960). Since that time only one further volume has come out: *Omoo* (Harrison Hayford and Walter Blair), dated 1969 (actually distributed in 1973) but consisting of work done between 1947 and 1951 (with scholarly references through 1957 added). Other scholars originally scheduled to edit other works were Charles R. Anderson (*Typee*), Merrell R. Davis (*Mardi*), Gordon Roper (*Typee, Israel Potter*), Merton M. Sealts, Jr. (*Stories and Sketches*), and Willard Thorp (*Redburn*), and further work was anticipated from Mansfield (*Mardi*) and Vincent (*White-Jacket*). A quarter-century after the Constable Edition, the time was overdue for a complete edition that would give serious attention to textual matters; as Stanley T. Williams said in 1956 (in his essay for *Eight American Authors*), the edition had become "a case of hope deferred" (p. 209).

One must now acknowledge, however, that the hope of this edition was never fulfilled—partly, of course, because the edition was never completed but also because what was completed does not attain the necessary level of textual scholarship. Inaccuracies abound in some of the volumes, beginning with the *Collected Poems*; in the *Moby-Dick*, for instance, the list of differences in wording between the American and English texts is far from complete (though fuller than William S. Ament's 1932 account), and the list of twenty emendations made by the editors in their copy-text (the original American edition) does not in fact record all the departures of their text from that American edition. (William H. Hutchinson in 1954 noted what in his view were twenty more emendations and 108 typographical errors, and more have since been discovered.) In any case, aside from questions of accuracy, the textual policy was not very sophisticated, emphasizing emendation for consistency and for the correction of what Henry A. Murray (who found the Constable *Pierre* "a decided improvement on the original") called "indubitable errors" (pp. v-vi); one regrets that further thought was not given to the bearing of authorial revision on emendation and to the precise purpose for which emendation was being undertaken. Nevertheless, the Hendricks House volumes gave more attention to textual matters than the works covered had previously received (offering such pioneer works as Foster's on the *Confidence-Man* fragments), and they provided some lists of variants that have had an interim usefulness. Their lasting contribution, however, is not in their texts or textual apparatus but in their historical and explanatory notes (the fullest yet offered) and their introductions (some of them book-length treatments); the extensive notes to *Moby-Dick* and *Omoo*, the admirable introductions to *The Confidence-Man* and *Clarel*, and the remarkable essay preceding *Pierre* (the most celebrated part of the whole Edition) are among the permanently valuable features of these volumes, but they could have been published separately from the texts and are peripheral to the main business of an edition.

Two more editions of *Moby-Dick* from this period and one from the early 1960s include some comment on textual matters (Arvin's Rinehart edition of 1948, Kazin's Riverside edition of 1956, and Feidelson's Bobbs-Merrill edition of 1964); but these editions nevertheless are unreliable textually, and unfortunately they are characteristic, in that unreliability, of the majority of classroom editions of Melville's works. In his 1973 examination of the "practical editions" of *Moby-Dick*, Hershel Parker found, for example, that both the Kazin and the Feidelson editions had been set from the Hendricks House text (and thus incorporated some of its errors), even though both editions have prefatory notes stating that the text is that of the first American edition. At least these editors did attempt, however inexpertly, to deal with textual problems; frequently, scholars and critics write introductions without paying any attention—or being allowed by the publishers to pay attention—to the source and accuracy of the texts they are introducing.

Classroom editions of Melville's books appeared in considerable numbers during the 1960s (only *Redburn*, of Melville's first ten books, failing to be set in type at least once during the decade), but few of them demand notice for their textual scholarship. (The production of five new editions of *The Confidence-Man*, plus a facsimile, within the five-year period 1964–68 is of interest as a reflection of the belated recognition of that book, but only two of the editions—Cohen's Rinehart edition of 1964 and Franklin's Bobbs-Merrill edition of 1967—state that some emendations have been undertaken.) Two editions of "Benito Cereno" appeared in 1965 in collections of material for classroom study (one edited by Seymour L. Gross, the other by John P. Runden), both of them providing some notes on textual variants. It also happens that the two editions of *White-Jacket* published in these years examine the text of this work more attentively than had previously been done and record some of the variants between the American and English editions, but they are faulty for different reasons: A. R. Humphreys's edition (Oxford University Press, 1966) takes the English text as copy-text on the incorrect assumption that it is earlier and often emends it with readings from the American; Hennig Cohen's Rinehart edition (1967) properly takes the American text as copy-text but does not emend it with those English variants judged to be Melville's revisions, instead claiming to record the English variants in brackets in the text (and actually noting about a third of them). Harold Beaver's Penguin edition (1967) of *Billy Budd, Sailor and Other Stories*, though it contains a note on the text, can be dismissed because Beaver has "deleted a comma, or even added one, as sense demanded" (p. 51). Far more significant was the textual work appearing in dissertations at this time: Norman E. Jarrard's edition of the published poems (1960), Robert C. Ryan's of the unpublished "Weeds and Wildings Chiefly" (1967), and Wilson Walker Cowen's of the marginalia (1965).

Harrison Hayford's Signet edition of *Typee* (1964) uses brackets in the text to mark passages Melville deleted or revised (with the revisions given in notes), but following the publisher's policy it indicates only major changes. This edition represents the most serious textual work on *Typee* to that time; but it is not on a level with Hayford's two other editorial projects of the 1960s, prior to the NN edition. These two projects—the Hayford-Sealts *Billy Budd, Sailor* (1962) and the Hayford-Parker *Moby-Dick* (1967)—are primary landmarks of Melville textual scholarship (the chief ones, indeed, before the NN edition). The *Billy Budd* has become not only the classic example of a "genetic" text, but also an often-cited demonstration of how a single edition can treat a text two ways, as a document and as a work of art. Hayford and Sealts offer two texts, the first a literal transcription of the complex manuscript, showing with the aid of symbols the stages of revision it contains, and the second a reading text, largely consisting of the final readings of the manuscript but also incorporating emendations when the editors deem them necessary. There will never be complete agreement on every detail of what the reading text of this work, or any other critical edition, should contain (the policy of regularizing punctuation and spelling, for example, can legitimately be objected to, as it is by the NN editors); but the genetic text will remain valuable as a record of the documentary evidence on which any reading text must be based. The Hayford-Parker *Moby-Dick*, in the series of "Norton Critical Editions," pushed the textual study of that work far ahead of what anyone else had done and provided by far the finest critical edition that any of Melville's published books had received. Through an examination of all available evidence, Hayford and Parker came to recognize that some of the variants in the English text result from Melville's revision and that a truly critical edition would require the editors to judge the authority of each English variant. This edition is the first, therefore, to emend the American copy-text with those English readings judged to be authorial (Hayford and Parker adopt ninety-nine of the English substantive variants), in addition to correcting readings in which both the American and English tests appear to be erroneous. The editors also supply discussions of the textual history of the work and their editorial policy, along with lists of the variants between the American and English editions, of their emendations, and of further possible emendations considered but not adopted. (This edition also furnishes, among its supplementary materials, the first scholarly edition of "Hawthorne and His *Mosses*" to use the manuscript as copy-text, though presenting it in "a slightly normalized reading text.")

It is not surprising, given this history, that Harrison Hayford should have been the guiding force in the major event of the decade, the inauguration of the NN edition of *The Writings of Herman Melville*. Although the project was formally instituted—in rooms at the Northwestern University Library and The Newberry Library—in the summer of 1965 (following a meeting of Melville scholars in September 1963 and the circulation of Hayford's "Brief Account of Plans" in July 1964) and the first volume was published in 1968, the origins of the edition lie earlier. One can trace the whole editorial movement of the 1960s, resulting in the establishment of textually authoritative editions of a number of American writers, to the 1947–48 academic year, when a Committee on Definitive Editions was set up, under Willard Thorp, by the American Literature Group of the Modern Language Association of America. A more immediate antecedent—a belated product of that committe—was a June 1962 discussion (again led by Willard Thorp) followed by the Gould House conference of October 1962 on the establishment of a Center for Editions of American Authors (CEAA). Such a Center was actually created the following spring, with an executive board that was to be a formal committee of the Modern Language Association and with William M. Gibson as its director. The textual guidelines adopted by the CEAA have a separate, but converging, history. For the English Institute of 1949 W. W. Greg wrote a paper on "The Rationale of Copy-Text" (published in *Studies in Bibliography* for 1950–51), which Fredson Bowers immediately championed in various essays and put into practice in his edition of Dekker. In November 1962—just when the CEAA was being organized—Bowers read a paper at the South Atlantic Modern Language Association conference on "Some Principles for Scholarly Editions of Nineteenth-Century American Authors" (published in *Studies in Bibliography* for 1964), showing how Greg's advice for handling Renaissance drama could be extended to this later body of literature; and in the essay on "Textual Criticism" in the MLA's widely circulated pamphlet on *The Aims and Methods of Scholarship in Modern Languages and Literatures* (edited by James Thorpe in 1963), Bowers further elaborated on Greg's rationale. With this persuasive argument at hand, the CEAA essentially followed Bowers's adaptation of Greg, setting forth its position in a *Statement of Editorial Principles* in 1967.

The extensive editorial work that followed, and the mixed reception accorded it (the chief criticism coming from those who hold that Greg's rationale cannot appropriately be adapted to the conditions under which later literature was produced), gave the textual scholarship of modern literature more attention than it had previously received and placed the editing of American literature at the center of the debate. Although some critics suggested that the CEAA was oppressively monolithic, its reliance on Greg's general approach actually meant that the emphasis was on individual editors' judgments, and the resulting editions are by no means uniform. It is true, however, that this editing focused on authorial intention (precisely which of an author's several intentions, when more than one existed, is a separate question), rather than on the social and collaborative result of the publishing process. In advocating that normally an author's finished manuscript, when it survives (or the edition closest to it, when it does not survive), should provide copy-text, to be emended by readings in later texts that can convincingly be declared authorial, the CEAA was not denying the legitimate interest that attaches, for the study of cultural history, to the documentary texts that in fact were available to readers at particular times; it was simply asserting the desirability of having, among other possibilities, eclectic texts that resulted from informed critical judgment as to what their authors (in isolation from their printers or publishers) intended at one finished stage or another. (I have offered a history and critical assessment of these developments in three essays, "Greg's Theory of Copy-Text and the Editing of American Literature" [1975] "Recent Editorial Discussion and the Central Questions of Editing" [1981], and "Historicism and Critical Editing" [1986], and have provided a record of much of the associated literature to 1977 in the announcement of the CEAA's successor, *The Center for Scholarly Editions: An Introductory Statement.*)

Hayford, who was a member of the first CEAA executive committee, naturally and rightly envisaged the new Melville edition in this context. The aim of the edition was to establish texts that reflected Melville's final intentions, as faithfully as the editors' judgment of all surviving evidence would allow. That evidence includes, in addition to such documents as letters, manuscript drafts, and publishers' records, the results of collations of multiple copies of all authorized editions of Melville's writings during his lifetime. Although textual decisions must obviously grow out of an understanding (and thus an interpretation) of the meaning of the texts and therefore of a knowledge of historical allusions in them, it was not part of the purpose of the Edition to provide historical or explanatory annotation or to engage in critical analysis. Each volume was to contain, in addition to a critical text, only such supplementary material as was directly relevant to understanding the textual history of the work and the editors' treatment of the textual problems it raised: a historical essay setting forth the history of the composition, publication, and reception of the work (this essay also includes somewhat fuller comment on posthumous editions than I have provided here); a textual essay explaining the editorial principles followed and their application to specific situations arising in the texts involved; a series of textual notes discussing particular cruxes not covered in detail by the textual essay; lists of all emendations made in the copy-text and all substantive variants between authorized texts during Melville's lifetime; and reproductions and analyses of related documents, such as surviving manuscript fragments or important source works.

Copy-texts in each case are the printed texts closest to the missing manuscripts (thus the English edition of *Typee*, the American magazine texts of *Israel Potter* and *The Piazza Tales*, and the American book editions of the remaining commercially published books) or the manuscripts when they survive (as for some of the periodical pieces and poems and for *Billy Budd, Sailor* and other unpublished work). Emendations are made in these copy-texts whenever the editors are convinced that a variant in another authorized text during Melville's lifetime results from his revision and whenever they believe that they have discovered (and know how to replace) other erroneous copy-text readings; inconsistencies in spelling and punctuation are not generally considered errors, and emendations are not normally made in order to produce consistency. Hayford invited Hershel Parker and me to join him as principal editors, and the three of us have been assisted over the years by various associates and contributing scholars, among them the Bibliographical Associate, Richard Colles Johnson, present from the beginning, and the expert Editorial Coordinator of recent years, Alma A. MacDougall. The textual work has been centralized (except that other editors, such as Robert C. Ryan and Howard C. Horsford, are primarily responsible for some of the volumes of manuscript material), and the scholars who write the historical essays are not involved in textual decisions (except when they happen also to be members of the editorial staff).

As of mid-1986, eight volumes had appeared: *Typee* (1968), *Omoo* (1968), *Redburn* (1969), *Mardi* (1970), *White-Jacket* (1970), *Pierre* (1971), *Israel Potter* (1982), and *The Confidence-Man* (1984). Two more volumes, *The Piazza Tales and Other Prose Pieces 1839–1860* and *Moby-Dick*, are in late stages of production, leaving five volumes (all well advanced in preparation) to follow: *Clarel*, journals, letters, shorter published poems, and late manuscript material (both poetry and prose). (The *Moby-Dick* text differs somewhat from that in the Norton edition as a result of more conservative emendation policy and of evidence—especially regarding the texts of Melville's sources—discovered since it was published.) Because the texts of the NN volumes are critical texts, incorporating the editors' critical judgments, readers will not necessarily be in agreement with every decision made in them; no single critical text can ever be the only responsible text. But one can fairly say that the NN texts emerge from the most thorough study of the printing, publishing, and textual history of Melville's works yet undertaken and that the volumes place on public record, in their essays and lists, a fuller assemblage of the resulting evidence than has ever before been available.

Since the beginning of the Northwestern-Newberry project, Melville has been the subject of considerable textual discussion, not only in the pages of this edition but also in separate essays, often written by the NN editors themselves. For example, Hayford in 1978 published an essay—now regarded as a classic—called "Unnecessary Duplicates," brilliantly building on his study of Melville's texts to suggest an approach to the composition of *Moby-Dick*; Parker has cited Melville prominently in "Melville and the Concept of 'Author's Final Intentions' " (1971), "Regularizing Accidentals: The Latest Form of Infidelity" (1973), "Evidence for 'Late Insertions' in Melville's Works" (1975), "The 'New Scholarship' " (1981), and *Flawed Texts and Verbal Icons* (1984); and I have drawn many examples from Melville in "Textual Study and Literary Judgment" (1971), "The Editorial Problem of Final Authorial Intention" (1976), and "External Fact as an Editorial Problem" (1979), in addition to taking up, more explicitly, "Bibliographical Problems in Melville" (1974). Only three of the newly edited texts to appear after the first NN volume deserve mention here for their textual contribution: Watson Branch's facsimile of the American edition of *The Confidence-Man* with emendations and notes (his 1970 Northwestern University dissertation), Parker's Norton edition of *The Confidence-Man* (1971), and his Merrill edition of *Shorter Works of Hawthorne and Melville* (1972). In addition, a list of the variants between the magazine and book texts of "Bartleby, the Scrivener" is presented (without a reading text) in Appendix B of George R. Petty, Jr., and William M. Gibson's description of a program for computerized collation, *Project OCCULT* (1970). Harold Beaver's 1972 Penguin edition of *Moby-Dick* does contain an eighteen-page section on textual matters, but its listings are derived from the Norton edition, though many of the Norton emendations from the English edition are rejected. Similarly, Milton Stern's 1975 Bobbs-Merrill edition of *Billy Budd, Sailor*—with forty-four pages of textual appendix—is an offshoot of the Hayford-Sealts edition, based on its genetic text but offering an "alternative" reading text "that in some cases makes consistency and grammatical correctness secondary to what Melville actually wrote" (p. 144); the differences between this text and the Hayford-Sealts are given considerable, but rather naive, attention in Thomas J. Scorza's 1979 book on *Billy Budd*. Tyrus Hillway, in his 1973 *Mardi*, mistakenly believes that the "modern reader" requires the excision of "some hundreds of unnecessary commas and several scores of semicolons."

Other editions are of interest for their critical commentary, even when they make no great contribution to textual scholarship—a prime example being Robert Penn Warren's edition of *Selected Poems of Herman Melville* (1970), which does in fact contain a number of notes reporting manuscript variants. Concordances are not editions, but they are necessarily dependent on editions and ought to reflect careful textual investigation; it is therefore sad to report that, although we now have two concordances to *Moby-Dick*, neither is based on the proper text—the Hennig Cohen-James Cahalan concordance of 1978 (see Watson Branch's incisive review) uses Feidelson's text, and the Eugene F. Irey of 1982 (see Hershel Parker's review) uses the Mansfield-Vincent text (the publisher of the Cohen-Cahalan promising to supply "a conversion table" after the NN text appears). Nor do they include variant readings that are possibly Melville's and that should therefore be available to students of his language. However, Larry Edward Wegener's concordance (1979) to *Clarel* uses the first edition, incorporates Melville's corrections entered on a set of sheets now at Harvard, and records in an appendix the first-edition readings at these points; and his concordance (1985) to *Pierre* follows the NN text (with an appendix on NN hyphenation), as does Jill B. Gidmark's concordance to Melville's sea language (1982).

Some of the NN texts themselves have reappeared under other publishers' imprints, both in photoreproduction and in new typesettings. One oddity—which can scarcely be classified as a use of the NN text—is George Woodcock's Penguin edition (1972) of *Typee*; although that text is its starting point, it restores most of the English spellings, a course of action puzzlingly regarded as "doubly justified" because "the English edition appeared first and the present edition is intended primarily for English readers" (p. 29). Of the resettings of NN texts thus far produced, the only accurate ones are those published by the Library of America, a not-for-profit undertaking founded in 1979 with initial grants from the Ford Foundation and the National Endowment for the Humanities. The aim of the Library of America series (the lineage of which goes back to Edmund Wilson, and no doubt beyond) is to make responsible texts of important American writings available to a wide audience in the form of handsome uniform volumes, compact but containing a large amount of material; it is conceived of as a publishing rather than an editing project, reprinting whatever text of each work is judged by the textual committee (after extensive research and collation by the office staff) to be the most defensible choice among those available, whether it is the text of a scholarly edition or that of an authorized edition from the author's lifetime. As reprinted by the Library of America, the chosen texts are altered in one respect, by the correction of typographical errors (verified, for texts from scholarly editions, by the original scholarly editors; or determined, for texts from contemporary editions, by the textual committee). A good account of the genesis and operation of the Library's textual policy has been published by Jo Ann Boydston, a member—with Don L. Cook and me—of the textual committee.

The first four volumes of the series appeared in the spring of 1982, with a Melville volume (containing *Typee*, *Omoo*, and *Mardi*) among them. A second Melville volume (*Redburn*, *White-Jacket*, and *Moby-Dick*) followed in 1983, and a third (*Pierre*, *Israel Potter*, *The Piazza Tales*, *The Confidence-Man*, and uncollected prose, including *Billy Budd, Sailor*) in 1984. For the first two, I prepared the notes (which, following Library policy, are kept brief and do not provide a comprehensive historical record of variants), and for the third, Harrison Hayford wrote them. The text of *Billy Budd, Sailor* is the reading text from the Hayford-Sealts edition; all the other texts are from the NN edition (those of *Moby-Dick* and the short prose pieces appearing here in advance of their publication in that Edition). In the space of three volumes (totaling 4,247 pages), therefore, one now has reliable texts of the bulk of Melville's prose—incorporating (and listing) the correction of eight typographical errors, which will also be corrected in future printings of the relevant volumes of the NN edition. Any errors in the Library of America texts will be corrected and noted in the next printing after they are discovered. Melville's poems are scheduled to fill a fourth Library of America volume.

Of the events chronicled in these pages, there is no doubt who the hero is: Harrison Hayford has been responsible for more basic work—from the maintenance of a file of secondary material to the production of critical editions—than anyone else. I have tried here to show in words, as he has demonstrated in deeds, the interrelationship of all these activities and their centrality to the other pursuits that historians and critics engage in. (Bibliographers and editors are, if they do their work well, both historians and critics.) A whale ship may have been Melville's Yale College and his Harvard, but his further studies were largely pursued in books, and what he gleaned from them affected what he learned from life. We can now know Melville only through books—his own and those others have written about him—and these books in turn affect our own lives. It is not easy to separate books from life, nor is it any easier to disentangle, in the texts of books, what got there through the processes of book production from what is there because the author wished it to be. The various studies that can be called bibliographical and textual—those, that is, concerned in one way or another with the world of books—are fundamental to understanding what Melville read, what he wrote, what those who came after him thought he wrote, and what they have written about it. We can feel fortunate that so much work in recent years has focused on these matters; but it is clear that much remains to be done if we, in our own bowers of the Arsacides, are to be adequately prepared for the attempt to measure Melville himself.

WORKS CITED

Abbott, Jacob. *The Harper Establishment; or, How the Story Books Are Made.* New York: Harper, 1855. Rpt.: Introd. Jacob Blanck. Hamden: Shoe String Press, 1956.

Altick, Richard D. *The English Common Reader: A Social History of the Mass Reading Public, 1800–1900.* Chicago: University of Chicago Press, 1957.

Ament, William S. "Bowdler and the Whale: Some Notes on the First English and American Editions of *Moby-Dick*." *American Literature* 4 (March 1932): 39–46.

American Academy of Arts and Letters. *The Great Decade in American Writing, 1850–1860.* New York: American Academy of Arts and Letters and National Institute of Arts and Letters, 1954.

American Book Prices Current. New York: Dodd, Mead et al., 1895–   .

Anderle, Donald L. "Not Just Another Old Trunk Story." *American Book Collector* n.s. 5 (November-December 1984): 3–10.

Barber, Edwin, and Virginia Price. "A Description of Old Harper and Brothers Publishing Records Recently Come to Light." *Bulletin of Bibliography* 25 (1966–68): 1–6, 29–34, 39–40.

Barber, Giles. "Galignani's and the Publication of English Books in France from 1800 to 1852." *Library* 5th ser. 16 (1961): 267–86.

Barnes, James J. *Authors, Publishers and Politicians: The Quest for an Anglo-American Copyright Agreement, 1815–1854.* London: Routledge & Kegan Paul, 1974.

Barnes, Warner. "A Critical Survey of Authors Represented in Blanck's *Bibliography of American Literature*." Ph.D. Diss., University of Texas, 1962.

Bebb, Bruce. " 'Bartleby': An Annotated Checklist of Criticism." *Bartleby the Inscrutable.* Ed. M. Thomas Inge. Hamden: Archon, 1979, pp. 199–229. (With "Supplement" by Elizabeth Williamson, 230–34.)

Beebe, Maurice, Harrison Hayford, and Gordon Roper. "Criticism of Herman Melville: A Selected Checklist." *Modern Fiction Studies* 8 (1962): 312–46.

Bennett, Whitman. *A Practical Guide to American Book Collecting (1663–1940).* New York: Bennett, 1941.

Bentley, Richard, & Son. *A List of the Principal Publications Issued from New Burlington Street During the Year [1829–98].* London: Bentley, 1893–1920.

Berkshire Athenaeum. *General Inventory of the Collections in the Melville Room.* Pittsfield: Berkshire Athenaeum, 1953. Rev. ed.: 1955.

———. "The Melville Room in the Berkshire Athenaeum." *Bay State Librarian* 47.1 (1957): 9.

Bibliographical Society of the University of Virginia. "Harper Records." *Secretary's News Sheet* 37 (September 1957): 6.

Billson, James. "Some Melville Letters." *Nation and Athenaeum* 29 (13 August 1921): 712–13.

Birss, John H. "A Book Review by Herman Melville." *New England Quarterly* 5 (April 1932): 346–48.

———. " 'A Mere Sale to Effect' with Letters of Herman Melville." *New Colophon* 1 (July 1948): 239–55.

Blanck, Jacob. "Herman Melville." *Bibliography of American Literature*. 7 vols. to date. New Haven, Conn.: Yale University Press, 1955– . 6: 152–81.

———. "News from the Rare Book Sellers." *Publishers' Weekly* 152 (1947): B121–22.

Bonner, Paul Hyde. *Sale Catalogue of the Private Library of Paul Hyde Bonner*. New York: E. P. Dutton, 1931.

Book Auction Records. London: Karslake (later Stevens, Son & Stiles; then Dawson), 1903– .

Boswell, Jeanetta. *Herman Melville and the Critics: A Checklist of Criticism, 1900–1978*. Scarecrow Author Bibliographies 53. Metuchen, N.J.: Scarecrow Press, 1981.

Bowen, James K., and Richard VanDerBeets. *A Critical Guide to Herman Melville: Abstracts of Forty Years of Criticism*. Glenview, Ill.: Scott, Foresman, 1971.

Bowers, Fredson. "Some Principles for Scholarly Editions of Nineteenth-Century American Authors." *Studies in Bibliography* 17 (1964): 223–28.

———. "Textual Criticism." *The Aims and Methods of Scholarship in Modern Languages and Literatures*. Ed. James Thorpe. New York: Modern Language Association of America, 1963, pp. 23–42. Rev. ed.: 1970, pp. 29–54.

Bowman, David H., and Ruth L. Bohan. "Herman Melville's *Mardi, and a Voyage Thither*: An Annotated Checklist of Criticism." *Resources for American Literary Study* 3 (1973): 27–72.

Boydston, Jo Ann. "Editing the Library of America." *Scholarly Publishing* 16 (1984): 121–32.

Branch, Watson G. "An Annotated Bibliography." *The Confidence-Man: His Masquerade*. Ed. Hershel Parker. New York: W.W. Norton, 1971, pp. 361–76.

———, ed. *Melville: The Critical Heritage*. London: Routledge & Kegan Paul, 1974.

———. Rev. of Cohen-Cahalan concordance to *Moby-Dick* (1978). *Computers and the Humanities* 13 (1979): 141–46.

Brewer, Reginald. *The Delightful Diversion: The Whys and Wherefores of Book Collecting*. New York: Macmillan Co., 1935.

Brussel, I. R. *Anglo-American First Editions, Part Two: West to East, 1786–1930*. London: Constable, 1936.

Bryant, John. *Melville Dissertations, 1924–1980: An Annotated Bibliography and Subject Index*. Westport, Conn.: Greenwood Press, 1983.

Cahoon, Herbert. "Herman Melville: A Check List of Books and Manuscripts in the Collections of the New York Public Library." *Bulletin of the New York Public Library* 55 (June and July 1951): 263–75, 325–38. Rpt.: New York: New York Public Library, 1951.

———, Thomas V. Lange, and Charles Ryskamp. *American Literary Autographs from Washington Irving to Henry James*. New York: Dover, with The Pierpont Morgan Library, 1977.

Carter, John. *More Binding Variants*. London: Constable, 1938.

————. *Taste and Technique in Book-Collecting.* New York: Bowker, 1948.

Center for Editions of American Authors. *Statement of Editorial Principles.* New York: Modern Language Association of America, 1967. Rev. ed.: *Statement of Editorial Principles and Procedures,* 1972.

The Center for Scholarly Editions: An Introductory Statement. New York: Modern Language Association of America, 1977. Also in *PMLA* 92 (September 1977): 583–97.

Charvat, William. *Literary Publishing in America, 1790–1850.* Rosenbach Lectures 1958. Philadelphia: University of Pennsylvania Press, 1959.

————. "Melville and the Common Reader." *Studies in Bibliography* 12 (1959): 41–57.

————. "Melville's Income." *American Literature* 15 (November 1943): 251–61.

————. *The Profession of Authorship in America, 1800–1870: The Papers of William Charvat.* Ed. Matthew J. Bruccoli. Columbus: Ohio State University Press, 1968.

[Chew, Beverly.] *The Longfellow Collectors' Hand-Book.* New York: W. E. Benjamin, 1885.

Cohen, Hennig, and James Cahalan. *A Concordance to Melville's Moby-Dick.* 3 vols. N.p.: Melville Society, 1978.

Curle, Richard. *Collecting American First Editions: Its Pitfalls and Its Pleasures.* Indianapolis: Bobbs-Merrill, 1930.

Current Co. *An Illustrated Catalogue of Books and Other Printed Material by and about Herman Melville, Including a Long Run of Editions of Moby-Dick.* Chapter & Verse 30. Bristol, R.I.: Current Co., 1980.

Davis, Merrell R. *Melville's Mardi: A Chartless Voyage.* New Haven, Conn.: Yale University Press, 1952.

Davis, Susan. "More for the NYPL's Long Vaticans." *Melville Society Extracts* 57 (February 1984): 5–7.

De Voto, Bernard. "Editions of 'Typee.'" *Saturday Review of Literature* 5 (24 November 1928): 406.

Duban, James. *Melville's Major Fiction: Politics, Theology, and Imagination.* DeKalb: Northern Illinois University Press, 1983.

Durham, Philip. "Prelude to the Constable Edition of Melville." *Huntington Library Quarterly* 21 (May 1958): 285–89.

Ewing, Douglas C. "The Harper Archive at the Pierpont Morgan Library." *Manuscripts* 20.2 (1968): 40–42.

————. "The Three-Volume Novel." *Papers of the Bibliographical Society of America* 61 (1967): 201–207.

Exman, Eugene. *The Brothers Harper.* New York: Harper & Row, 1965.

————. *The House of Harper.* New York: Harper & Row, 1967.

Fiene, Donald M. "A Bibliography of Criticism of 'Bartleby the Scrivener.'" *Melville Annual 1965: A Symposium, Bartleby the Scrivener.* Ed. Howard P. Vincent. Kent, Ohio: Kent State University Press, 1966, pp. 140–90.

Foley, Patrick K. *American Authors, 1795–1895: A Bibliography of First and Notable Editions Chronologically Arranged with Notes.* Boston: Printed for subscribers, 1897.

————. *A Catalogue of First and Notable Editions of American Authors.* Catalogue 13. Boston: Foley, 1903.

Fullerton, B. M. *Selective Bibliography of American Literature, 1775–1900.* New York: Payson, 1932.

Gettmann, Royal A. *A Victorian Publisher: A Study of the Bentley Papers.* Cambridge, Mass.: Cambridge University Press, 1960.

Gidmark, Jill B. *Melville Sea Dictionary: A Glossed Concordance and Analysis of the Sea Language in Melville's Nautical Novels.* Westport, Conn.: Greenwood Press, 1982.

Goodspeed Book Shop. *Rare Books and First Editions.* Catalogue 209. Boston: Goodspeed, [1931].

Gordan, John D. "An Anniversary Exhibition: The Henry W. and Albert A. Berg Collection, 1940–1965." *Bulletin of the New York Public Library* 69 (1965): 537–54, 597–608, 665–77.

Greg. W. W. "The Rationale of Copy-Text." *Studies in Bibliography* 3 (1950–51): 19–36. Rpt.: *Collected Papers.* Ed. J. C. Maxwell. Oxford: Clarendon Press, 1966, pp. 374–91.

Gretchko, John M.J. "Supplement to Higgins." *Melville Society Extracts* 60 (November 1984): 12–13.

Griest, Guinevere L. *Mudie's Circulating Library and the Victorian Novel.* Bloomington: Indiana University Press, 1970.

Grolier Club. *One Hundred Influential American Books Printed Before 1900: Catalogue and Addresses.* New York: Grolier Club, 1947.

Gross, Theodore L. "Herman Melville." *Hawthorne, Melville, Stephen Crane: A Critical Bibliography.* By Gross and Stanley Wertheim. New York: Free Press, 1971, pp. 101–201.

Hart, James D. *The Popular Book: A History of America's Literary Taste.* New York: Oxford University Press, 1950.

Hawthorne, Julian. *Nathaniel Hawthorne and His Wife.* 2 vols. Boston: Osgood, 1884.

Hayford, Harrison. "An Appeal for Information from Librarians and Owners of Melville Editions." Evanston, Ill.: Mimeographed, 1 August 1964.

———. "Brief Account of Plans for a New Melville Edition." Evanston, Ill.: Mimeographed, 20 July 1964.

———. "Contract: *Moby-Dick*, by Herman Melville." *Proof* 1 (1971): 1–7.

———. *Dimensions of Moby-Dick.* Chicago: The Newberry Library, R.R. Donnelley, and Library of America, [1983].

———. "Unnecessary Duplicates." *New Perspectives on Melville.* Ed. Faith Pullin. Kent, Ohio and Edinburgh: Kent State University Press, and Edinburgh University Press, 1978, pp. 128–61.

[Head, Francis Bond.] "The Printer's Devil." *Quarterly Review* 65 (1839–40): 1–30.

Heflin, Wilson L. "New Light on Herman Melville's Cruise in the *Charles and Henry.*" *Historic Nantucket* 22 (October 1974): 6–27. Rpt.: Glassboro, N.J.: Melville Society, [1976].

Hetherington, Hugh W. *Melville's Reviewers, British and American, 1846–1891.* Chapel Hill: University of North Carolina Press, 1961.

———. "The Reputation of Herman Melville in America." Ph.D. Diss., University of Michigan, 1933. [*Mel. Diss.*, #4].

Higgins, Brian. *Herman Melville: An Annotated Bibliography*. Vol. 1: 1846–1930. Boston: Hall, 1979.

———. "Supplement to *Herman Melville: An Annotated Bibliography*." *Melville Society Extracts* 37 (February 1979): 10–15.

———, and Hershel Parker. Introduction. *Critical Essays on Herman Melville's Pierre; or, The Ambiguities*. Ed. Higgins and Parker. Boston: Hall, 1983, pp. 1–27.

Hillway, Tyrus. *Doctoral Dissertations on Herman Melville: A Chronological Summary (1933–1952)*. Greeley, Colo.: [Melville Society], 1953.

———, and Hershel Parker. *Directory of Melville Dissertations*. Evanston, Ill.: Melville Society, 1962.

Hutchinson, William H. " A Definitive Edition of *Moby-Dick*." *American Literature* 25 (November 1953): 472–78.

Irey, Eugene F. *A Concordance to Herman Melville's Moby-Dick*. 2 vols. New York: Garland, 1982.

Ives, Sidney. "A Melville Ghost." *Papers of the Bibliographical Society of America* 59 (1965): 318.

———, ed. *The Parkman Dexter Howe Library*. Gainesville: University of Florida, 1983–

Jarrard, Norman E. *Melville Studies: A Tentative Bibliography*. [Melville Society Special Publication 1.] Austin, Tenn.: [Melville Society], 1958. Rpt. with addenda: 1959.

Jenkins Co. *Rare Books and Documents*. Catalogue 144. Austin: Jenkins, [1982].

Jerman, Bernard R. " 'With Real Admiration': More Correspondence Between Melville and Bentley." *American Literature* 25 (November 1953): 307–13.

Johnson, Merle, ed. *American First Editions: Bibliographic Check Lists of the Works of One Hundred and Five American Authors*. New York: Bowker, 1929. 2d ed.: 1932. 3d ed.: Rev. Jacob Blanck. 1936. 4th ed.: Rev. Jacob Blanck. 1942.

———. *High Spots of American Literature*. New York: Bennett, 1929.

Johnson, Richard Colles. "An Attempt at a Union List of Editions of Melville, 1846–91." *Book Collector* 19 (1970): 333–47.

———. "Melville in Anthologies." *American Book Collector* 21,8 (1971): 7–8.

Johnson, Thomas H. "Herman Melville." *Literary History of the United States: Bibliography*. Ed. Robert E. Spiller, et al. New York: Macmillan Co., 1948, pp. 647–54. Supplemented by Richard M. Ludwig. *Bibliography Supplement*, 1959, pp. 164–68. And by Ludwig. *Bibliography Supplement II*, 1972, pp. 218–22.

Jones, Buford. "Some 'Mosses' from the *Literary World*: Critical and Bibliographical Survey of the Hawthorne-Melville Relationship." *Ruined Eden of the Present: Hawthorne, Melville, and Poe*. Ed. G. R. Thompson, and Virgil L. Lokke. West Lafayette, Ind.: Purdue University Press, 1981, pp. 173–203.

Kennedy, Frederick James. "Dr. Samuel Arthur Jones and Herman Melville." *Melville Society Extracts* 32 (November 1977): 3–7.

Kohn, John S. Van E. *Herman Melville*. New York: Seven Gables Bookshop, [1952].

Lauterbach, Charles E., and Edward S. Lauterbach. "The Nineteenth Century

Three-Volume Novel." *Papers of the Bibliographical Society of America* 51 (1957): 263–302.

Leary, Lewis. *Articles on American Literature, 1900–1950.* Durham, N.C.: Duke University Press, 1954. [Subsequent volumes cover 1950–1967 (1970) and, with John Auchard, 1968–1975 (1979).]

Leon & Brother. *Catalogue of First Editions of American Authors.* New York: Leon, 1885.

Leyda, Jay. *The Melville Log.* 2 vols. New York: Harcourt, Brace, 1951. Rpt. with supplement: New York: Gordian Press, 1969.

Longman, publishers. [Entry for *The Confidence-Man.*] *Notes on Books* 1 (30 May 1857): 135.

McGrath, Daniel F. *Bookman's Price Index.* Detroit: Gale, 1964–

Maeno, Shigeru. *The Sources of Melville's Quotations.* Tokyo: Kaibunsha, [1981].

Maggs Brothers Ltd. *The Novel from Antiquity to the Present Day.* Catalogue 621. London: Maggs, 1936.

Madison, Mary K. *Books on Melville 1891–1981: A Checklist.* Evanston, Ill.: Loose-Fish Books, 1982.

———. "Melville's Sources: A Checklist." Ph.D. Diss., Northwestern University, 1984.

Mailloux, Steve, and Hershel Parker. *Checklist of Melville Reviews.* N.p.: Melville Society, 1975.

Mansfield, Luther S. "Melville's Comic Articles on Zachary Taylor." *American Literature* 9 (January 1938): 411–18.

Matthiessen, F. O. *American Renaissance: Art and Expression in the Age of Emerson and Whitman.* New York: Oxford University Press, 1941.

[Melville Elizabeth.] "Herman Melville's Works." *New York Times Saturday Review of Books and Art,* (5 October 1901): 706–707.

Melville, Gansevoort. "Gansevoort Melville's 1846 London Journal." Ed. Hershel Parker. *Bulletin of the New York Public Library* 69 (1965): 633–54; 70 (1966): 36–49, 113–31. Rpt. with additions: *Gansevoort Melville's 1846 London Journal and Letters from England, 1845.* New York: New York Public Library, 1966.

Melville Society. *Melville Society Newsletter* (1945–60); *Melville Society "Extracts"* (1969–71); *Extracts* (1972–February 1978); *Melville Society Extracts* (May 1978–   ).

Mills, Gordon H. "American First Editions at TxU: VII. Herman Melville (1819–1891)." *University of Texas Library Chronicle* 4.2 (1951): 89–92.

Minnigerode, Meade. "Herman Melville, 1819–1891." *Publishers' Weekly* 102 (18 November 1922): 1866.

———. *Some Personal Letters of Herman Melville and a Bibliography.* New York: Brick Row Book Shop, 1922.

Mumey, Nolie. *A Study of Rare Books.* Denver: Clason, 1930.

Myerson, Joel. "How Stands the Cause? The *Bibliography of American Literature* after a Quarter of a Century." *Papers of the Bibliographical Society of America* 78 (1984): 45–56.

———, and Arthur H. Miller, Jr. *Melville Dissertations: An Annotated Directory.* N.p.: Melville Society, 1972.

Newton, A. Edward. *The Format of the English Novel*. Cleveland: Rowfant Club, 1928.

———. *This Book-Collecting Game*. Boston: Little, Brown, 1928.

Nichol, John W. "Melville's ' "Soiled" Fish of the Sea.' " *American Literature* 21 (November 1949): 338–39.

Nowell-Smith, Simon. *International Copyright Law and the Publisher in the Reign of Queen Victoria*. Oxford: Clarendon Press, 1968.

Paltsits, Victor Hugo, ed. "Family Correspondence of Herman Melville, 1830–1904." *Bulletin of the New York Public Library* 33 (1929): 507–25, 575–625. Rpt.: New York: New York Public Library, 1929.

———. "Herman Melville's Background and New Light on the Publication of *Typee*." *Bookmen's Holiday: Notes and Studies Written and Gathered in Tribute to Harry Miller Lydenberg*. Ed. Deoch Fulton. New York: New York Public Library, 1943. 248–68.

Parke-Bernet Galleries. *The William E. Stockhausen Collection of English and American Literature*. Part I. New York: Parke-Bernet, 1974.

Parker, Hershel. "Contract: *Pierre*, by Herman Melville." *Proof* 5 (1977): 27–44.

———. "Evidence for 'Late Insertions' in Melville's Works." *Studies in the Novel* 7 (1975): 407–24.

———. "Five Reviews Not in *Moby-Dick as Doubloon*." *English Language Notes* 9 (1972): 182–85.

———. *Flawed Texts and Verbal Icons: Literary Authority in American Fiction*. Evanston, Ill.: Northwestern University Press, 1984.

———. "Melville and the Concept of 'Author's Final Intentions.' " *Proof* 1 (1971): 156–68.

———. "The 'New Scholarship': Textual Evidence and Its Implications for Criticism, Literary Theory, and Aesthetics." *Studies in American Fiction* 9 (Autumn 1981): 181–97.

———. "Practical Editions: Herman Melville's *Moby-Dick*." *Proof* 3 (1973): 371–78.

———, ed. *The Recognition of Herman Melville: Selected Criticism since 1846*. Ann Arbor: University of Michigan Press, 1967.

———. "A Reexamination of *Melville's Reviewers*." *American Literature* 42 (1970): 226–32.

———. "Regularizing Accidentals: The Latest Form of Infidelity." *Proof* 3 (1973): 1–20.

———. Rev. of Irey Concordance to *Moby-Dick* (1982). *Analytical & Enumerative Bibliography* 7 (1983): 54–57.

———. "Why *Pierre* Went Wrong." *Studies in the Novel* 8 (1976): 7–23.

———, and Harrison Hayford, eds. *Moby-Dick as Doubloon: Essays and Extracts (1851–1970)*. New York: W.W. Norton, 1970.

Petty, George R., Jr., and William M. Gibson. *Project OCCULT: The Ordered Computer Collation of Unprepared Literary Text*. New York: New York University Press, 1970.

Phelps, Leland R. *A Preliminary Check-List of Foreign Language Materials on the Life and Works of Herman Melville*. Melville Society Special Publication 2. [Evanston, Ill.: Melville Society,] 1960.

———. *A Preliminary Check-List of the Works of Herman Melville in Translation*.

Melville Society Special Publication 2, part 2. [Evanston, Ill.: Melville Society,] 1961.

————, with Kathleen McCullough. *Herman Melville's Foreign Reputation: A Research Guide*. Boston: G.K. Hall, 1983.

Phillips, Son & Neale. *Autograph Letters, Documents and Manuscripts*. Catalogue 529. New York: Phillips, 1984.

Phillpotts, Eden. *The Red Redmaynes*. New York: Macmillan Co., 1922.

Potter, David. "The Brodhead Diaries 1846–1849." *Journal of the Rutgers University Library* 11 (1947): 21–27.

Quaritch, Booksellers. *Miscellany 6 of English Literature with Some American Books and Some Manuscripts*. Bulletin n.s. 20. London: Quaritch, 1984.

Randall, David A. *Dukedom Large Enough*. New York: Random House, 1969.

————, and John T. Winterich. "One Hundred Good Novels . . . 'Moby-Dick.' " *Publishers' Weekly* 137 (1940): 255–57.

Rice, Howard C., Jr., Alexander D. Wainwright, Julie Hudson, and Alexander P. Clark. "Moby-Dick by Herman Melville: A Century of an American Classic, 1851–1951, A Catalogue of an Exhibition." *Princeton University Library Chronicle* 13.2 (Winter 1952): 63–118.

Ricks, Beatrice, and Joseph D. Adams. *Herman Melville: A Reference Bibliography, 1900–1972, with Selected Nineteenth Century Materials*. Boston: G.K. Hall, 1973.

Roper, Gordon. "Bibliography of Works by and on Herman Melville." N.p.: Mimeographed, [1950].

Sabin, Joseph. "Melville, Herman." *Bibliotheca Americana: A Dictionary of Books Relating to America*. 29 vols. New York: Sabin (later Bibliographical Society of America), 1868–1936; vol. 11 (1879): 577.

Sadleir, Michael. "Bibliography of the First Editions of the Prose Works of Herman Melville." *The Works of Herman Melville*. 16 vols. London: Constable, 1922–24. 12 (1923): 337–58.

————. "Herman Melville." *Excursions in Victorian Bibliography*. London: Chaundy & Cox, 1922. pp. 217–33.

————. *XIX Century Fiction; A Bibliographical Record Based on His Own Collection*. 2 vols. London: Constable; Berkeley: University of California Press, 1951.

Scharnhorst, Gary. "Addenda to the Melville Bibliography, 1850–1928." *Melville Society Extracts* 47 (September 1981): 15–16.

Schwartz, Jacob. *1100 Obscure Points: The Bibliographies of 25 English and 21 American Authors*. London: Ulysses Bookshop, 1931.

Scorza, Thomas J. *In the Time Before Steamships: Billy Budd, the Limits of Politics, and Modernity*. DeKalb: Northern Illinois University Press, 1979.

Sealts, Merton M., Jr. "The Chronology of Melville's Short Fiction, 1853–1856." *Harvard Library Bulletin* 28 (1980): 391–403.

————. *The Early Lives of Melville: Nineteenth-Century Biographical Sketches and Their Authors*. Madison: University of Wisconsin Press, 1974.

————. "Melville's Reading: A Check-List of Books Owned and Borrowed." *Harvard Library Bulletin* 2 (1948): 141–63, 378–92; 3 (1949): 119–30, 268–77, 407–21; 4 (1950): 98–109. Supplemented by "Melville's Reading: A Supplementary List of Books Owned and Borrowed." 6 (1952): 239–47.

————. *Melville's Reading: A Check-List of Books Owned and Borrowed*. Madison:

University of Wisconsin Press, 1966. Supplemented by "A Supplementary Note to *Melville's Reading* (1966)." *Harvard Library Bulletin* 19 (1971): 280–84. And by "A Second Supplementary Note. . . ." 27 (1979): 330–35.

———. "The Publication of Melville's *Piazza Tales*." *Modern Language Notes* 59 (1944): 56–59.

———. *Pursuing Melville 1940–1980*. Madison: University of Wisconsin Press, 1982.

Sherman, Stuart, John H. Birss, and Gordon Roper. *Annual Melville Bibliography 1951*. Providence, R.I.: Public Library, [1952].

———. *Melville Bibliography 1952–1957*. Providence, R.I.: Public Library, 1959.

Simon, Jean. *Herman Melville: Marin, métaphysicien et poète*. Paris: Boivin, 1939.

Smiles, Samuel. *A Publisher and His Friends: Memoir and Correspondence of the Late John Murray*. 2 vols. London: Murray, 1891.

Stafford, William T. "An Annotated Checklist of Studies of *Billy Budd*." *Melville's Billy Budd and the Critics*. Ed. Stafford. San Francisco: Wadsworth, 1961. 2d ed.: Belmont, Calif.: Wadsworth, 1968, pp. 263–72.

Starosciak, Kenneth. *Re: Herman Melville*. New Brighton, Minn.: Starosciak, [1973].

Stern, Milton R. *The Fine-Hammered Steel of Herman Melville*. Urbana: University of Illinois Press, 1957.

Stone, Herbert Stuart. *First Editions of American Authors: A Manual for Book-Lovers*. Cambridge, Mass.: Stone & Kimball, 1893.

Storm, Colton, and Howard Peckham. *Invitation to Book Collecting: Its Pleasures and Practices*. New York: Bowker, 1947.

Sutherland, J. A. *Victorian Novelists and Publishers*. London: Athlone, 1976.

Tanselle, G. Thomas. "BAL Addenda: Melville." *Papers of the Bibliographical Society of America* 72 (1978): 243–45.

———. "Bibliographical Problems in Melville." *Studies in American Fiction* 2 (1974): 57–74.

———. *A Checklist of Editions of Moby-Dick, 1851–1976*. Evanston and Chicago: Northwestern University Press and the Newberry Library, 1976.

———. "The Editorial Problem of Final Authorial Intention." *Studies in Bibliography* 29 (1976): 167–211. Rpt.: *Selected Studies*, pp. 309–54.

———. "External Fact as an Editorial Problem." *Studies in Bibliography* 32 (1979): 1–47. Rpt.: *Selected Studies*, pp. 355–402.

———. "Greg's Theory of Copy-Text and the Editing of American Literature." *Studies in Bibliography* 28 (1975): 167–229. Rpt.: *Selected Studies*, pp. 245–308.

———. *Guide to the Study of United States Imprints*. 2 vols. Cambridge, Mass.: Belknap Press of Harvard University Press, 1971.

———. Letter on reprints in the *BAL*. *Papers of the Bibliographical Society of America* 73 (1979): 371.

———. "Non-Firsts." In *Collectible Books: Some New Paths*. Ed. Jean Peters. New York: Bowker, 1979, pp. 1–31.

———. "Recent Editorial Discussion and the Central Questions of Editing." *Studies in Bibliography* 34 (1981): 23–65.

———. "The Sales of Melville's Books." *Harvard Library Bulletin* 17 (1969): 195–215.

————. *Selected Studies in Bibliography.* Charlottesville: University Press of Virginia, 1979.

————. "Textual Study and Literary Judgment." *Papers of the Bibliographical Society of America* 65 (1971): 109–22.

————. "Two Melville Association Copies: The Hubbard *Whale* and the Jones *Moby-Dick.*" *Book Collector* 31 (1982): 170–86, 309–30.

————. "*Typee* and De Voto: A Footnote." *Papers of the Bibliographical Society of America* 64 (1970): 207–209.

————. "*Typee* and De Voto Once More." *Papers of the Bibliographical Society of America* 62 (1968): 601–604.

Taylor, Walter Fuller. *A History of American Letters.* Bibliographies by Harry Hartwick. New York: American Book Co., 1936.

Tsunematsu, Masao, and Sanford E. Marovitz. "A Bibliography of Herman Melville Studies in Japan." *Memoirs of the Faculty of Law and Literature: Literature* [Shimane University] 2 (1979): 13–68.

Van Doren, Carl. "Fiction II: Comtemporaries of Cooper." *The Cambridge History of American Literature.* Ed. W. P. Trent et al. 4 vols. New York: Putnam, 1917–21. 1: 307–25, 536–38.

————. "A Note of Confession." *Nation* 127 (1928): 622.

Vann, J. Don. "A Selected Checklist of Melville Criticism, 1958–1968." *Studies in the Novel* 1 (Winter 1969): 507–35.

Vincent, Howard P. *The Merrill Checklist of Herman Melville.* Columbus, Ohio: Merrill, 1969.

————. *The Tailoring of Melville's White-Jacket.* Evanston, Ill.: Northwestern University Press, 1970.

————. *The Trying-Out of Moby-Dick.* Boston: Houghton Mifflin, 1949.

Weaver, Raymond M. *Herman Melville: Mariner and Mystic.* New York: Doran, 1921.

Wenke, Joseph. "An Annotated Bibliography of *Typee* Studies." *Critical Essays on Herman Melville's Typee.* Boston: G.K. Hall, 1982, pp. 259–314.

Wegelin, Oscar. "Herman Melville as I Recall Him." *Colophon* n.s. 1 (1935–36): 21–24.

Wegener, Larry Edward. *A Concordance to Herman Melville's Clarel: A Poem and Pilgrimage in the Holy Land.* 3 vols. N.p.: Melville Society, 1979.

————. *A Concordance to Herman Melville's Pierre; or, The Ambiguities.* New York: Garland, 1985.

Wells, Daniel A. "Melville Allusions in *Harper's New Monthly Magazine,* 1850–1900." *Melville Society Extracts* 48 (November 1981): 12–13.

Whitcomb, Selden L. *Chronological Outlines of American Literature.* New York: Macmillan Co., 1894.

Williams, Mentor L. "Some Notices and Reviews of Melville's Novels in American Religious Periodicals, 1846–1849." *American Literature* 22 (May 1950): 119–27.

Williams, Stanley T. "Melville." *Eight American Authors: A Review of Research and Criticism.* Ed. Floyd Stovall. New York: Modern Language Association, 1956, pp. 207–70. Rpt. with "Bibliographical Supplement" by J. Chesley Matthews. New York: W.W. Norton, 1963, pp. 438–45.

Wilson, Carroll A. "Herman Melville." *Thirteen Author Collections of the Nineteenth*

Century and Five Centuries of Familiar Quotations. Ed. Jean C. S. Wilson and David A. Randall. 2 vols. New York: Privately printed for Scribner, 1950, pp. 305–16.

Wilson, James C. "The Hawthorne-Melville Relationship: An Annotated Bibliography." *American Transcendental Quarterly* 45/46 (1982): 1–79. Rpt.: Kingston, R.I.: American Transcendental Quarterly, University of Rhode Island, 1982.

Winterich, John T. *Collector's Choice*. New York: Greenberg, 1928.

———. *A Primer of Book Collecting*. New York: Greenberg, 1926. Rev. ed.: 1935.

Wolf, Edwin, 2nd, with John F. Fleming. *Rosenbach: A Biography*. Cleveland: World, 1960.

Woodress, James, ed. (later alternating with J. Albert Robbins; 1983 vol. ed. Warren French). *American Literary Scholarship: An Annual*. Durham, N.C.: Duke University Press, 1965–   .

Wright, Nathalia. "Herman Melville." *Eight American Authors: A Review of Research and Criticism*. Rev. ed. Ed. James Woodress. New York: W.W. Norton, 1971, pp. 173–224.

Zimmerman, Michael P. "Herman Melville in the 1920's: A Study in the Origins of the Melville Revival, with an Annotated Bibliography." Ph.D. Diss., Columbia University, 1963. [*Mel. Diss.*, #121.]

———. "Herman Melville in the 1920's: An Annotated Bibliography." *Bulletin of Bibliography* 24 (1963–66): 117–20, 106, 139–44.

Works by Melville

Collected Sets

The Works of Herman Melville. 16 vols. London: Constable, 1922–24. [Vol. 13, edited by Raymond M. Weaver, is *Billy Budd and Other Prose Pieces*, 1924.] Rpt.: New York: Russell & Russell, 1963. Tokyo: Meicho Fukyu Kai, 1983.

The Complete Works of Herman Melville. Ed. Howard P. Vincent et al. 7 vols. to date. Chicago (later New York): Hendricks House, 1947–   .

The Writings of Herman Melville: The Northwestern-Newberry Edition. Ed. Harrison Hayford, Hershel Parker, G. Thomas Tanselle, et al. 8 vols. to date. Evanston, Ill.: Northwestern University Press; Chicago: The Newberry Library, 1968–   . [The historical essays in the volumes thus far published are by Leon Howard (*Typee*, 1968), Gordon Roper (*Omoo*, 1968), Elizabeth S. Foster (*Mardi*, 1970), Hershel Parker (*Redburn*, 1969), Willard Thorp (*White-Jacket*, 1970), Leon Howard and Hershel Parker (*Pierre*, 1971), Walter E. Bezanson (*Israel Potter*, 1982), and Watson Branch, Hershel Parker, and Harrison Hayford, with Alma A. MacDougall (*The Confidence-Man*, 1984).]

Herman Melville. Notes by G. Thomas Tanselle (vols. 1, 2) and Harrison Hayford (vol. 3). 3 vols. to date. New York: Library of America, 1982–

Composite Volumes

The Piazza Tales. New York: Dix & Edwards, 1856.

Battle-Pieces. New York: Harper, 1866.

John Marr and Other Sailors. New York: De Vinne Press, 1888.

Timoleon. New York: Caxton Press, 1891.

The Apple-Tree Table and Other Sketches. Ed. Henry Chapin. Princeton, N.J.: Princeton University Press, 1922.

John Marr and Other Poems. Ed. Henry Chapin. Princeton, N.J.: Princeton University Press, 1922.

Romances of Herman Melville. New York: Pickwick, 1928.

Shorter Novels. Ed. Raymond M. Weaver. Black & Gold Library. New York: Liveright, 1928.

Herman Melville: Representative Selections. Ed. Willard Thorp. New York: American Book Co., 1938.

Selected Poems. Ed. William Plomer. New Hogarth Library 10. London: Hogarth Press, 1943.

Selected Poems. Ed. F. O. Matthiessen. Poets of the Year Series. Norfolk, Conn.: New Directions, 1944.

The Complete Stories of Herman Melville. Ed. Jay Leyda. New York: Random House, 1949.

Selected Tales and Poems. Ed. Richard Chase. Rinehart Editions. New York: Rinehart, 1950.

The Portable Melville. Ed. Jay Leyda. New York: Viking Press, 1952.

"Texts of Lectures, with Commentary." Ed. Merton M. Sealts, Jr. *Melville as Lecturer*. By Sealts. Cambridge, Mass.: Harvard University Press, 1957, pp. 125–85.

The Letters of Herman Melville. Ed. Merrell R. Davis and William H. Gilman. New Haven, Conn.: Yale University Press, 1960.

"Poems by Herman Melville: A Critical Edition of the Published Verse." Ed. Norman E. Jarrard. Ph.D. Diss., University of Texas, 1960. [*Mel. Diss.*, #92.]

"Melville's Marginalia." Ed. Wilson Walker Cowen. Ph.D. Diss., Harvard University, 1965. [*Mel. Diss.*, #134.]

Billy Budd, Sailor and Other Stories. Ed. Harold Beaver. Penguin English Library. Harmondsworth: Penguin Books, 1967.

"*Weeds and Wildings Chiefly: With a Rose or Two* by Herman Melville: Reading Text and Genetic Text." Ed. Robert C. Ryan. Ph.D. Diss., Northwestern University, 1967. [*Mel. Diss.*, #167.]

Selected Poems of Herman Melville. Ed. Robert Penn Warren. New York: Random House, 1970.

Shorter Works of Hawthorne and Melville. Ed. Hershel Parker. Columbus, Ohio: Merrill, 1972.

Volumes Containing Single Works

Narrative of a Four Month's Residence Among the Natives of a Valley of the Marquesas Islands. London: Murray, 1846.

———. [With "The Story of Toby."] London: Murray, 1846.

Typee. New York: Wiley & Putnam, 1846.

———. Rev. ed. New York: Wiley & Putnam, 1846.

———. London: Gibbs, 1850.

———. London: Routledge, 1850.

———. Ed. and introd. Arthur Stedman. New York: United States Book Co., 1892.

———. With memoir by Henry S. Salt. London: Murray, 1893.

———. Introd. W. P. Trent. Boston: Heath, 1902.

———. London: Lane, 1904.

———. Everyman's Library. London: Dent, 1907.

———. The World's Classics. London: Oxford University Press, 1924.

———. Ed. Harrison Hayford. Signet Classics. New York: New American Library, 1964.

———. Ed. George Woodcock. Penguin English Library. Harmondsworth: Penguin Books, 1972.

Omoo. London: Murray, 1847.

———. New York: Harper, 1847.

———. London: Routledge, 1850.

———. [Ed. Arthur Stedman.] New York: United States Book Co., 1892.

———. With memoir by Henry S. Salt. London: Murray, 1893.

———. London: Lane, 1904.

———. Everyman's Library. London: Dent, 1908.

———. The World's Classics. London: Oxford University Press, 1924.

Mardi. 3 vols. London: Bentley, 1849.

———. 2 vols. New York: Harper, 1849.

———. Ed. Raymond M. Weaver. Pequod Edition. New York: Boni, 1925.

———. Ed. Tyrus Hillway. New Haven, Conn.: College & University Press, 1973.

Redburn. 2 vols. London: Bentley, 1849.

———. New York: Harper, 1849.

———. Baudry's European Library. Paris: Galignani, 1850.

———. Ed. Raymond M. Weaver. Pequod Edition. New York: Boni, 1924.

White-Jacket. 2 vols. London: Bentley, 1850.

———. New York: Harper, 1850.

———. [Ed. Arthur Stedman.] New York: United States Book Co., 1892.

———. The World's Classics. London: Oxford University Press, 1924.

———. Ed. A. R. Humphreys. London: Oxford University Press, 1966.

———. Ed. Hennig Cohen. Rinehart Editions. New York: Rinehart, 1967.

The Whale. 3 vols. London: Bentley, 1851.

Moby-Dick. New York: Harper, 1851.

———. [Ed. Arthur Stedman.] New York: United States Book Co., 1892.

———. New York: Scribner, 1899.

———. Introd. Louis Becke. London: Putnam, 1901.

———. Everyman's Library. London: Dent, 1907.

———. Introd. Viola Meynell. The World's Classics. London: Oxford University Press, 1920.

———. Ed. Raymond M. Weaver. Pequod Edition. New York: Boni, 1925.

———. New York: Modern Library, 1926.

―――. Ill. Rockwell Kent. Chicago: Lakeside Press, 1930.

―――. Ed. Willard Thorp. New York: Oxford University Press, 1947.

―――. Ed. Newton Arvin. Rinehart Editions. New York: Rinehart, 1948.

―――. Ed. Alfred Kazin. Riverside Editions. Boston: Houghton Mifflin, 1956.

―――. Ed. Charles Feidelson. Library of Literature. Indianapolis: Bobbs-Merrill, 1964.

―――. Ed. Harrison Hayford and Hershel Parker. Norton Critical Editions. New York: W.W. Norton, 1967.

―――. Ed. Harold Beaver. Penguin English Library. Harmondsworth: Penguin Books, 1972.

Pierre. New York: Harper, 1852.

―――. London: Sampson Low, 1852.

―――. Ed. Robert S. Forsythe. Americana Deserta Series. New York: Alfred A. Knopf, 1930.

The Encantadas. Ed. Victor Wolfgang von Hagen. Burlingame, Calif.: Wreden, 1940.

"Benito Cereno." *A Benito Cereno Handbook.* Ed. Seymour L. Gross. Belmont, Calif.: Wadsworth, 1965, pp. 1–70.

―――. Melville's Benito Cereno: A Textbook for Guided Research. Ed. John P. Runden. Boston: D.C. Heath, 1965, pp. 1–75.

Israel Potter. New York: Putnam, 1855.

―――. London: Sampson Low, 1855.

―――. London: Routledge, 1855.

[―――.] *The Refugee.* Philadelphia: Peterson, 1865.

―――. Ed. Raymond M. Weaver. Pequod Edition. New York: Boni, 1924.

The Confidence-Man. New York: Dix & Edwards, 1857.

―――. London: Longman, 1857.

―――. London: Lehmann, 1948.

―――. New York: Grove Press, 1949.

―――. Ed. Hennig Cohen. Rinehart Editions. New York: Rinehart, 1964.

―――. Ed. H. Bruce Franklin. Library of Literature. Indianapolis: Bobbs-Merrill, 1967.

―――. Ed. Watson Branch. Ph.D. Diss., Northwestern University, 1970. [*Mel. Diss.*, #223.]

―――. Ed. Hershel Parker. Norton Critical Editions. New York: W.W. Norton, 1971.

Clarel. New York: Putnam, 1876.

Melville's Billy Budd. Ed. F. Barron Freeman. Cambridge, Mass.: Harvard University Press, 1948. With Elizabeth Treeman's *Corrigenda*, 1953.

Billy Budd, Sailor. Ed. Harrison Hayford and Merton M. Sealts, Jr. Chicago: University of Chicago Press, 1962.

―――. Ed. Milton Stern. Library of Literature. Indianapolis: Bobbs-Merrill, 1975.

[Journals.] "Journal of Melville's Voyage in a Clipper Ship." *New England Quarterly* 2 (1929): 120–39.

―――. *Journal up the Straits.* Ed. Raymond M. Weaver. New York: Colophon, 1935.

————. *Journal of a Visit to London and the Continent.* Ed. Eleanor Melville Metcalf. Cambridge, Mass.: Harvard University Press, 1948.

————. *Journal of a Visit to Europe and the Levant.* Ed. Howard C. Horsford. Princeton, N.J.: Princeton University Press, 1955.

GENERAL INDEX

Arabic Translations, 761
Arac, Jonathan, 470 n.20
Archer, Lewis Franklin, 656
Archetypal symbols, 527
Archie, 720
Architecture, 654
Arcturion (*Mardi*), 171
Arcturus, 72. *See also* Mathews,
  Charles
Arendt, Hannah, 688
Aristocracy, 747
Aristotelian Tragedy, 357. *See also*
  Elizabethan Drama; Tragedy
Aristotle, 544–45, 568, 569, 592
Arms, George, 422
Arnold, Armin, 670
Arnold, Fritz Volquard, 757
Arnold, Matthew, 393, 568, 592, 595
  n.2, 644, 650, 657
Arrowhead, 178
Art of Concealment, 249
"Art," 364, 463, 556, 650; as guide to
  HM's aesthetics, 626
Articles on American Literature (Leary),
  800
Artist, 643; alienated, 683
Arvin, Newton, 24–25, 107, 137, 147,
  151, 191, 236 n.1, 249, 261, 265,
  266, 287, 303, 308, 351, 352, 389,
  393, 412, 422, 469 n.15, 470 n.15,
  524, 596 n.8, 813; scorn for tales,
  248
"At Melville's Tomb" (Hart Crane),
  674
"At the Hostelry," 410, 654
Atkins, Thomas, 703
Auden, W. H., 202, 616, 676–78;
  post-romantic christian ideology,
  676; use of *MD*, 676; and *BBS*,
  676–77; his didacticism, 677
Auld, Jedediah B., 100
Aurelius, Marcus, 568, 592
Austria, 757
"Authentic Edens in a Pagan Sea,"
  411
Authenticity: problem of fact vs. fiction, 170
Authority, 258, 439, 446, 448, 453,

455, 465, 498, 639; denunciation
  of 7; in *Omoo*, 110, 164; as joke,
  446
Autobiography 146, 149, 154, 220,
  221, 253, 747; Anderson's opposition to, 104; problem of, in HM's
  work, 3, 15, 19, 20–21, 40
Avallone, C. Sherman, 270
Avallone, Charlene, 229, 231
Avicenna, 563 n.3
Axelrod, Steven, 686

Mrs. B., 222. *See also* Mrs., A.M.A.;
  Melvill, Allan
B.C., 716
Babbalanja (*Mardi*), 124, 127, 129,
  447, 571, 574, 577, 581, 589, 587,
  619; as frantic Socrates, 575; as
  relativist, 575; as precursor to Ish-
  mael, 575
Babin, James L., 112
Babo ("Benito Cereno"), 105
Bach, Bert C., 471 n.23, 646
Bacon, Francis, 545, 593
Bagley, Carol L., 524
Bahlke, George W., 677
Baiae (Italy), 53
Baird, James, 100, 102, 103, 106,
  138, 196, 392, 502, 503, 639
Bakeless, John 467 n.1
Baker, James, R., 689
Bakhtin, Mikhail, 342
Baldini, Gabriele, 765
Ballard, Mister: as Falsgrave (*Pierre*),
  221
Ballenger, Sara Elizabeth, 756
Balzac, Honoré, 649
Banta, Martha, 596 n.8
Banvard, John, 329
Barbarow, George, 705
Barber Shop Motif, 329
Barber, Edwin and Virginia Price,
  787
Barber, Giles, 787
Barbour, James, 176, 331, 595 n.2
Barbour, John D., 498
Baritz, Loren, 467 n.1
Barker-Benfield, G. J., 229

not autobiography, 21; biographical parallels in, 149; invented scenes in, 150; sources and composition, 150; reviews of, 150–51, 743; editions of, 151; HM's contempt for, 145; as autobiography, 146, 149; internationalism of, 451; Launcelott's-Hey scene, 148; narrative structure, 147; spiritual hunger in, 147; awakening of HM's tragic sense, 151; characterization in, 151; greenhorn sailor tradition, 21; Jackson as Cain, 148; guide books in, 48; immigrants in, 149; oppressed masses in, 451; temperance society, 148; aristocracy in, 151; humor in, 151; inconsistent archetypal myth in, 151; initiation theme, 152; Adamic myth, 152; symbolism in, 153; Ishmael in, 187; narrative voice in, 152, 223; translations of, French (pirated), 750; German, 754; future study, 164

Redeemer Figure: in poems, 353

Redfield, Justus, 69, 79n.8, 226. *See also* Duyckincks

Reed, Henry, 718–19

Rees, Robert A., 139

Reeves, Paschal, 331

Reeves, Randall R., 195

Reformation, 495

Regelson, Abraham, 763

Regent's Park, 46

Reich, Charles A., 464, 498

Relativism, 575, 584–87; Winters's reaction to, 679

Religio Medici (Browne), 574

Religion: as varied phenomena, 481–82; varied conceptions of, 482–83; partial view of, 482; normative view, 483; critical bias in discussion of, 483–84; confusion of expression and belief, 484; normative Christian bias, 484; and imaginative context, 485; development of 19th protestantism, 486–87; as social experience, 487; pious fiction,

492; theories of, 500–506; and psychology, 528

Religion and Melville: Pacific experience, 490; Skepticism, 494; prophetic tradition, 494; jeremiad, 494; Millennialism, 494; traditional protestantism, 494–95; use of the Bible, 495–97; in the social and literary context, 498–99, 504 n.1; civil religion, 498–99, 508 n.5; aesthetics and theories of religious expression, 500–506, 508 n.6; imagination and models of religion, 501, 508 n.9; psychological approach, 502, 528; theories of consciousness, 503; language and style, 503–504; cognition, cosmology, and epistemology, 504–505. *See also* Calvinism; Protestantism; Puritanism; Religion; individual denominations.

Repose, 649

The Republic (Plato), 463, 579, 592

Reputation, xviii; at death, 16; and study of editions, 805. *See also* Readers; Reception

Reputation Abroad: post-WWII trends, 742; British, 743–50; French, 750–54; German, 754–58; Spanish and Portuguese, 758–60; Greek, 760–61; Turkish, 761; Arabic, 761–62; Indian, 762; Hebrew, 762–63; Italian, 763–66; Dutch and Scandanavian, 767; Japanese, Chinese, Korean, and Southeast Asian, 768–70; Eastern European, 771–73; Russian, 773–75

Rescher, Nicholas, 563 n.3

"Resolution and Independence," 254

Restaurants, 724

Reveille, 72. *See also* Mathews, Charles

Revivalism, 342, 486, 490, 492. *See also* Apocalypse; Millennialism

Revolution, 637, 648, 686, 690; in *Clarel*, 400

Revolutionary War, 282

Reynolds, David S., 492

Reynolds, J. N., 195

INDEX OF AUTHORS CITED

Master list of authors cited in the *Companion* bibliographies.

ABOUT THE CONTRIBUTORS

JAMES BARBOUR, Associate Professor of English at the University of New Mexico, is co-editor of *American Literary Realism: 1870–1910* and *Critical Essays in American Literature: Realism*. Winner of the 1975 Norman Foerster Award, he has published articles in *American Literature, New England Quarterly, ESQ, Studies in Short Fiction* and other journals. Currently he is editing a collection of essays on the composition of certain American classics.

JOHANNES D. BERGMANN is Chair of the American Studies Faculty at George Mason University. He has published articles on Melville and the nineteenth-century American city in *American Literature, American Quarterly, Prospects*, and *Melville Society Extracts*. He is working on *God in the Street*, a book on perceptions of New York City in the 1840s and 1850s, and (with Harriet Bergmann) on *The Literary Contents of the New York Tribune, 1841–1851*.

WALTER E. BEZANSON was born in New England. His graduate study at Yale and combat duty in the Pacific aboard the carrier *Intrepid* jointly encouraged an interest in Melville. Since then he has taught American Studies and English at Yale, Dartmouth, Harvard, Liège (Fulbright chair) and has recently retired from Rutgers. He has edited the Hendricks House *Clarel* (1960) and provided the historical note for the Northwestern-Newberry edition of *Israel Potter* (1982). His critical essays include "Moby-Dick: Work of Art" reprinted in the Norton Critical Edition.

MARTIN BICKMAN is Associate Professor of English at the University of Colorado, where he won the Teaching Excellence Award in 1984. He is author of *The Unsounded Centre: Jungian Studies in American Romanticism* (1980) and editor of the MLA volume *Approaches to Teaching Melville's Moby-Dick* (1985). His reviews appear regularly in *Library Journal*.

WATSON BRANCH has taught at the University of California at Santa Barbara, the University of Cincinnati, and Upsala University, where he was Fulbright Professor of American Literature from 1983 to 1985. Now he lives with his wife and two sons in La Jolla where he spends his mornings writing and his afternoons managing the household. Editor of *Melville: The Critical Heritage* (1974), he has also published essays on Melville, Hawthorne, Twain, James, Howells, and Faulkner.

JOHN BRYANT, editor of this volume, is Associate Professor of English at Hofstra University. A graduate of the University of Chicago, he has taught at Chicago, the Universities of Genoa and Turin (as a Fulbright Lecturer), Widener College, and the Pennsylvania State University. He published *Melville Dissertations, 1926–1980* (1983) and has written articles on Melville in *American Literature, Nineteenth-Century Fiction, Philological Quarterly, ELN*, and *Melville Society Extracts*, and on composition in the *Journal of General Education*. Once his pre-occupation with *A Companion to Melville Studies* ceases, he plans to complete his book *Melville, Humor and the Aesthetics of Repose*.

HENNIG COHEN is the John Welsh Centennial Professor in the History of English Literature at the University of Pennsylvania. A native of Darlington, South Carolina, and graduate of Tulane University, he has served as Executive Secretary of the American Studies Association, Editor of *American Quarterly*, and Secretary and President of the Melville Society. His publications include editions of *Battle-Pieces, Selected Poems, White-Jacket*, and *The Confidence-Man*, as well as numerous articles on Melville. He has received fellowships from the National Endowment for the Humanities, the Guggenheim Foundation, and the Newberry Library. His Fulbright appointments include the Universities of London and Budapest.

SHIRLEY M. DETTLAFF is English Teacher and Department Chairperson at Glendale High School in California, where she has taught since 1963. She received her doctorate in 1978 from the University of Southern California. Her publications include "The Concept of Beauty in 'The Artist of the Beautiful' and Hugh Blair's *Rhetoric*" in *Studies in Short Fiction* and "Ionian Form and Esau's Waste: Melville's View of Art in *Clarel*" in *American Literature*.

THOMAS FAREL HEFFERNAN received his doctorate from Columbia University and is a Professor of English at Adelphi University. He is the author of *Stove by a Whale: Owen Chase and the Essex* (1981), a study of the episode that furnished Melville with the climactic action of *Moby-Dick*. He has also written "Melville and Wordsworth," and a variety of scholarly and popular articles on Melville and other subjects.

WILSON HEFLIN, whose death in November 1985 came shortly after the completion of his contribution to this volume, earned his doctorate from Vanderbilt University and was a Professor of English at the United States Naval Academy. He is the author of a number of important scholarly articles on Melville including "Melville's Third Whaler," in which he identified the *Charles and Henry* as the ship on which Melville served in 1842–43. Professor Heflin's major work, *Melville's Whaling Years*, is to be published posthumously.

BRIAN HIGGINS is Associate Professor of English at the University of Illinois at Chicago. Among his publications are *Herman Melville: An Annotated Bibliography* (1979) and *Critical Essays on Herman Melville's Pierre: Or, The Ambiguities* (1983; edited with Hershel Parker). Since 1984 he has written the annual chapter on Melville for *American Literary Scholarship*.

M. THOMAS INGE is Robert Emory Blackwell Professor of Humanities at Randolph-Macon College where he teaches American studies and interdisciplinary courses. As a Fulbright Lecturer, he has taught in Spain, Argentina, and the Soviet Union, and as Resident Scholar in American Studies with the USIA, he lectured in some twenty countries abroad. His publications on American literature and culture include Greenwood's three-volume *Handbook of American Popular Culture* (1981). He has edited a volume on "Bartleby" and is writing a book-length study of Melville in popular culture.

VINCENT KENNY is Professor Emeritus at Marymount College, Tarrytown, New York. His work on Melville includes *Herman Melville's CLAREL* (1973) and two articles in *ATQ*. He has also written a study of the North Carolina novelist and playwright Paul Green (1971) and a profile of a minor New York poet Abigail Cole (1981). He is now attending to Emily Dickinson, Walker Percy, peach trees, people, and Cape Cod.

SANFORD E. MAROVITZ, Professor of English at Kent State University, where he has taught since 1967, earned his doctorate from Duke University. He has been a Woodrow Wilson Fellow (1960–1), a Fulbright Teaching Grantee in English (Greece, 1965–7), and a Visiting Professor of English at Shimane University, Japan (1976–7). In 1985 he received the Distinguished Teaching Award at Kent State. Co-editor of *Artful Thunder: Versions of the Romantic Tradition in American Literature in Honor of Howard P. Vincent* (1975) and co-compiler of *Bibliographical Guide to the Study of the Literature of the U.S.A.*, 5th ed. (1984), Professor Marovitz has published widely in critical collections and professional journals, mostly on nineteenth- and twentieth-century American topics including Melville, the American Renaissance, and Jewish fiction.

HERSHEL PARKER is H. Fletcher Brown Professor of American Romanticism at the University of Delaware. An Associate General Editor of the Northwestern-Newberry edition of *The Writings of Herman Melville*, he has published critical editions of *Moby-Dick* (with Harrison Hayford) and *The Confidence-Man*, and is editor of the 1820–1865 period in *The Norton Anthology of American Literature*. His recent book *Flawed Texts and Verbal Icons: Literary Authority in American Fiction* (1984) attempts to bring together literary, editorial, creativity, and cognitive theories.

EDWARD H. ROSENBERRY is Professor Emeritus at the University of Delaware, where he has served as Chairman of the English Department and Acting Dean of the College of Arts and Sciences. Among his publications are *Melville and the Comic Spirit* (1955), *Melville* (1979), and critical essays on Melville and other American authors in periodicals such as *PMLA*, *New England Quarterly*, and *American Literature*. He was president of the Melville Society in 1981. His post-retirement travel and study have focused on Biblical history and language.

MERTON M. SEALTS, Jr., is Henry A. Pochmann Professor of English, Emeritus, University of Wisconsin-Madison. Co-editor of Melville's *Billy Budd, Sailor* (1962), he is also the author of *Melville as Lecturer* (1957), *Melville's Reading* (1966), *The Early Lives of Melville* (1974), and *Pursuing Melville, 1940–1980: Chapters and Essays* (1982); he contributed the annual chapters on Melville to *American Literary Scholarship* for 1967–1971. He is currently writing books on both Melville and Emerson.

ROWLAND A. SHERRILL is Associate Professor of Religious Studies and American Studies at Indiana University, Indianapolis. The author of *The Prophetic Melville* (1979) and an essay on "The Bible and Twentieth-Century American Fiction" in *The Bible and American Arts and Letters*

(1983; ed. Giles Gunn), he has also published numerous articles and reviews in religious studies and literature journals. He is presently the editor of a forthcoming collection of essays on religion and American culture.

EDWIN S. SHNEIDMAN, who received his doctorate at the University of Southern California, is Professor of Thanatology at UCLA. He has been Chief of the Center for the Study of Suicide Prevention at the National Institute of Mental Health (in Bethesda), Visiting Professor at Harvard and at the Ben Gurion University of the Negev (in Beersheva), and a Fellow at the Center for the Advanced Study in the Behavioral Sciences (at Stanford). The author of *Deaths of Man* (nominated for a 1973 National Book Award), *Voices of Death* (1980), and *Definition of Suicide* (1985), he has also published on Melville in several journals of psychology, in *Melville and Hawthorne in the Berkshires*, and in *Melville Society Extracts*. Currently he teaches a course on Melville at UCLA.

WILLIAM H. SHURR is Lindsay Young Professor of English at the University of Tennessee. He has written books on Melville's poetry (a SAMLA award winner), on Calvinism in American Literature, and on the fascicle poetry of Emily Dickinson. He has published articles on such authors as Emerson, Gerard Manley Hopkins, Robert Frost and Anne Sexton. He serves on the advisory boards of *ESQ* and *Poe Studies* and is currently writing a biographical study of Walt Whitman.

MILTON R. STERN is Distinguished Alumni Professor in the English Department of the University of Connecticut. A former Fulbright Professor at the University of Warsaw, he has taught at Michigan State University (where he received his doctorate), Harvard University, the University of Illinois, Smith College, and the University of Wyoming. A Guggenheim Fellow and a Fellow of the National Humanities Institute at Yale, he has written or edited approximately twenty books, including *The Fine Hammered Steel of Herman Melville* (1957), *The Golden Moment: The Novels of F. Scott Fitzgerald* (1970), and (with S. L. Gross) the four volumes of the Viking-Penguin *American Literature Survey*. His essays and reviews have appeared in *Nation, JEGP*, and *PMLA*.

G. THOMAS TANSELLE, Vice President of the John Simon Guggenheim Memorial Foundation, is an Adjunct Professor of English and Comparative Literature at Columbia University and one of the editors of the Northwestern-Newberry Edition of *The Writings of Herman Melville*. Currently president of the Grolier Club and the Bibliographical Society of America, he has published a *Guide to the Study of United States*

Imprints (1971) and numerous essays on bibliography and textual criticism, some of which are collected in his *Selected Studies in Bibliography* (1979).

BETTE S. WEIDMAN is an Associate Professor of English at Queens College of the City University of New York. Her major publications include *White on Red: Images of the American Indian*, with Nancy B. Black (1976); "The Pinto Letters of Charles F. Briggs," in the 1979 annual volume of *Studies in the American Renaissance*, ed. Joel Myerson, and two volumes of historic photographs of Long Island with explanatory captions, published by Dover Publications. Current research interests focus on Hawthorne and Melville, regional history, Native American Studies and oral history.

JOHN WENKE teaches American literature at Salisbury State College, Maryland. His essays on Melville have appeared in *ESQ, Essays in Literature, American Transcendental Quarterly, Critical Essays on Melville's Typee* (ed. Milton R. Stern), and *Melville Society Extracts*. He has also published scholarly articles on Thomas Nashe, James Joyce, Gelett Burgess and J. D. Salinger. Wenke is currently writing a book on Melville's transformations of philosophical materials.

KINGSLEY WIDMER has published eight books on modernism and such authors as D. H. Lawrence, Henry Miller, Paul Goodman, and Nathanael West. He has also written *The Ways of Nihilism* (1970), a study of Melville's short novels. His articles on poetry, social and cultural issues, and literary criticism have appeared in numerous journals. He has been Professor of English at San Diego State University for many years.

DONALD YANNELLA, Professor of English at Glassboro (N.J.) State College, has written a number of articles and reviews, edited several collections of essays, and co-authored *American Prose to 1820* (1979). His most recent book is *Ralph Waldo Emerson* (1982), and his edition of the Duyckinck diaries is forthcoming. Since 1975, he has edited *Melville Society Extracts* and has served that organization as an officer since 1972. He is also a member of the Advisory Council of the American Literature Section of the Modern Language Association.